ESSENTIALS OF Psychology

ESSENTIALS OF Psychology

FOURTH EDITION

SPENCER A. RATHUS
St. John's University

HARCOURT BRACE COLLEGE PUBLISHERS

Fort Worth Philadelphia San Diego New York Orlando Austin San Antonio

Toronto Montreal London Sydney Tokyo

Publisher	Ted Buchholz
Acquisitions Editor	Eve Howard
Developmental Editor	John Haley
Project Editor	Mark Hobbs
Production Manager	Debra Jenkin
Art Director	Burl Sloan
Photo Research	Sue Howard, Annette Coolidge

Address for Editorial Correspondence: Harcourt Brace College Publishers, 301 Commerce Street, Suite 3700, Fort Worth, TX 76102.

Address for Orders: Harcourt Brace & Company, 6277 Sea Harbor Drive, Orlando, Florida 32887. 1-800-782-4479, or 1-800-433-0001 (in Florida).

ISBN: 0-15-500739-4

Library of Congress Catalog Card Number: 93- 79351

Printed in the United States of America

4 5 6 7 8 9 0 1 2 069 9 8 7 6 5 4 3 2

Contents in Brief

To my daughter, Taylor,
who had the nerve to ask her father
why some were sad or glad or bad,
and to my wife, Lois,
who had the audacity to encourage her.

Preface

"a forward-looking combination of elements that

- foster a knowledge base consisting of important psychological theories, research findings, and issues,
- help students function in and appreciate the multicultural America of the twenty-first century, and
- provide the intellectual tools with which students can continue to teach themselves for a lifetime. . . . ."

Voltaire, the French man of letters, once apologized to a friend for writing such a long letter. He had not the time, he lamented, to write a brief one. Similarly, the writing of *Essentials of Psychology* has been a very special challenge for me. The inclusion of various topics and studies in an "essentials" textbook implies that those topics and studies that were omitted were *not* essential—that they were, perhaps, the antonym of *essential,* or "superfluous." It is likely, however, that no two psychologists would fully agree on everything that is essential and everything that is superfluous. It was thus necessary to make difficult decisions about what to include and what to exclude. In the process, I learned to share Voltaire's lament that the creation of a brief work is, indeed, difficult and time-consuming.

Having made the difficult decisions as to what to cover, however, nothing was spared in the explication of topics. Psychological subjects ranging from research methods and biological psychology to developmental and social psychology are given the depth that they require. The textbook, moreover, is a complete teaching and learning tool, with motivational features and a thorough, built-in study guide that aims to put the student on an equal footing with the subject matter.

As the author of the fourth edition of a successful textbook, I also challenged that homely piece of folklore that maintains, "If it ain't broke, don't fix it." Earlier editions of the book were clearly not "broke," but I chose to tamper with the successful and "fix" the book, anyhow. The fourth edition differs from earlier editions in its increased attention to human diversity, critical thinking, research methods, states of consciousness, and health psychology. It presents a forward-looking combination of elements that are intended to

- foster a knowledge base consisting of important psychological theories, research findings, and issues,
- help students function in and appreciate the multicultural America of the twenty-first century, and
- provide the intellectual tools with which students can continue to teach themselves for a lifetime.

ORIENTATION OF *ESSENTIALS OF PSYCHOLOGY*

The fourth edition of *Essentials of Psychology,* as earlier editions, was deliberately written with the needs of students in mind. *Essentials* maintains an engaging, stimulating quality without descending into frivolity and condescension.

Essentials was written explicity for the instructor who requires a textbook that

- communicates the true scientific nature of psychology through in-depth coverage of critical thinking, research methods, and classic studies in psychology and
- reflects the importance of human diversity in psychology and in students' lives.

Yet it also retains the stylistic "essentials" that gave earlier editions their unique flavor:

- the abundant use of humor, personal anecdotes, and *Truth-or-Fiction?* items to help motivate students, and
- the use of energetic, accessible prose in the presentation of abstract, complex concepts.

WHAT'S NEW IN THIS EDITION

The fourth edition of *Essentials* makes major advances in coverage over the third.

New Chapters

a knowledge base consisting of important psychological theories, research findings, and issues . . .

The central improvements in coverage are found in the fourth edition's three new chapters: "Research Methods in Psychology," "States of Consciousness," and "Health Psychology." The addition of these chapters allows for new or expanded discussion of

- human diversity and psychology,
- critical thinking and psychology,
- the scientific method,
- samples and populations,
- kinds of research methods used by psychologists,
- meanings of *consciousness,*
- effects of various substances on consciousness,
- meditation,
- biofeedback training,
- hypnosis,
- stress,
- moderators of the impact of stress,
- the immune system,
- psychological factors in the origins and treatments of headaches, hypertension, cardiovascular disorders, asthma, cancer, and AIDS, and
- psychological factors in compliance with medical advice.

Consider the coverage of human diversity and critical thinking.

Coverage of Human Diversity

to help students function in and appreciate the multicultural America of the twenty-first century . . .

The fourth edition of *Essentials* emphasizes the discussion of human diversity and its place in psychology. There are several reasons:

- The profession of psychology is committed to the dignity of the individual, and we cannot understand individuals without an awareness of the richness of human deversity.
- The ethnic composition of the United States is changing dramatically. In 1992, according to the U.S. Bureau of the Census, 74–75 percent of the U.S. population was composed of non-Hispanic white Americans. The Bureau of the Census projected that by the year 2050, however, only 53 percent of the population will consist of non-Hispanic white Americans.
- The study of human diversity enables students to appreciate the cultural heritages and historical problems of various ethnic groups.
- Psychologists are called on to help people of all ethnic groups solve personal problems. However, psychologists cannot hope to understand the aspirations and problems of individuals from an ethnic group without understanding the history and cultural heritage of that group.

To enhance students' knowledge of human diversity as it relates to psychology, the fourth edition of *Essentials* contains:

A Major Section on Human Diversity in Chapter 1. This section explores the meanings of human diversity (ethnic diversity, gender, and so on), informs students why psychologists study human diversity, and provides information on members of ethnic minority groups and women who have made significant contributions to the development of psychology as a science.

Discussions of Human Diversity Throughout the Text. Discussions of human diversity are integrated within the subject matter of the text and also highlighted in "World of Diversity" features that are new to this edition. Topics include

- the representation of ethnic minority groups in psychological research studies,
- ethnicity and substance abuse among adolescents,
- the influence of ethnic stereotypes on our perceptions and memories,
- Black English,
- bilingualism,
- ethnic differences in intelligence test scores—their implications and possible origins,
- ethnic differences in prenatal care,
- ethnic differences in vulnerability to various physical problems and disorders, ranging from obesity to hypertension and cancer,
- ethnic differences in the utilization of health care for physical and psychological problems,
- differential patterns of diagnosis of psychological disorders among various ethnic groups,

- the prevalence of suicide among people of different ethnic minority groups,
- considerations in the practice of psychotherapy with clients from different ethnic groups,
- machismo/marianismo stereotypes and Hispanic culture,
- interracial dating and marital relationships, and
- prejudice.

"ESL—Bridging-the-Gap" Sections in the Built-In Study Guide. ESL (English as a Second Language) sections, described below, not only assist and encourage students whose second language is English, they also heighten the sensitivity of students whose native tongue is English to the situations of bilingual students.

Coverage of Critical Thinking

> *the intellectual tools with which students can continue to teach themselves for a lifetime. . . .*

Higher education is a broadening experience not only because of exposure to intellectual disciplines and human diversity but also because it encourages students to think critically. By thinking critically, students can challenge widely accepted but erroneous beliefs, including some of their own most cherished beliefs. The textbook's emphasis on critical thinking reflects the author's belief that a college education should do more than provide students with a data bank of knowledge. It should also supply intellectual tools that allow students to analyze information independently so that they can continue to educate themselves for a lifetime.

To enhance students' critical thinking skills as they relate to psychology, the fourth edition of *Essentials* offers two features:

A Major Section on Critical Thinking in Chapter 1. This section explains eight principles of critical thinking, from encouraging an attitude of skepticism to examining the definitions of terms to exercising caution in the interpretation of research findings. It also points out four common fallacies found in arguments, such as *ad hominem* arguments (arguments directed against the person) and *ad verecundiam* arguments (appeals to authority).

Pretest (Truth-or-Fiction?) Items That Challenge Students to Reconsider Common Knowledge. Students reexamine commonly held beliefs in the light of psychological research findings. Such items include beliefs that

- alcohol causes aggression,
- we tend to act out our forbidden fantasies in our dreams,
- we must make mistakes in order to learn,
- some people have photographic memories,
- the best way to solve a frustrating problem is to keep plugging away at it,
- misery loves company,
- people who threaten suicide are only seeking attention,
- we value things more when we have to work for them, and
- beauty is in the eye of the beholder.

Improvements in Pedagogy

The central improvement in pedagogy is the fourth edition's inclusion of an "ESL—Bridging the Gap" section in each chapter's built-in "Study Guide." Although the ESL sections are designed to aid students whose first language is not English, they will help native English speakers become more conversant with the idioms of their own tongue and sensitize them to the needs of bilingual students.

BUILT-IN, SELF-SCORING, STUDENT STUDY GUIDE

We are particularly proud of *Essentials'* built-in "Study Guide" as a vehicle for promoting students learning. The study guide contains the following features:

Learning Objectives. Each chapter begins with a list of learning objectives that are organized according to the major topics withing the chapter. For this reason, the learning objectives also serve as advance organizers, providing an overview of the chapter "at a glance."

Pretests (the "Truth or Fiction?" Feature). In each chapter, a pretest follows the learning objectives. These strings of true-or-false items, as noted, stimulate students' interest by challenging folklore and their own preconceptions about psychology and human behavior. This feature also prompts critical thinking and primes students for scientific exploration of issues that have previously received biased or unscientific consideration.

Truth-or-Fiction Revisited. These inserts are found in the text at the places where discussions of the pretest topics occur. In this way, students are intermittently prompted to reflect on their answers to the pretests, and their motivation to continue to compare their preconceptions with scientific knowledge is maintained and amplified.

Running Glossary. Key terms are defined in the margins at the points at which they are introduced in the text, where they appear in boldface. Research shows that many students fail to take advantage of a glossary placed at the back of a book. Other students find that the need to flip back and forth between the text and an end-of-book glossary disrupts their concentration.

To heighten the utility of this study aid, definitions are repeated in other chapters as needed. In this way, instructors are given flexibility in the order of reading assignments, and, for students, the meanings of key terms are reinforced.

Exercises. At the end of each chapter are found one or more exercises. Exercises vary according to the nature of the material covered in the chapter. For example, Chapter 1 features an exercise on prominent people in psychology. Chapter 4 features exercises that address the anatomy of the eye and the ear. Answers follow the exercises.

ESL-Bridging the Gap: Not Just for Those Whose Second Language is English. ESL stands for "English as a second language." Not all introductory psychology students grew up speaking English in their homes. Some students, in fact, may have emigrated to the United States only recently and may have been speaking English for only a few months or years before entering college. The "Bridging-the Gap" feature in each chapter's study guide helps such students (and other students) in the following ways:

- It lists and explains *idioms* that are found in the chapter . Idioms are usages of a language—in this case, English—that may not be directly or literally, translatable into other languages. Examples of such idioms, as listed and explained in the Chapter 1 study guide, include "look upon," "took over," "spare time," "bear on," "sort out," and "breaking it down." Many English speakers will immediately grasp the meanings of these phrases, but people for whom English is a second language—and some for whom English is the first language—may profit from the explanations provided in the "bridging-the-gap" feature.

- It lists and explains *cultural references.* These are people, places, things, and activities that may be familiar to most people whose first language is English. Other people may not recognize them, however; so they—as well as the (intended) subject matter of the course—pose obstacles. Examples that are listed and explained in Chapter 1 of the study guide include "uppers" and "Mark Twain." Again, you can see how many people whose first language is English may nevertheless profit from such a list. Does everyone know who Mark Twain is or what the word *uppers* means, for example?
- It lists and explains *phrases and expressions* in which words have meanings that differ from their usual meanings or are used as metaphors. Examples from Chapter 1 of the study guide include "That's you to a 't,'" "surprised at ourselves," "out of character," "tip of the tongue," and "do their bidding." Again, many English speakers will immediately perceive the meanings of such phrases, but others will not. This feature, like the others, will be of help to many, many students—not just those for whom English is a second language.

Students whose first language is English are encouraged to read the bridging-the-gap sections for several reasons. These sections, for example, will

- enhance their ability to use idiomatic English,
- remind them of the material in the textbook from which the words, phrases, and references were taken, and
- increase their sensitivity to the language problems of people whose first language is not English.

Chapter Review. Chapter review sections are organized according to the major heads in the chapter. They repeat the learning objectives, and they are programmed to provide students with the opportunity to fill in information as they read. Unique "prompts" (a letter or group of letters from the missing word or phrase) help students recall items to be filled in. Answers follow the chapter reviews.

Posttests. Most psychologists use multiple-choice questions in their assessment of student knowledge. For this reason, each chapter concludes with a 20-item multiple-choice test that allows students to check their knowledge following the chapter review. These tests provide students with a numerical measure of their mastery and, perhaps, with a reasonably accurate basis for predicting their performance on the instructor's quizzes and tests. Answers follow the tests.

End-of-Book Glossary. Students reap the benefits of a running glossary and of an end-of-book glossary. They are able to find the meanings of key terms in the running glossary without interrupting their reading of the chapters. However, they can also find definitions of terms presented in a traditional, alphabetized format. Moreover, those students who enjoy browsing through a glossary will be gratified.

THE ANCILLARIES

The needs of contemporary instructors and students demand a full and broad array of ancillary materials that facilitate teaching and learning. *Essentials of Psychology* is accompanied by a complete, convenient, and carefully conceived package.

For the Student

Built-In Study Guide. *Essentials* features a fully revised, built-in study guide at no additional cost to the student. The study guide includes (a) learning objectives and pretests ("Truth-or-Fiction?" items) at the start of the chapters, (b) a running glossary of key terms, and (c) exercises, chapter review sections in which students fill in the blanks, and multiple-choice posttests at the end of the chapters.

Interactive Software. *PsychLearn (IBM and Apple®):* Students can use this interactive software program to review important concepts and participate in five experiments: Schedules of Reinforcement; Short-Term Memory; Reaction Time; Self-Consciousness Scale; and Social Dilemma. The full-color program comes with an instructional guide, including questions for each lesson.

IBM, 5¼", ISBN: 0-03-004864-8
Apple, ISBN: 0-03-008109-2

BrainStack (Macintosh): This interactive software program takes students on a self-guided tour of the cerebral cortex, giving them valuable information on topics such as memory, thinking, pattern recognition, and language. ISBN: 0-15-505542-9

The Psychology Experimenter (IBM): Users can perform experiments and record and analyze data with this interactive program. It also duplicates four classic memory and perception experiments and allows users to modify experiments of their own design. ISBN: 0-15-572674-9

SuperShrink I: Victor and SuperShrink II: Jennifer (IBM): In these interactive programs, users adopt the role of counselor at a helpline clinic and interview clients, Victor and Jennifer. These programs offer extremely valuable experience to introductory psychology students learning concepts in psychotherapy, personality, and assessment.

Victor, 5¼" 0-15-584761-9
Jennifer, 5¼" 0-15-584763-5
Jennifer, 3½" 0-15-584764-3
Price: $16.00 NET

For the Instructor

Test Bank. The *Test Bank,* by Linda Hjorth of DeVry Technical Institute, consists of over 2,000 multiple-choice questions, organized according to learning objectives. All questions are coded to question type, difficulty, and text page number. ISBN: 0-15-500741-6

Instructor's Manual. The *Instructor's Manual,* by Linda Hjorth, includes learning objectives, lecture suggestions, classroom activities, and suggestions for incorporating diversity into class presentations. A videodisc coordination section, prepared by Alicia Goldner-Ortiz of Long Beach City College, provides suggestions for using the Harcourt Brace videodisc, **Dynamic Concepts in Psychology,** in conjunction with the text. ISBN: 0-15-500740-8

EXAMaster + ™ Computerized Test Bank. The computerized test bank offers easy-to-use options for test creation:

EasyTest creates a test from a single screen in just a few easy steps. Instructors choose parameters, then select questions from the data base or let EasyTest randomly select them.

FullTest offers a range of options that includes selecting, editing, adding, or linking questions or graphics; random selection from a wide range of criteria; creating criteria; blocking questions; and printing up to 99 different versions of the same test and answer sheet.

IBM®, 5¼" ISBN: 0-15-500743-2
IBM, 3½" ISBN: 0-15-500742-4
Macintosh®, ISBN: 0-15-500744-0

EXAMRecord™records, curvers, graphs, and prints out grades according to criteria the instructor selects. Grade distribution displays as a bar graph or plotted graph.

IBM, 5¼", ISBN: 0-03-039653-0
Macintosh 0-03-039652-2

RequesTest is a service for instructors without access to a computer. A software specialist will compile questions according to the instructor's criteria and mail or fax the test master within 48 hours! Call 1-800-447-9457.

The Software Support Hotline is available to answer questions Monday through Friday, 9 a.m. to 4 p.m. Central Time at 1-800-447-9457.

The Whole Psychology Catalog. Instructors can easily supplement course work and assignments with this manual of perforated pages containing experimental exercises, questionnaires, lecture outlines, and visual aids. ISBN: 0-03-030429-6

Overhead Transparency Acetates. More than 200 full-color acetates, with accompanying guide, enhance classroom lectures and *supplement* (not duplicate) material in the text. ISBN: 0-03-007717-6

ACKNOWLEDGMENTS

The discipline of psychology owes its progress and its scientific standing to experts who formulate theories and conduct research in many different areas. Similarly, *Essentials of Psychology* owes a great deal of its substance and form to my colleagues, who provided expert suggestions and insights at various stages in its development. My sincere thanks to the following:

John Benson, Texarkana College; Ervin L. Betts, Norwalk Community College; Richard L. Cahoon, Cape Cod Community College; Albert Cohoe, Ohio Northern University; Philip W. Compton, Ohio Northern University; Bridget Coughlin, Hocking Technical Insitute; James R. Council, North Dakota State University; R. Scott Ditsel, Tiffin University; George J. Downing, Gloucester County College; Barbara Engler, Union County College; Mary Farkas, Lansing Community College; Barry Fish, Eastern Michigan University; Ajaipal S. Gill, Anne Arundel Community College; Brian Gladue, North Dakota State University; John N. Goodwin, School of the Ozarks; Charles S. Grunder, University of Maine; Barbara Gryzlo, Illinois Technical College; John R. Haig, Philadelphia College of Textiles and Science; Tom Hailen, Northwestern College; George Hampton, University of Houston; James E. Hart, Edison State Community College; Kathryn Jennings, College of the Redwoods; Grace Leonard, University of Maine—Augusta; Kenneth LeSure, Cuyahoga Community College—Metro Campus; Peter C. Murrell, Milwaukee Area Technical College; Carroll S. Perrino, Morgan State University; Richard L. Port, University of Pittsburgh; Valda Robinson, Hillsborough Community College; John Roehr, Hudson Valley Community College; Laurie M. Rotando, Westchester Community College; David L. Salmond, Vincennes University; Keith Schirmer, Kellogg Community College; Linda Schwandt, Western Wisconsin Technical

Institute; Joe M. Tinnin, Richland College; Carol Vitiello, Kirkwood Community College; Ann Weber, University of North Carolina; Kenneth N. Wildman, Ohio Northern University; Michael Witmer, Skagit Valley College; Cecelia K. Yoder, Oklahoma City Community College; David Zehr, Plymouth State College.

The publishing professionals at Harcourt Brace & Company are a particularly able group of individuals, and many of them have become good friends over the years.

First among these is Eve Howard, Psychology Editor. Her enthusiasm and her concrete suggestions have made key contributions to the evolution of this textbook. Mark Hobbs and Debra Jenkin, with Barbara Moreland and Deanna Johnson, coordinated the editing, design, and production activities that were necessary to transform my typo-ridden manuscript and floppy diskettes into a beautiful bound book. Burl Sloan is responsible for the splendid revised design of the fourth edition and for the cover design. The management team at Harcourt Brace has been a continuous source of support, inspiration, and good lunches. My gratitude to Carl Tyson, President; to Ted Buchholz, Publisher; to John Haley, Developmental Editor; and to Lee Sutherlin, Marketing Director. Thanks, pals.

Contents

Chapter 2

Chapter 3

Chapter 5 States of Consciousness 165

Chapter 6 Learning 205

Chapter 8

Chapter 9

Chapter 11

Chapter 12

Chapter 14

Chapter 15

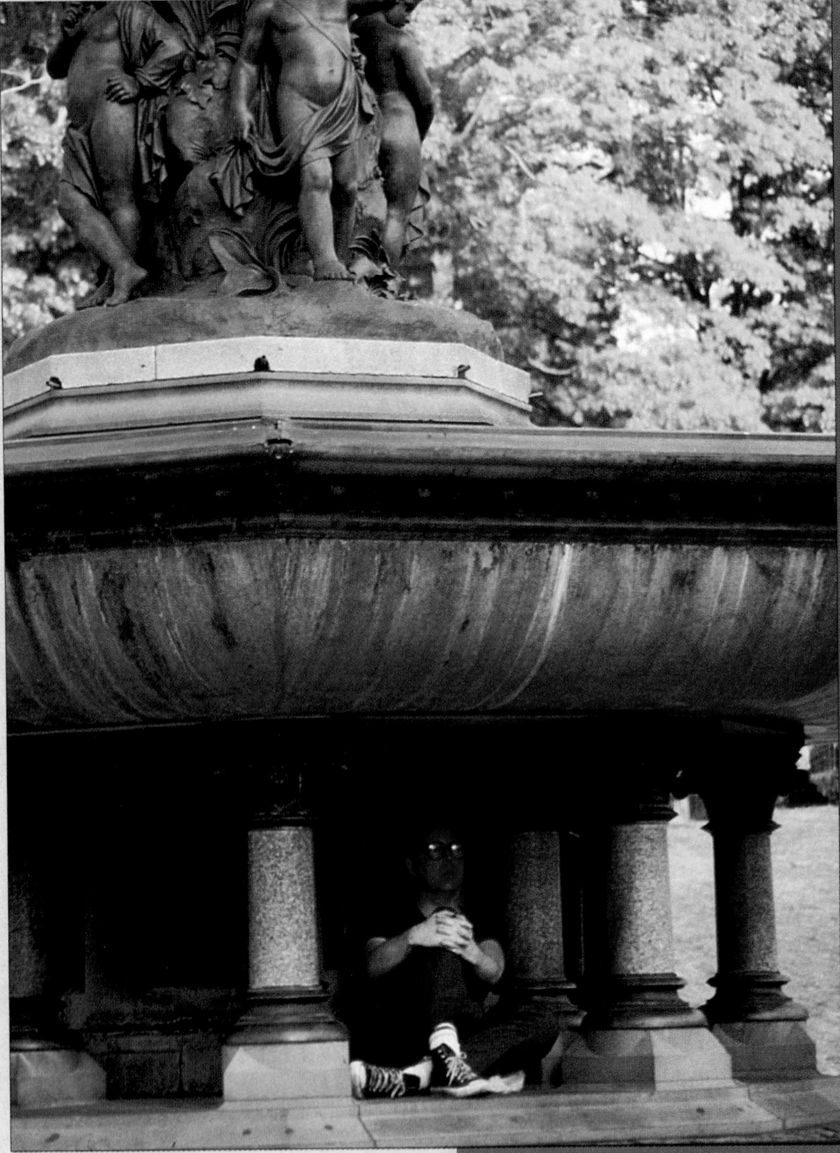

- Psychologists attempt to control behavior.
- Some psychologists measure the effectiveness of television commercials.
- Other psychologists serve as expert witnesses in court.
- Still other psychologists guide people into eating more healthful diets.
- A book on psychology, whose contents are similar to those of the book you are now holding in your hands, was written by Aristotle more than 2,000 years ago.
- The ancient Greek philosopher Socrates suggested a research method that is still used in psychology.
- Some psychologists look upon our strategies for solving problems as "mental programs" operated by our very "personal computers"—our brains.
- The numbers of students from ethnic minority groups have increased dramatically on college campuses in the past decade.
- Women were not permitted to attend college in the United States until 1833.
- Men receive the majority of doctoral degrees in psychology.
- 50 million French people cannot be wrong.

What Is Psychology?

Learning Objectives

When you have finished studying Chapter 1, you should be able to:

Psychology as a Science

1. Define *psychology*.
2. List and discuss the goals of psychology.

What Psychologists Do

3. Explain the functions of different types of psychologists, including clinical, counseling, school, educational, developmental, personality, social, experimental, industrial, organizational, consumer, forensic, and health psychologists.

Where Psychology Comes From: A Brief History

4. Outline the history of psychology.

How Today's Psychologists View Behavior

5. Compare and contrast the five major theoretical perspectives in contemporary psychology: the biological, cognitive, humanistic–existential, psychodynamic, and learning perspectives.

Human Diversity and Psychology

6. Discuss some of the issues concerning psychological research, practice, and people of ethnic minority groups.
7. Discuss women and members of ethnic minority groups who have contributed to the development of psychology.

Critical Thinking and Psychology

8. Discuss the principles of critical thinking, and explain how they may be applied to the subject matter of psychology.

"What a piece of work is man!" wrote William Shakespeare. How noble in reason! how infinite in faculty! in form and moving how express and admirable! in action how like an angel! in apprehension how like a god! the beauty of the world! the paragon of animals!"

You probably had no trouble recognizing yourself in Shakespeare's description—"noble in reason," "admirable," godlike in understanding, head and shoulders above all other animals. That's you to a *tee,* isn't it? Human behavior varies greatly, however, and much of it is not so admirable. A good deal of human behavior, even familiar behavior, is puzzling. Consider these examples:

Most adults on crowded city streets will not stop to help a person lying on the sidewalk or to help a lost child. Why?

While most of us watch television, ride a bicycle, jog, or go for a swim, some people seek excitement by driving motorcycles at breakneck speed, skydiving, or taking "uppers." Why?

Most adults who overeat or smoke cigarettes know that they are jeopardizing their health. Yet they continue in their hazardous habits. Why?

Some children seem capable of learning more in school than other children. Their teachers scan their records and find that the more capable children usually have received higher scores on intelligence tests. But what is intelligence? How is intelligence measured? Why do some people have, or seem to have, more of it than others?

A rapist or murderer claims to have committed his crime because another "personality" dwelling in him took over or because a dog prompted him with mental messages. What is wrong with such people? Should they be found guilty of their crimes or be judged not guilty by reason of insanity? Should they go to prison or to a psychiatric facility?

Human behavior has always fascinated other human beings. Sometimes we are even surprised at ourselves because we have thoughts or impulses that seem to be out of character or we can't recall something on the "tip of the tongue." Psychologists, like other people, are intrigued by the mysteries of behavior and make an effort to answer questions such as these. Most people try to satisfy their curiosities about behavior in their spare time. (Perhaps they ask a friend for an opinion or make some casual observations.) Psychologists, however, make the scientific study of behavior their life's work.

Psychology is the scientific study of behavior and mental processes. Topics of interest to psychologists have included the nervous system, sensation and perception, learning and memory, language, thought, intelligence, growth and development, personality, stress, abnormal behavior, ways of treating abnormal behavior, sexual behavior, and the behavior of people in social settings such as groups and organizations.

Not all psychologists will be satisfied by our definition of psychology as the science of behavior and mental processes. Many psychologists, especially **behaviorists,** prefer to limit the scope of psychology to *overt,* or observable, behavior—to activities such as pressing a lever; turning left or right; eating and mating; or even involuntary body functions such as heart rate, dilation of the pupils of the eyes, blood pressure, or emission of brain waves. All these behaviors are *public.* They can be measured by simple observation or by laboratory instruments. Even the emission of brain waves is made public by scientific instruments (see Chapters 3 and 5), and diverse observers would readily agree about their existence and characteristics. Other psychologists, some of whom are **cognitive** psychologists, focus on our mental representations of the world, our memories, our strategies for solving problems, even our biases and prejudices.

Behaviorists are concerned that mental processes are private, not public, events that cannot be verified by observation or laboratory instruments. Sometimes, mental processes are accepted as being present on the basis of the **self-report** of the person experiencing them. Other times, however, mental processes can be indirectly verified by laboratory instruments, as in the case of dreams. Psychologists have learned that dreams are most likely to occur when particular brain waves are being emitted (see Chapter 5). A report of dreaming in the absence of these brain waves might thus be viewed with suspicion. Similarly, strong emotions tend to be accompanied by increases in the heart and respiration rates (see Chapter 9). So psychologists who study mental processes can often tie them to observable changes, allowing them to corroborate self-reports. Moreover, cognitive psychologists do not believe that we can understand much about human nature unless we are willing to venture into the realm of the intellect.

As a science, psychology brings carefully designed methods of observation such as the survey and the experiment to bear on its subject matter. Although most psychologists are interested primarily in human behavior, many others focus on the behavior of animals ranging from sea snails and pigeons to rats and gorillas. Some psychologists believe that research findings with lower animals can be applied, or **generalized,** to humans. Other psychologists argue that people are so distinct that we can only learn about people by studying people. Each view holds some merit. For example, laboratory studies of the nerve cells of squids have afforded insight into the workings of human nerve cells. Experiments in teaching sign language to chimpanzees and gorillas have sparked innovations in teaching language to severely retarded people. Only by studying people, however, can we learn about human qualities such as morality, values, and romantic love. Still, many psychologists study lower animals because they enjoy doing so. They are under no obligation to justify their curiosities on the basis of applicability to people.

Psychology The science that studies behavior and mental processes.

Behaviorist A psychologist who believes that psychology should address observable behavior and the relationships between stimuli and responses.

Cognitive Having to do with mental processes such as sensation and perception, memory, intelligence, language, thought, and problem-solving.

Self-report A subject's testimony about his or her own thoughts, feelings, or behaviors.

Generalize To go from the particular to the general; to extend.

Theory A formulation of relationships underlying observed events.

PSYCHOLOGY AS A SCIENCE

Psychology, like other sciences, seeks to describe, explain, predict, and control the events it studies. Psychology thus seeks to describe, explain, predict, and control the processes involved in areas such as perception, learning, memory, motivation, emotion, intelligence, personality, and the formation of attitudes.

When possible, descriptive terms and concepts are interwoven into **theories,** which are related sets of statements about events. Theories are based on certain assumptions, and they allow us to derive explanations and predictions. Many psychological theories combine statements about psychological concepts (such as learning and motivation), behavior (such as eating or problem-solving), and anatomical structures or biological processes. For instance, our responses to drugs such as alcohol and marijuana reflect the biochemical actions of these drugs and our (psychological) expectations of their effects.

A satisfactory psychological theory allows us to predict behavior. For instance, a satisfactory theory of hunger will allow us to predict when people will or will not eat. A broadly satisfying, comprehensive theory should have a wide range of applicability. A broad theory of hunger might apply to human beings and lower animals, to normal-weight and overweight people, and to people who have been deprived of food for differing lengths of time. If our observations cannot be adequately explained by, or predicted from, a given theory, we should consider revising or replacing that theory.

In psychology, many theories have been found to be incapable of explaining or predicting new observations. As a result, they have been revised extensively. For example, the theory that hunger results from stomach contractions may be partially correct for normal-weight individuals, but it is inadequate as an explanation for feelings of hunger among the overweight. In Chapter 9 we shall see that stomach contractions are only one of many factors, or **variables,** involved in hunger. Contemporary theories also focus on biological variables (such as the body's muscle-to-fat ratio) and situational variables (such as the presence of other people who are eating and the time of day).

The notion of controlling behavior and mental processes is controversial. Some people erroneously think that psychologists seek ways to make people do their bidding—like puppets on strings. This is not so. Psychologists are committed to a belief in the dignity of human beings, and human dignity demands that people be free to make their own decisions and choose their own behavior. Psychologists are learning more all the time about the various influences on human behavior, but they implement this knowledge only upon request and in ways they believe will be helpful to an individual or organization.

It is true that psychologists attempt to control behavior. However, in practice, this means helping clients engage in behavior that will help them meet their own goals.

The remainder of this chapter provides an overview of psychology and psychologists.

WHAT PSYCHOLOGISTS DO

Psychologists share a keen interest in behavior, but in other ways, they may differ markedly. Some psychologists engage primarily in basic research, or **pure research.** Pure research has no immediate application to personal or social problems and has thus been characterized as research for its own sake. Other psychologists engage in **applied research,** which is designed to find solutions to specific personal or social problems. Although pure research is spurred onward by curiosity and the desire to know and understand, today's pure research frequently enhances tomorrow's way of life. For example, pure research into learning and motivation with lower animals early in the century has found widespread applications in today's school systems. Pure research into the workings of the nervous system has enhanced knowledge of disorders such as epilepsy, Parkinson's disease, and Alzheimer's disease.

Many psychologists do not engage in research at all. Instead, they apply psychological knowledge to help people change their behavior so that they can meet

Variable A condition that is measured or controlled in a scientific study. A variable can vary in a measurable manner.

Pure research Research conducted without concern for immediate applications.

Applied research Research conducted in an effort to find solutions to particular problems.

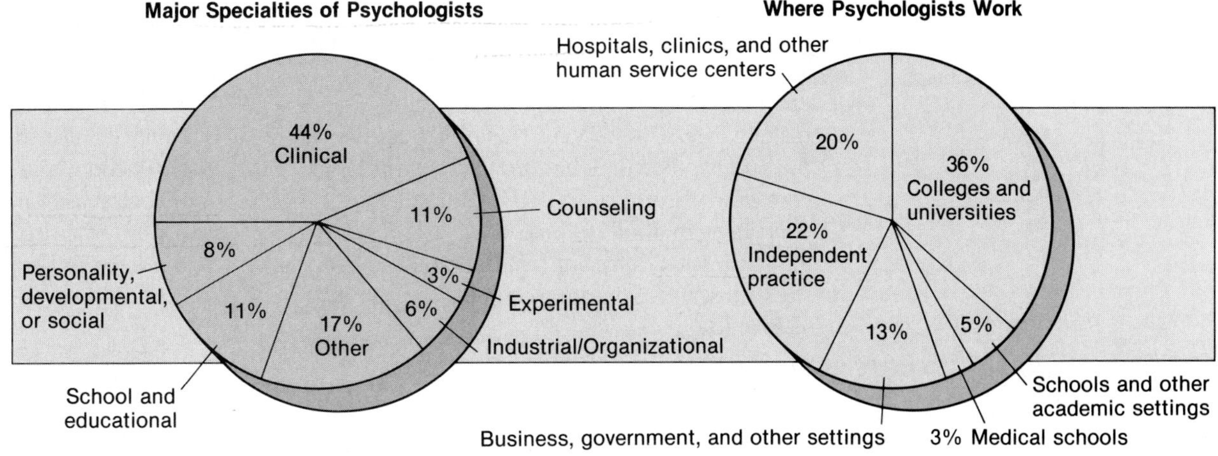

FIGURE 1.1
Specialties and Work Settings of Psychologists.

A survey of doctoral-level psychologists by the American Psychological Association (Stapp, Tucker, & VandenBos, 1985) showed that 44 percent identified themselves as clinical psychologists (see chart at left). The single largest group of psychologists works in colleges and universities, while large numbers of psychologists also work in independent practice and in hospitals, clinics, and other human-service settings (see chart at right).

their own goals more effectively. Numerous psychologists engage primarily in teaching. They disseminate psychological knowledge in classrooms, seminars, and workshops. Figure 1.1 shows that a large percentage of psychologists are employed by colleges and universities, but some of these psychologists counsel students rather than teach.

Many psychologists are involved in all of these activities: research, **consultation,** and teaching. For example, professors of psychology usually conduct pure or applied research and consult with individuals or industrial clients as well as teach. Full-time researchers may be called on to consult with industrial clients and to organize seminars or workshops to help clients develop skills. Practitioners, such as clinical and industrial psychologists, may also engage in research—which is usually applied—and teach in the classroom or workshop. Unfortunately for psychologists who teach, conduct research, and also carry on a practice, research into expanding the week to 250 hours does not look promising.

Let us now explore some of the specialties of psychologists.

Clinical and Counseling Psychologists

Clinical psychologists specialize in helping people with psychological problems adjust to the demands of life. Clients' problems may range from anxiety and depression to sexual dysfunctions to loss of goals. Clinical psychologists are trained to evaluate problems through structured interviews and psychological tests. They help their clients resolve their problems and change maladaptive behavior through techniques of **psychotherapy** and **behavior therapy**. Clinical psychologists may work in institutions for the mentally ill or mentally retarded, in outpatient clinics, in college and university clinics, or in private practices.

Clinical psychologists are the largest subgroup of psychologists (see Figure 1.1), so most people think of clinical psychologists when they hear the term *psychologist.* Many clinical psychologists divide their time among clinical practice, teaching, and research.

Consultation The provision of professional advice or services.

Psychotherapy The systematic application of psychological knowledge to the treatment of problem behavior.

Behavior therapy Application of principles of learning to the direct modification of problem behavior.

Counseling psychologists, like clinical psychologists, use interviews and tests to define their clients' problems. Clients of counseling psychologists typically have adjustment problems but do not behave in seriously abnormal ways. Clients may encounter difficulty in making academic or vocational decisions or difficulty in making friends in college. They may experience marital or family conflicts, have physical handicaps, or have adjustment problems such as those encountered by a convict who is returning to the community. Counseling psychologists use various counseling methods to help clients clarify their goals and find ways of surmounting obstacles. Counseling psychologists are often employed in college and university counseling and testing centers. They are also found in rehabilitation agencies.

School and Educational Psychologists

School psychologists are employed by school systems to help identify and assist students who encounter problems that interfere with learning. These range from social and family problems to emotional disturbances and learning disabilities such as **dyslexia**. School psychologists define students' problems through interviews with teachers and parents and with students themselves; through psychological tests such as intelligence and achievement tests; and through direct observation of behavior in the classroom. They consult with teachers, school officials, parents, and other professionals to help students overcome obstacles to learning. They also help make decisions about placement of students in special education and remediation programs.

Educational psychologists, like school psychologists, are concerned with optimizing classroom conditions to facilitate learning. They usually focus, however, on improvement of course planning and instructional methods for a school system rather than on identification of, and assistance to, children with learning problems.

Educational psychologists are usually more concerned than school psychologists about theoretical issues relating to learning, measurement, and child development. They are more likely to do research and to hold faculty posts in colleges and universities. Their research interests include the ways in which variables such as motivation, personality, intelligence, rewards and punishments, and teacher characteristics influence learning. Some educational psychologists specialize in preparing standardized tests such as the Scholastic Aptitude Tests.

Developmental Psychologists

Developmental psychologists study the changes—physical, emotional, cognitive, and social—that occur throughout the life span. They attempt to sort out the relative influences of heredity (nature) and the environment (nurture) on specific types of growth and to discover the origins of developmental abnormalities.

We find developmental psychologists conducting research on a variety of issues. These include the effects of maternal use of aspirin or heroin on an unborn child, the outcomes of various patterns of child rearing, children's concepts of space and time, adolescent conflicts, and factors that contribute to adjustment among the elderly.

Personality, Social, and Environmental Psychologists

Personality psychologists attempt to define human traits; to determine influences on human thought processes, feelings, and behavior; and to explain both normal and abnormal patterns of behavior. They are particularly concerned with human

Dyslexia Severely impaired reading ability.

Environmental Psychology. Environmental psychologists focus on the ways in which we affect and are affected by the physical environment. Among the concerns of environmental psychologists are the effects of crowding and "stimulus overload" on city dwellers.

issues such as anxiety, aggression, the assumption of gender roles, and learning by observing others. Other topics of interest to personality psychologists include **repression** as a way in which we defend ourselves from feelings of anxiety and guilt, and the effects of television violence.

Social psychologists are primarily concerned with the nature and causes of individuals' thoughts, feelings, and overt behavior in social situations. Whereas personality psychologists tend to look within the person for explanations of behavior, social psychologists tend to focus on social or external influences. The fact of the matter, of course, is that behavior is influenced from within and from without. Both avenues of research are valid.

Social psychologists have historically focused on topics such as attitude formation and attitude change, interpersonal attraction and liking, the nature of gender roles and **stereotypes,** obedience to authority, conformity to group norms, and group decision-making processes. Social psychologists, like personality psychologists, study the problem of human aggression.

Environmental psychologists focus on the ways in which behavior influences, and is influenced by, the physical environment. Like social psychologists, environmental psychologists are concerned with the effects of crowding on the behavior of city dwellers. Environmental psychologists study ways in which buildings and cities can be designed to better serve human needs. They also investigate the effects of extremes of temperature, noise, and air pollution on people and lower animals.

Experimental Psychologists

Psychologists in all specialties may conduct experimental research. However, those called experimental psychologists conduct research into fundamental processes relevant to more applied specialties. These basic processes include the functions of the nervous system, sensation and perception, learning and memory, thought, motivation, and emotion, to name but a few. Experimental psychologists who focus on the biological foundations of behavior and seek to understand the relationships between biological changes and psychological events are called biological psychologists.

Experimental psychologists are more likely than other psychologists to engage in basic or pure research. Their findings are often applied by other specialists in practice. Pure research in motivation, for example, has helped clinical and counseling psychologists devise strategies for helping people control weight problems. Pure research in learning and memory has helped school and educational psychologists enhance learning conditions in the schools.

Repression In psychodynamic theory, the automatic ejection of anxiety-evoking ideas from awareness.

Stereotype A fixed, conventional idea about a group.

Experimental Psychology. Experimental psychologists conduct research into fundamental psychological processes, such as the functions of the nervous system, sensation and perception, learning and memory, thinking, language, motivation, and emotion. Some of their research is carried out with lower animals, such as laboratory rats, but they also engage in research with humans.

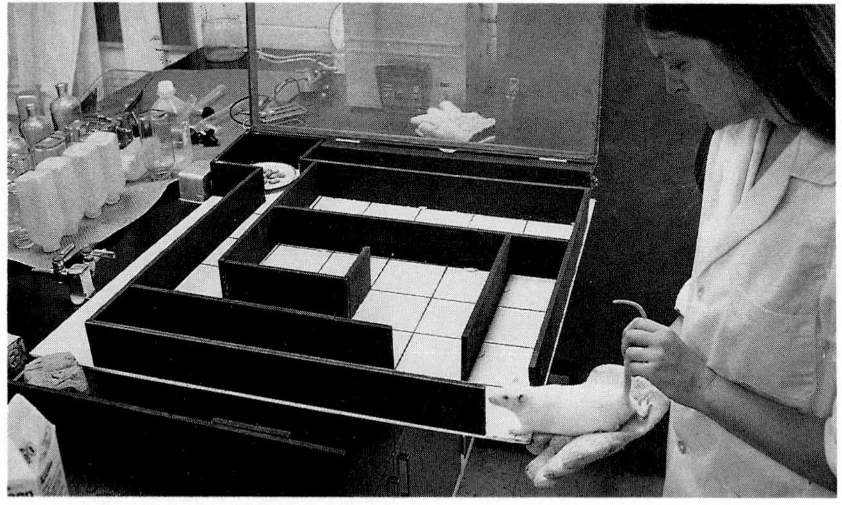

Psychologists in Industry

Industrial and organizational psychology are closely related fields. Industrial psychologists focus on the relationships between people and work, whereas organizational psychologists study the behavior of people in organizations such as business firms. However, many psychologists are trained in both areas. Industrial and organizational psychologists are employed by business firms to improve working conditions, enhance productivity, and—if they have counseling skills—work with employees who encounter problems on the job. They assist in the processes of hiring, training, and promotion. They devise psychological tests to ascertain whether job applicants have the abilities, interests, and traits that predict successful performance of various jobs. They innovate concepts such as **job sharing** and **flextime,** and their research skills equip them to evaluate the results. They also conduct research concerning job motivation, job satisfaction, the psychological and physical well-being of employees, and ways of making technical systems such as automobile dashboards and computer keyboards more user friendly.

Industrial psychology is a rapidly expanding specialization. Businesses have been learning that psychological expertise can help them increase productivity and simultaneously abate employee turnover and absenteeism.

Consumer psychologists study the behavior of shoppers in an effort to predict and influence their behavior. They advise store managers about how to lay out the aisles of a supermarket to boost impulse buying and how to arrange window displays to attract customers. They devise strategies for enhancing the persuasiveness of newspaper ads and television commercials.

Some psychologists do measure the effectiveness of television commercials. They are consumer psychologists.

Job sharing Sharing of a full-time job by two or more workers.

Flextime A flexible work schedule that attempts to meet worker as well as company needs.

Emerging Fields

There are many other fields and subfields in psychology. The behavior problems that affect children can be very different from those encountered by adults. Clinical child psychologists assess these problems and work with parents and teachers, and the children themselves, to help children overcome or adjust to problems.

Forensic psychologists apply psychological expertise within the criminal-justice system. They may serve as expert witnesses in the courtroom, testifying about the competence of defendants to stand trial or describing mental disorders and how they may affect criminal behavior. Psychologists are employed by police departments to assist in the selection of stable applicants; to counsel officers on how to cope with stress; and to train police in the handling of suicide threats, hostage crises, family disputes, and other human problems.

Other psychologists do serve as expert witnesses in court. They are forensic psychologists.

Health psychologists examine the ways in which behavior and mental processes such as attitudes are related to physical health. They study the effects of stress on health problems such as high blood pressure, heart disease, diabetes, and cancer. Health psychologists investigate the factors that contribute to patient compliance with medical advice. Health psychologists also guide clients to undertake more healthful behavior patterns such as exercise, quitting smoking, and eating a more healthful diet.

Still other psychologists guide people into eating more healthful diets. Health psychologists do so, as well as clinical and counseling psychologists.

Psychologists are continually finding new areas in which to apply their knowledge and skills. Table 1.1 provides more insight into the diverse interests of psychologists.

WHERE PSYCHOLOGY COMES FROM: A BRIEF HISTORY

Psychology is as old as history and as modern as today. Knowledge of the history of psychology allows us to appreciate psychology's theoretical conflicts, its place among the sciences, the evolution of its methods, and its social and political roles (McGovern et al., 1991).

Although research findings and theoretical developments seem to change the face of psychology every few years, the outline for this textbook could have been written by the Greek philosopher Aristotle (ca. 384–322 B.C.). One of Aristotle's works was called *Peri Psyches*, which translates as "About the Psyche." *Peri Psyches*, like this book, began with a history of psychological thought and historical perspectives on the nature of the mind and behavior. Given his scientific approach, Aristotle made the case that human behavior, like the movements of the stars and the seas, was subject to rules and laws. Then Aristotle delved into his subject matter topic by topic: personality, sensation and perception, thought, intelligence, needs and motives, feelings and emotion, and memory. This book reorganizes these topics, but each is here.

It is true that a book on psychology, whose contents are similar to this one, was written by Aristotle more than 2,000 years ago. Its name is *Peri Psyches*.

TABLE 1.1: Divisions of the American Psychological Association

General Psychology	Society for Community Research and Action
Teaching of Psychology	Psychopharmacology and Substance Abuse
Experimental Psychology	Psychotherapy
Evaluation and Measurement	Psychological Hypnosis
Physiological and Comparative Psychology	State and Provincial Psychological Associations
Developmental Psychology	Humanistic Psychology
Personality and Social Psychology	Mental Retardation and Developmental Disabilities
Society for the Psychological Study of Social Issues	Population and Environmental Psychology
Psychology and the Arts	Psychology of Women
Clinical Psychology	Psychologists Interested in Religious Issues
Society for Industrial and Organizational Psychology	Child, Youth, and Family Services
Educational Psychology	Health Psychology
School Psychology	Psychoanalysis
Counseling Psychology	Clinical Neuropsychology
Psychologists in Public Service	American Psychology and Law
Military Psychology	Psychologists in Independent Practice
Adult Development and Aging	Family Psychology
Division of Applied Experimental & Engineering Psychology	Society for the Psychological Study of Lesbian and Gay Issues
Rehabilitation Psychology	Society for the Psychological Study of Ethnic Minority Issues
Consumer Psychology	Media Psychology
Theoretical and Philosophical Psychology	Exercise and Sport Psychology
Experimental Analysis of Behavior	Peace Psychology
History of Psychology	Group Psychology & Group Psychotherapy

This evolving list reflects the diversity of interests among psychologists, as well as specialties and areas of social concern. Many psychologists are active in several divisions.

Aristotle also declared that people are basically motivated to seek pleasure and avoid pain, a view that has been employed in modern psychodynamic and learning theories.

There are other contributors from ancient Greece. Democritus, for instance, suggested around 400 B.C. that we could think of behavior in terms of a body and a mind. (Contemporary psychologists still talk about the interaction of biological and cognitive processes.) Democritus also pointed out that our behavior was influenced by external stimulation, and he was one of the first to raise the issue of whether or not there is such a thing as free will or choice. After all, if we are influenced by external forces, can we be said to control our own behavior? Putting it another way, where do the influences of others end and our "real selves" begin?

Plato (ca. 427–347 B.C.), the disciple of Socrates, recorded Socrates' advice "Know thyself," which has remained one of the mottos of psychological thought ever since. Socrates claimed that we could not attain reliable self-knowledge through our senses because the senses do not exactly mirror reality. Because the senses provide imperfect knowledge, Socrates suggested that we should rely on processes such as rational thought and **introspection** to achieve self-knowledge.

Socrates did suggest a research method that is still used in psychology today—introspection.

Socrates also stressed the importance of social psychology. He pointed out that people are social creatures who influence one another profoundly.

Had we room enough and time, we could trace psychology's roots to thinkers more distant than the ancient Greeks, and we could trace its develop-

Introspection An objective approach to describing one's mental content.

Wilhelm Wundt

ment through the great thinkers of the Renaissance. We could point to nineteenth-century influences such as theories about evolution, the movements of the atoms, transmission of neural messages in the brain, and the association of thoughts and memories. We could also describe the development of statistics, which, as you will see in Appendix A, is used by psychologists to help judge the results of their research.

As it is, we must move to the development of psychology as a laboratory science during the second half of the nineteenth century. There are so many controversies in psychology that it seems excessive to debate when modern psychology had its debut as an experimental science. Yet some historians set the marker date at 1860, when Gustav Theodor Fechner (1801–1887) published his *Elements of Psychophysics.* Fechner's book showed how physical events (such as lights and sounds) were related to psychological sensation and perception, and he showed how we could scientifically measure the effect of these events. Most historians, however, set the birth of psychology as a science in the year 1879, when Wilhelm Wundt (1832–1920) established the first psychological laboratory in Leipzig, Germany.

Structuralism

Wilhelm Wundt, like Aristotle, claimed that the mind was a natural event and could be studied scientifically, just like light, heat, and the flow of blood. Wundt used the method of introspection, recommended by Socrates, to try to discover the basic elements of experience. When presented with various sights and sounds, he and his colleagues tried to look inward as objectively as possible to describe their sensations and feelings.

Wundt and his students—among them Edward Bradford Titchener, who brought Wundt's methodology to Cornell University—founded the school of psychology known as **structuralism**. Structuralism attempted to define the makeup of conscious experience, breaking it down into **objective** sensations such as sight or taste, and **subjective** feelings such as emotional responses, will, and mental images (for example, memories or dreams). Structuralists believed that the mind functioned by creatively combining the elements of experience.

Another of Wundt's American students was G. Stanley Hall (1844–1924), whose main interests included the psychological developments of childhood, adolescence, and old age. Hall is usually credited with originating the discipline of child psychology, and he founded the American Psychological Association. The development of child psychology altered the widespread belief that children were simply miniature adults.

Structuralism The school of psychology that argues that the mind consists of three basic elements—sensations, feelings, and images—which combine to form experience.

Objective Of known or perceived objects rather than existing only in the mind; real.

Subjective Of the mind; personal; determined by thoughts and feelings rather than by external objects.

Functionalism

> *I wished, by treating Psychology like a natural science, to help her become one.*
>
> William James

Toward the end of the nineteenth century, William James (1842–1910), brother of the novelist Henry James, adopted a broader view of psychology that focused on the relation between conscious experience and behavior. James was a major figure in the development of psychology in the United States. He received an M.D. degree from Harvard University but never practiced medicine. He made his career in academia, teaching at Harvard—first in physiology, then in philosophy, and finally in psychology. He described his views in the first modern psychology textbook, *The Principles of Psychology,* which was published in 1890. Though it is a century old, James's book is still considered by some to be the "single greatest

William James

John B. Watson

Functionalism The school of psychology that emphasizes the uses or functions of the mind rather than the elements of experience.

Habit A response to a stimulus that becomes automatic with repetition.

Behaviorism The school of psychology that defines psychology as the study of observable behavior and studies relationships between stimuli and responses.

work in American psychology" (Adelson, 1982, p. 52). In *Principles,* which became known to students as the "Jimmy," James argued that the stream of consciousness is fluid and continuous. His experiences with introspection assured him that experience cannot be broken down into units as readily as the structuralists maintained.

James was also one of the founders of the school of **functionalism,** which dealt with overt behavior as well as consciousness. The American philosopher and educator John Dewey (1842–1910) also contributed to functionalist thought. Functionalism addressed the ways in which experience permits us to function more adaptively in our environments, and it used behavioral observation in the laboratory to supplement introspection. The structuralists tended to ask, "What are the parts of psychological processes?" The functionalists tended to ask, "What are the purposes (functions) of overt behavior and mental processes? What difference do they make?"

Dewey and James were influenced by the English naturalist Charles Darwin's (1809–1882) theory of evolution. Earlier in the nineteenth century, Darwin had argued that organisms with adaptive features survive and reproduce, whereas those without such features are doomed to extinction. This doctrine is known as the "survival of the fittest." It suggests that as the generations pass, organisms whose behavior and physical traits (weight, speed, coloring, size, and so on) are best suited to their environments are most likely to survive until maturity and to transmit these traits to future generations.

Functionalists adapted Darwin's view to behavior and proposed that more adaptive behavior patterns are learned and maintained. Less adaptive behavior patterns tend to drop out, or to be discontinued. The "fittest" behavior patterns survive. Adaptive actions tend to be repeated and become **habits**. James wrote that "habit is the enormous flywheel of society." Habit maintains civilization from day to day.

The formation of habits is seen in acts such as lifting forks to our mouths and turning doorknobs. At first, these acts require full attention. If you are in doubt, stand by with paper towels and watch a baby's first efforts at self-feeding. Through repetition, the acts that make up self-feeding become automatic, or habitual. The multiple acts involved in learning to drive a car also become routine through repetition. We can then perform them without much attention, freeing ourselves to focus on other matters such as our clever conversation and the cultured sounds issuing from the radio. The idea of learning by repetition is also basic to the behavioral tradition.

Behaviorism

Think of placing a hungry rat in a maze. It meanders down a pathway that comes to an end. It can then turn left or right. If you consistently reward the rat with food for turning right at this choice-point, it will learn to turn right when it arrives there, at least when it is hungry. But what does the rat *think* when it is learning to turn right? "Hmm, last time I was in this situation and turned to the right, I was given some food. Think I'll try that again"?

Does it seem absurd to try to place yourself in the "mind" of a rat? So it seemed to John Broadus Watson (1878–1958), the founder of American **behaviorism**. But Watson was asked to consider just such a question as one of the requirements for his doctoral degree, which he received from the University of Chicago in 1903. Functionalism was abroad in the land and dominant at the University of Chicago, and functionalists were concerned with the stream of consciousness as well as observable behavior. Watson bridled at the introspective struggles of the functionalists to study consciousness, especially the consciousness of lower animals. He asserted that if psychology was to be a natural science, like physics or chemistry, it must limit itself to observable, measurable events—

that is, to behavior. It must not concern itself with "elements of consciousness" that are accessible only to the organism perceiving them.

Watson agreed with the functionalist focus on the importance of learning, however, and suggested that psychology address the learning of measurable **responses** to environmental **stimuli**. He pointed to the laboratory experiments being conducted by Ivan Pavlov in Russia as a model. Pavlov had found that dogs will learn to salivate when a bell is rung, if ringing the bell has been repeatedly associated with feeding. Pavlov explained the salivation in terms of the laboratory conditions, or **conditioning**, that led to it, not in terms of the imagined mental processes of the dogs. Moreover, the response that Pavlov chose to study, salivation, was a public event that could be measured by laboratory instruments. It was absurd to try to determine what a dog, or person, was thinking.

Watson went to Johns Hopkins University in 1908, where behaviorism took root and soon became firmly planted in American psychology. In 1920 Watson got a divorce so that he could marry a former student, and the scandal forced him to leave academic life. For a while Watson sold coffee and worked as a clerk in a department store. Then he undertook a second productive career in advertising, and he eventually became vice president of a New York agency.

Harvard University psychologist B. F. Skinner (1904–1990) took up the behaviorist call and introduced the concept of **reinforcement** to behaviorism. Organisms, Skinner maintained, learn to behave in certain ways because they have been reinforced for doing so. He demonstrated that laboratory animals will carry out various simple and complex behaviors because of reinforcement. They will peck buttons (Figure 1.2), turn in circles, climb ladders, and push toys across the floor. Many psychologists adopted the view that, in principle, one could explain intricate human behavior as the summation of instances of learning through reinforcement. Nevertheless, as a practical matter, they recognized that trying to account for all of a person's behaviors by enumerating her or his complete history of reinforcement would be a hopeless task.

Response A movement or other observable reaction to a stimulus.

Stimuli Plural of *stimulus.* (1) A feature in the environment that is detected by an organism or leads to a change in behavior (a response). (2) A form of physical energy such as light or sound that impinges on the sensory receptors.

Conditioning A simple form of learning in which stimuli come to signal other stimuli by means of association.

Reinforcement A stimulus that follows a response and increases the frequency of the response.

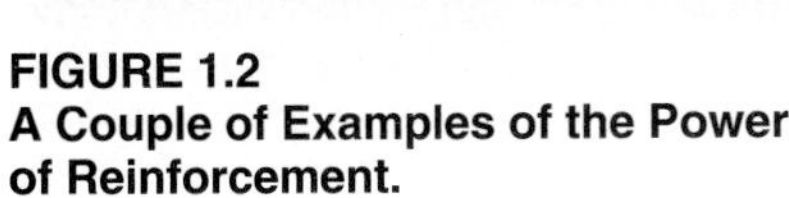

FIGURE 1.2
A Couple of Examples of the Power of Reinforcement.

In the photo on the left, we see how our feathered gift to city life has earned its keep in many behavioral experiments on the effects of reinforcement. Here, the pigeon pecks the blue button because pecking this button has been followed (reinforced) by the dropping of a food pellet into the cage. In the photo on the right, the raccoon shoots a basket. Behaviorists teach animals complex behaviors such as shooting baskets by first reinforcing approximations to the goal (or target behavior). As time progresses, closer approximations are demanded before reinforcement is given.

Max Wertheimer

Gestalt Psychology

In the 1920s, another school of psychology—**Gestalt psychology**—was quite prominent in Germany. In the 1930s, the three founders of the school—Max Wertheimer (1880–1943), Kurt Koffka (1886–1941), and Wolfgang Köhler (1887–1967)—left Europe to escape the Nazi threat. They carried on their work in the United States, giving further impetus to American ascendance in psychology.

Wertheimer and his colleagues focused on perception and on how perception influences thinking and problem-solving. In contrast to the behaviorists, Gestalt psychologists argued that one cannot hope to understand human nature by focusing on clusters of overt behavior alone. In contrast to the structuralists, they claimed that one cannot explain human perceptions, emotions, or thought processes in terms of basic units. Perceptions were *more* than the sums of their parts: Gestalt psychologists saw our perceptions as wholes that give meaning to parts.

Gestalt psychologists illustrated how we tend to perceive separate pieces of information as integrated wholes, including the contexts in which they occur. Consider Figure 1.3. The dots in the centers of the configurations at the left are the same size, yet we may perceive them as being of different sizes because of the contexts in which they appear. The inner squares in the center figure are equally bright, but they may look different because of their contrasting backgrounds. The second symbol in each line at the right is identical, but in the top row we may perceive it as a B and in the bottom row as the number 13. The symbol has not changed, only the context in which it appears. In *The Prince and the Pauper,* Mark Twain dressed a peasant boy as a prince, and the kingdom bowed to him. Do clothes sometimes make the man or woman?

Gestalt psychologists believed that learning could be active and purposeful, not merely responsive and mechanical as in Pavlov's experiments. Wolfgang Köhler and the others demonstrate that much learning, especially in learning to solve problems, is accomplished by **insight,** not by mechanical repetition. Köhler was marooned by World War I on one of the Canary Islands, where the Prussian Academy of Science kept a colony of apes, and his research on the island lent him, well, insight into the process of learning by insight.

Gestalt psychology The school of psychology that emphasizes the tendency to organize perceptions into wholes and to integrate separate stimuli into meaningful patterns.

Insight In Gestalt psychology, the sudden reorganization of perceptions, allowing the sudden solution of a problem.

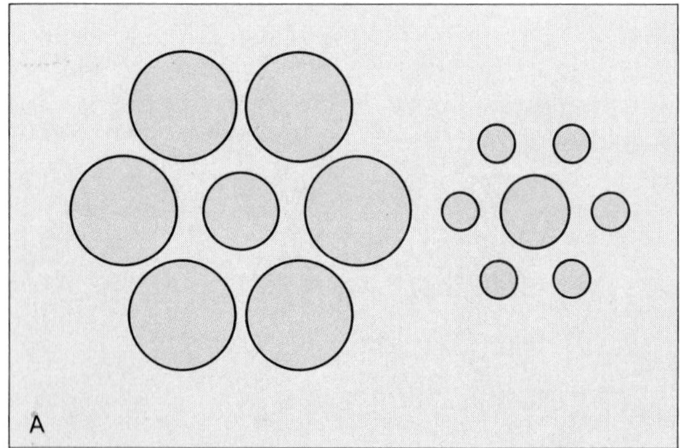

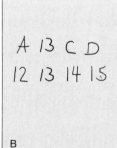

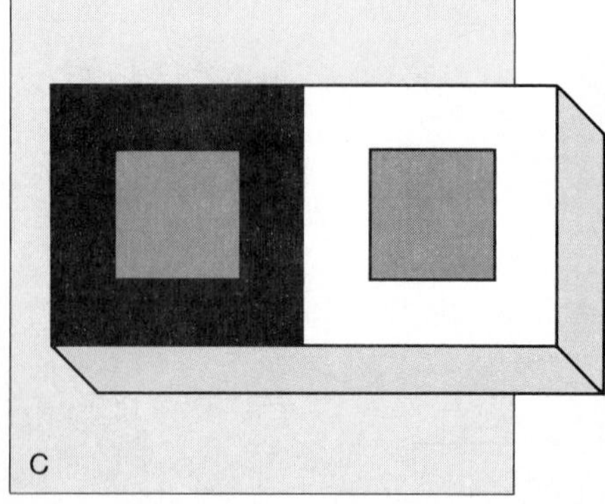

FIGURE 1.3
The Importance of Context.

(A) Are the dots in the center of the configuration the same size? Why not take a ruler and measure their diameters? (B) Is the second symbol in each line the letter B or the number 13? (C) Which of the gray squares is brighter? Gestalt psychologists have shown that our perceptions depend not only on our sensory impressions but also on the context of our impressions. They argue that human perception cannot be explained in terms of basic units because we tend to interpret our perceptions of things as wholes, in terms of the contexts in which they occur. You will interpret a man running toward you very differently depending on whether you are on a deserted street at night or at a track in the morning.

FIGURE 1.4
Some Insight into the Role of Insight.

At first, the chimpanzee cannot reach the bananas hanging from the ceiling. After some time has passed, it suddenly piles the boxes on top of one another to reach the fruit, behavior suggestive of a "flash of insight." Gestalt psychologists argue that behavior is often too complex to be explained in terms of learning mechanical responses to environmental stimulation.

Consider the chimpanzee in Figure 1.4. At first, the ape is unsuccessful in reaching for bananas suspended from the ceiling. Then it suddenly piles the boxes atop one another and climbs them to reach the bananas. It seems that the chimp has experienced a sudden reorganization of the mental elements that represent the problem—that is, it has had a "flash of insight." Köhler's findings suggest that we often manipulate the mentally represented elements of problems until we group them in such a way that we believe we will be able to reach a goal. The manipulations may take quite some time as mental trial and error proceeds. Once the proper grouping has been found, however, we seem to perceive it all at once.

Psychoanalysis The school of psychology that emphasizes the importance of unconscious motives and conflicts as determinants of human behavior.

Have you ever sat pondering a problem for quite a while and then, suddenly, the solution appeared? Did it seem to come out of nowhere? In a flash? Was it difficult at that point to understand how it could have taken so long?

Gestalt principles of perceptual organization will be discussed in Chapter 4, and learning by insight will be elaborated on in Chapter 6.

Sigmund Freud

Psychoanalysis

Psychoanalysis, the school of psychology founded by Sigmund Freud, is very different from the other schools in its background and approach. Freud's theory, more than the others, has invaded the popular culture, and you may already be familiar with a number of its concepts. For example, an emotionally unstable person is likely to go on a killing spree on at least one television crime show each season. At the show's conclusion, a psychiatrist typically explains that the killer was "unconsciously" doing away with his own mother or father. Or perhaps a friend has tried to "interpret" a slip of the tongue you made or has asked you what you thought might be the symbolic meaning of a dream.

The notions that people are driven by deeply hidden impulses and that verbal slips and dreams represent unconscious wishes largely reflect the influence of

Sigmund Freud (1856–1939), a Viennese physician who fled to England in the 1930s to escape the Nazi tyranny. In contrast to the academic psychologists, who conducted research mainly in the laboratory, Freud gained his understanding of human thoughts, emotions, and behavior through clinical interviews with patients. He was astounded at how little insight his patients seemed to have into their motives. Some patients justified, or rationalized, the most abominable behavior with absurd explanations. Others, in contrast, seized the opportunity to blame themselves for nearly every misfortune that had befallen the human species.

Freud came to believe that unconscious processes, especially primitive sexual and aggressive impulses, were more influential than conscious thought in determining human behavior. Freud thought that most of the mind was unconscious, consisting of a seething cauldron of conflicting impulses, urges, and wishes. People were motivated to gratify these impulses, ugly as some of them were, but at the same time, people were motivated to judge themselves as being decent. Thus, they would often delude themselves about their real motives. Because of the assumed motion of underlying forces in personality, Freud's theory is referred to as **psychodynamic.**

Freud devised a method of psychotherapy called psychoanalysis. Psychoanalysis aims to help patients gain insight into many of their deep-seated conflicts and find socially acceptable ways of expressing wishes and gratifying needs. Psychoanalytic therapy is a process that can extend for years. We describe psychoanalysis at length (but not for years) in Chapter 14.

Now let's turn to the "top ten"—psychology's golden oldies. Table 1.2 ranks the top ten ("most important") historic figures in psychology according to historians of psychology and chairpersons of psychology departments (Korn et al., 1991). The historians and chairpersons concur on seven of their top ten. (We shall have more to say about the people who populate this table in our discussion of human diversity and psychology.)

Today we no longer find psychologists who describe themselves as structuralists or functionalists. Although the school of Gestalt psychology gave birth to current research approaches in perception and problem-solving, few would consider themselves Gestalt psychologists. The numbers of orthodox behaviorists and psychoanalysts have also been declining. Many contemporary psychologists in the behaviorist tradition look on themselves as social-learning theorists, and many psychoanalysts consider themselves neoanalysts rather than traditional Freudians. Still, the historical traditions of psychology find expression in many contemporary fields and schools of psychology.

Psychodynamic Referring to Freud's theory, which proposes that the motion of underlying forces of personality determines our thoughts, feelings, and behavior. (From the Greek *dynamis,* meaning "power.")

Hormone A chemical substance that promotes development of body structures and regulates various body functions.

Genes The basic building blocks of heredity.

TABLE 1.2: Historians' and Chairpersons' Rankings of the Importance of Figures in the History of Psychology

Historians			Chairpersons		
Rank	**Figure**	**Area of Contribution**	**Rank**	**Figure**	**Area of Contribution**
1.	Wilhelm Wundt	Structuralism	1.	B. F. Skinner	Operant Conditioning
2.	William James	Functionalism	2.	Sigmund Freud	Psychoanalysis
3.	Sigmund Freud	Psychoanalysis	3.	William James	Functionalism
4.	John B. Watson	Behaviorism	4.	Jean Piaget	Cognitive Development
5.	Ivan Pavlov	Conditioning	5.	G. Stanley Hall	Development
6.	Hermann Ebbinghaus	Memory	6.	Wilhelm Wundt	Structuralism
7.	Jean Piaget	Cognitive Development	7.	Carl Rogers	Self Theory, Person-Centered Therapy
8.	B. F. Skinner	Operant Conditioning	8.	John B. Watson	Behaviorism
9.	Alfred Binet	Assessment of Intelligence	9.	Ivan Pavlov	Conditioning
10.	Gustav Theodor Fechner	Psychophysics	10.	Edward L. Thorndike	Learning—Law of Effect

Rankings based on data from Korn, J. H., Davis, R., & Davis, S. F. (1991). Historians' and chairpersons' judgments of eminence among psychologists. *American Psychologist, 46,* 789–792.

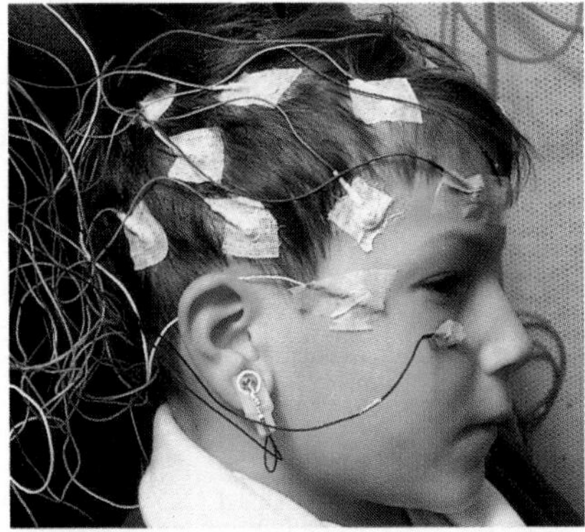

A

B

The Biological Perspective. Psychologists with a biological perspective investigate the connections between biological processes, overt behavior, and mental processes. They may use methods such as Brain Electrical Activity Mapping (BEAM), in which electrodes measure the electrical activity of parts of the brain while subjects are exposed to various stimuli (A). The left-hand column of B shows the average level of electrical activity of the brains of 10 normal people at four time intervals. The right-hand column shows the average activity of 10 schizophrenic people. (Schizophrenia is a severe psychological disorder.) The more intense the activity, the brighter the color (white is most intense). The bottom diagram summarizes similarities and differences between normal people and schizophrenics: areas in blue reflect smaller differences; white areas, larger differences.

HOW TODAY'S PSYCHOLOGISTS VIEW BEHAVIOR

First a new theory is attacked as absurd; then it is admitted to be true, but obvious and insignificant; finally it is seen to be so important that its adversaries claim that they themselves discovered it.

William James

The history of psychological thought has taken many turns, and contemporary psychologists also differ in their approaches. Today, there are five broad, influential perspectives in psychology: the biological, cognitive, humanistic–existential, psychodynamic, and learning perspectives. Each perspective emphasizes different topics of investigation, and each tends to approach its topics in its own ways.

The Biological Perspective

Psychologists assume that our thoughts, fantasies, dreams, and mental images are made possible by the nervous system and especially by that pivotal part of the nervous system, the brain. Biologically oriented psychologists seek the links between events in the brain—such as the activity of brain cells—and mental processes. They use techniques such as CAT scans, PET scans, and electrical stimulation of sites in the brain to show that these sites are involved in intellectual activity and emotional and behavioral responses (see Chapter 3). Through biological psychology, we have discovered parts of the brain that are highly active when we listen to music, solve math problems, or suffer from certain mental disorders. We have learned how the production of chemical substances in certain parts of the brain is essential to the storage of information—that is, the formation of memories. Among some lower animals, electrical stimulation of parts of the brain prompts the expression of innate, or built-in, sexual and aggressive behaviors.

Biological psychologists are also concerned about the influences of hormones and genes. For instance, in humans, the **hormone** prolactin stimulates production of milk; but in rats, prolactin also sparks maternal behavior. In lower animals and people, sex hormones stimulate development of the sex organs. In some lower animals, they also determine whether mating behavior will follow stereotypical masculine or feminine behavior patterns. In people, hormones seem to play a subtler role.

Genes are the basic units of heredity. Psychologists are vitally interested in the extent of genetic influences on human traits such as intelligence, abnormal behaviors, criminal behaviors, and even the tendency to become addicted to substances such as alcohol and narcotics. Identical twins (who share the same genetic endowment) are more likely than fraternal twins (who are no more closely related than other brothers and sisters) to share such broad personality traits as sociability, emotionality, and level of activity (see Chapter 3). In Chapter 8 we shall see that the degree to which intelligence reflects heredity (nature) or environmental influences (nurture) is a hotly debated issue, with political implications.

The Cognitive Perspective

In man there is nothing great but mind.

Sir William Hamilton, *Lecture on Metaphysics*

Psychologists with a cognitive perspective focus on our mental processes. They investigate the ways in which we perceive and mentally represent the world, how we go about solving problems, how we dream and daydream. Cognitive psychologists, in short, attempt to study those things we refer to as the *mind*.

The cognitive tradition has roots in Socrates' advice "Know thyself" and in Socrates' suggested method of looking inward (introspection) to find truth. We also find cognitive psychology's roots in structuralism, functionalism, and Gestalt psychology, each of which, in its own way, addressed issues of interest to cognitive psychologists.

Cognitive-Developmental Theory. Today, the cognitive perspective has many faces. One is the cognitive-developmental theory advanced by the Swiss biologist Jean Piaget (1896–1980). Piaget's innovative study of the intellectual or cognitive development of children has inspired thousands of research projects by developmental and educational psychologists. The focus of this research is to learn how children and adults mentally represent and reason about the world.

According to Piaget and his intellectual descendants, the child's conception of the world grows more sophisticated as the child matures (see Chapter 10). Although experience is essential to children, their perception and understanding of the world unfolds as if guided by an inner clock.

Information Processing. Another face of the cognitive perspective is information processing. Psychological thought has been influenced by the status of the physical sciences of the day. For example, Freud's psychodynamic theory was related to the development of thermodynamics in the last century. Many of today's cognitive psychologists have been influenced by concepts of computer science. Computers process information to solve problems. Information is first fed into the computer (encoded so that it can be accepted by the computer as input). Then it is placed in *memory*—or working memory—while it is manipulated. You can also store the information more permanently in *storage*—on a floppy disk, a hard disk, or another device. In Chapter 7, we shall see that many psychologists also speak of people as having working memories (short-term memories) and storage (long-term memories). If information has been placed in storage (or in long-term memory), it must be retrieved before we can work on it again. To retrieve information from computer storage, we must know the code or name for the data file and the rules for retrieving data files. Similarly, note psychologists, we must have appropriate cues to retrieve information from our own long-term memories, or else the information is lost to us. The data in a computer's storage is usually retrieved in a more exact state than human memories. Our memories tend to be colored by our biases and our expectations.

Many cognitive psychologists thus focus on information processing in people—the processes by which information is encoded (input), stored (in long-term memory), retrieved (placed in working memory), and manipulated to solve problems (output). Our strategies for solving problems are sometimes referred to as our "mental programs" or "software." In this computer metaphor, our brains are translated into the "hardware" that runs our mental programs. Our brains, that is, become *very* personal computers.

It is true that some psychologists see our strategies for solving problems as "mental programs" that are operated by our "personal computers," or brains. They are cognitive psychologists, who investigate the ways in which we process information.

Psychologists in the behaviorist tradition argue that cognitions are not directly observable and that cognitive psychologists do not place adequate emphasis on the situational determinants of behavior. Cognitive psychologists counter that human behavior cannot be understood without reference to cognition.

The Humanistic–Existential Perspective

The humanistic–existential perspective is related to Gestalt psychology and is cognitive in flavor. **Humanism** stresses the human capacity for self-fulfillment and the central roles of human consciousness, self-awareness, and the capacity to make choices. Consciousness is seen as the force that unifies our personalities. **Existentialism** views people as free to choose and responsible for choosing ethical conduct.

Humanistic psychology considers subjective or personal experience to be the most important event in psychology. Humanists believe that self-awareness, experience, and choice permit us, to a large extent, to "invent ourselves"—to fashion our growth and our ways of relating to the world—as we progress through life.

There is a debate in psychology about whether we are free to choose or whether our behavior is determined by external factors. John Watson's behaviorism was a deterministic stance that assumed that our behavior reflected the summation of the effects of the stimuli impinging upon us. The humanistic–existential approach of American psychologists such as Carl Rogers (1902–1987), Rollo May (born 1909), and Abraham Maslow (1916–1972) asserts that we are basically free to determine our own behavior. Humanistic–existential psychologists suggest that we are engaged in quests to discover our personal identities and the meanings of our lives.

The goals of humanistic–existential psychology have been more applied than academic. Humanistic–existential psychologists have devised ways to help people "get in touch" with their feelings and realize their potentials, for example. Humanistic–existential psychology reached the peak of its popularity in the 1970s with encounter groups, gestalt therapy, meditation, and a number of other methods that have been stamped collectively as the Human Potential Movement.

Critics, including those in the behaviorist tradition, insist that psychology must be a natural science and address itself to observable events. They argue that our experiences are subjective events that are poorly suited to objective observation and measurement. Humanistic–existential psychologists such as Carl Rogers (1985) may agree that the observation methods of humanists have sometimes been less than scientific. They argue, however, that subjective human experience remains vital to the understanding of human nature. Rogers would have us improve the research methods used to study humanistic–existential concepts rather than remove them from serious scientific consideration.

The Psychodynamic Perspective

In the 1940s and 1950s, psychodynamic theory dominated the practice of psychotherapy and was also widely influential in scientific psychology and the arts. Most psychotherapists were psychodynamically oriented, and many renowned artists and writers sought ways to liberate the expression of their unconscious ideas. "Automatic painting" and "automatic writing" were major movements in the humanities.

Today, the influence of psychoanalytic thought continues to be felt, although it no longer dominates psychology, and its influence has apparently subsided in the humanities as well. Psychologists who follow Freud today are likely to consider themselves to be **neoanalysts**. Neoanalysts such as Karen Horney, Erich Fromm, and Erik Erikson tend to focus less on the roles of unconscious sexual and aggressive impulses in human behavior and more on deliberate choice and self-direction.

Many Freudian ideas are retained in sort of watered-down form by the population at large. Sometimes we have ideas or inclinations that seem foreign to us. We may say, in the vernacular, that it seems as if something is trying to get the better

Humanism The philosophy and school of psychology that asserts that people are conscious, self-aware, and capable of free choice, self-fulfillment, and ethical behavior.

Existentialism The view that people are completely free and responsible for their own behavior.

Neoanalysts Contemporary followers of Freud who focus less on the roles of unconscious impulses and more on conscious choice and self-direction.

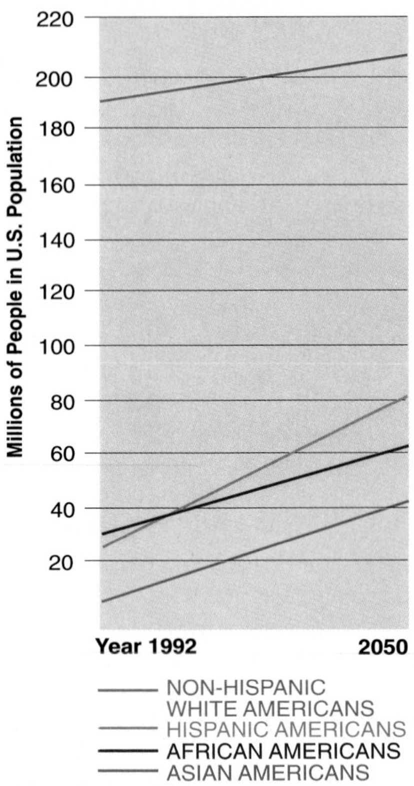

FIGURE 1.5
Projected Growth of Ethnic Groups in the United States, 1992-2050. Although non-Hispanic white Americans are more numerous than the other ethnic groups within the United States that are shown in this figure, their growth rate is projected to be lower.

of us. In the Middle Ages, such thoughts and impulses were usually magically attributed to the Devil or an agent of his. Dreams, likewise, were thought to enter us magically from the spirit world beyond. Today, largely because of Sigmund Freud, many people ascribe uncharacteristic or "improper" ideas and dreams to "unconscious processes" that are assumed to reside deep within. Although people may still consider the wellsprings of the ideas and dreams to be inaccessible, at least their existence and expression is not so likely to be viewed as magical.

Research and philosophical analysis has been somewhat hard on some of the theoretical aspects of the psychodynamic perspective. Many psychoanalytic concepts cannot be confirmed by scientific means (see Chapter 11). On the other hand, the reviews of psychoanalytic forms of psychotherapy have been generally positive (see Chapter 14).

Learning Perspectives

Many psychologists today study the effects of experience on behavior. Learning, to them, is the essential factor in describing, explaining, predicting, and controlling behavior. The term *learning* has different meanings to psychologists of different persuasions, however. Some students of learning find roles for consciousness and insight. Others do not. This distinction is found among those who adhere to the behavioral and social-learning perspectives.

The Behavioral Perspective. For John B. Watson, behaviorism was an approach to life as well as a broad guideline for psychological research. Not only did Watson despair of measuring consciousness and mental processes in the laboratory, he also applied behavioral analysis to virtually all situations in his daily life. He viewed people as doing things because of their learning histories, situational influences, and the rewards involved rather than because of conscious choice.

Learning, for Watson and his followers, is exemplified by experiments in conditioning. The results of conditioning are explained in terms of external laboratory procedures, not in terms of changes that have occurred within the organism. Behaviorists do not attempt to find out what an organism has come to "know" through learning. Cognitive psychologists, in contrast, view conditioning as a process that alters the organism's mental representation of the environment—one that may encourage but does not compel changes in behavior (Rescorla, 1988).

The Social-Learning Perspective. Since the early 1960s, **social-learning theorists** have gained influence in the areas of personality development, abnormal behavior, and methods of therapy. Theorists such as Albert Bandura, Julian Rotter, and Walter Mischel see themselves as being within the behaviorist tradition because of their focus on the role of learning in human behavior. Yet they also return to their functionalist roots by theorizing a key role for cognition. Behaviorists emphasize the importance of environmental influences and focus on the learning of habits through repetition and reinforcement. Social-learning theorists, in contrast, suggest that people can modify or create their environments. People also engage in intentional learning by observing others. Through observational learning, we acquire a storehouse of responses to life's situations. Social-learning theorists are also humanistic in that they believe that our expectations and values help determine whether we shall *choose* to do what we have learned how to do.

Let us now consider two ways in which higher education is a broadening experience—by exposing us to human diversity and by fostering critical thinking.

Social-learning theory A school of psychology in the behaviorist tradition that includes cognitive factors in the explanation and prediction of behavior.

HUMAN DIVERSITY AND PSYCHOLOGY

The profession of psychology focuses mainly on individual people and is committed to the dignity of the individual. We cannot understand individuals without an awareness of the richness of human diversity, however (Bronstein & Quina, 1988; Goodchilds, 1991). People diverge, or differ, from one another in many ways.

Ethnic Diversity

The nation and the world at large contain more kinds of people and more ways of doing and viewing things than most of us might imagine. One kind of diversity involves people's **ethnic groups,** which tend to unite them according to features such as their cultural heritage, their race, their language, and their common history. One reason for studying ethnic diversity is the changing ethnic makeup of the United States.

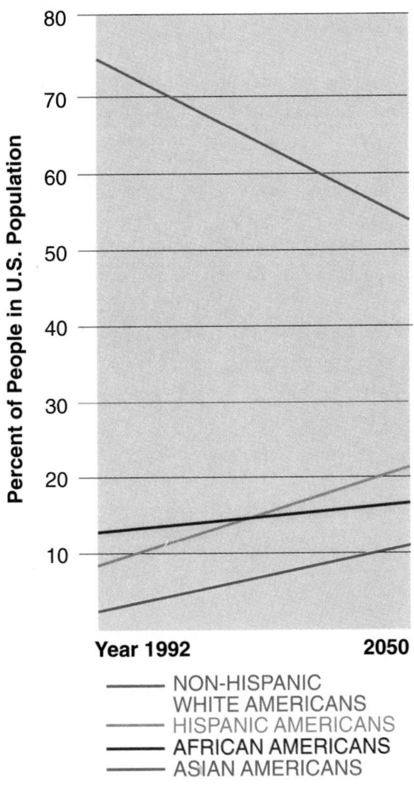

FIGURE 1.6
Changes in the Ethnic Makeup of the United States, According to the Numbers of Each Ethnic Group as a Percentage of the Overall Population, 1992–2050. Although the numbers of non-Hispanic white Americans will increase between 1992 and 2050, trends in reproduction and immigration suggest that non-Hispanic white Americans will make up a much smaller percentage of the overall U.S. population by the year 2050. Asian Americans are currently the most rapidly growing ethnic group in the United States.

Figures 1.5 and 1.6 highlight the dramatic changes under way in the United States due to reproductive patterns and immigration. The U.S. Bureau of the Census projects, for example, that the nation's non-Hispanic white population will increase from 191 million in 1992 to 202 million in the year 2050, an increase of 11 million people (*The Outlook,* 1993; see Figure 1.5). Because, however, the populations of other ethnic groups in the United States are projected to increase relatively more rapidly, the *percentage* of non-Hispanic white Americans in the total population will *decrease* from 74–75 percent in 1992 to 53 percent in 2050 (see Figure 1.6). The fastest growing ethnic group consists of Asians and Pacific Islanders (to whom we refer as Asian Americans). In 1992 there were 9 million Asian Americans in the United States, and they are expected to increase to 41 million by 2050 (Figure 1.5), rising from 3 percent to 11 percent of the U.S. population (Figure 1.6). As shown in Figures 1.5 and 1.6, the numbers of African Americans and Hispanic Americans (who may be white, Black, or Native American Indian in racial origin) are also growing more rapidly than those of non-Hispanic white Americans. The African-American population is expected to grow from 32 million people (12% of the current population) in 1992 to 62 million people (16%) by the year 2050. The Hispanic-American population is expected to increase from 24 million people (9% of the current population) to 81 million people (21% of the projected overall population) by the year 2050. The cultural heritages, languages, and histories of ethnic minority groups are thus likely to have increasing impacts on the cultural life of the United States.

Figure 1.7 reveals the ethnic diversity to be found in the United States' college population. The non-Hispanic white majority accounts for fewer than 80 percent of the nation's more than 13 million college students overall. As noted in the *Chronicle of Higher Education* (1992), the percentage of Asian Americans increased by 67 percent between 1980 and 1990 (from 2.4% to 4.0%), and the percentage of Hispanic Americans increased by nearly 40 percent (from 3.9% to 5.5%). The percentages of African Americans (8.9% versus 9.2%) and Native Americans (0.8% versus 0.7%) remained relatively stable, and the percentage of non-Hispanic white Americans declined (to 77.9% from 81.3%).

Actually, the number of only Asian Americans and Hispanic Americans have increased dramatically on U.S. college campuses over the past decade. The numbers of African Americans and Native Americans have remained relatively stable.

Ethnic group A group characterized by common features such as cultural heritage, history, race, and language.

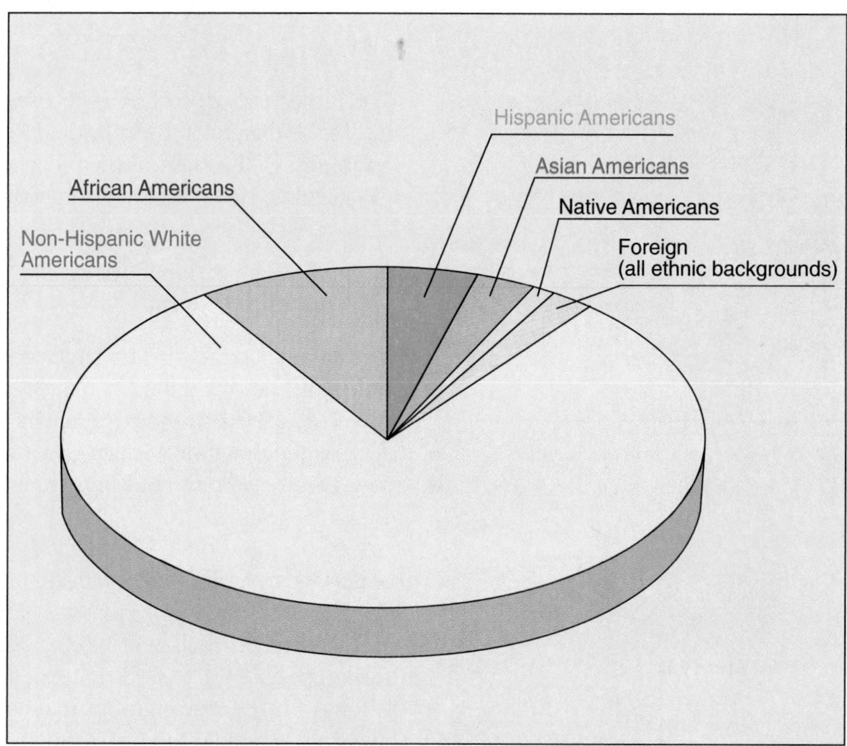

FIGURE 1.7
Ethnic Diversity in the U.S. College Population. About 78 percent of the nation's more than 13 million post-secondary students consist of non-Hispanic white Americans. The percentages of Hispanic Americans and Asian Americans in higher education have been increasing rapidly in recent years. Source of data: *The Chronicle of Higher Education*, March 18, 1992, p. A35.

Another reason for studying human diversity is to enable students to appreciate the cultural heritages and historical problems of various ethnic groups. Too often throughout our history, the traditions, languages, and achievements of ethnic minority groups have been judged by majority standards or denigrated (Jones, 1991; Sue, 1991). Consider two issues that we address in Chapter 8: Black English and bilingualism. Black English has been erroneously considered inferior to standard English, and bilingualism has been erroneously deemed to be inferior to being reared to speak English only. Psychological investigation of these issues debunks these myths.

Still another reason for studying diversity concerns psychological intervention and consultation. Psychologists are called upon to help people of all ethnic groups solve personal problems, for example. How can psychologists hope to understand the aspirations and problems of individuals from an ethnic group without understanding the history and cultural heritage of that group (Jones, 1991; Nevid, Rathus, & Greene, 1994; Sue, 1991)? How can psychologists understand African Americans or Hispanic Americans, for example, without sensitivity to the histories of prejudice to which members of these ethnic groups have been exposed? Moreover, should psychologists from the white majority attempt to practice psychotherapy with people from ethnic minority groups? If so, what kinds of special education or training might they need to do so? What is meant by "culturally sensitive" forms of psychotherapy? We deal with issues such as these in Chapters 12, 13, and 14.

Throughout the text we will consider many issues that address ethnic minority groups and psychology. Just a handful include:

- The representation of ethnic minority groups in psychological research studies
- Ethnicity and substance abuse among adolescents
- The influence of ethnic stereotypes on our perceptions and memories
- Black English

- Bilingualism
- Ethnic differences in intelligence test scores—their implications and possible origins
- Ethnic differences in vulnerability to various physical problems and disorders, ranging from obesity to hypertension and cancer
- Ethnic differences in prenatal care
- Ethnic differences in the utilization of health care for physical and psychological problems
- Differential patterns of diagnosis of psychological problems (mental disorders) among various ethnic groups
- The prevalence of suicide among members of different ethnic minority groups
- Considerations in the practice of psychotherapy with clients from different ethnic groups
- Machismo/Marianismo stereotypes and Hispanic culture
- Interracial dating and marital relationships
- Prejudice

Gender

Another way in which people differ concerns their **gender**—that is, the state of being male or being female. Gender is not simply a matter of anatomic sex; it involves a complex web of cultural expectations and social roles that affect people's self-concepts and hopes and dreams as well as their overt behavior. How can sciences such as psychology and medicine hope to understand the particular viewpoints, qualities, and problems of women if most research is conducted with men and by men?

Just as there have been historic prejudices against members of ethnic minority groups, so too have there been prejudices against women. The careers of women have been traditionally channeled into domestic chores, regardless of their wishes as individuals. Not until relatively modern times were women generally considered suitable for higher education (and women are still considered unsuited to education in many parts of the world!) Women have attended college in the United States only since 1833, when Oberlin opened its doors to women. Today, however, more than half (54½%) of U.S. post-secondary students are women. As noted in Figure 1.8, African Americans and Native Americans contributed relatively higher percentages of women.

It is true that women were not permitted to attend college in the United States until 1833, when Oberlin began to accept women students.

Contemporary women today are also making inroads into academic and vocational spheres such as medicine, law, and engineering that were traditionally male preserves. Women now make up about 40 percent of U.S. medical students, for example, although fewer women physicians are currently in practice. Women make up about 40 percent of Harvard Law School's students and about 40 percent of new associates in the 250 largest U.S. legal firms. Because women have only recently increased their numbers in the legal profession, their numbers are lower among lawyers in practice today (Goldstein, 1988). Women now make up nearly

Gender The state of being female or being male.

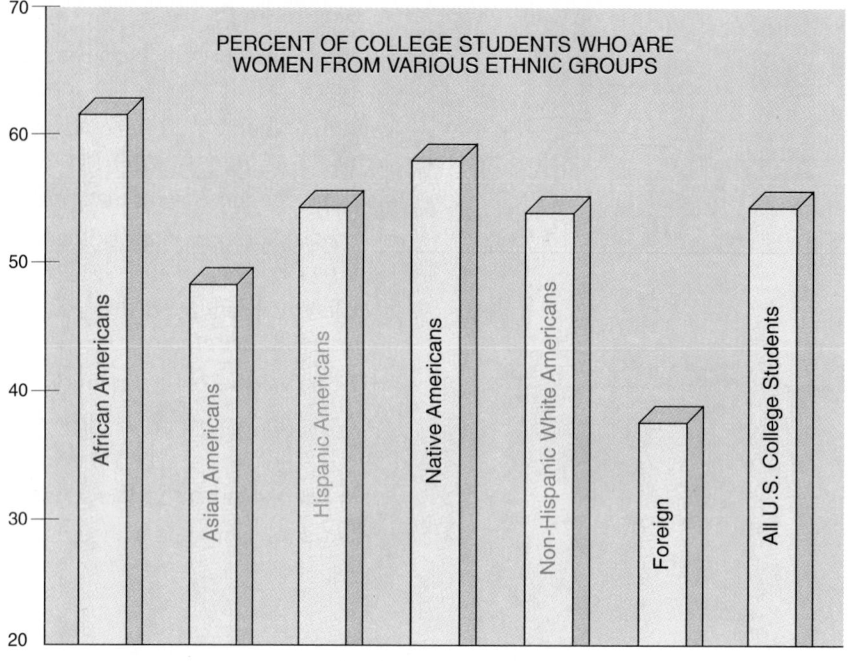

FIGURE 1.8
The Percentages of Women Post-secondary Students in the United States, According to Ethnic Group. Note that the percentages of African-American and Native-American women among postsecondary students are relatively high, whereas the percentages of Asian-American and foreign women are relatively low. Why do you think this is so? Source of data: *The Chronicle of Higher Education*, March 18, 1992, p. A35.

15 percent of engineering graduates. Although this figure is relatively low, history provides some perspective. Only 20 years ago, women accounted for some 4 percent of engineering graduates (Adelson, 1988; Morrison & Von Glinow, 1990)! Obvious trends are in place—and overdue.

Others Kinds of Diversity

Human diversity also touches upon differences in age, physical ability, and sexual orientation. The elderly, the differently abled, and gay males and lesbians have all suffered from discrimination, and the mainstream culture has from time to time been loath to consider and profit from the particular sensitivities and perspectives afforded by individuals from each of these groups.

Our focus on human diversity throughout the text will help us to better understand and fully appreciate the true extent of human behavior and mental processes. This broader view of psychology—and the world—is enriching for its own sake and heightens the accuracy and scope of our presentation.

The Diversity of People Who Have Contributed to the Development of Psychology

Now let us return to psychology's "golden oldies," as listed in Table 1.2 on page 16. Did you notice something they have in common? They are all white males. Critics assert that such lists create the erroneous impression that women and people of color have not made major contributions to the history of psychology (Russo, 1990a; Guthrie, 1990).

Consider some of the women. Christine Ladd-Franklin was born in 1847, during an era in American history during which women were expected to remain in the home and were excluded from careers in science (Furumoto, 1992). She nevertheless pursued a career in psychology, taught at Johns Hopkins and Columbia Universities, and formulated a theory of color vision. Mary Whiton Calkins (born in 1863), a student of William James, pioneered research in memory. She introduced the method of paired associates and discovered the primacy and recency effects (see Chapter 7) (Madigan & Ohara, 1992). She was also the first woman

Human Diversity. How can psychologists comprehend the aspirations and problems of individuals from an ethnic group without understanding the history and cultural heritage of that group? Not only does the study of human diversity help us to understand and appreciate the true scope of human behavior and mental processes, it is enriching for its own sake.

Margaret Floy Washburn

Kenneth B. Clark

president of the American Psychological Association in 1905. Margaret Floy Washburn (born in 1871) was the first woman to receive a PhD in psychology. Washburn also wrote *The Animal Mind,* a work that presaged behaviorism.

Then there are psychologists of different ethnic backgrounds. Back in 1901, African-American Gilbert Haven Jones received his PhD in psychology in Germany. J. Henry Alston engaged in research in the perception of heat and cold and was the first African-American psychologist to be published in a key psychology journal (the year was 1920). A more contemporary African-American psychologist, Kenneth B. Clark, studied ethnicity and influenced a key Supreme Court decision on desegregation (Korn et al., 1991).

Hispanic-American and Asian-American psychologists have also made their mark. Jorge Sanchez, for example, was among the first to show how intelligence tests are culturally biased—to the detriment of Mexican-American children. Asian-American psychologist Stanley Sue (see Chapter 8) has engaged in prominent research in racial differences in intelligence and academic achievement and has discussed these differences in terms of adaptation to discrimination, among other factors.

True—psychology was once the province of white males. Today, however, more than half (53%) of the PhDs in psychology are awarded to women (Women's Programs Office, 1988). African-Americans and Hispanic-Americans each receive only 3 percent of the PhDs awarded in psychology (Jones, 1991), however. This percentage is far below their representation in the general population, unfortunately. Even so, fewer than two psychology PhDs in five are now received by white males. Psychology, like the world in which it is housed, is showing diversification.

Women actually receive the majority of PhD's in psychology today.

Put it another way: psychology is for everyone.

By challenging our sometimes narrow views of the world, the study of human diversity is also used by many post-secondary institutions as one pathway toward encouraging critical thinking (Celis, 1993).

CRITICAL THINKING AND PSYCHOLOGY

The object of education is to prepare the young to educate themselves throughout their lives.

Robert M. Hutchins

A great many people think they are thinking when they are merely rearranging their prejudices.

William James

Higher education is a broadening experience not only because of exposure to intellectual disciplines and human diversity, but also because it encourages students to learn to think critically. By thinking critically, people can challenge widely accepted but erroneous beliefs, including some of their own most cherished beliefs. **Critical thinking** helps make us into active, astute judges of other people and their points of view, rather than passive recipients of the latest intellectual fads and tyrannies.

Critical thinking fosters skepticism so that we no longer so readily take certain "truths" for granted. Consider the widespread assumptions that authority figures like doctors and government leaders usually provide us with factual information and are generally best equipped to make the decisions that affect our lives. But when doctors disagree as to whether or not surgery is necessary to cure a health problem, how can they all be correct? When political leaders who all claim to have the "best interests" of the nation at heart fling accusations and epithets at one another, how can we know whom to trust? If we are to be conscious, productive citizens of the nation, and of the world, we need to learn to seek pertinent information to make our own decisions and to rely on our analytical abilities to judge the accuracy of this information. This textbook will help you learn to seek and analyze information that lies within the province of psychology, but the critical thinking skills you acquire will be broadly applicable in all of your courses and all of your adult undertakings.

Critical thinking helps students to evaluate other people's claims and arguments, and to reconsider and, when necessary, dispute widely held beliefs. Critical thinking has many meanings. On one level, critical thinking means taking nothing for granted. It means not believing things just because they are in print or because they were uttered by authority figures or celebrities. On another level, critical thinking refers to a process of thoughtfully analyzing and probing the questions, statements, and arguments of others. It means examining the definitions of terms, examining the premises or assumptions behind arguments, and scrutinizing the logic with which arguments are developed.

Goals for an Undergraduate Education in Psychology

Psychologists have been working with the Association of American Colleges to establish goals and guidelines for undergraduate education. One psychology task force listed several goals for undergraduate education in psychology (McGovern, 1989). The first was to foster a knowledge base consisting of important psychological theories, research findings, and issues. This goal seems obvious enough.

Critical thinking An approach to thinking characterized by skepticism and thoughtful analysis of statements and arguments—for example, probing arguments' premises and the definitions of terms.

Critical Thinking. Critical thinking means taking nothing for granted and refers to a process of thoughtfully analyzing and probing the questions, statements, and arguments of others. It means examining the definitions of terms, examining the premises or assumptions behind arguments, and scrutinizing the logic with which arguments are developed. Critical thinking skills provide the keys not only to a college education, but to a lifetime of self-education.

But the second goal was to promote skills in critical thinking and reasoning. These thinking skills involve:

- Development of skepticism about explanations and conclusions
- The ability to inquire about causes and effects
- Refinement of curiosity about behavior
- Knowledge of research methods
- The ability to critically analyze arguments

The emphasis on critical thinking reflects the widespread belief that your college education is intended to do more than provide you with a data bank of useful knowledge. It is also meant to supply intellectual tools that allow you to analyze information independently. With these tools, you can continue to educate yourself for the rest of your life.

Principles of Critical Thinking

Many of the Truth-or-Fiction? items presented in this textbook are intended to encourage you to apply principles of critical thinking to the subject matter of psychology. Some of them reflect "truisms," or beliefs that are often taken for granted within our culture. Consider a sampling of Truth-or-Fiction? items from several chapters:

- Alcohol causes aggression.
- Messages travel in the brain by means of electricity.
- Onions and apples have the same taste.
- We tend to act out our forbidden fantasies in our dreams.
- We must make mistakes in order to learn.
- Some people have photographic memories.
- The best way to solve a frustrating problem is to keep plugging away at it.
- Head Start programs have raised children's IQs.
- Misery loves company.
- Most elderly people are dissatisfied with their lives.
- Too much of a good thing can make you ill.
- You can never be too rich or too thin.
- People who threaten suicide are only seeking attention.
- Drugs are never of help in treating people with abnormal behavior.
- We value things more when we have to work for them.
- Beauty is in the eye of the beholder.

You will have the opportunity to agree or disagree with these items in the following chapters. We will refer to a number of them as we elaborate the principles of critical thinking, however. We won't give you the answers to the items—not yet—but we will certainly provide hints, and we will illustrate some principles of critical thinking as we whet your appetite for psychology:

1. *Be skeptical.* Politicians and advertisers strive to convince you of their points of view. Even research reported in the media or in textbooks may take a certain slant. Have the attitude that you will accept nothing as true until you have personally examined the evidence. It is also desirable, however, to extend this principle to yourself.

   After all, you might just discover that some of your own attitudes and beliefs are superficial or unfounded if you examine them critically.

2. *Examine definitions of terms.* Some statements are true when a term is defined in one way but not another. Consider the statement "Head Start programs have raised children's IQs." Although I won't drop the answer in your lap, I'll tell you that the correctness of the statement depends on the definition of "IQ." (In Chapter 8, you will see that the term *IQ* has a specific meaning and that it is not synonymous with *intelligence.*)

   One of the strengths of psychology is the use of *operational definitions* of concepts. Operational definitions are framed in terms of the ways in which we measure concepts. In interpreting research, pay attention to how the concepts are defined. The truth of the following statement also rests on the definitions of terms: "Onions and apples have the same taste." What, in other words, does *taste* mean? Also consider the widely heard "Beauty is in the eye of the beholder." What does *in the eye of* mean? What of the statement that "Some people have photographic memories"? What is a *photographic memory*? (Turn to Chapter 7 to find out.)

3. *Examine the assumptions or premises of arguments.* Consider the controversial abortion issue and the statement that "Abortion is murder." Murder is a legal term that my dictionary defines as "the unlawful and malicious or premeditated killing of one human being by another." If one accepts this definition of murder as one's premise, then abortion is murder only when several conditions are met: when the embryo or fetus is a "human being," when the act of abortion is unlawful, and when the abortion is malicious (having evil intention) or premeditated (planned). Legally speaking, then, would abortion fit the definition of murder under circumstances in which it is lawful? The question as to whether or not an embryo or fetus is a human being, or exactly when an embryo or fetus becomes a human being or a human life, also sparks considerable controversy, of course.

   Also consider the statement "You cannot learn about human beings by engaging in research with animals." One premise in the statement seems to be that human beings are not animals. We are, of course—thoroughly delightful animals, I might add. (Would you rather be a plant?)

4. *Be cautious in drawing conclusions from evidence.* Studies for many years had shown that most clients who receive psychotherapy improve. It was therefore generally assumed that psychotherapy worked. Some 40 years ago, however, a psychologist named Hans Eysenck pointed out that most psychologically troubled people who did *not* receive psychotherapy also improved! The question thus becomes whether people receiving psychotherapy are *more* likely to improve than those who do not. More recent research into the effectiveness of psychotherapy thus carefully compares the benefits of therapy techniques to those of other techniques or to those of no treatment at all. Be skeptical, moreover, when your friend swears by the effectiveness of megavitamin therapy for colds or acupuncture for headaches. What is the nature of the "evidence"? Is it convincing?

   Correlational evidence is also inferior to experimental evidence as a way of determining cause and effect. Consider the statement "Alcohol causes aggression" in the following principle.

5. *Consider alternative interpretations of research evidence.* Does alcohol cause aggression? Is the assertion that it does so truth or fiction? Evidence certainly shows a clear *connection* or "correlation" between alcohol and aggression. That is, many people who commit violent crimes have been drinking. Does the evidence show that this connection is *causal,* however? Tune into Chapter 2's discussion of the differences between the correlational and experimental methods to find out. You will see that rival explanations can be employed to explain correlational evidence.

   As another example, consider the research finding that people who live together (cohabit) before getting married are more likely to get divorced after they marry. Can we conclude that cohabitation *causes* divorce? What rival explanations are possible?

6. *Do not oversimplify.* Consider the issue as to whether or not psychotherapy helps people with psychological problems. In Chapter 14 you will see that a broad answer to this question—a simple yes or no—might be oversimplifying the matter and thus misleading. It is more worthwhile to ask, What *type* of psychotherapy, practiced by *whom,* is most helpful for *what kind of problem*?

   Also consider the statements "We must make mistakes in order to learn" and "Misery loves company." Both statements have the superficial ring of truth, but we need to specify the kinds of behavior patterns we are talking about. Moreover, as noted in your textbook's discussions of language, intelligence, and development, most behavior patterns involve complex interactions of genetic and environmental influences.

7. *Do not overgeneralize.* Consider the statement "Misery loves company." In Chapter 8 you will see that the statement is accurate under certain circumstances. Also consider the statement "You cannot learn about human beings by engaging in research with animals." Is the truth of the matter an all-or-nothing issue, or are there certain kinds of information we can obtain about people from research with animals? What types of things about people might you be able to learn from animal research? What kinds of things are you likely to be able to learn only by conducting research with people?

   Also consider: "Messages travel in the brain by means of electricity." What does Chapter 3 say about how messages travel in the brain? (Hint: Do messages within and between neurons travel in the same manner?)

8. *Apply critical thinking to all areas of life.* A skeptical attitude and a demand for evidence are not simply academic exercises that serve in introductory psychology and other college courses. They are of value in all areas of life. Be skeptical when you are bombarded by TV commercials, when political causes try to sweep you up, when you see the latest cover stories about Elvis and UFOs on the tabloids at the supermarket. How many times have you heard the claim, "Studies have shown that . . ."? Perhaps such claims sound convincing, but ask yourself, Who ran the studies? Were the researchers neutral scientists or biased toward obtaining certain results? Did the studies possess all of the controls described in the discussion of experiments in Chapter 2?

As noted by the educator Robert M. Hutchins, "The object of education is to prepare the young to educate themselves throughout their lives." One of the primary ways of educating yourself is through critical thinking.

Recognizing Common Fallacies in Arguments

Another aspect of critical thinking is learning to recognize the fallacies in other people's claims and arguments. Consider the following examples.

1. Arguments Directed to the Person (*Argumentum ad Hominem*): Psychological theories and research enterprises have met with historic upheavals. The views of Sigmund Freud, for example, the founder of psychodynamic theory, were assaulted almost as soon as they were publicized both by members of his inner circle, such as Carl Jung, and by psychologists of other schools, such as behaviorists. Freud has been alternately referred to as an ingenious, compassionate scientist and as an elitist faker who spun his theories out of the fabric of the fantasy lives of bored, wealthy women. Both extremes are examples of *ad hominem* arguments. Freud's personality and his motives are certainly of historic interest, but neither of them addresses the accuracy of his views. Freud's theories, in other words, are to be judged on whether or not there is scientific support for them, not on Freud's character.

2. Appeals to Force (*Argumentum ad Baculum*): Galileo invented the telescope in the seventeenth century and discovered that the Earth revolved around the sun, rather than vice versa. The Church had taught that the Earth was at the center of the universe, however. Galileo was condemned for heresy and warned that he would be burned to death if he did not confess the error of his ways. Galileo apparently agreed with Shakespeare's words in *King Henry IV, Part I* that "The better part of valour is discretion" and recanted his views, but the facts of course are as they are. Social approval and, at the opposite extreme, threats of violence do not make arguments correct or incorrect.
3. Appeals to Authority (*Argumentum ad Verecundiam*): You have heard arguments to this effect many times: "Well, my mother/teacher/minister says this is true, and I think that he/she knows more about it than you do." Appeals to authority can be persuasive or infuriating, depending on whether or not you agree with them. It matters not *who* makes an assertion, however—even if that person is a psychological luminary like Sigmund Freud, William James, or John B. Watson. An argument is true or false on its own merits. Consider the evidence presented in arguments, not the person making the argument, no matter how exalted. As noted in Chapter 15's discussion of the Milgram studies on obedience, unfortunately, most people have alarmingly strong tendencies to follow the dictates of authority figures.
4. Appeals to Popularity (*Argumentum ad Populum*): The appeal to popularity is cousin to the appeal to authority. It is perhaps best (and most often) illustrated by the TV commercial or newspaper ad. If Bill Cosby advertises Jello, for example, can Jello be bad? Bill Cosby is a highly popular public figure. (His TV role as *Doctor* Huxtable also makes him appear to be an authority figure.) The people making the pitches in TV commercials are usually very popular—either because they are good looking or because they are celebrities. Again, critically evaluate the evidence being presented and ignore the appeal of the person making the pitch.

   The argument that you should do something or believe something because "everyone's doing it" is another type of appeal to popularity—one that gets some people involved in activities they later regret. A majority vote may pass a bill in the legislature, but it does not mean that the arguments in favor of the bill are correct—even if the vote is unanimous. Similarly, the fact that cognitive-behavioral psychotherapy methods are the ones being taught most commonly in graduate schools does not make them the best methods. Only evidence that compares them to other psychotherapy methods can do that.

Despite the familiarity of this "truism," 50 million French people certainly can be wrong. So can the entire human population for that matter. Principles of critical thinking inform us that the evidence, and not appeals to popularity, determines the correctness or incorrectness of arguments.

In sum, be skeptical of claims and arguments. Critically examine the evidence presented rather than focusing on the authority, force, or appeal of the people making the argument. Acquiring an education means more than memorizing data bases and learning how to solve problems in courses such as chemistry and calculus—it also means acquiring the tools to think critically, so that you can continue to educate yourself for a lifetime.

We have concluded this chapter by urging students to examine the evidence before accepting the truth or falseness of other people's claims and arguments. In the following chapter, we explain how psychologists conduct research to gather evidence for their points of view.

STUDY GUIDE

EXERCISE 1: Matching—Names to Know

Instructions: The names of a number of persons who are important to psychology are placed in the first column. Schools of psychology and other identifying information are placed in the second column. Place the letter of the item that is best associated with the person in the blank space to the left of the person's name. Answers are given below.

_____ 1. Aristotle
_____ 2. Plato
_____ 3. Wolfgang Köhler
_____ 4. Gustav Theodor Fechner
_____ 5. Erik Erikson
_____ 6. Edward B. Titchener
_____ 7. Abraham Maslow
_____ 8. B. F. Skinner
_____ 9. Mary Whiton Calkins
_____ 10. Carl Rogers
_____ 11. Socrates
_____ 12. John B. Watson
_____ 13. Wilhelm Wundt
_____ 14. Jean Piaget
_____ 15. Ivan Pavlov
_____ 16. Max Wertheimer
_____ 17. G. Stanley Hall
_____ 18. Kurt Koffka
_____ 19. Sigmund Freud
_____ 20. Karen Horney
_____ 21. Kenneth B. Clark
_____ 22. William James
_____ 23. Christine Ladd-Franklin

A. Humanistic Perspective
B. Behaviorism
C. Gestalt Psychology
D. Studied ethnicity and influenced a Supreme Court decision on desegregation
E. Psychodynamic Perspective
F. Author, *Elements of Psychophysics*
G. Structuralism
H. Founder of American Psychological Association
I. Introspection
J. Formulated a theory of color vision
K. Functionalism
L. Cognitive Perspective
M. Author, *Peri Psyches*
N. Said "Know thyself"
O. Introduced the method of paired associates and discovered the primacy and recency effects
P. Disciple of Socrates

Answer Key to Exercise 1

1. M
2. P
3. C
4. F
5. E
6. G
7. A
8. B
9. O
10. A
11. I, N
12. B
13. G, I
14. L
15. B
16. C
17. H
18. C
19. E
20. E
21. D
22. K
23. J

EXERCISE 2: Prominent Figures in the History of Psychology

This exercise is based on Table 1.2 in the chapter and provides you with the opportunity to recall people whom psychological historians' and department chairpersons' rank as having made notable contributions to psychology. Write the missing name in the blank space and check your answers against the key that follows the exercise.

HISTORIANS			CHAIRPERSONS		
RANK	FIGURE	AREA OF CONTRIBUTION	RANK	FIGURE	AREA OF CONTRIBUTION
1.	Wilhelm (1) W________	Structuralism	1.	B. F. (2) S________	Operant Conditioning
2.	William (3) J________	Functionalism	2.	Sigmund (4) F________	Psychoanalysis
3.	(5) S________ Freud	Psychoanalysis	3.	(6) W________ James	Functionalism
4.	John B. (7) W________	Behaviorism	4.	Jean (8) P________	Cognitive Development
5.	Ivan (9) P________	Conditioning	5.	G. Stanley (10) H________	Development
6.	Hermann (11) E________	Memory	6.	(12) W________ Wundt	Structuralism
7.	(13) J________ Piaget	Cognitive Development	7.	Carl (14) R________	Self Theory, Person-Centered Therapy
8.	B. F. (15) S________	Operant Conditioning	8.	(16) J________ B. Watson	Behaviorism
9.	Alfred (17) B________	Assessment of Intelligence	9.	(18) I________ Pavlov	Conditioning
10.	Gustav Theodor (19) F________	Psychophysics	10.	Edward L. (20) T________	Learning—Law of Effect

Answer Key to Exercise 2

1. Wundt
2. Skinner
3. James
4. Freud
5. Sigmund
6. William
7. Watson
8. Piaget
9. Pavlov
10. Hall
11. Ebbinghaus
12. Wilhelm
13. Jean
14. Rogers
15. Skinner
16. John
17. Binet
18. Ivan
19. Fechner
20. Thorndike

ESL—BRIDGING THE GAP

This part is divided into

1. cultural references
2. phrases and expresssions in which words are used differently from their regular meaning, or are used as metaphors

Cultural References

uppers (2)—pills (drugs) which cause a person to feel good, elated, excited

Mark Twain (24)—a famous American writer, a novelist and humorist

Phrases and Expressions (Different Usage)

That's you to a "tee" (2)—that is an exact description of you

"surprised at ourselves" (2)—we discover that we think in ways that we do not expect and are surprised

out of character (2)—an action or thought is not what we expect

tip of the tongue (2)—almost remember something, but cannot

do their bidding (4)—do what they want

differ markedly (4)—be extremely different

spurred onward (4)—encouraged to continue

wear more than one hat (5)—do more than one job

stand trial (9)—to be judged innocent or guilty in a court of law

free will (10)—people can decide what they will do or be

not . . . mirror reality (10)—not the same as reality; not a reflection of reality

founded a school (11)—started a movement (unorganized institution)

a broader view (11)—a greater range of ideas

a major figure (11)—an important person

stream of consciousness (12)—the continuation of our thoughts without deciding what we will or will not think
doomed to extinction (12)—definitely will not continue to live as a species
best suited (12)—the most appropriate to
fittest (12)—the best in every way
"flywheel" (12)—a wheel which drives a machine
comes to an end (12)—stops
abroad in the land (12)—known all over the country
clothes . . . make the man or woman (14)—success in business or a career depends upon how a person looks, or the clothes that he or she wears
trial and error (15)—to try different methods until one method succeeds
all at once (15)—together; in one moment
go on a killing spree (15)—kill a lot of people in a short time
verbal slips (15)—words spoken which were not meant to be spoken
seething cauldron (16)—angry (a cauldron is a container of fire)
has taken many turns (17)—has gone in many different directions; there have been a lot of changes in ideas
in flavor (19)—related in the basic ideas
to a large extent (19)—in most ways
to fashion our growth (19)—to determine what we will become
"get in touch" (19)—know what they feel
realize their potential (19)—become the best, most creative and productive person that is possible for that person

CHAPTER REVIEW

SECTION 1: Psychology as a Science

Objective 1: Define *psychology*.

Psychology is defined as the study of (1) b__________ and mental processes.

(2) __________ists limit their investigations to observable behaviors, such as muscular responses or measurement of heart rate. Cognitive psychologists include (3) m__________ processes, such as images, concepts, thoughts, and dreams. Behaviorists argue that the difficulty in studying mental processes is that they are private events, usually assumed to be present on the basis of the (4) self-report__________ of the person experiencing them.

Objective 2: List and discuss the goals of psychology.

Psychology seeks to describe, explain, (5) p__________, and (6) control__________ behavior. But psychologists do not attempt to (7) c__________ the behavior of other people against their wills. Instead, they help clients (8) modify__________ their own behavior for their own benefit.

Behavior is explained through psychological (9) t__________, which are sets of statements that involve assumptions about behavior. Explanations and (10) p__________ are derived from theories. Theories are revised, as needed, to accommodate new (11) ob__________. If necessary, theories are discarded.

SECTION 2: What Psychologists Do

Objective 3: Explain the functions of different types of psychologists, including clinical, counseling, school, educational, developmental, personality, social, experimental, industrial, organizational, consumer, forensic, and health psychologists.

Some psychologists engage in basic or (12) pure__________ research, which has no immediate applications. Other psychologists engage in (13) applied__________ research, which seeks solutions to specific problems. In addition to research, many psychologists are found in (14) __________ching.

(15) Clinical__________al psychologists comprise the largest subgroup of psychologists. Clinical psychologists help people who are behaving (16) __________ally adjust to the demands of life. Clinical psychologists help clients resolve problems through (17) PsychoThero__________rapy and (18) behavior__________ __________ therapy. (19) Counseling__________ psychologists work with individuals who have adjustment problems but do not show seriously abnormal behavior.

School psychologists assist students with problems that interfere with (20) __________ing. School psychologists help make decisions about placement of students in (21) sp__________ __________ education and (22) rem__________ programs. (23) Ed__________ psychologists are more concerned with theoretical issues concerning human learning.

(24) D_Developmental_ psychologists study the changes that occur throughout the life span. They attempt to sort out the relative influences of heredity and the (25) en__________ on growth. Personality psychologists to define human (26) __________its. They study influences on our thought processes, feelings, and (27) b__________. (28) S__________ psychologists study the nature and causes of our thoughts, feelings, and behavior in social situations. Environmental psychologists study the ways in which behavior influences and is influenced by the (29) p__________ environment.

(30) E__________ psychologists conduct research into basic psychological processes, such as sensation and perception, learning and memory, and motivation and emotion. Experimental psychologists who seek to understand the relationships between biological changes and psychological events are called (31) b__________ psychologists.

Industrial psychologists focus on the relationships between people and (32) w__________. (33) __________nal psychologists study the behavior of people in organizations. Consumer psychologists attempt to predict and influence the behavior of (34) c__________.

Health psychologists are concerned with the ways in which (35) s__________ and other psychological factors can contribute to diseases. Forensic psychologists apply psychological expertise within the (36) c__________ j__________ system.

SECTION 3: Where Psychology Comes From: A Brief History

Objective 4: Outline the history of psychology.

The Greek philosopher (37) A__________ was among the first to argue that human behavior is subject to rules and laws. Socrates proclaimed "Know thyself" and suggested the use of (38) __________tion to gain self-knowledge.

Wilhelm (39) W__________ established the first psychological laboratory in 1879. Wundt also founded the school of (40) __________alism and used introspection to study the objective and subjective elements of experience.

William James founded the school of (41) __________alism. Functionalism dealt with observable behavior as well as conscious experience, and focused on the importance of (42) h__________, to which James referred as the "enormous flywheel of society."

John B. Watson founded the school of (43) b__________. Behaviorists argue that psychology must limit itself to (44) ob__________ behavior and forgo excursions into subjective consciousness. Watson pointed to Pavlov's experiments in (45) __________ning as a model for psychological research. Behaviorism focused on learning by conditioning, and B. F. Skinner introduced the concept of (46) __________ment as an explanation of how learning occurs.

Gestalt psychology focused on (47) p__________. Gestalt psychologists saw our perceptions as (48) wh__________ that give meaning to parts. They argued that learning can be active and (49) __________ful, not merely responsive and (50) __________ical as in Pavlov's experiments.

Sigmund Freud founded the school of (51) p__________. According to psychodynamic theory, people are driven by hidden impulses and distort reality in order to protect themselves from (52) a__________.

SECTION 4: How Today's Psychologists View Behavior

Objective 5: Compare and contrast the five major theoretical perspectives in contemporary psychology: the biological, cognitive, humanistic–existential, psychodynamic, and learning perspectives.

The five major perspectives in contemporary psychology include the biological, (53) co__________, (54) hu__________–existential, psychodynamic, and learning perspectives. Biologically oriented psychologists study the links between behavior and biological events, such as the firing of cells in the (55) b__________ and the release of hormones.

Cognitive psychologists study the ways in which we perceive and mentally (56) r__________ the world. Piaget's study of the (57) c__________ development of children has inspired many developmental and educational psychologists. Cognitive psychologists also study (58) in__________ processing—the processes by which information is perceived, stored, and (59) re__________.

Humanistic–existential psychologists stress the importance of human (60) ex________________. They also assert that people have the freedom to make responsible (61) ch________________.

Contemporary psychoanalysts are likely to consider themselves (62) ________________-analysts. They generally follow Freud's views, but focus less on the roles of (63) un________________ sexual and aggressive impulses and see people as more capable of making conscious choices.

Watson and his followers are referred to as (64) ________________ists. Social-learning theorists are in the behaviorist tradition because of their strong focus on the role of (65) ________________ing in human behavior. Social-learning theorists also find roles for (66) ob________________ learning, expectations, and values in explaining human behavior, however.

SECTION 5: Human Diversity and Psychology

Objective 6: Discuss the importance of awareness of human diversity in the study of psychology.

The profession of psychology is committed to the dignity of the (67) ________________dual, but we cannot understand individuals without an awareness of the richness of human (68) ________________sity. People's (69) ________________nic groups are defined by features such as their common cultural heritage, race, language, and history. People also differ according to their (70) ________________er—that is, the state of being male or being female. Today (71: Circle one: Men or Women?) account for 54½% of U.S. post-secondary students.

Objective 7: Discuss women and members of ethnic minority groups who have contributed to the development of psychology.

Psychology's "golden oldies," as listed in Table 1.2, are all white (72: Circle one: Females or Males?). Christine (73) Ladd-F________________ formulated a theory of color vision. Mary Whiton (74) C________________ introduced the method of paired associates and discovered the primacy and recency effects. Margaret Floy (75) W________________ wrote *The Animal Mind.* African-American psychologist J. Henry (76) A________________ engaged in research in the perception of heat and cold. Kenneth B. (77) C________________ influenced a key Supreme Court decision on desegregation. Jorge (78) S________________ was among the first to show how intelligence tests are culturally biased.

SECTION 6: Critical Thinking and Psychology

Objective 8: Discuss the principles of critical thinking, and explain how they may be applied to the subject matter of psychology.

Critical thinking is intended to foster an attitude of (79) skep________________. Critical thinking refers to thoughtfully (80) ________________yzing and probing the questions, statements, and arguments of others. It means examining the (81) def________________s of terms, examining the (82) pre________________s or assumptions behind arguments, and scrutinizing the logic with which arguments are developed. Critical thinking within the science of psychology also refers to the ability to inquire about causes and (83) ________________cts, and to knowledge of (84) re________________ methods. Critical thinkers are also cautious in drawing conclusions from (85) ________________ence. Critical thinkers do not (86) over________________ or (87) over________________.

Critical thinkers also learn to recognize the logical (88) fal________________s in other people's claims and arguments. Critical thinkers, for example, recognize the fallacies in arguments directed to the person [Argumentum ad (89) ________________inem], arguments employing force [Argumentum ad Baculum], appeals to authority [Argumentum ad (90) ________________diam], and appeals to popularity [Argumentum ad (91) ________________lum].

Answers to Chapter Review

1. Behavior
2. Behaviorists
3. Mental
4. Self-report
5. Predict
6. Control
7. Control
8. Modify
9. Theories
10. Predictions
11. Observations
12. Pure
13. Applied
14. Teaching
15. Clinical
16. Abnormally
17. Psychotherapy
18. Behavior therapy
19. Counseling
20. Learning
21. Special education
22. Remediation
23. Educational
24. Developmental
25. Environment
26. Traits
27. Behaviors
28. Social
29. Physical
30. Experimental
31. Biological
32. Work
33. Organizations
34. Consumers
35. Stress
36. Criminal justice
37. Aristotle
38. Introspection
39. Wundt
40. Structuralism
41. Functionalism
42. Habit
43. Behaviorism
44. Observable
45. Conditioning
46. Reinforcement
47. Perception
48. Wholes
49. Purposeful
50. Mechanical
51. Psychoanalysis
52. Anxiety
53. Cognitive
54. Humanistic
55. Brain
56. Represent
57. Cognitive
58. Information
59. Retrieved
60. Experience
61. Choices
62. Neoanalysts (or Ego analysts)
63. Unconscious
64. Behaviorists
65. Learning
66. Observational
67. Individual
68. Diversity
69. Ethnic
70. Gender
71. Women
72. Males
73. Franklin
74. Calkins
75. Washburn
76. Alston
77. Clark
78. Sanchez
79. Skepticism
80. Analyzing
81. Definitions
82. Premises
83. Effects
84. Research
85. Evidence
86. Oversimplify (or Overgeneralize)
87. Overgeneralize (or Oversimplify)
88. Fallacies
89. Hominem
90. Verecundiam
91. Populum

POSTTEST

1. If you wanted to run a study in which you learned about another person's _______, you would have to rely on that person's self-report.
   (a) heart rate,
   (b) mental images,
   (c) emission of a brain wave,
   (d) muscular responses.

2. Applied research is best described as research undertaken
   (a) with human beings,
   (b) with lower animals,
   (c) to find solutions to specific problems,
   (d) for its own sake.

3. If you knew someone who was having an adjustment problem, you would be best-advised to refer that person to a(n) _______ psychologist.
   (a) educational,
   (b) developmental,
   (c) personality,
   (d) counseling.

4. If you were to read an article comparing the values of breast-feeding and bottle-feeding, it would probably report research that had been carried out by _______ psychologists.
   (a) clinical,
   (b) personality,
   (c) developmental,
   (d) school.

5. _______ psychologists are most directly concerned with the investigation of issues related to gender roles, processes such as repression, and the development of traits.
   (a) Personality,
   (b) Clinical,
   (c) Organizational,
   (d) School.

6. Industrial/organizational psychologists are most likely to be consulted to
   (a) assist in the processes of hiring and promotion,
   (b) help workers make educational decisions,
   (c) treat workers showing abnormal behavior,
   (d) investigate the political and social attitudes of workers.

7. The earliest author of a book about psychology is
   (a) Democritus,
   (b) Darwin,
   (c) Sophocles,
   (d) Aristotle.

8. Which of the following schools of psychology was originated in Germany?
   (a) Functionalism,
   (b) Structuralism,
   (c) Behaviorism,
   (d) Psychoanalysis.

9. Who argued that the mind, like light or sound, was a natural event?
   (a) Carl Rogers,
   (b) Sigmund Freud,
   (c) B. F. Skinner,
   (d) Wilhelm Wundt.

10. The school of psychology that focused most directly on perceptual processes is
    (a) psychoanalysis,
    (b) behaviorism,
    (c) humanistic psychology,
    (d) Gestalt psychology.

11. Who founded the American Psychological Association?
    (a) William James,
    (b) Edward Bradford Titchener,
    (c) G. Stanley Hall,
    (d) Mary Whiton Calkins.

12. ________ is a neoanalyst.
    (a) Christine Ladd-Franklin,
    (b) Erik Erikson,
    (c) Albert Bandura,
    (d) Carl Rogers.

13. Social-learning theorists differ from behaviorists in that social-learning theorists focus on the role of ________ in behavior.
    (a) unconscious processes,
    (b) cognition,
    (c) reinforcement,
    (d) learning.

14. Which of the following wrote *The Animal Mind*?
    (a) Margaret Floy Washburn,
    (b) Elizabeth Loftus,
    (c) Christine Ladd-Franklin,
    (d) Mary Whiton Calkins.

15. Which of the following introduced the methods of paired associates?
    (a) Margaret Floy Washburn,
    (b) Elizabeth Loftus,
    (c) Christine Ladd-Franklin,
    (d) Mary Whiton Calkins.

16. Which of the following engaged in research on the perception of heat and cold?
    (a) B. F. Skinner,
    (b) J. Henry Alston,
    (c) Jorge Sanchez,
    (d) Kenneth B. Clark.

17. Which of the following influenced a key Supreme Court decision on desegregation?
    (a) B. F. Skinner,
    (b) J. Henry Alston,
    (c) Jorge Sanchez,
    (d) Kenneth B. Clark.

18. Which of the following was among the first to show how intelligence tests are culturally biased?
    (a) B. F. Skinner,
    (b) J. Henry Alston,
    (c) Jorge Sanchez,
    (d) Kenneth B. Clark.

19. A key value of critical thinking is that it
    (a) provides a data base of knowledge,
    (b) makes individuals argumentative,
    (c) provides people with skills to educate themselves for a lifetime,
    (d) teaches people how to criticize works of art, literature, and music.

20. A student says, "I know this is true because my psychology professor says that it is true." This argument is an example of the *Argumentum ad*
    (a) *Hominem,*
    (b) *Baculum,*
    (c) *Verecundiam,*
    (d) *Populum.*

ANSWER KEY TO POSTTEST

1. B
2. C
3. D
4. C
5. A
6. A
7. D
8. B
9. D
10. D
11. C
12. B
13. B
14. A
15. D
16. B
17. D
18. C
19. C
20. C

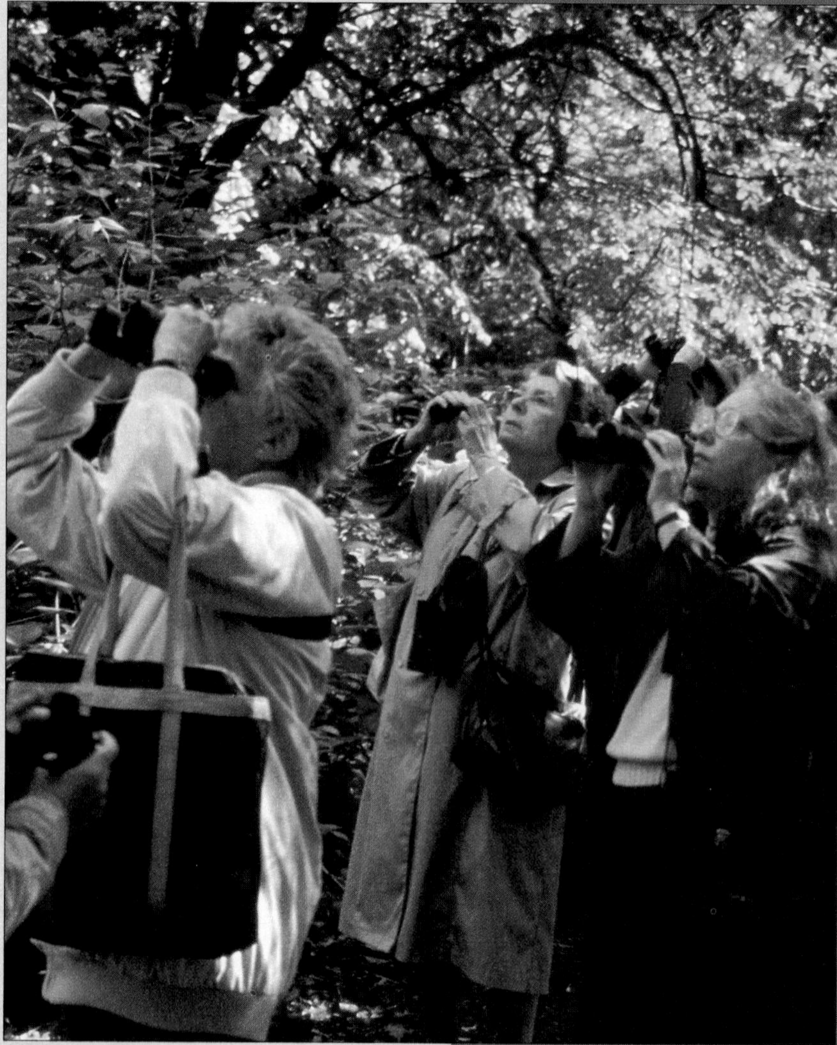

- You could survey 20 million Americans and still not predict accurately the outcome of a presidential election.

- Only people use tools.

- In many experiments, neither the subjects in the experiment nor the researchers who are running the experiment know which subjects have received the real treatment and which subjects have received a placebo ("sugar pill").

- Alcohol causes aggression.

- Psychologists would not be able to carry out certain research studies without deceiving participants as to the purposes and methods of the studies.

- Human subjects may not be pressured into participating in psychological research.

Research Methods in Psychology

Learning Objectives

When you have finished studying Chapter 2, you should be able to:

The Scientific Method

1. Describe the features of the scientific method.

Samples and Populations: Representing Human Diversity

2. Explain how psychologists use samples in an effort to represent populations.
3. Discuss the use of sampling in psychology to represent human diversity.

Methods of Observation: The Better To See You With

4. Discuss the strengths and weaknesses of the case-study method.
5. Discuss the strengths and weaknesses of the survey method.
6. Discuss the strengths and weaknesses of the testing method.
7. Discuss the strengths and weaknesses of the naturalistic-observation method.
8. Discuss the strengths and weaknesses of the laboratory-observation method.

The Correlational Method: Seeing What Goes Up and What Comes Down

9. Define the *correlational method.*
10. Discuss the limitations of the correlational method.

The Experimental Method: Trying Things Out

11. Define the *experimental method*.
12. Discuss the use of independent and dependent variables in the experimental method.
13. Discuss the use of experimental and control groups in the experimental method.
14. Discuss the use of blinds and double blinds in the experimental method.

Ethics in Psychological Research and Practice

15. Discuss ethical issues conducting research and practice with human subjects.
16. Discuss ethical issues concerning research with animal subjects.

Do only people use tools? Does alcohol cause aggression? Why do some people hardly ever think of food while others are obsessed with it and snack all day long? Why do some unhappy people attempt suicide whereas other unhappy people seek alternate ways to cope with their problems? Does having people of different ethnic backgrounds work together serve to decrease or increase feelings of prejudice?

Many of us have expressed opinions on questions such as these at one time or another, and different psychological theories suggest a number of possible answers. Psychology is an **empirical** science, however. Within an empirical science, assumptions about the behavior of cosmic rays, chemical compounds, cells, or people must be supported by evidence. Strong arguments, reference to authority figures, even tightly knit theories are not adequate as scientific evidence. As noted in Chapter 1's discussion of critical thinking, psychologists and other scientists make it their business—literally and figuratively speaking—to be skeptical.

Scientific evidence is obtained by means of the **scientific method.**

THE SCIENTIFIC METHOD

The scientific method is an organized way of going about expanding and refining knowledge. Psychologists do not necessarily place a list of steps of the scientific method on the counter and follow them as they might follow a cookbook when they go about their work. They are principles that generally guide scientists' research endeavors, however.

Psychologists usually begin by *formulating a research question.* Research questions can have many sources. Our daily experiences, psychological **theory,** even folklore all help to generate questions for research. Consider some questions that may arise from daily experience. Daily experience in using day-care centers may motivate us to conduct research into whether day care influences development of social skills or the bonds of attachment between children and their mothers.

Or consider questions that might arise from psychological theory (see Figure 2.1). Social-learning principles of observational learning may prompt research into the effects of televised violence. Sigmund Freud's psychoanalytic theory may prompt research into whether or not the verbal expression of feelings of anger helps relieve feelings of depression.

Folklorish statements such as "Misery loves company," "Opposites attract," and "Beauty is in the eye of the beholder"—statements that we consider in Chapters 9 and 15—may also give rise to research questions. That is, *does* misery love company? *Do* opposites attract? *Is* beauty in the eye of the beholder?

A research question may be studied in its question format, or it may be reworded into a **hypothesis** (see Figure 2.1). A hypothesis is a specific statement about behavior or mental processes that is tested through research. One

Empirical Emphasizing or based on observation and experiment.

Scientific method A method for obtaining scientific evidence in which research questions or hypotheses are formulated and tested.

Theory A formulation of the relationships and principles that underlie observed events. Theories allow us to explain and predict behavior.

Hypothesis In psychology, a specific statement about behavior or mental processes that is tested through research.

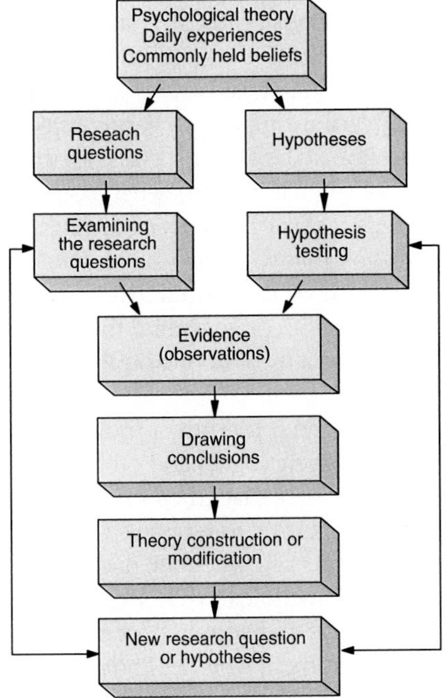

FIGURE 2.1
The Scientific Method. The scientific method is a systematic way of organizing and expanding scientific knowledge. Daily experiences, cultural beliefs, and scientific observations all foster the development of scientific theory. Theory explains observations and leads to hypotheses about events—in the case of psychology, behavior and mental processes. Our observations of hypothesized events can confirm the theory, lead to the refinement of the theory, or disconfirm the theory and possibly suggest the formulation of a new theory.

hypothesis about day care might be that preschoolers placed in day care will acquire greater social skills in relating to peers than preschoolers who are cared for in the home. A hypothesis about TV violence might be that elementary school children who watch more violent TV shows tend to behave more aggressively toward their peers. A hypothesis that addresses Freudian theory might be that the verbal expression of feelings of anger will decrease feelings of depression.

Psychologists next examine the research question or *test the hypothesis* through carefully controlled methods such as naturalistic or laboratory observation and the experiment. For example, we could introduce day-care and non-day-care children to a new child in a college child-research center and observe how each group fares with the new acquaintance.

To undertake research we must provide **operational definitions** for the variables under study. Concerning the effects of TV violence, we could have parents help us tally which TV shows their children watch and rate the shows for violent content. Each child could receive a composite "exposure-to-TV-violence score." We could also operationally define aggression in terms of teacher reports on how aggressively the children act toward their peers. Then we could determine whether more-aggressive children also watch more violence on television.

Testing the hypothesis that the verbal expression of feelings of anger decreases feelings of depression might be more complex. Researchers would have to decide, for example, whether they should use feelings of anger that people already have or to use a standardized set of angry statements that address common areas of parent-child conflict. Would their **subjects** include people undergoing psychoanalysis or, say, introductory psychology students? What would be the operational definition of feelings of depression? Self-ratings of depression according to a numerical scale? Scores on psychological tests of depression? Reports of depressive behavior by informants such as spouses? Psychologists frequently use a combination of definitions to increase their chances of tapping into targeted behavior patterns and mental processes.

Psychologists draw conclusions about their research questions or the accuracy of their hypotheses on the basis of their research observations or findings. When their observations do not bear out their hypotheses, they may modify the theories from which the hypotheses were derived (see Figure 2.1). Research findings often suggest refinements to psychological theories and, consequently, new avenues of research.

In our research on day care, we would probably find that day-care children show somewhat greater social skills than children cared for in the home (Berns, 1993). We would probably also find that more aggressive children spend more time watching TV violence (see Chapter 6). Research into the effectiveness of psychoanalytic forms of therapy is usually based on case studies, as we shall see in Chapter 14.

As psychologists draw conclusions from research evidence, they are guided by principles of critical thinking. For example, they try not to confuse connections between the findings with cause and effect. Although more-aggressive children apparently spend more time watching TV violence, it may be erroneous to conclude from this kind of evidence that TV violence *causes* aggressive behavior. Perhaps there is a **selection factor** at work, for example, such that more-aggressive children are more likely than less-aggressive children to tune into violent TV programs.

To better understand the potential effects of the selection factor, consider a study on the relationship between exercise and health. If we were to compare a group of people who exercised regularly to a group who did not, we might find that the exercisers were physically healthier than the couch potatoes. Could we conclude from this research approach that exercise is a causal factor in good health? Perhaps not. The selection factor—the fact that one group chose to exercise and the other did not—could also suggest that healthy people are more apt

Operational definition A definition of a variable in terms of the methods used to create or measure that variable.

Subjects Participants in a scientific study.

Selection factor A source of bias that may occur in research findings when subjects are allowed to determine for themselves whether or not they will receive a treatment condition in a scientific study. Do you think, for example, that there are problems in studying the effects of a diet or of smoking cigarettes when we allow study participants to choose whether or not they will try the diet or smoke cigarettes? Why or why not?

to choose to exercise[1]. Later we shall consider the kinds of research studies that do permit us to draw conclusions about cause and effect.

As critical thinkers, psychologists similarly attempt to avoid oversimplifying or overgeneralizing their results. The effects of day care are apparently very complex, for example. Although children in day care usually exhibit better social skills than children who are not, there is also a tendency for them to be somewhat more aggressive. If we conducted our research into the benefits of expressing feelings of anger with clients in psychoanalysis, do you think that we would be justified in generalizing the results to the population at large? If we conducted that research with introductory psychology students, could we extend or generalize the results to people who sought psychotherapy to relieve feelings of depression? Why or why not?

Some psychologists include publication of research reports in professional journals as a crucial part of the scientific method. Psychologists and other scientists are obligated to provide enough details of their work that other scientists will be able to repeat or **replicate** it. Psychologists may attempt to replicate a study in all its details in order to corroborate the findings, especially when the findings are significant for people's health or general welfare. Sometimes psychologists replicate research methods with different kinds of subjects to determine, for example, whether findings with women can be generalized to men, whether findings with non-Hispanic white Americans can be generalized to ethnic minority groups, or whether findings with people who have sought psychotherapy can be generalized to people at large.

Publication of data and researchers' interpretations of data also permit the scientific community at large to evaluate, and perhaps criticize, the methods and conclusions of other scientists. A bruised ego here and there is considered a reasonable price to pay for the advancement of scientific knowledge.

Let us now consider the research methods used by psychologists: methods of sampling, methods of observation, the use of correlation, and the queen of the empirical approach—the experiment.

SAMPLES AND POPULATIONS: REPRESENTING HUMAN DIVERSITY

Consider a piece of history that never quite happened: the Republican candidate Alf Landon defeated the incumbent president, Franklin D. Roosevelt, in 1936. Or at least Landon did so in a poll conducted by a popular magazine of the day, the *Literary Digest.* In the actual election, however, Roosevelt routed Landon in a landslide of 11 million votes. How, then, could the *Digest* predict a Landon victory? How was so great a discrepancy possible?

The *Digest,* you see, had phoned the voters it surveyed. Today, telephone sampling is a widely practiced and reasonably legitimate technique. But the *Digest* poll was taken during the Great Depression, when Americans who had telephones were much wealthier than those who did not. Americans at higher income levels are also more likely to vote Republican. No surprise, then, that the overwhelming majority of those sampled said that they would vote for Landon.

The principle involved here is that samples must accurately *represent* the population they are intended to reflect, if we are to be able to **generalize** from research samples to populations.

In surveys such as that conducted by the *Literary Digest,* and in other research methods, the individuals, or subjects, who are studied are referred to as a

Replicate Repeat, reproduce, copy. What are some reasons that psychologists replicate the research conducted by other psychologists?

Generalize To extend from the particular to the general; to apply observations based on a sample to a population.

[1] I am not trying to suggest that exercise does *not* make a contribution to health. I am merely pointing out that research that compares people who have chosen to exercise to people who have not is not a valid way to study the issue.

A Population? Psychologists and other scientists attempt to select their research samples so that they will represent target populations. What population is suggested by the people in this photograph? How might you go about sampling them? How do people who agree to participate in research differ from those who refuse?

sample. A sample is a segment of a **population.** Psychologists and other scientists need to ensure that the subjects they observe *represent* their target population, such as Americans, and not subgroups such as southern California Yuppies or non-Hispanic white members of the middle class.

Science is a conservative enterprise, and scientists are cautious about generalizing experimental results to populations other than those from which their samples were drawn.

Representing Human Diversity: Problems in Generalizing from Psychological Research

All generalizations are dangerous, even this one.

Alexandre Dumas

Many factors must be considered in interpreting the accuracy of the results of scientific research. One is the nature of the research sample. Later in the chapter we shall consider research in which the subjects were drawn from a population of college men who were social drinkers. That is, the subjects tended to drink at social gatherings but not when alone. Whom do college men represent, other than themselves? To whom can we extend, or generalize, the results? For one thing, the results may not extend to women, not even to college women. In Chapter 5, for example, we shall learn that alcohol goes more quickly to "women's heads" than to men's.

College men also tend to fall within a certain age range (about 18 to 22) and are more intelligent than the general population. We cannot be certain that the findings extend to older men of average intelligence, although it seems reasonable to **infer** that they do. Social drinkers may also differ biologically and psychologically from alcoholics, who have difficulty controlling their drinking. Nor can we be certain that college social drinkers represent people who do not drink at all.

Women's groups and health professionals argue that there is a historic bias in favor of conducting research with men (DeAngelis, 1991). Inadequate resources have been devoted to conducting health-related research with women subjects. For example, most of the large-sample research into life style and health has been conducted with male subjects (see Chapters 5 and 12). Former APA president Bonnie Strickland (1991) cites three areas in which there is a crucial deficiency of research with women subjects: the promotion of women's health (including disease prevention); women and depression; and women and chemical dependence. More research with women subjects is also needed in areas such as AIDS and the effects of violence on women.

Research samples have also tended to underrepresent minority ethnic groups in the population. Personality tests completed by non-Hispanic white Americans and by African Americans may need to be interpreted in diverse ways if accurate conclusions are to be drawn, for example (Rathus, Nevid, & Greene, 1994). The well-known Kinsey studies on sexual behavior (Kinsey et al., 1948, 1953) did not adequately represent African Americans, poor people, the elderly, and diverse other groups.

One way to achieve a representative sample is by means of **random sampling.** In a random sample, each member of a population has an equal chance of being selected to participate. Researchers can also use a **stratified sample,** which is drawn so that identified subgroups in the population are represented proportionately in the sample. For instance, 12 percent of the American population is African American (Barringer, 1991). Thus, a stratified sample would be 12 percent African American. As a practical matter, a large, randomly selected sample will show reasonably accurate stratification. A random sample of 1,500 people will represent the general American population reasonably well. A haphazardly drawn sample of 20 million, however, might not.

Sample Part of a population.

Population A complete group of organisms or events.

Infer Draw a conclusion.

Random sample A sample that is drawn so that each member of a population has an equal chance of being selected to participate.

Stratified sample A sample that is drawn so that identified subgroups in the population are represented proportionately in the sample. How can stratified sampling be carried out to ensure that a sample represents the ethnic diversity we find in the population at large?

WORLD OF DIVERSITY

The Wyatt Survey of African-American and White Women in Los Angeles County

Although Alfred Kinsey and his colleagues, the authors of the "Kinsey Reports," gathered some data on the sexual behavior of African-American people, they did not report it because African-American people were significantly underrepresented in their samples. In more recent years, however, UCLA researcher Gail Wyatt and her colleagues (Wyatt, 1989, 1990; Wyatt et al., 1988a, 1988b, 1990) studied the sexual behavior of a sample of 122 white and 126 African-American women aged 18 to 36 in Los Angeles County. She recruited her subjects at random from telephone listings. Women who agreed to participate were selected to try to balance the sample in terms of demographic variables such as age, education, socioeconomic status, marital status, and number of children. One in three women called refused to cooperate, so a volunteer bias was clearly at work in her final samples. The subjects were interviewed face-to-face.

Wyatt's work is important because it deals with changes in sexual behavior that have occurred in U.S. society since the years just following World War II, with prominent social issues such as childhood sexual abuse, and is one of the few studies of sexual behavior among African-American women (Rathus et al., 1993). A striking difference between the Kinsey data and Wyatt's was that contemporary women—both African-American and white—reported engaging in initial sexual intercourse at earlier ages than women in Kinsey's sample reported. Only about one woman in five in Kinsey's sample reported engaging in premarital intercourse by the age of 20 (Kinsey et al., 1953, p. 286). By contrast, 98 percent of Wyatt's subjects (African-American and white) reported engaging in premarital intercourse by the age of 20 (Wyatt, 1989). When social class differences were mathematically considered, the ages of initial intercourse for the African-American and white women in Wyatt's sample were very much alike.

What of it? Can we conclude that in our liberated times, 98 percent of single women throughout the United States engage in premarital intercourse by the age of 20? Clearly not. Wyatt's research was limited to the Los Angeles area. One out of three women contacted by Wyatt refused to participate, introducing a volunteer bias. Moreover, to balance her white and African-American samples for factors such as socioeconomic status, marital status, and level of education, Wyatt limited her pool of subjects to women who were comparable according to them. Her final sample of African-American women matched the population of African-American women in Los Angeles County, but her final sample of white women did not match the population of white women in Los Angeles County. Her sample contained a disproportionate number of white women of lower socioeconomic status, for example.

African-American and White Women. Gail Wyatt and her colleagues at UCLA studied the sexual behavior of African-American and white women in Los Angeles County. How did Wyatt achieve samples who were comparable according to socioeconomic status, marital status, and other demographic factors? How did Wyatt's findings differ from those of Kinsey and his colleagues, which were reported some 40 years earlier? How representative are Wyatt's samples of her target populations?

Wyatt's samples thus did not fully represent the targeted populations. Remember, however, that when factors such as socioeconomic status, marital status, and level of education were held constant, the African-American and white women in her samples exhibited highly similar patterns of sexual behavior. May we conclude, then, that sexual behavior is influenced more by such demographic factors than it is by race *per se*? What do you think?

You could, in fact, survey 20 million Americans and still not predict accurately the outcome of a presidential election. Samples must accurately represent the populations from which they are drawn if we are to be able to extend our findings from the sample to the population.

Large-scale magazine surveys of sexual behavior such as those run by *Redbook* (Tavris & Sadd, 1977) and *Cosmopolitan* (Wolfe, 1981) have asked readers to fill out and return questionnaires. Although many thousands of readers completed the questionnaires and sent them in, did they represent the general American population? Probably not. These studies and similar ones may have influenced by **volunteer bias.** The concept behind volunteer bias is that people who offer to participate in research studies differ systematically from people who do not. In the case of research into sexual behavior, volunteers may represent subgroups of the population—or of readers of the magazines in question—who are willing to disclose intimate information (Rathus, Nevid, & Fichner-Rathus, 1993). Volunteers may also be more interested in research than nonvolunteers, as well as having more spare time. How might such volunteers differ from the population at large? How might such differences slant or bias the research outcomes?

METHODS OF OBSERVATION: THE BETTER TO SEE YOU WITH

Many people consider themselves experts on behavior and mental processes on the basis of their life experiences. How many times have grandparents, for example, told us what they have seen in their lives and what it means about human nature?

We see much indeed during our lifetimes. Our personal observations tend to be fleeting and uncontrolled, however. We sift through experience for the minutia that interest us. We often ignore the obvious because it does not fit our preexisting ideas (or "schemes") of the ways that things ought to be.

Scientists, however, have devised more controlled ways of observing others. Let us consider the case-study, survey, testing, naturalistic-observation, and laboratory-observation methods (see Figure 2.2).

Volunteer bias A source of bias or error in research that reflects the prospect that people who offer to participate in research studies differ systematically from people who do not.

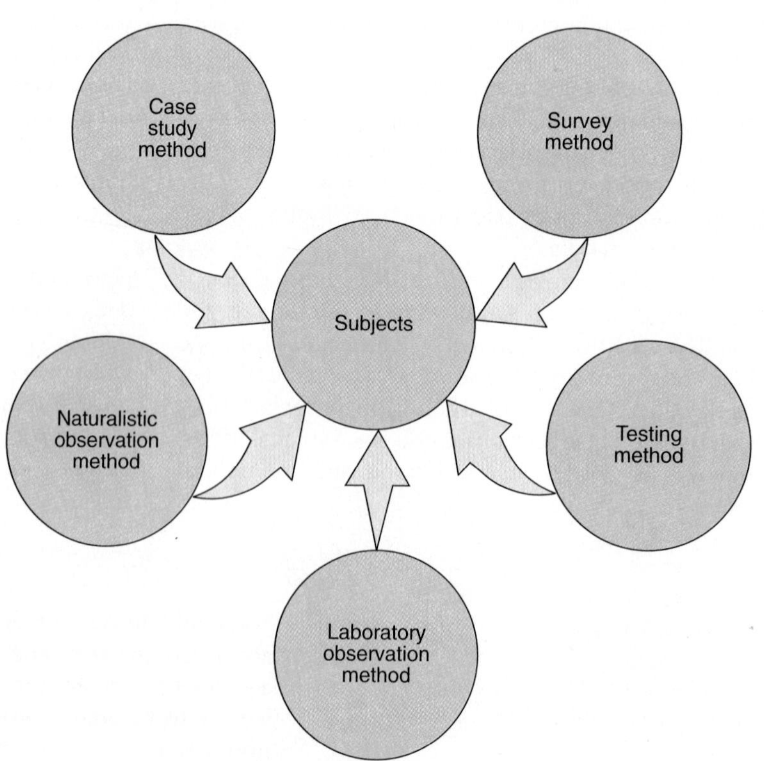

FIGURE 2.2
Methods of Observation in Psychology.

The Case-Study Method

We begin with the case-study method because our own informal ideas about human nature tend to be based on **case studies,** or information we collect about individuals and small groups. But most of us gather our information haphazardly. Often, we see what we want to see. Unscientific accounts of people's behavior are referred to as *anecdotes.* Psychologists attempt to gather information about individuals more carefully.

Sigmund Freud developed psychodynamic theory largely on the basis of case studies. Freud studied his patients in great depth, seeking factors that seemed to contribute to notable patterns of behavior. He followed some patients for many years, meeting with them several times a week.

Of course, there are bound to be gaps in memory when people are questioned. People may also distort their pasts because of social desirability and other factors. Interviewers may also have certain expectations and subtly encourage their subjects to fill in gaps in ways that are consistent with their theoretical perspectives. Psychoanalysts have been criticized, for example, for guiding their patients into viewing their own lives from the psychodynamic perspective (e.g., Bandura, 1986). No wonder, then, that many patients provide "evidence" that is consistent with psychodynamic theory. However, interviewers and other kinds of researchers who hold *any* theoretical viewpoint run the risk of indirectly prodding their subjects into producing what they want to hear.

Case studies are often used to investigate rare occurrences, as in the cases of "Eve" and "Genie." "Eve" (in real life, Chris Sizemore) was an example of a multiple personality (see Chapter 13). "Eve White," as we shall see, was a mousy, well-intentioned woman who had two other "personalities" living inside her. One was "Eve Black," a promiscuous personality who now and then emerged to take control of her behavior.

"Genie's" father locked her in a small room at the age of 20 months and kept her there until she was discovered at the age of 13½ (Curtiss, 1977; Rymer, 1992). Her social contacts were limited to her nearly blind mother, who entered the room only to feed her, and to beatings at the hands of her father. No one spoke to her throughout this period. After her rescue, Genie's language development followed the normal sequence, as outlined in Chapter 8, suggesting the universality of this sequence. Genie did not reach normal proficiency in her use of language, however. Perhaps there is a "sensitive period" for learning language in early childhood.

The case study is also used in psychological consultation. Psychologists learn whatever they can about individuals, agencies, and business firms so that they can suggest ways in which these clients can more effectively meet their challenges. Psychologists base their suggestions on laboratory research whenever possible, but psychological practice is also sometimes an art in which psychologist and client agree that a suggestion or a treatment has been helpful on the basis of the client's self-report.

The Survey Method

In the good old days, when being "sound as a dollar" was a sign of good health, one had to wait until the wee hours of the morning to learn the results of local and national elections. Throughout the evening and early morning hours, suspense would build as ballots from distant neighborhoods and states were tallied. Nowadays, one is barely settled with an after-dinner cup of coffee on election night when the news-show computer cheerfully announces (computers do not, of course, have emotions or make "cheerful" announcements, but they do seem rather smug at times) that it has examined the ballots of a "scientifically selected sample" and then predicts the next president of the United States. All this may

Case study A carefully drawn biography that may be obtained through interviews, questionnaires, and psychological tests.

occur with less than 1 percent of the vote tallied. Pre-election polls also do their share of eroding wonderment and doubt—so much so that some supporters of projected winners must be encouraged to actually vote on Election Day so that predictions will be borne out.

Just as computers and pollsters predict election results and report national opinion on the basis of scientifically selected samples, psychologists conduct **surveys** to learn about behavior and mental processes that cannot be observed in the natural setting or studied experimentally. Psychologists making surveys may employ questionnaires and interviews or examine public records. By distributing questionnaires and analyzing answers with a computer, psychologists can survey many thousands of people at a time.

We alluded to the "Kinsey reports," in which Alfred Kinsey of Indiana University and his colleagues published two surveys of sexual behavior, based on interviews, that shocked the nation: these were *Sexual Behavior in the Human Male* (1948) and *Sexual Behavior in the Human Female* (1953). Kinsey reported that masturbation was virtually universal in his sample of men at a time when masturbation was still widely thought to impair physical or mental health. He also reported that about one woman in three still single at age 25 had engaged in premarital intercourse. In addition to compiling self-reports of behavior, surveys are also used to learn about people's mental processes, including their opinions, attitudes, and values.

Interviews and questionnaires are not foolproof, of course. People may inaccurately recall their behavior or purposefully misrepresent it. Some people try to ingratiate themselves with their interviewers by answering in what they perceive to be the socially desirable direction. The Kinsey studies all relied on male interviewers, for example. It has been speculated that women interviewees might have been more open and honest with women interviewers. Similar problems may occur when interviewers and those surveyed are from different ethnic or socioeconomic backgrounds. Other people may falsify attitudes and exaggerate problems to draw attention to themselves or just to try to foul up the results.

The results of a survey of 210,739 first-year students entering two- and four-year postsecondary institutions in the fall of 1991 are instructive. The students were asked to identify themselves as either far left, liberal, middle of the road, conservative, or far right in their political views. As you can see in Table 2.1, about one student in four (25.7%) rated herself or himself as liberal or very liberal ("far left"); about one student in five (20.3%), as conservative or very conservative ("far right"); and slightly more than half (54%) rated themselves as middle of the road.

Table 2.2 shows the results of a survey of the political views of the same students on specific issues. The students were asked to respond to the statements shown, and others, according to a commonly used five-point scale:

__ Agree strongly

__ Agree

__ No opinion

__ Disagree

__ Disagree strongly

One could say the that students neared a consensus on the statements that "Just because a man thinks that a woman has led him on does not entitle him to have sex with her," and "Government is not doing enough to control pollution." Only about one student in four agreed with the traditionalist stance that "Married women's activities are best confined to home and family." Although nearly four students out of five rated themselves as middle of the road or liberal, consider their responses to statements that could be considered liberal: Only about one student in five agreed that "Marijuana should be legalized," and only about one student in four agreed that "Taxes should be raised to reduce the federal deficit."

TABLE 2.1: Political Views of First-Year Students

Far left	2.1%
Liberal	23.6
Middle of the road	54.0
Conservative	19.1
Far right	1.2

Source of data: A. W. Astin, "The American Freshman: National Norms for Fall 1991." Published by The American Council on Education and University of California at Los Angeles. Reprinted from *The Chronicle of Higher Education* (1992, August 26), p. 13.

TABLE 2.2: Percentage of First-Year Students Who Agree Strongly or Somewhat That—	
Government is not doing enough to protect the consumer from faulty goods and services	69.1%
Government is not doing enough to control pollution	85.5
Taxes should be raised to reduce the federal deficit	25.5
There is too much concern in courts for the rights of criminals	65.3
Military spending should be increased	26.0
Abortion should be legal	63.0
The death penalty should be abolished	21.1
It is all right for two people who really like each other to have sex even if they've known each other for a very short time	50.1
Married women's activities are best confined to home and family	26.0
Marijuana should be legalized	20.9
Busing to achieve racial balance in schools is all right	54.7
It is important to have laws prohibiting homosexual relationships	42.2
The chief benefit of college is that it increases one's earning power	71.0
Employers should be allowed to require employees or job applicants to take drug tests	80.8
The best way to control AIDS is through widespread, mandatory testing	66.4
Just because a man thinks that a woman has "led him on" does not entitle him to have sex with her	87.1
The government should do more to control the sale of handguns	78.1
A national health-care plan is needed to cover everybody's medical costs	75.8
Nuclear disarmament is attainable	63.7
Racial discrimination is no longer a major problem in America	20.3
The federal government should do more to discourage energy consumption	78.5
Realistically, an individual can do little to bring about changes in our society	31.3

Source of data: A. W. Astin, "The American Freshman: National Norms for Fall 1991." Published by The American Council on Education and University of California at Los Angeles. Reprinted from *The Chronicle of Higher Education* (1992, August 26), p. 13.

The death penalty is supported by a clear majority of students (only about one student in five would like to see it abolished), although one might consider support of the death penalty to represent a conservative political view. Only one student in five, moreover, agreed that "Racial discrimination is no longer a major problem in America." Ethnic diversity is unfortunately still connected with a great deal of prejudice and social friction. Fortunately, fewer than one-third of the students surveyed (31.3%) agreed with the statement that "Realistically, an individual can do little to bring about changes in our society." If the majority of students believe in their capacity to bring about meaningful social changes, perhaps they will apply themselves to doing so.

I noted that this survey was conducted with 210,739 students. This vast number allowed the investigators to obtain information that allows them to compare and contrast the views and opinions of first-year students at many colleges and universities across the United States. If their sole intention had been to obtain a sample that represented the entire entering first-year class of 1991, however, a random sample of 1500 or so first-year students would have sufficed.

The Testing Method

Psychologists also use psychological tests—such as intelligence, aptitude, and personality tests—to measure various traits and characteristics among a population. There is a wide range of psychological tests, and they measure traits ranging from verbal ability and achievement to anxiety, depression, the need for social dominance, musical aptitude, and vocational interests.

Psychological test results, like the results of surveys, can be distorted by respondents who answer in a socially desirable direction or attempt to exaggerate problems. For these reasons, some commonly used psychological tests have items built into them called **validity scales.** Validity scales are sensitive to misrepresentations and alert the psychologist when test results may be deceptive.

Survey A method of scientific investigation in which a large sample of people is questioned about their attitudes or behavior.

Validity scales Groups of test items that suggest whether or not the test results are valid (measure what they are supposed to measure).

FIGURE 2.3
The Naturalistic-Observation Method.

Jane van Lawick Goodall has used the naturalistic-observation method with chimpanzees, quietly observing them for many years in their natural environments. In using this method, scientists try to avoid interfering with the animals or people they observe, even though this sometimes means allowing an animal to be mistreated by other animals or to die from a curable illness. We learn from Goodall that tools are used by primates other than human beings. The chimp in the left-hand photo is using a stick as a tool to poke around in a termite hill for food. Goodall's observations have also taught us that not only humans use kissing as a social greeting (see right-hand photo). Male chimps have even been observed greeting females by kissing their hands. Very European?

The Naturalistic-Observation Method

You use **naturalistic observation** every day of your life. That is, you observe people in their natural habitats.

So do psychologists. The next time you opt for a fast-food burger lunch, look around. Pick out slender people and overweight people and observe whether they eat their burgers and fries differently. Do the overweight eat more rapidly? Chew less frequently? Leave less food on their plates? This is precisely the type of research psychologists have recently used to study the eating habits of normal-weight and overweight people. In fact, if you notice some mysterious people at McDonald's peering out over sunglasses and occasionally tapping the head of a partly concealed microphone, perhaps they are recording their observations of other people's eating habits, even as you watch.

In naturalistic observation, psychologists and other scientists observe behavior in the field, or "where it happens." They try to avoid interfering with the behaviors they are observing by using **unobtrusive** measures. Jane Goodall has observed the behavior of chimpanzees in their natural environment to learn about their social behavior, sexual behavior, use of tools, and other facts of chimp life (see Figure 2.3). Her observations have shown us that (1) we were incorrect to think that only people use tools; and (2) kissing, as a greeting, is used by chimpanzees as well as people.

The naturalistic-observation method has, in fact, taught us that not only people use tools.

Naturalistic observation A scientific method in which organisms are observed in their natural environments.

Unobtrusive Not interfering.

Do not conclude, however, that using tools or kissing are inborn, or **instinctive,** behaviors among primates. Chimps, like people, can learn from experience. It may be that they learned how to use tools and to kiss. The naturalistic-observation method provides descriptive information, but it is not the best method for determining the causes of behavior.

There are many problems with the naturalistic-observation method. For instance, sometimes we see what we want to see. Kissing behavior among chimps seems to serve a social function similar to human kissing, but "kissing" by the kissing gourami, a tropical fish, seems to be a test of strength. We must be cautious in our interpretations.

Finally, it is difficult to determine the causes of behavior through naturalistic observation. After visiting a few bars near the university where I teach, you might conclude, as you duck to avoid the flying ashtrays and chairs, that alcohol causes aggressive behavior. There is little doubt that aggression often accompanies drinking, as we shall see in the following sections, but it is not so certain that alcohol causes aggression—at least among college men who are social drinkers.

The Laboratory-Observation Method: Under the Microscope?

I first became acquainted with the laboratory-observation method when, as a child, I was given tropical fish. My parents spent a small fortune to keep my new dependents in sound health. My laboratory for observation—my tank—was an artificial sea world. I filtered impurities out of the water with an electric pump. I warmed the water with a heater with an angry orange eye. I regularly assessed and regulated the acidity (pH) of the water. All this enabled me to while away the hours watching the fish swim in and out of protecting leaves, establish and defend territories, and, sometimes, court mates and breed. I even noted how the fish became conditioned to swim to the surface of the water when the light was turned on in the room. They apparently came to associate the light with the appearance of food.

By bringing the fish into my home, I did not have to voyage to the reefs of the Caribbean or the mouth of the Amazon to make my observations. I also created just the conditions I wished, and I observed how my subjects reacted to them.

Something like wondering children, psychologists at times place lower animals and people into controlled laboratory environments where they can be

Instinctive Inborn, natural, unlearned.

The Naturalistic-Observation Method. In the naturalistic-observation method, psychologists study behavior in the field, "where it happens." For example, psychologists have recorded eating behavior in fast-food restaurants to learn whether or not obese people eat more rapidly or take larger bites than other people.

readily observed and where the effects of specific conditions can be discerned. Figure 1.2 on page 13 shows one such environment, which is constructed so that pigeons receive reinforcers for pecking buttons.

With people, the **laboratory** takes many forms. Do not confine your imagination to rows of Bunsen burners and the smell of sulfur or to rats and pigeons in wire cages being reinforced with food pellets from heaven.

Figure 15.4 (see p. 599), for example, diagrams a laboratory set-up at Yale University, where human subjects (the "Teacher" in the diagram) were urged to deliver electric shock to other people (so-called Learners) as a way of signalling them that they had made errors on a learning task. You will see that this study was inspired by the atrocities committed by apparently typical German citizens during World War II, and its true purpose was to determine how easy it would be to induce normal people to hurt others. In studies on sensation and perception, human subjects may be placed in dark or quiet rooms in order to learn how bright or loud a stimulus must be before it can be detected.

Intelligence and Achievement. Correlations between intelligence test scores and academic achievement—as measured by school grades and achievement tests—tend to be positive and strong. Does the correlational method allow us to say that intelligence *causes* or *is responsible for* academic achievements? Why, or why not?

THE CORRELATIONAL METHOD: SEEING WHAT GOES UP AND WHAT COMES DOWN

Are people with higher intelligence more likely to do well in school? Are people with a stronger need for achievement likely to climb higher up the corporate ladder? What is the relationship between stress and health?

Correlation follows observation. By using the **correlational method,** psychologists investigate whether one observed behavior or measured trait is related to, or correlated with, another. Consider the variables of intelligence and academic performance. The variables of intelligence and academic performance are assigned numbers such as intelligence test scores and academic averages. Then the numbers or scores are mathematically related and expressed as a **correlation coefficient.** A correlation coefficient is a number that varies between +1.00 and –1.00.[2]

Numerous studies report **positive correlations** between intelligence and achievement. Generally speaking, the higher people score on intelligence tests, the better their academic performance is likely to be. The scores attained on intelligence tests are positively correlated (about +0.60 to +0.70) with overall academic achievement (see Figure 2.4).

What of the need for achievement and getting ahead? The need for achievement can be assessed by rating stories told by subjects for the presence of this need (see Chapter 9). Getting ahead can be assessed in many ways—salary and the prestige of one's occupation or level within the corporation are just a few of them.

There is a **negative correlation** between stress and health. As the amount of stress affecting us increases, the functioning of our immune systems decreases (see Chapter 12). Under high levels of stress, many people show poorer health.

Correlational research may suggest but does not show cause and effect. For instance, it may seem logical to assume that high intelligence makes it possible for children to profit from education. Research has also shown, however, that education contributes to higher scores on intelligence tests. Children placed in richly stimulating Head Start programs at an early age do better later on intelligence tests than age mates who did not have this experience. The relationship between intelligence and academic performance may not be as simple as you might have thought. What of the link between stress and health? Does stress impair health, or is it possible that people in poorer health encounter higher levels of stress?

Thus, correlational research does not allow us to place clear "cause" and "effect" labels on variables. Nevertheless, correlational research can point the way to

[2]The mathematics of the correlation coefficient are discussed further in Appendix A.

Laboratory A place in which theories, techniques, and methods are tested and demonstrated.

√**Correlational method** A scientific method that studies the relationships between variables.

Correlation coefficient A number between +1.00 to −1.00 that expresses the strength and direction (positive or negative) of the relationship between two variables.

Positive correlation A relationship between variables in which one variable increases as the other also increases.

Negative correlation A relationship between two variables in which one variable increases as the other decreases.

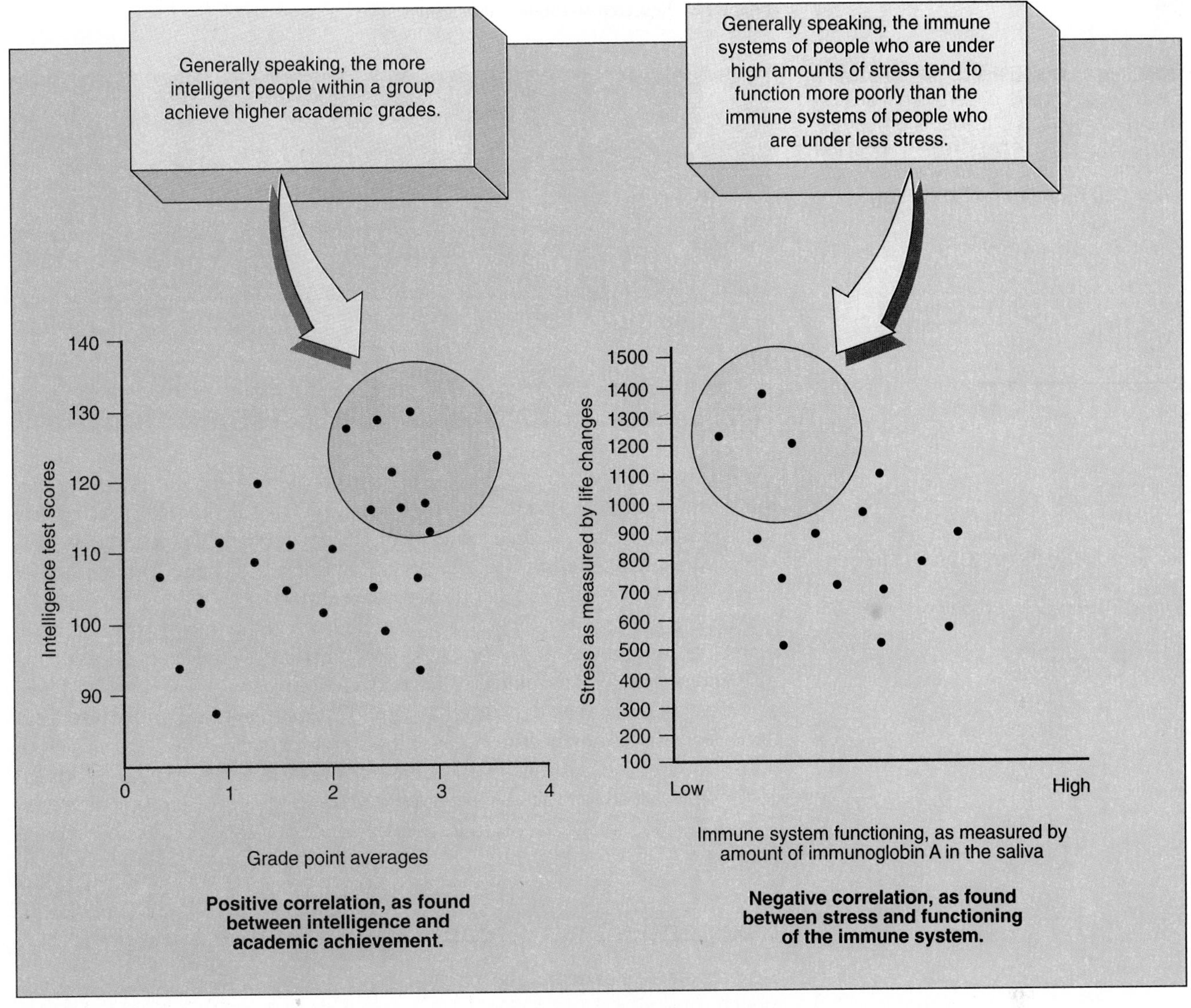

FIGURE 2.4
Positive and Negative Correlations.

When there is a positive correlation between variables, as there is between intelligence and achievement, one tends to increase as the other increases. By and large, the higher people score on intelligence tests, the better their academic performance is likely to be, as in the diagram to the left. (Each dot is located to represent an individual's intelligence test score and grade point average.) Similarly, there is a positive correlation between engaging in exercise and physical health, as we shall see in Chapter 12. On the other hand, there is a negative correlation between stress and health. As the amount of stress we experience increases, the functioning of our immune systems tends to decrease. Correlational research may suggest but does not demonstrate cause and effect.

profitable experimental research. That is, if there were no correlation between intelligence and achievement, there would be little purpose in running experiments to determine causal relationships. If there were no relationship between the need for achievement and success, it would be pointless to ask whether the need for achievement contributes to success.

Experiment A scientific method that seeks to confirm cause-and-effect relationships by introducing independent variables and observing their effects on dependent variables.

Treatment In experiments, a condition received by participants so that its effects may be observed.

THE EXPERIMENTAL METHOD: TRYING THINGS OUT

Most psychologists would agree that the preferred method for answering questions concerning cause and effect is the experimental method. In an **experiment,** a group of participants receives a **treatment,** such as a dose of alcohol.

What are the Effects of Alcohol? Psychologists have undertaken research to determine alcohol's effects on behavior. Questions have been raised about the soundness of research in which subjects *know* they have drunk alcohol. Why?

The participants, or subjects, are then observed carefully to determine whether the treatment makes a difference in their behavior. Does alcohol affect their ability to take tests, for example? In another example, environmental psychologists have varied room temperatures and the background levels of noise to see whether these treatments have an effect on subjects' behavior.

Experiments are used whenever possible in contemporary psychological research because they allow psychologists to control directly the experiences of animals and people to determine the effects of a treatment.

A psychologist may theorize that alcohol leads to aggression because it reduces fear of consequences or because it generally energizes the activity levels of drinkers. He or she may then hypothesize that the treatment of a specified dosage of alcohol will lead to increases in aggression. Let us follow the example of the effects of alcohol on aggression to further our understanding of the experimental method.

Independent and Dependent Variables

In an experiment to determine whether or not alcohol causes aggression, experimental subjects would be given a quantity of alcohol, and its effects would be measured. Alcohol would be considered an **independent variable.** The presence of an independent variable is manipulated by the experimenters so that its effects may be determined. The independent variable of alcohol may be administered at different levels, or doses, from none or very little, to enough to cause intoxication, or drunkenness.

The measured results or outcomes in an experiment are called **dependent variables.** The presence of dependent variables presumably depends on the independent variables. In an experiment to determine whether alcohol influences aggression, aggressive behavior would be a dependent variable. Other dependent variables of interest in an experiment on the effects of alcohol might include sexual arousal, visual-motor coordination, and performance on intellectual tasks such as defining words or doing numerical computations.

In an experiment on the relationships between temperature and aggression, temperature would be an independent variable and aggressive behavior would be a dependent variable. We might use various temperature settings, from below freezing to blistering hot, and study the effects of each. We might also use a second independent variable such as social provocation and insult certain subjects but not others. Then we could also study the interaction between temperature and social provocation as they influence aggression.

Experiments can be quite complex, with several independent and dependent variables. Psychologists often use complex experimental designs and sophisticated statistical techniques to determine the effect of each independent variable, as that variable acts alone and in combination with others, on each dependent variable.

Independent variable A condition in a scientific study that is manipulated so that its effects may be observed.

Dependent variable A measure of an assumed effect of an independent variable.

Experimental and Control Groups

Ideal experiments use experimental and control subjects or groups. **Experimental subjects** receive the treatment, whereas **control subjects** do not. Every effort is made to ensure that all other conditions are held constant for both experimental and control subjects. In this way, researchers can have confidence that the experimental outcomes reflect the treatments and not chance factors or chance fluctuations in behavior.

In an experiment concerning the effects of alcohol on aggression, experimental subjects would be given alcohol and control subjects would not. In a complex experiment, different experimental groups might receive (1) different dosages of alcohol and (2) different types of social provocations.

Blinds and Double Blinds

One experiment on the effects of alcohol on aggression (Boyatzis, 1974) reported that men at parties where beer and liquor were served acted more aggressively than control subjects at parties where only soft drinks were served. But we must be cautious in interpreting these findings because the experimental subjects *knew* that they had drunk alcohol, and the control subjects *knew* that they had not. Aggression that appeared to result from alcohol might not have reflected drinking per se; instead, it might have reflected subjects' expectations about the effects of alcohol. People tend to act in stereotypical ways when they believe that they have been drinking alcohol. For instance, men tend to become less anxious in social situations, more aggressive, and more sexually aroused.

A **placebo,** or "sugar pill," often results in the behavior that people expect. Physicians now and then give sugar pills to demanding, but healthy, patients; and many patients who receive placebos report that they feel better. When subjects in psychological experiments are given placebos—such as tonic water—but think that they have drunk alcohol, we can conclude that changes in behavior stem from their beliefs about alcohol, not the alcohol itself.

Well-designed experiments control for the effects of expectations by creating conditions under which subjects are unaware of, or **blind** to, the treatment they have received. Yet researchers may also have expectations. They may, in effect, be "rooting for" a certain treatment. For instance, tobacco-company executives may wish to show that cigarette smoking is harmless. It is thus useful if the people measuring the experimental outcomes are also unaware of who has received the treatment. Studies in which both subjects and experimenters are unaware of who has received the treatment are called **double-blind studies.**

Double-blind studies are required by the Food and Drug Administration before they will allow the marketing of new drugs (Margraf et al., 1991). The drug and the placebo look and taste alike. Subjects are assigned to the drug or placebo at random, and neither the subjects nor the people who measure their progress know who has received the drug and who has received the placebo. After the final measurements are made, an impartial panel judges whether the effects of the drug differed from those of the placebo.

It is true that in many experiments, neither the subjects in the experiment nor the researchers who are running the experiment know which subjects have received the real treatment and which subjects have received a placebo ("sugar pill"). Such experiments are referred to as double-blind studies, and they control for the effects of subjects' and researchers' expectations.

Experimental subjects Subjects receiving a treatment in an experiment.

Control subjects Experimental participants who do not receive the experimental treatment but for whom all other conditions are comparable to those of experimental subjects.

Placebo A bogus treatment that has the appearance of being genuine.

Blind In experimental terminology, unaware of whether or not one has received a treatment.

Double-blind study A study in which neither the subjects nor the persons measuring results know who has received the treatment.

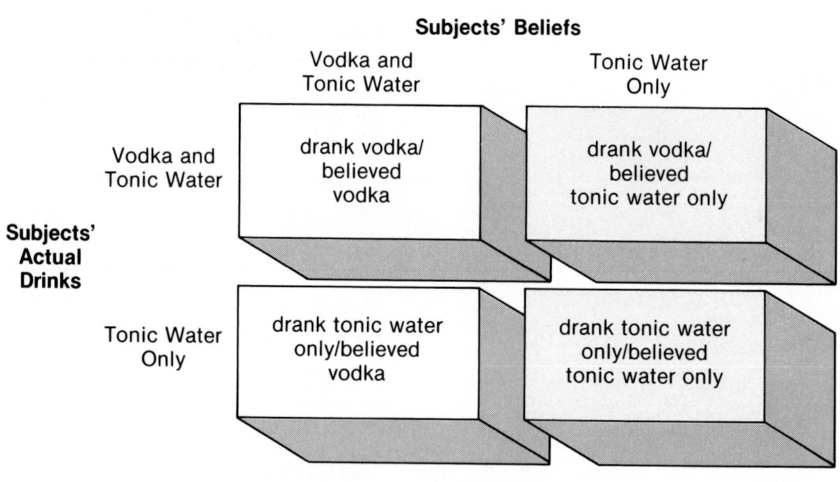

FIGURE 2.5
The Experimental Conditions in the Lang Study. The taste of vodka cannot be discerned when vodka is mixed with tonic water. For this reason, it was possible for subjects in the Lang study on the effects of alcohol to be kept "blind" as to whether or not they had actually drunk alcohol. Blind studies allow psychologists to control for the effects of subject expectations.

In one double-blind study on the effects of alcohol, Alan Lang and his colleagues (1975) pretested a highball of vodka and tonic water to determine that it could not be discriminated by taste from tonic water alone. They recruited as subjects college men who described themselves as social drinkers. Some subjects received vodka and tonic water, whereas others received tonic water only. Of subjects who received vodka, half were misled into believing that they had drunk tonic water only (Figure 2.5). Of subjects receiving tonic water only, half were misled into believing that their drink contained vodka. Thus, half the subjects were blind to the treatment they received. Experimenters who measured aggressive responses were also blind concerning which subjects had received vodka.

The research team found that men who believed that they had drunk vodka responded more aggressively to a provocation than men who believed that they had drunk tonic water only. The actual content of the drink was immaterial. That is, men who had actually drunk alcohol acted no more aggressively than men who had drunk tonic water only. The results of the Lang study differ dramatically from those reported by Boyatzis, perhaps because the Boyatzis study did not control for the effects of expectations or beliefs about alcohol.

Note that in the Lang study on alcohol and aggression, alcohol was operationally defined as a certain dose of vodka. Other types of drinks and other dosages of vodka might have had different effects. Aggression was operationally defined as selecting a certain amount of electric shock and administering it to another student participating in a psychological experiment. College men might behave differently when they drink in other situations—for example, when they are insulted by a supporter of an opposing football team or are threatened outside a bar.

Is it possible, as the results of the Lang study suggest, that alcohol does not cause aggression, that centuries of folklore have been in error? Yes, quite possible. Other studies (replications) that control for the effects of expectations suggest that drinking alcohol increases aggressive behavior only when drinkers believe that aggression is the appropriate response for them (Jeavons & Taylor, 1985; Taylor & Sears, 1988).

Although alcohol is frequently linked to aggression, there is *no* scientific evidence that alcohol causes aggression.

Psychology is an empirical science. Centuries of folklore may stimulate research into certain topics, but folklore is not acceptable evidence within science.

What, then, do we make of these findings? Why does belief that one has drunk alcohol increase aggression, whereas alcohol itself may not? Perhaps alcohol gives one a certain social role to play in our culture—the role of the uninhibited social mover. Perhaps alcohol also provides an excuse for aggressive or other antisocial behavior. After all, the drinker can always claim, "It wasn't me; it was the alcohol." What will you think the next time someone says, "It was the alcohol?"

To properly study behavior, psychologists must not only be skilled in the uses and limitations of research methods, they must also treat research subjects ethically.

ETHICS IN PSYCHOLOGICAL RESEARCH AND PRACTICE

Psychologists adhere to a number of **ethical** standards that are intended to promote the dignity of the individual, foster human welfare, and maintain scientific integrity (McGovern et al., 1991). They also assure that psychologists do not undertake research methods or treatments that are harmful to subjects or clients (American Psychological Association, 1992). Exceptions come into play, however, as we shall see.

Research with Human Subjects

We described how Lang and his colleagues (1975) gave small doses of alcohol to college students who were social drinkers. Other researchers, however, have paid alcoholics—people who have difficulties limiting their alcohol consumption—to drink in the laboratory so that they could study their reactions and those of family members (e.g., Jacob et al., 1991). Practices such as these raise more complex ethical questions (Beutler & Kendall, 1991; Stricker, 1991). For example, paying the alcoholics to drink in the laboratory, and providing the alcohol, could be construed as encouraging them to engage in self-destructive behavior (Koocher, 1991).

In order to help avoid harming subjects, human subjects must provide **informed consent** before they participate in research programs. Having a general overview of the research and the opportunity to choose not to participate apparently gives subjects a sense of control and decreases the stress of participating (Dill et al., 1982).

It is true that human subjects may not be pressured into participating in psychological research. Such pressuring would be considered unethical and unacceptable within the profession of psychology.

Psychologists treat the records of research subjects and clients as **confidential.** This is because psychologists respect people's privacy and also because people are more likely to express their true thoughts and feelings when researchers or therapists keep their disclosures confidential (Blanck et al., 1992). Sometimes conflicts of interest arise, however, as when a client threatens a third party and the psychologist feels an obligation to warn the third party (Rathus et al., 1994).

Ethical standards tend to limit the types of research that psychologists may conduct. For example, how can we determine whether early separation from

---

Ethical Moral; referring to one's system of deriving standards for determining what is moral.

Informed consent The term used by psychologists to indicate that a person has agreed to participate in research after receiving information about the purposes of the study and the nature of the treatments.

Confidential Secret; not to be disclosed.

one's mother impairs social development? One research direction is to observe the development of children who have been separated from their mothers from an early age. It is difficult to draw conclusions from such research, however, because the same factors that led to the separation, such as family tragedy or irresponsible parents, instead of the separation itself, may have led to the observed outcomes. Scientifically, it would be more sound to run experiments in which children are purposefully separated from their mothers at an early age and compared with children who are not. Psychologists would not seriously consider such research because of ethical standards. However, experiments in which infants are purposefully separated from mothers have been run with lower animals.

The Use of Deception. A number of psychological experiments could not be run without deceiving their human subjects. However, the use of deception raises ethical issues. Before we explore them, however, consider the Lang (Lang et al., 1975) study on alcohol and aggression. In that study, the researchers had to (1) misinform subjects about the beverage they were drinking and (2) mislead subjects into believing that they were giving other participants electric shocks when they were actually only pressing switches on a dead control board. (Pressing these switches was the operational definition of aggression in the study.) In the Lang study, students who believed they had drunk vodka were more aggressive than students who believed they had not. The actual content of the beverages was immaterial. This study could not have been run without deceiving the subjects. Foiling their expectations or beliefs was crucial to the experiment, and the potential benefits of the research may well outweigh the possible harmful effects of the deceptions. Certainly it seems preferable that subjects only thought they were shocking other people. After all, would we prefer them actually to deliver painful electric shocks?

Yet some psychologists are opposed to using deception—period. Diana Baumrind (1985) argues, for example, that deception-based research can harm not only research subjects but also the reputation of the profession of psychology. In a study that supports Baumrind's views, one group of students participated in experiments in which they were deceived. Afterward, they regarded psychologists as being less trustworthy than did students who were not deceived (Smith & Richardson, 1983). Baumrind argues that deception might eventually cause the public to lose trust in psychologists and other professionals.

In any event, many studies continue to employ deception (Adair et al., 1985). Psychological ethics require that research subjects who are deceived be **debriefed** afterward to help eliminate misconceptions and anxieties about the research and to leave them with their dignity intact (Blanck et al., 1992). After the Lang study was completed, the subjects were informed of the deceptions and of the rationale for them. Students who had actually drunk alcohol were given coffee and a **breathalyzer** test so that the researchers could be sure they were not leaving the laboratory in an intoxicated state.

It is true that psychologists cannot carry out certain research studies without deceiving participants as to their purposes and methods. However, subjects are debriefed after such studies are completed.

Psychologists use deception in research only when the research could not be run without it. As with other ethical dilemmas, deception is used when the psychologist believes that the benefits will outweigh the harm.

Debrief To receive information about a just-completed procedure.

Breathalyzer A device that measures the quantity of alcohol in the body by analyzing the breath.

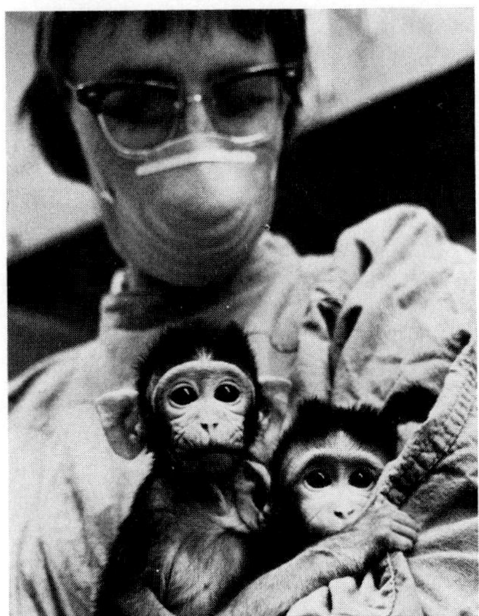

The Ethics of Animal Research. Now and then, psychologists and other scientists harm animals to answer research questions that may yield important benefits for people. Justifying such harm poses a major ethical dilemma.

Lesion An injury that results in impaired behavior or loss of a function.

Research with Animal Subjects

Psychologists and other scientists frequently turn to animal subjects to conduct research that cannot be carried out with humans. For example, experiments on the effects of early separation from the mother have been done with monkeys and other animals. Such research has helped psychologists investigate the formation of parent–child bonds of attachment (see Chapter 10).

Experiments with infant monkeys highlight some of the dilemmas faced by psychologists and other scientists who contemplate potentially harmful research with people or lower animals. Psychologists and biologists who study the workings of the brain destroy sections of the brains of laboratory animals to learn how they influence behavior. For instance, a **lesion** in one part of a brain structure will cause a rat to overeat (see Chapter 9). A lesion elsewhere will cause the rat to go on a crash diet. Psychologists generalize to people from experiments such as these in the hope that we may find solutions to persistent human problems such as eating disorders. Proponents of the use of animals in research argue that major advances in medicine and psychology could not have taken place without them (Fowler, 1992; Martinez, 1992; Pardes et al., 1991).

Psychologists must still face the ethical dilemma of subjecting animals to harm. As with human subjects, psychologists follow the principle that animals should be subjected to harm only when there is no alternative and they believe that the benefits of the research will justify the harm (American Psychological Association, 1992).

Psychologists are human, of course, and capable of error. Human and animal subjects are occasionally exposed to more harm than anticipated. Psychologists generally make every effort to minimize the potential harm of their research, however.

STUDY GUIDE

EXERCISE: True or False?

Circle the T or F for each of the following, to indicate whether the item is true or false. Check your answers in the key given below. It is more important at this time for you to understand why each item is true or false than to get them all right.

T F 1. In the scientific method, subjects are randomly selected and assigned to experimental groups or control groups.

T F 2. A hypothesis is a formulation of the relationships and principles that underlie observed events that allows us to explain and predict behavior.

T F 3. A hypothesis is a specific statement about behavior or mental processes that is tested through research.

T F 4. A subject is a person who volunteers to participate in a scientific study.

T F 5. In the Lang study on the effects of alcohol on aggression, aggression was operationally defined as selection of a level of shock to deliver to another person.

T F 6. The most important factor about a sample is that it is very large.

T F 7. If a sample is not randomly selected, the results of the study are inaccurate.

T F 8. A random sample is selected by picking out telephone numbers in a directory by chance.

T F 9. People who volunteer to participate in research studies differ from people who refuse to participate.

T F 10. There is a positive correlation between intelligence and academic achievement.

T F 11. There is a negative correlation between two variables. We can conclude that increasing one variable causes the other to decrease.

T F 12. Researchers attempt to use unobtrusive measures in the naturalistic-observation method so that they do not influence the behavior they are observing.

T F 13. Experimental blinds aim at controlling for the effects of expectations.

T F 14. Case studies differ from surveys in the numbers of subjects studied.

T F 15. It is unethical for a psychologist to breach confidentiality with a client, even when the client states that she or he is going to kill a third party.

Answer Key to True-False Exercise

1. F. This statement describes an experiment. The scientific method is a way of obtaining scientific evidence in which research questions or hypotheses are formulated and tested.

2. F. The statement defines a theory, not a hypothesis.

3. T.

4. F. A subject is a participant in a scientific study. Whether or not the subject volunteers is immaterial to the definition of the term.

5. T. The operational definition of a variable is defined in terms of the methods used to create or measure that variable.

6. F. The most important factor about a sample is that it represent the targeted population.

7. F. The results of the study may be accurate enough for the sample in the study. The results may not be able to be generalized to a target population, however.

8. F. A random sample is defined as a sample that is drawn so that each member of a population has an equal chance of being selected to participate. Telephone numbers may be used in random sampling, but are not essential to the definition of random sampling.

9. T. Sure they do. They may be more willing to help other people, more interested in research, or simply have more time. In the case of sex surveys, they may also be more willing to disclose intimate information. Factors such as these may introduce volunteer bias into the results of a study.

10. T. That is, people who are more intelligent, for example, speaking, also tend to obtain better grades in school. Such a correlation does not delve into matters of cause and effect, however.

11. F. We can assume that as one variable increases, the other is *likely* to decrease. Correlation does not demonstrate cause and effect, however.

12. T.

13. T True. Double-blind studies, which are the standard for demonstrating the effectiveness of new drugs, attempt to control for the expectations of both the subjects and the researchers.

14. T Case studies usually address an individual or a small group, whereas surveys may address thousands of people. Ways of acquiring information may be similar, however, including interviews and questionnaires.

15. F. As pointed out in the text, such situations create ethical dilemmas, but many psychologists—and many states—require that a psychologist warn the threatened party of the danger.

ESL—BRIDGING THE GAP

This part is divided into

1. idioms
2. cultural references
3. phrases and expressions in which words are used differently from their regular meaning, or are used as metaphors

Idioms

drawing conclusions (41)—reaching conclusions; arriving at conclusions; coming to conclusions
bear out (41)—prove
borne out (48)—proved
built into (49)—already in

Cultural References

southern California Yuppies (44)—people between about 25 and 45 who are concerned primarily with money and career
tonic water (56)—non-alcoholic carbonated water

Phrases and Expressions (Different Usage)

to climb higher up the corporate ladder (52)—continual promotion in a large business
cause and effect (52)—something happens and as a result something else happens
running experiments (53)—doing experiments
further our understanding (54)—help us to understand more
outcomes (54)—results
are held constant (55)—remain the same
chance factors . . . fluctuations (55)—occurrences which are not predictable or expected
"rooting for" (55)—hoping for; encouraging and wanting
at random (55)—not in a predetermined or planned manner
social mover (57)—one who is socially aggressive and influential
target population (44)—the people whom the experimenters wish to study
samples were drawn (44)—samples were gotten from
"sound as a dollar" (47)—dependable
to foul up the results (48)—to cause the results to be invalid
workings of the brain (59)—how the brain operates
crash diet (59)—when a person almost stops eating for a short period of time for the purpose of losing weight
face the ethical dilemma (59)—consider carefully the moral problem

CHAPTER REVIEW

SECTION 1: The Scientific Method

Objective 1: Describe the features of the scientific method.

The (1) ______________fic method is an organized way of going about expanding and refining knowledge. Psychologists usually begin by formulating a (2) r______________ question. A research question may be studied in its question format, or it may be reworded into a (3) ______________sis, which is a specific statement about behavior or mental processes that is tested through research. Psychologists next examine the research question or (4) t______________ the hypothesis through carefully controlled methods such as naturalistic or laboratory observation and the experiment. Psychologists draw (5) ______________sions about their research questions or the accuracy of their hypotheses on the basis of their research (6) ob______________s or findings. Research findings often suggest refinements to psychological (7) ______________ries and, consequently, new avenues of research.

As psychologists draw conclusions from research evidence, they are guided by principles of (8) cr______________ thinking. For example, they try not to confuse connections (correlations) between the findings with (9) c______________ and effect. As critical thinkers, psychologists similarly attempt to avoid (10) over______________ing or overgeneralizing their results.

Some psychologists include (11) ______________cation of research reports in professional journals as a crucial part of the scientific method. Psychologists and other scientists are obligated to provide enough details of their work that other scientists will be able to repeat or (12) ______________cate it. Publication also permits the scientific community at large to (13) ev______________, and perhaps criticize, the methods and conclusions of other scientists.

SECTION 2: Samples and Populations

Objective 2: Explain how psychologists use samples in an effort to represent populations.

Samples must accurately (14) rep______________ the population they are intended to reflect. Otherwise, we cannot (15) ______________lize from research samples to populations.

The individuals, or (16) ______________jects, who are studied are referred to as a sample. A sample is a segment of a (17) ______________ation.

Objective 3: Discuss the use of sampling in psychology to represent human diversity.

Women's groups and health professionals argue that there is a historic bias in favor of conducting research with (18: Circle one: Men or Women). Most large-sample research conducted into life style and health has been conducted with (19: Circle one: Men or Women). Research samples have also tended to (20: Circle one: Overrepresent or Underrepresent) minority ethnic groups in the population. The Kinsey studies on sexual behavior did not adequately represent (21) Af______________ Americans, poor people, the elderly, and diverse other groups.

In a (22) r______________ sample, each member of a population has an equal chance of being selected to participate. Researchers can also use a (23) ______________fied sample, which is drawn so that identified subgroups in the population are represented proportionately in the sample. A large, randomly selected sample (24: Circle one: Will or Will not) show reasonably accurate stratification.

The concept behind (25) ______________teer bias is that people who offer to participate in research studies differ systematically from people who do not.

Gail Wyatt conducted a survey to compare the sexual behavior of white women and (26) ______________-American women. When social class differences were mathematically considered, Wyatt found that the ages of initial intercourse for the African-American and white women in her sample were (27: Circle one: Similar or Dissimilar). The white women in Wyatt's sample (28: Circle one: Did or Did not) match the population of white women in Los Angeles County.

SECTION 3: Methods of Observation: The Better To See You With

Objective 4: Discuss the strengths and weaknesses of the case-study method.

Sigmund (29) ______________d developed psychodynamic theory largely on the basis of case studies. Problems with the case study include gaps in (30) m______________ and purposeful distortion of the past. Interviewers may also have certain expectations and subtly guide their subjects to fill in gaps in ways that are (31: Circle one: Consistent or Inconsistent) with their theoretical perspectives.

Objective 5: Discuss the strengths and weaknesses of the survey method.

Psychologists conduct surveys to learn about behavior and mental processes that cannot be observed in the natural setting or studied (32) ex__________ally. Psychologists making surveys may employ questionnaires and interviews or examine public (33) re__________s. In responding to surveys, people may inaccurately recall their behavior or purposefully (34) mis__________ it. Some people try to ingratiate themselves with their interviewers by answering in what they perceive to be the (35) __________ly desirable direction. Other people may falsify attitudes and exaggerate problems to draw (36) at__________ to themselves or try to foul up the results.

Objective 6: Discuss the strengths and weaknesses of the testing method.

Psychologists also use psychological tests to measure various (37) t__________s and characteristics among a population. Psychological test results, like the results of surveys, can be distorted by respondents who answer in a socially (38) __________able direction or attempt to exaggerate problems. For these reasons, some psychological tests have (39) v__________ scales built into them.

Objective 7: Discuss the strengths and weaknesses of the naturalistic-observation method.

The (40) __________istic-observation method observes subjects in their natural habitats. Psychologists and other scientists try to avoid interfering with the behaviors they are observing by using (41) __________sive measures. Jane (42) __________ has extensively observed the behavior of chimpanzees in their natural environment. It is difficult to determine cause and (43) __________ through naturalistic observation.

Objective 8: Discuss the strengths and weaknesses of the laboratory-observation method.

Psychologists place lower animals and people into controlled laboratory environments where they can be readily observed and where the effects of specific (44) con__________s can be discerned.

SECTION 4: The Correlational Method: Seeing What Goes Up and What Comes Down

Objective 9: Define the *correlational method.*

Psychologists use the correlational method to investigate whether one observed behavior or measured trait is related to, or (45) __________lated with, another. A number called the correlation (46) co__________ indicates the direction and the magnitude of a correlation between variables. A correlation coefficient can vary between +1.00 and (47) __________.

When variables are (48) __________ly correlated one increases as the other increases. When variables are (49) __________ly correlated one increases as the other decreases. Numerous studies report (50) __________tive correlations between intelligence and achievement.

Objective 10: Discuss the limitations of the correlational method.

Correlational research may suggest but does not show cause and (51) __________. Nevertheless, correlational research can point the way to profitable experimental research.

SECTION 5: The Experimental Method: Trying Things Out

Objective 11: Define the *experimental method.*

An (52) __________ment is considered the best research method for answering questions concerning cause and effect. In an experiment, a group of participants receives a (53) __________ment, such as a dose of alcohol. The participants, or subjects, are then observed carefully to determine whether the treatment makes a difference in their behavior. Experiments allow psychologists to (54) con__________ the experiences of subjects to determine the effects of a treatment.

Objective 12: Discuss the use of independent and dependent variables in the experimental method.

The presence of an (55) ______________dent variable is manipulated by the experimenters so that its effects may be determined. The measured results or outcomes in an experiment are called (56) ______________dent variables. The presence of (57) ______________dent variables presumably depends on the (58) ______________dent variables.

Objective 13: Discuss the use of experimental and control groups in the experimental method.

Ideal experiments use both experimental and (59) con______________ subjects or groups. (60) ______________tal subjects receive the treatment, whereas (61) ______________ol subjects do not. Every effort is made to ensure that all other (62) ______________tions are held constant for both experimental and control subjects. In this way, researchers can have confidence that the experimental outcomes reflect the (63) ______________ments and not chance factors or chance fluctuations in behavior.

Objective 14: Discuss the use of blinds and double blinds in the experimental method.

A (64) p______________, or "sugar pill", often results in the behavior that people expect. When subjects in psychological experiments are given placebos but think that they have received the real (65) tr______________, we can conclude that changes in behavior and mental processes stem from their (66) ______________fs about the treatment, and not from the treatment itself.

Well-designed experiments control for the effects of expectations by creating conditions under which subjects are unaware of, or (67) ______________ to, the treatment they have received. Yet researchers may also have expectations. Studies in which both subjects and experimenters are unaware of who has received the treatment are called (68) ______________-______________ studies.

SECTION 6: Ethics in Psychological Research and Practice

Objective 15: Discuss ethical issues conducting research and practice with human subjects.

Psychologists adhere to a number of (69) ______________cal standards that are intended to promote the dignity of the individual, foster human welfare, and maintain scientific integrity. They also assure that psychologists (70: Circle one: Do or Do not) undertake research methods or treatments that are harmful to subjects or clients.

In order to help avoid harming subjects, human subjects must provide (71) ______________ consent before they participate in research programs. Psychologists treat the records of research subjects and clients as (72) ______________tial because they respect people's privacy and because people are more likely to express their true thoughts and feelings when researchers or therapists keep their disclosures confidential.

Many experiments like the Lang study on the effects of alcohol cannot be run without (73) de______________ing subjects. Psychological ethics require that research subjects who are deceived be (74) ______________fed afterward to help eliminate misconceptions and anxieties about the research and to leave them with their dignity intact.

Objective 16: Discuss ethical issues concerning research with animal subjects.

Psychologists and other scientists frequently turn to (75) ______________mal subjects to conduct harmful or potentially harmful research that cannot be carried out with humans. Psychologists still face the (76) eth______________ dilemma of subjecting animals to harm. As with human subjects, psychologists follow the principle that animals should be subjected to (77) h______________ only when there is no alternative and they believe that the benefits of the research will justify the harm.

Answers to Chapter Review

1. Scientific
2. Research
3. Hypothesis
4. Test
5. Conclusions
6. Observations
7. Theories
8. Critical
9. Cause
10. Oversimplifying
11. Publication
12. Replicate
13. Evaluate
14. Represent
15. Generalize
16. Subjects
17. Population
18. Men
19. Men
20. Underrepresent
21. African
22. Random
23. Stratified
24. Will
25. Volunteer
26. African
27. Similar
28. Did not
29. Freud
30. Memory
31. Consistent
32. Experimentally
33. Records
34. Misrepresent (or Misstate)
35. Socially
36. Attention
37. Traits
38. Desirable
39. Validity
40. Naturalistic
41. Unobtrusive
42. Goodall
43. Effect
44. Conditions
45. Correlated
46. Coefficient
47. –1.00
48. Positively
49. Negatively
50. Positive
51. Effect
52. Experiment
53. Treatment
54. Control
55. Independent
56. Dependent
57. Dependent
58. Independent
59. Control
60. Experimental
61. Control
62. Conditions
63. Treatments
64. Placebo
65. Treatment
66. Beliefs
67. Blind
68. Double-blind
69. Ethical
70. Do not
71. Informed
72. Confidential
73. Deceiving
74. Debriefed
75. Animal
76. Ethical
77. Harm

POSTTEST

1. Unobtrusively observing diners at a fast-food restaurant in order to determine how frequently they take bites is an example of the
(a) experimental method.
(b) case-study method.
(c) survey method.
(d) naturalistic-observation method.

2. If you were to run an experiment on the effects of temperature on aggressive behavior, aggressive behavior would be the
(a) hypothesis.
(b) dependent variable.
(c) treatment.
(d) correlation coefficient.

3. In the Lang experiment on alcohol and aggression, the condition that led to the most aggressive behavior was
(a) drinking tonic water only.
(b) drinking vodka and tonic water.
(c) belief that one had drunk tonic water only.
(d) belief that one had drunk vodka and tonic water.

4. The Lang study on alcohol and aggression could *not* have been carried out without the _______ of subjects.
(a) informed consent
(b) confidentiality
(c) deception
(d) debriefing

5. Kinsey used _______ in his research on sexual behavior.
(a) laboratory observations of sexual behavior
(b) reports of former lovers of the subjects
(c) interview data
(d) psychological test data

6. A _______ sample is one in which every member of a population has an equal chance of being selected.
(a) biased
(b) chance
(c) random
(d) stratified

7. The development of psychodynamic theory relied largely on the
(a) case-study method.
(b) naturalistic-observation method.
(c) survey method.
(d) psychological testing method.

8. Wyatt's research compared the behavior of white women to that of
(a) white men.
(b) African-American women.
(c) Hispanic-American women.
(d) Native-American women.

9. Psychologists generally agree that the best research method for determining cause and effect is the
(a) naturalistic-observation method.
(b) case-study method.
(c) correlational method.
(d) experimental method.

10. According to the text,
    (a) there is a positive correlation between intelligence and academic achievement.
    (b) there is a negative correlation between intelligence and academic achievement.
    (c) intelligence provides the basis for academic achievement.
    (d) there is no relationship between intelligence and academic achievement.

11. Which of the following is/are the source(s) of research questions?
    (a) Psychological theory
    (b) Daily experiences
    (c) Folklore
    (d) All of the above

12. A specific statement about behavior or mental processes that is tested through research is termed a
    (a) research question.
    (b) hypothesis.
    (c) theory.
    (d) scientific principle.

13. Psychologists have observed that more-aggressive children spend more time watching TV violence than less-aggressive children. What can we conclude from this observation?
    (a) TV violence causes aggression.
    (b) Aggressive behavior causes the watching of violent TV shows.
    (c) There is a correlation between aggression and watching TV violence.
    (d) None of the above conclusions is possible.

14. According to the text, most of the large-sample research conducted into life style and health has been conducted with
    (a) female subjects.
    (b) male subjects.
    (c) a balance of male and female subjects.
    (d) subjects drawn from ethnic minority groups.

15. The concept behind ________ is that people who offer to participate in research studies differ systematically from people who do not.
    (a) the selection factor
    (b) blinds and double blinds
    (c) the use of placebos
    (d) volunteer bias

16. The case of ________ provides a valuable case study in the processes of language development.
    (a) Genie
    (b) Eve
    (c) Lang
    (d) Jane

17. Validity scales are most likely to be employed in the
    (a) naturalistic-observation method.
    (b) correlational method.
    (c) testing method.
    (d) experimental method.

18. Which of the following is apparently an effect of providing informed consent in psychological research?
    (a) A sense of control
    (b) Volunteer bias
    (c) Selection factor
    (d) Violation of ethical principles

19. Diana Baumrind argues that deception-based research
    (a) is necessary only with human subjects.
    (b) makes experiments less stressful.
    (c) can harm the reputation of the profession of psychology.
    (d) is ethical only when the benefits of the research outweigh the potential harm.

20. The most important factor about a sample is that it
    (a) be large.
    (b) be drawn at random.
    (c) represent the targeted population.
    (d) consist of people who are volunteers.

Answer Key To Posttest

1. D
2. B
3. D
4. C
5. C
6. C
7. A
8. B
9. D
10. A
11. D
12. B
13. C
14. B
15. D
16. A
17. C
18. A
19. C
20. C

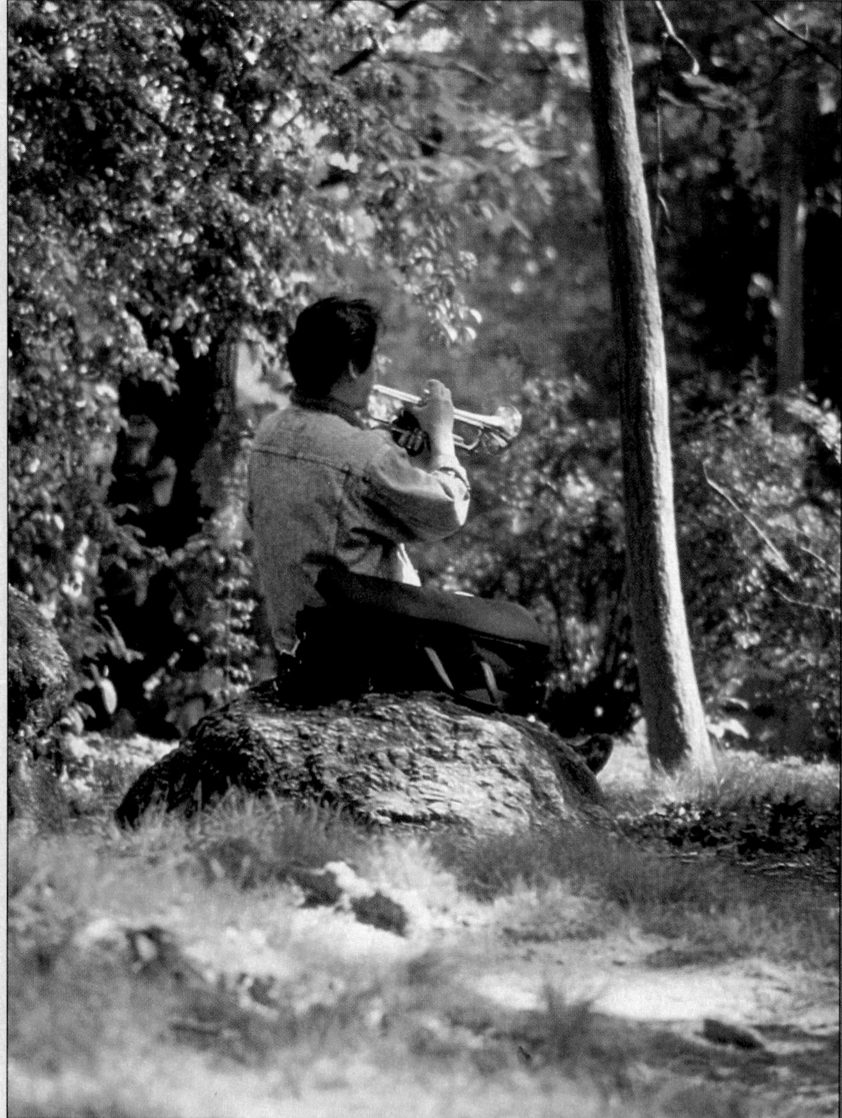

- ☐ Some cells in your body stretch all the way down your back to your big toe.
- ☐ Messages travel in the brain by means of electricity.
- ☐ Our bodies produce natural pain killers that are more powerful than morphine.
- ☐ The human brain is larger than that of any other animal.
- ☐ Fear can give you indigestion.
- ☐ If a surgeon were to stimulate a certain part of your brain electrically, you might swear in court that someone had stroked your leg.
- ☐ Rats will learn to do things that result in a "reward" of a burst of electricity in the brain.

Biology and Behavior

Learning Objectives

When you have finished studying Chapter 3, you should be able to:

Neurons

1. Describe the parts and functions of the neuron.
2. Differentiate between afferent and efferent neurons.
3. Explain the electrochemical process by which neural impulses travel.
4. Explain the "all-or-none principle."
5. Explain the functions of synapses and neurotransmitters.

The Nervous System

6. Explain what is meant by a nerve.
7. Explain the functions of the divisions of the nervous system.
8. Explain how spinal reflexes work.
9. Explain ways in which psychologists study the functions of the brain.
10. Describe the functions of the major structures of the hindbrain, midbrain, and forebrain.
11. Summarize the activities of the sympathetic and parasympathetic branches of the autonomic nervous system.

The Cerebral Cortex

12. Explain the functions of the lobes of the cerebral cortex.
13. Discuss divided-brain research.
14. Summarize research on electrical stimulation of the brain.

The Endocrine System

15. Explain the functions of various hormones.

Heredity

16. Define genes and chromosomes, and describe human chromosomal structure.
17. Discuss psychologists' use of various kinds of kinship studies.
18. Summarize the results of experiments in selective breeding.

According to the big bang theory, our universe began with an enormous explosion that sent countless particles hurtling into every corner of space. For billions of years, these particles have been amassing into immense gas clouds. Galaxies and solar systems have been condensing from the clouds, sparkling for some eons, then winking out. Human beings have only recently evolved on an unremarkable rock circling an average star in a typical spiral-shaped galaxy.

Since the beginning of time, the universe has been in flux. Change has brought life and death and countless challenges. Some creatures have adapted successfully to these challenges and continued to evolve. Others have not met the challenges and have become extinct, falling back into the distant mists of time. Some have left fossil records. Others have disappeared without a trace.

At first, human survival on planet Earth required a greater struggle than it does today. We fought predators like the leopard. We foraged across parched lands for food. We might have warred with creatures very much like ourselves—creatures who have since become extinct. We prevailed. The human species has survived and continues to transmit its unique traits through the generations by means of genetic material whose chemical codes are only now being cracked.

What is handed down through the generations? The answer is biological, or **physiological,** structures. There is no evidence that we inherit thoughts or ideas or images or plans. We do inherit physiological structures, however, and they serve as the material base for our observable behaviors, emotions, and cognitions (our thoughts, images, and plans).

Biological psychologists (or psychobiologists) work at the interfaces of psychology and biology (Dewsbury, 1991). They study the ways in which our mental processes and observable behaviors are linked to physiological structures and biological processes. In recent years, biological psychologists have been unlocking the mysteries of:

1. *Neurons.* Neurons are the building blocks of the nervous system. There are billions upon billions of neurons in the body—perhaps as many as there are stars in the Milky Way galaxy.
2. *The nervous system.* Neurons combine to form the structures of the nervous system. The nervous system has branches that are responsible for muscle movement, perception, automatic functions such as breathing and the secretion of hormones, and psychological phenomena such as thoughts and feelings.
3. *The cerebral cortex.* The cerebral cortex is the large, wrinkled mass inside your head that you think of as your brain. Actually, it is only one part of the brain—the part that is the most characteristically human.
4. *The endocrine system.* Through secretion of hormones, the endocrine system controls functions ranging from growth in children to production of milk in nursing women.
5. *Heredity.* Within every cell of your body there are about 100,000 genes. These chemical substances determine just what type of creature you are, from the color of your hair to your body temperature to the fact that you have arms and legs rather than wings or fins.

Physiological Having to do with the biological functions and vital processes of organisms.

Biological psychologists Psychologists who study the relationships between life processes and behavior.

Pablo Picasso at Work. The great artist's nervous system was composed of neurons like those of other people. Biological psychologists delve into how our behavior and mental processes are linked to the functioning of the nervous system and other biological processes.

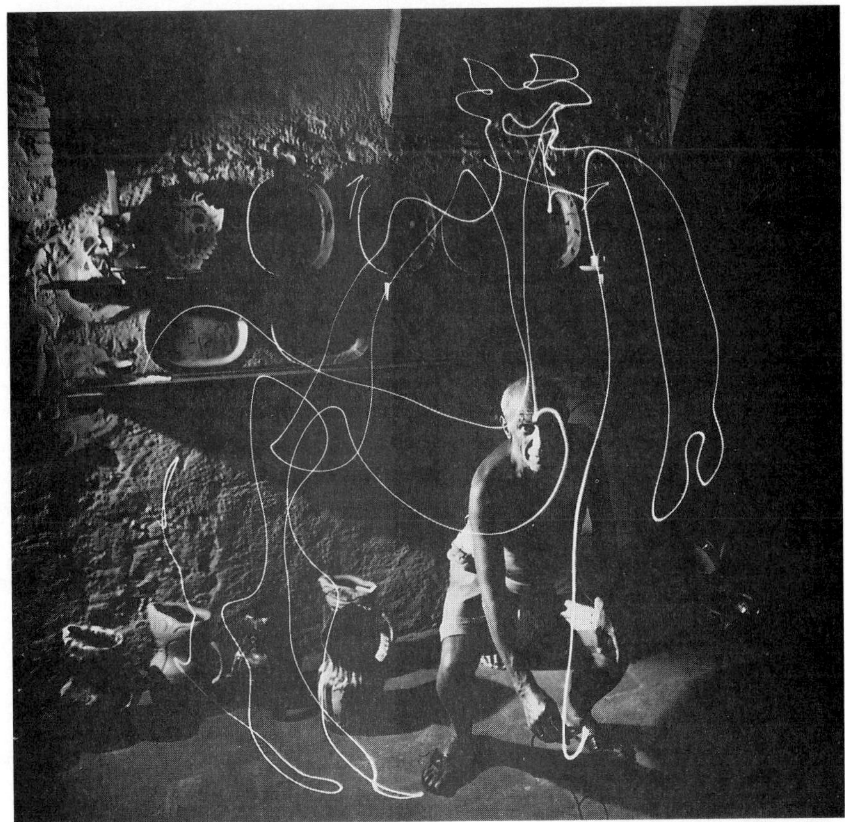

NEURONS

Let us begin our journey in a fabulous forest of nerve cells, or **neurons,** that can be visualized as having branches, trunks, and roots—something like trees. As in other forests, many nerve cells lie alongside one another like a thicket of trees. Neurons can also lie end to end, however, with their "roots" intertwined with the "branches" of neurons that lie below. Trees receive water and nutrients from the soil. Neurons receive "messages" from a number of sources such as other neurons, pressure on the skin, and light, and they can pass these messages along.

Neurons communicate by means of chemicals called **neurotransmitters.** Neurons release neurotransmitters that are taken up by other neurons, muscles, and glands. Neurotransmitters cause chemical changes in the receiving neuron so that the message can travel along its "trunk," be translated back into neurotransmitters in its "branches," and then travel through the small spaces between neurons to be received by the "roots" of yet other neurons.

Each neuron transmits and coordinates messages in the form of neural impulses. We are born with perhaps 100 billion neurons, most of which are found in the brain. The messages transmitted by neurons somehow account for phenomena ranging from perception of an itch from a mosquito bite to the coordination of a skier's vision and muscles to the composition of a concerto to the solution of an algebraic equation.

Neuron A nerve cell.

Neurotransmitters Chemical substances involved in the transmission of neural impulses from one neuron to another.

Soma A cell body.

The Makeup of Neurons

Neurons vary according to their functions and their location. Some in the brain are only a fraction of an inch in length, whereas others in the legs are several feet long. Every neuron is a single nerve cell with a cell body (or **soma**), dendrites, and an axon (see Figure 3.1). The cell body contains the nucleus of the cell. The cell

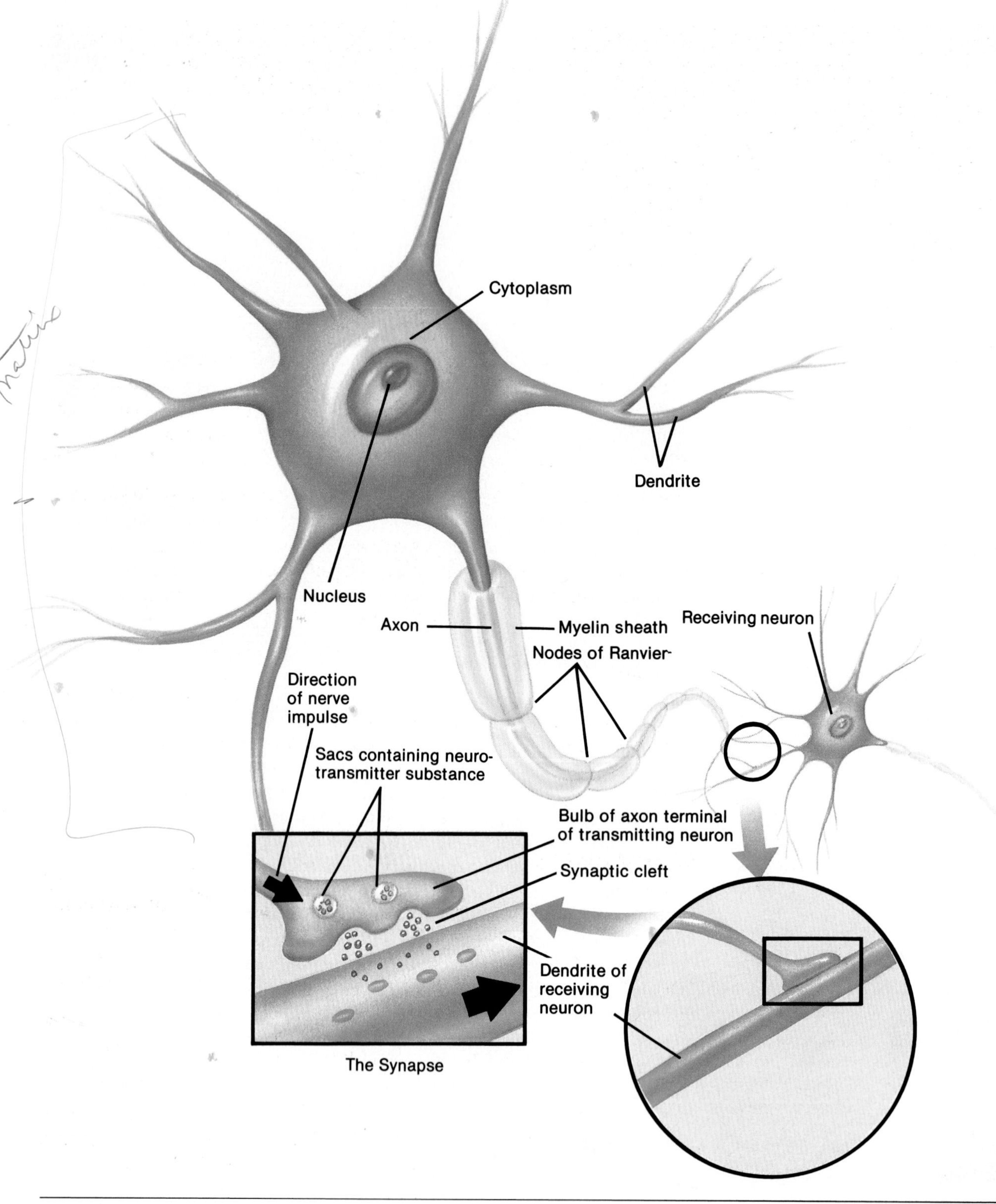

Figure 3.1
The Anatomy of a Neuron.

"Messages" enter neurons through dendrites, are transmitted along the trunklike axon, and then are sent through axon terminals to muscles, glands, and other neurons. A neuron relays its message to another neuron across a junction called a synapse, which consists of an axon terminal from the transmitting neuron, the membrane of the receiving neuron, and a small gap between the neurons referred to as the synaptic cleft. Axon terminals contain sacs of chemicals called neurotransmitters. Neurotransmitters are released by the transmitting neuron into the synaptic cleft, and many of them are taken up by receptor sites on the dendrites of the receiving neuron. Some neurotransmitters (called "excitatory") influence receiving neurons in the direction of firing; others (called "inhibitory") influence them in the direction of *not* firing. To date, a few dozen possible neurotransmitters have been identified.

body uses oxygen and nutrients to generate energy to carry out the work of the cell. Anywhere from a few to several hundred short fibers, or **dendrites,** extend rootlike from the cell body to receive incoming messages from up to 1,000 adjoining neurons. Each neuron has one **axon** that extends trunklike from the cell body. Axons are very thin, but those that carry messages from the toes to the spinal cord extend for several feet.

It is true that some cells in your body—neurons—stretch all the way down your back to your big toe.

Like tree trunks, axons too can divide and extend in different directions. Axons end in smaller branching structures called **terminals.** At the tips of the axon terminals are swellings called **knobs.** Neurons carry messages in one direction only: from the dendrites or cell body through the axon to the axon terminals. The messages are then transmitted from the axon terminals to other neurons.

Myelin. Many neurons are wrapped tightly with white, fatty **myelin sheaths.** The high fat content insulates the axon from electrically charged atoms, or ions, found in the fluids that encase the nervous system. Myelin minimizes leakage of the electric current being carried along the axon, thus allowing messages to be conducted more efficiently. Myelin does not uniformly coat the surface of an axon. It is missing at points called **nodes of Ranvier,** where the axon is exposed. Because of the insulation provided by myelin, neural messages, or impulses, travel rapidly from node to node.

Myelination is part of the maturation process that leads to the abilities to crawl and walk during the first year. Babies are not physiologically "ready" to engage in visual-motor coordination and other activities until the coating process reaches certain levels. In the disease multiple sclerosis, myelin is replaced with a hard fibrous tissue that throws off the timing of nerve impulses and disrupts muscular control. Affliction of neurons that control breathing can result in suffocation.

Afferent and Efferent Neurons. If someone steps on your big toe, the sensation is registered by receptors or sensory neurons near the surface of your skin. Then it is transmitted to the spinal cord and brain through **afferent neurons,** which are perhaps two- to three-feet long. In the brain, subsequent messages might be buffeted about by associative neurons that are only a few thousandths of an inch long. You experience the pain through this process and perhaps entertain some rather nasty thoughts about the perpetrator, who is now apologizing and begging for understanding. Long before you arrive at any logical conclusions, however, motor neurons **(efferent neurons)** send messages to your foot so that you withdraw it and begin an impressive hopping routine. Other efferent neurons stimulate glands so that your heart is now beating more rapidly, you are sweating, and the hair on the back of your arms has become erect! Being a sport, you say, "Oh, it's nothing." But considering all the neurons involved, it really is something, isn't it?

In case you think that afferent and efferent neurons will be hard to distinguish because they sound pretty much the SAME to you, remember that they *are* the "SAME." That is, *S*ensory = *A*fferent, and *M*otor = *E*fferent. But don't tell your professor I let you in on this **mnemonic** device.

Dendrites Rootlike structures, attached to the soma of a neuron, that receive impulses from other neurons.

Axon A long, thin part of a neuron that transmits impulses to other neurons from branching structures called terminals.

Terminals Small structures at the tips of axons.

Knobs Swellings at the ends of terminals. Also referred to as *bulbs* or *buttons*.

Myelin sheath A fatty substance that encases and insulates axons, facilitating transmission of neural impulses.

Node of Ranvier A noninsulated segment of a myelinated axon.

Afferent neurons Neurons that transmit messages from sensory receptors to the spinal cord and brain. Also called *sensory neurons*.

Efferent neurons Neurons that transmit messages from the brain or spinal cord to muscles and glands. Also called *motor neurons*.

Mnemonic Aiding memory, usually by linking chunks of new information to well-known schemes.

The Neural Impulse

In the eighteenth century, Italian physiologist Luigi Galvani (1737–1798) conducted a shocking experiment in a rainstorm. While his neighbors had the sense to remain indoors, Galvani and his wife were out on the porch connecting

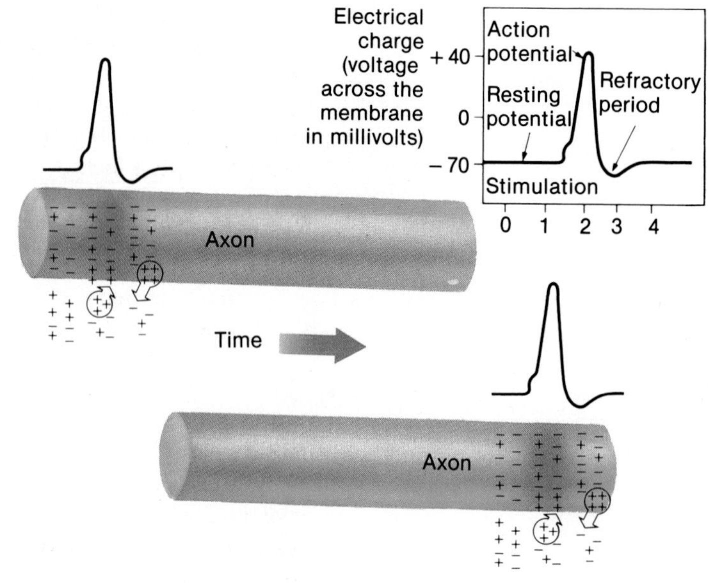

Figure 3.2
The Neural Impulse. When a section of a neuron is stimulated by other neurons, the cell membrane becomes permeable to sodium ions so that an action potential of about +40 millivolts is induced. This action potential is transmitted along the axon. Eventually the neuron fires (or fails to fire) according to the all-or-none principle.

lightning rods to the heads of dissected frogs whose legs were connected by wire to a well of water. When lightning blazed above, the frogs' muscles contracted repeatedly and violently. This is not a recommended way to prepare frogs' legs; Galvani was demonstrating that the messages **(neural impulses)** that travel along neurons are electrochemical in nature.

Neural impulses travel somewhere between 2 (in nonmyelinated neurons) and 225 miles an hour (in myelinated neurons). This speed is not impressive when compared with that of an electric current in a toaster oven or a lamp, which can travel at the speed of light—over 186,000 miles per second. Distances in the body are short, however, and a message will travel from a toe to the brain in perhaps 1/50th of a second.

An Electrochemical Process. The process by which neural impulses travel is electrochemical. Chemical changes take place within neurons that cause an electric charge to be transmitted along their lengths. In a resting state, when a neuron is not being stimulated by its neighbors, there are relatively greater numbers of positively charged sodium ions (Na+) and negatively charged chloride (Cl–) ions in the body fluid outside the neuron than in the fluid within the neuron. Positively charged potassium (K+) ions are more plentiful inside, but there are many other negative ions inside that are not balanced by negative ions on the outside, lending the inside an overall negative charge in relation to the outside. The difference in electrical charge **polarizes** the neuron with a negative **resting potential** of about –70 millivolts in relation to the body fluid outside the cell membrane.

When an area on the surface of the resting neuron is adequately stimulated by other neurons, the cell membrane in the area changes its **permeability** to allow sodium ions to enter. As a consequence, the area of entry becomes positively charged, or **depolarized** with respect to the outside (Figure 3.2). The permeability of the cell membrane changes again, allowing no more sodium ions to enter.

The inside of the cell at the disturbed area has an **action potential** of 110 millivolts. This action potential, added to the –70 millivolts that characterize the resting potential, brings the membrane voltage to a positive charge of +40 millivolts. This inner change causes the next section of the cell to become permeable

Neural impulse The electrochemical discharge of a nerve cell, or neuron.

Polarize To ready a neuron for firing by creating an internal negative charge in relation to the body fluid outside the cell membrane.

Resting potential The electrical potential across the neural membrane when it is not responding to other neurons.

Permeability The degree to which a membrane allows a substance to pass through it.

Depolarize To reduce the resting potential of a cell membrane from about –70 millivolts toward zero.

Action potential The electrical impulse that provides the basis for the conduction of a neural impulse along an axon of a neuron.

to sodium ions. At the same time, potassium ions are being pumped out of the area of the cell that was previously affected, which then returns to its resting potential. In this way, the neural impulse is transmitted continuously along an axon that is not myelinated. Because the impulse is created anew as it progresses, its strength does not change. Neural impulses are conducted more rapidly along myelinated axons because they jump from node to node.

It is true that messages travel in the brain by means of electricity. They also travel from neurons to other neurons, muscles, or glands by means of neurotransmitters.

The conduction of the neural impulse along the length of a neuron is what is meant by "firing." Some neurons fire in less than 1/1,000th of a second. In firing, neurons "attempt" to transmit the message to other neurons, muscles, or glands. However, other neurons will not fire unless the incoming messages combine to reach an adequate **threshold.** A weak message may cause a temporary shift in electrical charge at some point along a neuron's cell membrane, but this charge will dissipate if the neuron is not stimulated to threshold.

A neuron may transmit several hundred such messages in a second. In accord with the **all-or-none principle,** each time a neuron fires, it transmits an impulse of the same strength. Neurons fire more frequently when they have been stimulated by larger numbers of other neurons; stronger stimuli result in firing with greater frequency.

For a thousandth of a second or so after firing, a neuron enters an **absolute refractory period,** during which it will not fire in response to stimulation from other neurons. For another few thousandths of a second, the neuron is said to be in a **relative refractory period,** during which it will fire but only in response to messages that are stronger than usual. The refractory period is a time of recovery during which sodium is prevented from passing through the neuronal membrane. When we realize that such periods of recovery might take place hundreds of times per second, it seems a rapid recovery and a short rest indeed.

The Synapse

A neuron relays its message to another neuron across a junction called a **synapse.** A synapse consists of a "branch," or axon terminal from the transmitting neuron; a dendrite ("root"), or the soma of a receiving neuron; and a fluid-filled gap between the two that is called the synaptic cleft (see Figure 3.3). Although the neural impulse is electrical, it does not jump the synaptic cleft like a spark. Instead, when a nerve impulse reaches a synapse, axon terminals release chemicals into the synaptic cleft like myriad ships being cast off into the sea.

Neurotransmitters

In the axon terminals are sacs, or synaptic vesicles, that contain chemicals called neurotransmitters. When a neural impulse reaches the axon terminal, the vesicles release varying amounts of these neurotransmitters into the synaptic cleft. From there, they influence the receiving neuron.

A few dozen neurotransmitters have been identified. There may be hundreds (Snyder, 1980). Each neurotransmitter has its own chemical structure, and each can fit into a specifically tailored harbor, or **receptor site,** on the dendrite of the

Threshold The point at which a stimulus is just strong enough to produce a response.

All-or-none principle The fact that a neuron fires an impulse of the same strength whenever its action potential is triggered.

Absolute refractory period A phase following firing during which a neuron's action potential cannot be triggered.

Relative refractory period A phase following the absolute refractory period during which a neuron will fire in response to stronger-than-usual messages.

Synapse A junction between the axon terminals of one neuron and the dendrites or soma of another neuron.

Receptor site A location on a dendrite of a receiving neuron tailored to receive a neurotransmitter.

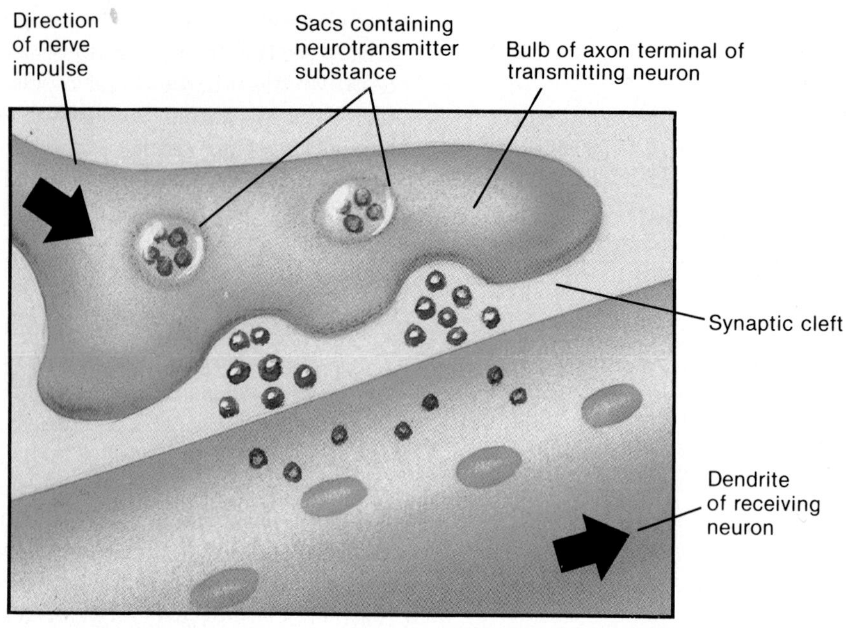

Figure 3.3
The Synapse. Neurons relay their messages to other neurons across junctions called synapses. A synapse consists of an axon terminal from the transmitting neuron, the membrane of the receiving neuron, and a small gap between the two which is referred to as the synaptic cleft. Molecules of neurotransmitters are released into the synaptic cleft from vesicles within the axon terminal. Many molecules are taken up by receptor sites on the receiving neuron. Others are broken down or taken up again by the transmitting neuron.

receiving cell. The analogy of a key fitting into a lock has been used. Once released, not all molecules of a neurotransmitter find their ways into receptor sites of other neurons. "Loose" neurotransmitters are usually either broken down or reabsorbed by the axon terminal. Reabsorption is called *re-uptake.*

Some neurotransmitters act to excite other neurons—that is, to influence receiving neurons in the direction of firing. The synapses between axon terminals with excitatory neurotransmitters and receiving neurons are called **excitatory synapses.** Other neurotransmitters inhibit receiving neurons; that is, they influence them in the direction of not firing. The synapses between axon terminals with inhibitory neurotransmitters and receiving neurons are called **inhibitory synapses.** Neurons may be influenced by neurotransmitters that have been released by up to 1,000 other neurons. The additive stimulation received from all these cells determines whether a particular neuron will also fire and which neurotransmitters will be released in the process.

Neurotransmitters are involved in processes ranging from muscle contraction to emotional response. Excesses or deficiencies of neurotransmitters have been linked to diseases and abnormal behavior.

Acetylcholine. **Acetylcholine** (ACh) is a neurotransmitter that controls muscle contractions. ACh is excitatory at synapses between nerves and muscles that involve voluntary movement but inhibitory at the heart and some other locations.

The effects of curare highlight the functioning of ACh. Curare is a poison that is extracted from plants by South American Indians and used in hunting. If an arrow tipped with curare pierces the skin and the poison enters the body, it prevents ACh from lodging within receptor sites inneurons, resulting in paralysis. The victim is prevented from contracting the muscles used in breathing and dies from suffocation.

ACh is also normally prevalent in a part of the brain called the **hippocampus,** a structure involved in the formation of memories. When the ACh available to the brain decreases, memory formation is impaired. **Alzheimer's disease** is associated with progressive deterioration of neurons that produce ACh (Teri & Wagner, 1992).

Excitatory synapse A synapse that influences receiving neurons in the direction of firing by increasing depolarization of their cell membranes.

Inhibitory synapse A synapse that influences receiving neurons in the direction of not firing by encouraging changes in their membrane permeability in the direction of the resting potential.

Acetylcholine A neurotransmitter that controls muscle contractions. Abbreviated *ACh.*

Hippocampus A part of the *limbic system* of the brain that is involved in memory formation.

Alzheimer's disease A progressive disorder characterized by loss of memory and other cognitive functions.

Dopamine. **Dopamine** is primarily an inhibitory neurotransmitter. Dopamine is involved in voluntary movements, learning and memory, and emotional arousal. Deficiencies of dopamine are linked to Parkinson's disease, a disorder in which patients progressively lose control over their muscles. They develop muscle tremors and jerky, uncoordinated movements. The drug L-dopa, a substance that the brain converts to dopamine, helps slow the progress of Parkinson's disease.

The psychological disorder schizophrenia (see Chapter 13) has also been linked to dopamine. Schizophrenic individuals may have more receptor sites for dopamine in an area of the brain that is involved in emotional responding. For this reason, they may "overutilize" the dopamine that is available in the brain. Overutilization leads to hallucinations and disturbances of thought and emotion. The phenothiazines, a group of drugs used in the treatment of schizophrenia, are thought to block the action of dopamine by locking some dopamine out of receptor sites (Snyder, 1984). Not surprisingly, phenothiazines may have Parkinson-like side effects, which are usually then treated by additional drugs, adjustment of the dose of phenothiazine, or switching to another drug.

Noradrenaline. **Noradrenaline** is produced largely by neurons in the brain stem. Noradrenaline acts both as a neurotransmitter and a hormone. It speeds up the heartbeat and other body processes and is involved in general arousal, learning and memory, and eating. Excesses and deficiencies of noradrenaline have been linked to mood disorders (see Chapter 13).

The stimulants cocaine and amphetamines ("speed") facilitate the release of dopamine and noradrenaline and also impede their re-uptake by the releasing synaptic vesicles. As a result, excesses of these neurotransmitters vastly increase the firing of neurons and lead to a persistent state of high arousal. The stimulant caffeine, found in coffee, is thought to prevent reabsorption of these neurotransmitters by blocking the action of the enzymes that break them down. Until the caffeine has been removed from the system, we may experience "coffee nerves."

Serotonin. Also primarily an inhibitory transmitter, **serotonin** is involved in emotional arousal and sleep. Deficiencies of serotonin have been linked to anxiety, mood disorders, and insomnia. The drug LSD (see Chapter 5) decreases the action of serotonin and may also influence the utilization of dopamine. With LSD, "two no's make a yes." By inhibiting an inhibitor, brain activity increases, in this case often causing hallucinations.

Endorphins. The word *endorphin* is the contraction of *endogenous morphine. Endogenous* means "developing from within." **Endorphins,** then, are similar to the narcotic morphine in their functions and effects and are produced by our own bodies. They occur naturally in the brain and in the bloodstream.

Endorphins are inhibitory neurotransmitters. They lock into receptor sites for chemicals that transmit pain messages to the brain. Once the endorphin "key" is in the "lock," pain-causing chemicals cannot transmit their (often unwelcome) messages. There are a number of endorphins.

It is true that our bodies produce natural pain killers that are more powerful than morphine. They are called endorphins.

In addition to relieving pain, endorphins play a role in regulating respiration, hunger, memory, sexual behavior, blood pressure, mood, and body temperature. Endorphins may also increase our sense of self-competence and may be connected with the "runner's high" reported by many long-distance runners.

Dopamine A neurotransmitter that is involved in Parkinson's disease and that appears to play a role in schizophrenia.

Noradrenaline A neurotransmitter whose action is similar to that of the hormone *adrenaline* and that may play a role in depression.

Serotonin A neurotransmitter, deficiencies of which have been linked to affective disorders, anxiety, and insomnia.

Endorphins Neurotransmitters that are composed of amino acids and that are functionally similar to morphine.

A View of the New York City Marathon. Why have thousands of people taken up long-distance running? Running, of course, promotes cardiovascular conditioning, firms the muscles, and helps us to control weight. But long-distance runners also report experiencing a "runner's high," which may be connected with the release of endorphins. Endorphins are naturally occurring substances similar in function to the narcotic morphine.

There you have it: a fabulous forest of neurons in which billions upon billions of vesicles are pouring neurotransmitters into synaptic clefts at any given time—when you are involved in strenuous activity, now as you are reading this page, or even as you are passively watching television. This microscopic picture is repeated several hundred times every second. The combined activity of all these neurotransmitters determines which messages will be transmitted and which will not. Your experience of sensations, your thoughts, and your psychological sense of control over your body are very different from the electrochemical processes we have described. Yet somehow these many electrochemical events underlie your psychological sense of yourself and of the world.

THE NERVOUS SYSTEM

As a child, I did not think it a good thing to have a "nervous" system. After all, if your system were not so nervous, you might be less likely to jump at strange noises.

I learned later that a nervous system is not a system that is nervous. It is a system of nerves involved in thought processes, heartbeat, visual-motor coordination, and so on. I also learned that the human nervous system is more complex than that of any other animal and that our brains are larger than those of any other animal. Now this last piece of business is not quite true. A human brain weighs about three pounds, but elephant and whale brains may be four times as heavy. Still, our brains compose a greater part of our body weight than do those of elephants or whales. Our brains weigh about 1/60th of our body weight. Elephant brains weigh about 1/1,000th of their total weight, and whale brains are a paltry 1/10,000th of their weight. So, if we wish, we can still find figures to make us proud.

Figure 3.4
The Divisions of the Nervous System. The nervous system contains two main divisions: the central nervous system and the peripheral nervous system. The central nervous system consists of the brain and spinal cord. The peripheral nervous system contains the somatic and autonomic systems. In turn, the autonomic nervous system is composed of sympathetic and parasympathetic divisions.

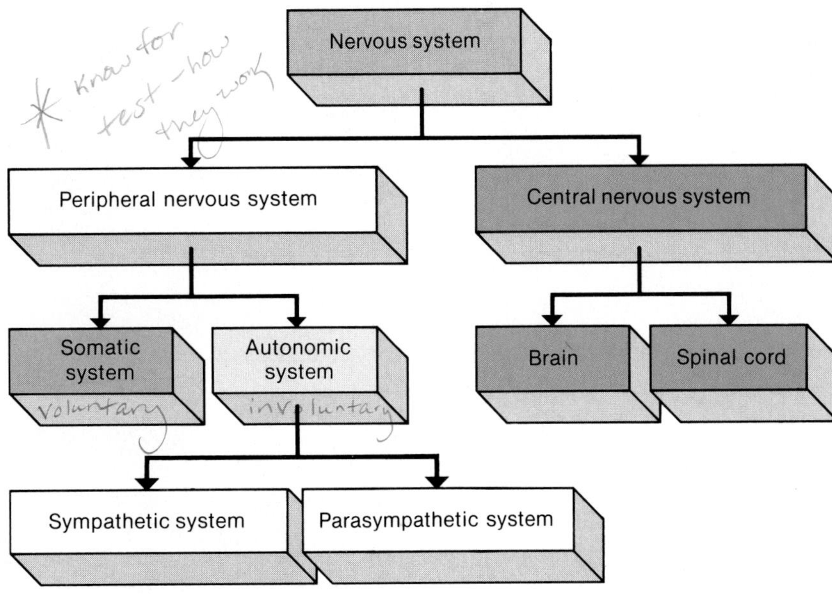

The human brain is *not* larger than that of any other animal. Elephants and whales have larger brains.

The brain is only one part of the nervous system. A **nerve** is a bundle of axons and dendrites. The cell bodies of these neurons are not considered to be part of the nerve. The cell bodies are gathered into clumps called **nuclei** in the brain and spinal cord and **ganglia** elsewhere.

The nervous system consists of the brain, the spinal cord, and the nerves linking them to receptors in the sensory organs and effectors in the muscles and glands. The brain and spinal cord make up what we refer to as the **central nervous system** (see Figure 3.4). The sensory (afferent) neurons, which receive and transmit messages to the brain and spinal cord, and the motor (efferent) neurons, which transmit messages from the brain or spinal cord to the muscles and glands, make up the **peripheral nervous system.** There is no deep, complex reason for labeling the two major divisions of the nervous system in this way. It is just geography. The peripheral nervous system extends more into the edges, or periphery, of the body.

Let us now examine the nature and functions of the central and peripheral nervous systems.

Nerve A bundle of axons and dendrites from many neurons.

Nuclei Plural of *nucleus*. A group of neural cell bodies found in the brain or spinal cord.

Ganglia Plural of *ganglion*. A group of neural cell bodies found elsewhere in the body (other than the brain or spinal cord).

Central nervous system The brain and spinal cord.

Peripheral nervous system The part of the nervous system consisting of the somatic nervous system and the autonomic nervous system.

Spinal cord A column of nerves within the spine that transmits messages from sensory receptors to the brain and from the brain to muscles and glands throughout the body.

The Central Nervous System

The central nervous system consists of the spinal cord and the brain.

The Spinal Cord. The **spinal cord** is a column of nerves about as thick as a thumb. It transmits messages from receptors to the brain and from the brain to muscles and glands throughout the body (Figure 3.5). The spinal cord is also capable of some "local government" of responses to external stimulation through

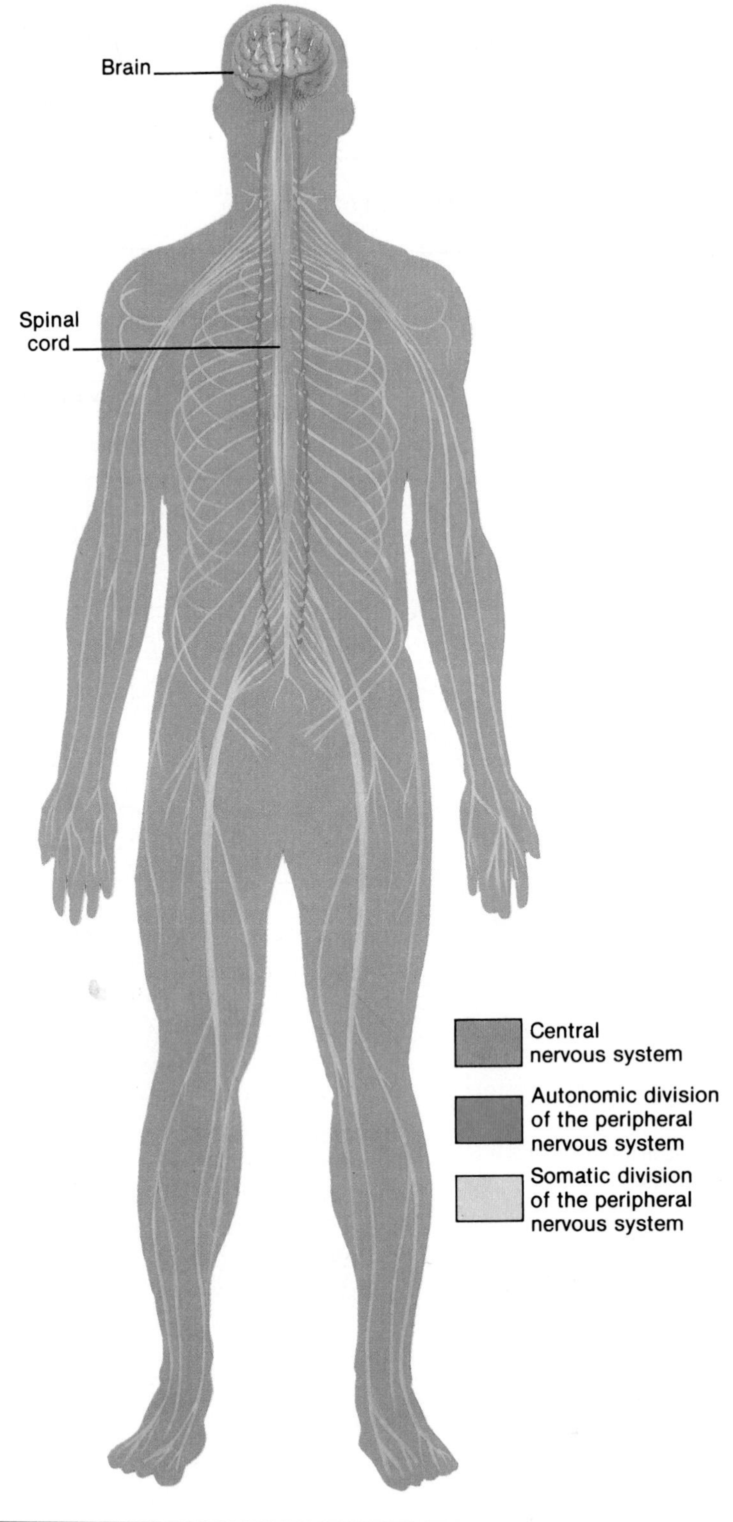

Figure 3.5
The Parts of the Nervous System. Note that the spinal cord is protected by a column of bones called vertebrae. The brain is protected by the skull.

Spinal reflex A simple, unlearned response to a stimulus that may involve only two neurons.

Interneuron A neuron that transmits a neural impulse from a sensory neuron to a motor neuron.

Gray matter In the spinal cord, the grayish neurons and neural segments that are involved in spinal reflexes.

spinal reflexes. A spinal reflex is an unlearned response to a stimulus that may involve only two neurons—a sensory (afferent) neuron and a motor (efferent) neuron (Figure 3.6). In some reflexes, a third neuron, called an **interneuron,** transmits the neural impulse from the sensory neuron through the spinal cord to the motor neuron.

The spinal cord (and the brain) consist of gray matter and white matter. The **gray matter** is composed of nonmyelinated neurons. Some of these nonmyeli-

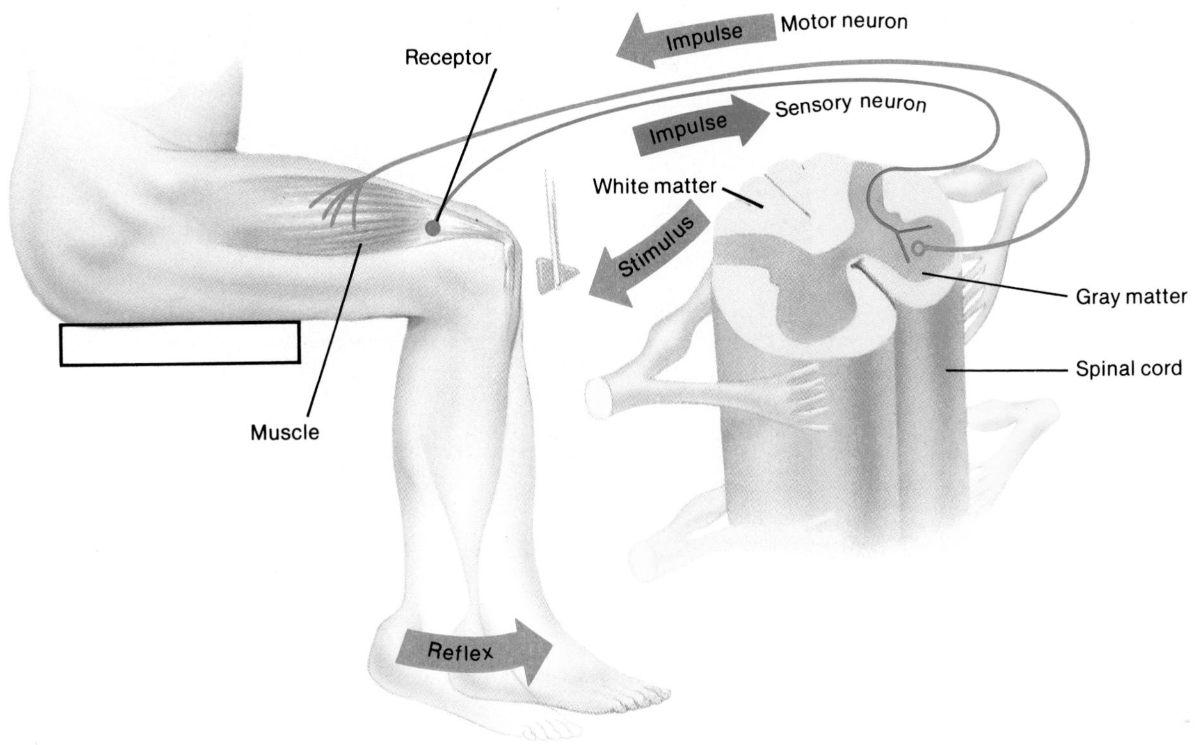

Figure 3.6
The Reflex Arc.

A cross-section of the spinal cord, showing a sensory neuron and a motor neuron, which are involved in the knee-jerk reflex. In some reflexes, interneurons link sensory and motor neurons.

nated neurons are involved in spinal reflexes, whereas others send axons to the brain. The **white matter** is composed of bundles of longer, myelinated (and thus whitish) axons that carry messages to and from the brain. As you can see in Figure 3.6, a cross section of the spinal cord shows the gray matter, which includes cell bodies, to be distributed in a butterfly pattern.[1]

We engage in many reflexes. We blink in response to a puff of air. We swallow when food accumulates in the mouth. A physician may tap the leg below the knee to elicit the knee-jerk reflex, a sign that the nervous system is operating adequately. Urinating and defecating are reflexes that occur in response to pressure in the bladder and the rectum. Parents often spend months toilet-training infants, or teaching them to involve their brains in the process of elimination. Learning to inhibit these reflexes makes civilization possible.

The Brain. Just where is that elusive piece of business you think of as your "mind"? Thousands of years ago, it was not generally thought that the mind had a place to hang its hat within the body. It was common to assume that the body was inhabited by demons or souls that could not be explained in terms of substance. After all, if you look inside a human being, the biological structures you find do not look all that different in quality from those of many lower animals. Thus, it seemed to make sense that those qualities that made us distinctly human—such as abstract thought, poetry, science, and the composition of music—were unrelated to substances that you could see, feel, and weigh on a scale.

White matter In the spinal cord, axon bundles that carry messages from and to the brain.

[1]If you turn to the Rorschach inkblot shown on page 436, you can see why many biology and nursing students report that it reminds them of the spinal cord.

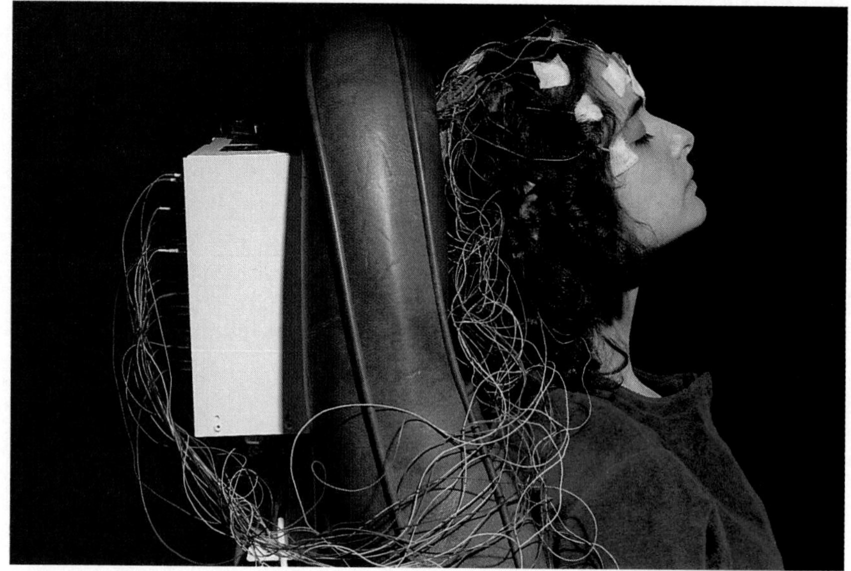

Figure 3.7
The Electroencephalograph. In this method of research, brain waves are detected by placing electrodes on the scalp and measuring the current that passes between them.

Lesion A brain injury that results in impaired behavior or loss of a function.

Electroencephalograph An instrument that measures electrical activity of the brain. Abbreviated *EEG.* ("Cephalo-" derives from the Greek *kephale,* meaning "head.")

Computerized axial tomography Formation of a computer-generated image of the anatomical details of the brain by passing a narrow X-ray beam through the head and measuring from different angles the amount of radiation that passes through. Abbreviated *CAT scan.*

Through a variety of accidents and research projects, we have come to recognize that mind, or consciousness, dwells essentially within the brain. From injuries to the head—some of them minimal, some horrendous—we have learned that brain damage can impair consciousness and awareness. People can lose their vision, hearing, or memory, or become confused. Loss of some large portions of the brain may ironically cause little loss of function. The loss of smaller, sensitively located portions can cause deficits in language or memory, even death.

Some Ways in Which Scientists Study the Brain. Experiments in electrical stimulation of areas in animal and human brains show that portions of the surface of the brain are associated with specific types of sensations (such as sensation of light or of a touch on the torso) or motor activities (such as movement of a leg). They show that a tiny group of structures near the center of the brain (the hypothalamus) is involved in sexual and aggressive behavior patterns, and that a rectangular structure that rises from the back part of the brain into the forebrain (the reticular activating system) is involved in wakefulness and sleep.

Whereas accidents have shown us how destruction of certain parts of the brain is related to behavioral changes in humans, intentional **lesions** in the brains of laboratory animals have yielded more specific knowledge. For example, destruction of one part of the limbic system causes rats and monkeys to show relatively docile behavior. Destruction of another part of the limbic system leads monkeys to show rage responses at the slightest provocation. Destruction of yet another area of the limbic system prevents animals from forming new memories.

The **electroencephalograph** (EEG) records the electrical activity of the brain. Electrodes are attached to the scalp with tape or paste (Figure 3.7). The EEG detects minute amounts of electrical activity—called brain waves—that pass between the electrodes (Wong, 1991). Certain brain waves are associated with feelings of relaxation and with various stages of sleep (see Chapter 5). Researchers and physicians use the EEG to locate the areas of the brain that respond to certain stimuli, such as lights or sounds, and to diagnose a number of kinds of abnormal behavior. The EEG also helps locate tumors.

The computer's capacity to generate images of the parts of the brain from various sources of radiation has sparked the development of imaging techniques that have been useful to researchers and physicians (Pollack, 1991). In one such technique, **computerized axial tomography** (the CAT scan), a narrow X-ray

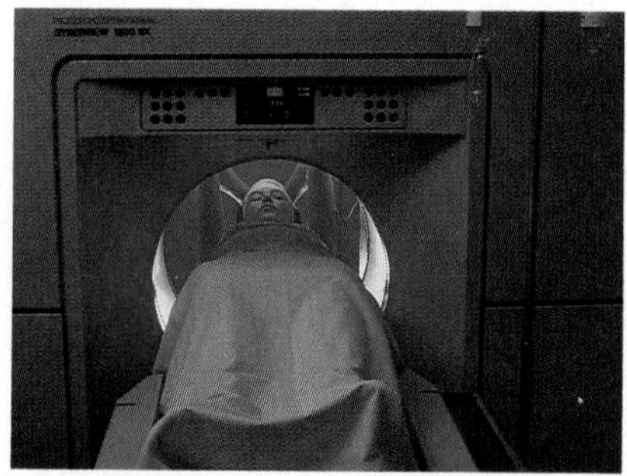

Figure 3.8
The Computerized Axial Tomograph Scan. In the CAT scan, a narrow X-ray beam is passed through the head, and the amount of radiation that passes through is measured simultaneously from various angles. The computer enables us to integrate these measurements into a view of the brain.

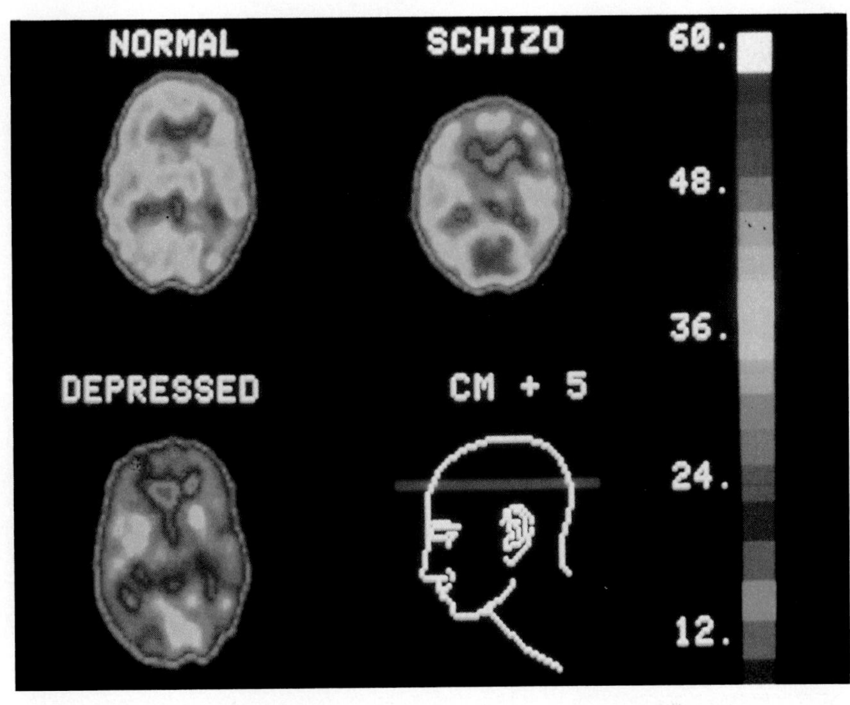

Figure 3.9
The Positron Emission Tomograph Scan. These PET scans of the brains of normal, schizophrenic, and depressed individuals are computer-generated images of the neural activity of parts of their brains, as formed by tracing the amount of glucose metabolized by these parts. Parts of the brain with greater neural activity metabolize more glucose. The metabolic activity ranges from low (blue) to high (red).

beam passes through the head. The amount of radiation that passes through is measured simultaneously from multiple angles (see Figure 3.8). The computer integrates these measurements into a three-dimensional view of the brain. As a result, brain damage and other abnormalities that years ago could be detected only by surgery can be displayed on a video monitor.

A second method, **positron emission tomography** (the PET scan), forms a computer-generated image of the neural activity of parts of the brain by tracing the amount of glucose used (or metabolized) by these parts. More glucose is metabolized in the parts of the brain in which neural activity is greater. To trace the metabolism of glucose, a harmless amount of a radioactive compound, called a tracer, is mixed with glucose and injected into the bloodstream. When the glucose reaches the brain, the patterns of neural activity are revealed by measurement of the positrons—positively charged particles—that are given off by the tracer. The PET scan has been used by researchers to see which parts of the brain are most active when we are, for example, listening to music, working out a math problem, or using language (Petersen et al., 1988). Neural activity also appears to differ in the brains of normal and schizophrenic people (see Figure 3.9). Researchers are exploring the meanings of these differences.

A third imaging technique is **magnetic resonance imaging** (MRI). In MRI, the person lies in a powerful magnetic field. The person is then also exposed to radio waves that cause parts of the brain to emit signals that are measured from multiple angles. As with the CAT scan, the signals are integrated into an anatomic image (see Figure 3.10).

Parts of the Brain. Now that we have explored some of the methods of biological psychologists, let us look at the brain (see Figure 3.11). We begin with the back of the head, where the spinal cord rises to meet the brain, and work our way forward. The lower part of the brain, or hindbrain, consists of three major structures: the medulla, the pons, and the cerebellum.

Many pathways that connect the spinal cord to higher levels of the brain pass through the **medulla.** The medulla regulates vital functions such as heart rate,

Positron emission tomography Formation of a computer-generated image of the neural activity of parts of the brain by tracing the amount of glucose used by the various parts. Abbreviated *PET scan.*

Magnetic resonance imaging Formation of a computer-generated image of the anatomy of the brain by measuring the signals emitted when the head is placed in a strong magnetic field.

Medulla An oblong area of the hindbrain involved in regulation of heartbeat and respiration.

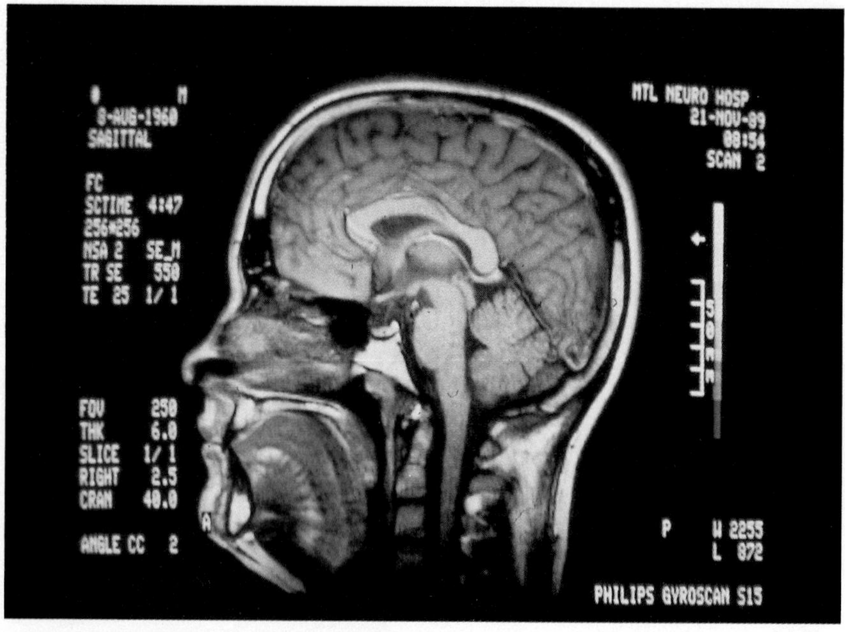

Figure 3.10
Magnetic Resonance Imaging. An image of the brain as produced by MRI.

blood pressure, and respiration. It also plays a role in sleep, sneezing, and coughing. The **pons** is a bulge in the hindbrain that lies forward of the medulla. *Pons* is the Latin word for "bridge." The pons is so named because of the bundles of nerves that pass through it. The pons transmits information about body movement. It is also involved in functions related to attention, sleep and alertness, and respiration.

Behind the pons lies the **cerebellum** ("little brain" in Latin). The two hemispheres of the cerebellum are involved in maintaining balance and in controlling motor (muscle) behavior. Injury to the cerebellum may lead to lack of motor coordination, stumbling, and loss of muscle tone.

The **reticular activating system** (RAS) begins in the hindbrain and ascends through the region of the midbrain into the lower part of the forebrain. The RAS is vital in the functions of attention, sleep, and arousal. Injury to the RAS may leave an animal **comatose.** Stimulation of the RAS causes it to send messages to the cortex, making us more alert to sensory information. Electrical stimulation of the RAS awakens sleeping animals, and certain drugs called central-nervous-system depressants (alcohol is one) are thought to lower RAS activity.

Sudden, loud noises stimulate the RAS and awaken a sleeping animal or person. But the RAS may become selective, or acquire the capacity to play a filtering role, through learning. It may allow some messages to filter through to higher brain levels and awareness while screening others out. For example, the parent who has primary responsibility for child care may be awakened by the stirring sounds of an infant, whereas louder sounds of traffic or street noise are filtered out. The other parent may usually sleep through even loud cries. If the first parent must be away for several days, however, the second parent's RAS may quickly acquire sensitivity to noises produced by the child. This sensitivity may rapidly fade again when the first parent returns.

Also located in the midbrain are areas involved in vision and hearing. These include the area that controls eye reflexes such as dilation of the pupils and eye movements.

Five major areas of the front-most part of the brain, or forebrain, are the thalamus, the hypothalamus, the limbic system, the basal ganglia, and the cerebrum.

The **thalamus** is located near the center of the brain. It consists of two joined egg- or football-shaped structures. The thalamus serves as a relay station for

Pons A structure of the hindbrain involved in respiration, attention, and sleep and dreaming.

Cerebellum A part of the hindbrain involved in muscle coordination and balance.

Reticular activating system A part of the brain involved in attention, sleep, and arousal.

Comatose In a coma, a state resembling sleep from which it is difficult to be aroused.

Thalamus An area near the center of the brain involved in the relay of sensory information to the cortex and in the functions of sleep and attention.

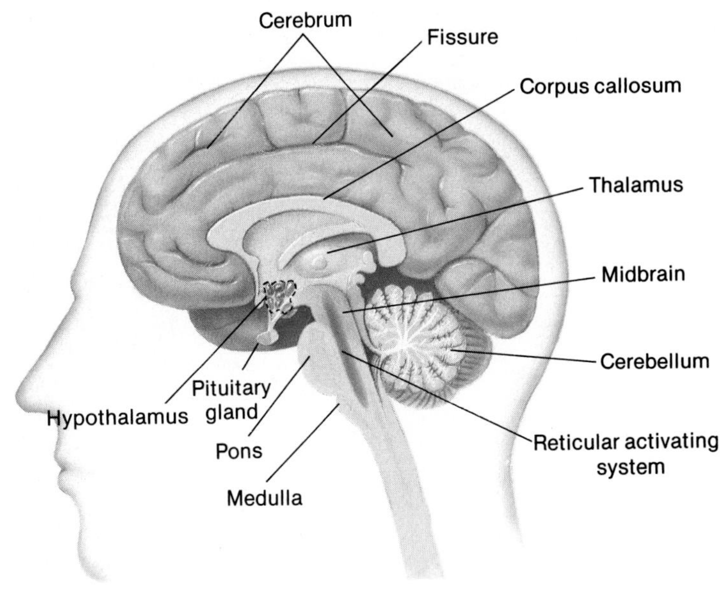

Figure 3.11
The Parts of the Human Brain. This view of the brain, split top to bottom, labels some of the most important structures.

sensory stimulation. Nerve fibers from our sensory systems enter from below; the information carried by them is then transmitted to the cerebral cortex by way of fibers that exit from above. For instance, the thalamus relays sensory input from the eyes to the visual areas of the cerebral cortex. The thalamus is also involved in controlling sleep and attention in coordination with other brain structures, including the RAS.

The **hypothalamus** lies beneath the thalamus and above the pituitary gland. It weighs only four grams, yet it controls the autonomic nervous system and the endocrine system. Thus, it is vital in the regulation of body temperature, the concentration of fluids, the storage of nutrients, and various aspects of motivation and emotion. Experimenters learn many of the functions of the hypothalamus by implanting electrodes in various parts of it and observing the behavioral effects when a current is switched on. In this way, it has been found that the hypothalamus is involved in hunger, thirst, sexual behavior, caring for offspring, and aggression. Among lower animals, stimulation of various areas of the hypothalamus can trigger stereotypical behaviors such as fighting, mating, or even nest building. The hypothalamus is just as important to people, but our behavior in response to messages from the hypothalamus is less stereotypical and relatively more influenced by cognitive functions such as thought, choice, and value systems.

The **limbic system** is made up of several structures, including the septum, amygdala, hippocampus, and parts of the hypothalamus (Figure 3.12) (Derryberry & Tucker, 1992). The limbic system lies along the inner edge of the cerebrum and is fully evolved in mammals only. It is involved in memory and emotion, and in the drives of hunger, sex, and aggression. People in whom operations have damaged the hippocampus can retrieve old memories but cannot permanently store new information. As a result, they may reread the same newspaper day in and day out without recalling that they have read it before. Or they may have to be perpetually reintroduced to people they have met just hours earlier (Squire, 1986). Destruction of an area within the **amygdala** leads monkeys and other mammals to show docile behavior (Carlson, 1986). Destruction of the **septum** leads some mammals to respond aggressively, even with slight provocation.

The limbic system thus provides a system of "checks and balances." The amygdala and the septum appear to allow us to inhibit stereotypical behaviors that are prompted by the hypothalamus. We then have the chance to mull over situations and are less likely, when threatened, to automatically flee or attack.

Hypothalamus A bundle of nuclei below the thalamus involved in body temperature, motivation, and emotion.

Limbic system A group of structures involved in memory, motivation, and emotion that forms a fringe along the inner edge of the cerebrum.

Amygdala A part of the limbic system that apparently facilitates stereotypical aggressive responses.

Septum A part of the limbic system that apparently restrains stereotypical aggressive responses.

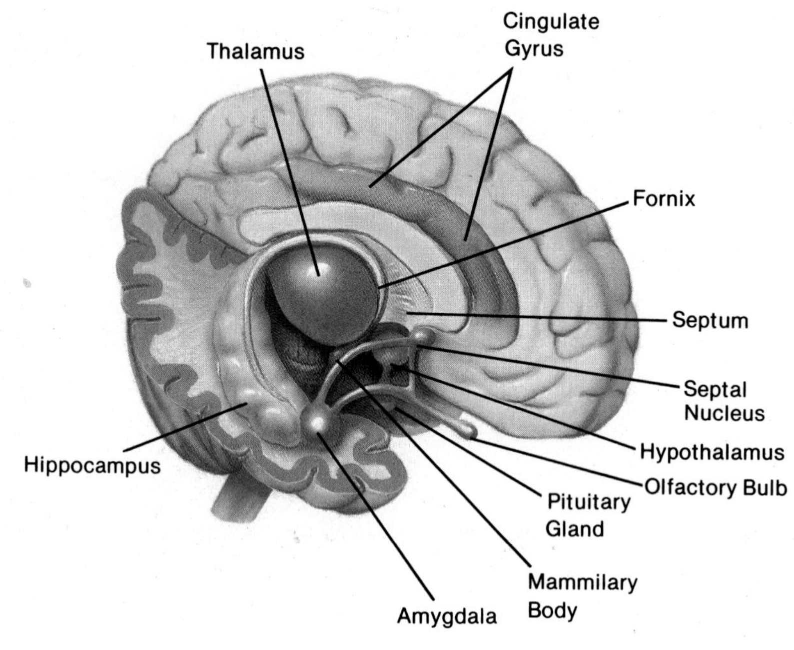

Figure 3.12
The Limbic System. The limbic system consists of the amygdala, hippocampus, septum and septal nuclei, fornix, cingulate gyrus, and parts of the hypothalamus.

The **basal ganglia** are buried beneath the cortex in front of the thalamus. The basal ganglia are involved in the control of postural movements and the coordination of the limbs. Most of the brain's dopamine is produced by neurons in the basal ganglia, and the degeneration of these neurons has been linked to Parkinson's disease. In novel approaches to the treatment of Parkinson's disease tried out in Sweden and Mexico, cells from the adrenal medulla, which produce small amounts of dopamine, have been transplanted to patients' basal ganglia, but results of these operations have been mixed (Kimble, 1988; Kolata, 1988). However, the transplanting of fetal dopamine-producing cells into the brains of rats with Parkinson-like symptoms has apparently improved control over movement (Bjorklund & Stenevi, 1984).

The **cerebrum** is the crowning glory of the brain. Only in human beings does the cerebrum compose such a large proportion of the brain (Figure 3.11). The surface of the cerebrum is wrinkled, or convoluted, with ridges and valleys. This surface is the **cerebral cortex.** The convolutions allow a great deal of surface area to be packed into the brain.

Valleys in the cortex are called **fissures.** A most important fissure almost divides the cerebrum in half. The hemispheres of the cerebral cortex are connected by the **corpus callosum** (Latin for "thick body" or "hard body"), a thick fiber bundle.

Basal ganglia Ganglia located between the thalamus and cerebrum that are involved in motor coordination.

Cerebrum The large mass of the forebrain, which consists of two hemispheres.

Cerebral cortex The wrinkled surface area (gray matter) of the cerebrum.

Fissures Valleys.

Corpus callosum A thick fiber bundle that connects the hemispheres of the cortex.

Somatic nervous system The division of the peripheral nervous system that connects the central nervous system with sensory receptors, skeletal muscles, and the surface of the body.

The Peripheral Nervous System

The peripheral nervous system consists of sensory and motor neurons that transmit messages to and from the central nervous system. Without the peripheral nervous system, our brains would be isolated from the world: they would not be able to perceive it, and they would not be able to act on it. The two main divisions of the peripheral nervous system are the somatic nervous system and the autonomic nervous system.

The Somatic Nervous System. The **somatic nervous system** contains sensory (afferent) and motor (efferent) neurons. It transmits messages about sights, sounds, smells, temperature, body positions, and so on, to the central nervous system. As a result, we can experience the beauties and the horrors of the world, its physical ecstasies and agonies. Messages from the brain and spinal cord to the somatic nervous system control purposeful body movements such as raising a hand, winking, or running as well as breathing and movements that we hardly attend to—movements that maintain our posture and balance.

The Autonomic Nervous System. *Autonomic* means "automatic." The **autonomic nervous system** (ANS) regulates the glands and the muscles of internal organs. Thus, the ANS controls activities such as heartbeat, respiration, digestion, and dilation of the pupils of the eyes. These activities can occur automatically, as we are asleep. But some of them can be overridden by conscious control. You can breathe at a purposeful pace, for example. Methods like biofeedback and yoga also help people gain voluntary control of functions such as heart rate and blood pressure.

The ANS has two branches or divisions: **sympathetic** and **parasympathetic.** These branches have largely opposing effects. Many organs and glands are stimulated by both branches of the ANS (Figure 3.13). When organs and glands are simultaneously stimulated by both divisions, their effects can average out to some degree. In general, the sympathetic division is most active during processes that involve the spending of body energy from stored reserves, such as in a fight-or-flight response to a predator or when you find out that your mortgage payment is going to be increased. The parasympathetic division is most active during processes that replenish reserves of energy, such as eating. When we are afraid, the sympathetic division of the ANS accelerates the heart rate. When we relax, it is the parasympathetic division that decelerates the heart rate. The parasympathetic division stimulates digestive processes, but the sympathetic branch inhibits digestion. Since the sympathetic division predominates when we feel fear or anxiety, fear or anxiety can cause indigestion.

It is true that fear can give you indigestion. Fear predominantly involves sympathetic activity, and digestion involves counteracting parasympathetic activity.

The ANS is of particular interest to psychologists because its activities are linked to various emotions such as anxiety and love. Some people may have overly reactive sympathetic nervous systems. Even in the absence of external threats, their bodies may respond as though they were faced with danger (see Chapter 13).

THE CEREBRAL CORTEX

Sensation and muscle activity involve many parts of the nervous system. The essential human activities of thought and language, however, involve the hemispheres of the cerebral cortex.

The Geography of the Cerebral Cortex

Each of the two hemispheres of the cerebral cortex is divided into four parts, or lobes, as shown in Figure 3.14. The **frontal lobe** lies in front of the central fissure, and the **parietal lobe** lies behind it. The **temporal lobe** lies below the side, or

Autonomic nervous system The division of the peripheral nervous system that regulates glands and activities such as heartbeat, respiration, digestion, and dilation of the pupils. Abbreviated *ANS.*

Sympathetic The branch of the ANS that is most active during emotional responses such as fear and anxiety that spend the body's reserves of energy.

Parasympathetic The branch of the ANS that is most active during processes such as digestion that restore the body's reserves of energy.

Frontal lobe The lobe of the cerebral cortex that lies to the front of the central fissure.

Parietal lobe The lobe of the cerebral cortex that lies just behind the central fissure.

Temporal lobe The lobe of the cerebral cortex that lies below the lateral fissure, near the temples of the head.

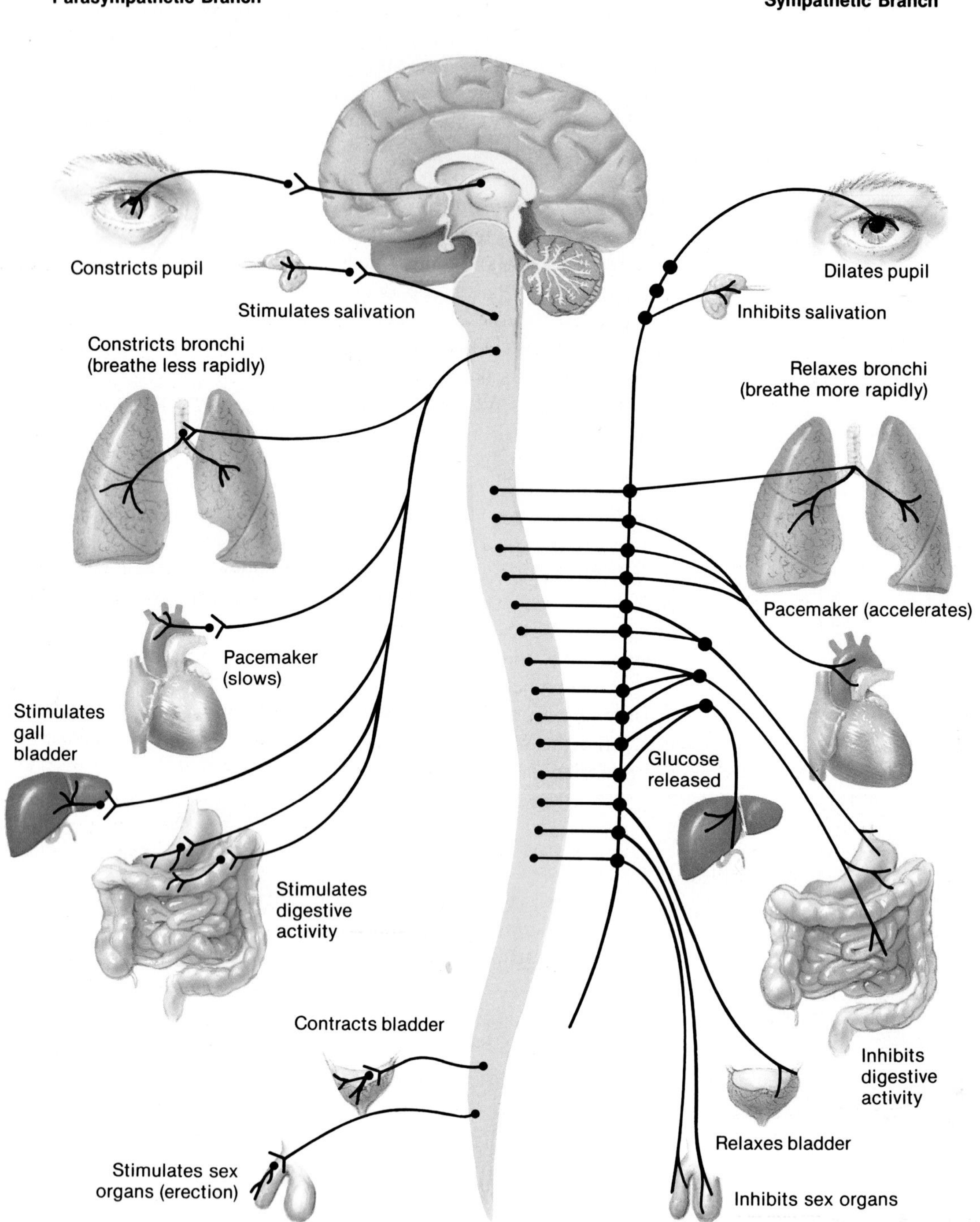

Figure 3.13
The Activities of the Two Branches of the Autonomic Nervous System (ANS).

The parasympathetic branch of the ANS generally acts to replenish stores of energy in the body. It is connected to organs by nerves that originate near the top and bottom of the spinal cord. The sympathetic branch is most active during activities that expend energy. Its neurons collect in clusters or chains of ganglia along the central portion of the spinal cord. The two branches of the ANS frequently have antagonistic effects on the organs they service.

lateral, fissure, across from the frontal and parietal lobes. The **occipital lobe** lies behind the temporal lobe and behind and below the parietal lobe.

When light strikes the retinas of the eyes, neurons in the occipital lobe fire, and we "see." Direct artificial stimulation of the occipital lobe also produces visual sensations. You would "see" flashes of light if neurons in the occipital region of the cortex were stimulated with electricity, even if it were pitch black or your eyes were covered. The hearing or auditory area of the cortex lies in the temporal lobe along the lateral fissure. Sounds cause structures in the ear to vibrate (see Chapter 4). Messages are relayed to the auditory area of the cortex, and when you hear a noise, neurons in this area are firing.

Just behind the central fissure in the parietal lobe lies an area of **somatosensory cortex,** in which the messages received from skin senses all over the body are projected. These sensations include warmth and cold, touch, pain, and movement. Neurons in different parts of the sensory cortex fire, depending on whether you wiggle your finger or raise your leg. If a brain surgeon were to stimulate the proper area of your somatosensory cortex with a small probe known as a "pencil electrode," it might seem as if someone were touching your arm or leg.

It is true that it might seem as though someone had stroked your leg if a surgeon were to stimulate a certain part of your brain with an electrode.

Figure 3.14 suggests how our faces and heads are overrepresented on this cortex as compared with, say, our trunks and legs. This overrepresentation is one of the reasons that our faces and heads are more sensitive to touch than other parts of the body.

People who have injuries in one hemisphere of the brain tend to show sensory or motor deficits on the opposite side of the body. Sensory and motor nerves cross in the brain and elsewhere. The left hemisphere controls functions on, and receives inputs from, the right side of the body. The right hemisphere controls functions on, and receives inputs from, the left side of the body.

The **motor cortex** lies in the frontal lobe, just across the valley of the central fissure from the somatosensory cortex. Neurons in the motor cortex fire when we move certain parts of our body. If a surgeon were to stimulate a certain area of the right hemisphere of the motor cortex with a pencil electrode, you would raise your left leg. Raising the leg would be sensed in the somatosensory cortex, and you might have a devil of a time trying to figure out whether you had "intended" to raise that leg!

Thought, Language, and the Cortex

Areas of the cerebral cortex that are not primarily involved in sensation or motor activity are called **association areas.** They make possible the breadth and depth of human learning, thought, memory, and language. Association areas, for example, involve memory functions required for simple problem-solving. Monkeys with lesions in certain association areas have difficulty remembering which of a pair of cups holds food when the cups have been screened off from them for a few seconds (Bauer & Fuster, 1976; French & Harlow, 1962). Stimulation of many association areas with pencil electrodes during surgery leads some people to report visual/auditory experiences that seem like memories, and sometimes they seem to be attended by appropriate emotions (Penfield, 1969).

Occipital lobe The lobe of the cerebral cortex that lies behind and below the parietal lobe and behind the temporal lobe.

Somatosensory cortex The section of cortex in which sensory stimulation is projected. It lies just behind the central fissure in the parietal lobe.

Motor cortex The section of cortex that lies in the frontal lobe, just across the central fissure from the sensory cortex. Neural impulses in the motor cortex are linked to muscular responses throughout the body.

Association areas Areas of the cortex involved in learning, thought, memory, and language.

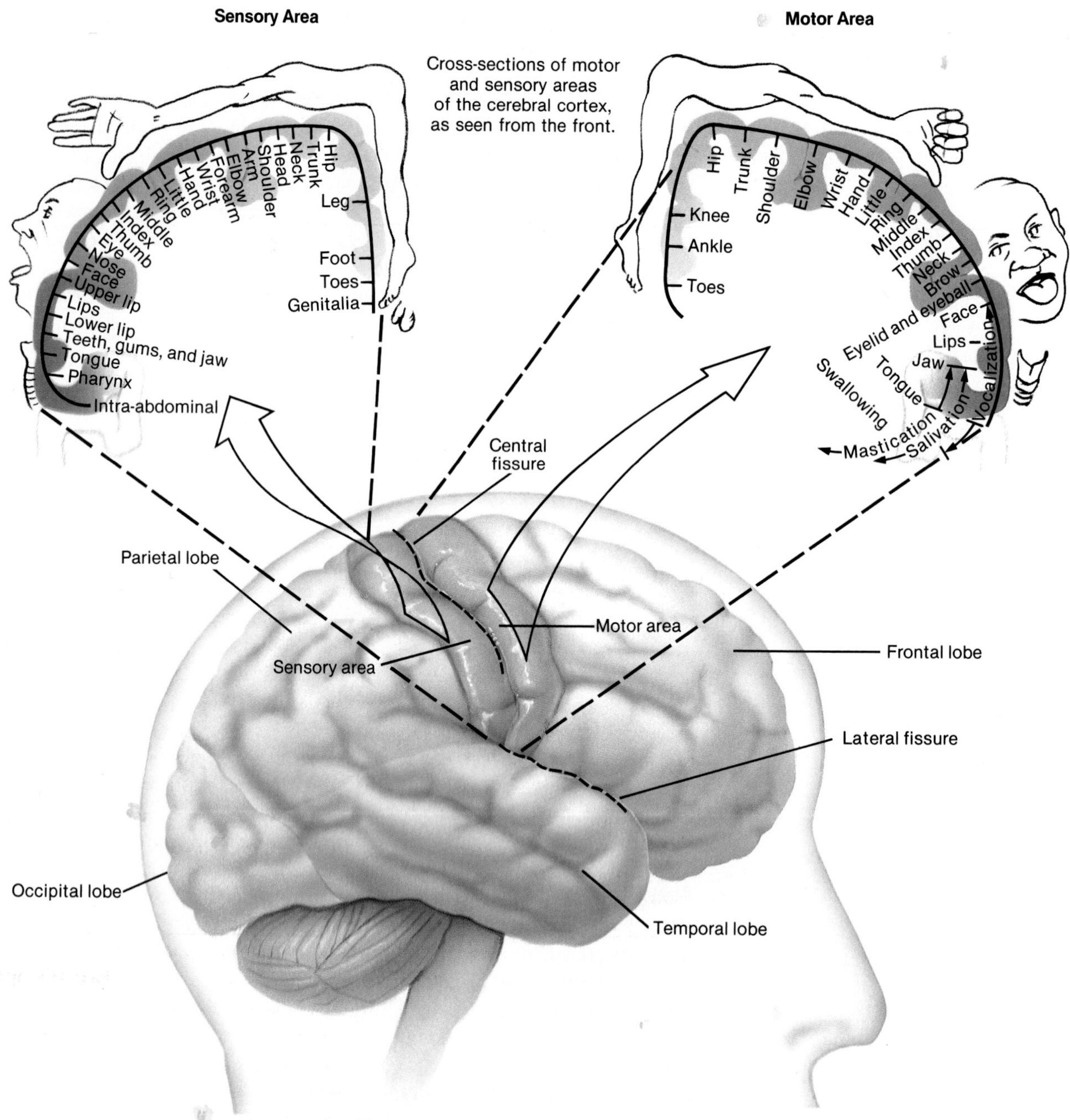

Figure 3.14
The Geography of the Cerebral Cortex.

The cortex is divided into four lobes: frontal, parietal, temporal, and occipital. The visual area of the cortex is located in the occipital lobe. The hearing or auditory cortex lies in the temporal lobe. The sensory and motor areas face each other across the central fissure. What happens when a surgeon stimulates areas of the sensory or motor cortex during an operation?

Some association areas are involved in the integration of sensory information. Certain neurons in the visual area of the occipital lobe fire in response to the visual presentation of vertical lines. Others fire in response to presentation of horizontal lines. Although one group of cells may respond to one aspect of the visual field and another group of cells may respond to another, association areas "put it all together." As a result, you see a box or an automobile or a road map and not a confusing array of verticals and horizontals.

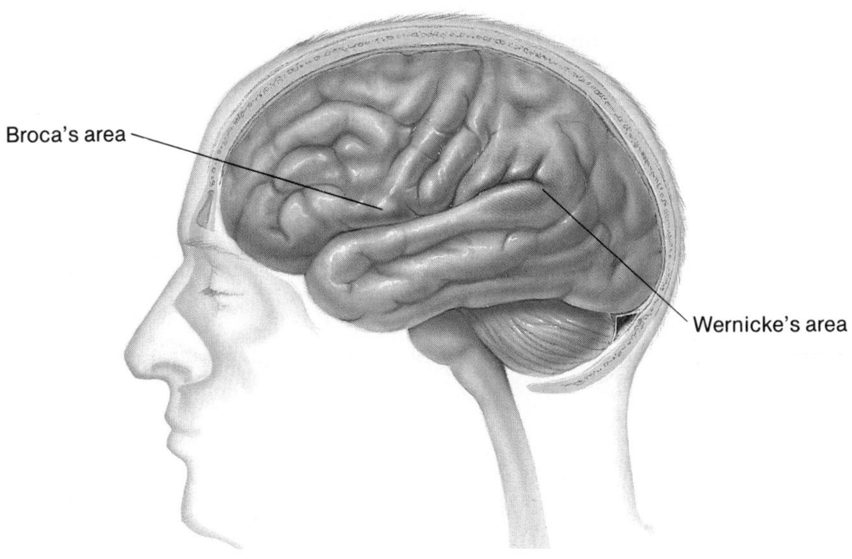

Figure 3.15
Broca's and Wernicke's Areas of the Cerebral Cortex. Areas of the dominant hemisphere most involved in speech are Broca's area and Wernicke's area. Damage to either can produce a characteristic aphasia—that is, a predictable disruption of the ability to understand or produce language.

Language Functions. In many ways, the left and right hemispheres of the brain tend to duplicate each other's functions, but they are not entirely equal. For most people, the left hemisphere contains language functions.

Dennis and Victoria Molfese (1979) found that even at birth, the sounds of speech elicit greater electrical activity in the left hemisphere than in the right, as indicated by the activity of brain waves. Sensory pathways cross over in the brain, so dominance of the left hemisphere is associated with dominance of the right ear, and vice versa.

Within the dominant (usually left) hemisphere of the cortex, the two areas most involved in speech are Broca's area and Wernicke's area (see Figure 3.15). Damage to either area is likely to cause an **aphasia**—that is, a disruption of the ability to understand or produce language.

Broca's area is located in the frontal lobe, near the section of the motor cortex that controls the muscles of the tongue and throat and of other areas of the face that are used when speaking. When Broca's area is damaged, people speak slowly and laboriously, with simple sentences—a pattern termed **Broca's aphasia.** Comprehension and use of syntax may be seriously impaired.

Wernicke's area lies in the temporal lobe near the auditory cortex. This area appears to be involved in the integration of auditory and visual information. Broca's area and Wernicke's area are connected by nerve fibers. People with damage to Wernicke's area may show **Wernicke's aphasia,** in which they usually speak freely and with proper syntax. Their abilities to comprehend other people's speech and to think of the proper words to express their own thoughts are impaired, however (Gardner, 1978). Wernicke's area thus seems to be essential to understanding the relationships between words and their meanings.

Aphasia Impaired ability to comprehend or express oneself through language.

Broca's aphasia A language disorder characterized by slow, laborious speech.

Wernicke's aphasia A language disorder characterized by difficulty comprehending the meaning of spoken language.

Left Brain, Right Brain?

In recent years, it has become popular to speak of people as being "left-brained" or "right-brained." The notion is that the hemispheres of the brain are involved in very different kinds of intellectual and emotional functions and responses, along the lines suggested in Figure 3.16. According to this view, people whose left brains are dominant would be primarily logical and intellectual. People whose right brains are dominant would be intuitive, creative, and emotional. Those of us

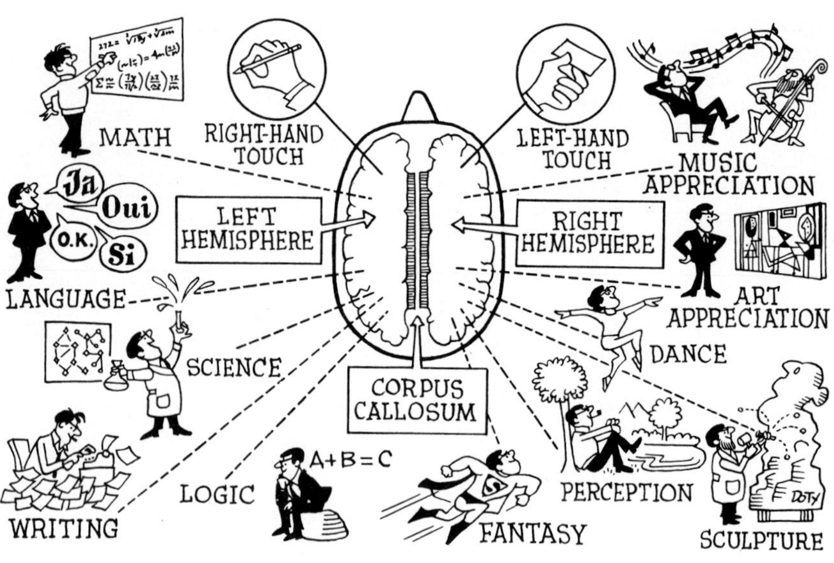

Figure 3.16
Some of the "Specializations" of the Left and Right Hemispheres of the Cerebral Cortex. This cartoon, which appeared in a popular magazine, exaggerates the "left brain–right brain" notion. The dominant (usually left) hemisphere is apparently somewhat more involved in intellectual undertakings that require logic and problem-solving, whereas the nondominant (usually right) hemisphere is relatively more concerned with decoding visual information, aesthetic and emotional responses, and imagination. Yet each hemisphere has some involvement with logic, creativity, and intuition.

fortunate enough to have our brains "in balance" would presumably have the best of it—the capacity for logic combined with emotional richness.

Like so many other popular ideas, the left-brain–right-brain notion is at best exaggerated. Research does suggest that in right-handed individuals, the left hemisphere is relatively more involved in intellectual undertakings that require logical analysis and problem solving, understanding syntax, associating written words with their sounds, the general comprehension and production of speech, and mathematical computation (Borod, 1992; J. Levy, 1985). The nondominant (usually right) hemisphere is relatively more concerned with spatial functions, aesthetic and emotional responses, imagination, understanding metaphors, and creative mathematical reasoning.

Despite these differences, however, it would be erroneous to think that the hemispheres of the brain act independently or that some people are left-brained and others are right-brained. The functions of the left and right hemispheres overlap to some degree, and the hemispheres tend to respond simultaneously as we focus our attention on one thing or another. The hemispheres are aided in their "cooperation" by myelination of the corpus callosum, the bundle of nerve fibers that connects them. Myelination of the corpus callosum proceeds rapidly during early and middle childhood and is largely complete by the age of 8. By that time, we apparently have greater ability to integrate logical and emotional functioning.

Biological psychologist Jerre Levy (1985) summarizes left-brain and right-brain similarities and differences as follows:

1. The hemispheres are similar enough that each can function quite well independently but not as well as they function in normal combined usage.
2. The left hemisphere does seem to play a special role in understanding and producing language, whereas the right hemisphere does seem to play a special role in emotional response.
3. Both hemispheres are involved in logic.
4. Creativity and intuition are not confined to the right hemisphere.
5. Both hemispheres are educated at the same time, even when instruction is intended to "appeal" to the right hemisphere (as in music) or the left (in a logic class).

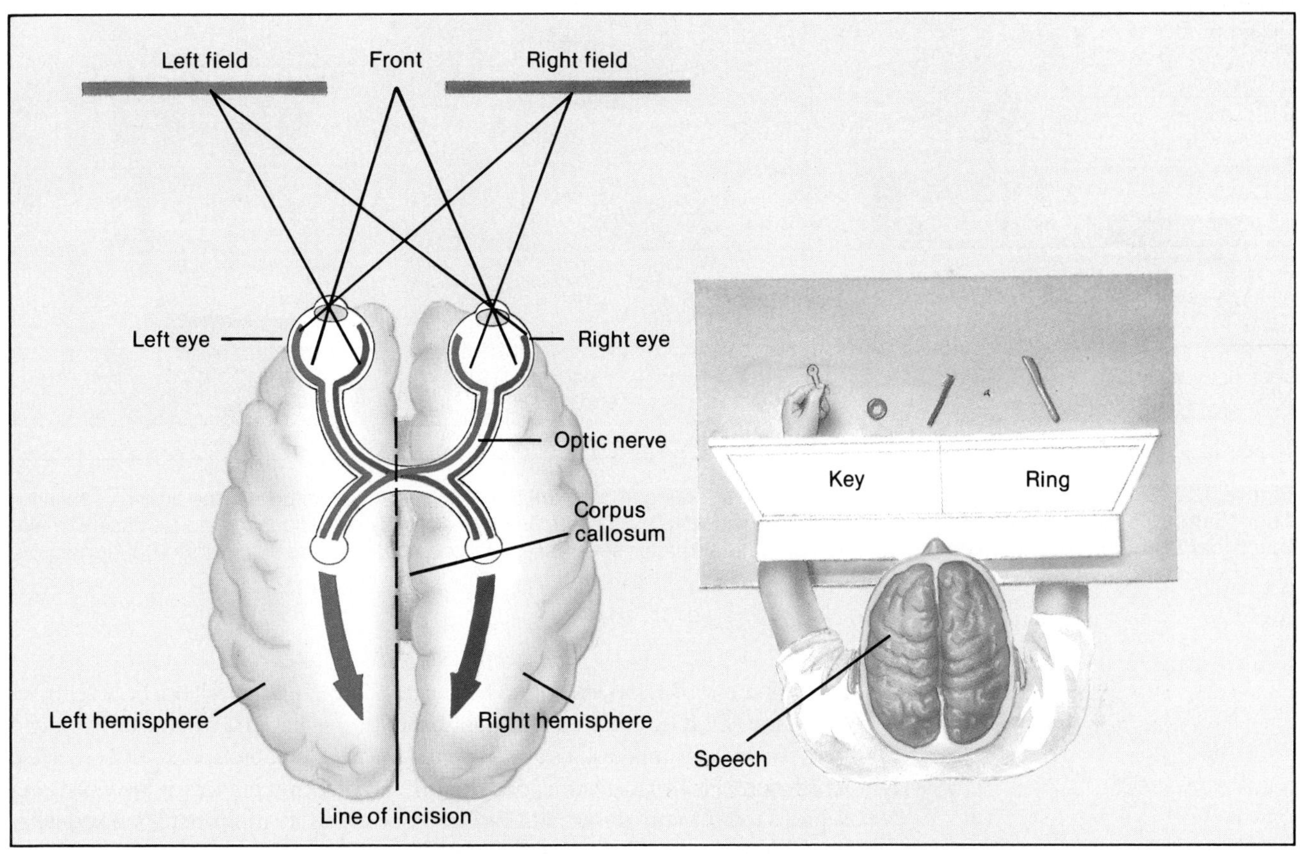

Figure 3.17
A Divided-Brain Experiment.

In the drawing on the left, we see that visual sensations in the left visual field are projected in the occipital cortex of the right hemisphere. Visual sensations from the right visual field are projected in the occipital cortex in the left hemisphere. In the divided-brain experiment diagrammed on the right, a subject with a severed corpus callosum handles a key with his left hand and perceives the written word *key* with his left eye. The word "key" is projected in the right hemisphere. Speech, however, is usually a function of the left (dominant) hemisphere. The written word "ring," perceived by the right eye, is projected in the left hemisphere. So, when asked what he is handling, the divided-brain subject reports "ring," not "key."

Split-Brain Experiments: When Hemispheres Stop Communicating

A number of patients suffering from severe cases of **epilepsy** have undergone **split-brain operations** in which the corpus callosum is severed. The purpose of the operation is to try to confine epilepsy to one hemisphere of the cerebral cortex rather than allowing a reverberating neural tempest. These operations do seem to be of help. People who have undergone them can bethought of as winding up with two brains, yet under most circumstances their behavior remains ordinary enough. Still, some aspects of hemispheres that have stopped talking to one another are intriguing.

Gazzaniga (1972, 1983, 1985) has shown that split-brain patients whose eyes are closed may be able to verbally describe an object such as a key that they hold in one hand, but they cannot do so when they hold the object in the other hand. As shown in Figure 3.17, if a split-brain patient handles a key with his left hand behind a screen, **tactile** impressions of the key are projected into the right

Epilepsy Temporary disturbances of brain functions that involve sudden neural discharges.

Split-brain operation An operation in which the corpus callosum is severed, usually in an effort to control epileptic seizures.

Tactile Of the sense of touch.

Figure 3.18
The "Taming" of a Brave Bull by Electrical Stimulation of the Brain.
Brave bulls are dangerous animals that will attack an intruder in the arena. Even in full charge, however, a bull can be stopped abruptly by radio-triggered electrical stimulation of the brain. After several stimulations, there is a lasting inhibition of aggressive behavior.

hemisphere, which has little or no language ability. Thus, he will not be able to describe the key. If he holds it in his right hand, he will have no trouble describing it because sensory impressions are projected into the left hemisphere of the cortex, which contains language functions. To further confound matters, if the word *ring* is projected into the dominant (left) hemisphere while the patient is asked what he is handling, he will say "ring," not "key."

However, this discrepancy between what is felt and what is said occurs only in split-brain patients. As noted earlier, most of the time the hemispheres work together, even when we are playing the piano or are involved in scientific thought.

In case you have ever wondered whether other people could make us play the piano or engage in scientific thinking by "pressing the right buttons," let us consider some of the effects of electrical stimulation of the brain.

Electrical Stimulation of the Brain

Some years ago, José Delgado astounded the scientific world by stepping into a bullring armed only with a radio transmitter, a cape, and, perhaps, crossed fingers (Figure 3.18). Describing his experiment in *Physical Control of the Mind* (1969), Delgado explained that he had implanted a radio-controlled electrode in the limbic system of a brave "bull"—a variety bred to respond with a raging charge when it sees any human being. When Delgado pressed a button on the transmitter, sending a signal to a battery-powered receiver attached to the bull's horns, an electrical impulse went into the bull's brain and the animal ceased his charge. After several repetitions, the bull no longer attempted to charge Delgado.

Another effect of electrical stimulation of the brain was discovered accidentally (how many important discoveries are made by accident!) during the 1950s by James Olds and Peter Milner (Olds, 1969). Olds and Milner found that electrical stimulation of an area of the hypothalamus of a rat induced the animal to increase the frequency of whatever it was doing at the time (Figure 3.19). Rats also rapidly learned to engage in behavior such as pressing a lever that resulted in more stimulation. Rats, in fact, will stimulate themselves in this area repeatedly, up to 100 times a minute and over 1,900 times an hour. For this reason, Olds and Milner labeled this area of the hypothalamus a pleasure center.

Figure 3.19
A "Pleasure Center" of the Brain. A rat with an electrode implanted in a section of the hypothalamus that has been termed a pleasure center learns to press a lever to receive electrical stimulation.

It is true that rats will learn to do things that result in a "reward" of a burst of electricity in the pleasure center of the brain.

In our discussion of the nervous system, we have described naturally occurring chemical substances that facilitate or inhibit the transmission of neural messages—neurotransmitters. Let us now turn our attention to other naturally occurring chemical substances that influence behavior—hormones. We shall see that some hormones also function as neurotransmitters.

THE ENDOCRINE SYSTEM

Here are some things you may have heard about hormones and behavior. Are they truth or fiction?

_______ Some overweight people actually eat very little, and their excess weight is caused by "glands."

_______ Injections of growth hormone have reversed some of the effects of aging in men in their 60s and 70s.

_______ A woman who becomes anxious and depressed just before menstruating is suffering from "raging hormones."

_______ Women who "pump iron" frequently use hormones to achieve the muscle definition that is needed to win body-building contests.

_______ People who receive injections of adrenaline may report that they feel as if they are about to experience some emotion, but they're not sure which one.

Let us consider each of these items. Some overweight people do eat relatively little but are "sabotaged" in their weight-loss efforts by hormonal changes that lower the rates at which they metabolize food (Brownell, 1988). A synthetic version of growth hormone, which is normally secreted by the **pituitary gland,** has helped many elderly people gain muscle, shed fat, and thicken the bone in their spines (Rudman et al., 1990). Their skin regained a youthful thickness, and the hormone may also have helped rebuild vital organs, including the heart and kidneys.[2] Women may become somewhat more anxious or depressed at the time of menstruation, but the effects of hormones have been exaggerated, and women's response to menstruation reflects their attitudes as well as biological changes. Many top women (and men) body-builders do use steroids (hormones that are produced by the **adrenal cortex**) and growth hormone to achieve muscle mass and definition (Leerhsen & Abramson, 1985). Steroids and growth hormone promote resistance to stress and muscle growth in both genders. Finally, adrenaline, a hormone produced by the **adrenal medulla,** does generally arouse people and heighten general emotional responsiveness. The specific emotion to which this arousal is attributed depends in part on the person's situation (see Chapter 8).

Ductless Glands. The body contains two types of glands: glands with **ducts** and glands without ducts. A duct is a passageway that carries substances to specific locations. Saliva, sweat, tears (the name of a new rock group?), and milk

Pituitary gland The gland that secretes growth hormone, prolactin, antidiuretic hormone, and others.

Adrenal cortex The outer part of the adrenal glands located above the kidneys. It produces steroids.

Adrenal medulla The inner part of the adrenal glands that produces adrenaline.

Duct Passageway.

[2] Such research is in its infancy, however, and medical experts also warn that excesses of growth hormone have been linked to arthritis, diabetes, heart failure, and other problems (Vance, 1990).

TABLE 3.1: An Overview of Some Major Glands of the Endocrine System

Gland	Hormone	Major Effects
Hypothalamus	Growth-hormone releasing factor	Causes pituitary gland to secrete growth hormone
	Corticotrophin-releasing hormone	Causes pituitary gland to secrete adrenocorticotrophic hormone
	Thyrotropin-releasing hormone	Causes pituitary gland to secrete thyrotropin
	Gonadotropin-releasing hormone	Causes pituitary gland to secrete follicle-stimulating hormone and luteinizing hormone
	Prolactin-releasing hormone	Causes pituitary gland to secrete prolactin
Pituitary		
Anterior Lobe	Growth hormone	Causes growth of muscles, bones, and glands
	Adrenocorticotrophic hormone (ACTH)	Regulates adrenal cortex
	Thyrotrophin	Causes thyroid gland to secrete thyroxin
	Follicle-stimulating hormone	Causes formation of sperm and egg cells
	Luteinizing hormone	Causes ovulation, maturation of sperm and egg cells
	Prolactin	Stimulates production of milk
Posterior Lobe	Antidiuretic hormone (ADH)	Inhibits production of urine
	Oxytocin	Stimulates uterine contractions during delivery and ejection of milk during nursing
Pancreas	Insulin	Enables body to metabolize sugar, regulates storage of fats
Thyroid	Thyroxin	Increases metabolic rate
Adrenal		
Cortex	Steroids (e.g., cortisol)	Increase resistance to stress; regulate carbohydrate metabolism
Medulla	Adrenaline (epinephrine)	Increases metabolic activity (heart and respiration rates, blood sugar level, etc.)
	Noradrenaline (norepinephrine)	Raises blood pressure, acts as neurotransmitter
Testes	Testosterone	Promotes growth of male sex characteristics
Ovaries	Estrogen	Regulates menstrual cycle
	Progesterone	Promotes growth of female reproductive tissues; maintains pregnancy
Uterus	(Several)	Maintain pregnancy

all reach their destinations by means of ducts. Psychologists are interested in the substances secreted by ductless glands because of their behavioral effects (see the summary in Table 3.1). The ductless glands constitute the **endocrine system** of the body, and they secrete **hormones** (from the Greek *horman,* meaning "to stimulate" or "to excite").

Hormones are released directly into the bloodstream. As is the case with neurotransmitters,[3] hormones have specific receptor sites. Although they are poured into the bloodstream and circulate throughout the body, they act only on hormone receptors in certain locations. Some hormones released by the hypothalamus influence only the pituitary gland. Some hormones released by the pituitary influence the adrenal cortex, others influence the testes and ovaries, and so on.

Let us consider several glands and hormone that are of interest to psychologists.

The Hypothalamus

The hypothalamus secretes a number of releasing hormones, or factors, that influence the anterior (front) lobe of the pituitary gland to secrete corresponding

Endocrine system Ductless glands that secrete hormones and release them directly into the bloodstream.

Hormone A substance secreted by an endocrine gland that regulates various body functions.

[3]Recall that some hormones, such as noradrenaline, also function as neurotransmitters.

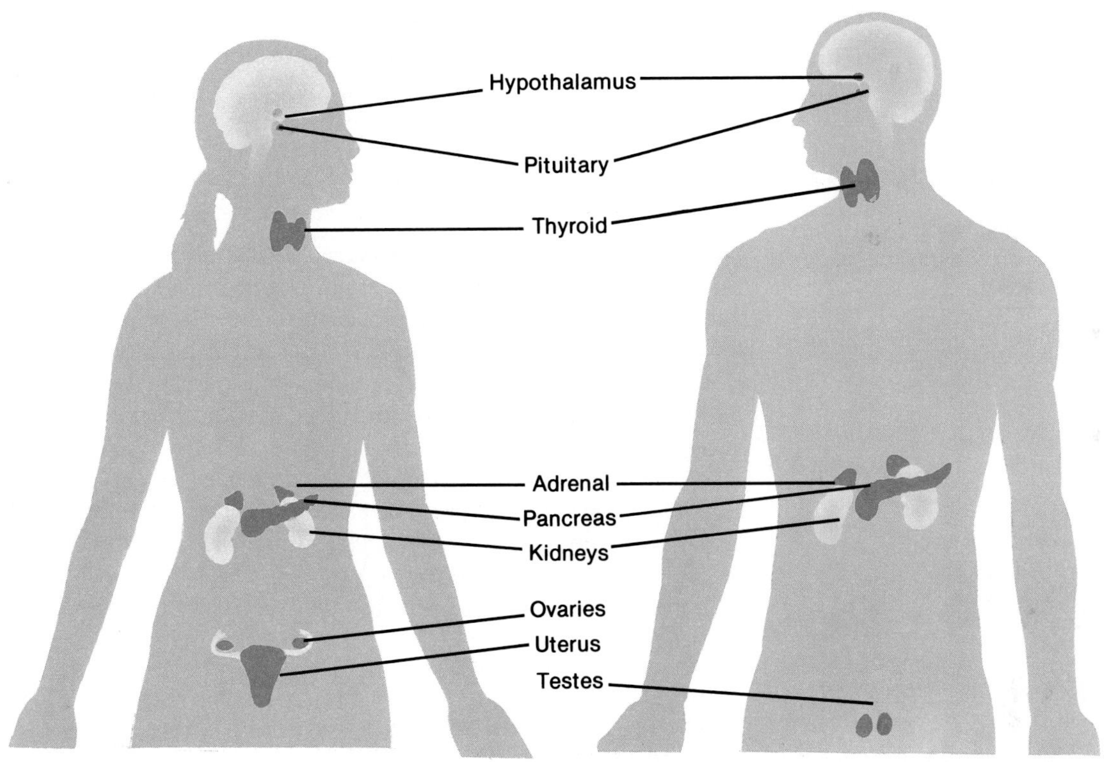

Figure 3.20
Major Glands of the Endocrine System.

The hypothalamus is a structure of the brain. Since it secretes hormones, however, it is also an endocrine gland.

hormones (Derryberry & Tucker, 1992). A dense network of blood vessels between the hypothalamus and the pituitary gland provides a direct route of influence.

The Pituitary Gland

The pituitary gland lies just below the hypothalamus (see Figure 3.20). It is about the size of a pea, but it is so central to the body's functioning that it has been referred to as the "master gland." Despite this designation, today we know that the hypothalamus regulates a good deal of pituitary activity.

Much hormonal action helps the body maintain steady states, as in fluid levels, blood sugar levels, and so on. Bodily mechanisms measure current levels and signal glands to release hormones when these levels deviate from optimal. The maintenance of steady states requires the feedback of bodily information to glands. This type of system is referred to as a **negative feedback** loop. That is, when enough of a hormone has been secreted, the gland is signaled to stop. With a negative feedback system in effect, even the master gland must serve a master—the hypothalamus. In turn, the hypothalamus responds to information from the body.

The anterior and posterior (back) lobes of the pituitary gland produce or secrete many hormones, some of which are listed in Table 3.1. **Prolactin** largely regulates maternal behavior in lower mammals such as rats and stimulates production of milk in women. Transfusion of blood from a new mother rat to another female rat will cause the recipient to display stereotypical mothering behaviors.

Oxytocin stimulates labor in pregnant women. Obstetricians may induce labor or increase the strength of uterine contractions during labor by injecting pregnant women with oxytocin. During nursing, stimulation of nerve endings in and around the nipple sends messages to the brain that cause oxytocin to be secreted. Oxytocin then causes contractile cells in the breast to eject milk.

Negative feedback Descriptive of a system in which information that a quantity (e.g., of a hormone) has reached a set point suspends action of the agency (e.g., a gland) that gives rise to that quantity.

Prolactin A pituitary hormone that regulates production of milk and, in lower animals, maternal behavior.

Oxytocin A pituitary hormone that stimulates labor and lactation.

Hypothalamic corticotrophin-releasing hormone (CRH) causes the pituitary gland to release **adrenocorticotrophic hormone** (ACTH). ACTH then incites the adrenal cortex to release **steroids** that help the body manage stress by fighting inflammation and allergic reactions.

The Pancreas

Endocrine cells within the **pancreas** regulate the level of sugar in the blood and the urine through **insulin** and other hormones. One form of diabetes (diabetes mellitus) is characterized by excess sugar in the blood—**hyperglycemia**—and in the urine, a condition that can lead to coma and death (Becker, 1990). Diabetes stems from inadequate secretion or utilization of insulin. People who do not secrete enough insulin of their own may need to inject this hormone daily in order to control diabetes.

The condition **hypoglycemia** is characterized by too little sugar in the blood. Symptoms of hypoglycemia include shakiness, dizziness, and lack of energy, a **syndrome** that is easily confused with anxiety. Many people have sought help for anxiety and learned through a series of blood tests that they are actually suffering from hypoglycemia. This disorder is generally controlled through dietary restrictions.

The Thyroid Gland

Thyroxin is produced by the thyroid gland. Thyroxin affects the body's **metabolism,** or rate of using oxygen and producing energy. Some people who are overweight are suffering from a condition known as **hypothyroidism,** which results from abnormally low secretions of thyroxin. Deficiency of thyroxin can lead to **cretinism** in children, which is symptomized by stunted growth and mental retardation. Adults who secrete too little thyroxin may feel tired and sluggish and may put on weight. People who produce excess amounts of thyroxin may develop **hyperthyroidism,** which is symptomized by excitability, insomnia, and weight loss (Becker, 1990).

The Adrenal Glands

The adrenal glands, located above the kidneys, have an outer layer, or cortex, and an inner core, or medulla. The adrenal cortex is regulated by pituitary ACTH. The cortex secretes as many as 20 different hormones known as **corticosteroids,** or cortical steroids. Cortical steroids (**cortisol** is one) increase resistance to stress; promote muscle development; and cause the liver to release stored sugar, making energy available for emergencies.

The **catecholamines** adrenaline and noradrenaline are secreted by the adrenal medulla. **Adrenaline,** also known as epinephrine, is manufactured exclusively by the adrenal glands. Noradrenaline (norepinephrine) is also produced elsewhere in the body. The sympathetic branch of the autonomic nervous system causes the adrenal medulla to release a mixture of adrenaline and noradrenaline that helps arouse the body in preparation for coping with threats and stress. Adrenaline is of interest to psychologists because of its emotional, as well as physiological, effects. Adrenaline may intensify most emotions and is crucial to the experience of fear and anxiety. Noradrenaline raises the blood pressure and, in the nervous system, it acts as a neurotransmitter.

The Testes and the Ovaries

Did you know that if it were not for the secretion of the male sex hormone **testosterone** about six weeks after conception, we would all develop external fe-

---

Adrenocorticotrophic hormone A pituitary hormone that regulates the adrenal cortex. Abbreviated *ACTH.*

Steroids A family of hormones including testosterone, estrogen, progesterone, and corticosteroids.

Pancreas An organ behind the stomach; endocrine cells in the pancreas secrete hormones that influence the blood sugar level.

Insulin A pancreatic hormone that stimulates the metabolism of sugar.

Hyperglycemia A disorder caused by excess sugar in the blood.

Hypoglycemia A disorder caused by too little sugar in the blood.

Syndrome A cluster of symptoms characteristic of a disorder.

Thyroxin The thyroid hormone that increases metabolic rate.

Metabolism In organisms, a continuous process that converts food into energy.

Hypothyroidism A condition caused by a deficiency of thyroxin and characterized by sluggish behavior and a low metabolic rate.

Cretinism A condition caused by thyroid deficiency in childhood and characterized by mental retardation and stunted growth.

Hyperthyroidism A condition caused by excess thyroxin and characterized by excitability, insomnia, and weight loss.

Corticosteroids Steroids produced by the adrenal cortex that regulate carbohydrate metabolism and increase resistance to stress by fighting inflammation and allergic reactions. Also called *cortical steroids.*

Cortisol A hormone (steroid) produced by the adrenal cortex that helps the body cope with stress by counteracting inflammation and allergic reactions.

Catecholamines A number of chemical substances produced from an amino acid that are important as neurotransmitters (dopamine and noradrenaline) and as hormones (adrenaline and noradrenaline).

Adrenaline A hormone produced by the adrenal medulla that stimulates sympathetic ANS activity. Also called *epinephrine.*

male sex organs? Testosterone is produced by the testes and, in smaller amounts, by the ovaries and adrenal glands. A few weeks after conception, testosterone stimulates prenatal differentiation of male sex organs. (The quantities produced by the ovaries and adrenal glands are normally insufficient to foster development of male sex organs.)

During puberty, testosterone stokes the growth of muscle and bone and the development of primary and secondary sex characteristics. **Primary sex characteristics** such as the growth of the penis and the sperm-producing ability of the testes are directly involved in reproduction. **Secondary sex characteristics** such as growth of the beard and deepening of the voice differentiate males and females but are not directly involved in reproduction.

Testosterone levels vary slightly with stress, time of the day or month, and other factors, but are maintained at fairly even levels by the hypothalamus, pituitary gland, and testes. Low blood levels of testosterone signal the hypothalamus to produce gonadotropin-releasing hormone (GnRH). GnRH, in turn, signals the pituitary to secrete luteinizing hormone (LH), which stimulates the testes to secrete testosterone and follicle-stimulating hormone (FSH), which causes sperm cells to develop (Conn & Crowley, 1991). The negative feedback loop is completed as follows: High blood levels of testosterone signal the hypothalamus not to secrete GnRH so that production of LH, FSH, and testosterone is suspended.

The ovaries produce **estrogen** and **progesterone.** (Estrogen is also produced in smaller amounts by the testes.) Estrogen is a generic name for several female sex hormones that foster female reproductive capacity and secondary sex characteristics such as accumulation of fat in the breasts and hips. Progesterone also has multiple functions. It stimulates growth of the female reproductive organs and maintains pregnancy. As with testosterone, estrogen and progesterone levels influence and are also influenced by GnRH, LH, and FSH. In women, FSH causes ova (egg cells) within follicles in the ovaries to ripen. Whereas testosterone levels remain fairly stable, estrogen and progesterone levels vary markedly and regulate the menstrual cycle.

Testosterone A male sex hormone produced by the testes that promotes growth of male sexual characteristics and sperm.

Primary sex characteristics Physical traits that distinguish males from females and are directly involved in reproduction.

Secondary sex characteristics Physical traits that differentiate males from females but are not directly involved in reproduction.

Estrogen A generic term for several female sex hormones that promote growth of female sex characteristics and regulate the menstrual cycle.

Progesterone A female sex hormone that promotes growth of the sex organs and helps maintain pregnancy.

Heredity The transmission of traits from one generation to another through genes.

Genetics The branch of biology that studies heredity.

Behavior genetics The study of the genetic transmission of structures and traits that give rise to behavior.

HEREDITY

Consider some of the facts of life:

- People cannot breathe underwater (without special equipment).
- People cannot fly (again, without rather special equipment).
- Fish cannot learn to speak French or do an Irish jig even if you rear them in enriched environments and send them to finishing school (which is why we look for tuna that tastes good, not for tuna with good taste).
- Chimpanzees and gorillas can use sign language but cannot speak.

People cannot breathe underwater or fly (without oxygen tanks, airplanes, or other devices) because of the structures they have inherited. Fish are similarly limited by their **heredity,** or the biological transmission of traits and characteristics from one generation to another. Because of their heredity, fish cannot speak French or do a jig. Chimpanzees and gorillas can understand and express some concepts through American Sign Language and other nonverbal symbol systems. However, apes show no ability to speak, even though they can make sounds. They have probably failed to inherit the humanlike speech areas of the cerebral cortex.

Heredity plays a momentous role in the determination of human and nonhuman traits. The structures we inherit at the same time make our behaviors possible and limit them (Kimble, 1989).The field within the science of biology that studies heredity is called **genetics. Behavior genetics** is a specialty that bridges the sciences of psychology and biology. It is concerned with the transmission of structures and traits that give rise to patterns of behavior.

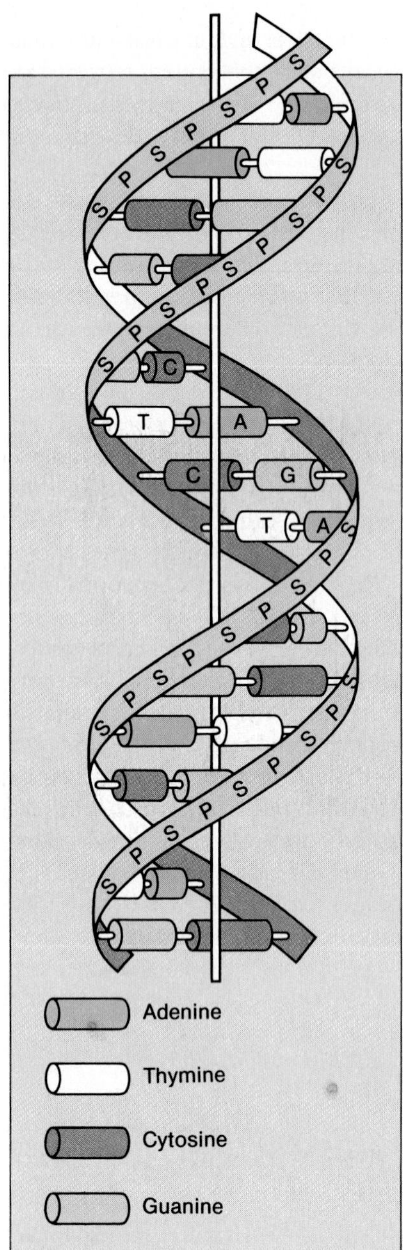

Figure 3.21
The Double Helix of DNA.

Extraversion A trait in which a person directs his or her interest to persons and things outside the self. Sociability.

Genes The basic building blocks of heredity, which consist of DNA.

Polygenic Determined by several genes.

Chromosomes Structures consisting of genes that are found in the nuclei of the body's cells.

Sex chromosomes The 23rd pair of chromosomes, which determine whether the child will be male or female.

Genetics are fundamental in the transmission of physical traits such as height, hair texture, and eye color. Genetics also appear to be factors in the origins of personality traits such as **extraversion** and anxiety (McCartney et al., 1990; Pedersen et al., 1988; Tellegen et al., 1988), shyness (Kagan, 1984; Plomin, 1989), social dominance, and aggressiveness (Goldsmith, 1983). Genetic influences are also implicated in psychological disorders such as schizophrenia (Gottesman, 1991), bipolar disorder (Vandenberg et al., 1986), and alcoholism (Newlin & Thomson, 1990); even in criminal behavior (DiLalla & Gottesman, 1991; Mednick et al., 1987).

Genes and Chromosomes

Genes are the basic building blocks of heredity. They are the biochemical materials that regulate the development of traits. Some traits, such as blood type, are transmitted by a single pair of genes—one of which is derived from each parent. Other traits, referred to as **polygenic,** are determined by complex combinations of genes.

Chromosomes, the genetic structures found in the nuclei of the body's cells, each consist of more than 1,000 genes. A normal human cell contains 46 chromosomes, which are organized into 23 pairs.

We have about 100,000 genes in every cell in our bodies. Genes occupy segments along the length of chromosomes. Chromosomes are large, complex molecules of deoxyribonucleic acid, which has several chemical components. You can breathe a sigh of relief, for this acid is usually referred to simply as DNA. The structure of DNA was first demonstrated in the 1950s by the team of James Watson and Francis Crick (1958). DNA takes the form of a double helix, similar in appearance to a twisting ladder (see Figure 3.21).

We receive 23 chromosomes from our fathers' sperm cells and 23 chromosomes from our mothers' egg cells (ova). When a sperm cell fertilizes an ovum, the chromosomes form 23 pairs (Figure 3.22). The 23rd pair consists of **sex chromosomes,** which determine our sex. We all receive an X sex chromosome (so called because of the "X" shape) from our mothers. If we also receive an X sex chromosome from our fathers, we develop into females. If we receive a Y sex chromosome (named after the "Y" shape) from our fathers, we develop into males.

Behavior geneticists are attempting to sort out the relative importance of **nature** (heredity) and **nurture** (environmental influences) in the origins of behavior. Psychologists are especially interested in the roles of nature and nurture in intelligence and abnormal behavior.

Behavior in general reflects the influences of both nature and nurture. Organisms inherit structures that set the stage for certain behaviors. But none of us, as we appear, is the result of heredity alone. Environmental factors such as nutrition, learning opportunities, cultural influences, exercise, and (unfortunately) accident and illness also determine whether genetically possible behaviors will be displayed. A potential Shakespeare who is reared in an impoverished neighborhood and never taught to read or write is unlikely to create a *Hamlet.* Thus, behavior appears to represent the interaction between nature and nurture.

Kinship Studies

Psychologists conduct kinship studies to help determine the role of genetic factors in behavior patterns and mental processes. They locate subjects who show the behavior pattern in question and then study the distribution of the behavior among relatives. The more closely people are related, the more genes they have in common. Parents and children have a 50 percent overlap in their genetic

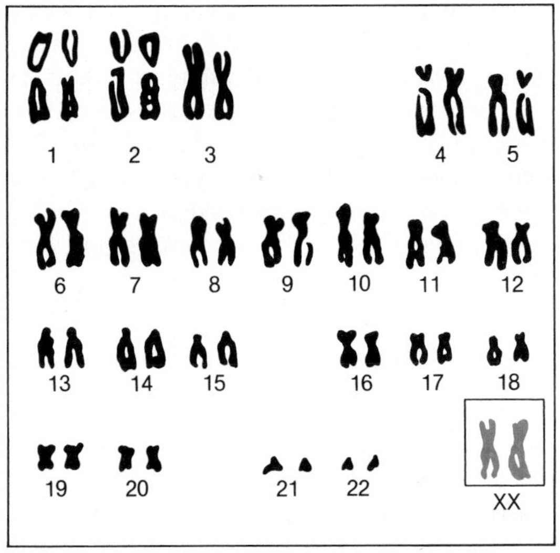

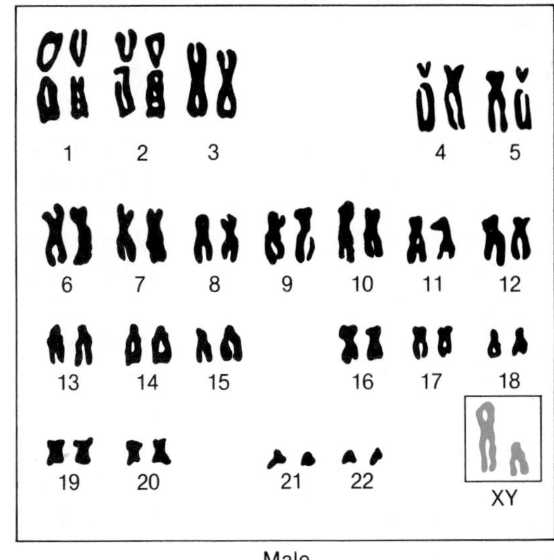

Figure 3.22
The 23 Pairs of Human Chromosomes. People normally have 23 pairs of chromosomes. Anatomic gender is determined by the 23rd pair of chromosomes. Females have two X sex chromosomes (part A), whereas males have an X and a Y sex chromosome (part B).

endowments, and so do siblings (brothers and sisters). Aunts and uncles related by blood have a 25 percent overlap with nieces and nephews; first cousins share 12.5 percent of their genetic endowment. So if genes are implicated in a behavior pattern, people more closely related should be more likely to share the pattern.

Twin Studies. The fertilized egg cell (ovum) that carries genetic messages from both parents is called a **zygote.** Now and then, a zygote divides into two cells that separate so that each develops into an individual with the same genetic makeup. Such people are identical twins, or **monozygotic (MZ) twins.** If the woman releases two ova in the same month, and they are both fertilized, they develop into fraternal twins, or **dizygotic (DZ) twins.** DZ twins are related as other siblings. MZ twins are important in the study of the relative influences of nature (heredity) and nurture (the environment) because differences between MZ twins are the result of nurture.

MZ twins look alike and are closer in height than DZ twins. MZ twins resemble one another more strongly than DZ twins in traits such as irritability and

Nature In behavior genetics, heredity.

Nurture In behavior genetics, environmental influences on behavior, such as nutrition, culture, socioeconomic status, and learning.

Zygote A fertilized egg cell.

Monozygotic twins Identical, or MZ, twins. Twins who develop from a single zygote, thus carrying the same genetic instructions.

Dizygotic twins Fraternal, or DZ, twins. Twins who develop from separate zygotes.

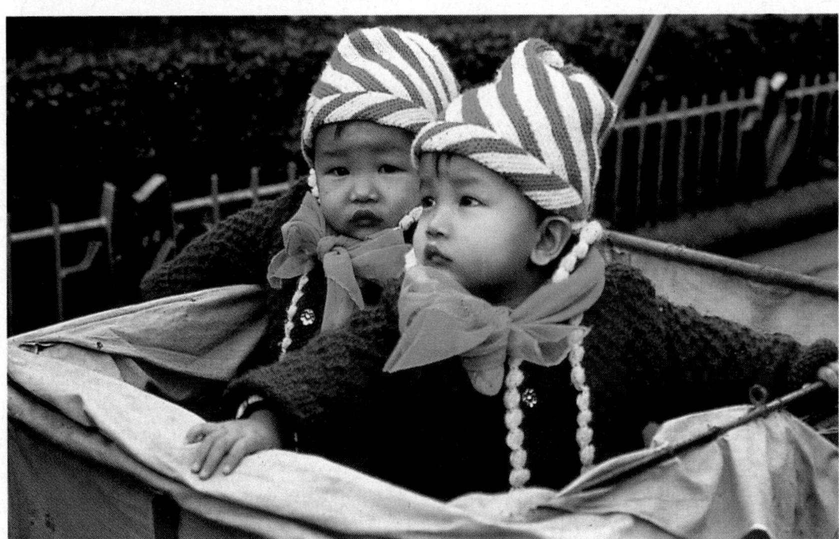

Monozygotic (Identical) Twins. Identical, or MZ, twins are important in the study of the relative influences of heredity and environment, because differences between MZ twins are the result of environmental influences (of nurture, not nature).

sociability, persistence in performing cognitive tasks, verbal and spatial skills, and perceptual speed (DeFries et al., 1987; Floderus-Myrhed et al., 1980; Matheny, 1983; Scarr & Kidd, 1983). MZ twins show more similarity than DZ twins in their early signs of attachment, such as smiling, cuddling, and expression of fear of strangers (Scarr & Kidd, 1983). Also, MZ twins are more likely than DZ twins to share psychological disorders such as **autism,** anxiety, substance dependence, and schizophrenia. In one study on autism, the **concordance** rate for MZ twins in one study was 96 percent (Ritvo et al., 1985). The concordance rate for DZ twins was only 24 percent.

Adoptee Studies. The interpretation of many kinship studies is confounded by the fact that relatives usually share common backgrounds as well as genes (Coon et al., 1990). This is especially true of identical twins, who are frequently dressed identically and encouraged to follow similar interests. Adoptee studies, in which children are separated from their parents at an early age (or in which identical twins are separated at an early age) and then reared apart, provide special opportunities for sorting out nature and nurture. As we shall see in discussions of the origins of intelligence (Chapter 8) and psychological disorders (Chapter 13), psychologists look for the relative similarities between children and their adoptive and natural parents. When children who are reared by adoptive parents are nonetheless more similar to their natural parents in a trait, a powerful argument is made for a genetic role in the appearance of that trait.

Experiments in Selective Breeding

You need not be a psychologist to know that animals can be selectively bred to enhance desired traits. Compare wolves with their descendants—varieties as diverse as the Great Dane; the tiny, nervous Chihuahua; and the pug-nosed bulldog. We breed our cattle and chickens to be bigger and fatter so that they provide more food calories for less feed. We can also selectively breed animals to enhance traits that are of more interest to psychologists, such as aggressiveness and intelligence—though "intelligence" in lower animals may not correspond to human intelligence. As dogs go, poodles and Shih-tzus are relatively intelligent, bulldogs are loyal, golden retrievers are docile and patient with children, and border collies show a compulsive herding instinct (Rosenthal, 1991). Even as puppies, border collies will attempt to corral people who are out on a lackadaisical stroll.

Chapter 8 extensively discusses the roles of heredity (nature) and the environment (nurture) in human intelligence. Here, let us illustrate the concept of selective breeding for intelligence with rats which have been bred selectively for maze-learning ability (Rosenzweig, 1969; Tryon, 1940) and many other traits such as preference for alcohol over water (Gatto et al., 1987).

In one study, an initial group of rats was tested for maze-learning ability as indicated by the number of mistakes they made in repeated efforts to find a food goal. Rats making the fewest mistakes were labeled B_1, signifying the first generation of "maze-bright" rats. "Maze-dull" rats were labeled D_1. The total distribution of errors, or blind-alley entrances, made by the first (parent) generation is shown in Figure 3.23. These errors were made over a series of 19 runs in the Tryon study.

Maze-bright rats from the first generation were then bred with other maze-bright rats, and maze-dull rats were similarly interbred. The second graph in Figure 3.23 shows how the offspring (B_2) of the maze-bright parents compared with the offspring (D_2) of the maze-dull parents in numbers of errors (blind-alley entrances). The offspring of the maze-bright rats, as a group, clearly made fewer errors than the offspring of the maze-dull, although there was considerable overlap between groups. The brightest offspring of the maze-bright were then interbred, as were the dullest of the maze-dull, for six consecutive generations. Fortunately for experimental psychologists, rat generations are measured in months, not

Autism A childhood disorder marked by problems such as failure to relate to others, lack of speech, and intolerance of change.

Concordance Agreement.

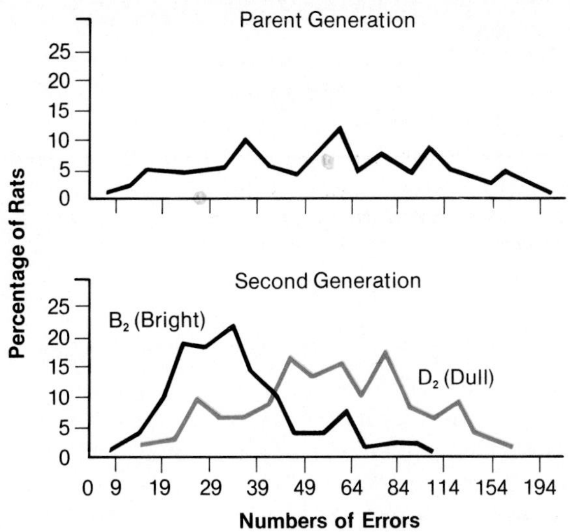

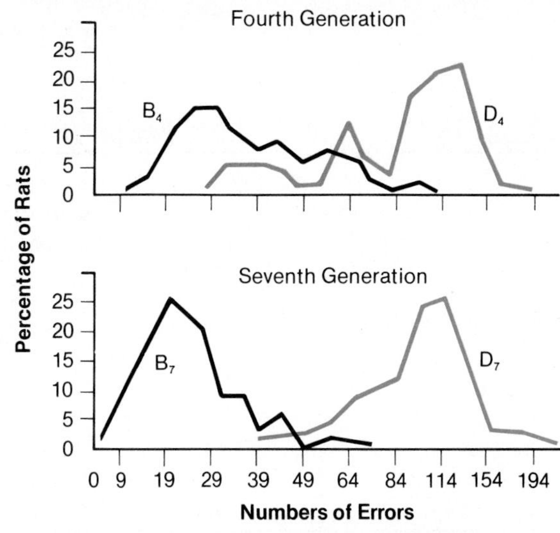

Figure 3.23
Selective Breeding for Maze-Learning Ability.

In the Tryon study, the offspring of maze-bright rats were inbred for six generations. So were the offspring of maze-dull rats. As the generations became further removed, there was progressively less overlap in the maze-learning ability of the offspring of the two groups, even though environmental influences were held as constant as possible for all offspring. Is maze-learning ability in rats similar to intelligence in human beings?

decades. Throughout these generations, the environments of the rats were kept as constant as possible. Dull rats were often raised by bright mothers, and vice versa, so that a critic could not argue that the maze-learning ability of bright offspring could be attributed to an enriched environment provided by a bright mother.

After six generations, there was little overlap in maze-learning performance between maze-bright and maze-dull rats. The (spatial relations) superiority of the maze-bright rats did not generalize to all types of learning tasks. We also cannot emphasize too strongly that maze-learning ability in rats is not comparable to the complex groupings of behavior that define human intelligence. Still, experiments such as these suggest that it would be foolhardy to completely overlook possible genetic influences on human intelligence.

Some breeds of dogs such as Doberman pinschers and German shepherds have been bred to be more aggressive than other varieties. Within breeds, however, dogs have been selectively bred to show high or low activity levels. Chickens have also been selectively bred for aggressiveness (consider the "sport" of cockfighting) and for level of sexual activity.

STUDY GUIDE

EXERCISE 1: Parts of the Brain

Fill in the names of the parts of the brain on the lines. Check your answers against Figure 3.11 in the chapter.

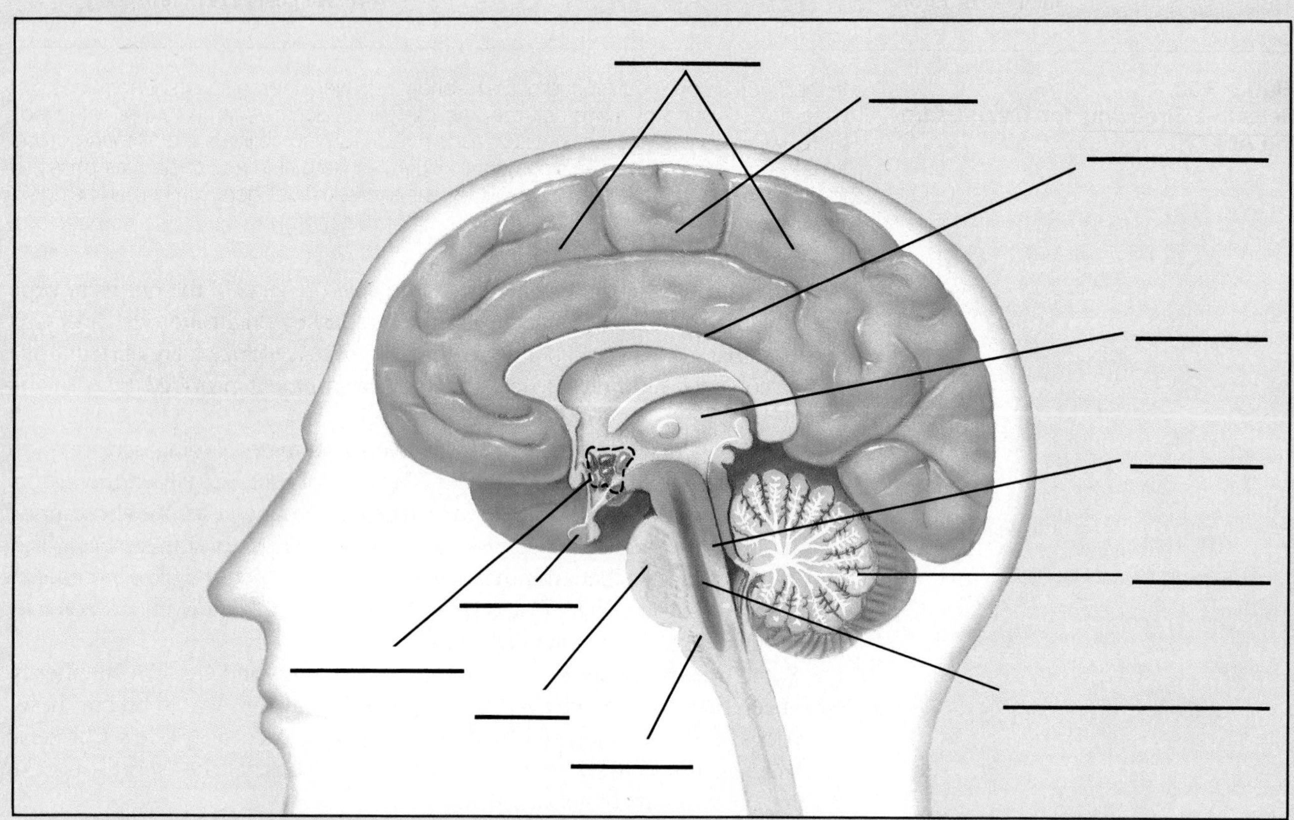

EXERCISE 2: Major Glands of the Endocrine System

Fill in the names of the glands of the endocrine system. Can you list the important hormones secreted by each gland and explain their functions? Check your answers against Figure 3.20 in the chapter.

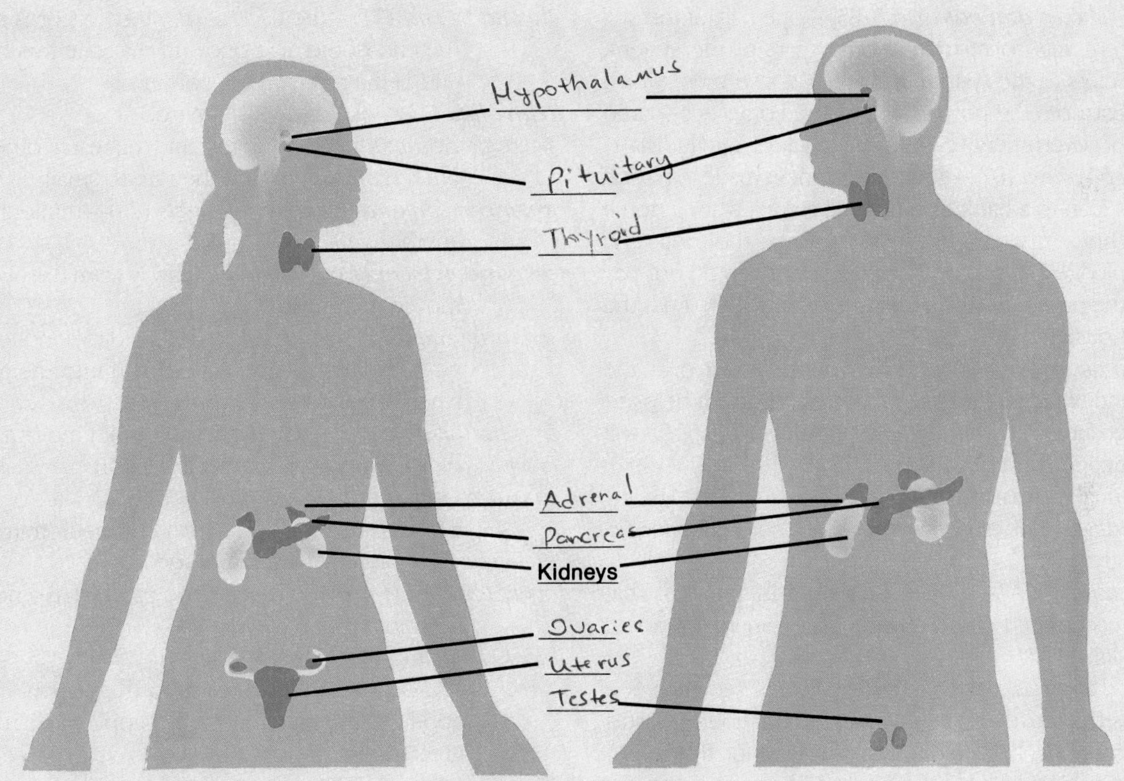

ESL—BRIDGING THE GAP

This part is divided into

1. cultural references,
2. phrases and expressions in which words are used differently from their regular meaning, or are used as metaphors.

Cultural References

Pablo Picasso (71)—born in 1881, a prolific (produced a lot) Spanish artist who lived in France after 1900

way to prepare frog's legs (74)—frog's legs are a delicacy (expensive and special food); served primarily in France

system of "checks and balances" (85)—one part of the system acts to restrain another part of the system; refers to the system of the U.S. government which balances the powers of the three branches (parts) of government (executive, legislative, and judicial)

mortgage payment (87)—monthly payment made to pay off a loan to a bank or mortgage company for a home (house) which you are buying; the house is pledged as security for the loan (if you do not pay the payments, the bank or company then owns the house).

crossed fingers (94)—to cross the middle finger over the index finger (first finger after the thumb) helps to ensure that what the person wants to happen will happen; a superstition

pump iron (95)—exercise strenuously

body-building contests (95)—contests of body muscle and strength

finishing school (99)—a kind of school in the U.S. that teaches and emphasizes good manners and social skills

tastes good/good taste (99)—"tastes" in this sentence is a verb; "taste" in this sentence is a noun. "Tastes good" = "a person likes the taste of the food." "Good taste" = "a person has appreciation for good clothes, food, art, and manners."

a potential Shakespeare (100)—a person who has the ability to become a great writer (he or she may or may not); Shakespeare was the English writer. He wrote many plays, including *Hamlet,* which is considered to be the greatest play in the English language.

Phrases and Expressions (Different Usage)

swear in court (68)—insist; be completely positive; refers to testifying in a court of law under oath

winking out (70)—disappearing

in flux (70)—always changing

fossil records (70)—fossils are the calcified bones of animals that existed and died millions of years ago

without a trace (70)—nothing remains to indicate that the creatures (people or animals) were here

now being cracked (70)—now being deciphered and understood

unlocking the mysteries of (70)—investigating and discovering what has not been understood previously

thicket of trees (71)—group of trees close together

lie end to end (71)—the back of one touches or is next to the end of the next one and that one touches the end of the next and this continues

trunk-like (73)—like the trunk of a tree

be buffeted about (73)—moved and hit each other and other neurons because they are so small

entertain some rather nasty thoughts (73)—think unpleasant thoughts

withdrawn them (73)—taken them away from the place; removed them

lightning rods (74)—a metal wire designed to conduct lightning (redirect it) away and down into the ground where it will do less harm

in a resting state (74)—when a neuron is not moving

created anew (75)—created again and again

into a specifically tailored harbor (75)—a site, or place, which is chemically unique for that neurotransmitter

highlight (76)—accentuate; emphasize

overutilize (77)—use too much ("too much" has a negative meaning)

block the action (77)—stop the action

"runner's high" (77)—"high" refers to the elation, or very good feeling, experienced by people while running great distances

There you have it (78)—Now you understand it

fabulous forest (78)—a dense and beautiful group of trees

piece of business (78)—item of information

make us proud (78)—that will cause us, as people, to feel good about ourselves; we are better than animals

It is just geography (79)—refers to the physical location of parts of the nervous system

capable of "local government" (79)—capable of responding to; refers to a localized response to stimuli over by the spinal cord and not to the rest of the nervous system also

knee-jerk reflex (81)—quick and sudden movement up of the leg in response to it having been hit just under the kneecap

place to hang its hat (81)—a specific location belonging especially to the mind

at the slightest provocation (82)—at something minor and not important
sparked the development (82)—caused the development
work our way forward (83)—move in a forward direction, studying the brain as we move
to play a filtering role (84)—to filter; to select
screening others out (84)—ignoring others
egg- or football-shaped (84)—shaped like an egg or football
day in and day out (85)—every day
perpetually reintroduced (85)—introduced to the same person many times
In novel approaches (86)—In some new and different treatments
the crowning glory (86)—the most beautiful and magnificent part
spending of body energy from stored reserves (87)—the body is using energy from what has been saved (reserved)
fight or flight response (87)—fight the predator or flee (go away from quickly)
pitch black (89)—completely dark, with no light
a devil of a time (89)—a very difficult time; a lot of trouble
screened off (89)—hidden
emotional richness (92)—emotional variety and intensity
stopped talking to one another (93)—stopped connecting and interacting
"sabotaged" in their weight-loss efforts (95)—hormonal changes restrict the person from losing weight
heighten general emotional responsiveness (95)—increase general emotional responses
it is so central to (97)—it is so important to
maintain steady states (97)—maintain (keep) the condition or level of activity
and so on (97)—etc.; continue with similar examples
In turn, (97)—the next step is that
put on weight (98)—increase weight; weight gain
sign language (99)—communication through hand and finger signals
breathe a sigh of relief (100)—make a sound to indicate that an unpleasant situation has been remedied or corrected
a twisting ladder (100)—steps that turn as they go up (see Figure 3.21 in the textbook)
set the stage (100)—prepare for the event
maze-learning ability (102)—ability to learn how to travel a maze in order to locate the exit
maze-bright (102)—intelligent about figuring out a maze
maze-dull (102)—unintelligent about figuring out a maze and not successful at it
to find a food goal (102)—to find the food by finding the route to the food
blind-alley entrance (102)—an entrance in a maze which stops and does not lead to the goal or to the exit

CHAPTER REVIEW

SECTION 1: Neurons

Objective 1: Describe the parts and functions of the neuron.

The (1) n____________ system contains billions of neurons. Neurons transmit messages to other neurons by means of chemical substances called (2) ____________mitters. Neurons have a cell body, or (3) s____________; (4) d____________, which receive transmissions; and (5) a____________, which extend trunklike from the cell body. Chemicals called neurotransmitters travel across (6) s____________ to transmit messages to other neurons.

Many neurons have a fatty myelin (7) s____________. These sheaths are missing at the nodes of (8) R____________. Neural impulses travel more rapidly along myelinated (9) a____________, where they can jump from (10) n____________ to node.

Objective 2: Differentiate between afferent and efferent neurons.

Sensory or (11) ____________ent neurons transmit sensory messages to the central nervous system. Motor or (12) ____________ent neurons conduct messages from the central nervous system that stimulate glands or cause muscles to contract.

Objective 3: Explain the electrochemical process by which neural impulses travel.

Neural transmission is an (13) e____________ process. An electric charge is conducted along an axon through a process that allows (14) s____________ions into the cell and then pumps them out. The neuron has a (15) r____________ potential of –70 millivolts in relation to the body fluid outside the cell membrane, and an (16) a____________ potential of +110 millivolts. The conduction of the neural impulse along the length of the neuron is what is meant by (17) ____________ing.

Objective 4: Explain the "all-or-none principle."

Neurons (18) f____________ according to an all-or-none principle. Neurons may fire (19) ____________s of times per second. Firing is first followed by an (20) ________________ refractory period, during which neurons do not fire in response to further stimulation. Then they undergo a (21) ________________ refractory period, during which they will fire, but only in response to stronger-than-usual messages.

Objective 5: Explain the functions of synapses and neurotransmitters.

A synapse consists of an axon (22) ________________al from the transmitting neuron; a (23) d________________ of a receiving neuron; and a small fluid-filled gap between them that is called the synaptic (24) c________________. (25) ________________tory synapses stimulate neurons to fire. (26) ________________tory neurons influence neurons in the direction of not firing.

Neurotransmitters are contained within synaptic (27) ________________s. These vesicles are found in the knobs at the tips of the axon (28) ________________als. Each neurotransmitter can fit into a specific (29) ________________tor site on the dendrite of the receiving neuron.

(30) Ace________________ (abbreviated ACh) is the neurotransmitter that controls muscle contractions. The poison (31) c________________ acts by preventing ACh from lodging within receptor sites. ACh is normally prevalent in a brain structure essential to the formation of memories: the (32) ________________pus. (33) ________________mer's disease is connected with deterioration of cells that produce ACh. The neurotransmitter (34) ________________ine is involved in voluntary movements, learning and memory, and emotional arousal. Deficiencies of dopamine are linked to (35) ________________son's disease. It is also theorized that schizophrenic individuals may (36) over________________ dopamine because of a greater-than-normal number of receptor (37) ________________s. Deficiencies of (38) ________________line have been linked to depression. Amphetamines act by increasing the release of the neurotransmitters (39) ________________ and (40) ________________. Deficiencies of (41) ________________nin are linked to anxiety, depression, and insomnia. The drug (42) ________________ decreases the action of serotonin, frequently leading to hallucinations.

"Runner's high" may be caused by the release of chains of amino acids called (43) ________________ns. Endorphins act like (44: Inhibitory or Excitatory?) neurotransmitters.

SECTION 2: The Nervous System

Objective 6: Explain what is meant by a nerve.

A nerve is composed of a bundle of (45) ________________ns of neurons.

Objective 7: Explain the functions of the divisions of the nervous system.

The first major division of the nervous system is into the central and (46) ________________al nervous systems. The brain and (47) s________________ ________________ compose the central nervous system. The peripheral nervous system is divided into the (48) ________________ic and (49) ________________ic nervous systems. The somatic nervous system transmits sensory information about muscles, skin, and joints to the (50) c________________ nervous system. The somatic nervous system also controls (51) ________________ar activity from the central nervous system. The autonomic nervous system is subdivided into sympathetic and (52) ________________tic branches.

Objective 8: Explain how spinal reflexes work.

A spinal (53) r________________ is an unlearned response to a stimulus that does not involve the brain. A spinal reflex may involve as few as two neurons: a sensory or (54) ________________ent neuron, and a motor or (55) ________________ent neuron. A third kind of neuron, an (56) ________________ron, may transmit the neural impulse from the sensory neuron through the spinal cord to the motor neuron.

In the spinal cord, (57: Gray or White?) matter consists of small, nonmyelinated neurons that are involved in reflexes. (58: Gray or White?) matter is composed of bundles of longer, myelinated axons that carry messages back and forth to and from the brain.

Objective 9: Explain ways in which psychologists study the functions of the brain.

There are numerous ways of studying the brain. The (59) ________________lograph records the electrical activity of the brain. In computerized (60) ________________ ________________ a narrow X-ray beam is passed through the head; measurements of the amount of radiation that passes through permits the computer to generate a three-dimensional image of the brain. Positron (61) ________________ ________________ translates the glucose metabolized by parts of the brain into an image. In magnetic (62) ________________ imaging, radio waves cause parts of the brain to emit signals that are integrated into an image of the brain.

Objective 10: Describe the functions of the major structures of the hindbrain, midbrain, and forebrain.

The hindbrain includes the (63) m________________, which is vital in heartbeat, blood pressure, and respiration; the pons, which transmits information concerning movement and is also involved in attention and respiration; and the (64) ________________lum, which is involved in maintaining balance and controlling motor behavior.

The (65) ________________ar activating system (RAS) begins in the hindbrain and continues through the midbrain into the forebrain and is vital in the functions of attention, sleep, and arousal.

Important structures of the forebrain include the thalamus, hypothalamus, limbic system, basal ganglia, and cerebrum. The (66) ________________mus serves as a relay station for sensory stimulation. The (67) ________________us is vital in the control of body temperature, motivation, and emotion. The (68) ________________ic system is involved in memory and in the drives of hunger, sex, and aggression. The basal (69) ________________ are involved in posture and muscle coordination, and their deterioration is linked to Parkinson's disease. The surface of the cerebrum is called the (70) ________________ ________________tex. The cortex is (71) ________________luted in shape. Valleys in the cortex are called (72) ________________sures. The hemispheres of the cerebral cortex are connected by the (73) ________________ ________________sum.

Objective 11: Summarize the activities of the sympathetic and parasympathetic branches of the autonomic nervous system.

The (74) ________________ic nervous system (ANS) regulates the glands and involuntary activities such as heartbeat, digestion, and (75) d________________ of the pupils. The (76) ________________tic division of the ANS dominates in activities that expend the body's resources, such as experiencing anxiety or fleeing a predator. The (77) ________________tic division dominates during processes that build the body's reserves, such as eating.

SECTION 3: The Cerebral Cortex

Objective 12: Explain the functions of the lobes of the cerebral cortex.

The ancient Egyptians attributed control of the person to a (78) hom________________, who they believed dwelled within the skull. The cerebral cortex is divided into the frontal, parietal, temporal, and (79) ________________al lobes. The visual cortex is in the (80) ________________al lobe, and the auditory cortex is in the (81) ________________al lobe. The sensory cortex lies behind the central fissure in the (82) ________________al lobe. The motor cortex lies in the (83) ________________al lobe, across the (84) ________________al fissure from the sensory cortex.

(85) A________________ areas of the cortex are involved in learning, thought, memory, and language. The (86) l________________ areas of the cortex lie near the intersection of the frontal, temporal, and parietal lobes in the dominant hemisphere. For the great majority of people, the (87: Left or Right?) hemisphere of the cortex contains language functions. In (88) ________________'s aphasia, people speak slowly and laboriously, in simple sentences. In (89) ________________'s aphasia, the ability to understand language is impaired. The (90: left or right?) hemisphere of the cortex seems to play a special role in understanding and producing language. The (91: left or right?) hemisphere of the cortex seems to play a special role in aesthetic and emotional response.

Objective 13: Discuss divided-brain research.

Split-brain operations are sometimes carried out in an effort to control (92) ________________sy. In such operations, the (93) ________________ ________________um is severed. Split-brain patients may be able to verbally describe a screened-off object like a pencil that is held in the hand connected to the (94) d________________ hemisphere, but cannot do so when the object is held in the other hand.

Objective 14: Summarize research on electrical stimulation of the brain.

José Delgado caused a brave bull to cease its charge by sending electrical impulses into the animal's (95) ________________ ________________tem. Olds and Milner's research suggests that a "pleasure center" exists in the (96) ________________mus of the rat.

SECTION 4: The Endocrine System

Objective 15: Explain the functions of various hormones.

The endocrine system consists of (97) ____________less glands that secrete hormones. The (98) ______________mus secretes a number of hormones that regulate the functions of other glands. The pituitary gland secretes (99) ______________in, which regulates maternal behavior in lower animals and stimulates production of (100) m______________ in women. ADH increases the reabsorption of (101) ______________e to conserve fluid. (102) ______________in stimulates labor in pregnant women.

The adrenal cortex produces (103) corticо______________s, which promote development of muscle mass and increase resistance to stress and activity level. The adrenal medulla secretes (104) ______________ine (also called epinephrine), which increases the metabolic rate and is involved in general emotional arousal.

Sex hormones secreted by the testes and (105) ______________es are responsible for prenatal sexual differentiation. Female sex hormones also regulate the (106) ______________al cycle. The female hormone (107) ______________one helps maintain pregnancy.

SECTION 5: Heredity

Objective 16: Define *genes* and *chromosomes,* and describe human chromosomal structure.

(108) ______________s are the basic building blocks of heredity. Genes consist of (109) ______________, which is abbreviated DNA. A large number of genes make up each (110) ______________e. People normally have (111: How many?) ______________ chromosomes. People receive (112: How many?) ______________ chromosomes from the father and 23 from the mother. The biological science that is concerned with the transmission of traits from generation to generation is called (113) ______________s. The specialty that is concerned with the transmission of traits that give rise to behavior is called (114) ______________ genetics.

Objective 17: Discuss psychologists' use of various kinds of kinship studies.

Psychologists use kinship studies to sort out the effects of heredity and the (115) ______________ment. There is reason to believe that heredity is a factor in the development of the trait when people who are (116: more or less?) similar in kinship exhibit the trait. A fertilized egg cell is called a (117) ______________e. Identical twins are formed from (118: One or Two?) zygote(s), and are termed (119) ______________zygotic. Fraternal twins are formed from (120: One or Two?) zygote(s), and are termed (121) ______________zygotic. It is assumed that differences between (122: Monozygotic or Dizygotic?) twins are determined by environmental factors.

Objective 18: Summarize the results of experiments in selective breeding.

Experiments show that animals can be selectively bred to heighten the influence of many (123) ______________s. Rats, for example, can be selectively bred for (124) ______________-learning ability. However, we cannot assume that maze-learning ability in rats corresponds directly to human (123) ______________gence.

Answers to Chapter Review

1. Nervous
2. Neurotransmitters
3. Soma
4. Dendrites
5. Axons
6. Synapses
7. Sheath
8. Ranvier
9. Axons
10. Node
11. Afferent
12. Efferent
13. Electrochemical
14. Sodium
15. Resting
16. Action
17. Firing
18. Fire
19. Hundreds
20. Absolute
21. Relative
22. Terminal
23. Dendrite
24. Cleft
25. Excitatory
26. Inhibitory
27. Vesicles
28. Terminals
29. Receptor
30. Acetylcholine
31. Curare
32. Hippocampus
33. Alzheimer's
34. Dopamine
35. Parkinson's
36. Overutilize
37. Sites
38. Noradrenaline
39. Dopamine (or noradrenaline)
40. Noradrenaline (or dopamine)
41. Serotonin
42. LSD
43. Endorphins
44. Inhibitory
45. Axons
46. Peripheral
47. Spinal cord
48. Somatic (or autonomic)
49. Autonomic (or somatic)
50. Central
51. Muscular
52. Parasympathetic
53. Reflex
54. Afferent
55. Efferent
56. Interneuron
57. Gray
58. White
59. Electroencephalograph
60. Axial tomography
61. Emission tomography
62. Resonance
63. Medulla
64. Cerebellum
65. Reticular
66. Thalamus
67. Hypothalamus
68. Limbic
69. Ganglia
70. Cerebral cortex
71. Convoluted
72. Fissures
73. Corpus callosum
74. Autonomic
75. Dilation
76. Sympathetic
77. Parasympathetic
78. Homunculus
79. Occipital
80. Occipital
81. Temporal
82. Parietal
83. Frontal
84. Central
85. Association
86. Language
87. Left
88. Broca's
89. Wernicke's
90. Left
91. Right
92. Epilepsy
93. Corpus callosum
94. Dominant
95. Limbic system
96. Hypothalamus
97. Ductless
98. Hypothalamus
99. Prolactin
100. Milk
101. Urine
102. Oxytocin
103. Corticosteroids
104. Adrenaline
105. Ovaries
106. Menstrual
107. Progesterone
108. Genes
109. Deoxyribonucleic acid
110. Chromosome
111. 46
112. 23
113. Genetics
114. Behavior
115. Environment
116. More
117. Zygote
118. One
119. Monozygotic
120. Two
121. Dizygotic
122. Monozygotic
123. Traits
124. Maze
125. Intelligence

POSTTEST

1. The _______ of the neuron uses oxygen to create energy to carry out the work of the cell.
   (a) axon
   (b) dendrite
   (c) soma
   (d) myelin

2. In the disease _______, myelin is replaced with a hard, fibrous tissue.
   (a) cebrebral palsy
   (b) multiple sclerosis
   (c) diabetes
   (d) acromegaly

3. When a neuron is polarized, it has a resting potential of about _______ millivolts in relation to the body fluid outside the cell membrane.
   (a) −70
   (b) −40
   (c) +40
   (d) +70

4. One of the neurons in your brain receives stimulation from a few neighboring neurons and, as a result, it fires. The same receiving neuron then receives messages from larger and larger numbers of neighboring neurons. As a consequence, the receiving neuron
   (a) fires more strongly.
   (b) fires more frequently.
   (c) shows no change in its pattern of firing.
   (d) releases more inhibitory than excitatory neurotransmitters.

5. Receptor sites for neurotransmitters are found on the _______ of receiving neurons.
   (a) dendrites
   (b) synaptic vesicles
   (c) clefts
   (d) axon terminals

6. _______ is excitatory at synapses between nerves and muscles that involve voluntary movements, but inhibitory at the heart and some other locations.
   (a) ADH
   (b) ACTH
   (c) ANS
   (d) ACh

7. _______ increase(s) the release of dopamine and noradrenaline, and also impede(s) their reabsorption after neurons have fired.
   (a) Phenothiazines
   (b) LSD
   (c) Amphetamines
   (d) Endorphins

8. You sit and cross your legs, and a physician taps your leg just below the knee. As a result, you kick reflexively. Which of the following is involved in your reflexive response?
   (a) White matter in the spinal cord
   (b) Sensory cortex
   (c) Afferent neurons
   (d) Motor cortex

9. The part of the brain that gives it its wrinkled, mushroom-like appearance is
   (a) the cerebellum.
   (b) Broca's area.
   (c) the occipital lobe.
   (d) the cerebrum.

10. You know someone who is going to have an operation to help control epilepsy. It is likely that a part of his _______ will be removed in this operation.
    (a) cerebellum
    (b) limbic system
    (c) hypothalamus
    (d) myelin sheath

11. Messages from the brain and spinal cord to the _______ nervous system control purposeful body movements, such as raising a hand or running.
    (a) autonomic
    (b) somatic
    (c) sympathetic
    (d) parasympathetic

12. The parasympathetic division of the autonomic nervous system stimulates
    (a) digestive processes.
    (b) the fight-or-flight response.
    (c) the heart rate.
    (d) ejaculation.

13. If a person's abilities to comprehend other people's speech and to think of the proper words to express his own thoughts were impaired, we should suspect damage to _______ area of the brain.
    (a) Levy's
    (b) Delgado's
    (c) Wernicke's
    (d) Gazzaniga's

14. Concerning the left brain–right brain controversy, it is most accurate to conclude that
    (a) the sounds of speech evoke a response in the dominant hemisphere only.
    (b) the sounds of speech evoke a response in the nondominant hemisphere only.
    (c) creativity and intuition are confined to the nondominant hemisphere.
    (d) the hemispheres are similar enough so that each can function quite well independently, but not as well as they function in normal combined usage.

15. Luteinizing hormone is secreted by the
    (a) posterior lobe of the pituitary gland.
    (b) anterior lobe of the pituitary gland.
    (c) adrenal medulla.
    (d) adrenal cortex.

16. In women, prolactin
    (a) regulates maternal behavior.
    (b) causes uterine contractions.
    (c) stimulates production of milk.
    (d) maintains pregnancy.

17. Psychologists conduct kinship studies to
    (a) learn of the origins of physical traits such as eye color and height.
    (b) help determine the role of genetic factors in behavior patterns and mental processes.
    (c) sort out the effects of cultural beliefs and personal attitudes on behavior.
    (d) learn how to correct abnormalities in the endocrine system.

18. Psychologists primarily engage in adoptee studies because
    (a) there are no other ways to determine the effects of selective breeding in rats and other laboratory animals.
    (b) they are easier to conduct than physiologically based studies.
    (c) adopted siblings share 50 percent of their inheritance.
    (d) many kinship studies are confounded by the fact that relatives usually share common backgrounds as well as genes.

19. Studies in selective breeding have shown that
    (a) people can be selectively bred for level of intelligence.
    (b) people can be selectively bred for level of aggressiveness.
    (c) rats can be selectively bred for level of verbal and spatial-relations abilities.
    (d) rats can be selectively bred for level of maze-learning ability.

20. The relationship between genetics and behavior, as expressed in the text, is that
    (a) genetics determines the behavior of rats but not of primates.
    (b) genetics determines the behavior of lower mammals, including lower primates, but not of humans.
    (c) genetics determines the level of aggressiveness but not intelligence in mammalian species.
    (d) genetics makes behaviors possible and also sets limits on them.

Answers to Posttest

1. C
2. B
3. A
4. B
5. A
6. D
7. C
8. C
9. D
10. B
11. B
12. A
13. C
14. D
15. B
16. C
17. B
18. D
19. D
20. D

- People have five senses.
- On a clear, dark night you could probably see the light from a candle burning 30 miles away.
- If we could see lights of slightly longer wavelengths, warmblooded animals would glow in the dark.
- Sometimes we fail to hear things because we don't want to hear them.
- White sunlight is actually composed of all the colors of the rainbow.
- When we mix blue light and yellow light, we attain green light.
- A $500 machine-made violin will produce the same musical notes as a $200,000 Stradivarius.
- Onions and apples have the same taste.
- We have a sense that keeps us upright.

Sensation and Perception

Learning Objectives

When you have finished studying Chapter 4, you should be able to:

Basic Concepts in Sensation and Perception

1. Define the terms *sensation* and *perception.*
2. Define *psychophysics,* and explain the contribution of Ernst Weber.
3. Define *absolute* and *difference thresholds.*
4. Discuss signal-detection theory.
5. Discuss sensory adaptation.

Vision

6. Explain the electromagnetic nature of light.
7. Describe the functions of the parts of the eye.
8. Describe the functions of rods and cones.
9. Define the color concepts of *hue, brightness,* and *saturation.*
10. Define *warm* and *cool* colors.
11. Define *complementary colors* and *analogous colors.*
12. Explain the trichromatic and opponent-process theories of color vision.

Visual Perception

13. Explain Gestalt rules of perceptual organization.
14. Describe perception of movement.
15. Describe monocular and binocular cues for depth.
16. Explain size, color, brightness, and shape constancy and show how they give rise to illusions.

Hearing

17. Explain the transmission and structure of sound waves.
18. Describe the functions of the parts of the ear.
19. Explain theories of pitch perception.
20. Describe three kinds of deafness.

Smell

21. Explain how we sense odors.

Taste

22. Explain how we sense tastes.

The Skin Senses

23. List the skin senses and explain how we perceive hotness and pain.

Kinesthesis

24. Describe kinesthesis.

The Vestibular Sense

25. Describe the vestibular sense.

Five thousand years ago in China, give or take a day or two, an arrow was shot into the air. Where did it land? Ancient records tell us precisely where: in the hand of a fierce warrior and master of the martial arts. As the story was told to me, the warrior had grown so fierce because of a chronic toothache. Incessant pain had ruined his disposition.

One fateful day, our hero watched as invading hordes assembled on surrounding hills. His troops were trembling in the face of their great numbers, and he raised his arms to boost their morale. A slender wooden shaft lifted into the air from a nearby rise, arced, and then descended—right into the warrior's palm. His troops cringed and muttered among themselves, but our hero said nothing. Although he saw the arrow through his palm, he did not scream. He did not run. He did not even complain.

He was astounded. His toothache had vanished. His whole jaw was numb.

Meanwhile the invaders looked on—horrified. They, too, muttered among themselves. What sort of warrior could regard an arrow through his hand with such indifference? Even with a smile? If this was the caliber of the local warrior, they'd be better off traveling west and looking for a brawl in ancient Sumer or in Egypt. They sounded the retreat and withdrew.

Our warrior received a hero's welcome back in town. A physician offered to remove the arrow without a fee—a tribute to bravery. But the warrior would have none of it. The arrow had done wonders for his toothache, and he would brook no meddling. He already had discovered that if the pain threatened to return, he need only twirl the arrow and it would recede once more.

All was not well on the home front, however. Yes, his wife was thrilled to find him jovial once more, but the arrow put a crimp in romance. When he put his arm around her, she was in danger of being stabbed. Finally, she gave him an ultimatum: it was she or the arrow.

Placed in deep conflict, our warrior consulted a psychologist, who then huddled with the physician and the village elders. After much to-do, they asked the warrior to participate in an experiment. They would remove the arrow and replace it with a pin that the warrior could twirl as needed. If the pin didn't do the trick, they could always fall back on the arrow, so to speak.

To the warrior's wife's relief, the pin worked. And here, in ancient China, lay the origins of the art of **acupuncture**—the use of needles to relieve pain and treat assorted ills.

I confess that this tale is not entirely accurate. To my knowledge, there were no psychologists in ancient China. (Their loss.) Moreover, the part about the warrior's wife is fictitious. It is claimed, however, that acupuncture as a means for dealing with pain originated in ancient China when a soldier was, in fact, wounded in a hand by an arrow and discovered that a chronic toothache had disappeared.

Pain is one of the many issues that interest psychologists who study the closely related concepts of sensation and perception. **Sensation** is the stimulation of sensory receptors and the transmission of sensory information to the

---

Acupuncture The ancient Chinese practice of piercing parts of the body with needles to deaden pain and treat illness.

Sensation The stimulation of sensory receptors and the transmission of sensory information to the central nervous system.

Sensation and Perception on a Summer's Day. These children are beating the heat of a sweltering afternoon by frolicking in the water. How many senses are alive to their surroundings and activity? How do they perceive each other and the water? How do they avoid crashing into one another?—or intentionally jostle one another? How do they hear each other laugh? How do they acquire information about the temperatures of the air and the water? How do they gather information about their own movements?

central nervous system (the spinal cord or brain). Sensory receptors are located in sensory organs such as the eyes and ears and, as we shall see, in the skin and elsewhere in the body. The stimulation of the senses is mechanical; it results from sources of energy like light and sound or from the presence of chemicals, as in smell and taste.

Perception is not mechanical. Perception is the process by which sensations are organized and interpreted, forming an inner representation of the world. Perception involves much more than sensation. It reflects learning and expectations and the ways in which we organize incoming information about the world. Perception is an active process through which we make sense of sensory stimulation. A human shape and a 12-inch ruler may stimulate paths of equal length among the sensory receptors in our eyes. Whether we interpret the human shape to be a foot-long doll or a full-grown person 15 to 20 feet away is a matter of perception.

In this chapter, you will see that your personal map of reality—your ticket of admission to a world of changing sights, sounds, and other sources of sensory input—depends largely on the so-called five senses: vision, hearing, smell, taste, and touch. We shall see, however, that touch is just one of several "skin senses," which also include pressure, warmth, cold, and pain. There are also other senses that alert you to your own body position without your literally having to watch every step you take. As we explore the nature of each of these senses, we shall find that highly similar sensations may lead to quite different perceptions in different people—or within the same person in different situations.

People actually have many more than five senses, as we shall see in this chapter.

First let us explore some of the ways in which psychologists gather information about the processes of sensation and perception.

Perception The process by which sensations are organized into an inner representation of the world.

BASIC CONCEPTS IN SENSATION AND PERCEPTION

Before we begin our journey through the senses, let us consider a number of concepts that apply to all the senses: absolute threshold, difference threshold, signal-detection theory, and sensory adaptation. In doing so, we shall learn why we might be able to dim the lights gradually to near darkness without people becoming aware of our mischief. We shall also learn why we might grow unaware of the most savory aromas of delightful dinners.

Absolute Threshold

The weakest amount of a stimulus that can be told apart from no stimulus at all is called the **absolute threshold** for that stimulus. For example, the amount of physical energy required to activate the visual sensory system is the absolute threshold for light. Beneath this threshold, detection of light is impossible (Haber & Hershenson, 1980).

Psychophysicists experiment to determine the absolute thresholds of the senses by presenting stimuli of progressively greater intensity. In the **method of constant stimuli,** researchers use sets of stimuli with magnitudes close to the expected threshold. The order of the stimuli is randomized. Subjects are asked to say yes if they detect a stimulus and no if they do not. The stimuli are then repeatedly presented to the subjects. A subject's absolute threshold for the stimulus is the lowest magnitude of the stimulus that he or she reports detecting 50 percent of the time. Weaker stimuli may be detected, but less than 50 percent of the time. Stronger stimuli, of course, will be detected more than 50 percent of the time.

The relationship between the intensity of a stimulus (a physical event) and its perception (a psychological event) is considered to be **psychophysical.** That is, it bridges psychological and physical events.

Absolute thresholds have been determined for the senses of vision, hearing, taste, smell, and touch (see Table 4.1). Naturally, there are individual differences in absolute thresholds. Some people, that is, are more sensitive to sensory stimuli than others. The same person may also differ somewhat in sensitivity to sensory stimuli from day to day or from occasion to occasion.

If our absolute thresholds were different, our daily experiences might be unrecognizable. Our ears are particularly sensitive, especially to sounds low in **pitch.** If they were any more sensitive, we might hear the collisions among molecules of air. If our eyes were sensitive to lights of slightly longer wavelengths, we would perceive infrared light waves. As a result, animals who are warmblooded and thus give off heat—including our mates—would literally glow in the dark.

It is true that on a clear, dark night you could probably see the light from a candle burning 30 miles away. This figure is in keeping with the absolute threshold for light.

It is true that if we could see lights of slightly longer wavelengths, warmblooded animals would glow in the dark.

Absolute threshold The minimal amount of energy that can produce a sensation.

Psychophysicist A person who studies the relationships between physical stimuli (such as light or sound) and their perception.

Method of constant stimuli A psychophysical method for determining thresholds in which the researcher presents stimuli of various magnitudes and asks the subject to report detection.

Psychophysical Bridging the gap between the physical and psychological worlds.

Pitch The highness or lowness of a sound, as determined by the frequency of the sound waves.

Difference threshold The minimal difference in intensity required between two sources of energy so that they will be perceived as being different.

Difference Threshold

How much of a difference in intensity between two lights is required before you will detect one as being brighter than the other? The minimum difference in the magnitude of two stimuli required to tell them apart is their **difference**

TABLE 4.1: Absolute Detection Thresholds and Other Characteristics of Human Sensory Systems

Sense	Stimulus	Receptors	Threshold
Vision	Electromagnetic energy	Rods and cones in the retina	A candle flame viewed from a distance of about 30 miles on a clear, dark night
Hearing	Sound pressure waves	Hair cells on the basilar membrane of the inner ear	The ticking of a watch from about 20 feet away in a quiet room
Taste	Chemical substances dissolved in saliva	Taste buds on the tongue in the mouth	About one teaspoon of sugar dissolved in two gallons of water
Smell	Chemical substances in the air	Receptor cells in the upper part of the nasal cavity (the nose)	About one drop of perfume diffused throughout a small house (1 part in 500 million)
Touch	Mechanical displacement or pressure on the skin	Nerve endings located in the skin	The wing of a fly falling on a cheek from a distance of about 0.4 inch

Source: Adapted from Galanter (1962).

threshold. As with the absolute threshold, psychologists have agreed to the criterion of a difference in magnitudes that can be detected 50 percent of the time.

Psychophysicist Ernst Weber discovered through laboratory research that the difference threshold for perceiving differences in the intensity of light is about 2 percent (actually closer to 1/60th) of their intensity. This fraction, 1/60th, is known as **Weber's constant** for light. A closely related concept is the **just noticeable difference** (jnd), or the minimal amount by which a source of energy must be increased or decreased so that a difference in intensity will be perceived. In the case of light, people can perceive a difference in intensity 50 percent of the time when the brightness of a light is increased or decreased by 1/60th. Weber's constant for light holds whether we are comparing two quite bright or rather dull lights. It becomes inaccurate, however, when we compare extremely bright or extremely dull lights. Weber's research in psychophysics touched on many senses (see Table 4.2).

Weber's constant The fraction of the intensity by which a source of physical energy must be increased or decreased so that a difference in intensity will be perceived.

Just noticeable difference The minimal amount by which a source of energy must be increased or decreased so that a difference in intensity will be perceived.

A little math will show you the practical importance of these jnd's. Consider weightlifting. Weber's constant for noticing differences in lifted weight is 1/53rd. (Round it off to 1/50th.) That means that one would probably have to increase the weight on a 100-pound barbell by about 2 pounds before the lifter would notice the difference. Now think of the 1-pound dumbbells used by many runners. Increasing the weight of each dumbbell by 2 pounds would be readily apparent to almost anyone because the increase would be threefold, not a small fraction. The increase is still "only" 2 pounds, however. Return to our power lifter. When he is pressing 400 pounds, a 2-pound difference is less likely to be noticeable than when he is pressing 100 pounds. This is because our constant 2 pounds has become a difference of only 1/200th.

The same principle holds for other senses: small changes are more apt to be noticed when we begin our comparisons with small stimuli. Some dieting programs suggest that dieters reduce calorie intake by "imperceptible" amounts on a daily or weekly basis. They will eventually reach sharply reduced calorie-intake goals, but they may not feel so deprived during the reduction process.

Sensory Thresholds. How much stimulation is necessary before you can detect a stimulus? How bright must the beacon from the lighthouse be to enable you to see it through the fog from several miles offshore?

TABLE 4.2: Weber's Constant for Various Sensory Discriminations

Sense	Type of Discrimination	Weber's Constant
Vision	Brightness of a light	1/60
Hearing	Pitch (frequency) of a tone	1/333
	Loudness of a tone	1/10
Taste	Difference in saltiness	1/5
Smell	Amount of rubber smell	1/10
Touch	Pressure on the skin surface	1/7
	Deep pressure	1/77
	Difference in lifted weights	1/53

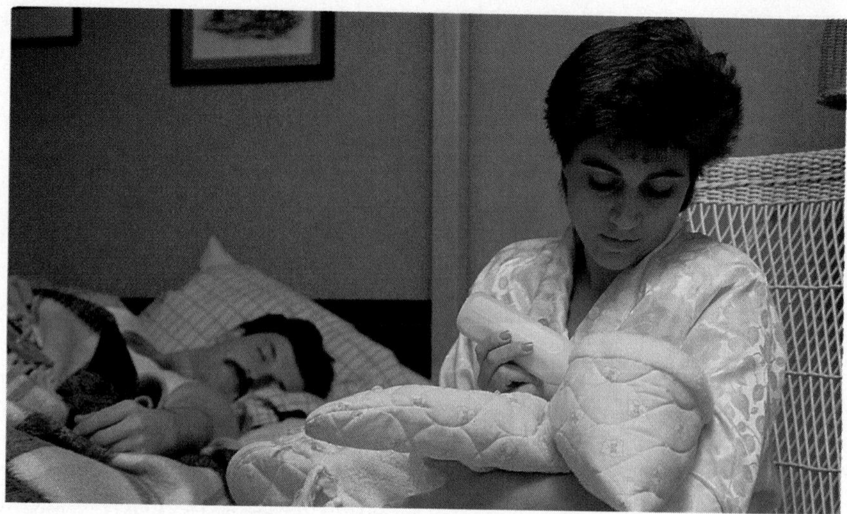

Signal Detection. He sleeps while she is awakened by the baby's crying. Detection of signals, such as a baby's crying, is determined not only by the physical characteristics of the signals but also by psychological factors, such as motivation and attention.

Signal-Detection Theory

Our discussion so far has been rather "inhuman." We have written about perception of sensory stimuli as if people are simply switched on by certain amounts of external stimulation. This is not quite the case. Although people are sensory instruments, they are influenced by psychological factors as well as external changes (Macmillan & Creelman, 1991). **Signal-detection theory** considers the human aspects of sensation and perception.

The intensity of the signal is just one of the factors that determine whether people will perceive sensory stimuli (signals) or a difference between two signals. Another is the degree to which the signal can be distinguished from background **noise.** It is easier to hear a friend in a quiet room than in one where people are conversing and clinking silverware and glasses. The quality of a person's biological sensory system is still another factor. Here, we are concerned with the sharpness or acuteness of the individual's sensory system. We consider whether sensory capacity is fully developed or diminished because of illness or advanced years.

Signal-detection theory also considers psychological factors such as motivation, expectations, and learning. The place in which you are reading this book may be abuzz with signals. If you are outside, perhaps there is a breeze against your face. Perhaps the shadows of passing clouds variegate the scene. If you are inside, the occasional clanks and hums of a heating system may vie for attention. Perhaps the odors of dinner are hanging in the air, or the voices from a TV set suggest a crowd in another room. Yet, you are focusing your attention on this page (I hope). The other signals thus recede into the backdrop of your consciousness. One psychological factor in signal detection is the focusing or narrowing of attention to signals the person deems important.

One parent may sleep through a baby's crying. The other parent may be awakened. This is not necessarily because one parent is innately more sensitive to the sounds of crying (although some men may assume that mothers are). Instead, it may be because one parent has been assigned the task of caring for the baby through the night and is thus more highly motivated to attend to the sounds. Because of training, an artist might notice the use of line or subtle colors that would go undetected by a lay person looking at the same painting.

It is true that we sometimes fail to hear things because we don't want to hear them. Psychological factors, as well as stimulus characteristics, influence perception.

Signal-detection theory The view that the perception of sensory stimuli involves the interaction of physical, biological, and psychological factors.

Noise (1) In signal-detection theory, any unwanted signal that interferes with perception of the desired signal. (2) More generally, a combination of dissonant sounds.

Signal-detection theory emphasizes the psychological aspects of detecting and responding to signals. The relationship between a physical stimulus and a sensory response is more than mechanical or mathematical. People's ability to detect stimuli such as meaningful blips on a radar screen depends not only on the intensity of the blips themselves but also on their training (learning), motivation (their desire to perceive meaningful blips), and psychological states such as fatigue or alertness.

Sensory Adaptation

There is a saying that the only thing that remains constant is change. It happens that our sensory systems are admirably suited to a changing environment. **Sensory adaptation** refers to the processes by which we become more sensitive to stimuli of low magnitude and less sensitive to stimuli of relatively constant magnitude.

Most of us are familiar with the process by which the visual sense adapts to lower intensities of light. When we first walk into a darkened theater, we see little but the images on the screen. As time elapses, however, we become increasingly sensitive to the faces of those around us and the inner features of the theater. The process of becoming more sensitive to stimulation is referred to as **sensitization,** or positive adaptation.

On the other hand, we become less sensitive to ongoing stimulation. Sources of light appear to grow dimmer as we adapt to them. In fact, if you could keep an image completely stable on the retinas of your eyes—which is virtually impossible to accomplish without a still image and stabilizing equipment—the image would fade within a few seconds and be very difficult to see. Similarly, at the beach we soon become less aware of the lapping of the waves. When we live in the city, we become desensitized to traffic sounds except for the occasional backfire or accident. As you may have noticed from experiences with freshly painted rooms, disagreeable odors fade quite rapidly. The process of becoming less sensitive to stimulation is referred to as **desensitization,** or negative adaptation.

Let us now examine how each of the human sensory systems perceives signals from the outer (and inner) environments.

Sensory adaptation The processes by which organisms become more sensitive to stimuli that are low in magnitude and less sensitive to stimuli that are constant or ongoing in magnitude.

Sensitization The type of sensory adaptation in which we become more sensitive to stimuli that are low in magnitude. Also called *positive adaptation.*

Desensitization The type of sensory adaptation in which we become less sensitive to constant stimuli. Also called *negative adaptation.*

Visual capture The tendency of vision to dominate the other senses.

Light The part of the electromagnetic spectrum that stimulates the eye and produces visual sensations.

Visible light See *light.*

VISION

Our eyes are our "windows on the world." Most of us find information from vision to be more essential than that from hearing, smell, taste, and touch. Consider the findings of one study in **visual capture.** When we look at a square object through lenses that distort it into a rectangle, we usually perceive it as a rectangle, even though we can feel it with our hands (Rock & Victor, 1964). Because vision is our dominant sense, we consider blindness our most debilitating sensory loss. An understanding of vision requires discussion of the nature of light and of the master of the sensory organs, the eye.

Light

In almost all cultures, **light** is a symbol of goodness and knowledge. We describe capable people as being "bright" or "brilliant." If we are not being complimentary, we label them as "dull." People who aren't in the know are said to be "in the dark." Just what is this stuff called light?

Visible light is the stuff that triggers visual sensations. It is just one small part of a spectrum of electromagnetic energy (see Figure 4.1) that is described in terms of wavelengths. These wavelengths vary from those of cosmic rays, which

FIGURE 4.1
The Visible Spectrum. By passing a source of white light, such as sunlight, through a prism, we break it down into the colors of the visible spectrum. The visible spectrum is just one part—and a narrow part indeed—of the electromagnetic spectrum. The electromagnetic spectrum also includes radio waves, microwaves, X-rays, cosmic rays, and many others. Different forms of electromagnetic energy have different wavelengths which vary from a few trillionths of a meter to thousands of miles. Visible light varies in wavelength from about 400 to 700 nanometers. What is a nanometer? One *billionth* of a meter. (A meter = 39.37 inches.)

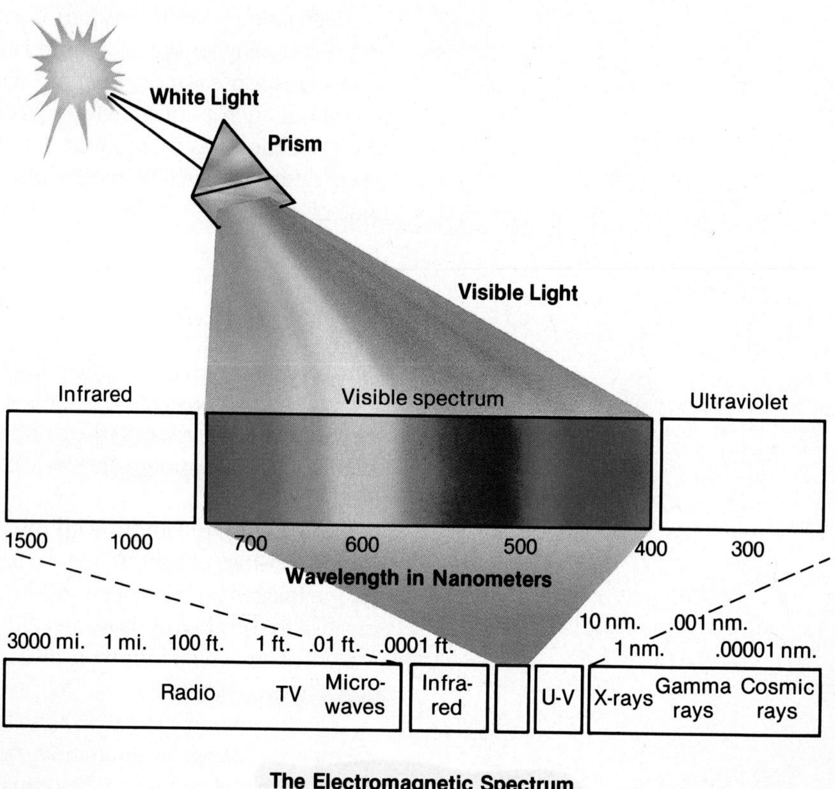

are only a few trillionths of an inch long, to some radio waves, which extend for many miles. Radar, microwaves, and X-rays are also forms of electromagnetic energy.

You have probably seen rainbows or light broken down into several colors as it filtered through your windows. Sir Isaac Newton, the British scientist, discovered that sunlight could be broken down into different colors by means of a triangular solid of glass called a **prism** (Figure 4.1). When I took introductory psychology, I was taught that I could remember the colors of the spectrum, from longest to shortest wavelengths, by using the mnemonic device *Roy G. Biv* (red, orange, yellow, green, blue, indigo, violet). I must have been a backward student because I found it easier to recall them in reverse order, using the meaningless acronym *vibgyor.*

It is true that white sunlight is composed of all the colors of the rainbow.

The wavelength of visible light determines its color, or **hue.** The wavelength for red is longer than that for orange, and so on through the spectrum.

Prism A transparent triangular solid that breaks down visible light into the colors of the spectrum.

Hue The color of light, as determined by its wavelength.

The Eye: Our Living Camera

Consider that magnificent invention called the camera, which records visual experiences. In the camera, light enters an opening and is focused onto a sensitive

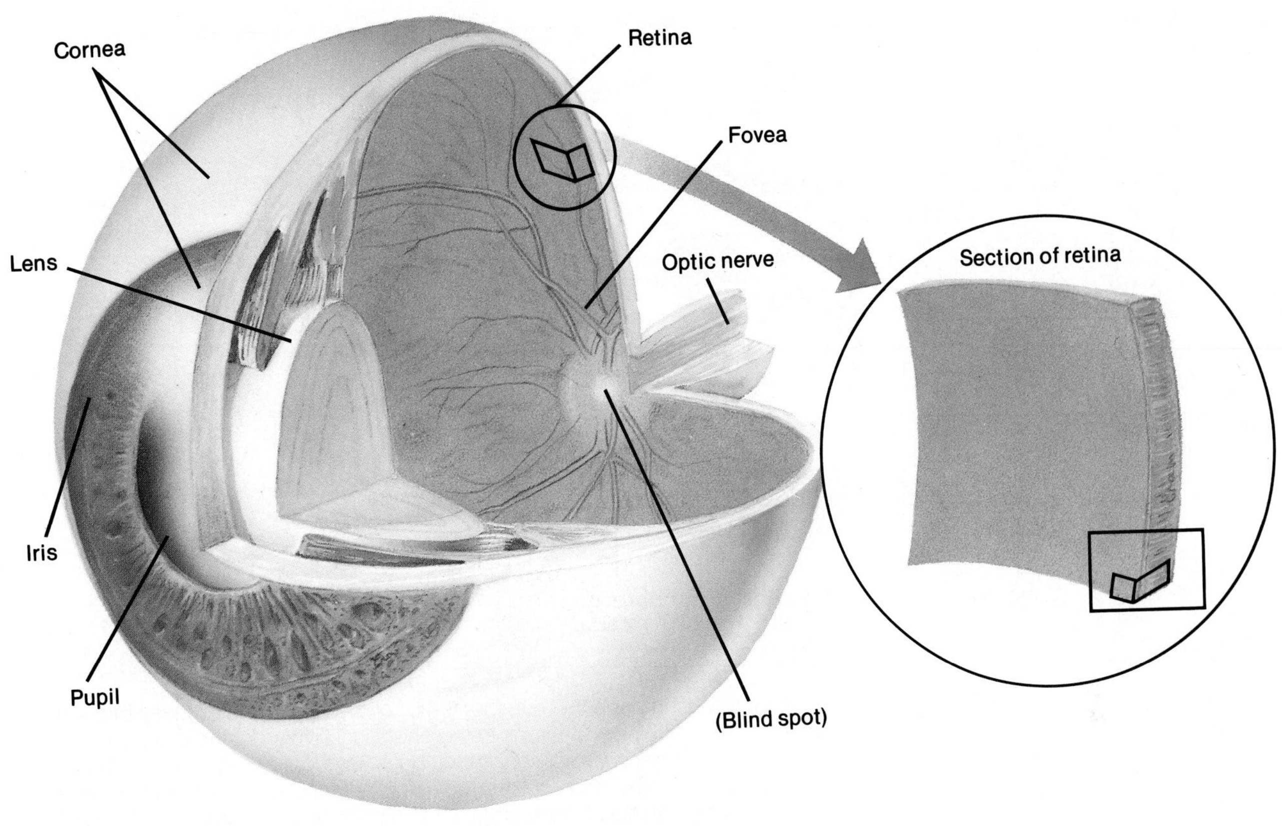

FIGURE 4.2
The Human Eye.

In both the eye and a camera, light enters through a narrow opening and is projected onto a sensitive surface. In the eye, the photosensitive surface is called the retina, and information concerning the changing images on the retina is transmitted to the brain. In a camera, the photosensitive surface is usually film, which captures a single image.

surface, or film. Chemicals on this surface create a lasting impression of the image that entered the camera.

The eye—our living camera—is no less remarkable (see Figure 4.2). As with a film or TV camera, light enters through a narrow opening and is projected onto a sensitive surface. Light first passes through the transparent **cornea,** which covers the front of the eye's surface. (The so-called white of the eye is composed of a hard protective tissue and is called the *sclera.)* The amount of light that passes through the cornea is determined by the size of the opening of the muscle called the **iris,** which is also the colored part of the eye. The opening in the iris is called the **pupil.** Pupil size adjusts automatically to the amount of light. You need not try to open the eye farther to see better in low lighting. The more intense the light, the smaller the opening. We similarly adjust the amount of light allowed into a camera according to its brightness. Pupil size is also sensitive to emotional response: we can literally be "wide-eyed with fear."

Once light passes through the iris, it encounters the **lens.** The lens adjusts or accommodates to the distance of the image by changing its thickness. Changes in thickness focus the light. They permit projection of a clear image of the object onto the retina. If you hold a finger at arm's length, then slowly bring it toward your nose, you will feel tension in the eye as the thickness of the lens accommodates to keep the retinal image in focus (Haber & Hershenson, 1980). When people squint to bring an object into focus, they are adjusting the thickness of the lens. The lens in a camera does not accommodate to the distance of objects.

Cornea Transparent tissue forming the outer surface of the eyeball.

Iris A muscular membrane whose dilation regulates the amount of light that enters the eye.

Pupil The apparently black opening in the center of the iris, through which light enters the eye.

Lens A transparent body behind the iris that focuses an image on the retina.

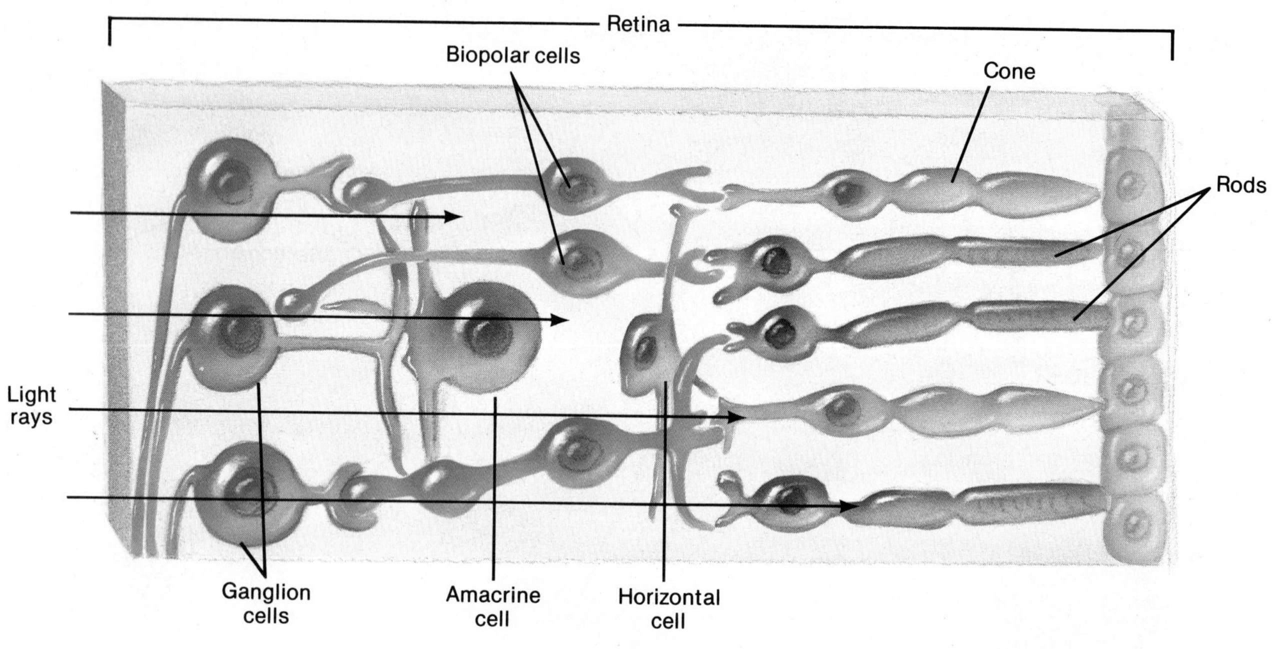

FIGURE 4.3
The Retina.

After light travels through the vitreous humor of the eye, it finds its way through ganglion neurons and bipolar neurons to the photosensitive rods and cones. These photoreceptors then transmit sensory input back through the bipolar neurons to the ganglion neurons. The axons of the ganglion neurons form the optic nerve, which transmits sensory stimulation through the brain to the visual cortex of the occipital lobe. Amacrine cells and horizontal cells make connections within layers that allow photoreceptors to funnel their information into the ganglion cells.

Retina The area of the inner surface of the eye that contains rods and cones.

Photoreceptors Cells that respond to light.

Bipolar cells Neurons that conduct neural impulses from rods and cones to ganglion cells.

Ganglion cells Neurons whose axons form the optic nerve.

Optic nerve The nerve that transmits sensory information from the eye to the brain.

Fovea An area near the center of the retina that is dense with cones and where vision is consequently most acute.

Blind spot The area of the retina where axons from ganglion cells meet to form the optic nerve.

Rods Rod-shaped photoreceptors that are sensitive only to the intensity of light.

Cones Cone-shaped photoreceptors that transmit sensations of color.

Instead, to focus the light that is projected onto the film, the camera lens is moved farther away from or closer to the film.

The **retina** is like the film or image surface of the camera. Instead of being composed of film that is sensitive to light (photosensitive), the retina has photosensitive cells, or **photoreceptors,** called *rods* and *cones.* The retina (Figure 4.3) contains several layers of cells: the rods and cones, **bipolar cells,** and **ganglion cells.** All of these cells are neurons. Light travels past the ganglion cells and bipolar cells and stimulates the rods and cones. The rods and cones then send neural messages through the bipolar cells to the ganglion cells. The axons of the million or so ganglion cells in our retinae form the **optic nerve.** The optic nerve conducts sensory input to the brain, where it is relayed to the visual area of the occipital lobe.

The **fovea** is the most sensitive area of the retina (see Figure 4.2). Receptors there are more densely packed. The **blind spot,** in contrast, is insensitive to visual stimulation. It is the part of the retina where the axons of the ganglion cells congregate to form the optic nerve (Figure 4.4).

Rods and Cones. **Rods** and **cones** are the photoreceptors in the retina (Figure 4.5). About 100 million rods and 5 million cones are distributed on the retina. The fovea is composed almost exclusively of cones. Cones become more sparsely distributed as you work forward from the fovea toward the lens. Rods, in contrast, are nearly absent at the fovea but become more dense as you approach the lens.

Rods are sensitive to the intensity of light. They allow us to see in black and white. Cones provide color vision. If you are a camera buff, you know that under conditions of extreme low lighting, it is possible to photograph a clearer image

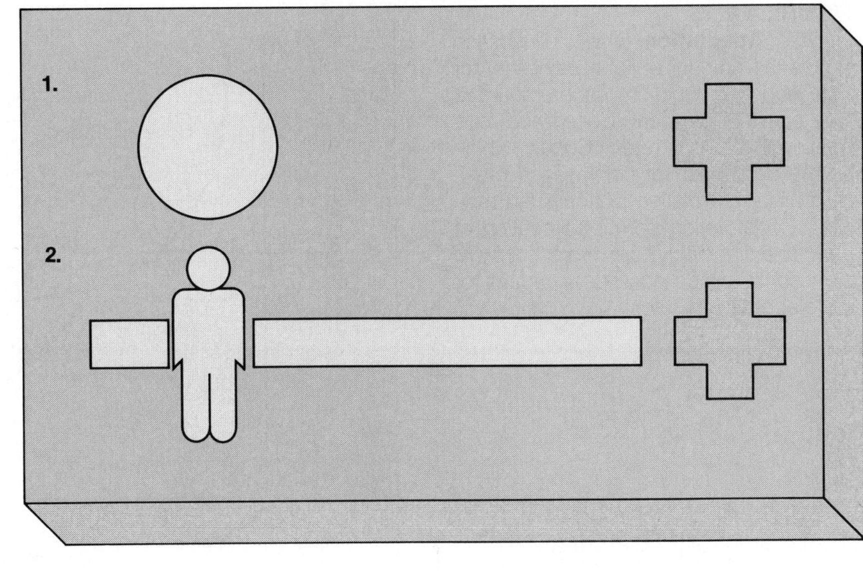

FIGURE 4.4
Locating the Blind Spots in Your Eyes. To try a "disappearing act," first look at Drawing 1. Close your right eye. Then move the book back and forth about one foot from your left eye while you stare at the plus sign. You will notice the circle disappear. When the circle disappears it is being projected onto the blind spot of your retina, the point at which the axons of ganglion neurons collect to form the optic nerve. Then close your left eye. Stare at the circle with your right eye and move the book back and forth. When the plus sign disappears, it is being projected onto the blind spot of your right eye. Now look at Drawing 2. You can make this figure disappear and "see" the black line continue through the spot where it was by closing your right eye and staring at the plus sign with your left. When this figure is projected onto your blind spot, your brain "fills in" the line, which is one reason that you're not usually aware that you have blind spots.

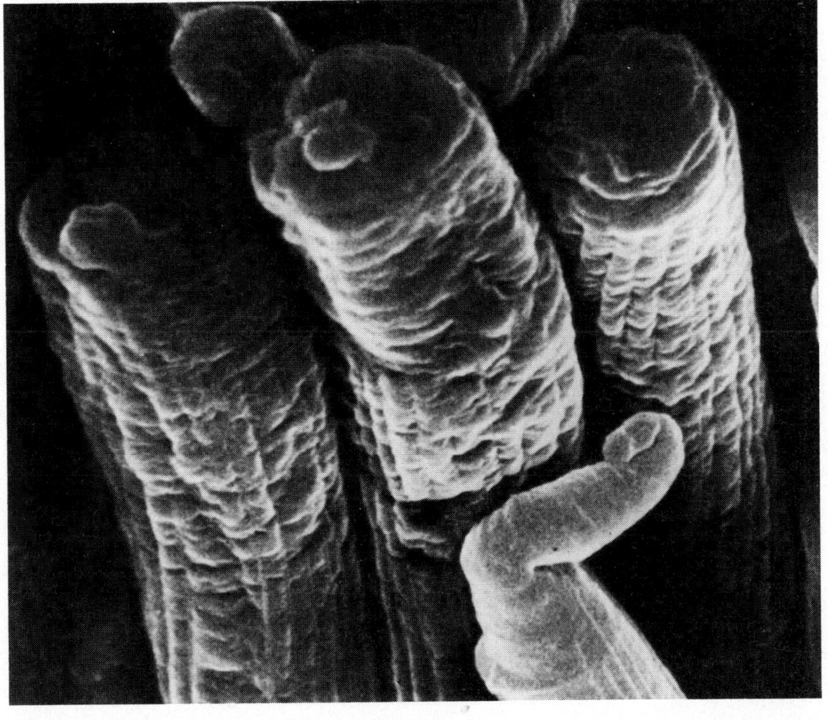

FIGURE 4.5
A Much (Much!) Enlarged Photograph of Several Rods and a Cone. Cones are usually upright fellows. However, the cone at the bottom right of this photo has been bent by the photographic process. You have about 100 million rods and 5 million cones distributed across the retina of each eye. Only cones provide sensations of color. The fovea of the eye is almost exclusively populated by cones, which are then distributed more sparsely as you work forward toward the lens. Rods, in contrast, are nearly absent at the fovea and become more densely packed as you work forward.

with black-and-white film than with color film. Similarly, rods are more sensitive to light than cones. As lighting grows dim, as in the evening hours, objects "lose" their color before their outlines fade from view.

Feature Detectors. The geography of the visual cortex corresponds to the world outside. When parts of the retina are stimulated by sensory input, they relay

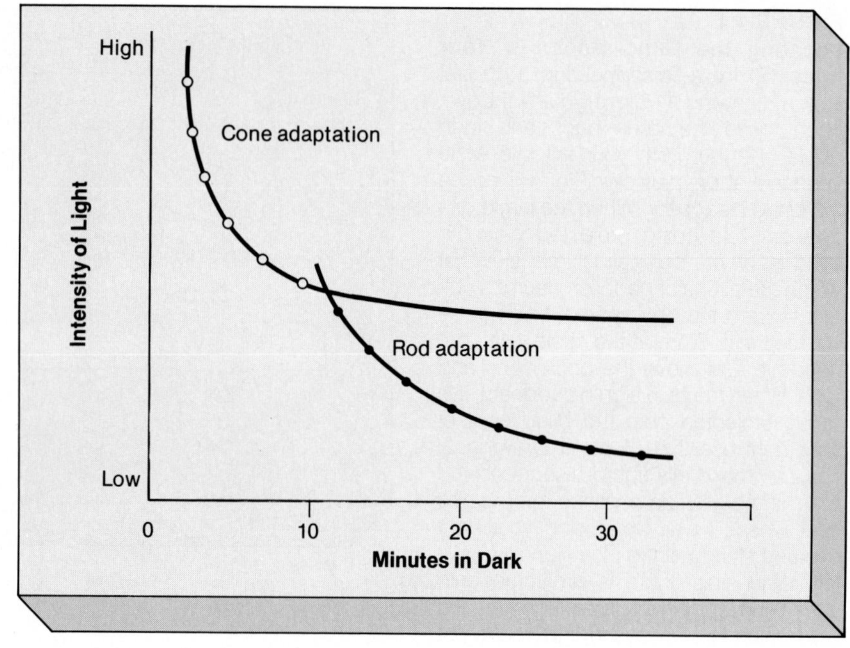

FIGURE 4.6
Dark Adaptation. This illustration shows the amount of light necessary for detection as a function of the amount of time spent in the dark. Cones and rods adapt at different rates. Cones, which permit perception of color, reach maximum dark adaptation in about ten minutes. Rods, which permit perception of dark and light only, are more sensitive than cones. Rods continue to adapt for up to about 45 minutes.

information to corresponding parts of the visual cortex in the brain. The brain thus maps the world outside.

Nobel prize winners David Hubel and Torsten Wiesel (1979) discovered that various neurons in the visual cortex fire in response to particular features of the visual input. Many cells, for example, fire in response to lines presented at various angles—vertical, horizontal, and in-between. Other cells fire in response to specific colors. Because they respond to different aspects or features of a scene, these cells are termed **feature detectors.**

We do not see just bits and pieces (features) of scenes, however; we see them in their entirety. In terms of information processing, a visual scene is transmitted to the brain as millions of pieces of information—information about edges and angles and shapes, information about colors. Millions of feature detectors in the visual cortex fire individually in response to these shards of information. Somehow, in higher brain centers, the bits of information are reassembled into a picture of the world outside. When you consider that millions of feature detectors are involved in vision, and that each fires many times per second to keep abreast of the changing scene, you can understand why mathematicians and computer scientists are in awe of the apparently effortless processes of sensation and perception.

Light Adaptation. A movie theater may at first seem too dark to allow us to find seats readily. But as time goes on, we come to see the seats and other people clearly. Adjusting to lower lighting is called **dark adaptation.**

Figure 4.6 shows the amount of light needed for detection as a function of the amount of time spent in the dark. The cones and rods adapt at different rates. The cones, which permit perception of color, reach their maximum adaptation to darkness in about 10 minutes. The rods, which allow perception of light and dark only, are more sensitive and continue to adapt to darkness for up to about 45 minutes.

Adaptation to brighter lighting occurs more rapidly. When you emerge from the theater into the brilliance of the afternoon, you may at first be painfully surprised by the featureless blaze around you. The visual experience is not unlike

Feature detectors Neurons in the visual cortex that fire in response to specific features of visual information such as lines or edges presented at particular angles.

Dark adaptation The process of adjusting to conditions of lower lighting by increasing the sensitivity of rods and cones.

turning the brightness of the TV set to maximum, in which case the edges of objects dissolve into light. Within a minute or so of entering the street, however, the brightness of the scene will have dimmed and objects will have regained their edges.

Color Vision

For most of us, the world is a place of brilliant colors—the blue-greens of the ocean, the red-oranges of the lowering sun, the deepened greens of June, the glories of rhododendron and hibiscus. Color is an emotional and aesthetic part of our everyday lives.

Psychological Dimensions of Color: Hue, Brightness, and Saturation

The wavelength of light determines its color, or hue. The brightness of a color is its degree of lightness or darkness. The brighter the color, the lighter it is.

If we bend the colors of the spectrum into a circle, we create a color wheel, as shown in Figure 4.7. Yellow is the lightest color on the color wheel. As we work our way around from yellow to violet-blue, we encounter progressively darker colors.

Warm and Cool Colors. Psychologically, the colors on the green-blue side of the color wheel are considered "cool," and the colors on the yellow-orange-red

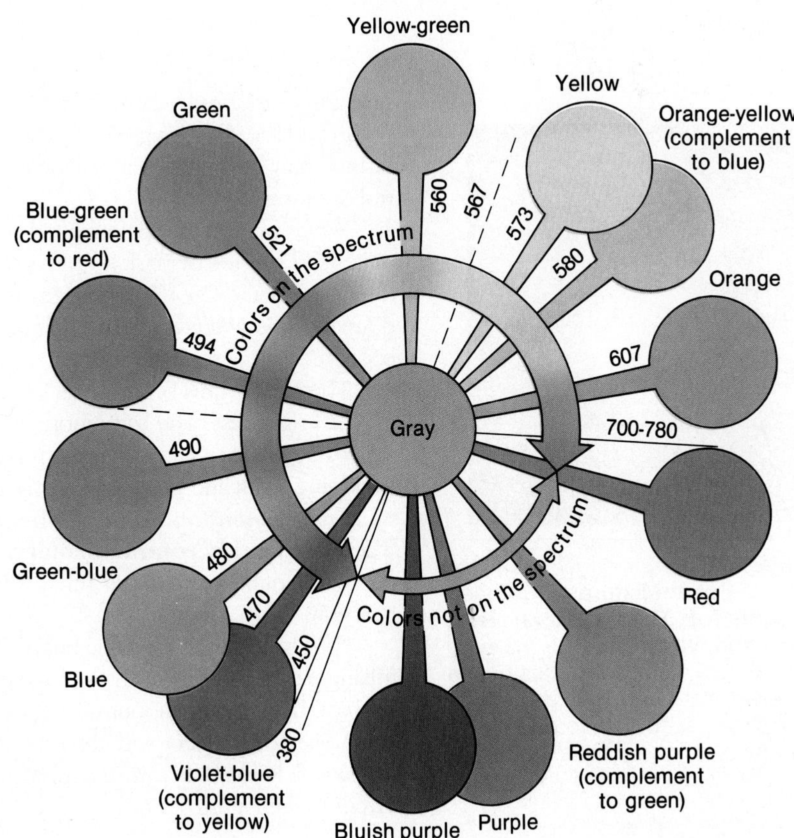

FIGURE 4.7
The Color Wheel. A color wheel can be formed by bending the colors of the spectrum into a circle and placing complementary colors across from one another. (A few colors between violet and red that are not found on the spectrum must be added to complete the circle.) When lights of complementary colors such as yellow and violet-blue are mixed, they dissolve into neutral gray. The afterimage of a color is also the color's complement.

FIGURE 4.8
Orange and Yellow. Warm colors such as orange and yellow seem to advance toward the viewer, while cool colors such as blue and green seem to recede. The oranges and yellows of Rothko's painting seem to pulsate toward the observer.

FIGURE 4.9
Highway No. 2. The "warm" Sunoco sign in d'Arcangelo's painting leaps out toward the viewer, while the "cool" blue sky recedes into the distance.

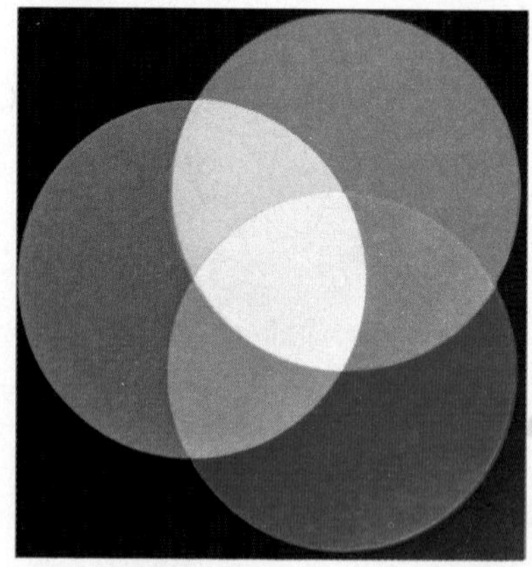

FIGURE 4.10
Additive Color Mixtures Produced by Lights of Three Colors: Red, Green, and Violet-Blue. In the early 1800s, British scientist Thomas Young discovered that white light and all the colors of the spectrum could be produced by adding various combinations of lights of three colors and varying their intensities.

side are considered "warm." Greens and blues may suggest the coolness of the ocean and the sky. Things tend to burn red or orange. A room decorated in green or blue may seem more appealing on a hot day in July than a room decorated in red or orange.

When we look at a painting, warm colors seem to advance toward us. The oranges and yellows of Mark Rothko's *Orange and Yellow* (Figure 4.8) seem to pulsate toward us. Cool colors seem to recede. The warm Sunoco sign in Allan d'Arcangelo's *Highway No. 2* (Figure 4.9) leaps out toward us. In contrast, the cool blue sky seems to recede into the distance.

The **saturation** of a color is its pureness. Pure hues have the greatest intensity, or brightness. The saturation, and thus the brightness, decreases when another hue or black, gray, or white is added. Artists produce shades of a given hue by adding black and produce tints by adding white.

Complementary Colors. The colors across from one another on the color wheel are labeled **complementary.** Red-green and blue-yellow are the major complementary pairs. If we mix complementary colors together, they dissolve into gray.

"But wait!" you say. "Blue and yellow cannot be complementary because by mixing pigments of blue and yellow we create green, not gray." True enough, but we have been talking about mixing *lights,* not *pigments.* Light is the source of all color. Pigments reflect and absorb different wavelengths of light selectively. The mixture of lights is an *additive* process, whereas the mixture of pigments is *subtractive* (see Figure 4.10).

Upclose detail of *Sunday Afternoon on the Island of La Grande Jatte*

FIGURE 4.11
Sunday Afternoon on the Island of La Grande Jatte.

The French painter Seurat molded his figures and forms from dabs of pure and complementary colors. Up close, the dabs of pure color are visible. From afar, they create the impression of color mixtures.

It is *not* true that we attain green light when we mix blue light and yellow light. We attain green when we mix *pigments* of blue and yellow.

Pigments attain their colors by absorbing light from certain segments of the spectrum and reflecting the rest. We see most plant life as green because the pigment in chlorophyll absorbs most of the red, blue, and violet wavelengths of light. The remaining green is reflected. A red pigment absorbs most of the spectrum but reflects red. White pigments reflect all colors equally. Black pigments reflect very little light.

Primary, Secondary, and Tertiary Colors. The pigments of red, blue, and yellow are the **primary colors**—those that cannot be produced by mixing pigments of other hues. **Secondary colors** are created by mixing pigments of primary colors. The three secondary colors are orange (derived from mixing red and yellow), green (blue and yellow), and purple (red and blue). **Tertiary colors** are created by mixing pigments of primary and adjoining secondary colors, as in yellow-green and bluish-purple.

In his *Sunday Afternoon on the Island of La Grande Jatte* (Figure 4.11), French painter Georges Seurat molded his figures and forms from dabs of pure and complementary colors. Instead of mixing his pigments, he placed points of pure color next to one another. The sensations are of pure color when the painting is viewed from very close (see detail, Figure 4.11). From a distance, the positioning of the pure colors creates the impression of mixtures of color.

Afterimages. Before reading on, why don't you try a brief experiment? Look at the strangely colored American flag in Figure 4.12 for at least half a

Saturation The degree of purity of a color.

Complementary Descriptive of colors of the spectrum that when combined produce white or nearly white light.

Primary colors Colors that cannot be produced by mixing pigments of other hues.

Secondary colors Colors derived by mixing primary colors.

Tertiary colors Colors derived by mixing primary and adjoining secondary colors.

Afterimage The lingering visual impression made by a stimulus that has been removed.

FIGURE 4.12
Three Cheers for the . . . Green, Black, and Yellow? Don't be concerned. We can readily restore Old Glory to its familiar hues. Place a sheet of white paper beneath the book, and stare at the center of the flag for 30 seconds. Then remove the book. You will see a more familiar image on the paper beneath. This is an afterimage. Afterimages such as this led Ewald Hering to doubt the trichromatic theory of color vision and to propose the opponent-process theory in its place. Both theories have received some empirical support.

minute. Then look at a sheet of white or gray paper. What has happened to the flag? If your color vision is working properly, and if you looked at the miscolored flag long enough, you should see a flag composed of the familiar red, white, and blue. The flag you perceive on the white sheet of paper is an **afterimage** of the first. (If you didn't look at the green, black, and yellow flag long enough the first time, you may wish to try it again. It will work any number of times.)

In afterimages, persistent sensations of color are followed by perception of the complementary color when the first color is removed. The same holds true for black and white; staring at one will create an afterimage of the others. Stare at d'Arcangelo's *Highway 1, No. 2* (Figure 4.9) for 30 seconds. Then look at a sheet of white paper. You are likely to perceive a black stripe down a white highway, along with a blue Sunoco sign and a yellow sky. The phenomenon of afterimages has contributed to one of the theories of color vision, as we shall soon see.

Analogous Colors. **Analogous** hues lie next to one another on the color wheel, forming families of colors like yellow and orange, orange and red, and green and blue. As we work our way around the wheel, the families intermarry, as blue with violet and violet with red. Works of art that use closely related families of color seem harmonious. For example, Rothko's *Orange and Yellow* draws on analogous oranges and yellows.

Theories of Color Vision

People can normally discriminate up to 150 differences in color (Bornstein & Marks, 1982). Different colors have different wavelengths. Although we can vary the physical wavelengths of light continuously from shorter to longer, changes in color seem to be discontinuous. Our perception of a color may thus shift suddenly from blue to green, even though the change in wavelength is smaller than that between two blues. People from different cultures may classify colors in ways that seem strange to us; the preliterate Hanunoo speak of "dark," "light," "dry," and "wet" colors, for example. People from all cultural backgrounds nevertheless divide the regions of the visible spectrum into similar groupings that correspond to reds, yellows, greens, and blues.

Color perception relies on the eye's transmission of different messages to the brain when lights of different wavelengths stimulate the cones in the retina. Let us consider two theories of how lights of different wavelengths are perceived as different colors: *trichromatic theory* and *opponent-process theory.*

Analogous Similar or comparable colors.

Trichromatic Theory. **Trichromatic theory** is based on an experiment that was run by British scientist Thomas Young in the early 1800s. Young projected three lights of different colors onto a screen so that they partly overlapped (see Figure 4.10). He found that he could create any color from the visible spectrum by varying the intensities of the lights. When all three lights fell on the same spot, they created white light, or the appearance of no color at all. The three lights manipulated by Young were red, green, and blue-violet.

German physiologist Hermann von Helmholtz saw in Young's discovery an explanation of color vision. Von Helmholtz suggested that the eye must have three different types of photoreceptors or cones. Some must be sensitive to red light, some to green, and some to blue. We see still other colors when two different types of color receptors are stimulated. The perception of yellow, for example, would result from the simultaneous stimulation of receptors for red and green. Trichromatic theory is also known as the Young-Helmholtz theory, after Thomas Young and Hermann von Helmholtz.

Opponent-Process Theory. In 1870, Ewald Hering proposed the **opponent-process theory** of color vision. Opponent-process theory also holds that there are three types of color receptors, but they are not theorized to be red, green, and blue. Hering suggested that afterimages (such as of the American flag shown in Figure 4.12) are made possible by three types of color receptors: red-green, blue-yellow, and a type that perceives differences in brightness from light to dark. A red-green cone could not transmit messages for red and green at the same time. Hering would perhaps have said that when you are staring at the green, black, and yellow flag for 30 seconds, you are disturbing the balance of neural activity. The afterimage of red, white, and blue would then represent the eye's attempt to reestablish a balance.

Evaluation. Both theories of color vision may be partially correct (Hurvich, 1981). Research with **microspectrophotometry** supports trichromatic theory. It shows that some cones are sensitive to blue, some to green, and some to yellow-red parts of the spectrum—consistent with trichromatic theory.

However, studies of the bipolar and ganglion neurons suggest that messages from the cones are transmitted to the brain and relayed by the thalamus to the occipital lobe in an opponent-process fashion (DeValois & Jacobs, 1984). Some neurons that transmit messages to the visual centers in the brain, for example, are excited or "turned on" by green light but inhibited or "turned off" by red light. Others can be excited by red light but are inhibited by green light. A "neural rebound effect" may explain afterimages. With such an effect, a green-sensitive ganglion that had been excited by green light for half a minute or so might switch briefly to inhibitory activity when the light is shut off. The effect would be to perceive red, even though no red light was being shone (Haber & Hershenson, 1980).

These theoretical updates allow for the afterimage effects with the green, black, and yellow flag and are also consistent with Young's experiments in mixing lights of different colors.

Trichromatic theory The theory that color vision is made possible by three types of cones, some of which respond to red light, some to green, and some to blue.

Opponent-process theory The theory that color vision is made possible by three types of cones, some of which respond to red or green light, some to blue or yellow, and some only to the intensity of light.

Microspectrophotometry A method for analyzing the sensitivity of single cones to lights of different wavelengths.

Trichromat A person with normal color vision.

Monochromat A person who is sensitive to black and white only and hence color blind.

Color Blindness

If you can discriminate the colors of the visible spectrum, you have normal color vision and are labeled a **trichromat.** This means that you are sensitive to red-green, blue-yellow, and light-dark. People who are totally color blind are called **monochromats** and are sensitive to light-dark only. Total color blindness is quite rare. The fully color blind see the world as trichromats would on a black-and-white TV set or in a black-and-white movie.

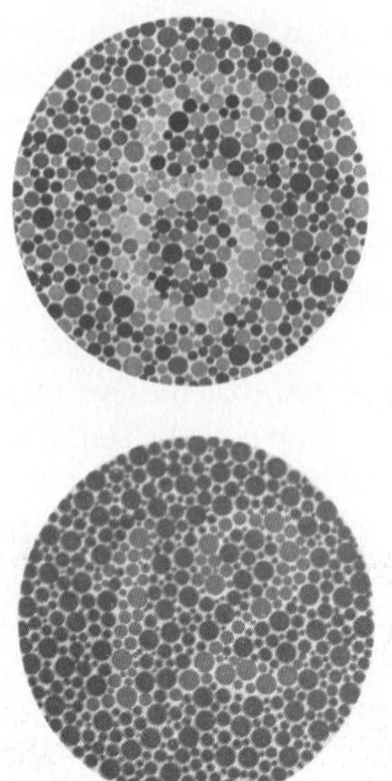

FIGURE 4.13
Plates from a Test for Color Blindness. Can you see the numbers in these plates from a test for color blindness? A person with red-green color blindness would not be able to see the 6, and a person with blue-yellow color blindness would probably not discern the 12. (Caution: These reproductions cannot be used for actual testing of color blindness.)

Partial color blindness is more common than total color blindness. Partial color blindness is a sex-linked trait that strikes mostly males. The recessive genes for the disorder are found on the X sex chromosome. In males they are thus unopposed by dominant genes that might be found on a second X sex chromosome (Nathans et al., 1986). The partially color blind are called **dichromats.** Dichromats can discriminate only two colors—red and green, or blue and yellow—and the colors that are derived from mixing these colors. Figure 4.13 shows the types of tests that are used to diagnose color blindness. Also see Figure 4.14.

A dichromat might put on one red sock and one green sock but would not mix red and blue socks. Monochromats might put on socks of any color. They would not notice a difference as long as the socks' color did not differ in intensity, or brightness.

When we selectively breed cats and dogs, we are interested in producing coats of certain colors. But if cats and dogs bred human beings, they would be less concerned about our color because their color vision is less well developed (Rosenzweig & Leiman, 1982). Cats, for example, can distinguish fewer colors and only on large surfaces.

VISUAL PERCEPTION

Perception is the process by which we organize or make sense of our sensory impressions. Although visual sensations are caused by electromagnetic energy, visual perception also relies on our knowledge, expectations, and motivations. Whereas sensation may be thought of as a mechanical process, perception is an active process by which we interpret the world around us.

For example, just what do you see in Figure 4.15? Do you see random splotches of ink or a rider on horseback? If you perceive a horse and rider, it is not just because of the visual sensations provided by the drawing. Each of the blobs is meaningless in and of itself, and the pattern they form is also less than clear. Despite the lack of clarity, however, you may still perceive a horse and rider. Why? The answer has something to do with your general knowledge and your desire to fit incoming bits and pieces of information into familiar patterns.

In the case of the "horse and rider," your integration of disconnected shards of information into a meaningful whole also reflects what Gestalt psychologists refer to as the principle of **closure,** or the tendency to perceive a complete or whole figure even when there are gaps in the sensory input. Put another way, in perception the whole can be very much more than the mere sum of the parts. Collecting parts alone can be meaningless; it is their configuration that matters.

Perceptual Organization

Earlier in the century, Gestalt psychologists noted consistencies in our integration of bits and pieces of sensory stimulation into meaningful wholes and attempted to formulate rules that governed these processes. Max Wertheimer, in particular, discovered many such rules. As a group, these rules are referred to as the laws of **perceptual organization.**

Figure–Ground Perception. If you look out your window, you may see people, buildings, cars, and streets, or perhaps grass, trees, birds, and clouds. In any event, the objects around you tend to be perceived as figures against backgrounds. Cars against the background of the street are easier to pick out than cars piled on each other in a junkyard. Birds against the sky are more likely to be perceived than, as the saying goes, birds in the bush. Figures are closer to us than their grounds.

Dichromat A person who is sensitive to black-white and either red-green or blue-yellow and hence partially color blind.

Closure The tendency to perceive a broken figure as being complete or whole.

Perceptual organization The tendency to integrate perceptual elements into meaningful patterns.

Ambiguous Having two or more possible meanings.

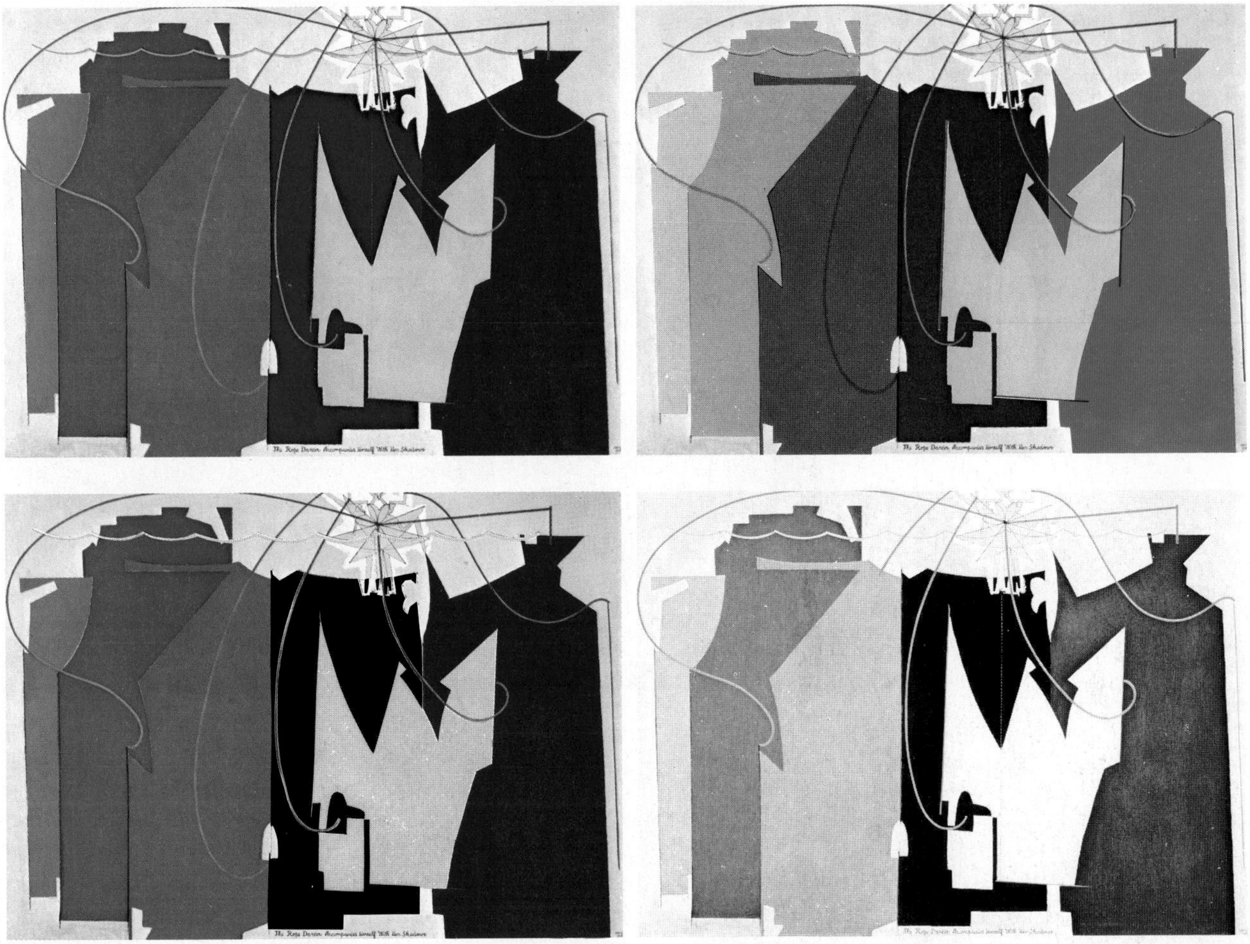

FIGURE 4.14
Color Blindness.

The painting in the upper left-hand panel—Man Ray's *The Rope Dancer Accompanies Herself with Her Shadows*—appears as it would to a person with normal color vision. If you suffered from red-green color blindness, the picture would appear as it does in the upper right-hand panel. The lower left-hand and lower right-hand panels show how the picture would look to viewers with yellow-blue or total color blindness, respectively. (Museum of Modern Art, New York. Gift of G. David Thompson.)

FIGURE 4.15
Closure. Meaningless splotches of ink or a horse and rider? This figure illustrates the Gestalt principle of closure.

When figure–ground relationships are **ambiguous,** our perceptions tend to be unstable. They shift back and forth. Take a look at Figure 4.16—a nice leisurely look. How many people, objects, and animals can you find in this Escher print? If your eye is drawn back and forth, so that sometimes you are perceiving light figures on a dark background and then dark figures on a light background, you are experiencing figure-ground reversals. In other words, a shift is occurring in your perception of what is figure and what is ground, or backdrop. Escher was able to have some fun with us because of our tendency to try to isolate geometric patterns or figures from a background. However, in this case the "background" is as meaningful and detailed as the "figure." Therefore, our perceptions shift back and forth.

The Rubin Vase. In Figure 4.17 we see a Rubin vase, one of psychologists' favorite illustrations of figure-ground relationships. The figure-ground relationship in part A of the figure is ambiguous. No cues suggest which area must be the figure. For this reason, our perception may shift from seeing the vase as the figure and then seeing two profiles as the figure.

FIGURE 4.16
Figure and Ground. How many animals and demons can you find in this Escher print? Do we have white figures on a black background or black figures on a white background? Figure-ground perception is the tendency to perceive geometric forms against a background.

Proximity Nearness. The perceptual tendency to group together objects that are near one another.

Similarity The perceptual tendency to group together objects that are similar in appearance.

There is no such problem in part B. Since it seems that a white vase has been brought forward against a colored ground, we are more likely to perceive the vase than the profiles. In part C, we are more likely to perceive the profiles than the vase because the profiles are whole, and the vase is broken against the background. Of course, we can still perceive the vase in part C, if we wish to, because experience has shown us where it is. Why not have fun with some friends by covering parts B and C and asking them what they see? (They'll catch on to you quickly if they can see all three drawings at once.)

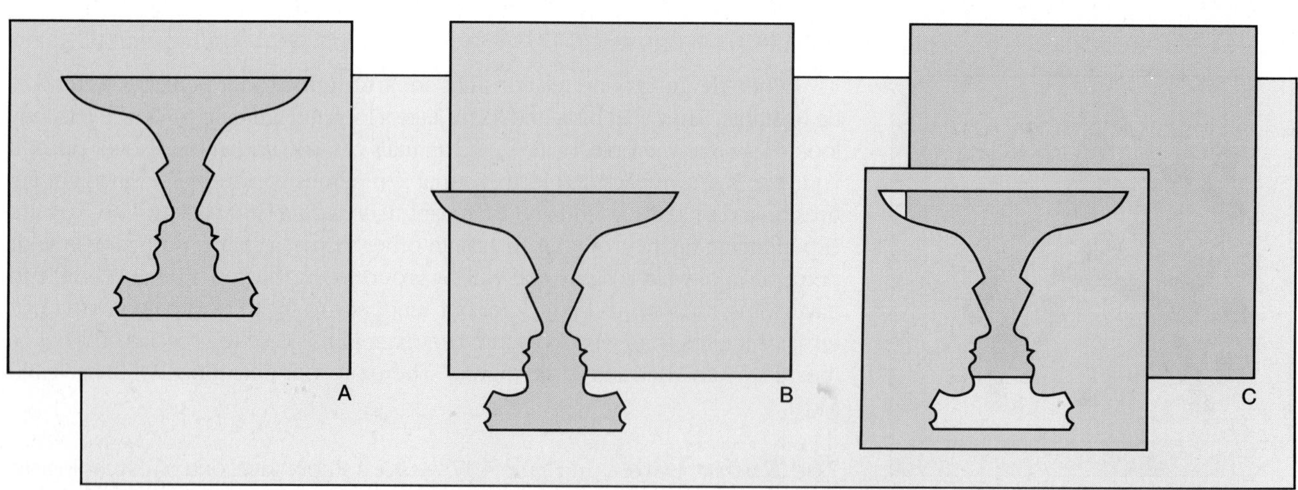

FIGURE 4.17
The Rubin Vase.

A favorite drawing used by psychologists to demonstrate figure-ground perception. Part A is ambiguous, with neither the vase nor the profiles clearly the figure or the ground. In part B, the vase is the figure; in part C, the profiles are.

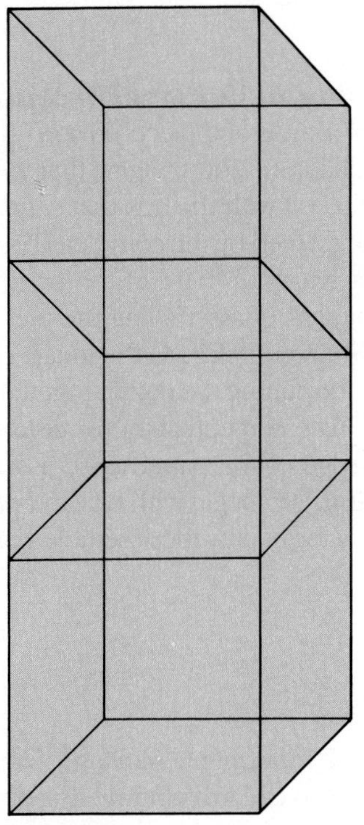

FIGURE 4.18
A Stack of Necker Cubes. Ambiguity in the drawing of the cubes makes perceptual shifts possible.

The Necker Cube. The Necker cubes (Figure 4.18) provide another example of how an ambiguous drawing can lead to perceptual shifts.

Hold this page at arm's length and stare at the center of the figure for 30 seconds or so. Allow your eye muscles to relax. (The feeling is of your eyes "glazing over.") After a while you will notice a dramatic shift in your perception of these "stacked boxes," so that what was once a front edge is now a back edge, and vice versa. Again, the dramatic perceptual shift is made possible by the fact that the outline of the drawing permits two interpretations.

Some Other Gestalt Rules for Organization. In addition to the law of closure, Gestalt psychologists have noted that our perceptions are guided by rules or laws of *proximity, similarity, continuity,* and *common fate.*

Verbally describe part A of Figure 4.19 without reading further. Did you say that part A consisted of six lines or of three groups of two parallel lines? If you said three sets of lines, you were influenced by the **proximity,** or nearness, of some of the lines. There is no other reason for perceiving them in pairs or subgroups: all lines are parallel and of equal length.

Now describe part B of the figure. Did you perceive the figure as a six-by-six grid, or as three columns of *x*'s and three columns of *o*'s? According to the law of **similarity,** we perceive similar objects as belonging together. For this reason, you may have been more likely to describe part B in terms of columns than rows or a grid.

What about part C? Is it a circle with two lines stemming from it, or is it a (broken) line that goes through a circle? If you saw it as a single (broken) line, you were probably organizing your perceptions according to the rule of **continuity.** That is, we perceive a series of points or a broken line as having unity.

According to the law of **common fate,** elements seen moving together are perceived as belonging together. A group of people running in the same direction appear unified in purpose. Birds that flock together seem to be of a feather. (Did I get that right?)

Part D of Figure 4.19 provides another example of the law of closure. The arcs tend to be perceived as a circle (or circle with gaps) rather than as just a series of arcs.

Continuity The tendency to perceive a series of points or lines as having unity.

Common fate The tendency to perceive elements that move together as belonging together.

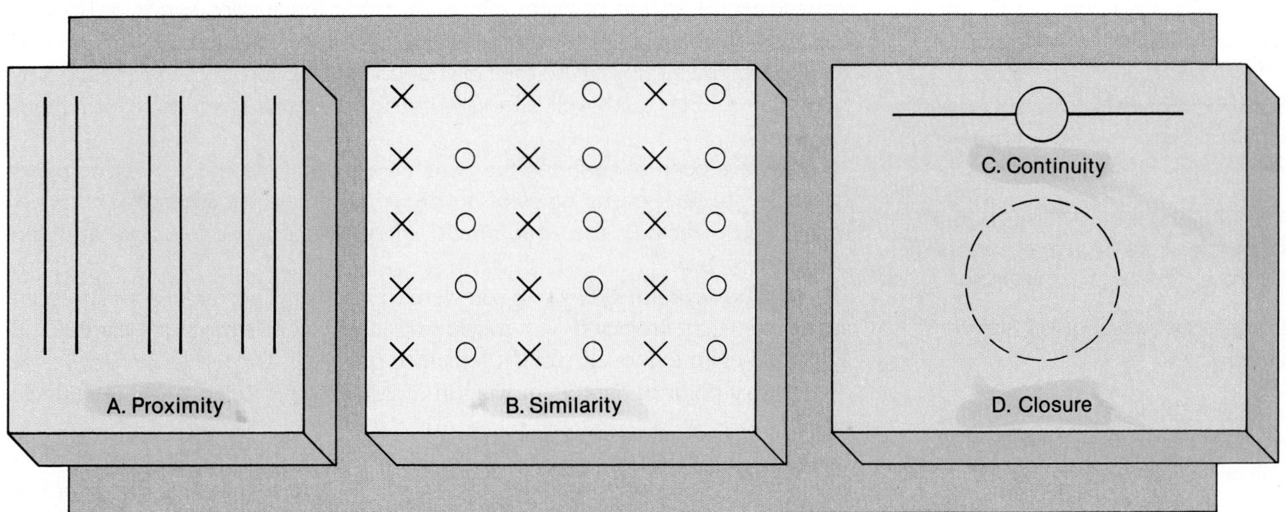

FIGURE 4.19
Some Gestalt Laws of Perceptual Organization.

These drawings illustrate the Gestalt laws of proximity, similarity, continuity, and closure.

Top-Down versus Bottom-Up Processing in Pattern Perception. Imagine that you are trying to piece together a thousand-piece puzzle—a task that I usually avoid, despite the cajoling of my children. Now imagine that you are trying to accomplish it after someone has walked off with the box that contained the pieces—you know, the box with the picture formed by the completed puzzle.

When you have the box—when you know what the "big picture" or pattern looks like—cognitive psychologists refer to the task of assembling the pieces as **top-down processing.** The "top" of the visual system refers to the image of the pattern in the brain, and the top-down strategy for putting the puzzle together implies that you use the pattern to guide subordinate perceptual-motor tasks such as hunting for proper pieces. Without knowledge of the pattern, the assembly process is referred to as **bottom-up processing.** You begin with bits and pieces of information and become aware of the pattern formed by the assembled pieces only after you have labored for a while.

Perception of Movement

Consider the importance of the perception of movement. Moving objects—whether they are other people, animals, cars, or tons of earth plummeting down a hillside—are vital sources of sensory information. Moving objects capture the attention of even newborn infants.

To understand how we perceive movement, recall what it is like to be on a train that has begun to pull out of the station while the train on the adjacent track remains stationary. If your own train does not lurch as it accelerates, you might think at first that the other train is moving. Or you might not be certain whether your train is moving forward or the other train is moving backward.

The visual perception of movement is based on change of position relative to other objects. To early scientists, whose only instrument for visual observation was the naked eye, it seemed logical that the sun circled the earth. You have to be able to imagine the movement of the earth around the sun as seen from a theoretical point in outer space—you cannot observe it directly.

How, then, do you determine which train is moving when your train is pulling out of the station (or that other train is pulling in)? One way is to look for objects you know are stable, such as station platform columns, houses, signs, or trees. If you are stationary in relation to them, your train is not moving. Observing people walking on the station platform may not provide the answer, however, because they are also changing their position relative to stationary objects. You might also try to sense the motion of the train in your body. You know from experience how to do these things quite well, although it may be difficult to phrase explanations for them.

We have been considering the perception of real movement. Psychologists have also studied several types of apparent movement, or **illusions** of movement. These include the *autokinetic effect, stroboscopic motion,* and the *phi phenomenon.*

The Autokinetic Effect. If you were to sit quietly in a dark room and stare at a point of light projected onto the far wall, after a while it might appear that the light had begun to move, even if it remained quite still. The tendency to perceive a stationary point of light as moving in a dark room is called the **autokinetic effect.**

Over the years, psychologists have run interesting experiments in which they have asked subjects, for example, what the light is "spelling out." The light has spelled out nothing, of course, and the words perceived by subjects have reflected their own cognitive processes, not external sensations.

Stroboscopic Motion. Stroboscopic motion makes motion pictures possible. In **stroboscopic motion,** the illusion of movement is provided by the

Top-down processing The use of contextual information or knowledge of a pattern in order to organize parts of the pattern.

Bottom-up processing The organization of the parts of a pattern to recognize, or form an image of, the pattern they compose.

Illusions Sensations that give rise to misperceptions.

Autokinetic effect The tendency to perceive a stationary point of light in a dark room as moving.

Stroboscopic motion A visual illusion in which the perception of motion is generated by a series of stationary images that are presented in rapid succession.

FIGURE 4.20
Stroboscopic Motion.

In a motion picture, viewing a series of stationary images at the rate of about 16 to 22 frames per second provides the illusion of movement. This form of apparent movement is termed stroboscopic motion.

presentation of a rapid progression of images of stationary objects (Beck et al., 1977). So-called motion pictures do not really consist of images that move. Rather, the audience is shown 16 to 22 pictures, or frames, per second, like those in Figure 4.20. Each frame differs slightly from that preceding it. Showing the frames in rapid succession then provides the illusion of movement.

At the rate of at least 16 frames per second, the "motion" in a film seems smooth and natural. With fewer than 16 or so frames per second, the movement looks jumpy and unnatural. That is why slow motion is achieved through filming perhaps 100 or more frames per second. When they are played back at about 22 frames per second, movement seems slowed down, yet smooth and natural.

The Phi Phenomenon. Have you seen news headlines spelled out in lights that rapidly wrap around a building? Have you seen an electronic scoreboard in a baseball or football stadium? When the hometeam scores, some scoreboards suggest the explosions of fireworks. What actually happens is that a row of lights is switched on, then off. As the first row is switched off, the second row is switched on, and so on for dozens, perhaps hundreds of rows. When the switching occurs rapidly, the **phi phenomenon** occurs: the on-off process is perceived as movement.

Phi phenomenon The perception of movement as a result of sequential presentation of visual stimuli.

Monocular cues Stimuli suggestive of depth that can be perceived with only one eye.

Perspective A monocular cue for depth based on the convergence (coming together) of parallel lines as they recede into the distance.

Like stroboscopic motion, the phi phenomenon is an example of apparent motion. Both stroboscopic motion and the phi phenomenon appear to occur because of the law of continuity. We tend to perceive a series of points as having unity, so the series of lights (points) is perceived as moving lines.

Depth Perception

Think of the problems you might have if you could not judge depth or distance. You might bump into other people, thinking them to be farther away than they are. An outfielder might not be able to judge whether to run toward the infield or the fence to catch a fly ball. You might give your front bumper a workout in stop-and-go traffic. Fortunately, both *monocular and binocular cues* help us perceive the depth of objects. Let us examine a number of them.

Monocular Cues. Now that you have considered how difficult it would be to navigate through life without depth perception, ponder the problems of the artist who attempts to portray three-dimensional objects on a two-dimensional surface. Artists use **monocular cues,** or cues that can be perceived by one eye, to create an illusion of depth. These cues—including perspective, clearness, interposition, shadows, and texture gradient—cause certain objects to appear to be more distant from the viewer than others.

Distant objects stimulate smaller areas on the retina than nearby objects. The amount of sensory input from them is smaller, even though they may be the same size. The spaces between distant objects also look smaller than equivalent spaces between nearby objects. These perceptual facts give rise to **perspective:** the tendency to perceive parallel lines as converging as they recede from us. However, as

The Phi Phenomenon. The phi phenomenon is an illusion of movement that is produced by lights blinking on and off in sequence, as with this New York Stock Exchange electronic "ticker."

FIGURE 4.21
What Is Wrong with These Pictures?

In *Waterfall,* to the left, how does Dutch artist M. C. Escher suggest that fallen water flows back upward, only to fall again? In *False Perspective,* to the right, how does English artist William Hogarth use monocular cues for depth perception to deceive the viewer?

we shall see when we discuss *size constancy,* experience teaches us that distant objects that look small will be larger when they are close. Their relative size thus becomes a cue to their distance from us.

The two engravings in Figure 4.21 represent impossible scenes in which the artists use principles of perspective to fool the viewer. In the engraving to the left, *Waterfall,* note that the water appears to be flowing away from the viewer in a zigzag because the stream becomes gradually narrower (that is, lines that we assume to be parallel are shown to be converging) and the stone sides of the aqueduct appear to be stepping down. However, given that the water arrives at the top of the fall, it must actually somehow be flowing upward. However, the spot from which it falls is no farther from the viewer than the collection point from which it appears to (but does not) begin its flow backward.

Again, distant objects look smaller than nearby objects of the same size. The paradoxes in the engraving to the right, *False Perspective,* are made possible by the fact that more-distant objects are not necessarily depicted as being smaller than nearby objects. Thus, what at first seems to be background suddenly becomes foreground, and vice versa.

The clearness of an object also suggests its distance from us. Experience shows us that we sense more details of nearby objects. For this reason, artists can suggest that certain objects are closer to the viewer by depicting them in greater detail. Note that the "distant" hill in the Hogarth engraving (Figure 4.21) is given less detail than the nearby plants at the bottom of the picture. Our perceptions

Interposition A monocular cue for depth based on the fact that a nearby object obscures a more distant object behind it.

Shadowing A monocular cue for depth based on the fact that opaque objects block light and produce shadows.

Texture gradient A monocular cue for depth based on the perception that closer objects appear to have rougher (more detailed) surfaces.

Motion parallax A monocular cue for depth based on the perception that nearby objects appear to move more rapidly in relation to our own motion.

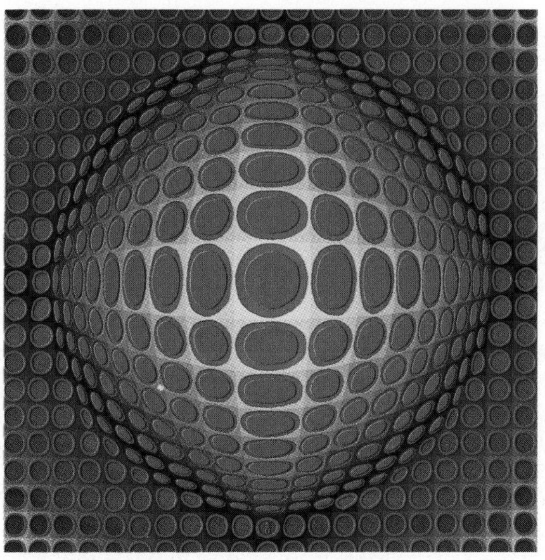

FIGURE 4.22
Creating the Illusion of Three Dimensions with Two. How does Op Artist Victor Vasarely use monocular cues for depth perception to lend this work a three-dimensional quality? (Work: *Vega-Tek,* wool Aubusson tapestry, 1969. 101 x 98½". Private collection.)

are mocked when a man "on" that distant hill in the background is shown conversing with a woman leaning out a window in the middle ground.

How does artist Viktor Vasarley use monocular cues to provide the illusion of a curving surface in his tapestry, *Vega-Tek* (Figure 4.22)?

We also learn that nearby objects can block our views of more-distant objects. Overlapping, or **interposition,** is the apparent placing of one object in front of another. Experience encourages us to perceive the partly covered objects as being farther away than the objects that hide parts of them from view (Figure 4.23). In the Hogarth engraving (Figure 4.21), which looks closer: the trees in the background (background?) or the moon sign hanging from the building (or is it buildings?) to the right? How does the artist use interposition to confound the viewer?

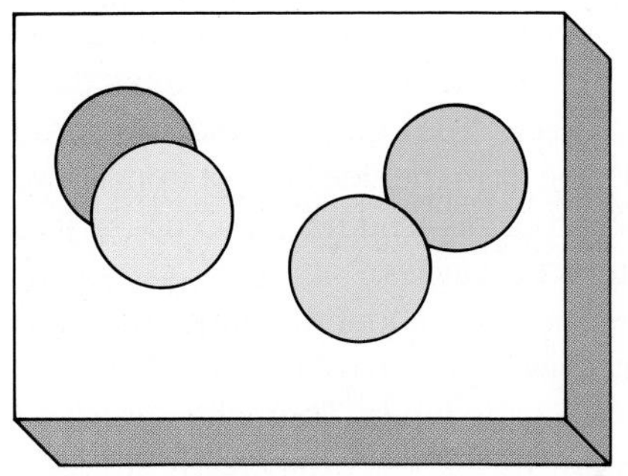

FIGURE 4.23
The Effects of Interposition. The four circles are all the same size. Which circles seem closer: the complete circles or the circles with chunks bitten out of them?

Additional information about depth is provided by **shadowing** and is based on the fact that opaque objects block light and produce shadows. Shadows and highlights give us information about objects' three-dimensional shapes and about their relationships to the source of light. The left part of Figure 4.24 is perceived as a two-dimensional circle, but the right part tends to be perceived as a three-dimensional sphere because of the highlight on its surface and the shadow underneath. In the "sphere," the highlighted central area is perceived as being closest to us, with the surface then receding to the edges.

Another monocular cue is **texture gradient.** A gradient is a progressive change, and closer objects are perceived as having progressively rougher textures. In the Hogarth engraving (Figure 4.21), the building just behind the large fisherman's head has a rougher texture and thus seems to be closer than the building with the window from which the woman is leaning. Our surprise is thus heightened when the moon sign is seen as hanging from both buildings.

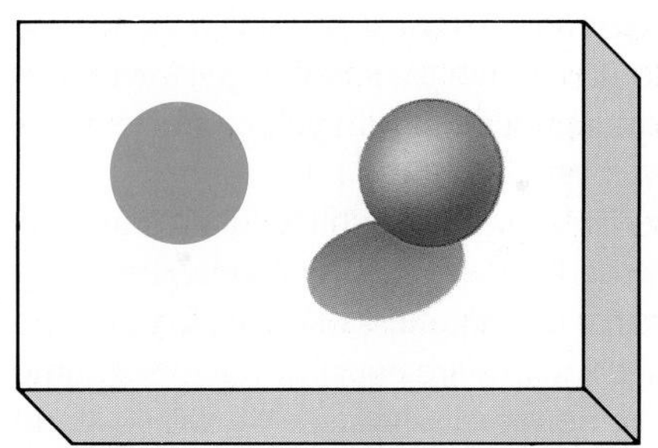

FIGURE 4.24
Shadowing as a Cue in the Perception of Depth. Shadowing lends the circle on the right a sense of three-dimensionality.

Motion Cues. If you have ever driven in the country, you have probably noticed that distant objects such as mountains and stars appear to move along with you. Objects at an intermediate distance seem to be stationary, but nearby objects such as roadside markers, rocks, and trees seem to go by quite rapidly. The tendency of objects to seem to move backward or forward as a function of their distance is known as **motion parallax.** We learn to perceive objects that appear to move with us as being at greater distances.

Earlier we noted that nearby objects cause the lens of the eye to accommodate or bend more to bring them into focus. The sensations of tension in the eye

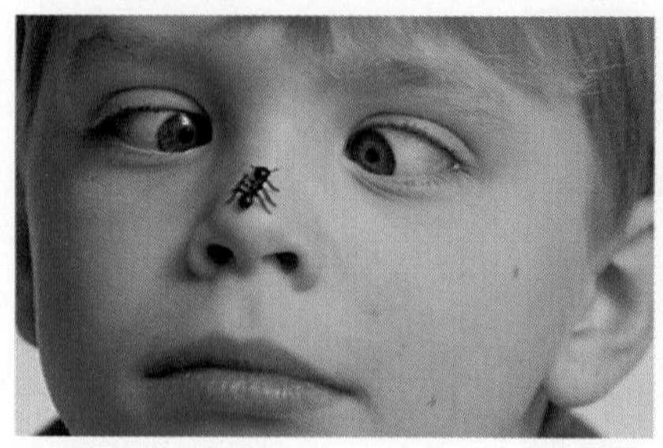

FIGURE 4.25
Retinal Disparity and Convergence as Cues for Depth. As an object nears your eyes, you begin to see two images of it because of retinal disparity. If you maintain perception of a single image, your eyes must converge on the object.

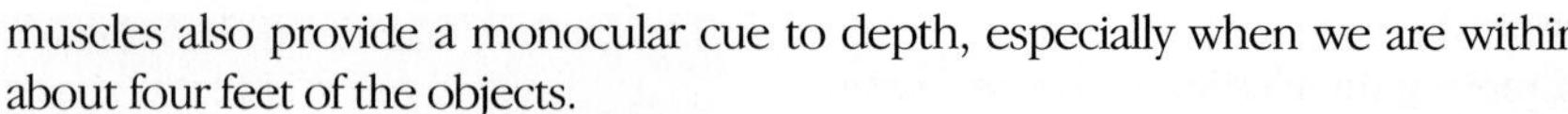

muscles also provide a monocular cue to depth, especially when we are within about four feet of the objects.

Binocular Cues. **Binocular cues,** or cues that involve both eyes, also help us perceive depth. Two binocular cues are *retinal disparity* and *convergence.*

Try a simple experiment. Hold your index finger at arm's length. Now, gradually bring it closer until it almost touches your nose. If you keep your eyes relaxed as you do so, you will see two fingers. An image of the finger will be projected onto the retina of each eye, and each image will be slightly different because the finger will be seen at different angles. The difference between the projected images is referred to as **retinal disparity** and serves as a binocular cue for depth perception (see Figure 4.25). Note that the closer your finger comes, the farther apart the "two fingers" appear to be. Closer objects have greater retinal disparity.

If we try to maintain a single image of the approaching finger, our eyes must turn inward, or converge on it, giving us a cross-eyed look. **Convergence** is associated with feelings of tension in the eye muscles and provides another binocular cue for depth. The binocular cues of retinal disparity and convergence are strongest at near distances.

Perceptual Constancies

The world is a constantly shifting display of visual sensations. What confusion would reign if we did not perceive a doorway to be the same doorway when seen from six feet as when seen from four feet. As we neared it, we might think that it was larger than the door we were seeking and become lost. Or consider the problems of the pet owner who recognizes his dog from the side but not from above, when the shapes differ. Fortunately, these problems tend not to occur—at least with familiar objects—because of perceptual constancies.

The image of a dog seen from 20 feet occupies about the same amount of space on your retina as an inch-long insect crawling in the palm of your hand. Yet, you do not perceive the dog to be as small as the insect. Through your experiences you have acquired **size constancy,** or the tendency to perceive the same object as being the same size, even though the size of its image on the retina varies as a function of its distance. Experience teaches us about perspective, that the same object seen at a great distance will appear to be much smaller than when it is nearby.

We also have **color constancy**—the tendency to perceive objects as retaining their color even though lighting conditions may alter their appearance. Your bright orange car may edge toward yellow-gray as the hours wend their way through twilight to nighttime. But when you finally locate it in the parking lot, you will still think of it as being orange. You expect an orange car and still judge it to be "more orange" than the (faded) blue and green cars to either side. However, it would be fiercely difficult to find it in a parking lot filled with yellow and red cars similar in size and shape.

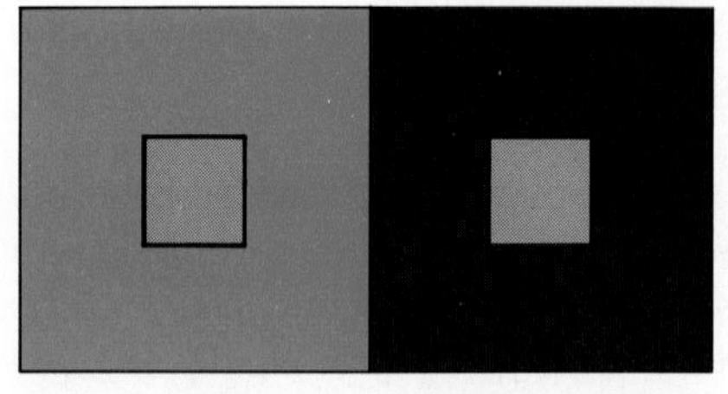

FIGURE 4.26
Color Constancy. The orange squares within the blue squares are the same hue, yet the orange within the dark blue square is perceived as being purer. Why?

Consider Figure 4.26. The orange squares within the blue squares are the same hue. However, the orange within the dark blue square is perceived as being purer. Why? Again, experience teaches us that the pureness of colors fades as the background grows darker. Since the orange squares are equally pure, we assume that the one in the dark background must be more saturated. We would stand ready to perceive the orange squares as being equal in purity if the square within the darker blue field actually had a bit of black mixed in with it.

Similar to color constancy is **brightness constancy.** The same gray square is perceived as brighter when placed within a black background than when placed within a white background (see Figure 1.3 on p. 14). Again, consider the role of

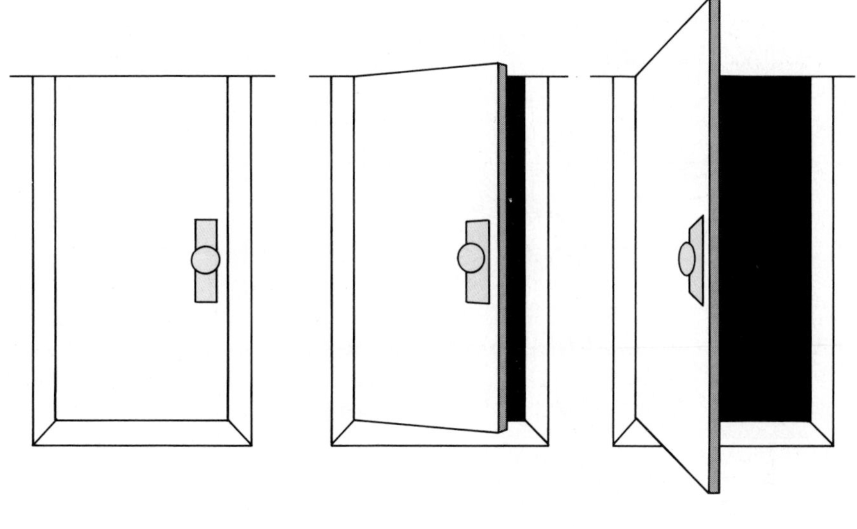

FIGURE 4.27
Shape Constancy. When closed, this door is a rectangle. When open, the retinal image is trapezoidal. But because of shape constancy, we still perceive the door as being rectangular.

experience. If it were nighttime, we would expect gray to fade to near blackness. The fact that the gray within the black square stimulates the eye with equal intensity suggests that it must be very much brighter than the gray within the white square.

We also perceive objects as maintaining their shapes, even if we perceive them from different angles so that the shape of the retinal image changes dramatically. This tendency is called **shape constancy.** You perceive the top of a coffee cup or a glass to be a circle even though it is a circle only when seen from above. When seen from an angle, it is an ellipse. When seen on edge, the retinal image of the cup or glass is the same as that of a straight line. So why do you still describe the rim of the cup or glass as being a circle? Perhaps for two reasons: One is that experience has taught you that the cup will look circular when seen from above. The second is that you may have labeled the cup circular or round. Experience and labels make the world a stable place. Can you imagine the chaos that would prevail if we described objects as they stimulated our sensory organs with each changing moment, rather than according to stable conditions?

In another example, a door is a rectangle only when viewed straight on (Figure 4.27). When we move to the side or open it, the left or right edge comes closer and appears to be larger, changing the retinal image to a trapezoid. Yet we continue to think of doors as being rectangles.

The principles of perceptual organization make possible some fascinating illusions.

Binocular cues Stimuli suggestive of depth that involve simultaneous perception by both eyes.

Retinal disparity A binocular cue for depth based on the difference in the image cast by an object on the retinas of the eyes as the object moves closer or farther away.

Convergence A binocular cue for depth based on the inward movement of the eyes as they attempt to focus on an object that is drawing nearer.

Size constancy The tendency to perceive an object as being the same size even as the size of its retinal image changes according to the object's distance.

Color constancy The tendency to perceive an object as being the same color even though lighting conditions change its appearance.

Brightness constancy The tendency to perceive an object as being just as bright even though lighting conditions change its intensity.

Shape constancy The tendency to perceive an object as being the same shape although the retinal image varies in shape as it rotates.

Visual Illusions

The principles of perceptual organization make it possible for our eyes to "play tricks on us." Psychologists, like magicians, enjoy pulling a rabbit out of the hat now and then, and I am pleased to be able to demonstrate how the perceptual constancies trick the eye through so-called visual illusions.

The Hering-Helmholtz and Müller-Lyer illusions (Figure 4.28, part A) are named after the people who originated them. In the Hering-Helmholtz illusion, the horizontal lines are straight and parallel. However, the radiating lines cause them to appear to be bent outward near the center. The two lines in the Müller-Lyer illusion are the same length, but the line on the left, with its reversed arrowheads, looks longer.

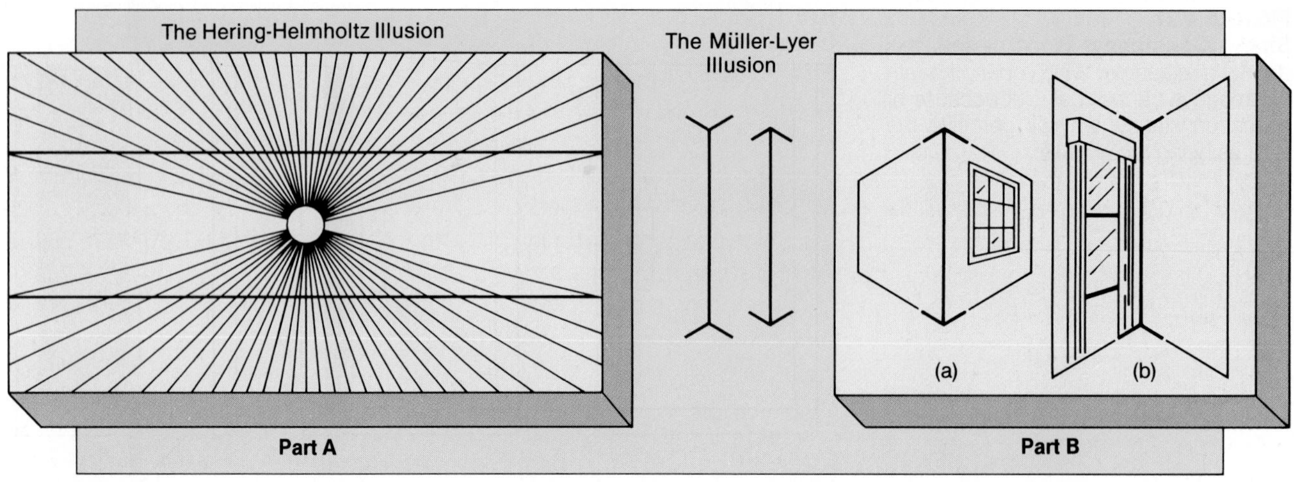

FIGURE 4.28
The Hering-Helmholtz and Müller-Lyer Illusions.

In the Hering-Helmholtz illusion, are the horizontal lines straight or curved? In the Müller-Lyer illusion, are the vertical lines equal in length?

Let us try to explain these illusions. Because of experience and lifelong use of perceptual cues, we tend to perceive the Hering-Helmholtz drawing as being three-dimensional. Because of the tendency to perceive bits of sensory information as figures against grounds, we perceive the white area in the center as being a circle in front of a series of radiating lines, all of which lies in front of a white ground. Next, because of our experience with perspective, we perceive the radiating lines as being parallel. We perceive the two horizontal lines as intersecting the "receding" lines, and we know that they would have to appear bent out at the center if they were to be equidistant at all points from the center of the circle.

Experience probably compels us to perceive the vertical lines in the Müller-Lyer illusion as being the corners of a room as seen from inside a house, at left, and outside a house, at right (see Figure 4.28, part B). In such an example, the reverse arrowheads to the left are lines where the walls meet the ceiling and the floor. We perceive such lines as extending toward us; they push the corner away from us. The arrowheads to the right are lines where exterior walls meet the roof and foundation. We perceive them as receding from us; they push the corner toward us. The vertical line to the left is thus perceived as being farther away. Since both vertical lines stimulate equal expanses across the retina, the principle of size constancy encourages us to perceive the line to the left as being longer.

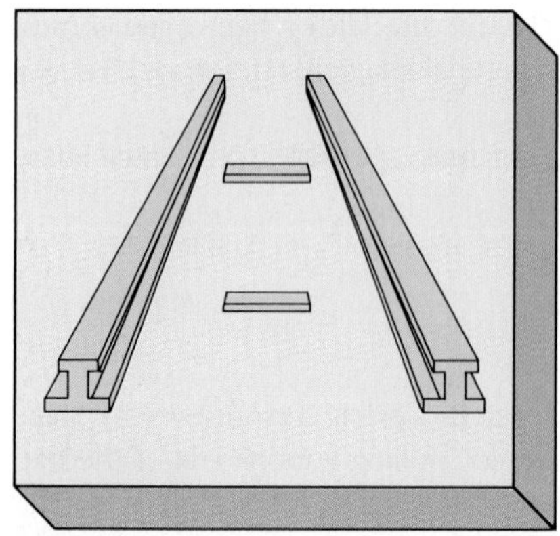

FIGURE 4.29
The Ponzo Illusion. The two horizontal lines in this drawing are equal in length, but the top line is perceived as being longer. Can you use the principle of size constancy to explain why?

Figure 4.29 is known as the Ponzo illusion. In this illusion, the two horizontal lines are the same length. However, do you perceive the top line as being longer? The rule of size constancy may also afford insight into this illusion. Perhaps the converging lines strike us as being parallel lines receding into the distance, like the train tracks in the drawing to the left. If so, we assume from experience that the horizontal line at the top is farther down the track—farther away from us. And again, the rule of size constancy tells us that if two objects appear to be the same size and one is farther away, the farther object must be larger. So we perceive the top line as being larger.

Now that you are an expert on these visual illusions, look at Figure 4.30. First take some bets from friends about whether the three cylinders are equal in height and width. Then get a ruler. Once you have made some money, however, try to explain why the cylinders to the right look progressively larger.

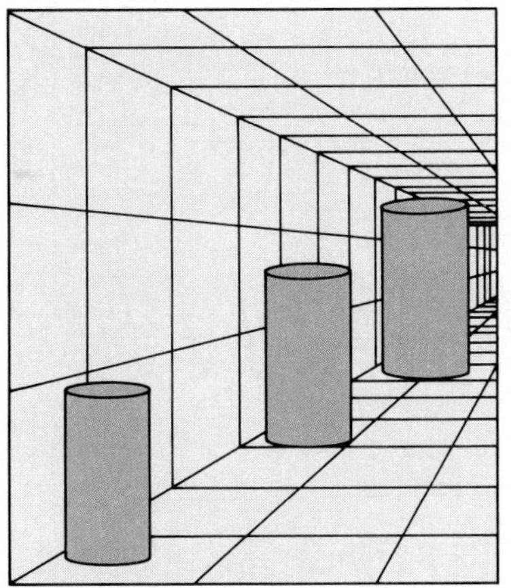

FIGURE 4.30
An Illusion Created by the Principle of Size Constancy. In this drawing, the three cylinders are the same size, yet they appear to grow larger toward the top of the picture. Can you use the principle of size constancy to explain why?

HEARING

Consider the advertising slogan for the science fiction film *Alien:* "In space, no one can hear you scream." It's true. Space is an almost perfect vacuum, and hearing requires a medium such as air or water through which sound can travel.

Sound, or **auditory** stimulation, travels through the air like waves. Sound is caused by changes in air pressure that result from vibrations. These vibrations, in turn, can be created by a tuning fork, your vocal cords, guitar strings, or the clap of a book thrown down on a desk.

Figure 4.31 suggests the way in which a tuning fork creates sound waves. During a vibration back and forth, the right prong of the tuning fork moves to the right. In so doing, it pushes together, or compresses, the molecules of air immediately to the right. Then the prong moves back to the left, and the air molecules to the right expand. By vibrating back and forth, the tuning fork actually sends air waves in many directions. A cycle of compression and expansion is considered to be one wave of sound. Sound waves can occur many times in one second. The human ear is sensitive to sound waves that vary from frequencies of 20 to 20,000 cycles per second.

Auditory Having to do with hearing.

Hertz A unit expressing the frequency of sound waves. One Hertz, or *1 Hz,* equals one cycle per second.

Amplitude Height.

Pitch and Loudness

Pitch and loudness are two psychological dimensions of sound.

Pitch. The pitch of a sound is determined by its frequency, or the number of cycles per second as expressed in the unit **Hertz** (Hz). One cycle per second is one Hz. The greater the number of cycles per second (Hz), the higher the pitch of the sound. The pitch of women's voices is usually higher than those of men because women's vocal cords are usually shorter and thus vibrate at a greater frequency. The strings of a violin are shorter than those of a viola or bass viol. They vibrate at greater frequencies, and we perceive them to be higher in pitch.

Loudness. The loudness of a sound is determined by the height, or **amplitude,** of sound waves. The higher the amplitude of the wave, the louder the sound. Figure 4.32 shows records of sound waves that vary in frequency and amplitude. Frequency and amplitude are independent dimensions. Sounds both high and low in pitch can be either high or low in loudness.

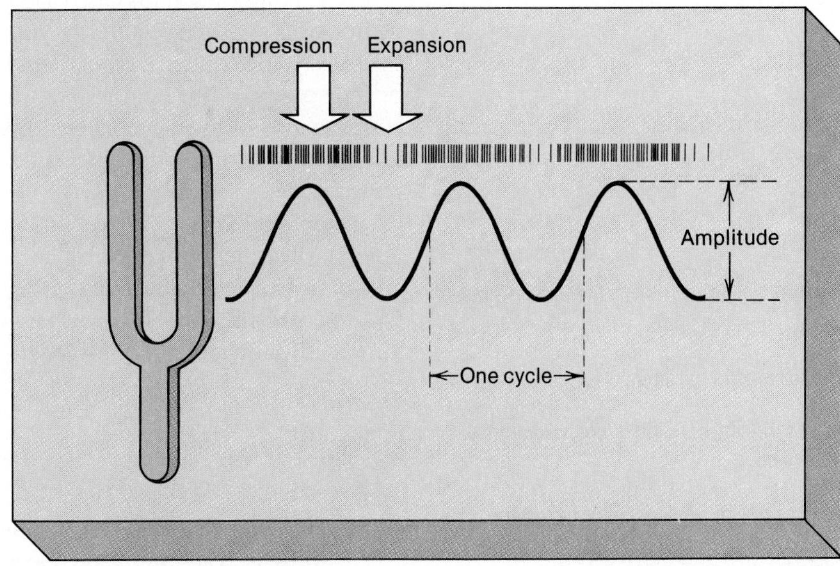

FIGURE 4.31
Creation of Sound Waves. The vibration of the prongs of a tuning fork alternately compresses and expands air molecules, sending forth waves of sound.

FIGURE 4.32
Sound Waves of Various Frequencies and Amplitudes. Which sounds have the highest pitch? Which are loudest?

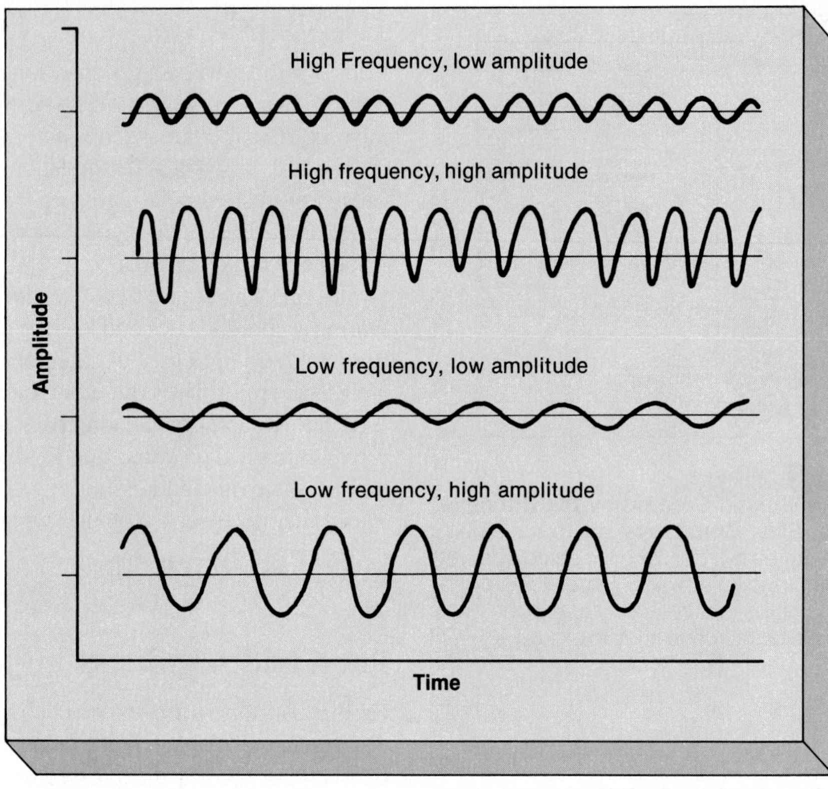

The loudness of a sound is usually expressed in the unit **decibel,** abbreviated *dB,* which is named after the inventor of the telephone, Alexander Graham Bell. Zero dB is equivalent to the threshold of hearing. How loud is that? It's about as loud as the ticking of a watch 20 feet away in a very quiet room (see Table 4.1).

The decibel equivalents of many familiar sounds are shown in Figure 4.33. Twenty dB is equivalent in loudness to a whisper at five feet. Thirty dB is roughly the limit of loudness at which your librarian would like to keep your college library. You may suffer hearing damage if exposed protractedly to sounds of 85 to 90 dB.

When musical sounds (also called tones) of different frequency are played together, we also perceive a third tone that results from the difference in their frequencies. If the combination of tones is pleasant, we say that they are in harmony, or **consonant** (from Latin roots meaning "together" and "sound"). Unpleasant combinations of tones are labeled **dissonant** ("the opposite of" and "sound"). The expression that something "strikes a dissonant chord" means that we find it disagreeable.

Overtones and Timbre. In addition to producing the specified musical note, an instrument like the violin also produces a number of tones that are greater in frequency. These more highly pitched sounds are called **overtones.** Overtones result from vibrations elsewhere in the instrument and contribute to the quality or richness—the **timbre**—of a sound.

Decibel A unit expressing the loudness of a sound. Abbreviated *dB.*

Consonant In harmony.

Dissonant Incompatible, not harmonious, discordant.

Overtones Tones of a higher frequency than those played that result from vibrations throughout a musical instrument.

Timbre The quality or richness of a sound.

It is true that a $500 machine-made violin will produce the same musical notes as a $200,000 Stradivarius. The Stradivarius has richer overtones, however, which give the instrument its greater value.

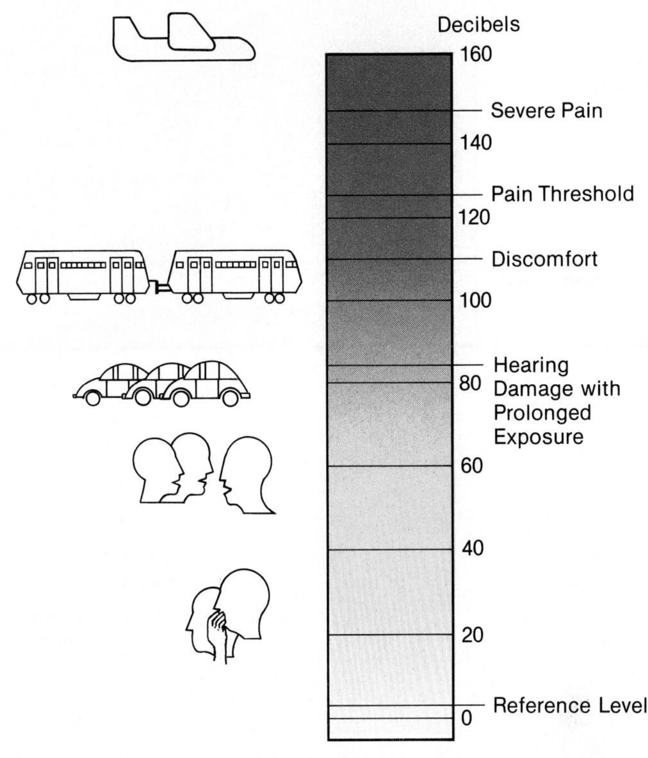

FIGURE 4.33
Decibel Ratings of Some Familiar Sounds. Zero dB is the threshold of hearing. You may suffer hearing loss if you incur prolonged exposure to sounds of 85–90 dB.

Professional musicians require more expensive instruments because of the richness of their overtones—their timbre.

Noise. In terms of the sense of hearing, noise is a combination of dissonant sounds.[1] When you place a spiral shell to your ear, you do not hear the roar of the ocean. Rather, you hear the reflected noise in your vicinity. **White noise** consists of many different frequencies of sound. Yet, this mixture can lull us to sleep if the loudness is not too great.

Now let us turn our attention to the marvelous instrument that senses all these different "vibes": the human ear.

The Ear

The human ear is good for lots of things—catching dust, combing your hair around, hanging jewelry from, and nibbling. It is also admirably suited for sensing sounds. The ear is shaped to capture sound waves, to vibrate in sympathy with them, and to transmit all this business to centers in the brain. In this way, you not only hear something, you can also figure out what it is. You have an outer ear, a middle ear, and an inner ear (see Figure 4.34).

The Outer Ear. The outer ear is shaped to funnel sound waves to the **eardrum,** a thin membrane that vibrates in response to sound waves and thereby transmits them to the middle and inner ears.

The Middle Ear. The middle ear contains the eardrum and three small bones—the hammer, the anvil, and the stirrup—which also transmit sound by vibrating. These bones were given their names (actually the Latin *malleus, incus,* and *stapes,* which translate as hammer, anvil, and stirrup) because of their shapes. The middle ear functions as an amplifier: it increases the magnitude of the air pressure.

White noise Discordant sounds of many frequencies, often producing a lulling effect.

Eardrum A thin membrane that vibrates in response to sound waves, transmitting the waves to the middle and inner ears.

[1]Within the broader context of signal-detection theory, *noise* has a different meaning, discussed earlier in the chapter.

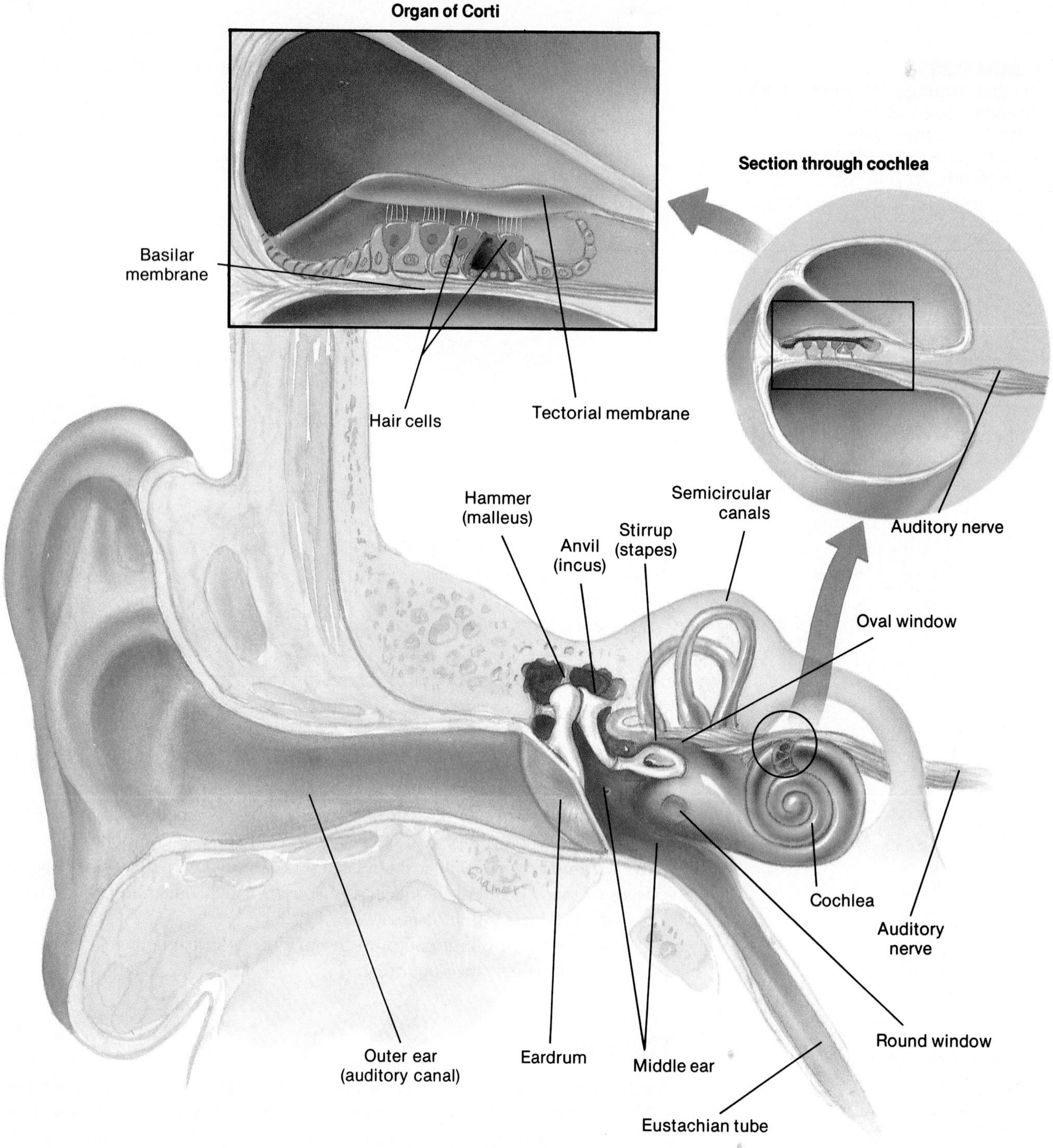

FIGURE 4.34
The Human Ear.

The outer ear funnels sound to the eardrum. Inside the eardrum, vibrations of the hammer, anvil, and stirrup transmit sound to the inner ear. Vibrations in the cochlea transmit the sound to the auditory nerve by way of the basilar membrane and the organ of Corti.

Oval window A membrane that transmits vibrations from the stirrup of the middle ear to the cochlea within the inner ear.

Cochlea The inner ear; the bony tube that contains the basilar membrane and the organ of Corti.

The stirrup is attached to another vibrating membrane, the **oval window.** The round window shown in Figure 4.34 pushes out when the oval window pushes in, and it is pulled in when the oval window vibrates outward, thus balancing the pressure in the inner ear.

The Inner Ear. The oval window transmits vibrations into the inner ear, the bony tube called the **cochlea** (from the Greek for "snail"). The cochlea, which has the shape of a snail shell, contains two longitudinal membranes that divide it into three fluid-filled chambers. One of the membranes that lies coiled within the cochlea is called the **basilar membrane.** Vibrations in the fluids within the chambers of the inner ear press against the basilar membrane.

The **organ of Corti,** sometimes referred to as the "command post" of hearing, is attached to the basilar membrane. Thousands of hair cells (receptor cells that project like hair from the organ of Corti) "dance" in response to the vibrations of the basilar membrane (Brownell, 1992). This up-and-down movement generates neural impulses that are transmitted to the brain via the 31,000 neurons that form the **auditory nerve** (Yost & Nielson, 1985). Within the brain, auditory input is projected onto the hearing areas of the temporal lobes of the cerebral cortex.

Locating Sounds

How do you balance the loudness of a stereo set? You sit between the speakers and adjust the volume until the sound seems to be equally loud in each ear. If the sound to the right is louder, the musical instruments will be perceived as being toward the right rather than straight ahead.

There is a resemblance between balancing a stereo set and locating sounds. A sound that is louder in the right ear is perceived as coming from the right. A sound from the right side also reaches the right ear first. Loudness and sequence of stimulating the ears both provide directional cues.

But it may not be easy to locate a sound that is directly in front, in back, or overhead. Such sounds are equally loud in and distant from each ear. So what do we do? Simple—usually we turn our heads slightly to determine in which ear the sound increases. If you turn your head a few degrees to the right and the loudness increases in your left ear, the sound must be in front of you. Of course we also use vision and general knowledge in locating the source of sounds. If you hear the roar of jet engines, most of the time you will make money by betting that the airplane is overhead.

Perception of Loudness and Pitch

We know that sounds are heard because they cause vibration in parts of the ear and information about these vibrations is transmitted to the brain. But what determines the loudness and pitch of our perceptions of these sounds?

The loudness and pitch of sounds appear to be related to the number of receptor neurons on the organ of Corti that fire and how often they fire. Psychologists generally agree that sounds are perceived as being louder when more of these sensory neurons fire. They are not so certain about the perception of pitch. Two of the theories that have been advanced to explain pitch discrimination are *place theory* and *frequency theory.*

Place Theory. According to **place theory,** the pitch of a sound is determined by the place along the basilar membrane that vibrates in response to it. In his classic research with guinea pigs and cadavers, von Békésy (1957) found that receptors at different sites along the membrane fire in response to tones of differing frequencies. By and large, the higher the pitch of a sound, the closer the responsive neurons lie to the oval window. However, the entire membrane appears to be responsive to tones that are low in frequency.

Frequency Theory. Place theory does not explain all the phenomena of hearing. For example, it has been found that impulses in the auditory nerve follow the pattern of the sound waves being detected. **Frequency theory** has been developed to account for such occurrences. In general, frequency theory proposes that pitch perception depends on the stimulation of neural impulses that match

Basilar membrane A membrane that lies coiled within the cochlea.

Organ of Corti The receptor for hearing that lies on the basilar membrane in the cochlea.

Auditory nerve The axon bundle that transmits neural impulses from the organ of Corti to the brain.

Place theory The theory that the pitch of a sound is determined by the section of the basilar membrane that vibrates in response to the sound.

Frequency theory The theory that the pitch of a sound is reflected in the frequency of the neural impulses that are generated in response to the sound.

the frequency of the sound waves. However, frequency theory breaks down for perception of pitches higher than 1,000 Hz because neural impulses are not able to follow the forms of the sound waves at those levels.

Duplicity theory advances the view that pitch perception depends both on the place and frequency of neural response. A more comprehensive theory of pitch perception will have to explain (1) why neurons at different sites on the basilar membrane fire in response to different pitches, (2) why impulses in the auditory nerve follow the patterns of sound waves at many frequencies, and (3) how we perceive pitches at above 1,000 Hz.

Unfortunately, not everyone perceives sound, and many of us do not perceive sounds of certain frequencies. Let us consider a number of kinds of hearing problems, or deafness.

Deafness. There are three major types of hearing problems or deafness, and each has a different source.

Conduction deafness occurs because of damage to the structures of the middle ear—either to the eardrum or to the three bones that conduct (and amplify) sound waves from the outer ear to the inner ear. People with conduction hearing loss have high absolute thresholds for detection of sounds at all frequencies. This is the type of hearing impairment frequently found among the elderly. People with conduction deafness often profit from hearing aids, which provide the amplification that the middle ear does not.

Sensory-neural deafness usually stems from damage to the structures of the inner ear, most often the loss of hair cells, which will not regenerate. Sensory-neural deafness can also stem from damage to the auditory nerve. In this form of deafness, people tend to be more sensitive to sounds of some pitches than others. Experimental cochlear implants, or "artificial ears," contain microphones that sense sounds and electronic equipment that transmits sounds past damaged hair cells to stimulate the auditory nerve directly. Multi-channel implants apply the place theory of pitch perception to enable hearing patients to discriminate sounds of high and low pitches. Such implants have helped many patients with sensory-neural deafness (Schmeck, 1988). However, they cannot assume the functions of damaged auditory nerves.

Can we really "make ourselves deaf" by listening to high-volume rock-and-roll concerts or tapes? Do construction workers really risk deafness when they fail to protect themselves from the sounds of pneumatic drills? Apparently these risks are very real and can account for the kind of deafness termed **stimulation deafness.** Stimulation deafness is caused by exposure to very loud sounds. As with sensory-neural deafness, some kinds of stimulation deafness, such as Hunter's notch, are limited to particular frequencies—in this case, the frequencies of the sound waves generated by a gun firing. Prolonged exposure to 85 dB can cause stimulation loss. People who attend high-volume rock concerts risk damaging their ears, as do workers who run pneumatic drills or drive high-volume transportation vehicles. The ringing sensation that may follow exposure to loud sounds probably means that hair cells have been damaged (McFadden & Wightman, 1983). If you find yourself suddenly exposed to loud sounds, remember that your fingertips serve as good emergency ear protectors.

SMELL

Smell and taste are the chemical senses. In the cases of vision and hearing, physical energy impacts on our sensory receptors. With smell and taste, we sample molecules of the substances being sensed.

You could say that we are underprivileged when it comes to the sense of smell. Dogs, for instance, devote about seven times as much area of the cerebral

Duplicity theory A combination of the place and frequency theories of pitch discrimination.

Conduction deafness The forms of deafness in which there is loss of conduction of sound through the middle ear.

Sensory-neural deafness The forms of deafness that result from damage to hair cells or the auditory nerve.

Stimulation deafness The forms of deafness that result from exposure to sounds that are excessively loud.

cortex to the sense of smell. Male dogs sniff to determine where the territories of other dogs leave off and to determine whether female dogs are sexually receptive. Dogs even make a living sniffing out marijuana in closed packages and suitcases.

Still, smell has an important role in human behavior. Smell makes a crucial contribution to the flavor of foods, for example (Brody, 1992). If you did not have a sense of smell, an onion and an apple would taste the same to you! People's senses of smell may be lacking when we compare them to those of a dog, but we can detect the odor of one one-millionth of a milligram of vanilla in a liter of air.

It is true that onions and apples have the same taste. Their *flavors* are very different, however.

Odor The characteristic of a substance that makes it perceptible to the sense of smell.

Olfactory Having to do with the sense of smell.

Olfactory nerve The nerve that transmits information concerning odors from olfactory receptors to the brain.

Anosmia Lack of sensitivity to a specific odor.

Taste cells Receptor cells that are sensitive to taste.

Taste buds The sensory organs for taste. They contain taste cells and are located on the tongue.

An **odor** is a sample of the actual substance being sensed. Odors are detected by sites on receptor neurons in the **olfactory** membrane high in each nostril. Receptor neurons fire when a few molecules of the substance in gaseous form come into contact with them. Firing transmits information about odors to the brain via the **olfactory nerve.** That is how the substance is smelled.

According to various theories, there are several basic odors: flowery, minty, musky, camphoraceous, ethereal, pungent, and putrid. Other odors can then be broken down into combinations of basic odors. According to one theory, we smell substances whose molecules fit the shapes of receptor sites (Amoore, 1970). This theory receives some support from the fact that we can develop an **anosmia,** or "smell blindness," for a particular odor—suggesting that one kind of receptor has been damaged or degenerated. However, we are not certain how many different types of receptors for odor there are. Too, each of our receptors seems to be responsive to two or more odorous substances.

The sense of smell tends to adapt rather rapidly to odors, even obnoxious ones. This might be fortunate if you are using a locker room or an outhouse. But it might not be so fortunate if you are being exposed to fumes from paints or other chemicals, since you may lose awareness of them even though they remain harmful. One odor may also be masked by another, which is how air fresheners work.

TASTE

Your cocker spaniel may jump at the chance to finish off your ice cream cone, but your Siamese cat may turn up her nose at this golden opportunity. Why? Dogs can perceive the taste quality of sweetness, as can pigs, but cats cannot (Dethier, 1978).

There are four primary taste qualities: sweet, sour, salty, and bitter. The *flavor* of a food involves its taste but is more complex. Apples and onions have the same taste—or the same mix of taste qualities—but their flavor differs vastly. (You wouldn't chomp into a nice cold onion on a warm day, would you?) The flavor of a food depends on its odor, texture, and temperature as well as its taste. If it were not for odor, heated tenderized shoe leather just might pass for your favorite steak.

Taste is sensed through **taste cells,** or receptor neurons that are located on **taste buds.** You have about 10,000 taste buds, most of which are located near the edges and back of your tongue. Taste buds tend to specialize (see Figure 4.35). Some, for example, are more responsive to sweetness, whereas others react to several tastes. Receptors for sweetness lie at the tip of the tongue, and receptors for bitterness lie toward the back of the tongue. Sourness is sensed along the

A Taste of . . . Well, Certainly Not Honey. The flavors of foods are determined not only by taste but also by their odor, texture, and temperature.

sides of the tongue, and saltiness overlaps the areas sensitive to sweetness and sourness (Figure 4.35). This is why people perceive a sour dish to "get them" at the sides of the tongue.

According to Bartoshuk, we live in "different taste worlds" (Sheraton, 1984). Some of us with a low sensitivity for the sweet taste may require twice the sugar to sweeten our food as others who are more sensitive to sweetness. Those of us who enjoy bitter foods may be taste-blind to them. Sensitivities to different tastes apparently have a strong genetic component.

By eating hot foods and scraping your tongue, you regularly kill off many taste cells. But you need not be alarmed at this inadvertent oral aggression. Taste cells are the rabbits of the sense receptors. They reproduce rapidly enough to completely renew themselves about once a week.

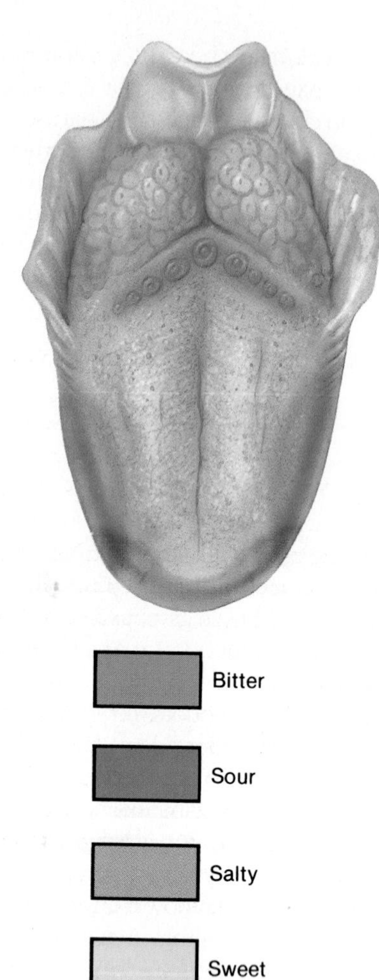

FIGURE 4.35
Location of Various Taste Buds on the Tongue. Taste buds on different areas of the tongue are sensitive to different primary taste qualities.

THE SKIN SENSES

Vision is usually the most dominant of the senses, but 6-month-old infants are sometimes so engrossed with the feel of objects that they may better remember changes in temperature than changes in color (Bushnell et al., 1985). Of course, on a hot, humid July day, we may all pay more attention to a cold breeze than to a change in the color of a neighbor's beach umbrella.

Changes in temperature are just one type of event we sense by means of nerve endings in the skin. We know that the skin discriminates among many kinds of sensations—touch, pressure, warmth, cold, and pain—but how it does so is not so clear. It now seems that we have distinct sensory receptors for pressure, temperature, and pain (Brown & Deffenbacher, 1979). It might also be that some nerve endings receive more than one type of sensory input.

Touch and Pressure

Sensory receptors located around the roots of hair cells appear to fire in response to touching the surface of the skin. You may have noticed that if you are trying to "get the feel of" a fabric or the texture of a friend's hair, you must move your hand over it (Loomis & Lederman, 1986). Otherwise, the sensations quickly fade. If you pass your hand over the skin and then hold it still, again sensations of touching will fade. This sort of "active touching" involves reception of information that concerns not only touch per se but also pressure, temperature, and feedback from the muscles that are involved in movements of our hands.

Other structures beneath the skin are apparently sensitive to pressure. All in all, there are about half a million receptors for touch and pressure spaced throughout the body. Different parts of the body are more sensitive to touch and pressure than others. Psychophysicists use methods such as the **two-point threshold** to assess sensitivity to pressure. This method determines the smallest distance by which two rods touching the skin must be separated before the (blindfolded) subject will report that there are two rods, not one. As revealed by this method, our fingertips, lips, noses, and cheeks are much more sensitive than our shoulders, thighs, and calves. That is, the rods can be closer together when they touch the lips than the shoulders and still be perceived as distinct. Differential sensitivity occurs for at least two reasons: First, nerve endings are more densely packed in the fingertips and face than in other locations. Second, a greater amount of sensory cortex is devoted to the perception of sensations in the fingertips and face.

Two-point threshold The least distance by which two rods touching the skin must be separated before the subject will report that there are two rods, not one, on 50 percent of occasions.

The sense of pressure, like the sense of touch, undergoes rather rapid adaptation. You may have undertaken several minutes of strategic movements to wind

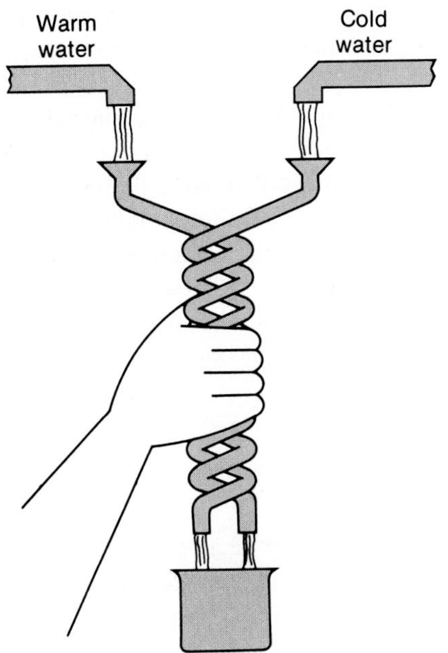

FIGURE 4.36
Paradoxical Hotness. The perception of hotness usually relies on the simultaneous firing of receptors for cold and pain. However, we also perceive hotness when receptors for warmth and coldness are stimulated simultaneously. Would you be able to hold on to the coils if you perceived intense heat, even if you knew that one coil was filled with warm water and the other with cold water?

up with your hand on the arm or leg of your date, only to discover that adaptation to this delightful source of pressure saps the sensation.

Temperature

The receptors for temperature are neurons just beneath the skin. When skin temperature increases, receptors for warmth fire. Decreases in skin temperature cause receptors for cold to fire.

Sensations of temperature are relative. When we are at normal body temperature, we might perceive another person's skin as being warm. When we are feverish, though, the other person's skin might seem cool to the touch. We also adapt to differences in temperature. When we walk out of an air-conditioned house into the desert sun, we at first feel intense heat. Then the sensations of heat tend to fade (although we still may be made terribly uncomfortable by high humidity). Similarly, when we first enter a swimming pool, the water may seem cool or cold because it is below body temperature. Yet after a few moments, an 80-degree-Fahrenheit pool may seem quite warm. In fact, we may chide the tentative newcomer for being overly sensitive.

Note that we have receptors that are sensitive to warmth and to coldness. Sensations of hotness, however, are *not* transmitted by rapid firing of warmth receptors, nor by firing of whole platoons of warmth receptors. Instead, in one of nature's unexpected twists, it turns out that so-called cold receptors fire not only when they are stimulated by objects below skin temperature but also when they are stimulated by objects above 45 degrees centigrade. Warmth receptors also fire in response to hot stimulation, so sensations of hotness rely on the simultaneous firing of receptors for cold and warmth. (In the case of actual burning, receptors for pain will also fire.)

A classic experiment showed that simultaneous firing of receptors for warmth and coldness are linked to sensations of hotness, regardless of the nature of the stimulus that is causing the cold receptors to fire. As shown in Figure 4.36, two coils were intertwined. Warm water was run through one of them and cold water through the other. Yet, people who grasped the coils simultaneously perceived heat so intense that they had to let go at once. Knowing that the heat was phony made no difference. Sensation was more convincing than knowledge. I'll bet my cash that you would let go of the coils on each trial, too.

Pain

Pain is a signal that something is wrong in the body. Pain is adaptive in the sense that it motivates us to do something about it. For some of us, however, chronic pain—pain that even lasts once injuries or illnesses have cleared up—saps our vitality and the pleasures of everyday life.

Pain originates at the point of contact, as with a stubbed toe (see Figure 4.37). The pain message to the brain is initiated by the release of various chemicals including prostaglandins, bradykinin (perhaps the most painful known substance), and the mysterious chemical called P (yes, *P* stands for "pain"). Prostaglandins not only facilitate transmission of the pain message to the brain, they also heighten circulation to the injured area, causing the redness and swelling we call inflammation. Inflammation attracts infection-fighting blood cells to the area to protect against invading bacteria. **Analgesic** drugs such as aspirin and ibuprofen (brand names such as Motrin, Medipren, Advil, and so on) work by inhibiting prostaglandin production.

Analgesic Giving rise to a state of not feeling pain though fully conscious.

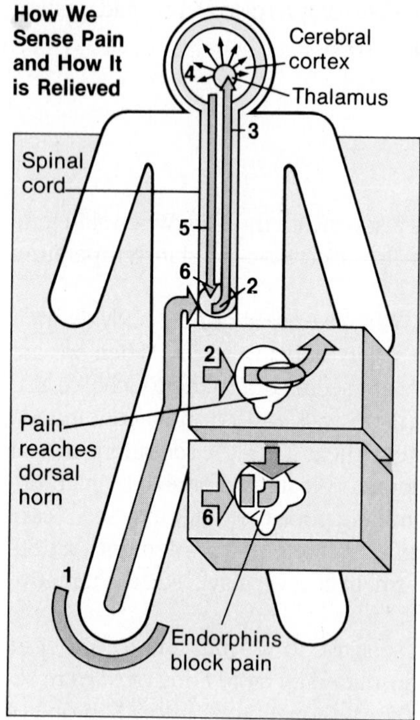

FIGURE 4.37
Perception of Pain. Pain originates at the point of contact, and the pain message to the brain is initiated by the release of prostaglandins, bradykinin, and substance *P*.

The pain message is relayed from the spinal cord to the thalamus and then projected to the cerebral cortex, where the location and intensity of the damage become apparent.

Gate Theory. Simple remedies like rubbing and scratching the injured toe frequently help. Why? One possible answer lies in the so-called gate theory of pain originated by Melzack (1980). From this perspective, only a limited amount of stimulation can be processed by the nervous system at a time. Rubbing or scratching the toe transmits sensations to the brain that, in a sense, compete for neurons. Numerous nerves are thus prevented from transmitting pain messages to the brain. The mechanism is analogous to shutting down a "gate" in the spinal cord. It is something like too many calls flooding a switchboard at once. Such flooding prevents any calls from getting through.

It is true that rubbing or scratching a sore toe can be an effective way of relieving pain. Rubbing or scratching may flood the gate with messages so that news of the pain does not get through.

Endorphins. In response to pain, the brain triggers the release of endorphins (see Chapter 3). Some people who have severe pain that cannot be relieved by available medical treatments have been found to have lower-than-normal concentrations of endorphins in their cerebrospinal fluid (Akil, 1978).

Acupuncture. Thousands of years ago, the Chinese began mapping the body to learn where pins might be placed to deaden pain elsewhere. Much of the Chinese practice of acupuncture was unknown in the West, even though Western powers occupied much of China during the 1800s. But early in the 1970s, *New York Times* columnist James Reston underwent an appendectomy in China, with acupuncture as the only anesthetic. He reported no discomfort.

Reston's evidence is anecdotal, of course. The question of whether or not acupuncture can be scientifically demonstrated to provide relief from pain has been controversial. For example, in 1975 the National Institutes of Health reported that acupuncture was no more effective than sugar pills, or **placebos.** Since then, however, a number of studies have suggested that acupuncture can relieve pain in humans, such as chronic back pain (Price et al., 1984). There is also experimental evidence that acupuncture reduces perception of pain in cats and mice (Levitt, 1981).

Some of the effects of acupuncture may be due to the release of endorphins (Kimble, 1988). There is supportive evidence. The drug *naloxone* is known to block the pain-killing effects of morphine. The analgesic effects of acupuncture are also blocked by naloxone. Therefore, it may well be that the analgesic effects of acupuncture can be linked to the morphinelike endorphins.

KINESTHESIS

Try a brief experiment. Close your eyes. Then touch your nose with your index finger. If you weren't right on target, I'm sure you came close. But how? You didn't see your hand moving, and you (probably) didn't hear your arm swishing through the air.

You were able to bring your finger to your nose through your kinesthetic sense. **Kinesthesis** derives from the Greek words for "motion" *(kinesis)* and "perception" *(aisthesis)*. When you "make a muscle" in your arm, the sensations of tightness and hardness are also provided by kinesthesis. Kinesthesis is the

Kinesthesis The sense that informs us about the positions and motion of parts of our bodies.

Vestibular sense The sense of equilibrium that informs us about our bodies' positions relative to gravity.

Semicircular canals Structures of the inner ear that monitor body movement and position.

Kinesthesis. This young acrobat at a Chinese academy receives information about the position and movement of the parts of his body through the sense of kinesthesis. Kinesthesis feeds sensory information to his brain from sensory organs in the joints, tendons, and muscles. He can follow his own movements intimately without visual self-observation.

sense that informs you about the position and motion of parts of your body. In kinesthesis, sensory information is fed back to the brain from sensory organs in the joints, tendons, and muscles.

Imagine going for a walk without kinesthesis. You would have to watch the forward motion of each leg to be certain that you had raised it high enough to clear the curb. And if you had tried our brief experiment without the kinesthetic sense, you would have had no sensory feedback until you felt the pressure of your finger against your nose (or cheek, or eye, or forehead), and you probably would have missed dozens of times.

Are you in the mood for another experiment? Close your eyes, again. Then "make a muscle" in your right arm. Could you sense the muscle without looking at it or feeling it with your left hand? Of course you could. Kinesthesis also provides information about muscle contractions.

THE VESTIBULAR SENSE

Your **vestibular sense** tells you whether you are upright—physically, not morally. Sensory organs located in the **semicircular canals** (Figure 4.34) and elsewhere in the ears monitor your body's motion and position in relation to gravity. They tell you whether you are falling and provide cues to whether your body is changing speeds such as when you are in an accelerating airplane or automobile.

We do have a sense that keeps us upright—physically upright, that is. It is the vestibular sense.

STUDY GUIDE

EXERCISE Parts of the Eye

Below is a drawing of the human eye. Can you label its parts and explain the function of each part? Check your answers against Figure 4.2.

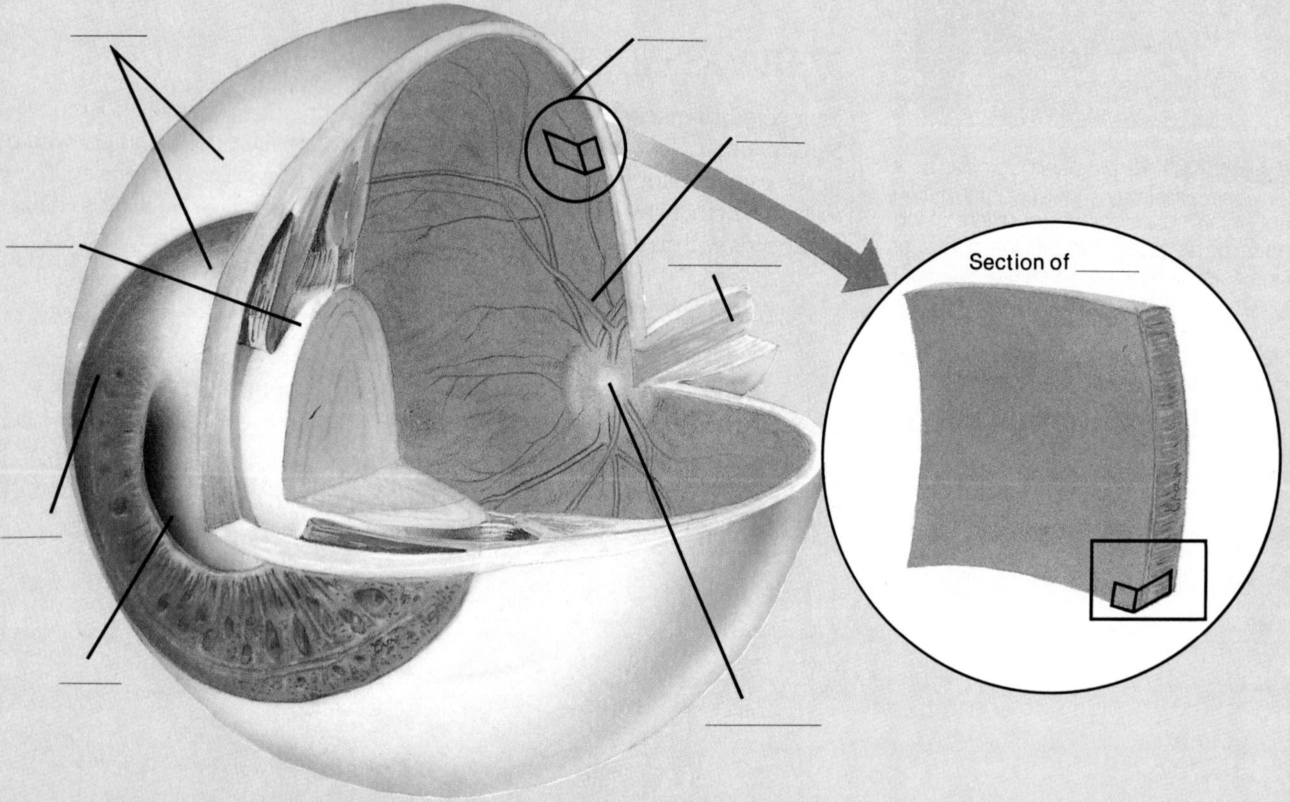

EXERCISE Parts of the Ear

Below is a drawing of the human ear. Can you label its parts and explain the function of each part? Check your answers against Figure 4.34.

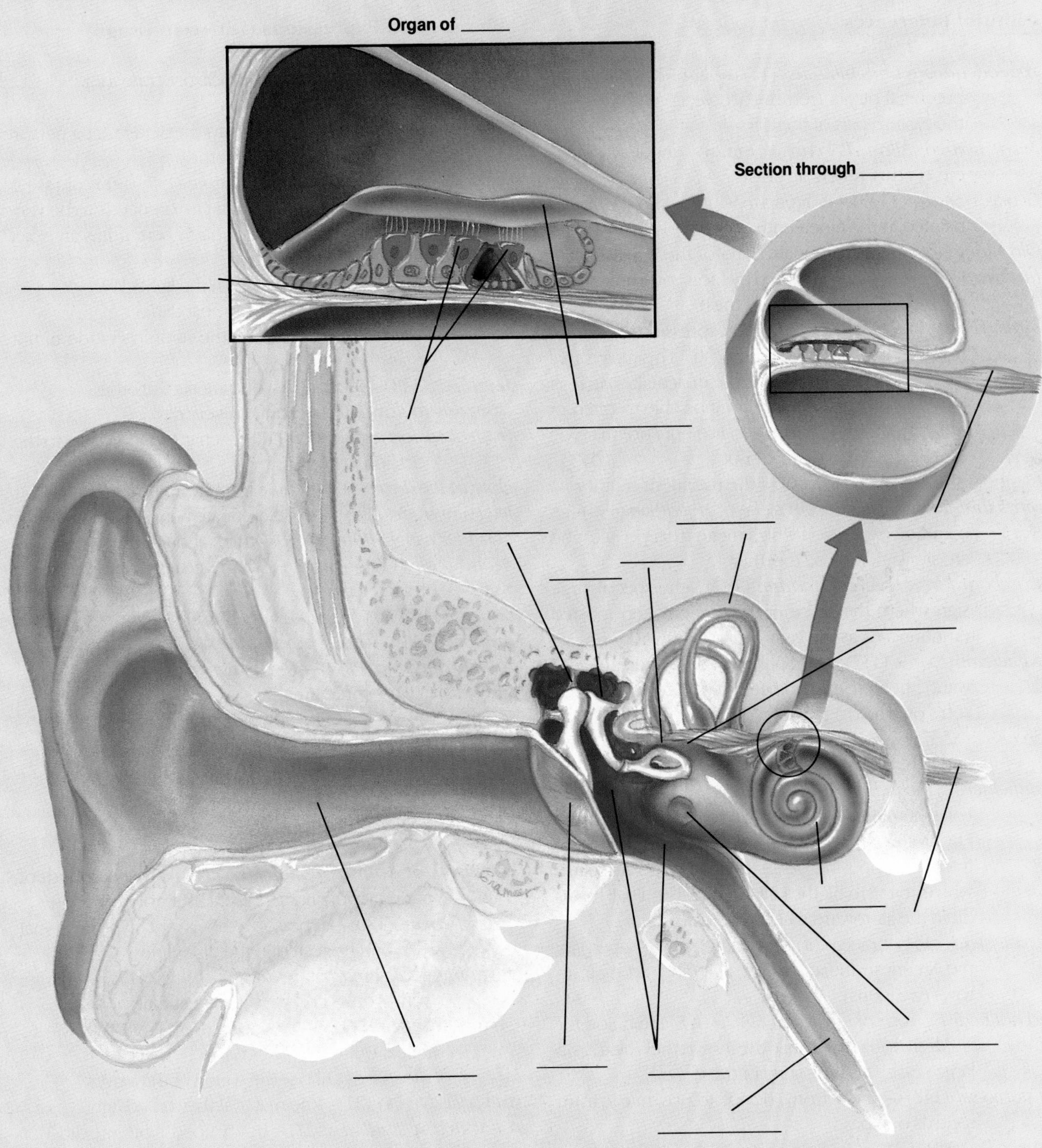

ESL—BRIDGING THE GAP

This part is divided into

1. cultural references,
2. phrases and expressions in which words are used differently from their regular meaning, or are used as metaphors.

Cultural References

rhododendron and hibiscus (127)—large bright-colored perennial plants (return each year) which grow in the eastern part of the U.S.

Mark Rothko, Allan d'Arcangelo, (128)—modern twentieth-century American artists

Georges Seurat (129)—a French painter who lived and painted in the nineteenth century

Old Glory (130)—an affectionate term for the U.S. flag

junkyard (132)—a space provided by local governments for disposing of large pieces of trash

birds in the bush (132)—part of the expression, "A bird in the hand is worth two in the bush." This means that it is better to take what you can actually catch or have rather than hope you will be able to catch or obtain something which you are not sure that you can obtain, and you might not.

Escher (133)—a European artist of the twentieth century

Birds that flock together seem to be of a feather (135)—A common expression which means that people who are similar like to be together

scoreboard in a baseball stadium (137)—the special large sign where the score of the game is kept posted (announced) as the game progresses

hometeam scores (137)—a popular event because people want "their" team (hometeam, the team in a person's own town) to win

fireworks (137)—explosives that are ignited for the noise and light that they produce

outfielder ... fly ball (137)—"outfield" is the place in baseball where the "outfielder" is positioned, or placed. He or she is farthest away (the greatest distance) from the opposing player (on the opposite team) who is trying to hit the ball. A "fly ball" is a ball that is hit in the air toward where the outfielder is.

arrowheads (141)—pieces of stone carved (cut, shaped) by the American Indians to use as points on their arrows (weapons).

do not hear the roar of the ocean (145)—it is a tradition for children to be told that the noise they hear in a large seashell is the sound of the ocean

a stereo set (147)—an electronic device to play music from records or tapes

James Reston (152)—a famous writer and an editor of the *New York Times*

Phrases and Expressions (Different Usage)

foot-long doll (117)—a doll that measures one foot

full-grown person (117)—an adult

ticket of admission (117)—refers to the ticket that a person needs to be admitted to a theater

literally ..., watch every step you take (117)—this phrase is often used to mean that a person needs to be very careful about everything (life); here it has an exact meaning

dim the lights (118)—gradually turn the lights low

near darkness (118)—until it is almost dark

randomized (118)—the order of the stimuli is random; not organized

it bridges (118)—it connects; one affects the other

from day to day (118)—changes every day

from occasion to occasion (118)—changes according to the occasion

glow in the dark (118)—shine brightly in the dark

tell them apart (118)—to differentiate between them

consider weight lifting (119)—think about lifting weights

round it off (119)—change it to the nearest whole number (not a fraction)

barbell (119)—a type of weight for exercising

dumbbell (119)—see "barbell"

readily apparent (119)—very noticeable

threefold (119)—three times

so far (120)—from the beginning of the chapter until now

background noise (120)—noise that is present but which is not the noise that we are paying attention to

advanced years (120)—old age

abuzz with signals (120)—a lot of background noise

hanging in the air (120)—noticeable

backdrop of your consciousness (120)—background of your consciousness; present, but not noticeable

a lay person (120)—a person who is not a professional artist, but interested in the discipline

only thing that remains constant is change (121)—change always occurs and we can expect that

On the other hand (121)—however, there is another way to think about it

lapping of the waves (121)—the sound of the waves

stuff called light (121)—the material they called light

a backward student (121)—not a good student; did not study

a lasting impression (121)—a permanent impression or condition

a camera buff (124)—a person who enjoys photography and knows a lot about cameras
a featureless blaze (126)—it is impossible to distinguish objects because the sun is so bright
the brighter the color, the lighter it is (127)—as the color gets brighter, the color also gets lighter
in contrast (127)—the opposite occurs
But wait! You say. (127)—But that does not seem (appear) right to me.
True enough (127)—This is true
is working properly (130)—is operating correctly
miscolored flag (130)—the flag has the wrong colors; ("mis" is a negative prefix)
the families intermarry (130)—the colors that are related mix with other colors
partly overlapped (131)—a piece of the color was over a piece of another color
theoretical updates (131)—recent research has changed the theory
shards of information (132)—pieces of information; amounts of information
meaningful whole (132)—a complete concept which has meaning
as the saying goes (132)—as we know the expression to be
in other words (133)—another way to say this is the following
jumpy (137)—not smooth
rapidly wrap around a building (137)—move fast around a building
stop and go traffic (137)—many cars on a busy street that has many stop lights and other reasons for cars to stop frequently
perceptions are mocked (138)—our perceptions are deceived
roadside markets (139)—markets by the side of the road, on the edge of the road
a cross-eyed look (140)—when the eyes both look toward the nose at the same time
confusion would reign (140)—there would be great confusion
As we neared it (140)—As we became closer to it
wend their way (140)—move slowly toward
fiercely difficult (140)—extremely difficult
stand ready to (140)—be ready to argue
seen from above (141)—when you look down on the top of it
to play tricks on (141)—to joke; we are victims of what our eyes see
lifelong (142)—all of life, to the end
take some bets from friends (142)—say to some friends, "You give me ten dollars (or any amount) if I am wrong when I say that the three cylinders are equal."
advertising slogan (143)—an expression which helps to advertise
in so doing (143)—when it does this
cycles per second (143)—a cycle is a period of time or space in which one round of events is completed. The event is one which occurs regularly
lull us to sleep (145)—make us sleepy and gradually cause us to go to sleep
in this way (145)—this is how it occurs
when it comes to the sense of smell (148)—when we think about our sense of smell
golden opportunity (149)—wonderful opportunity
taste cells are the rabbits of the sense receptors (150)—rabbits have a reputation of reproducing often
nerve endings (150)—the ends of nerves
per se (150)—by itself; that and no other
all in all (150)—when we consider all of them
spaced throughout (150)—in different places all through the body
whole platoons (151)—a great many groups
unexpected twists (151)—not what we expect; not logical
in the mood (153)—do you want to

CHAPTER REVIEW

Objective 1: Define *sensation* and *perception.*

Sensation refers to mechanical processes that involve the stimulation of (1) s________________ receptors (neurons) and the transmission of sensory information to the (2) c________________ nervous system. Perception is not mechanical. (3) P________________ is the active organization of sensations into a representation of the world. (4) P________________ reflects learning and expectations, as well as sensations.

SECTION 1: Basic Concepts in Sensation and Perception

Objective 2: Define *psychophysics,* and explain the contribution of Ernst Weber.

Objective 3: Define *absolute* and *difference thresholds.*

The (5) ________________ threshold for a stimulus, such as light, is the lowest intensity at which it can be detected. A person's absolute threshold for light is the lowest (6) ________________ty of light that he or she can see 50 percent of the time, according to the method of (7) ____________nt stimuli. The minimum difference in intensity that can be discriminated is the (8) ____________ threshold. Difference thresholds are expressed in fractions called (9) ____________'s constants. Weber's constant for light is 1/60th.

Objective 4: Discuss signal-detection theory.

According to (10) ____________al-detection theory, several factors determine whether a person will perceive a stimulus. The detection of a signal is determined by the sensory stimuli themselves, the biological (11) s____________ system of the person, and (12) psy____________ factors, such as motivation and attention.

Objective 5: Discuss sensory adaptation.

Sensory (13) ____________tion refers to the processes by which we become more sensitive to stimuli of low magnitude and less sensitive to stimuli relatively constant in magnitude. The process of becoming more sensitive to stimulation is referred to as (14) ____________tion, or positive adaptation. The process of becoming less sensitive to stimulation is referred to as (15) de____________, or (16) ____________tive adaptation.

SECTION 2: Vision

(17) V____________ is our dominant sense.

Objective 6: Explain the electromagnetic nature of light.

Visible light triggers visual (18) ____________s. Visible light is one part of a spectrum of (19) ____________netic energy. Electromagnetic energy is described in terms of (20) ____________s. The wavelength of visible light determines its color, or (21) h____________.

Objective 7: Describe the functions of the parts of the eye.

The eye senses and transmits visual stimulation to the (22) ____________tal lobe of the (23) ce____________ cortex. Light enters the eye through the transparent (24) c____________. The amount of light allowed in is determined by the size of the opening of the muscle called the (25) ____________s. The opening in the iris is called the (26) p____________. Once past the iris, light passes through the (27) ____________s, which accommodates to the image by changing its thickness. Accommodation of the lens focuses light so that a clear image is projected onto the (28) r____________. The retina is composed of (29) photo____________ called rods and (30) ____________s. The rods and cones send neural messages through the (31) ____________ar cells to ganglion cells. The axons of the ganglion cells constitute the (32) ____________ic nerve, which conducts the sensory input to the brain.

The (33) ____________a is the most sensitive part of the retina. The blind spot is the part of the retina where the axons of (34) ____________n cells congregate to form the optic nerve.

Objective 8: Describe the functions of rods and cones.

The fovea is populated almost exclusively by (35) ____________s, which permit perception of color. Rods are spaced most densely near the (36) ____________s, and they transmit sensations of light and (37) d____________ only. Rods are more (38) s____________ than cones to light. Rods continue to (39) a____________ to darkness once cones have reached peak adaptation.

SECTION 3: Color Vision

Objective 9: Define the color concepts of *hue, brightness,* and *saturation.*

White light or sunlight can be broken down into the colors of the visible (40) ____________m by using a triangular glass solid called a (41) ____________m. The wavelength of light determines its color or (42) h____________. The brightness of a color is its degree of lightness or (43) ____________ness. Brighter colors are (44: lighter or darker?). The saturation of a color is its (45) ____________ness. Pure hues have the greatest intensity or (46) b____________.

Objective 10: Define *warm* and *cool* colors.

Yellows, oranges, and reds are considered (47) w____________ colors. Blues and (48) ____________s are considered cool. In works of art, (49) ____________ colors seem to advance toward the viewer. (50) C____________ colors seem to recede.

Objective 11: Define *complementary colors* and *analogous colors.*

Colors across from one another on the color (51) w________________ are termed complementary. (52) Red-________________ and blue-yellow are the major complementary pairs. The mixture of lights is an (53) ________________tive process. When we mix lights of complementary colors, they dissolve into (54) ________________. In works of art, complementary colors clash when they are placed next to one another, and there seem to be (55) ________________tions where they meet. The (56) ________________image of a color is its complement.

The primary colors of red, blue, and (57) ________________ cannot be produced by mixing pigments of other hues. Secondary and (58) ________________ary colors are produced by mixing other colors. (59) A________________ colors lie next to one another on the color wheel. The color combinations of works of art using analogous colors are (60) ________________ious.

Objective 12: Explain the trichromatic and opponent-process theories of color vision.

According to the (61) ________________ theory of color vision, there are three types of cones. Some cones are sensitive to red, some to blue, and some to (62) ________________ light. Opponent-process theory proposes three types of color receptors: red-green, (63) ________________, and (64) ________________. (65) ________________-________________ theory better accounts for afterimages; however, both theories seem to have some validity.

People with normal color vision are called (66) ________________mats. Color-blind people who can see light and dark only are called (67) ________________mats. Dichromats are more common, and they can discriminate only two colors: red and (68) ________________, or blue and (69) ________________. Partial color blindness is a sex-linked trait that strikes mostly (70: males or females?).

SECTION 4: Visual Perception

Objective 13: Explain Gestalt rules of perceptual organization.

Gestalt rules of (71) ________________ ________________tion influence our grouping of bits of sensory stimulation into meaningful wholes. Rules of perceptual organization concern (72) ________________-ground relationships, proximity, similarity, continuity, common fate, and closure. Our perceptions seem to be unstable when figure-ground relationships are (73) ________________ous. The Rubin (74) ________________ and the Necker (75) ________________ are examples of ambiguous figures.

Objective 14: Describe perception of movement.

We perceive actual movement by sensing (76) m________________ across the retina, and by sensing change of (77) p________________ of an object in relation to other objects. The (78) ________________tic effect is the tendency to perceive a point of light in a darkened room as moving. (79) ________________opic motion, used in films, is the perception of a rapidly presented series of still pictures as moving.

Objective 15: Describe monocular and binocular cues for depth.

Depth perception involves monocular and (80) ________________lar cues. Monocular cues include perspective, in which we tend to perceive (81) p________________ lines as converging as they recede from us; clearness—(82: nearby or distant)? objects are perceived as clearer; interposition, shadowing, texture gradient, motion (83) p________________, and accommodation. According to motion parallax, distant objects appear to move more (84: rapidly or slowly?) than nearby objects. Binocular cues include retinal (85) ________________ and convergence of the eyes. Closer objects have (86: greater or lesser?) retinal disparity and require (87: greater or lesser?) convergence.

Objective 16: Explain size, color, brightness, and shape constancy and show how they give rise to visual illusions.

Through experience we develop a number of perceptual constancies. For example, we learn to assume that objects retain their size, (88) s________________, (89) b________________, and (90) c________________ despite their distance, their position, or changes in lighting conditions. In the case of size constancy, we tend to perceive an object as remaining the same size, although the size of the image on the (91) r________________ varies as a function of the object's (92) d________________ from the viewer.

Visual illusions use (93) p________________ cues as well as twists on rules for organization to deceive the eye. The effects of the Müller-Lyer and Ponzo illusions can probably be explained by using the principle of (94) ________________ constancy.

SECTION 5: Hearing

Objective 17: Explain the transmission and structure of sound waves.

(95) A________________ stimulation, or sound waves, require a medium such as air or water for transmission. Sound waves alternately (96) ________________ress and expand molecules of the medium, creating (97) ________________s.

The human ear can hear sounds varying in frequency from 20 to (98) ________________ cycles per second. The greater the frequency of the sound (99) ________________s, the higher the (100) p________________ of a sound.

The loudness of a sound is measured in (101) ________________els, which are abbreviated *dB*. We can suffer hearing loss if exposed to protracted sounds of (102) ________________ dB or more. In addition to producing specified notes, instruments may produce tones that are greater in frequency and referred to as (103) ________________s. Such overtones contribute to the richness or (104) t________________ of a sound. A combination of (105) ________________nt sounds is referred to as noise.

Objective 18: Describe the functions of the parts of the ear.

The ear consists of an outer, (106) m________________, and (107) ________________ ear. A thin membrane in the outer ear, called the (108) ________________, vibrates in response to sound waves, and transmits them to the middle and (109) ________________ ears. The middle ear contains the three bones, the "hammer," (110) ________________, and (111) ________________, which also vibrate and transmit sound waves to another membrane called the (112) ________________ window. The oval window then transmits sound waves to the bony tube of the inner ear called the (113) ________________a. Within the cochlea are fluids that vibrate against the (114) b________________ membrane. The "command post of hearing," or organ of (115) C________________, is attached to the basilar membrane. Sound waves travel from the organ of Corti to the brain by the (116) ________________ry nerve. Sounds are perceived as louder when more of the sensory neurons on the organ of (117) ________________ fire.

Objective 19: Explain theories of pitch perception.

Two of the major theories that have been advanced to account for the perception of pitch are place theory and (118) ________________ theory. According to place theory, the pitch of a sound is determined by the segment of the (119) ________________ ________________ne that vibrates in response to it. According to frequency theory, the frequency with which sensory neurons fire corresponds to the (120) ________________ of the sound. So-called (121) ________________ity theory advances the view that pitch perception depends both on the place and frequency of neural response.

Objective 20: Describe three kinds of deafness.

(122) ________________tion deafness occurs because of damage to the structures of the middle ear that conduct and amplify sound waves from the outer ear to the inner ear. (123) Sensory-________________ deafness stems from damage to the structures of the inner ear or to the auditory nerve. (124) ________________tion deafness stems from exposure to very loud sounds.

SECTION 6: Smell

Objective 21: Explain how we sense odors.

An odor is a sample of a number of (125) ________________ules of the substance being smelled. Odors are detected by the (126) ________________ membrane in each nostril. The sense of smell adapts rapidly to odors, even unpleasant ones.

SECTION 7: Taste

Objective 22: Explain how we sense tastes.

There are four primary taste qualities: sweet, sour, (127) ________________, and (128) ________________. Flavor involves not only the taste of food, but also its (129)

_______________, texture, and temperature. The receptor neurons for taste are called (130) _______________ cells. Taste cells are located in (131) _______________ _______________s on the tongue.

The "taste loss" found among the elderly is probably due to a decline in the sense of (132) _______________.

SECTION 8: The Skin Senses

Objective 23: List the skin senses and explain how we perceive hotness and pain.

There are five skin senses: touch, pressure, warmth, (133) _______________, and (134) _______________.

The (135) _______________-_______________nt threshold method allows psychophysicists to assess sensitivity to pressure by determining the distance by which two rods touching the skin must be separated before the subject will report that there are two rods, not one. Sensations of (136) _______________ture are relative; when we are feverish, another person's skin may seem cool to the touch. The perception of hotness relies on the simultaneous firing of receptors for cold and (137) _______________.

Pain originates at the point of contact and is transmitted to the brain by various chemicals, including prostaglandins, (138) br_______________, and substance *P.* According to (139) _______________ theory, rubbing and scratching painful areas may reduce pain by sending competing messages to the brain. Naturally occurring (140) _______________ins also help relieve pain.

SECTION 9: Kinesthesis

Objective 24: Describe kinesthesis.

Kinesthesis is the sensing of bodily (141) p_______________ and movement. Kinesthesis relies on sensory organs in the joints, (142) t_______________, and (143) _______________s.

SECTION 10: The Vestibular Sense

Objective 25: Describe the vestibular sense.

The vestibular sense informs us as to whether we are in an (144) _______________ position or changing speeds. The vestibular sense is housed primarily in the (145) s_______________ _______________ of the ears.

Answers to Chapter Review

1. Sensory
2. Central
3. Perception
4. Perception
5. Absolute
6. Intensity
7. Constant
8. Difference
9. Weber's
10. Signal
11. Sensory
12. Psychological
13. Adaptation
14. Sensitization
15. Desensitization
16. Negative
17. Vision
18. Sensations
19. Electromagnetic
20. Wavelengths
21. Hue
22. Occipital
23. Cerebral
24. Cornea
25. Iris
26. Pupil
27. Lens
28. Retina
29. Photoreceptors
30. Cones
31. Bipolar
32. Optic
33. Fovea
34. Ganglion
35. Cones
36. Lens
37. Dark
38. Sensitive
39. Adapt
40. Spectrum
41. Prism
42. Hue
43. Darkness
44. Lighter
45. Pureness
46. Brightness
47. Warm
48. Greens
49. Warm
50. Cool
51. Wheel
52. Green
53. Additive
54. Gray
55. Vibrations
56. Afterimage
57. Yellow
58. Tertiary
59. Analogous
60. Harmonious
61. Trichromatic
62. Green
63. Blue-yellow (or light-dark)
64. Light-dark (or blue-yellow)
65. Opponent-process
66. Trichromats
67. Monochromats
68. Green
69. Yellow
70. Males
71. Perceptual organization
72. Figure
73. Ambiguous
74. Vase
75. Cube
76. Movement
77. Position
78. Autokinetic
79. Stroboscopic
80. Binocular
81. Parallel
82. Nearby
83. Parallax
84. Slowly
85. Disparity
86. Greater
87. Greater
88. Shape
89. Brightness
90. Color
91. Retina
92. Distance
93. Perceptual
94. Size
95. Auditory
96. Compress
97. Vibrations
98. 20,000

99. Waves
100. Pitch
101. Decibels
102. 85–90
103. Overtones
104. Timbre
105. Dissonant
106. Middle
107. Inner
108. Eardrum
109. Inner
110. Anvil (or stirrup)
111. Stirrup (or anvil)
112. Oval
113. Cochlea
114. Basilar
115. Corti
116. Auditory
117. Corti
118. Frequency
119. Basilar membrane
120. Frequency
121. Duplicity
122. Conduction
123. Sensory-neural
124. Stimulation
125. Molecules
126. Olfactory
127. Salty (or bitter)
128. Bitter (or salty)
129. Odor (or aroma, etc.)
130. Taste
131. Taste buds
132. Smell
133. Cold (or pain)
134. Pain (or cold)
135. Two-point
136. Temperature
137. Warmth
138. Bradykinin
139. Gate
140. Endorphins
141. Position
142. Tendons
143. Muscles
144. Upright
145. Semicircular canals

POSTTEST

1. Of the following, _______ have the shortest wavelengths of the spectrum of electromagnetic energy.
(a) cosmic rays
(b) X-rays
(c) sound waves
(d) visible colors

2. Weber's constant for the pitch of a tone is closest to
(a) 1/7th.
(b) 1/53rd.
(c) 1/333rd.
(d) 1/20,000th.

3. You look at a lamp ten feet away and it is clearly in focus. As you walk toward it, the lamp remains in focus. The lamp remains in focus because the _______ of your eyes are accommodating to the image of the lamp by changing their thickness.
(a) corneas
(b) irises
(c) lenses
(d) pupils

4. The cones reach their maximum adaptation to darkness in about _______ minutes.
(a) 5
(b) 10
(c) 30
(d) 45

5. Colors across from one another on the color wheel are labeled
(a) primary.
(b) afterimage.
(c) analogous.
(d) complementary.

6. _______ suggested that the eye must have three different types of cones, some sensitive to red, some to green, and some to blue.
(a) Thomas Young
(b) Sir Isaac Newton
(c) Hermann von Helmholtz
(d) Ewald Hering

7. The Rubin vase is used by psychologists to demonstrate rules of
(a) perceptual organization.
(b) perceptual constancy.
(c) depth perception.
(d) visual illusions.

8. You attend a motion picture, and it seems to you as if the people and objects being projected onto the screen are moving. Actually, your impression that the people and objects are moving is made possible by
(a) the phi phenomenon.
(b) stroboscopic motion.
(c) the autokinetic effect.
(d) motion parallax.

9. When we are driving along a dark road at night, the Moon may appear to move along with us. This is an example of
(a) the autokinetic effect.
(b) perspective.
(c) motion parallax.
(d) the phi phenomenon.

10. The unit for expressing the loudness of a sound is named after
(a) Bell.
(b) Hertz.
(c) Helmholtz.
(d) Newton.

11. A combination of dissonant sounds is referred to as
(a) timbre.
(b) overtones.
(c) noise.
(d) white noise.

12. Hairlike receptor cells on the organ of Corti bend in response to vibrations of the
(a) eardrum.
(b) oval window.
(c) stirrup.
(d) basilar membrane.

13. Within the ears are found organs for
    (a) vision.
    (b) kinesthesis.
    (c) the vestibular sense.
    (d) extrasensory perception.

14. Duplicity theory advances the view that
    (a) people cannot perceive pitches at above 1,000 Hz.
    (b) neurons at different sites on the basilar membrane fire in response to different pitches.
    (c) impulses in the auditory nerve follow the patterns of sound waves at many frequencies.
    (d) pitch perception depends both on the place and frequency of neural response.

15. We have about ________ taste buds.
    (a) 10
    (b) 100
    (c) 10,000
    (d) 10,000,000

16. ________ is sensed along the sides of the tongue.
    (a) Sweetness
    (b) Bitterness
    (c) Saltiness
    (d) Sourness

17. Sensory receptors located ________ appear to fire in response to touching the surface of the skin.
    (a) on the surface of the skin
    (b) around the roots of hair cells
    (c) at the tips of hair cells
    (d) in tendons, joints, and muscle

18. All of the following are involved in the perception of pain with the *exception* of
    (a) prostaglandins.
    (b) bradykinin.
    (c) amacrine cells.
    (d) *P.*

19. The view that pain messages may not get through to the brain when the "switchboard" that transmits pain messages becomes "flooded" is termed
    (a) gate theory.
    (b) opponent-process theory.
    (c) volley principle.
    (d) acupuncture.

20. Organs in the ________ alert you as to whether your body is changing speeds.
    (a) joints
    (b) tendons
    (c) ears
    (d) olfactory membrane

Answers To Posttest

1. A
2. C
3. C
4. B
5. D
6. C
7. A
8. B
9. C
10. A
11. C
12. D
13. C
14. D
15. C
16. D
17. B
18. C
19. A
20. C

- ☐ People who sleep nine hours or more a night tend to be lazy and happy-go-lucky.
- ☐ We tend to act out our forbidden fantasies in our dreams.
- ☐ Many people have insomnia because they try too hard to get to sleep at night.
- ☐ It is dangerous to awaken a sleepwalker.
- ☐ Alcohol goes to women's heads more quickly than to men's.
- ☐ Some people drink because alcohol provides them with an excuse for failure.
- ☐ Heroin was once used as a cure for addiction to morphine.
- ☐ Coca-Cola once "added life" through a powerful but now illegal stimulant.
- ☐ Cigarette smokers tend to smoke more when they are under stress.
- ☐ People have managed to bring high blood pressure under control through meditation.
- ☐ You can learn to increase or decrease your heart rate just by thinking about it.
- ☐ People who are easily hypnotized have positive attitudes toward hypnosis.

States of Consciousness

Learning Objectives

When you have finished studying Chapter 5, you should be able to:

The $64,000 Question: What *Is* Consciousness?

1. Discuss the controversy concerning the inclusion of consciousness as a topic in the science of psychology.
2. Define *consciousness* as sensory awareness, the selective aspect of attention, direct inner awareness, personal unity, and the waking state.

Altering Consciousness Through Sleep and Dreams

3. List the four stages of NREM sleep, and discuss the features of each.
4. Describe REM sleep, and explain why it is also referred to as paradoxical sleep.
5. Summarize research concerning the functions of sleep, focusing on the effects of sleep deprivation, and on long versus short sleepers.
6. Discuss dreams, including theories of dream content.

Altering Consciousness Through Drugs

7. Define *substance abuse* and *substance dependence*.

Altering Consciousness Through Depressants

8. Summarize research concerning the effects of alcohol.
9. Discuss the effects of opiates and opioids, and explain how methadone is used to treat heroin dependence.
10. Discuss the effects of barbiturates and methaqualone.

Altering Consciousness Through Stimulants

11. Discuss the effects of amphetamines.
12. Discuss the effects of cocaine.
13. Discuss the effects of the ingredients in cigarette smoke, and explain how stress influences the desire for smokers to increase their usage of cigarettes.

Altering Consciousness Through Hallucinogenics

14. Discuss the effects of marijuana.
15. Discuss the effects of LSD, and summarize research concerning the flashback controversy.

Altering Consciousness Through Meditation: When Eastern Gods Meets Western Technology

16. Summarize research concerning the effects of meditation.

Altering Consciousness Through Biofeedback: Getting in Touch with the Untouchable

17. Summarize research concerning the effects of biofeedback.

Altering Consciousness Through Hypnosis

18. Describe the history of hypnosis.
19. Discuss the changes in consciousness that can be brought about by means of hypnosis.
20. Explain the role and neodissociation theories of hypnosis.

In 1904, William James wrote an intriguing article entitled "Does Consciousness Exist?" Think about that. *Does consciousness exist?* Do *you* have consciousness? Are *you* conscious or aware of yourself? Of the world around you? Would you bear witness to being conscious of, or experiencing, thoughts and feelings? I would bet that you would. So, to be sure, would William James. But James did not think that consciousness was a proper area of study for psychologists, because no scientific method could be devised to directly observe or measure another person's consciousness.

John Watson, the "father of modern behaviorism," also insisted that only observable, measurable behavior was the proper province of psychology. In "Psychology as the Behaviorist Views It," published in 1913, Watson declared, "The time seems to have come when psychology must discard all references to consciousness" (p. 163). The following year, Watson was elected president of the American Psychological Association, which further cemented these ideas in the minds of many psychologists.

THE $64,000 QUESTION: WHAT *IS* CONSCIOUSNESS?

Despite such objections, and despite the problems involved in defining (much less measuring) consciousness, we will attempt to explore the meanings and varieties of this intriguing concept. Many psychologists, especially cognitive psychologists, believe that we cannot meaningfully discuss human behavior without referring to consciousness.

The Meanings of Consciousness

The word *consciousness* has several meanings. Let's have a look at a few of them.

Consciousness as Sensory Awareness. One meaning of consciousness is **sensory awareness** of the environment. The sense of vision permits us to be conscious of, or to see, the sun gleaming in the snow on the rooftops. The sense of hearing allows us to be conscious of, or to hear, a concert.

Consciousness as the Selective Aspect of Attention. We are not always aware of sensory stimulation, however. We can be unaware, or unconscious of, sensory stimulation when we do not pay attention to it (Greenwald, 1992). The world is abuzz with signals, yet you are conscious of, or focusing on, the words on this page (I hope).

The focusing of one's consciousness on a particular stimulus is referred to as **selective attention.** Since the world is abuzz with myriad stimuli, the concept of

Sensory awareness Knowledge of the environment through perception of sensory stimulation—one definition of consciousness.

Selective attention The focus of one's consciousness on a particular stimulus.

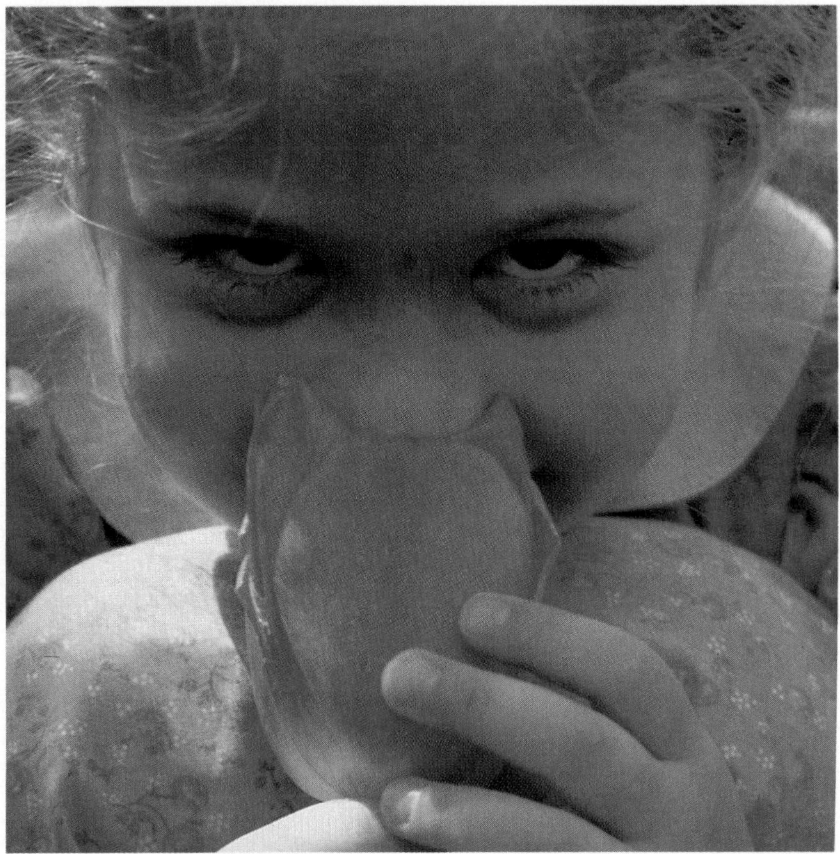

Sensory Awareness. One of the definitions of consciousness is sensory awareness of the world around us.

selective attention is important in psychology, and, indeed, to self-regulation. In order to pay attention in class, you must screen out the pleasant aroma of the cologne or perfume from the person in the next seat. In order to keep your car on the road, you must pay more attention to driving conditions than to your hunger pangs or your feelings about an argument with your family. If you are out in the woods at night, attending to rustling in the brush may be crucial to your very survival.

Part of our adaptation to our environments involves learning which stimuli must be attended to and which can be safely ignored. Selective attention markedly enhances our perceptual abilities (Johnston & Dark, 1986; Moran & Desimone, 1985), to the point where we can pick out the speech of a single person across a room at a cocktail party. (This phenomenon has been suitably labeled the *cocktail party effect.*)

Although we to a large extent determine where and when we shall focus our attention, various kinds of stimuli also tend to capture attention. Such stimuli include:

- Sudden changes, as when a cool breeze enters a sweltering room, or we receive a particularly high or low grade on a returned exam
- Novel stimuli, as when a dog enters the classroom, or a person has an unusual hairdo
- Intense stimuli, such as bright colors, loud noises, or sharp pain, and
- Repetitive stimuli, as when the same TV commercial is played a dozen times throughout the course of a football game

Consciousness as Direct Inner Awareness. Close your eyes. Imagine spilling a can of bright red paint across a black tabletop. Watch it spread across the black, shiny surface, then spill onto the floor. Although this image may be vivid, you

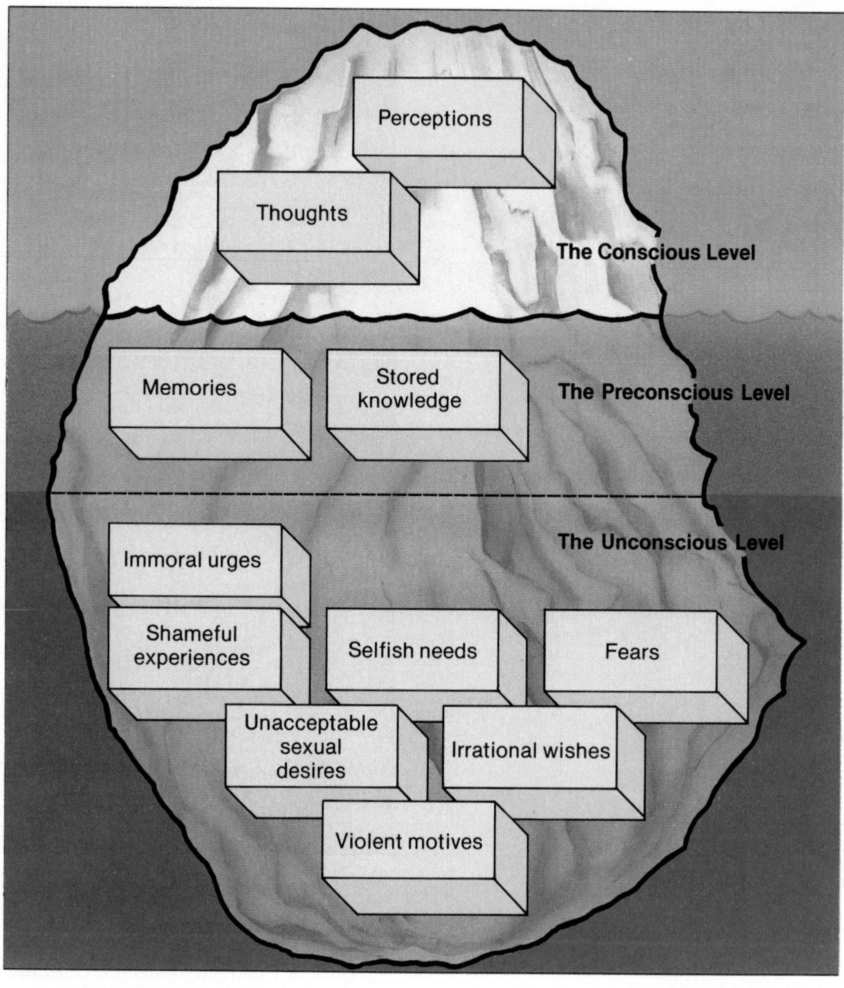

FIGURE 5.1
Levels of Consciousness, According to Sigmund Freud. According to Freud, many memories, impulses, and feelings exist below the level of conscious awareness. We could note that any film that draws an audience seems to derive its plot from items that populate the unconscious.

Direct inner awareness Knowledge of one's own thoughts, feelings, and memories without use of sensory organs—another definition of consciousness.

Preconscious In psychodynamic theory, descriptive of material that is not in awareness but can be brought into awareness by focusing one's attention. (The Latin root *prae-* means "before.")

Unconscious In psychodynamic theory, descriptive of ideas and feelings that are not available to awareness.

Repress In psychodynamic theory, to eject anxiety-provoking ideas, impulses, or images from awareness, without knowing that one is doing so.

Suppression The deliberate, or conscious, placing of certain ideas, impulses, or images out of awareness.

did not "see" it literally. Neither your eyes nor any other sensory organs were involved. You were conscious of the image through **direct inner awareness.**

We are conscious of—or have direct inner awareness of—thoughts, images, emotions, and memories. We are conscious of, or know of, the presence of these cognitive processes without using our senses.

Sigmund Freud, the founder of psychoanalysis, differentiated between thoughts and feelings of which we are conscious, or aware, and those which are preconscious and unconscious (see Figure 5.1). **Preconscious** material is not currently in awareness but is readily available. As you answer the following questions, you will summon up "preconscious" information: What did you eat for dinner yesterday? About what time did you wake up this morning? What's happening outside the window or down the hall right now? What's your phone number? You can make these preconscious bits of information conscious simply by directing your inner awareness, or attention, to them.

According to Freud, still other mental events are **unconscious,** or unavailable to awareness under most circumstances. Freud believed that certain memories were painful, and certain impulses (primarily sexual and aggressive impulses) were unacceptable. Therefore, people would place them out of awareness, or **repress** them, to escape feelings of anxiety, guilt, and shame.

Still, people do sometimes choose to stop thinking about distracting or unacceptable ideas. This conscious method of putting unwanted mental events out of awareness is termed **suppression.** We may suppress thoughts of a date when we need to study for a test. We may also try to suppress thoughts of an unpleasant test when we are on a date, so that the evening will not be ruined.

Some bodily processes are **nonconscious**—incapable of being experienced either through sensory awareness or direct inner awareness. The growing of hair and the carrying of oxygen in the blood are nonconscious. We can see that our hair has grown, but we have no sense receptors that provide sensations related to the process. We can feel the need to breathe but do not directly experience the exchange of carbon dioxide and oxygen.

Consciousness as Personal Unity: The Sense of Self. As we develop, we differentiate us from that which is not us. We develop a sense of being persons, individuals. There is a totality to our impressions, thoughts, and feelings that makes up our conscious existence—our continuing sense of **self** in a changing world.

In this usage of the word, consciousness *is* self. Cognitive psychologists view a person's consciousness as an important determinant of the person's behavior. Humanistic psychologists view consciousness as the essence of being human. Traditional psychoanalysts tend to stress the relative importance of *un*conscious processes in determining human behavior. Behaviorists stress the importance of environmental or situational determinants of behavior.

Consciousness as the Waking State. The word *conscious* also refers to the waking state as opposed, for example, to sleep. From this perspective, sleep, meditation, the hypnotic "trance," and the distorted perceptions that can accompany use of consciousness-altering drugs are considered **altered states of consciousness.**

For the remainder of this chapter, we explore various states of consciousness and the agents that bring them about. These states and agents include sleep and dreams, various drugs, meditation, biofeedback, and hypnosis.

ALTERING CONSCIOUSNESS THROUGH SLEEP AND DREAMS

Sleep has always been a fascinating topic. After all, we spend about one-third of our adult lives asleep. Most of us complain when we do not sleep at least six hours or so each night. Some people sleep for an hour or less a day, however, and lead otherwise healthy and normal lives.

Why do we sleep? Why do we dream? Why do some of us have trouble getting to sleep, and what can we do about it? Although we don't have all the answers to these questions, we have learned a great deal in the past couple of decades.

The Stages of Sleep

The **electroencephalograph,** or EEG, is one of the major tools of sleep researchers. The EEG measures the electrical activity of the brain, or brain waves. Figure 5.2 shows some scrawls produced by the EEG that reflect the frequency and strength of brain waves that occur during the waking state, when we are relaxed, and when we are in one of the stages of sleep.

Brain waves are cyclical. During the various stages of sleep, our brains emit waves of different frequencies and amplitudes. The printouts in Figure 5.2 show what happens during a period of 15 seconds or so. Brain waves high in frequency are associated with wakefulness. The amplitude of brain waves reflects their strength. The strength or energy of brain waves is expressed in the electric unit **volts.**

Figure 5.2 shows five stages of sleep: four stages of **non-rapid-eye-movement** (NREM) sleep, and one stage of **rapid-eye-movement** (REM) sleep.

Nonconscious Descriptive of bodily processes such as the growing of hair, of which we cannot become conscious. We may "recognize" that our hair is growing but cannot directly experience the biological process.

Self The totality of impressions, thoughts, and feelings. The sense of self is another definition of consciousness.

Altered states of consciousness States other than the normal waking state, including sleep, meditation, the hypnotic trance, and the distorted perceptions produced by use of some drugs.

Electroencephalograph An instrument that measures electrical activity of the brain. Abbreviated *EEG.*

Volt A unit of electrical potential.

Non-rapid-eye-movement sleep Stages of sleep 1 through 4. Abbreviated *NREM* sleep.

Rapid-eye-movement sleep A stage of sleep characterized by rapid eye movements, which have been linked to dreaming. Abbreviated *REM* sleep.

Awake

Awake—beta waves
(low amplitude, high frequency)

Drowsy—alpha waves
(higher amplitude, slower frequency)

NREM Sleep

Stage 1 sleep—theta waves
(low frequency, low amplitude)

Stage 2 sleep—sleep spindles
and the K complex

sleep spindle K complex

Stage 3 sleep—beginning of delta waves
(low frequency, high amplitude)

Stage 4 sleep—delta waves continue to
increase in amplitude

REM sleep—brain-wave patterns are very
similar to those of initial NREM Stage 1

REM Sleep
(occurs when we re-enter
Stage 1, about 90
minutes after falling asleep—
frequently called "paradoxical sleep"

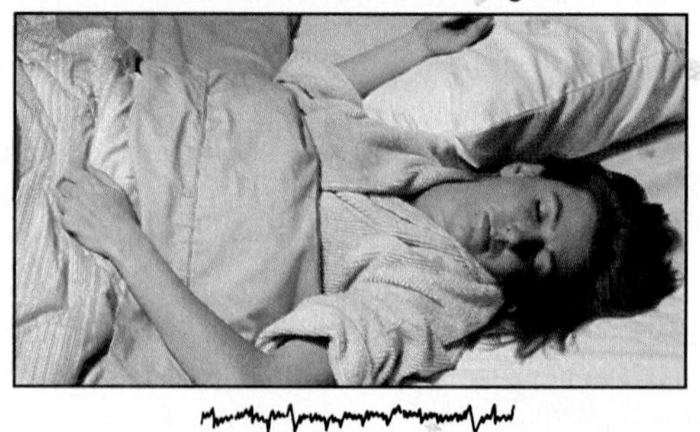

FIGURE 5.2
The Stages of Sleep.

This figure illustrates typical EEG patterns for the stages of sleep. During REM sleep, EEG patterns resemble those of the lightest stage of sleep, stage 1 sleep. For this reason, REM sleep is often termed *paradoxical sleep.* As sleep progresses from stage 1 to stage 4, brain waves become slower and their amplitude increases. Dreams, including normal nightmares, are most vivid during REM sleep. More disturbing sleep terrors tend to occur during deep stage 4 sleep.

When we close our eyes and begin to relax before going to sleep, our brains emit many **alpha waves.** Alpha waves are low-amplitude brain waves of about 8 to 13 cycles per second. (Through biofeedback training, discussed later in the chapter, people have been taught to relax by purposefully emitting alpha waves.)

As we enter stage 1 sleep, our brain waves slow down from the alpha rhythm and enter a pattern of **theta waves.** Theta waves, which have a frequency of about 6 to 8 cycles per second, are accompanied by slow, rolling eye movements. The transition from alpha waves to theta waves may be accompanied by a **hypnagogic state,** during which we may experience brief hallucinatory, dreamlike images that resemble vivid photographs. These images may be related to creativity. Stage 1 sleep is the lightest stage of sleep. If we are awakened from stage 1 sleep, we may feel that we have not slept at all.

After 30 to 40 minutes of stage 1 sleep, we undergo a rather steep descent into sleep stages 2, 3, and 4 (see Figure 5.3). During stage 2, brain waves are medium in amplitude and have a frequency of about 4 to 7 cycles per second, but these are punctuated by **sleep spindles.** Sleep spindles have a frequency of 12 to 16 cycles per second and represent brief bursts of rapid brain activity. During stage 2, we also experience instances of the so-called **K complex.** This complex occurs in response to external stimuli such as the sound of a book dropped in the room, or internal stimuli such as muscle tightness in the leg.

During deep-sleep stages 3 and 4, our brains produce slower **delta waves.** During stage 3, the delta waves are of about one to three cycles per second. Delta waves reach relatively great amplitude as compared to other brain waves. Stage 4 is the deepest stage of sleep, from which it is most difficult to be awakened. During stage 4 sleep, the delta waves slow to about 0.5 to 2 cycles per second, and their amplitude is greatest.

After perhaps half an hour of deep stage 4 sleep, we begin a relatively rapid journey back upward through the stages until we enter REM sleep (Figure 5.3). REM sleep derives its name from the *r*apid *e*ye *m*ovements, observable beneath our closed lids, that characterize this stage. During REM sleep, we produce relatively rapid, low-amplitude brain waves that resemble those of light stage 1 sleep. REM sleep is also called paradoxical sleep. This is because the EEG patterns observed during REM sleep suggest a level of arousal similar to that of the waking state (Figure 5.2). However, there are important chemical differences between REM sleep and the waking state. During REM sleep, there is a heightened level of acetylcholine in the brain and lowered levels of noradrenaline and serotonin (Schmeck, 1987). REM sleep is also "deep" in the sense that we are difficult to awaken during these periods. When we are awakened during REM sleep, as is the practice in sleep research, about 80 percent of the time we report that we have been dreaming. (We also dream during NREM sleep, but less frequently. We report dreaming only about 20 percent of the time when awakened during NREM sleep.)

We undergo about five trips through the stages of sleep each night (see Figure 5.3). These trips include about five periods of REM sleep. Our first journey through stage 4 sleep is usually longest. Sleep tends to become lighter as the night wears on. Our periods of REM sleep tend to become longer, and, toward morning, our last period of REM sleep may last close to half an hour.

Now that we have some idea of what sleep is like, let us examine the issue of *why* we sleep.

Alpha waves Rapid, low-amplitude brain waves that have been linked to feelings of relaxation.

Theta waves Slow brain waves produced during the hypnagogic state.

Hypnagogic state The drowsy interval between waking and sleeping, characterized by brief, hallucinatory, dreamlike experiences.

Sleep spindles Short bursts of rapid brain waves that occur during stage 2 sleep.

K complex Bursts of brain activity that occur during stage 2 sleep and reflect external stimulation.

Delta waves Strong, slow brain waves usually emitted during stage 4 sleep.

REM dream stage

Functions of Sleep

One outdated theory of the reasons for sleep suggested that sleep allowed the brain to rest and recuperate from the stresses of working all day. The EEG has shown that the brain is active all night long, however. Moreover, at least during REM sleep, the brain waves are quite similar to those of light sleep and the waking state. So the power isn't switched off at night.

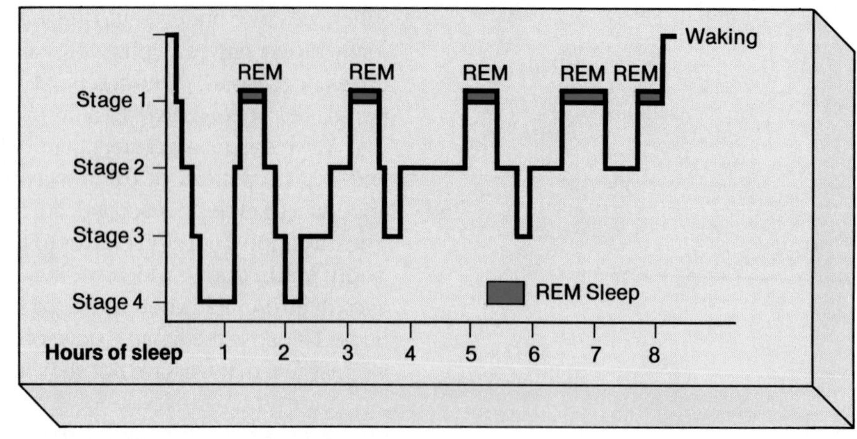

FIGURE 5.3
Sleep Cycles. This figure illustrates the alternation of REM and non-REM sleep for the typical sleeper. There are about five periods of REM sleep during an eight-hour night. Sleep is deeper earlier in the night, and REM sleep tends to become prolonged toward morning.

What of sleep and the rest of the body? Sleep helps rejuvenate a tired body (Donatelle et al., 1991). Most of us have had the experience of going without sleep for a night and feeling "wrecked" the following day. Perhaps the next evening we went to bed early to "catch up on our sleep." Research also suggests that increased physical exertion leads to a greater proportion of time spent in NREM sleep (Walker et al., 1978). Hartmann (1973) suggests that many proteins are synthesized during NREM sleep.

Let us continue our study of the functions of sleep by turning to research concerning long versus short sleepers and the effects of sleep deprivation.

Long versus Short Sleepers. Ernest Hartmann (1973) compared people who slept 9 hours or more a night (long sleepers) with people who slept 6 hours or less (short sleepers). He found that short sleepers tended to be more happy-go-lucky. They spent less time ruminating and were energetic, active, and relatively self-satisfied. The long sleepers were more concerned about personal achievement and social causes. They tended to be more creative and thoughtful, but they were also more anxious and depressed. Hartmann also found that, in general, people tend to need more sleep during periods of change and stress such as a change of jobs, an increase in work load, or an episode of depression. So it may be that sleep helps us recover from the stresses of life.

It is *not* true that people who sleep 9 hours or more a night tend to be lazy and happy-go-lucky. They are actually more industrious and anxious than short sleepers.

Hartmann also found that long sleepers spend proportionately more time in REM sleep than short sleepers. Subtracting the amount of REM sleep experienced by both types of sleepers dramatically closed the gap between them. Perhaps REM sleep is at least partially responsible for the restorative function. Since much REM sleep is spent in dreaming, it has been speculated that dreams may somehow promote recovery.

Sleep Deprivation. What will happen to you if you miss sleep for one night? For several nights? If you cut down from, say, your normal 7 to 10 hours to just $5^1/_2$? Anecdotal and research evidence offers some suggestions.

In 1959, disc jockey Peter Tripp remained awake for eight days. Toward the end of this episode, he became so paranoid that he could not be given psychological tests (Dement, 1972). However, 17-year-old Randy Gardner remained awake for 264 consecutive hours (11 days), and he did not show serious psychological disturbance (Levitt, 1981).

In another anecdote, 10 of 11 military cadets who were ordered to engage in strenuous activity for 100 hours developed visual hallucinations, and most developed problems in balance and movement (Opstad et al., 1978). But these cadets were also deprived of rest and food, not just sleep (Levitt, 1981). According to sleep researcher Wilse Webb, carefully controlled experiments with people who remain sleepless for several consecutive days result in few serious disturbances. Most often, participants show temporary problems in attention, confusion, or misperception (Goleman, 1982). These cognitive lapses may reflect brief episodes of borderline sleep. Participants may also show fine hand tremors, droopy eyelids, problems in focusing the eyes, and heightened sensitivity to pain. There are few, if any, horror stories.

What if we were to decide that we wanted to spend a bit more of our lives in the waking state—to work, to study, to play, perchance to daydream? Would ill effects attend curtailing our sleep to, say, 5½ hours a night? Webb followed 15 college men who restricted their sleep to five and a half hours for 60 days. For the first few weeks, these men showed an increase in deep sleep but a decrease in REM sleep. By the end of the first 30 days, they returned to the original level of deep sleep. The amount of REM sleep remained below normal, however.

During the 60 days, the men showed little drop-off in ability to remember or to compute numbers. They did show less vigilance on one psychological test, as measured in terms of numbers of responses. However, Webb suggests that this deficit may have reflected decreased motivation to perform well rather than a falling off of perceptual sharpness. It is particularly interesting that the men reported falling asleep in class or feeling drowsy during the first week only. After that, they reported *less* drowsiness than prior to the study. Did the study encourage them to permanently change their life styles? No. Despite the lack of ill effects of restricting sleep, all participants returned to their normal 7 or 8 hours when the study was complete.

Deprivation of REM Sleep. In some studies, animals or people have been deprived of REM sleep. Animals deprived of REM sleep learn more slowly and forget what they have learned more rapidly (Winson, 1992). Rats deprived of REM sleep for 10 days begin to eat voraciously but die of starvation (Hobson, 1992). REM sleep would appear to be essential to brain metabolism and body temperature regulation (Hobson, 1992).

In people, REM sleep may foster brain development during prenatal and infant development (McCarley, 1992). REM sleep may also help to maintain neurons in adults by "exercising" them at night (McCarley, 1992). REM-sleep deprivation is accomplished in human subjects by monitoring EEG records and eye movements and waking subjects during REM sleep. There is too much individual variation to conclude that people deprived of REM sleep learn more poorly than they otherwise would (McGrath & Cohen, 1978). It does seem, though, that such deprivation interferes with human memory—that is, the retrieval of information that has been learned previously (Winson, 1992). In any event, people and lower animals deprived of REM sleep tend to show *REM-rebound.* They spend more time in REM sleep during subsequent sleep periods. They catch up.

There is some research concerning possible links between REM sleep and various forms of abnormal behavior, such as hallucinations and depression. For example, in severe cases of depression, REM sleep often appears earlier than usual in the sleep cycle. Moreover, drugs that act to alleviate depression—by elevating the amounts of noradrenaline and serotonin available to the brain—also tend to delay REM sleep (Blakeslee, 1992).

Dream Images? In *Winter Night in Vitebsk,* Marc Chagall seems to depict images born in dreams.

It is during REM sleep that we tend to dream. Let us now turn our attention to dreams, a mystery about which people have theorized for centuries.

Dreams

Just what is the stuff of **dreams**? Like vivid memories and daytime fantasies, dreams involve imagery in the absence of external stimulation. Some dreams are so realistic and well organized that we feel they must be real—that we simply cannot be dreaming this time. You may have had such a dream on the night before a test. The dream would have been that you had taken the test and now it is all over. (Ah, what disappointment then prevailed when you woke up to realize that such was not the case!) Other dreams are disorganized and unformed.

Dreams are most vivid during REM sleep. Then they are most likely to have clear imagery and coherent plots, even if some of the content is fantastic. Plots are vaguer and images more fleeting during NREM sleep. You may well have a dream every time you are in REM sleep. Therefore, if you sleep for eight hours and undergo five sleep cycles, you may have five dreams. Upon waking, you may think that time seemed to expand or contract during your dreams so that during 10 or 15 minutes, your dream content ranged over days or weeks. But dreams tend to take place in "real time": 15 minutes of events fills about 15 minutes of dreaming. Your dream theater is quite flexible: you can dream in black and white and in full color.

Dreams A sequence of images or thoughts that occur during sleep. Dreams may be vague and loosely plotted or vivid and intricate.

Theories of the Content of Dreams. You may recall dreams involving fantastic adventures, but most dreams are simple extensions of the activities and problems of the day (Reiser, 1992). If we are preoccupied with illness or death, sexual or aggressive urges, or moral dilemmas, we are likely to dream about them. The characters in our dreams are more likely to be friends and neighbors than spies, monsters, and princes.

The Freudian View. Sigmund Freud theorized that dreams reflected unconscious wishes and urges. He argued that through dreams, we could express impulses that we would censor during the day. Moreover, he said that the content of dreams was symbolic of unconsciously fantasized objects such as genital organs. Freud devoted much time to analyzing his clients' dreams. Freud also believed that dreams "protected sleep" by providing imagery that would help keep disturbing, repressed thoughts out of awareness.

The view that dreams protect sleep has been challenged by the observation that disturbing events of the day tend to be followed by related disturbing dreams—not protective imagery (Reiser, 1992). Our behavior in dreams is also generally consistent with our waking behavior. Most dreams, then, are unlikely candidates for the expression (even disguised) of repressed urges. The person who leads a moral life tends to dream moral dreams.

It is *not* true that we tend to act out our forbidden fantasies in our dreams.

The Activation-Synthesis Model. According to the **activation-synthesis model** proposed by J. Allan Hobson and Robert W. McCarley (1977), dreams primarily reflect biological, not psychological, activity. According to this view, an abundance of acetylcholine in the brain and a time-triggered mechanism in the pons stimulate a number of responses that lead to dreaming. One is *activation* of the reticular activating system (RAS), which arouses us but not to the point of waking. During the waking state, firing of these cells in the reticular formation is linked to movement, particularly the semiautomatic movements found in walking, running, and other physical acts. During REM sleep, however, neurotransmitters generally inhibit motor (muscular) activity, so we don't thrash about as we dream (Steriade, 1992). In this way, we save ourselves (and our bed partners) some wear and tear. The eye muscles are also stimulated, and they show the rapid eye movement associated with dreaming. In addition, the RAS stimulates neural activity in the parts of the cortex involved in vision, hearing, and memory. The cortex then automatically *synthesizes,* or puts together, these sources of stimulation to yield the substances of dreams.

The activation-synthesis model explains why there is a strong tendency to dream about events of the day: the most current neural activity of the cortex would be that which represented the events or concerns of the day. Even so, Hobson (1992) concludes that "There are many theories but little data" about the functions of REM sleep and dreams, although "everybody loves to speculate."

Nightmares. Have you ever dreamed that something heavy was on your chest and watching as you breathed? Or that you were trying to run from a terrible threat but couldn't gain your footing or coordinate your leg muscles?

In the Middle Ages, such nightmares were thought to be the work of demons called incubi and succubi (singular: **incubus** and **succubus**). By and large, they were seen as a form of retribution. That is, they were sent to make you pay for your sins. They might sit on your chest and observe you fiendishly (how else would a fiend observe, if not "fiendishly"?), as suggested in Fuseli's *Nightmare,* or they might try to suffocate you. If you were given to sexual fantasies or behavior, they might have sexual intercourse with you.

Nightmares, like most pleasant dreams, are generally products of REM sleep. College students keeping dream logs report an average of two nightmares a month (Wood & Bootzin, 1990). Traumatic events can spawn nightmares, as reported in a study of survivors of the San Francisco earthquake of 1989 (Wood et al., 1992). People who suffer frequent nightmares are more likely than other people to also suffer from anxieties, depression, and other kinds of psychological discomfort (Berquier & Ashton, 1992).

Activation-synthesis model The view that dreams reflect activation by the reticular activating system and synthesis by the cerebral cortex.

Incubus (1) A spirit or demon thought in medieval times to lie on sleeping people, especially on women for sexual purposes. (2) A nightmare.

Succubus A female demon thought in medieval times to have sexual intercourse with sleeping men.

Nightmare. In the Middle Ages, nightmares were thought to be the work of demons who were sent to pay sleepers for their sins. In this picture, *Nightmare,* by Fuseli, a demon sits upon a woman who is dreaming a nightmare and threatens to suffocate her.

Insomnia. **Insomnia** refers to three types of sleeping problems: difficulty falling asleep (sleep-onset insomnia), difficulty remaining asleep through the night, and early morning awakening (Lacks & Morin, 1992). About one-third of American adults are affected by insomnia in any given year (Gillin, 1991). Women complain of the disorder more frequently than men.

As a group, people who suffer from insomnia show greater restlessness and muscle tension than nonsufferers (Lacks & Morin, 1992). Insomnia sufferers also have greater "cognitive arousal" than nonsufferers; they are more likely to worry and have "racing thoughts" at bedtime (White & Nicassio, 1990). Insomnia comes and goes with many people, increasing during periods of anxiety and tension (Gillin, 1991).

Insomniacs tend to compound their sleep problems through their efforts to force themselves to get to sleep (Bootzin et al., 1991). Their concern heightens autonomic activity and muscle tension. You cannot force or will yourself to get to sleep. You can only set the stage for it by lying down and relaxing when you are tired. If you focus on sleep too closely, it will elude you. Yet, millions go to bed each night dreading the possibility of sleep-onset insomnia.

It is true that many people have insomnia because they try too hard to get to sleep at night. *Trying* to get to sleep heightens tension and anxiety, both of which counteract the feelings of relaxation that help induce sleep.

Insomnia A term for three types of sleeping problems: (1) difficulty falling asleep, (2) difficulty remaining asleep, and (3) waking early. (From the Latin *in-,* meaning "not," and *somnus,* meaning "sleep.")

Psychoactive Descriptive of drugs that have psychological effects such as stimulation or distortion of perceptions.

ALTERING CONSCIOUSNESS THROUGH DRUGS

The world is a supermarket of **psychoactive** substances, or drugs. The United States is flooded with drugs that distort perceptions and change mood—drugs

TABLE 5.1: Percentage of College Students Who Report Drug Use "During the Last 30 Days," 1981–1991

Drug	1981	1982	1983	1984	1985	1986	1987	1988	1989	1990	1991
Alcohol	81.9	82.8	80.3	79.1	80.3	79.7	78.4	77.0	76.2	74.5	74.7
Cigarettes	25.9	24.4	24.7	21.5	22.4	22.4	24.0	22.6	21.1	21.5	23.2
Marijuana	33.2	26.8	26.2	23.0	23.6	22.3	20.3	16.8	16.3	14.0	14.1
Cocaine	7.3	7.9	6.5	7.6	6.9	7.0	4.6	4.2	2.8	1.2	1.0
(Crack)	NA*	NA	NA	NA	NA	NA	0.4	0.5	0.2	0.1	0.3
Other stimulants	12.3	9.9	7.0	5.5	4.2	3.7	2.3	1.8	1.3	1.4	1.0
Sedatives Barbiturates Methaqualone	3.4	2.5	1.1	1.0	0.7	0.6	0.6	0.6	0.2	0.2	0.3
Hallucinogens	2.3	2.6	1.8	1.8	1.3	2.2	2.0	1.7	2.3	1.4	1.2
Heroin	0.0	0.0	0.0	0.0	0.0	0.0	0.1	0.1	0.1	0.0	0.1

*NA = Not available.

Source of table: Johnston, L. D., Bachman, J. G., & O'Malley, P. M. (1992).

that take you up, let you down, and move you across town. Some people use drugs because their friends do, or because their parents tell them not to. Some are seeking pleasure, others are seeking inner truth.

Alcohol is the most popular drug on high school and college campuses (Johnston et al., 1992). Most college students have tried marijuana, and perhaps one in five smokes it regularly. Many Americans take **depressants** to get to sleep at night and **stimulants** to get going in the morning. Karl Marx charged that "religion . . . is the opium of the people," but heroin is the real opium of the people. Cocaine was, until recently, the toy of the well-to-do, but price breaks have brought it into the lockers of high school students. Given laws, moral pronouncements, medical warnings, and an occasional horror story, drug use actually seems to have declined in recent years (Johnston et al., 1992). Table 5.1 shows an 11-year trend for college students, according to University of Michigan surveys.

Substance Abuse and Substance Dependence

Where does drug use end and abuse begin? The borderline is not always clear, and even professionals do not always agree on definitions (Helzer & Schuckit, 1990). Many psychologists and other professionals define **substance abuse** as persistent use of a substance despite the fact that it is causing or compounding social, occupational, psychological, or physical problems. If you are missing school or work because you are drunk or "sleeping it off," you are abusing alcohol. The amount you drink is not as crucial as the fact that your pattern of use disrupts your life.

Dependence is more severe than abuse, although the borderline can be confusing here as well (Helzer & Schuckit, 1990; Schuckit, 1990). Dependence has behavioral and physiological aspects. Behaviorally, dependence is often characterized by loss of control over the substance, as in organizing one's life around getting it and using it. Physiologically, dependence is typified by tolerance, withdrawal symptoms, or both. **Tolerance** is the body's habituation to a substance so that with regular usage, higher doses are required to achieve similar effects. There are characteristic withdrawal symptoms, or an **abstinence syndrome,** when the level of usage suddenly drops off.[1] The abstinence syndrome for alcohol includes anxiety, tremors, restlessness, weakness, rapid pulse, and high blood pressure.

Depressant A drug that lowers the rate of activity of the nervous system. (From the Latin *de-*, meaning "down," and *premere,* meaning "to press.")

Stimulant A drug that increases activity of the nervous system.

Substance abuse Persistent use of a substance even though it is causing or compounding problems in meeting the demands of life.

Tolerance Habituation to a drug, with the result that increasingly higher doses of the drug are needed to achieve similar effects.

Abstinence syndrome A characteristic cluster of symptoms that results from sudden decrease in an addictive drug's level of usage. (From the Latin *abstinere,* meaning "to hold back.")

[1]The lay term *addiction* is usually used to connote physiological dependence, but here, too, there may be inconsistency. After all, some people speak of being "addicted" to work or to love.

When doing without a drug, people who are *psychologically* dependent show signs of anxiety (shakiness, rapid pulse, and sweating are three) that overlap abstinence syndromes. Because of these signs, they may believe that they are physiologically dependent on a drug when they are psychologically dependent. Still, symptoms of abstinence from certain drugs are unmistakably physiological. One is **delirium tremens** ("the DTs"), encountered by some chronic alcoholics when they suddenly lower intake. The DTs are characterized by heavy sweating, restlessness, general **disorientation,** and terrifying **hallucinations**—often of creepy, crawling animals.

Causal Factors in Substance Abuse and Substance Dependence

There are many reasons for substance abuse and dependence. A handful include curiosity, use by peers and parents, rebelliousness, and escape from boredom or pressure (Botvin et al., 1990; Johnson et al., 1990; Rhodes & Jason, 1990; Sher et al., 1991). Another reason is self-handicapping: by using alcohol or another drug when we are faced with a difficult task, we can blame failure on the alcohol, not ourselves. Similarly, alcohol and other drugs have been used as excuses for behaviors such as aggression, sexual forwardness, and forgetfulness.

Psychological and biological theories also account for substance abuse in the following ways.

Psychodynamic Views. Psychodynamic explanations of substance abuse propose that drugs help people control or express unconscious needs and impulses. Alcoholism, for example, may reflect the need to remain dependent on an overprotective mother or the effort to reduce emotional conflicts or to cope with unconscious sexual impulses.

Learning Views. Social-learning theorists suggest that people commonly try tranquilizing agents such as Valium and alcohol on the basis of observing others or a recommendation. Expectancies about the effects of a substance are powerful predictors of its use (Schafer & Brown, 1991; Stacy et al., 1991). Subsequent use may be reinforced by the drug's positive effects on mood and its reduction of unpleasant sensations such as anxiety, fear, and tension. For people who are physiologically dependent, avoidance of withdrawal symptoms is also reinforcing. Carrying the substance around is reinforcing, because then one need not worry about having to go without it. Some people, for example, will not leave the house without taking Valium along.

Parents who use drugs such as alcohol, tranquilizers, and stimulants may increase their children's knowledge of drugs and, in effect, show them when to use them—for example, when they are seeking to reduce tension or to "lubricate" social interactions (Sher et al., 1991; Stacy et al., 1991).

Genetic Predispositions. There is some evidence that people may have a genetic predisposition toward physiological dependence on various substances, including alcohol (Goodwin, 1985; Schuckit, 1987; Vaillant, 1982) and nicotine (Hughes, 1986). For example, the biological children of alcoholics who are reared by adoptive parents seem more likely to develop alcohol-related problems than the natural children of the adoptive parents (Goodwin, 1985).

An inherited tendency toward alcoholism may involve a combination of greater sensitivity to alcohol (enjoyment of it) and greater biological tolerance (Newlin & Thomson, 1990). For example, college-age children of alcoholics exhibit better muscular control and visual-motor coordination when they drink. They feel less intoxicated when they drink low to moderate doses of alcohol and show lower hormonal response to alcohol (Pihl et al., 1990).

Let us now consider the effects of some frequently used depressants, stimulants, and hallucinogenics.

Delirium tremens A condition characterized by sweating, restlessness, disorientation, and hallucinations. The "DTs" occurs in some chronic alcohol users when there is a sudden decrease in usage. (From the Latin *de-*, meaning "from," and *lira,* meaning "line" or "furrow"—suggesting that one's behavior is away from the beaten track or norm.)

Disorientation Gross confusion. Loss of sense of time, place, and the identity of people.

Hallucinations Perceptions in the absence of sensation. (From the Latin *hallucinari,* meaning "to wander mentally.")

WORLD OF DIVERSITY

Ethnicity and Adolescent Substance Abuse

Adolescent substance abuse increased through 1981, but has since been in more or less of a decline (Johnston et al., 1992). Substance abuse is generally higher among African-, Hispanic-, and Native-American adolescents than among non-Hispanic white American adolescents. However, the extent of substance abuse also depends on where these adolescents live. The highest rates of abuse occur where economically disadvantaged minority groups live in segregated enclaves. African Americans who live in the "ghetto," Hispanic Americans who dwell in the barrio, and Native Americans who live on the reservation all have high rates of use. Youth who dwell in such enclaves are more likely to encounter social isolation, unemployment, poverty, and deviant role models, some of which take the form of gangs (Oetting & Beauvais, 1990).

Yet, when we survey *high-school seniors* only, African Americans and Hispanic Americans apparently abuse substances no more than their non-Hispanic white counterparts (Oetting & Beauvais, 1990). How do we account for this discrepancy? It seems that the adolescents who are at greatest risk for substance abuse also tend to drop out of school before the senior year. School-based surveys thus systematically underestimate substance abuse by some minority groups (Oetting & Beauvais, 1990).

Native Americans and Irish Americans have the highest rates of alcoholism in the United States (Lex, 1987; Moncher et al., 1990). Jews have relatively low rates of alcoholism, and a cultural explanation is usually offered. Jews tend to expose children to alcohol (wine) early in life, within a strong family or religious context. Wine is offered in small quantities, with consequent low blood alcohol levels. Alcohol is thus not connected with rebellion, aggression, or failure in Jewish culture.

There are biological explanations for low levels of drinking among some ethnic groups such as Asian Americans. Asians are more likely than white people to show a "flushing response" to alcohol, as evidenced by rapid heart rate, dizziness, and headaches (Ellickson et al., 1992). Particular sensitivity to alcohol may inhibit immoderate drinking among Asian Americans.

Alcohol and tobacco appear to be taking their heaviest toll on Native Americans. Native Americans are the American ethnic group at greatest risk of incurring alcohol-related diabetes, fetal abnormalities, cirrhosis of the liver, and accident fatalities (Moncher et al., 1990). Tobacco of the smoked and smokeless varieties also places Native Americans at high risk of cardiovascular disorders and several kinds of cancer. However, these overall high rates of substance use mask the great variability in rates among Native Americans in various tribes and geographical settings (Moncher et al., 1990).

It is not enough to say that overall substance use and abuse is in a general decline in the United States. We must attend to the types of people who volunteer to participate in the surveys and to ethnic diversity among participants.

ALTERING CONSCIOUSNESS THROUGH DEPRESSANTS

Depressant drugs generally act by slowing the activity of the central nervous system, although there are a number of other effects specific to each drug. In this section we consider the effects of alcohol, opiates and opioids, barbiturates, and methaqualone.

Alcohol

No drug has meant so much to so many as alcohol. Alcohol is our dinnertime relaxant, our bedtime **sedative,** our cocktail-party social facilitator. We celebrate holy days, applaud our accomplishments, and express joyous wishes with alcohol. The young assert their maturity with alcohol. It is used at least occasionally by four out of five high school students (Johnston et al., 1992). The elderly use alcohol to stimulate circulation in peripheral areas of the body. Alcohol even kills germs on surface wounds.

Alcohol is the tranquilizer you can buy without prescription. It is the relief from anxiety you can swallow in public without criticism or stigma. A man who

Sedative A drug that soothes or quiets restlessness or agitation. (From the Latin *sedare,* meaning "to settle.")

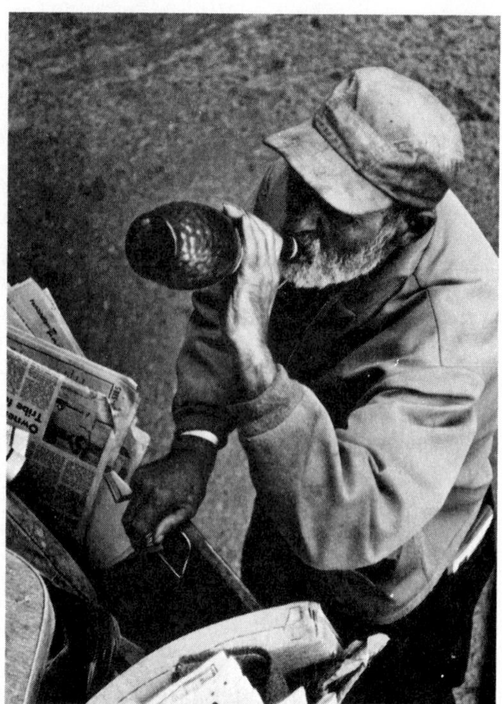

Two Facets of Alcohol. No drug has meant so much to so many as alcohol. Yet for many, alcohol is a central problem of life.

pops a Valium tablet may look weak. A man who chugalugs a bottle of beer may be perceived as "macho."

No drug has been so abused as alcohol. Ten to twenty million Americans are alcoholics. In contrast, 500,000 use heroin regularly, and 300,000 to 500,000 abuse sedatives. Excessive drinking has been linked to lower productivity, loss of employment, and downward movement in social status (Baum-Baicker, 1984; Mider, 1984; Vaillant & Milofsky, 1982). Yet, half of all Americans use alcohol, and despite widespread marijuana use, it is the drug of choice among adolescents.

Effects of Alcohol. The effects of drugs vary from individual to individual (Erwin et al., 1984). Generally speaking, however, our response to a substance reflects (1) the physiological effects of that substance and (2) our interpretations of those effects. Our interpretations of the drug's effects are, in turn, influenced by our expectations. As noted by Cox and Klinger (1988), we decide whether or not to drink alcohol according to our expectation that the positive emotional consequences will outweigh those of not drinking. Our past experiences with drinking, our situations, and our biological reactivity to alcohol all help form our expectations.

What do people expect from alcohol? Adolescent and adult American samples tend to report the beliefs that alcohol reduces tension, enhances performance, enhances pleasure, increases social ability, and transforms experiences for the better (Brown et al., 1985; Sher et al., 1991). These are expectations. What *does* alcohol do?

The effects of alcohol vary with the dose and the duration of use. Low doses of alcohol may be stimulating, but higher doses of alcohol have a sedative effect (Niaura et al., 1988), which is why alcohol is classified as a depressant. Ironically, short-term use of alcohol may lessen feelings of depression, but regular use over a year or more may augment feelings of depression (Aneshensel & Huba, 1983).

Alcohol relaxes and deadens minor aches and pains. Alcohol also intoxicates: it impairs cognitive functioning, slurs the speech, and reduces motor coordination. Alcohol is implicated in about half of our automobile accidents.

Men are much more likely than women to become alcoholics. A cultural explanation is that tighter social constraints are usually placed on women. A biological explanation is that alcohol hits women harder. If, for example, you have the impression that alcohol "goes to women's heads" more quickly than to men's, you are probably correct. Women seem to be more affected by alcohol because they metabolize very little of it in the stomach. Thus, alcohol reaches women's bloodstreams and brains relatively intact. (Women have less of an enzyme that metabolizes alcohol in the stomach than men do [Lieber, 1990].) Women mainly metabolize alcohol in the liver. For women, reports one health professional, "drinking alcohol has the same effect as injecting it intravenously" (Lieber, 1990). Powerful stuff, indeed.

Alcohol does appear to "go to women's heads" more quickly than to men's.

Despite their greater responsiveness to small quantities of alcohol, women who drink heavily are apparently as likely as men to become alcoholics.

Drinkers may do things they would not do if sober (Lang et al., 1980; Lansky & Wilson, 1981), such as linger over sexually explicit pictures in the presence of researchers. Why? One possibility is that alcohol impairs the information-processing needed to inhibit impulses (Hull et al., 1983; Steele & Josephs, 1990). When intoxicated, people may be less able to foresee the negative consequences of misbehavior and may be less likely to recall social and personal standards for behavior. Alcohol also induces feelings of elation and **euphoria** that may help wash away self-doubts and self-criticism. Also, do not forget that alcohol is associated with a liberated social role in our culture and that it provides an external excuse for otherwise unacceptable behavior.

Drinking Your Troubles Away: Drinking as a Strategy for Coping with Stress and Failure. Adolescent involvement with alcohol has been linked repeatedly to poor school grades and other negative life events (Chassin et al., 1988; Mann et al., 1987; Wills, 1986). Drinking can, of course, contribute to poor grades and other problems, but drinking may also help reduce academic and other stresses. Some researchers, in fact, find that drinking in order to cope with stress and as an excuse for failure are powerful predictors of alcohol abuse (Abrams & Wilson, 1983; Cooper et al., 1988).

Some people do drink because alcohol provides them with an excuse for failure.

Regardless of how or why one starts drinking, regular drinking can lead to physiological dependence. Once one has become physiologically dependent on alcohol, one will be motivated to drink in order to avoid withdrawal symptoms. Still, even when alcoholics have been "dried out"—withdrawn from alcohol—many return to drinking. Perhaps they still want to use alcohol as a way of coping with stress or as an excuse for failure.

Euphoria Feelings of well-being, elation. (From the Greek *euphoros,* meaning "healthy.")

Opiates and Opioids

Opiates are **narcotics** derived from the opium poppy. The ancient Sumerians gave this poppy its name: It means "plant of joy." The opiates include morphine, heroin, codeine, Demerol, and similar drugs whose major medical application is **analgesia.** Opiates appear to stimulate centers in the brain that lead to pleasure and to physiological dependence (Goeders & Smith, 1984; Ling et al., 1984).

In this section, we discuss morphine, heroin, and the **opioid** methadone. Opioids are similar to opiates in chemical structure and effect but are artificial (synthesized in the laboratory).

Morphine. **Morphine** was introduced at about the time of the Civil War in the United States and the Franco-Prussian War in Europe. It was used liberally to deaden pain from wounds. Physiological dependence on morphine became known as the "soldier's disease." There was little stigma attached to dependence until morphine became a restricted substance.

Heroin. **Heroin** was so named because it made people feel "heroic" and was hailed as the "hero" that would cure physiological dependence on morphine.

It is true that heroin was once used as a cure for addiction to morphine. Today, methadone is used to help addicts avert withdrawal symptoms from heroin.

Heroin, like the other opiates, is a powerful depressant that can also provide a euphoric rush. Users of heroin claim that it is so pleasurable it can eradicate any thought of food or sex. Soon after its initial appearance, heroin was used to treat so many problems that it became known as G.O.M. ("God's own medicine").

Morphine and heroin can have distressing abstinence syndromes, beginning with flu-like symptoms and progressing through tremors, cramps, chills alternating with sweating, rapid pulse, high blood pressure, insomnia, vomiting, and diarrhea. However, the syndrome can be quite variable from person to person. Many soldiers who used heroin regularly in Vietnam are reported to have suspended usage with relatively little trouble when they returned to the United States.

Heroin is illegal. Because the penalties for possession or sale are high, it is also expensive. For this reason, many physiologically dependent people support their habits through dealing (selling heroin), prostitution, or selling stolen goods. But the chemical effects of heroin do not directly stimulate criminal or aggressive behavior. On the other hand, people who use heroin regularly may be more likely than nonusers to engage in *other* risky criminal behaviors as well.

Although regular users develop tolerance for heroin, high doses can cause drowsiness, stupor, altered time perception, and impaired judgment.

Methadone. The synthetic narcotic **methadone** has been used to treat physiological dependence on heroin in the same way that heroin was used to treat physiological dependence on morphine. Methadone is slower acting than heroin and does not provide the thrilling rush. Most people treated with it simply swap dependence on one drug for dependence on another. Because they are unwilling to undergo withdrawal symptoms or to contemplate a life style devoid of drugs, they must be maintained on methadone indefinitely.

If methadone is injected rather than taken orally, it can provide sensations similar to those of heroin. Another drug, *naloxone,* prevents users from becoming high if they later take heroin. Some people are placed on naloxone after being

Opiates A group of addictive drugs derived from the opium poppy that provide a euphoric rush and depress the nervous system.

Narcotics Drugs used to relieve pain and induce sleep. The term is usually reserved for opiates. (From the Greek *narke,* meaning "numbness" or "stupor.")

Analgesia A state of not feeling pain, although fully conscious.

Opioid A synthetic (artificial) drug similar in chemical composition to opiates.

Morphine An opiate introduced at about the time of the U.S. Civil War.

Heroin An opiate. Heroin, ironically, was used as a "cure" for morphine addiction when first introduced.

Methadone An artificial narcotic that is slower acting than, and does not provide the rush of, heroin. Methadone use allows heroin addicts to abstain from heroin without experiencing an abstinence syndrome.

"Shooting Up" Heroin. Users of heroin claim that the drug is so pleasurable that it can eradicate any thought of food or sex. Many users remain dependent on heroin because they are unwilling to undergo withdrawal symptoms or to contemplate a life devoid of drugs.

withdrawn from heroin. However, former addicts can simply choose not to take naloxone. Drugs like naloxone also do not motivate former users to undertake a heroin-free life style.

Barbiturates and Methaqualone

Barbiturates such as amobarbital, phenobarbital, pentobarbital, and secobarbital are depressants with a number of medical uses including relief of anxiety and tension, deadening of pain, and treatment of epilepsy, high blood pressure, and insomnia. Barbiturates lead rapidly to physiological and psychological dependence.

Methaqualone, sold under the brand names Quaalude and Sopor, is a depressant similar in effect to barbiturates. Methaqualone also leads to physiological dependence and is quite dangerous.

Psychologists generally oppose using barbiturates and methaqualone for anxiety, tension, and insomnia. These drugs lead rapidly to dependence and do nothing to teach the individual how to alter disturbing patterns of behavior. Many physicians, too, have become concerned about barbiturates. They now prefer to prescribe minor tranquilizers such as Valium and Librium for anxiety and tension and other drugs for insomnia. However, it is now thought that minor tranquilizers may also create physiological dependence. Tranquilizers also do nothing to help people change the relationships or other factors that distress them.

Barbiturates and methaqualone are popular as street drugs because they relax the muscles and produce a mild euphoric state. High doses of barbiturates result in drowsiness, motor impairment, slurred speech, irritability, and poor judgment. A physiologically dependent person who is withdrawn abruptly from barbiturates may experience severe convulsions and die. High doses of methaqualone may cause internal bleeding, coma, and death. Because of additive effects, it is dangerous to mix alcohol and other depressants at bedtime, or at any time.

ALTERING CONSCIOUSNESS THROUGH STIMULANTS

All stimulants increase the activity of the nervous system. Stimulants' other effects vary somewhat from drug to drug, and some seem to contribute to feelings of euphoria and self-confidence.

Amphetamines

Amphetamines are a group of stimulants that were first used by soldiers during World War II to help them remain alert through the night. Truck drivers have used them to drive through the night. Amphetamines have become perhaps more widely known through students, who have used them for all-night cram sessions, and through dieters, who use them because they reduce hunger.

Called speed, uppers, bennies (for Benzedrine), and dexies (for Dexedrine), these drugs are often used for the euphoric rush they can produce, especially in high doses. (The so-called antidepressant drugs, discussed in Chapter 14, do not produce a euphoric rush.) Some people swallow amphetamines in pill form or inject liquid Methedrine, the strongest form, into their veins. They may stay awake and "high" for days on end. Such highs must come to an end. People who have been on prolonged highs sometimes "crash," or fall into a deep sleep or depression. Some people commit suicide when crashing.

A related stimulant, methylphenidate (Ritalin), is widely used to treat **hyperactivity** in children (Wolraich et al., 1990). Ritalin has been shown to increase self-control, increase the attention span, decrease fidgeting, and lead to academic

Barbiturate An addictive depressant used to relieve anxiety or induce sleep.

Methaqualone An addictive depressant. Often called "ludes."

Amphetamines Stimulants derived from *a*lpha-*m*ethyl-beta-*ph*enyl-*et*hyl-*amine,* a colorless liquid consisting of carbon, hydrogen, and nitrogen. speed

Hyperactive More active than normal.

"Snorting" Cocaine. Cocaine is a powerful stimulant whose use has become widespread because of recent price breaks. Health professionals have become concerned about cocaine's stimulation of sudden rises in blood pressure, its constriction of blood vessels, and its acceleration of the heart rate. Several well-known athletes have recently died from cocaine overdoses.

gains in these children (Abikoff & Gittelman, 1985; Barkley, 1989; Rapport, 1987). The paradoxical calming effect of stimulants on hyperactive children may be explained by assuming that a cause of hyperactivity is immaturity of the cerebral cortex. Stimulants may spur the cortex to exercise control over more primitive centers in the lower brain. A combination of stimulants and cognitive-behavior therapy may treat hyperactivity most effectively (Pelham & Murphy, 1986; Whalen & Henker, 1991).

People can become psychologically dependent on amphetamines, especially when they are used to cope with depression. Tolerance develops rapidly, but opinion is mixed as to whether they lead to physiological dependence. High doses may cause restlessness, insomnia, loss of appetite, hallucinations, paranoid delusions, and irritability. In the amphetamine psychosis, there are hallucinations and delusions that mimic the symptoms of paranoid schizophrenia (see Chapter 13). In addition to causing restlessness and loss of appetite with hyperactive children, Ritalin may also suppress growth and give rise to tics and cardiovascular changes. These side effects are usually reversible with "drug holidays" or dosage decreases (Whalen & Henker, 1991).

Cocaine

No doubt you've seen commercials claiming that Coke adds life. Given its caffeine and sugar content, "Coke"—Coca-Cola, that is—should provide quite a lift. But Coca-Cola hasn't been "the real thing" since 1906. At that time, the manufacturers discontinued the use of cocaine in its formula, which is derived from coca leaves—the plant from which the soft drink derived its name.

It is true that Coca-Cola once "added life" through a powerful but now illegal stimulant. That stimulant is cocaine.

Coca leaves contain **cocaine,** a stimulant that produces a state of euphoria, reduces hunger, deadens pain, and bolsters self-confidence. Cocaine's popularity with college students seems to have peaked in the mid-1980s (see Table 5.1). Today, perhaps 1 percent use it regularly. The great majority of high-school seniors now believe that regular use of cocaine is harmful (Johnston et al., 1992). However, questions remain about the prevalence of cocaine use among minority youth, high-school dropouts, and young people who do not attend college. (Oetting & Beauvais, 1990; Rhodes & Jason, 1990).

Cocaine is brewed from coca leaves as a "tea," breathed in through the nose ("snorted") in powder form, and injected ("shot up") in liquid form. Repeated snorting constricts blood vessels in the nose, drying the skin and, at times, exposing cartilage and perforating the nasal septum. These problems require cosmetic surgery. Of course, people who take cocaine intravenously and share contaminated needles risk becoming infected by the AIDS virus. The potent derivatives "crack" and "bazooka" have received much attention in the media. These derivatives are inexpensive because they are unrefined and may be contaminated with toxic substances.

On a physiological level, cocaine stimulates sudden rises in blood pressure, tightening of the blood vessels (decreasing the oxygen supply to the heart), and quickening of the heart rate (Altman, 1988). There are occasional reports of respiratory and cardiovascular collapse, as with the deaths of the athletes Len Bias, Don Rogers, and Dave Croudip. Overdoses can lead to restlessness and insomnia, tremors, headaches, nausea, convulsions, hallucinations, and delusions. Cocaine gradually lowers the brain threshold for seizures in laboratory rats (Bales, 1986).

Cocaine A powerful stimulant.

A Vial of Crack. Crack "rocks" resemble white pebbles and produce a powerful rush when smoked. Crack is found only rarely on college campuses but appears to be having more of an impact in inner cities.

That is, individual moderate doses of cocaine had no apparent harmful effect, but there was a cumulative "kindling effect" for brain seizures and, in some cases, sudden death. Use of crack has also been connected with strokes (S. R. Levine et al., 1990).

Cocaine—also called *snow* and *coke,* like the slang term for the soft drink—has been used as a local anesthetic since the early 1800s. It came to the attention of one Viennese neurologist in 1884, a young chap named Sigmund Freud, who used it to fight his own depression and published an early supportive article, "Song of Praise." Freud's early ardor was soon tempered by awareness that cocaine was habit-forming and could cause hallucinations and delusions.

Despite media and government claims that cocaine is addictive, some question remains as to whether cocaine does cause physiological dependence. Users may not develop tolerance for the drug, and it is not clear that there is a specific abstinence syndrome for cocaine (Van Dyke & Byck, 1982). There is no doubt, however, that users can readily become psychologically dependent.

Although cocaine has been unavailable to the general public since the Harrison Narcotic Act of 1914, it is still commonly the anesthetic of choice for surgery on the nose and throat. Cocaine, by the way, *is* a stimulant, not a narcotic. Its classification as a narcotic was only a legality—bringing the drug under the prohibitions of the narcotics act.

Cigarettes (Nicotine)

Smoking: a "custome lothesome to the Eye, hatefull to the Nose, harmefull to the Braine, dangerous to the Lungs."

King James I, 1604 (Barry, 1991)

The perils of smoking are no secret. All cigarette packs sold in the United States carry messages such as: "Warning: The Surgeon General Has Determined That Cigarette Smoking Is Dangerous to Your Health." Cigarette advertising has been banned on radio and television. About half a million Americans die from smoking-related illnesses each year. This is nearly ten times the number who die from motor-vehicle accidents.

The average life reduction of smokers is about five to eight years (Fielding, 1985). The carbon monoxide in cigarette smoke impairs the blood's ability to carry oxygen, causing shortness of breath. The **hydrocarbons** ("tars") in cigarette smoke cause several kinds of cancer in laboratory animals: cancers of the

Hydrocarbons Chemical compounds consisting of hydrogen and carbon.

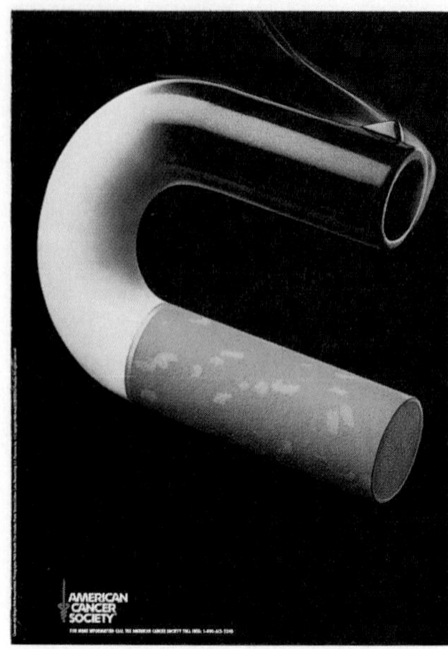

Cigarettes: Smoking Guns? The perils of cigarette smoking are widely known today. Former Surgeon General C. Everett Koop declared that cigarette smoking is the chief preventable cause of death in the United States. The numbers of Americans who die from smoking are comparable to three jumbo jets crashing *every day.* If flying were that unsafe, would the government ground all flights? Would the public continue to book airline reservations?

lungs, larynx, oral cavity, and esophagus. They may contribute to cancer of the bladder, pancreas, and kidneys. Cigarette smoking is linked to death from heart disease (Epstein & Perkins, 1988), chronic lung and respiratory diseases, and other illnesses. Pregnant women who smoke risk miscarriage, premature birth, and birth defects—as well as the other ills of smoking.

Because of health concerns, the percentage of American adults who smoke declined from 42.2 in 1966 to 25.5 in 1990 (*New York Times,* 1992). (At the same time, tobacco companies are raking in money from increased overseas sales [Barry, 1991].) According to a 1992 report of the Centers for Disease Control, the prevalence of smoking is about the same for African and white Americans. The prevalence of smoking is highest among Native Americans and high-school dropouts.

Passive smoking is also connected with respiratory illnesses and other diseases (USDHHS, 1991). Prolonged childhood and adolescent exposure to tobacco smoke in the household is a risk factor for lung cancer (Janerich et al., 1990). Because of the noxious effects of second-hand smoke, smoking has been banished from public places such as airplanes and elevators. Many restaurants reserve sections for nonsmokers. Forty-four states and Washington, DC, have restricted smoking in public places (*New York Times,* 1992).

Why, then, do people smoke? For many reasons—such as the desires to look sophisticated (though smokers may be more likely to be judged foolish than sophisticated these days), to have something to do with their hands, and to take in *nicotine.*

Nicotine. **Nicotine** is the stimulant in cigarettes. Nicotine can cause cold, clammy skin, faintness and dizziness, nausea and vomiting, and diarrhea—all of which account for the discomforts of the novice smoker. Nicotine also incites discharge of the hormone adrenaline. Adrenaline creates a burst of autonomic activity including rapid heart rate and release of sugar into the blood. Nicotine suppresses the appetite and provides a sort of mental "kick" (Grunberg, 1991). Some people smoke as a method of weight control (Klesges et al., 1991). Moderate and heavy female smokers weigh less than nonsmokers and light smokers (0–4 cigarettes a day), even when we take their diets and levels of physical activity into consideration (Klesges et al., 1991). Moderate male smokers also have lower body weights than male nonsmokers and light smokers. However, heavy male smokers weigh as much as male nonsmokers. It may be that regular doses of nicotine lead to weight loss by raising the metabolism, but the reasons for the gender difference are unclear (Klesges et al., 1991).

Nicotine is the agent that creates physiological dependence on cigarettes (Lichtenstein & Glasgow, 1992). Regular smokers adjust their smoking to maintain fairly even levels of nicotine in their bloodstream. Symptoms for withdrawal from nicotine include nervousness, drowsiness, energy loss, headaches, fatigue, irregular bowels, lightheadedness, insomnia, dizziness, cramps, palpitations, tremors, and sweating. Since many of these symptoms mimic anxiety, it was believed for many years that cigarette smoking might be a habit rather than an addiction.

Nicotine is excreted more rapidly when the urine is highly acidic. Stress increases the amount of acid in the urine. For this reason, smokers may need to smoke more when under stress to maintain the same blood nicotine level, even though they may *believe* that smoking is helping them cope with stress.

It is true that cigarette smokers tend to smoke more when they are under stress. That is because nicotine is excreted more rapidly when they are under stress.

Passive smoking Inhaling of smoke from the tobacco products and exhalations of other people; also called *second-hand smoking.*

Nicotine A stimulant found in tobacco smoke. (From the French name for the tobacco plant, *nicotiane.*)

ALTERING CONSCIOUSNESS THROUGH HALLUCINOGENICS

Hallucinogenic drugs are so named because they produce hallucinations—that is, sensations and perceptions in the absence of external stimulation. But hallucinogenic drugs may also have additional effects such as relaxing the individual, creating a sense of euphoria, or, in some cases, causing panic. We shall focus on the effects of marijuana and LSD.

Marijuana

Marijuana is produced from the *Cannabis sativa* plant, which grows wild in many parts of the world. Marijuana helps some people relax and can elevate their mood. It also sometimes produces mild hallucinations, which is why marijuana is classified as a **psychedelic,** or hallucinogenic, drug. The major psychedelic substance in marijuana is **delta-9-tetrahydrocannabinol,** or THC. THC is found in the branches and leaves of male and female plants, but it is highly concentrated in the **resin** of the female plant. **Hashish,** or "hash," is derived from this sticky resin. Hashish is more potent than marijuana, although the effects are similar.

In the nineteenth century, marijuana was used almost as aspirin is used today for headaches and minor aches and pains. It could be bought without prescription in any drugstore. Today, marijuana use and possession are illegal in most states, but medical applications are being explored. Marijuana is known to decrease nausea and vomiting among cancer patients receiving chemotherapy (Grinspoon, 1987). It appears to help **glaucoma** sufferers by reducing fluid pressure in the eye. It may even offer some relief from asthma. However, there are also causes for concern, as noted in 1982 by the Institute of Medicine of the National Academy of Sciences. For example, marijuana impairs motor coordination and perceptual functions used in driving and the operation of other machines. It also impairs short-term memory and slows learning. Although it causes positive mood changes in many people, there are also disturbing instances of anxiety and confusion and occasional reports of psychotic reactions. Marijuana increases the heart rate up to 140–150 beats per minute and, in some people, raises blood pressure. This rise in workload poses a threat to persons with hypertension and cardiovascular disorders.

Today marijuana is used by about 14 percent of college students, down from about one-third in 1981 (Johnston et al., 1992).

Psychoactive Effects of Marijuana. Marijuana smokers report different sensations at different levels of intoxication. The early stages of intoxication are frequently characterized by restlessness, which gives way to calmness. Fair to strong intoxication is linked to reports of heightened perceptions and increases in self-insight, creative thinking, and empathy for the feelings of others. Strong intoxication is linked to perceiving time as passing more slowly. A song, for example, might seem to last an hour rather than a few minutes. There is increased awareness of bodily sensations such as heart beat. Smokers also report that strong intoxication heightens sexual sensations. Visual hallucinations are not uncommon. Strong intoxication may cause smokers to experience disorientation. If the smoker's mood is euphoric, loss of identity may be interpreted as harmony with the universe.

However, some smokers encounter negative experiences when they are highly intoxicated. An accelerated heart rate and heightened awareness of bodily sensations leads some smokers to fear that their hearts will "run away" with them. Some smokers find disorientation threatening, and they fear failure to regain their identities. High levels of intoxication occasionally induce nausea and vomiting. Needless to say, smokers with such experiences smoke infrequently, or just once.

Hallucinogenic Giving rise to hallucinations.

Marijuana The dried vegetable matter of the *Cannabis sativa* plant. (A Mexican-Spanish word.)

Psychedelic Causing hallucinations, delusions, or heightened perceptions.

Delta-9-tetrahydrocannabinol The major active ingredient in marijuana. Abbreviated *THC*. Its name describes its chemical composition.

Resin The saplike substance of plants.

Hashish A drug derived from the resin of *Cannabis sativa.* Often called "hash."

Glaucoma An eye disease characterized by increased fluid pressure within the eye. A cause of blindness. (From the Greek *glaukos,* meaning "gleaming"—referring to the appearance of the diseased eye.)

Some people report that marijuana helps them socialize at parties. However, the friendliness characteristic of early stages of intoxication may give way to self-absorption and social withdrawal as the smoker becomes higher (Fabian & Fishkin, 1981).

There is controversy about whether or not marijuana causes physiological dependence. People can become psychologically dependent on marijuana, as on any other drug, but many psychologists maintain that marijuana does not cause physiological dependence. Tolerance is a sign of dependence, and with marijuana, **reverse tolerance** has been reported. That is, with marijuana, regular usage frequently leads to the need for less of the substance to achieve similar effects. It may be that some of the psychoactive substances in marijuana smoke take a long time to be metabolized by the body. The effects of new doses then would be added to those of the chemicals remaining in the body. But regular users also expect certain effects. These expectations may interact with even mild bodily cues or sensations to produce effects previously achieved only through higher doses.

Marijuana's entire story has not yet been told. Whereas certain horror stories about marijuana may have been exaggerated, one cannot assume that smoke containing 50 percent more carcinogenic hydrocarbon than tobacco smoke is completely harmless.

LSD

LSD is the abbreviation for lysergic acid diethylamide, a synthetic hallucinogenic drug. Users of "acid" claim that it "expands consciousness" and opens new worlds. Sometimes people believe they have achieved great insights while using LSD, but when it wears off they often cannot apply or recall these discoveries.

LSD and similar hallucinogenics are used by about 6 percent of the high school population (Johnston et al., 1992). As a powerful hallucinogenic, LSD produces vivid and colorful hallucinations. LSD "trips" can be somewhat unpredictable. Some regular users have only good trips. Others have one bad trip and swear off. Regular users who have had no bad trips argue that people with bad trips were psychologically unstable prior to using LSD. In fairness, Barber's review of the literature (1970) suggests that rare psychotic symptoms are usually limited to people with a history of psychological problems.

Reverse tolerance Requirement of less of a substance to achieve the same effects that were previously attained with higher doses.

Amotivational syndrome Loss of ambition or motivation to achieve.

LSD Lysergic acid diethylamide. A hallucinogenic drug.

An LSD "Trip"? This hallucinogenic drug can give rise to a vivid parade of colors and visual distortions. Some users claim to have arrived at great insights while "tripping," but afterward they have been typically unable to recall or apply them.

Flashbacks. Some LSD users have **flashbacks**—distorted perceptions or hallucinations that occur days, weeks, or longer after usage but mimic the LSD trip. It has been speculated that flashbacks stem from chemical changes in the brain produced by LSD, but Heaton and Victor (1976) and Matefy (1980) offer a psychological explanation for flashbacks.

Heaton and Victor (1976) found that users who have flashbacks are more oriented toward fantasy and allowing their thoughts to wander. They are also more likely to focus on internal sensations. If they should experience sensations similar to a past trip, they may readily label them flashbacks and allow themselves to focus on them indefinitely, causing an entire replay of the experience to unfold.

Matefy (1980) found that users who have flashbacks show greater capacity to become fully engrossed in role-playing and hypothesized that flashbacks may be nothing more than enacting the role of being on a trip. This does not necessarily mean that people who claim to have flashbacks are lying. They may be more willing to surrender personal control in response to internal sensations for the sake of altering their consciousness and having peak experiences. Users who do not have flashbacks prefer to be more in charge of their thought processes and have greater concern for meeting the demands of daily life.

Other Hallucinogenics

Other hallucinogenic drugs include **mescaline** (derived from the peyote cactus) and **phencyclidine** (PCP). Regular use of hallucinogenics may lead to tolerance and psychological dependence. But hallucinogenics are not known to lead to physiological dependence. High doses may induce frightening hallucinations, impaired coordination, poor judgment, mood changes, and paranoid delusions.

Let us now consider a number of ways of altering consciousness that do not involve drugs.

ALTERING CONSCIOUSNESS THROUGH MEDITATION: WHEN EASTERN GODS MEET WESTERN TECHNOLOGY

There are many kinds of **meditation,** but they seem to share similar psychological threads: through rituals, exercises, and passive observation, the normal person-environment relationship is altered. Problem-solving, planning, worry, awareness of the events of the day are all suspended. In this way, consciousness—that is, the normal focuses of attention—is altered, and a state of relaxation is often induced. Scientifically speaking, it is reasonable to suggest that the effects of meditation, like the effects of drugs, reflect whatever bodily changes are induced by meditation *and* one's expectations about meditation.

Transcendental Meditation, or TM, is a simplified form of Far Eastern meditation that was brought to the United States by the Maharishi Mahesh Yogi in 1959. Hundreds of thousands of Americans practice TM by repeating and concentrating on **mantras**—words or sounds that are claimed to have the capacity to help one achieve an altered state of consciousness.

TM has a number of spiritual goals such as expanding consciousness, but there are also more worldly goals such as healthful effects on the blood pressure. Herbert Benson (1975) of Harvard Medical School studied TM practitioners and found no scientific evidence that TM expanded consciousness, despite the claims of many practitioners. However, TM did produce what Benson labeled a **relaxation response.** During TM, the body's metabolic rate dramatically decreased. The blood pressure of people with hypertension decreased (Benson et al., 1973). In fact, people who meditated twice daily tended to show normalized blood

Flashbacks Distorted perceptions or hallucinations that occur days or weeks after LSD usage but mimic the LSD experience.

Mescaline A hallucinogenic drug derived from the mescal (peyote) cactus. In religious ceremonies, Mexican Indians chew the buttonlike structures at the tops of the rounded stems of the plant.

Phencyclidine Another hallucinogenic drug whose name is an acronym for its chemical structure. Abbreviated *PCP.*

Meditation Within psychology, a systematic way of narrowing one's attention that slows the metabolism and helps produce feelings of relaxation. (There are also metaphysical definitions.)

Transcendental meditation The simplified form of meditation brought to the United States by the Maharishi Mahesh Yogi. Abbreviated *TM.*

Mantra A word or sound that is repeated in TM. (A Sanskrit word that has the same origin as the word *mind.)*

Relaxation response Benson's term for a group of responses that can be brought about by meditation. They involve lowered activity of the sympathetic branch of the autonomic nervous system.

Meditation. People use many forms of meditation to try to expand inner awareness and experience inner harmony. The effects of meditation, like the effects of drugs, reflect both the bodily changes induced by meditation *and* the meditator's expectations.

pressure through the day. Meditators produced more frequent alpha waves—brain waves associated with feelings of relaxation but infrequent during sleep. Benson's subjects also showed lower heart and respiration rates and a decrease in blood lactate, a substance whose presence has been linked to anxiety.

It is true that people have managed to bring high blood pressure under control through meditation.

Other researchers agree that TM lowers a person's level of arousal, but they argue that the same relaxing effects can be achieved by engaging in other relaxing activities (West, 1985), even by resting quietly for the same amount of time (Holmes et al., 1983; Holmes, 1984, 1985). The Holmes group (1983) found no differences between experienced meditators and novice "resters" in heart rate, respiration rate, blood pressure, and sweat in the palms of the hands (that is, galvanic skin response, or GSR). Most critics of meditation do not argue that meditation is useless but rather that meditation may have no special effects as compared with a restful break from a tension-producing routine.

Note that formerly anxious and tense individuals who practice TM have also *chosen* to alter their stress-producing life styles by taking time out for themselves once or twice a day. Just taking this time out may be quite helpful.

The final word on meditation is not in (Suler, 1985). Still, if you wish to meditate, the following instructions may be of help.

How To Meditate

There is controversy concerning the effects of meditation. Although psychologists tend to agree that meditation helps us relax and can also normalize our blood pressure, it has not been shown that the effects of meditation are superior to those of resting quietly. However, if you want to gather some first-hand knowledge of the effects of meditation, you can try it out by using the following measures:

1. Meditate once or twice daily for 10 to 20 minutes at a time.
2. Adopt a passive, "what happens, happens" attitude. (What you *don't* do is more important than what you *do* do.)
3. Create a quiet, nondisruptive environment. For example, don't face a light directly.
4. Do not eat for an hour beforehand. Avoid caffeine for at least two.
5. Assume a comfortable position. Change it as needed. It's okay to scratch or yawn.
6. For a concentrative device, you may focus on your breathing or seat yourself before a calming object such as a plant or burning incense. Benson suggests "perceiving" (rather than mentally saying) the word *one* on every outbreath. This means thinking the word, but "less actively" than usual. Others suggest thinking or perceiving the word *in* as you are inhaling and *out,* or *ah-h-h,* as you are exhaling. Mantras such as *ah-nam, shi-rim,* and *ra-mah* may also be used.
7. If you are using a mantra, you can prepare for meditation and say the mantra out loud several times. Enjoy it. Then say it more and more softly. Close your eyes and think only the mantra. Allow yourself to perceive, rather than actively think, the mantra. Adopt a passive attitude. Continue to perceive the mantra. It may grow louder or softer, or disappear for a while, then return.

Biofeedback. Biofeedback is a system that provides, or "feeds back," information about a bodily function to an organism. Through biofeedback training, people have learned to gain voluntary control over a number of functions that are normally involuntary.

8. If disruptive thoughts come in as you are meditating, allow them to "pass through." Don't get wrapped up in trying to squelch them.
9. Allow yourself to drift. (You won't go too far.) What happens, happens.
10. Above all, take what you get. You cannot force the effects of meditation. You can only set the stage for them and allow them to happen.

ALTERING CONSCIOUSNESS THROUGH BIOFEEDBACK: GETTING IN TOUCH WITH THE UNTOUCHABLE

There is little we can take for granted in life. A few decades ago, however, psychologists were reasonably secure with the distinction between *voluntary* and *involuntary* functions. Voluntary functions, like lifting an arm or leg, were conscious. They could be directly willed. But other functions such as heart rate and blood pressure were involuntary or autonomic. They were beyond conscious control. We could no more consciously control blood pressure than, say, purposefully emit alpha waves.

Once in a while, to be sure, we heard tales of yogis (practitioners of yoga) or other exotics who could make their hair stand literally on end or "will" their cheeks to stop bleeding after a nail had been put through. But such episodes were viewed as horror stories or stage tricks. Serious scientists went back to serious research—except for a handful of pioneering psychologists like Neal E. Miller of Rockefeller University. In classic research of the 1960s, Miller trained laboratory rats to increase or decrease their heart rates voluntarily (Miller, 1969). His procedure was simple. There is a "pleasure center" in the hypothalamus of the rat. A small burst of electricity in this center is strongly reinforcing: rats will do whatever they can to reap this bit of shock, such as learning to press a lever.

Miller implanted electrodes in the rats' pleasure centers. Then some rats were given an electric shock whenever their heart rates happened to increase. Other rats received shock when their heart rates went lower. In other words, one group of rats was consistently "rewarded" (that is, shocked) when the rats' heart rates showed an increase. The other group was consistently rewarded for a decrease. After a single 90-minute training session, rats learned to alter their heart rates by as much as 20 percent in the direction for which they had been rewarded.

Miller's research was an early example of **biofeedback training** (BFT). Biofeedback is simply a system that provides, or "feeds back," information about a bodily function to an organism. Miller used electrical stimulation of the brain to feed-back information to rats when they had engaged in a targeted bodily response (in this case, raised or lowered their heart rates). Somehow the rats then used this information to raise or lower their heart rates.

Similarly, people have learned to voluntarily change various bodily functions, including heart rate, that were once considered to be beyond their control.

It is true that you can learn to increase or decrease your heart rate just by thinking about it. Biofeedback training can help you realize this aim.

Biofeedback training The systematic feeding back to an organism of information about a bodily function so that the organism can gain control of that function. Abbreviated *BFT.*

However, electrodes are not implanted in people's brains. Rather, people hear a "blip" or observe some other signal that informs them when the targeted response is being displayed.

BFT is used in many ways. BFT can be used to help people regain control over various functions when nerve pathways have been damaged. For example, a signal informs them when nervous impulses cause targeted muscles to contract, and they learn to make such control reliable by trying to cause the signal to be sounded again.

BFT can also help people combat stress, tension, and anxiety (Budzynski & Stoyva, 1984). In one example, people can learn to emit alpha waves (and feel somewhat more relaxed) through feedback from an EEG. A blip may increase in frequency whenever alpha waves are being emitted. The psychologist's instructions are simply to "make the blip go faster." An **electromyograph** (EMG), which monitors muscle tension, is commonly used to help people become more aware of muscle tension in the forehead and elsewhere and to learn to lower this tension. Through the use of other instruments, people have learned to lower their heart rates, their blood pressure, and the amount of sweat in the palm of the hand. All of these changes are relaxing. Biofeedback is widely used today by sports psychologists to teach athletes how to relax muscle groups that are unessential to the task at hand so that they can control anxiety and tension (Nelson, 1990).

People have also learned to elevate the *temperature* of a finger. Why bother, you ask? It happens that limbs become subjectively warmer when more blood flows into them. Increasing the temperature of a finger—that is, altering patterns of blood flow in the body—helps some people control migraine headaches, which may be caused by dysfunctional circulatory patterns.

ALTERING CONSCIOUSNESS THROUGH HYPNOSIS

Perhaps you have seen films in which Count Dracula hypnotized resistant victims into a stupor. Then he could get on with a bite in the neck with no further nonsense. Perhaps a fellow student labored to place a friend in a "trance" after reading a book on hypnosis. Or perhaps you have seen an audience member hypnotized in a nightclub act. If so, chances are this person acted as if he or she had returned to childhood, imagined that a snake was about to have a nip, or lay rigid between two chairs for a while.

A Brief History

Hypnosis, a term derived from the Greek word for sleep, has only recently become a respectable subject for psychological inquiry. Modern hypnosis seems to have begun with the ideas of Franz Mesmer in the eighteenth century. Mesmer asserted that the universe was connected by forms of magnetism—which may not be far from the mark. He claimed that people, too, could be drawn to one another by "animal magnetism." (No bullseye here.) Mesmer used bizarre props to bring people under his "spell." He did manage a respectable cure rate for minor ailments. But we skeptics are more likely to attribute his successes to the placebo effect than to animal magnetism.

Hypnosis. Only recently has hypnosis become a respectable subject for psychological inquiry. Hypnotized subjects become passive and tend to deploy their attention according to the instructions of the hypnotist.

During the second half of the last century, hypnosis contributed to the formation of psychoanalytic theory. Jean Martin Charcot, a French physician, had assumed that **hysterical disorders** such as hysterical blindness and paralysis were caused by physical problems. When students were able to stimulate a normal woman to display hysterical symptoms through hypnosis, however, Charcot began to pursue psychological causes for hysterical behavior. One of his students, Pierre Janet, suggested that hysterical symptoms represented subconscious thoughts breaking through a "weakness in the nervous system."

The notion of subconscious roots for hysterical disorders was developed in Vienna, Austria. The physician Josef Breuer discovered that a patient felt better about personal problems as a result of talking and expressing feelings under hypnosis. Sigmund Freud later suggested that hypnosis was one avenue to the unconscious. (He believed that dreams were another.) Freud used hypnosis to uncover what he thought were the unconscious roots of his patients' problems. Under hypnosis, for example, a number of his patients recalled traumatic childhood experiences, such as being seduced by a parent, that they could not otherwise remember. But after a while, Freud switched from hypnosis to free association. One reason is that he came to believe that some of his patients were recalling childhood fantasies, not actual events.

Hypnotism Today. Today, hypnotism retains its popularity in nightclubs, but it is also used as an anesthetic in dentistry, childbirth, even surgery. Psychologists may use hypnosis to teach clients how to relax or help them imagine vivid imagery in techniques like systematic desensitization (see Chapter 13). Police use hypnosis to prompt the memories of witnesses.

Hypnotic Induction

The state of consciousness called the hypnotic trance is traditionally induced by asking subjects to narrow their attention to a small light, a spot on the wall, an object held by the hypnotist, or just the hypnotist's voice. There are usually suggestions that the limbs are becoming warm, heavy, and relaxed. Subjects may also be told that they are becoming sleepy or falling asleep. Hypnosis is *not* sleep, however, as shown by differences in EEG recordings for the hypnotic trance and the stages of sleep. Still, the word *sleep* is understood by subjects to suggest a hypnotic trance and has a track record of success.

It is also possible to induce hypnosis through instructions that direct subjects to remain active and alert (Clkurel & Gruzelier, 1990; Miller et al., 1991). The effects of hypnosis are thus unlikely to be attributable to relaxation.

People who are readily hypnotized are said to have *hypnotic suggestibility.* Part of hypnotic suggestibility is knowledge of what is expected during the "trance state." Suggestible subjects also usually have positive attitudes and expectations about hypnosis and want to be hypnotized (Barber et al., 1974). Liking and trusting the hypnotist also contribute to suggestibility (Gfeller et al., 1987).

It is true that people who are easily hypnotized have positive attitudes toward hypnosis. They look forward to the experience and cooperate with the hypnotist.

Like LSD users who claim to have flashbacks, people with high hypnotic suggestibility enjoy daydreaming and have vivid and absorbing imaginations (Crawford, 1982).

Changes in Consciousness Brought About by Hypnosis

Hypnotists and hypnotized subjects report that hypnosis can bring about some or all of the following changes in consciousness. As you read them, bear in mind that all changes in "consciousness" are inferred from changes in observable behavior and self-reports.

Passivity. When being hypnotized, or in a trance, subjects await instructions and appear to suspend planning.

Electromyograph An instrument that measures muscle tension. Abbreviated *EMG.* (From the Greek *mys,* meaning "mouse" and "muscle"—reflecting similarity between the movement of a mouse and the contraction of a muscle.)

Hypnosis A condition in which people appear to be highly suggestible and behave as though they are in a trance. (From the Greek *hypnos,* meaning "sleep.")

Hysterical disorders Disorders in which a bodily function is lost because of psychological rather than biological reasons. (Now referred to as conversion disorders; see Chapter 13.)

Narrowed Attention. Subjects may focus on the hypnotist's voice or a spot of light and avoid attending to background noise or intruding thoughts. It is claimed that subjects may not hear a loud noise behind the head if they are directed not to. (However, objective measures of hearing *do* suggest that subjects do not show any reduction in auditory sensitivity; rather they *report* greater deafness [Spanos et al., 1982].)

Pseudomemories and Hypermnesia. Subjects may be instructed to show **pseudomemories** or **hypermnesia.** In police investigations, witnesses' memories are usually heightened by instructing them to focus on selected details of a crime and then to reconstruct the entire scene. Studies suggest, however, that although subjects may report recalling more information when they are hypnotized (Orne et al., 1984), such information is often incorrect (Dwyan & Bowers, 1983; Nogrady et al., 1985; Weekes et al., 1992). But hypnotized subjects often report false information with conviction (Sheehan & Tilden, 1983; Weekes et al., 1992) so that police investigators or juries are misled.

Suggestibility. Subjects may respond to suggestions that an arm is becoming lighter and will rise or that the eyelids are becoming heavier and must close. They may act as though they cannot unlock hands clasped by the hypnotist or bend an arm "made rigid" by the hypnotist. Hypnotized subjects serving as witnesses are also highly open to the suggestions of their interviewers. They may incorporate ideas and images presented by interviewers into their "memories" and report them as facts (Laurence & Perry, 1983).

Playing Unusual Roles. Most subjects expect to play sleepy, relaxed roles, but they may also be able to play roles calling for increased strength or alertness, such as riding a bicycle with less fatigue than usual (Banyai & Hilgard, 1976). In **age regression,** subjects may play themselves as infants or children. Research shows that many supposed childhood memories and characteristics are played inaccurately. Nonetheless, some subjects show excellent recall of such details as hair style or speech pattern. A subject may speak a language forgotten since childhood.

Perceptual Distortions. Hypnotized subjects may act as though hypnotically induced hallucinations and delusions are real. In the "thirst hallucination," for example, subjects act as if they are parched, even if they have just had a drink. Subjects may behave as though they cannot hear loud noises, smell odors (Zamansky & Bartis, 1985), or sense pain.

Posthypnotic Amnesia. Many subjects apparently cannot recall events that take place under hypnosis (Davidson & Bowers, 1991), or even that they were hypnotized—if so directed. Subjects can usually recall these things if they are rehypnotized and instructed by the hypnotist to do so, however (Kihlstrom et al., 1985).

The results of at least one experiment suggest that it may be advisable to take the phenomenon of posthypnotic amnesia with a grain of salt. Subjects are more likely to report recalling events while "in a trance" when they are subjected to a lie-detector test and led to believe that they will be found out if they are faking (Coe & Yashinski, 1985).

Posthypnotic Suggestion. Subjects may follow instructions according to prearranged cues of which they are supposedly unaware. For instance, a subject may be directed to fall again into a deep trance upon the single command, "Sleep!" Smokers frequently seek the help of hypnotists to break their habits, and they are frequently given the suggestion that upon "waking," cigarette smoke will become aversive. They may also be instructed to forget that this idea originated with the hypnotist.

Pseudomemories Hypnotically induced false memories.

Hypermnesia Greatly enhanced or heightened memory.

Age regression In hypnosis, taking on the role of childhood, commonly accompanied by vivid recollections of one's past.

Regression Return to a form of behavior characteristic of an earlier stage of development.

Theories of Hypnosis

Hypnotism is no longer explained in terms of animal magnetism, but psychodynamic theory and learning theory have offered explanations. According to Freud, the hypnotic trance represents **regression.** Hypnotized adults suspend "ego functioning," or conscious control of their behavior. They permit themselves to return to childish modes of responding that emphasize fantasy and impulse rather than fact and logic. Other theorists focus on concepts such as role playing and dissociation.

Role Theory. Theodore Sarbin (1972) offers a **role-theory** view of hypnosis (Sarbin & Coe, 1972). He points out that the changes in behavior that are attributed to the hypnotic trance can be successfully imitated when subjects are instructed to behave *as though* they were hypnotized. For example, people can lie rigid between two chairs whether or not they are hypnotized. People also cannot be hypnotized unless they are familiar with the hypnotic "role"—the behavior that constitutes the trance. Sarbin is not saying that hypnotic subjects *fake* the hypnotic role. He is suggesting, instead, that they allow themselves to enact this role under the hypnotist's directions.

Research findings that "suggestible" hypnotic subjects are motivated to enact the hypnotic role, are good role players, and have vivid and absorbing imaginations would all seem to support role theory. The fact that the behaviors shown by hypnotized subjects can be mimicked by role players means that we need not resort to the concept of the "hypnotic trance"—an unusual and mystifying altered state of awareness—to explain hypnotic events.

Dissociation. Runners frequently get through the pain and tedium of long-distance races by *dissociating*—by imagining themselves elsewhere, doing other things. My students inform me that they manage the pain and tedium of *other* instructors' classes in the same way. Ernest Hilgard (1977) similarly explains hypnotic phenomena through **neodissociation theory.** This is the view that we can selectively focus our attention on one thing (like hypnotic suggestions) and dissociate ourselves from the things going on around us.

In one experiment related to neodissociation theory, participants were hypnotized and instructed to submerse their arms in ice water—causing "cold pressor pain" (Miller et al., 1991). Participants were given suggestions to the effect that they were not in pain, however. Highly hypnotizable subjects reported dissociative experiences that allowed them to avoid the perception of pain, such as imagining that they were at the beach or imagining that their limbs were floating in air above the ice water.

Though hypnotized people may be focusing on the hypnotist's suggestions and perhaps imagining themselves to be somewhere else, they still tend to perceive their actual surroundings peripherally. In a sense, we do this all the time. We are not fully conscious, or aware, of everything going on about us. At any moment we selectively focus on events such as tests, dates, or TV shows that seem important or relevant. While taking a test, we may nevertheless be peripherally aware of the color of the wall or of the sound of rain.

Consider posthypnotic amnesia. When told to forget that they were hypnotized, subjects may focus on other matters. But the experience of hypnosis can be focused on afterward. Let us assume a person in a "trance" is given the posthypnotic suggestion to fall into a trance again upon hearing "Sleep!" but not to recall the fact that he or she was given this command. Upon "waking," the person does not focus on the posthypnotic suggestion. However, hearing the command "Sleep!" leads to rapid refocusing of attention and return to the trance. These thoughts are all, in a sense, separated or dissociated from each other. Yet, the person's attention can focus rapidly on one, then another.

Role theory and neodissociation theory do not suggest that the phenomena of hypnosis are phony. Instead, they suggest that we do not need to explain these events through an altered state of awareness called a trance. Hypnosis may not be special at all. Rather, it is *we* who are special—through our great imaginations, our role-playing ability, and our capacity to divide our consciousness—concentrating now on one event we deem important, concentrating later on another.

Role theory A theory that explains hypnotic events in terms of the person's ability to act *as though* he or she were hypnotized. Role theory differs from faking in that subjects cooperate and focus on hypnotic suggestions instead of pretending to be hypnotized.

Neodissociation theory A theory that explains hypnotic events in terms of the splitting of consciousness.

STUDY GUIDE

EXERCISE: Types of Drugs

Below are the names of several types of drugs that are discussed in the text. Indicate whether each drug is a depressant (D), stimulant (S), or hallucinogenic (H) by writing the appropriate letter—D, S, or H—in the blank space to the left of the drug. The answers are given at the end of the exercise.

_____ 1. Codeine
_____ 2. Benzedrine
_____ 3. Lysergic acid (LSD)
_____ 4. Cocaine
_____ 5. Demerol
_____ 6. Nicotine
_____ 7. Mescaline
_____ 8. Methadone
_____ 9. Quaalude
_____ 10. Ritalin
_____ 11. Phenobarbital
_____ 12. Valium
_____ 13. Dexedrine
_____ 14. Alcohol
_____ 15. Marijuana
_____ 16. Morphine
_____ 17. Phencyclidine (PCP)
_____ 18. Heroin
_____ 19. Secobarbital
_____ 20. Methedrine

ANSWERS TO MATCHING EXERCISE

1. D
2. S
3. H
4. S
5. D
6. S
7. H
8. D
9. D
10. S
11. D
12. D
13. S
14. D
15. H
16. D
17. H
18. D
19. D
20. S

ESL—BRIDGING THE GAP

This part is divided into

1. cultural references,
2. phrases and expressions in which words are used differently from their regular meaning, or are used as metaphors.

Cultural References

Marc Chagall (174)—a Russian artist born in 1887 who became a French citizen in 1922 and painted for the rest of his life there

supermarket (176)—a large indoor market where customers choose from a great amount of items

Karl Marx (177)—(1818–1883): a German socialist and political economist who lived in London; author of *Communist Manifesto* and *Das Kapital*

Civil War (182)—(1861–1865); The American Civil War, or War Between the States, was a tragic war between the northern states and the southern states that caused much suffering

Franco-Prussian War (182)—(1870–1871); a war between France and Prussia (Germany) in which the Germans were the victors

nightclub act (192)—entertainment in a restaurant which is known for its entertainment and not for its food

lie-detector test (194)—a mechanism that measures blood pressure and other physiological responses to determine if a person who is being questioned is telling the truth (being honest)

Phrases and Expressions (Different Usage)

the $64,000 question (166)—the biggest question there is

a proper area (166)— a correct area; an appropriate area

the proper province (166)—the correct or appropriate area for the study of psychology to have control
further cemented (166)—increased and made permanent
readily available (168)—easily received
summon up (168)—remember; look for and get
after all (169)— When you think about it
essence of (169)—basis; the basic or most important element
bring them about (169)—cause them
some scrawls (169)—movements of pencil or pen
printout (169)— prints or pages that have printing on them from a computer
a rather steep descent (171)—extreme decline
brief bursts (171)—short small explosions
outdated theory (171)—a theory that does not have support now
power isn't switched off (171)—(a reference to turning off the electric current)
contest the view (171)—argue that
"wrecked" the following day (172)—very bad or terrible the next day
"catch up on our sleep" (172)—get the sleep which we did not get before
long versus short sleepers (172)—how people who sleep many hours are different from people who sleep few hours
happy-go-lucky (172)—an attitude of happiness without concern for problems which may occur later; without worry
self-satisfied (172)—happy with oneself
closed the gap (172)—there was not any difference
horror stories (173)—terrible incidents
droopy eyelids (174)—eyelids that are closing slowly over the eyeballs
dream theater (175)—the way that you dream; dream arena
unlikely candidates (175)—probably not good means or methods
time-triggered mechanism (175)—a mechanism which acts at a specific time
thrash about (175)—move with energy
wear and tear (175)—a little physical damage; (from the idiom, "wear out" which means becoming unusable)
gain your footing (175)—remain balanced
that is, (175)—this means that
sleep-onset (176)—the point at which sleep begins
set the stage (176)—prepare
take you up (177)—make you feel good, or euphoric
let you down (177)—make you feel calm and sometimes depressed
toy of the well-to-do (177)—plaything of the wealthy
price breaks (177)—the cost has greatly decreased
"sleeping it off" (177)—the great length of time someone sometimes sleeps after having had a lot of alcohol
a handful (178)—a few, not all
in effect (178)—in reality; what actually happens, although we do not plan it that way
meant so much to so many (179)—the most important for a large number of people
drug of choice (180)—the drug which most adolescents prefer
short-term use (180)—use for a brief period of time
slurs the speech (181)—speech is not clear; words are not pronounced carefully
street drugs(183)—drugs which are sold illegally on the street
poor judgment(183)—bad judgment
from drug to drug (183)—the effects of one drug may be different from the effects of another
all-night cram sessions (183)—remaining awake all night in order to study for an exam
opinion is mixed (184)—there are different opinions
deadens pain (184)—causes a person to not feel pain
quickening of the heart rate (184)—the rate of the beat of the heart increases suddenly
came to the attention (185)—was noticed by
habit-forming (185)—a person might acquire a habit for it; become dependent on
novice smoker (186)—new and inexperienced smoker, or person who is beginning to smoke
mental "kick" (186)—a sudden elation or good feeling
light-headedness (186)—a feeling that there is air in one's head
grows wild (187)—grows without anyone cultivating it or planting and caring for it
short-term memory (187)—memory of recent events
rise in workload (187)—increase in the work that the heart will have to do
opens new worlds (188)—makes new experience available
LSD "trips" (188)—journeys (fantasies and imagery) of the mind caused by LSD
swear off (188)—make a positive decision to not use it or do it anymore
thoughts . . . wander (189)—uncontrolled thoughts
replay of the experience (189)—unfold, or repeat the experience
for the sake of (189)—deprive oneself of one experience in order to have another
peak experiences (189)—experiences of euphoria
similar psychological threads (189)—they are connected
normal person-environment relationship (190)—the normal relationship of the person to the environment
Just taking this time out (190)—Doing nothing else except to change activities, relax or do nothing
the final word on meditation is not yet in (190)—there are no conclusive research findings on meditation yet
gather some first-hand knowledge (190)—acquire some knowledge by doing it yourself
try it out (190)—attempt it
outbreath (190)—a breath that you breathe out of your mouth
wrapped in (191)—completely involved
to squelch them (191)—to eliminate them
above all (191)—the important thing is

can take for granted in life (191)—assume, accept and not think about or pay attention to

Once in a while(191)—it happens but not often

to be sure (191)—it is true

hair stand literally on end (191)—the hair on the head rises in a vertical position; (this phrasing is common for expressing fear)

not be far from the mark (192)—it may be almost accurate

avenue to the unconscious (193)—a method of reaching the unconscious

to narrow attention (193)—to focus

a track record (193)—has had some success in the past which indicates there will be more success

to take . . . with a grain of salt (194)—to consider it as not very important and also to not believe it

CHAPTER REVIEW

SECTION 1: The $64,000 Question: What *Is* Consciousness?

Objective 1: Discuss the controversy concerning the inclusion of consciousness as a topic in the science of psychology.

In 1904, William (1) ________________ wrote an article, "Does Consciousness Exist?" John (2) ________________, the father of modern behaviorism, argued that only observable (3) b________________ should be studied by psychologists. However, (4) cog________________ psychologists believe that we cannot discuss meaningful human behavior without referring to consciousness.

Objective 2: Define *consciousness* as sensory awareness, the selective aspect of attention, direct inner awareness, personal unity, and the waking state.

Consciousness has several meanings, including sensory awareness; the selective aspect of attention; direct (5) ________________r awareness of cognitive processes; personal (6) ________________y, or the sense of self; and the waking state. Sensory (7) ________________ness refers to consciousness of the environment. (8) D________________ inner awareness refers to consciousness of thoughts, images, emotions, and memories.

Sigmund Freud differentiated among ideas that are conscious; (9) ________________scious, that is, available to awareness by focusing on them; and (10) ________________scious, that is, unavailable to awareness under ordinary circumstances.

SECTION 2: Altering Consciousness Through Sleep and Dreams

Objective 3: List the four stages of NREM sleep, and discuss the features of each.

(11) Electro________________ (EEG) records show different stages of sleep. Different stages of sleep are characterized by different (12) b________________ waves. We have four stages of (13) non________________ (NREM) sleep. Stage (14) ________________ sleep is lightest, and stage (15) ________________ sleep is deepest.

The strength of brain waves is measured in the unit (16) ________________s. When we close our eyes and relax, before going to sleep, our brains emit (17) ________________a waves. As we enter stage 1 sleep, we enter a pattern of (18) ________________a waves. The transition from alpha to theta waves may be accompanied by brief hallucinatory, dream-like images referred to as the (19) ________________gic state. During stage 2 sleep, sleep (20) ________________les appear. We emit slow, strong (21) ________________a waves during stages 3 and 4 sleep.

Objective 4: Describe REM sleep, and explain why it is also referred to as paradoxical sleep.

After a half hour or so of stage (22) ________________ sleep, we journey upward through the stages until we enter REM sleep. REM sleep is characterized by rapid (23) ________________ movements beneath closed lids, and by the emission of brain waves that resemble those of light stage (24) ________________ sleep. Because EEG patterns during REM sleep resemble those of the waking state, REM sleep is also referred to as (25) ________________ical sleep. During REM sleep we dream about (26) ________________ percent of the time. We dream about (27) ________________ percent of the time during NREM sleep.

During a typical eight-hour night, we undergo about (28:

How many?) ________________ trips through the different stages of sleep. Our first journey through stage 4 sleep is usually (29: longest or shortest?). Sleep tends to become (30: lighter or deeper?) as the night wears on. Periods of REM sleep tend to become (31: longer or shorter?) toward morning.

Objective 5: Summarize research concerning the functions of sleep, focusing on the effects of sleep deprivation, and on long versus short sleepers.

Sleep apparently helps restore a tired body, but we do not know exactly how sleep restores us, or how much sleep we need. People who sleep nine or more hours a day are called long sleepers. Long sleepers are more concerned about (32) ________________ment than short sleepers are. Long sleepers are more creative than short sleepers, but also more anxious and (33) ________________ed. Long sleepers spend proportionately more time in (34: REM or NREM?) sleep than short sleepers do.

People who are sleep-deprived show temporary problems in (35) ________________tion, which may reflect episodes of (36) ________________line sleep. People deprived of REM sleep show (37) REM-________________nd during subsequent sleep periods.

Objective 6: Discuss the nature of dreams, including theories of dream content.

Dreams are most vivid during (38: REM or NREM?) sleep. Freud theorized that dreams reflect (39) ________________scious wishes and serve the function of protecting sleep. According to the activation-synthesis model, dreams reflect activation by the (40) ________________s, and automatic integration of resultant neural activity by the (41) cerebral co________________. The content of most dreams is an extension of the events or concerns of the day.

SECTION 3: Altering Consciousness Through Drugs

Objective 7: Define *substance abuse* and *substance dependence.*

Various substances or drugs alter consciousness. Substance use is considered abuse when it is continued for at least one (42) ________________ despite the fact that it is causing or compounding a social, (43) oc________________, psychological, or (44) ph________________ problem. The (45) am________________ of the substance used is not the crucial factor. Substance dependence is characterized by (46: Increased or Decreased?) use despite efforts to cut down and by (47) ________________cal dependence. Physiological dependence is evidenced by tolerance or by an (48) ab________________ syndrome upon withdrawal.

People usually first try drugs because of (49) ________________ity, but usage can be reinforced by anxiety reduction, feelings of euphoria, and other sensations. People are also motivated to avoid (50) ________________wal symptoms once they become physiologically dependent. Some people may have genetic predispositions to become physiologically dependent on certain substances.

SECTION 4: Altering Consciousness Through Depressants

Objective 8: Summarize research concerning the effects of alcohol.

The group of substances called depressants acts by slowing the activity of the (51) ________________ nervous system.

Alcohol is an intoxicating depressant that leads to (52) phy________________ dependence. Alcohol impairs (53) cog________________ functioning, slurs the (54) s________________, and reduces (55) m________________coordination. Alcohol provides people with an excuse for (56) ________________re or for (57) anti________________ behavior, but alcohol has not been shown to induce antisocial behavior directly. As a depressant, alcohol also (58: Increases or Decreases?) sexual response, although many people expect alcohol to have the opposite effect.

Objective 9: Discuss the effects of opiates and opioids, and explain how methadone is used to treat heroin dependence.

Opiates are a group of (59) ________________cs derived from the opium poppy. (60) ________________ds are similar to opiates in chemical structure, but are synthesized in the laboratory. The opiates (61) mor________________ and (62) h________________ are depressants that reduce pain, but they are also bought on the street because of the euphoric rush they provide. Opiates and opioids can lead to (63) ph________________ dependence and distressing (64) ab________________ syndromes. The synthetic narcotic

(65) ______done has been used to treat heroin dependence. The drug (66) ______one blocks the "high" of heroin.

Objective 10: Discuss the effects of barbiturates and methaqualone.

Barbiturates are (67) ______nts with many medical uses. These uses include treatment of (68) ep______, of high (69) ______ pressure, and of anxiety and insomnia. Barbiturates lead rapidly to (70) ph______ dependence.

SECTION 5: Altering Consciousness Through Stimulants

Objective 11: Discuss the effects of the amphetamines.

Stimulants act by (71: increasing or decreasing?) the activity of the nervous system.

(72) ______ines are stimulants that produce feelings of euphoria when taken in high doses. But high doses of amphetamines may also cause restlessness, insomnia, psychotic symptoms, and a "crash" upon (73) ______al. Amphetamines and a related stimulant, (74) R______, are commonly used to treat hyperactive children.

Objective 12: Discuss the effects of cocaine.

The stimulant (75) c______ was used in Coca-Cola prior to 1906. Now it is an illegal drug that provides feelings of (76) ______ia and bolsters self-confidence. As with the amphetamines, overdoses can lead to (77) ______ness, (78) in______, and psychotic reactions. There is controversy as to whether stimulants lead to (79) ______cal dependence, although it is generally agreed that any drug can lead to (80) ______cal dependence.

Objective 13: Discuss the effects of the ingredients in cigarette smoke, and explain how stress influences the desire for smokers to increase their usage of cigarettes.

Cigarette smoke contains carbon (81) ______ide, hydrocarbons, and the stimulant (82) ______ine. Regular smokers adjust their smoking to maintain a consistent blood level of nicotine, suggestive of (83) ______cal dependence. Cigarette smoking has been linked to death from heart disease, cancer, and many other disorders.

SECTION 6: Altering Consciousness Through Hallucinogenics

Objective 14: Discuss the effects of marijuana.

Hallucinogenic substances produce (84)______tions, or sensations and perceptions in the absence of external stimulation that become confused with reality.

Marijuana is a (85) ______genic drug. Marijuana's psychoactive ingredients including (86) delta ______inol, or THC. THC often produces heightened and distorted (87) ______tions, relaxation, feelings of (88) em______, and reports of new insights. Hallucinations are possible.

Objective 15: Discuss the effects of LSD, and summarize research concerning the flashback controversy.

LSD is a hallucinogenic drug that produces vivid (89) ______tions. So-called LSD (90) ______cks may reflect psychological rather than physiological factors. Persons prone to flashbacks are more oriented toward (91) ______sy and toward allowing their thoughts to (92) ______der. Regular use of hallucinogenics may lead to psychological (93) ______dence and to (94) tol______. However, hallucinogenics are not known to lead to (95) ______cal dependence.

SECTION 7: Altering Consciousness Through Meditation

Objective 16: Summarize research concerning the effects of meditation.

In meditation, one focuses "passively" on an object or a (96) m______ in order to alter the normal person-environment relationship. In this way consciousness (that is, the normal focuses of attention) is altered and a (97) re______ ______ is often induced. (98) Tr______ Meditation (TM) and other forms of meditation appear to reduce high blood pressure along with producing relaxation. There is controversy as to whether meditation is more relaxing or effective in reducing (99) b_______________ pressure than is simple quiet sitting or resting.

SECTION 8: Altering Consciousness Through Biofeedback

Objective 17: Summarize research concerning the effects of biofeedback.

Biofeedback is a system that (100) _______________s back information about a bodily function to an organism. Neal Miller taught rats to increase or decrease their (101) _______________ _______________s by giving them an electric shock in their "pleasure centers" when they performed the targeted response. Through biofeedback training, people and lower animals have learned to consciously control a number of (102) _______________tary or autonomic functions. The (103) _______________graph (EMG) monitors (104) m_______________ tension and helps people become more aware of muscle tension in the forehead and elsewhere.

SECTION 9: Altering Consciousness Through Hypnosis

Objective 18: Describe the history of hypnosis.

Hypnosis in its modern form was originated by Franz (105) M_______________. Mesmer explained the hypnotic "trance" through his concept of animal (106) _______________ism. In the second half of the nineteenth century, hypnotism contributed to the development of (107) _______________tic theory. By means of hypnosis, Charcot and Janet found that so-called (108) _______________ical disorders had psychological roots. Freud suggested that hypnosis was one avenue to the (109) _______________scious mind.

Today hypnotism is used in night club acts and thus has its sensationalistic aspects. However, psychologists responsibly use hypnosis to help clients relax, to help them (110) _______________ine vivid imagery, and to help them cope with (111) p_______________. Police use hypnosis to prompt the (112) m_______________ of witnesses.

Objective 19: Discuss the changes in consciousness that can be brought about by means of hypnosis.

People who are readily hypnotized are said to have hypnotic (113) _______________lity. Suggestible people have (114) _______________tive attitudes toward hypnosis, and are highly (115) _______________ed to become hypnotized.

Hypnosis typically brings about the following changes in consciousness: passivity, narrowed (116) _______________tion, (117) _______________sia (heightened memory), suggestibility, assumption of unusual roles, perceptual distortions, (118) post_______________ amnesia, and posthypnotic suggestion.

Objective 20: Explain the role and neodissociation theories of hypnosis.

According to Freud's psychoanalytic theory, the hypnotic trance represents (119) _______________sion.

Current theories of hypnosis do not rely on the existence of a special (120) t_______________ state. According to role theory, hypnotized subjects enact the (121) _______________ of being in a hypnotic trance. In order to enact this role, they must be aware of the (122) _______________iors that constitute the trance, and motivated to imitate these behaviors.

According to (123) neo_______________tion theory, hypnosis involves the selective deployment of attention.

Answers To Chapter Review

1. James
2. Watson
3. Behavior
4. Cognitive
5. Inner
6. Unity
7. Awareness
8. Direct
9. Preconscious
10. Unconscious
11. Electroencephalograph
12. Brain
13. Non-rapid-eye-movement
14. 1
15. 4
16. Volts
17. Alpha
18. Theta
19. Hypnagogic
20. Spindles
21. Delta
22. 4
23. Eye
24. 1
25. Paradoxical
26. 80
27. 20
28. Five
29. Longest
30. Lighter
31. Longer
32. Achievement
33. Depressed
34. REM
35. Attention

36. Borderline
37. REM-rebound
38. REM
39. Unconscious
40. Pons
41. Cortex
42. Month
43. Occupational
44. Physical
45. Amount
46. Increased
47. Physiological
48. Abstinence
49. Curiosity
50. Withdrawal
51. Central
52. Physiological
53. Cognitive
54. Speech
55. Motor
56. Failure
57. Antisocial
58. Decreases
59. Narcotics
60. Opioids
61. Morphine
62. Heroin
63. Physiological
64. Abstinence
65. Methadone
66. Naloxone
67. Depressants
68. Epilepsy
69. Blood
70. Physiological
71. Increasing
72. Amphetamines
73. Withdrawal
74. Ritalin
75. Cocaine
76. Euphoria
77. Restlessness
78. Insomnia
79. Physiological
80. Psychological
81. Monoxide
82. Nicotine
83. Physiological
84. Hallucinations
85. Hallucinogenic
86. -9-tetrahydro-cannabinol
87. Perceptions
88. Empathy
89. Hallucinations
90. Flashbacks
91. Fantasy
92. Wander
93. Dependence
94. Tolerance
95. Physiological
96. Mantra
97. Relaxation response
98. Transcendental
99. Blood
100. Feeds
101. Heart rates
102. Involuntary
103. Electromyograph
104. Muscle
105. Mesmer
106. Magnetism
107. Psychodynamic (or psychoanalytic)
108. Hysterical
109. Unconscious
110. Imagine
111. Pain
112. Memory
113. Suggestibility
114. Positive
115. Motivated
116. Attention
117. Hypermnesia
118. Posthypnotic
119. Regression
120. Trance
121. Role
122. Behaviors
123. Neodissociation

POSTTEST

1. Sigmund Freud labeled mental events that are unavailable to awareness under most circumstances as
   (a) preconscious.
   (b) unconscious.
   (c) repressed.
   (d) dissociated.

2. According to the text, the least controversial meaning of the word "consciousness" refers to
   (a) direct inner awareness.
   (b) sensory awareness.
   (c) the normal waking state.
   (d) the sense of self.

3. Brain waves are measured by means of the
   (a) electrocardiogram.
   (b) electroencephalograph.
   (c) electromyograph.
   (d) thermistor.

4. During stage 4 sleep, the brain emits ________ waves.
   (a) alpha
   (b) beta
   (c) delta
   (d) theta

5. Sleep spindles appear during stage ________ sleep.
   (a) 1
   (b) 2
   (c) 3
   (d) 4

6. Jim usually sleeps eight hours a night. About how many dreams is he likely to have during the night?
   (a) None
   (b) One
   (c) Five
   (d) Twenty-five or more

7. Freud believed that dreams "protected sleep" by
   (a) causing us to emit alpha waves.
   (b) inhibiting the reticular activating system.
   (c) producing rapid eye movements.
   (d) keeping disturbing ideas out of awareness.

8. When they drink, the college-age children of alcoholics ________ than the children of nonalcoholics.
   (a) show lower tolerance
   (b) develop withdrawal symptoms more rapidly
   (c) show better visual-motor coordination
   (d) are more likely to become physically ill

9. In terms of its action on the body, cocaine is correctly categorized as a
   (a) depressant.
   (b) hallucinogenic.
   (c) narcotic.
   (d) stimulant.

10. The most widely used drug on college campuses is
   (a) cocaine.
   (b) marijuana.
   (c) LSD.
   (d) alcohol.

11. According to the text, ________ prevents users from becoming "high" if they take heroin afterward.
(a) antabuse
(b) naloxone
(c) methadone
(d) imipramine

12. Which of the following is *not* part of the abstinence syndrome for alcohol?
(a) Rapid pulse
(b) Low blood pressure
(c) Anxiety
(d) Tremors

13. Methaqualone is a(n) ________ drug.
(a) depressant
(b) stimulant
(c) antidepressant
(d) hallucinogenic

14. Which of the following is least likely to cause physiological dependence?
(a) Barbiturates
(b) LSD
(c) Methaqualone
(d) Methadone

15. TM was introduced by
(a) Maharishi Mahesh Yogi.
(b) Franz Mesmer.
(c) Herbert Benson.
(d) Neal Miller.

16. Biofeedback is defined as a system that feeds back information about ________ to an organism.
(a) autonomic functions
(b) heart rate
(c) voluntary functions
(d) a body function

17. A friend tells you that he has learned how to raise the temperature in a finger through biofeedback training. Your friend probably acquired this skill in order to
(a) relax the muscles of the forehead.
(b) control headaches.
(c) lower acid secretion in the gastrointestinal tract.
(d) emit alpha waves.

18. According to neodissociation theory,
(a) hypnotized subjects are aware of many things going on around them, even though they are focusing primarily on the hypnotist.
(b) the trance state is induced by age regression.
(c) only subjects who are highly motivated to be hypnotized can be hypnotized.
(d) one cannot enter a hypnotic trance unless one is suggestible.

19. Who first encouraged a patient to talk and express her feelings freely while she was hypnotized?
(a) Sigmund Freud
(b) Pierre Janet
(c) Josef Breuer
(d) Jean Martin Charcot

20. Arnold knows that you are taking a psychology course and asks you if you think he would be a "good subject" for hypnosis. You point out that research suggests that hypnosis is most successful with people who
(a) understand what is expected of them during the "trance state."
(b) are seeking the approval of the hypnotist.
(c) are unfamiliar with hypnosis.
(d) are below average in intelligence.

Answer Key To Posttest

1. B
2. A
3. B
4. C
5. B
6. C
7. D
8. C
9. D
10. D
11. B
12. B
13. A
14. B
15. A
16. D
17. B
18. A
19. C
20. Aq

- A single nauseating meal can give rise to a food aversion that persists for years.
- Dogs can be trained to salivate when a bell is sounded.
- Psychologists helped a young boy overcome fear of rabbits by having him eat cookies while a rabbit was brought nearer.
- During World War II, a psychologist devised a plan for training pigeons to guide missiles to their targets.
- Punishment does not work.
- You can "hook" people on gambling by allowing them to win some money in the early stages and then tapering off with the payoffs.
- Psychologists successfully fashioned a method to teach an emaciated 9-month-old infant to stop throwing up.
- We must make mistakes in order to learn.
- Only people are capable of insight.

Learning

Learning Objectives

When you have finished studying Chapter 6, you should be able to:

Learning

1. Discuss controversies in defining learning.

Classic Conditioning

2. Describe the role of Ivan Pavlov in the history of the psychology of learning.
3. Describe the roles of US, CS, UR, and CR in classical conditioning.
4. Describe various types of classical conditioning.
5. Explain how contingency theory challenges the traditional explanation of classical conditioning.
6. Describe the processes of extinction and spontaneous recovery within classical conditioning.
7. Describe the processes of generalization and discrimination within classical conditioning.
8. Discuss applications of classical conditioning.

Operant Conditioning

9. Describe the roles of Edward Thorndike and B. F. Skinner in the history of the psychology of learning.
10. Explain the process of operant conditioning.
11. Distinguish between various kinds of reinforcers.
12. Describe the processes of extinction and spontaneous recovery within operant conditioning.
13. Differentiate between reinforcers and rewards and punishments.
14. Define *discriminative stimulus.*
15. Describe the effects of various schedules of reinforcement.
16. Describe shaping.
17. Discuss applications of operant conditioning.

Cognitive Learning

18. Describe evidence that supports the view that learning can occur by insight.
19. Define *latent learning* and describe evidence that supports this kind of learning.
20. Discuss observational learning, including the effects of media violence.
21. Discuss prototypes and concept learning.

When I was a child in The Bronx, my friends and I would go to the movies on Saturday mornings. There would be a serial ("Rocketman" was my favorite) followed by a feature film, and admission was a quarter. We would also eat candy (I loved Nonpareils and Raisinets) and popcorn. One morning, my friends dared me to eat two large containers of buttered popcorn by myself. For reasons that I label "youth," I rose to the challenge. Down went an enormous container of buttered popcorn. More slowly—much more slowly—I stuffed down the second. Predictably, I felt bloated and nauseated. The taste of the butter, corn, and salt lingered in my mouth and nose, and my head spun with the repulsive sensations. It was obvious to me that I would have no more popcorn that day. However, I was surprised that I could not face buttered popcorn again for a year.

Years later, I learned that psychologists referred to my response to buttered popcorn as a *taste aversion.* Although I could not analyze my reaction in a sophisticated fashion at the time, I recognized that there was something strange about it. As I thought of it then, my "head" was telling me one thing about the popcorn while my "stomach" was telling me another. On a cognitive level, I recognized that my feelings stemmed from eating too much buttered popcorn and that smaller amounts would be safe. But something had also apparently been learned on a "gut level" that overrode my belief that I should be able to eat and enjoy reasonable amounts of buttered popcorn.

Now I know that a **taste aversion** is an example of *classical conditioning.* Classical conditioning leads organisms to anticipate events. An "overdose" of buttered popcorn had made me queasy. Afterward, the sight and odor of buttered popcorn—even the thought of it—was sufficient to make me anticipate nausea. In fact, they induced sensations of nausea in my throat and stomach. My aversion seemed silly at the time, but it is adaptive for organisms to develop taste aversions readily. Often when foods make us ill, it is because they are poisoned or unhealthful for other reasons. A taste aversion serves the adaptive function of keeping us away from them.

After I had acquired my taste aversion, I stayed away from buttered popcorn. My avoidance could be explained in terms of another kind of learning, *operant conditioning,* in which organisms learn to do things—and not to do other things—because of the consequences of their behavior. I stayed away from buttered popcorn in order to avoid anticipated nausea. But we also seek fluids when thirsty, sex when aroused, and an ambient temperature of 68 to 70 degrees Fahrenheit because we anticipate pleasant consequences. Put briefly, classical conditioning focuses on how organisms form anticipations about their environments. Operant conditioning focuses on what they do about them.

By the way, more than 30 years have now passed—how many more is my business. But I still prefer my popcorn *un*buttered.

It is true that you can develop an aversion to a food that lasts for months or years on the basis of one nauseating meal.

Taste aversion A kind of classical conditioning in which a previously desirable or neutral food becomes repugnant because it is associated with aversive stimulation.

How Do We Learn How to Play Chess? Games like chess are learned, but how? Can we explain playing chess as the summation of myriad instances of conditioning or must we turn to notions of mental representations and cognitive maps? What developments in the nervous system make us "ready" to learn the right moves? What biological changes register the memories of games long past?

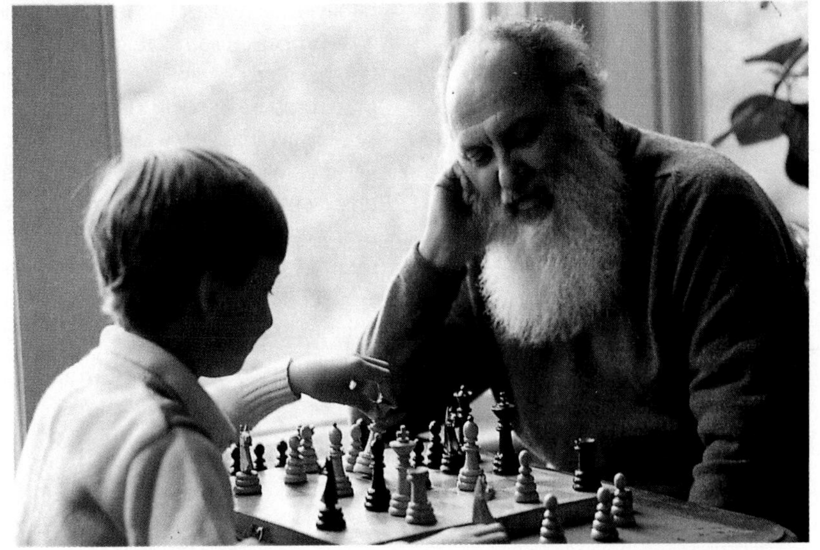

Classical and operant conditioning are two forms of learning, which is the subject of this chapter. In lower organisms, much behavior is instinctive, or inborn. Fish are born "knowing" how to swim. Salmon instinctively return to spawn in the streams of their birth after they have matured and spent years roaming the deep seas. Robins instinctively know how to sing the songs of their species and to build nests. Rats instinctively mate and rear their young. Among people, however, the variety and complexity of behavior patterns are largely learned through experience. Experience is essential in our learning to walk and in our acquisition of the languages of our parents and communities. We learn to read, to do mathematical computations, and to symbolically rotate geometric figures. We learn to seek out the foods valued in our cultures when we are hungry. We get into the habit of starting our days with coffee, tea, or other beverages. We learn which behavior patterns are deemed socially acceptable and which are considered wrong. And, of course, our families and communities use verbal guidance, set examples, and apply rewards and punishments in an effort to teach us to stick to the straight and narrow.

Sometimes our learning experiences are direct, as was my taste aversion for buttered popcorn. But we can also learn from the experiences of others. For example, I warn my children against the perils of jumping from high places and running wild in the house. (Occasionally they heed me.) We learn about the past, about other peoples, and about how to put things together from books and visual media. And we learn as we invent ways of doing things that have never been done before.

Having noted these various ways of learning, let me admit that the very definition of **learning** stirs controversy in psychology. The concept may be defined in different ways.

From the behaviorist perspective, learning is defined as a relatively permanent change in behavior that arises from experience. Changes in behavior also arise from maturation and physical changes, but they are not considered to reflect learning. The behaviorist definition is operational. Learning is defined in terms of the measurable events or changes in behavior by which it is known. From the behaviorist perspective, buttered popcorn came to evoke nausea because it was temporally associated with nausea. I also learned to avoid popcorn because of the temporal consequences of consuming it—simple and not-so-sweet.

Learning (1) According to behaviorists, a relatively permanent change in behavior that results from experience. (2) According to cognitive theorists, the process by which organisms make relatively permanent changes in the way they represent the environment because of experience. These changes influence the organism's behavior but do not fully determine it.

From the cognitive perspective, learning involves processes by which experience contributes to relatively permanent changes in the way organisms mentally represent the environment. Changes in representation may influence, but do not cause, changes in behavior. From this perspective, learning is *made evident* by behavioral change, but learning is defined as an internal and not directly observable process. From the cognitive perspective, my gorging on buttered popcorn taught me to regard, or mentally represent, buttered popcorn in a different way. My altered image of buttered popcorn then encouraged me to avoid it for a while. But my avoidance was not mechanical or imperative.

Behaviorists do not concern themselves with the ways in which I mentally represent buttered popcorn. (And who can fault them?) They argue that there is no direct way of measuring my mental imagery, only my overt behavior. Why, then, try to embrace imagery in a scientific theory?

Let us now focus on some of the particulars of a number of kinds of learning, beginning with classical conditioning. We shall return to these theoretical matters from time to time as well.

CLASSICAL CONDITIONING

Classical conditioning involves some of the ways in which we learn to associate events. Consider: We have a distinct preference for having instructors grade our papers with A's rather than F's. We are also (usually) more likely to stop our cars for red than green traffic lights. Why? We are not born with instinctive attitudes toward the letters A and F. Nor are we born knowing that red means stop and green means go. We learn the meanings of these symbols because they are associated with other events. A's are associated with instructor approval and the likelihood of getting into graduate school. Red lights are associated with avoiding accidents and traffic citations.

Ivan Pavlov Rings a Bell

Lower animals also learn relationships among events, as Russian physiologist Ivan Pavlov (1849–1936) discovered in research with laboratory dogs. Pavlov was attempting to identify neural receptors in the mouth that triggered a response from the salivary glands. But his efforts were hampered by the dogs' salivating at undesired times such as when a laboratory assistant inadvertently clanged a food tray.

Because of its biological makeup, a dog will salivate if meat powder is placed on its tongue. Salivation in response to meat powder is unlearned, a **reflex.** Reflexes are elicited by a certain range of stimuli. A **stimulus** is an environmental condition that evokes a response from an organism, such as meat powder on the tongue or a traffic light's changing colors. Reflexes are simple unlearned responses to stimuli. Pavlov discovered that reflexes can also be learned, or conditioned, through association. His dogs began salivating in response to clinking

Reflex A simple unlearned response to a stimulus.

Stimulus An environmental condition that elicits a response.

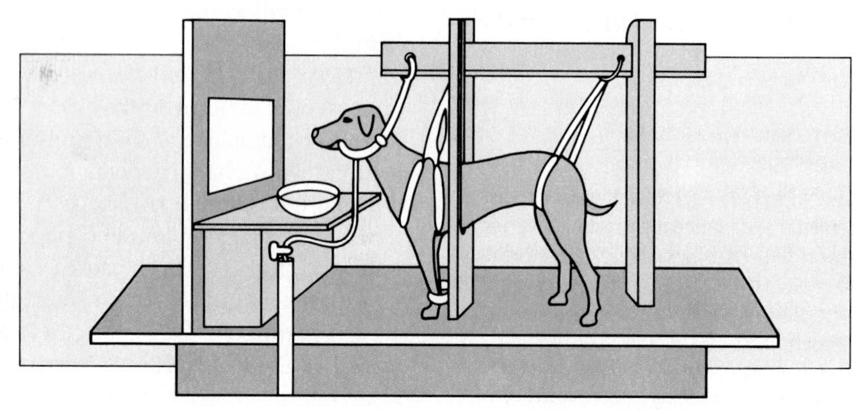

FIGURE 6.1 Pavlov's Demonstration of Conditioned Reflexes in Laboratory Dogs. From behind the two-way mirror at the left, a laboratory assistant rings a bell and then places meat powder on the dog's tongue. After several pairings, the dog salivates in response to the bell alone. A tube collects saliva and passes it to a vial. The quantity of saliva is taken as a measure of the strength of the animal's response.

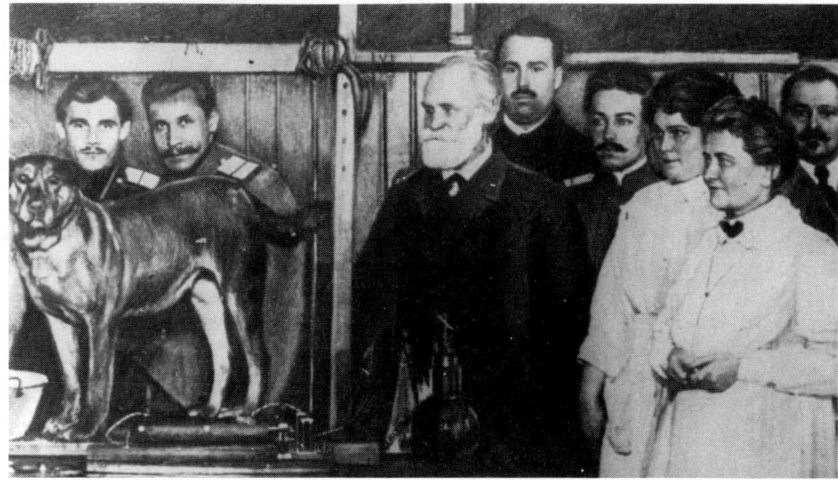

Ivan Pavlov. Pavlov, his assistants, and a professional salivator (the dog) at a Russian academy early in the century.

food trays because this noise, in the past, had been paired repeatedly with the arrival of food. The dogs would also salivate when an assistant entered the laboratory. Why? In the past, the assistant had brought food.

When we are faced with novel events, we sometimes have no immediate way of knowing whether or not they are important. When we are striving for concrete goals, we often ignore the unexpected, even when the unexpected is just as important, or more important, than the goal. So it was that Pavlov at first saw this uncalled-for canine salivation as an annoyance, a hindrance to his research. But in 1901, he decided that his "problem" was worth looking into. He then set about to show that he could train, or condition, his dogs to salivate when he wished and in response to any stimulus he chose.

Pavlov termed these trained salivary responses "conditional reflexes." They were *conditional* upon the repeated pairing of a previously neutral stimulus (such as the clinking of a food tray) and a stimulus (in this case, food) that predictably evoked the target response (in this case, salivation). Today, conditional reflexes are more generally referred to as **conditioned responses** (CRs). They are responses to previously neutral stimuli that are learned, or conditioned.

Pavlov demonstrated conditioned responses by strapping a dog into a harness such as the one in Figure 6.1. When meat powder was placed on the dog's tongue, the dog salivated. Pavlov repeated the process several times, with one difference. He preceded the meat powder by half a second or so with the sounding of a bell on each occasion. After several pairings of meat powder and bell, Pavlov sounded the bell but did *not* follow the bell with the meat powder. Still the dog salivated. It had learned to salivate in response to the bell.

It is true that dogs can be trained to salivate when a bell is rung, a buzzer is sounded, a light is shone, and so on.

Why did the dog learn to salivate in response to the bell? Behaviorists and cognitive psychologists explain the learning process in very different ways.

Behaviorists explain the outcome of **classical conditioning** in terms of the publicly observable conditions of learning. They define classical conditioning as a simple form of learning in which one stimulus comes to evoke the response usually evoked by a second stimulus by being paired repeatedly with the second stimulus. In Pavlov's demonstration, the dog learned to salivate in response to the bell

Conditioned response (CR) In classical conditioning, a learned response to a conditioned stimulus.

Classical conditioning (1) According to behaviorists, a form of learning in which one stimulus comes to evoke the response usually evoked by a second stimulus by being paired repeatedly with the second stimulus. (2) According to cognitive theorists, the learning of relationships among events so as to allow an organism to represent its environment. Also referred to as *respondent conditioning* or *Pavlovian conditioning.*

because the sounding of the bell had been paired with meat powder. That is, in classical conditioning, the organism forms associations between stimuli because the stimuli are **contiguous.** Behaviorists do *not* say that the dog "knew" that food was on the way. They argue that we cannot speak meaningfully about what a dog "knows." We can only outline the conditions under which targeted behaviors will reliably occur. The behaviorist focus is on the mechanical acquisition of the conditioned response.

Cognitive psychologists view classical conditioning as the learning of relationships among events. The relationships allow organisms to mentally represent their environments and make predictions (Holyoak et al., 1989; Rescorla, 1988). In Pavlov's demonstration, the dog salivated in response to the bell because the bell—from the cognitive perspective—became mentally connected with the meat powder. The cognitive focus is on the information gained by organisms. Organisms are viewed as seekers of information who generate and test rules about the relationships among events (Weiner, 1991).

Behaviorists might counter that organisms can learn to engage in conditioned responses without any evidence that they are aware of what they are learning. There are any number of classic experiments in which people learn conditioned responses that are presumably too small to perceive. In one example, people learned to engage in apparently imperceptible thumb contractions that involved only 25–30 microvolts of energy (Hefferline & Keenan, 1963). Learners, in other words, are not necessarily privy to all of their changes in behavior.

Stimuli and Responses in Classical Conditioning: US, CS, UR, and CR

In the demonstration just described, the meat powder is an unlearned or **unconditioned stimulus** (US). Salivation in response to the meat powder is an unlearned or **unconditioned response** (UR). The bell was at first a meaningless or neutral stimulus. It might have produced an **orienting reflex** in the dog because of its distinctness. But it was not yet associated with food. Then, through repeated association with the meat powder, the bell became a learned or **conditioned stimulus** (CS) for the salivation response. Salivation in response to the *bell* (or CS) is a learned or conditioned response (CR). A CR is a response similar to a UR, but the response elicited by the CS is by definition a CR, not a UR (see Figure 6.2).

Contiguous Next to one another.

Unconditioned stimulus (US) A stimulus that elicits a response from an organism prior to conditioning.

Unconditioned response (UR) An unlearned response to an unconditioned stimulus.

Orienting reflex An unlearned response in which an organism attends to a stimulus.

Conditioned stimulus (CS) A previously neutral stimulus that elicits a conditioned response because it has been paired repeatedly with a stimulus that already elicited that response.

Delayed conditioning A classical conditioning procedure in which the CS is presented before the US and left on until the response occurs.

Simultaneous conditioning A classical conditioning procedure in which the CS and US are presented at the same time.

Trace conditioning A classical conditioning procedure in which the CS is presented and then removed before the US is presented.

Types of Classical Conditioning

Classical conditioning tends to occur most efficiently when the conditioned stimulus (CS) is presented about 0.5 second before the unconditioned stimulus (US) and is continued until the learner responds to the US. This is an example of **delayed conditioning,** in which the CS (for example, a light) can be presented anywhere from a fraction of a second to several seconds before the US (in this case, meat powder) and is left on until the response (salivation) is shown. Conditioning can also take place via **simultaneous conditioning,** in which a CS such as a light is presented along with a US such as meat powder. In **trace conditioning,** the CS (for example, a light) is presented and then removed (or turned off) prior to presentation of the US (meat powder). Therefore, only the memory trace of the CS (light) remains to be conditioned to the US.

Conditioning occurs most effectively in delayed conditioning, perhaps because it is most adaptive. That is, in delayed conditioning, the CS signals the consequent appearance of the US. As a result, organisms can learn to make predictions about their environments. Predictability is adaptive because it allows organisms to prepare for future events. Learning is inefficient and may not take

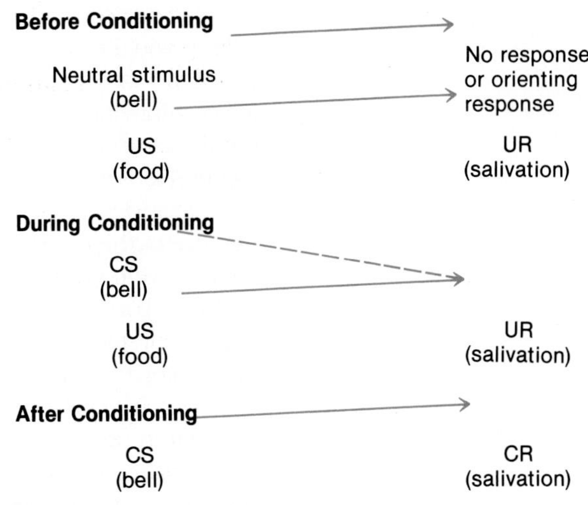

FIGURE 6.2 A Schematic Representation of Classical Conditioning. Prior to conditioning, food elicits salivation. The bell, a neutral stimulus, elicits either no response or an orienting response. During conditioning, the bell is rung just before meat powder is placed on the dog's tongue. After several repetitions, the bell, now a CS, elicits salivation, the CR.

place at all when the US is presented before the CS (Hall, 1989), a sequence referred to as **backward conditioning.** Backward conditioning may not permit organisms to make useful predictions about their environments.

Contingency Theory: Contiguity or Contingency? What "Really" Happens During Classical Conditioning?

Behaviorists and cognitive psychologists interpret the events of the conditioning process in different ways. Behaviorists explain the outcomes of classical conditioning in terms of the contiguous presentation of stimuli. Cognitive psychologists explain classical conditioning in terms of the ways in which stimuli provide information that allows organisms to form and revise mental representations of their environments.

In classical-conditioning experiments with dogs, Robert Rescorla (1967) obtained some results that are difficult to explain without reference to cognitive concepts. Each phase of his work paired a tone (CS) with electric shock (US) but in different ways. With one group of animals, the shock was presented consistently after the tone. That is, the US followed on the heels of the CS as in Pavlov's studies. The dogs in this group learned to show a fear response when the tone was presented.

A second group of dogs heard an equal number of tones and received an equal number of electric shocks, but the shock never immediately followed the tone. In other words, the tone and shock were unpaired. Now, from the behavioral perspective, the dogs should not have learned to associate the tone and the shock, since one did not presage the other. Actually, the dogs learned quite a lot: they learned that they had nothing to fear when the tone was sounded! The dogs showed vigilance and fear when the laboratory was quiet—for apparently the shock could come at any time—but they were calm in the presence of the tone.

The third group of dogs also received equal numbers of tones and shocks, but these were presented at purely random intervals. Occasionally they were paired, but most often they were not. According to Rescorla, behaviorists might argue that intermittent pairing of the tones and shocks should have brought about some learning. Yet it did not. The animals showed no fear in response to the tone. Rescorla suggests that the animals in this group learned nothing because the tones provided no information about the prospect of being shocked.

Backward conditioning A classical conditioning procedure in which the unconditioned stimulus is presented prior to the conditioned stimulus.

Rescorla concluded that contiguity—that is, the co-appearance of two events (the US and the CS)—cannot in itself explain classical conditioning. Instead, learning occurs only when the conditioned stimulus (in this case, the tone) provides information about the unconditioned stimulus (in this case, the shock). According to so-called **contingency theory,** learning occurs because a conditioned stimulus indicates that the unconditioned stimulus is likely to ensue.

Behaviorists might counter, of course, that for the second group of dogs, the *absence* of the tone became the signal for the shock. Shock may be a powerful enough event that the fear response becomes conditioned to the laboratory environment. For the third group of dogs, the shock was as likely in the presence of the neutral stimulus as in its absence. Therefore, many behaviorists would expect no learning to occur.

So, behaviorists and cognitive psychologists will probably interpret Rescorla's research in different ways. What "really" happens during classical conditioning may remain somewhat speculative for generations to come. During that period, behaviorists may suggest that we stick to a description of laboratory conditions as our most scientific explanation. Cognitive psychologists may continue to insist that we do violence to the dignity of the individual when we fail to refer to mentalistic concepts.

Now let us consider some findings concerning taste aversion. We shall try to see why I developed an aversion to buttered popcorn but not to the Rocketman serial.

Contingency theory The view that learning occurs when stimuli provide information about the likelihood of the occurrence of other stimuli.

Taste Aversion

Taste aversions serve the adaptive function of motivating organisms to avoid potentially harmful foods. Although taste aversions are acquired by association, they differ from other kinds of classical conditioning in a couple of ways. First, only one association may be required. I did not have to go back for seconds at the movies to develop my aversion for buttered popcorn! Second, whereas most kinds of classical conditioning require that the US and CS be contiguous, in taste aversion the US (nausea) can occur hours after the CS (flavor of food).

Formation of a Taste Aversion? Taste aversions may be acquired by just one association of the US and the CS. Most kinds of classical conditioning require that the US and CS be contiguous, but in a taste aversion, the US (nausea) can occur hours after the CS (flavor of food).

Sad to say, taste aversion can further impair the health of people being treated with chemotherapy for cancer. The chemotherapy often induces nausea, and a taste aversion can develop for foods eaten earlier in the day. Thus, cancer patients, who may already be losing weight because of their illness, may find that taste aversion compounds the problems associated with lack of appetite. To combat taste aversion in such patients, Bernstein (1985) recommends giving them unusual foods prior to chemotherapy. If a taste aversion develops, it will then be to the unusual food, and patients' appetites for dietary staples may be unaffected.

Research in taste aversion also challenges the behaviorist view that organisms learn to associate any stimuli that are contiguous. Not all stimuli are created equal. Instead, it seems that organisms are biologically predisposed to develop aversions that are adaptive in their environmental settings (Garcia et al., 1989). In a classic study, Garcia and Koelling (1966) conditioned two groups of rats. Each group was exposed to the same three-part CS: a taste of sweetened water, a light, and a clicker. Afterward, one group was presented a US of nausea (induced by poison or radiation), and the other group was presented a US of electric shock.

After conditioning, the rats who had been nauseated showed an aversion for sweetened water but not to the light or clicker. Although all three stimuli had been presented at the same time, *they had acquired only the taste aversion.* After conditioning, the rats who had been shocked avoided both the light and the clicker, *but they did not show a taste aversion to the sweetened water.* For each group of rats, the conditioning that took place was adaptive. In the natural scheme of things, nausea is more likely to stem from poisoned food than from lights or sounds. And so, for nauseated rats, acquiring the taste aversion was appropriate. Sharp pain, in contrast, is more likely to stem from natural events involving lights (fire, lightning) and sharp sounds (twigs snapping, things falling). Therefore, it was more appropriate for the shocked animals to develop an aversion to the light and the clicker than to the sweetened water.

This finding fits my experience as well. My nausea led to a taste aversion to buttered popcorn—but not to an aversion to the Rocketman serial (which, in retrospect, was more deserving of nausea) or the movie theater. I returned every Saturday morning to see what would happen next. Yet, the serial and the theater, as much as the buttered popcorn, had been associated (contiguous) with my nausea.

Extinction and Spontaneous Recovery

Extinction and *spontaneous recovery* are aspects of conditioning that help organisms adapt by updating their expectations or revising their representations of the changing environment. A dog may learn to associate a new scent (CS) with the appearance of a dangerous animal. It can then take evasive action when it whiffs the scent. A child may learn to connect hearing a car pull into the driveway (CS) with the arrival of his or her parents (US). The child may thus come to squeal with delight (CR) when the car is heard.

Times change. The once dangerous animal may no longer be a threat. (What a puppy perceives to be a threat may lose its power to menace once the dog matures.) After moving to a new house, the child's parents may commute by means of public transportation. The sounds of a car in a nearby driveway may signal a neighbor's, not a parent's, homecoming. When conditioned stimuli (such as the scent or the sound of a car) are no longer followed by unconditioned stimuli (a dangerous animal, a parent's homecoming), they lose their ability to elicit conditioned responses. In this way, the organism adapts to a changing environment.

Extinction. In classical conditioning, **extinction** is the process by which conditioned stimuli (CSs) lose the ability to elicit conditioned responses (CRs) because the CSs are no longer associated with unconditioned stimuli (USs). From the cognitive perspective, extinction teaches the organism to modify its representation of the environment because the CS no longer serves its predictive function.

In experiments in the extinction of CRs, Pavlov found that repeated presentations of the CS (or bell) without the US (meat powder) led to extinction of the CR (salivation in response to the bell). Figure 6.3 shows that a dog conditioned by Pavlov began to salivate (show a CR) in response to a bell (CS) after only a couple of pairings—referred to as **acquisition trials**—of the bell with meat powder (the US). Continued pairings of the stimuli led to increased salivation as measured in number of drops of saliva. After seven or eight trials, salivation leveled off at 11 to 12 drops.

Then, salivation to the bell (CR) was extinguished through several trials—referred to as **extinction trials**—in which the CS (bell) was presented without the meat powder (US). After about ten extinction trials, the CR (salivation in response to the bell) was no longer shown.

What would happen if we were to allow a day or two to pass after we had extinguished the CR (salivation response to a bell) in a laboratory dog, and then we again presented the CS (bell)? Where would you place your money? Would the dog salivate or not?

If you bet that the dog would again show the CR (salivate in response to the bell), you were correct. Organisms tend to show **spontaneous recovery** of extinguished CRs merely as a function of the passage of time. For this reason, the term *extinction* may be a bit misleading. When a species of animal becomes extinct, all members of that species capable of reproducing have died. The species vanishes permanently. But the experimental extinction of CRs does not lead to the

---

Extinction An experimental procedure in which stimuli lose their ability to evoke learned responses because the events that had followed the stimuli no longer occur. (The learned responses are said to be *extinguished*.)

inhibited

Acquisition trial In conditioning, a presentation of stimuli such that a new response is learned and strengthened.

Extinction trial In conditioning, a performance of a learned response in the absence of its predicted consequences so that the learned response becomes inhibited.

Spontaneous recovery The recurrence of an extinguished response as a function of the passage of time.

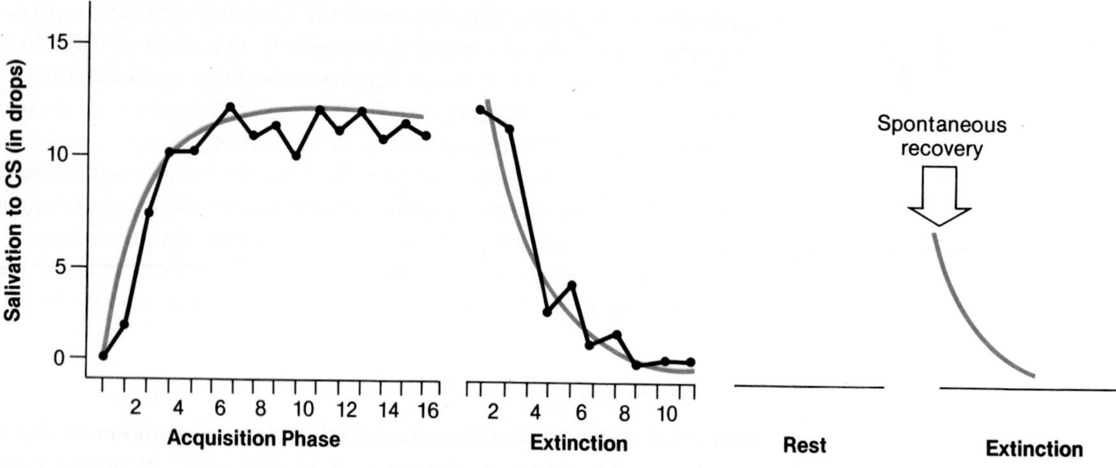

FIGURE 6.3
Learning and Extinction Curves.
Actual data from Pavlov (1927) compose the jagged line, and the curved lines are idealized. In the acquisition phase, a dog salivates (shows a CR) in response to a bell (CS) after only a few trials in which the bell is paired with meat powder (the US). Afterward, the CR is extinguished in about ten trials in which the CS is not followed by the US. After a rest period, the CR recovers spontaneously. A second series of extinction trials then leads to more rapid extinction of the CR.

permanent eradication of CRs. Rather, it seems that they inhibit that response. The response does remain available for future performance.

Consider Figure 6.3 again. When spontaneous recovery of the CR does occur, the strength of the response (in this case, the number of drops of saliva) is not as great as it was at the end of the series of acquisition trials. A second set of extinction trials will also extinguish the CR more rapidly than the first series of extinction trials. Although the CR is at first weaker the second time around, pairing the CS with the US once more will build response strength rapidly.

Spontaneous recovery, like extinction, is adaptive. What would happen if the child heard no car in the driveway for several months? It could be that the next time a car entered the driveway, the child would associate the sounds with a parent's homecoming (rather than the arrival of a neighbor). This expectation could be appropriate. After all, *something* had systematically changed in the neighborhood when no car had entered the nearby driveway for so long. In the wilds, a waterhole may contain water for only a couple of months during the year. But it is useful for animals to associate the waterhole with the thirst drive from time to time so that they will return to it at the appropriate time.

As time passes and the seasons change, things sometimes follow circular paths and arrive at a place where they were before. Spontaneous recovery seems to provide a mechanism whereby organisms are capable of rapidly adapting to intermittently recurring situations.

Generalization at the Crossroads. Chances are that you have never seen this particular traffic light in this particular setting. Because of generalization, however, we can safely bet that you would know what to do if you were to drive up to it.

Generalization and Discrimination

No two things are quite alike. Traffic lights are hung at slightly different heights, and shades of red and green differ a little. The barking of two dogs differs, and the sound of the same animal differs slightly from bark to bark. Adaptation requires that we respond similarly to stimuli that are equivalent in function and that we respond differently to stimuli that are not.

Generalization. Pavlov noted that responding to different stimuli as though they are functionally equivalent is adaptive for animals. Rustling sounds in the undergrowth differ, but rabbits and deer do well to flee when they perceive any of many varieties of rustling. Sirens differ, but people do well to become vigilant or to pull their cars to the side of the road when any siren is heard.

In a demonstration of **generalization,** Pavlov first conditioned a dog to salivate when a circle was presented. During each acquisition trial, the dog was shown a circle (CS), then given meat powder (US). After several trials, the dog exhibited the CR of salivating when presented with the circle alone. Pavlov demonstrated that the dog also exhibited the CR (salivation) in response to closed geometric figures such as ellipses, pentagons, and even squares. The more closely the figure resembled a circle, the greater the strength of the response (the more drops of saliva that flowed).

Discrimination. Organisms must also learn (1) that many stimuli perceived as being similar are functionally different and (2) to respond adaptively to each. During the first couple of months of life, babies can discriminate the voices of their mothers from those of others. They will often stop crying when they hear their mother but not when they hear a stranger's voice.

Pavlov showed that a dog conditioned to salivate in response to circles could be trained *not* to salivate in response to ellipses. The type of conditioning that trains an organism to show a CR in response to a narrow range of stimuli (in this case, circular rather than elliptical geometric figures) is termed **discrimination training.** Pavlov trained the dog by presenting it with circles and ellipses but associating the meat powder (US) with circles only. After a while, the dog no longer showed the CR (salivation) in response to the ellipses. Instead, the animal showed **discrimination.** It displayed the CR in response to circles only.

Pavlov then discovered that he could make the dog behave as though it were tormented by increasing the difficulty of the discrimination task. After the dog exhibited stimulus discrimination, Pavlov showed the animal progressively rounder ellipses. Eventually, the dog could no longer discriminate them from circles. The animal then put on an infantile show. It urinated, defecated, barked profusely, and snapped at laboratory personnel.

How do we explain the dog's belligerent behavior? In a classic work written half a century ago, *Frustration and Aggression,* a group of behaviorally oriented psychologists suggested that frustration induces aggression (Dollard et al., 1939). Why is failure to discriminate circles from ellipses frustrating? For one thing, in such experiments, rewards—such as meat powder—are usually made contingent on correct discrimination. That is, if the dog errs, it forgoes the meat. Cognitive theorists, however, propose that organisms are motivated to construct realistic maps of the world. In building their overall images of the world, organisms—including dogs—adjust their representations to reduce discrepancies and accommodate new information (Rescorla, 1988). In the Pavlovian experiment, the dog lost the ability to meaningfully adjust its representation of the environment as the ellipses grew more circular, and so it was frustrated. Behaviorists counter that it is fruitless to speculate on what goes on in the "mind" of another organism because there is no scientific way to verify our conjectures, whether the organism is a person or a lower animal such as a dog.

In any event, the capacity to make discriminations is important. Most of us would grow concerned if we could no longer make the discriminations necessary for survival. Consider how you might behave if you could barely discriminate between a greenish-red and a reddish-green traffic light, but a person dressed in unmistakable blue was ready to hand you a ticket every time you made an error.

Daily living requires appropriate generalization and discrimination. No two hotels are alike, but when traveling from one city to another, it is adaptive to expect to stay in some hotel. It is encouraging that green lights in Washington, D.C., have the same meaning as green lights in Honolulu. But returning home in the evening requires the ability to discriminate between our homes or apartments and those of others. If we could not readily tell our spouses apart from those of others, we might land in divorce court.

Generalization In conditioning, the tendency for a conditioned response to be evoked by stimuli that are similar to the stimulus to which the response was conditioned.

Discrimination training Teaching an organism to show a learned response in the presence of only one of a series of similar stimuli, accomplished by alternating the stimuli but following only the one stimulus with the unconditioned stimulus.

Discrimination In conditioning, the tendency for an organism to distinguish between a conditioned stimulus and similar stimuli that do not forecast an unconditioned stimulus.

Higher-Order Conditioning

In **higher-order conditioning,** a previously neutral stimulus comes to serve as a CS after being paired repeatedly with a stimulus that has already become a CS. Pavlov demonstrated higher-order conditioning by first conditioning a dog to salivate (show a CR) in response to a bell (a CS). He then paired the shining of a light repeatedly with the bell. After several pairings, shining the light (the higher-order CS) came to elicit the response (salivation) that had been elicited by the bell (the first-order CS).

Consider children who learn that their parents are about to arrive when they hear a car in the driveway. It may be the case that a certain TV cartoon show starts a few minutes before the car enters the driveway. The TV show can begin to elicit the expectation that the parents are coming by being paired repeatedly with the car's entering the driveway. In another example, a boy may burn himself by touching a hot stove. After this experience, the sight of the stove may serve as a CS for eliciting a fear response. And because hearing the word *stove* may evoke a cognitive image of the stove, hearing the word alone may also elicit a fear response.

Applications of Classical Conditioning

Classical conditioning is a major avenue of learning in our daily lives. It is how stimuli come to serve as signals for other stimuli. It is why we come to expect that someone will be waiting outside when the doorbell is rung, or why we expect a certain friend to appear when we hear a characteristic knock. In this section, we explore a number of applications of classical conditioning.

The Bell-and-Pad Method for Bedwetting. By the ages of 5 or 6, children normally awaken in response to the sensations of a full bladder. They inhibit urination, which is an automatic or reflexive response to bladder tension, and go to the bathroom. But bedwetters tend not to respond to sensations of a full bladder while asleep. And so they remain asleep and frequently wet their beds.

By means of the bell-and-pad method, children are taught to wake up in response to bladder tension. They sleep on a special sheet or pad that has been placed on the bed. When the child starts to urinate, the water content of the urine causes an electrical circuit in the pad to be closed. Closing of the circuit triggers a bell or buzzer, and the child is awakened. In terms of principles of classical conditioning, the bell is a *US* that wakes the child (waking up is the *UR*). By means of repeated pairings, stimuli that precede the bell become associated with the bell and also gain the capacity to awaken the child. What stimuli are these? The sensations of a full bladder. In this way, bladder tension (the CS) gains the capacity to awaken the child *even though the child is asleep during the classical conditioning procedure.*

The bell-and-pad method provides a superb example of why behaviorists prefer to explain the effects of classical conditioning in terms of the pairing of stimuli and not in terms of what the learner knows. The behaviorist may argue that we cannot assume that a sleeping child "knows" that wetting the bed will cause the bell to ring. We can only note that by repeatedly pairing bladder tension with the bell, the child eventually *learns* to wake up in response to bladder tension alone. *Learning* is demonstrated by the change in the child's behavior. What the child *knows* about the learning process is a private matter and one on which others can only speculate.

Similar buzzer circuits have also been built into training pants as an aid to toilet training.

The Story of Little Albert: A Case Study in the Classical Conditioning of Emotional Responses. In 1920, John B. Watson and his future wife, Rosalie Rayner, published an article describing their demonstration

Know

Higher-order conditioning (1) According to behaviorists, a classical conditioning procedure in which a previously neutral stimulus comes to elicit the response brought forth by a *conditioned* stimulus by being paired repeatedly with that conditioned stimulus. (2) According to cognitive psychologists, the learning of relationships among events, none of which evokes an unlearned response.

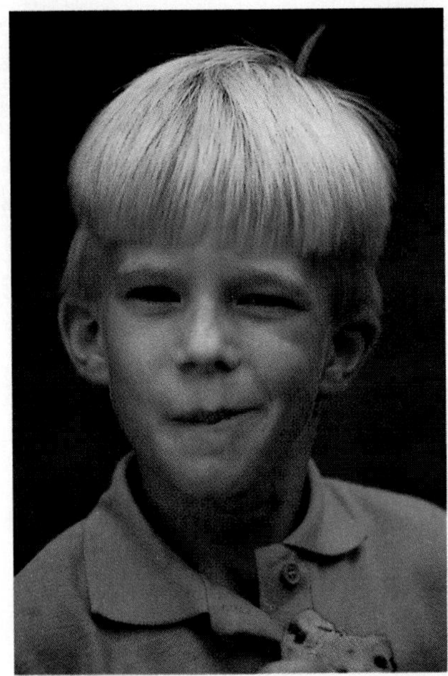

Can Chocolate Chip Cookies Countercondition Fears? Yes, they taste good, but do they have the capacity to countercondition fears? At Berkeley in the 1920s, the Joneses helped a boy overcome his fear of rabbits by having him munch away as the animal was brought closer. Are contemporary behavior therapists sort of keeping up with the Joneses?

that emotional reactions such as fears can be acquired through principles of classical conditioning. The subject of their demonstration was a lad known in the psychological literature by the name of Little Albert. Albert was a phlegmatic fellow at the age of 11 months, not given to ready displays of emotion. But he did enjoy playing with a laboratory rat. Such are the playmates to be found in psychologists' laboratories.

Using a method that some psychologists have criticized as unethical, Watson startled Little Albert by clanging steel bars behind his head when the infant played with the rat. After seven pairings, Albert showed fear of the rat even though clanging was suspended. Albert's fear was also generalized to objects similar in appearance to the rat, such as a rabbit and the fur collar on a woman's coat. Albert's conditioned fear of rats may never have become extinguished. Extinction would have required perceiving rats (the conditioned stimuli) without painful consequences (in the absence of the unconditioned stimuli). Fear, however, might have prevented Albert from facing rats. And, as we shall see in the section on operant conditioning, avoiding rats might have been *reinforced* by reduction of fear.

We must also note that other experiments in conditioning fears (e.g., by English, 1929) have not always been successful. As mentioned in our discussion of taste aversions, it may be that people are more biologically predisposed to learn fears of some objects and situations than others.

In any event, Watson and Rayner did not attempt to reverse, or undo, the effects of Little Albert's conditioning. (Somewhere there may be a gentleman in his 70s who cringes when he sees furry puppies or muffs protecting the hands of girls in winter and, of course, whenever rats are discussed on television.) But, as we shall see in the following sections, other psychologists have used principles of classical conditioning to do just that.

Counterconditioning. Early in the century, University of California professors Harold Jones and Mary Cover Jones (Jones, 1924) reasoned that if fears could be conditioned by painful experiences, it should be possible to *countercondition* them by pleasant experiences. In **counterconditioning,** a pleasant stimulus is paired repeatedly with a fear-evoking object, in this way counteracting the fear response.

Two-year-old Peter feared rabbits intensely. The Joneses arranged for a rabbit to be gradually brought closer to Peter while he engaged in some of his favorite activities such as munching merrily away on candy and cookies. As opposed to flooding, the rabbit was not plopped in Peter's lap. Had they done so, the cookies on the plate and those already eaten might have decorated the walls. At first, they placed the rabbit in a far corner of the room while Peter munched and crunched. Peter, to be sure, cast a wary eye, but he continued to consume the treats. Gradually the animal was brought closer. Eventually, Peter ate treats and touched the rabbit at the same time. The Joneses theorized that the pleasure of eating was incompatible with fear and thus counterconditioned the fear.

It is true that psychologists helped a young boy overcome fear of rabbits by having him eat cookies while a rabbit was brought nearer.

Through classical conditioning, we learn to associate stimuli so that a simple, usually passive, response made to one is then made in response to the other. In the case of Little Albert, clanging noises were associated with a rat, so the rat came to elicit the fear response brought forth by the noise. However, classical conditioning is only one kind of learning that occurs in these situations. According to O. Hobart Mowrer's two-factor theory of learning, classical conditioning in the study with Little Albert suffices to explain the involuntary acquisition of the fear

Counterconditioning A fear-reduction technique in which pleasant stimuli are associated with fear-evoking stimuli so that the fear-evoking stimuli lose their aversive qualities.

response. The boy's voluntary behavior also changed, however. He avoided the rat as a way of reducing his fear. Little Albert thus engaged in another kind of learning—operant conditioning.

In operant conditioning, as we see in the next section, organisms learn to engage in certain behaviors because of their effects. The sight of a hypodermic syringe, for example, may elicit a fear response because a person once had a painful injection. The subsequent avoidance of injections is *operant behavior.* It has the effect of reducing fear. In other cases, we engage in operant behavior to attain rewards, not to avoid unpleasant outcomes.

OPERANT CONDITIONING

In **operant conditioning**—also referred to as **instrumental conditioning**—an organism learns to engage in certain behavior because of the effects of that behavior. We begin this section with the historic work of psychologist Edward L. Thorndike. Then we shall examine the more recent work of B. F. Skinner.

Edward L. Thorndike and the Law of Effect

In the 1890s, stray cats were mysteriously disappearing from the streets and alleyways of Harlem. Many of them, it turned out, were being brought to the quarters of Columbia University doctoral student Edward Thorndike. Thorndike was using them as subjects in experiments in learning by trial and error.

Thorndike placed the cats in so-called puzzle boxes. If the animals managed to pull a dangling string, a latch would be released, allowing them to jump out and reach a bowl of food.

When first placed in a puzzle box, a cat would try to squeeze through any opening and would claw and bite at the confining bars and wire. It would claw at any feature it could reach. Through such **random trial-and-error** behavior, it might take three to four minutes before the cat would chance on the response of pulling the string. Pulling the string would open the cage and allow the cat to reach the food. When placed back in the cage, it might again take several minutes for the animal to pull the string. But as these trials were repeated, it would take progressively less time for the cat to pull the string. After seven or eight trials, it might pull the string immediately when placed back in the box.

The Law of Effect. Thorndike explained the cat's learning to pull the string in terms of his **law of effect.** According to this law, a response (such as string pulling) is "stamped in" or strengthened in a particular situation (such as being inside a puzzle box) by a reward (escaping from the box and eating). Rewards, that is, stamp in S–R (stimulus–response) connections. Punishments, in contrast, "stamp out" stimulus–response connections. Organisms would learn *not* to engage in punished responses. Later we shall see that the effects of punishment on learning are not so certain.

B. F. Skinner and Reinforcement

"What did you do in the war, Daddy?" is a question familiar to many who served during America's conflicts. Some stories involve heroism, others involve the unusual. When it comes to unusual war stories, few will top that of Harvard University psychologist B. F. Skinner. For, as he relates the tale in his autobiography, *The Shaping of a Behaviorist* (1979), one of Skinner's wartime efforts was "Project Pigeon."

During World War, II Skinner proposed that pigeons be trained to guide missiles to their targets. In their training, the pigeons would be **reinforced** with food

---

Operant conditioning A simple form of learning in which an organism learns to engage in behavior because it is reinforced.

Instrumental conditioning A term similar to *operant conditioning,* reflecting the fact that the learned behavior is *instrumental* in achieving certain effects.

Random trial-and-error behavior Behavior that occurs in a novel situation prior to the reception of rewards or reinforcements.

Law of effect Thorndike's principle that responses are "stamped in" by rewards and "stamped out" by punishments.

Reinforce To follow a response with a stimulus that increases the frequency of the response.

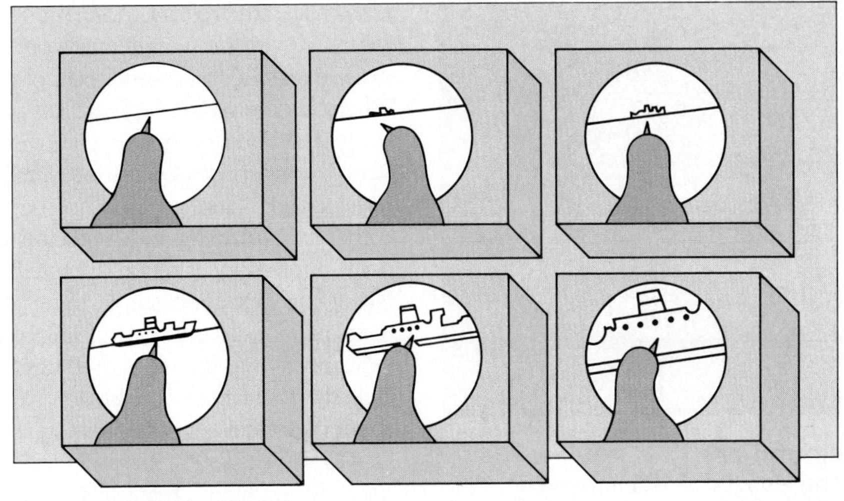

FIGURE 6.4
Project Pigeon. During World War II, B. F. Skinner suggested training pigeons to guide missiles to their targets. In an operant conditioning procedure, the pigeons would be reinforced for pecking at targets projected on a screen. Afterward, in combat, pecking at the on-screen target would keep the missile on course.

pellets for pecking at targets projected onto a screen (see Figure 6.4). Once trained, the pigeons would be placed in missiles. Pecking at similar targets displayed on a screen within the missile would correct the flight path of the missile, resulting in a "hit" and a sacrificed pigeon. However, plans for building the necessary missile—for some reason called the *Pelican* and not the *Pigeon*—were scrapped. The pigeon equipment was too bulky, and as Skinner lamented, his suggestion was not taken seriously. Apparently the Defense Department concluded that Project Pigeon was for the birds.

It is true that a psychologist did conceive a plan for training pigeons to guide missiles to their targets during World War II. That psychologist was B. F. Skinner.

Project Pigeon may have been scrapped, but the principles of learning Skinner applied to the project have found wide applications in operant conditioning. In classical conditioning, an organism learns about the relationships among events. In other words, it learns to associate stimuli. As a laboratory procedure, one previously neutral stimulus (the CS) comes to elicit the response brought forth by another stimulus (the US) because they have been paired repeatedly. In operant conditioning, an organism learns to *do* something because of its effects or consequences.

This is **operant behavior,** behavior that operates on, or manipulates, the environment. In classical conditioning, involuntary responses such as salivation or eyeblinks are often conditioned. In operant conditioning, *voluntary* responses such as pecking at a target, pressing a lever, or many of the athletic skills required in playing tennis are acquired, or conditioned.

In operant conditioning, organisms engage in operant behaviors, also known simply as **operants,** that result in presumably desirable consequences such as food, a hug, an A on a test, attention, or social approval. Some children learn to conform their behavior to social codes and rules to earn the attention and approval of their parents and teachers. Other children, ironically, may learn to "misbehave," since misbehavior also results in attention from other people. Children may especially learn to be "bad" when their "good" behavior is routinely ignored.

Operant behavior Voluntary responses that are reinforced.

Operant The same as an operant behavior.

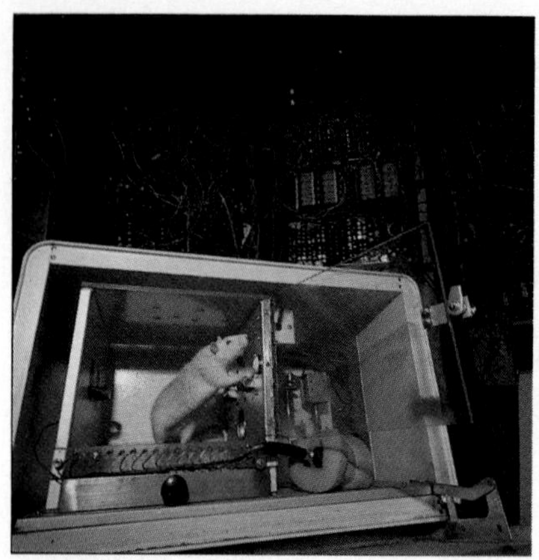

FIGURE 6.5
The Effects of Reinforcement. One of the luminaries of modern psychology, an albino laboratory rat, earns its keep in a Skinner box. The animal presses a lever because of reinforcement—in the form of food pellets—delivered through the spout of the feeder. The habit strength of this operant can be measured as the frequency of lever pressing.

Units of Behavior, "Skinner Boxes," and Cumulative Recorders. In his most influential work, *The Behavior of Organisms,* Skinner (1938) made many theoretical and technological innovations. Among them was his focus on discrete behaviors such as lever-pressing as the unit, or type, of behavior to be studied. Whereas other psychologists might focus on how organisms think or "feel," Skinner focused on measurable things that they do. Many psychologists have found Skinner's kinds of behaviors inconsequential, especially when it comes to explaining and predicting human behavior. But Skinner's supporters point out that focusing on discrete behavior creates the potential for helpful behavior changes. For example, in helping people combat depression, one psychologist might focus on their "feelings." The Skinnerian would focus on cataloguing (and modifying) the types of things that people who complain of depression *do.* Directly modifying depressive behavior might also brighten clients' self-reports about their "feelings of depression" of course.

To study operant behavior efficiently, Skinner also devised an animal cage (or "operant chamber") that was dubbed the *Skinner box* by psychologist Clark Hull. (Skinner himself repeatedly requested that his operant chamber *not* be called a Skinner box. It remains to be seen whether history will honor his wishes.) Such a box is shown in Figure 6.5. The cage is ideal for laboratory experimentation because experimental conditions (treatments) can be carefully introduced and removed, and the results on laboratory animals (defined as changes in the rate of lever pressing) can be carefully observed. The operant chamber (or Skinner box) is also energy-efficient—in terms of the energy of the experimenter. In contrast to Thorndike's puzzle box, a "correct" response does not allow the animal to escape and thus have to be recaptured and placed back in the box.

The rat in Figure 6.5 was deprived of food and placed in a Skinner box with a lever at one end. At first it sniffed its way around the cage and engaged in random behavior. When organisms are behaving in a random manner, responses that meet with favorable consequences tend to occur more frequently. Responses that do not meet with favorable consequences tend to be performed less frequently.

The rat's first pressing of the lever was inadvertent. However, because of this action, a food pellet dropped into the cage. The food pellet increased the probability that the rat would press the lever again. The pellet is thus said to have served as a reinforcement for the lever pressing.

Skinner further mechanized his laboratory procedure by making use of a turning drum, or **cumulative recorder** (see Figure 6.6). The cumulative recorder provides a precise measure of operant behavior. The experimenter need not even be present to record correct responses. In the example used, the lever in the Skinner box is connected to the recorder so that the recording pen moves upward with each correct response. The paper moves continuously to the left at a slow but regular pace. In the sample record shown in Figure 6.6, lever pressings (which record correct responses) were at first few and far between. But after several reinforced responses, lever pressing came fast and furious. When the rat is no longer hungry, the lever pressing will drop off and then stop.

The First "Correct" Response. In operant conditioning, it matters little how the first response that is reinforced comes to be made. The organism can happen on it by chance, as in random learning. The organism can also be physically guided into the response. You may command your dog to "Sit!" and then press its backside down until it is in a sitting position. Finally, you reinforce sitting with food or a pat on the head and a kind word.

Animal trainers use physical guiding or coaxing to bring about the first "correct" response. Can you imagine how long it would take to train your dog if you waited for it to sit or roll over and then seized the opportunity to command it to sit or roll over? You would both age significantly in the process.

Cumulative recorder An instrument that records the frequency of an organism's operants (or "correct" responses) as a function of the passage of time.

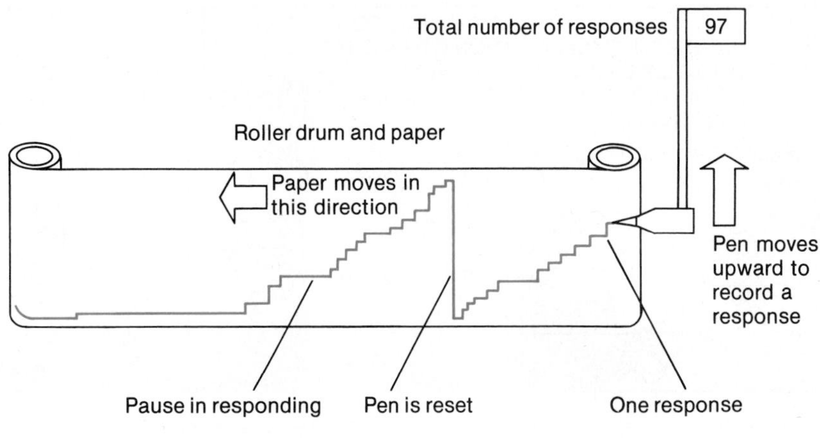

FIGURE 6.6
The Cumulative Recorder. In the cumulative recorder, paper moves continuously to the left while a pen automatically records each targeted response by moving upward. When the pen reaches the top of the paper, it is automatically reset to the bottom.

People, of course, can be verbally guided into desired responses when they are learning tasks such as running a machine, spelling, or adding numbers. But they then need to be informed when they have made the correct response. Knowledge of results is often all the reinforcement that motivated people need to learn new skills.

Types of Reinforcers

Any stimulus that increases the probability that responses preceding it will be repeated serves as a reinforcer. Reinforcers include food pellets when an organism has been deprived of food, water when it has been deprived of liquid, the opportunity to mate, and the sound of a bell that has been previously associated with eating.

Positive and Negative Reinforcers. Skinner distinguished between positive and negative reinforcers. **Positive reinforcers** increase the probability that an operant will occur when they are applied. Food and approval usually serve as positive reinforcers. **Negative reinforcers** increase the probability that an operant will occur when they are *removed.* People often learn to plan ahead so that they need not fear that things will go wrong. Fear acts as a negative reinforcer, because *removal* of fear increases the probability that the behaviors preceding it (such as planning ahead or fleeing a predator) will be repeated.

Greater reinforcers prompt more-rapid learning than do lesser reinforcers. You will probably work much harder for $1,000 than for $10. (If not, get in touch with me—I have some chores that need to be taken care of.) With sufficient reinforcement, operants become a **habit.** They show a high probability of recurrence in a certain situation.

Primary and Secondary Reinforcers. We can also distinguish between primary and secondary, or conditioned, reinforcers. **Primary reinforcers** are effective because of the biological makeup of the organism. Food, water, adequate warmth (positive reinforcers), and pain (a negative reinforcer) all serve as primary reinforcers. **Secondary reinforcers** acquire their value through being associated with established reinforcers. For this reason, they are also termed **conditioned reinforcers.** We may seek money because we have learned that it may be exchanged for primary reinforcers. Money, attention, social approval—all are conditioned reinforcers in our culture. We may be suspicious of, or not

Positive reinforcer A reinforcer that when *presented* increases the frequency of an operant.

Negative reinforcer A reinforcer that when *removed* increases the frequency of an operant.

Primary reinforcer An unlearned reinforcer.

Secondary reinforcer A stimulus that gains reinforcement value through association with established reinforcers.

Conditioned reinforcer Another term for a secondary reinforcer.

FIGURE 6.7
Secondary Reinforcers.

Understanding other people includes being able to predict what they will find reinforcing. In this "Blondie" cartoon, Dagwood apparently finds money more reinforcing than the praise of his boss, Mr. Dithers.

"understand," people who are not interested in money or the approval of others. Part of understanding others lies in being able to predict what they will find reinforcing (see Figure 6.7).

Extinction and Spontaneous Recovery in Operant Conditioning

In operant conditioning, as in classical conditioning, extinction is a process in which stimuli lose the ability to evoke learned responses because the events that had followed the stimuli no longer occur. In classical conditioning, however, the "events" that normally follow and confirm the appropriateness of the learned response (that is, the conditioned response) are the unconditioned stimuli. In Pavlov's experiment, the meat powder was the event that followed and confirmed the appropriateness of salivation. In operant conditioning, the ensuing events are reinforcers. Thus, in operant conditioning, the extinction of learned responses (that is, operants) results from repeated performance of operant behavior without reinforcement. After a number of trials, the operant behavior is no longer shown.

When some time is allowed to pass after the extinction process, an organism will usually perform the operant again when placed in a situation in which the operant had been reinforced previously. Spontaneous recovery of learned responses occurs in operant conditioning as well as in classical conditioning. If the operant is reinforced at this time, it quickly regains its former strength. Spontaneous recovery of extinguished operants suggests that they are inhibited or suppressed by the extinction process and not lost permanently.

Reinforcers versus Rewards and Punishments

Rewards, like reinforcers, are stimuli that increase the frequency of behavior. But rewards are also considered to be pleasant events. Skinner preferred the concept of reinforcement to that of reward because reinforcement does not suggest trying to "get inside the head" of an organism (person or lower animal) to guess what it would find pleasant or unpleasant. A list of reinforcers is arrived at **empirically,** by observing what sorts of stimuli will increase the frequency of the behavior.

Reward A pleasant stimulus that increases the frequency of the behavior it follows.

Empirically By trial or experiment rather than by logical deduction.

However, it should be noted that some psychologists consider the term *reward* to be synonymous with positive reinforcement.

Punishments are aversive events that suppress or decrease the frequency of the behavior they follow.[1] Punishment can rapidly suppress undesirable behavior and may be warranted in "emergencies" such as when a child tries to run out into the street.

It is *not* true that punishment doesn't work. Strong punishment suppresses the behavior it follows. The issues pertaining to punishment concern its limitations and its side effects.

Despite the fact that punishment works, many learning theorists agree that punishment is usually undesirable, especially in rearing children, for reasons such as the following:

1. Punishment does not in itself suggest an alternative acceptable form of behavior.
2. Punishment tends to suppress undesirable behavior only under circumstances in which its delivery is guaranteed. It does not take children long to learn that they can "get away with murder" with one parent, or one teacher, but not with another.
3. Punished organisms may withdraw from the situation. Severely punished children may run away, cut class, or drop out of school.
4. Punishment can create anger and hostility. Adequate punishment will almost always suppress unwanted behavior—but at what cost? A child may express accumulated feelings of hostility against other children.
5. Punishment may generalize too far. The child who is punished severely for bad table manners may stop eating altogether. Overgeneralization is more likely to occur when children do not know exactly why they are being punished and when they have not been shown alternative acceptable behaviors.
6. Punishment may be modeled as a way of solving problems or coping with stress. We shall see that one way children learn is by observing others. Even though children may not immediately perform the behavior they observe, they may perform it later on, even as adults, when their circumstances are similar to those of the **model.**
7. Finally, children learn responses that are punished. Whether or not children choose to perform punished responses, punishment draws their attention to them.

It is usually preferable to focus on rewarding children for desirable behavior than on punishing them for unwanted behavior. By ignoring their misbehavior, or by using **time out** from positive reinforcement, we can consistently avoid reinforcing children for misbehavior.

To reward or positively reinforce children for desired behavior takes time and care. Simply never using punishment is not enough. First, we must pay attention to children when they are behaving well. If we take their desirable behavior for granted, and act as if we are aware of them only when they misbehave, we may be encouraging misbehavior. Second, we must be certain that children are aware of, and capable of performing, desired behavior. It is harmful and fruitless merely to

Punishment An unpleasant stimulus that suppresses the behavior it follows.

Model An organism that engages in a response that is then imitated by another organism.

Time out Removal of an organism from a situation in which reinforcement is available when unwanted behavior is shown.

[1] Recall that *negative reinforcers* are defined in terms of *increasing* the frequency of behavior, although the increase occurs when the negative reinforcer is *removed.* A punishment *decreases* the frequency of a behavior when it is *applied.*

A Discriminative Stimulus. You might not think that pigeons are very discriminating, yet this gift to city life readily learns that pecking will not bring food in the presence of a discriminative stimulus such as a red light.

punish children for unwanted behavior. We must also carefully guide them physically or verbally into making the desired responses and then reward them. We cannot teach children table manners by waiting for them to exhibit proper responses at random and then reinforcing them. If we waited by holding a half-gallon of ice cream behind our backs as a reward, we would have slippery dining room floors long before we had children with table manners.

Discriminative Stimuli

B. F. Skinner might not have been able to get his pigeons into the drivers' seats of missiles during the war, but he had no problem training them to respond to traffic lights. Try the following experiment for yourself.

Find a pigeon. Or sit on a park bench, close your eyes, and one will find you. Place it in a Skinner box with a button on the wall. Drop a food pellet into the cage whenever the pigeon pecks the button. (Soon it will learn to peck the button whenever it has not eaten for a while.) Now place a small green light in the cage. Turn it on and off intermittently throughout the day. Reinforce button pecking with food whenever the green light is on but not when the light is off. It will not take long for this clever city pigeon to learn that it will gain as much by grooming itself or squawking and flapping around as it will by pecking the button when the light is off.

The green light will have become a **discriminative stimulus.** Discriminative stimuli act as cues. They provide information about when an operant (in this case, pecking a button) will be reinforced (in this case, by a food pellet being dropped into the cage).

As previously noted, operants that are not reinforced tend to become extinguished. For the pigeon in our experiment, pecking the button *when the light is off* becomes extinguished.

A moment's reflection will suggest many ways in which discriminative stimuli influence our behavior. Would you rather ask your boss for a raise when she is smiling or when she is frowning? Wouldn't you rather answer the telephone when it is ringing? Do you think it is wise to try to get smoochy when your date is blowing smoke in your face or chugalugging a bottle of antacid tablets? One of the factors involved in gaining social skills is learning to interpret social discriminative stimuli (smiles, tones of voice, body language) accurately.

Schedules of Reinforcement

In operant conditioning, some responses are maintained by **continuous reinforcement.** You probably become warmer every time you put on heavy clothing. You probably become less thirsty every time you drink water. Yet, if you have ever watched people throwing money down the maws of slot machines, or "one-armed bandits," you know that behavior can also be maintained by **partial reinforcement.**

Some folklore about gambling is based on solid learning theory. You can get a person "hooked" on gambling by fixing the game to allow heavy winnings at first. Then you gradually space out the gambling behaviors that are reinforced until the gambling is maintained by infrequent winning—or even no winning at all.

It is true that you can hook people on gambling by allowing them to win some money in the early stages and then tapering off with the payoffs. Partial reinforcement schedules can maintain behavior for a great deal of time, even though it goes unreinforced.

Discriminative stimulus In operant conditioning, a stimulus that indicates that reinforcement is available.

Continuous reinforcement A schedule of reinforcement in which every correct response is reinforced.

Partial reinforcement One of several reinforcement schedules in which not every correct response is reinforced.

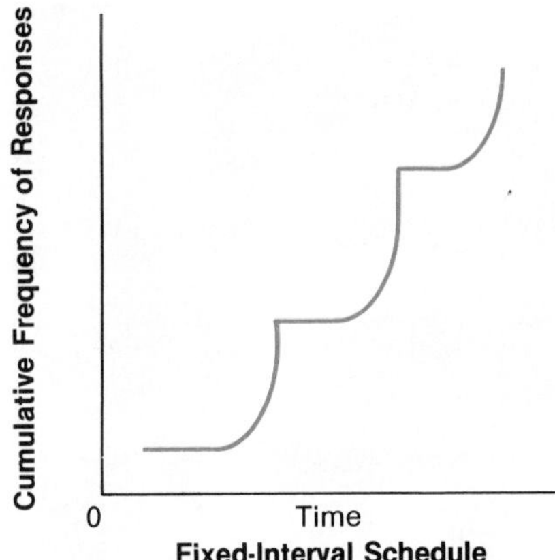

FIGURE 6.8
The "Fixed-Interval Scallop." Organisms who are reinforced on a fixed-interval schedule tend to slack off in responding after each reinforcement. The rate of response then picks up as they near the time when reinforcement will again become available. The results on the cumulative recorder look like an upward-moving series of waves, or scallops.

New operants or behaviors are acquired most rapidly through continuous reinforcement or, in some cases, through "one-trial learning" that meets with great reinforcement. So-called **pathological gamblers** often had big wins at the racetrack or casino or in the lottery in their late teens or early 20s (Greene, 1982). But once the operant has been acquired, it can be maintained by tapering off to a schedule of partial reinforcement.

There are four basic schedules of reinforcement. They are determined by changing either the *interval* of time that must elapse between correct responses before reinforcement is made available or the *ratio* of correct responses to reinforcements. If the interval that must elapse between correct responses, before reinforcement becomes available, is zero seconds, the reinforcement schedule is continuous. A larger interval of time, such as 1 or 30 seconds, is a partial-reinforcement schedule. A one-to-one (1:1) ratio of correct responses to reinforcements is a continuous-reinforcement schedule. A higher ratio such as 2:1 or 5:1 would be a partial-reinforcement schedule.

The four basic types of schedules of reinforcement are *fixed-interval, variable-interval, fixed-ratio,* and *variable-ratio* schedules.

In a **fixed-interval schedule,** a fixed amount of time, say one minute, must elapse between the previous and subsequent times that reinforcement is made available for correct responses. In a **variable-interval schedule,** varying amounts of time are allowed to elapse between making reinforcement available. In a three-minute variable-interval schedule, the mean amount of time that would elapse between reinforcement opportunities would be three minutes. Each interval might vary, however, from one to five minutes.

With a fixed-interval schedule, an organism's response rate falls off after each reinforcement, then picks up as it nears the time when reinforcement, will be dispensed. For example, in a one-minute fixed-interval schedule, a rat will be reinforced with, say, a food pellet for the first operant—for example, the first pressing of a lever—that occurs after a minute has elapsed. After each reinforcement, the rat's rate of lever pressing slows down, but as the end of the one-minute interval draws near, lever pressing increases in frequency, as suggested by Figure 6.8. It is as if the rat has learned that it must wait a while before reinforcement will be made available. The resultant record on the cumulative recorder (Figure 6.8) shows a series of characteristic upward-moving waves or scallops, which is referred to as a *fixed-interval scallop.*

In the case of the more unpredictable variable-interval schedule, the response rate is steadier but lower. If the boss calls us in for a weekly report, we will probably work hard to pull the pieces together just before the report is to be given, just as we might cram the night before a weekly quiz. But if we know that the boss might call us in for a report on the progress of a project at any time (variable-interval schedule), we are likely to keep things in a state of reasonable readiness at all times. However, our efforts are unlikely to have the intensity they would in a fixed-interval (for example, weekly) schedule. Similarly, we are less likely to cram for a series of unpredictable "pop quizzes" than for regularly scheduled quizzes. But we are likely to do at least some studying on a regular basis.

Note the effects of the reduced prices and rebates automobile companies usually offer during the period between July and September to make way for the new models. Aren't they encouraging buyers to wait for the summer and then buy in a flurry?

In a **fixed-ratio schedule,** reinforcement is provided after a fixed number of correct responses has been made. In a **variable-ratio schedule,** reinforcement is provided after a variable number of correct responses has been made. In a 10:1 variable-ratio schedule, the mean number of correct responses that would have to be made before a subsequent correct response would be reinforced is 10, but the ratio of correct responses to reinforcements might be allowed to vary from, say, 1:1 to 20:1 on a random basis.

Pathological gambler A person who gambles habitually despite consistent losses.

Fixed-interval schedule A schedule in which a fixed amount of time must elapse between the previous and subsequent times that reinforcement is available.

Variable-interval schedule A schedule in which a variable amount of time must elapse between the previous and subsequent times that reinforcement is available.

Fixed-ratio schedule A schedule in which reinforcement is provided after a fixed number of correct responses.

Variable-ratio schedule A schedule in which reinforcement is provided after a variable number of correct responses.

Taking the Pledge. Operant conditioning appears to play a role in the socialization of children. Parents and teachers tend to reward children for expressing attitudes that coincide with their own and to punish or ignore them when they express deviant attitudes.

Fixed-ratio and variable-ratio schedules maintain a high response rate. With a fixed-ratio schedule, it is as if the organism learns that it must make several responses before being reinforced. It then "gets them out of the way" as rapidly as possible. Consider the example of piecework. If a worker must sew five shirts to receive a ten dollar bill, he or she is on a fixed-ratio (5:1) schedule and is likely to sew at a uniformly high rate, although there might be a brief pause following each reinforcement. With a variable-ratio schedule, reinforcement can come at any time. This unpredictability also maintains a high response rate. Slot machines tend to pay off on variable-ratio schedules, and players can be seen popping coins into their maws and pulling their "arms" with barely a pause. I have seen players who do not even stop to pick up their winnings. Instead, they continue to smoothly pop in the coins, whether from their original stack or from the winnings tray.

Shaping. If you are teaching break dancing to people who have never danced, do not wait until they have performed a perfect moon walk before telling them they're on the right track. The foxtrot will be back in style before they have learned a thing.

We can teach complex behaviors by **shaping,** or at first reinforcing small steps toward the behavioral goals. In the beginning it may be wise to smile and say "Good" when a reluctant newcomer gathers the courage to get out on the dance floor, even if your feet get flattened by his initial clumsiness. If you are teaching someone to drive a car with a standard shift, at first generously reinforce the learner simply for shifting without stalling.

As training proceeds, we come to expect more before dispensing reinforcement. We reinforce **successive approximations** to the goal. If you want to train a rat to climb a ladder, first reinforce it (with a food pellet) when it turns toward the ladder. Then wait until it approaches the ladder before using reinforcement. Then do not drop a food pellet into the cage until the rat touches the ladder. In this way, the rat will reach the top of the ladder more quickly than if you had waited until the target behavior had first occurred at random.

Learning to drive a new standard-shift automobile to a new job also involves a complex sequence of operant behaviors. At first, we actively seek out all the discriminative stimuli or landmarks that cue us when to turn—signs, buildings, hills, and valleys. We also focus on shifting to a lower gear as we slow down so that the car won't stall. After many repetitions, though, these responses, these chains of behavior, become "habitual" and we need to pay very little attention to them.

Shaping A procedure for teaching complex behaviors that at first reinforces approximations to the target behavior.

Successive approximations Behaviors that are progressively closer to a target behavior.

Have you ever driven home from school or work and been suddenly unsettled as you got out of your car because you couldn't recall exactly how you had returned home? Your entire trip may seem "lost." Were you in great danger? How could you allow such a thing to happen? Actually, it may be that your responses to the demands of the route and to driving your car had become so habitual that you did not have to focus much awareness on them. You were able to think about dinner, a problem at work, or the weekend as you drove. But if something unusual such as hesitation in your engine or a severe rainstorm had occurred on the way, you would have deployed as much attention as was needed to arrive home. Your trip was probably quite safe, after all.

Applications of Operant Conditioning

Habit is the enormous flywheel of society.

William James

Operant conditioning, like classical conditioning, is not just an exotic laboratory procedure. We use operant conditioning every day in our efforts to influence other people. Parents and peers incline children to acquire "gender-appropriate" behavior patterns through the elaborate use of rewards and punishments. Parents also tend to praise their children for sharing with others and to punish them for being too aggressive. Peers participate in the **socialization** process by playing with children who are generous and nonaggressive and, often, by avoiding those who are not.

Operant conditioning may also play a role in attitude formation. Parents tend to reward their children for expressing attitudes that coincide with their own and to punish or ignore them for expressing attitudes that deviate. Many children are also placed in religious schools that provide instruction and a system of rewards and punishments to shape behavior patterns from an early age.

Principles of operant conditioning have also permitted psychologists and educators to develop many beneficial innovations such as interventions with young children, behavior modification in the classroom, and programmed learning.

Using Avoidance Learning to Save a Baby's Life. The techniques of avoidance learning have found real-life—perhaps real-life-saving—applications with children who are too young or distressed to respond to verbal forms of therapy. In one example, reported by Lang and Melamed (1969), a 9-month-old infant vomited regularly within 10 to 15 minutes after eating. Diagnostic workups found no medical basis for the problem, and medical treatments were to no avail. When the case was brought to the attention of Lang and Melamed, the infant weighed only 9 pounds and was in critical condition, being fed by a pump.

The psychologists monitored the infant for the first physical indications (local muscle tension) that vomiting was to occur. When the child tensed prior to vomiting, a tone was sounded and followed by painful but (presumably) harmless electric shock. After two one-hour treatment sessions, the infant's muscle tensions ceased in response to the tone alone, and vomiting soon ceased altogether. At a 1-year follow-up, the infant was still not vomiting and had caught up in weight.

Psychologists did successfully fashion a method to teach an emaciated 9-month-old infant to stop throwing up. They employed principles of classical and operant conditioning to do so.

Socialization Guidance of people into socially desirable behavior by means of verbal messages, the systematic use of rewards and punishments, and other methods of teaching.

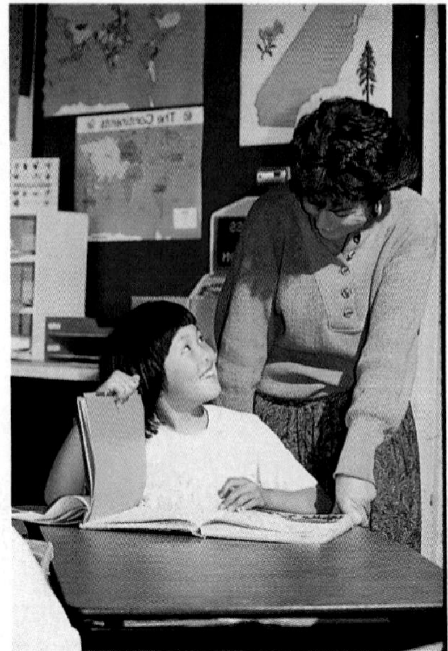

Praise. Teacher praise reinforces desirable behavior in most children. Behavior modification in the classroom applies principles of operant conditioning.

How do we explain this remarkable procedure? It appears to be an example of two-factor learning, as theorized by Mowrer (1947). The first factor was classical conditioning. Through repeated pairings, the tone (CS) came to elicit expectation of electric shock (US), so the psychologists could use the painful shock sparingly.

The second factor was operant conditioning. The electric shock and, after classical conditioning, the tone were aversive stimuli. The infant soon learned to suppress the behaviors (muscle tensions) that were followed with aversive stimulation. By so doing, the aversive stimuli were removed. And so, the aversive stimuli served as negative reinforcers.

This learning occurred at an age long before any sort of verbal intervention could have been understood, and it apparently saved the infant's life. Similar procedures have been used to teach very young autistic children to avoid mutilating and otherwise injuring themselves.

Behavior Modification and Education. Remember that reinforcers are defined as stimuli that increase the frequency of behavior—not as pleasant events. Ironically, adults frequently reinforce undesirable behavior in children by attending to them, or punishing them, when they misbehave but by ignoring them when they behave in desirable ways. Similarly, teachers who raise their voices when children misbehave may be unintentionally conferring hero status on their pupils in the eyes of their peers. Some children may go out of their way to earn teacher disapproval, frequently to the teacher's surprise.

Teacher-preparation programs and in-service programs now usually show teachers how to use behavior modification in the classroom in order to reverse these response patterns. Teachers are taught to pay attention to children when they are behaving appropriately and, when possible, to ignore (avoid reinforcing) their misbehavior (Lahey & Drabman, 1981). The younger the school child, the more powerful teacher attention and approval seem to be.

Among older children and adolescents, peer approval is often a more powerful reinforcer than teacher approval. Peer approval may maintain misbehavior, and ignoring misbehavior may only allow peers to become more disruptive. In such cases, it may be necessary to separate troublesome children.

Teachers also frequently use time out from positive reinforcement to discourage misbehavior. In this method, children are placed in drab, restrictive environments for a specified time period, usually about 10 minutes, when they behave disruptively. When isolated, they cannot earn the attention of peers or teachers, and no reinforcing activities are present.

It may strike you that these techniques are not startlingly new. Perhaps we all know parents who have ignored their children's misbehavior and have heard of teachers making children "sit facing the corner." What is novel is the focus on (1) avoiding punishment and (2) being consistent so that undesirable behavior is not partially reinforced. It should be noted, however, that punishment can also decrease undesirable behavior in the classroom. For example, after-school detention has been found to reduce disruptive classroom behavior (Brigham et al., 1985).

Programmed Learning. B. F. Skinner developed an educational practice called **programmed learning** that is based on operant conditioning. Programmed learning assumes that any complex task involving conceptual learning as well as motor skills can be broken down into a number of small steps. These steps can be shaped individually and combined in sequence to form the correct behavioral chain.

Programmed learning does not punish errors. Instead, correct responses are reinforced. All children earn "100," but at their own pace. Programmed learning also assumes that it is the task of the teacher (or program) to structure the learning experience in such a way that errors will not be made.

Programmed learning A method of learning in which complex tasks are broken down into simple steps, each of which is reinforced. Errors are not reinforced.

It is *not* true that we must make mistakes if we are to learn. This idea that we must make mistakes derives from folklore to the effect that we learn from (bad) experience. However, as pointed out in the chapter, we also learn from good (positively reinforced) experiences and from the experiences of others.

COGNITIVE LEARNING

Classical and operant conditioning are relatively simple forms of learning. Much of conditioning's appeal has been that it can be said to meet the behaviorist objective of explaining behavior in terms of public, observable events—in this case, laboratory conditions. Building on this theoretical base, some psychologists have suggested that the most complex human behavior involves the summation of so many instances of conditioning. However, many psychologists believe that the conditioning model is too mechanical to explain all instances of learned behavior, even in laboratory rats (Glover et al., 1990; Hayes, 1989; Weiner, 1991). They have turned to cognitive kinds of learning to describe and explain additional findings.

In addition to concepts such as *association* and *reinforcement,* cognitive psychologists use concepts such as *mental structures, schemas, templates,* and *information processing.* Cognitive psychologists see people as searching for information, weighing evidence, and making decisions. The kinds of learnings of most interest to cognitive psychologists include insight learning, latent learning, observational learning, and concept learning. These kinds of cognitive learnings are not necessarily limited to humans, although people, of course, are the only species that can talk about them.

Now let us consider some classic psychological studies and what they suggest about the nature of learning. We begin with a German psychologist who was stranded with some laboratory subjects on a Canary Island during World War I: Wolfgang Köhler.

Insight Learning

Gestalt psychologist Wolfgang Köhler became convinced that not all forms of learning could be explained by conditioning when one of his chimpanzees, Sultan, "went bananas." Sultan had learned to use a stick to rake in bananas placed outside his cage. But now Herr Köhler (pronounced *hair curler*) placed the banana beyond the reach of the stick. He gave Sultan two bamboo poles that could be fitted together to make a single pole long enough to retrieve the delectable reward. The setup was similar to that shown in Figure 6.9.

As if to make this historic occasion more dramatic, Sultan at first tried to reach the banana with one pole. When he could not do so, he returned to fiddling with the sticks. Köhler left the laboratory after an hour or so of frustration (his own as well as Sultan's). An assistant was assigned the thankless task of observing Sultan. Soon afterward, Sultan happened to align the two sticks as he fiddled, however. In what seemed to be a flash of inspiration, Sultan then fitted them together and pulled in the elusive banana.

Köhler was summoned to the laboratory. When he arrived the sticks fell apart, as if on cue. Sultan regathered them, fit them firmly together, and tested the strength of the fit before retrieving another banana.

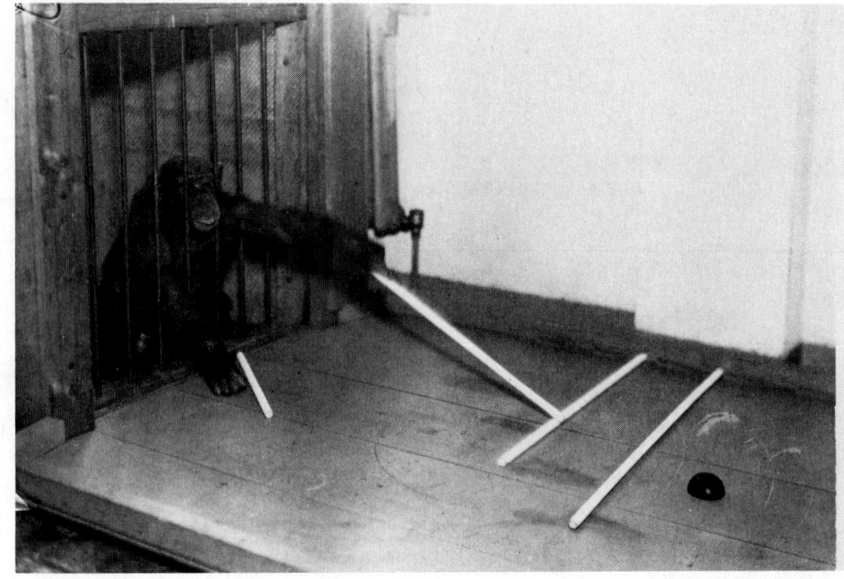

FIGURE 6.9
A Demonstration of Insight or Just Some Fiddling with Sticks? Gestalt psychologist Wolfgang Köhler ran experiments with chimpanzees that suggest that not all learning is mechanical. This chimp must retrieve a stick outside the cage and attach it to a stick he already has before he can retrieve the distant circular object. While fiddling with two such sticks, Sultan, another chimp, seemed to suddenly recognize that the sticks could be attached. This is an example of learning by insight.

Köhler was impressed by Sultan's rapid "perception of relationships" and used the term **insight** to describe it. He noted that such insights were not learned gradually through reinforced trials. Rather, they seemed to occur "in a flash" when the elements of a problem had been arranged appropriately. Sultan also proved himself to be immediately capable of stringing several sticks together to retrieve various objects, not just bananas. This seemed to be no mechanical generalization. It appeared that Sultan understood the principle of the relationship between joining sticks and reaching distant objects.

Rescorla (1988) argues that even the events that occur in conditioning suggest that learning is not as mechanical as behaviorists believe. Rescorla suggests that at some point, for animals, that is, something akin to insight occurs. Animals may fail to grasp the relationships among events during several trials as measured by display of the targeted response. But then they may suddenly display the intended response as if something had "clicked."

Soon after Köhler's findings were reported, psychologists in the United States demonstrated that not even the behavior of rats was fully mechanical. E. C. Tolman (1948), a University of California psychologist, showed that rats behaved as if they had acquired **cognitive maps** of mazes. Although they would learn many paths to a food goal, they would typically choose the shortest. If the shortest path was blocked, they would quickly switch to another. The behavior of the rats suggested that they learned *places in which reinforcement was available,* not a series of mechanical motor responses.

Bismarck, one of University of Michigan psychologist N. R. F. Maier's laboratory rats, provided further evidence for learning by insight (Maier & Schneirla, 1935). Bismarck had been trained to climb a ladder to a tabletop where food was placed. On one occasion, Maier used a mesh barrier to prevent Bismarck from reaching his goal. As shown in Figure 6.10, a second ladder to the table was provided. The second ladder was in clear view of the animal. At first, Bismarck sniffed and scratched and made every effort to find a path through the mesh barrier. Bismarck then spent some time washing his face, an activity that signals frustration in rats. Suddenly, Bismarck jumped into the air, turned, ran down the familiar ladder around to the new ladder, ran up the new ladder, and then claimed his just desserts.

It is difficult to explain Bismarck's behavior in terms of conditioning. It seems that Bismarck suddenly perceived the relationships between the elements of his

Insight In Gestalt psychology, a sudden perception of relationships among elements of the "perceptual field," permitting the solution of a problem.

Cognitive map A mental representation or "picture" of the elements in a learning situation such as a maze.

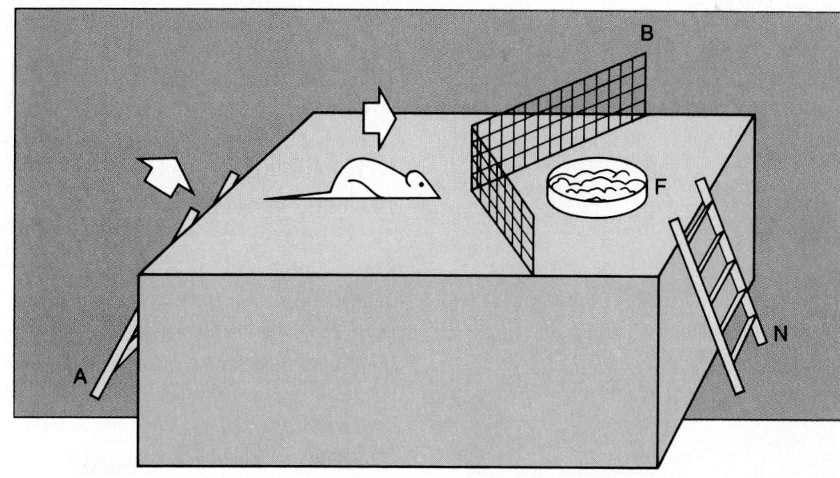

FIGURE 6.10
Bismarck Uses a Cognitive Map to Claim His Just Desserts. Bismarck has learned to reach dinner by climbing ladder *A*. But now the food goal (*F*) is blocked by a wire mesh barrier *B*. Bismarck washes his face for a while, but then, in an apparent flash of insight, runs back down ladder *A* and up new ladder *N* to reach reinforcement.

problem so that the solution occurred by insight. He seems to have had what Gestalt psychologists have termed an "Aha! experience."

It is *not* true that only people are capable of insight. Lower animals, including apes and rats, have also apparently shown insight in classic experiments.

Latent Learning

I'm all grown up. I know the whole [shopping] mall.

The author's daughter Jordan at age 7

Many behaviorists argue that organisms acquire only those responses, or operants, for which they are reinforced. E. C. Tolman, however, showed that rats also learn about their environments in the absence of reinforcement.

Tolman trained some rats to run through mazes for standard food goals. Other rats were permitted to explore the same mazes for several days without food goals or other rewards. The rewarded rats could be said to have found their ways through the mazes with fewer errors (fewer "wrong turns") on each trial run. In a sense, there were no correct or incorrect turns for the unrewarded rats, since no response led to a reward.

After the unrewarded rats had been allowed to explore the mazes for 10 days, food rewards were placed in a box at the far end of the maze. The previously unrewarded explorers reached the food box as quickly as the rewarded rats after only one or two reinforced trials (Tolman & Honzik, 1950).

Tolman concluded that rats learned about mazes in which they roamed even when they were unrewarded for doing so. He distinguished between learning and performance. Rats would acquire a cognitive map of a maze, and even though they would not be motivated to follow an efficient route to the far end, they would learn rapid routes from end to end just by roaming about within the maze. Such learning might remain hidden, or **latent,** however, until they were motivated to follow the rapid routes for food goals.

Latent Hidden or concealed.

Observational Learning

Observational Learning. People acquire a variety of skills by means of observational learning. Here, students learn how to "throw" a pot.

How many things have you learned from watching other people in real life, in films, and on television? From films and television, you may have gathered vague ideas about how to sky dive, ride surfboards, climb sheer cliffs, run a pattern to catch a touchdown pass in the Superbowl, and dust for fingerprints, even if you have never tried these activities.

In his studies on social learning, Albert Bandura has run experiments (e.g., Bandura et al., 1963) that show we can acquire operants by observing the behavior of others. We may need some practice to refine the operants, but we can acquire the required knowledge by observation alone. We may also choose to allow these operants or skills to lie latent. For example, we may not imitate aggressive behavior unless we are provoked and believe that we are more likely to be rewarded than punished for it.

Observational learning may account for most human learning. It occurs when, as children, we observe parents cook, clean, or repair a broken appliance. There is evidence that observational learning for simple tasks such as opening the halves of a toy barrel to look at a smaller barrel within occurs as early as age 1 (Abravanel & Gingold, 1985). As I wrote this sentence, my 10-month-old daughter, Taylor, was imitating clapping hands, making wow-wow sounds by batting her mouth with her hand, making other sounds that may be euphemistically referred to as "raspberries," and an assortment of other useful behaviors. Observational learning takes place when we watch teachers solve problems on the blackboard or hear them speak in a foreign language. Observational learning is not mechanically acquired through reinforcement. We can learn by observation without engaging in overt responses at all. It appears sufficient to pay attention to the behavior of others.

In the terminology of observational learning, a person who engages in a response to be imitated is a *model.* When observers see a model being reinforced for displaying an operant, the observers are said to be *vicariously* reinforced. Display of the operant thus becomes more likely for the observer as well as the model.

Observational Learning and Media Violence. Observational learning extends to observing parents and peers, classroom learning, reading books, and—in one of the more controversial aspects of modern life—learning from media such as television and films. Nearly all of us have been exposed to television, videotapes, and films in the classroom. Children in day-care centers often watch *Sesame Street.* There are filmed and videotaped versions of great works of literature such as Orson Welles' *Macbeth* or Laurence Olivier's *Hamlet.* Nearly every school shows films of laboratory experiments. Sometimes we view "canned lectures" by master teachers.

What of our viewing *outside* of the classroom? Television is also one of our major sources of informal observational learning. American preschoolers average four hours of viewing a day (Pearl et al., 1982; Singer & Singer, 1981). During the school years, they spend more hours at the TV set than in school (Singer, 1983). And many of the shows they watch—from Saturday morning cartoons to evening drama series—brim with violence. There have also been harrowing news stories, such as the following:

There is the case of a 9-year-old California girl who was raped with a bottle by four girls who admitted that they had gotten the idea from the TV film *Born Innocent.* The victim's family sued the network and the local station that had screened the film. The courts, however, decided not to award damages. They argued that such a precedent might infringe upon the right of free expression as guaranteed by the First Amendment to the Constitution.

Observational learning Acquiring operants by observing others engage in them.

In the 1990s, audiences at films such as *Colors, Boyz N the Hood,* and *Juice* have gotten into fights, shot one another, and gone on rampages after the showings. These films have been about violent urban youth and, perhaps not ironically, the subjects of the films are generally the ones who have gone on violent sprees afterward. Psychologists, educators, and parent groups have therefore raised questions about the effects of media violence.

Some of these examples seem compelling, yet let me insert a comment before proceeding. Media violence does not in itself directly *cause* violence. If it did, there would be millions of *daily* incidents in which viewers imitate the aggression that they observe.

Still, the links between media violence and aggressive behavior are not to be ignored. In study after study, children and adults who view violence in the media later show higher levels of aggressive behavior than people who are not exposed to media violence (Liebert et al., 1989). Aggressive video games apparently serve a similar purpose. In one study, 5- to 7-year-olds played one of two video games (Schutte et al., 1988)—one ("Karateka") in which villains were destroyed by being hit or kicked; the other ("Jungle Hunt") in which the character swung nonviolently from vine to vine to cross a jungle. Afterward the children were observed in a playroom. Those who had played "Karateka"—both boys and girls—were significantly more likely to hit their playmates and an inflated doll. Most psychologists thus agree that media violence *contributes* to aggression (NIMH, 1982; Rubinstein, 1983). Consider a number of ways in which depictions of violence make this contribution.

In terms of social-learning concepts, TV violence supplies *models* of aggressive "skills." Acquisition of these skills, in turn, enhances children's aggressive *competencies.* In fact, children are more likely to imitate what their parents do than to heed what they say. If adults say they disapprove of aggression but smash furniture or slap each other when frustrated, children are likely to develop the notion that aggression is the way to handle frustration. Classic experiments have shown that children tend to imitate the aggressive behavior they see on television, whether the models are cartoons or real people (Bandura et al., 1963) (see Figure 6.11).

The expression of operants or skills may be inhibited by punishment or by the expectation of punishment. Conversely, media violence may disinhibit the expression of aggressive impulses that would otherwise have been controlled, especially when media characters "get away" with violence or are rewarded for it. In fact, "bad guys" were invariably punished in Hollywood movies through most of the 1950s for this reason. Only since the 1960s have many violent characters managed to escape the law on the silver screen.

Bandura's research has shown that the probability of aggression increases when the models are similar to the observers and when the models are rewarded for aggression. Viewers have been theorized to be *vicariously* reinforced when they observe another person being reinforced for engaging in operants. And perhaps observers of rewarded aggressors are more likely to come to believe that aggression may be appropriate for them as well.

Media violence and aggressive video games increase viewers' levels of arousal. In the vernacular, television "works them up." We are more likely to engage in dominant forms of behavior, including aggressive behavior, when we are highly aroused.

Media violence has cognitive effects that parallel those of biological arousal. It primes or arouses aggressive ideas and memories (Berkowitz, 1988). Media violence also provides viewers with aggressive *scripts*—that is, ideas as to how to behave in situations that seem to parallel those they have observed (Huesmann, 1988).

We also become used, or habituated, to many stimuli that impinge on us repeatedly. Repeated TV violence may therefore decrease viewers' emotional response to real violence (Geen, 1981; Thomas et al., 1977). If children come to perceive violence as the norm, their own attitudes toward violence may become less condemnatory and they may place less value on constraining aggressive urges (Eron, 1987).

FIGURE 6.11
A Classic Experiment in the Imitation of Aggressive Models.
Research by Albert Bandura and his colleagues has shown that children frequently imitate the aggressive behavior that they observe. In the top row, an adult model strikes a clown doll. The lower rows show a boy and a girl imitating the aggressive behavior.

Although media violence encourages aggression in viewers, it has its greatest impact on children who are *already* considered the most aggressive by their teachers (Josephson, 1987). There thus seems to be a circular relationship between viewing media violence and aggressive behavior (Eron, 1982, 1987; Fenigstein, 1979). TV violence contributes to aggressive behavior, but aggressive children are also more likely to tune in and stay tuned to it. The viewers of films such as *Colors, Boyz N the Hood,* and *Juice* who later went on sprees were often violent gang members to begin with. In fact, the audiences often packed in gangs that were hostile toward one another.

Eron and other psychologists find that aggressive children are less popular than nonaggressive children—at least within the middle-class culture. Eron theorizes that aggressive children watch more television because their peer relationships are less fulfilling and because the high incidence of TV violence tends to confirm their encoding of aggressive behavior as being normal (1982). Media violence interacts with other contributors to violence. Eron has found that parental rejection and the use of physical punishment by parents also increases the likelihood of aggression in children (Eron, 1982). Harsh home life may further confirm the viewer's encoding of the world as a violent place and further encourage reliance on television for companionship.

In any event, our children are going to be exposed to a great deal of media violence—if not in Saturday morning cartoon shows, then in evening dramas and in the news. Or they'll learn of violence in *Hamlet, Macbeth,* and even in the Bible. It is impractical to believe that children can be sheltered from exposure to violent models.

What, then, is there to do? Huesmann and his colleagues (1983) have shown that we as parents and educators can do many things to mitigate the impact of media violence. For example, children who watch violent shows are rated by peers as being significantly less aggressive when they are informed of the following:

1. The violent behavior they observe in the media does *not* represent the behavior of most people.
2. The apparently aggressive behaviors they watch are not real. They reflect camera tricks, special effects, and stunts.
3. Most people resolve conflicts by nonviolent means.

In observational learning, the emphasis is on the cognitive. If children consider violence inappropriate for them, they will probably not act aggressively, even if they have acquired aggressive skills.

Concept Learning

What's black and white and read all over? This riddle was heard quite often when I was younger. Since the riddle was spoken and involved the colors black and white, you would probably think that "read" meant "red" when you heard it. And so, in seeking an answer, you might scan your memory for an object that was red although it also managed to be black and white. The answer to the riddle, "a newspaper," was sure to be met with a good groan.

The word *newspaper* is a **concept.** *Red, black,* and *white* are also concepts—color concepts. Concepts are symbols that stand for groups of objects, events, or ideas that have common properties.

Prototypes. **Prototypes** of concepts are schemas or templates that contain the essential features of the concept. In less technical terms, prototypes are good examples of a particular category (Rosch, 1978). Many lower animals appear to possess instinctive or inborn prototypes of various concepts. Male robins instinctively attack round reddish objects that apparently match the prototype of the breasts of other male robins—even when they have been reared in isolation and have not seen such objects until they achieve physical maturity.

People, however, apparently begin to acquire many prototypes on the basis of experience. Many simple prototypes such as *dog* and *red* can be taught by association. We can simply point to a dog and say "dog" or "This is a dog" to a child. Dogs are considered to be **positive instances** of the dog concept. **Negative instances**—that is, things that are not dogs—are then shown to the child while one says, "This is *not* a dog."

Things that are negative instances of one concept may be positive instances of another. So, in teaching a child, one may be more likely to say "This is not a dog—it's a cat," than simply, "This is not a dog."

Children may at first include horses and other four-legged animals within the dog schema or concept until the differences between dogs and horses are pointed out. (To them, the initial category could be more appropriately labeled "fuzzy-wuzzies.") In language development, the overinclusion of instances in a category (reference to horses as dogs) is labeled *overextension.* Children's prototypes become refined as the result of being shown positive and negative instances and being given verbal explanations.

Abstract concepts such as *uncle* or *square root* may have to be learned through verbal explanations that involve more basic concepts. If one points to *uncles* (positive instances) and *not uncles* (negative instances) repeatedly, a child may eventually learn that uncles are males or even that they are males that are somehow parts of their extended families. However, it is doubtful that this show-and-tell method would ever teach them that uncles are brothers of a parent. The

Concept A symbol that stands for a group of objects, ideas, or events with common properties.

Prototype A concept of a category of objects or events that serves as a good example of the category.

Positive instance An example of a concept.

Negative instance An idea, event, or object that is *not* an example of a concept. Concept formation is aided by presentation of positive and negative instances.

concept *uncle* is best taught by explanation after the child understands the more basic concepts *parent* (or at least *Mommy* and *Daddy*) and *brother*.

Still more abstract concepts like *justice, goodness,* and *beauty* may require complex explanations and the presentation of many positive and negative instances. These concepts are so abstract and instances so varied that no two people may agree on their definition. Or, if their definitions coincide, they may argue over positive versus negative instances (what is beautiful and what is ugly). What seems to be a beautiful work of art to me may impress you as meaningless jumbles of color. This is an example of the old adage, "Beauty is in the eye of the beholder."

Hypothesis Testing. Psychologists have also shown that children are not merely passive recipients of information about the meanings of concepts. They—and we as adults—also engage in the active process of **hypothesis testing** in attempting to ferret out the meanings of concepts.

A parent may point to a small, elongated fish in a tank and tell a child "That's a guppy." The child may hypothesize that "things that move in water" are guppies. Then the parent points to a large fish with flowing fins and says, "That's an angel fish." Now the child will probably modify his or her hypothesis about what makes up a guppy or an angel fish. The child may focus on the shapes, sizes, and colors of the fish and try to generalize to other fish, pointing and asking, "Is this a guppy, too?" The parent will answer yes or no and perhaps begin to explain that guppies are small, sort of cigar-shaped fish that come in various colors. The child may then wonder if the small, cigar-shaped fish with the black and white stripes are also guppies and continue to ask, "Is this a guppy, too?" When the parent says, "No, that's a zebra fish," the child may restrict his or her concept of guppies to the fish that are gray or have blue or red patches. The parent's responding yes or no gives the child further feedback as to the accuracy of his or her hypotheses.

There are thus many different kinds of learning. We have touched on a number of them in this chapter. We have seen that psychologists disagree about what learning is, what is learned, and whether organisms are basically active or passive as they participate in the processes of learning. Nonetheless, most psychologists agree that the capacity to learn is at the heart of organisms' abilities to adapt to their environments. Some psychologists also believe that organisms, especially humans, can learn to fashion their environments in ways that enable them to meet their needs better.

It would be of little use to discuss how we learn if we were not capable of remembering what we learn from second to second, from day to day, or, in many cases, for a lifetime. In the next chapter, we turn our attention to the subject of memory. And, in Chapter 8, we shall see how learning is intertwined with language development, problem-solving, and a concept that many people think of as learning ability: intelligence.

Hypothesis testing In concept formation, a process in which we attempt to ferret out the meanings or salient features of concepts by testing our assumptions.

STUDY GUIDE

EXERCISE: Classical Versus Operant Conditioning

Below are a number of terms that are used in discussions of conditioning. Some terms apply to classical conditioning, some to operant conditioning, and some to both. For each term place a checkmark in the appropriate blank space, or spaces, to show the type(s) of learning to which it applies. The answer key is given below.

Classical Conditioning	Operant Conditioning	Term	Classical Conditioning	Operant Conditioning	Term
_____	_____	1. Discriminative stimulus	_____	_____	15. Operant
_____	_____	2. Unconditioned stimulus	_____	_____	16. Spontaneous recovery
_____	_____	3. Conditioned response	_____	_____	17. Shaping
_____	_____	4. Extinction	_____	_____	18. Cumulative recorder
_____	_____	5. Reinforcer	_____	_____	19. Conditional reflex
_____	_____	6. Backward conditioning	_____	_____	20. Variable-ratio schedule
_____	_____	7. Generalization	_____	_____	21. Response
_____	_____	8. Instrumental conditioning	_____	_____	22. Higher-order conditioning
_____	_____	9. Bell-and-pad method	_____	_____	23. Successive approximations
_____	_____	10. Contingency theory	_____	_____	24. Programmed learning
_____	_____	11. Trial and error	_____	_____	25. Rewards and punishments
_____	_____	12. Stimulus	_____	_____	26. Trace conditioning
_____	_____	13. Neutral stimulus	_____	_____	27. Simultaneous conditioning
_____	_____	14. Skinner box			

Answer Key To Exercise

1. O	8. O	15. O	22. C
2. C	9. C	16. C, O	23. O
3. C	10. C	17. O	24. O
4. C, O	11. O	18. O	25. O
5. O	12. C, O	19. C	26. C
6. C	13. C	20. O	27. C
7. C, O	14. O	21. C, O	

ESL—BRIDGING THE GAP

This part is divided into

1. cultural references
2. phrases and expresssions in which words are used differently from their regular meaning, or are used as metaphors.

Cultural References

Rocketman serial (206)—adventure movie about a man who flew with a rocket on his back; a chapter was shown at the theater every week (serial)

buttered popcorn (206)—a popular food sold at movie theaters, baseball games, and other entertainment events; made from corn

person dressed in unmistakable blue (215)—a policeman (it is impossible not to recognize the color of the uniform)

tennis (219)—a game in which two or four players hit a ball across a net with a racket; it is played on a court

maws of slot machines (224)—jaws (mouths, openings) of gambling machines

"one-armed bandits" (224)—slot machines operated by pulling a lever; bandits are robbers or thieves

big wins at the racetrack or casino or in the lottery (225)—a lot of money won from betting (wagering) on racehorses, at gambling houses, and from choosing the same number that an official or licensed gambling organization has chosen *rebates* (225)—a refund (money returned after having been delivered) of a portion (part) of a payment already made

break dancing; moon walk (226)—popular and current dance steps

fox-trot (226)—a dance step which was popular before 1950; the music required slow dancing

standard shift (226)—in old cars, a person operated a lever by hand in order to change the ratio of the gears that connected the motor and the transmission; some newer cars also have standard shift, but most are automatic shift

shifting without stalling (226)—see "standard shift"; it used to be difficult to shift gears (change the gear)—the car would often stall, or stop, before the shift had occurred completely

sky dive (232)—jump from the top of a mountain or from an airplane and "fly" with the aid of a glider or a parachute

ride a surfboard (232)—stand on boards at the edge of the ocean and move on the waves (surf)

run a pattern to catch a touchdown pass in the Superbowl (232)—run on the field in order to make a touchdown (a score) in football in the final contest of the champions of a year

dust for fingerprints (232)—spread a chemical powder which will reveal the fingerprints (the imprint which the ends of the fingers make on surfaces); this is done in order to discover the identity of a person

Sesame Street (232)—a popular TV educational program for young children

Orson Welles' Macbeth *or Laurence Olivier's* Hamlet (232)—two famous twentieth-century actors; two famous plays by Shakespeare

right to free expression as guaranteed by the First Amendment (232)—The First Amendment to the Constitution provides that the government may not restrict the right of a person to say anything he or she wishes to say

a good groan (235)—when a joke is heard, a person often groans (makes a long low sound)

Phrases and Expressions (Different Usage)

dared me (206)—said, "We dare you,"; tried to persuade me to do something that I did not want to do and that they did not want to do themselves

rose to the challenge (206)—agreed

Down went (206)—ate

stuffed down (206)—ate with difficulty

head spun (206)—felt sick

not face (206)—not look at; not eat

on a "gut level" (206)—on an emotional level; from strong feeling

queasy (206)—nauseous

"get into the habit" (207)—become accustomed to; do the same thing at the same time regularly

deemed socially acceptable (207)—thought to be the right ones by most people

stick to the straight and narrow (207)—behave correctly; be good

likelihood (208)—probability

traffic citations (208)—tickets to indicate that a fine (money) must be paid for violating rules for correct driving

triggered (208)—caused

hampered by (208)—hindered by; made difficult by

biological makeup (209)—biological composition

paired repeatedly (209)—accompanied many times

faced with novel events (209)—confronted with "new" events, ones we have not experienced

concrete goals (209)—specific goals; tangible goals; goals that we know we want

uncalled-for (209)—not asked for; not wanted

worth looking into (209)—important enough to investigate

target response (209)—the response which we are looking for, or expecting

may not take place at all (210)—may not occur or happen

purely random (211)—completely random; completely by chance

in a couple of ways (212)—in two ways

Sad to say (212)—Unfortunately

further impair (212)—damage more

dietary staples (212)—necessary foods for health

scheme of things (212)—plan of events

fits (213)—corresponds to

updating (213)—causing their expectation to change according to the current environment

whiffs the scent (213)—smells the scent

pull into the driveway (213)—drive into the driveway

squeal with delight (213)—make a happy noise

times change (213)—the old rules and concerns do not apply now

homecoming (213)—arrival home

led to (213)—caused; resulted in

leveled off at (213)—stopped at

Where would you place your money? (213)—What do you think? (How would you bet?); Which do you think would happen?

a bit misleading (213)—difficult to understand; it appears to have one meaning, but actually has another

In the wilds (214)—in the forest or desert; in the natural area

follow circular paths (214)—go around in a circle

from bark to bark (214)—each time the same dog barks, it sounds different

Rustling sounds in the undergrowth (214)—noise in the forest

a narrow range (215)—a limited range

After a while (215)—After time passes

put on an infantile show (215)—acted like a baby

snapped at (215)—tried to bite

errs (215)—makes a mistake
forgoes the meat (215)—does not receive the meat
tell our spouses apart (215)—recognize *our* spouse (husband or wife) as being different from another spouse
land in divorce court (215)—our spouse would divorce us
major avenue (216)—major method
come to serve (216)—act as
characteristic knock (216)—the person knocks with his or her style, or his or her personality, and we recognize that
bed-wetters . . . wet their beds (216)—children . . . urinate in their beds at night
training pants . . . toilet training (216)—underwear that is thicker than usual in order to absorb urine; it is worn by one- to three-year-old children while they are learning how to use the toilet
not given to ready displays of emotion (217)—who did not reveal, or let people see, how he felt
undo (217)—correct; make something right that has been wrong
to do just that (217)—to do *that* specifically
munching merrily away (217)—eating without paying attention to what is occurring
not plopped in Peter's lap (217)—not suddenly dropped in Peter's lap (the position of the thighs when sitting) without gradual introduction
cast a wary eye (217)—looked at so that he could defend himself if he had to
consume the treat (217)—eat the candy and cookies
stray cats (218)—cats that have no homes and live on the street
so-called puzzle boxes (218)—the box is called this because it is a "puzzle" to the cat; the cat has to solve puzzles (problems that are like games) to get to the food
few will top that off (218)—few people have a more unusual story about the war
were scrapped (219)—were not continued or practiced
was for the birds (219)—was useless
found wide applications (219)—been applied by many people
brought forth by (219)—created by
routinely ignored (219)—ignored regularly
point out that (220)—emphasize
sniffed its way around (220)—walked around in the cage and sniffing (smelling) at the same time as he walked
few and far between (220)—not often
came fast and furious (220)—was very frequent
it matters little (220)—it is not important
comes to be made (220)—occurs
backside (220)—haunches
age significantly in the process (220)—get a lot older while it happens
to plan ahead (221)—to plan what to do in the future (sooner or later)
lies in (222)—is in
"gets inside the head of" an (222)—think like an
"get away with murder" (223)—do a negative act and not be corrected
withdraw from (223)—leave
run away (223)—leave home without telling parents and not returning
cut class (223)—not attend class
drop out off school (223)—stop attending school
at what cost (223)—the other results might be worse
later on, (223)—in the future
draws their attention to (223)—causes them to pay attention to
take . . . for granted (223)—accept it but ignore it
slippery dining room floors (224)—the ice cream would melt, would become cream and cause the floor to be "slippery" (a person could slide on it easily)
A moment's reflection will suggest (224)—If we think for a moment, we can think of many ways
get smoochy (224)—become romantic
chugalugging a bottle of antacid tablets (224)—eating pills which are for indigestion
body language (224)—movements of the body which communicate (without speech)
"hooked" on gambling (224)—addicted to gambling
by tapering off (225)—by reducing gradually
cram the night before (225)—study a lot the night before a test
state of reasonable readiness (225)—a condition of always being ready
in a flurry (225)—a lot at the same time as opposed to a small amount at other times
gathers the courage (226)—acquires courage
to get out on the dance floor (226)—to start dancing
to no avail (227)—did not correct the problem
conferring hero status (228)—creating heroes
in the eyes of their peers (228)—the way in which the peers see
broken down into (228)—separated
"went bananas" (229)—became insane (crazy)
setup (229)—arrangement
the thankless task (229)—the task (a specific job) for which no appreciation would be given
flash of inspiration (229)—sudden inspiration
as if on cue (229)—as if the sticks behaved from direction
"in a flash" (230)—suddenly
akin to (230)—similar to
as if something had "clicked" (230)—as if something had suddenly been understood
to a food goal (230)—to reach the goal where there was food
switch to (230)—change to
just desserts (230)—reward that he deserved
"Aha-experience" (231)—a sudden understanding inspiration
on each trial run (231)—on each previous attempt to go through the maze

latent (231)—not used
"canned lectures" (232)—lectures on video tape
brim with violence (232)—have a lot of violence
not to award damages (232)—the family was not entitled to any money from the TV station
In the vernacular (233)—What I am going to say is colloquial, not formal English
"works them up" (233)—causes them to be aroused or excited and want to act
the norm (233)—normal
tune in (234)—turn on and watch TV
stay tuned in (234)—continue to watch TV violence
what, then, is there to do? (235)—So, what shall we do?
beholder (236)—the one who looks or sees
ferret out (236)—dig out; search out; try to understand
at the heart of (236)—the essence of; at the base of

CHAPTER REVIEW

Objective 1: Discuss controversies in defining learning.

From the behaviorist perspective, learning is defined as a relatively permanent change in behavior that arises from (1) ________ence. From the cognitive perspective, learning involves processes by which experience contributes to relatively permanent changes in the way organisms mentally (2) ________sent the environment.

SECTION 1: Classical Conditioning

Objective 2: Describe the role of Ivan Pavlov in the history of the psychology of learning.

Classical conditioning is defined as a simple form of learning in which an originally (3) ________al stimulus comes to bring forth, or (4) e________, the response usually brought forth by another stimulus by being paired repeatedly with that stimulus.

When Pavlov discovered conditioning, he was attempting to identify neural receptors in the mouth that triggered a response from the (5) ________ary glands. Salivation in response to meat is unlearned, a (6) ____ex. Reflexes are elicited by (7) ____li. A stimulus may be defined as an (8)________mental condition that evokes a response from an organism. Pavlov discovered that reflexes can also be learned or conditioned, through (9) ________tion. Pavlov called learned reflexes (10) ________nal reflexes. Today conditional reflexes are termed (11) ____ ________ses.

Objective 3: Describe the process of classical conditioning, referring to the roles of the US, CS, UR, and CR.

In classical conditioning, a previously neutral stimulus, called the (12) ________ned stimulus (or CS) comes to elicit the response evoked by a second stimulus, called the (13) ________ned stimulus (or US) by being paired repeatedly with the second stimulus. A response to a US is called an (14) ________ned response (UR), and a response to a CS is termed a (15) ________ned response (CR).

Objective 4: Describe various types of classical conditioning.

Classical conditioning occurs efficiently when the (16) ________ned stimulus (CS) is presented about 0.5 seconds before the (17) ________ned stimulus (US). In (18) ________neous conditioning the CS is presented at the same time as the US and left on until the response occurs. In (19) ________ed conditioning the CS is presented before the US and is left on until the response is shown. In trace conditioning the CS is presented and removed (20: prior to? or after?) presentation of the US. In (21) ________ard conditioning the US is presented prior to the CS.

Objective 5: Explain how contingency theory poses a challenge to the traditional explanation for classical conditioning.

According to contingency theory, the (22) con________ presentation of stimuli—that is, the co-appearance of the US and the CS—does not explain classical conditioning. Instead, learning occurs only when the CS provides (23) ________tion about the US. According to (24) con________ theory, learning occurs because a CS indicates that the US stimulus is likely to ensue.

Taste aversions differ from other kinds of classical conditioning in a couple of ways: First, (25: only one association? or several associations?) may be required. Second, the US and CS need not be presented (26) ________uously; the US (nausea) can occur hours after the CS (flavor of food).

Research intaste aversion also challenges the (27) _______________rist view that organisms learn to associate any stimuli that are contiguous. Instead, it seems that organisms are biologically predisposed to develop aversions that are (28) _______________tive in their environmental settings.

Objective 6: Describe the processes of extinction and spontaneous recovery within classical conditioning.

After a US–CS association has been learned, repeated presentation of the (29) _______________ned stimulus (for example, a bell) without the US (meat) will extinguish the CR (salivation). But extinguished responses may show (30) _______________neous recovery as a function of time that has elapsed since the end of the extinction process.

Objective 7: Describe the processes of generalization and discrimination within classical conditioning.

In stimulus (31) _______________ation, organisms show a CR in response to a range of stimuli similar to the CS. In stimulus (32) _______________ation, organisms learn to show a CR in response to a more limited range of stimuli by pairing only the limited stimulus with the US.

In higher-order conditioning, a previously neutral stimulus comes to serve as a (33) _______________ned stimulus after being paired repeatedly with a stimulus that has already been established as a CS.

Objective 8: Discuss applications of classical conditioning.

Classical conditioning involves ways in which (34) _______________uli come to serve as signals for other stimuli.

In the (35) bell-and-_______________ method for teaching children to stop bedwetting, a (36) b_______________ is sounded when the child urinates in bed, waking the child. Urine is detected by a (37) _______________ placed beneath the sheets and then the bell is sounded. The bell is paired repeatedly with fullness in the child's (38) bl_______________. In this way, sensations of a full bladder (the conditioned stimulus) gain the capacity to wake the child just as the bell (the [39] _______________ned stimulus) did.

In the case of Little (40) _______________, a young boy was taught to fear rats. In this case study, John (41) _______________ and Rosalie (42) _______________ clanged steel bars behind Albert's head as Albert played with a rat.

In the fear-reduction method of (43)_______________tioning, a pleasant stimulus is paired repeatedly with a fear-evoking object, in this way counteracting the fear response.

SECTION 2: Operant Conditioning

Objective 9: Describe the roles of Edward Thorndike and B. F. Skinner in the history of the psychology of learning.

Edward L. Thorndike used so-called (44) p_______________ boxes to study learning in cats. Thorndike also originated the law of (45) _______________ct, which holds that responses are "stamped in" by rewards and "stamped out" by (46) _______________ments. B. F. Skinner introduced the concept of (47) _______________ment. Skinner also devised a kind of cage, which has been dubbed the (48) S_______________ _______________, which could be used to study discrete operant behaviors in animals. Skinner's use of the (49) _______________tive recorder also permitted precise measurement of operant behavior, even in the absence of the researcher.

Objective 10: Explain the process of operant conditioning.

In operant conditioning, behaviors that manipulate the environment in order to attain reinforcers are termed (50) _______________ts. In operant conditioning, an organism learns to emit an operant because it is (51) _______________ed. Initial "correct" responses may be performed by random trial and (52) _______________r, or by physical or verbal guiding. A reinforcement is a stimulus that increases the (53) _______________cy of an operant.

Objective 11: Distinguish between various kinds of reinforcers.

Positive reinforcers increase the probability that operants will occur when they are (54: applied or removed?). Negative reinforcers (55: increase or decrease?) the probability that operants will occur when they are (56: applied or removed?). (57) _______________ary reinforcers have their value because of the biological makeup of the organism. (58) _______________ary reinforcers, such as money and approval, acquire their value through association with established reinforcers. Secondary reinforcers are also referred to as (59) ________ned reinforcers.

Objective 12: Describe the processes of extinction and spontaneous recovery within operant conditioning.

In operant conditioning, (60) ________tion results from repeated performance of operant behavior in the absence of reinforcement. In operant conditioning, the (61) ________nt is extinguished. (62) Sp________ recovery of learned responses can occur as a function of the passage of time following extinction.

Objective 13: Differentiate between reinforcers and rewards and punishments.

Rewards, like reinforcers, are (63) ________li that increase the frequency of behavior. But rewards differ from reinforcers in that rewards are considered (64) pl________ stimuli. Punishments are defined as (65) ________sive stimuli that suppress the frequency of behavior. Skinner preferred the term *reinforcer* because *reinforcement* has to do with effects on observable (66) ________ior.

Many learning theorists prefer treating children's misbehavior by ignoring it or using time out from (67) ________ment rather than by using punishment. Strong punishment (68: will or will not?) suppress undesired behavior. However, punishment also has some "side effects." One is that punishment (69: does or does not?) teach acceptable, alternative behavior. Punishment (70) sup________ undesired behavior only when its delivery is guaranteed. Punishment also may cause the organism to (71) w________from the situation, as in the child's running away from home, cutting classes, or dropping out of school. Moreover, punishment can create anger and hostility, can lead to overgeneralization, and can serve as a (72) m________ for aggression. Finally, children (73) l________ punished responses, whether or not they perform them.

Objective 14: Define *discriminative stimulus.*

A (74) ________ative stimulus indicates when an operant will be reinforced.

Objective 15: Describe the effects of various schedules of reinforcement.

A (75) co________-reinforcement schedule leads to most rapid acquisition of new responses, but operants are maintained most economically through (76) ________tial reinforcement. Partial reinforcement also makes responses more resistant to (77) ________tion.

There are four basic schedules of reinforcement. In a (78) ________-________ schedule, a specific amount of time must elapse since a previous correct response before reinforcement again becomes available. In a variable-interval schedule, the amount of (79) ________ is allowed to vary. With a (80) ________-interval schedule, an organism's response rate falls off after each reinforcement, then picks up as it nears the time when reinforcement will be dispensed. The resultant record on the cumulative recorder shows a series of characteristic upward-moving waves, which are referred to as fixed-interval (81) ________lops. In a (82) ________-________ schedule, a fixed number of correct responses must be performed before one is reinforced. In a variable-ratio schedule, the (83) ________ of correct responses that must be performed before reinforcement becomes available is allowed to vary. Payment for piecework is an example of a (84) ________-________schedule. The unpredictability of (85: fixed or variable?) schedules maintains a high response rate. Slot machines tend to pay off on (86) ________-ratio schedules.

Objective 16: Describe shaping.

In shaping, we at first (87) r________ small steps toward behavioral goals. We reinforce (88) ________sive approximations to the goal. Eventually we reinforce organisms for performing complex behavioral (89)________s, with each link performed in proper sequence.

Objective 17: Discuss applications of operant conditioning.

Parents and peers socialize children into acquiring (90) "gender-________iate" behavior patterns through the elaborate use of rewards and punishments. Parents and peers also tend to (91: reward or punish?) their children for sharing with others and to (92: reward or punish?) them for being too aggressive.

Lang and Melamed used (93) ________ance learning to save the life of a baby that repeatedly threw up after eating. When the child tensed prior to vomiting, a tone was sounded and followed by painful but (presumably) harmless electric shock. We can explain this procedure through Mowrer's (94) ________________-factor learning. Through (95) ________________cal conditioning, the tone (CS) came to elicit expectation of electric shock (US), so that shock could be used sparingly. But the shock and, after classical conditioning, the tone were aversive stimuli. Through (96) ________________nt conditioning the infant learned to suppress the behaviors (muscle tensions) that were followed with aversive stimulation. By so doing, the aversive stimuli were removed. And so, the aversive stimuli served as (97: positive or negative?) reinforcers.

In using behavior (98) ________________tion in the classroom, teachers usually reinforce desired behavior and attempt to (99) ex________________ undesired behavior by ignoring it. (100) ________________med learning is based on the assumption that learning tasks can be broken down into a number of small steps. Correct performance of each small step is (101) ________________ced.

SECTION 3: Cognitive Learning

Objective 18: Describe evidence that supports the view that learning can occur by insight.

Not all learning can be explained through conditioning. Gestalt psychologist Wolfgang Köhler showed that apes can learn through sudden reorganization of (102) ________________al relationships, or insight.

E. C. Tolman's work with rats suggests that they develop (103) ________________ive maps of the environment. Tolman's work also suggests that operant conditioning teaches organisms where (104) rein________________ may be found, rather than mechanically increasing the frequency of (105) ________________nts.

Objective 19: Define *latent learning* and describe evidence that supports this kind of learning.

Tolman's work in (106) l________________ learning also found that organisms learn in the absence of reinforcement. Tolman also distinguished between learning and (107) ________________ance, and found that organisms do not necessarily perform all the behaviors that they have learned.

Objective 20: Discuss observational learning, including the effects of media violence.

Albert (108) B________________ and other social-learning theorists have shown that people can also learn by observing others. In observational learning, it is not necessary that people emit (109) ________________nses of their own, nor that their behavior be (110) ________________orced, in order for learning to take place. Learners may then choose to (111) p________________ the behaviors they have observed when "the time is ripe"—that is, when they believe that they will be rewarded.

People may (112) im________________ aggressive models if they believe that aggression is appropriate for them under a specific set of conditions. Media violence may contribute to aggressive behavior by increasing the level of (113) ar________________ of viewers, by (114) dis________________ of aggressive impulses, by providing models for development of aggressive skills, and (115) hab________________ of viewers to violence.

Objective 21: Discuss prototypes and concept learning.

Concepts are (116) ________________ols. Concepts stand for groups of objects, events, or ideas that have (117) c________________ properties. (118) ________________ types of concepts are schemas or templates that contain the essential features of the concept. Prototypes are good (119) ex________________s of a particular category. Many lower animals appear to possess instinctive or inborn (120) p________________s of various concepts.

Answers To Chapter Review

1. Experience
2. Represent
3. Neutral
4. Elicit (or evoke)
5. Salivary
6. Reflex
7. Stimuli
8. Environmental
9. Association
10. Conditional
11. Conditioned responses
12. Conditioned
13. Unconditioned
14. Unconditioned
15. Conditioned
16. Conditioned
17. Unconditioned
18. Simultaneous
19. Delayed
20. Prior to
21. Backward
22. Contiguous
23. Information
24. Contingency
25. Only one association
26. Contiguously
27. Behaviorist
28. Adaptive
29. Conditioned
30. Spontaneous
31. Generalization
32. Discrimination

33. Conditioned
34. Stimuli
35. Pad
36. Bell
37. Pad
38. Bladder
39. Unconditioned
40. Albert
41. Watson
42. Rayner
43. Counterconditioning
44. Puzzle
45. Effect
46. Punishments
47. Reinforcement
48. Skinner box
49. Cumulative
50. Operants
51. Reinforced
52. Error
53. Frequency
54. Applied
55. Increase
56. Removed
57. Primary
58. Secondary
59. Conditioned
60. Extinction
61. Operant
62. Spontaneous
63. Stimuli
64. Pleasant
65. Aversive
66. Behavior
67. Reinforcement
68. Will
69. Does not
70. Suppresses
71. Withdraw
72. Model
73. Learn
74. Discriminative
75. Continuous
76. Partial
77. Extinction
78. Fixed-interval
79. Time
80. Fixed
81. Scallops
82. Fixed-ratio
83. Number
84. Fixed-ratio
85. Variable
86. Variable
87. Reinforce
88. Successive
89. Chains
90. Appropriate
91. Reward
92. Punish
93. Avoidance
94. Two
95. Classical
96. Operant
97. Negative
98. Modification
99. Extinguish
100. Programmed
101. Reinforced
102. Perceptual
103. Cognitive
104. Reinforcement
105. Operants
106. Latent
107. Performance
108. Bandura
109. Responses
110. Reinforced
111. Perform
112. Imitate
113. Arousal
114. Disinhibition
115. Habituation
116. Symbols
117. Common
118. Prototypes
119. Examples
120. Prototypes

POSTTEST

1. Ivan Pavlov is known for his contribution to the understanding of
   (a) learning to engage in voluntary behavior.
   (b) observational learning.
   (c) classical conditioning.
   (d) contingency theory.

2. Which school of psychologists would define learning as a change in behavior that results from experience?
   (a) Behaviorists
   (b) Cognitive psychologists
   (c) Gestalt psychologists
   (d) Psychoanalysts

3. In Pavlov's experiments, salivation in response to meat was a
   (a) CR.
   (b) CS.
   (c) UR.
   (d) US.

4. In using the bell-and-pad method for overcoming bedwetting, the sensations of a full bladder are the
   (a) CR.
   (b) CS.
   (c) UR.
   (d) US.

5. Extinction in classical conditioning occurs because of repeated presentation of the
   (a) CR in the absence of the CS.
   (b) UR in the absence of the US.
   (c) CS in the absence of the US.
   (d) US in the absence of the CS.

6. In higher-order conditioning, a previously neutral stimulus comes to serve as a CS after being paired with a
   (a) CR.
   (b) CS.
   (c) UR.
   (d) US.

7. Little Albert learned to fear rats as a result of
   (a) clanging of steel bars in the presence of a rat.
   (b) observing a rat attack another animal.
   (c) being informed that rats carry certain harmful diseases.
   (d) being personally bitten by a rat.

8. Who originated the use of puzzle boxes?
   (a) Ivan Pavlov
   (b) John Watson
   (c) B. F. Skinner
   (d) Edward Thorndike

9. According to the law of effect, ________ has the effect of stamping out stimulus-response connections.
   (a) forgetting
   (b) negative reinforcement
   (c) extinction
   (d) punishment

10. Pain is an example of a
   (a) primary positive reinforcer.
   (b) primary negative reinforcer.
   (c) secondary positive reinforcer.
   (d) secondary negative reinforcer.

11. Which of the following statements about punishment is *false?*
    (a) Children learn responses that are punished.
    (b) Punishment increases the frequency of undesired behavior.
    (c) Punished children may withdraw from the situation.
    (d) Punishment may be modeled as a way of solving problems.

12. With a ________-________ schedule, an organism's response rate falls off after each reinforcement.
    (a) fixed-interval
    (b) fixed-ratio
    (c) variable-interval
    (d) variable-ratio

13. According to the text, the best way for teachers to use behavior modification in the classroom is to
    (a) pay attention to children when they are misbehaving.
    (b) pay attention to children when they are behaving correctly.
    (c) punish children when they are misbehaving.
    (d) reward children when they are misbehaving.

14. An experiment with Sultan provided evidence for
    (a) classical conditioning.
    (b) operant conditioning.
    (c) learning by insight.
    (d) latent learning.

15. In order for observational learning to take place,
    (a) stimuli must be paired repeatedly.
    (b) a stimulus must elicit a response.
    (c) an organism must be reinforced.
    (d) an organism must observe another organism.

16. The text defines a stimulus as
    (a) a change in the environment.
    (b) a condition that evokes a response from an organism.
    (c) any change that is learned.
    (d) an environmental condition that evokes a response from an organism.

17. A parent encourages a reluctant child to enter the water of a swimming pool by hugging and petting the child and murmuring "It's really nice," "You'll love it." This method is most similar to the behavior-therapy technique of
    (a) extinction.
    (b) systematic desensitization.
    (c) counterconditioning.
    (d) flooding.

18. According to contingency theory, learning occurs because
    (a) a conditioned stimulus indicates that the unconditioned stimulus is likely to ensue.
    (b) stimuli are contiguous.
    (c) of repeated trial and error.
    (d) organisms observe the outcomes of the behaviors of other organisms and act when they expect that the reinforcement contingencies will be rewarding.

19. In order to demonstrate that people can learn conditioned responses that are presumably too small to perceive, Hefferline and Keenan conditioned subjects to engage in apparently imperceptible
    (a) eyeblinks.
    (b) knee jerks.
    (c) galvanic skin responses.
    (d) thumb contractions.

20. An important way in which the learning of taste aversions differs from other kinds of classical conditioning is that
    (a) often only one pairing of the stimuli is required.
    (b) learning rapidly decays.
    (c) taste aversions are arbitrary, whereas other kinds of conditioning are adaptive.
    (d) there is no reward for learning.

Answers To Posttest

1. C
2. A
3. C
4. B
5. C
6. B
7. A
8. D
9. D
10. B
11. B
12. A
13. B
14. C
15. D
16. D
17. C
18. A
19. D
20. A

- Some people have photographic memories.
- It may be easier for you to recall the name of your first-grade teacher than of someone you just met at a party.
- All of our experiences are permanently imprinted on the brain so that proper stimulation can cause us to remember them exactly.
- Our memories are distorted by our prejudices.
- There is no practical limit to the amount of information you can store in your memory.
- Learning must be meaningful if we are to remember it.
- We are more likely to recall happy events while we are feeling happy and sad events while we are feeling sad.
- We can remember important events that took place during the first two years of life.
- If a certain part of your brain were damaged, you would retain remembrances of things past, but you would not be able to form new memories.

Memory

Learning Objectives

When you have finished studying Chapter 7, you should be able to:

Three Kinds of Memory

1. Describe the three kinds of memory.

Three Processes of Memory

2. Describe the three processes of memory.
3. Define *memory*.

Three Stages of Memory

4. Describe the functioning of sensory memory.
5. Describe the functioning of short-term memory.
6. Describe the functioning of long-term memory.

The Levels-of-Processing Model of Memory

7. Describe the levels-of-processing model of memory.

Forgetting

8. Explain the origin of the use of nonsense syllables in the study of memory and forgetting.
9. Explain the types of memory tasks that are used in measuring forgetting.
10. Explain the role of interference theory in forgetting.
11. Explain the possible role of repression in forgetting.
12. Explain the roles of anterograde and retrograde amnesia in forgetting.
13. Describe some methods for improving memory.

The Biology of Memory

14. Describe some views of the biology of memory.

My oldest daughter Jill was talking about how she had run into a friend from elementary school. She said they had a splendid time recalling the goofy things they had done. Her sister Allyn, age 6 at the time, was not to be outdone. "I can remember when I was born," she put in.

The family's ears perked up. Being a psychologist, I knew exactly what to say. "You can remember when you were born?" I said.

"Oh, yes," she insisted. "Mommy was there."

So far she could not be faulted. I cheered her on, and she elaborated a remarkably meticulous account of how it had been snowing in the wee hours of a bitter December morning when Mommy had to go to the hospital. You see, she said, her memory was so good that she could also summon up what it had been like *before* she was born. She wove a wonderful patchwork quilt, integrating details we had given her with her own recollections of the events surrounding the delivery of her younger sister, Jordan. All in all, she seemed quite satisfied that she had pieced together a faithful portrait of her arrival on the world stage.

Later in the chapter, we shall see that children usually cannot recall events prior to the age of 2 years, much less those of the first hours. But Allyn's tale dramatized the way in which we "remember" many of the things that have happened to us. When it comes to long-term memories, truth can take a back seat to drama and embellishment. Very often, our memories are like the bride's apparel—there's something old, something new, something borrowed, and, from time to time, something blue.

Memory is what this chapter is about. Without memory, there is no past. Without memory, experience is trivial and learning cannot abide. We shall soon contemplate what psychologists have learned about the ways in which we remember things, but first try to meet the following challenges to your memory.

Find four sheets of blank paper and number them 1 through 4. Then follow the directions given below.

1. Following are ten letters. Look at them for 15 seconds. Later in the chapter, I shall ask you if you can write them on sheet number 1. (No cheating! Don't do it now.)

THUNSTOFAM

2. Look at these nine figures for 30 seconds. Then try to draw them in the proper sequence on sheet number 2. (Yes, right after you've finished looking at them. We'll talk about your drawings later.)

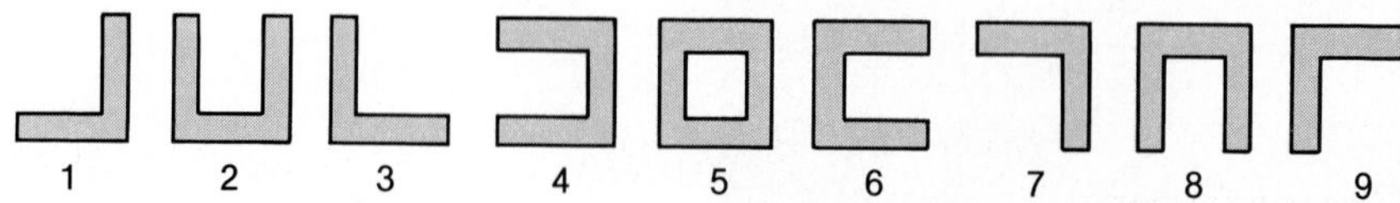

3. Okay, here's another list of letters, 17 this time. Look at the list for 60 seconds and then see whether you can reproduce it on sheet number 3. (I'm being generous this time—a full minute.)

GMC–BSI–BMA–TTC–IAF–BI

4. Which of these pennies is an accurate reproduction of the Lincoln penny you see every day? This time there's nothing to draw on another sheet; just circle or put a checkmark by the penny you think resembles the ones you throw in the back of the drawer.

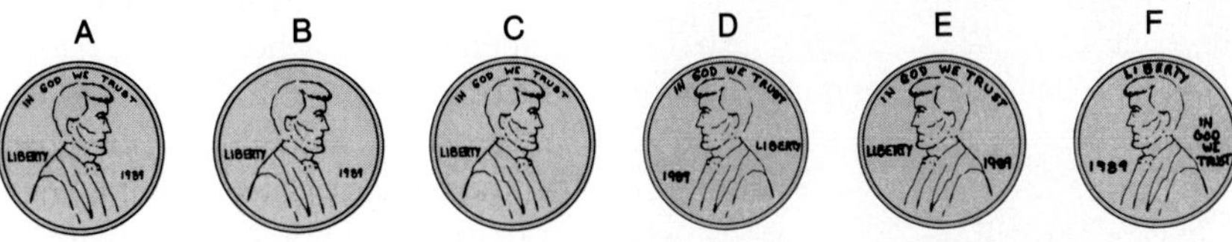

5. Examine the following drawings for 1 minute. Then copy the names of the figures on sheet number 4. When you're finished, just keep reading. Soon I'll be asking you to draw those figures.

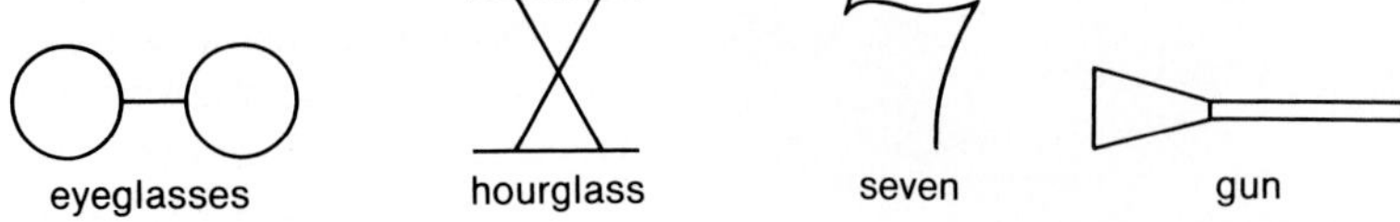

THREE KINDS OF MEMORY

Memories contain different kinds of information, and some theorists classify memories according to the kind of material they hold (Brewer & Pani, 1984; Tulving, 1972, 1982, 1985). Return to Allyn's "recollection." Of course Allyn could not really remember her own birth. That is, she could not recall the particular event in which she had participated.

Episodic Memory

> *Memory requires more than mere dating of a fact in the past. It must be dated in* my *past. In other words, I must think that I directly experienced its occurrence. It must have that "warmth and intimacy" . . . as characterizing all experiences "appropriated" by the thinker as his own.*
>
> William James

Memories of the events that happen to a person or take place in the person's presence are referred to as **episodic memory.** Your memory of what you ate for breakfast and of what your professor said in class this afternoon are examples of episodic memory.

What Allyn did recount is more accurately characterized as generalized knowledge than as visions of that important event in her young life. From listening to her parents, and from her personal experience with the events surrounding Jordan's birth, Allyn had gained extensive knowledge of what happens during childbirth. She had erroneously represented this knowledge as a precise portrayal of her birth.

Semantic Memory

Generalized knowledge is referred to as **semantic memory.** *Semantics* concerns meanings, and Allyn was reporting her understanding of the meaning of childbirth rather than an episode in her own life. You "remember" that the United States has 50 states without necessarily visiting all of them and personally adding them up. You "remember" who authored *Hamlet,* although you were not looking over Shakespeare's shoulder as he did so. These, too, are examples of semantic memory.

Episodic memory Memories of incidents experienced by a person; of events that occur to a person or take place in the person's presence.

Semantic memory General knowledge as opposed to episodic memory.

Procedural Memory. Procedural memory—also referred to as skill memory—involves knowledge of how to do things. Memories of how to ride a bicycle, how to type, how to turn on and off the lights, and how to drive a car are procedural memories. Procedural memories tend to persevere even when we have not used them for many years. Here, an elderly Jean Piaget, the famed cognitive-developmental theorist discussed in Chapter 9, demonstrates that we may never forget how to ride a bicycle.

Your future recollection that there are three kinds of memory is more likely to be semantic than episodic. In other words, you are more likely to "know" that there are three types of memory than to recall the date on which you learned about them, exactly where you were and how you were sitting, and whether or not you were also thinking about dinner at the time. We tend to use the phrase "I remember . . ." when we are referring to episodic memories, as in "I *remember* the blizzard of 1988" (Tulving, 1972). But we are more likely to say "I know . . ." in reference to semantic memories, as in "I *know* about—" (or, "I heard about—") "—the blizzard of 1888." Put it another way: You may *remember* that you wrote your mother, but you *know* that Shakespeare wrote *Hamlet.*

Procedural Memory

The third type of memory is **procedural memory,** also referred to as *skill memory.* Procedural memory involves knowledge of how to do things. You have learned and "remember" how to ride a bicycle, how to swim or swing a bat, how to type (or in the case of my hunting and pecking, the approximate location of the typewriter keys), how to turn the lights on and off, and how to drive a car. Procedural memories tend to persevere even when we have not used them for many, many years. For example, it is said that we never forget how to ride a bicycle. On the other hand, procedural memories may concern skills that we cannot readily describe in words. Would you be able to explain to another person just how you manage to keep from falling when you ride a bike? When you're teaching someone how to use a manual shift, do you stick to words, or do you move your arm both to remember and to illustrate the technique?

Do you think it would help for a person to have "ESP" to remember the three types of memory? That is, E = episodic, S = semantic, and P = procedural. As we proceed, we shall see that a good deal of information about memory comes in threes. We shall also learn more about **mnemonic devices**, such as "ESP." By the way, is your use of the **acronym** *ESP* to help remember the kinds of memory an instance of episodic, semantic, or procedural memory?

Before proceeding to the next section, why don't you turn to that piece of paper on which you wrote the names of the four figures—that is, sheet number 4—and draw them from memory as exactly as you can. Then hold on to the drawings, and we'll talk about them a bit later.

THREE PROCESSES OF MEMORY

Psychologists and computer scientists both speak in terms of the processing of information. Think of using a minicomputer to write a term paper. Once the system is operating, you begin to type in information. You place information into the computer's memory by typing letters on a keyboard. If you were to practice grisly surgery on your computer (which I am often tempted to do) and open up its memory, however, you wouldn't find these letters inside. This is because the computer is programmed to change the letters, the information you have typed, into a form that can be placed in its electronic memory. Similarly, when we perceive information, we must convert it into a form that can be remembered if we are to place it in memory.

Encoding

The first stage of information processing, or changing information so that we can place it in memory, is called **encoding.** Information about the world outside reaches our senses as physical and chemical stimulation. When we encode this

Procedural memory Knowledge of ways of doing things; skill memory.

Mnemonic devices Systems for remembering in which items are related to easily recalled sets of symbols such as acronyms, phrases, or jingles.

Acronym A word that is composed of the first letters of the elements of a phrase.

Encoding Modifying information so that it can be placed in memory. The first stage of information processing.

information, we convert it into psychological formats that can be mentally represented. To do so, we commonly use *visual, acoustic,* and *semantic codes.*

Let us illustrate the uses of coding by referring to the list of letters you first saw in the box on challenges to memory. Try to write the letters down now on sheet number 1, and then we'll talk about them. Go on, take a minute, and then come back.

Okay, now; if you had used a **visual code** to try to remember the list, you would have mentally represented it as a picture. That is, you would have maintained—or attempted to maintain—a mental image of the letters. Some artists and art historians seem to maintain marvelous visual mental representations of works of art, so that they recognize at once whether a photograph of a work is authentic.

You may also have decided to read the list of letters to yourself—that is, to silently say them in sequence: "t," "h," "u," and so on. By so doing, you would have been using an **acoustic code,** or representing the stimuli as a sequence of sounds. You may also have read the list as a three-syllable word, "thun-sto-fam." This is an acoustic code, but it also involves the "meaning" of the letters, in the sense that you are interpreting the list as a word. And so this approach has elements of a semantic code.

Semantic codes represent stimuli in terms of their meaning. How can you use a semantic code to help remember the three colors blue, yellow, and gray? You may recall from Chapter 4 that blue and yellow are complementary, and when we mix lights of complementary colors we attain gray. Using this relationship among the colors to remember them lends the grouping meaning and, for this reason, is an example of a semantic code.

Our ten letters were meaningless in and of themselves. However, they can also serve as an acronym for the familiar phrase "THe UNited STates OF AMerica," an observation that lends them meaning.

Storage

The second process of memory is **storage,** or the maintenance of information over time. If you were given the task of storing the list of letters (told to remember it), how would you attempt to place it in storage? One way would be by **maintenance rehearsal**—by mentally repeating the list, or saying it to yourself. Our awareness of the functioning of our memory, referred to by psychologists as **metamemory,** becomes more sophisticated as we develop. We become more likely to use rehearsal as we develop.

You could also have condensed the amount of information you were rehearsing by reading the list as a three-syllable word; that is, you could have rehearsed three syllables rather than ten letters. In either case, repetition would have been the key to memory. (We'll talk more about such condensing, or "chunking," very soon.) However, if you had encoded the list semantically, as an acronym for "The United States of America," storage might have been instantaneous and permanent, as we shall see.

Retrieval

The third memory process is **retrieval,** or locating stored information and returning it to consciousness. With well-known information such as our names and occupations retrieval is effortless and, for all practical purposes, immediate. But when we are trying to remember massive quantities of information, or information that is not perfectly understood, retrieval can be tedious and not always successful. To retrieve stored information in a computer, we need to know the name

---

Visual code Mental representation of information as a picture.

Acoustic code Mental representation of information as a sequence of sounds.

Semantic code Mental representation of information according to its meaning.

Storage The maintenance of information over time. The second stage of information processing.

Maintenance rehearsal Mental repetition of information in order to keep it in memory.

Metamemory Self-awareness of the ways in which memory functions, allowing the person to encode, store, and retrieve information effectively.

Retrieval The location of stored information and its return to consciousness. The third stage of information processing.

of the file. Similarly, retrieval of information from our memories requires knowledge of the proper cues.

If you had encoded THUNSTOFAM as a three-syllable word, your retrieval strategy would involve recollection of the word and rules of decoding. In other words, you would say the "word" *thun-sto-fam* and then decode it by spelling it out. You might err in that "thun" sounds like "thumb" and "sto" could also be spelled "stow." Using the semantic code, or recognition of the acronym for "The United States of America," could lead to flawless recollection, however.

I stuck my neck out by predicting that you would immediately and permanently store the list if you recognized it as an acronym. Here, too, there would be recollection (of the name of our country) and decoding rules. To "remember" the ten letters, that is, you would have to envision the phrase and read off the first two letters of each word. Since using this semantic code is more complex than simply seeing the entire list (using a visual code), it may take a while to recall (actually, to reconstruct) the list of ten letters. By using the phrase, however, you are likely to remember the list of letters perpetually and flawlessly.

Now, what if you were not able to remember the list of ten letters? What would have gone wrong? In terms of the three processes of memory, it could be that you had (1) not encoded the list in a useful way, (2) not entered the encoded information into storage, or (3) stored the information but lacked the proper cues for remembering it—such as the phrase "The United States of America" or the rule for decoding the phrase.

You may have noticed, now that we have been drawn well into the chapter, that I have discussed three kinds of memory and three processes of memory, but I have not yet *defined* memory. No apologies—we weren't ready. Now that we have explored some basic concepts, let us have a try: **Memory** is defined as the processes by which information is encoded, stored, and retrieved. These processes allow us to maintain information over the passage of time. How much time? From a fraction of a second to a lifetime. Memory is responsible for your recollection of the previous word as your eyes scan this page. Memory is equally responsible for your recollection of the names of your elementary school classmates.

Now let us turn our attention to two psychological models of memory—memory as stages and memory as levels of processing information.

THREE STAGES OF MEMORY

Before the turn of the century, a Harvard University professor was intrigued by the fact that some memories were unreliable, "going in one ear and out the other," whereas others could be recalled for a lifetime:

> *The stream of thought flows on, but most of its elements fall into the bottomless pit of oblivion. Of some, no element survives the instant of their passage. Of others, it is confined to a few moments, hours, or days. Others, again, leave vestiges which are indestructible, and by means of which they may be recalled as long as life endures.*
>
> William James, *Principles of Psychology*, 1890

Yes, the world is a constant display of sights and sounds and other sources of sensory stimulation, but only some of these things are remembered. James observed correctly that we remember various "elements of thought" for different lengths of time and many not at all. Atkinson and Shiffrin (1968) propose that there are three stages of information processing and that the progress of information through these stages determines whether (and how long) it will be retained (see Figure 7.1). These stages are *sensory memory, short-term memory (STM),* and *long-term memory (LTM).* Let us try to make *sense* of the *short* and the *long* of memory.

Memory The processes by which information is encoded, stored, and retrieved.

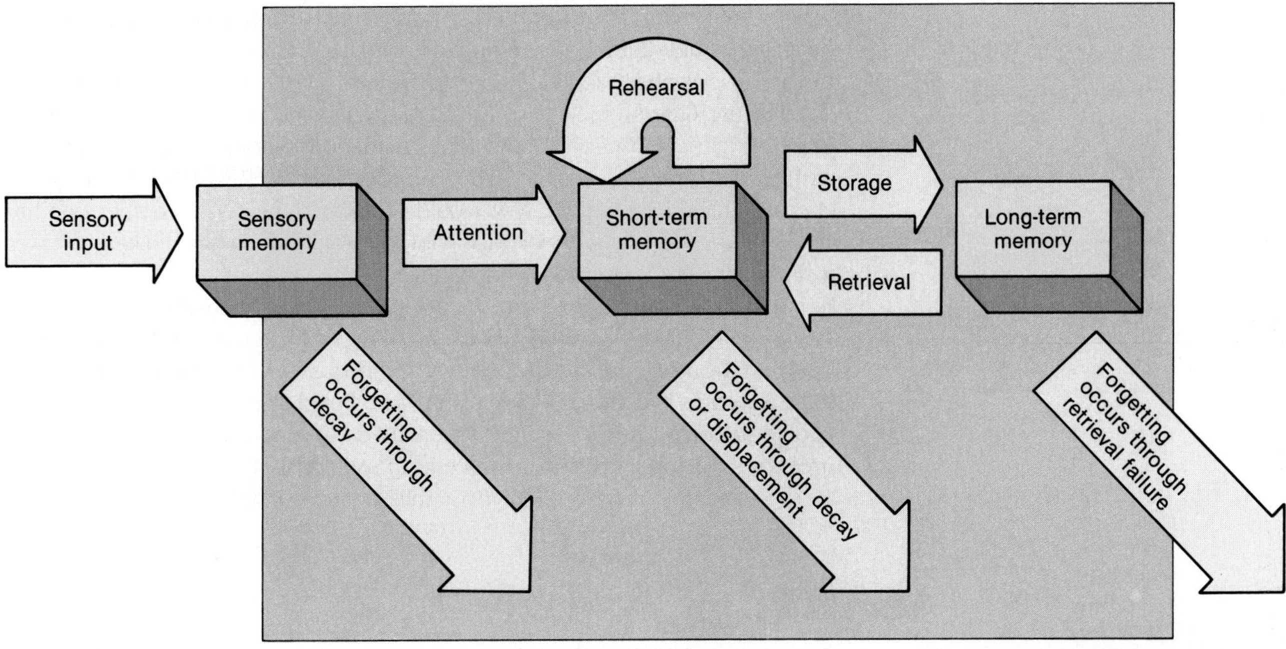

FIGURE 7.1
Three Stages of Memory.

A number of psychologists hypothesize that there are three distinct stages of memory. Sensory information impacts upon the registers of sensory memory, where memory traces are held briefly before decaying. If we attend to the information, much of it is transferred to short-term memory (STM). Information in STM may decay or be displaced if it is not transferred to long-term memory (LTM). We usually use rehearsal to transfer memories to LTM. Once in LTM, memories may be retrieved through appropriate search strategies. But if information is organized poorly, or if we cannot find cues to retrieve it, it may be lost.

Sensory Memory

Consciousness . . . does not appear to itself chopped up in bits. A "river" or a "stream" are the metaphors by which it is most naturally described. In talking of it hereafter, let us call it the stream of thought, of consciousness, or of subjective life.

William James

Thus wrote William James of the stream of thought, or of consciousness. When we look at a visual stimulus, our impressions may seem fluid enough. Actually, they consist of a series of eye fixations referred to as **saccadic eye movement.** These movements jump from one point to another about four times each second. The visual sensations seem continuous, or streamlike, however, because of **sensory memory.** Sensory memory is the type or stage of memory first encountered by a stimulus. Although it holds impressions briefly, it is long enough so that series of perceptions seem to be connected.

Return to our example of the list of letters: THUNSTOFAM. If the list were flashed on a screen for a fraction of a second, the visual impression, or **memory trace,** of the stimulus would also last for only a fraction of a second afterward. Psychologists speak of the memory trace of the list as being held in a visual **sensory register.** Sensory memory, in other words, consists of registers that can briefly hold information that is entered by means of our senses.

If the letters had been flashed on a screen for, say, one-tenth of a second, your ability to remember them on the basis of sensory memory alone would be

Saccadic eye movement The rapid jumps made by a person's eyes as they fixate on different points.

Sensory memory The type or stage of memory first encountered by a stimulus. Sensory memory holds impressions briefly, but long enough so that series of perceptions are psychologically continuous.

Memory trace An assumed change in the nervous system that reflects the impression made by a stimulus. Memory traces are said to be "held" in sensory registers.

Sensory register A system of memory that holds information briefly, but long enough so that it can be processed further. There may be a sensory register for every sense.

meager. Your memory would be based on a single eye fixation, and the trace of the image would vanish before a single second had passed. At the turn of the century, the social psychologist William McDougall (1904) engaged in research in which he presented subjects 1 to 12 letters arranged in rows—just long enough to allow a single eye fixation. Under these conditions, subjects could typically remember only four or five letters. Thus, recollection of *THUNSTOFAM,* a list of ten letters arranged into a single row, would probably depend on whether one had successfully transformed or encoded it into a form in which it could be processed by further stages of memory.

George Sperling (1960) modified McDougall's experimental method and showed that there is a difference between what people can see and what they can report. McDougall had used a *whole-report procedure,* in which subjects were asked to report every letter seen in the array. Sperling used a modified *partial-report procedure,* in which subjects were asked to report the contents of one of three rows of letters. In a typical procedure, Sperling flashed three rows of letters like those that follow on a screen for 50 milliseconds (1/20th of a second):

A G R E

V L S B

N K B T

Using the whole-report procedure, subjects could report an average of four letters from the entire display (one out of three). But if Sperling pointed an arrow immediately after presentation at a row he wanted viewers to report, they usually reported most of the letters in the row successfully.

If Sperling presented six letters arrayed in two rows, subjects could usually report either row without error. If subjects were flashed 3 rows of 4 letters each—a total of 12—they reported correctly an average of 3 of 4 of the designated row, suggesting that about 9 letters of the 12 had been perceived.

Sperling found that the amount of time that elapsed before indicating the row to be reported was crucial. If he delayed pointing the arrow for a few fractions of a second after the display, subjects were much less successful in reporting the target row. If he allowed a full second to elapse, the arrow did not aid recall at all. From these data, Sperling concluded that the memory trace of visual stimuli *decays* within a second in the visual sensory register (see Figure 7.1). With a single eye fixation, subjects can *see* most of a display of 12 letters clearly, as shown by their ability to immediately read off most of the letters in a designated row. Yet, as the fractions of a single second are elapsing, the memory trace of the letters is fading. By the time a second has elapsed, the trace has vanished.

Iconic Memory. Psychologists believe there is a sensory register for each one of our senses. The mental representations of visual stimuli are referred to as **icons.** The sensory register that holds icons is labeled **iconic memory.** Iconic memories are accurate, photographic memories. So those of us who can see—who mentally represent visual stimuli—have "photographic memories." However, they are very brief. What most of us normally think of as a photographic memory—the ability to retain exact mental representations of visual stimuli over long periods of time—is referred to by psychologists as eidetic imagery.

Eidetic Imagery. Visual stimuli, or icons, persist for remarkably long periods of time among a few individuals. About 5 percent of children can look at a detailed picture, turn away, and several minutes later recall the particulars of the picture with exceptional clarity—as if they were still viewing it. This extraordinary visual memory is referred to as **eidetic imagery** (Haber, 1980). Among the minority of children who have this ability, it declines with age, all but disappearing by adolescence.

Figure 7.2 provides an example of a test of eidetic imagery. Children are asked to look at the first drawing in the series for 20 to 30 seconds, after which it is removed. The children then continue to gaze at a neutral background. Several

Icon A mental representation of a visual stimulus that is held briefly in sensory memory.

Iconic memory The sensory register that briefly holds mental representations of visual stimuli.

Eidetic imagery The maintenance of detailed visual memories over several minutes.

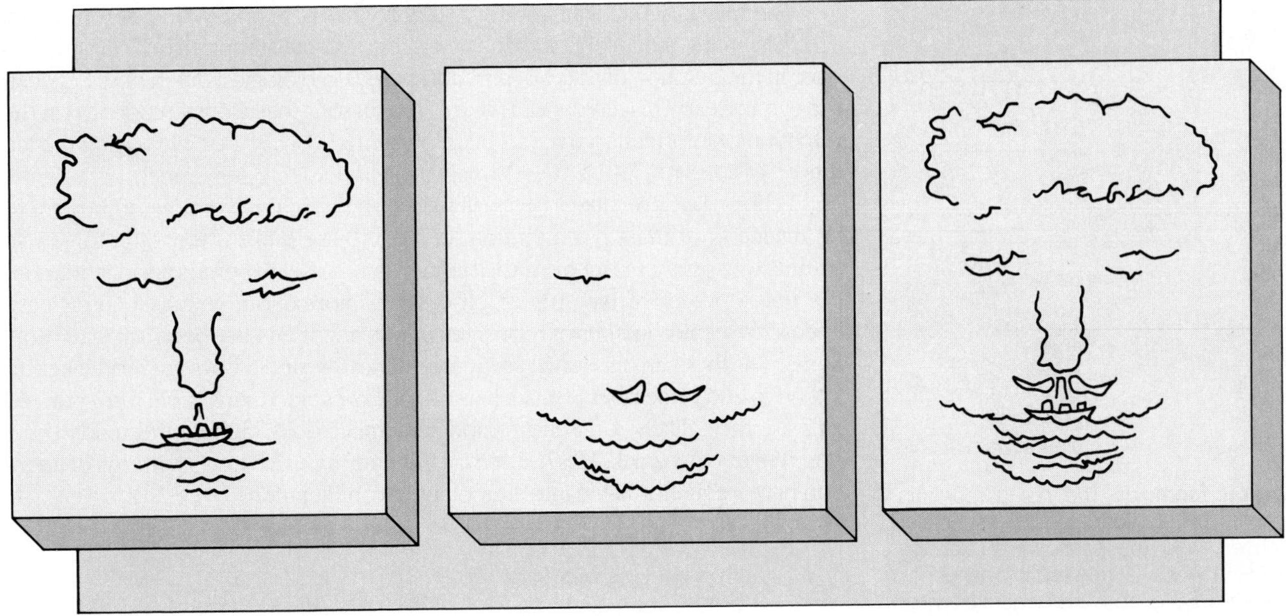

FIGURE 7.2
A Research Strategy for Assessing Eidetic Imagery.
Children look at the first drawing for 20 to 30 seconds, after which it is removed. Next, the children look at a neutral background for several minutes. They are then shown the second drawing. When asked what they see, children with the capacity for eidetic imagery report seeing a face. The face is seen only by children who retain the first image and fuse it with the second, thus perceiving the third image.

minutes later, the drawing in the center is placed on the backdrop. When asked what they see, many report "a face." A face would be seen only if the children had retained a clear image of the first picture and fused it with the second so that they are, in effect, perceiving the third picture in Figure 7.2 (Haber, 1980).

Eidetic imagery appears remarkably clear and detailed. It seems to be essentially a perceptual phenomenon in which coding is not a factor.

Those of us who can see actually have photographic, or iconic, memories. However, only a few of us have eidetic imagery, and this capacity usually disappears by adolescence.

Although eidetic imagery is rare, iconic memory, as we see in the following section, universally transforms visual perceptions into smoothly unfolding impressions of the world.

Iconic Memory and Saccadic Eye Movements: Smoothing Out the Bumps in the Visual Ride. Saccadic eye movements occur about four times every second. Iconic memory, however, holds icons for up to a second. As a consequence, the flow of visual information seems smooth and continuous. Your impression that the words you are reading flow across the page, rather than jump across in spurts, is a product of your iconic memory. Similarly, motion pictures present 16 to 22 separate frames, or still images, each second. Iconic memory allows you to perceive the imagery as being seamless (Loftus, 1983).

Echoic Memory. The mental representations of sounds, or auditory stimuli, are called **echoes.** The sensory register that holds echoes is referred to as **echoic memory.**

Echo A mental representation of an auditory stimulus (sound) that is held briefly in sensory memory.

Echoic memory The sensory register that briefly holds mental representations of auditory stimuli.

Echoic Memory. The mental representations of auditory stimuli are called echoes, and the sensory register that holds echoes is referred to as echoic memory. By encoding visual information as echoes and rehearsing the echoes, we commit them to memory. The drama student is memorizing the script by encoding typed words as echoes (placing them in echoic memory) and rehearsing them.

The memory traces of auditory stimuli (that is, echoes) can last for several seconds, many times longer than the traces of visual stimuli (icons). The difference in the duration of traces is probably based on biological differences between the eye and ear. This difference is one of the reasons that acoustic codes aid in the retention of information that has been presented visually—or why saying the letters or syllables of THUNSTOFAM makes the list easier to remember.

Echoes, however, like icons, will fade with the passage of time. If they are to be retained, we must pay attention to them. By selectively attending to certain stimuli, we sort them out from the background noise. For example, in studies on the development of patterns of processing information, young children have been shown photographs of rooms full of toys and then have been asked to recall as many as they can. One such study found that 2-year-old boys are more likely to attend to and remember toys such as cars, puzzles, and trains, whereas 2-year-old girls are more likely to attend to and remember dolls, dishes, and teddy bears (Renninger & Wozniak, 1985). Even by this early age, children's patterns of attention have frequently fallen into stereotypical configurations.

Short-Term Memory

> *We have . . . not memory so much as memories. . . . We can set our memory as it were to retain things for a certain time, and then let them depart.*
>
> William James

If you focus attention on a stimulus in the sensory register, you will tend to retain it in **short-term memory**—also referred to as **working memory**—for a minute or so after the trace of the stimulus decays. When you are given a phone number by the information operator and then write it down or dial the number, you are retaining the number in your short-term memory. When you are told the name of someone at a party and then use that name immediately in addressing the person, you are retaining the name in short-term memory. In short-term memory, the image tends to fade significantly after 10 to 12 seconds if it is not repeated or rehearsed. It is possible to focus on maintaining a visual image in the short-term memory, but it is more common to encode visual stimuli as sounds, or auditory stimulation. The sounds can then be rehearsed, or repeated.

As noted, most of us know that a way of retaining information in short-term memory—and possibly storing it permanently—is to rehearse it. When an information operator tells me a phone number, I usually rehearse it continuously while I am dialing it or running around frantically searching for a pencil and a scrap of paper. Most of us also know that the more times we rehearse information, the more likely we are to remember it. We have the capacity (if not the will or the time) to rehearse information and thereby keep it in short-term memory indefinitely.

Encoding. Let us now return to the task of remembering the first list of letters in my challenge to memory. If you had coded the letters as the three-syllable word THUN-STO-FAM, you would probably have recalled them by mentally rehearsing (saying to yourself) the three-syllable "word" and then spelling it out from the sounds. A few minutes later, if someone asked whether the letters had been upper case (THUNSTOFAM) or lower case (thunstofam), you might not have been confident of an answer. You had used an acoustic code to help recall the list, and upper- and lower-case letters sound alike.

Because it can be pronounced, THUNSTOFAM is not too difficult to retain in short-term memory. But what if the list of letters had been TBXLFNTSDK? This list of letters cannot be pronounced as it is. You would have had to find a complex acronym in order to code these letters, and within a fraction of a second—most

---

Short-term memory The type or stage of memory that can hold information for up to a minute or so after the trace of the stimulus decays. Also called *working memory.*

Working memory See *short-term memory.*

likely an impossible task. To aid recall, you would probably have tried to repeat or rehearse the letters rapidly—to read each one as many times as possible before the memory trace faded. You might have visualized each letter as you said it and tried to get back to it (that is, to run through the entire list) before it decayed.

Let us assume that you encoded the letters as sounds and then rehearsed the sounds. When asked to report the list, you might mistakenly say T-V-X-L-F-N-T-S-T-K. This would be an understandable error because the incorrect *V* and *T* sounds are similar, respectively, to the correct *B* and *D* sounds.

The Serial-Position Effect. Note that you would also be likely to recall the first and last letters in the series, *T* and *K,* more accurately than the others. Why? The tendency to recall more accurately the first and last items in a series is known as the **serial-position effect.** This effect may occur because we pay more attention to the first and last stimuli in a series. They serve as the visual or auditory boundaries for the other stimuli. It may also be that the first items are likely to be rehearsed more frequently (repeated more times) than other items (Rundus, 1971). The last items are likely to have been rehearsed most recently and so are most likely to be retained in short-term memory.

According to cognitive psychologists, the tendency to recall the initial items in a list is referred to as the **primacy effect.** Social psychologists also note a powerful primacy effect in our formation of impressions of other people. Our first impressions tend to last. The tendency to recall the last items in a list is referred to as the **recency effect.** If we are asked to recall the last items in a list soon after we have been shown the list, they may still be in short-term memory. As a result, they can be "read off." Earlier items, in contrast, may have to be retrieved from long-term memory.

Chunks of Information: Is Seven a Magic Number or Did the Phone Company Get Lucky? Rapidly rehearsing ten meaningless letters is not an easy task. With TBXLFNTSDK there are ten discrete elements, or **chunks,** of information that must be kept in short-term memory. When we encode *THUNSTOFAM* as three syllables, there are only three chunks to swallow at once—a memory task that is much easier on the digestion.

Psychologist George Miller noted that the average person was comfortable with digesting about seven integers at a time, the number of integers in a telephone number. In an article appearing in the *Psychological Review,* he wrote,

> *My problem is that I have been persecuted by an integer. For seven years this number has followed me around, has intruded in my most private data, and has assaulted me from the pages of our most public journals (1956).*

In public, yet. Most people have little trouble recalling five chunks of information, as in a zip code. Some can remember nine, which is, for all but a few, an upper limit. Seven chunks, plus or minus one or two, is thus the "magic" number—in Germany (Ebbinghaus, 1885) and China (Yu et al., 1985) as well as in the English-speaking world.

How, then, you ask, do we successfully include the area codes in our recollections of telephone numbers, hence making them ten digits long? The truth of the matter is that we usually don't. We tend to recall the area code as a single chunk of information derived from our general knowledge of where a person lives. We are thus more likely to remember (or "know") the ten-digit numbers of acquaintances who reside in locales with area codes we use frequently.

Businesses pay the phone company hefty premiums so that they can attain numbers with two or three zeroes—for example, 592-2000 or 614-3300. These numbers have fewer chunks of information and hence are easier to remember. Customer recollection of business phone numbers increases sales. One financial services company uses the toll-free number CALL-IRA, which reduces the task to

Serial-position effect The tendency to recall more accurately the first and last items in a series.

Primacy effect The tendency to recall the initial items in a series of items.

Recency effect The tendency to recall the last items in a series of items.

Chunk A stimulus or group of stimuli that are perceived as a discrete piece of information.

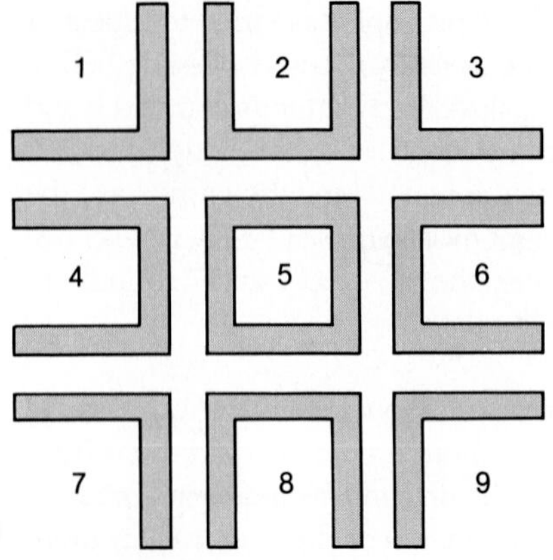

FIGURE 7.3
A Familiar Grid. The nine drawings in the second challenge to memory form this familiar tic-tac-toe grid when the numbers are placed inside them and they are arranged in numerical order, three shapes to a line. This method for recalling the shapes collapses nine chunks of information into two. One is the tic-tac-toe grid. The second is the rule for decoding the drawings from the grid.

two chunks of information that also happen to be meaningfully related (semantically coded) to the nature of the business. Similarly, a clinic in my area that helps people quit smoking arranged for a telephone number that can be reached by dialing the letters NO SMOKE. Do you use meaningful words to assist you in remembering codes that must be punched in to use your bank cash card or the combination on a lock? I once used my first address in The Bronx as the combination number of a lock, and now I use one of my publishers' names as the code for my bank cash card. (Was publishing the last bit of information a mistake?)

Return to the third challenge to memory presented on page 248. Were you able to remember the six groups of letters? Would your task have been simpler if you had grouped them differently? How about moving the dashes forward by a letter, so that they read GM-CBS-IBM-ATT-CIA-FBI? We have exactly the same list of letters, but we suddenly have six chunks of information that can be coded semantically. You may have also been able to generate the list by remembering a rule, such as "big corporations and government agencies."

If we can recall seven or perhaps nine chunks of information, how, then, do children remember the alphabet? The alphabet contains 26 discrete pieces of information. How do children learn to encode the letters of the alphabet, presented visually, as spoken sounds? The 26 letters of the alphabet cannot be pronounced like a word or phrase—despite the existence of that impossible *Sesame Street* song, "Ab k'defkey jekyl m'nop kw'r stoov w'ksizz." There is nothing about the shape of an *A* that suggests its sound. Nor does the visual stimulus *B* sound "B-ish." Children learning the alphabet and learning to associate visually presented letters with their spoken names do so by **rote.** It is mechanical associative learning that requires time and repetition. If you think that learning the alphabet by rote is a simple child's task, now that it is behind you, try learning the Russian or Hebrew alphabet.

Now, if you had recognized THUNSTOFAM as an acronym for the first two letters of each word in the phrase "THe UNited STates OF AMerica," you also would have reduced the number of chunks of information that had to be recalled. You could have considered the phrase to be a single chunk of information, and the rule that you must use the first two letters of each word of the phrase to be another chunk.

Reconsider the second challenge to memory on page 248. You were asked to remember nine chunks of visual information. Perhaps you could have used the acoustic codes "L" and "Square" for chunks three and five, but no obvious codes are available for the seven other chunks. Now look at Figure 7.3. If you had recognized that the elements in the challenge could be arranged as the familiar tic-tac-toe grid, remembering the nine elements might have required two chunks of information. The first would have been the mental image of the grid and the second would have been the rule for decoding: each element corresponds to the shape of a section of the grid if read like words on a page (from upper left to lower right). The number sequence 1 through 9 would not in itself present a problem, because you learned this series by rote many years ago and have rehearsed it in countless calculations since.

Interference in Short-Term Memory. I mentioned that I often find myself running around looking for a pencil and a scrap of paper to write down a telephone number that has been given to me. If I keep on rehearsing the number while I'm looking, I'm okay. However, I have also cursed myself repeatedly for failing to keep a pad and pencil by the telephone, and sometimes the mental dressing down interferes with my recollection of the number. (The moral of the story? Avoid self-reproach.) It has also happened that I have actually looked up a phone number for myself and been about to dial it when someone has asked me for the time or where I said we were going to dinner. Unless I say, "Now hold on a minute!" and manage to jot down the number on something, it's back to the

Rote Mechanical associative learning that is based on repetition.

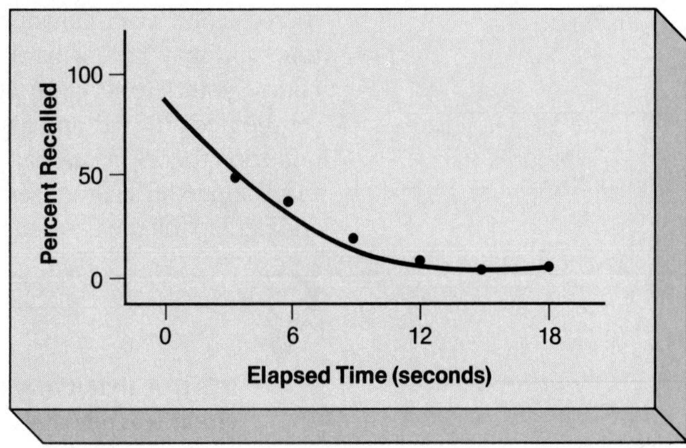

FIGURE 7.4
The Effect of Interference on Information in Short-Term Memory. In this experiment, college students were asked to maintain a series of three letters in their memories while they counted backward by three's from an arbitrary number. After just three seconds, retention was cut by half. Ability to recall the words was almost completely lost by 15 seconds.

phone book. Attending to distracting information, even briefly, prevents me from rehearsing the number, so it falls between the cracks of my short-term memory.

In an experiment with college students, Lloyd and Margaret Peterson (1959) demonstrated how prevention of rehearsal can wreak havoc with short-term memory. They asked students to remember three-letter combinations, such as HGB—normally, three easy chunks of information. They then had the students count backward from an arbitrary number, such as 181, by threes (that is, 181, 178, 175, 172, and so on). The students were told to stop counting and to report the letter sequence after the passage of the intervals of time shown in Figure 7.4. The percentage of letter combinations recalled correctly fell precipitously within seconds. After 18 seconds of interference, counting had dislodged the letter sequences in almost all of these bright young students' memories.

Psychologists say that the appearance of new information in short-term memory **displaces** the old information. Remember: only a few bits of information at a time can be retained in short-term memory. Klatzky (1980) likens short-term memory to a shelf or workbench. Once it is full, some things fall off when new items are shoved on. Here, we have another possible explanation for the recency effect: The most recently learned bit of information is least likely to be displaced by additional information.

Displace In memory theory, to cause chunks of information to be lost from short-term memory by adding new items.

Displacement occurs at cocktail parties, and I'm not referring to the jostling of one's body by others in the crowd. The point is this: When you meet Jennifer or Jonathan at the party, there should be little trouble remembering the name. But

Displacement. Information can be lost to short-term memory by means of displacement. We may have little trouble remembering the names of the first one or two people we meet at a party. But as introductions continue, new names may displace the old, and we may forget the names of people we met only a few minutes earlier.

then you may meet Tamara or Timothy and, still later, Stephanie or Steven. By that time you may have a hard time dredging up Jennifer or Jonathan—unless, of course, you were very, very attracted to one of them. A passionate response would set the person apart and inspire a good deal of selective attention. Recall signal-detection theory from Chapter 4: If you were enamored enough, we may predict that the person's name (sensory signals) would be "detected" with a vengeance, and perhaps all the ensuing names would dissolve into background noise.

It is true that it may be easier for you to recall the name of your first-grade teacher than of someone you just met at a party. Your first-grade teacher's name is stored in long-term memory, whereas you may soon be juggling your new acquaintance's name with many others in short-term memory.

Long-Term Memory

Long-term memory is the third stage of processing of information. Think of your long-term memory as a vast storehouse of information containing names, dates, places, what Johnny did to you in second grade, and what Susan said about you when you were 12.

Some psychologists (Sigmund Freud was one) used to believe that nearly all of our perceptions and ideas were stored permanently. Of course, we might not be able to retrieve all of them, but such memories might be "lost" because of the unavailability of the proper cues, or they might be kept beneath the surface of conscious awareness by the forces of **repression.** Adherents to this view often pointed to the work of neurosurgeon Wilder Penfield (1969). When parts of their brain were electrically stimulated, many of Penfield's patients reported the appearance of images that had something of the feel of memories.

Most psychologists today view this notion as exaggerated. Memory researcher Elizabeth Loftus, for example, notes that the "memories" stimulated by Penfield's probes were impoverished in detail and not necessarily factual (Loftus & Loftus, 1980; Loftus, 1983).

It is *not* true that all of our experiences are permanently imprinted on the brain.

Evidence is far from compelling that we store all of our experiences. To the contrary, we appear to be more likely to store incidents that have a greater impact on us—events more laden with personal meaning.

Now let us consider some important questions about long-term memory.

How Accurate Are Long-Term Memories?—Memory as Reconstructive.

False memories are by no means rare occurrences in most of us. The most frequent source of false memory is the accounts we give to others of our experiences.

William James

Long-term memory The type or stage of memory capable of relatively permanent storage.

Repression In Freud's psychodynamic theory, the ejection of anxiety-evoking ideas from conscious awareness.

Reconstructive Based on the piecing together of memory fragments with general knowledge and expectations rather than a precise picture of the past.

WORLD OF DIVERSITY

Memory and Ethnic Stereotypes

Our ethnic stereotypes also influence our perceptions and our memories. Consider an experiment in which Elizabeth Loftus showed subjects pictures of an African-American man holding a hat and a white man carrying a razor. Now white Americans often stereotype African Americans as aggressive criminals. Thus, when asked what they had seen, Loftus's subjects often erroneously recalled the razor as being in the hands of the African American. Our prejudices and biases, in other words, also serve as schemas according to which we organize our perceptions. And again, our schemas color our memories.

The point here is that retrieving information from long-term memory is not like scanning an old photograph. We don't have accurate snapshots in our long-term memories. When we recall the past, we don't just locate and read off faithful mental representations. Instead, memory tends to be **reconstructive** and less than wholly reliable. And we reconstruct our recollections according to our schemas, some of which may be ethnic stereotypes.

It is true that our memories are distorted by our prejudices, as well as by other kinds of schemas.

Elizabeth Loftus notes that memories are distorted by our biases and needs—by the ways in which we conceptualize our worlds. Cognitive psychologists speak of much of our knowledge of the world as being represented in terms of **schemas.**

To understand better what is meant by the schema, consider the problems of travelers who met up with the legendary highwayman of ancient Greece, Procrustes. Procrustes had a quirk. He was not only interested in travelers' pocketbooks but also in their height. He had a concept—a schema—of just how tall people should be, and when people did not fit his schema, they were in for it. You see, Procrustes also had a very famous bed, a bed that comes down to us in history as a "Procrustean bed." He made his victims lie down in the bed, and when they were too short for it, he stretched them to make them fit. When they were too long for it, he is said to have practiced surgery on their legs. Many unfortunate passersby failed to survive.

Although the myth of Procrustes may sound absurd, it reflects a quirky truth about each of us. We all carry our cognitive Procrustean beds around with us—our unique ways of perceiving the world—and we try to make things and people fit.

Let me give you an example. Why don't you "retrieve" the fourth sheet of paper you prepared according to the instructions for the challenges to memory. The labels you wrote on the sheet will remind you of the figures. Please take a minute or two to draw them now. Then continue reading.

Now that you made your drawings, turn to Figure 7.5 on page 262. Are your drawings closer in form to those in Group 1 or those in Group 2? I wouldn't be surprised if they were more like those in Group 1. After all, they were labeled like the drawings in Group 1. The labels serve as *schemas* for the drawings—ways of organizing your knowledge of them—and these schemas may have influenced your recollections.

Consider another example of the power of schemas in processing information. Loftus and Palmer (1974) showed subjects a film of a car crash and then asked them to fill out questionnaires that included a question about how fast the

Schema A way of mentally representing the world, such as a belief or an expectation, that can influence perception of persons, objects, and situations.

How Fast Were These Cars Going When They Collided? Our schemas influence our processing of information. When shown pictures such as these, subjects who were asked how fast the cars were going when they *smashed* into one another offer higher estimates than subjects told they *hit* one another.

cars were going at the time. The language of the question varied subtly, however. Some subjects were asked to estimate how fast the cars were going when they "hit" one another. Other subjects were asked to estimate their speed when they "smashed" into one another. Subjects reconstructing the scene on the basis of the cue "hit" estimated a speed of 34 mph. Subjects who watched the same film but reconstructed the scene on the basis of the cue "smashed" estimated a speed of 41 mph! In other words, the use of the word *hit* or *smash* caused subjects to organize their knowledge about the crash in different ways. That is, the words served as diverse schemas that fostered the development of very different ways of processing information about the crash.

Subjects in the same study were questioned again a week later: "Did you see any broken glass?" Since there was no broken glass shown in the film, positive replies were errors. Of subjects who had earlier been encouraged to process information about the accident in terms of one car "hitting" the other, 14 percent in-

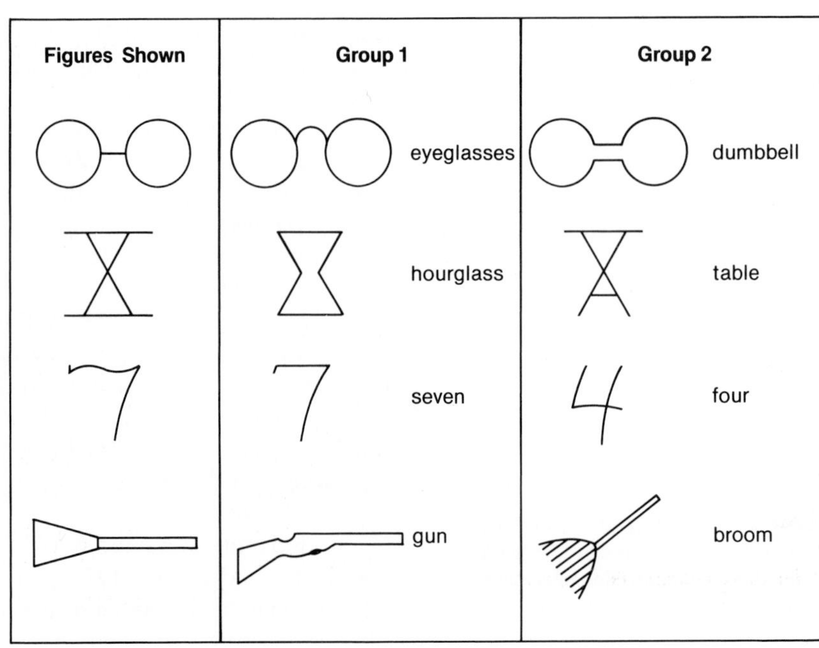

FIGURE 7.5
Memory as Reconstructive. In their classic experiment, Carmichael, Hogan, and Walter (1932) presented subjects the figures in the left-hand box and made remarks as suggested in the other boxes. For example, the experimenter might say, "This drawing looks like eyeglasses [or a dumbbell]." When subjects later reconstructed the drawings, it was clear that their drawings had been influenced by the experimenters' labels. That is, the experimenters had provided schemas according to which the subjects organized their experiences and reconstructed their memories.

correctly answered yes. But 32 percent of the subjects who had processed information about the crash in terms of one car "smashing" the other reported, incorrectly, that they had seen broken glass.

How Much Information Can Be Stored in Long-Term Memory?

There is no evidence for any limit to the amount of information that can be stored in long-term memory. New information may replace older information in short-term memory, but there is no evidence that memories in long-term memory are lost by displacement. Long-term memories may last days, years, or for all practical purposes, a lifetime. From time to time, it may seem as if we have forgotten, or "lost," a long-term memory such as the names of elementary- or high-school classmates. It may be that we cannot find the proper cues to help us retrieve the information, however. If it is lost, it usually becomes lost only in the same way as when we misplace an object but know that it is still somewhere in the house or apartment. It is misplaced, but not eradicated or destroyed.

It is true that there is no practical limit to the amount of information you can store in your memory. At least no limit has been discovered to date.

Transferring Information from Short-Term to Long-Term Memory. How is information transferred from short-term to long-term memory? By and large, the more often chunks of information are rehearsed, the more likely they are to be transferred to long-term memory (Rundus, 1971). We noted that repeating information over and over to prevent it from decaying or being displaced is termed *maintenance rehearsal.* Making no attempt to give information meaning by linking it to past learning, maintenance rehearsal is no guarantee of permanent storage (Craik & Watkins, 1973).[1]

A more effective method is to purposefully relate new material to information that has already been solidly acquired. (Recall that the nine chunks of information in the second challenge were made easier to reconstruct once they were associated with the familiar tic-tac-toe grid in Figure 7.3.) Relating new material to well-known material is known as **elaborative rehearsal** (Postman, 1975). For example, have you seen this word before?

FUNTHOSTAM

Say it aloud. Do you know it? If you had used an acoustic code alone to memorize THUNSTOFAM, the list of letters you first saw on page 248, it might not have been easy to recognize FUNTHOSTAM as an incorrect spelling. Let us assume, however, that by now you have encoded THUNSTOFAM semantically as an acronym for "The United States of America." Then you would have been able to scan the spelling of the words in the phrase "The United States of America" to determine the correctness of FUNTHOSTAM. Of course, you would have found it to be incorrect.

Pure repetition of a meaningless group of syllables, such as *thun-sto-fam,* would be relying on maintenance rehearsal for permanent storage. The process might be tedious (continued rehearsal) and unreliable. But usage of elaborative rehearsal—tying *THUNSTOFAM* to the name of a country—might make storage instantaneous and retrieval foolproof.

Elaborative rehearsal A method for increasing retention of new information by relating it to information that is well-known.

[1]Maintenance rehearsal, however, is responsible for rote learning.

It is *not* true that learning must be meaningful if we are to remember it. However, elaborative rehearsal, which is based on meaning, is more efficient than maintenance rehearsal, which is based on repetition.

You may recall that English teachers encouraged you to use new vocabulary words in sentences to help you remember them. Each new usage is an instance of elaborative rehearsal. Usage helps you build extended semantic codes that will help you retrieve their meanings in the future. When I was in high school, foreign-language teachers told us that learning classical languages "exercises the mind" so that we would understand English better. Not exactly. The mind is not analogous to a muscle that responds to exercise. However, the meanings of many English words are based on foreign tongues. A person who recognizes that *retrieve* stems from roots meaning "again" (*re-*) and "find" (*trouver* in French) is less likely to forget that *retrieval* means "finding again" or "bringing back."

Think, too, of all the algebra and geometry problems we were asked to solve in high school. Each problem is an application of a procedure and, perhaps, of certain formulas and theorems. By repeatedly applying the procedures, formulas, and theorems in different contexts, we rehearse them elaboratively. As a consequence, we are more likely to remember them. Knowledge of the ways in which a formula or an equation is used helps us remember the formula. Also, by building theorem upon theorem in geometry, we relate new theorems to theorems that we already understand. As a result, we process information about them more deeply and remember them better,

Before proceeding to the next section, let me ask you to cover the preceding paragraph. Now, which of the following words is correctly spelled: *retrieval* or *retreival?* The spellings sound alike, so an acoustic code for reconstructing the correct spelling would fail. A semantic code, however, such as the spelling rule *"i* before *e* except after *c,"* would allow you to reconstruct the correct spelling: retr *ie* val.

Flashbulb Memories Where were you and what were you doing when you learned that the space shuttle *Challenger* exploded in 1986? When you learned that the War in the Persian Gulf had started or that Magic Johnson had been infected with the AIDS virus in 1991? Major happenings can illuminate everything about them, so that we clearly recall all the personal surrounding events. Many of us who are middle-aged or older will never forget where we were or what we were doing when we heard that President Kennedy had been shot.

Flashbulb Memories.

> *The attention which we lend to an experience is proportional to its vivid or interesting character; and it is a notorious fact that what interests us most vividly at the time is, other things equal, what we remember best. An impression may be so exciting emotionally as almost to leave a scar upon the cerebral tissues.*
>
> William James

Do you remember the first time you were "in love"? Can you remember how the streets and the trees looked somehow transformed? The vibrancy in your step? How generous you felt? How all of life's problems suddenly seemed to be solved?

Psychologists have learned that we tend to remember more clearly the events that occur under unusual, emotionally arousing circumstances. For example, those of us who are middle-aged and older tend to remember what we were doing when we heard that President John F. Kennedy had been shot in November 1963. Younger people tend to recall the events surrounding them on the day the space shuttle *Challenger* exploded in January 1986, when the war in the Persian Gulf broke out in January 1991, or when Magic Johnson announced that he was infected with the AIDS virus in November of the same year. Similarly, we may remember in detail what we were doing when we learned of a relative's death. These are all examples of "flashbulb memories," because they preserve experiences in such detail (Brown & Kulik, 1977; Thompson & Cowan, 1986).

Why does the memory become etched when the "flashbulb" goes off? One factor is the distinctness of the memory. It is easier to discriminate stimuli that stand out. Such events are salient in themselves, and the feelings that are engendered by them are also rather special. It is thus relatively easy to pick them out from the storehouse of memories. However, major events such as the assassination of a president or the loss of a close relative also tend to have important effects on our lives. As a result, we are likely to dwell on them and form networks of associations; that is, we are likely to rehearse them elaboratively. Our rehearsal may include great expectations about, or deep fears for, the future.

Organization in Long-Term Memory. The storehouse of long-term memory is usually well organized. Items are not just piled on the floor or thrown into closets. We tend to gather information about rats and cats into a certain section of the storehouse, perhaps the animal or mammal section. We put information about oaks, maples, and eucalyptus into the tree section.

Categorization is a basic cognitive function. Categorizing stimuli allows us to make predictions about specific instances and store information efficiently (Corter & Gluck, 1992).

Preschoolers tend to organize their memories by grouping objects that share the same function (Lucariello & Nelson, 1985). At first, "toast" is grouped with "peanut butter sandwich" because both are eaten. Only during the early elementary-school years are toast and peanut butter sandwich categorized as kinds of foods. Similarly, preschoolers and first graders may associate dogs and cats because they are often found together around the house (Bjorklund & de Marchena, 1984). Dogs and rabbits, however, are usually not placed in the same category until the concept "animal" is used to include them, which may not happen for a few more years.

As we develop, we tend to organize information according to a *hierarchical structure,* as shown in Figure 7.6. A hierarchy is an arrangement of items (or chunks of information) into groups or classes according to common or distinct features. As we work our way up the hierarchy shown in Figure 7.6, we find more encompassing, or **superordinate,** classes to which the items below belong. For example, all mammals are animals, but there are many types of animals other than mammals.[2]

When items are correctly organized in long-term memory, you are more likely to recall—or know—accurate information about them. For instance, do you remember whether whales breathe under water? If you did not know that whales

Superordinate Descriptive of a higher (including) class or category in a hierarchy.

[2]A note to biological purists: Figure 7.6 is not intended to represent phyla, classes, orders, and so on accurately. Rather, it shows how an individual's classification scheme might be organized.

A Whale Nurses Her Young. Are whales categorized as mammals or fish in your memory? If the answer is fish, the content of this photograph may be of some surprise.

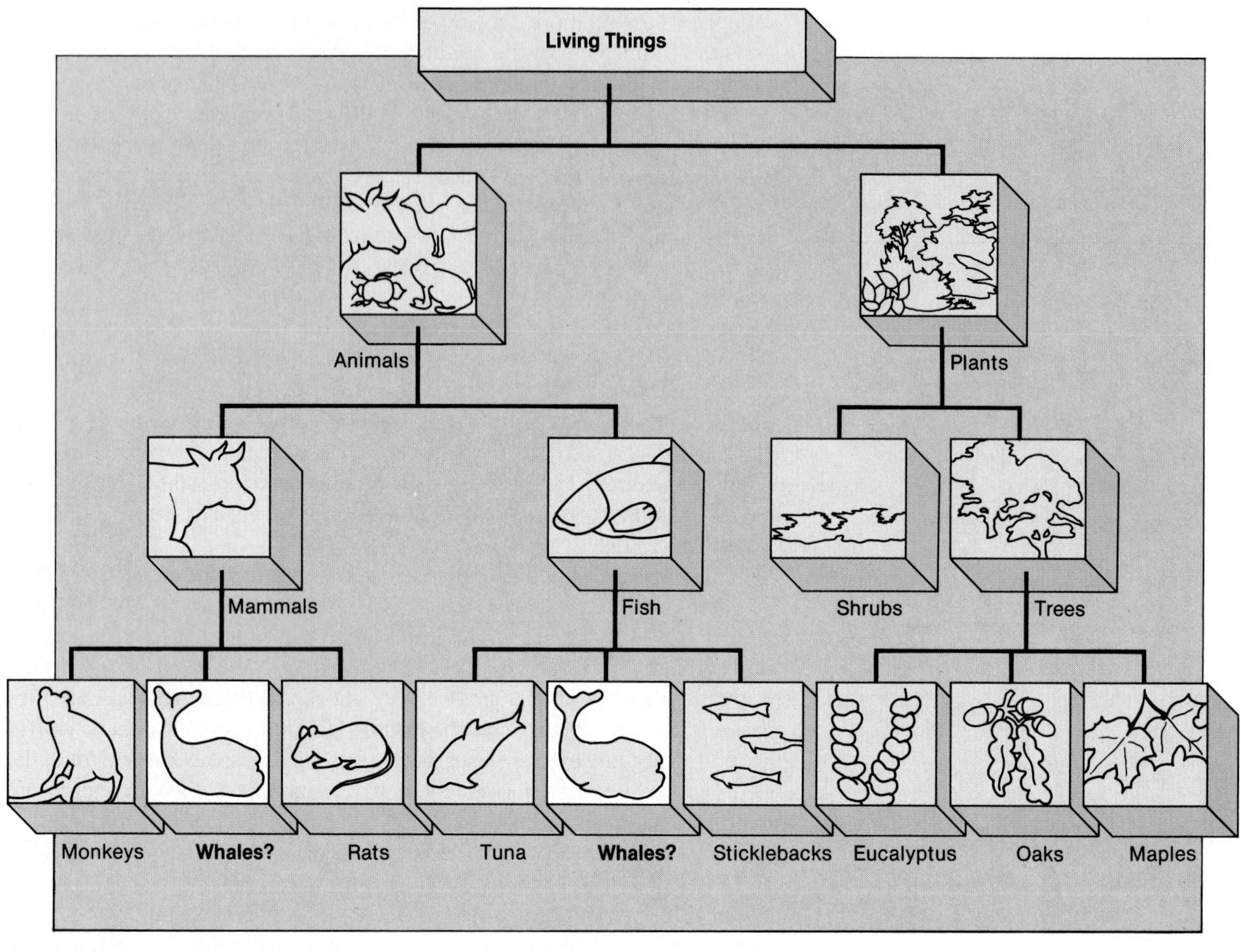

FIGURE 7.6
The Hierarchical Structure of Long-Term Memory.

Where are whales filed in the hierarchical cabinets of your memory? Your classification of whales may influence your answers to these questions: Do whales breathe under water? Are they warm-blooded? Do they nurse their young?

are mammals (or, in Figure 7.6, **subordinate** to mammals), or if you knew nothing about mammals, a correct answer might depend on some remote instance of rote learning. That is, you might be depending on chancy episodic memory rather than on reliable semantic memory. For example, you might recall some details from a Public Broadcasting System documentary on whales. If you *did* know that whales are mammals, however, you would also know—or remember—that whales do not breathe under water. How? You would reconstruct information about whales from knowledge about mammals, the group to which whales are subordinate. Similarly, you would know, or remember, that whales, because they are mammals, are warmblooded, nurse their young, and are a good deal more intelligent than, say, tunas and sticklebacks, which are fish. Had you incorrectly classified whales as fish, you might have searched your memory and constructed the incorrect answer that they do breathe under water.

Let us now consider some issues in the retrieval of information from long-term memory: the tip-of-the-tongue phenomenon, state-dependent memory, and context-dependent memory.

Subordinate Descriptive of a lower (included) class or category in a hierarchy.

The Tip-of-the-Tongue Phenomenon. Have you ever been so close to retrieving information that it seemed to be on "on the tip of your tongue"? Still, you could not quite remember it? This is a frustrating experience, similar to reeling in a fish but having it drop off the line just before it breaks the surface of the water. Psychologists term this experience the **tip-of-the-tongue (TOT) phenomenon,** or the **feeling-of-knowing experience.**

In one TOT experiment, Brown and McNeill (1966) defined some rather unusual words for students, such as *sampan,* which is a small riverboat used in China and Japan. Students were then asked to recall the words they had learned. Some of the students often had the right word "on the tips of their tongues" but reported words similar in meaning such as *junk, barge,* or *houseboat.* Still other students reported words that sounded similar such as *Saipan, Siam, sarong,* and *sanching.* Why?

To begin with, the words were unfamiliar, so elaborative rehearsal did not take place. The students, that is, did not have the opportunity to relate the words to other things that they knew. Brown and McNeill also suggested that our storage systems are indexed according to cues that include both the sounds and the meanings of words—according to both acoustic and semantic codes. By scanning words that are similar in sound and meaning to the word that is on the tip of the tongue, we sometimes find a useful cue and retrieve the word for which we are searching.

The feeling-of-knowing experience also seems to reflect incomplete or imperfect learning. In such cases, our answers may be "in the ballpark" if not on the mark. In some feeling-of-knowing experiments, subjects are often asked trivia questions. When they do not recall an answer, they are then asked to guess how likely it is that they will recognize the right answer if it is among a group of possibilities. People turn out to be very accurate in their estimations about whether or not they will recognize the answer. Similarly, Brown and McNeill found that the students in their TOT experiment proved to be very good at estimating the number of syllables in words they could not recall. The students often correctly guessed the initial sounds of the words and sometimes recognized words that rhymed with them.

Our sense that an answer is on the tips of our tongues thus often reflects incomplete knowledge. We may not know the exact answer, but we know something. As a matter of fact, if we have good writing skills, we may present our incomplete knowledge so forcefully that we earn a good grade on an essay question on the topic! At such times, the problem lies not in retrieval but in the original encoding and storage.

Context-Dependent Memory. The context in which we acquire information can also play a role in retrieval. I remember walking down the halls of The Bronx apartment building where, as a child, I had lived many years earlier. I was suddenly assaulted by images of playing under the staircase, of falling against a radiator, of the shrill voice of a former neighbor calling for her child at dinnertime. Have you ever walked the halls of an old school and been assaulted by memories of faces and names that you would have guessed had been lost forever? Have you ever walked through your old neighborhood and recalled the faces of people or the aromas of cooking that were so real you salivated?

These are examples of **context-dependent memory.** Being in the proper context, that is, can dramatically enhance recall (Estes, 1972; Watkins et al., 1976). One classic experiment in context-dependent memory included a number of subjects who were "all wet." Members of a university swimming club were asked to learn lists of words either while they were submerged or literally high and dry (Godden & Baddeley, 1975). Students who learned the list underwater showed superior recall of the list when immersed. Those who had rehearsed the list ashore, similarly, showed better retrieval on terra firma.

Other studies have found that students do better on tests when they study in the room where the test is to be given (Smith et al., 1978). When police are interviewing witnesses to crimes, they have the witnesses verbally paint the scene as

Tip-of-the-tongue phenomenon The feeling that information is stored in memory although it cannot be readily retrieved. Also called the *feeling-of-knowing experience.*

Feeling-of-knowing experience See *tip-of-the-tongue phenomenon.*

Context-dependent memory Information that is better retrieved in the context in which it was encoded and stored, or learned.

vividly as possible, or they visit the scene of the crime with the witnesses. People who mentally place themselves back in the context in which they encoded and stored information frequently retrieve it more accurately.

State-Dependent Memory. **State-dependent memory** is an extension of context-dependent memory. It sometimes happens that we retrieve information better when we are in a physiological or emotional state that is similar to the one in which we encoded and stored the information. Drugs, for example, alter our physiological response patterns. They can influence the production and uptake of neurotransmitters involved in learning and memory and can modify the general state of alertness of the body. It also happens that material that is learned "under the influence" of a drug may be most readily retrieved when the person is again under the influence of that drug (Overton, 1985).

Our moods may also serve as cues that aid in the retrieval of memories. Feeling the rush of love may trigger images of other times when we had fallen in love. The grip of anger may prompt memories of frustration and rage. Gordon Bower (1981) ran experiments in which happy or sad moods were induced in people by hypnotic suggestion, and the subjects then learned lists of words. People who learned a list while in a happy mood showed better recall when a happy state was induced again. But people who had learned the list when a sad mood had been induced showed superior recall when they were saddened again. Bower suggests that in day-to-day life, a happy mood influences us to focus on positive events. As a result, we will have better recall of these happy events in the future. A sad mood, unfortunately, leads us to focus on and recall the negative. Happiness may feed on happiness, but sadness under extreme circumstances can develop into a vicious cycle.

It is true that we are more likely to recall happy events when we are feeling happy and sad events when we are feeling sad.

THE LEVELS-OF-PROCESSING MODEL OF MEMORY

Not all psychologists view memory in terms of stages (Denton, 1988). Fergus Craik and Robert Lockhart (1972) suggest that we do not have a sensory memory, a short-term memory, and a long-term memory per se. Instead, our ability to remember things can also be viewed in terms of a single stage or dimension—the degree to which we process information. Put it another way: According to Craik and Lockhart, we don't form enduring memories by getting information into long-term memory. Rather, memories tend to endure when information is processed deeply—when it is attended to, encoded carefully, pondered, and rehearsed elaboratively or related to things we already know well.

Consider our familiar list of letters, THUNSTOFAM. In an experiment, we could ask one group of people to remember the list by repeating it aloud a few times, a letter at a time. Another group could be informed that it is an acronym for "The United States of America." If several months later each group were shown several similar lists of words and asked to select the correct list, which group do you think would be more likely to pick out THUNSTOFAM from the pack? It ought to be the group given the acronym, because the information in that group would have been processed more deeply. It would have been semantically encoded and rehearsed elaboratively. The group engaging in more superficial information processing would be sticking to acoustic coding and maintenance

State-dependent memory Information that is better retrieved in the physiological or emotional state in which it was encoded and stored, or learned.

rehearsal. In another example, consider why so many people have difficulty selecting the accurate drawing of the Lincoln penny. Is it perhaps because they have processed information about the appearance of a penny rather superficially? If they knew they were going to be quizzed about the features of a penny, however, wouldn't they process information about its appearance more deeply? That is, wouldn't they study the features and purposefully note whether the profile is facing left or right, what the lettering says, and where the date goes?

Earlier in the chapter, we noted that 2-year-old boys are more likely to remember stereotypical "boys' toys" in photographs, and girls at the same age are more likely to recall "girls' toys." Why do we find this gender difference? Perhaps cultural conditioning has already encouraged boys to process information about transportation toys more deeply than information about dolls. Girls have been pushed in the opposite direction.

Consider an experiment with children. Pictures of objects that fell into four categories (animals, clothes, furniture, and transportation) were placed on a table before first through sixth graders (Neimark et al., 1971). The children were allowed three minutes to arrange the pictures as they wished and to remember as many of them as they could. Children in older groups made a greater effort to categorize the pictures and showed greater recall of them. However, among children in each grade group, those who categorized the pictures also showed greater recall. By categorizing the pictures, they were engaging in greater semantic coding and elaborative rehearsal; that is, they were processing information about them more deeply.

Also weigh a fascinating experiment with three groups of college students, all of whom were asked to study a picture of a living room for one minute (Bransford et al., 1977). Their examination entailed different approaches, however. Two groups were informed that small x's were imbedded in the picture. The first of these groups was asked to find the x's by scanning the picture horizontally and vertically. The second group was informed that the x's could be found in the edges of the objects in the room and was asked to look for them there. The third group was asked, instead, to think about how it would use the objects pictured in the room. As a result of the divergent sets of instructions, the first two groups (the *x* hunters) processed information about the objects in the picture superficially. But the third group rehearsed the objects elaboratively—that is, the group members thought about the objects in terms of their meanings and uses. It should not be surprising that the third group remembered many times more objects than the first two groups.

Note that the levels-of-processing model finds uses for most of the concepts employed by those who think of memory in terms of stages. For example, adherents to this model also speak of the basic memory processes (encoding, storage, and retrieval) and of different kinds of rehearsal. The essential difference is that they view memory as consisting of a single dimension or entity that varies according to depth.

We have been discussing remembering for quite some time. Since variety is supposed to be the spice of life, let's consider forgetting for a while.

FORGETTING

What do DAL, RIK, BOF, and ZEX have in common? They are all **nonsense syllables.** Nonsense syllables are meaningless sets of two consonants with a vowel sandwiched in between. They were first used by German psychologist Hermann Ebbinghaus (1850–1909) and have since been used by many psychologists to study memory and forgetting.

Nonsense syllables Meaningless sets of two consonants, with a vowel sandwiched in between, that are used to study memory.

Because nonsense syllables are intended to be meaningless, remembering them should depend on simple acoustic coding and maintenance rehearsal rather than on elaborative rehearsal, semantic coding, or other ways of making

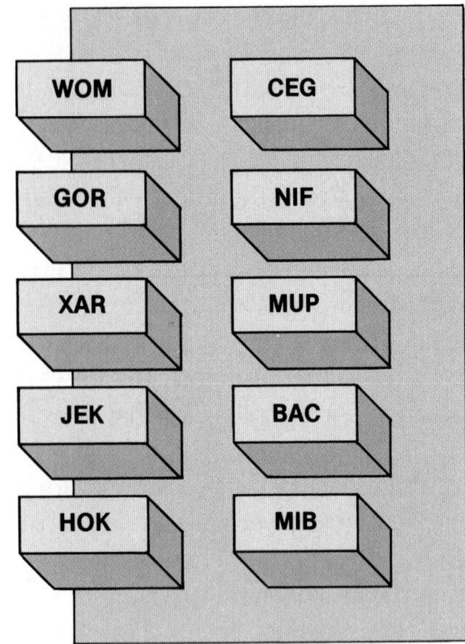

FIGURE 7.7
Paired Associates. Psychologists often use paired associates, like the above, to measure recall. Retrieving CEG in response to the cue WOM is made easier by an image of a WOMan smoking a "CEG-arette."

learning meaningful. Nonsense syllables provide a means of measuring simple memorization ability in studies of the three basic memory tasks of *recognition, recall,* and *relearning.* Studying these memory tasks has led to several conclusions about the nature of forgetting.

Memory Tasks Used in Measuring Forgetting

Recognition. There are many ways of measuring **recognition.** In one study of high-school graduates, Harry Bahrick and his colleagues (1975) interspersed photos of classmates with four times as many photos of strangers. Recent graduates correctly recognized persons who were former schoolmates 90 percent of the time, whereas subjects who had been out of school for 40 years recognized former classmates 75 percent of the time. A chance level of recognition would have been only 20 percent (one photo in five was of an actual classmate), so even older subjects showed rather solid long-term recognition ability.

In many studies of recognition, psychologists ask subjects to read a list of nonsense syllables. The subjects then read a second list of nonsense syllables and indicate whether they recognize any of the syllables as having appeared on the first list. Forgetting is defined as failure to recognize a nonsense syllable that has been read before.

Recognition is the easiest type of memory task. This is why multiple-choice tests are easier than fill-in-the-blank or essay tests. We can recognize or identify photos of former classmates more easily than we can recall their names (Tulving, 1974).

Recall. In his own studies of **recall,** another kind of memory task, Ebbinghaus would read lists of nonsense syllables aloud to the beat of a metronome and then see how many he could produce from memory. After reading through a list once, he usually would be able to recall seven nonsense syllables—the typical limit for short-term memory.

Psychologists also often use lists of pairs of nonsense syllables, called **paired associates,** to measure recall. A list of paired associates is shown in Figure 7.7. Subjects read through the lists pair by pair. Later, they are shown the first member of each pair and are asked to recall the second. Recall is more difficult than recognition. In a recognition task, one simply indicates whether an item has been seen before or which of a number of items is paired with a stimulus (as in a multiple-choice test). In a recall task, the person must retrieve a syllable with another syllable serving as a cue.

Retrieval is made easier if the two syllables can be meaningfully linked—encoded semantically—even if the "meaning" is stretched a bit. Consider the first pair of nonsense syllables in Figure 7.7. The image of a WOMan smoking a CEG-arette may make CEG easier to retrieve when the person is presented with the cue WOM.

As we develop throughout childhood, our ability to recall information increases. This memory improvement is apparently linked to our growing ability to process (categorize) stimulus cues quickly (Howard & Polich, 1985). In one study, Robert Kail and Marilyn Nippold (1984) asked 8-, 12-, and 21-year-olds to name as many animals and pieces of furniture as they could during separate 7-minute intervals. The number of items recalled increased with age for both animals and furniture. For all age groups, items were retrieved according to classes. For example, in the animal category, a series of fish might be named, then a series of birds, and so on.

It is easier to recall vocabulary words from foreign languages if you can construct a meaningful link between the foreign and English words (Atkinson, 1975). The *peso,* pronounced *pay-so,* is a unit of Mexican money. A link can be formed by

Recognition In information processing, the easiest memory task, involving identification of objects or events encountered before.

Recall Retrieval or reconstruction of learned material.

Paired associates Nonsense syllables presented in pairs in experiments that measure recall.

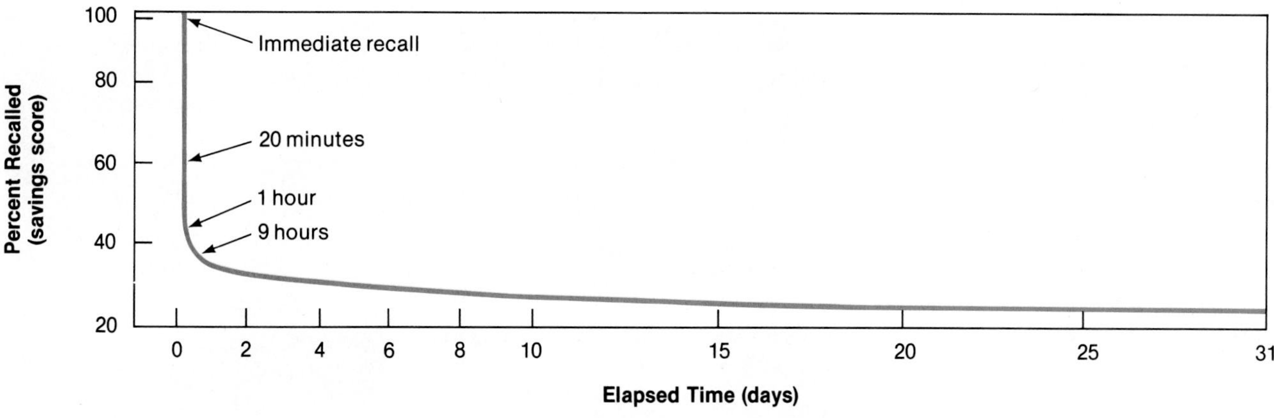

FIGURE 7.8
Ebbinghaus's Classic Curve of Forgetting.

Recollection of lists of words dropped precipitously during the first hour after learning. Losses of learning then became more gradual. Whereas retention dropped by half within the first hour, it took a month (31 days) for retention to be cut in half again.

finding a part of the foreign word, such as the *pe-* (pronounced *pay*) in *peso,* and constructing a phrase such as "You pay with money." When you read or hear the word *peso* in the future, you recognize the *pe-* and retrieve the link or phrase. From the phrase, you then reconstruct the translation, "a unit of money."

Some people who have been hypnotized show **posthypnotic amnesia.** They are unable, for example, to recall previously learned word lists (Kihlstrom, 1980). Spanos and his colleagues (1980, 1982) hypothesize that posthypnotic amnesia occurs when hypnotized subjects interpret the suggestion not to recall information as an "invitation" to refrain from attending to retrieval cues. A hypnotized person might be told that he or she would not be able to recall the colors of the spectrum upon awakening. This suggestion might be interpreted as an invitation *not* to focus on the acronym Roy G. Biv (red, orange, yellow, etc.).

Relearning: Is Learning Easier the Second Time Around? **Relearning** is a third method of measuring retention. Do you remember having to learn all of the state capitals in grade school? What were the capitals of Wyoming and Delaware? Even when we cannot recall or recognize material that had once been learned, we can relearn it more rapidly the second time, such as Cheyenne for Wyoming and Dover for Delaware. Similarly, as we go through our thirties and forties we may forget a good deal of our high-school French or geometry. Yet, we could learn what took months or years much more rapidly the second time around.

To study the efficiency of relearning, Ebbinghaus (1885) devised the **method of savings.** First, he recorded the number of repetitions required to learn a list of nonsense syllables or words. Then, he recorded the number of repetitions required to relearn the list after a certain amount of time had elapsed. Next, he computed the difference between the number of repetitions required to arrive at the **savings.** If a list had to be repeated 20 times before it was learned, and 20 times again after a year had passed, there were no savings. Relearning, that is, was as tedious as the initial learning. However, if the list could be learned with only ten repetitions after a year had elapsed, half the number of repetitions required for learning had been saved. (Ten is half of twenty.)

Figure 7.8 is Ebbinghaus's classic curve of forgetting. As you can see, there was no loss of memory as measured by savings immediately after a list had been learned. However, recollection dropped precipitously during the first hour after learning a list. Losses of learning then became more gradual. Whereas retention

Posthypnotic amnesia Inability to recall material presented while hypnotized, following the suggestion of the hypnotist.

Relearning A measure of retention. Material is usually relearned more quickly than it is learned initially.

Method of savings A measure of retention in which the difference between the number of repetitions originally required to learn a list and the number of repetitions required to relearn the list after a certain amount of time has elapsed is calculated.

Savings The difference between the number of repetitions originally required to learn a list and the number of repetitions required to relearn the list after a certain amount of time has elapsed.

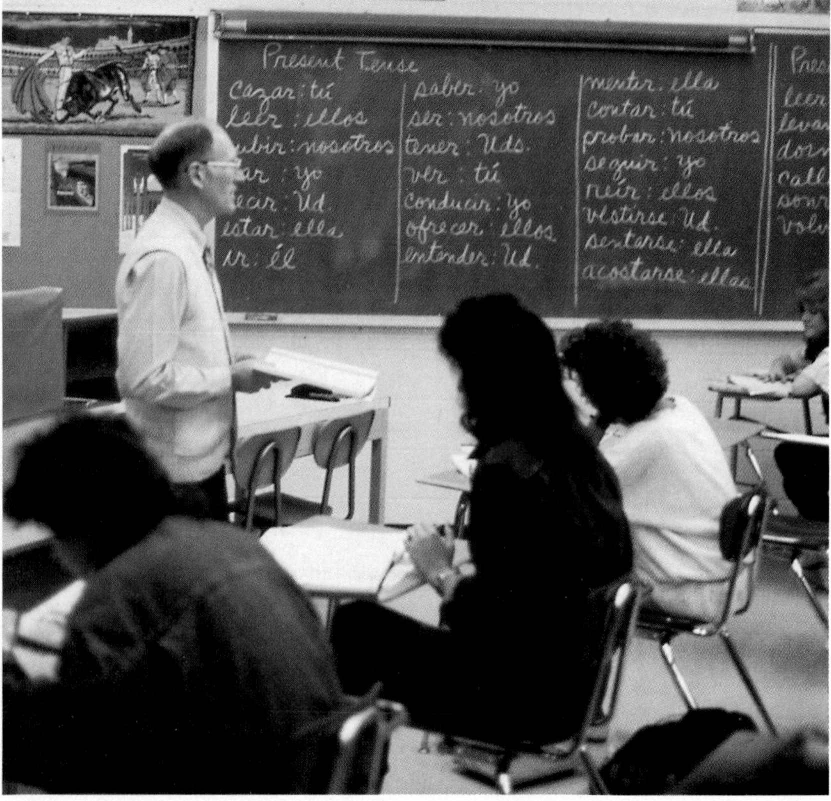

Interference. In retroactive interference, new learning interferes with the retrieval of old learning. In proactive interference, older learning interferes with the capacity to retrieve more recently learned material. High-school French vocabulary may "pop in," for example, when you are trying to retrieve Spanish words learned for a test in college.

dropped by half within the first hour, it took a month (31 days) for retention to be cut in half again. In other words, forgetting occurred most rapidly right after material was learned. We continue to forget material as time elapses but at a relatively slower rate.

Before leaving this section, I have one question for you: What are the capitals of Wyoming and Delaware?

Interference Theory

When we do not attend to, encode, and rehearse sensory input, we may forget it through decay of the trace of the image. Material in short-term memory, like material in sensory memory, can be lost through decay. It can also be lost through displacement, as may happen when we try to remember several new names at a party.

According to **interference theory,** we also forget material in short-term and long-term memory because newly learned material interferes with it. The two basic types of interference are *retroactive interference* (also called *retroactive inhibition)* and *proactive interference* (also called *proactive inhibition.*)

Interference theory The view that we may forget stored material because other learning interferes with it.

Retroactive interference The interference of new learning with the ability to retrieve material learned previously.

Proactive interference The interference by old learning with the ability to retrieve material learned recently.

Psychogenic amnesia Amnesia thought to stem from psychological conflict or trauma.

Retroactive Interference. In **retroactive interference,** new learning interferes with the retrieval of old learning. A medical student may memorize the names of the bones in the leg through rote repetition. Later, he or she may find that learning the names of the bones in the arm makes it more difficult to retrieve the names of the leg bones, especially if the names are similar in sound or in relative location on each limb.

Proactive Interference. In **proactive interference,** older learning interferes with the capacity to retrieve more recently learned material. High-school Spanish may pop in when you are trying to retrieve college French or Italian words. All three are Romance languages, with similar roots and spellings. Old German vocabulary words probably would not interfere with your ability to retrieve more-recently learned French or Italian, because many German roots and sounds differ considerably from those of the Romance languages.

In terms of motor skills, you may learn how to drive a standard shift on a car with three forward speeds and a clutch that must be let up slowly after shifting. Later, you learn to drive a car with five forward speeds and a clutch that must be released rapidly. For a while, you make a number of errors on the five-speed car because of proactive interference. (Old learning interferes with new learning.) If you return to the three-speed car after driving the five-speed car has become natural, you may stall it a few times. This is because of retroactive interference (new learning interfering with the old).

Repression

According to Sigmund Freud, we are motivated to forget painful memories and unacceptable ideas because they produce anxiety, guilt, and shame. (In terms of operant conditioning, anxiety, guilt, and shame serve as negative reinforcers. We learn to do that which is followed by their removal—in this case, to avoid thinking about certain events and ideas.) Psychoanalysts believe that repression is at the heart of disorders such as **psychogenic amnesia.**

Childhood Amnesia

In his clinical investigations of patients' early experiences, Freud discovered that patients could not recall events that happened prior to the age of 3 and that recall was very cloudy through the age of 5. Freud labeled this phenomenon **childhood amnesia.** Many of us have the impression that we have vivid recollections of events during the first two or three years after birth, but studies in which attempts are made to verify these memories by interviewing independent older witnesses show that they are inaccurate (e.g., Sheingold & Tenney, 1982).

Childhood amnesia has nothing to do with the fact that the events are of the distant past. Those of us who are in our thirties, forties, and older have many vivid memories of childhood events that occurred between the ages of 6 and 10, although they are many decades old. But 18-year-olds show steep declines in memory once they attempt to recall events earlier than the age of 6, even though these events are fewer than 18 years away (Wetzler & Sweeney, 1986).

Freud attributed childhood amnesia to the repression of the aggressive and sexual impulses that he believed young children had toward their parents. However, the events lost to childhood amnesia are not weighted in the direction of such "primitive" impulses; they include the most pedestrian, emotionally bland incidents. The effects of childhood amnesia are too broad, too nonselective, for Freud's hypothesis to hold water.

Childhood amnesia probably reflects the interaction of physiological and cognitive factors rather than psychoanalytic factors. For example, a structure of the limbic system (the **hippocampus**) that is involved in the storage of memories does not become mature until we are about 2 years old. Also, myelination of brain pathways is still occurring for the first several years after birth, contributing to the efficiency of memory functioning for the general processing of information. From a cognitive perspective, children usually cannot use language until about the age of 2. Since they are lacking language, they are impaired in their ability to construct hierarchies of concepts. Therefore, their ability to classify objects and events in their environments is also limited. As a result, their ability to *encode* sensory input—that is, to apply auditory and semantic codes—is severely restricted.

Childhood amnesia Inability to recall events that occurred prior to the age of 3.

Hippocampus A structure in the limbic system that plays an important role in the formation of new memories.

It is *not* true that we can remember important events that took place during the first two years of life. (Really, Allyn, believe me.)

Those early childhood memories that we are so certain we can see today are probably reconstructed and mostly inaccurate. Or else they may stem from a time when we were older than we think.

Anterograde and Retrograde Amnesia

In **anterograde amnesia,** there are memory lapses for the period following a traumatic event such as a blow to the head, an electric shock, or an operation. In some cases, it seems that the trauma interferes with all the processes of memory. The ability to pay attention, the encoding of sensory input, and rehearsal are all impaired. A number of investigators have linked certain kinds of brain damage—such as that to the hippocampus—to amnesia (Corkin et al., 1985; Squire et al., 1984).

Consider the often-cited case of a man with the initials H.M. Parts of the brain are sometimes lesioned to help epilepsy patients (see Chapter 3). In H.M.'s case, a section of the hippocampus was removed (Milner, 1966). Right after the operation, the man's mental functioning appeared to be normal. As time went on, however, it became quite clear that he had severe problems in the processing of information. For example, two years after the operation, H.M. believed that he was 27—his age at the time of the operation. When his family relocated to a new address, H.M. could not find his new home or remember the new address. He responded with appropriate grief to the death of his uncle, yet he then began to ask about his uncle and why he did not visit. Each time he was informed of his uncle's passing, he grieved as though he had first heard of it. All in all, it seems that H.M.'s operation prevented him from transferring information from short-term memory to long-term memory.

In **retrograde amnesia,** the source of trauma prevents people from remembering events that took place before the accident. A football player who is knocked unconscious or a victim of an auto accident may be unable to recall events for several minutes prior to the trauma. The football player may not recall taking to the field. The accident victim may not recall entering the car. It also sometimes happens that the victim cannot remember events that occurred for several years prior to the traumatic incident.

In one well-known case of retrograde amnesia, a man received a head injury in a motorcycle accident (Baddeley, 1982). When he regained consciousness, he had lost memory for all events after the age of 11. In fact, he appeared to believe that he was still 11 years old. During the next few months, he gradually recovered more knowledge of his past. He moved toward the present year by year, up until the critical motorcycle ride. He never did recover the events just prior to the accident, however. The accident had apparently prevented the information that was rapidly unfolding before him from being transferred to long-term memory.

In terms of stages of memory, it may be that our perceptions and ideas need to **consolidate,** or rest undisturbed for a while, if they are to be transferred to long-term memory (Gold & King, 1974). Let us now turn our attention to some of the biological events that appear to be involved in the formation of memories.

Anterograde amnesia Failure to remember events that occur after physical trauma because of the effects of the trauma.

Retrograde amnesia Failure to remember events that occur prior to physical trauma because of the effects of the trauma.

Consolidation The fixing of information in long-term memory.

THE BIOLOGY OF MEMORY

Psychologists assume that changes in the brain accompany the encoding, storage, and retrieval of information—that is, memory.

Changes at the Neural Level

Rats who are reared in richly stimulating environments develop more dendrites and synapses in the cerebral cortex than rats reared in relatively impoverished environments (Rosenzweig et al., 1972). It also has been shown that the level of visual stimulation rats receive is associated with the number of synapses they develop in the visual cortex (Turner & Greenough, 1985). In sum, there is reason to believe that the storage of experience requires that the number of avenues of communication among brain cells be increased.

Thus, changes occur in the visual cortex as a result of visual experience. Changes are also likely to occur in the auditory cortex as a result of heard experiences. Information received through the other senses is just as likely to lead to corresponding changes in the cortical regions that represent them. And so the storage of experiences that are perceived by several senses is likely to involve numerous areas of the brain (Squire, 1986). The recollection of these experiences is also likely to require neural activity in the affected areas of the brain.

When sea snails are conditioned, more of the neurotransmitter serotonin is released at certain synapses. As a consequence, transmission at these synapses becomes more efficient as trials (learning) progress (Goelet et al., 1986; Kandel & Schwartz, 1982). The hormone adrenaline generally stimulates bodily arousal and activity. It also strengthens memory when it is released into the bloodstream following instances of learning (Delanoy et al., 1982; Laroche & Bloch, 1982; McGaugh, 1983). The neurotransmitter acetylcholine (ACh) is also vital in memory formation, as is highlighted by the study of **Alzheimer's disease.**

Alzheimer's disease is associated with the degeneration of cells in an area of the hippocampus that normally produces large amounts of ACh (Coyle et al., 1983). The neurons involved collect plaques of amyloid protein—dark areas of cellular "garbage"—and die off in large numbers. The disease may be ultimately caused by a mutation in the gene that directs nerve cells to produce the protein (Hardy et al., 1991). Early viral infections and brain accumulations of metals such as zinc and aluminum may also be involved.

The affected area of the brain and ACh are involved in the formation of new memories. For this reason, one of the cardinal symptoms of Alzheimer's disease is inability to consolidate new learning (such as recalling a change of address) and disorientation. Memories for remote events are usually less affected, however.

Another hormone that can play a role in memory is antidiuretic hormone (ADH), also known as vasopressin. Volunteers have received a synthetic form of ADH through nasal sprays and have shown significant improvement in recall (McGaugh, 1983). Excess vasopressin, unfortunately, can have serious side effects such as constriction of the blood vessels. Research into the effects of similar chemicals which may have fewer side effects is under way.

Changes at the Structural Level

Certain parts of the brain such as the hippocampus also appear to be involved in the formation of new memories—or the transfer of information from short-term memory to long-term memory. The hippocampus does not comprise the "storage bins" for memories themselves, because H.M.'s memories prior to the operation were not destroyed. Rather, the hippocampus is involved in relaying incoming sensory information to parts of the cortex. Therefore, it appears to be vital to the storage of new information even if old information can be retrieved without it (Murray & Mishkin, 1985; Squire, 1986).

In just one of the many surprises that confront and invigorate researchers, it turns out that persons with hippocampal damage can form new procedural memories, even though they cannot form new episodic memories. For example, they can acquire the skill of reading words backwards even though they cannot recall individual practice sessions (Squire, 1986).

Alzheimer's disease A progressive disease that is associated with degeneration of hippocampal cells that produce acetylcholine and symptomized by confusion and inability to form new memories.

The thalamus, a structure near the center of the brain, appears to be involved in the formation of verbal memories. Part of the thalamus of an unfortunate Air Force cadet, known as N. A., was lesioned in a freak fencing accident. Following the episode, N. A. could no longer form verbal memories. However, his ability to form visual memories was unimpaired (Squire, 1986).

It is true that if a certain part of your brain were damaged, you would indeed retain remembrance of things past, but you would not be able to form new memories. One such part in the brain is the hippocampus. Another is a section of the thalamus.

The encoding, storage, and retrieval of information thus involves biological activity on several levels. As we learn, new synapses are developed, and changes occur at existing synapses. Various parts and structures of the brain are also involved in the formation of different kinds of memories.

A Final Challenge to Memory

Now that you've become an expert on memory, let us end the chapter with a sixth and final challenge to your memory:

At the stroke of midnight on December 31, 2000, I challenge you to remember to say the following list of letters to yourself: *T-H-U-N-S-T-O-F-A-M.* As you join in the mass reveling of that special New Year's Eve—the one when we usher in the new millennium—repeat that list of letters silently to yourself. Oh, you may also kiss your partner, toot a horn, throw confetti into the air, and any number of other things. But also think *T-H-U-N-S-T-O-F-A-M.*

Why do I have such confidence in you? Why would I be willing to gamble that you'll be able to set aside other concerns for a few seconds so many years hence? There are two reasons. The first is that you'll surely be able to retrieve the letter list because of your enduring knowledge that it remains an acronym for "The United States of America." The second is that this challenge is so unusual—so distinct from the other happenings in your life—that you may just store it deeply enough to jar your memory a decade into the future.

And if you don't meet this challenge, might you have the nagging thought that there was something you were going to do as the third millennium displaces the second? Might the challenge be—as some psychologists say—right on the tip of your tongue? And on that same New Year's Eve, my daughter Allyn—who will refuse to think *T-H-U-N-S-T-O-F-A-M* no matter what—will probably still be insisting that she can remember being born.

STUDY GUIDE

EXERCISE: Names to Remember

In the column to the left are a number of concepts in the psychology of memory. In the column to the right are the names of individuals who have had an impact on the psychology of memory. Write the name(s) of the proper persons in the blank spaces to the left of the concepts.

	Concepts		Names
_____	1. Curve of forgetting	A.	Atkinson & Shiffrin
_____	2. Sensory memory	B.	Brown & McNeill
_____	3. Nonsense syllables	C.	Craik & Lockhart
_____	4. Repression	D.	Ebbinghaus
_____	5. Method of savings	E.	Freud
_____	6. Levels-of-processing theory	F.	Loftus
_____	7. Eyewitness testimony	G.	McDougall
_____	8. Stages of memory	H.	Penfield
_____	9. Neurosurgery	I.	The Petersons
_____	10. Tip-of-the-Tongue phenomenon	J.	Sperling
_____	11. Childhood amnesia		
_____	12. Inference		
_____	13. Partial-report procedure		
_____	14. Psychogenic amnesia		
_____	15. Whole-report procedure		

Answer Key to Exercise

1. D
2. I, J
3. D
4. E
5. D
6. C
7. F
8. A
9. H
10. B
11. E
12. I
13. J
14. E
15. G

ESL–BRIDGING THE GAP

This part is divided into

1. cultural references,
2. phrases and expressions in which words are used differently from their regular meaning, or are used as metaphors.

Cultural References

bride's apparel (248)—a tradition exists which indicates that a bride should always wear something old, something new, something borrowed and something blue for future happiness to be ensured

blizzard of 1988 (250)—extremely heavy (strong winds and a lot of snow) snowstorm occurred in 1988 in the northeast part of the United States

elementary school (252)—all children in the U.S. must attend school from age 6 to age 16 or grade 1 to grade 8. Elementary school is from grade 1 to 6 or grade 1 to 5.

zip code (257)—the number at the end of an address which indicates the postal region where a person lives

bank cash card (258)—a plastic credit card which allows you to take out money from a bank money machine

GM-CBS-IBM-ATT-CIA-FBI . . . (258)—GM = General Motors; CBS = Columbia Broadcasting System; IBM = International Business Machines; ATT = AT&T = American Telephone and Telegraph; CIA = Central Intelligence Agency (government agency); FBI = Federal Bureau of Investigation (government agency)
cocktail parties (259)—late afternoon or evening parties where many people gather to talk and drink alcohol and meet new people. It usually does not include dinner.
toast/peanut butter sandwich (265)—a peanut butter sandwich is probably the most common lunch food for children in the U.S.
Public Broadcasting System documentary (266)—"PBS" is a TV channel which has no advertising and specializes in educational programs and documentaries (non-fiction informational stories)
"in the ballpark" (267)—the rules that everybody agrees upon; (a reference to baseball—a ball that goes out of the ballpark is out of bounds, or has broken a rule (not abided by a rule)
Wyoming and Delaware (271)—Wyoming is a state in the western part of the U.S. and Delaware is a state in the eastern part
kiss your partner (276)—a custom in the U.S. and probably other places, is to kiss the person you love at midnight on New Year's Eve

Phrases and Expressions (Different Usage)

goofy (248)—unconventional; silly
not to be outdone (248)—did not want to have anyone tell better stories than she could; wanted attention
ears perked up (248)—listened intently and suddenly
not to be faulted (248)—no one could argue with her; she was right
wee hours (248)—early morning hours, but still night
wove a wonderful patchwork quilt (248)—told a wonderful intricate story; refers to bed covers that are made by hand and have intricate patterns
prior (248)—before
much less those (248)—not even those (an emphatic statement)
take a back seat (248)—become not important
No cheating! (248)—I don't want you to cheat (be unfair)
material they hold (249)—content they have
not looking over Shakespeare's shoulder (249)—not standing next to Shakespeare and watching him
Put it another way (250)—Say it another way; in different words
manual shift (250)—standard shift; see Chapter 6, Cultural References, page 376B
stick to words (250)—explain only in words
a bit later (250)—a little later; a short time later
to practice grisly surgery (250)—to dismantle your computer, remove the mechanism
Go on, take a minute (251)—Please, stop reading for a minute and do what I say
come back (251)—return to reading
By so doing (251)—By doing this
lends the grouping meaning (251)—the grouping (the way they are grouped together) then has meaning
over time (252)—for a long period of time
err in that (252)—make a mistake because
gone wrong? (252)—you have done wrong?
been drawn well into (252)—become involved in
No apologies (252)—I am not apologizing
Let us have a try (252)—Let us try; make an attempt
a lifetime (252)—the complete life of a person
going in one ear and out the other (252)—not retaining information
stream of thought, or of consciousness (252)—continuous thought without thinking about what is being thought
streamlike (252)—like a stream or river, a continuous flow
holds impressions briefly (253)—maintains impressions for a short time
flashed on a screen (253)—put quickly on a screen and then removed
subjects could typically remember (254)—all of them could usually remember
read off (254)—read
remarkably long periods (254)—unusually long periods; longer than expected
turn away (254)—stop looking at it
jump across in spurts (255)—be irregular in movement
being seamless (255)—continuous without interruption
sort them out (256)—organize and distinguish
fallen into (256)—become (in a negative manner)
declines with age, all but disappearing (256)—as the child gets older, the ability decreases and almost disappears
frantically searching (256)—looking in a busy and upset manner
tried to get back to it (257)—tried to do it again
first impressions tend to last (257)—what we notice or what we feel about a person the first time we meet the person is the way we tend to continue to think and feel about the person
easier on the digestion (257)—easier to undertake, or do
upper limit (257)—the maximum
truth of the matter (257)—actually
hefty premiums (257)—a lot of extra money
toll-free (258)—no money (toll) is required to make the call
nature of the business (258)—what kind of business it is
behind you (258)—you have already done it and don't have to do it again, or think about it again
cursed myself (258)—became angry with myself
mental dressing down (258)—telling myself how terrible I am and that I should change
self-reproach (259)—reproach myself
falls between the cracks (259)—is not retained; it is lost
wreak havoc (259)—greatly disrupt

shoved on (259)—put on carelessly
dredging up (260)—remembering
with a vengeance (260)—emphatically, definitely; acutely and strongly
juggling your new acquaintance's name (260)—trying to retain your new acquaintance's name
vast storehouse (260)—a very large storage area
evidence is far from compelling (260)—there is no substantial evidence
had a quirk (261)—a particular habit that was different from other people's habits
in for it (261)—had to suffer because of it
color our memories (261)—have an effect on our memories
indeed distorted by (261)—definitely distorted by (emphasis)
less than wholly reliable (261)—not completely reliable
to date (263)—so far
Not exactly (264)—This is not exactly true
The vibrancy in your step (264)—How vibrant you felt; how wonderful you felt, which makes you walk in a happy manner
to pick them out (265)—to choose them
on chancy episodic memory (266)—unreliable episodic memory
"in the ballpark" if not on the mark (267)—in the correct general area, but not completely accurate
assaulted by images (267)—received strong images
high and dry (267)—out of the water (a slang expression to mean without help when you need it)
ashore (267)—on land; the edge of the water
on terra firma (267)—on the land; firm ground (Latin)
"under the influence" (268)—while the drug is in the body and affecting functions
grip of anger (268)—the feel of strong anger
feed on happiness (268)—cause and also be the result of happiness
a vicious cycle (268)—occurs when the result of one act produces a bad result which again produces another bad result and so on (etc.)
pushed in (269)—influenced in
fell into (269)—could be organized into
sandwiched in between (269)—put in between
long-term (270)—over a long period of time
CEG-arette (270)—"cigarette" is spelled "cig . . .", however the pronunciation is similar so the association is appropriate
pop in (272)—enter the mind without trying to retrieve it
stall it (273)—cause the engine to stop operating because the car is in the wrong gear
very cloudy (273)—very unclear; not very clear
not weighted in the direction of (273)—does not support
too broad (273)—too wide; there are too many effects ("too" is negative here)
to hold water (273)—to be true (it cannot be true)
often-cited (273)—the incident is told often
uncle's passing (274)—uncle's death
was rapidly unfolding (274)—was quickly occurring
turn our attention to (274)—attend to
nasal sprays (275)—medicine which is sprayed (sent with force) into the nose
a freak fencing accident (276)—an unusual and strange fencing accident (fencing is a sport involving two people fighting each other with swords)
jar your memory (276)—cause you to remember
might you have the nagging thought that (276)—I hope you have a disturbing thought that

CHAPTER REVIEW

SECTION 1: Three Kinds of Memory

Objective 1: Describe the three kinds of memory.

Memories of the events that happen to a person or take place in the person's presence are referred to as (1) ________________dic memory. Generalized knowledge is referred to as (2) ________________tic memory. We tend to use the phrase "I remember . . ." when we are referring to (3) ________________dic memories, but we are more likely to say "I know . . ." in reference to (4) ________________tic memories. (5) Pro________________ memory involves knowledge of how to do things. Procedural memory is also referred to as (6) ________________ memory.

SECTION 2: Three Processes of Memory

Objective 2: Describe the three processes of memory.

The first stage of (7) ________________ation processing, or changing information so that we can place it in memory, is called (8) ________________ding. When we (9) en________________ information, we convert it into psychological formats that can be mentally represented. To do so, we commonly use (10) ________________ual, (11) ________________ory, and (12) ________________tic codes. A visual code mentally (13) ________________sents information as a picture. An acoustic code represents information as a sequence of (14) ________________nds. Semantic codes represent stimuli in terms of their (15) ________________ing.

The second process of memory is (16) s______________, or the maintaining of information over time. One way of storing information is by (17) ______________nance rehearsal, or by mentally repeating it ("saying it to yourself").

The third memory process is (18) ______________val, or locating stored information and returning it to consciousness. Retrieval of information from memory requires knowledge of the proper (19) ______________es.

Objective 3: Define *memory*.

Memory is defined as the processes by which information is (20) ______________ded, stored, and (21) ______________ved.

SECTION 3: Three Stages of Memory

The three stages of memory proposed by Atkinson and Shiffrin are (22) ______________sory memory, (23) ______________-______________ memory (STM), and (24) ______________-______________ (LTM).

Objective 4: Describe the functioning of sensory memory.

Sensory memory is the stage of memory first encountered by a (25) ______________lus. It holds impressions briefly, but long enough so that series of (26) ______________tions seem connected. The memory (27) t______________ of a stimulus lasts for only a fraction of a second. Memory traces are "held" in sensory (28) ______________ters. Sensory (29) m______________ consists of registers that can briefly hold information that is entered by means of our senses.

Sperling used the (30) ______________-report procedure to show that there is a difference between what people can see and what they can report in the visual sensory register. Sperling concluded that the memory trace of visual stimuli (31) d______________ within a second in the visual sensory register.

The mental representations of visual stimuli are referred to as (32) ______________ns. The sensory register which holds icons is labeled (33) ______________ory. Iconic memories are accurate, (34) ______________aphic memories. The ability to retain exact mental representations of visual stimuli over long amounts of time is referred to by psychologists as (35) ______________tic imagery. The mental representations of (36) ______________ory stimuli are called echoes. The sensory register which holds echoes is referred to as (37) ______________ ______________ory. The memory (38) ______________ces of echoes can last for several seconds, many times longer than the traces of icons.

Objective 5: Describe the functioning of short-term memory.

By focusing attention on a stimulus in the sensory register, you will retain it in (39) ______________-______________ memory for a minute or so after the trace of the stimulus decays. Short-term memory is also referred to as (40) ______________ing memory. Most of us know that a way of retaining information in short-term memory—and possibly storing it permanently—is to (41) re______________ it. Rote repetition is referred to as (42) ______________ance rehearsal.

According to the (43) ______________-position effect, we are most likely to recall the first and last items in the series. First items are likely to be rehearsed (44: more or less?) frequently than other items. Last items are likely to have been rehearsed (45: most or least?) recently. The tendency to recall the initial items in a list is referred to as the (46) ______________cy effect. The tendency to recall the last items in a list is referred to as the (47) ______________cy effect.

Miller noted that the average person can maintain about (48: how many?) ______________ chunks of information in short-term memory at a time. Children learn the alphabet by (49) r______________—that is, by mechanical associative learning that requires time and (50) re______________.

The Petersons showed that information can be displaced from short-term memory by means of (51) ______________ence.

Objective 6: Describe the functioning of long-term memory.

Long-term memory is the third stage of processing of (52) ______________tion.

Sigmund (53) F______________ believed that nearly all of our perceptions and ideas were stored permanently, but memories are not complete. Moreover, our memories are distorted by our (54) ______________as, or ways of conceptualizing our worlds. That is, we (55) re________________ our recollections according to our schemas.

There (56: is or is not?) evidence for a limit to the amount of information that can be stored in long-term memory. New information may displace older information in (57: long or short?) -term memory, but there is no evidence that memories in long-term memory are lost by displacement. However, we need the proper (58) c________________s to help us retrieve information in long-term memory.

Information may be transferred from short-term to long-term memory by several means, including rote repetition—also referred to as (59) ________________ance rehearsal. In (60) ________________tive rehearsal, new information is related to what is already known.

Psychologists have learned that we tend better to remember the events that occur under (61: usual or unusual?) emotionally arousing circumstances. We retain such detailed memories of events like these that they are referred to as (62) "fl________________ memories." One explanation for flashbulb memory is the (63) dis________________ of the memory. But major events, such as the assassination of a president or the loss of a close relative, also have important impacts on our lives. And so we are likely to form networks of associations to other pieces of information—that is, to rehearse them (64) ________________tively.

We tend to organize information in long-term memory according to a (65) ________________cal structure.

The (66) ________________-of-the-(67) ________________ phenomenon—also referred to as the feeling-of-knowing experience—seems to reflect incomplete or imperfect learning. The classic "TOT" experiment by Brown and McNeill also suggests that our storage systems are indexed according to cues that include both the sounds and the meanings of words—that is, according to both (68) ________________tic and (69) ________________tic codes.

(70) C________________-dependent memory refers to information that is better retrieved under the circumstances in which it was encoded and stored, or learned. State-dependent memory is an extension of (71) ________________-dependent memory and refers to the finding that we sometimes retrieve information better when we are in a (72) phys________________ or emotional state that is similar to the one in which we encoded and stored the information.

SECTION 4: The Levels-of-Processing Model of Memory

Objective 7: Describe the levels-of-processing model of memory.

Craik and Lockhart suggest that we (73: do or do not?) "have" a sensory memory, a short-term memory, and a long-term memory per se. They view our ability to remember in terms of a single stage or dimension—the degree to which we (74) pr________________ information. Put it another way: According to the (75) ________________-of-processing model, memories tend to endure when information is processed deeply—when it is attended to, encoded carefully, pondered, and rehearsed elaboratively or related to things we already know well.

SECTION 5: Forgetting

Objective 8: Explain the origin of the use of nonsense syllables in the study of memory and forgetting.

German psychologist Hermann (76) ________________aus originated the use of nonsense syllables in the study of memory and forgetting. Nonsense syllables are (77: meaningful or meaningless?). Thus their retention is based on (78) ac________________ coding and maintenance (79) ________________sal.

Objective 9: Explain the types of memory tasks that are used in measuring forgetting.

The three memory tasks listed in the text are (80) ________________ition, (81) ________________ll, and relearning. (82) Re________________ is the easiest type of memory task. In his own studies of recall, Ebbinghaus would read lists of (83) ________________ ________________bles aloud to the beat of a metronome and then see how many he could produce from memory. Psychologists also often use lists of pairs of nonsense syllables, called (84) ________________ed ________________ates, to measure recall.

People who show posthypnotic (85) ________________a cannot recall previously learned word lists following hypnosis. Spanos and his colleagues hypothesize that posthypnotic amnesia occurs when hypnotized subjects interpret the suggestion not to recall information as an "invitation" to refrain from attending to (86) re________________ cues.

Ebbinghaus devised the method of (87) ________ings to study the efficiency of relearning. First he would record the number of repetitions required to learn a list of (88) n________ syllables or words. Then he would record the number of repetitions required to (89) re________ the list after a certain amount of time had elapsed. He would compute the difference between the numbers of (90) ________tions required to arrive at the savings. According to Ebbinghaus's classic curve of (91) ________ting, there is no loss of memory as measured by savings immediately after a list has been learned. Recollection drops (92: gradually or precipitously?) during the first hour after learning a list. Losses of learning then become more (93: gradual or precipitous?).

Objective 10: Explain the role of interference theory in forgetting.

According to (94) ________ence theory, we forget material in short-term and long-term memory because newly learned material interferes with it. In (95) ________tive interference new learning interferes with the retrieval of old learning. In (96) ________tive interference older learning interferes with the capacity to retrieve more recently learned material.

Objective 11: Explain the possible role of repression in forgetting.

According to Sigmund Freud, we repress many painful memories and unacceptable ideas because they produce (97) an________, guilt, and shame. Psychoanalysts believe that repression is at the heart of disorders such as (98) ________nic amnesia.

Freud discovered that we usually cannot remember events that took place prior to the age of (99) ________. Freud labeled this phenomenon childhood (100) am________, and attributed it to (101) re________. However, the text suggests that childhood amnesia probably reflects the interaction of physiological and (102) ________tive factors. For example, the (103) hip________, which is involved in memory formation, does not mature until about the age of 2. Moreover, infants' lack of language impairs their ability to (104) en________ information.

Objective 12: Explain the roles of anterograde and retrograde amnesia in forgetting.

In (105) ________rade amnesia there are memory lapses for the period following a traumatic event, such as a blow to the head, electric shock, or an operation. In (106) ________rade amnesia the source of trauma prevents people from remembering events that took place beforehand.

Objective 13: Describe some methods for improving memory.

One way to improve memory is by rote (107) ________ance rehearsal, otherwise referred to as (108) dr________ and practice. A method based on the concept of elaborative rehearsal is to (109) r________ new information to that which is already known. It is also helpful to form unusual, exaggerated (110) ________tions. So-called (111) ________ic devices combine chunks of information into formats such as acronyms or phrases.

SECTION 6: The Biology of Memory

Objective 14: Describe some views of the biology of memory.

The storage of experience apparently requires that the number of avenues of communication among brain cells be increased by means of development of (112) ________ites and (113) ________pses. Research with sea snails has shown that more of the (114) ________mitter serotonin is released at certain synapses when they are conditioned. As a result, transmission at these synapses becomes (115: more or less?) efficient as trials (learning) progress.

The hormone (116) ________line generally stimulates bodily arousal and activity. Adrenaline and (117) ________uretic hormone (ADH) strengthen memory when they are released following learning.

The hippocampus is involved in relaying incoming sensory information to parts of the (118) cor________. Therefore, it appears vital to the storage of (119: new or old?) information, even if (120: new or old?) information can be retrieved without it. Persons with hippocampal damage can form new (121) ________ral memories, even though they cannot form new (122) ________ic memories.

The (123) ________mus, a structure near the center of the brain, seems involved in the formation of verbal memories.

Answers To Chapter Review

1. Episodic
2. Semantic
3. Episodic
4. Semantic
5. Procedural
6. Skill
7. Information
8. Encoding
9. Encode
10. Visual
11. Auditory
12. Semantic
13. Represents
14. Sounds
15. Meaning
16. Storage
17. Maintenance
18. Retrieval
19. Cues
20. Encoded
21. Retrieved
22. Sensory
23. Short-term
24. Long-term
25. Stimulus
26. Perceptions
27. Trace
28. Registers
29. Memory
30. Partial
31. Decays
32. Icons
33. Iconic memory
34. Photographic
35. Eidetic
36. Auditory
37. Sensory memory
38. Traces
39. Short-term
40. Working
41. Rehearse (or repeat)
42. Maintenance
43. Serial
44. More
45. Most
46. Primacy
47. Recency
48. Seven
49. Rote
50. Repetition
51. Interference
52. Information
53. Freud
54. Schemas
55. Reconstruct
56. Is not
57. Short
58. Cues
59. Maintenance
60. Elaborative
61. Unusual
62. Flashbulb
63. Distinctness (or discriminability)
64. Elaboratively
65. Hierarchical
66. Tip
67. Tongue
68. Acoustic
69. Semantic
70. Context
71. Context
72. Physiological
73. Do not
74. Process
75. Levels
76. Ebbinghaus
77. Meaningless
78. Acoustic
79. Rehearsal
80. Recognition
81. Recall
82. Recognition
83. Nonsense syllables
84. Paired associates
85. Amnesia
86. Retrieval
87. Savings
88. Nonsense
89. Relearn
90. Repetitions
91. Forgetting
92. Precipitously
93. Gradual
94. Interference
95. Retroactive
96. Proactive
97. Anxiety
98. Psychogenic
99. Three
100. Amnesia
101. Repression
102. Cognitive
103. Hippocampus
104. Encode
105. Anterograde
106. Retrograde
107. Maintenance
108. Drill
109. Relate
110. Associations
111. Mnemonic
112. Dendrites
113. Synapses
114. Neurotransmitter
115. More
116. Adrenaline
117. Antidiuretic
118. Cortex
119. New
120. Old
121. Procedural
122. Episodic
123. Thalamus

POSTTEST

1. Tim remembers that Shakespeare wrote *Hamlet.* This type of memory is referred to as a(n)
   (a) episodic memory.
   (b) metamemory.
   (c) procedural memory.
   (d) semantic memory.

2. George Sperling used the _______ method in his studies of sensory memory.
   (a) partial-report
   (b) savings
   (c) paired-associates
   (d) whole-report

3. Visual impressions last for _______ in the sensory memory.
   (a) up to a second
   (b) about 2–5 seconds
   (c) about half a minute
   (d) several minutes or longer

4. Only about 5 percent of children show
   (a) metamemory.
   (b) iconic memory.
   (c) photographic memory.
   (d) eidetic imagery.

5. Echoic memory is defined as
   (a) an acoustic code.
   (b) the pathways between the thalamus and the auditory cortex.
   (c) the sensory register that holds auditory stimuli.
   (d) a type of procedural memory.

6. Working memory is another term for
   (a) iconic memory.
   (b) semantic memory.
   (c) elaborative rehearsal.
   (d) short-term memory.

7. You are given the task of remembering the written phrase, "Every good boy does fine." You "say" the phrase "mentally," or "to yourself," and then you repeat it to yourself ten times. Which of the following methods have you employed?
(a) visual encoding and elaborative rehearsal
(b) acoustic encoding and maintenance rehearsal
(c) semantic encoding and maintenance rehearsal
(d) episodic memory and procedural memory

8. You are asked to memorize this list of letters: TBJKZMGXTR. You repeat the list several times. Which letters are you most likely to recall?
(a) the sequence JKM
(b) the sequence ZM
(c) the Z and the X
(d) the first T and the R

9. A student studies for a test in the room in which the test will be administered. The student is apparently hoping that performance will be facilitated by
(a) context-dependent memory.
(b) state-dependent memory.
(c) photographic memory.
(d) iconic memory.

10. Information is least likely to be lost through decay in
(a) iconic memory.
(b) echoic memory.
(c) short-term memory.
(d) long-term memory.

11. Which of the following has been compared to a shelf or workbench so that once it is full, some things fall off when new items are shoved on?
(a) episodic memory
(b) sensory memory
(c) short-term memory
(d) long-term memory

12. Which of the following is most likely to remain firmly "embedded" in your memory over the decades?
(a) the name of your second-grade teacher
(b) a sonnet you memorized in high school
(c) how you celebrated your eleventh birthday
(d) how to ride a bicycle

13. John forgets a dental appointment about which he had been extremely anxious. Freud would probably attribute his forgetting to
(a) repression.
(b) anterograde amnesia.
(c) proactive interference.
(d) decay of the memory trace.

14. Loftus and Palmer showed subjects a film of a car crash and then asked them to fill out questionnaires that included a question about how fast the cars were going at the time. Subjects who reported that the car was going fastest had been asked to estimate how fast the cars were going when they ________ one another.
(a) "hit"
(b) "smashed" into
(c) "bumped" into
(d) "touched"

15. Which of the following does the text state is the most effective way of transferring information from STM into LTM?
(a) eidetic imagery
(b) maintenance rehearsal
(c) elaborative rehearsal
(d) becoming emotionally aroused

16. According to the text, the feeling-of-knowing experience seems to reflect
(a) lack of visual retrieval cues.
(b) incomplete or imperfect learning.
(c) skill memory rather than semantic memory.
(d) STM displacement by anxiety-evoking information.

17. A parent knows that you are taking a psychology course and asks how he can teach his young child the alphabet. You note that children usually learn the alphabet by
(a) mechanical associative learning.
(b) use of elaborative rehearsal.
(c) semantic coding.
(d) chunking.

18. Information in short-term memory tends to be forgotten by means of
(a) psychogenic amnesia.
(b) failure to use appropriate retrieval cues.
(c) displacement.
(d) retrograde amnesia.

19. The easiest type of memory task is
(a) recall.
(b) recognition.
(c) relearning.
(d) savings.

20. When sea snails are conditioned, more of the neurotransmitter ________ is released at certain synapses. As a result, transmission at these synapses becomes more efficient as trials (learning) progress.
(a) acetylcholine
(b) dopamine
(c) norepinephrine
(d) serotonin

Answer Key to Posttest

1. D
2. A
3. A
4. D
5. C
6. D
7. B
8. D
9. A
10. D
11. C
12. D
13. A
14. B
15. C
16. B
17. A
18. C
19. B
20. D

- Crying is the child's earliest use of language.
- Children babble only the sounds of their parents's language.
- A 3-year-old says "Daddy goed away" instead of "Daddy went away" because the child does not yet understand rules of grammar.
- The majority of people around the world speak at least two languages.
- It may be boring, but using the "tried and true" formula is the most efficient way to solve a problem.
- The best way to solve a frustrating problem is to keep plugging away at it.
- Intelligent people are also creative.
- Two children can answer exactly the same items on an intelligence test correctly, yet one can be above average and the other below average in intelligence.
- Head Start programs have raised children's IQs.

Language, Thought, and Intelligence

Learning Objectives

When you have finished studying Chapter 8, you should be able to:

Language

1. Define *language*.
2. Explain the three properties of language

Patterns of Language Development

3. Trace the development of language.

Language and Thought

4. Discuss the relationships between language and thought.

Problem Solving

5. Describe the stages of problem solving.
6. Explain the roles of algorithms and heuristic devices in problem solving.
7. Define *incubation effect.*
8. Explain how mental sets and functional fixedness impede problem solving.
9. Discuss the relationships between problem solving, creativity, and intelligence.

Intelligence

10. Define intelligence.

Theories of Intelligence

11. Discuss factor theories of intelligence.
12. Discuss cognitive theories of intelligence.

Measurement of Intelligence

13. Show how the concepts of reliability and validity are applied to the measurement of intelligence.
14. Describe the features of the Stanford-Binet and Wechsler scales.
15. Explain the concept of cultural bias and how psychologists have tried to create culture-fair intelligence tests.

The Determinants of Intelligence

16. Summarize research concerning genetic and environmental influences on intelligence.

When I was in high school, I was taught that people differ from other creatures that run, swim, or fly because only we use tools and language. Then I learned that lower animals also use tools. Otters use rocks to open clam shells. Chimpanzees toss rocks as weapons and use sticks to dig out grubs for food.

In recent years, our exclusive claim to language has also been questioned, because chimps and gorillas have been taught to use **symbols** to communicate. Some communicate by making signs with their hands. Others use plastic symbols or press keys on a computer keyboard. (See Figure 8.1.)

Language is the communication of thoughts and feelings by means of symbols that are arranged according to rules of grammar. Language makes it possible for one person to communicate knowledge to another and for one generation to communicate to another. According to **psycholinguist** Roger Brown, "The important thing about language is that it makes life experiences cumulative, across generations and within one generation, among individuals. Everyone can know much more than he [or she] could possibly learn by direct experience" (1970, p. 212).

Language provides many of the basic units of thought, and thought is central to intelligent behavior. Language is one of our great strengths. Other species may be stronger, run faster, smell more keenly, even live longer, but only we have produced literature, music, mathematics, and science. Language ability has made all this possible.

In this chapter, we explore the interrelated cognitive processes of language, thought, and intelligence. We discuss the structure of language, chronicle language development, and explore theories of language acquisition. This will prepare us for a discussion of how language and thought are intertwined in problem solving. Finally, we turn to intelligence. As you may have gathered from publicity over IQ tests, the definition and measurement of intelligence are controversial issues.

Symbol Something that stands for or represents another object, event, or idea.

Language The communication of information by means of symbols arranged according to rules of grammar.

Psycholinguist A scientist who specializes in the study of the relationships between psychological processes and language.

FIGURE 8.1.
An Ape Uses Signs to Communicate. Apes at Emory University's Yerkes Primate Center have been taught to express simple ideas by pressing keys on a computer-controlled keyboard.

LANGUAGE

Teach me half the gladness
  That thy brain must know,
Such harmonious madness
  From my lips would flow,
The world should listen then, as I am listening now.

Percy Bysshe Shelley, "To a Skylark"

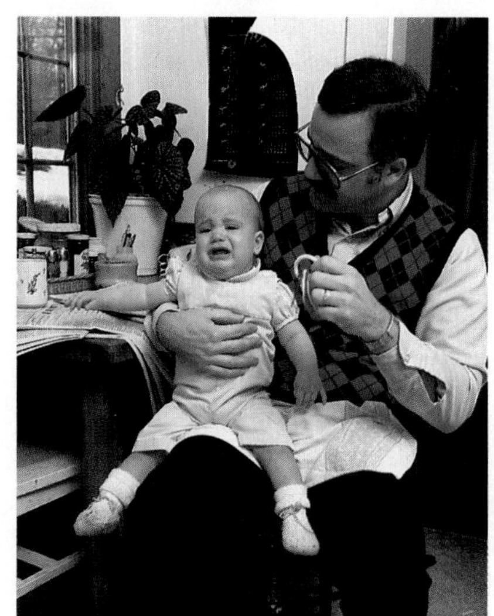

Crying. Crying is a prelinguistic vocalization that most adults find aversive and strive to bring to an end.

Many species, including skylarks, have systems of communication. Birds warn other birds of predators. They communicate that they have taken possession of a certain tree or bush through particular chirps and shrieks. The "dances" of bees inform other bees of the location of a food source or a predator. Vervet monkeys make sounds that signal the distance and species of predators. But these are all inborn communication patterns. Swamp sparrows reared in isolation, for example, produce songs very similar to those produced by birds reared naturally in the wild (Brody, 1991a).

According to Roger Brown (1973), three properties distinguish true language from the communication systems of lower animals: *semanticity, productivity,* and *displacement.* **Semanticity** refers to the fact that words serve as symbols for actions, objects, relational concepts (over, in, more, and so on), and other ideas. The communications systems of the birds and the bees lack semanticity. Specific sounds and—in the case of bees—specific waggles do *not* serve as symbols.

Productivity refers to the capacity to combine words into original sentences. An "original" sentence is *not* one that has never been spoken before. Rather, it is a sentence that is produced by the individual instead of being imitated. To produce original sentences, children must have a basic understanding of **syntax,** or the structure of grammar. Two-year-old children string signs (words) together in novel combinations. Although psychologists have been able to use sign language to communicate with chimpanzees and gorillas, it remains unclear whether the apes possess people's capacities for productivity and use of syntax.

Displacement is the capacity to communicate information about events and objects in another time or place.[1] Language makes possible the efficient transmission of complex knowledge from one person to another and from one generation to another. Displacement permits parents to warn children of their own mistakes. Displacement allows children to tell their parents what they did in school.

Now that we have explored the properties of language, let us chronicle the "child's task"of acquiring language.

Semanticity Meaning. The quality of language in which words are used as symbols for objects, events, or ideas.

Productivity The capacity to combine words into original sentences.

Syntax The rules in a language for placing words in proper order to form meaningful sentences.

Displacement The quality of language that permits one to communicate information about objects and events in another time and place.

Prelinguistic Prior to the development of language.

Cooing Prelinguistic, articulated, vowel-like sounds that appear to reflect feelings of positive excitement.

Language Development

Children appear to develop language in an invariant sequence of steps. Because the sequence is the same from child to child, many psycholinguists believe that people have an innate tendency—called by some a "language acquisition device"—to perceive and develop language in certain ways. We begin with the **prelinguistic** vocalizations of crying, cooing, and babbling.

Newborn children, as parents are well aware, have an unlearned but highly effective form of verbal expression: crying and more crying. Crying is about the only sound that babies make during the first month. During the second month, they also begin **cooing.** Babies use their tongues when they coo. For this reason, coos are more articulated than cries. Coos are often vowel-like and may resemble extended "oohs" and "ahs." Cooing appears to be linked to feelings of pleasure or positive excitement. Babies do not coo when they are hungry, tired, or in pain.

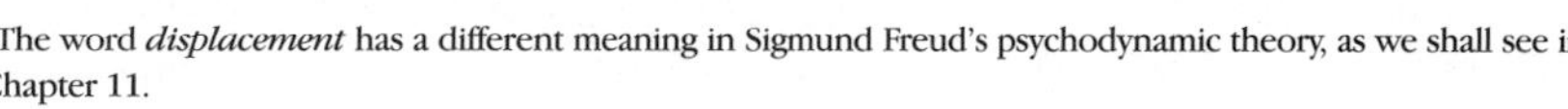

[1]The word *displacement* has a different meaning in Sigmund Freud's psychodynamic theory, as we shall see in Chapter 11.

Black English

Black English is spoken by segments of the African-American community. A study in which an audiotape of standard English was played to poor African-American children who were asked to repeat what they had heard will give you a taste of Black English. The taped sentence was "I asked him if he did it, and he said he didn't do it." One 5-year-old girl recast the sentence in Black English as follows: "I asks him if he did it, and he says he didn't did it, but I knows he did" (Anastasiow & Hanes, 1976, p. 3).

As the example suggests, the major differences between Black English and standard English lie in the use of verbs. Tenses are formed differently in Black English. For example, "She-ah hit us" may be used in the place of the standard English "She will hit us." Consider the verb "to be." In Black English, "He be gone" indicates the standard "He has been gone for a long while," and "He gone" signifies "He is gone right now" in standard English.

Some observers have thought that standard English verbs are used haphazardly in Black English, as if the bare bones of English are being adapted and downgraded. As a result, some school systems have reacted to Black English with contempt. Yet, many linguists, such as William Labov (1972), have argued that Black English is just one dialect of English. The grammatical rules of Black English differ from those of standard English. However, Black English has consistent rules, and they allow for the expression of thoughts that are as complex as those permitted by standard English. In other words, Black English is different but not inferior.

"To Be or Not to Be": Use of the Verb "to be" in Black English

Let us consider a couple of examples of rules in Black English—rules involving use of the verb "to be" and negation. In standard English, "be" is part of the infinitive form of the verb used in the formation of the future tense, as in "I'll be angry tomorrow." Thus, "I be angry" is incorrect. In Black English, "be" is used to denote a continuing state of being. "I am angry" would be perfectly good standard English *and* Black English. But the Black English sentence "I be angry" means in standard English, "I have been angry for a while," and is good Black English.

Black English also *omits* the verb *to be* in some cases (Rebok, 1987), usually when standard English would use a contraction. For example, "She's the one I'm talking about" could be translated as "She the one I talking about." Omitting the verb in Black English is no more careless than contracting it in standard English.

"Not to Be or Not to Be Nothing": Negation in Black English

Black English also differs in the use of the double negative. Consider the sentence, "I don't want no trouble," which is, of course, commendable. Middle-class white children would be corrected for this instance of double negation and encouraged to say either "I don't want any trouble" or "I want no trouble." Double negation is acceptable in Black English, but teachers who use standard English are likely to "jump on" African-American children who speak this way.

Some African-American children switch readily from standard English to Black English. They use standard English in a conference with their teacher or in a job interview, but Black English "in the neighborhood." Other children cannot switch back and forth. For them, the ever-present frowns of standard-English-speaking teachers become an academic burden.

Parents soon learn that different cries and coos can indicate different things: hunger, gas, or pleasure at being held or rocked. Cries can be highly irritating, and psychologists are analyzing infants' cries as aids to diagnosing developmental disorders.

True language has *semanticity.* Sounds (or signs, in the case of sign language) are symbols. Cries and coos do not represent objects or events, so they are prelinguistic.

It is *not* true that crying is the child's earliest use of language. Crying is a prelinguistic event.

By about 8 months, cooing decreases markedly. By about the fifth or sixth month, children have begun to babble. **Babbling** is the first vocalizing that sounds like human speech. Children babble **phonemes** of several languages, including the throaty German *ch,* the clicks of certain African tribes, and rolling *r*'s. In babbling, babies frequently combine consonants and vowels, as in "ba," "ga," and, sometimes, the much valued "dada."

Babbling, like crying and cooing, appears to be inborn. Children from different cultures, where languages sound very different, all seem to babble the same sounds, including many that they could not have heard (Oller, 1981).

It is *not* true that children babble only the sounds of their parents' language. Children babble sounds heard in languages around the world.

Children seem to single out the types of phonemes used in the home within a few months. By the age of 9 or 10 months, these phonemes are repeated regularly. Foreign phonemes begin to drop out, so there is an overall reduction in the variety of phonemes that infants produce.

Babbling, like crying and cooing, is a prelinguistic event, but infants usually understand much of what others are saying well before they utter their first words. Comprehension precedes production, and infants demonstrate comprehension with their actions and gestures.

Development of Vocabulary. Ah, that long-awaited first word! What a thrill! What a milestone! Sad to say, many parents miss it. They are not quite sure when their infants utter their first word, often because the first word is not pronounced clearly or because pronunciation varies from usage to usage. *Ball* may be pronounced "ba," "bee," or even "pah" on separate occasions (Ferguson & Farwell, 1975).

Vocabulary acquisition is slow at first. It may take children three to four months to achieve a ten-word vocabulary after their first word is spoken (Nelson, 1973). By about 18 months, children are producing nearly two dozen words. Many words such as *no, cookie, mama, hi,* and *eat* are quite familiar. Others, like *allgone* and *bye-bye,* may not be found in the dictionary, but they function as words.

Children try to talk about more objects than they have words for, and so they often extend the meaning of one word to refer to things and actions for which they do not have words. This phenomenon is termed **overextension.** At some point many children refer to horses as *doggies.* My daughter Allyn, at age 6, counted by tens as follows: sixty, seventy, eighty, ninety, *tenty.*

Development of Syntax. Although children first use one-word utterances, these utterances appear to express the meanings of sentences. Roger Brown (1973) calls brief expressions that have the meanings of sentences telegraphic speech. When we as adults write telegrams, we use principles of syntax to cut out all the "unnecessary" words. "Home Tuesday" might stand for "I expect to be home on Tuesday." Similarly, only the essential words are used in children's telegraphic speech—in particular, nouns, verbs, and some modifiers.

Single words that are used to express complex meanings are called **holophrases.** For example, *mama* may be used by the child to signify meanings as varied as "There goes Mama," "Come here, Mama," and "You are my Mama." Similarly, *poo-cat* can signify "There is a pussycat," "That stuffed animal looks just like my pussycat," or "I want you to give me my pussycat right now!" Most children readily teach their parents what they intend by augmenting their

Babbling The child's first vocalizations that have the sounds of speech.

Phoneme A basic sound in a language.

Overextension Overgeneralizing the use of words to objects and situations to which they do not apply—a normal characteristic of the speech of young children.

Holophrase A single word used to express complex meanings.

holophrases with gestures, intonations, and reinforcers. That is, they act delighted when parents do as requested and howl when they do not.

Toward the end of the second year, children begin to speak in telegraphic two-word sentences. In the sentence "That ball," the words *is* and *a* are implied. Two-word utterances seem to appear at about the same time in the development of all languages (Slobin, 1973). Also, the sequence of emergence of the types of two-word utterances (for example, first, agent–action; then action–object, location, and possession) is the same in languages as diverse as English, Luo (an African tongue), German, Russian, and Turkish (Slobin, 1983).

Two-word utterances, although brief, show understanding of syntax. The child will say, "Sit chair" to tell a parent to sit in a chair, not "Chair sit." The child will say, "My shoe," not "Shoe my," to show possession. "Mommy go" means Mommy is leaving, whereas "Go Mommy" expresses the wish for Mommy to go away. For this reason, "Go Mommy" is not heard often.

Toward More Complex Language. Between the ages of 2 and 3, children's sentence structure usually expands to include the missing words in telegraphic speech. During the third year children usually add articles (*a, an, the*), conjunctions (*and, but, or*), possessive and demonstrative adjectives (*your, her, that*), pronouns (*she, him, one*), and prepositions (*in, on, over, around, under, through*). Their grasp of syntax is shown in language oddities such as *your one* instead of *yours* and *his one* instead of, simply, *his.*

One of the more intriguing language developments is **overregularization.** To understand children's use of overregularization, consider the formation of the past tense and of plurals in English. We add *d* or *ed* phonemes to regular verbs and *s* or *z* phonemes to regular nouns. Thus, *walk* becomes *walked* and *look* becomes *looked. Pussycat* becomes *pussycats* and *doggy* becomes *doggies.* There are also irregular verbs and nouns. For example, *see* becomes *saw, sit* becomes *sat,* and *go* becomes *went. Sheep* remains *sheep* (plural) and *child* becomes *children.*

At first, children learn a small number of these irregular verbs by imitating their parents. Two-year-olds tend to form them correctly—temporarily (Kuczaj, 1982)! Then they become aware of the syntactic rules for forming the past tense and plurals in English. As a result, they tend to make charming errors (Bowerman, 1982). Some 3- to 5-year-olds, for example, are more likely to say "I seed it" than "I saw it" and more likely to say "Mommy sitted down" than "Mommy sat down." They are likely to talk about the "gooses" and "sheeps" they "seed" on the farm and about all the "childs" they ran into at the playground. This tendency to regularize the irregular is what is meant by overregularization.

A 3-year-old actually says "Daddy goed away" instead of "Daddy went away" because the child *does* understand rules of grammar. Because of knowledge of grammar, the child is overregularizing the irregular verb "to go."

Some parents recognize that their children were forming the past tense of irregular verbs correctly and that they then began to make errors. The thing to remember is that overregularization *does represent an advance in the development of syntax.* Overregularization reflects knowledge of grammar—not faulty language development. In another year or two, *mouses* will be boringly transformed into *mice,* and Mommy will no longer have *sitted* down. Parents might as well enjoy overregularization while they can.

By the fourth year, children are asking questions, taking turns talking, and engaging in lengthy conversations. By the age of 6, their vocabularies have expanded

Overregularization The application of regular grammatical rules for forming inflections (e.g., past tense and plurals) to irregular verbs and nouns.

to 10,000 words, give or take a few thousand. By 7 to 9, most children realize that words can have more than one meaning, and they are entertained by riddles and jokes that require semantic sophistication ("What's black and white, but read all over?"). Between the elementary-school and high-school years, vocabulary continues to grow rapidly. There are also subtle advances in articulation and the capacity to use complex syntax.

Individual Differences in Language Development. Although the sequences of development are invariant, there are individual, social-class, and gender differences in the rate of language development. Girls are slightly superior to boys in their language development. Children from families of lower socioeconomic status tend to have poorer vocabularies than children from middle- or upper-class families. Knowledge of the meanings of words is the single strongest predictor of overall scores on intelligence tests.

LANGUAGE AND THOUGHT

According to the **linguistic-relativity hypothesis** proposed by Benjamin Whorf (1956), language structures the ways in which we perceive the world. Consider our perceptions of microcomputers. People who understand terms such as *640 K, megabyte,* and *RAM* can think about microcomputers with greater sophistication than those who do not.

According to the linguistic-relativity hypothesis, most English speakers' ability to think about snow may be rather limited when compared to that of the Inuit people. We have only a few words for snow, whereas the Inuit people have many words, related, for example, to whether the snow is hard-packed, falling, melting, or covered by ice. When we think about snow, we have fewer words to choose from and have to search for descriptive adjectives. The Inuit people, however, can readily find a single word that describes a complex weather condition. It might then be easier for them to think about this variety of snow in relation to other aspects of their world. Similarly, the Hanunoo people of the Philippines use 92 words for rice, depending on whether the rice is husked or unhusked and on how it is prepared. And we have one word for camel, whereas Arabs have more than 250.

In English, we have hundreds of words to describe different colors, but those who speak Shona use only three words for colors. People who speak Bassa use only two words for colors (Gleason, 1961), corresponding to light and dark. The Hopi Indians had two words for flying objects, one for birds and an all-inclusive word for anything else that may be found traveling through the air.

Does this mean that the Hopi were limited in their ability to think about bumblebees and airplanes? Are English speakers limited in their ability to think about skiing conditions? Are those who speak Shona and Bassa "color-blind" for practical purposes?

Probably not. People who use only a few words to distinguish colors seem to perceive the same color variations as people with dozens of words (Bornstein & Marks, 1982). For example, the Dani of New Guinea, like the Bassa, have just two words for colors: *mola,* which refers to warm colors, and *mili,* which refers to cool colors. Still, tasks in matching and memory show that the Dani can discriminate the many colors of the spectrum when they are motivated to do so. English-speaking skiers who are concerned about different skiing conditions have developed a comprehensive special vocabulary about snow, including the terms *powder, slush, ice, hard-packed,* and *corn snow,* that might enable them to communicate and think about snow with the facility of the Inuit people. When a need to expand a language's vocabulary arises, the speakers of that language apparently have little difficulty in meeting the need.

Linguistic relativity hypothesis
The view that language structures the way in which we view the world.

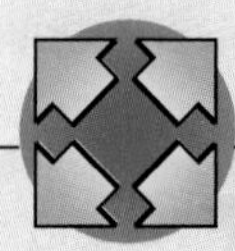

WORLD OF DIVERSITY
Bilingualism

It may seem strange to Americans, but most people throughout the world speak two or more languages (Grosjean, 1982). Most countries have minority populations whose languages differ from the national tongue. Nearly all Europeans are taught English and the languages of neighboring nations. Consider the Netherlands. Dutch is the native tongue, but all children are also taught French, German, and English and expected to become fluent in each of them.

The majority of people around the world do speak at least two languages.

For millions of U.S. children, English is a second language. Spanish, Russian, Chinese, or Arabic is spoken in the home and, perhaps, the neighborhood. Some of these children receive no training in English until they enter school.

A few decades ago, it was widely believed that children reared in bilingual homes were retarded in their cognitive and language development (Rebok, 1987). However, recent analysis of older studies in bilingualism shows that the families observed were also often low in socioeconomic status and level of education. Lack of education, not bilingualism, is the problem. Today, most linguists consider it advantageous for children to be bilingual (Diaz, 1985). For one thing, knowledge of more than one language expands children's awareness of different cultures and broadens their perspectives.

In terms of cognitive development, bilingual children learn early to distinguish between words and their meanings. Linguist Dan Slobin's English-speaking daughter was taught German in the homes of relatives beginning at the age of 2. By age 3, she was asking what things were called in the other language (Slobin, 1978). Despite fears that learning two languages at a young age can confuse children, the evidence suggests that bilingual children perform at least as well as monolingual children on intelligence tests and related tests of cognitive functioning (Segalowitz, 1981).

Bilingual Education

Despite the positive aspects of bilingualism, many U.S. children who speak a different language in the home have problems learning English in school. Early in the century, the educational approach to teaching English to non-English-speaking children was simple: sink or swim. Children weretaught in English from the outset. It was incum-

Critics of the linguistic-relativity hypothesis argue that a language's vocabulary only suggests the range of concepts that the speakers of the language have traditionally found important. Yet, people can make distinctions for which there are no words. Hopi Indians flying from New York to San Francisco nowadays would not think that they are flying inside a bird or a bumblebee, even if they have no word for airplane.

Although language may not be necessary for all thought, it does help. In the section on problem-solving, however, we shall see that our labels for things can sometimes impair our problem-solving abilities.

PROBLEM-SOLVING

One of the pleasures I derived from my own introductory psychology course lay in showing friends the textbook and getting them involved in the problems in the section on problem-solving. First, of course, I struggled with the problems myself. It's that time, now. And it's your turn. Get some scrap paper, take a breath, and have a go at the following problems. The answers will be discussed in the following pages, but don't peek. *Try* the problems first.

1. Provide the next two letters in the series for each of the following:
   - **a.** ABABABAB??
   - **b.** ABDEBCEF??
   - **c.** OTTFFSSE??

bent upon them to catch on as best they could. Most children swam. Some sank.

A more formal term for the sink-or-swim method is total immersion. Total immersion has a checkered history. There are, of course, many successes with total immersion, but there are also more failures than the U.S. educational system is willing to tolerate. For this reason, bilingual education has been adopted in many school systems.

Bilingual-education legislation requires that non-English-speaking children be given the chance to study in their own language in order to smooth the transition into U.S. life. The official purpose of federal bilingual programs is to help foreign-speaking children use their native tongue to learn English rapidly, then switch to a regular school program. Yet, the degree of emphasis on English differs markedly from program to program.

So-called transitional programs shoot their students into regular English-speaking classrooms as quickly as possible. Under a second technique, called the maintenance method, rapid mastery of English is still the goal. But students continue studying their own culture and language. A third approach, being tried in areas with large Hispanic enclaves, such as New York, Florida, and Southern California, is bilingual and bicultural: the programs encourage native-born U.S. citizens to achieve fluency in a foreign language even as their counterparts are learning English. In Miami's Coral Way Elementary School, which inaugurated the bicultural method to cope with the huge influx of refugees from Cuba, all students study for half a day in Spanish and for the other half in English.

Rotberg (1982) suggests that bilingual education has been most successful when four criteria have been met: (1) The child begins with mastery of the language spoken in the home, providing a secure linguistic base. (2) The bilingual program focuses specifically on teaching English and does not just start teaching other subjects in English, even at a low level. (3) The child's parents understand and support the goals and methods of the program. (4) Teachers, parents, and other members of the community have mutual respect for one another and for each others' languages.

When in.struction in a second language is carried out carefully, there is little evidence to suggest that it interferes with the first language (McLaughlin, 1984; Rebok, 1987). Under such circumstances, children show little confusion between the languages.

All in all, it seems that Rotberg's principles accomplish more than teaching children English. They help ensure that bilingual children will be proud of the ethnic heritage they bring into the mainstream culture. Children may attain the language skills necessary to forge ahead in today's workplace and participate in political and social processes, while they retain a sense of ethnic identity and self-esteem.

2. Draw straight lines through all the points in part A of Figure 8.2, using only *four* lines. Do not lift your pencil from the paper or retrace your steps. (Answers are given in Figure 8.4.)
3. Move three matches in part B of Figure 8.2 to make four squares of the same size. You must use *all* the matches. (Answer shown on p. 300.)
4. You have three jars, A, B, and C, which hold the amounts of water, in ounces, shown in Table 8.1. For each of the seven problems in Table 8.1, use the jars in any way you wish to arrive at the indicated amount of water. Fill or empty any jar as often as you wish. How do you obtain the desired amount of water in each problem? (The solutions are discussed on p. 298.)

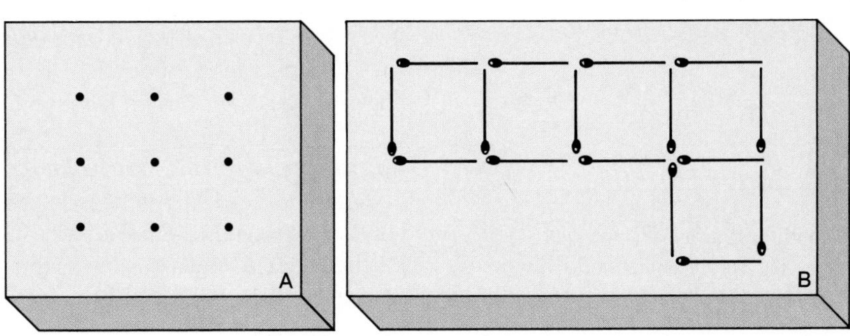

FIGURE 8.2
Two Problems. Draw straight lines through all the points in Part A, using only four lines. Do not lift your pencil or retrace your steps. Move three matches in Part B to make four squares equal in size. Use all the matches.

TABLE 8.1: Water Jar Problems

Problem Number	Three Jars Are Present with the Listed Capacity (in Ounces) Jar A	Jar B	Jar C	Obtain This Amount of Water
1	21	127	3	100
2	14	163	25	99
3	18	43	10	5
4	9	42	6	21
5	20	59	4	31
6	23	49	3	20
7	10	36	7	3

For each problem, how can you use some combination of the three jars given, and a tap, to obtain precisely the amount of water shown?

Adapted from ***Rigidity of Behavior*** (p.109) by Abraham S. Luchins and Edith H. Luchins, 1959, Eugene: University of Oregon Press.

Stages in Problem-Solving

If you are like most other problem-solvers, you used three steps to solve parts a and b of problem 1. First, you sought to define the elements of the problems by discovering the structure of the *cycles* in each series. Series *1a* has repeated cycles of two letters: *AB, AB,* and so on. Series *1b* may be seen as having four cycles of two consecutive letters: *AB, DE, BC,* and so on.

Then you tried to produce *rules* that governed the advance of each series. In series *1a,* the rule is simply to repeat the cycle. Series *1b* is more complicated, and different sets of rules can be used to describe it. One correct set of rules is that odd-numbered cycles (*1* and *3,* or *AB* and *BC*) simply repeat the last letter of the previous cycle (in this case *B*) and then advance by one letter according to the alphabet. The same rule applies to even-numbered cycles (*2* and *4,* or *DE* and *EF*).

Then you used your rules to produce the next letters in the series: *AB* in series *1a,* and *CD* in series *1b.* Finally, you evaluated the effectiveness of the rules by checking your answers against the solutions in the preceding paragraphs.

Question: What alternate sets of rules could you have found to describe these two series? Would you have generated the same answers from these rules?

Preparation, Production, Trial, and Evaluation. People tend to use four stages in solving problems, whether the problem concerns dieting, selecting a house, or moving matchsticks about to create a design. These stages include (1) preparation, (2) production, (3) trial, and (4) evaluation.

We prepare ourselves to solve a problem by familiarizing ourselves with its elements and clearly defining our goals. We prepare to solve high-school algebra and geometry problems by outlining all the givens and trying to picture the answers as best we can. Part of preparation is proper classification of the problem. "Does this problem involve a right triangle? Does it seem to be similar to problems I've solved by using the quadratic equation?"

In parts a and b of problem 1, the search for cycles and for the rules governing the cycles served as preparation for producing possible solutions.

Algorithms versus Heuristics. In solving problems, we sometimes turn to *algorithms* or *heuristic devices.* An **algorithm** is a specific procedure for solving a certain type of problem that will lead to the solution if it is used properly. Mathematical formulas—such as the Pythagorean Theorem—are examples of algorithms. They will yield correct answers to problems *as long as the right*

Algorithm A systematic procedure for solving a problem that works invariably when applied correctly.

formula is used. Finding the right formula to solve a problem may require scanning one's memory for all formulas that contain variables that represent one or more of the elements in the problem. The Pythagorean Theorem, for example, concerns triangles with right angles. Therefore, it is appropriate to consider using this formula for problems concerning right angles but not for others.

Consider anagram problems, in which we try to reorganize groups of letters into words. In seeing how many words we can make from *DWARG,* we can use the algorithm of simply listing every possible letter combination, using from one to all five letters, and then checking to see whether each result is, in fact, a word. The method might be plodding, but it would work.

Heuristics are rules of thumb that help us simplify and solve problems. Heuristics, in contrast to algorithms, do not guarantee a correct solution to a problem, but when they work, they tend to allow for more rapid solutions. A heuristic device for solving the anagram problem would be to look for letter combinations that are found in words and then to check the remaining letters for words that include these combinations. In *DWARG,* for example, we can find the familiar combinations *dr* and *gr.* We may then quickly find *draw, drag,* and *grad.* The drawback to this method, however, is that we might miss some words.

It is *not* true that using the "tried and true" formula (that is, an algorithm) is invariably the most efficient way to solve a problem. Sometimes a heuristic device leads to a more rapid solution.

One type of heuristic device is the **means–end analysis,** in which we evaluate the difference between our current situation and our goals at various steps along the way and then do what we can to reduce this discrepancy at each step. Let's say that you are lost, but you know that your goal is west of your current location and on the "other side of the tracks." A heuristic device would be to drive toward the setting sun (west) and, at the same time, to remain alert for railroad tracks. If your road comes to an end and you must turn left or right, you can scan the distance in either direction for tracks. If you don't see any, turn right or left, but then, at the next major intersection, turn toward the setting sun again. Eventually you may get there. If not, you could use that most boring of algorithms: ask people for directions until you find someone who knows the route.

Incubation. Let us return to the problems at the beginning of the section. How did you do with problem 1, part c, and problems 2 and 3? If you produced and then tried out solutions that did not meet the goals, you may have become frustrated and thought, "The heck with it! I'll come back to it later." This attitude suggests another avenue to problem-solving: **incubation.** An incubator warms chicken eggs for a while so that they will hatch. Incubation in problem-solving refers to standing back from the problem for a while as some mysterious process in us seems to continue to work on it. Later, the answer may occur to us as "in a flash." Standing back from the problem might provide us with some distance from unprofitable but persistent mental sets.

It is *not* necessarily true that the best way to solve a frustrating problem is to keep plugging away at it. It may be better to distance oneself from the problem for a while and allow it to incubate.

Heuristics Rules of thumb that help us simplify and solve problems.

Means–end analysis A heuristic device in which we try to solve a problem by evaluating the difference between the current situation and the goal.

Incubation In problem-solving, a hypothetical process that sometimes occurs when we stand back from a frustrating problem for a while and the solution "suddenly" appears.

Mental Sets

Let us return to problem 1, part c. To try to solve this problem, did you seek a pattern of letters that involved cycles and the alphabet? If so, it may be because parts a and b were solved by this approach.

The tendency to respond to a new problem with the same approach that helped solve earlier, similar-looking problems is termed a **mental set.** Mental sets usually make our work easier, but they can mislead us when the similarity between problems is illusory, as in part c of problem 1. Here is a clue: Part c is no alphabet series. Each of the letters in the series *stands* for something. If you can discover what they stand for (that is, discover the rule), you will be able to generate the ninth and tenth letters. (The answer is in Figure 8.4 on p. 300.)

Let us now have another look at the possible role of incubation in helping us get around hampering mental sets. Consider the seventh water-jar problem. What if we had tried all sorts of solutions involving the three water jars, and none had worked? What if we were then to stand back from this water-jar problem for a day or two? Is it not possible that with a little distance we might suddenly recall a 10, a 7, and a 3—three elements of the problem—and realize that we can arrive at the correct answer by using only two water jars? Our solution might seem too easy, and we might check Table 8.1 cautiously to make certain that the numbers are there as remembered. Perhaps our incubation period would have done nothing more than unbind us from the mental set that the case 7 *ought* to be solved by the formula *B–A–2C.*

While we are discussing mental sets and the water-jar problems, have another look at water-jar case number 6. The formula *B–A–2C* will solve this problem. Is that how you solved it? Note also that the problem could have been solved more efficiently by using the formula *A–C.* If the second formula did not occur to you, it may be because of the mental set you acquired from solving the first five problems.

Functional Fixedness

Functional fixedness may also impair your problem-solving efforts. For example, first ask yourself what a pair of pliers is. Is it a tool for grasping, a paperweight, or a weapon? A pair of pliers could function as any of these, but your tendency to think of it as a grasping tool is fostered by your experience with it. You have probably only used a pair of pliers for grasping things. Functional fixedness is the tendency to think of an object in terms of its name or its familiar usage. Functional fixedness can be similar to a mental set in that it can make it difficult for you to use familiar objects to solve problems in novel ways.

In a classic experiment in functional fixedness, Birch and Rabinowitz (1951) placed subjects in a room with electrical equipment, a switch, and a relay, and asked them to solve the Maier two-string problem. In this problem, a person is asked to tie together two dangling strings. But, as shown in Figure 8.3, they cannot be reached simultaneously.

In the experiment, either the switch or the relay can be used as a weight for one of the strings. If the weighted string is sent swinging, the subject can grasp the unweighted string and then wait for the weighted string to come his or her way. Subjects given prior experience with the switch as an electrical device were significantly more likely to use the relay as the weight. Subjects given prior experience with the intended function of the relay were significantly more likely to use the switch as a weight. Subjects given no prior experience with either device showed no preferences for using one or the other as the weight.

You may know that soldiers in survival training in the desert are taught to view insects and snakes as sources of food rather than as pests or threats. But it

Mental set The tendency to respond to a new problem with an approach that was successfully used with problems similar in appearance.

Functional fixedness The tendency to view an object in terms of its name or familiar usage.

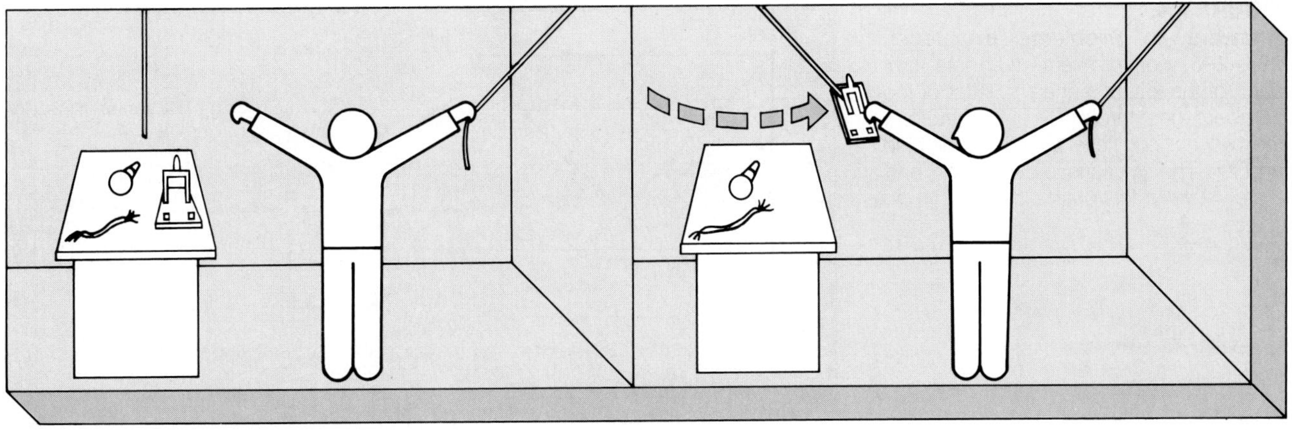

FIGURE 8.3.
The Two-String Problem.

A person is asked to tie two dangling strings together, but he cannot reach them both at once. He is allowed to use any object in the room to help him—paper clips, tissue paper, a pair of pliers, a chair, tape. He can solve the problem by taping the pliers to one string and sending it swinging back and forth. Then he grabs the stationary string and catches the moving string when it swings his way. After removing the pliers, the strings are tied together. Functional fixedness could impede solution of the problem by causing the person to view the pliers as only a grasping tool and not as a weight.

would be understandable if you chose to show civilian functional fixedness for as long as possible if you were stuck in the desert.

Creativity in Problem-Solving

A creative person may be more capable of solving problems to which there are no preexisting solutions, no tried and tested formulas.

Creativity is an enigmatic concept. According to Sternberg (1985), we tend to perceive creative people as:

Willing to take chances

Unaccepting of limitations; trying to do the impossible

Appreciating art and music

Capable of using the materials around them to make unique things

Questioning social norms and assumptions

Willing to take an unpopular stand

Inquisitive

A professor of mine once remarked that there is nothing new under the sun, only novel combinations of old elements. To him, the core of creativity was the ability to generate novel combinations of existing elements. My professor's view of creativity was similar to that of many psychologists—that creativity is the ability to make unusual, sometimes remote, associations to the elements of a problem so that new combinations that meet the goals are generated. An essential aspect of a creative response is the leap from the elements of the problem to the novel solution (Amabile, 1983). A predictable solution is not particularly creative, even if it is difficult to arrive at.

Creativity The ability to generate novel solutions to problems.

In the two-string problem, the ability to associate a switch or a relay with the quality of weight rather than with their intended electronic functions requires

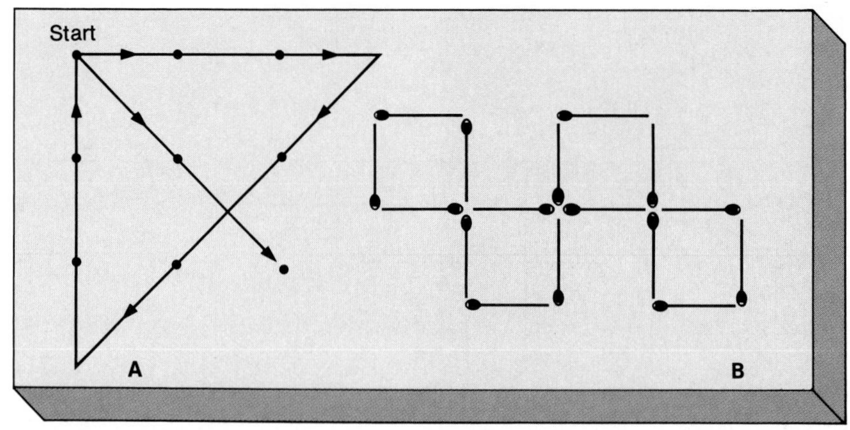

FIGURE 8.4.
Answers to Problems on pages 294–295. For problem 1C, note that each of the letters is the first letter of the numbers one through eight. Therefore, the two missing letters are *NT*, for *n*ine and *t*en. The solutions to problems 2 and 3 are shown in this illustration.

some creativity. Tying the switch or relay to the end of the string is a new combination of the familiar elements in the problem, one that meets the requirements of the situation.

Convergent Thinking and Divergent Thinking. According to Guilford (1959; Guilford & Hoepfner, 1971), creativity demands divergent thinking rather than convergent thinking. In **convergent thinking,** thought is limited to present facts as the problem-solver tries to narrow thinking to find the best solution. In **divergent thinking,** the problem-solver associates more fluently and freely to the various elements of the problem. The problem-solver allows "leads" to run a nearly limitless course to determine whether they will eventually combine as needed. *Brainstorming* is a popular term for divergent thinking when carried out by a group.

Successful problem-solving may require both divergent and convergent thinking. First, divergent thinking generates many possible solutions; then, convergent thinking is used to select the most probable solutions and reject the others.

Factors in Creativity. What factors contribute to creativity? Guilford (1959) noted that creative people show flexibility, fluency (in generating words and ideas), and originality. Getzels and Jackson (1962) found that creative schoolchildren tend to express, rather than inhibit, their feelings and to be playful and independent. Conger and Petersen (1984) concur that creative people tend to be independent and nonconformist. But independence and nonconformity do not necessarily make a person creative. Stereotypes of the creative personality have led to individual exaggerations of nonconformity.

Nevertheless, creative children are often at odds with their teachers because of their independence. Faced with the chore of managing as many as 30 pupils, teachers too often label quiet and submissive children as "good" children. These studies of creativity may also explain in part why there have been many more male than female artists throughout history, even though Maccoby and Jacklin (1974) found no sex differences in creativity. Over the years, traits like independence and nonconformity are more likely to have been discouraged in females than in males, because such traits are inconsistent with the passive and compliant social roles traditionally ascribed to females. Because of the women's movement, the number of women in the creative arts and sciences is growing rapidly today. In the past, the creativity of many girls may have been nipped in the bud.

Convergent thinking A thought process that attempts to narrow in on the single best solution to a problem.

Divergent thinking A thought process that attempts to generate multiple solutions to problems.

Creativity and Intelligence

Creativity and intelligence sometimes, but not always, go hand in hand. Persons low in intelligence are often low in creativity as well, but high intelligence is no

Creativity. Henry Moore creates one of his figurative sculptures. What traits are connected with creativity? What is the relationship between intelligence and creativity?

guarantee of creativity. However, it sometimes happens that people of only moderate intelligence excel in creativity, especially in fields like art and music.

It is *not* necessarily true that intelligent people are also creative. Many intelligent people are relatively unimaginative.

A Canadian study found that highly intelligent ("gifted") boys and girls aged 9 to 11 were as a group more creative than less intelligent children, but not all the gifted children were more creative than their less intelligent peers (Kershner & Ledger, 1985). The girls in the study were significantly more creative than the boys, especially on verbal tasks.

Tests that measure intelligence are not useful in measuring creativity. As you will see on the following pages, intelligence-test questions usually require convergent thinking to focus in on the answer. On an intelligence test, an ingenious answer that differs from the designated answer is wrong. Tests of creativity are oriented toward determining how flexible and fluent thinking can be. Here, for example, is an item from a test used by Getzels and Jackson (1962) to measure associative ability, a factor in creativity: "Write as many meanings as you can for each of the following words: (a) duck; (b) sack; (c) pitch; (d) fair." Those who write several meanings for each word, rather than only one, are rated as being potentially more creative.

INTELLIGENCE

What form of life is so adaptive that it can survive in desert temperatures of 120 degrees Fahrenheit or Arctic climes of –40 degrees Fahrenheit? What form of life can run, walk, climb, swim, live under water for months on end, and fly to the moon and back? I won't keep you in suspense any longer. We are that form of life. Yet, our unclad bodies do not allow us to adapt to these extremes of temperature. Brute strength does not allow us to live under water or travel to the moon. Rather, it is our **intelligence** that permits us to adapt to these conditions and to challenge our physical limitations.

The term *intelligence* is familiar enough. At an early age, we gain impressions of how intelligent we are compared to others. We associate intelligence with academic success, advancement on the job, and appropriate social behavior. Psychologists use intelligence as a **trait** that may explain, at least in part, why people do (or fail to do) things that are adaptive and inventive.

Despite our familiarity with the concept of intelligence, it cannot be seen, touched, or measured physically. Intelligence is thus subject to various interpretations. In this section, we shall discuss different ways of looking at intelligence. We shall see how intelligence is measured and discuss group differences in intelligence. Finally we shall examine the determinants of intelligence: heredity and the environment.

THEORIES OF INTELLIGENCE

Psychologists generally distinguish between **achievement** and intelligence. Achievement refers to knowledge and skills gained from experience. It involves specific content such as English, history, and math. The relationship between achievement and experience seems obvious: we are not surprised to find that a student who has taken Spanish, but not French, does better on a Spanish achievement test than on a French achievement test.

Intelligence A complex and controversial concept. According to David Wechsler (1975), the "capacity . . . to understand the world [and] resourcefulness to cope with its challenges."

Trait A distinguishing characteristic that is presumed to account for consistency in behavior.

Achievement That which is attained by one's efforts and made possible by one's abilities.

Going for a "Walk." Our human intelligence permits us to live under water for months on end or to fly to the moon and back. Physically we are weaker than many other organisms. Our intelligence permits us to adapt successfully to the physical environment, however—to create new environments and to go for leisurely "spacewalks."

The meaning of *intelligence* is more difficult to pin down. Most psychologists agree that intelligence somehow provides the cognitive basis for academic achievement. Intelligence is usually perceived as underlying competence or learning ability, whereas achievement involves acquired competencies or performance. Psychologists disagree, however, about the nature and origins of underlying competence or learning ability.

There are two broad approaches to understanding intelligence: factor and cognitive theories.

Factor Theories

Many investigators have viewed intelligence as consisting of one or more mental abilities, or **factors.** Alfred Binet, the Frenchman who developed intelligence-testing methods at the turn of the century, believed that intelligence consisted of several related factors. Other investigators have argued that intelligence consists of from one to hundreds of factors.

In 1904, British psychologist Charles Spearman suggested that the behaviors we consider to be intelligent have a common underlying factor. He labeled this factor **g,** for "general intelligence." *G* represented broad reasoning and problem-solving abilities. Spearman supported this view by noting that people who excel in one area can usually excel in others. But he also noted that even the most capable people are relatively superior in some areas—whether in music or business or poetry. For this reason, he suggested that specific, or **s** factors account for specific abilities.

American psychologist Louis Thurstone (1938) used mathematical techniques to analyze tests of specific abilities and concluded that Spearman had

Factor A cluster of related items such as those found on an intelligence test.

g Spearman's symbol for general intelligence, which he believed underlay more specific abilities.

s Spearman's symbol for *specific* factors, or *s factors,* that he believed accounted for individual abilities.

A Musical Prodigy. According to Gardner's theory of multiple intelligences, there are seven intelligences, not one, and each is based in a different area of the brain. Two of these involve language ability and logic, which are familiar components of intelligence functions. But Gardner also refers to bodily talents, musical ability, spatial-relations skills, and two kinds of personal intelligence—sensitivity to one's own feelings and sensitivity to the feelings of others. According to this view, one could compose symphonies or advance mathematical theory while remaining average in, say, language skills.

oversimplified the concept of intelligence. Thurstone's data suggested the presence of nine specific factors, which he labeled **primary mental abilities.** Thurstone suggested, for example, that we might have high word fluency, enabling us to rapidly develop lists of words that rhyme yet not enabling us to be efficient at solving math problems (Thurstone & Thurstone, 1963).

Gardner's Theory of Multiple Intelligences. Howard Gardner (1983) proposes that there are seven factors in intelligence, although he refers to each as "an intelligence." Each factor, or in Gardner's terms, each intelligence, is based in a different area of the brain. Two such "intelligences" involve language ability and logical-mathematical ability, which are familiar aspects of intelligence. Gardner also refers to bodily-kinesthetic talents (of the sort shown by dancers, mimes, and athletes), musical talent, spatial-relations skills, and two kinds of personal intelligence: awareness of one's own inner feelings, and sensitivity to other people's feelings and the ability to respond to them appropriately. According to Gardner, one can compose symphonies or advance mathematical theory yet be average in, say, language and personal skills. (Are not some academic "geniuses" foolish in their personal lives?)

Cognitive Theories

Cognitive theorists tend to view intelligence in terms of information processing. They focus on how information "flows" through us and is modified by us as we adapt to and act to change our environments. Let us consider Yale University psychologist Robert Sternberg's cognitive triarchic theory.

Triarchic Theory. Sternberg's (1985) **triarchic** model of intelligence (see Figure 8.5) contains three levels: *contextual, experiential,* and *componential.* Individual differences are found at each level. The **contextual level** concerns the environmental setting. It is assumed that intelligent behavior permits people to adapt to the demands of their environments. For example, keeping a job by "adapting" one's behavior to the requirements of one's employer is adaptive. But if the employer is making unreasonable demands, reshaping the environment (by changing the employer's attitudes) or selecting an alternate environment (finding a more suitable job) is also adaptive.

Primary mental abilities According to Thurstone, the basic abilities that make up intelligence.

Triarchic Governed by three.

Contextual level Those aspects of intelligent behavior that permit people to adapt to their environment.

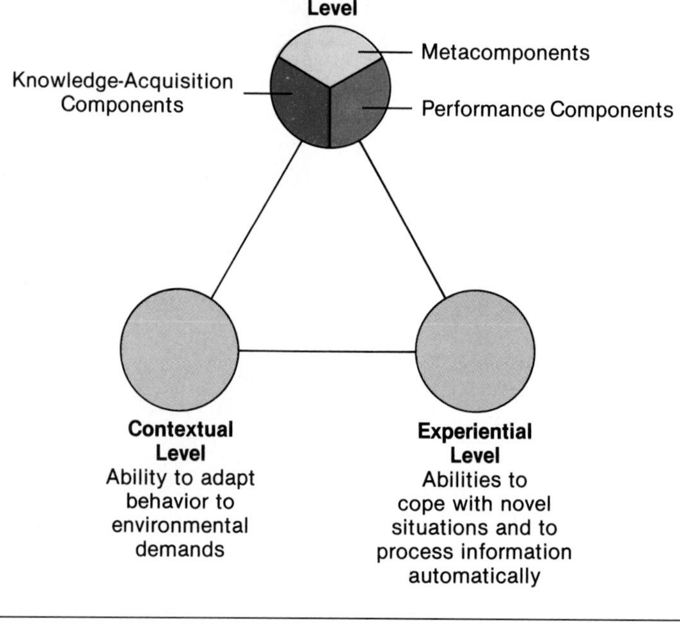

FIGURE 8.5.
Sternberg's Triarchic Model of Intelligence. Robert Sternberg views intelligence as consisting of contextual, experiential, and componential levels. The componential level consists of metacomponents, performance components, and knowledge-acquisition components.

On the **experiential level,** intelligent behavior is defined by the abilities to cope with novel situations and to process information automatically. The ability to quickly relate novel situations to familiar situations (to perceive the similarities and differences) fosters adaptation. Moreover, as a result of experience, we come to solve problems more rapidly. Intelligence and experience in reading permit the child to process familiar words more or less automatically and to decode new words efficiently. In sum, it is "intelligent" to profit from experience.

The **componential level** of intelligence consists of three processes: *metacomponents, performance components,* and *knowledge-acquisition components.* **Metacomponents** concern our awareness of our own intellectual processes. Metacomponents are involved in deciding what problem to solve, selecting appropriate strategies and formulas, monitoring the solution, and changing performance in the light of knowledge of results.

Performance components are the mental operations or skills used in solving problems or processing information. Performance components include encoding information, combining and comparing pieces of information, and generating a solution. Consider Sternberg's (1979) analogy problem:

Washington is to *one* as *Lincoln* is to
(a) 5 (c) 15
(b) 10 (d) 50

To solve the analogy, we must first correctly *encode* the elements—*Washington, one,* and *Lincoln*—by identifying them and comparing them to other information. We must first encode *Washington* and *Lincoln* as the names of presidents,[2] and then try to combine *Washington* and *one* in a meaningful manner. Two possibilities quickly come to mind. Washington was the first president, and his picture is on the one dollar bill. We can then generate two possible solutions and try them out. First, what number president was Lincoln? Second, on what bill is Lincoln's picture found? (Do you need to consult a history book or peek into your wallet at this point?)

Knowledge-acquisition components are used in gaining new knowledge. These include encoding information (for example, Roger Smith as the founder of

Experiential level Those aspects of intelligence that permit people to cope with novel situations and process information automatically.

Componential level The level of intelligence that consists of metacomponents, performance components, and knowledge-acquisition components.

Metacomponents Components of intelligence that are based on self-awareness of our intellectual processes.

Performance components The mental operations used in processing information.

Knowledge-acquisition components Components used in gaining knowledge, such as encoding and relating new knowledge to existing knowledge.

[2]There are other possibilities. Both are the names of memorials and cities, for example.

TABLE 8.2: Interpretations of Some Correlation Coefficients

Correlation Coefficient	Interpretations
+1.00	Perfect positive correlation, as between temperature in Fahrenheit and centigrade
+0.90	High positive correlation, adequate for test reliability
+0.60 to +0.70	Moderate positive correlation, usually considered adequate for test validity
+0.30	Weak positive correlation, unacceptable for test reliability or validity
0.00	No correlation between variables (no association indicated)
−0.30	Weak negative correlation
−0.60 to −0.70	Moderate negative correlation
−0.90	High negative correlation
−1.00	A perfect negative correlation

Rhode Island or as the past president of General Motors), combining pieces of information, and comparing new information with what is already known.

Sternberg's model is complex, but it does a promising job of capturing what most investigators mean by intellectual functioning. David Wechsler, the originator of a series of widely used intelligence tests, described intelligence in terms that are simpler but, I think, consistent with Sternberg's view. Intelligence, wrote Wechsler, is the "capacity of an individual to understand the world [and the] resourcefulness to cope with its challenges" (1975, p. 139). Intelligence, to Wechsler, involves accurate representation of the world (which Sternberg discusses as encoding, comparing new information to old information, and so on) and effective problem solving (adapting to one's environment, profiting from experience, selecting the appropriate formulas and strategies, and so on).

THE MEASUREMENT OF INTELLIGENCE

There may be disagreements about the nature of intelligence, but thousands of intelligence tests are administered by psychologists and educators every day. Let us explore some basic characteristics of intelligence tests.

Characteristics of Intelligence Tests

Because important decisions are made on the basis of intelligence tests, they must be *reliable* and *valid*. Psychologists use statistical techniques such as the **correlation coefficient** to determine reliability and validity. For a test to be considered reliable, correlations between a group's test results on separate occasions should be positive and high: about +0.90 (see Table 8.2).

The **reliability** of a measure is its consistency. A measure of height would not be reliable if a person appeared to be taller or shorter every time a measurement was taken. A reliable measure of intelligence, like a good tape measure, must yield similar results on different testing occasions.

There are different ways of showing a test's reliability, all of which rely on the correlation coefficient. One of the most commonly used is **test–retest reliability,** which is shown by comparing scores of tests taken on different occasions. The measurement of test–retest reliability may be confused in tests of intelligence and **aptitude** by the fact that people often improve their scores from one occasion to the next because of familiarity with the test items and the testing procedure.

The **validity** of a test is the degree to which it measures what it is supposed to measure. To determine whether a test is valid, we see whether it actually

Correlation coefficient A number that indicates the direction (positive or negative) and strength of the relationship between two variables.

Reliability Consistency.

Test–retest reliability A method for determining the reliability of a test by comparing (correlating) test takers' scores from separate occasions.

Aptitude An ability or talent to succeed in an area in which one has not yet been trained.

Validity The degree to which a test measures what it is supposed to measure.

predicts an outside standard, or external criterion. A proper standard, or criterion, for determining the validity of a test of musical aptitude is the ability to learn to play a musical instrument. Tests of musical aptitude, therefore, should correlate highly with the ability to learn to play a musical instrument. Most psychologists assume that intelligence is one of the factors responsible for academic prowess. Intelligence test scores should thus correlate positively with school grades. They do—about +0.60 or so (Sattler, 1988). Other indexes of academic prowess include scores on achievement tests and teacher ratings of cognitive ability.

Because we would expect people who are more intelligent to be placed in white collar and professional jobs, there should also be a positive correlation between intelligence test scores attained during childhood and the status of one's occupation as an adult. In one longitudinal study, intelligence test scores attained after the age of 7 were indeed shown to correlate moderately positively with occupational status (McCall, 1977).

A correlation of about +0.60 to +0.70 is generally considered to be adequate for purposes of assessing test validity. However, such a correlation does not approach a perfect positive relationship. This finding suggests that factors *other* than performance on intelligence tests contribute to academic and occupational success. Motivation to do well and one's general level of personal adjustment are two of them (Anastasi, 1983; Hrncir et al., 1985; Scarr, 1981).

By these standards, the Stanford-Binet Intelligence Scale (SBIS) and the Wechsler scales for children and adults have adequate reliability and validity.

Individual Intelligence Tests

The Stanford-Binet Intelligence Scale. The SBIS originated through the work of Frenchmen Alfred Binet and Theodore Simon early in this century. The French public school system sought an instrument that could identify children who were unlikely to profit from the regular classroom so that they could receive special attention. The Binet-Simon scale came into use in 1905. Since that time, it has undergone great revision and refinement.

Despite his view that many factors are involved in intellectual functioning, Binet constructed his test to yield a single overall score so that it could be more easily used by the school system. He also assumed that intelligence increased with age. Therefore, older children should get more items right than younger children. Thus, Binet included a series of age-graded questions, as in Table 8.3, and he arranged them in order of difficulty.

The Binet-Simon scale yielded a score called a **mental age,** or MA. The MA shows the intellectual level at which a child is functioning. A child with an MA of 6 is functioning, intellectually, like the average child aged 6. In taking the test, children earned "months" of credit for each correct answer. Their MA was determined by adding the years and months of credit they attained.

Louis Terman adapted the Binet-Simon scale for use with American children. The first version of the *Stanford*-Binet Intelligence Scale (SBIS)[3] was published in 1916. The SBIS included more items than the original test and was used with children aged 2 to 16. The SBIS also yielded an **intelligence quotient (IQ)** rather than an MA. American educators developed interest in learning the IQs of their pupils. The current version of the SBIS is used with children from the age of 2 upward and with adults.

The IQ reflects the relationship between a child's mental age and actual age, or chronological age (CA). Use of this ratio reflects the fact that the same MA score has different implications for children of different ages. That is, an MA of 8 is an above-average score for a 6-year-old, but an MA of 8 is below average for a 10-year-

Mental age The accumulated months of credit that a person earns on the Stanford-Binet Intelligence Scale. Abbreviated *MA.*

Intelligence quotient (IQ) (1) Originally, a ratio obtained by dividing a child's score (or mental age) on an intelligence test by his or her chronological age. (2) Generally, a score on an intelligence test.

[3]The test is so named because Terman carried out his work at Stanford University.

TABLE 8.3: Items Similar to Those on the Stanford-Binet Intelligence Scale

Level (years)	Item
2 years	1. Children show knowledge of basic vocabulary words by identifying parts of a doll such as the mouth, ears, and hair.
	2. Children show counting and spatial skills along with visual-motor coordination by building a tower of four blocks to match a model.
4 years	1. Children show word fluency and categorical thinking by filling in the missing words when they are asked questions such as: "Father is a man; mother is a __________?" "Hamburgers are hot; ice cream is __________?"
	2. Children show comprehension by answering correctly when they are asked questions such as: "Why do people have automobiles?" "Why do people have medicine?"
9 years	1. Children can point out verbal absurdities, as in this question: "In an old cemetery, scientists unearthed a skull which they think was that of George Washington when he was only five years of age. What is silly about that?
	2. Children show fluency with words, as shown by answering the questions: "Can you tell me a number that rhymes with snore?" "Can you tell me a color that rhymes with glue?"
Adult	1. Adults show knowledge of the meanings of words and conceptual thinking by correctly explaining the differences between word pairs like "sickness and misery," "house and home," and "integrity and prestige."
	2. Adults show spatial skills by correctly answering questions like: "If a car turned to the right to head north, in what direction was it heading before it turned?"

old. The German psychologist Wilhelm Stern in 1912 suggested use of the IQ to handle this problem.

Stern computed IQ by the formula IQ = (Mental Age/Chronological Age) × 100, or

$$IQ = \frac{MA}{CA} \times 100$$

According to this formula, a child with an MA of 6 and a CA of 6 would have an IQ of 100. Children who can handle intellectual problems as well as older children will have IQs above 100. For instance, an 8-year-old who does as well on the SBIS as the average 10-year-old will attain an IQ of 125. Children who do not answer as many items correctly as other children of their age will attain MAs lower than their CAs, and their IQ scores will be below 100.

Today, IQ scores on the SBIS are derived by seeing how children's and adults' performances deviate from those of other people of the same age. People who get more items correct than average attain IQ scores above 100, and people who answer fewer items correctly attain scores below 100.

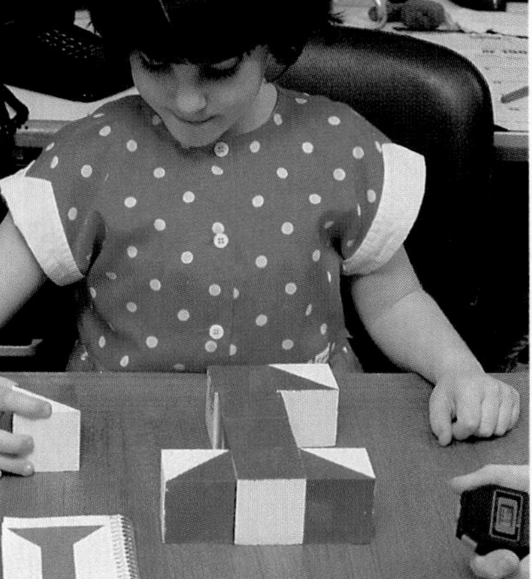

Taking the Wechsler. The Wechsler intelligence scales consist of verbal and performance subtests such as the one shown in this photograph.

It is true that two children can answer exactly the same items on an intelligence test correctly, yet one can be above average and the other below average in intelligence. The more intelligent child would be the younger of the two.

We pursue the concept of the deviation IQ in our discussion of the Wechsler scales.

The Wechsler Scales. David Wechsler developed a series of scales for use with children and adults. The Wechsler scales group test questions into a number of separate subtests (such as those shown in Table 8.4). Each subtest measures a different type of intellectual task. For this reason, the test shows how well a person does on one type of task (such as defining words) as compared with another

TABLE 8.4: Subtests from the Wechsler Adult Intelligence Scale (WAIS)

Verbal Subtests	Performance Subtests
1. *Information:* "What is the capital of the United States?" "Who was Shakespeare?"	7. *Digit Symbol:* Learning and drawing meaningless figures that are associated with numbers.
2. *Comprehension:* "Why do we have zip codes?" "What does 'A stitch in time saves 9' mean?"	8. *Picture Completion:* Pointing to the missing part of a picture.
3. *Arithmetic:* "If 3 candy bars cost 25 cents, how much will 18 candy bars cost?"	9. *Block Design:* Copying pictures of geometric designs using multicolored blocks.
4. *Similarities:* "How are good and bad alike?" "How are peanut butter and jelly alike?"	10. *Picture Arrangement:* Arranging cartoon pictures in sequence so that they tell a meaningful story.
5. *Digit Span:* Repeating a series of numbers forwards and backwards.	11. *Object Assembly:* Putting pieces of a puzzle together so that they form a meaningful object.
6. *Vocabulary:* "What does canal mean?"	

Items for verbal subtests 1, 2, 3, 4, and 6 are similar but not identical to actual test items on the WAIS.

(such as using blocks to construct geometric designs). In this way, the Wechsler scales highlight children's relative strengths and weaknesses, as well measure overall intellectual functioning.

As you can see in Table 8.4, Wechsler described some of his scales as measuring *verbal* tasks and others as assessing *performance* tasks. In general, verbal subtests require knowledge of verbal concepts, whereas performance subtests require familiarity with spatial-relations concepts. (Figure 8.6 shows items similar to those found on the performance scales of the Wechsler tests.) But the two groupings are not that easily distinguished. For example, associating to the name of the object being pieced together in subtest 11—a sign of word fluency and general knowledge as well as of spatial-relations ability—helps the person construct it rapidly. In any event, Wechsler's scales permit the computation of verbal and performance IQs. It is not unusual for nontechnically oriented college students to attain higher verbal than performance IQs.

Wechsler also introduced the concept of the deviation IQ. Instead of using mental and chronological ages to compute an IQ, he based IQ scores on how a person's answers compared with (or deviated from) those attained by people in

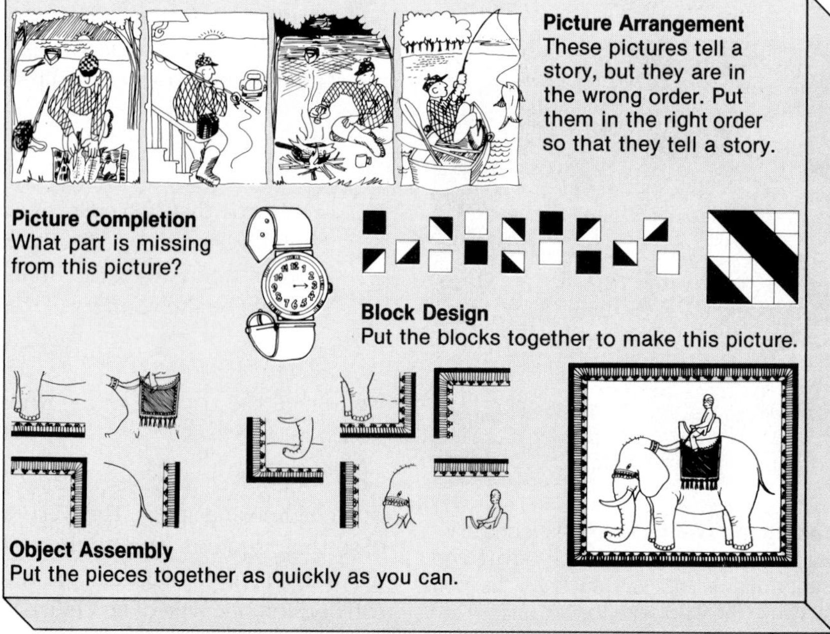

FIGURE 8.6. Performance Items of an Intelligence Test. This figure shows a number of items that resemble those in the performance subtests of the Wechsler Adult Intelligence Scale.

TABLE 8.5: Variations in IQ Scores

Range of Scores	Percent of Population	Brief Description
130 and above	2	Very superior
120–129	7	Superior
110–119	16	Above average
100–109	25	High average
90–99	25	Low average
80–89	16	Slow learner
70–79	7	Borderline
Below 70	2	Intellectually deficient

the same age group. The average test result at any age level is defined as an IQ score of 100. Wechsler then distributed IQ scores so that the middle 50 percent of them would fall within the "broad average range" of 90 to 110.

As you can see in Figure 8.7, most IQ scores cluster around the average. Only 5 percent of the population have IQ scores of above 130 or below 70. Table 8.5 indicates the labels that Wechsler assigned to various IQ scores and the approximate percentages of the population who attain IQ scores at those levels.

Group Tests

The SBIS and Wechsler scales are administered to one person at a time. This one-to-one ratio is optimal. It allows the examiner to facilitate performance (within the limits of the standardized directions) and to observe the test taker closely. Examiners are thus alerted to factors that impair performance, such as language difficulties, illness, or a noisy or poorly lit room. But large institutions with few trained examiners, such as the public schools and armed forces, have also wished to estimate the intellectual functioning of their charges. They require tests that can be administered simultaneously to large groups of people.

Group tests for children, first developed during World War I, were administered to 4 million children by 1921, a couple of years after the war had ended (Cronbach, 1975). At first, these tests were heralded as remarkable instruments because they eased the huge responsibilities of school administrators. However, as the years passed they came under increasing attack, because many administrators relied on them completely to track children. The administrators did not seek other sources of information about the children's abilities and achievements (Reschly, 1981).

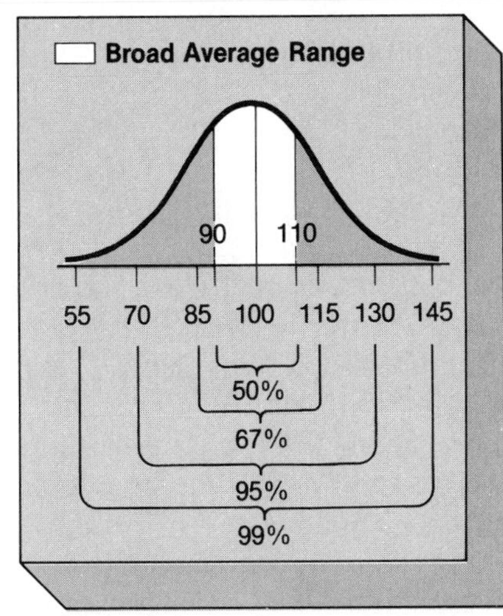

FIGURE 8.7. Approximate Distribution of IQ Scores. Wechsler defined the deviation IQ so that 50 percent of scores would fall within the broad average range of 90–110. This bell-shaped curve is referred to as a *normal curve* by psychologists. It describes the distribution of many traits, including height.

THE DETERMINANTS OF INTELLIGENCE: WHERE DOES INTELLIGENCE COME FROM?

In 1969, Arthur Jensen published an article called "How Much Can We Boost IQ and Scholastic Achievement?" in the *Harvard Educational Review.* It gained national visibility because of the assertion that 80 percent of the variability in IQ scores is inherited. This may sound like nothing much to get excited about, but Jensen became the focus of campus demonstrations and was sometimes booed loudly in class. *Why?*

It turns out that African Americans score below white Americans on intelligence tests. Jensen had asserted that this difference was largely genetically determined. If so, the difference could never be decreased. Protests from the African-American community were echoed by many whites, including many prominent psychologists and other scientists. Crawford (1979) suggested that Jensen's views

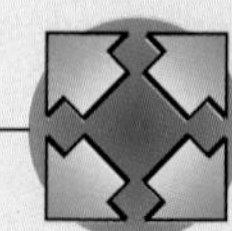

WORLD OF DIVERSITY

Social-Class, Racial, and Ethnic Differences in Intelligence

There is a body of research suggestive of differences between social, racial, and ethnic groups. Lower-class American children attain IQ scores some 10 to 15 points lower than those of middle- and upper-class children. African-American children tend to attain IQ scores some 15 points lower than their white agemates (Helms, 1992). As groups, Hispanic-American and Native-American children also score significantly below norms of whites.

Several studies on IQ have confused the factors of social class and race because disproportionate numbers of African, Hispanic, and Native Americans are found among the lower socioeconomic classes. When we limit our observations to particular racial groups, however, we still find an effect for social class. That is, middle-class whites outscore lower-class whites. Middle-class African, Hispanic, and Native Americans also all outscore lower-class members of their own racial groups.

Research has also discovered differences between Asians and white people. Asian Americans, for example, frequently outscore white Americans on the math section of the Scholastic Aptitude Test. Students in China (Taiwan) and Japan also outscore Americans on standardized achievement tests in math and science (Stevenson et al., 1986). British psychologist Richard Lynn (1977, 1982) has reported that Japanese (residing in Japan) attain higher IQ scores than white Britishers or Americans. The mean Japanese IQ was 111, which exceeds the top of the high average range in the United States by a point. In the United States, moreover, people of Asian-Indian, Korean, Japanese, Filipino, and Chinese extraction are more likely to graduate high school and complete four years of college than white, African, and Hispanic Americans (Sue & Okazaki, 1990). Asian Americans are vastly overrepresented in competitive colleges and universities. They make up only 2.4 percent of the American population but account for 12 percent of the undergraduates at MIT, and 24 and 33 percent, respectively, at the University of California campuses at Berkeley and Irvine (Butterfield, 1990).

Lynn (1991) argues that the greater intellectual accomplishments of Asian students are at least in part genetically determined. According to Sue and Okazaki (1990), however, the higher scores of Asian students may reflect different values in the home, the school, or the culture at large rather than differences in underlying competence. They argue that Asian Americans have been discriminated against in careers that do not require advanced education, so they place relatively greater emphasis on the value of education. Looking to other environmental factors, Steinberg and his colleagues (1992) claim that parental encouragement and supervision in combination with peer support for academic achievement partially explain the superior performances of white and Asian Americans as compared to African and Hispanic Americans.

The controversy over group differences in IQ scores has led many psychologists to ask the question: Just what do intelligence tests measure?

The Testing Controversy: Just What Do Intelligence Tests Measure?

> *I was almost one of the testing casualties. At 15 I earned an IQ test score of 82, three points above the track of the special education class. Based on this score, my counselor suggested that I take up bricklaying because I was "good with my hands." My low IQ, however, did not allow me to see that as desirable.*

This testimony, offered by African-American psychologist Robert L. Williams (1974, p. 32), echoes the sentiments of many psychologists. A survey of psychologists and educational specialists by Mark Snyderman and Stanley Rothman (1987, 1990) found that most consider intelligence tests somewhat biased against African Americans and members of the lower classes. Elementary and secondary schools may also place too much emphasis on them in making educational placements.

During the 1920s, intelligence tests were misused to prevent the immigration of many Europeans and others into the United States (Kamin, 1982; Kleinmuntz, 1982). For example, test pioneer H. H. Goddard (1917) assessed 178 newly arrived immigrants at Ellis Island and claimed that "83 percent of the Jews, 80 percent of the Hungarians, 79 percent of the Italians, and 87 percent of the Russians were 'feeble-minded' " (Kleinmuntz, 1982, p. 333). Apparently it was of little concern to Goddard that these immigrants by and large did not understand English—the language in which the tests were administered.

Questions about the effects of social class on test performance, the role of tests in enhancing or inhibiting social mobility, and the like, have been asked at least since the use of mental testing in China 2,000 years ago (Matarazzo, 1990). Twentieth-century misuse of intelligence tests has led psy-

---

Cultural bias A factor that provides an advantage for test takers from certain cultural or ethnic backgrounds.

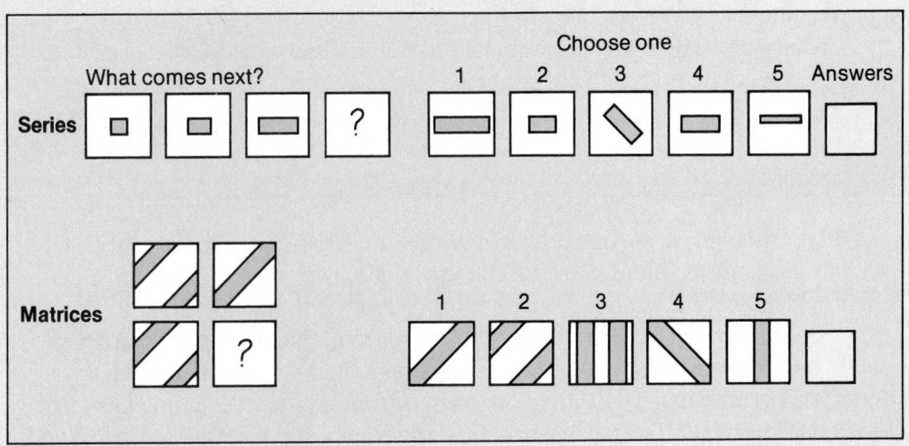

FIGURE 8.8. Sample Items from Raymond Cattell's Culture-Fair Intelligence Test. Culture-fair tests attempt to exclude items that discriminate on the basis of cultural background rather than intelligence.

Who's Smart? Asian children and Asian-American children frequently outscore other American children on intelligence tests. Can we attribute the difference to genetic factors or to Asian parents' emphasis on acquiring the kinds of cognitive skills that enable children to fare well on such tests and in school? Sue and Okazaki (1990) suggest that Asian-Americans place great value on education because they have been discriminated against in careers that do not require advanced education.

chologists such as Leon Kamin to complain, "Since its introduction to America the intelligence test has been used more or less consciously as an instrument of oppression against the underprivileged—the poor, the foreign born, and racial minorities" (in Crawford, 1979, p. 664).

Intelligence tests, as pointed out by critics such as Robert Williams, measure traits that are required in modern, high-technology societies (Anastasi, 1983; Pearlman et al., 1980; Schmidt et al., 1981). The vocabulary and arithmetic subtests on the Wechsler scales, for example, clearly reflect achievements in language skills and computational ability. It is generally assumed that the broad achievements measured by these tests reflect intelligence, but they might also reflect cultural familiarity with the concepts required to answer test questions correctly. In particular, the tests seem to reflect middle-class white culture in the United States (Garcia, 1981).

Is It Possible to Develop Culture-Free Intelligence Tests?

If scoring well on intelligence tests requires a certain type of cultural experience, the tests are said to have a **cultural bias.** Children reared in African-American neighborhoods could be at a disadvantage, not because of differences in intelligence but because of cultural differences and economic deprivation. For this reason, psychologists such as Raymond B. Cattell (1949) and Florence Goodenough (1954) have tried to construct **culture-free** intelligence tests.

Cattell's Culture-Fair Intelligence Test evaluates reasoning ability through the child's ability to comprehend the rules that govern a progression of geometric designs, as shown in Figure 8.8. Goodenough's Draw-A-Person test is based on the premise that children from all cultural backgrounds have had the opportunity to observe people and note the relationships between the parts and the whole. Her instructions simply require children to draw a picture of a man or woman.

Culture-free tests have not lived up to their promise, however. Middle-class white children still outperform African-American children, perhaps because they are more likely to be familiar with materials such as blocks and pencils and paper. They are more likely than disadvantaged children to have arranged blocks into various designs (practice relevant to the Cattell test) and more likely to have sketched animals, people, and inanimate objects (practice relevant to the Goodenough test). Too, culture-free tests do not predict academic success as well as other intelligence tests.

Motivation to do well might also be a cultural factor. Because of socioeconomic differences, African-American children often do not have the same motivation as white children to do well on tests. Highly motivated children attain higher scores on intelligence tests than less-well-motivated children do (Zigler & Butterfield, 1968). Perhaps there is no such thing as a culture-free intelligence test.

Culture-free Describing a test in which cultural biases have been removed.

met with such opposition because they fly in the face of the belief that American children are supposed to be able to grow up to be whatever they want to be, even president.

What do psychologists know about the **determinants** of intelligence? What are the roles of heredity and environment?

Genetic Influences on Intelligence

Let us return to experiments with laboratory animals to point up some of the difficulties and shortcomings of research on genetic influences on *human* intelligence. Then we shall examine correlational research with human subjects.

Rats have been selectively bred for maze-learning ability (see Chapter 3). Maze-bright parent rats tend to have maze-bright litters, whereas maze-dull parents tend to have maze-dull litters. We must be cautious in generalizing from rats to people, however. The (spatial-relations) superiority of the maze-bright rats did not generalize to all learning tasks, even for the rats. And it cannot be emphasized too strongly that maze-learning ability in rats is not comparable to the complex cognitive tasks that define human intelligence. However, the selective-breeding technique provides a model worth noting because it *cannot* be replicated with people for ethical, legal, and practical reasons. Research on genetic influences on human intelligence must thus employ different strategies, such as kinship studies, MZ–DZ twin studies, and adoptee studies.

We can examine the IQ scores of closely and distantly related people who have been reared together or apart, for example. If heredity is involved in human intelligence, closely related people ought to have more similar IQs than distantly related or unrelated people, even when they are reared separately.

Figure 8.9 is a composite of the results of more than 100 studies of IQ and heredity in human beings, as reported by Bouchard and associates (1990). The IQ

Determinants Factors that set limits.

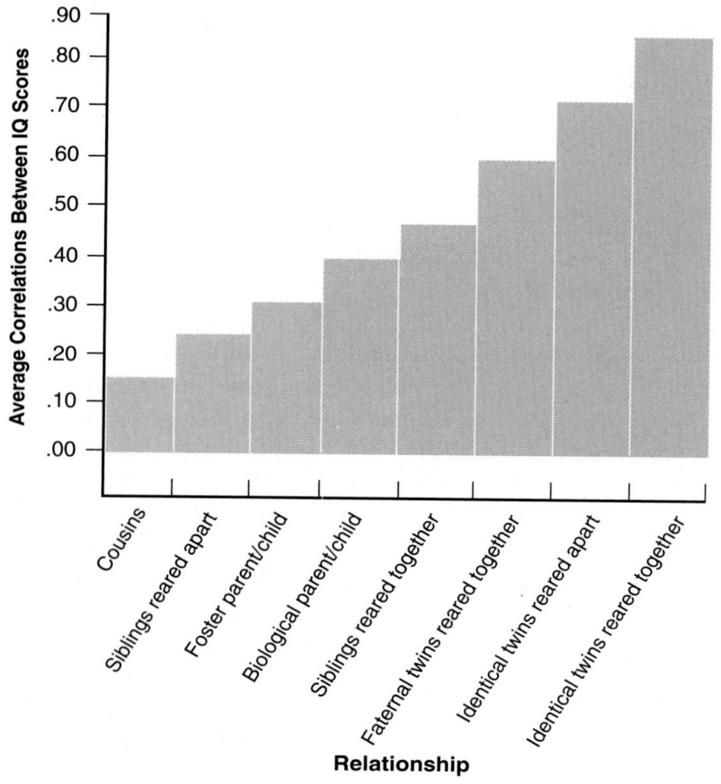

FIGURE 8.9.
Findings of Studies of the Relationship Between IQ Scores and Heredity. The data are a composite of hundreds of studies summarized in *Science* magazine (Bouchard et al., 1990). By and large, correlations grow stronger for persons who are more closely related. Persons reared together or living together have more similar IQ scores than persons reared or living apart. Such findings support genetic and environmental hypotheses of the origins of intelligence.

scores of identical (MZ) twins are more alike than the scores for any other pairs, even when the twins have been reared apart. Correlations between the IQ scores of fraternal (DZ) twins, siblings, and parents and children are moderate. Correlations between children and their foster parents and between cousins are weak.

Large-scale twin studies are consistent with the data in Figure 8.9. For instance, a study of 500 pairs of MZ and DZ twins in Louisville, Kentucky (Wilson, 1983), found that the correlations in intelligence between MZ twins were about the same as that for MZ twins in Figure 8.9. The correlations in intelligence between DZ twin pairs was the same as that between other siblings.

All in all, these studies appear to provide evidence for a role for heredity in IQ scores. Note, however, that genetic pairs (such as MZ twins) reared together show higher correlations between IQ scores than similar genetic pairs (such as other MZ twins) who were reared apart. This finding holds for MZ twins, siblings, parents and children, and unrelated people. *For this reason, the same group of studies suggests that the environment may play a role in IQ scores.*

Another strategy for exploring genetic influences on intelligence is to compare the correlations between adopted children and their biological and adoptive parents (Coon et al., 1990). When children are separated from their biological parents at early ages, one can argue that strong relationships between their IQs and those of their natural parents reflect genetic influences. Strong relationships between their IQs and those of their adoptive parents might reflect environmental influences.

Several studies with 1- and 2-year-old children in Colorado (Baker et al., 1983), Texas (Horn, 1983), and Minnesota (Scarr & Weinberg, 1983) have found a stronger relationship between the IQ scores of adopted children and their biological parents than with their adoptive parents. The Scarr and Weinberg report concerns African-American children reared by white adoptive parents, and we shall return to its findings in the section on environmental influences on intelligence.

There thus may be a genetic influence on intelligence. We shall see that there is also probably an environmental influence, however.

Environmental Influences on Intelligence

Studies on environmental influences employ various research strategies. One approach simply focuses on the situational factors that determine IQ scores. Remember that an IQ is a score on a test. The testing situation itself can explain part of the social-class difference in IQ in some cases. In one study, the experimenters (Zigler et al., 1982) simply made children as comfortable as possible during the test. Rather than being cold and impartial, the examiner was warm and friendly, and care was taken to see that the children understood the directions. As one result, children's test anxiety was markedly reduced. As another, the children's IQ scores were six points higher than those for a control group treated in a more indifferent manner, and disadvantaged children made relatively greater gains from the procedure. *By doing nothing more than make testing conditions more optimal for* all *children, we may narrow the IQ gap between white and African-American children.*

Ironically, the studies of the rats selectively bred for maze-learning ability have also provided evidence for the importance of experience. Cooper and Zubek (1958) provided young rats descended from maze-bright and maze-dull parents with different early environments. Some rats from each group were reared in a dull, featureless environment. Others were reared in rat amusement parks with ramps, ladders, wheels, and toys. Rats reared in the impoverished environment did poorly on maze learning tasks in adulthood, regardless of their parentage. But rats reared in the amusement park later learned mazes relatively rapidly. An enriched early environment narrowed the gap between the performances of rats with maze-dull and maze-bright parents.

Head Start. Preschoolers placed in Head Start programs have made dramatic increases both in readiness for elementary school and in IQ scores.

The early home environment and styles of parenting also appear to have an effect on IQ (Coon et al., 1990; Hoffman, 1985). Children of mothers who are emotionally and verbally responsive, who provide appropriate play materials, who are involved with their children, and who provide varied daily experiences during the early years attain higher IQ scores later on (Bradley & Caldwell, 1976; Elardo et al., 1975, 1977; Gottfried, 1984). The extent of home organization and safety has also been linked to higher IQs at later ages and to higher achievement test scores during the first grade (Bradley & Caldwell, 1984).

Dozens of other studies support the view that the child's early environment is linked to IQ scores and academic achievement. For example, McGowan and Johnson (1984) found that good parent-child relationships and maternal encouragement of independence were both positively linked to Mexican-American children's IQ scores by the age of 3. A number of studies have also found that high levels of maternal restrictiveness and punishment at 24 months are linked to *lower* IQ scores later on (Bee et al., 1982; Yeates et al., 1983).

Government-funded efforts to provide preschoolers with enriched early environments have also led to intellectual gains. Head Start programs, for example, enhance the IQ scores, achievement test scores, and academic skills of poor children (Barnett & Escobar, 1990; Hauser-Cram et al., 1991; Zigler et al., 1992) by exposing them to materials and activities that middle-class children take for granted. These include letters and words, numbers, books, exercises in drawing, pegs and pegboards, puzzles, toy animals, and dolls. Children whose IQ scores are initially lowest make the greatest gains in IQ. In addition to boosting IQ scores, early childhood intervention also decreases the likelihood of juvenile delinquency (Zigler et al., 1992).

Head Start programs have in fact raised children's IQs.

The Minnesota adoption studies reported by Scarr and Weinberg suggest a genetic influence on intelligence. The same studies (Scarr & Weinberg, 1976, 1977) also suggest a role for environmental influences, however. African-American children who were adopted during the first year by white parents above average in income and education showed IQ scores some 15 to 25 points higher than those attained by African-American children reared by their natural parents (Scarr & Weinberg, 1976). Still, the adoptees' average IQ scores, about 106, remained somewhat below those of their adoptive parents' natural children—117 (Scarr & Weinberg, 1977). Even so, the adoptive early environment closed a good deal of the IQ gap.

On Race and Intelligence: A Concluding Note

Many psychologists believe that heredity and environment interact to influence intelligence. Forty-five percent of Snyderman and Rothman's (1987, 1990) sample of 1,020 psychologists and educational specialists believe that African-American–white differences in IQ are a "product of both genetic and environmental variation, compared to only 15 percent who feel the difference is entirely due to environmental variation. Twenty-four percent of experts do not believe there are sufficient data to support any reasonable opinion, [and 1 percent] indicate a belief in an entirely genetic determination" (1987, p. 141).

Perhaps we need not be so concerned with "how much" of a person's IQ is due to heredity and how much is due to environmental influences. Psychology has traditionally supported the dignity of the individual. It might be more appropriate for us to try to identify children *of all races* whose environments place them at risk for failure and to do what we can to enrich them.

STUDY GUIDE

EXERCISE: MATCHING

In the first column are the names of some individuals who have had an impact on cognitive psychology. In the second column are names and concepts with which they are associated. Match the concepts in the second column with the names in the first by writing as many letters as apply to the left of the names. Check your answers against those in the key, which is given below.

_____	1. Alfred Binet	A. Multiple intelligences
_____	2. Robert Sternberg	B. **g**
_____	3. Arthur Jensen	C. Stanford-Binet Intelligence Scale
_____	4. Sandra Scarr	D. Deviation IQ
_____	5. Charles Spearman	E. Determinants of intelligence
_____	6. Louis Terman	F. **s**
_____	7. Louis Thurstone	G. Triarchic theory
_____	8. David Wechsler	H. Primary mental abilities
_____	9. Benjamin Whorf	L. Word fluency
_____	10. Robert Williams	M. Linguistic-relativity hypothesis
_____	11. Raymond Cattell	N. Measurement of intelligence
_____	12. Howard Gardner	O. Mental age
_____	13. Florence Goodenough	P. Metacomponents
		Q. Culture-fair test
		R. WAIS
		S. Word fluency

Answers To Matching Exercise

1. C, N, O
2. G, P
3. N
4. E
5. B, F
6. C, N
7. H, L, N
8. D, N, R
9. M
10. E, N
11. N, Q
12. A, N
13. N, Q

ESL—BRIDGING THE GAP

This part consists of phrases and expresssions in which words are used differently from their regular meaning, or are used as metaphors.

Phrases and Expressions

our exclusive claim . . . has been questioned (288)—we say that humans are the only species that uses language, but it is possible that we are not

standard English (290)—English which is spoken with accepted grammar

barebones (290)—basics

downgraded (290)—made inferior

"To Be or Not to Be" (290)—In Shakespeare's *Hamlet,* the protagonist asks himself this question: "Is it better to be alive or dead?"

double negative (290)—two negatives in one sentence, not including "no", at the beginning of a sentence that is in answer to a question

much valued (291)—greatly appreciated

bi (292)—bye (goodbye)

allgone (292)—all gone; finished; there is no more

charming errors (292)—children's errors that amuse adults
playground (292)—a park for children which contains play equipment
boringly transformed (292)—will become uninteresting; no longer a "charming error"
taking turns (292)—not interrupting; on talking when the other is not
"color-blind" (293)—unable to distinguish colors
probably not, (293)—It probably is not true
meeting the need (293)—satisfying the need to
lay in (294)—was in
Now it's your turn (294)—I have done it and you could not, but now you have the opportunity to do it
scrap paper (294)—paper which is to be disposed of
take a breath (294)—relax and prepare yourself
have a go (294)—try it
don't peek (294)—don't look
"mainstream" linguistic alternative (295)—standard English
retrace your steps (295)—go back and draw over the same lines again
problem solvers (296)—people who solve problems
matchsticks (296)—matches
all the givens (296)—all the accepted hypotheses
as long as (296)—if
method . . . plodding (297)—the method might be slow and a little difficult
rules of thumb (297)—practical rules for solving problems
the drawback to (297)—the disadvantage to
"tried and true" (297)—different alternatives or actions have been tried, and this is the one that is best and is now accepted
Let's say that (297)—We shall imagine that
major intersection (297)—large and important area where many (at least four) streets meet or cross
most boring (297)—uninteresting
"The heck with it! . . . " (297)—I will dismiss it because I am not interested anymore
keep plugging away at it (297)—continue trying
stands for something (298)—is a symbol for something
hampering mental sets (298)—mental sets that hinder us
Is it not possible (298)—Isn't it possible
unbind us from (298)—allowed us to be free from
take an unpopular stand (299)—have a very definite opinion about something which is different from what other people have
nothing new under the sun (299)—everything has been said and done
difficult to arrive at (299)—difficult to achieve
allows "leads" to run a nearly limitless course (300)—follows ideas to their limit
Brainstorming (300)—Two or more people discussing ideas which may be opposing in order to achieve a conclusion
go hand in hand (300)—exist together
is no guarantee of (300–301)—does not promise to include
climes (301)—climate
keep you in suspense (301)—prevent you from knowing the answer
unclad bodies (301)—unclothed bodies; naked
Brute strength (301)—great strength; very strong
taken Spanish . . . taken French (301)—has studied Spanish . . . has studied French
to pin down (302)—to analyze and understand
somehow (302)—in some way, we don't know how
peek into your wallet (304)—look into the place where you keep your money
of capturing what (305)—of explaining what
tape measure (305)—a standard device for measuring short distances
unlikely to profit from (306)—probably not benefit from
spatial-relations (308)—see Table 8.5, numbers 8–11
fall within (309)—be included in the
test taker (309)—a person who is taking a test
poorly lit (309)—not enough light
charges (309)—the people they are responsible for
heralded (309)—praised
eased (309)—made easier
sound like nothing much to get excited about (309)—appears to be not important
booed loudly (309)—verbally expressed scorn and displeasure
It turns out (309)—The reason was
If so, (309)—If this is true
were echoed by (309)—were agreed to by
outscore (310)—get higher scores
mean . . . IQ (310)—average IQ
bricklaying (310)—constructing buildings with brick
"feeble-minded" (310)—retarded; did not have average intelligence
lived up to their promise (311)—have not achieved what people expected
outperform (311)—getting better scores
met with such opposition (312)—people were opposed to his views
fly in the face of (312)—contradict established opinion
to point up (312)—to illustrate; to prove
shortcomings of research (312)—does not prove what it is supposed to prove
does not generalize to (312)—does not transfer to
cannot be emphasized too strongly that (312)—it must be emphasized that
worth noting (312)—that we have to recognize the importance of
cold and impartial (313)—unfriendly and not appearing to care
later on (314)—when they are older
Still, the (314)—But, the
Even so (314)—Even with this being true, they anyway; in spite of
closed a good deal of the IQ gap (314)—made the discrepancy less; reduced the difference

CHAPTER REVIEW

Section 1: Language

Objective 1: Define *language.*

Language is the communication of thoughts and feelings through (1) s________________. These symbols are arranged according to rules of (2) ________________ar.

Objective 2: Explain the three properties of language.

Language has the properties of (3) sem________________, productivity, and (4) ________________ment. Semanticity means that words serve as (5) ________________ls for actions, objects, and relational concepts. Productivity refers to the capacity to combine (6) ________________s into original sentences. Displacement is the capacity to communicate (7) in________________ about objects or events in another time or place.

SECTION 2: Patterns of Language Development

Objective 3: Trace the development of language.

Children cry at birth and begin to (8) c________________ by about two months. (9) ________________s are frequently vowel-like and may resemble repeated "oohs" and "ahs." Cooing appears associated with feelings of (10) ________________sure.

(11) ________________ling is the first kind of vocalization that has the sound of speech. Babbling appears at about six months and contains (12) ________________emes found in many languages. Babbling is innate, although it can be modified by learning. Crying, cooing, and babbling are all (13) pre________________ events. They are prelinguistic because they lack (14) ________________city.

Children speak their first words at about the age of (15) ________________. Children try to talk about more objects than they have words for, and so they often (16) over________________ the meaning of one word to refer to things and actions for which they do not have words.

Children first use (17) ________________-word utterances. These utterances express the meanings found in complete sentences and are referred to as (18) ________________phic speech. Two-word telegraphic utterances appear toward the end of the (19)________________d year.

Children also use (20) over________________izations, as in "I seed it" and "Mommy sitted down." The "errors" made in overregularizing indicate a grasp of the rules of (21) ________________ar.

SECTION 3: Language and Thought

Objective 4: Discuss the relationships between language and thought.

Thought is possible without (22) ________________age, but language facilitates thought. According to the (23) ________________-relativity hypothesis, language structures (and limits) the way in which we perceive the world. Critics argue that a (24) ________________lary may suggest the concepts deemed important by the users of a language; however, vocabulary limits do not necessarily prevent language users from making distinctions for which there are no (25) ________________ds.

SECTION 4: Problem Solving

Objective 5: Describe the stages of problem solving.

Problem solving involves stages of preparation, (26) ________________tion, trial, and (27) ________________tion. We prepare ourselves to solve a problem by (28) ________________izing ourselves with its elements and clearly defining our (29) ________________s. Then we try to produce alternate (30) ________________tions. We try them out (overtly or cognitively) and (31) ________________ate whether a solution has met our goals.

Objective 6: Explain the roles of algorithms and heuristic devices in problem solving.

(32) ________________thms are specific procedures for solving problems (such as formulas) that will work invariably, so long as they are applied correctly. (33) ________________tics are rules of thumb that help us simplify and solve problems. (34) H________________ are less reliable than algorithms, but they allow us to solve problems more rapidly when they are effective.

Objective 7: Define *incubation effect.*

When we cannot find a solution to a problem, distancing ourselves from the problem sometimes allows the solution to (35) ________bate. Incubation may permit the breaking down of misleading mental (36) ________s.

Objective 8: Explain how mental sets and functional fixedness impede problem solving.

A (37) ________ set is the tendency to solve a new problem in ways in which similar problems were solved in the past. Functional (38) ________ss is the tendency to perceive an object in terms of its intended function or name, and can prevent novel use of familiar objects.

Objective 9: Discuss the relationships between problem solving, creativity, and intelligence.

Creativity is the ability to make unusual and sometimes remote (39) ________tions to the elements of a problem in order to generate new combinations that meet the goals. Creative people show (40) fl________, fluency, and (41) ________ence. Creativity demands (42) ________gent thinking rather than (43) ________gent thinking.

There is only a moderate relationship between creativity and (44) ________gence. Persons low in intelligence are usually also low in (45) cr________. However, high (46) int________ is no guarantee of creativity.

SECTION 5: Intelligence

Objective 10: Define *intelligence.*

Intelligence is a (47) t________ that helps explain why people do things that are adaptive and inventive. (48) ________ment is what a person has learned, the knowledge and skills gained through experience. (49) In________is presumed to make academic achievement possible. Wechsler defined intelligence as "capacity . . . to (50) u________ the world [and] resourcefulness to cope with its challenges."

SECTION 7: Theories of Intelligence

Objective 11: Discuss factor theories of intelligence.

Spearman believed that a common factor called (51) ________ underlay all intelligent behavior. He also theorized that people also have specific abilities, or (52) ________ factors.

Thurstone suggested that there are nine (53) p________ ________al abilities. His primary mental abilities included (54) w________ fluency and numerical ability.

Objective 12: Discuss cognitive theories of intelligence.

Cognitive theorists view intelligence in terms of (55) ________tion processing.

Sternberg has constructed a (56) ________ level, or triarchic, model of intelligence. The three levels are (57) ________tual, experiential, and (58) ________tial. The contextual level allows people to adapt to the demands of the social and physical (59) ________ments. On the (60) ________tial level, intelligent behavior is defined by the abilities to cope with novel situations and to process information automatically. The componential level consists of three processes: (61) m________nents, performance components, and (62) ________-acquisition components. Metacomponents are involved in deciding what (63) ________lem to solve, selecting appropriate strategies and formulas, and (64) ________ring the solution. Performance components include (65) ________ding information, combining and comparing pieces of information, and generating a solution. (66) ________-acquisition components are used in gaining new knowledge. They include encoding (67) ________tion, combining pieces of information, and comparing new information with what is already known.

SECTION 7: Measurement of Intelligence

Objective 13: Show how the concepts of reliability and validity are applied to the measurement of intelligence.

Intelligence tests must be reliable and valid, features that are expressed in terms of (68) ________tion coefficients. Reliability is the (69) ________ency of a test. A commonly used measure of reliability is (70) ________-retest reliability, which is shown by comparing scores of tests taken on different occasions. (71)

__________ity is the degree to which a test measures that which it is supposed to measure. Validity is usually assessed by comparing test scores to an external (72) __________ion. One frequently used external criterion is (73) __________ic success.

Objective 14: Describe the features of the Stanford-Binet and Wechsler scales.

Intelligence tests yield scores called intelligence (74) __________nts, or *IQs.* The Stanford-Binet Intelligence Scale (SBIS) was originated by the Frenchman Alfred (75) __________ to identify children that needed special attention. The SBIS derives IQ scores by dividing children's (76) __________-age scores by their chronological ages, then multiplying by 100.

The Wechsler scales use (77) __________tion IQs, which are derived by comparing a person's performance to that of agemates. Wechsler scales contain verbal and (78) __________ance subtests. The average (mean) IQ score on a Wechsler test is (79) __________, and (80) __________ percent of the scores fall within the broad average range of 90–110.

Objective 15: Explain the concept of cultural bias and how psychologists have tried to create culture-fair intelligence tests.

Intelligence test scores reflect (81) m__________ to do well and (82) ad__________ in the school setting as well as learning ability. Some psychologists argue that intelligence tests are (83) __________ally biased in favor of middle-class white children. As a consequence, efforts have been made to develop (84) __________-fair or culture-free tests. However, culture-fair tests are (85: better or worse?) predictors of academic success.

SECTION 8: The Determinants of Intelligence

Objective 16: Summarize research concerning genetic and environmental influences on intelligence.

Research into the genetic determinants of human intelligence tends to rely on kinship studies and studies of the intelligence of (86) __________ees. The IQ scores of (87) __________al (MZ) twins are more alike than the scores for any other pairs. This finding holds even when identical twins have been (88) __________red apart. There is a (89: stronger or weaker?) relationship between the IQ scores of adopted children and their biological parents than there is with their adoptive parents.

Evidence for the importance of environmental factors stems from research into the effects of the early environment, including school (90) __________ Start programs, and studies of adoptees. Maternal factors that contribute to IQ scores include (91) __________nal and verbal responsiveness, personal involvement, and provision of varied daily experiences. Children in Head (92) __________ programs make significant and lasting intellectual gains. African-American children who are adopted by white parents before the age of one year show (93: higher or lower?) IQ scores than those attained by African-American children who are reared by their natural parents.

The largest group of psychologists and educational specialists conclude that black–white differences in IQ are a "product of both (94) __________tic and (95) __________mental variation."

Answers To Chapter Review

1. Symbols
2. Grammar
3. Semanticity
4. Displacement
5. Symbols
6. Words
7. Information
8. Coo
9. Coos
10. Pleasure
11. Babbling
12. Phonemes
13. Prelinguistic
14. Semanticity
15. One (12 months)
16. Overextend
17. One
18. Telegraphic
19. Second
20. Overgeneralizations
21. Grammar
22. Language
23. Linguistic
24. Vocabulary
25. Words
26. Production
27. Evaluation
28. Familiarizing
29. Goals
30. Solutions
31. Evaluate
32. Algorithms
33. Heuristics
34. Heuristics
35. Incubate
36. Sets
37. Mental
38. Fixedness
39. Associations
40. Flexibility
41. Independence
42. Divergent
43. Convergent
44. Intelligence

45. Creativity
46. Intelligence
47. Trait
48. Achievement
49. Intelligence
50. Understand
51. **g**
52. **s**
53. Primary mental
54. Word
55. Information
56. Three
57. Contextual
58. Componential
59. Environments
60. Experiential
61. Metacomponents
62. Knowledge
63. Problem
64. Monitoring
65. Encoding
66. Knowledge
67. Information
68. Correlation
69. Consistency
70. Test
71. Validity
72. Criterion
73. Academic
74. Quotients
75. Binet
76. Mental
77. Deviation
78. Performance
79. 100
80. 50
81. Motivation
82. Adjustment
83. Culturally
84. Culture
85. Worse
86. Adoptees
87. Identical
88. Reared
89. Stronger
90. Head
91. Emotional
92. Start
93. Higher
94. Genetic
95. Environmental

POSTTEST

1. According to Roger Brown, the "important thing about language" is that
   (a) only people can use language.
   (b) thought is not possible without language.
   (c) language is made possible by a language-acquisition device.
   (d) language makes life experiences cumulative.

2. The language characteristic of semanticity means that
   (a) words can mean whatever we want them to mean.
   (b) sentences have surface and deep structures.
   (c) words serve as symbols.
   (d) children have an intuitive grasp of meaning.

3. Which of the following occurs first?
   (a) babbling
   (b) holophrases
   (c) cooing
   (d) overextension

4. Which of the following is true about two-word utterances?
   (a) The order of appearance of types of two-word utterances is the same for such diverse languages as Russian, Luo, and Turkish.
   (b) The order of appearance of types of two-word utterances is the same for different European languages only.
   (c) The appearance of two-word utterances shows that conditioning does not play a role in language development.
   (d) The word order in two-word utterances tends to be haphazard.

5. A 3-year-old old says, "Mommy goed away." This statement is an example of
   (a) failure to understand grammar.
   (b) overregularization.
   (c) overextension.
   (d) understanding of deep structure, but not surface structure.

6. Which of the following considers musical talent to be a form of intelligence?
   (a) Jensen
   (b) Gardner
   (c) Sternberg
   (d) Binet

7. According to the linguistic relativity hypothesis,
   (a) language structures the ways in which we perceive the world.
   (b) different cultures have different numbers of words for snow.
   (c) concepts are innate.
   (d) words are relative to linguistics.

8. Which of the following developed the linguistic relativity hypothesis?
   (a) Spearman
   (b) Whorf
   (c) Terman
   (d) Thurstone

9. An algorithm is a(n)
   (a) grammatical marker.
   (b) example of a heuristic device.
   (c) specific procedure for solving a problem.
   (d) mental set.

10. The Maier two-string problem is a demonstration of the role of ________ in problem solving.
    (a) mental sets
    (b) the incubation effect
    (c) means-end analysis
    (d) functional fixedness

11. Joan says that Jane must be extremely intelligent because she has created a number of original musical compositions. You show off your knowledge of introductory psychology by making an accurate statement of the relationship between creativity and intelligence. You note that

(a) high intelligence suggests at least moderate creativity.
(b) high intelligence suggests high creativity.
(c) high creativity suggests at least moderate intelligence.
(d) high creativity suggests low intelligence.

12. The symbol **g** was used by Spearman to signify
(a) general intelligence.
(b) primary mental abilities.
(c) the ability to do well on intelligence tests.
(d) IQ, but not intelligence.

13. According to Sternberg, deciding what problem to solve and selecting appropriate strategies and formulas are examples of the _______ of intellectual functioning.
(a) performance components
(b) experiential level
(c) metacomponents
(d) contextual level

14. The reliability of an intelligence test is its
(a) relationship to an external criterion.
(b) ability to predict academic performance.
(c) means-end analysis.
(d) consistency.

15. A friend says, "We run experiments to find out everything else, so why can't we run experiments to find out exactly how much of a person's intelligence is due to heredity and how much is due to the environment?" You point out that we do not have experimental evidence concerning the genetic determinants of human intelligence because
(a) it would be unethical to selectively breed people.
(b) it is theoretically impossible to separate the effects of heredity and the environment.
(c) data from kinship and adoptee studies has been faked.
(d) psychologists have not been able to agree on the definition of intelligence in humans.

16. The Stanford-Binet IQ was computed by the formula:
(a) (CA/MA) × 100.
(b) (CA–MA) × 100.
(c) (MA/CA) × 100.
(d) (MA–CA) × 100.

17. Arthur Jensen has become known for
(a) constructing culture-fair intelligence tests.
(b) asserting that intelligence is largely genetically determined.
(c) research in Head Start programs.
(d) falsifying data in identical-twin studies of intelligence.

18. The IQ scores of _______ show the highest correlations.
(a) identical twins reared together
(b) fraternal twins reared together
(c) identical twins reared apart
(d) fraternal twins reared apart

19. You are visiting your old high school, and a former teacher says to you, "You're taking psychology. Does it matter how children are treated while they are taking intelligence tests?" You clear your throat and say, "In a study by Zigler and his colleagues, children were made as comfortable as possible during intelligence testing. The results showed that
(a) test scores decreased for children made most comfortable."
(b) test scores were 15 points higher than those for a control group."
(c) middle-class children made relatively greater gains from this procedure."
(d) disadvantaged children made relatively greater gains from this procedure."

20. The largest group of psychologists and educational specialists voice the opinion that
(a) intelligence reflects the interaction of heredity and environmental influences.
(b) only heredity really influences intelligence.
(c) only environmental influences really affect the development of intelligence.
(d) neither heredity nor the environment has a meaningful influence on intelligence.

Answers To Pretest

1. D	**6.** B	**11.** C	**16.** C
2. C	**7.** A	**12.** A	**17.** B
3. C	**8.** B	**13.** C	**18.** A
4. A	**9.** C	**14.** D	**19.** D
5. B	**10.** D	**15.** A	**20.** A

- Baseball pitchers with multiyear contracts perform just as well as pitchers who have to scrap for raises from season to season.
- Americans overeat by enough to feed the nation of Germany.
- Homosexuals suffer from hormonal imbalances.
- Getting away from it all by going on a vacation from all sensory input for a few hours is relaxing.
- If quarterbacks get too "psyched up" for a big game, their performance on the field may suffer.
- Misery loves company.
- You may be able to fool a lie detector by squiggling your toes.

Motivation and Emotion

Learning Objectives

When you have finished studying Chapter 9, you should be able to:

Motives, Needs, Drives, and Incentives

1. Define *motives, needs, drives,* and *incentives*.
2. Discuss various theories of motivation.

Physiological Drives

3. Define *homeostasis.*
4. Discuss contributors to the hunger drive.
5. Summarize research concerning obesity.
6. Explain the organizing and activating effects of sex hormones.
7. Discuss the origins of homosexuality.

Stimulus Motives

8. Define *stimulus motive.*
9. Describe the effects of sensory deprivation.
10. Define *optimal arousal,* and explain the Yerkes-Dodson law.

Social Motives

11. Define *social motive.*
12. Discuss the need for achievement.
13. Discuss the need for affiliation.

Emotion

14. Describe the role of emotions in human behavior.
15. Discuss lie detectors.
16. Discuss whether or not ways of expressing emotions are universal.
17. Explain the facial-feedback hypothesis.
18. Evaluate the James-Lange, Cannon-Bard, and cognitive-appraisal theories of emotion.

Pitchers Dwight Gooden and Roger Clemens each hurl $5 million a year into their treasure chests, whether they win 20 games or 2. Sluggers José Canseco and Bobby Bonilla each smack millions into their bank accounts each year, whether they hit .350 or .200. Because players cannot be bound indefinitely to the teams that first sign them, owners try to tie up their stars for as many years as they can. And the stars often receive salaries so high in their multiyear contracts that they are enriched whether they help the team to win or lose in a given season.

Richard O'Brien and his colleagues at Hofstra University compiled statistical evidence that suggests that multiyear contracts take some of the hustle out of professional baseball players—especially pitchers. They examined the records of 38 pitchers for three years before and after they signed multiyear contracts, and they compared their play to that of 38 randomly chosen pitchers who had signed single-season contracts for the same period.

As long as they had to get their contracts renewed each year, the players who eventually won long-term berths improved steadily, from an average of 3.66 earned runs scored against them per game to 2.91. After signing their long-term agreements, however, their earned run averages (ERAs) climbed to an average of 4.04 three years later. Pitchers with one-year contracts showed no consistent pattern over the same period. Multiyear contracts apparently sap the motivation of professional athletes.

Actually, the performance of pitchers with multiyear contracts declines in comparison to that of pitchers with single-season contracts. Could it be that guaranteed wealth saps the motivation of pitchers with multiyear contracts?

The researchers recommend that owners combine a base salary with incentive payments for achieving goals such as a specified ERA or batting average. Negotiated performance targets, they say, "would allow equitable rewards for productive seasons for all players." Many owners do just this, but the base salaries are often so high that the incentives aren't much of an . . . incentive.

Incentives are only one kind of motive. In this chapter, we explore motivation and the closely related topic of emotion. Five million dollars a year might strike you as rather motivating—at least under most normal circumstances. Five "mill" a year also gives rise to some rather powerful emotional responses—especially among fans. Seventy-one percent of the American people believe that baseball players make too much (Thomas, 1991). How many think that baseball players receive too little for their services? One percent.

The psychology of motivation is concerned with the *whys* of behavior. Why do we eat and drink? Why do some of us ride motorcycles at breakneck speeds? Why do we try new things or strive to get ahead?

Let us begin with some definitions.

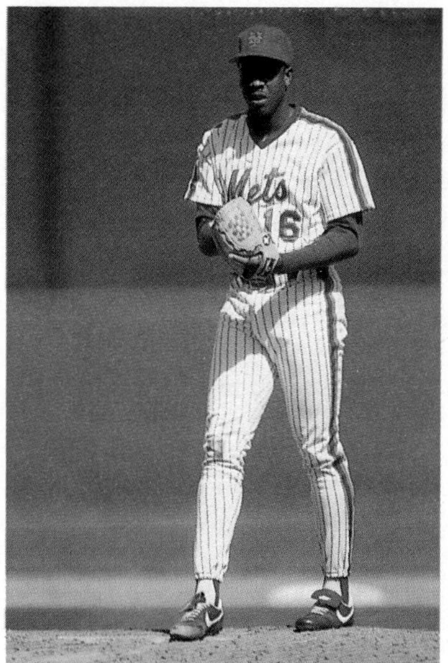

They May Be Rich, But Are They Motivated? Mets' ace Dwight Gooden (left) gets ready to hurl a fast ball. Athletics' slugger José Canseco (right) slams one into the stands. When professional athletes receive lucrative multiyear contracts, do they have sufficient incentive to offer their best game after game?

MOTIVES, NEEDS, DRIVES, AND INCENTIVES

The word *motive* derives from the Latin *movere,* meaning "to move." **Motives** are defined as hypothetical states within organisms that activate behavior and propel the organisms toward goals. Why do we say "hypothetical states"? We say so because motives are not seen and measured directly. Like many other psychological concepts, they are inferred from behavior. Psychologists assume that behavior does not occur at random. We assume that behavior is caused; the behavior of organisms is assumed to be largely caused by motives. *Needs, drives,* and *incentives* are closely related concepts.

The term **need** has been used in at least two different ways by psychologists. We speak of both physiological needs and psychological needs. Certain physiological needs must be met if we are to survive. They include oxygen, food, drink, pain avoidance, proper temperature, and the elimination of waste products. Some physiological needs such as hunger and thirst are states of physical deprivation. For instance, when we have not eaten or drunk for a while, we develop needs for food and water. We speak of the body as having needs for oxygen, fluids, calories, vitamins, minerals, and so on.

Psychological needs include needs for achievement, power, self-esteem, social approval, and belonging, among others. Psychological needs differ from physiological needs in two important ways: First, psychological needs are not necessarily based on states of deprivation; a person with a strong need for achievement may have a history of consistent success. Second, psychological needs may be acquired through experience, or learned, whereas physiological needs reside in the physical makeup of the organism. Because our biological makeups are similar, we would assume that people share similar physiological needs. And because our learning experiences differ, we would expect that people differ markedly in their psychological needs. In the section on social motives, we shall see that this is indeed the case.

Needs are said to give rise to **drives.** Depletion of food gives rise to the hunger drive, and depletion of liquids gives rise to the thirst drive. Physiological drives are the psychological counterparts of physiological needs. When we have gone without food and water, our bodies may *need* these substances; however, our *experience* of drives of hunger and thirst is psychological in nature. Drives

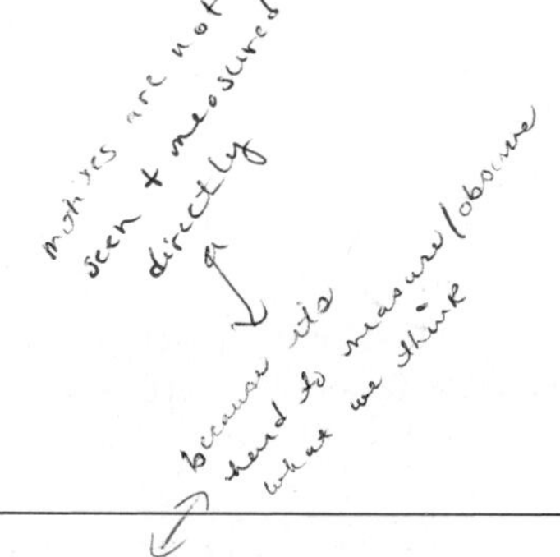

Motive A hypothetical state within an organism that propels the organism toward a goal.

Need A state of deprivation.

Drive A condition of arousal in an organism that is associated with a need.

arouse us to action. Our drive levels tend to increase with the length of time we have been deprived. We are usually more highly aroused by the hunger drive when we have not eaten for several hours than when we have not eaten for, say, 5 minutes.

Our psychological needs for approval, achievement, and belonging also give rise to drives. We can be driven to get ahead in the world of business just as surely as we can be driven to eat. For many of us, the drives for achievement and power consume our daily lives.

An **incentive** is an object, person, or situation perceived as being capable of satisfying a need or desirable for its own sake. Money, food, a sexually attractive person, social approval, and attention all can act as incentives that motivate behavior. Needs and incentives can interact to influence the strength of drives. Strong needs combined with enticing incentives create the most powerful drives. Even a person who has just eaten may be tempted by a chocolate dessert. A colleague with whom I eat lunch once said, "That pie looks so good it creates its own drive." A rat will run down a maze more rapidly when it whiffs Limburger cheese than when it has learned to expect Purina Rat Chow. The Limburger cheese acts as an incentive that heightens the hunger drive. A dog will eat steak more rapidly than it will eat Purina Dog Chow. I'll show that I have nothing against the Purina folks by adding that you are probably more motivated to buy Purina Dog Chow when it is on a limited-time-only, half-price sale. That is, you may respond to the financial *incentive.*

In the following section, we explore theories of motivation—that is, we ask the question: Just what is so motivating about motives? Psychologists and others have spawned very different views of the motives that propel us.

THEORETICAL PERSPECTIVES ON MOTIVATION

Although psychologists agree that it is important to understand why people and lower animals do things, they do not agree about the nature of motivation. Let us consider four theoretical perspectives on motivation: the instinct, drive-reduction, humanistic, and cognitive theories.

Instinct Theory

Animals are born with preprogrammed tendencies to respond to certain situations in certain ways. Birds reared in isolation from other birds build nests during the mating season even though they have never observed another bird building a nest (or, for that matter, seen a nest). Siamese fighting fish reared in isolation assume stereotypical threatening stances and attack other males when they are introduced into their tanks.

Behaviors such as these are characteristic of particular species (species-specific) and do not rely on learning. They are called **instincts.** Spiders spin webs. Bees "dance" to communicate the location of food to other bees. All this activity is inborn. It is genetically transmitted from generation to generation.

Ethologists label instincts **fixed-action patterns** (or FAPs). FAPs occur in response to stimuli that ethologists call **releasers.** Male members of many species are sexually aroused by pheromones secreted by females. Pheromones "release" the FAP of sexual response.

At the turn of the century, psychologists William James (1890) and William McDougall (1908) argued that people have instincts that foster self-survival and social behavior. James asserted that we have social instincts such as love, sympathy, and modesty. McDougall compiled 12 "basic" instincts, including hunger, sex, and self-assertion. Other psychologists have catalogued longer lists.

Incentive An object, person, or situation perceived as being capable of satisfying a need.

Instinct An inherited disposition to activate specific behavior patterns that are designed to reach certain goals.

Ethologist A scientist who studies the behavior patterns characteristic of different species.

Fixed-action pattern An instinct; abbreviated FAP.

Releaser In ethology, a stimulus that elicits a FAP.

A Fixed-Action Pattern. In the presence of other males, Siamese Fighting Fish assume instinctive threatening stances in which they circle one another while they extend their fins and gills. If neither male retreats, there will be conflict.

The psychoanalyst Sigmund Freud also used the term *instincts* to refer to physiological needs within people. Freud believed that the instincts of sex and aggression give rise to *psychic energy,* which is perceived as a feeling of tension. Tension motivates us to restore ourselves to a calmer, resting state. The behavior patterns we use to reduce the tension are largely learned.

The psychodynamic views of Sigmund Freud also coincide reasonably well with those of a group of learning theorists who presented a drive-reduction theory of learning.

Drive-Reduction Theory

Rewards are defined as pleasant events that increase the frequency of behavior. But what makes them pleasant?

According to **drive-reduction theory,** as framed by psychologist Clark Hull at Yale University in the 1930s, rewards are pleasant because they reduce drives. Hull argued that **primary drives** such as hunger, thirst, and pain trigger arousal (tension) and activate behavior. We learn responses that partially or completely reduce the drives. Through association, we also learn **acquired drives.** We may acquire a drive for money because money enables us to attain food, drink, and homes that protect us from predators and extremes of temperature. We might acquire drives for social approval and affiliation because other people, and their good will, also help us to reduce primary drives, especially when we are infants. In all cases, tension reduction is the goal.

Drive-reduction theory The view that organisms learn to engage in behaviors that have the effect of reducing drives.

Primary drives Unlearned, or physiological, drives.

Acquired drives Drives that are acquired through experience, or learned.

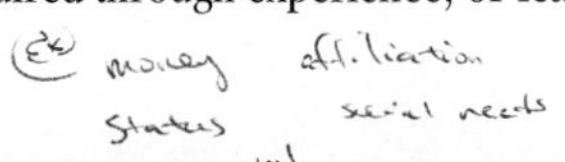

Humanistic Theory

Humanistic psychologists, particularly Abraham Maslow, note that the instinct and drive-reduction theories of motivation are basically defensive. These theories suggest that human behavior occurs in rather mechanical fashion and is aimed toward survival and tension reduction. As a humanist, Maslow asserted that behavior is also motivated by the conscious desire for personal growth. Humanists note that people will tolerate pain, hunger, and many other sources of tension to achieve what they perceive as personal fulfillment.

Abraham Maslow and the Hierarchy of Needs. Maslow was fond of asking graduate students, "How many of you expect to achieve greatness

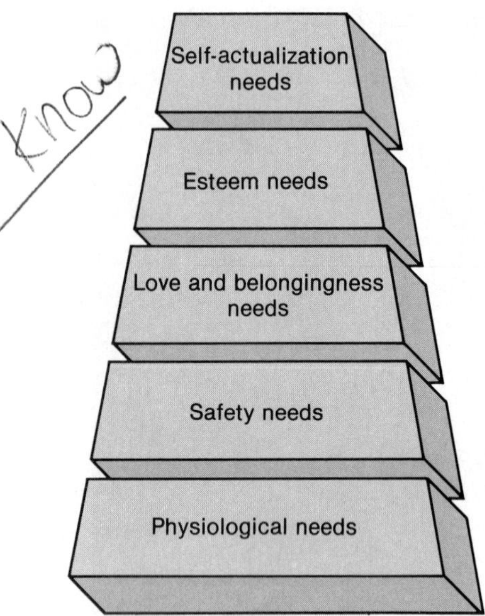

FIGURE 9.1
Maslow's Hierarchy of Needs. Maslow believed that we progress toward higher psychological needs once basic survival needs have been net. Where do you fit in this picture?

in your careers?" He would prod them to extend themselves, because he believed that people are capable of doing more than responding to drives. Maslow believed that we are separated from lower animals by our capacity for **self-actualization,** or self-initiated striving to become whatever we believe we are capable of being. In fact, Maslow saw self-actualization to be as essential a human need as hunger.

Maslow (1970) organized human needs into a hierarchy, from physiological needs such as hunger and thirst, through self-actualization (see Figure 9.1.) He believed that in our lives we would naturally travel up through this hierarchy as long as we did not encounter insurmountable social or environmental hurdles. Maslow was optimistic about human nature. Whereas some psychologists believed in aggressive instincts, Maslow believed that people acted aggressively only when needs were frustrated, particularly the needs for love and acceptance.

Maslow's needs hierarchy includes the following:

1. *Physiological needs:* hunger, thirst, elimination, warmth, fatigue, pain avoidance, sexual release.
2. *Safety needs:* protection from the environment through housing and clothing; security from crime and financial hardship.
3. *Love and belongingness needs:* love and acceptance through intimate relationships, social groups, and friends. Maslow believed that in a generally well-fed society such as ours, much frustration stemmed from failure to meet needs at this level.
4. *Esteem needs:* achievement, competence, approval, recognition, prestige, status.
5. *Self-actualization:* fulfillment of our unique potentials. For many individuals, self-actualization involves needs for cognitive understanding (novelty, exploration, knowledge) and aesthetic needs (music, art, poetry, beauty, order).

Cognitive Theory

According to cognitive theorists such as Robert Rescorla (1988), Jean Piaget, and George Kelly (1955), people mentally represent the world around them. Piaget and Kelly hypothesize that people are born "scientists" who innately strive to understand the world around them so that they can predict and control events. Social-learning theorists Albert Bandura (1989, 1991) and Julian Rotter (1972, 1990) assert that people are motivated by their expectations. On the basis of experience and reasoning, people expect that certain behaviors will lead to certain outcomes, and they behave in ways that will enable them to achieve (or avert) these outcomes.

Other cognitive theorists such as Leon Festinger (1957) assert that people are also motivated to achieve cognitive consistency. Festinger believed that people are motivated to hold harmonious beliefs and to justify their behavior (see Chapter 15). That is why we are more likely to appreciate things we must work for.

Evaluation

Instinct theory has been criticized for yielding circular explanations of behavior. If we say that mothers love and care for their children because of a maternal instinct, and then we take maternal care as evidence for such an instinct, we have come full circle. But we have explained nothing. We have only repeated ourselves.

Instincts are also species-specific. That is, they occur within a given species. They give rise to stereotypical behaviors in all members of a class (such as adult females) within that species. There is so much variation in human behavior that it seems unlikely that much of it is instinctive. Consider William James's notion that sympathy is an instinct. Many people are cruel and cold-hearted; are we to assume

Self-actualization According to Maslow and other humanistic psychologists, self-initiated striving to become what one is capable of being. The motive to reach one's full potential, to express one's unique capabilities.

that they somehow possess less of this instinct? If so, this assumption is incompatible with the definition of an instinct.

Drive-reduction theory appears to apply in many situations involving physiological drives such as hunger and thirst. It runs aground, however, when we consider the evidence that we often act to increase, rather than decrease, the tensions acting on us. Even when hungry, we might go to lengthy efforts to prepare a meal instead of a snack, although the snack would reduce the hunger drive as well. We drive fast cars, ride roller coasters, and sky-dive for sport—all activities that heighten rather than decrease arousal. We often seek novel ways of doing things because of the stimulation they afford, shunning the tried and true. Yet, the tried and true would lead to tension reduction more reliably. Other psychologists have theorized the existence of "stimulus motives" that surmount the limitations of drive-reduction theory.

Critics of Maslow argue that there is too much individual variation for the hierarchy of motivation to apply to everyone. Some people whose physiological, safety, and love needs are met show little interest in achievement and recognition. Others seek distant, self-actualizing goals while exposing themselves to great danger. Some artists, musicians, and writers devote themselves fully to their art, even at the price of poverty.

Some psychologists criticize cognitive theory for its reliance on unobservable concepts such as expectations, rather than observable behavior. Other psychologists question whether the motives to understand and manipulate the environment are inborn or acquired as we learn that understanding allows us to satisfy physiological drives such as hunger and thirst.

Perhaps no theory of motivation explains all of psychologists' observations or satisfies all objections. Yet, there is a wealth of research on motivation. Let us first consider drives that arise from physiological needs. Then we shall turn our attention to stimulus motives and social motives.

PHYSIOLOGICAL DRIVES

Physiological needs give rise to **physiological drives**—aroused conditions within the organism that activate behavior that will reduce these needs. Because physiological drives are unlearned, they are also referred to as primary drives. Though sexual behavior allows survival of the species instead of survival of the individual, sex is also considered a primary drive.

Primary drives are inborn, but learning influences the *behavior* that satisfies them. Eating meat or fish, drinking coffee or tea, kissing lips or rubbing noses are all learned preferences.

Homeostasis. Physiological drives operate largely according to principles of drive reduction. Mechanisms in the body are triggered when we are in a state of deprivation. These mechanisms then motivate us—through sensations such as hunger, thirst, and cold—to act to restore the balance. The bodily tendency to maintain a steady state is called **homeostasis.**

Homeostasis works much like a thermostat. When the room temperature drops below the set point, the heating system is triggered. The heat stays on until the set point is reached. The body's homeostatic systems involve fascinating interactions between physiological and psychological processes.

HUNGER

Some of us bounce up and down in weight because of cycles of binge eating and dieting, but most of us maintain remarkably constant weights over the years (Keesey, 1986). What bodily mechanisms regulate the hunger drive? What psychological processes are at work?

Physiological drives Unlearned drives with a biological basis, such as hunger, thirst, and avoidance of pain.

Homeostasis The tendency of the body to maintain a steady state.

Hunger. How do *you* feel while you wait for someone to carve the meat? Hunger is a physiological drive that motivates us to eat. What makes us feel hungry? What makes us feel satiated? Why do many of us continue to eat when we have already supplied our bodies with the needed nutrients?

The Mouth. Let us begin with the mouth—an appropriate choice since we are discussing eating. Chewing and swallowing provide some sensations of **satiety.** If they did not, we might eat for a long time after we had taken in enough food; it takes the digestive tract time to metabolize food and provide signals of satiety to the brain by way of the bloodstream.

In classic "sham-feeding" experiments with dogs, a tube was implanted in the animals' throats so that any food swallowed fell out of the body. Even though no food arrived at the stomach, the animals stopped feeding after a brief period (Janowitz & Grossman, 1949). However, they resumed feeding sooner than animals whose food did reach the stomach.

Let us proceed to the stomach, too, as we seek other regulatory factors in hunger.

Stomach Contractions.

> *I go by tummy-time and I want my dinner.*
>
> Sir Winston Churchill

An empty stomach will lead to stomach contractions, which we call hunger pangs. These pangs are not as influential as had once been thought. People and animals whose stomachs have been removed still regulate food intake to maintain a normal weight level. This finding led to the discovery of many other regulatory mechanisms including blood sugar level, the hypothalamus, and even receptors in the liver.

Blood-Sugar Level. When we are deprived of food, the level of sugar in the blood drops. The deficit is communicated to the hypothalamus (see Chapter 3). The drop in blood sugar apparently indicates that we have been burning energy and need to replenish it by eating.

Experiments with the Hypothalamus: The Search for "Start-Eating" and "Stop-Eating" Centers in the Brain. If you were just reviving from a surgical operation, fighting your way through the fog of the anesthesia, food would probably be that last thing on your mind. But when rats are operated on and a **lesion** in the **ventromedial nucleus** (VMN) of the hypothalamus is made, they will grope toward their food supplies as soon as their eyes open. Then they eat vast quantities of Purina Rat Chow or whatever else they can find.

Satiety The state of being satisfied; fullness.

Lesion An injury that results in impaired behavior or loss of a function.

Ventromedial nucleus A central area on the underside of the hypothalamus that appears to function as a stop-eating center.

FIGURE 9.2
A Hyperphagic Rat. This rodent winner of the basketball look-alike contest went on a binge after it received a lesion in the ventromedial nucleus (VMN) of the hypothalamus. It is as if the lesion pushed the "set point" for body weight up several notches, and the rat's weight is now about five times normal. But now it eats only enough to maintain its pleasantly plump stature, so you need not be concerned that it will eventually burst. If the lesion had been made in the lateral hypothalamus, the animal might have become the "Twiggy" of the rat world.

The VMN might function like a stop-eating center in the rat's brain (Novin et al., 1976). If the VMN is electrically stimulated—that is, "switch it on"—a rat will stop eating until the current is turned off. When the VMN is lesioned, the rat becomes **hyperphagic.** It will continue to eat until it has about doubled its normal weight (see Figure 9.2). Then it will level off its eating and maintain the higher weight. It is as if the set point of the stop-eating center has been raised to a higher level (Keesey & Powley, 1986).

VMN-lesioned rats are also more finicky about their food. They will eat more fats or sweet-tasting food, but they will actually eat less if their food is salty or bitter (Kimble, 1988).

The **lateral hypothalamus** might be a start-eating center in the rat's brain. If you electrically stimulate the lateral hypothalamus, the rat will start to eat. If you make a lesion in the lateral hypothalamus, the rat may stop eating altogether—that is, become **aphagic.** If you force-feed an aphagic rat for a while, however, it will begin to eat on its own and level off at a relatively low body weight. You have lowered the rat's set point. It is like turning the thermostat down from, say, 70 degrees Fahrenheit to 40 degrees Fahrenheit.

Receptors in the Liver. Other research suggests that receptors in the liver are also important in regulating hunger (Friedman & Stricker, 1976). These receptors appear to be sensitive to the blood-sugar level. In a state of food deprivation, blood sugar is low, and these receptors send rapid messages to the brain. After a meal, the blood-sugar level rises, and the receptors' rate of firing decreases (Novin et al., 1983).

Although many areas of the body work in concert to regulate the hunger drive, this is only part of the story. In human beings, the hunger drive is more complex. Psychological as well as physiological factors play an important role, as we see in our discussion of obesity.

Obesity

Consider a few facts about obesity:

Forty percent of Americans consider themselves overweight (Burros, 1988), and 35 percent want to lose at least 15 pounds (Toufexis et al., 1986).

One out of four American adults is obese—that is, weighs more than 20 percent above his or her recommended weight (Kuczmarski, 1992).

Eleven million American adults are severely obese (Wallis, 1985), exceeding their desirable body weight by at least 40 percent.

Americans consume 815 billion calories of food each day, which is 200 billion calories more than are necessary to maintain their weight (Jenkins, 1988). The excess calories could feed a nation of 80 million people (Jenkins, 1988).

Americans do overeat by enough to feed the nation of Germany—80 million people!

At any given time, 25 to 50 percent of the adult American population is on a diet (Bouchard, 1991), and they use about 30,000 different approaches (Blumenthal, 1988).

The number of women dieters significantly exceeds men (Toufexis et al., 1986).

Within one year after dieting, the average dieter regains 36 percent of the weight that had been lost (Brownell & Wadden, 1986).

Hyperphagic Characterized by excessive eating.

Lateral hypothalamus An area at the side of the hypothalamus that appears to function as a start-eating center.

Aphagic Characterized by undereating.

Within a few years, at least two-thirds of "successful" dieters regain every pound they have lost—and then some (Toufexis et al., 1986).

Obesity is pervasive, yet the obese encounter more than their fair share of illnesses, including cardiovascular diseases, diabetes, gout, respiratory problems, even certain kinds of cancer (Leary, 1991; Manson et al., 1990; Sorlie et al., 1980). If obesity is connected with health problems and unhappiness with the image reflected in the mirror, why do so many people overeat? Psychological research has made major and sometimes startling contributions to our knowledge concerning why so many people are obese and what we can do about it.

Heredity. Obesity runs in families. It used to be the conventional wisdom that obese parents encouraged their children to be overweight by having fattening foods in the house and setting poor examples. However, a recent study of Scandinavian adoptees by Stunkard and his colleagues (1990) found that children bear a closer resemblance in weight to their biological parents than to their adoptive parents. Heredity, then, appears to play a role. However, we shall see that environmental factors also play a role. Since we are sort of "stuck" with our heredity, that is encouraging. We *can* exert an influence over the situational factors that affect us.

Fat Cells. The efforts of obese people to maintain a slender profile might be sabotaged by microscopic units of life within their own bodies: *fat cells.* No, fat cells are not overweight cells. They are adipose tissue, or cells that store fat. Hunger might be related to the amount of fat stored in these cells. As time passes after a meal, the blood-sugar level drops. Fat is then drawn from these cells to provide further nourishment. At some point, referred to as the *set point,* the hypothalamus is signaled of the fat deficiency in these cells, triggering the hunger drive.

People with more adipose tissue than others feel food-deprived earlier, even though they may be equal in weight. This might be because more signals are being sent to the brain. Obese people, and *formerly* obese people, tend to have more adipose tissue than people of normal weight (Braitman et al., 1985). For this reason, many people who have lost weight complain that they are always hungry when they try to maintain normal weight levels.

Fatty tissue also metabolizes food more slowly than muscle. For this reason, a person with a high fat-to-muscle ratio will metabolize food more slowly than a person of the same weight with a lower fat-to-muscle ratio. In other words, two people identical in weight will metabolize food at different rates, according to their bodies' distribution of muscle and fat. Obese people are therefore doubly handicapped in their efforts to lose weight—not only by their extra weight but by the fact that much of their body is composed of adipose tissue.

In a sense, the normal distribution of fat cells is sexist. The average man is 40 percent muscle and 15 percent fat, whereas the average woman is 23 percent muscle and 25 percent fat. Therefore, if a man and woman with typical distributions of muscle and fat are of the same weight, the woman—who has more fat cells—will have to eat less in order to maintain the same weight.

Compensating Metabolic Forces that Affect Dieters. In addition, people who are dieting and people who have lost substantial amounts of weight usually do not eat enough to satisfy the set points in their hypothalamuses (Keesey, 1986). As a consequence, compensating metabolic forces are set in motion; that is, fewer calories are burned.

Fat cells might play a role in triggering internal sensations of hunger, but they cannot compel us to eat. Below we shall review evidence that obese people are actually *less* sensitive than normal-weight people to internal sensations of hunger.

The Perils of Yo-Yo Dieting. Repeated cycles of dieting and regaining lost weight—"yo-yo dieting"—may be harmful to one's physical health (Lissner et

Obesity: Why the Racial Gap?

African Americans are more likely than non-Hispanic white Americans to be obese. Why the racial gap in weight?

For one thing, obesity is found most often among people who dwell at the low end of the socioeconomic spectrum (Ernst & Harlan, 1991). African Americans are more likely than white Americans to be poor. The prevalence of obesity also increases with age, especially in women (Williamson et al., 1990), so that 60 percent of African-American women between the ages of 45 and 75 are obese (Van Itallie, 1985).

For many non-Hispanic white Americans—particularly women—the ideal figure has been losing weight rapidly in recent years, so that most of them diet at one time or another. Many African Americans belong to cultural groups in which many people associate obesity with happiness and health, however. This connection is made by some Haitian groups (Laguerre, 1981) and some Puerto Rican groups (Harwood, 1981), for example.

There are other reasons as well. Health-consciousness is linked to socioeconomic status, and, being poorer, many African Americans make little effort to avoid high-fat, high-cholesterol foods that are not only connected with weight but also with heart problems and cancer (see Chapter 12). Fried foods, especially fried chicken and fried high-fat meats, are also heavily promoted in the urban ghetto. Moreover, many ghetto residents choose eating as a way of coping with the stresses of the social ills they encounter, such as poverty and crime (Freeman, 1991).

al., 1991) and particularly traumatic to one's set point. Such cycles may teach the body that it will be intermittently deprived of food, slowing the metabolism whenever future food intake is restricted (Brownell & Wadden, 1992). For this reason, *to maintain a slim profile, formerly obese people must usually eat much less than people of the same weight who have always been slender.*

Kelly Brownell suggests a second effect of yo-yo dieting that hampers repeated dieting efforts:

> *Consider a hypothetical dieter, Christine, who drops from 140 pounds down to 120 pounds. She might lose 15 pounds of fat and 5 pounds of muscle. If she regains the 20 pounds, will she replace all 5 pounds of muscle? [Animal studies] suggest that she won't, so Christine may replace 18 pounds of fat and only 2 pounds of muscle. She may be the same weight before and after this cycle, but her metabolic rate would be lower after the cycle because she has more fat, which is less metabolically active than muscle (Brownell, 1988, p. 22).*

In other words, it will be more difficult for Christine to merely maintain the 140 pounds the second time around. In fact, if she eats as many calories as she had eaten earlier at 140 pounds, she will probably go above 140. Moreover, now that her body is overall somewhat "less metabolically active," it will be harder for her to lose the same 20 pounds again.

Other factors, such as emotional state, might also play a role in obesity. Dieting efforts may be impeded by negative emotional states such as depression (Baucom & Aiken, 1981; Ruderman, 1985) and anxiety (Pine, 1985).

Methods of Weight Control

Sound weight-control programs do not involve fad diets such as fasting, eliminating carbohydrates, or eating excessive amounts of grapefruit or rice. Instead, they involve major changes in life style that include improving nutritional knowledge, decreasing calorie intake, exercising, and modifying behavior (Brownell & Wadden, 1992).

Nutritional knowledge helps assure that we will not deprive ourselves of essential food elements and suggests strategies for losing weight without making us feel overly deprived. For example, eating foods that are low in saturated fats and cholesterol is not only good for the heart. Because dietary fat is converted to bodily fat more efficiently than carbohydrates are, a low-fat diet also leads to weight loss (Brownell & Wadden, 1992; Wood et al., 1991). Nutritional knowledge also leads to suggestions for taking in fewer calories, which is a common avenue to reduction. Taking in fewer calories doesn't only mean eating smaller portions. It includes switching to some lower-calorie foods—relying more on fresh, unsweetened fruits and vegetables (eating apples rather than apple pie), lean meats, fish and poultry, and skim milk and cheese products. It means cutting down on—or eliminating—butter, margarine, oils, and sugar.

Dieting plus exercise is more effective than dieting alone for shedding pounds (Epstein et al., 1984; Wood et al., 1991) and for maintaining weight losses (Perri et al., 1988). Exercise burns calories in itself and increases the body's muscle tissue. Fat (adipose tissue) metabolizes food more slowly than muscle. By building muscle, exercise thus heightens the quantity of tissue that will burn calories rapidly. Keesey (1986) also hypothesizes that a long-term exercise program may lower the set point for body weight.

Here are a number of suggestions for losing weight that rely on behavior modification:

Establish calorie-intake goals and heighten awareness of whether or not you are meeting them. Get a book that shows how many calories are found in various foods and keep a diary of your calorie intake.

Use low-calorie substitutes for high-calorie foods. Fill your stomach with celery rather than cheesecake and enchiladas. Eat preplanned low-calorie snacks instead of binging on a jar of peanuts or a container of ice cream.

Establish eating patterns similar to those of internal eaters. Take small bites. Chew thoroughly. Use smaller plates. Put down your utensils between bites. Remove or throw out leftover foods quickly. Take a 5-minute break between helpings. Ask yourself whether you're still hungry. If not, stop eating.

Avoid sources of external stimulation (temptations) to which you have succumbed in the past. Shop at the mall with the Alfalfa Sprout, not the Gushy Gloppy Shoppe. Plan your meal before entering a restaurant and avoid ogling that tempting, full-color menu. Attend to your own plate, not to the sumptuous dish at the next table. Shop from a list. Walk briskly through the supermarket, preferably after dinner when you're no longer hungry. Don't be sidetracked by pretty packages (fattening things may come in them). Keep out of the kitchen. Study, watch TV, or write letters elsewhere. Keep fattening foods out of the house. Prepare only enough food to remain within your calorie goals.

Reward yourself for meeting calorie goals (but not with food). Imagine how great you'll look in that new swimsuit next summer. Do not go to see that great new film unless you have met your weekly calorie goal. Each time you meet your weekly calorie goal, put cash in the bank toward a vacation or new camera.

Use imagery to help yourself lose weight. Tempted by a fattening dish? Imagine that it's rotten, that you would be nauseated by it and have a sick taste in your mouth for the rest of the day. Tempted to binge? Strip before the mirror and handle a fatty area of your body. Ask yourself if you *really* want to make it larger or if you would prefer to exercise self-control? When tempted, you can also think of the extra work your heart must do for every pound of extra weight. Imagine your arteries clogging up with dreaded substances (not far off base!).

Mentally rehearse solutions to problem situations. Consider how you will politely refuse when cake is handed out at the office party. Rehearse your next visit to "the relatives"—the ones who tell you how painfully thin you look and try to stuff you like a pig. Imagine how you'll politely (but firmly) refuse seconds, and thirds, despite all their protestations.

Above all, if you slip from your plan for a day, don't blow things out of proportion. Dieters are often tempted to binge, especially when they rigidly see themselves either as perfect successes or complete failures (Polivy & Herman, 1985), or when they experience powerful emotions—either positive or negative (Cools et al., 1992). Consider the weekly or monthly trend, not just the day. Credit yourself for the long-term trend. If you do binge, resume dieting the next day.

SEX

We may describe people as "hungering" or "thirsting" for sex. The sex drive differs from the hunger and thirst drives, however, in that sex may be necessary for the survival of the species but not the individual (despite occasional claims to the effect, "I'll simply *die* unless you . . . .").

There are, however, important similarities among these drives. All three can be triggered by external cues as well as internal processes. The sex drive can be tripped by the sight (or memory) of an attractive person, a whiff of perfume, provocative photographs, even a wink. In this section, we focus on issues in sexual motivation, including sex hormones and homosexuality.

Organizing and Activating Effects of Sex Hormones

Sex hormones have many effects. They promote biological sexual differentiation, regulate the menstrual cycle, and affect sexual behavior.

Sexual behavior among many lower animals is almost completely governed by hormones (Crews & Moore, 1986). Sex hormones have organizing and activating effects (Buchanan et al., 1992). They predispose lower animals toward masculine or feminine mating patterns (a directional or *organizing effect*). Hormones also influence the sex drive and facilitate sexual response (*activating effects*).

Consider the influences of sex hormones on the mating behavior of rats. Male rats who have been castrated at birth—and thus deprived of *testosterone*—make no effort to mate as adults. But when they receive *female* sex hormones in adulthood, they become receptive to the sexual advances of other males and assume female mating stances (Harris & Levine, 1965). Male rats who are castrated in adulthood do not engage in sexual activity. However, if they receive injections of testosterone, which replaces the testosterone that would have been secreted by their own testes, they resume stereotypical male sexual behavior patterns.

The sex organs of female rodents exposed to large doses of testosterone in utero (which occurs naturally when they share the uterus with many brothers or artificially as a result of hormone injections) become masculinized in appearance. Such females are also predisposed toward masculine mating behaviors. If they are given additional testosterone as adults, they attempt to mount other females about as often as males do (Goy & Goldfoot, 1976). Prenatal testosterone might have organized the brains of these females in the masculine direction, predisposing them toward masculine sexual behaviors in adulthood. Testosterone in adulthood would then activate the masculine behavior patterns.

Testosterone is also important in the behavior of human males. Men who are castrated or given drugs that decrease the amount of androgens in the bloodstream (antiandrogens) usually show gradual loss of sexual desire and of the capacities for erection and orgasm. Still, many castrated men remain sexually active for years, suggesting that for many people, fantasies, memories, and other cognitive stimuli are as important as hormones in sexual motivation. Beyond minimal levels, there is no clear link between testosterone level and sexual arousal. For example, sleeping men are *not* more likely to have erections during surges in the testosterone level (Schiavi et al.,1977).

Female mice, rats, cats, and dogs are receptive to males only during *estrus,* when female sex hormones are plentiful. During estrus, female rats respond to males by hopping, wiggling their ears, and arching their backs with their tails to one side, thus making penetration possible. But, as noted by Kimble (1988),

> *. . . if we were to observe this same pair of animals one day [after estrus], we would see very different behaviors. The male would still be interested (at least at first), but his advances would not be answered with hopping, ear wiggling, and [back arching]. The female would be much more likely to "chatter" her teeth at the male (a sure sign of hostility if you are a rat). If the male were to be slow to grasp her meaning, she might turn away from him and kick him in the head, mule fashion. Clearly, it is over between them. (p. 271)*

Women, in contrast, are sexually responsive during all phases of the menstrual cycle, even during menstruation itself, when hormone levels are low, and after *menopause*. Androgens influence female as well as male sexual response (Sherwin et al., 1985). Women whose adrenal glands and ovaries have been removed (so that they no longer produce androgens) may gradually lose sexual interest and the capacity for sexual response. An active and enjoyable sexual history seems to ward off loss of sexual capacity, suggestive of the importance of cognitive and experiential factors in human sexual motivation.

Sex hormones thus play a role in human sexual behavior, but our sexual behavior is far from mechanical. Sex hormones initially promote the development of our sex organs, and, as adults, we need minimal levels of sex hormones to become sexually aroused. Psychological factors also influence our sexual behavior, however. In human sexuality, biology apparently is not destiny.

Homosexuality

Homosexuality, or a homosexual orientation, is an erotic response to members of one's own gender. Sexual activity with members of one's own gender is not in itself evidence of homosexuality. It may reflect limited sexual opportunities or even ritualistic cultural practices, as in the case of the New Guinean Sambian people. American adolescent males may manually stimulate one another while fantasizing about girls. Men in prisons may similarly turn to each other as sexual outlets. Sambian male youths engage exclusively in homosexual practices with older males, since it is believed that they must drink "men's milk" to achieve the fierce manhood of the head hunter (Money, 1987). But their behavior turns exclusively *heterosexual* once they reach marrying age.

About 8 percent of the men and 3 percent of the women surveyed by Kinsey and his colleagues (1948, 1953) reported being exclusively homosexual or "almost" exclusively homosexual in their sexual activities. About 2 percent of the men and 1 percent of the women in a more recent survey reported a homosexual orientation (Hunt, 1974). The numbers of homosexuals in the population remain unknown, but homosexuals have become more visible, more self-accepting, and more willing to talk openly about their sexual orientation.

Origins of Homosexuality. The origins of homosexuality are complex and controversial. Developmentally speaking, about two gay males in three report gender nonconformity as children. That is, they preferred playing with girls and "girls' toys" to transportation toys, guns, and rough-and-tumble play. These preferences frequently led to their being called "sissies" (Adams & Chiodo, 1983; Bell et al., 1981; Green, 1987). On the other hand, about one in three homosexuals shows gender conformity—for example, "masculine" aggressiveness. Some homosexuals have played professional football. Let us consider a number of psychological and biological theories concerning the origins of homosexuality.

Psychodynamic theory ties homosexuality to identification with male or female figures. Identification, in turn, is related to resolution of the Oedipus and Electra complexes. In men, faulty resolution of the Oedipus complex would stem from a "classic pattern" in which there is a "close-binding" mother and a "detached-hostile" father. Boys reared in such a family environment would identify with their mothers and not their fathers. Psychodynamic theory has been criticized, however, because many gay males have had excellent relationships with both parents. The childhoods of many heterosexuals also fit the "classic pattern."

From the perspective of learning theory, early reinforcement of sexual behavior (as by orgasm achieved through interaction with members of one's own gender) can influence one's sexual orientation. Many gay males and lesbians, however, are aware of their orientations before they have sexual contacts (Bell et al., 1981). We thus cannot attribute their orientations to early reinforcement of sexual behavior by persons of the same gender. Nor can we point to the power of observational learning. In a society that denigrates homosexuality, children are unlikely to develop the expectancy that homosexual behavior will be reinforcing for them. In other words, they are unlikely to strive to imitate homosexual models. Remember the Sambian youth as well: Even repeated homosexual experiences do not sway them from their eventual exclusive heterosexuality.

Biological theories focus on genetic and hormonal factors. It was once thought that homosexuality might be genetically transmitted. Kallmann (1952) found a 95 percent *concordance* rate for homosexuality among the *probands* of 40 identical twin pairs, but only 12 percent among pairs of fraternal twins. More recent studies have found much lower concordance rates for identical twins (Eckert et al., 1986; McConaghy & Blaszczynski, 1980). Still, MZ twins do appear to have a higher concordance rate for homosexuality than DZ twins (52% for MZ twins versus 22% for DZ twins, according to Bailey and Pillard [1991]). Although genetic factors may partly determine sexual orientation, psychologist John Money, who has specialized in sexual behavior, concludes that homosexuality is "not under the direct governance of chromosomes and genes" (1987, p. 384).

Because sex hormones influence the mating behavior of lower animals, it has been wondered whether gay males might be deficient in testosterone or whether lesbians might have lower-than-normal levels of estrogen and higher-than-normal levels of androgens in their bloodstreams. However, homosexuality has not been reliably linked to current (adult) levels of male or female sex hormones (Feder, 1984).

It is *not* true that homosexuals suffer from hormonal imbalances.

Another possibility concerns the prenatal effects of sex hormones. Prenatal sex hormones can masculinize or feminize the brains of laboratory animals in the ways that they direct the development of brain structures. Research suggests that parts of the brain, whose development would have been affected by sex hormones, may differ in structure in heterosexual and homosexual men (Angier, 1992).

Lee Ellis (1990; Ellis & Ames, 1987) theorizes that sexual orientation is hormonally determined prior to birth and is affected by genetic factors, drugs (such as androgens), and maternal stress. Why maternal stress? Stress causes the release of hormones such as adrenaline and cortisol, which can interact with testosterone and affect the prenatal development of the brain. Perhaps the brains of some gay males have been prenatally feminized, and the brains of some lesbians have been masculinized (Money, 1987). Even so, Money argues that prenatal hormonal influences would not induce a robotlike sexual orientation in humans and that socialization—or early learning experiences—would probably also play a role.

The causes of human homosexuality are mysterious and complex. Current research suggests that they may involve prenatal hormone levels—which can be affected by factors such as heredity, drugs, and maternal stress—and postnatal socialization. The precise interaction of these influences has eluded detection, however.

STIMULUS MOTIVES

Physical needs give rise to drives such as hunger and thirst. In such cases, organisms are motivated to *reduce* the tension or stimulation that impinges on them. In the case of **stimulus motives,** however, organisms seek to *increase* stimulation. Stimulus motives include sensory stimulation, activity, exploration, and manipulation of the environment. People may be motivated to seek the level of stimulation that produces an *optimal level of arousal*—that is, a general level of activity or motivation at which they feel their best and behave most effectively.

Some stimulus motives provide a clear evolutionary advantage. People and lower animals who are motivated to learn about and manipulate the environment are more likely to survive. Learning about the environment increases awareness of resources and of potential dangers, and manipulation permits one to change the environment in beneficial ways. Learning and manipulation increase the chances of survival until sexual maturity and of transmitting whatever genetic codes may underlie these motives to future generations.

Sensory Stimulation and Activity

During the 1950s, "The $64,000 Question" was a hit TV show. The prize doubled with each correct answer, and, as contestants neared the big one—the $64,000 question—they were placed in an "isolation booth." They could not hear the audience from the booth, and it supposedly prevented cheating. Psychologist Dr. Joyce Brothers first became known to the public by winning a $64,000 prize—in the category of boxing.

At the time, I was unaware that some lucky students at McGill University in Montreal were being paid $20 a day (which, with inflation, would be well above $100 today) for entering another kind of isolation booth. In the booth, they did absolutely nothing. Would you like such "work" for $100 a day? Don't answer too quickly. According to the results of such experiments in **sensory deprivation,** you might not like it much at all.

Student volunteers were blindfolded in quiet cubicles (Bexton et al, 1954). Their arms were bandaged, and they could hear nothing but the dull, continuous hum of air conditioning (Figure 9.3). With nothing to do, many students slept for a while. After a few hours of sensory-deprived wakefulness, most felt bored and irritable. As time went on, many of them grew more uncomfortable, and some reported hallucinations, as of images of dots and geometric shapes (Zubek, 1973).

Many subjects quit during the first day despite the financial incentive and the desire to contribute to science. Many of those who remained for a few days found it temporarily difficult to concentrate on simple problems afterward. For many, the experimental conditions did not provide a relaxing vacation. Instead, they instigated boredom and disorientation.

Stimulus motives Motives to increase the stimulation impinging upon an organism.

Sensory deprivation Referring to a research method for systematically decreasing the amount of stimulation that impinges upon sensory receptors.

It is *not* true that "getting away from it all" by going on a vacation from all sensory input for a few hours is necessarily relaxing. If carried out as done at McGill University, the "vacation" may be highly stressful.

Individual Differences in Desire for Stimulation. Some people seek higher levels of stimulation and activity than others. John is a "couch potato," content to sit by the TV set all evening. Marsha doesn't feel right unless she's out on the tennis court or jogging. Cliff isn't content unless he has ridden his motorcycle over back trails at breakneck speeds, and Janet feels exuberant when she's catching the big wave or diving freefall from an airplane. One's preference for tennis, motorcycling, or skydiving reflects one's geographical location, social class, and learning experiences. It may just be that the levels of arousal at which we are comfortable would be too high or too low for other people, however. It also may be that these levels are determined to some degree by innate factors.

Exploration and Manipulation

Have you ever brought a dog or cat into a new home? At first, it may show general excitement. New kittens are also known to hide under a couch or bed for a few hours. But then they will begin to explore every corner of the new environment. When placed in novel environments, many animals appear to possess an innate motive to engage in exploratory behavior.

Once they are familiar with the environment, lower animals and people appear to be motivated to seek **novel stimulation.** For example, when they have not been deprived of food for a great deal of time, rats will often explore unfamiliar arms of mazes rather than head straight for the section of the maze in which they have learned to expect food. Animals who have just **copulated** and thereby reduced their sex drives will often show renewed interest in sexual behavior when presented with a novel sex partner. Monkeys will learn how to manipulate gadgets for the incentive of being able to observe novel stimulation through a window (see Figure 9.3). Children will spend hour after hour manipulating the controls of video games for the pleasure of zapping video monsters.

The question has arisen whether people and animals seek to explore and manipulate the environment *because* these activities help them reduce primary drives such as hunger and thirst or whether they engage in these activities for their own sake. Many psychologists do believe that such stimulating activities are reinforcing in and of themselves. Monkeys do seem to get a kick out of "monkeying around" with gadgets (see Figure 9.4). They learn how to manipulate hooks and eyes and other mechanical devices without any external incentives whatsoever (Harlow et al., 1950). Children engage in prolonged play with "busy boxes"—boxes filled with objects that honk, squeak, rattle, and buzz. They seem to find discovery of the cause-and-effect relationships in these gadgets pleasurable even though they are not rewarded with food, ice cream, or even hugs from parents.

Novel stimulation (1) An unusual source of arousal or excitement. (2) A hypothesized primary drive to experience new or different stimulation.

Copulate To engage in sexual intercourse.

Arousal A general level of activity or motivation in an organism.

The Search for Optimal Arousal

Some drives such as hunger and thirst are associated with higher levels of **arousal** within an organism. When we eat or drink to reduce these drives, we are also lowering the associated level of arousal. At other times, we act to increase our levels of

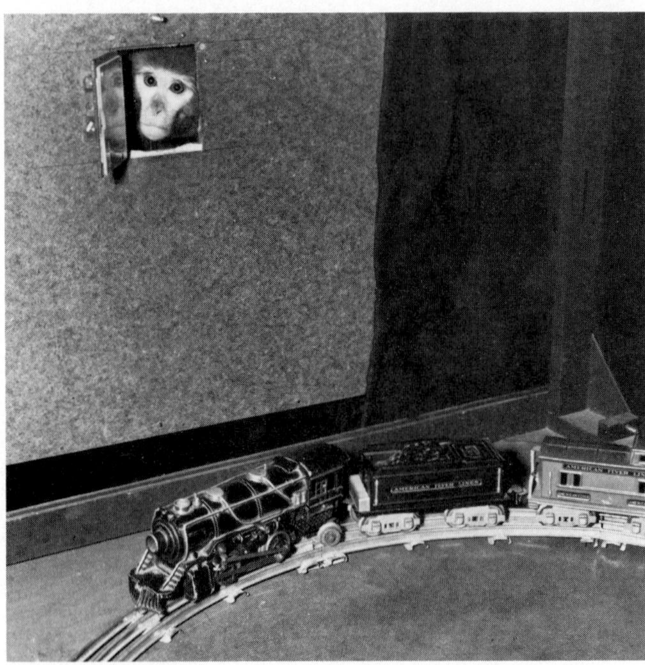

FIGURE 9.3
The Allure of Novel Stimulation. People and many lower animals are motivated to explore the environment and to seek novel stimulation. This monkey has learned to unlock a door for the privilege of viewing a model train.

FIGURE 9.4
A Manipulation Drive? These young rhesus monkeys appear to monkey around with gadgets for the sheer pleasure of monkeying around. No external incentives or reinforcements are needed. Children similarly enjoy manipulating gadgets that honk, squeak, rattle, and buzz, even though the resultant honks and squeaks do not satisfy physiological drives such as hunger or thirst.

arousal, as in going to a horror film, engaging in athletic activity, or seeking a new sex partner.

How can we explain the apparently contradictory observations that organisms sometimes act to reduce arousal and at other times to increase it? Some psychologists reconcile these differences by suggesting that we are motivated to seek **optimal arousal**—that is, levels of arousal that are optimal for us as individuals at certain times of the day.

Our levels of arousal can vary from quite low (see Figure 9.5), as when we are sleeping, to quite high, as when we are frightened or enraged. Psychologists also hypothesize that we each have optimal levels of arousal at which we feel best and function most efficiently. People whose optimal levels of arousal are relatively low may prefer sedentary lives. People whose optimal levels are high may seek activities such as skydiving and motorcycling, intense problem-solving (such as a difficult crossword puzzle), or vivid daydreaming. Psychologists Donald Fiske and Salvatore Maddi argue that people try to increase the impact of stimulation when their levels of arousal are too low and to decrease it when their levels are too high (Maddi, 1980). The types of activity they engage in depend on other aspects of their personalities.

Optimal arousal The level of arousal at which we feel and function best.

Yerkes-Dodson law The principle that a high level of motivation increases efficiency in the performance of simple tasks, whereas a lower level of motivation permits greater efficiency in the performance of complex tasks.

The Yerkes-Dodson Law. A former National Football League linebacker was reported to work himself into such a frenzy before a game that other players gave him a wide berth in the locker room. Linebacking is a relatively simple football job, requiring brute strength and something called "desire" more so than does, say, quarterbacking. This particular linebacker was no stronger than

FIGURE 9.5
Level of Arousal and Efficiency of Performance. Our optimal levels of arousal may differ somewhat, but they tend to lie somewhere in between sleep and a state of panic. People whose optimal levels of arousal are high will seek more stimulation than people whose optimal levels are low.

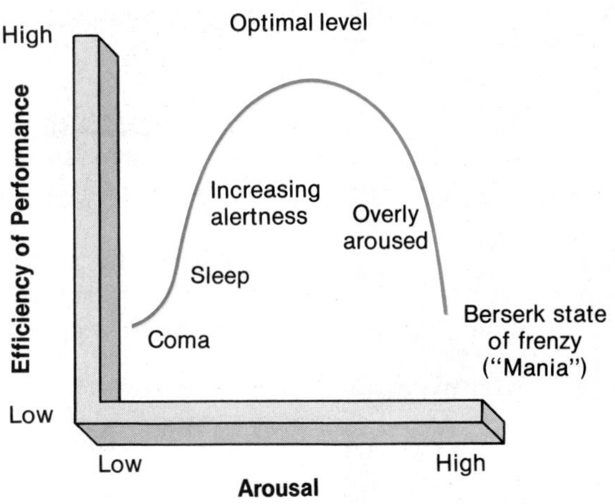

many others, but his level of arousal—or desire—helped his team reach several Superbowls.

According to the **Yerkes-Dodson law** (see Figure 9.6), a high level of arousal enhances performance of relatively simple tasks, whether they are linebacking or solving simple math problems. When tasks are complex, it seems helpful to keep one's arousal at lower levels. True, there are some complexities to the linebacker's job. Through experience, the linebacker must acquire the capacity to predict, or "read," the play. But the quarterback's job is more complex. He must call the plays, sometimes change them at the line of scrimmage because of an unexpected defensive realignment, and "keep a cool head" as his receivers try to break into the open and the defenders try to tackle him. Similarly, it is worthwhile to try to remain somewhat relaxed on the eve of a demanding (complex) "big test."

"Cool" linebackers and "hotheaded" quarterbacks don't fare well in the professional ranks. Instead, linebackers must "psych" themselves up, and quarterbacks must "keep cool."

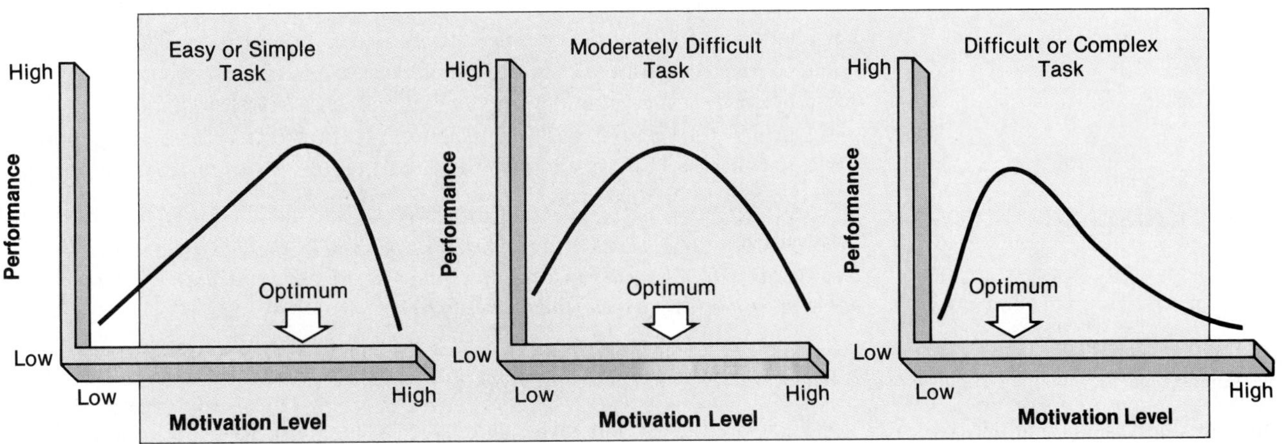

FIGURE 9.6.
The Yerkes-Dodson Law.

A simple task may be facilitated by a high level of arousal or motivation. A highly aroused 118-pound woman is reported to have lifted the front end of a two-ton Cadillac in order to rescue a child. However, a complex task such as quarterbacking a football team or attempting to solve a math problem requires attending to many variables at once. For this reason, a complex task is usually carried out more efficiently at a lower level of arousal.

Keeping a Cool Head. If quarterbacks are to be effective, they must remain reasonably composed under pressure, as when their pockets of protection are collapsing around them. Rushing defenders, whose tasks are relatively simpler, can afford to get more worked up.

It is true that quarterbacks' field performance may suffer if they get too "psyched up" for a big game.

What motivates people to get involved in contact sports such as football in the first place? Stimulus motives may be a part of the answer, but learned or social motives may also have a good deal to do with it.

SOCIAL MOTIVES

Money, achievement, social approval, power, aggression—these are examples of **social motives.** Social motives differ from primary motives in that they are acquired through social learning. Like other motives, however, social motives arouse us and prompt goal-directed behavior.

Harvard University psychologist Henry Murray (1938) referred to social motives as psychological needs. He compiled a list of 21 important psychological needs, including needs for achievement, affiliation, aggression, autonomy, dominance, **nurturance,** and understanding. Because we undergo different learning experiences, we may develop different levels of these needs or give them different priorities. Let us now consider some findings concerning the needs for achievement and affiliation.

The Need for Achievement

We all know people who strive persistently to get ahead, to "make it," to earn vast sums of money, to invent, to accomplish the impossible. These people have a high need for achievement, abbreviated ***n* Ach.**

Psychologist David McClelland (1958) helped pioneer the assessment of *n* Ach through people's reported fantasies. One assessment method involves the **Thematic Apperception Test** (TAT), which was developed by Henry Murray. The TAT contains cards with pictures and drawings that are subject to various interpretations (see Chapter 11). Subjects are shown one or more TAT cards and asked to construct stories about the pictured theme: to indicate what led up to it, what the characters are thinking and feeling, and what is likely to happen.

One TAT card is similar to that in Figure 9.7. The boy may be sleeping, thinking about the book, or wishing he were out playing. Consider two stories that could be told about this card:

Story 1: "He's upset that he's got to read the book because he's behind in his assignments and doesn't particularly like to work. He'd much rather be out playing with the other kids, and he'll probably sneak out to do just that."

Story 2: "He's thinking, 'Someday I'll be a great scholar. I'll write books like this, and everybody will be proud of me.' He reads all the time."

There are formal standards that enable psychologists to derive *n* Ach scores from stories such as these, but you need not be acquainted with them to see that the second story suggests more achievement motivation than the first. McClelland (1985) has found that motives as measured by the TAT permit the prediction of long-term behavior patterns.

Behavior of Individuals with High n Ach. Classic studies find that people with high *n* Ach earn higher grades than people of comparable learning ability but low *n* Ach. They are more likely to earn high salaries and be promoted

Social motives Learned or acquired motives.

Nurturance The quality of nourishing, rearing, fostering the development of children, animals, or plants.

***n* Ach** The need for achievement—the need to master, to accomplish difficult things.

Thematic Apperception Test A test devised by Henry Murray to measure needs through fantasy production.

FIGURE 9.7
Tapping Fantasies in Personality Research This picture is similar to a thematic Apperception Test card that is frequently used to measure the need for achievement. What is happening in this picture? What is the person thinking and feeling? What is going to happen? Your answers to these questions reflect your own needs as well as the content of the picture itself.

than are low-*n*-Ach people with similar opportunities. They perform better at math problems and unscrambling anagrams such as decoding the letters RSTA into STAR, TARS, ARTS, or RATS.[1]

McClelland (1965) found that 83 percent of high-*n*-Ach college graduates took positions characterized by risk, decision-making, and the chance for great success, such as business management, sales, or businesses of their own making. Seventy percent of the graduates who chose nonentrepreneurial positions showed low *n* Ach. High-*n*-Ach individuals seem to prefer challenges and are willing to take moderate risks to achieve their goals. They see their fate as being in their own hands (McClelland et al., 1953). Workers with higher *n* Ach are also more likely to find satisfaction on the job (Reuman et al., 1984).

Development of n Ach. Mothers with high *n* Ach tend to encourage their children to think and act independently, whereas low-*n*-Ach mothers tend to be more protective and restrictive. Winterbottom (1958) found that mothers of sons with high *n* Ach made more demands and imposed more restrictions on their sons during the early elementary school years than did mothers of sons with low *n* Ach. Even during the preschool years, the mothers of high-*n*-Ach sons demanded that they keep their rooms and possessions neat, that they make their own decisions concerning clothes, that they select their own friends, compete as needed, and undertake difficult tasks and persist at them. But mothers of high-*n*-Ach sons also showed warmth and praised their sons profusely for their accomplishments.

In sum, it may be that children who develop high *n* Ach are encouraged to show independence and responsibility at early ages and that their parents respond warmly to their efforts.

The Need for Affiliation

The need for **affiliation,** abbreviated *n* Aff, prompts us to make friends,join groups, and to prefer to do things with others rather than go it alone. *N* Aff contributes to the social glue that creates families and civilizations. In this sense, it is

Affiliation Association or connection with a group.

[1]You can count on a psychologist not to miss an opportunity to throw a few rats into his book.

certainly a healthful trait. Yet, some people have such strong *n* Aff that they find it painful to make their own decisions or even to be by themselves over extended periods of time. Research by Stanley Schachter suggests that high *n* Aff may indicate anxiety, such as when people "huddle together" in fear of some outside force.

The Schachter Studies on Anxiety and n Aff. In a classic experiment on the effects of anxiety on *n* Aff, Stanley Schachter (1959) manipulated subjects' anxiety by leading them to believe that they would receive either painful electric shocks (the high-anxiety condition) or mild electric shocks (the low-anxiety condition). Subjects were then asked to wait while the shock apparatus was supposedly being set up. Subjects could choose to wait alone or in a room with others. The majority (63 percent) of subjects who expected a painful shock chose to wait in a room with other people. Only one-third (33 percent) of the subjects who expected a mild shock chose to wait with others.

In a related experiment, Schachter found that "misery loves company," but only company of a special sort. Highly anxious subjects were placed in two social conditions. In the first, they could choose either to wait alone or with other subjects who would also receive painful shocks. Sixty percent of these subjects chose to affiliate—that is, to wait with others. In the second condition, highly anxious subjects could choose to wait alone or with people they believed were not involved with the study. In this second condition, no one chose to affiliate.

It is true that misery loves company—as long as the company is miserable, too!

Why did Schachter's subjects wish to affiliate only with people who shared their misery? Schachter explained their choice through the **theory of social comparison.** This theory holds that in an ambiguous situation—that is, a situation in which we are not certain about what we should do or how we should feel—we will affiliate with people with whom we can compare feelings and behaviors. Schachter's anxious recruits could compare their reactions with those of other "victims," but not with people who had no reason to feel anxious. His highly anxious subjects may also have resented uninvolved people for "getting away scot-free."

EMOTION

Emotions color our lives. We are green with envy, red with anger, blue with sorrow. The poets paint a thoughtful mood as a brown study. Positive emotions such as love and desire can fill our days with pleasure, but negative emotions such as fear, depression, and anger can fill us with dread and make each day a chore.

An emotion can at once be a response to a situation (in the way that fear is a response to a threat) and have motivating properties (in the way that anger can motivate us to act aggressively). An emotion can also be a goal in itself. We may behave in ways that will lead us to experience joy or feelings of love.

Emotions are states of feeling that have cognitive, physiological, and behavioral components (Carlson & Hatfield, 1992; Fischer et al., 1990; Haaland, 1992). Many strong emotions spark activity in the autonomic nervous system (LeDoux, 1986). Fear, which usually occurs in response to a threat, involves cognitions that one is in danger, predominantly **sympathetic** arousal (rapid heartbeat and breathing, sweating, muscle tension), and tendencies to avoid or escape from the situation (see Table 9.1). As a response to a social provocation, anger involves

Theory of social comparison The view that people look to others for cues about how to behave when they are in confusing or unfamiliar situations.

Emotion A state of feeling that has cognitive, physiological, and behavioral components.

Sympathetic Of the sympathetic division of the autonomic nervous system.

TABLE 9.1: Components of Three Common Emotions

Emotion	Components: Cognitive	Physiological	Behavioral
Fear	Belief that one is in danger	Sympathetic arousal	Avoidance tendencies
Anger	Frustration or belief that one is being mistreated	Sympathetic and parasympathetic arousal	Attack tendencies
Depression	Thoughts of helplessness, hopelessness, worthlessness	Parasympathetic arousal	Inactivity, possible self-destructive tendencies

cognitions that a provocateur should be paid back, both sympathetic and **parasympathetic** arousal, and tendencies to attack. Depression usually involves cognitions of helplessness and hopelessness, predominantly parasympathetic arousal, and behavioral tendencies toward inactivity or—sometimes—self-destruction. Joy, grief, jealousy, disgust, embarrassment, liking—all have cognitive, physiological, and behavioral components. Generally speaking, the greater the autonomic arousal, the more intense the emotion (Chwalisz et al., 1988).

Let us now consider whether knowledge of emotional responses can be used to detect lies.

"Lie Detectors"

One may smile, and smile, and be a villain.

Shakespeare, *Hamlet*

Lying—for better and for worse—is an integral part of life (Saxe, 1991a). Political leaders lie to work their will (Caro, 1989). Some students lie about why they have not completed assignments (Greene & Saxe, 1990). ('Fess up!) The great majority of us lie to our lovers—most often about other relationships (Shusterman & Saxe, 1990). (Is it really true that you never held anyone's hand before?) People also lie about their qualifications to obtain jobs and, of course, to deny guilt for crimes. Although we are unlikely to subject our political leaders, students, and lovers to "lie-detector" tests, such tests are frequently used in hiring and police investigative work.

Facial expressions often offer clues to deceit (Ekman, 1985), but as noted by Shakespeare, some people can "smile and smile" and still have malice within. The use of devices to sort out smiles from villainy—truth from lies—has a lengthy, if not laudable, history:

The Bedouins of Arabia . . . until quite recently required conflicting witnesses to lick a hot iron; the one whose tongue was burned was thought to be lying. The Chinese, it is said, had a similar method for detecting lying: Suspects were forced to chew rice powder and spit it out; if the powder was dry, the suspect was guilty. A variation of this test was used during the Inquisition. The suspect had to swallow a "trial slice" of bread and cheese; if it stuck to the suspect's palate or throat he or she was not telling the truth. (Kleinmuntz & Szucko, 1984, pp. 766–767)

These methods may sound primitive, even bizarre, but they are consistent with modern knowledge. Anxiety concerning being caught in a lie is linked to sympathetic arousal, and one sign of sympathetic arousal is lack of saliva, or dryness in the mouth. The emotions of fear and guilt are also linked to sympathetic arousal and, hence, dryness in the mouth.

Modern lie detectors, or polygraphs (see Figure 9.8), monitor four indicators of sympathetic arousal while a witness or suspect is being examined: heart rate, blood pressure, respiration rate, and electrodermal response (sweating). Questions have been raised about the validity of the polygraph, however.

Parasympathetic Of the parasympathetic division of the autonomic nervous system.

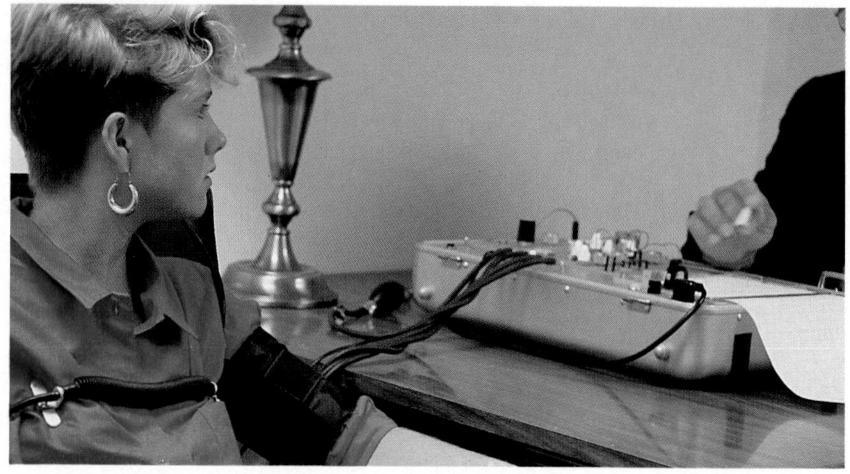

FIGURE 9.8
What do "Lie Detectors" Detect? The polygraph monitors heart rate, blood pressure, respiration rate, and sweat in the palms of the hands. Is the polygraph sensitive to lying only? Is it foolproof? Because of the controversy surrounding these questions, many courts no longer admit polygraph evidence.

The American Polygraph Association (1992) claims that the polygraph is 85 to 95 percent accurate. Critics, however, find polygraphs less accurate and sensitive to more than lies (Furedy, 1990; Kleinmuntz & Szucko, 1984; Saxe, 1991b; Steinbrook, 1992; U.S. Congress, 1983). Studies have found that factors such as tensing muscles, drugs, and previous experience with polygraph tests all significantly reduce the accuracy rate (Steinbrook, 1992). In one experiment, subjects were able to reduce the accuracy rate to about 50 percent by biting their tongues (to produce pain) or pressing their toes against the floor (to tense muscles) while being interviewed (Honts et al., 1985).

It is true that you may be able to fool a lie detector by squiggling your toes.

In a review of the literature, the government Office of Technology Assessment (OTA) found that there was little valid research into the use of the polygraph in preemployment screening, "dragnet" investigations (attempts to ferret out the guilty from many subjects), or determining who should be given access to classified information (U.S. Congress, 1983). OTA also looked into studies involving investigations of specific indictments. The studies' conclusions varied widely. In 28 studies judged to have adequate methodology, accurate detections of guilt ranged from 35 to 100 percent. Accurate judgments of innocence ranged from 12.5 to 94 percent.

In sum, there may be no such thing as a lie detector per se (Saxe, 1991b; Steinbrook, 1992). Because of validity problems, results of polygraph examinations are no longer admitted as evidence in many courts. Polygraph interviews are still often conducted in criminal investigations and in job interviews, but these practices are also being questioned.

The Expression of Emotions

The face of man is the index to joy and mirth, to severity and sadness.

Pliny the Elder (A.D. 62–113)

There's no art
To find the mind's construction in the face.

Shakespeare, *Macbeth*

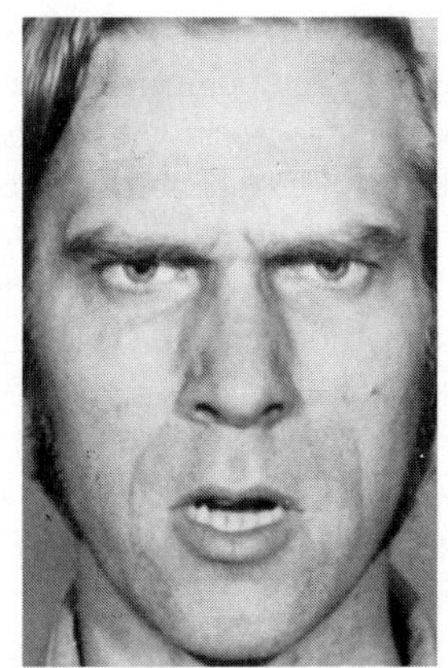
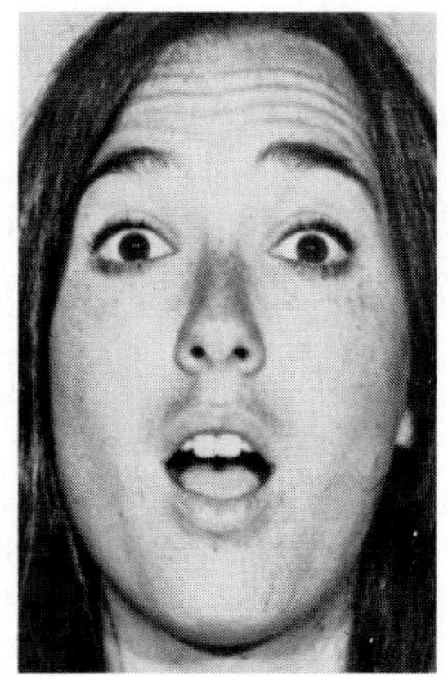
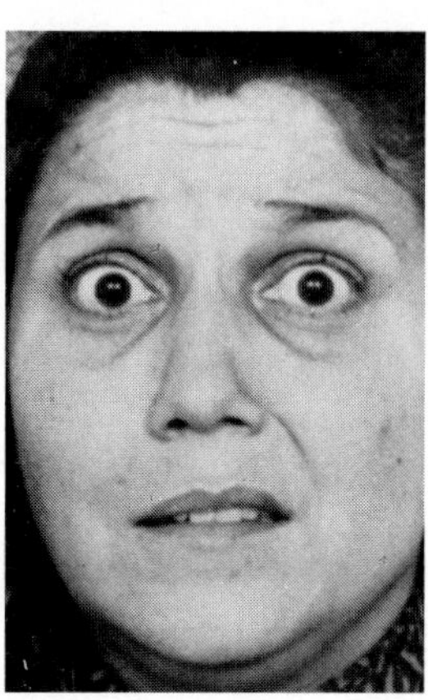

FIGURE 9.9
The Universality of the Expression of Emotions.
Ekman's research suggests that there are several basic emotions (including those shown in these photographs) whose expression is recognized around the world. These include happiness, anger, surprise, and fear.

Joy and sadness are found in diverse cultures around the world, but how can we tell when other people are happy or despondent? It turns out that the expression of many emotions is also universal (Rinn, 1991). Smiling, for instance, appears to be a universal sign of friendliness and approval (Ekman & Oster, 1979). Baring the teeth, as noted by Charles Darwin (1872) in the last century, may be a universal sign of anger. As the originator of the modern theory of evolution, Darwin believed that the universal recognition of facial expressions would have survival value. For example, facial expressions could signal the approach of enemies (or friends) even in the absence of language.

Research by psychologist Paul Ekman and his colleagues also supports the universality of the facial expression of emotions. In one study, Ekman (1980) took a number of photographs of people posing the emotions of anger, disgust, fear, happiness, sadness, and surprise, similar to those shown in Figure 9.9, and asked subjects throughout the world to indicate what emotions they depicted. Subjects ranged from European college students to the Fore, an isolated tribe who dwell in the highlands of New Guinea. All groups, including the Fore, who had almost no contact with Western culture, correctly identified the emotions being portrayed. Moreover, even the Fore displayed familiar facial expressions when asked how they would respond if they were the characters in stories that called for basic emotional responses. Ekman and his colleagues (1987) obtained similar results in a study of ten cultures in which subjects were permitted to report that multiple emotions were shown by facial expressions. The subjects generally agreed on which two emotions were being shown and which emotion was most intense.

The Facial-Feedback Hypothesis

We generally recognize that facial expressions reflect emotional states. In fact, various emotional states give rise to certain patterns of electrical activity in the facial muscles and in the brain (Cacioppo et al., 1988; Ekman et al., 1990).

The **facial-feedback hypothesis** argues, however, that the causal relationship between emotions and facial expressions can also work in the opposite direction. Consider Darwin's words:

> *The free expression by outward signs of an emotion intensifies it. On the other hand, the repression, as far as possible, of all outward signs softens our emotions.*
>
> Charles Darwin, 1872, p. 22

Can smiling give rise to feelings of good will, for example, or frowning, to anger?

Facial-feedback hypothesis The view that stereotypical facial expressions can contribute to stereotypical emotions.

Psychological research has given rise to some interesting findings concerning the facial-feedback hypothesis. Inducing experimental subjects to smile, for example, leads them to report more positive feelings (Kleinke & Walton, 1982; McCanne & Anderson, 1987) and to rate cartoons as being more humorous (Laird, 1974, 1984). When subjects are induced to frown, they rate cartoons as being more aggressive (Laird, 1974; 1984). When subjects pose expressions of pain, they rate electric shocks as being more painful (Colby et al., 1977; Lanzetta et al., 1976).

What are the possible links between facial feedback and emotion? One link is arousal. Intense contraction of facial muscles such as those used in signifying fear heightens arousal (Zuckerman et al., 1981). Our perception of heightened arousal then leads to self-report of heightened emotional activity. Other links may involve changes in brain temperature and the release of neurotransmitters (Ekman, 1985; Zajonc, 1985). Kinesthetic feedback of the contraction of facial muscles may also induce us to perceive heightened emotional activation (McCaul et al., 1982).

Critics of the research on the facial-feedback hypothesis have argued that experimenters have not controlled for subjects' expectations. For example, a subject who is asked to smile may be more likely to focus on positive feelings, and vice versa. To control for this methodological problem, Strack and his colleagues (1988) asked subjects to hold pens in their mouths in certain ways, rather than smile or frown. The method of holding the pen facilitated or inhibited muscles involved in smiling without subject awareness of the purpose of the study. Subjects who held the pens in such a way as to facilitate smiling did rate cartoons as being more humorous than subjects who held the pens in the other way.

In yet another approach, McCanne and Anderson (1987) suppressed facial response and, as one consequence, decreased subjects' enjoyment of an experimental task. But the researchers admit that the lessened enjoyment might have been the result of distraction from the tasks at hand and not from the suppression of facial muscle activity itself. A reviewer of research on the facial-feedback hypothesis recently analyzed a large body of research and concluded that the effects of modifying facial behavior on self-reported emotional response are small to moderate (Matsumoto, 1987). But they do seem to exist.

You may have heard the British expression "to keep a stiff upper lip" as a recommended way of handling stress. It might be that a "stiff" lip suppresses emotional response—as long as the lip is relaxed rather than quivering with fear or tension. But when a lip is stiffened through strong muscle tension, facial feedback may heighten autonomic activity and the perception of emotional response. In the following section, we shall see that the facial-feedback hypothesis is related to the James-Lange theory of emotion.

THEORIES OF EMOTION

Emotions have physiological, situational, and cognitive components, but psychologists have disagreed about how these components interact to produce feeling states and actions. Some psychologists argue that physiological arousal is a more basic component of emotional response than cognition and that the type of arousal we experience strongly influences our cognitive appraisal and our labeling of the emotion (e.g., Izard, 1984; Zajonc, 1984). Other psychologists argue that cognitive appraisal and physiological arousal are so strongly intertwined that cognitive processes may determine the emotional response (e.g., Lazarus, 1984; 1991a).

The common sense theory of emotions is that something happens (situation) that is cognitively appraised (interpreted) by the person and the feeling state (a combination of arousal and thoughts) follows. For example, you meet someone new, appraise that person as being delightful, and feelings of attraction follow. Or you flunk a test, recognize that you're in trouble, and feel down in the dumps.

However, historic and contemporary theories of how the components of emotions interact are at variance with the commonsense view. Let us consider a number of more important theories and see if we can arrive at some useful conclusions.

The James-Lange Theory

At the turn of the century, William James suggested that our emotions follow, rather than cause, our behavioral responses to events. This view was also proposed by a contemporary of James's, the Danish physiologist Karl G. Lange. It is thus termed the James-Lange theory of emotion.

According to James and Lange (see Figure 9.10, part A), certain external stimuli instinctively trigger specific patterns of arousal and action such as fighting or fleeing. We then become angry *because* we act aggressively. We then become afraid *because* we run away. Emotions are simply the cognitive representations (or by-products) of automatic physiological and behavioral responses.

Walter Cannon (1927) criticized the James-Lange assertion that each emotion has distinct physiological correlates. Cannon argued that the physiological arousal that accompanies emotion A is not as distinct from the arousal that accompanies emotion B as the theory asserts. We can also note that the James-Lange view ascribes a meager function to human cognition; it denies the roles of cognitive appraisal, personal values, and personal choice.

The Cannon-Bard Theory

Walter Cannon was not content to criticize the James-Lange theory. He (Cannon, 1927) and Philip Bard (1934) suggested that an event would trigger bodily responses (arousal and action) and the experience of an emotion simultaneously. As shown in Figure 9.10 (part B), when an event is perceived (processed by the brain), the brain stimulates autonomic and muscular activity (arousal and action) *and* cognitive activity (experience of the emotion). According to the Cannon-Bard theory, emotions *accompany* bodily responses. Emotions are not *produced by* bodily changes, as in the James-Lange theory.

The central criticism of the Cannon-Bard theory focuses on whether bodily responses (arousal and action) and emotions are actually stimulated simultaneously. For example, pain or the perception of danger may trigger arousal before we begin to feel distress or fear. Also, many of us have had the experience of having a "narrow escape" and then becoming aroused and shaky afterward, when we have finally had time to consider the damage that might have occurred.

What is needed is a theory that allows for an ongoing interaction of external events, physiological changes (such as autonomic arousal and muscular activity), and cognitive activities. We do not need to be overly concerned with which comes first—the chicken, the egg, or the egg salad.

The Theory of Cognitive Appraisal

The ancestor of every action is a thought.

Ralph Waldo Emerson

According to Campos and Stenberg (1981), "The recent history of the study of emotion has been dominated by approaches stressing cognitive factors" (p. 273). Among those psychologists who argue that thinking comes first are Gordon Bower, Richard Lazarus, Stanley Schachter, and Robert Zajonc.

Stanley Schachter (1971) asserts that emotions have generally similar patterns of bodily arousal. The essential way in which they vary is along a

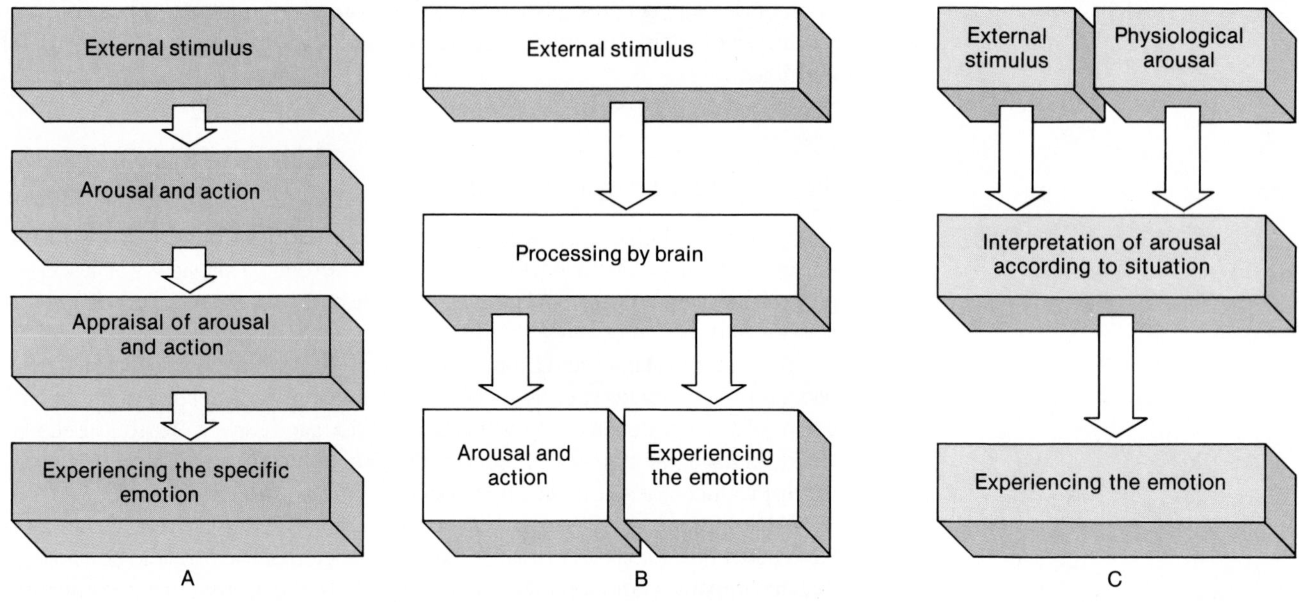

FIGURE 9.10
What Are the Major Theories of Emotion?

Several theories of emotion have been advanced, each of which proposes a different role for the components of emotional response. According to the James-Lange theory (part A), events trigger specific arousal patterns and actions. Emotions result from our appraisal of our body responses. According to the Cannon-Bard theory (part B), events are first processed by the brain. Body patterns of arousal, action, and our emotional responses are then triggered simultaneously. According to the theory of cognitive appraisal (part C), events and arousal are appraised by the individual. The emtional response stems from the person's appraisal of the situation and his or her level of arousal.

weak–strong dimension that is determined by one's level of arousal. The label we *attribute* to an emotion largely depends on our cognitive appraisal of our situation. Cognitive appraisal is based on many factors, including our perception of external events and the ways in which other people seem to respond to those events (see Figure 9.10, part C). Given the presence of other people, we engage in *social comparison* (see p. 344) to arrive at an appropriate response.

In a classic experiment, Schachter and Jerome Singer (1962) showed that arousal can be labeled quite differently depending on a person's situation. The investigators told subjects that their purpose was to study the effects of a vitamin on vision. Half of the subjects received an injection of adrenaline, a hormone that increases autonomic arousal (see Chapter 3). A control group received an injection of an inactive solution. Subjects given adrenaline then received one of three "cognitive manipulations," as shown in Table 9.2. Group 1 was told nothing about possible emotional effects of the "vitamin." Group 2 was deliberately misinformed; group members were led to expect itching, numbness, or other irrelevant symptoms. Group 3 was informed accurately about the increased arousal they would experience.

After receiving injections and cognitive manipulations, subjects were asked to wait, in pairs, while the experimental apparatus was being set up. Subjects did not know that the person with whom they were waiting was a confederate of the experimenter. The confederate's purpose was to model a response that the subject would believe resulted from the injection.

Some subjects waited with a confederate who acted in a happy-go-lucky manner. He flew paper airplanes about the room and tossed paper balls into a wastebasket. Other subjects waited with a confederate who acted angry, complaining about the experiment, tearing up a questionnaire, and departing the waiting room in a huff. As the confederates worked for their Oscars, real subjects were

TABLE 9.2: Injected Substances and Cognitive Manipulations in the Schachter-Singer Study

Group	Substance	Cognitive Manipulation
1	Adrenaline	No information given about effects
2	Adrenaline	Misinformation given: itching, numbness, etc.
3	Adrenaline	Accurate information: physiological arousal
4	(Inactive)	None

Source: Schachter & Singer, 1962.

observed through a one-way mirror.

Subjects in groups 1 and 2 were likely to imitate the behavior of the confederate. Those exposed to the **euphoric** confederate acted jovial and content. Those exposed to the angry confederate imitated that person's complaining, aggressive ways. But groups 3 and 4 were less influenced by the confederate's behavior.

Schachter and Singer concluded that groups 1 and 2 were in an ambiguous situation. The subjects felt arousal from the adrenaline injection but had no basis for attributing it to any event or emotion. Social comparison with the confederate led them to attribute their arousal either to happiness or to anger, whichever was displayed by the confederate. Group 3 expected arousal from the injection with no particular emotional consequences. These subjects did not imitate the confederate's display of happiness or anger because they were not in an ambiguous situation. Group 4 had no physiological arousal for which they needed an attribution, except perhaps for some induced by observing the confederate. Group 4 subjects also failed to imitate the confederate.

Now, happiness and anger are quite different emotions. Happiness is a positive emotion, and anger, for most of us, is a negative emotion. Yet, Schachter and Singer suggest that any physiological differences between these two emotions are so slight that opposing cognitive appraisals of the same situation can lead one person to label arousal as happiness and another person to label arousal as anger. A supportive experiment suggests that it is similarly possible for people to confuse feelings of fear with feelings of sexual attraction (Dutton & Aron, 1974).

The Schachter-Singer view could not be farther removed from the James-Lange theory, which holds that each emotion has specific and readily recognized body sensations. The truth, it turns out, may lie somewhere in between.

In science, it must be possible to attain identical or similar results when experiments are replicated. The Schachter and Singer study has been replicated with *different* results. For instance, in studies by Rogers and Deckner (1975) and Maslach (1978), subjects were less likely to imitate the behavior of the confederate and were more likely to apply negative emotional labels to their arousal, even when exposed to a euphoric confederate.

Evaluation

What do we make of all this? Research by Paul Ekman and his colleagues (1983) suggests that the patterns of arousal that lead us to believe we are experiencing certain emotions may be more specific than suggested by Schachter and Singer but less specific than suggested by James and Lange. It seems that there are some reasonably distinct patterns of arousal, patterns that are not fully interchangeable. Yet our perceived situations, and our cognitive appraisals of our situations, also affect our emotional responses. And when our situations are ambiguous, we may be somewhat more likely to interpret them by social comparison.

In sum, various components of an experience—cognitive, physiological, and behavioral—contribute to our responses. The fact that none of the theories we discussed applies to all people in all situations is comforting. Our emotions are not as easily understood or manipulated as theorists have suggested.

Euphoric Characterized by feelings of well-being, elation.

STUDY GUIDE

Exercise: Matching Scientists and Concepts

Here are a number of statements that express various concepts or positions that concern the psychology of motivation and emotion. Below them are the names of a number of psychologists and other scientists discussed in Chapter 9. Write the number of the statement to the left of the name of the appropriate scientist. The answer key follows the exercise.

1. When our levels of arousal are too low, we engage in activity that will elevate them. When our levels of arousal are too high, we engage in activity that will lower them.
2. People have twelve basic instincts, including hunger, sex, and self-assertion.
3. Once people have met their lower-level needs, they naturally try to find personal fulfillment by actualizing their unique potentials.
4. When people are in an ambiguous situation, they tend to look to other people in the same situation for information as to how they ought to behave.
5. The reason that people and lower animals find rewards to be pleasant is that rewards have the effect of reducing primary or acquired drives.
6. There are 21 important social motives or psychological needs, including the needs for achievement, affiliation, nurturance, and aggression.
7. External events trigger instinctive patterns of arousal and action such as fighting or fleeing. We then become angry *because* we fight, or we become afraid *because* we run away.
8. The instincts of hunger, sex, and aggression give rise to psychic energy which is perceived as tension. This tension motivates us to find ways to restore ourselves to a calmer, resting state.
9. The free expression by outward signs of an emotion intensifies it. On the other hand, the repression, as far as possible, of all outward signs softens our emotions.
10. Yo-yo dieting may teach the body that it will be intermittently deprived of food, slowing the metabolism whenever future food intake is restricted.

_____ A. Charles Darwin
_____ B. Sigmund Freud
_____ C. Clark Hull
_____ D. William James
_____ E. Salvatore Maddi
_____ F. Abraham Maslow
_____ G. William McDougall
_____ H. Henry Murray
_____ I. Stanley Schachter
_____ J. Kelly Brownell

Answers To Matching Exercise

A. 9
B. 8
C. 5
D. 7
E. 1
F. 3
G. 2
H. 6
I. 4
J. 10

ESL—BRIDGING THE GAP

This part consists of phrases and expresssions in which words are used differently from their regular meaning, or are used as metaphors.

Phrases and Expressions (Different Usage)

Misery loves company (344)—people who are feeling unhappy want to be with other people who are feeling unhappy

must be met (325)—must be attended to

this is indeed the case (325)—this is certainly true (emphatic)

limited-time-only, half-price sale (326)—a sale of half the original prices for a very short time

multiyear contracts (324)—contracts for more than one year

berths (324)—positions

climbed (324)—rose; increased

largely learned (327)—predominantly learned; primarily learned

prod them to extend themselves (328)—encourage them to try to exert great effort

a wink (335)—the rapid lowering and raising of one eyelid; it is a signal of affection or interest

"sissies" (336)—boys who are perceived as acting like girls; a derogatory term

assume female mating stances (335)—become receptive to the males

slow to grasp her meaning (336)—not understanding (reluctant to stop his advances)

it is over between them (336)—they do not have a love relationship anymore

far from (336)—not (emphatic)

biology apparently is not destiny (336)—biology apparently does not determine our behavior

yielding circular explanations (328)—producing explanations which are circular, or start in one place and end in the same place

come full circle (328)—started at one point (place), moved and then ended at the same point

runs aground (329)—develops problems

at the price of poverty (329)—that means they will be poor (not have a career that produces money)

bounce up and down in weight (329)—gain and lose weight

binge eating (329)—eating very large amounts in a very short time

the last thing on your mind (330)—not what you would think about at that moment

grope toward (330)—move toward in an uncertain manner

finicky about their food (331)—careful about what they eat; very particular

work in concert (331)—operate together, at the same time

Don't answer too quickly (338)—Think about it before you answer because what you think now might not be what you would think later, or after the activity

As time went on (338)—As time progressed; As the moments passed

question has arisen (339)—question has been asked

"monkeying around" with (339)—playing with

whatsoever (339)—at all (emphatic)

on the eve of (341)—the night before

"psych" themselves up (341)—become enthusiastic and aroused

unscrambling (343)—deciphering; solving the anagram puzzle

took positions (343)—accepted jobs

nonentrepreneurial positions (343)—jobs that did not involve business risk or important decision concerns

see their fate as being in their own hands (343)—think of their future as something they can control

made more demands (343)—required more performance

go it alone (343)—do things alone

social glue (343)—social structure that joins people together ("glue" is adhesive)

"huddle together" (344)—stay closely together

leading them to believe (344)—causing them to think

supposedly (344)—it was not occurring but it was supposed to be occurring

"getting away scot-free" (344)—not having to suffer

color our lives (344)—provide our lives with variety, interest, enjoyment and feeling

fill our days . . . pleasure (344)—cause us to feel pleasure during our lives; cause each day to be pleasurable

fill us with (344)—cause us to have

paid back (345)—punished

lengthy, if not laudable (345)—has been occurring for a long time and can be criticized

squiggling your toes (346)—moving your toes

Baring the teeth (347)—holding the lips up and over the teeth, revealing the teeth; an angry expression in animals

as far as possible (347)—as much as possible

outward signs (347)—external indications

softens our emotions (347)—calms our emotions

"to keep a stiff upper lip" (348)—to maintain the upper lip in an unmovable position—the opposite of crying; thus, the expression means to not reveal emotion and be calm

down in the dumps (348)—depressed

having a "narrow escape" (349)—getting out of a dangerous position

shaky (349)—scared; fearful; afraid

the chicken, the egg, or the egg salad (349)—There is an expression which is the question: "Which came first, the chicken or the egg?" which means that there are some questions which cannot be answered and are not as important as the fact that the result exists.

classic experiment (350)—a famous experiment

confederate of the experimenter (350)—an accomplice of the experimenter; he or she had been told by the experimenter how to act

in a huff (350)—angrily

worked for their Oscars (350)—acted, worked as actors (Oscars are awards for acting in the movies very well.)

The truth, it turns out, may lie somewhere in between. (351)—The truth, we discovered later, may be not one or the other, but in between.

CHAPTER REVIEW

SECTION 1: Motives, Needs, Drive, and Incentives

Objective 1: Define *motives, needs, drives,* and *incentives.*

Motives can be defined as hypothetical states within organisms that (1) ________vate behavior and direct organisms toward (2) ________s. Physiological needs generally reflect states of physical (3)________tion. Psychological needs (4: are or are not?) necessarily based on states of deprivation and may be learned, or acquired through (5) ex________. Needs give rise to (6) ________s, which are psychological in nature and arouse us to action. An (7) ________tive is an object, person, or situation that is perceived as being capable of satisfying a need.

SECTION 2: Theoretical Perspectives on Motivation

Objective 2: Discuss various theories of motivation.

According to the (8) in________ theory of motivation, animals are born with preprogrammed tendencies to behave in certain ways in certain situations. Within instinct theory, stimuli called (9) ________sers elicit innate fixed (10) ________ patterns, or *FAPs.* William James and William (11) Mc________ argued that people have various instincts that lead not only to survival, but also to (12) s________ behavior.

According to Clark (13) ________'s drive-reduction theory of motivation, (14) ________ds are pleasant because they reduce drives. As a consequence, we are motivated to engage in (15) be________ that leads to rewards. Drive-reduction theorists differentiate between (16) pr________ (innate) drives and (17) ________red (learned) drives.

(18) ________istic psychologists argue that behavior can be growth-oriented. Humanists believe that people are motivated to consciously strive for personal (19) ________ment. Abraham (20) M________ hypothesized that people have a hierarchy of needs, including an innate need for self-actualization. Maslow's hierarchy includes physiological needs, safety needs, love and (21) ________ness needs, esteem needs, and, at the top, the need for (22) self-________ation.

SECTION 3: Physiological Drives

Objective 3:Define *homeostasis.*

Physiological drives are unlearned and thus also referred to as (23) ________ry drives. Physiological drives generally function according to the principle of (24) ________sis, which is the body's tendency to maintain a steady state.

Objective 4: Discuss contributors to the hunger drive.

Hunger is regulated by several internal mechanisms, including (25) ________ch contractions, blood (26) s________ level, receptors in the mouth and liver, and the responses of the hypothalamus. Chewing and swallowing provide some sensations of (27) ________ty. The (28) ________al nucleus (VMN) of the hypothalamus apparently functions as a stop-eating center. Lesions in this area lead to (29) ________gia in rats, a condition in which the animals grow to several times their normal body weight, but then level off. It is as if lesions in the VMN raise the (30) _______________t point of the stop-eating center to be triggered at a much higher level. The (31) _______________al hypothalamus apparently functions as a start-eating center. Lesions in the lateral hypothalamus can lead to (32) _______________gia in rats.

Objective 5: Summarize research concerning obesity.

Obesity (33: runs or does not run?) in families. A study of Scandinavian adoptees by Stunkard found that children bear a closer resemblance in weight to their (34: adoptive or biological?) parents than to their (35: adoptive or biological?) parents.

One reason that obese people may desire to eat more than normal-weight people is that they have larger numbers of (36) f_______________ cells, or adipose tissue. As time passes after eating, the (37) _______________d sugar level drops, causing fat to be drawn off from these cells in order to provide further nourishment. The resultant fat deficiency is signalled to the (38) _______________amus, triggering the hunger drive. Obese people may send (39: stronger or weaker?) signals to the hypothalamus because of the larger number of fat cells.

Fatty tissue metabolizes food more (40: rapidly or slowly?) than muscle. For this reason, a person with a high fat-to-muscle ratio will metabolize food (41: less or more?) slowly than a person of the same weight with a (42: higher or lower?) fat-to-muscle ratio. The average man has a (43: higher or lower?) fat-to-muscle ratio than the average woman.

Keesey notes that people who are dieting and people who have lost significant amounts of weight usually do not eat enough to satisfy the (44) _______________t points in their hypothalamuses. As a consequence, compensating metabolic forces are set in motion; that is, (45: fewer or more?) calories are burned. Repeated cycles of dieting and regaining lost weight—referred to as (46) "_______________ _______________" dieting—might be particularly traumatic to one's set point. Brownell points out that yo-yo dieting may teach the body that it will be intermittently deprived of food, thereby (47: accelerating or slowing down?) the metabolism whenever future food intake is restricted.

Effective diets tend to use combinations of the following four elements: improving (48) nu_______________al knowledge; decreasing intake of (49) _______________ries; (50) exer_______________; and behavior (51) _______________cation.

Objective 6: Explain the organizing and activating effects of sex hormones.

Sex hormones promote biological sexual (52) _______________tiation, regulate the menstrual cycle, and influence sexual behavior. Sexual behavior among many lower animals is almost completely governed by (53) _______________ones. Hormones predispose lower animals toward (54) _______________line or feminine mating patterns (an organizing effect) and influence the sex drive and facilitate sexual (55) re_______________ (activating effects).

Male rats who have been castrated at birth—and thus deprived of (56) _______________erone—make no effort to mate as adults. When male rats are castrated in adulthood, injections of testosterone cause them to resume stereotypical (57) _______________ine sexual behavior patterns. Men who are castrated or given antiandrogens usually show gradual loss of sexual desire and of the capacities for (58) _______________tion and orgasm. Female mice, rats, cats, and dogs are receptive to males only during (59) _______________us. But women are sexually responsive during all phases of the menstrual cycle and even after (60) _______________pause.

Objective 7: Discuss the origins of homosexuality.

Homosexuality, or a homosexual (61) _______________ation, is an erotic response to members of one's own sex. Psychodynamic theory ties homosexuality to a "classic pattern" of a (62) "close-_______________ing" mother and a (63) "_______________ed-hostile" father. From the perspective of learning theory, early reinforcement of sexual behavior can influence sexual orientation. Homosexuality (64: has or has not?) been reliably linked to current (adult) levels of male or female sex hormones. But homosexuality may be connected with (65) _______________tal exposure to sex hormones.

SECTION 4: Stimulus Motives

Objective 8: Define *stimulus motive*.

Stimulus motives are like physiological needs in that they are also (66) _______________nate. Physiological needs motivate us to (67: increase or reduce?) the stimulation that impinges upon us. Stimulus motives, by contrast, motivate us to (68: increase or decrease?) the stimulation impinging upon us. People and many lower animals have needs for stimulation and activity, for exploration and manipulation.

Objective 9: Describe the effects of sensory deprivation.

Studies in sensory (69) ________ation show that lack of stimulation is aversive. After a few hours, subjects in these studies become bored and (70) ________table. As time goes on, some of them report visual (71) ________ations, which tend to be limited to geometric figures. After a few days, subjects find it difficult to (72) co________ on problems.

Objective 10: Define optimal arousal, and explain the Yerkes-Dodson law.

There is evidence that we feel best and function most efficiently at our (73) ________al levels of arousal. Sensation seekers may have unusually (74: high or low?) levels of optimal arousal.

According to the Yerkes-Dodson Law, high levels of motivation facilitate performance on (75: simple or complex?) tasks. However, high levels of motivation impede performance on (76: simple or complex?) tasks.

SECTION 5: Social Motives

Objective 11: Define *social motive*.

Social motives differ from primary motives in that they are (77) ________ired through social learning experiences. Harvard University psychologist Henry (78) M________ referred to social motives as (79) ________ical needs. Murray compiled 21 important psychological needs, including needs for (80) ________, or *n* Ach, affiliation, and nurturance.

Objective 12: Discuss the need for achievement.

Psychologist David (81) Mc________ pioneered the assessment of *n* Ach through fantasy. In doing so, McClelland used Murray's Thematic (82) ________tion Test, or TAT.

People with high *n* Ach attain (83: higher or lower?) grades and earn (84: more or less?) money than people of comparable ability with lower *n* Ach. Mothers with high *n* Ach tend to encourage their children to think and act (85) ________dently.

Objective 13: Discuss the need for affiliation.

The need for (86) ________ation prompts us to join groups and make friends. Stanley Schachter found that anxiety tends to (87: increase or decrease?) the need for affiliation. When anxious, we prefer to affiliate with people who (88: share or do not share?) our predicaments. Schachter explains this preference through the theory of social (89) ________ison. This theory holds that when we are in (90) ________guous situations, we seek to affiliate with people with whom we can compare feelings and behaviors.

SECTION 6: Emotion

Objective 14: Describe the role of emotions in human behavior.

An emotion is a state of (91) ________ing. Emotions have physiological, (92) ________al, and cognitive components. Emotions motivate behavior, but can also serve as (93) ________nses to situations and as goals in themselves. The emotion of anxiety involves predominantly (94) ________etic arousal. The emotion of depression involves predominantly (95) ________etic arousal.

Objective 15: Discuss lie detectors.

So-called lie detectors are known technically as (96) ________aphs. Polygraphs assess sympathetic (97) ________al rather than lies per se. Polygraphs monitor four bodily functions: heart rate; blood (98) ________e; respiration rate; and (99) ________dermal response, which is an index of sweating. Supporters of the polygraph claim that it is successful in over (100) ________ percent of cases. However, subjects can reduce the accuracy rate of polygraphs, as lie detectors, by thinking about disturbing events during the interview, biting their tongues, or creating (101) ________etic arousal in other ways.

Objective 16: Discuss whether or not ways of expressing emotions are universal.

The expression of many emotions appears to be (102) ________sal. (103) Sm________ appears to be a universal sign of friendliness and approval. Psychologist

Paul (104) E____________ showed subjects throughout the world photographs of people posing emotions such as anger, disgust, fear, happiness, sadness, and surprise. All groups correctly identified the emotions being portrayed.

Objective 17: Explain the facial-feedback hypothesis.

According to the (105) f____________-f____________ hypothesis, posing intense facial expressions can heighten emotional response. Inducing (106) ____________ing leads subjects to report more positive feelings. Subjects who are induced to frown rate cartoons as more (107) ag____________. It seems that intense expressions heighten (108) ____________al; they may also provide muscular feedback that is characteristic of certain feeling states.

Objective 18: Evaluate the James-Lange, Cannon-Bard, and cognitive-appraisal theories of emotion.

Psychologists are not agreed as to the relative importance of physiological arousal and (109) co____________ appraisal in activating particular emotions. According to the James-Lange theory, emotions have specific patterns of (110) ar____________ and (111) ac____________ that are triggered by certain external events. Emotions follow, rather than cause, the overt behavioral (112) re____________s to events.

The Cannon-Bard theory proposes that processing of events by the brain gives rise simultaneously to (113) ____________nomic activity (arousal), (114) ____________lar activity (action), and cognitive activity (the mental experiencing of the emotion). From this view, emotions (115) ac____________ bodily responses, but are not produced by bodily changes.

According to the theory of cognitive appraisal, emotions have largely similar patterns of (116) ____________al. Emotions essentially vary along a (117) ____________g to weak dimension that is determined by one's level of arousal. The emotion a person will experience in response to an external stimulus reflects that person's (118) ap____________ of the stimulus—that is, the meaning of the stimulus to him or her. A classic study by (119) Sch____________ and Singer suggested that a similar pattern of arousal can be labeled quite differently, depending on a person's situation. However, the Schachter and Singer study has been replicated with different results.

Research seems to suggest that patterns of arousal are more specific than suggested by the theory of (120) ____________tive appraisal, but that cognitive appraisal does play an important role in determining our responses to events.

Answers To Chapter Review

1. Motivate
2. Goals
3. Deprivation
4. Are not
5. Experience
6. Drives
7. Incentive
8. Instinct
9. Releasers
10. Action
11. McDougall
12. Social
13. Hull
14. Rewards
15. Behavior
16. Primary
17. Acquired
18. Humanistic
19. Fulfillment
20. Maslow
21. Belongingness
22. Self-actualization
23. Primary
24. Homeostasis
25. stomach
26. Sugar
27. Satiety
28. Ventromedial
29. Hyperphagia
30. Set
31. Lateral
32. Aphagia
33. Runs
34. Biological
35. Adoptive
36. Fat
37. Blood
38. Hypothalamus
39. Stronger
40. Slowly
41. More
42. Lower
43. Lower
44. Set
45. Fewer
46. Yo-yo
47. Slowing down
48. Nutritional
49. Calories
50. Exercise
51 Modification
52. Differentiation
53. Hormones
54. Masculine
55. Response
56. Testosterone
57. Masculine
58. Erection
59. Estrus
60. Menopause
61. Orientation
62. Close-binding
63. Detached-hostile
64. Has not
65. Prenatal
66. Innate
67. Reduce
68. Increase
69. Deprivation
70. Irritable
71. Hallucinations
72. Concentrate
73. Optimal
74. High
75. Simple
76. Complex
77. Acquired
78. Murray
79. Psychological
80. Achievement

81. McClelland
82. Apperception
83. Higher
84. More
85. Independently
86. Affiliation
87. Increase
88. Share
89. Comparison
90. Ambiguous
91. Feeling
92. Situational
93. Responses
94. Sympathetic
95. Parasympathetic
96. Polygraphs
97. Arousal
98. Pressure
99. Electrodermal
100. 90
101. Sympathetic
102. Universal
103. Smiling
104. Ekman
105. Facial-feedback
106. Smiling
107. Aggressive
108. Arousal
109. Cognitive
110. Arousal
111. Action
112. Responses
113. Autonomic
114. Muscular
115. Accompany
116. Arousal
117. Strong
118. Appraisal
119. Schachter
120. Cognitive

POSTTEST

1. Physiological ______ are the psychological counterparts of physiological needs.
   (a) drives
   (b) incentives
   (c) responses
   (d) behaviors

2. Inherited dispositions that activate behavior patterns designed to reach specific goals are referred to as
   (a) motives.
   (b) drives.
   (c) instincts.
   (d) releasers.

3. A reward of $1,000 for returning a wallet would serve as a(n)
   (a) need.
   (b) incentive.
   (c) drive.
   (d) social motive.

4. Drive-reduction theory has the greatest difficulty explaining
   (a) sensation seeking.
   (b) the thirst drive.
   (c) the hunger drive.
   (d) avoidance of extremes in temperature.

5. When the ventromedial nucleus of a rat's hypothalamus is lesioned, the animal becomes
   (a) hyperglycemic.
   (b) hyperphagic.
   (c) hypoglycemic.
   (d) aphagic.

6. Classic sham feeding experiments with dogs have provided evidence for a role for the ______ in the regulation of the hunger drive.
   (a) hypothalamus
   (b) stomach
   (c) mouth
   (d) liver

7. A friend has managed to lose 30 pounds, but now complains that he is hungry "all the time." According to the text, obese and formerly obese people may be hungry more often than people who have always been normal weight because of
   (a) a higher blood sugar level.
   (b) lack of adequate nutritional information.
   (c) a higher level of adipose tissue.
   (d) a lesion in the lateral hypothalamus.

8. Which of the following is recommended by the text as a way of losing weight?
   (a) Fasting
   (b) Eating no fats
   (c) Going on an extremely low-calorie diet
   (d) Behavior modification.

9. Participants in sensory-deprivation experiments are reported to have experienced all of the following *except* for
   (a) boredom.
   (b) irritability.
   (d) hallucinations.
   (d) delusions.

10. High sensation seekers are less tolerant of ______ than other people.
    (a) high-risk activities
    (b) sensory deprivation
    (c) novel experiences
    (d) sexual experiences

11. A person's optimal level of arousal is
    (a) the level of arousal at which that person functions most efficiently.
    (b) equivalent to the greatest amount of stimulation that the person can tolerate.
    (c) equivalent to the smallest amount of stimulation that the person can tolerate.
    (d) the level of arousal that is associated with novel stimulation.

12. David McClelland assessed *n* Ach by using the
   (a) MMPI.
   (b) Rorschach inkblot test.
   (c) TAT.
   (d) California Psychological Inventory.

13. Social motives differ from primary motives in that they
   (a) affect the group, but not the individual.
   (b) are acquired through social learning.
   (c) are helpful or prosocial rather than selfish.
   (d) seek to reduce rather than increase the amount of stimulation impinging on the individual.

14. Stanley Schachter explains the findings of his research into anxiety and *n* Aff by means of
   (a) James-Lange theory.
   (b) cognitive dissonance theory.
   (c) the theory of social comparison.
   (d) drive reductionism.

15. According to the text, the emotion of ______ involves predominantly sympathetic arousal.
   (a) depression
   (b) anger
   (c) acceptance
   (d) fear

16. Observations of the sexual behavior of Sambian youth suggest that
   (a) youthful sexual behavior patterns have lasting effects on sexual orientation.
   (b) hormone levels vary according to the individual's pattern of sexual activity.
   (c) sexual repression leads to hostility and occasional aggressive outbursts.
   (d) cultural expectations can lead to turnabouts in sexual behavior patterns.

17. It is theorized that the facial-feedback hypothesis may influence the experience of emotions in all of the following ways, with the exception of
   (a) kinesthetic feedback.
   (b) feedback from other people.
   (c) release of neurotransmitters.
   (d) modifying the person's level of arousal.

18. Which of the following noted that baring the teeth may be a universal sign of anger?
   (a) Charles Darwin
   (b) Robert Zajonc
   (c) Stanley Schachter
   (d) William James

19. A person tries to get herself out of a state of depression by engaging in behaviors that were once enjoyable. This approach to overcoming depression is most consistent with a theory proposed by
   (a) William James.
   (b) Walter Cannon.
   (c) Henry Murray.
   (d) Stanley Schachter.

20. Which of the following statements contradicts the theory of emotion proposed by Schachter and Singer?
   (a) Strong arousal is associated with stronger emotions.
   (b) Situations influence the experience of emotions.
   (c) In ambiguous situations, we may try to determine how we should feel by observing others in the same situation.
   (d) There are some reasonably distinct patterns of arousal that are not exchangeable.

Answers To Posttest

1. A	**6.** C	**11.** A	**16.** D
2. C	**7.** C	**12.** C	**17.** B
3. B	**8.** D	**13.** B	**18.** A
4. A	**9.** D	**14.** C	**19.** A
5. B	**10.** B	**15.** D	**20.** D

- ☐ Fertilization takes place in the uterus.
- ☐ Your heart started beating when you were only one-fifth of an inch long and weighed a fraction of an ounce.
- ☐ Infants triple their birth weight by the time they reach their first birthday.
- ☐ The way to a baby's heart is through its stomach—that is, babies become emotionally attached to those who feed them.
- ☐ The highest level of moral reasoning involves relying on our own views of what is right and wrong.
- ☐ Boys are more aggressive than girls.
- ☐ Children's preferences for gender-typed toys and activities do *not* remain flexible until the ages of 5 or 6.
- ☐ Girls are capable of becoming pregnant when they have their first menstrual periods.
- ☐ Menopause brings the end of a woman's childbearing years.
- ☐ Mothers suffer from the "empty nest syndrome" when the youngest child leaves home.
- ☐ Most elderly people are dissatisfied with their lives.

Developmental Psychology?

Learning Objectives

When you have finished studying Chapter 10, you should be able to:

Controversies in Developmental Psychology

1. Discuss the nature-nuture controversy.
2. Discuss the issue as to whether development is continuous or discontinuous.

Physical Development

3. Describe the process of conception.
4. Discuss the sequences of physical development.
5. Describe the reflexes that are present at birth.

Perceptual Development

6. Describe the processes of perceptual development.

Attachment

7. Describe Ainsworth's views on attachment.
8. Explain various theoretical perspectives on attachment.

Cognitive Development

9. Define Piaget's concepts of *scheme, assimilation,* and *accommodation.*
10. Describe Piaget's stages of cognitive development.
11. Evaluate Piaget's theory.

Moral Development

12. Describe Kohlberg's levels and stages of moral development.

Gender-Typing

13. Summarize gender differences in cognition and aggression.
14. Discuss perspectives on gender-typing.

Adolescence

15. Describe the major changes that take place during adolescence.

Adult Development

16. Describe the challenges and crises of young adulthood.
17. Describe the challenges and crises of middle adulthood.
18. Describe the challenges and crises of late adulthood.

There is no cure for birth or death save to enjoy the interval.

George Santayana

On a summerlike day in October, Megan and her husband Michael rush out to their jobs as usual. While Megan, a buyer for a New York department store, is arranging for dresses from the Chicago manufacturer to arrive in time for the spring line, a very different drama is unfolding in her body. Hormones are causing a follicle (egg container) in one of her ovaries to rupture and release an egg cell, or ovum. Megan, like other women, possessed from birth all the egg cells she would ever have. How this ovum was selected to ripen and be released this month is unknown. In any case, Megan will be capable of becoming pregnant for only a couple of days following ovulation.

When it is released, the ovum begins a slow journey down a 4-inch-long fallopian tube to the uterus. It is within this tube that one of Michael's sperm cells will unite with the egg.

It is *not* true that fertilization takes place in the uterus. It normally occurs in a fallopian tube.

Like many other couples, Megan and Michael engaged in sexual intercourse the night before. Unlike most other couples, however, their timing and methodology were preplanned. Megan used a kit bought in a drug store to predict when she would ovulate. She chemically analyzed her urine for the presence of luteinizing hormone, which surges one to two days prior to ovulation. The results suggested that Megan would be most likely to conceive today.

When Megan and Michael made love, he ejaculated hundreds of millions of sperm, with about equal numbers of Y and X sex chromosomes. By the time of conception, only a few thousand had survived the journey to the fallopian tubes. Several bombarded the ovum, attempting to penetrate. Only one succeeded. It carried a Y sex chromosome, so the couple conceived a boy. The fertilized ovum, or **zygote,** is 1/175th of an inch across—a tiny stage for the drama yet to unfold.

Developmental psychologists would be pleased to study the development of Michael and Megan's new son from conception throughout his lifetime. There are several reasons for this. One approach to the explanation of adult behavior lies in the discovery of early influences and developmental sequences. An answer to the question of *why* we behave in certain ways lies in outlining the development of behavior patterns over the years. There also is interest in the effects of genetics, of early interactions with parents and **siblings,** and of the school and the community on traits such as aggressiveness and intelligence.

Developmental psychologists also seek insight into the causes of developmental abnormalities. This avenue of research can contribute to children's health and psychological well-being. For instance, should pregnant women abstain from

Zygote A fertilized ovum.

Siblings Brothers and sisters.

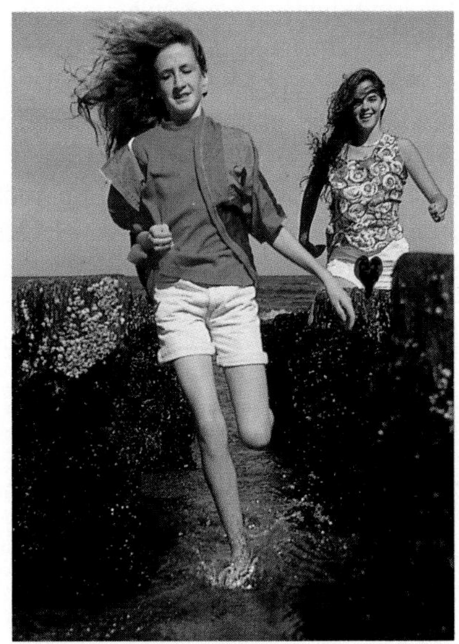

Which Aspects of Development Are Continuous, and Which Are Discontinuous? The adolescent growth spurt is an example of discontinuity in development. Psychologists debate whether or not other aspects of development—such as cognitive development—are most accurately described as continuous or discontinuous.

smoking and drinking? Is it safe for the **embryo** for pregnant women to take aspirin for a headache or tetracycline to ward off a bacterial invasion? Need we be concerned about placing our children in day care? What factors contribute to child abuse? Developmental psychologists are also concerned about issues in adult development. For example, what conflicts and disillusionments can we expect as we journey through our thirties, forties, and fifties? The information acquired by developmental psychologists can help us make decisions about how we rear our children and lead our own lives.

Of course, there is another very good reason for studying development. Thousands of psychologists enjoy it.

CONTROVERSIES IN DEVELOPMENTAL PSYCHOLOGY

Throughout this textbook, we have seen that psychologists see things in very different ways. Diverse views give rise to controversies in developmental psychology as well.

Does Development Reflect Nature or Nurture?

What aspects of behavior originate in a person's genes—that is, nature—and are biologically "programmed" to unfold in the child as long as minimal nutrition and social experience are provided? What aspects of behavior can be largely traced to environmental influences such as nutrition and learning—that is, nurture?

Psychologists seek to understand the influences of nature in our genetic heritage, in the functioning of the nervous system, and in the process of **maturation.** Psychologists look for the influences of nurture in our nutrition, cultural and family backgrounds, and opportunities to learn about the world, including early cognitive stimulation and formal education. The American psychologist Arnold Gesell (1880–1961) leaned heavily toward natural explanations of development, arguing that all areas of development are self-regulated by the unfolding of natural plans and processes. John Watson and other behaviorists leaned heavily toward environmental explanations. (Watson, of course, was focusing primarily on adaptive behavior patterns, whereas Gesell was focusing on many aspects of development, including physical and motor growth and development.) Today, most researchers would agree that nature and nurture interact as children develop.

Is Development Continuous or Discontinuous?

Do developmental changes occur gradually (continuously) or in major qualitative leaps (discontinuously) that dramatically alter our bodies and behavior?

Watson and other behaviorists have viewed human development as being a continuous process in which the effects of learning mount gradually, with no major sudden qualitative changes. Maturational theorists, in contrast, believe that there are a number of rapid qualitative changes that usher in new **stages** of development. Maturational theorists point out that the environment, even when enriched, profits us little until we are ready, or mature enough, to develop in a certain direction. For example, newborn babies will not imitate their parents' speech, even when parents speak clearly and deliberately. Nor does aided practice in "walking" during the first few months after birth significantly accelerate the emergence of independent walking.

Stage theorists such as Sigmund Freud and Jean Piaget saw development as being discontinuous. Both theorists saw biological changes as providing the

Embryo The baby from the third through the eighth weeks following conception, during which time the major organ systems undergo rapid differentiation.

Maturation The orderly unfolding of traits, as regulated by the genetic code.

Stage A distinct period of life that is qualitatively different from other stages.

potential for psychological changes. Freud focused on the ways in which physical sexual developments might provide the basis for personality development. Piaget centered on the ways in which maturation of the nervous system permitted cognitive advances. Stage theorists see the sequences of development as being invariant, although they allow for individual differences in timing.

Certain aspects of physical development do appear to occur in stages. For example, from the age of 2 to the onset of **puberty,** children gradually grow larger. Then the adolescent growth spurt occurs, ushered in by hormones and characterized by rapid biological changes in structure and function (as in the development of the sex organs) as well as in size. So it would appear that a new stage of life has begun. Psychologists disagree more strongly on whether aspects of development such as cognitive development, attachment, and gender typing occur in stages.

Let us now turn to physical development, in which there is clearly a crucial role for maturation.

PHYSICAL DEVELOPMENT

Physical development includes gains in height and weight; maturation of the nervous system; and development of bones, muscles, and the sex organs.

The most dramatic gains in height and weight occur during prenatal development. Although these changes occur literally "out of sight," within nine months, a child develops from a nearly microscopic cell to a **neonate** about 20 inches in length. Weight increases by the billions.

Prenatal Development

During the months following conception, the single cell formed by the union of sperm and egg will multiply—becoming two, then four, then eight, and so on. By the time a **fetus** is ready to be born, it will contain trillions of cells. Prenatal development is divided into three periods: the germinal stage (approximately the first two weeks), the embryonic stage (which lasts from two weeks to about two months after conception), and the fetal stage.

The zygote divides repeatedly as it proceeds on its three- to four-day journey to the uterus. The ball-like mass of multiplying cells wanders about the uterus for another three to four days before beginning to become implanted in the uterine wall. Implantation takes another week or so. The period from conception to implantation is called the **germinal stage,** or the **period of the ovum.** Prior to implantation, the dividing ball of cells is nourished solely by the yolk of the original egg cell, and it does not gain in mass.

The embryonic stage lasts from implantation until about the eighth week of development. During this stage, the major body organ systems differentiate. Development follows two general trends—**cephalocaudal** and **proximodistal.** The growth of the head precedes the growth of the lower parts of the body. If you also think of the body as containing a central axis that coincides with the spinal cord, the growth of the organ systems close to this axis (that is, *proximal*) takes precedence over the growth of the extremities (*distal* areas). Relatively early maturation of the brain and the major organ systems allows them to participate in the nourishment and further development of the embryo.

During the third week after conception, the head and the blood vessels begin to form. During the fourth week, a primitive heart begins to beat and pump blood—in an organism that is one-fifth of an inch long. The heart will continue to beat without rest every minute of every day for perhaps 80 or 90 years.

Puberty The period of early adolescence during which hormones spur rapid physical development.

Neonate A newly born child

Fetus The baby from the third month following conception through childbirth, during which time there is maturation of organ systems and dramatic gains in length and weight.

Germinal stage The first stage of prenatal development during which the dividing mass of cells has not become implanted in the uterine wall.

Period of the ovum Another term for the *germinal stage.*

Cephalocaudal Proceeding from top to bottom.

Proximodistal Proceeding from near to far.

It is true that your heart started beating when you were only one-fifth of an inch long and weighed a fraction of an ounce.

WORLD OF DIVERSITY

Some Notes on Prenatal Care: A Tale of Three Neighborhoods

The United States is many nations, not one. The United States may have the world's most sophisticated medical technology, yet the care that is received by poor people—and, often, middle-class people—places many of us in the "Third World."

Consider Table 10.1, which shows infant health statistics obtained from public records in New York City in 1990. Note that residents of the relatively wealthy white Kips Bay-Yorkville area have healthier newborns than residents of East Harlem (a low-income neighborhood made up mostly of African Americans and Hispanic Americans) or of middle-income and mainly white Astoria-Long Island City. East Harlem mothers, like other low-income mothers (McLaughlin et al., 1992), were more likely than their middle- and upper-income counterparts to have babies with low birth weights and babies who died during infancy. Maternal malnutrition and use of chemical substances such as alcohol and tobacco during pregnancy have all been linked to low birth weights and increased mortality during the first year of life (Barr et al., 1990; McLaughlin et al., 1992; Wardlaw & Insel, 1990).

The differences in infant health shown in the table are also connected with the incidence of prenatal care received by the mothers in the three neighborhoods. According to 1990 New York City Department of Health records, nearly 36 percent of East Harlem mothers receive either late prenatal care or none at all, as compared with about 6 percent in Kips Bay-Yorkville and about 10 percent in Astoria-Long Island City. Research has shown, however, that comprehensive prenatal care is connected with higher birth weights (McLaughlin et al., 1992).

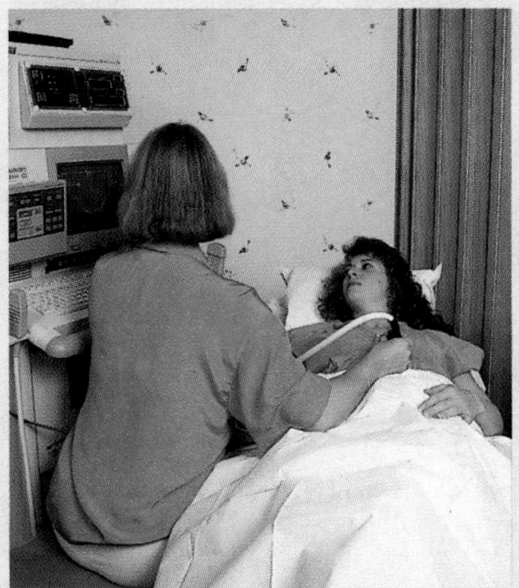

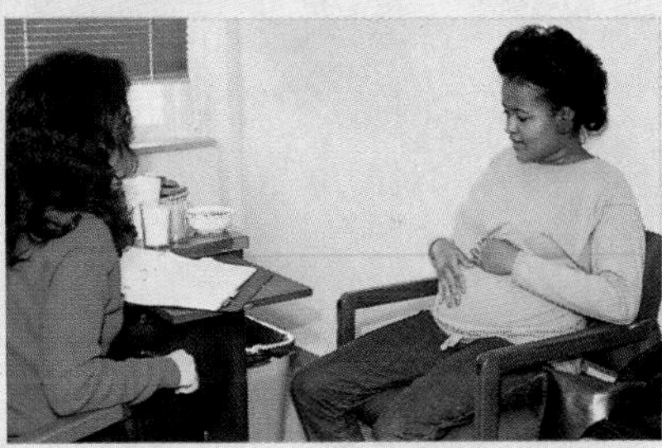

Prenatal Care—Nations Within Nations. Although the United States has the world's most advanced medical technology, this technology is not equally available to all people who live in the United States. Affluent people are highly likely to receive a comprehensive prenatal care program (see photo at top), whereas less affluent people receive more sporadic care, if they receive care at all (photo on bottom).

TABLE 10.1: Infant Health Statistics for Three New York City Neighborhoods

Infant Health Statistics	East Harlem	Astoria-Long Island City	Kips Bay-Yorkville
Infant deaths per 1,000 live births	23.4	14.9	7.3
Low birth-weight babies per 100 live births (less than 5.5 pounds)	18.5	6.1	6.0
Very low birth-weight babies per 100 live births (less than 3.3 pounds)	3.8	0.98	0.87
Live births per 100 in which mothers received late or no prenatal care	35.8	10.4	6.1

This table shows infant health statistics for three New York City neighborhoods. East Harlem is a heavily studied inner-city area that is characterized by poverty and a high proportion of minority residents. The Astoria-Long Island City area is populated by middle-income residents. Kips Bay-Yorkville is a high-income area. Source of data: Department of Health, City of New York, 1990.

A Child-Development Toy Receives an Examination. As children develop, their muscles and neural functions mature, and they learn to coordinate sensory and motor activity. Reflexes such as the grasping reflex drop out of their storehouse of responses and are replaced by voluntary behavior such as intentional holding and manipulation.

The fetal stage lasts from the beginning of the third month until birth. By the end of the third month, all the major organ systems have been formed. During the last three months, the organ systems of the fetus continue to mature. The heart and lungs become increasingly capable of sustaining independent life. Newborn boys average about 7½ pounds and newborn girls about 7 pounds.

Childhood

During infancy, dramatic gains continue. Babies usually double their birth weight in about five months and triple it by the first birthday. Their height increases by about 10 inches in the first year. Children grow another 4 to 6 inches during the second year and gain some 4 to 7 pounds.

It is true that infants triple their birth weight by the time they reach their first birthday. They also make dramatic gains in height.

Following the gains of infancy, children gain about 2 to 3 inches a year until they reach the adolescent growth spurt. Weight gains also remain fairly even at about 4 to 6 pounds per year.

In one of the more fascinating aspects of the development of the nervous system, newborn babies show a number of automatic behavior patterns that are essential to survival—reflexes.

Reflexes

Soon after you were born, a doctor or a nurse probably pressed her fingers against the palms of your hands. Although you would have had no "idea" as to what to do, most likely your grasped the fingers firmly—so firmly that you could actually have been lifted from your cradle by holding on! Grasping at birth is inborn, just one of the neonate's many **reflexes.** Reflexes are simple, unlearned, stereotypical responses that are elicited by specific stimuli. They do not involve higher brain functions. They occur automatically, without thinking.

Many reflexes such as the breathing reflex have survival value. The breathing rate is regulated by body levels of oxygen and carbon dioxide. We take in oxygen and give off carbon dioxide. Newborns normally take their first breath before the umbilical cord is cut. The breathing reflex continues to work for a lifetime, though we can take conscious control of breathing when we choose to do so.

Newborn children do not "know" that it is necessary to eat to survive, so it is fortunate that they have **rooting** and sucking reflexes. Neonates will turn their heads (root) toward stimuli that prod or stroke the cheek, chin, or corners of the mouth. They will suck objects that touch their lips. Neonates reflexively withdraw from painful stimuli (the withdrawal reflex), and they draw up their legs and arch their backs in response to sudden noises, bumps, or loss of support while being held (the startle, or Moro, reflex). They reflexively grasp objects that press against the palms of their hands (the grasp, or palmar, reflex). They spread their toes when the soles of their feet are stimulated (the Babinski reflex). Babies also show sneezing, coughing, yawning, blinking, and many other reflexes. It is guaranteed that you will learn about the **sphincter** reflex if you put on your best clothes and hold an undiapered neonate on your lap for a while. Pediatricians assess the adequacy of babies' neural functioning largely by testing their reflexes.

As children develop, their muscles and neural functions mature, and they

Reflex A simple unlearned response to a stimulus.

Rooting The turning of an infant's head toward a touch, such as by the mother's nipple.

Sphincter A ringlike muscle that circles a body opening such as the anus. An infant will exhibit the sphincter reflex (have a bowel movement) in response to intestinal pressure.

learn to coordinate sensory and motor activity. Many reflexes drop out of their storehouse of responses. Many processes, such as the elimination of wastes, come under voluntary control. Some highlights of children's motor development are chronicled in Figure 10.1.

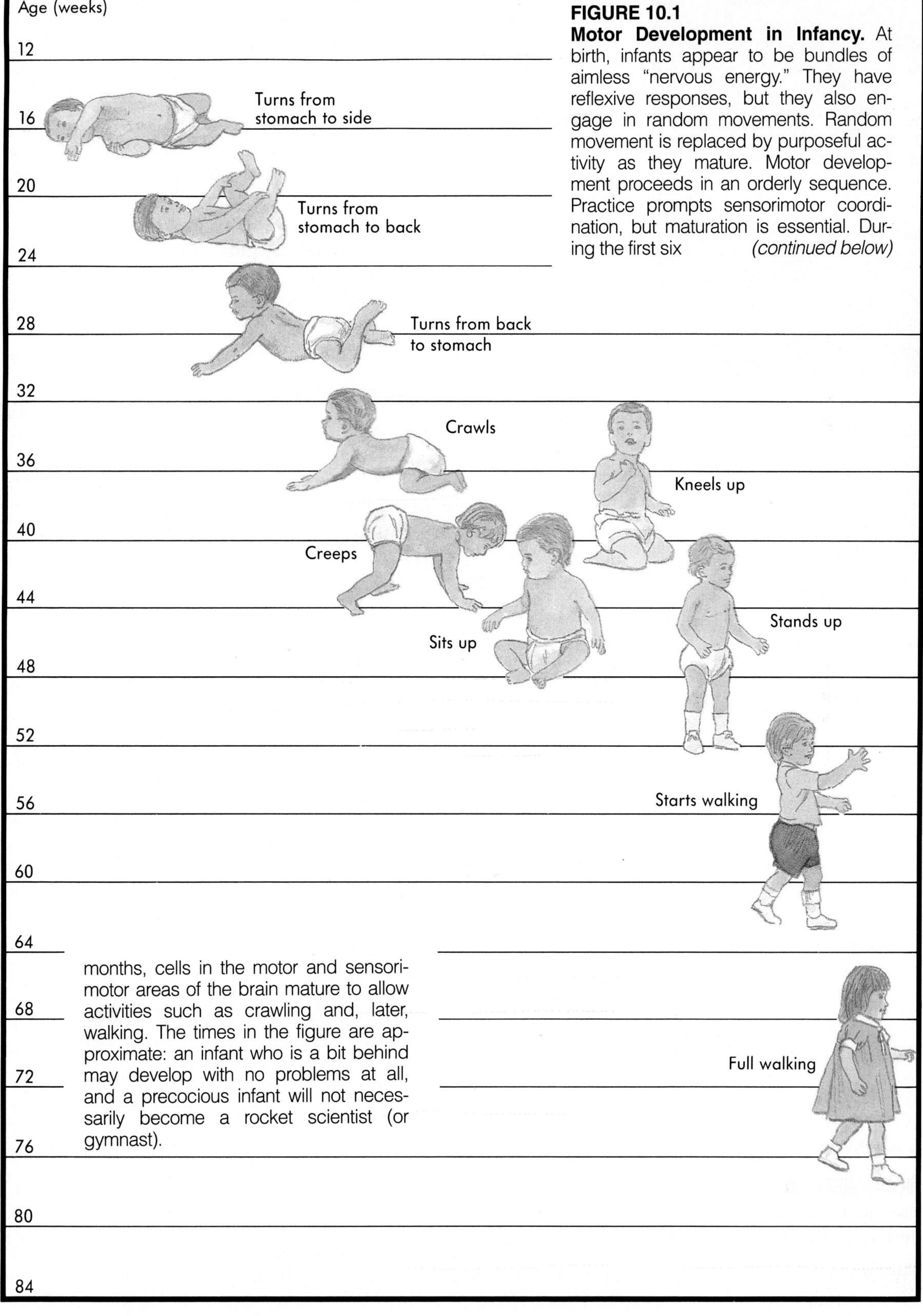

FIGURE 10.1
Motor Development in Infancy. At birth, infants appear to be bundles of aimless "nervous energy." They have reflexive responses, but they also engage in random movements. Random movement is replaced by purposeful activity as they mature. Motor development proceeds in an orderly sequence. Practice prompts sensorimotor coordination, but maturation is essential. During the first six *(continued below)* months, cells in the motor and sensorimotor areas of the brain mature to allow activities such as crawling and, later, walking. The times in the figure are approximate: an infant who is a bit behind may develop with no problems at all, and a precocious infant will not necessarily become a rocket scientist (or gymnast).

FIGURE 10.2
The Classic Visual Cliff Experiment. This young explorer has the good sense not to crawl out onto an apparently unsupported surface, even when Mother beckons from the other side. Rats, pups, kittens, and chicks also will not try to walk across to the other side. (So don't bother asking why the chicken crossed the visual cliff.)

PERCEPTUAL DEVELOPMENT

William James (1890) wrote that the newborn baby must sense the world as "one great booming, buzzing confusion." The neonate emerges from being literally suspended in a temperature-controlled environment to being—again, in James's words—"assailed by eyes, ears, nose, skin, and entrails at once." Despite his eloquence, James may have exaggerated the disorganization of the neonate's world.

Newborn children spend about 16 hours a day sleeping and do not have much opportunity to learn about the world. Yet, they are capable of perceiving the world reasonably well soon after birth (Haber & Hershenson, 1980).

Vision. The **pupillary reflex** is present at birth. Infants may be able to discriminate most, if not all, of the colors of the visible spectrum by 2 to 3 months of age. By age 4 months, they prefer red and blue to other colors (Bornstein & Marks, 1982; Fagen, 1980). Newborns can fixate on a light. Within a couple of days, they can follow, or track, a moving light with their eyes (McGurk et al., 1977).

Neonates do not show **visual accommodation.** They see as though looking through a fixed-focus camera. They are thus nearsighted and see objects 7 to 9 inches away most clearly (Banks & Salapatek, 1981). By about the age of 4 months, however, infants seem able to focus about as well as adults can. Visual acuity makes dramatic gains during the first six months and approaches adult levels within a few years.

Response to Complex Visual Stimulation and the Human Face. The visual preferences of infants are measured by the amount of time, termed **fixation time,** that they spend looking at one stimulus instead of another. In classic research by Robert Fantz (1961), 2-month-old infants preferred visual stimuli that resembled the human face as compared to newsprint, a bull's-eye, and featureless disks colored red, white, and yellow. Subsequent research suggests that the complexity of facelike patterns may be more important than their content at this age. For example, babies have been shown facelike patterns that differ either according to the number of elements or the degree to which they are organized to match the human face. Five- to ten-week-old babies fixate longer on patterns that have high numbers of elements. The organization of the elements—that is, the degree to which they resemble the face—is less important. By 15 to 20 weeks, the organization of the pattern also matters. Babies then dwell longer on facelike patterns (e.g., Haaf et al., 1983).

Infants thus seem to have an inborn preference for complex visual stimulation. However, preference for faces as opposed to other equally complex stimuli may not emerge until infants have had experience with people. Nurture as well as nature appears to influence infants' preferences.

Depth Perception. Infants generally respond to cues for depth by the time they are able to crawl about (6 to 8 months of age or so), as well as having the good sense to avoid crawling off ledges and tabletops into open space (Campos et al., 1978). Note the setup (Figure 10.2) in the classic "visual cliff" experiment run by Walk and Gibson (1961). An 8-month-old infant crawls freely above the portion of the glass with a checkerboard pattern immediately beneath but hesitates to crawl over the portion of the glass beneath which the checkerboard has been dropped a few feet. Since the glass alone would support the infant, this is a "visual cliff," not an actual cliff.

Psychologists can assess infants' "emotional" responses to the visual cliff long before they can crawl. For example, Joseph Campos and his colleagues (1970) found that 1-month-old infants showed no emotional response, as measured by changes in heart rate, when placed face-down on the visual cliff. At about 2 months of age, the infants showed decreases in heart rate when so placed, which psychologists interpret as interest. The heart rates of 9-month-olds accelerated when the infants were placed on the cliff, which is interpreted as a fear response. Moreover, eight of ten crawling infants studied by Walk and Gibson refused to venture onto the visually unsupported glass surface, even when their mothers beckoned.

Pupillary reflex The automatic adjustment of the irises to permit more or less light to enter the eye.

Visual accommodation Automatic adjustment of the thickness of the lens in order to focus on objects.

Fixation time The amount of time spent looking at a visual stimulus.

Hearing. Months before they are born, fetuses respond to sounds. Fetuses' middle and inner ears normally reach their mature sizes and shapes before birth (Aslin et al., 1983). During the seventh to ninth months, fetuses respond to sounds of different frequencies by movements and changes in the heart rate, suggesting that they can discriminate pitch.

Most neonates reflexively turn their heads toward unusual sounds and suspend other activities. This finding, along with findings about visual tracking, suggests that infants are preprogrammed to survey their environments. Neonates cannot hear sounds as high or low as those perceived by older children and adults, but they hear pitches of speech about as well as adults do. Hearing is thus a good medium for parent-child communication. Pitch discrimination gradually extends to 20 to 20,000 cycles per second in the adult.

Three-day-old babies prefer their mothers' voices to those of other women, but they do not show similar preferences for the voices of their fathers (DeCasper & Fifer, 1980; Prescott & DeCasper, 1981). By birth, of course, babies have had many months of "experience" in the uterus. For at least two or three months, babies have been capable of sensing sounds. Because they are predominantly exposed to sounds produced by their mothers, learning may contribute to neonatal preferences.

Smell: The Nose Knows Early. Neonates can discriminate distinct odors such as those of onions and licorice. Newborns breathe more rapidly and are more active when presented with powerful odors—and they turn away from unpleasant odors (Rieser et al., 1976). They can become used to even powerful odors, as can adults. The nasal preferences of babies are similar to those of adults (Steiner, 1979). Newborn infants spit, stick out their tongues, and literally wrinkle their noses at the odor of rotten eggs. But they smile and show licking motions in response to chocolate, strawberry, vanilla, and honey.

Taste. Shortly after birth, infants show the ability to discriminate taste. They suck liquid solutions of sugar and milk but grimace and refuse to suck salty or bitter solutions. Infants can clearly discriminate sweetness on the day following birth. The tongue pressure of 1-day-old infants sucking on a nipple correlates with the amount of sugar in their liquid diet.

Touch. Newborn babies are sensitive to touch. Many reflexes (rooting and sucking are two) are activated by pressure against the skin. Newborns are relatively insensitive to pain, however, which may be adaptive considering the squeezing of the birth process. Sensitivity increases dramatically within a few days.

The sense of touch is an important avenue of learning and communication for babies. Not only do the skin senses provide information, but sensations of skin against skin also appear to provide feelings of comfort and security that may contribute to the formation of affectionate bonds between infants and caregivers, as we shall see in the section on attachment.

vision is last to be developed. In the uterus.

Attachment. Feelings of attachment bind most parents tightly to their children. According to Ainsworth, attachment is an emotional bond between one animal or person and another specific individual. Secure attachment paves the way for healthy social development.

ATTACHMENT

At just 2 years, my daughter Allyn almost succeeded at preventing publication of an earlier edition of this book. When I locked myself into my study, she positioned herself outside the door and called, "Daddy, oh Daddy." Next came, "Pencer, oh Pencer." At other times, she would bang on the door or cry outside. When I would give in (several times a day) and open the door, she would run in and say, "I want you to pick up me" and hold out her arms or climb into my lap. Then she would say, "I want to play." I would beg, "I'm in the middle of something. Just give me a second to finish it." Then, when I would look back at my monitor, she would try to turn my face to hers or turn the computer off. Or, if I were trying to jot down some notes from a journal, she would try to yank them from my hands and toss them across the room. (I have sometimes wanted to do that to the journals, too.)

I am a psychologist. Solutions thus came easily. For example, I could write outside the home. But this solution had the drawback of distancing me from my family. Another solution was to let my daughter cry and ignore her. If I refused to reinforce crying, crying would become extinguished. There were only two problems with this solution. First, I was incapable of ignoring her crying. Second, I didn't *want* to extinguish her efforts to get to me. **Attachment,** you see, is a two-way street.

Mary Ainsworth (1989), one of the preeminent researchers in attachment, defines attachment as an emotional tie that is formed between one animal or person and another specific individual. Attachment keeps organisms together and tends to endure. Attachment is essential to the very survival of the infant (Bowlby, 1988).

The behaviors that define attachment include (1) attempts to maintain contact or nearness and (2) shows of anxiety when separated. Babies and children try to maintain contact with caregivers to whom they are attached. They engage in eye contact, pull and tug at them, ask to be picked up, and may even jump in front of them in such a way that they will be "run over" if they are not picked up!

Attachment is one measure of the care that infants receive (Bretherton & Waters, 1985; Sroufe, 1985). **Securely attached** babies cry less frequently than **insecurely attached** babies (Ainsworth & Bowlby, 1991). They are more likely to show affection toward their mothers, cooperate with them, and use them as a base for exploration (Bowlby, 1988). Securely attached children are more likely to be emotionally warm, socially mature, and popular with peers (LaFreniere & Sroufe, 1985). They are happier, more enthusiastic, and more socially active. In school, they show more leadership, academic persistence, curiosity, and self-reliance than insecurely attached agemates (Frodi et al., 1985; Sroufe, 1983).

Stages of Attachment

The study of attachment is greatly indebted to the individual and collaborative efforts of Mary D. Salter Ainsworth and John Bowlby (1991)—whose "partnership [has] endured for 40 years across time and distance" (p. 333). In a review of their research, they refer to critical cross-cultural studies such as one conducted by Ainsworth in Uganda, which led to a theory of stages of attachment.

Ainsworth tracked the attachment behaviors of Ugandan infants. She noted their efforts to maintain contact with the mother, their protests when separated, and their use of the mother as a base for exploring the environment. At first, the Ugandan infants showed **indiscriminate attachment.** That is, they preferred being held or being with someone to being alone, but they showed no preferences. Specific attachment to the mother began to develop at about 4 months of age and grew intense by about 7 months of age. Fear of strangers, if it developed at all, followed by one or two months.

From studies such as these, Mary Ainsworth (1984, 1985) identified three stages of attachment:

1. The **initial-preattachment phase,** which lasts from birth to about 3 months and is characterized by indiscriminate attachment.
2. The **attachment-in-the-making phase,** which occurs at about 3 or 4 months and is characterized by preference for familiar figures.
3. The **clear-cut-attachment phase,** which occurs at about 6 or 7 months and is characterized by intensified dependence on the primary caregiver—usually the mother.

Bowlby noted that children's attachment behaviors are also characterized by fear of strangers ("stranger anxiety"). But not all children show fear of strangers.

Attachment The enduring affectional tie that binds one person to another.

Secure attachment A type of attachment characterized by positive feelings toward attachment figures and feelings of security.

Insecure attachment A negative type of attachment, in which children show indifference or ambivalence toward attachment figures.

Indiscriminate attachment Showing attachment behaviors toward any person.

Initial-preattachment phase The first phase in forming bonds of attachment, characterized by indiscriminate attachment.

Attachment-in-the-making phase The second phase in forming bonds of attachment, characterized by preference for familiar figures.

Clear-cut-attachment phase The third phase in forming bonds of attachment, characterized by intensified dependence on the primary caregiver.

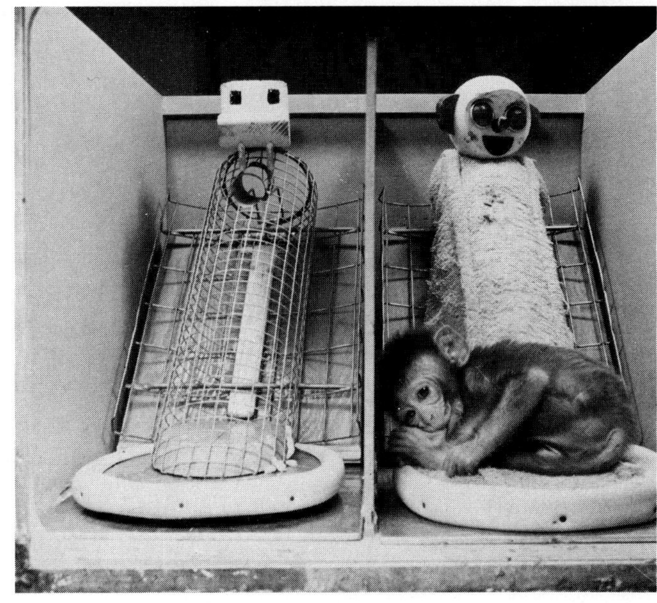

Time on cloth mother
Time on wire mother
Hours per Day
0 6 12 18
5 25 85 105 125 145 165
Mean Age (days)

FIGURE 10.3
Attachment in Infant Monkeys. Although this rhesus monkey infant is fed by the "wire mother," it spends most of its time clinging to the soft, cuddly "terry-cloth mother." It knows where to get a meal, but contact comfort is apparently a more central determinant of attachment in infant monkeys (and infant humans?) than is the feeding process.

Theoretical Views of Attachment

Attachment, like so many other behavior patterns, seems to develop as a result of the interaction of nature and nurture.

A Behavioral View of Attachment: Mother as a Reinforcer. Early in the century, behaviorists argued that attachment behaviors are learned through conditioning. Caregivers feed their infants and tend to their other physiological needs. Thus, infants associate their caregivers with gratification and learn to approach them to meet their needs. From this perspective, a caregiver becomes a conditioned reinforcer. The feelings of gratification that are associated with meeting basic needs generalize into feelings of security when the caregiver is present.

Harlow's View of Attachment: Mother as a Source of Contact Comfort. Classic research by psychologist Harry F. Harlow cast doubt on the behaviorist view that attachment is learned mechanically. Harlow had noted that infant rhesus monkeys reared without mothers or companions became attached to pieces of cloth in their cages. They maintained contact with them and showed distress when separated from them. Harlow conducted a series of experiments to find out why (Harlow, 1959).

In one study, Harlow placed rhesus monkey infants in cages with two surrogate mothers, as shown in Figure 10.3. One "mother" was made from wire mesh from which a baby bottle was extended. The other surrogate mother was made of soft, cuddly terry cloth. Infant monkeys spent most of their time clinging to the cloth mother, even though "she" did not gratify the need for food (see Figure 10.3). Harlow concluded that monkeys—and perhaps humans—have a primary

FIGURE 10.4
Security. With its terry-cloth surrogate mother nearby, this infant rhesus monkey apparently feels secure enough to explore the "bear monster" placed in its cage. But infants with only wire surrogate mothers, or with no mothers, remain cowering in a corner when the bear or other "monsters" are introduced.

(unlearned) need for **contact comfort** that is as basic as the need for food. Gratification of the need for contact comfort, rather than food, might be why infant monkeys (and humans) cling to their mothers.

It is *not* necessarily true that babies become emotionally attached to those who feed them. Contact comfort might be a stronger wellspring of attachment.

Let's put it another way: The path to a monkey's heart may be through its skin, not its stomach.

Harlow and Zimmerman (1959) found that a surrogate mother made of terry cloth could also serve as a comforting base from which a rhesus infant could explore the environment. Toys such as stuffed bears (see Figure 10.4) and oversized wooden insects were placed in cages with rhesus infants and their surrogate mothers. When the infants were alone or had wire surrogate mothers for companions, they cowered in fear as long as the "bear monster" or "insect monster" was present. But when the terry-cloth mothers were present, the infants clung to them for a while, then explored the intruding "monster." With human infants, too, bonds of mother-infant attachment appear to provide a secure base from which infants feel encouraged to express their curiosity motives.

Imprinting: An Ethological View of Attachment. Ethologists note that for many animals, attachment is an inborn fixed action pattern (FAP). The FAP of attachment, like other FAPs, is theorized to occur in the presence of a species-specific releasing stimulus and during a **critical period** of life.

Some animals become attached to the first moving object they encounter. The unwritten rule seems to be, "If it moves, it must be mother." It is as if the image of the moving object becomes "imprinted" on the young animal, and so the formation of an attachment in this manner is called **imprinting.**

Ethologist Konrad Lorenz (1981) became well known when pictures of his "family" of goslings were made public (see Figure 10.5). How did Lorenz acquire his following? He was present when the goslings hatched, during their critical periods, and he allowed them to follow him. The critical period for geese and some other animals is bounded, at the younger end, by the age at which they first engage in locomotion and, at the older end, by the age at which they develop fear of strangers. The goslings followed Lorenz persistently, ran to him when frightened, honked with distress at his departure, and tried to overcome barriers between them. If you substitute crying for honking, it all sounds rather human.

If imprinting occurs with children, it does not follow the mechanics that apply to waterfowl. Not all children develop fear of strangers. When they do, it occurs at about 6 to 8 months of age—*prior to* independent locomotion, or

Contact comfort A hypothesized primary drive to seek physical comfort through contact with another.

Critical period A period of time when a fixed action pattern can be elicited by a releasing stimulus.

Imprinting A process occurring during a critical period in the development of an organism, in which that organism responds to a stimulus in a manner that will afterward be difficult to modify.

FIGURE 10.5
Imprinting. Quite a following? Konrad Lorenz may not look like Mommy to you, but these goslings became attached to him because he was the first moving object they perceived and followed. This type of attachment process is referred to as imprinting.

crawling, which usually occurs one or two months later. Yet, Ainsworth and Bowlby (1991) also hold an ethological view of human attachment, though the critical period with humans would be quite extended.

COGNITIVE DEVELOPMENT

At 2½, Allyn found another way of preventing me from writing. She demanded that I continue to play Billy Joel on the stereo. Put aside the issue of her taste in music. My problem stemmed from the fact that when she asked for Billy Joel (the name of the singer), she could be satisfied only by my playing the first song ("Moving Out") on the album. When "Moving Out" ended and the next song, "The Stranger," began to play, she would insist that I play "Billy Joel" again. "That *is* Billy Joel," I would protest. "No! No!" she would insist, "I want Billy Joel!"

We went around in circles until it dawned on me that "Billy Joel," to her, symbolized the song "Moving Out," not the name of the singer. My daughter was conceptualizing *Billy Joel* as a *property* of a given song, not as the name of a person who could sing many songs. From the ages of 2 to 4, children tend to show confusion between symbols and the objects they represent. At their level of cognitive development, they do not recognize that words are arbitrary symbols for objects and events and that people could get together and decide to use different words for things. Instead, they tend to think of words as inherent properties of objects and events.

The developing thought processes of children—their cognitive development—is explored in this section. Cognitive functioning develops over a number of years, and children have ideas about the world that differ considerably from those of adults. Many of these ideas are charming but illogical. Swiss psychologist Jean Piaget (1896–1980) contributed significantly to our understanding of children's cognitive development.

Jean Piaget's Cognitive-Developmental Theory

In his early twenties, Jean Piaget obtained a job at the Binet Institute in Paris. His initial task was to develop a standardized version of the Binet intelligence test in French. In so doing, he questioned many children using potential items and became intrigued by their *incorrect* answers. Another investigator might have shrugged them off and forgotten them. Young Piaget realized that there were methods to his children's madness. The wrong answers reflected consistent, if illogical, cognitive processes.

Piaget hypothesized that children's cognitive processes develop in an orderly sequence of stages (1963). Although some children may be more advanced than others at particular ages, the developmental sequence is invariant. Piaget identified four major stages of cognitive development (see Table 10.1): *sensorimotor, preoperational, concrete–operational,* and *formal–operational.*

Piaget regarded children as natural physicists who actively intend to learn about and manipulate their worlds. In the Piagetian view, children who squish their food and laugh enthusiastically, for example, are often acting as budding scientists. In addition to enjoying a response from parents, they are studying the texture and consistency of their food. (Parents, of course, often wish that their children would practice these experiments in the laboratory, not the dining room.)

Piaget's view differs markedly from the behaviorist view that people merely react to environmental stimuli rather than intending to interpret and act on the world. Piaget saw people as actors, not reactors. Piaget believed that people purposefully form cognitive representations of, and seek to manipulate, the world.

TABLE 10.1: Piaget's Stages of Cognitive Development

Stage	Age	Description
Sensorimotor	Birth–2 years	Child lacks language and initially does not use symbols or mental representations of objects in the environment. Simple responding to the environment (through reflexive schemes) draws to an end, and intentional behavior—such as making interesting sights last—begins. The child develops the object concept and acquires the basics of language.
Preoperational	2–7 years	The child begins to represent the world mentally, but thought is egocentric. The child does not focus on two aspects of a situation at once and therefore lacks conservation. The child shows animism, artificialism, and immanent justice.
Concrete–operational	7–12 years	The child shows conservation concepts, can adopt the viewpoint of others, can classify objects in series (for example, from shortest to longest), and shows comprehension of basic relational concepts (such as one object being larger or heavier than another).
Formal–operational	12 years and above	Mature, adult thought emerges. Thinking seems to be characterized by deductive logic, consideration of various possibilities before acting to solve a problem (mental trial and error), abstract thought (for example, philosophical weighing of moral principles), and the formation and testing of hypotheses.

Piaget's Basic Concepts: Assimilation and Accommodation. Piaget described human thought or intelligence in terms of *assimilation* and *accommodation.* **Assimilation** is responding to a new stimulus through a reflex or existing habit. Infants, for example, usually try to place new objects in their mouths to suck, feel, or explore. Piaget would say that the child is assimilating a new toy to the sucking **scheme.** A scheme is a pattern of action or a mental structure that is involved in acquiring or organizing knowledge.

Accommodation is the creation of new ways of responding to objects or looking at the world. In accommodation, children transform existing schemes—action patterns or ways of organizing knowledge—in order to incorporate new events. Children (and adults) accommodate to objects and situations that cannot be integrated into existing schemes. The ability to accommodate to novel stimulation advances as a result of both maturation and learning, or experience.

Most of the time, newborn children assimilate environmental stimulation according to reflexive schemes, although adjusting the mouth to contain the nipple is a primitive kind of accommodation. Reflexive behavior, to Piaget, is not characteristic of "true" intelligence. True intelligence involves dealing with the world through a smooth, fluid balancing of the processes of assimilation and accommodation. As the child matures, accommodation becomes more sophisticated in that the child comes to imitate the ways in which other people cope with novel events. Let us now return to the stages of cognitive development.

The Sensorimotor Stage. The newborn infant is capable of assimilating novel stimulation only to existing reflexes (or ready-made schemes) such as the rooting and sucking reflexes. But by the time an infant reaches the age of 1 month, it will already show purposeful behavior by repeating behavior patterns that are pleasurable such as sucking its hand. During the first month or so, an infant apparently does not connect stimulation perceived through different senses. Crude turning toward sources of auditory and olfactory stimulation has a ready-made look about it that can not be considered purposeful searching. But within the first few months, the infant begins to coordinate vision with grasping so that it simultaneously looks at what it is holding or touching.

A 3- or 4-month-old infant may be fascinated by its own hands and legs. It may become absorbed in watching itself open and close its fists. The infant becomes increasingly interested in acting on the environment to make interesting results (such as the sound of a rattle) last. Behavior becomes increasingly intentional and purposeful. Between 4 and 8 months of age, the infant explores cause-and-effect relationships such as the thump that can be made by tossing an object or the way kicking can cause a hanging toy to bounce.

Assimilation According to Piaget, the inclusion of a new event into an existing scheme.

Scheme According to Piaget, a hypothetical mental structure that permits the classification and organization of new information.

Accommodation According to Piaget, the modification of schemes so that information inconsistent with existing schemes can be integrated or understood.

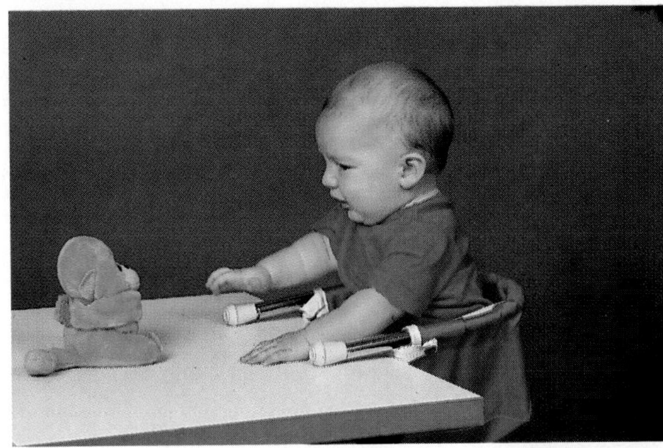

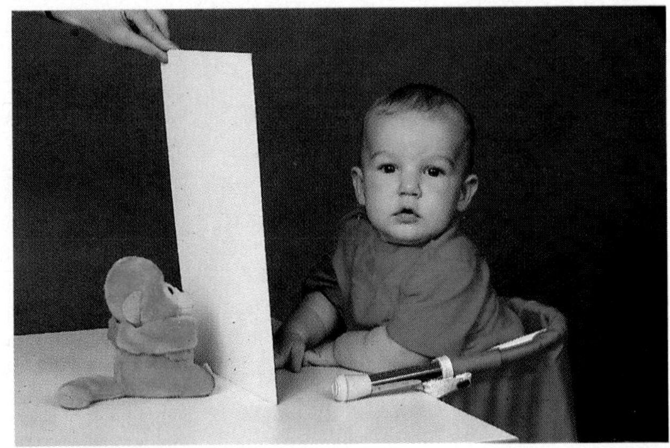

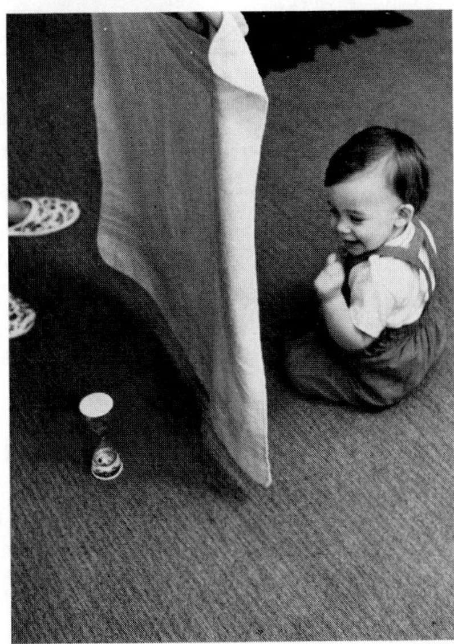

FIGURE 10.6
Object Permanence.

To the infant at the top, who is in the early part of the sensorimotor stage, out of sight is truly out of mind. Once a sheet of paper is placed between the infant and the toy elephant, the infant loses all interest in the toy. From evidence of this sort, Piaget concluded that the toy is not mentally represented. The bottom series of photos shows a child in a later part of the sensorimotor stage. This child does mentally represent objects and pushes through a towel to reach an object that has been screened from sight.

Prior to the age of 6 months or so, out of sight is literally out of mind. Objects are not yet mentally represented. For this reason, as you can see in Figure 10.6, a child will make no effort to search for an object that has been removed or placed behind a screen. By the ages of 8 to 12 months, however, infants realize that objects removed from sight still exist and attempt to find them. In this way, they show what is known as **object permanence.**

During the second year of life, children begin to show interest in how things are constructed. It may be for this reason that they persistently touch and finger their parents' and their own faces. Toward the end of the second year, children begin to engage in mental trial and error before they try out overt behavior. For instance, when they look for an object you have removed, they will no longer begin their search in the last place it was seen. Rather, they may follow you, assuming that you are carrying the object even though it is not visible. It is as though they are anticipating failure in searching for the object in the place where it was most recently seen.

Object permanence Recognition that objects removed from sight still exist, as demonstrated in young children by continued pursuit.

TABLE 10.2: Preoperational Thought

Type of Thought	Sample Questions	Typical Answers
Egocentrism	Why does it get dark out? Why does the sun shine? Why is there snow? Why is grass green? What are TV sets for?	So I can go to sleep. To keep me warm. For me to play in. Because that's my favorite color. To watch my favorite shows and cartoons.
Animism (attributing life to inanimate objects)	Why do trees have leaves? Why do stars twinkle? Why does the sun move in the sky? Where do boats go at night?	To keep them warm. Because they're happy and cheerful. To follow children and hear what they say. They sleep like we do.
Artificialism (assuming that environmental features have been fashioned by people)	What makes it rain? Why is the sky blue? What is the wind? What causes thunder? How does a baby get in Mommy's tummy?	Someone emptying a watering can. Somebody painted it. A man blowing. A man grumbling. Just make it first. (How?) You put some eyes on it, put the head on, etc.

Because the first stage of development is dominated by learning to coordinate perception of the self and of the environment with motor (muscular) activity, Piaget termed it the **sensorimotor stage.** The sensorimotor stage comes to a close at about the age of 2, with the acquisition of the basics of language.

The Preoperational Stage. The **preoperational stage** is characterized by children's early use of words and symbols to represent objects and the relationships among them. But be warned—any resemblance between the logic of children between the ages of 2 to 7 and your own logic very often appears to be purely coincidental. Children may use the same words as adults do, but this does not mean that their views of the world are similar to adults'. A major limit on preoperational children's thinking is that it tends to be one-dimensional—to focus on one aspect of a problem or situation at a time.

One consequence of one-dimensional thinking is **egocentrism.** Preoperational children cannot understand that other people do not see things as they do. When Allyn was 2½, I asked her to tell me about a trip to the store with her mother. "You tell me," she replied. Upon questioning, it seemed that she did not understand that I could not see the world through her eyes.

To egocentric preoperational children, all the world's a stage that has been erected to meet their needs and amuse them. When asked, "Why does the sun shine?" they may say, "To keep me warm." If asked, "Why is the sky blue?" they may respond, "'Cause blue's my favorite color." Preoperational children also show **animism.** They attribute life and intentions to inanimate objects like the sun and the moon. They also show **artificialism.** They believe that environmental features like rain and thunder were designed and constructed by people. Asked why the sky is blue, 4-year-olds may answer, "Cause Mommy painted it." Examples of egocentrism, animism, and artificialism are shown in Table 10.2.

To gain further insight into preoperational thinking, consider these problems:

1. Imagine that you pour water from a tall, thin glass into a low, wide glass. Now, does the low, wide glass contain more, less, or the same amount of water as was in the tall, thin glass? I won't keep you in suspense. If you said the same amount of water (with possible minor exceptions for spillage and evaporation), you were correct. Now that you're rolling, here is the other problem:
2. If you flatten a ball of clay into a pancake, do you wind up with more, less, or the same amount of clay? If you said the same amount of clay, you are correct once more.

To arrive at the correct answers to these questions, you must understand the law of **conservation.** This law holds that basic properties of substances such as mass,

Sensorimotor stage The first of Piaget's stages of cognitive development, characterized by coordination of sensory information and motor activity, early exploration of the environment, and lack of language.

Preoperational stage The second of Piaget's stages, characterized by illogical use of words and symbols, spotty logic, and egocentrism.

Egocentric According to Piaget, assuming that others view the world as one does oneself.

Animism The belief that inanimate objects move because of will or spirit.

Artificialism The belief that natural objects have been created by human beings.

Conservation According to Piaget, recognition that basic properties of substances such as weight and mass remain the same when superficial features change.

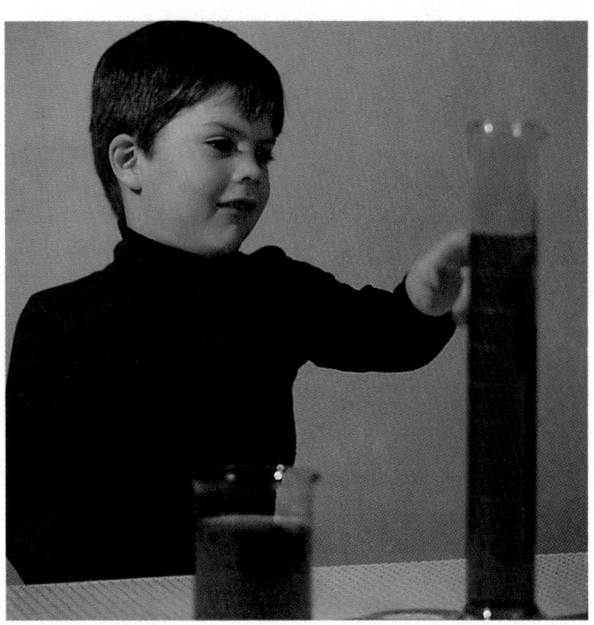

FIGURE 10.7 Conservation.

The boy in these photographs agreed that the amount of water in two identical containers is equal. He then watched as water from one container was poured into a tall, thin container. In the left-hand photograph, he is examining one of the original containers and the new container. When asked whether he thinks that the amounts of water in the two containers are now the same, he says no. Apparently, he is impressed by the height of the new container, and, prior to the development of conservation, he focuses on only one dimension of the situation at a time—in this case, the height of the new container.

weight, and volume remain the same—or are *conserved*—when you change superficial properties such as their shape or arrangement.

Conservation requires the ability to think about, or **center** on, two aspects of a situation at once, such as height and width. Conserving the mass, weight, or volume of a substance requires recognition that a change in one dimension can compensate for a change in another. But the preoperational boy in Figure 10.7 focuses on just one dimension at a time. First, he is shown two tall, thin glasses of water and agrees that they have the same amount of water. Then, while he watches, water is poured from one tall glass into a squat glass. Now, he is asked which glass has more water. After mulling over the problem, he points to the tall glass. Why? When he looks at the glasses, he is "overwhelmed" by the fact that the thinner glass is taller. The preoperational child focuses on the most apparent dimension of the situation—in this case, the greater height of the thinner glass. He does not realize that the gain in width in the squat glass compensates for the loss in height. By the way, if you ask him whether any water has been added or taken away in the pouring process, he will readily reply no. But if you then repeat the question about which glass has *more* water, he will again point to the taller glass.

If all this sounds rather illogical, that is because it is illogical–or to be precise, preoperational.

After you have tried the experiment with the water, try the following. Make two rows with five pennies each. In the first row, place the pennies about half an inch apart. In the second row, place the pennies two to three inches apart. Ask a 4- to 5-year-old child which row has more pennies. What do you think the child will say? Why?

Piaget (1962) found that the moral judgment of preoperational children is also one-dimensional. Five-year-olds are slaves to rules and authority. When you

Center According to Piaget, to focus one's attention.

ask them why something should be done in a certain way, they may insist "Because that's the way to do it!" or "Because my Mommy says so!" Right is right and wrong is wrong. Why? "Because!"—that's why.

According to most older children and adults, an act is a crime only when there is criminal intent. Accidents may be hurtful, but the perpetrators are usually seen as blameless. But in the court of the one-dimensional, preoperational child, there is **objective responsibility.** People are sentenced (and harshly!) on the basis of the amount of damage they have done, not their motive or intentions.

To demonstrate objective responsibility, Piaget would tell children stories and ask them which character was naughtier and why. John, for instance, accidentally breaks 15 cups when he opens a door. Henry breaks one cup when he sneaks into a kitchen cabinet to find forbidden jam. The preoperational child usually judges John to be naughtier. Why? He broke more cups.

The Concrete-Operational Stage. By about the age of 7, the typical child is entering the stage of **concrete operations.** In this stage, which lasts until about the age of 12, children show the beginnings of the capacity for adult logic. However, their logical thought, or operations, generally involves tangible objects rather than abstract ideas. Concrete operational children are capable of **decentration;** they can center simultaneously on two dimensions of a problem. This attainment has implications for moral judgments, conservation, and other intellectual undertakings.

Children now become **subjective** in their moral judgments. They center on the motives of wrongdoers as well as the amount of damage done when assigning guilt. Concrete-operational children judge Henry more harshly than John, since John's misdeed was an accident.

Concrete-operational children understand the laws of conservation. The boy in Figure 10.7, now a few years older, would say that the squat glass still has the same amount of water. If asked why, he might reply, "Because you can pour it back into the other one." An answer to this effect also suggests awareness of the concept of **reversibility**—recognition that many processes can be reversed or undone so that things can be restored to their previous condition. Centering simultaneously on the height and the width of the glasses, the boy recognizes that the loss in height compensates for the gain in width.

Concrete-operational children can conserve *number* as well as weight and mass. They recognize that there is the same number of pennies in each of the rows described earlier, even though one row may be spread out to look longer than the other.

Children in this stage are less egocentric. They are able to take on the roles of others and to view the world, and themselves, from other peoples' perspectives. They recognize that people see things in different ways because of different situations and different sets of values.

During the concrete-operational stage, children's own sets of values begin to emerge and acquire stability. Children come to understand that feelings of love between them and their parents can endure even when someone feels angry or disappointed at the moment.

The Formal-Operational Stage. The stage of **formal operations** is the final stage in Piaget's theory. It begins at about the time of puberty and is the stage of cognitive maturity. Not all children enter this stage at puberty, and some people never reach it.

Formal-operational children (and adults) think abstractly. They become capable of solving geometric problems about circles and squares without reference to what the circles and squares may represent in the real world. Children derive rules for behavior from general principles and can focus, or center, on many aspects of a situation at once in arriving at judgments and solving problems.

Objective responsibility According to Piaget, the assignment of blame according to the amount of damage done rather than the motives of the actor.

Concrete-operational stage Piaget's third stage, characterized by logical thought concerning tangible objects, conservation, and subjective morality.

Decentration Simultaneous focusing on more than one dimension of a problem, so that flexible, reversible thought becomes possible.

Subjective moral judgment According to Piaget, moral judgments that are based on the motives of the perpetrator.

Reversibility According to Piaget, recognition that processes can be undone, that things can be made as they were.

Formal-operational stage Piaget's fourth stage, characterized by abstract logical thought; deduction from principles.

In a sense, it is during the stage of formal operations that people tend to emerge as theoretical scientists—even though they may see themselves as having little or no interest in science. It is in this stage that children discover the world of the hypothetical. They become aware that situations can have many different outcomes, and they can think ahead, systematically trying out different possibilities. Children—adolescents by now—also conduct experiments to determine whether their hypotheses are correct. These experiments are not carried out in the laboratory. Rather, adolescents may experiment with different tones of voice, ways of carrying themselves, and ways of treating others to see which sorts of behavior are most effective for them.

Children in this stage can reason deductively, or draw conclusions about specific objects or people once they have been classified accurately. Adolescents can be somewhat proud of their new logical abilities. A new sort of egocentrism can develop in which adolescents emotionally press for acceptance of their logic without recognition of the exceptions or practical problems that are often considered by adults. Consider this **syllogism:** "It is wrong to hurt people. Industry A occasionally hurts people (perhaps through pollution or economic pressures). Therefore, Industry A must be severely punished or dismantled." This thinking is logical. By impatiently pressing for immediate major changes or severe penalties, however, one may not fully consider various practical problems such as thousands of resultant layoffs.

Evaluation of Piaget's Cognitive-Developmental Theory. A number of questions, such as the following, have been raised concerning the accuracy of Piaget's views:

1. *Was Piaget's timing accurate?* It seems that Piaget's methodology led him to underestimate the abilities of children. American researchers have used different methods and have found, for example, that preschoolers are less egocentric and that children are capable of conservation at earlier ages than Piaget believed.
2. *Is cognitive development discontinuous?* The most damaging criticism leveled at Piaget is that cognitive skills such as egocentrism and conservation appear to develop more continuously than Piaget thought—not in general stages. Cognitive psychologist John Flavell (1982) argues that cognitive development is "*not* very stage-like" at all (Flavell, 1982, p. 17). Flavell admits that "later cognitive acquisitions build on or are otherwise linked to earlier ones, and in their turn similarly prepare the ground for later ones" (1982, p. 18). However, the "acquisitions" process may be gradual, not discontinuous.
3. *Are developmental sequences invariant?* Here, Piaget's views have fared better. It seems that the sequences of development are indeed invariant, as Piaget believed. I also think it is fair to say that the sequences of development might be more essential to Piaget's theory than their timing.

In sum, Piaget's theoretical edifice has been rocked, but it has not been dashed to rubble. Research continues to wear away at his timing and at his belief that the stages of cognitive development are discontinuous, but his views on the sequences of development remain relatively inviolate.

Let us now turn our attention to Lawrence Kohlberg's theory of moral development and see how children process information that leads to judgments of right and wrong.

MORAL DEVELOPMENT

Psychologist Lawrence Kohlberg (1981) originated a cognitive-developmental theory of children's moral reasoning. Before we describe Kohlberg's views, read the following tale he used in his research and answer the questions that follow.

Syllogism A form of reasoning in which a conclusion is drawn from two statements or premises.

TABLE 10.3: Kohlberg's Levels and Stages of Moral Development

Stage of Development	Examples of Moral Reasoning That Support Heinz's Stealing the Drug	Examples of Moral Reasoning That Oppose Heinz's Stealing the Drug
	Level I: Preconventional	
STAGE 1: Judgments guided by obedience and the prospect of punishment (the consequences of the behavior)	It isn't wrong to take the drug. After all, Heinz tried to pay the druggist for it, and it's only worth $200, not $2,000.	It's wrong to take the drug because taking things without paying is against the law; Heinz will get caught and go to jail.
STAGE 2: Naively egoistic, instrumental orientation (things are right when they satisfy people's needs)	Heinz ought to take the drug because his wife really needs it. He can always pay the druggist back.	Heinz shouldn't take the drug. If he gets caught and winds up in jail, it won't do his wife any good.
	Level II: Conventional	
STAGE 3: "Good-boy orientation" (that which helps others and is socially approved is right)	Stealing is a crime, so it's bad, but Heinz should take the drug to save his wife or else people would blame him for letting her die.	Stealing is a crime. Heinz shouldn't just take the drug because his family will be dishonored and they will blame him.
STAGE 4: Law-and-order orientation (doing one's duty and showing respect for authority are right)	Heinz must take the drug to do his duty to save his wife. Eventually, he has to pay the druggist for it, however.	If everybody took the law into their own hands, civilization would fall apart, so Heinz shouldn't steal the drug.
	Level III: Postconventional	
STAGE 5: Contractual, legalistic orientation (it is moral to weigh pressing human needs against society's need to maintain the social order)	This thing is complicated because society has a right to maintain law and order, but Heinz has to take the drug to save his wife.	I can see why Heinz feels he has to take the drug, but laws exist for the benefit of society as a whole and can't simply be cast aside.
STAGE 6: Universal ethical principles orientation (people must act in accord with universal ethical principles and their own conscience, even if they must break the law in doing so)	This is a case in which the law comes into conflict with the principle of the sanctity of human life. Heinz must take the drug because his wife's life is more important than the law.	If Heinz, in his own conscience, believes that stealing the drug is worse than letting his wife die, he should not take it. People have to make sacrifices to do what they believe is right.

In Europe a woman was near death from a special kind of cancer. There was one drug that the doctors thought might save her. It was a form of radium that a druggist in the same town had recently discovered. The drug was expensive to make, but the druggist was charging ten times what the drug cost him to make. He paid $200 for the radium and charged $2,000 for a small dose of the drug. The sick woman's husband, Heinz, went to everyone he knew to borrow the money, but he could only get together about $1,000, which was half of what it cost. He told the druggist that his wife was dying and asked him to sell it cheaper or let him pay later. But the druggist said: "No, I discovered the drug and I'm going to make money from it." So Heinz got desperate and broke into the man's store to steal the drug for his wife. (Kohlberg, 1969)

What do you think? Should Heinz have tried to steal the drug? Was he right or wrong? As you can see from Table 10.3, the issue is more complicated than a simple yes or no. Heinz is caught up in a moral dilemma in which a legal or social rule (in this case, laws against stealing) is pitted against a strong human need (Heinz's desire to save his wife). According to Kohlberg's theory, children and adults arrive at yes or no answers for different reasons. These reasons can be classified according to the level of moral development they reflect.

As a stage theorist, Kohlberg argues that the stages of moral reasoning follow an invariant sequence. Children progress at different rates, and not all children (or adults) reach the highest stage. But children must go through stage 1 before they enter stage 2, and so on. According to Kohlberg, there are three levels of moral development and two stages within each level.

Preconventional level According to Kohlberg, a period during which moral judgments are based largely on expectation of rewards or punishments.

The Preconventional Level. The **preconventional level** applies to most children through about the age of 9. Children at this level base moral judgments on the consequences of behavior. For instance, stage 1 is oriented toward obedience and punishment. Good behavior is obedient and allows one to avoid punishment.

South African Anti-Apartheid Leader Nelson Mandela at a Rally. Mandela spent 27 years in prison in South Africa because his personal sense of morality required him to confront the Apartheid system and break the law. Post-Conventional morality is characterized by adhering to one's personal sense of ethics even if it requires conflict with the law.

In stage 2, good behavior allows people to satisfy their needs and those of others. (Heinz's wife needs the drug; therefore, stealing the drug—the only way of attaining it—is not wrong.)

The Conventional Level. In the **conventional level** of moral reasoning, right and wrong are judged by conformity to conventional (family, church, societal) standards of right and wrong. According to the stage 3 "good-boy orientation," it is moral to meet the needs and expectations of others. Moral behavior is what is "normal"—what the majority does. (Heinz should steal the drug because that is what a "good husband" would do. It is "natural" or "normal" to try to help one's wife. *Or,* Heinz should *not* steal the drug because "good people do not steal.")

In stage 4, moral judgments are based on rules that maintain the social order. Showing respect for authority and doing one's duty are valued highly. (Heinz must steal the drug; it would be his responsibility if he let his wife die. He would pay the druggist when he could.) Many people do not mature beyond the conventional level.

The Postconventional Level. In the **postconventional level,** moral reasoning is based on the person's own moral standards. In each instance, moral judgments are derived from personal values, not from conventional standards or authority figures. In stage 5's contractual, legalistic orientation, it is recognized that laws stem from agreed-upon procedures and that many laws have great value and should not be violated. But under exceptional circumstances, laws cannot bind the individual. (Although it is illegal for Heinz to steal the drug, in this case it is the right thing to do.)

Stage 6 thinking relies on supposed universal ethical principles such as those of human life, individual dignity, justice, and **reciprocity.** Behavior that is consistent with these principles is moral. If a law is unjust or contradicts the rights of the individual, it is wrong to obey it.

Postconventional people look to their consciences as the highest moral authority. This point has created confusion. To some it suggests that it is right to break the law when it is convenient. But this interpretation is incorrect. Kohlberg means that postconventional people must do what they believe is right even if it counters social rules or laws or requires personal sacrifice.

Not all people reach the postconventional level of moral reasoning. By age 16, stage 5 reasoning is shown by about 20 percent and stage 6 reasoning by about 5 percent of U.S. adolescents. Stage 3 and 4 judgments are made more frequently at all ages, 7 through 16, studied by Kohlberg and other investigators (Colby et al., 1983; Rest, 1983).

Evaluation of Kohlberg's Theory. Research suggests that moral reasoning does follow a developmental sequence (Snarey et al., 1985), even though most children do not reach postconventional thought. Postconventional thought, when found, first occurs during adolescence. It seems that formal operational thinking is a precedent for postconventional reasoning, which requires the capacities to understand abstract moral principles and to empathize with the attitudes and emotional responses of other people (Flavell, 1985).

Consistent with Kohlberg's theory, children do not appear to skip stages as they progress (Flavell, 1985). When children are exposed to adult models who enact a lower stage of moral reasoning, they can be induced to follow along (Bandura & McDonald, 1963). Children exposed to examples of moral reasoning above and below their own stage generally prefer the higher stage, however (Rest, 1976, 1983). The thrust of moral development is thus from lower to higher, even if children can be sidetracked by social influences.

Kohlberg believed that his stages of moral development followed the natural unfolding of inborn sequences. Their orderly emergence would thus be found by

---

Conventional level According to Kohlberg, a period during which moral judgments largely reflect social conventions. A "law-and-order" approach to morality.

Postconventional level According to Kohlberg, a period during which moral judgments are derived from moral principles and people look to themselves to set moral standards.

means of cross-cultural evidence. Cross-cultural investigators have found that postconventional thinking is virtually absent in tribal and village societies, however. Stages 1 through 4 are present in about 90 percent of cultures studied around the world and postconventional thought in only 64 percent (Snarey, 1987). Even within the United States, postconventional thinking is more likely to be voiced by persons of higher socioeconomic status. Longitudinal evidence shows that higher education also tends to foster higher levels of moral reasoning (Rest & Thoma, 1985).

Kohlberg's critics have suggested that postconventional reasoning, especially stage 6 reasoning, may reflect Kohlberg's personal ideals and not a natural, universal stage of development. Stage 6 reasoning is based on supposedly omnipresent ethical principles. The principles of justice, equality, integrity, and reverence for life may have a high appeal to you, but you were reared in a culture that idealizes them. They are not universal, however—witness the brutality of Adolf Hitler, Joseph Stalin, and Saddam Hussein. These principles are more reflective of Western ideals than of cognitive development. In his later years, Kohlberg virtually dropped stage 6 reasoning from his theory, in recognition of these problems.

Moreover, some cultures tend to follow moral principles not covered by Kohlberg's theory at all (Snarey, 1987). For example, natives of Papua New Guinea and persons living on Israeli kibbutzim have developed a principle of collective moral responsibility. According to one aspect of this principle, Heinz should take the drug because all resources should be available to the community at large.

It is true, *within our culture,* that the highest level of moral reasoning involves relying on our own views of what is right and wrong (that is, postconventional moral reasoning). However, postconventional thought is not found in all cultures, and there is more support for stage 5 reasoning than for stage 6 reasoning.

GENDER-TYPING

Cultural expectations of men and women involve complex clusters of stereotypes, called **gender roles,** that define the ways in which men and women are expected to behave. People tend to see the traditional feminine stereotype as dependent, gentle, helpful, kind, mild, patient, submissive (Cartwright et al., 1983), and interested in the arts. The typical masculine gender-role stereotype is tough, protective, gentlemanly (Myers & Gonda, 1982), logical, and competent at business, math, and science. Females are more often viewed as being warm and emotional, whereas males are more frequently seen as being independent and competitive. Women are more often expected to care for the kids and cook the meals.

Gender-role stereotypes reflect popular impressions. What are the actual differences in cognition and personality between males and females and how do they develop?

Gender Differences

It was once believed that males were more intelligent than females because of their greater knowledge of world affairs and their skill in science and industry. We now recognize that greater male knowledge and skill reflected not differences in intelligence but the systematic exclusion of females from world affairs, science, and industry. Studies in the assessment of intelligence do not show overall

Gender role A complex cluster of behaviors that characterizes traditional male or female behaviors.

differences in cognitive abilities between males and females. Researchers such as Maccoby and Jacklin (1974) have found, however, persistent suggestions that girls are somewhat superior to boys in verbal ability. Males, on the other hand, seem to be somewhat superior in visual–spatial abilities. Differences in mathematical ability are more complex. Girls excel in computational ability in elementary school, for example, and boys excel in mathematical problem solving in high school and in college (Hyde et al., 1990).

Three factors should caution us not to attach too much importance to these cognitive gender differences, however:

1. In most cases they are small, and in the case of verbal abilities and mathematics, getting smaller (Deaux, 1984; Hyde, 1981; Hyde et al., 1990; Maccoby, 1990).
2. These gender differences are *group* differences. Variation in these skills is larger *within* than between males and females (Maccoby, 1990). Millions of females outdistance the "average" male in math and spatial abilities.
3. The small differences that appear to exist may largely reflect cultural expectations and environmental influences (Tobias, 1982). Spatial and math abilities are stereotyped as masculine in our culture. Female introductory psychology students given just three hours of training in various visual-spatial skills, such as rotating geometric figures, showed no performance deficit in these skills when compared to men (Stericker & LeVesconte, 1982).

Most psychological studies of aggression have found that male children and adults behave more aggressively than females (Eagly, 1987; Maccoby, 1990; Maccoby & Jacklin, 1980). Ann Frodi and her colleagues (1977) reviewed 72 studies concerning gender differences in aggression and found that females are more likely to act aggressively under some circumstances than others:

1. Males are more likely than females to report physical aggression in their behavior, intentions, and dreams.
2. Females are more likely to feel anxious or guilty about behaving aggressively. These feelings tend to inhibit aggression.
3. Females behave as aggressively as males when they have the means to do so and believe that their behavior is justified. For example, women act as aggressively as men in experiments in which they are given the physical capacity to do so and believe that they should act aggressively.
4. Females are more likely to empathize with the victim—to put themselves in the victim's place.
5. Gender differences in aggression decrease when the victim is anonymous. Anonymity may prevent females from empathizing with their victims.

Boys do behave more aggressively than girls do. The question is, *Why?*

Gender-Typing: The Development of Gender Differences

There are thus a number of gender differences in cognition and personality. They include minor differences in cognitive functioning and differences in aggressiveness. In this section, we consider the biological and psychological factors that appear to contribute to the development of these gender differences.

Biological Influences. Biological views on gender differences tend to focus on the role of sex hormones. Sex hormones are responsible for prenatal differentiation of sex organs. Prenatal sex hormones may also "masculinize" or "feminize" the brain by creating predispositions that are consistent with some gender-role stereotypes (Diamond, 1977; Money, 1977, 1987).

Diamond takes an extreme view. She suggests that prenatal brain masculinization can cause tomboyishness and assertiveness—even preferences for trousers over skirts and for playing with "boys' toys." Money agrees that predispositions may be created prenatally but argues that social learning plays a stronger role in the development of **gender identity,** personality traits, and preferences. Money claims that social learning is powerful enough to counteract many prenatal predispositions.

Some evidence for the possible role of hormonal influences derives from animal studies. Male rats are generally superior to females in maze-learning ability, for example, a task that requires spatial skills. Female rats who are exposed to androgens in the uterus or soon after birth learn maze routes as rapidly as males, however (Beatty, 1979; Goy & McEwen, 1982).

Sex hormones also spur sexual maturation during adolescence, and there are some interesting suggestions that sexual maturation is linked to development of cognitive skills. Girls usually reach sexual maturity earlier than boys. Researchers have found that late maturers, whether boys or girls, show the "masculine pattern" of exceeding early maturers on math and spatial-relations tasks (Sanders & Soares, 1986; Sanders et al., 1982; Waber et al., 1985). Early-maturing boys exceed late-maturing boys in verbal skills and also show the "feminine pattern" of higher verbal than math and spatial-relations skills (Newcombe & Bandura, 1983). Early maturation seems to favor development of verbal skills, whereas late maturation may favor development of math and spatial-relations skills.

Let us now consider psychological views of the development of gender differences.

Psychological Influences. Sigmund Freud explained the acquisition of gender roles in terms of **identification.** Freud believed that gender identity remains flexible until the resolution of the Oedipus and Electra complexes at about the age of 5 or 6. Appropriate gender-typing requires that boys identify with their fathers and surrender the wish to possess their mothers. Girls have to surrender the wish to have a penis and identify with their mothers.

Boys and girls develop stereotypical preferences for toys and activities much earlier than might be predicted by psychodynamic theory, however. Even within their first year, boys are more explorative and independent. Girls are relatively more quiet, dependent, and restrained (Goldberg & Lewis, 1969). By 18 to 36 months, girls are more likely to play with soft toys and dolls and to dance. Boys of this age are more likely to play with blocks and toy cars, trucks, and airplanes (Fagot, 1974).

Children's preferences for gender-typed toys and activities do *not* remain flexible until the ages of 5 or 6. They become rather fixed by the age of 3.

Gender identity One's sense of being male or female. (The first stage in the cognitive-developmental theory of the assumption of sex roles.)

Identification In psychodynamic theory, unconscious incorporation of the personality of another person.

Social-learning theorists explain the acquisition of gender roles and gender differences in terms of observational learning, identification,[1] and socialization.

[1]But the social-learning concept of identification differs from the psychodynamic concept, as noted in this section.

Children learn much of what is considered masculine or feminine by observational learning, as suggested by an experiment conducted by David Perry and Kay Bussey (1979). In this study, children learned how behaviors are gender-typed by observing the *relative frequencies* with which men and women performed them. However, the adult role models expressed arbitrary preferences for one item from each of 16 pairs of items—pairs such as oranges versus apples and toy cows versus toy horses—as 8- and 9-year-old boys and girls observed. The children were then asked to show their own preferences. Boys selected an average of 14 of 16 items that agreed with the "preferences" of the men. Girls selected an average of only 3 of 16 items that agreed with the choices of the men.

Popular media—magazines, books, film, and television—also impart gender stereotypes (Remafedi, 1990). The media generally depict women and men in traditional roles (Signorielli, 1990). Men more often play attorneys, police officers, and doctors; women more often portray teachers, secretaries, nurses, and paralegals. Even when women play police officers or attorneys, they are more likely than men to deal with family disputes. The male police officer is more likely to play action roles. The male attorney is more likely to hold the court spellbound with his probing rhetoric. Working women are also more likely to be depicted as encountering role conflict—as being pulled in opposite directions by the family and the job. Despite contemporary awareness of sexism, "Women are often still depicted on television as half-clad and half-witted, and needing to be rescued by quick-thinking, fully clothed men" (Adelson, 1990).

Social-learning theorists view identification as a broad, continuous learning process in which children are influenced by rewards and punishments to imitate adults of the same gender—particularly the parent of the same gender (Storms, 1980). In identification, as opposed to imitation, children do not simply imitate a certain behavior pattern. They also try to become broadly like the model.

Socialization also plays a role. Parents and other adults—even other children—inform children about how they are expected to behave. They reward children for behavior they consider gender-appropriate. They punish (or fail to reinforce) children for behavior they consider inappropriate. Girls, for example, are given dolls while they still sleep in cribs. They are encouraged to rehearse care-taking behaviors in preparation for traditional feminine adult roles.

Social-learning theory has helped outline the ways in which rewards, punishments, and modeling foster "gender-appropriate" behavior. Critics of social-learning theory focus on theoretical issues such as how reinforcers influence us. Do reinforcers mechanically increase the frequency of behavior, or, as suggested by gender-schema theory, do they provide us with information that we process in making decisions?

Gender-schema theory holds that children use gender as one way of organizing their perceptions of the world (Bem, 1981, 1985). Gender has a great deal of prominence, even to young children (Maccoby, 1988). Therefore, children mentally group people of the same gender together.

As in social-learning theory, children learn "appropriate" behavior by observation. Children's processing of information also contributes to their gender-typing, however.

Consider the example of the strength–weakness construct or dimension. Children learn that strength is linked to the male gender-role stereotype and weakness to the female stereotype. They also learn that some dimensions, such as strength–weakness, are more relevant to one gender than the other—in this case, to males. Bill will learn that the strength he displays in weight training or wrestling affects the way others perceive him. Most girls do not find this dimension to be important, unless they are competing in sports such as gymnastics, tennis, or swimming. Even so, boys are expected to compete in these sports, and girls are not. Jane is likely to find that her gentleness and neatness are more important in the eyes of others than her strength.

Children thus learn to judge themselves according to the traits, or constructs, considered to relevant to their genders. In so doing, their self-concepts become blended with the gender schema of their culture. The gender schema provides standards for comparison. Children whose self-concepts are consistent with their society's gender schema are likely to have higher self-esteem than children whose self-concepts are not.

From the viewpoint of gender-schema theory, gender identity is sufficient to prompt "gender-appropriate" behavior. No external reinforcement is required. As soon as children understand the labels *boy* and *girl,* they have a basis for blending their self-concepts with the gender schema of their society. Children who have developed a sense of being male or being female, which usually occurs by the age of 3, will actively seek information about the gender schema. Their self-esteem will soon become wrapped up in the ways in which they measure up to the gender schema.

In one study, Carol Martin and Charles Halverson (1983) showed 5- and 6-year-old boys and girls pictures of actors engaged in "gender-consistent" or "gender-inconsistent" activities. The gender-consistent pictures showed boys in activities such as playing with trains or sawing wood and girls in activities such as cooking and cleaning. Gender-inconsistent pictures showed actors of the opposite gender engaged in these gender-typed activities. Each child was shown a randomized collection of pictures that included only one picture of each activity. One week later, the children were asked who had engaged in a pictured activity, a male or a female. Boys and girls both replied incorrectly significantly more often when the picture they had seen showed gender-inconsistent activity. The processing of information had been distorted to conform to the gender schema.

In sum, biological influences may contribute to gender-typed behavior and play a role in verbal ability, math skills, and aggression, but social learning can be strong enough to counteract most prenatal biological influences. Social-learning theory outlines the environmental factors that influence children to assume "gender-appropriate" behavior. However, social-learning theory may pay insufficient attention to children's active roles as seekers of information. Gender-schema theory integrates the strengths of social-learning theory with the ways in which children process information so as to blend their self-concepts with the gender schema of their culture.

Adolescents. In our culture, adolescents are "neither fish nor fowl." Although they may be old enough to reproduce and may be as large as their parents, adolescents are often treated like children.

ADOLESCENCE

In the last century, psychologist G. Stanley Hall described **adolescence** as a time of *Sturm und Drang*—storm and stress. Hall attributed the conflicts and distress of adolescence to biological changes. The evidence suggests that the hormonal changes of adolescence may have some effect on the activity levels, mood swings, and aggressive tendencies of many adolescents (Buchanan et al., 1992). Overall, however, it would appear that cultural influences and social expectations may have a greater impact on adolescents than hormonal changes or patterns of physical growth (Buchanan et al., 1992).

Adolescence is heralded by puberty. Puberty begins with the appearance of **secondary sex characteristics** such as body hair, deepening of the voice in males, and rounding of the breasts and hips in females. Puberty ends when the long bones make no further gains in length so that full height is attained. But adolescence ends with psychosocial markers such as assumption of adult responsibilities. Adolescence is a psychological concept with biological aspects, but puberty is a biological concept.

The Growth Spurt

The stable growth patterns in height and weight that characterize early and middle childhood come to an abrupt end with the adolescent growth spurt. Girls begin to spurt at about 10 years, 3 months and boys at about 11 years, 9 months. The spurts last between two and three years, with boys' spurts lasting about a half year longer than girls'. Adolescents add some 8 to 12 inches in height. Most boys wind up taller and heavier than most girls.

In boys, the muscle mass increases notably in weight, and there are gains in shoulder width and chest circumference. At age 20 or 21, men stop growing taller because testosterone prevents the long bones from making further gains in length. Estrogen brakes the female growth spurt earlier than testosterone brakes that of males. Girls deficient in estrogen during their late teens may grow quite tall, but most tall girls reach their heights because of genetically determined variations. Adolescents often eat enormous quantities of food to fuel their growth spurts. Adults fighting the battle of the bulge stare at them in wonder as they wolf down french fries and shakes at the fast-food counter and later go out for pizza.

Puberty

At puberty, pituitary hormones in boys stimulate the testes to increase the output of testosterone, causing the penis and testes to grow and pubic hair to appear. By age 13 or 14, erections become frequent, and boys may ejaculate. Ejaculatory ability usually precedes the presence of mature sperm by at least a year, so ejaculation is not evidence of reproductive capacity. Axillary, or underarm, hair appears at about age 15. At age 14 or 15, the voice deepens because of growth of the larynx, or voice box.

In girls, pituitary secretions cause the ovaries to begin to secrete estrogen, which stimulates growth of breast tissue as early as age 8 or 9. Estrogen promotes growth of fatty and supportive tissue in the hips and buttocks and widens the pelvis, rounding the hips. Small amounts of androgens produced by the adrenal glands, along with estrogen, stimulate growth of pubic and axillary hair. Estrogen and androgens work together to stimulate the growth of female sex organs. Estrogen production becomes cyclical in puberty and regulates the menstrual cycle. First menstruation, or **menarche,** usually occurs between the ages of 11 and 14.

Adolescence The period of life bounded by puberty and the assumption of adult responsibilities.

Secondary sex characteristics Characteristics that differentiate the sexes, such as distribution of body hair and depth of voice, but that are not directly involved in reproduction.

Menarche The beginning of menstruation.

Girls cannot become pregnant until they begin to ovulate, however, which may occur as much as two years later.

It is *not* usually true that girls are capable of becoming pregnant after they have their first menstrual periods. Menarche can precede ovulation by a year or more.

Adolescent Behavior and Conflicts

In our society, adolescents are "neither fish nor fowl," as the saying goes—neither children nor adults. Although adolescents may be old enough to reproduce and are as large as their parents, they are often treated quite differently. They may not be eligible for driver's licenses until they are 16 or 17, and they cannot attend R-rated films unless accompanied by an adult. They are prevented from working long hours. They are required to remain in school usually through age 16. They may not marry until they reach the "age of consent."

Adults overall tend to regard adolescents as an emotional, impulsive lot who must be restricted for their own good. The National Association of State Boards of Education reports that many American teenagers abuse drugs, have unplanned pregnancies, contract sexually transmitted diseases, become involved in violence, and encounter psychological and social problems that are connected with academic failure and suicide attempts (Leary, 1990). Nearly one in ten adolescent girls becomes pregnant each year. Nearly 10 percent of teenaged boys and 20 percent of teenaged girls attempt suicide. Alcohol-related incidents are the overall leading cause of death among adolescents. Among 15- to 19-year-old African Americans, homicide is the most common cause of death.

According to Roger Gould's (1975) research with 524 men and women of various age groups, a major concern of 16- to 18-year-olds is a yearning for independence from parental domination. Given the restrictions placed on adolescents, their yearning for independence, and a sex drive heightened by high levels of sex hormones, it is not surprising that many adolescents are in conflict with their families.

Despite their needs for dominance, independence, and personal responsibility, adolescents generally report that their current relationships with their parents involve more love and closeness than in earlier years (Pipp et al., 1985). Sandra Pipp and her colleagues interpret this finding as suggesting that adolescents view their relationships with their parents in a way that is consistent with their growing need for separation *and* their continued need for a close emotional tie.

Ego Identity versus Role Diffusion. According to psychoanalyst Erik Erikson, the major challenge of adolescence is the creation of an adult identity. This is accomplished primarily through choosing and developing a commitment to an occupation or a role in life.

Erikson (1963) theorizes that adolescents experience a life crisis of *ego identity versus role diffusion.* If this crisis is resolved properly, adolescents develop a firm sense of who they are and what they stand for. This sense of **ego identity** can carry them through difficult times and color their achievements with meaning. If they do not resolve this life crisis properly, they may experience **role diffusion.** They then spread themselves thin, running down one blind alley after another and placing themselves at the mercy of leaders who promise to give them the sense of identity they cannot mold for themselves.

Ego identity Erikson's term for a firm sense of who one is and what one stands for.

Role diffusion Erikson's term for lack of clarity in one's life roles—a function of failure to develop ego identity.

Establishing Intimate Relationships. According to Erik Erikson, establishing intimate relationships is a central task of young adulthood.

One aspect of attaining ego identity is learning "how to connect the roles and skills cultivated earlier with the occupational prototypes of the day" (Erikson, 1963, p. 261)—that is, with jobs. Ego identity also extends to sexual, political, and religious beliefs and commitments.

Now let us turn our attention to development during adulthood.

ADULT DEVELOPMENT

Development continues throughout a lifetime. Many theorists, including Erik Erikson and Daniel Levinson, believe that adult concerns and involvements are patterned so that we can speak of stages of adult development. Let us consider the adult years according to three broad categories: young adulthood, middle adulthood, and late adulthood.

Young Adulthood

Young or early adulthood covers the two decades from ages 20 to 40. Our chronicling of these years is based primarily on the views of Erik Erikson and Daniel Levinson and his colleagues. There are other noted views such as Roger Gould's "transformations" and Carol Gilligan's insights into the factors that influence women, and we refer to them as well.

Intimacy versus Isolation. According to Erik Erikson (1963), young adulthood is the stage of **intimacy versus isolation.** Erikson saw the establishment of intimate relationships as central to young adulthood. Young adults who have evolved a firm sense of identity during adolescence are now ready to "fuse" their identities with those of other people through marriage and abiding friendships.

Erikson warns that we may not be able to commit ourselves to others until we have achieved ego identity, or established stable life roles. Achieving ego identity is the central task of adolescence. Lack of personal stability is connected with the high divorce rate in teenage marriages.

Erikson argues that people who do not reach out to develop intimate relationships risk retreating into isolation and loneliness.

Intimacy versus isolation Erikson's life crisis of young adulthood, which is characterized by the task of developing abiding intimate relationships.

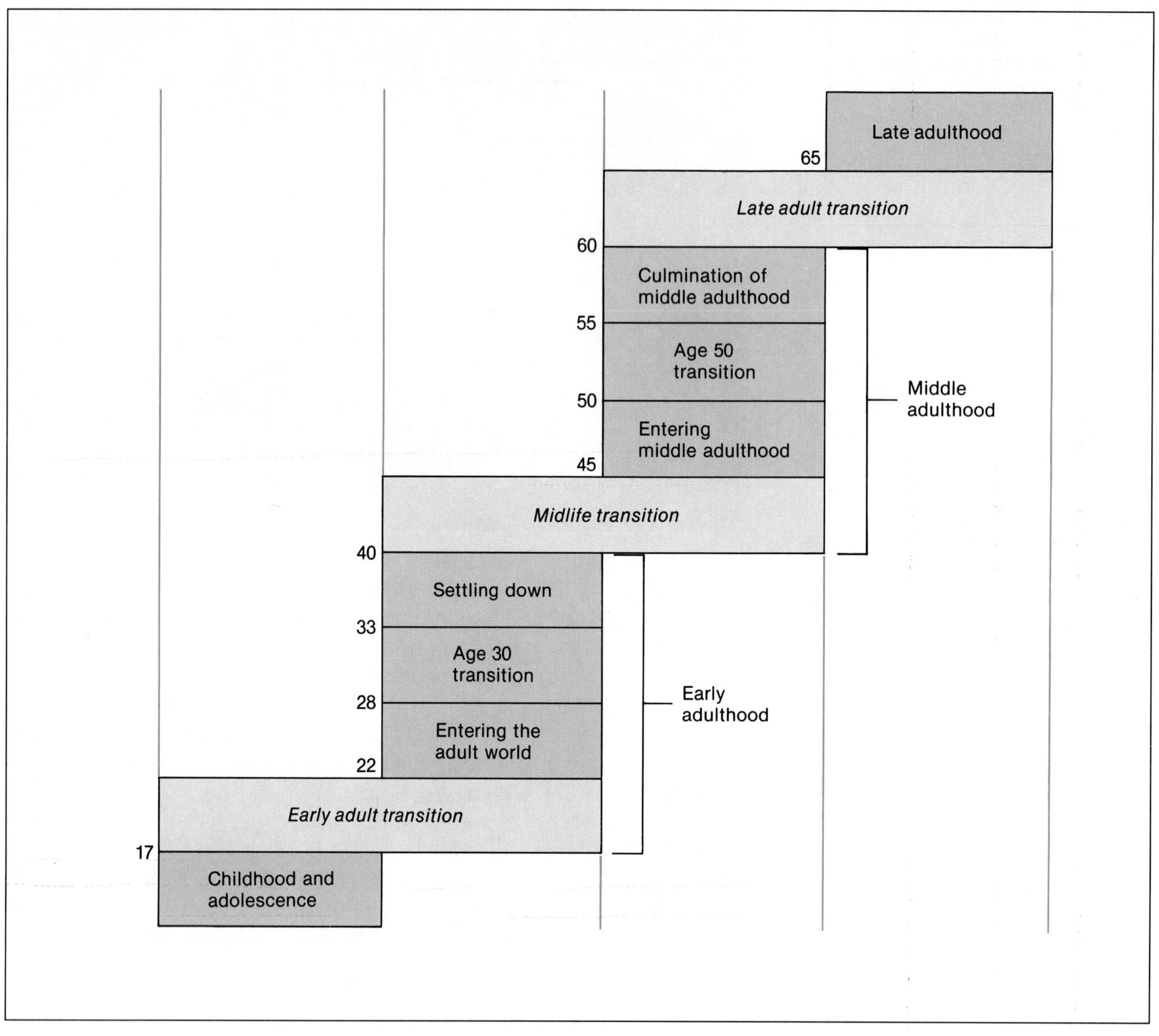

FIGURE 10.8
The Seasons of a Man's Life.

Daniel Levinson and his colleagues break young, middle, and late adulthood down into a number of developmental periods, including several transitions. Our major tasks as we enter the adult world are to explore and to establish some stability in our adult roles. During the age-30 transition, we reevaluate our earlier choices. How does women's adult development differ from men's?

Levinson's Seasons. According to Daniel Levinson's in-depth study of 40 men, which was published in 1978 as *The Seasons of a Man's Life,* we enter the adult world in our early twenties (see Figure 10.8). Upon entry, we are faced with the tasks of exploring adult roles (in terms of careers, intimate relationships, and so on) and of establishing stability in the chosen roles. At this time, we also often adopt a **dream**—the drive to "become" someone, to leave our mark on history—which serves as a tentative blueprint for our lives.

Adults in their twenties tend to be fueled by ambition as they strive to establish their pathways in life (Gould, 1975; Sheehy, 1976). Journalist Gail Sheehy labeled the twenties the **Trying 20s**—a period during which people basically strive to advance themselves in the career world. Young adults, according to Sheehy (1976, 1981), are concerned about establishing their pathways in life, finding their

Dream In this usage, Levinson's term for the overriding drive of youth to become someone important, to leave one's mark on history.

Trying 20s Sheehy's term for the third decade of life, when people are frequently occupied with advancement in the career world.

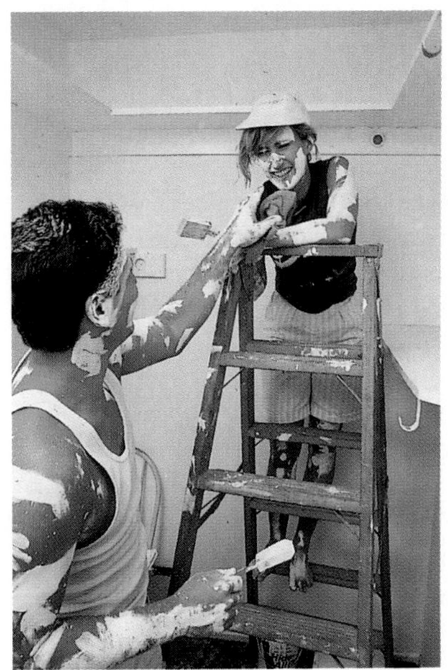

Settling Down. According to some chroniclers of adult development, the thirties are often characterized by settling down, or planting roots, as in taking on the responsibilities of a home.

places in the world. They are generally responsible for their own support, made their own choices, and are largely free from parental influences.

During our twenties, many of us feel "buoyed by powerful illusions and belief in the power of the will [so that] we commonly insist . . . that what we have chosen to do is the one true course in life" (Sheehy, 1976, p. 33). This "one true course" usually turns out to have many swerves and bends. As we develop, what seemed to be important one year can lose some of its allure in the next. That which we hardly noticed can gain prominence.

Gender Differences in Developmental Patterns of Young Adulthood. On the basis of his samples drawn from psychiatric clinics, psychiatrist Roger Gould (1975) suggested that men's development seems to be generally guided by needs for individuation (separation from others) and autonomy (self-direction). Psychologists such as Judith Bardwick (1980) and Carol Gilligan (1982), who have focused on the development of women, have found that women are relatively more likely to be guided by changing patterns of attachment and caring. In becoming adults, men are likely to undergo a transition from restriction to control. Women, as pointed out by Gilligan (1982), are relatively more likely to undergo a transition from being cared for to caring for others, however.

Levinson has recognized that he was remiss in studying only men in earlier years, and he has recently become involved in research into the "seasons" of women's lives. One of his findings is that many young, successful businesswomen differ from their male counterparts in that they are less likely to have long-term business goals: "They want to be independent but they are conflicted about ambition" (cited in Brown, 1987). Some of the conflict stems from concerns about whether ambition is compatible with femininity. Other conflicts stem from practical concerns about balancing a career with a home life and child-rearing.

Although there are very important differences in the development of women and men, a study by Ravenna Helson and Geraldine Moane (1987) of the University of California found that between the ages of 21 and 27, college women do develop in terms of individuation and autonomy. That is, they, like men, tend to assert increasing control over their own lives. College women, of course, are relatively liberated and career-oriented in comparison to their less-well-educated peers.

The Age-30 Transition. Levinson labeled the ages of 28 to 33 the **age-30 transition.** For many, this is a period of reassessment of the choices made during their early twenties. A number of researchers have noted that women frequently encounter a crisis that begins between the ages of 27 and 30 (Reinke et al., 1985). During the early thirties, many of the women studied by Helson and Moane (1987) felt exploited by others, alone, weak, limited, and as if they would "never get myself together." Concerns about nearing the end of the fertile years, opportunities closing down, and heightened responsibilities at home and work all make their contributions.

For men and women, the late twenties and early thirties are commonly characterized by self-questioning: "Where is my life going?" "Why am I doing this?" Sheehy (1976) labeled the thirties the **Catch 30s** because of such reassessment. During our thirties, we often find that the life styles we adopted during our twenties do not fit as comfortably as we had anticipated.

One response to the disillusionments of the thirties, according to Sheehy,

> *is the tearing up of the life we have spent most of our 20s putting together. It may mean striking out on a secondary road toward a new vision or converting a dream of "running for president" into a more realistic goal. The single person feels a push to find a partner. The woman who was previously content at home with children chafes to venture into the world. The childless couple reconsiders children. And almost everybody who is married . . . feels a discontent. (1976, p. 34)*

Age 30 transition Levinson's term for the ages from 28 to 33, which are characterized by reassessment of the goals and values of the twenties.

Catch 30s Sheehy's term for the fourth decade of life, when many people undergo major reassessments of their accomplishments and goals.

Settling Down. According to Levinson, the ages of about 33 to 40 are characterized by settling down. Men during this period still strive to forge ahead in their careers, their interpersonal relationships, and their communities. During the latter half of their thirties, men are also concerned about "becoming one's own man." That is, they desire independence and autonomy in their careers and adult relationships. Promotions and pay increases are important as signs of success.

Sheehy found that young adults who had successfully ridden out the storm of reassessments of the Catch 30s begin the process of "rooting" at this time. They feel a need to put down roots, to make a financial and emotional investment in their homes. Their concerns become more focused on promotion or tenure, career advancement, and long-term mortgages.

Is Middle Age the End of Young Adulthood? How do the middle-aged differ from young adults? To what extent are the biological changes of aging inevitable? How much control can we exert over our own aging?

Middle Adulthood

Middle adulthood spans the years from 40 to 60 or 65. Some authors, such as Levinson and his colleagues (1978), consider the years from 60 to 65 separately as a transition to late adulthood.

Generativity versus Stagnation. Erikson (1963) labels the life crisis of the middle years that of **generativity versus stagnation.** In other words, are we still striving to produce or to rear our children well, or are we marking time, treading water? Generativity by and large requires doing things that we believe are worthwhile. In so doing, we enhance and maintain our self-esteem. Generativity also involves the Eriksonian ideal of helping shape the new generation. This shaping may involve rearing our own children or generally working to make the world a better place. Many of us find great satisfaction in these tasks.

Levinson's Seasons. According to Levinson, there is a **midlife transition** at about age 40 to 45 that is characterized by a dramatic shift in psychological perspective. Previously, we had thought of our ages largely in terms of the number of years that have elapsed since birth. Once the midlife transition takes place, however, there is a tendency to think of our ages in terms of the number of years we have left.

Men in their thirties still think of themselves as part of the Pepsi Generation, older brothers to "kids" in their twenties. At about age 40 to 45, however, some marker event—illness, a change on the job, the death of a friend or of a parent, or being beaten at tennis by one's child—leads men to realize that they are a full generation older than 20-year-olds.

During this transition, it strikes men that life may be more than halfway over. There may be more to look back on than forward to. It dawns on men that they'll never be president or chairperson of the board. They'll never play shortstop for the Dodgers. They mourn their own youth and begin to adjust to the specter of old age and the finality of death.

The Midlife Crisis. The midlife transition may trigger a crisis referred to as the **midlife crisis.** The middle-level, middle-aged businessperson looking ahead to another 10 to 20 years of grinding out accounts in a Wall Street cubbyhole may encounter severe depression. The homemaker with two teenagers, an empty house from 8:00 to 4:00, and a fortieth birthday on the way might feel that she is coming apart at the seams. Both feel entrapment and loss of purpose. Some people are propelled into extramarital affairs at this time by the desire to prove to themselves that they remain attractive.

Until midlife, the men studied by the Levinson group were largely under the influence of their dream—the overriding drive of youth to "become," to be the great scientist or novelist, to leave one's mark on history. At midlife, they found they must come to terms with the discrepancies between their dream and their

Generativity versus stagnation Erikson's term for the crisis of middle adulthood, characterized by the task of being productive and contributing to younger generations.

Midlife transition Levinson's term for the ages from 40 to 45, which are characterized by a shift in psychological perspective from viewing ourselves in terms of years lived to viewing ourselves in terms of the years we have left.

Midlife crisis A crisis experienced by many people during the midlife transition when they realize that life may be more than halfway over, and they reassess their achievements in terms of their dreams.

actual achievements. Middle-aged people who free themselves from their dream find it easier to enjoy the passing pleasures of the day.

Levinson's study was carried out with men. Women, as suggested by Sheehy and other writers (e.g., Reinke et al., 1985) may undergo a midlife transition a number of years earlier. Sheehy (1976) writes that women enter midlife about five years earlier than men, at about age 35 instead of 40. Once they turn 35, women are usually advised to have their fetuses routinely tested for Down syndrome and other chromosomal disorders. At age 35, women also enter higher risk categories for side effects from birth-control pills.

Entering midlife triggers a sense of urgency, of a "last chance" to do certain things, and so Sheehy refers to the years between 35 and 45 as the **Deadline Decade.** This decade is characterized by recognition of one's own mortality among women and men. There is reevaluation of youthful illusions and, often, turmoil.

The study of college women by Helson and Moane (1987) suggests that many women in their early forties may already be emerging from some of the fears and uncertainties that are first confronting men. For example, they found that women at age 43 are more likely than women in their early thirties to feel confident; to exert an influence on their communities; to feel secure and committed; to feel productive, effective, and powerful; and to extend their interests beyond their own families.

Menopause usually occurs during the late forties or early fifties, although there are wide variations. Menopause is the final stage of a broader female experience, the climacteric, which is caused by a falling off in the secretion of the hormones estrogen and progesterone. The climacteric begins with irregular periods and ends with menopause.[2] With menopause, ovulation also draws to an end. There is some atrophy of breast tissue and a decrease in the elasticity of the skin. There can also be a loss of bone density that leads to osteoporosis in late adulthood.

Menopause also used to be the end of a woman's reproductive capacity. Today, this is no longer necessarily the case. After menopause, women no longer produce ova. Ova from donors have been fertilized in laboratory dishes, however, and the developing embryos have become successfully implanted in the uteruses of a number of post-menopausal women (Sauer et al., 1990).

It is no longer necessarily true that menopause brings the end of a woman's child-bearing years!

During the climacteric, some 50 to 85 percent of women encounter symptoms such as hot flashes (uncomfortable sensations characterized by heat and perspiration), insomnia, fatigue, labored breathing, and mood changes as a result. However, in most cases these symptoms are relatively mild, and menopause does not signal the end of a woman's sexual interests (Sarrell & Sarrell, 1984; Skalka, 1984). Physical changes that stem from falloff in hormone production are frequently controlled by estrogen-replacement therapy (ERT). Perhaps a more important issue is the meaning of menopause to the individual. Women who equate menopause with loss of femininity are likely to encounter more distress than those who do not (Rathus et al., 1993).

The Empty-Nest Syndrome. In earlier decades, psychologists placed great emphasis on a concept referred to as the **empty-nest syndrome** that

Deadline Decade Sheehy's term for the ages of 35 to 45, which are characterized by recognition of mortality, turmoil, and reassessment of youthful dreams.

Menopause The cessation of menstruation.

[2]There are many other reasons for irregular periods, and women who encounter them are advised to discuss them with their doctors.

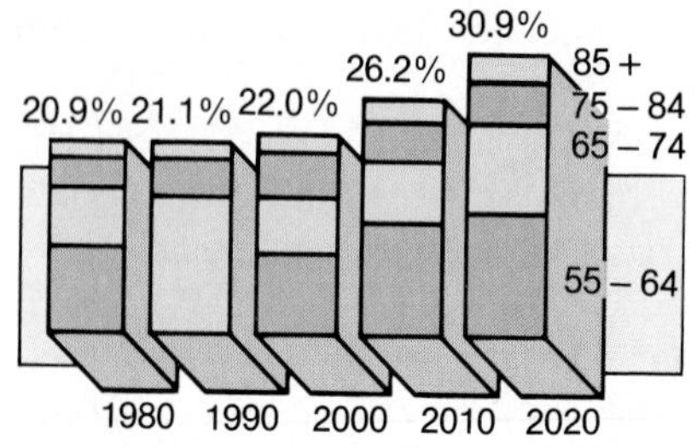

FIGURE 10.9
The Aging of America. Because of factors such as improved health care, diet, and exercise, Americans are living longer. By the year 2020, for example, about 31 percent of us will be at least 55 years old, as compared to about 21 percent today.

applied to women in particular. It was assumed that women experienced a profound sense of loss when the youngest child went off to college, got married, or moved into an apartment. Research findings paint more of a mixed and optimistic picture, however. Certainly there can be problems, and these apply to both parents. Perhaps the largest of these is letting go of one's children after so many years of mutual interdependence (Bell, 1983). The stresses of letting go can be compounded when the children are also ambivalent about becoming independent.

However, many mothers report increased marital satisfaction and personal changes such as greater mellowness, self-confidence, and stability after the children have left home, (Reinke et al., 1985). Middle-aged women show increased dominance and assertiveness, an orientation toward achievement, and greater influence in the worlds of politics and work (Serlin, 1980; Sheehy, 1976). It is as if they are cut free from traditional shackles by the knowledge that their child-bearing years are behind them.

In fact, the "empty nest" signals a time of increased freedom for both parents (Dyer, 1983). They have frequently become free of financial worries and are now also free to travel. Slightly more than half the women whose children have left the nest are now in the work force. Some have returned to college.

Most mothers (and fathers) actually do *not* suffer from the "empty-nest syndrome" when the youngest child leaves home.

Late Adulthood

The same space of time seems shorter as we grow older.
William James

How old would you be if you didn't know how old you was?
Satchel Paige, ageless baseball pitcher

The true test of maturity is not how old a person is but how he reacts to awakening in the midtown area in his shorts.
Woody Allen, *Without Feathers*

Late adulthood begins at age 65. One reason that developmental psychologists have become concerned about the later years is that with improved health care and knowledge of the importance of diet and exercise, more Americans than ever before are 65 or older—in excess of 33 million (Lonergan & Krevans, 1991). In 1900, only 1 American in 30 was over 65, as compared to 1 in 9 in 1970. By the year 2020, perhaps 1 American in 5 will be 65 or older (Figure 9.10). Another reason for the increased interest in aging is the recognition that, in a sense, *all* development involves aging. A third reason for studying the later years is to learn how we can further promote the health and psychological well-being of the elderly.

Physical Development. Various changes—some of them problematic—do occur during the later years. Changes in calcium metabolism lead to increased brittleness in the bones and heightened risk of breaks from accidents like falls. The skin becomes less elastic and subject to wrinkles and folds.

The senses become less acute. The elderly see and hear less acutely (Belsky, 1984b). Because of a decline in the sense of smell, they may use more spice to flavor their food. The elderly require more time (called **reaction time**) to respond to stimuli. Elderly drivers need more time to respond to traffic lights, other vehicles, and changing road conditions.

Empty-nest syndrome A sense of depression and loss of purpose felt by some parents when the youngest child leaves home.

Reaction time The amount of time required to respond to a stimulus.

As we grow older, our immune systems also function less effectively, leaving us more vulnerable to disease.

Cognitive Development. The elderly show some decline in general intellectual ability as measured by scores on intelligence tests. The drop-off is most acute on timed items such as those on many of the performance scales of the Wechsler Adult Intelligence Scale (see Chapter 8).

Although changes in reaction time, intellectual functioning, and memory are common, we understand very little about *why* they occur (Storandt, 1983). Losses of sensory acuity and of motivation to do well may contribute to lower scores. In his later years, psychologist B. F. Skinner (1983) argued that much of the falloff is due to an "aging environment" rather than an aging person. That is, in many instances the behavior of elderly people goes unreinforced. Note that nursing home residents who are rewarded for remembering recent events show improved scores on tests of memory (Langer et al., 1979; Wolinsky, 1982).

In some cases, supposedly irreversible cognitive changes reflect psychological problems such as depression (Albert, 1981). Such changes are neither primarily cognitive nor irreversible. If the depression is treated effectively, intellectual performance may also improve.

Theories of Aging. Although it may be hard to believe that it will happen to us, everyone who has so far walked the Earth has aged—which may not be a bad fate, considering the alternative. Why do we age? Various factors, some of which are theoretical, apparently contribute to aging.

Heredity plays a role. **Longevity** runs in families. People whose parents and grandparents lived into their eighties and nineties have a better chance of reaching these years themselves.

Environmental factors also influence aging. People who exercise regularly seem to live longer. Disease, stress, obesity, and cigarette smoking can contribute to an early death. Fortunately, we can exert control over some of these factors.

Elderly people show better health and psychological well-being when they do exert control over their own lives (Rodin, 1986; Wolinsky, 1982). About 29 percent of the elderly will spend at least some time in a nursing home (Kemper & Murtaugh, 1991), however, where many of them surrender much of their independence. Even in the nursing home, the elderly fare better when they are kept well-informed and allowed to make decisions on matters that affect them.

Disturbances in the abilities of cells to regenerate and repair themselves accompany aging. It is unclear whether these disturbances are genetically preprogrammed or are caused by external factors (such as ultraviolet light) or by an accumulation of random internal changes. More research is needed into the basic processes of aging, including the relationships between biological processes, life-style factors, and psychological problems such as confusional states and Alzheimer's disease (Lonergan & Krevans, 1991).

Ego Integrity versus Despair. According to Erikson, late adulthood is the stage of **ego integrity versus despair.** The basic challenge is to maintain the belief that life is meaningful and worthwhile in the face of the inevitability of death. Ego integrity derives from wisdom, as well as from the acceptance of one's life span as occurring at a certain point in the sweep of history and as being limited. We spend most of our lives accumulating things and relationships. Erikson also argues that adjustment in the later years requires the wisdom to be able to let go.

Erikson was optimistic. He believed that we can maintain a sense of trust through life and avoid feelings of despair.

Adjustment of the Elderly. Aging is not without its problems. One key problem experienced by the elderly, however, concerns the stereotypes that younger people tend to have of them. One such stereotype is that elderly people

---

Longevity A long span of life.

Ego integrity versus despair Erikson's term for the crisis of late adulthood, characterized by the task of maintaining one's sense of identity despite physical deterioration.

tend to be crotchety, irritable, and difficult to satisfy. However, a study of people retired for 18 to 120 months found that 75 percent rated retirement as mostly good (Hendrick et al., 1982a). Over 90 percent were generally satisfied with life, and more than 75 percent reported their health as good or excellent.

Despite the stereotype, the majority of the elderly are actually quite satisfied with their lives.

Adjustment among the elderly, as at any age, is related to financial security and physical health. The sicker we are, the less likely we are to be well-adjusted. There is also a link between financial status and physical health. Poor elderly people are more likely to report ill health than the financially secure (Birren, 1983). This finding would seem to call for better health care for the aged, and it does. But it may also be that people who have been healthier over the years are also better able to provide for their own financial security.

There are some stereotypes concerning living arrangements for the elderly. One has them living with children; another, in institutions. Still another has them buying recreational vehicles and taking off for condominiums or retirement communities in the sunbelt. First, let us put to rest the stereotype that elderly people are generally dependent on others. According to the U.S. Bureau of the Census, nearly 70 percent of heads of households aged at least 65 own their own homes.

Despite the stereotype of taking off for the sunbelt, the majority of the elderly remain in their home towns and cities. Moving is stressful at any age. Most of the elderly apparently prefer to remain in familiar locales. When elderly people do decide to move, however, careful plans and adequate finances decrease the stress of moving (Hendrick et al., 1982a).

Here, too, there are some stereotypes. Often the elderly are portrayed as living in poverty or at the mercy of their children and external forces such as government support. Unfortunately, some of these stereotypes are based on reality. People who no longer work are usually dependent on savings and fixed incomes such as pensions and social security payments. The flip side of the coin is that nationwide, only about 13 percent of those aged 65 and above live below the poverty level. But the financial status of elderly African Americans is worse. Two out of three live below the poverty level.

On Death and Dying.

Of all the wonders that I yet have heard,
It seems to me most strange that men should fear;
Seeing that death, a necessary end,
Will come when it will come.

Shakespeare, *Julius Caesar*

Death is the last great taboo. Psychiatrist Elisabeth Kübler-Ross commented on our denial of death in her landmark book *On Death and Dying:*

We use euphemisms, we make the dead look as if they were asleep, we ship the children off to protect them from the anxiety and turmoil around the house if the [person] is fortunate enough to die at home, [and] we don't allow children to visit their dying parents in the hospitals. (1969, p. 8)

From her work with terminally ill patients, Kübler-Ross found some common responses to news of impending death. She identified five stages of dying through which many patients pass, and she suggests that elderly people who suspect that death is approaching may under go similar emotional and cognitive responses. The stages are as follows:

1. *Denial.* In the denial stage, people feel, "It can't be me. The diagnosis must be wrong." As noted by Carroll (1985), denial can be flat and absolute, or it can fluctuate so that now the patient accepts the medical verdict and then the patient starts chatting animatedly about distant plans.
2. *Anger.* Denial usually gives way to anger and resentment toward the young and healthy and, sometimes, toward the medical establishment—"It's unfair. Why me?"
3. *Bargaining.* Next, people may try to bargain with God to postpone death, promising, for example, to do good deeds if they are given another six months, another year.
4. *Depression.* With depression come feelings of loss and hopelessness—grief at the specter of leaving loved ones and life itself.
5. *Final acceptance.* Ultimately, an inner peace may come, a quiet acceptance of the inevitable. Such "peace" does not resemble contentment; it is nearly devoid of feeling.

Psychologist Edwin Shneidman (1984), who has specialized in the concerns of suicidal and dying individuals, acknowledges the presence of feelings such as those described by Kübler-Ross, but he does not perceive them to be linked in sequence. Instead, Shneidman suggests that dying people show a variety of emotional and cognitive responses that tend to be fleeting or relatively stable, to ebb and flow, and to reflect pain and bewilderment. He also points out that the kinds of responses shown by individuals reflect their personality traits and their philosophies of life.

Research is more supportive of Shneidman's views than Kübler-Ross's. Reactions to nearing death turn out to be quite varied. For example, Kastenbaum (1977) found that some people are reasonably accepting of the inevitable; others are despondent; still others are terrorized. Some people show a rapid shifting of emotions ranging from rage to surrender, from envy of those who are younger and healthier to moments of yearning for the inevitable (Shneidman, 1984). Kalish and Reynolds (1976) questioned several hundred young adults, middle-aged persons, and elderly people in the Los Angeles area about their feelings concerning death. Generally speaking, the elderly thought more about death, but death was somewhat less frightening for them than it was for the younger groups.

"Lying Down to Pleasant Dreams . . ." The American poet William Cullen Bryant is best known for his poem "Thanatopsis," which he composed at the age of 18. "Thanatopsis" expresses Erik Erikson's goal of ego integrity—optimism that we can maintain a sense of trust through life. By meeting squarely the challenges of our adult lives, perhaps we can take our leave with dignity. When our time comes to "join the innumerable caravan"—the billions who have died before us—perhaps we can depart life with integrity.

Live, wrote the poet, so that

> . . . when thy summons comes to join
> The innumerable caravan that moves
> To that mysterious realm, where each shall take
> His chamber in the silent halls of death,
> Thou go not, like the quarry-slave at night,
> Scourged to his dungeon, but, sustained and soothed
> By an unfaltering trust, approach thy grave
> Like one that wraps the drapery of his couch
> About him, and lies down to pleasant dreams.

Bryant, of course, wrote "Thanatopsis" at age 18, not at 85, the age at which he died. At that advanced age, his feelings—and his verse—might have differed. But literature and poetry, unlike science, need not reflect reality. They can serve to inspire and warm us.

STUDY GUIDE

EXERCISE 1: Stages and Ages in Piaget's Theory

Directions: List the names of each of Piaget's stages of cognitive development and the approximate ages at which they take place.

	STAGE	APPROXIMATE AGES
1.	______________	______________
2.	______________	______________
3.	______________ ______________	______________
4.	______________ ______________	______________

EXERCISE 2: Events That Take Place During Piaget's Stages of Development

Directions: Following are a number of events that take place during Piaget's stages of cognitive development. In the blank space to the left of each event, write the letter A, B, C, or D that indicates the stage during which the event first takes place:

A = Sensorimotor
B = Preoperational
C = Concrete operational
D = Formal operational

_____ 1. Artificialism
_____ 2. Subjective moral judgments
_____ 3. Abstract thinking
_____ 4. Object permanence
_____ 5. Children emerge as theoretical scientists
_____ 6. Animism
_____ 7. Conservation
_____ 8. Assimilation of novel stimulation to ready-made schemes
_____ 9. Objective moral judgments
_____ 10. Reversibility

Answer Key to Exercise 1

1. Sensorimotor stage: First 2 years
2. Preoperational stage: Ages 2–6
3. Concrete operational stage: Ages 7–12
4. Formal operational stage: Adolescence and adulthood

Answer Key to Exercise 2

1. B **2.** C **3.** D **4.** A **5.** D **6.** B **7.** C **8.** A **9.** B **10.** C

ESL—BRIDGING THE GAP

This part consists of phrases and expresssions in which words are used differently from their regular meaning, or are used as metaphors.

Phrases and Expressions (Different Usage)

their timing (362)—the time that they choose
a very different drama was unfolding (362)—the exciting occurrence was happening
psychological well-being (362)—psychological health
Need we be concerned (363)—Should we worry
Diverse views (363)—Different opinions
biologically "programmed" (363)—biologically planned
be largely traced to (363)—predominantly caused by
leaned heavily toward (363)—believed that
major . . . leaps (363)—important periods of growth that are separate from each other
saw development as being (363)—believed that development was
as well as (364)—and it also happens
booming, buzzing (368)—loud; noisy
facelike patterns (368)—designs that look like faces
checkerboard (368)—pattern of black and white squares that alternate
placed face down (368)—placed with the face looking at the surface
when so placed (368)—when they were placed this way
to venture onto (368)—to go onto
beckoned (368)—indicated with hand movements
caregivers (370)—the people who care for the infants
pull and tug (370)—pull their arms and clothes
"run over" (370)—"stepped on"
tracked their attachment (370)—followed, watched and studied their attachment
grew intense (370)—became intense
soft, cuddly terry cloth (371)—"terry cloth" is "towel" material
path to a monkey's heart (372)—the way to make a monkey happy
a comforting base (372)—comfortable place
oversized (372)—a lot bigger than normal size
unwritten rule (372)—informal and nonscientific rule, but accepted
were made public (372)—were publicized; were put in national magazines or newspapers
waterfowl (372)—ducks and geese
Put aside the issue of (373)—We will not think about
it dawned on me (373)—it occurred to me; I realized
shrugged them off (373)—not paid attention to them
methods to his children's madness (373)—reasons for the incorrect answers
Crude turning (374)—inexperienced movement
out of sight is literally out of mind (375)—if the baby cannot see the object or person, the baby cannot think about it
try out (375)—attempt
But be warned (376)—But do not expect there to be
a squat glass (377)—a short and wide glass
wrongdoer (378)—a person who does something wrong
center on (378)—notice particularly
judge . . . more harshly (378)—are more judgmental; criticise . . . much more
in arriving at (378)—in deciding
trying out (379)—experimenting with
ways of carrying themselves (379)—methods of dressing, walking, talking and acting
layoffs (379)—loss of jobs; firing people
or are otherwise linked (379)—are in some other way connected
have fared better (379)—have been proved more
it is fair to say (379)—it is reasonable to say
edifice has been rocked (379)—structure has been questioned
dashed to rubble (379)—destroyed
to wear away at (379)—to question and to criticize
agreed-upon (381)—procedures that everyone (society) agrees to
the thrust of (381)—the direction of
storm and stress (387)—discontent and stress
wind up (387)—become; when they are finished growing
growth spurts (387)—short, separate periods of growing
fighting the battle of the bulge (387)—trying not to gain weight
wolf down (387)—eat a lot in a short period
"neither fish nor fowl" (388)—neither children nor adults; neither one definite group or the other, in between
for their own good (388)—so they do not physically or psychologically hurt themselves
a yearning for independence (388)—a great desire to be independent
a role in life (388)—a position or way of living which is accepted by the person and society
a firm sense (388)—a strong feeling
carry them through (388)—help them through
color their achievements with meaning (388)—give their achievements meaning
spread themselves thin (388)—do too many things
blind alley (388)—an endeavor that does not result in interest
mold for themselves (388)—create for themselves
central task (389)—important action
Upon entry (390)—When we enter the adult world
our mark on history (390)—do something that future generations will notice and appreciate
fueled by ambition (390)—motivated by the desire to succeed

pathways in life (390)—directions in life
for their own support (391)—for earning the money themselves for rent and food
swerves and bends (391)—frequently changing direction
lose some of its allure in the next (391)—not feel important in the next year
remiss (391)—was not correct
would "never get myself together" (391)—would never organize myself and my life
nearing the end of the fertile years (391)—arriving at the end of the times when a woman can get pregnant
closing down (391)—not available anymore
settling down (392)—becoming settled in a job and a family
forge ahead (392)—try to succeed
ridden out the storm (392)—survived the difficult years
to put down roots (392)—to settle in a place, a job and with a family
marking time, treading water (392)—not moving forward; not progressing in a job or career
a dramatic shift (392)—a noticeable and important change
some marker event (392)—an important event that symbolizes a change
it strikes men that (392)—men suddenly think that
dawns on men (392)—men think; men realize
the specter of old age (392)—the unpleasant idea of old age
middle-level (392)—middle position (job); not at the top and not at the bottom
grinding out accounts (392)—engaging in a boring activity
coming apart at the seams (392)—feels very unhappy, depressed and not able to figure out how to feel better
loss of purpose (392)—that there is no goal
extramarital affairs (392)—"love" and sexual attachments that are not with the spouse, but with someone else
overriding drive (392)—predominant effort
come to terms with (392)—understand that the dream may not be fulfilled
free themselves from their dreams (393)—decide that their unrealistic dream will not occur
a sense of urgency (393)—a feeling that the women must be quick
a "last chance" (393)—something must be accomplished *now* or it will never be accomplished
a falling off (393)—decrease
does not signal the end (393)—is not an indication that the end is near
It was once believed (382)—people used to believe
caution us not to attach too much importance to (383)—warn us not to believe completely
small (383)—small difference; not a lot of difference
means to do so (383)—ability to do it
tomboyishness (384)—traits of a young male in a young female
wrapped up in the ways (386)—concerned with the ways
flip side of the coin (396)—the other side of the issue
paint more of a mixed and optimistic picture (394)—indicate that the problems can be solved more easily
letting go of one's children (394)—allowing one's children to become independent
cut free from (394)—freed from
traditional shackles (394)—traditional confinements
times items (672)—items that have a time limit
so far walked the Earth (395)—lived up to this time; lived before us
fare better (395)—act and feel better
the sweep of history and (395)—the many years in the past and in the future
to call for (396)—demand
in her landmark book (396)—in her important book which many people paid attention to
terminally ill (396)—those people who will die from the illness
chatting animatedly (397)—talking happily
". . . Why me?" (397)—Why did this happen to me and not to someone else?
to ebb and flow (397)—to not occur and to occur
meeting squarely the challenges (397)—accepting and acting on the challenges

CHAPTER REVIEW

Section 1: Controversies in Developmental Psychology

Objective 1: Discuss the nature-nurture controversy.

Those aspects of behavior that originate in our genes and unfold in the child as long as minimal nutrition and social experience are provided are referred to as our (1) ____________ure. Those aspects of behavior that can be largely traced to environmental influences such as nutrition and learning are said to reflect our (2) ____________ure. Psychologist Arnold (3) G____________ endorsed natural explanations of development. Gesell argued that development is self-regulated by the unfolding of natural plans and processes, or by (4) ____________ation. John Watson and other behaviorists leaned heavily toward (5) ____________mental explanations. (6) W____________ focused primarily on adaptive behavior patterns, whereas (7) ____________ell focused on including physical and motor growth and development.

Objective 2: Discuss the issue as to whether development is continuous or discontinuous.

Psychologists argue as to whether developmental changes occur gradually—that is, (8) ______________ously, or in major qualitative leaps that dramatically alter the ways in which we are structured and behave—that is, (9) ______________ously. Behaviorists view development as a (10) ______________ous process in which the effects of learning mount gradually, with no major sudden qualitative changes. (11) ______________tional theorists, by contrast, believe that there are periods of life during which development occurs so dramatically that we can speak of its occurring in (12) ______________ges.

Section 2: Physical Development

Objective 3: Describe the process of conception.

It is possible to become pregnant for a day or so following (13) ______________tion. Ovulation is defined as the releasing of an (14) ______________ from an ovary. A person begins to grow and develop when a sperm cell combines with an ovum to become a (15) z______________. Sperm cells can carry X or (16) ______________ sex chromosomes. If a sperm cell with (17: an X or a Y?) sex chromosome fertilizes an ovum, a boy is conceived.

Objective 4: Describe the sequences of physical development.

Prenatal development may be divided into (18: How many?) ______________ stages or periods. These are the (19) ______________nal stage (approximately the first two weeks), the (20) em______________ stage (which lasts from two weeks to about two months after conception), and the (21) f______________ stage. During the germinal stage, the zygote divides repeatedly as it travels through the (22) f______________ tube and then within the uterus. Then the zygote becomes implanted in the wall of the (23) u______________.

The (24) ______________ic period lasts from implantation until the end of the second month. During the embryonic period, the major (25) o______________ systems of the unborn child undergo rapid development. Development follows two general trends: (26) ______________caudal and (27) prox______________.

The most dramatic gains in height and weight occur during (28) ______________tal development. Babies usually double their birth weight in about (29: how many?) ______________ months and triple it by the (30: which?) ______________ birthday. Following the gains of infancy, children gain about (31: how many?) ______________ to three inches a year and (32: how many?) ______________ to six pounds a year until they reach the adolescent growth spurt.

Objective 5: Describe the reflexes that are present at birth.

Infants are born with a number of reflexes. Reflexes are (33) ______________typical responses elicited by specific stimuli. Reflexes occur automatically; they do not involve higher (34) b______________ functions. The most basic reflex for survival is (35) ______________hing. In the (36) ______________ing reflex, infants turn their heads toward stimuli that touch the cheek. In the (37) ______________ing reflex, infants suck objects that touch the lips. In the (38) s______________, or Moro reflex, infants arch their backs and draw up their legs in response to sudden noises and bumps. In the grasp, or (39) ______________r reflex, infants grasp objects pressed against the palms of the hands. In the (40) B______________ reflex, they spread their toes when the soles of the feet are stimulated. Reflexes like rooting and sucking promote survival and phase out as neural functioning (41) ______________ures and many previously automatic processes come under (42) vol______________ control.

Section 3: Perceptual Development

Objective 6: Describe the processes of perceptual development.

Newborn children sleep about (43: how many?) ______________ hours a day. The (44) ______________ary reflex is present at birth, so the irises widen automatically to admit more light when it is dark, and vice versa. Neonates do not show visual (45) ______________dation; they see as through a fixed-focus camera. Estimates place their visual (46) ac______________ at about 20/600. Visual acuity makes the most dramatic gains between the ages of birth and (47: how many?) ______________ months.

Infants appear to have an inborn preference for (48: simple or complex?) visual stimulation. Infants are generally capable of depth perception, as measured by behavior on the visual cliff, by the time they are able to (49) c________________.

Most newborns (50) ________________xively turn their heads toward unusual sounds. Three-day-old babies prefer their (51) ________________rs' voices to those of other women, but do not show similar preferences for the voices of their fathers. Newborns can discriminate different odors, and they breathe (52: more or less?) rapidly and are (53: more or less?) active when presented with powerful odors. Newborns can discriminate sweet tastes. The tongue pressure of neonates sucking on a nipple correlates with the amount of (54) s________________ in their liquid diet. Newborns are sensitive to touch, but relatively insensitive to (55) p________________, which may reflect an adaptive response to the process of birth.

Section 4: Attachment

Objective 7: Describe Ainsworth's views on attachment.

Ainsworth defines attachment "as an (56) ________________tional tie that one person or animal forms between himself and another specific one—a tie that binds them together in (57) s________________ and endures over time." Securely attached babies cry (58: more or less?) frequently and are (59: more or less?) likely to show affection toward their mothers than insecurely attached babies.

Ainsworth identified three stages of attachment: the (60) ________________-________________chment phase, which lasts from birth to about 3 months and is characterized by indiscriminate attachment; the (61) attachment-in-the-________________ing phase, which occurs at about 3 or 4 months and is characterized by preference for familiar figures; and the (62) c________________-cut-attachment phase, which occurs at about 6 or 7 months and is characterized by intensified dependence on the primary caregiver.

Objective 8: Explain various theoretical perspectives on attachment.

Behaviorists argue that children become attached to mothers through (63) ________________ning, because their mothers feed them and attend to other primary needs. From this view, mothers serve as conditioned (64) ________________ers.

The Harlow studies with rhesus monkeys suggest that an innate motive, referred to as (65) c________________ comfort, is more important than conditioning in the development of attachment. Harlow's infant monkeys spent more time on soft terry-cloth (66) su________________ "mothers" than on wire "mothers," even when their feeding bottles protruded from the wire mothers. His infant monkeys were also more willing to explore the environment in the presence of (67: terry-cloth or wire?) surrogate mothers.

Ethologists argue that attachment occurs during a (68) c________________ period. During this critical period, young animals such as ducks and geese form (69) ________________ive attachments to the first moving objects they encounter. The process of forming an attachment in this manner is called (70) ________________ing. Attachment in these animals is bounded at the early end by the age at which they first engage in (71) lo________________ and, at the upper end, by the development of (72) ________________r of strangers.

Section 5: Cognitive Development

Objective 9: Define Piaget's concepts of *scheme*, *assimilation*, and *accommodation*.

Jean Piaget has advanced our knowledge of children's (73) c________________ development. Piaget saw children as budding (74) ________________ists who actively strive to make sense of the perceptual world. Piaget referred to action patterns and mental structures that are involved in acquiring or organizing knowledge as (75) ________________s. He defined intelligence as involving processes of (76) ________________tion, or responding to events according to existing schemes; and (77) ________________tion, or the changing of schemes to permit effective responses to new events.

Objective 10: Describe Piaget's stages of cognitive development.

Piaget's view of cognitive development includes (78: how many?) ________________ stages or periods. First comes the (79) ________________or period, which occurs prior to use of symbols and language. During the sensorimotor period, the child comes to mentally represent objects, and thus develops object (80) per________________. Second is the (81) ________________tional period, which is characterized by egocentric thought (or inability to see the world as it is seen by others); animism; artificialism; inability to (82) ______ter on more than one aspect of a situation at a time; and (83: objective or subjective?) moral judgments. Third is the (84) ______-operational period, which is characterized by conservation; less egocentrism; reversibility; and (85: objective or subjective?) moral judgments. The fourth period is the (86) ______-operational period, which is characterized by capacity for abstract logic.

Objective 11: Evaluate Piaget's theory.

Various issues have been raised about Piaget's views. For example, Piaget's methodology led him to (87: overestimate or underestimate?) the ages at which children can carry out certain kinds of tasks. Also, cognitive skills such as egocentrism and conservation may develop (88: more or less?) continuously than Piaget thought—not in general stages. On the positive side, it seems that the sequences of development are indeed (89: variant or invariant?), as Piaget believed.

Section 6: Moral Development

Objective 12: Describe Kohlberg's levels and stages of moral development.

Kohlberg's theory of cognitive development focuses on the development of (90) ______al reasoning. Kohlberg hypothesizes that the processes of moral reasoning develop through (91: how many?) ______ "levels" and (92: how many?) ______ stages within each level. In the (93) ______tional level, judgments are based on expectation of rewards or punishments. Stage 1 is oriented toward obedience and (94) ______ment. In stage 2, good behavior is equated with what will allow people to satisfy (95) ______ds. Conventional-level moral judgments reflect the need to conform to conventional standards of right or wrong. According to the stage 3 (96) "______ orientation," it is good to meet the needs and expectations of others. In stage 4, moral judgments are based on rules that maintain the social (97) ______r. The third level in Kohlberg's theory is termed (98) ______tional, and it consists of stages 5 and 6. In stage 5's (99) co______, legalistic orientation, it is recognized that laws stem from agreed-upon procedures, and that existing laws cannot bind the individual's behavior in unusual circumstances. In stage 6's conscience or (100) ______ed orientation, people consider behavior that is consistent with their own ethical standards as right.

Critics suggest that postconventional reasoning, especially stage (101) ______ reasoning, may be more reflective of Kohlberg's philosophical ideals than of a natural stage of cognitive development.

Section 7: Gender-Typing

Objective 13: Summarize gender differences in cognition and aggression.

Studies in the assessment of intelligence (102: show or do not show?) overall differences in cognitive abilities between the sexes. Maccoby and Jacklin find persistent suggestions that (103: boys or girls?) are somewhat superior in verbal ability. Males seem somewhat superior in (104) ______-spatial abilities and (105) ______tics.

Three factors should caution us not to attach too much importance to these cognitive gender differences: First, in most cases they are (106: large or small?). Second, these gender differences are (107) g______ differences. Third, they may largely reflect cultural (108) ______tions.

Most psychological studies of aggression have found that (109: males or females?) behave more aggressively.

Objective 14: Discuss perspectives on gender-typing.

(110) Pre______ sex hormones may "masculinize" or "feminize" the brain by creating predispositions that are consistent with some gender-role stereotypes. (111: Male or Female?) rats generally excel in maze-learning ability, a task that requires spatial skills. But female rats who are exposed to (112) ______gens early in life learn maze routes as rapidly as males.

(113: Early or Late?) maturers, whether boys or girls, tend to show the "masculine pattern" of excelling on math and spatial-relations tasks. (114: Early or Late?) maturation seems to favor development of verbal skills. Since females usually mature (115: earlier or later?) than boys, their verbal skills would usually be favored.

Freud believed that gender identity remains flexible until the resolution of the (116) O______ and Electra complexes. Appropriate gender-typing requires that boys (117) i__________ with their fathers and surrender the wish to possess their mothers. Girls would have to surrender the wish to have a (118) p__________ and identify with their mothers.

Social-learning theorists explain the acquisition of gender roles and gender differences in terms such as (119) __________tional learning, identification, and (120) so__________tion. Children learn much of what is considered masculine or feminine behaviors by (121) ob__________nal learning of the relative frequencies with which men and women perform them.

Social-learning theorists view (122) __________ation as a broad, continuous learning process in which children are influenced by rewards and punishments to imitate adults of the same gender. In socialization, parents and others (123) re__________ children for behavior they consider gender-appropriate.

According to cognitive theory, rewards provide children with (124) __________tion as to when they are behaving in ways that other people find appropriate. (125) Gender-__________ theory holds that children use gender as one way of organizing their perceptions of the world. As in social-learning theory, children learn "appropriate" behavior patterns by (126) __________tion. But children's active cognitive processing of (127) __________tion also contributes to gender-typing.

Children learn to judge themselves according to the traits, or constructs, considered relevant to their (128) __________er. In so doing, their (129) self-__________s become blended with the gender schema of their culture.

Section 8: Adolescence

Objective 15: Discuss the major changes that take place during adolescence.

Adolescence begins at (130) p__________ and ends with assumption of adult responsibilities. Puberty begins with the appearance of (131) __________ary sex characteristics, such as the growth of bodily hair, deepening of the (132) __________ in males, and rounding of the breasts and hips in females. Changes that lead to reproductive capacity and secondary sex characteristics are stimulated by (133) __________rone in the male and by (134) __________en and androgens in the female. Testosterone causes the penis and (135) __________es to grow and pubic hair appears. Small amounts of (136) __________gens, along with estrogen, stimulate growth of pubic and axillary hair in the female. First menstruation is termed (137) __________che.

Gould and other researchers have found that adolescents frequently yearn for (138) __________ence from parents. Erikson considers ego (139) __________y, or the defining of a life role, the major challenge of adolescence. Adolescents who do not develop ego identity may encounter role (140) d__________.

Section 9: Adult Development

Objective 16: Describe the challenges and crises of young adulthood.

Adulthood can be divided into young, middle, and (141) __________ adulthood. According to writers such as Gould and Sheehy, young adulthood is generally characterized by striving to advance in the (142) c__________ world. Men's development during this period is largely guided by needs for (143) ind__________ and (144) au__________, while women are more likely to be guided by shifting patterns of (145) at__________ and caring. Erikson considers the development of (146) __________te relationships a central task of young adulthood. Erikson labels young adulthood the stage of intimacy vs. (147) i__________. According to Levinson, young adults often adopt a (148) __________, which serves as a tentative blueprint for their lives and is characterized by the drive to "become" someone, to leave their mark on history.

During the late 20s and 30s, many women encounter a crisis involving concerns about nearing the end of the (149) f__________ years, closing opportunities, and heightened responsibilities. Sheehy labels the 30s the (150) __________ 30s, because many adults encounter disillusionment and reassess their lives at this time. According to Levinson and Sheehy, the second half of the 30s is frequently characterized by (151) __________ing down.

Objective 17: Describe the challenges and crises of middle adulthood.

Many middle-aged people encounter feelings of entrapment and loss of purpose that are termed the (152) mi________ ________. According to Levinson, at about age 40, some marker event causes men to realize that they are a full (153) ________ion older than 20-year-olds. Women may undergo a midlife transition about (154) ________ years earlier than men, at about 35 rather than 40.

Erikson labels middle age the stage of (155) ________ vs. stagnation. Middle adulthood is a time when we must come to terms with the discrepancies between our (156) ________ments and the dreams of youth.

Some middle-aged people become depressed when the youngest child leaves home; they experience the so-called (157) "e________-________ syndrome." However, many women at this time show increased (158) dom________ and (159) ________iveness. It is as if the children's leaving home has freed them from (160) tr________ expectations of how women are supposed to behave.

Objective 18: Describe the challenges and crises of late adulthood.

Late adulthood begins at age (161) ________. One reason psychologists have become more concerned about late adulthood is the (162) ________ic imperative; that is, more of us are joining the ranks of the elderly all the time.

In late adulthood, changes occuring in (163) ________m metabolism lead to increased brittleness in the bones. The senses become (164: more or less?) acute, and so the elderly frequently spice their food more heavily. The time required to respond to stimuli—that is, (165) ________ion time—increases. Presumed cognitive deficits among the elderly may actually reflect declining (166) mot________ or psychological problems such as (167) de________. On the job, years of experience frequently compensate for most kinds of age-related deficits.

Heredity plays a role in having a long life span, or (168) ________ity. According to the (169) ________ar aging theory, the ability to repair DNA within cells decreases as we age. Environmental factors such as exercise, proper diet, and the maintenance of (170) c________ over one's life can all apparently delay aging to some degree.

Kübler-Ross identifies five stages of dying among the terminally ill: (171) de________, anger, bargaining, (172) de________, and final (173) ________ance. Research by other investigators finds that psychological reactions to approaching death are (174: more or less?) varied than Kübler-Ross suggests.

Erikson terms late adulthood the stage of ego (175) ________ty vs. despair. Ego integrity is the ability to maintain one's sense of identity in spite of progressive physical deterioration. Erikson argues that ego integrity is derived from (176) w________, and he argues that adjustment in the later years requires the wisdom to be able to let go.

ANSWERS TO CHAPTER REVIEW

1. Nature
2. Nurture
3. Gesell
4. Maturation
5. Environmental
6. Watson
7. Gesell
8. Continuously
9. Discontinuously
10. Continuous
11. Maturational
12. Stages
13. Ovulation
14. Ovum (egg cell)
15. Zygote
16. Y
17. a Y
18. Three
19. Germinal
20. Embryonic
21. Fetal
22. Fallopian
23. Uterus
24. Embryonic
25. Organ
26. Cephalocaudal
27. Proximodistal
28. Prenatal
29. Five
30. First
31. Two
32. Four
33. Stereotypical
34. Brain
35. Breathing
36. Rooting
37. Sucking
38. Startle
39. Palmar
40. Babinski
41. Matures
42. Voluntary
43. 16
44. Pupillary
45. Accommodation
46. Acuity
47. Six
48. Complex
49. Crawl
50. Reflexively
51. Mothers'
52. More
53. More
54. Sugar
55. Pain
56. Affectional

57. Space
58. Less
59. More
60. Initial-preattachment
61. Attachment-in-the-making
62. Clear-cut-attachment
63. Conditioning
64. Reinforcers
65. Contact
66. Surrogate
67. Terry-cloth
68. Critical
69. Instinctive
70. Imprinting
71. Locomotion
72. Fear
73. Cognitive
74. Scientists
75. Schemes
76. Assimilation
77. Accommodation
78. Four
79. Sensorimotor
80. Permanence
81. Preoperational
82. Center
83. Objective
84. Concrete
85. Subjective
86. Formal
87. Underestimate
88. More
89. Invariant
90. Moral
91. Three
92. Two
93. Preconventional
94. Punishment
95. Needs
96. Good-boy
97. Order
98. Postconventional
99. Contractual
100. Principled
101. Six
102. Do not show
103. Girls
104. Visual-spatial
105. Mathematics
106. Small
107. Group
108. Expectations
109. Males
110. Prenatal
111. Male
112. Androgens
113. Late
114. Early
115. Earlier
116. Oedipus
117. Identify
118. Penis
119. Observational
120. Socialization
121. Observational
122. Identification
123. Reinforce (or Reward)
124. Information
125. Schema
126. Observation
127. Information
128. Gender
129. Self-concepts
130. Puberty
131. Secondary
132. Voice
133. Testosterone
134. Estrogen
135. Testes
136. Androgens
137. Menarche
138. Independence
139. Identity
140. Diffusion
141. Late
142. Career
143. Individuation
144. Autonomy
145. Attachment
146. Intimate
147. Isolation
148. Dream
149. Fertile
150. Catch
151. Settling
152. Midlife crisis
153. Generation
154. Five
155. Generativity
156. Achievements
157. Empty-nest
158. Dominance
159. Assertiveness
160. Traditional
161. 65
162. Demographic
163. Calcium
164. Less
165. Reaction
166. Motivation
167. Depression
168. Longevity
169. Cellular
170. Control
171. Denial
172. Depression
173. Acceptance
174. More
175. Integrity
176. Wisdom

POSTTEST

1. Conception normally takes place in the
   (a) uterus.
   (b) fallopian tube.
   (c) ovary.
   (d) vagina.

2. Development tends to be continuous, according to the views of
   (a) Sigmund Freud.
   (b) Erik Erikson.
   (c) John Watson.
   (d) Jean Piaget.

3. The embryonic period lasts from ________ until about the eighth week of prenatal development.
   (a) implantation
   (b) conception
   (c) ovulation
   (d) the time the zygote reaches the uterus

4. There is a sudden noise in the nursery, and a newborn baby draws up his legs and arches his back in response. This response is an example of the ________ reflex.
   (a) Babinski
   (b) palmar
   (c) sphincter
   (d) Moro

5. Which of the following is true of perception in babies?
   (a) They prefer the voices of their fathers to those of other men.
   (b) They cannot hear until they are two to three weeks old.
   (c) They can perceive depth within a few days after birth.
   (d) They are born with the pupillary reflex.

6. Which of the following is *not* known for research in the area of attachment?
   (a) Konrad Lorenz
   (b) Mary Ainsworth
   (c) Jown Bowlby
   (d) Sandra Bem

7. In Harlow's experiments, infant rhesus monkeys showed preference for surrogate mothers
   (a) of their own species.
   (b) that were made from soft material.
   (c) that fed them.
   (d) that were present when they wanted to explore the environment.

8. Piaget viewed children as
   (a) reacting mechanically to environmental stimuli.
   (b) at the mercy of instinctive impulses.
   (c) budding scientists.
   (d) having a hierarchy of needs.

9. According to Piaget, children first show object permanence during the
   (a) sensorimotor period.
   (b) preoperational period.
   (c) concrete operational period.
   (d) formal operational period.

10. According to Piaget, children first center on the motives of wrongdoers, as well as the amount of damage done, during the
    (a) sensorimotor period.
    (b) preoperational period.
    (c) concrete operational period.
    (d) formal operational period.

11. Which of the following stages of moral development comes earliest, according to Kohlberg?
    (a) good-boy orientation
    (b) contractual, legalistic orientation
    (c) naively egoistic orientation
    (d) obedience-and-punishment orientation

12. According to Kohlberg, stage ________ moral judgments are characterized by respect for authority and social order.
    (a) 1
    (b) 2
    (c) 3
    (d) 4

13. According to gender-schema theory, children
    (a) blend their self-concepts with the gender schema of their culture.
    (b) normally identify with the parent of the same gender.
    (c) mechanically imitate the behavior patterns of children and adults of the same gender.
    (d) form mental templates or concepts of gender-appropriate behavior, but do not usually act in accord with these concepts.

14. The period of adolescence is defined by
    (a) biological changes only.
    (b) psychosocial changes only.
    (c) both biological and psychosocial changes.
    (d) neither biological nor psychosocial changes.

15. Which of the following biological events usually occurs *last* in males?
    (a) ejaculatory ability
    (b) presence of mature sperm
    (c) growth of bodily hair
    (d) deepening of the voice

16. Menarche is defined as
    (a) the beginning of puberty in girls.
    (b) the appearance of secondary sex characteristics in girls.
    (c) the complete maturation of secondary sex characteristics in girls.
    (d) first menstruation.

17. According to Erikson, adolescence is characterized by the crisis of
    (a) ego identity vs. role diffusion.
    (b) intimacy vs. isolation.
    (c) autonomy vs. doubt.
    (d) ego integrity vs. despair.

18. Sheehy labels the 30s the "Catch 30s," because
    (a) the long bones make no further gains in length.
    (b) of disillusionments and reassessments.
    (c) women enter midlife at about age 35.
    (d) we reach the halfway point of the typical life span.

19. Research shows that middle-aged women
    (a) frequently show increased dominance and assertiveness.
    (b) most often report decreased marital satisfaction.
    (c) cannot make the transition from motherhood to socially useful occupations.
    (d) come under the influence of the dream.

20. According to the cellular aging theory, the ability to repair ________________ decreases as we age.
    (a) the cell wall
    (b) the myelin sheath
    (c) DNA
    (d) RNA

ANSWERS TO POSTTEST

1. B
2. C
3. A
4. D
5. D
6. D
7. B
8. C
9. A
10. C
11. D
12. D
13. A
14. C
15. B
16. D
17. A
18. B
19. A
20. C

- According to Sigmund Freud, the human mind is like a vast submerged iceberg, only the tip of which rises above the surface into conscious awareness.

- According to Freud, biting one's fingernails or smoking cigarettes as an adult is a sign of conflict during very early childhood.

- According to Carl Jung, you have inherited mysterious memories that date back to ancient times.

- We are more likely to persist at difficult tasks when we believe that we shall succeed.

- Psychologists can determine whether a person has told the truth on a personality test.

- There is a psychological test made up of inkblots, and one of them looks like a bat.

Personality: Theories and Measurement

Learning Objectives

When you have finished studying Chapter 11, you should be able to:

Personality and Personality Theories

1. Define *personality*.

Psychodynamic Theories

2. Describe the "mental structures" theorized by Sigmund Freud in his psychodynamic theory.
3. List Freud's stages of psychosexual development, and describe the major events that occur during each stage.
4. Describe the psychodynamic views of Carl Jung.
5. Describe the psychodynamic views of Alfred Adler.
6. Describe the psychodynamic views of Karen Horney.
7. Describe the psychodynamic views of Erik Erikson.
8. Evaluate psychodynamic theory.

Trait Theories

9. Define *trait*.
10. Describe the contribution of Gordon Allport to trait theory.
11. Describe the trait-theory views of Raymond Cattell.
12. Describe the trait-theory views of Hans Eysenck.
13. Evaluate trait theory.

Learning Theories

14. Describe the behaviorist approach to understanding personality.
15. Describe the social-learning-theory approach to understanding personality, emphasizing the roles of person and situational variables.
16. Evaluate the learning theory of personality.

Humanistic-Existential Theories

17. Describe Vikor Frankl's humanistic-existential views on personality.
18. Describe Abraham Maslow's humanistic-existential views on personality.
19. Describe Carl Rogers's humanistic-existential views on personality.
20. Evaluate humanistic-existential theory.

Measurement of Personality

21. Differentiate between objective and projective measures of personality.
22. Describe some of the major objective measures of personality.
23. Describe some of the major projective measures of personality.

I was reading Dr. Seuss's *One Fish, Two Fish* to my 2-year-old daughter, Taylor. The sneaky author set up a trap for fathers. A part of the book reads that "Some [fish] are sad. And some are glad. And some are very, very bad. Why are they sad and glad and bad? I do not know. Go ask your dad."

Thanks, Dr. Seuss.

For many months I had been just reciting this section and then moving on. On one particular day, however, Taylor's cognitive development apparently flowered, and she would not let me get away with glossing this over. Why, indeed, she wanted to know, were some fish sad, whereas others were glad and bad. I paused, and then, being a typical American dad, I gave the answer I'm sure has been given by thousands of other fathers:

"Uh, some fish are sad and others are glad or bad because of, uh, the interaction of nature and nurture—I mean, you know, heredity and environmental factors."

To which Taylor laughed and replied "Not!"

I'm still not certain whether Taylor thought my words came out silly or that my psychological theorizing was simplistic or off base. But this question, when applied to people—that is, why people are sad or glad or bad—is the kind of question that is of interest to psychologists who investigate matters of personality.

Personality theorists define **personality** as the reasonably stable patterns of emotions, motives, and behavior that distinguish people from one another (Prigatano, 1992). Psychologists seek to explain how personality develops—that is, why some (people) are sad or glad or bad—and to predict how people with certain features of personality will respond to life's demands. In this chapter, we explore four approaches to personality: psychodynamic, trait, learning, and humanistic–existential theories. Then we discuss methods of measuring whether people are sad, glad, bad, and lots of other things—personality tests.

PSYCHODYNAMIC THEORIES

There are several **psychodynamic theories** of personality, but they have a number of things in common. Each teaches that personality is characterized by a dynamic struggle. Drives such as sex, aggression, and the need for superiority come into conflict with laws, social rules, and moral codes. The laws and social rules become internalized: we make them parts of ourselves. After doing so, the dynamic struggle becomes a clashing of opposing *inner* forces. At a given moment, our behavior, thoughts, and emotions represent the outcome of these inner contests.

Each psychodynamic theory also owes its origin to the thinking of Sigmund Freud.

Personality The distinct patterns of behavior, thoughts, and feelings that characterize a person's adaptation to life.

Psychodynamic theory Sigmund Freud's perspective, which emphasizes the importance of unconscious motives and conflicts as forces that determine behavior.

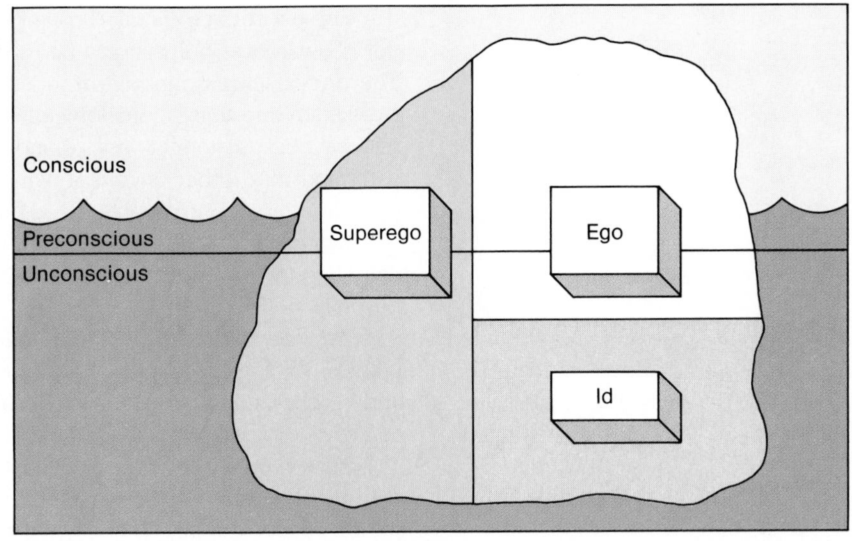

FIGURE 11.1
The Human Iceberg According to Freud. According to psychoanalytic theory, only the tip of human personality rises above the surface of the mind into conscious awareness. Material in the preconscious can become conscious if we direct our attention to it, but unconscious material tends to remain shrouded in mystery.

Sigmund Freud's Theory of Psychosexual Development

He was born with a shock of dark hair—in Jewish tradition, the sign of a prophet. In 1856, in a Czechoslovakian village, an old woman told his mother that she had given birth to a great man. The child was reared with great expectations. His sister, in fact, was prohibited from playing the piano when Freud was reading or reflecting in his room. In manhood, Sigmund Freud himself would be cynical about the prophecy. Old women, after all, would earn greater favors by forecasting good tidings than doom. But the forecast about Freud was not pure fantasy. Few have influenced our thinking about human nature so deeply.

Freud was trained as a physician. Early in his practice, he was astounded to find that some people apparently experienced loss of feeling in a hand or paralysis of the legs in the absence of any medical disorder. These odd symptoms often disappeared once patients had recalled and discussed distressful events and feelings of guilt or anxiety that seemed to be related to the symptoms. For a long time, these events and feelings had been hidden beneath the surface of awareness. Even so, they had the capacity to influence patients' behavior.

From this sort of clinical evidence, Freud concluded that the human mind is like an iceberg (Loftus & Klinger, 1992). Only the tip of an iceberg rises above the surface of the water, while the great mass of it darkens the deep (see Figure 11.1). Freud came to believe that people, similarly, were only aware of a small number of the ideas and impulses that dwelled within their minds. Freud argued that the greater mass of the mind—our deepest images, thoughts, fears, and urges—remained beneath the surface of conscious awareness, where little light illumined them.

It is true that Freud thought of the mind as being like a vast submerged iceberg, only the tip of which rises above the surface into conscious awareness.

Freud labeled the region that poked through into the light of awareness the **conscious** part of the mind. He called the regions that lay below the surface the preconscious and the unconscious.

Conscious Self-aware.

The **preconscious** mind contains elements of experience that are presently out of awareness but that can be made conscious simply by focusing on them. The **unconscious** mind is shrouded in mystery. It contains biological instincts such as sex and aggression. Some unconscious urges cannot be experienced consciously because mental images and words could not portray them in all their color and fury. Other unconscious urges may be kept below the surface by repression.

Repression is the automatic ejection of anxiety-evoking ideas from awareness. Repression protects us from identifying impulses we would consider inappropriate in light of our moral values.

The unconscious is the largest part of the mind. Here, the dynamic struggle between biological drives and social rules is fiercest. As drives seek expression, and internalized values exert counterpressures, the resultant conflict can precipitate psychological problems and behavioral outbursts.

Since we cannot view the unconscious mind directly, Freud developed a method of mental detective work called **psychoanalysis.** In psychoanalysis, people are prodded to talk about anything that "pops" into their minds while they remain comfortable and relaxed. People may gain **self-insight** by pursuing some of the thoughts that pop into awareness. But they are also motivated to evade threatening subjects. The same repression that has ejected unacceptable thoughts from awareness prompts **resistance,** or the desire to avoid thinking about or discussing them. Repression and resistance can make psychoanalysis a tedious process that lasts for years, even decades.

The Structure of Personality. When is a structure not a structure? When it is a mental or **psychic structure.** Sigmund Freud labeled the clashing forces of personality psychic structures. They could not be seen or measured directly, but their presence was suggested by observable behavior, expressed thoughts, and emotions. Freud hypothesized the existence of three psychic structures: the *id, ego,* and *superego.*

The **id** is present at birth. It represents physiological drives and is fully unconscious. Freud described the id as "a chaos, a cauldron of seething excitations" (1964, p. 73). The conscious mind might find it inconsistent to love and hate a person at the same time, but Freud believed that conflicting emotions could dwell side by side in the id. In the id, we could feel hatred for our mothers for failing to immediately gratify all of our needs even as we sense love for them.

The id follows what Freud termed the **pleasure principle.** It demands instant gratification of instincts without consideration of law, social custom, or the needs of others.

The **ego** begins to develop during the first year of life, largely because a child's demands for gratification cannot all be met immediately. The ego "stands for reason and good sense" (Freud, 1964, p. 76), for rational ways of coping with frustration. It curbs the appetites of the id and makes plans that are compatible with social convention so that a person can find gratification yet avert the censure of others. The id lets you know that you are hungry. The ego formulates the idea of walking to the refrigerator, warming up some enchiladas, and pouring a glass of milk.

The ego is guided by the **reality principle.** It takes into account what is practical and possible, as well as what is urged. Within Freudian theory, it is the ego that provides the conscious sense of self.

Although most of the ego is conscious, some of its business is carried out unconsciously. For instance, the ego also acts as a censor that screens the impulses of the id. When the ego senses that improper impulses are rising into awareness, it may use psychological defenses to deter them from surfacing. Repression is one such psychological defense, or **defense mechanism.** Various defense mechanisms are described in Table 11.1.

Preconscious Capable of being brought into awareness by the focusing of attention.

Unconscious In psychodynamic theory, not available to awareness by simple focusing of attention.

Repression A defense mechanism that protects the person from anxiety by ejecting anxiety-evoking ideas and impulses from awareness.

Psychoanalysis In this usage, Freud's method of exploring human personality.

Self-insight Accurate awareness of one's motives and feelings.

Resistance A blocking of thoughts whose awareness could cause anxiety.

Psychic structure In psychodynamic theory, a hypothesized mental structure that helps explain different aspects of behavior.

Id The psychic structure, present at birth, that represents physiological drives and is fully unconscious.

Pleasure principle The governing principle of the id—the seeking of immediate gratification of instinctive needs.

Ego The second psychic structure to develop, characterized by self-awareness, planning, and delay of gratification.

Reality principle Consideration of what is practical and possible in gratifying needs; the governing principle of the ego.

Defense mechanism In psychodynamic theory, an unconscious function of the ego that protects it from anxiety-evoking material by preventing accurate recognition of this material.

Dr. Jekyll and Mr. Hyde. Freud suggested that each of us is influenced by an id that demands instant gratification without regard for moral scruples and the needs of others. Robert Louis Stevenson had a dream in which a similar idea was expressed, and he developed it into the novel *Dr. Jekyll and Mr. Hyde.* In one film version of the tale, Dr. Jekyll, shown at right, is a loving, considerate person—suggestive of ego functioning. The monstrous Mr. Hyde, shown at left, is suggestive of the id. Stevenson's wife was horrified by the concept and destroyed an early version of the manuscript. But Stevenson was so enthralled by the idea that he rewrote the book.

TABLE 11.1: Some Defense Mechanisms of the Ego, According to Psychodynamic Theory

Defense Mechanism	Definition	Examples
Repression	The ejection of anxiety-evoking ideas from awareness.	A student forgets that a difficult term paper is due. A patient in therapy forgets an appointment when anxiety-evoking material is to be discussed.
Regression	The return, under stress, to a form of behavior characteristic of an earlier stage of development.	An adolescent cries when forbidden to use the family car. An adult becomes highly dependent on his parents following the breakup of his marriage.
Rationalization	The use of self-deceiving justifications for unacceptable behavior.	A student blames her cheating on her teacher for leaving the room during a test. A man explains his cheating on his income tax by saying "Everyone does it."
Displacement	The transfer of ideas and impulses from threatening or unsuitable objects to less threatening objects.	A worker picks a fight with her spouse after being criticized sharply by her supervisor.
Projection	The thrusting of one's own unacceptable impulses onto others so that others are assumed to harbor them.	A hostile person perceives the world as being a dangerous place. A sexually frustrated person interprets innocent gestures of others as sexual advances.
Reaction formation	Assumption of behavior in opposition to one's genuine impulses in order to keep impulses repressed.	A person who is angry with a relative behaves in a "sickly sweet" manner toward that relative. A sadistic individual becomes a physician.
Denial	Refusal to accept the true nature of a threat.	Belief that one will not contract cancer or heart disease although one smokes heavily. "It can't happen to me."
Sublimation	The channeling of primitive impulses into positive, constructive efforts.	A person paints nudes for the sake of "beauty" and "art." A hostile person becomes a tennis star.

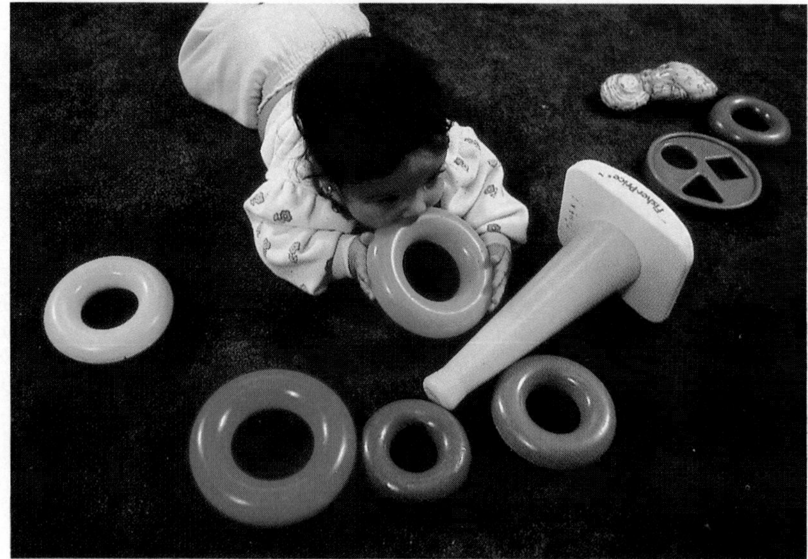

The Oral Stage? According to Sigmund Freud, the first year is the oral stage of development. If it fits, into the mouth it goes. What, according to Freud, are the effects of insufficient or excessive gratification during the oral stage? Is there evidence for his views?

The **superego** develops throughout early childhood, usually incorporating the moral standards and values of parents and important members of the community through **identification.** The superego functions according to the **moral principle.** The superego holds forth shining examples of an ideal self and also acts like the conscience, an internal moral guardian. Throughout life, the superego monitors the intentions of the ego and hands out judgments of right and wrong. It floods the ego with feelings of guilt and shame when the verdict is negative.

The ego hasn't an easy time of it. It stands between id and superego, braving the arrows of each. It strives to satisfy the demands of the id and the moral sense of the superego. The id may urge, "You are sexually aroused!" But the superego may warn, "You're not married." The poor ego is caught in the middle.

From the Freudian perspective, a healthy personality has found ways to gratify most of the id's demands without seriously offending the superego. Most of the id's remaining demands are contained or repressed. If the ego is not a good problem-solver, or if the superego is too stern, the ego will have a hard time of it.

Stages of Psychosexual Development

> *Freud found sex an outcast in the outhouse, and left it in the living room an honored guest.*
>
> W. Bertram Wolfe

Freud stirred controversy within the medical establishment of his day by arguing that sexual impulses and their gratification were pivotal factors in personality development, even among children. Freud saw children's basic ways of relating to the world, such as sucking their mothers' breasts and moving their bowels, as entailing sexual feelings.

Freud believed that a major instinct, which he termed **Eros,** aimed at preserving and perpetuating life. Eros was fueled by psychological, or psychic, energy which Freud labeled **libido.** Libidinal energy involved sexual impulses, so Freud considered it to be *psychosexual.* Libidinal energy would be expressed through sexual feelings in different parts of the body, or **erogenous zones,** as the child developed. To Freud, human development involved the transfer of libidinal energy from one zone to another. He hypothesized five periods of **psychosexual development:** oral, anal, phallic, latency, and genital.

Superego The third psychic structure, which functions as a moral guardian and sets forth high standards for behavior.

Identification In psychodynamic theory, the unconscious assumption of the behavior of another person.

Moral principle The governing principle of the superego, which sets moral standards and enforces adherence to them.

Eros In psychodynamic theory, the basic instinct to preserve and perpetuate life.

Libido (1) In psychodynamic theory, the energy of Eros; the sexual instinct. (2) Generally, sexual interest or drive.

Erogenous zone An area of the body that is sensitive to sexual sensations.

Psychosexual development In psychodynamic theory, the process by which libidinal energy is expressed through different erogenous zones during different stages of development.

During the first year of life, a child experiences much of its world through the mouth. If it fits, into the mouth it goes. This is the **oral stage.** Freud argued that oral activities such as sucking and biting bring the child sexual gratification as well as nourishment.

Freud believed that children would encounter conflicts during each stage of psychosexual development. During the oral stage, conflict would center around the nature and extent of oral gratification. Early **weaning** could lead to frustration. Excessive gratification, on the other hand, could lead an infant to expect that it would routinely be handed everything in life. Insufficient or excessive gratification in any stage could lead to **fixation** in that stage and to the development of traits characteristic of that stage. Oral traits include dependency, gullibility, and optimism or pessimism.

Freud theorized that adults with an **oral fixation** could experience exaggerated desires for "oral activities," such as smoking, overeating, alcohol abuse, and nail biting.

It is true that Freud interpreted biting fingernails or smoking as an adult to be a sign of conflict during very early childhood.

Like the infant whose very survival depends on the mercy of an adult, adults with oral fixations may be disposed toward clinging, dependent interpersonal relationships.

Note that according to psychodynamic theory, people are largely at the mercy of events that occurred long before they can weigh alternatives and make decisions about how to behave. Freud's own "oral fixation," cigar smoking, seems to have advanced the cancer of the mouth and jaw that killed him in 1939.

During the **anal stage,** sexual gratification is attained through contraction and relaxation of the muscles that control elimination of waste products. Elimination, which was controlled reflexively during most of the first year of life, comes under voluntary muscular control, even if such control is not reliable at first. The anal stage is said to begin in the second year of life.

During the anal stage, children learn to delay the gratification of eliminating as soon as they feel the urge. The general issue of self-control may become a source of conflict between parent and child. **Anal fixations** may stem from this conflict and lead to two sets of anal traits. **Anal-retentive** traits involve excessive use of self-control. They include perfectionism, a strong need for order, and exaggerated neatness and cleanliness. **Anal-expulsive** traits, on the other hand, "let it all hang out." They include carelessness, messiness, even **sadism.**

Children enter the **phallic stage** during the third year of life. During this stage, the major erogenous zone is the phallic region (the **clitoris** in girls). Parent–child conflict is likely to develop over masturbation, which parents may treat with punishment and threats. During the phallic stage, children may develop strong sexual attachments to the parent of the opposite gender and begin to view the same-gender parent as a rival for the other parent's affections. Boys may want to marry Mommy, and girls may want to marry Daddy.

Feelings of lust and jealousy are difficult for children to handle. Home life would be tense indeed if they were aware of them. So these feelings remain unconscious, although their influence is felt through fantasies about marriage and hostility toward the parent of the same gender. Freud labeled this conflict in boys the **Oedipus complex.** Oedipus is the legendary Greek king who unwittingly killed his father and married his mother. Similar feelings in girls give rise to the **Electra complex.** According to Greek legend, Electra was the daughter of the

---

Oral stage The first stage of psychosexual development, during which gratification is hypothesized to be attained primarily through oral activities.

Weaning Accustoming a child not to suck the mother's breast or a baby bottle.

Fixation In psychodynamic theory, arrested development. Attachment to objects of an earlier stage.

Oral fixation Attachment to objects and behaviors characteristic of the oral stage.

Anal stage The second stage of psychosexual development, when gratification is attained through anal activities.

Anal fixation Attachment to objects and behaviors characteristic of the anal stage.

Anal-retentive Descriptive of behaviors and traits that have to do with "holding in," or self-control.

Anal-expulsive Descriptive of behaviors and traits that have to do with unregulated self-expression such as messiness.

Sadism Attaining gratification from inflicting pain on, or humiliating, others.

Phallic stage The third stage of psychosexual development, characterized by a shift of libido to the phallic region.

Clitoris An external female sex organ which is highly sensitive to sexual stimulation.

Oedipus complex A conflict of the phallic stage in which the boy wishes to possess his mother sexually and perceives his father as a rival in love.

Electra complex A conflict of the phallic stage in which the girl longs for her father and resents her mother.

king Agamemnon. She longed for him after his death and sought revenge against his slayers: her mother and her mother's lover.

The Oedipus and Electra complexes become resolved by about the ages of 5 or 6. Children then repress their hostilities toward, and identify with, the parent of the same gender. Identification leads to playing the social and sexual roles of the same-gender parent and internalizing that parent's values. Sexual feelings toward the opposite-gender parent are repressed for a number of years. When the feelings emerge during adolescence, they are **displaced,** or transferred, to socially appropriate members of the opposite gender.

Freud believed that by the age of 5 or 6, children would have been in conflict with their parents over sexual feelings for several years. The pressures of the Oedipus and Electra complexes would motivate them to repress all sexual urges and enter **latency.** Latency is a period of life during which sexual feelings remain unconscious. They would use latency to focus on schoolwork and to consolidate earlier learning, most notably of appropriate gender-role behaviors. During latency, children would typically prefer playmates of their own gender.

Freud wrote that we enter the final stage of psychosexual development, or **genital stage,** at puberty. Adolescent males again experience sexual urges toward their mothers and adolescent females toward their fathers. However, the **incest taboo** provides ample motivation for keeping these impulses repressed and displacing them onto other adults or adolescents of the opposite gender. Boys still might seek girls "just like the girl that married dear old Dad." Girls still might be attracted to men who resemble their fathers.

People in the genital stage prefer, by definition, to find sexual gratification through intercourse with a member of the opposite gender. In Freud's view, oral or anal stimulation, masturbation, and homosexual activity would all represent **pregenital** fixations and immature forms of sexual conduct. They would not be consistent with the life instinct Eros.

Several personality theorists are intellectual heirs of Sigmund Freud. Their theories, like Freud's, include roles for unconscious motivation, for motivational conflict, and for defensive responses to anxiety that involve repression and cognitive distortion of reality (Wachtel, 1982). In other respects, theories differ considerably. We discuss the psychodynamic views of Carl Jung, Alfred Adler, Karen Horney, and Erik Erikson.

Carl Jung

The brain is viewed as an appendage of the genital glands.

Carl Jung (on Freud's psychodynamic theory)

Carl Jung (1875–1961) was a Swiss psychiatrist who had been a member of Freud's inner circle. He fell into disfavor with Freud when he developed his own psychodynamic theory—**analytical psychology.** As suggested by the above quotation, Jung down played the importance of the sexual instinct. He saw it as but one of several important instincts.

Jung, like Freud, was intrigued by unconscious processes. He believed that we not only have a *personal* unconscious which contains repressed memories and impulses, but also an inherited **collective unconscious.** The collective unconscious contains primitive images, or **archetypes,** which are reflections of the history of our species.

It is true that Jung believed that you have inherited mysterious memories that date back to ancient times.

Displaced Transferred.

Latency A phase of psychosexual development characterized by repression of sexual impulses.

Genital stage The mature stage of psychosexual development, characterized by preferred expression of libido through intercourse with an adult of the opposite gender.

Incest taboo The cultural prohibition against marrying or having sexual relations with a close blood relative.

Pregenital Characteristic of stages less mature than the genital stage.

Analytical psychology Jung's psychodynamic theory, which emphasizes the collective unconscious and archetypes.

Collective unconscious Jung's hypothesized store of vague racial memories.

Archetypes Basic, primitive images or concepts hypothesized by Jung to reside in the collective unconscious.

Archetypes include vague, mysterious mythical images. Examples of archetypes are the All-Powerful God, the young hero, the fertile and nurturing mother, the wise old man, the hostile brother, even fairy godmothers, wicked witches, and themes of rebirth or resurrection. Archetypes themselves remain unconscious, but Jung declared that they influence our thoughts and emotions and render us responsive to cultural themes in stories and films. Archetypes are somewhat accessible through the interpretation of dreams.

Jung believed that within each of us reside shadowy parts of the personality that may unfold gradually as we mature. He believed that women, who are feminine in most of their behavior patterns, have an **animus,** a masculine, aggressively competitive aspect of personality. Men, despite their masculinity, possess an **anima,** an aspect of personality that is feminine, soft, supportive, and passive. This is the way in which Jung accounted for the fact that women and men frequently display behaviors that are inconsistent with cultural stereotypes.

Despite all of his interest in the collective unconscious, Jung actually granted more importance to conscious motives than Freud did. Jung believed that one of the archetypes is a **Self,** a unifying force of personality that gives direction and purpose to human behavior. According to Jung, the Self aims to provide the personality with wholeness or fullness.

Alfred Adler

Alfred Adler (1870–1937), another follower of Freud, also believed that Freud had placed too much emphasis on sexual impulses. Adler believed that people are basically motivated by an **inferiority complex.** In some people, feelings of inferiority may be based on physical problems and the need to compensate for them. Adler believed, however, that all of us encounter some feelings of inferiority because of our small size as children, and these feelings give rise to a **drive for superiority.** For instance, the English poet Lord Byron, who had a deformed foot, became a champion swimmer. Beethoven's encroaching deafness may have spurred him on to greater musical accomplishments. Adler was crippled by rickets as a child and suffered from pneumonia, and it may be that his theory developed in part from his own childhood striving to overcome repeated bouts of illness. However, there is no empirical support for the view that all of us harbor feelings of inferiority.

Adler, like Jung, believed that self-awareness plays a major role in the formation of personality. Adler spoke of a **creative self,** a self-aware aspect of personality that strives to overcome obstacles and develop the individual's potential. Because this potential is uniquely individual, Adler's views have been termed **individual psychology.** Adler also introduced the term *sibling rivalry* to describe the jealousies that are found among brothers and sisters.

Karen Horney

Karen Horney (1885–1952) was born in Germany and emigrated to the United States before the outbreak of World War II. Horney agreed with Freud that childhood experiences played a major role in the development of adult personality, but, like many other neoanalysts, she believed that sexual and aggressive impulses took a back seat in importance to social relationships. Moreover, she disagreed with Freud that anatomical differences between the genders led girls to feel inferior to boys.

Horney, like Freud, saw parent–child relationships to be of paramount importance. Small children are completely dependent: when their parents treat them with indifference or harshness, they develop feelings of insecurity and what Horney terms **basic anxiety.** Children also resent neglectful parents, and Horney

---

Animus Jung's term for a masculine archetype of the collective unconscious.

Anima Jung's feminine archetype.

Self In analytical psychology, a conscious, unifying force to personality that provides people with direction and purpose.

Inferiority complex Feelings of inferiority hypothesized by Adler to serve as a central motivating force.

Drive for superiority Adler's term for the desire to compensate for feelings of inferiority.

Creative self According to Adler, the self-aware aspect of personality that strives to achieve its full potential.

Individual psychology Adler's psychodynamic theory, which emphasizes feelings of inferiority and the creative self.

Basic anxiety Horney's term for lasting feelings of insecurity that stem from harsh or indifferent parental treatment.

theorized that a **basic hostility** would accompany basic anxiety. Horney agreed with Freud that children would repress rather than express feelings of hostility toward their parents because of fear of reprisal and, just as important, fear of driving them away. On the other hand, it should be noted that Horney was more optimistic than Freud about the effects of early childhood traumatic experiences. She believed that genuine and consistent love could mitigate the effects of even the most traumatic childhoods (Quinn, 1987).

Later in life, basic anxiety and repressed hostility would lead to the development of one of three neurotic ways of relating to other people: moving toward others, moving against others, or moving away from others. Of course, it is healthful to relate to other people, but the neurotic person who moves toward others has feelings of insecurity and an excessive need for approval that render him or her compliant and overly anxious to please. People who move against others are also insecure, but they attempt to cope with their insecurity by asserting power and dominating social interactions. People who move away from others cope with their insecurities by withdrawing from social interactions. By remaining aloof from others, they attempt to prevent themselves from getting hurt by them. The price, of course, is perpetual loneliness.

Erik Erikson

Erik Erikson also believed that Freud had placed undue emphasis on sexual instincts, and he asserted that social relationships are more crucial determinants of personality. To Erikson, the general climate of the mother–infant relationship is more important than the details of the feeding process or the sexual feelings that might be stirred by contact with the mother. Erikson also argued that, to a large degree, we are the conscious architects of our own personalities—a view that grants more powers to the ego than Freud had allowed. Within Erikson's theory, it is possible for us to make real choices. Within Freud's theory, we might think that we are making choices, but we are probably only rationalizing the compromises forced upon us by intrapsychic warfare.

Erikson, like Freud, is known for devising a comprehensive developmental theory of personality. But whereas Freud proposed stages of psycho*sexual* development, Erikson proposed stages of psycho*social* development. In other words, rather than labeling a stage after an erogenous zone, Erikson labeled stages after the traits that might be developed during that stage (see Table 11.2). Each stage is named according to the possible outcomes, which are polar opposites. For example, the first stage of **psychosocial development** is named the stage of trust versus mistrust because of the two possible major outcomes. (1) A warm, loving relationship with the mother (and others) during infancy might lead to a sense of basic trust in people and the world. (2) A cold, nongratifying relationship might generate a pervasive sense of mistrust. Erikson believed that most of us would wind up with some blend of trust and mistrust—hopefully more trust than mistrust. A basic sense of mistrust could mar the formation of relationships for a lifetime unless we came to realize its presence and challenge its suitability.

Adolescent and Adult Development. Erikson extended Freud's five developmental stages to eight. Whereas Freud's developmental theory ends with adolescence, in the form of the genital stage, Erikson's theory includes the changing concerns of adulthood.

For Erikson, the goal of adolescence is the attainment of **ego identity,** not genital sexuality. Adolescents who attain ego identity develop a firm sense of who they are and what they stand for. One aspect of ego identity is learning how to "connect the roles and skills cultivated [during the elementary-school years] with

Basic hostility Horney's term for lasting feelings of anger that accompany basic anxiety but are directed toward nonfamily members in adulthood.

Psychosocial development Erikson's theory of personality and development, which emphasizes social relationships and eight stages of growth.

Ego identity A firm sense of who one is and what one stands for.

TABLE 11.2: Erik Erikson's Stages of Psychosocial Development

Time Period	Life Crisis	The Developmental Task
Infancy (0–1)	Trust versus mistrust	Coming to trust the mother and the environment—to associate surroundings with feelings of inner goodness
Early childhood (2–3)	Autonomy versus shame and doubt	Developing the wish to make choices and the self-control to exercise choice
Preschool years (4–5)	Initiative versus guilt	Adding planning and "attacking" to choice, becoming active and on the move
Grammar school years (6–12)	Industry versus inferiority	Becoming eagerly absorbed in skills, tasks, and productivity; mastering the fundamentals of technology
Adolescence	Identity versus role diffusion	Connecting skills and social roles to formation of career objectives
Young adulthood	Intimacy versus isolation	Committing the self to another; engaging in sexual love
Middle adulthood	Generativity versus stagnation	Needing to be needed; guiding and encouraging the younger generation; being creative
Late adulthood	Integrity versus despair	Accepting the timing and placing of one's own life cycle; achieving wisdom and dignity

Source: Erikson, 1963, pp. 247–269.

the occupational prototypes of the day" (Erikson, 1963, p. 261)—that is, with jobs. Ego identity also extends to sexual, political, and religious beliefs and commitments. According to Erikson, adolescents who do not develop a firm sense of identity are especially subject to peer influences and short-sighted hedonism.

Evaluation

Psychodynamic theories have had tremendous appeal. They are rich theories; that is, they involve many concepts and explain many varieties of human behavior and traits. Let us evaluate them by considering some of their strengths and weaknesses.

Strengths of Psychodynamic Approaches

1. *Psychic Determinism: Toward a More Scientific View of Behavior.* One of the basic tenets of psychodynamic theory is that behavior is determined by the outcome of intrapsychic conflict. Today, concepts such as "intrapsychic conflict" and "psychic energy" strike many psychologists as being unscientific. In his day, however, Freud fought for the idea that human personality and behavior were subject to scientific analysis.

2. *The Importance of Childhood.* Freud's psychodynamic theory also focused the attention of scientists and helping professionals on the far-reaching effects of childhood events. Freud's inquiries helped show how children differ from adults. The developmental theories of Freud and Erikson suggest ways in which early childhood traumas can color our perceptions and influence our behavior for a lifetime.

3. *The Importance of "Primitive" Impulses.* Freud is in part responsible for "getting people talking" about the importance of sexuality in their lives and about the prevalence of aggressive impulses and urges. Freud has helped us recognize that sexual and aggressive urges are commonplace and that there is a difference between acknowledging these urges and acting on them.

4. *The Role of Cognitive Distortion.* Freud also noted that people have defensive ways of looking at the world. He developed a list of defense mechanisms that have become part of everyday parlance. Whether or not we attribute these cognitive distortions to unconscious ego functioning, our thinking is

apparently distorted by our efforts to avert anxiety and guilt. If these concepts no longer strike us as being innovative, it is largely because of the influence of Sigmund Freud.

5. *Innovation of Methods of Psychotherapy.* Freud and other psychodynamic theorists innovated many of the methods of therapy that we consider in Chapter 14.

Weaknesses of Psychodynamic Approaches. Despite their richness, psychodynamic theories, particularly the original psychodynamic views of Sigmund Freud, have met with criticism for reasons such as the following:

1. *Overemphasis on Sexuality and Underemphasis on Social Relationships.* Some followers of Freud, such as Horney and Erikson, have argued that Freud placed too much emphasis on human sexuality and neglected the importance of social relationships. Other followers, such as Adler and Erich Fromm, have argued that Freud placed too much emphasis on unconscious motives. Adler and Fromm assert that people consciously seek self-enhancement and intellectual pleasures. They do not merely try to gratify the dark demands of the id.

2. *The Lack of Substance of "Psychic Structures".* A number of critics note that "psychic structures" such as the id, ego, and superego have no substance. They are little more than useful fictions—poetic ways to express inner conflict. It is debatable whether Freud ever attributed substance to the psychic structures. He, too, may have seen them more as poetic fictions than as "things." If so, his critics have the right to use other descriptive terms and write better "poems."

3. *Resistance to Disproof.* Sir Karl Popper (1985) has argued that Freud's hypothetical mental processes fail as scientific concepts because they can neither be observed nor can they predict observable behavior with precision. Scientific propositions must be capable of being proved false. But, as argued by Popper, Freud's statements about mental structures are unscientific because no conceivable type of evidence can disprove them; any behavior can be explained in terms of these hypothesized (but unobservable) "structures."

4. *Inaccuracies in Developmental Theories.* The stages of psychosexual development have not escaped criticism. Children begin to masturbate as early as the first year, not in the phallic stage. As parents know from discovering their children play "doctor," the latency stage is not as sexually latent as Freud believed.

   The evidence for some of Erikson's developmental views seems somewhat sturdier. For example, it may well be that infants who do not develop a sense of trust have a relatively hard time developing autonomy and industry in subsequent stages of psychosocial development. Moreover, adolescents who fail to develop ego identity also seem to have problems in intimate relationships later on.

5. *Possible Biases in the Gathering of Evidence.* Freud's method of gathering evidence from the clinical session is also suspect. Therapists may subtly influence clients to produce what they expect to find (Bandura, 1986; Grünbaum, 1985). Therapists may also fail to separate reported facts from their own interpretations.

Freud and many other psychodynamic theorists also restricted their evidence gathering to case studies with individuals who sought therapy for adjustment problems. Persons seeking therapy do not represent the population at large. They are likely to have more problems than the general population.

One of the richer aspects of the psychodynamic theories is the way in which they account for the development of various traits. Let us now consider trait theories, which address traits from a different perspective.

TRAIT THEORIES

In most of us by the age of thirty, the character has set like plaster, and will never soften again.

William James

I believe the best definition of man is the ungrateful biped.

Fyodor Dostoyevski

The notion of **traits** is very familiar. If I asked you to describe yourself, you would probably do so in terms of your traits. We also tend to describe other people in terms of traits.

Traits are elements of personality that are inferred from behavior. If you describe a friend as being "shy," it may be because you have observed social anxiety or withdrawal in the friend's encounters. Traits are also assumed to be enduring and to account for consistent behavior in diverse situations. You probably expect your "shy" friend to be retiring in most social confrontations—"all across the board," as the saying goes. The concept of traits also finds a place in other approaches to personality. Recall that throughout Freud's stages of psychosexual development, he linked development of certain traits to children's experiences.

Gordon Allport

Psychologist Gordon Allport (1937, 1961) thought of traits as being embedded in our nervous systems. He argued that traits "steer" or guide us to behave consistently. For example, the trait of sociability may steer us to invite friends along when going out, to share confidences in letters, and to make others feel at home at gatherings. A person who "lacks" sociability would be disposed to behave differently in these situations.

More than 50 years ago, Allport and Oddbert (1936) catalogued some 18,000 human traits from a search through word lists of the sort found in dictionaries. Some were physical traits such as short, black, and brunette. Others were behavioral traits such as shy and emotional. Still others were moral traits such as honest. This exhaustive list has served as the basis for personality research by many other psychologists, including Raymond Cattell.

Raymond Cattell

– 16 source traits

Psychologists such as Raymond Cattell (1965) have used statistical techniques to reduce this universe of innumerable traits to smaller lists of traits that show commonality. Cattell also distinguished between surface traits and source traits. **Surface traits** describe characteristic ways of behaving—for example, cleanliness, stubbornness, thrift, and orderliness. We may observe that these traits form meaningful patterns that are suggestive of underlying traits. (Cleanliness, stubbornness, and so on, were all referred to as *anal retentive* traits by Freud.)

Cattell refined the Allport catalogue by removing unusual terms and grouping the remaining traits under **source traits**—the underlying traits from which surface traits are derived. Cattell argued that psychological measurement of a person's source traits would enable us to predict his or her behavior in various situations.

Cattell's research led him to suggest the existence of 16 source traits, and these traits can be measured by means of his Sixteen Personality Factors Scale. The "16 PF" is frequently used in psychological research that explores differences between groups of people and individuals.

Trait An aspect of personality that is inferred from behavior and assumed to give rise to behavioral consistency.

Surface traits Cattell's term for characteristic, observable ways of behaving.

Source traits Cattell's term for underlying traits from which surface traits are derived.

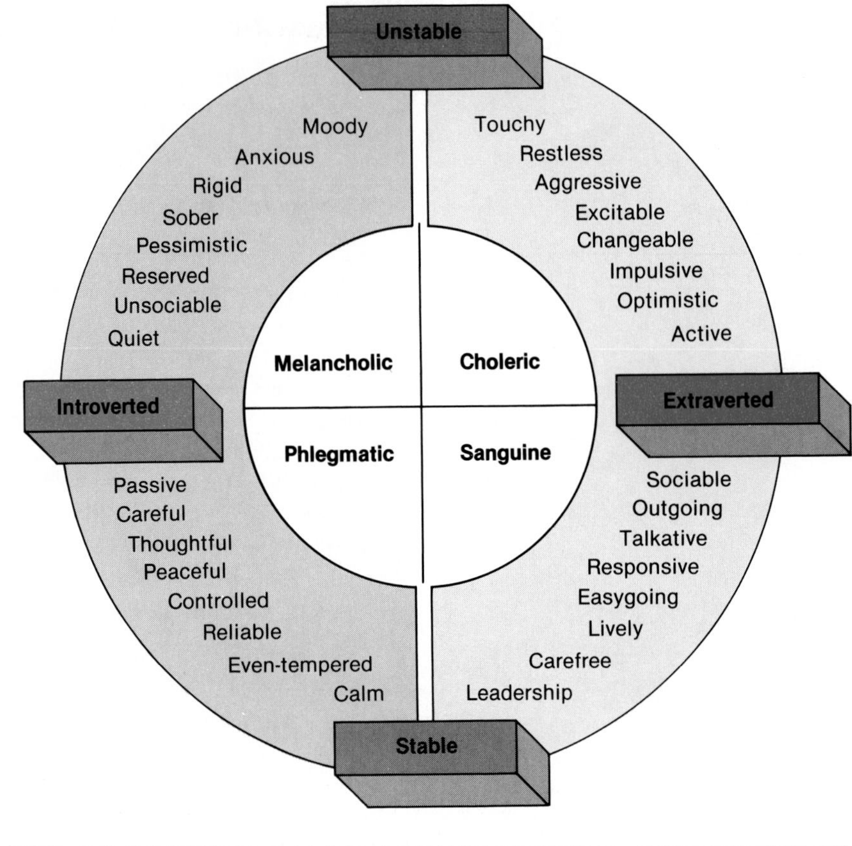

FIGURE 11.2
Eysenck's Personality Dimensions and Hippocrates' Personality Types. Various personality traits shown in the outer ring fall within the two major dimensions of personality suggested by Hans Eysenck. The inner circle shows how Hippocrates' four major personality types—choleric, sanguine, phlegmatic, and melancholic—fit within Eysenck's modern dimensions.

Hans Eysenck

British psychologist Hans J. Eysenck (1960; Eysenck & Eysenck, 1985) has focused much of his research on the relationships between two important traits: **introversion–extraversion** and emotional stability–instability, the latter otherwise called **neuroticism.** Carl Jung was first to distinguish between introverts and extraverts. Eysenck added the dimension of neuroticism to introversion–extraversion. He has catalogued various personality traits according to where they are "situated" along these dimensions (see Figure 11.2). For instance, an anxious person would be high both in introversion and in neuroticism—that is, preoccupied with his or her own thoughts and emotionally unstable.

Eysenck notes that his scheme is reminiscent of that suggested by Hippocrates (ca. 460–377 B.C.), the physician of the Golden Age of Greece. Hippocrates suggested that there are four basic personality types: choleric (quick-tempered), sanguine (warm, cheerful, confident), phlegmatic (sluggish, calm, cool), and melancholic (gloomy, pensive). The terms *choleric, sanguine,* and so on, remain in common use. According to Eysenck's dimensions, the choleric type would be extraverted and unstable; the sanguine type, extraverted and stable; the phlegmatic type, introverted and stable; and the melancholic type, introverted and unstable. Hippocrates believed that these types, and mixtures of these types, depend on the balance of the four "basic fluids," or humors, in the body. Yellow bile was associated with a choleric disposition; blood, a sanguine one; phlegm, a phlegmatic disposition; and black bile, a melancholic temperament.

Where would you place athletes and artists in terms of the dimensions of introversion–extraversion and neuroticism? Where would you place yourself?

Introversion A source trait characterized by intense imagination and the tendency to inhibit impulses.

Extraversion A source trait characterized by tendencies to be socially outgoing and to express feelings and impulses freely.

Neuroticism Eysenck's term for emotional instability.

Evaluation

Trait theories, like psychodynamic theories, have their strengths and weaknesses.

Strengths of Trait Theories

1. *Developing Psychological Tests.* Trait theorists have focused a good deal of their attention on the development of tests such as Cattell's Sixteen Personality Factors Scale to measure traits. Others are discussed in the section on measurement of personality.

2. *Spawning Theories Concerning the Fit between Personality and Jobs.* Because most of us spend some 40 hours a week on the job (and a good deal of the rest of the time thinking about our work!), it is important to our well-being that we "fit" our jobs. The qualities that suit us for various kinds of work can be expressed in terms of our abilities, our personality traits, and our interests. By using interviews and tests to learn about our abilities and our traits, testing and counseling centers can make valuable suggestions about the likelihood for our success and fulfillment in various kinds of jobs.

3. *Identifying of Basic Traits.* Freud developed his theories about "oral," "anal," and other traits on the basis of clinical case studies. However, trait theorists have administered broad personality tests to thousands of people and have used sophisticated statistical techniques to identify the basic traits, or factors, that tend to describe us.

   Empirical studies (Digman, 1990; Trull, 1992) suggest that there may be five basic personality factors. These include the two found by Eysenck—introversion–extraversion and emotional stability–instability (neuroticism)—and three suggested by Cattell: conscientiousness (self-discipline), agreeableness, and openness to new experience (akin to Cattell's experimenting–conservative dimension).

4. *Pointing Out that Traits Are Reasonably Stable.* Research has shown that numerous personality traits are stable over many years. James Conley (1984, 1985), for example, studied psychological tests taken by a sample of adults during the 1930s, the 1950s, and again during the 1980s. Their scores on the traits of extraversion, neuroticism, and impulsiveness showed significant consistency across five decades.

Weaknesses of Trait Theories

1. *Trait Theory Is Descriptive, Not Explanatory.* Trait theory focuses on describing existing traits rather than tracing their origins or investigating how they may be modified.

2. *Circular Explanations.* The explanations provided by trait theory are often criticized as being **circular.** They restate what is observed and do not explain what is observed. Saying that John failed to ask Marsha on a date *because* of shyness is an example of a circular explanation; all we have done is to restate John's (shy) behavior as a trait (shyness).

3. *Situational Variability in Behavior.* The trait concept requires that traits show stability. Although many personality traits seem to do so, behavior may vary more from situation to situation than trait theory would allow (Bem & Allen, 1974; Mischel, 1977, 1986). People who are high in **private self-consciousness** try to show consistent behavior from situation to situation (Fenigstein et al., 1975; Scheier et al., 1978; Underwood & Moore, 1981). Other people show more variable behavior.

Circular explanation An explanation that merely restates its own concepts instead of offering additional information.

Private self-consciousness The tendency to take critical note of one's own behavior, even when unobserved by others.

LEARNING THEORIES

Learning theorists also have studied issues relating to personality. We shall focus on two learning approaches: behaviorism and social-learning theory.

Behaviorism

You have freedom when you're easy in your harness.

Robert Frost

At Johns Hopkins University in 1924, psychologist John B. Watson announced the battle cry of the behaviorist movement:

Give me a dozen healthy infants, well-formed, and my own specified world to bring them up in and I'll guarantee to take any one at random and train him to become any type of specialist I might suggest—doctor, lawyer, merchant-chief and, yes, even beggar-man and thief, regardless of his talents, penchants, tendencies, abilities, vocations, and the race of his ancestors. (p. 82)

So it was that Watson proclaimed that situational variables or environmental influences—not internal, person variables—are the important shapers of human preferences and behaviors. As a counterbalance to the psychoanalysts and structuralists of his day, Watson argued that unseen, undetectable mental structures must be rejected in favor of that which can be seen and measured. In the 1930s, Watson's hue and cry was taken up by B. F. Skinner, who agreed that we should avoid trying to see within the "black box" of the organism and emphasized the effect that reinforcements have on behavior.

The views of John B. Watson and B. F. Skinner largely discard the notions of personal freedom, choice, and self-direction. Most of us assume that our wants originate within us. But Skinner suggests that environmental influences such as parental approval and social custom shape us into *wanting* certain things and *not wanting* others. To Watson and Skinner, even our telling ourselves that we have free will is determined by the environment as surely as is our becoming startled at a sudden noise.

In his novel *Walden Two,* Skinner (1948) describes a Utopian society in which people are happy and content, because they are allowed to do as they please. However, they have been trained or conditioned from early childhood to engage in **prosocial** behavior and to express prosocial attitudes. Because of their reinforcement histories, they *want* to behave in a decent, kind, and unselfish way. They see themselves as being free because society makes no effort to force them to behave as they do as adults.

Skinner elaborated on his beliefs about people and society in *Beyond Freedom and Dignity* (1972). According to Skinner, adaptation to the environment requires acceptance of behavior patterns that ensure survival. If the group is to survive, it must construct rules and laws that foster social harmony. Other people are then rewarded for following these rules and punished for disobeying them. None of us is really free, even though we think of ourselves as coming together freely to establish the rules and as choosing to follow them.

Some object to behaviorist notions because they sidestep the roles of human consciousness and choice. Others argue that people are not so blindly ruled by pleasure and pain. People have rebelled against the so-called necessity of survival by choosing pain and hardship over pleasure, or death over life. Many people have sacrificed their own lives to save those of others.

The behaviorist defense might be that the apparent choice of pain or death is forced on the altruist as inevitably as conformity to social custom is forced on others. The altruist was also shaped by external influences, but those influences differed from those that affect most of us.

Prosocial Behavior that is characterized by helping others and making a contribution to society.

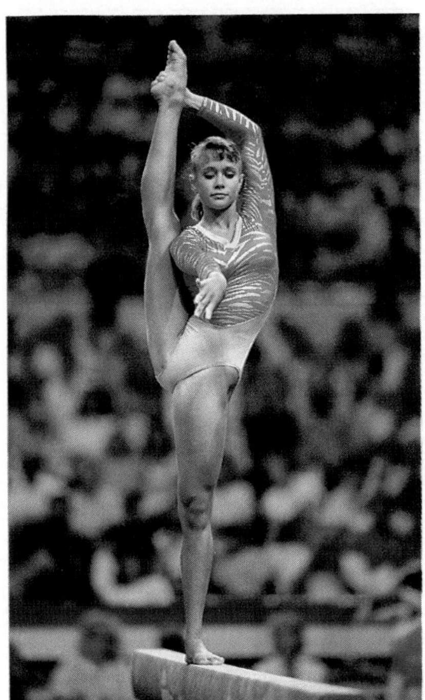

How Do Competencies Contribute to Performance? There are great individual differences in our competencies, based on genetic variation, nourishment, differences in learning opportunities, and other environmental factors. What factors contribute to this girl's performance on the balance beam?

Social-Learning Theory

Social-learning theory is a contemporary view of learning developed by Albert Bandura (1986, 1989, 1991) and other psychologists. It focuses on the importance of learning by observation and on the role of cognitive activity in human behavior. Social-learning theorists see people as influencing the environment just as the environment influences them. Social-learning theorists agree with behaviorists that discussions of human nature should be tied to observable experiences and behaviors. They assert, however, that variables within the person—**person variables**—must also be considered if we are to understand people.

One goal of all psychological theories is the prediction of behavior. Social-learning theorist Julian B. Rotter (1972) argues that we cannot predict behavior from situational variables alone. Whether or not a person will behave in a certain way also depends on the person's **expectancies** about that behavior's outcomes and the perceived or **subjective values** of those outcomes. **Generalized expectancies** are broad expectations that reflect extensive learning and that are relatively enduring. Their consistency and stability make them the equivalent of traits within social-learning theory.

To social-learning theorists, people are self-aware and engage in purposeful learning. People are not simply at the mercy of the environment. Instead, they seek to learn about their environment. They alter and construct the environment to make reinforcers available.

Social-learning theorists also note the importance of rules and symbolic processes in learning. Children, for example, learn more effectively how to behave in specific situations when parents explain the rules involved. In inductive methods of discipline, parents use the situation to teach children about general rules and social codes that should govern their behavior.

Observational Learning. Observational learning (also termed **modeling**) refers to the acquisition of knowledge by observing others. For operant conditioning to occur, an organism must engage in a response, and that response must be reinforced. But observational learning occurs even when the learner does not perform the observed behavior pattern. Therefore, direct reinforcement is not required either. Observing others extends to reading about them or perceiving what they do and what happens to them in media such as radio, television, and film.

Our expectations of what will happen if we do something stem from our observations of what happens to others, as well as our own experiences. For example, teachers are more accepting of "calling out" in class from boys than girls (Sadker & Sadker, 1985). As a result, boys frequently expect to be rewarded for calling out in class. Girls, however, are more likely to expect to be reprimanded for behaving in what traditionalists might refer to as an "unladylike" manner.

Let us now consider a number of the person variables in social-learning theory that account for individual differences in behavior.

Person Variables in Social-Learning Theory. Social-learning theorists view behavior as stemming from a fluid, ongoing interaction between person variables and situational variables. Person variables include competencies, encoding strategies, expectancies, subjective values, and self-regulatory systems and plans (Bandura, 1989; Mischel, 1993). (See Figure 11.3.)

1. *Competencies: What Can You Do?* **Competencies** include knowledge and skills. Competencies include knowledge of the physical world, cultural codes of conduct, and the behavior patterns expected in certain situations. They include academic skills such as reading and writing, athletic skills such as swimming and tossing a football properly, social skills such as knowing how to ask someone out on a date, job skills, and many others. Individual differences in

---

Social-learning theory A cognitively oriented learning theory in which observational learning, values, and expectations play major roles in determining behavior.

Person variables Factors within the person, such as generalized expectancies and competencies, that influence behavior.

Expectancies Personal predictions about the outcomes of potential behaviors.

Subjective value The desirability of an object or event.

Generalized expectancies Broad expectations that reflect extensive learning and that are relatively resistant to change.

Model In social-learning theory, an organism who exhibits behaviors that others will imitate or acquire through observational learning.

Competencies Knowledge and skills.

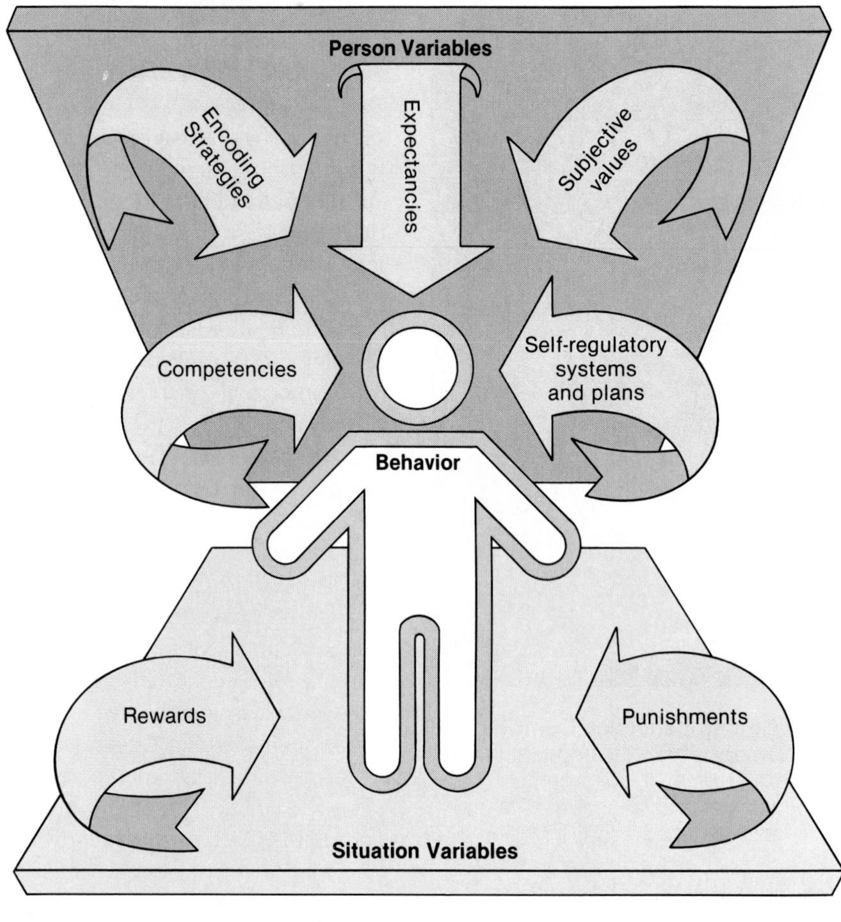

FIGURE 11.3
Person Variables and Situational Variables in Social-Learning Theory. According to social-learning theory, person variables and situational variables interact to influence behavior.

competencies are based on genetic variation, nourishment, learning opportunities, and other environmental factors.

2. *Encoding Strategies: How Do You See It?* Different people **encode** (symbolize or represent) the same situations in different ways, and their encoding strategies are an important factor in their overt behavior. One person might encode a tennis game as a chance to bat the ball back and forth and have some fun. Another might encode the game as a demand to perfect her or his serve. One person might encode a date that doesn't work out as a sign of personal incompetence; another might encode the experience as reflective of the fact that most people are not "made for each other."
3. *Expectancies: What Will Happen?* Expectancies are "if-then" statements, or personal predictions about the outcome (or reinforcement contingencies) of engaging in a response. Competencies influence expectancies, and expectancies, in turn, influence motivation to perform. People who believe that they have the competencies required to perform effectively are more likely to try difficult tasks than people who do not believe that they can master them (Bandura, Reese, & Adams, 1982). Albert Bandura (1989) refers to beliefs that one can handle certain tasks as **self-efficacy expectancies.**

We are in fact more likely to persist at difficult tasks when we believe that we shall succeed.

Encode Interpret; transform.

Self-efficacy expectations Beliefs that one can handle a task.

4. *Subjective Values: What Is It Worth?* Because of our different learning histories, we each may place a different value on the same outcome. What is frightening to one person may entice another. What is somewhat desirable to one may be irresistible to another. From the social-learning perspective, in contrast to behaviorist perspective, we are not controlled by stimuli. Instead, stimuli have various meanings for us, and these meanings are one factor in influencing our behavior.
5. *Self-Regulatory Systems and Plans: How Can You Achieve It?* Social-learning theory recognizes that one of the features of being human is our tendency to regulate our own behavior, even in the absence of observers and external constraints. We set goals and standards for ourselves, construct plans for achieving them, and congratulate or criticize ourselves, depending on whether or not we reach them (Bandura, 1991). Self-regulation amplifies our opportunities for influencing our environment. We can select the situations to which we expose ourselves and the arenas in which we shall contend. Based on our expectancies, we may choose to enter the academic or athletic worlds. We may choose marriage or the single life. When we cannot readily select our environment, we can to some degree select our responses within an environment—even an aversive one. For example, if we are undergoing an uncomfortable medical procedure, we may try to focus on something else—the cracks in the tiles on the ceiling or an inner fantasy—to reduce the stress.

Evaluation

Learning theorists have made important contributions to the understanding of behavior, but they have also left some psychologists dissatisfied. Let us consider the strengths and weaknesses of learning theory.

Strengths of Learning Approaches

1. *Focus on Observable Behavior.* Psychodynamic theorists and trait theorists propose the existence of psychological structures that cannot be seen and measured directly. Learning theorists—particularly behaviorists—have dramatized the importance of referring to publicly observable variables, or behaviors, if psychology is to be accepted as a science.
2. *Focus on the Situation.* Psychodynamic theorists and trait theorists focus on internal variables such as intrapsychic conflict and traits to explain and predict behavior. Learning theorists have emphasized the importance of environmental conditions, or situational variables, as determinants of behavior.
3. *Outlining the Conditions of Learning.* Learning theorists have elaborated on the conditions that foster learning—even automatic kinds of learning. They have shown that involuntary responses—including fear responses—may be conditioned, that we can learn to do things because of reinforcements, and that many broad behavior patterns are acquired by observing others.
4. *Innovation of Therapy Methods.* Learning theorists have devised methods for helping individuals solve adjustment problems that probably would not have been derived from any other theoretical perspective. These include the behavioral, extinction-based fear-reduction methods of flooding and systematic desensitization and the operant-conditioning method of biofeedback training.
5. *General Impact on Psychology.* Learning theories have probably had the broadest effect on psychology as a whole. They address issues ranging from learning per se, animal behavior, and motivation to child development, psychological disorders, therapy methods, and even attitude formation and change.

Weaknesses of Learning Approaches

1. *Problems with Behaviorism.* Behaviorism is limited in its ability to explain personality. For example, behaviorism does not describe or explain the richness of inner human experience. We experience thoughts and feelings and peruse our complex inner maps of the world, and behaviorism does not deal with these phenomena. To be fair, however, the limitations of behaviorism are self-imposed. Personality theorists have traditionally dealt with thoughts, feelings, and behavior, whereas behaviorism, in its insistence on studying only that which is observable and measurable, deals with behavior alone.
2. *Problems with Social-Learning Theory.* Critics of social-learning theory may not accuse its supporters of denying the importance of cognitive activity and feelings. But they may contend that social-learning theory has not derived satisfying statements about the development of traits and accounted for self-awareness. Social-learning theory—like its intellectual forebear, behaviorism—may also not have always paid sufficient attention to genetic variation in explaining individual differences in behavior. Learning theories have done very little to account for the development of traits or personality types.

   Social-learning theorists seem to be working on these theoretical flaws. Today's social-learning theorists see people as being active, not as reacting mechanically to environmental pressures (as Watson saw them). Cognitive functioning is an appropriate area of study for social-learning theorists (Bandura, 1986; Wilson, 1982). In the area of abnormal behavior, many social-learning theorists grant that inherited or physiological factors may interact with situational stress to give rise to abnormal behavior (Nevid, Rathus, & Greene, 1994).

   Now let us consider theories that begin with the assumption of consciousness and dwell on the importance of our cognitive functioning.

HUMANISTIC–EXISTENTIAL THEORIES

> *My experience in therapy and in groups makes it impossible for me to deny the reality and significance of human choice. To me it is not an illusion that man is to some degree the architect of himself.*
>
> Carl Rogers (1974, p. 119)

> *You are unique, and if that is not fulfilled, then something has been lost.*
>
> Martha Graham

> *Man . . . is the particular being who has to be aware of himself, be responsible for himself, if he is to become himself. He also is that particular being who knows that at some future moment he will not be; he is the being who is always in a dialectical relation with non-being, death. And he not only knows he will sometime not be, but he can, in his own choices, slough off and forfeit his being.*
>
> Rollo May (1958, p. 42)

High tech, artificial intelligence, space exploration—these are a few of the artifacts of modern life. Genocide and world war are others. Amid upheaval, humanists and existentialists dwell on the meaning of life. Their self-awareness of their being in the world is the hub of the humanistic–existential search for meaning. Because of their focus on conscious, subjective experience, humanistic–existential theories have also been referred to as **phenomenological.**

The term **humanism** has a lengthy history and diverse meanings. It became a third force in American psychology in the 1950s and 1960s, in part as a reply to the predominant psychodynamic and behavioral models. Humanism also

Phenomenological Having to do with conscious, subjective experience. self-awareness

Humanism The view that people are capable of free choice, self-fulfillment, and ethical behavior.

represented a reaction to the "rat race" spawned by industrialization and automation. Humanists opposed the posting of people on the gray, anonymous treadmills of industry. "Alienation" from inner sources of meaning distressed them. Against this backdrop emerged the humanistic views of Abraham Maslow and Carl Rogers.

Existentialism in part reflects the horrors of mass destruction of human life through war and genocide. The term *existentialism* implies that our existence or being in the world is more central to human nature than theories or abstractions about human nature.

The European existentialist philosophers Jean-Paul Sartre and Martin Heidegger saw human life as trivial in the grand scheme of things, leading to feelings of alienation. The Swiss psychiatrists Ludwig Binswanger and Medard Boss framed these philosophical ideas in more psychological terms. They argued that seeing human existence as meaningless could give rise to withdrawal and apathy—even suicide. Psychological salvation requires implanting personal meaning on things and making personal choices. Yes, there is pain in life, and yes, life sooner or later comes to an end, but people can see the world for what it is and make real, **authentic** choices.

Humanists and existentialists share a search for meaning in life and a belief that freedom and personal responsibility are the essence of being human. In this section, we consider the views of the European existentialist Viktor Frankl and two American humanistic theorists, Abraham Maslow and Carl Rogers.

Viktor Frankl and the Search for Meaning

Austrian psychiatrist Viktor Frankl (1959) endured the Nazi concentration camps—the starvation, the hard labor, the brutality, the cold, the typhus, the question as to whether any of his family remained alive. Despite intermittent feelings of apathy, now and then he saw a crimson sunrise. Now and then, he cracked a joke. Throughout his internment, he questioned, *Why?* Although death was everywhere, he came to think that while one remains alive, one is free to choose one's own attitude.

Frankl survived. He thought that his personal quest for meaning had helped him to do so. People can endure meaningful suffering. People, he came to believe, have basic wills to meaning and love. Psychology thus overlaps with people's philosophies of life. By clarifying or creating meaning, people can gain control over their lives. Without meaning, people are prone to existential frustration. Frankl believed that we are all unique. He believed that psychologists must learn to see the world through others' eyes, that they must be patient and develop a sense of empathy. Notions about clients' frames of references and empathy were also embraced by the American Carl Rogers, as we see later.

Frankl did not establish a pointed list of assumptions about human nature, but his writings seem to postulate the following points. They also recount much of humanistic–existential thought:

1. *People can see the world for what it is. Our consciousnesses are the true centers of our universes.* Personal, subjective experience is the most significant facet of human nature.
2. *People have unique potentials that they can recognize and use to steer their behavior.* People can consciously create their own personalities. They are also their own best experts on themselves, when they look inward.
3. *People are in the world; what they do about it is up to them.* People are responsible for themselves and make real choices, whether their choices help them develop as individuals or aim to avoid anxiety by following the paths created by others.
4. *People labor hard when their work is meaningful to them.*

Existentialism The view that people are completely free and responsible for their own behavior.

Authentic Genuine; consistent with one's values and beliefs.

Unique. According to humanistic psychologists like Carl Rogers, each of us views the world and ourselves from a unique frame of reference. What is important to one individual may hold little meaning for another.

5. *When their lives are meaningful, people can be caring and loving.*
6. *People need to behave authentically to find personal fulfillment.* Pressures to adapt and conform surround us. They were felt by death-camp inmate and Nazi storm trooper alike. When external forces prevent people from acting authentically—as outer constraints kept Frankl in the camps—people fare best by remembering their own values.
7. *People become alienated and apathetic when they are prevented from striving to reach their potentials.*
8. *People can be compelled to behave in ways that contradict their genuine feelings, as did the concentration camp* Capos, *inmates who served as watchdogs over fellow inmates. Their sense of self becomes distorted by incompatible behavior, however, and their lives feel wrong.*

Abraham Maslow and the Challenge of Self-Actualization

Humanists see Freud as preoccupied with the "basement" of the human condition. Freud wrote that people are basically motivated to gratify defensive, biological drives. (Maslow's theoretical *hierarchy of needs* is discussed in Chapter 9.) Humanistic psychologist Abraham Maslow argued that people also have growth-oriented needs for **self-actualization**—to become all that they can be. Because people are unique, they must follow unique paths to self-actualization. Self-actualization requires risk-taking. People who adhere to the "tried and true" may find their lives degenerating into monotony and predictability.

Carl Rogers' Self Theory

Carl Rogers (1902–1987) was a minister before he became a psychologist. Like Frankl and Maslow, he wrote that people shape themselves through free choice and action.

Rogers defines the *self* as an "organized, consistent, conceptual **gestalt** composed of perceptions of the characteristics of the 'I' or 'me' and the perceptions of the relationships of the 'I' or 'me' to others and to various aspects of life, together with the values attached to these perceptions" (1959, p. 200). Your self is your center of experience. It is your ongoing sense of who and what you are, your sense of how and why you react to the environment and how you choose to act on the environment. Your choices are made on the basis of your values, and your values are also parts of your self.

To Rogers, the sense of self is inborn, or innate. The self provides the experience of being human in the world. It is the guiding principle behind personality structure and behavior.

The Self-Concept and Frames of Reference. Our self-concepts comprise our impressions of ourselves and our evaluations of our adequacy. It may be helpful to think of us as rating ourselves according to various scales or dimensions such as good–bad, intelligent–unintelligent, strong–weak, and tall–short.

Rogers states that we all have unique ways of looking at ourselves and the world, or unique **frames of reference.** It may be that we each use a different set of dimensions in defining ourselves and that we judge ourselves according to different sets of values. To one person, achievement–failure may be the most important dimension. To another person, the most important dimension may be decency–indecency. A third person may not even think in terms of decency.

Self-actualization In humanistic theory, the innate tendency to strive to realize one's potential.

Gestalt In this usage, a quality of wholeness.

Frame of reference One's unique patterning of perceptions and attitudes according to which one evaluates events.

Self-Esteem and Positive Regard

The solar system has no anxiety about its reputation.
Ralph Waldo Emerson

Rogers assumes that we all develop a need for self-regard, or **self-esteem,** as we develop and become aware of ourselves. At first, self-esteem reflects the esteem in which others hold us. Parents help children develop self-esteem when they show them **unconditional positive regard**—that is, when they accept them as having intrinsic merit regardless of their behavior at the moment. But when parents show children **conditional positive regard**—accept them only when they behave in a desired manner—children may learn to disown the thoughts, feelings, and behaviors that parents have rejected. Conditional positive regard may lead children to develop **conditions of worth,** or to think that they are worthwhile only if they behave in certain ways.

Because each of us has a unique potential, children who develop conditions of worth must be somewhat disappointed in themselves. We cannot fully live up to the wishes of others and remain true to ourselves. This does not mean that the expression of the self inevitably leads to conflict. Rogers was optimistic about human nature. He believed that we hurt others or act in antisocial ways only when we are frustrated in our efforts to develop our potential. However, when parents and others are loving and tolerant of our differentness, we, too, are loving—even if some of our preferences, abilities, and values differ from those of our parents.

Children in some families learn that it is bad to have ideas of their own, especially about sexual, political, or religious matters. When they perceive their parents' disapproval, they may come to see themselves as rebels and label their feelings as being selfish, wrong, or evil. If they wish to retain a consistent self-concept and self-esteem, they may have to deny many of their genuine feelings, or disown parts of themselves. In this way, the self-concept becomes distorted. According to Rogers, anxiety often stems from partial perception of feelings and ideas that are inconsistent with the distorted self-concept. Since anxiety is unpleasant, such individuals may deny that these feelings and ideas exist.

Psychological Congruence and the Self-Ideal. When we accept our feelings as our own, we experience psychological integrity or wholeness. There is a "fit" between our self-concept and our behavior, thoughts, and emotions, which Rogers calls **congruence.**

According to Rogers, the path to self-actualization requires getting in touch with our genuine feelings, accepting them as ours, and acting on them. This is the goal of Rogers' method of psychotherapy, person-centered therapy, which we discuss in Chapter 14. Here, suffice it to say that person-centered therapists provide an atmosphere in which clients can cope with the anxieties of focusing on disowned parts of the self.

Rogers also believes that we have mental images of what we are capable of becoming, or **self-ideals.** We are motivated to reduce the discrepancy between our self-concepts and our self-ideals. As we undertake the process of actualizing ourselves, our self-ideals may gradually grow more complex. Our goals may become higher or change in quality. The self-ideal is something like a carrot dangling from a stick strapped to a burro's head. The burro strives to reach the carrot, as though it were a step or two away, without recognizing that its own progress also causes the carrot to advance. Rogers believes that the process of striving to meet meaningful goals, the good struggle, yields happiness.

Self-esteem One's evaluation and valuing of oneself.

Unconditional positive regard A persistent expression of esteem for the value of a person, but not necessarily an unqualified acceptance of all of the person's behaviors.

Conditional positive regard Judgment of another person's value on the basis of the acceptability of that person's behaviors.

Conditions of worth Standards by which the value of a person is judged.

Congruence According to Rogers, a fit between one's self-concept and one's behaviors, thoughts, and feelings.

Self-ideal A mental image of what we believe we ought to be.

Evaluation

Humanistic–existential theories usually have tremendous appeal for college students because of their optimistic views of human nature and their focus on the importance of personal experience. These ideas invaded the popular culture during the 1970s, which has been referred to by some as the "Me Decade." These views gave birth to the so-called Human-Potential Movement, which was particularly well-received in California and New York. A spate of humanistic–existential therapies and groups entered our consciousness, including movements based on Maslow's and Rogers's ideas, Gestalt therapy, transactional analysis (TA), encounter groups, microgroups, marathon groups, and so on. Hundreds of thousands of people went off in a flurry of directions to "get in touch" with their "genuine" feelings and talents and to actualize their potentials.

But the same factors that account for the appeal of humanistic–existential theories have led them to be censured by many psychologists as unscientific. Let us examine some of the strengths and weaknesses of these approaches.

Strengths of Humanistic–Existential Approaches

1. *Focus on Conscious Experience.* We tend to treasure our conscious experiences (our "selves") and those of the people we care about. For lower organisms, to be alive is to move, to process food, to exchange oxygen and carbon dioxide, and to reproduce one's kind. But for human beings, an essential aspect of life is conscious experience—the sense of one's self as progressing through space and time. Humanistic–existential theorists grant consciousness the cardinal role it occupies in our daily lives.
2. *Humanistic–Existential Theory Sets Us Free.* Psychodynamic theories see us largely as victims of our childhoods, whereas learning theories, to some degree, see us as "victims of circumstances"—or, at least, as victims of situational variables. But humanistic–existential theorists envision us as being free to make choices. Psychodynamic theorists and learning theorists wonder whether our sense of freedom is merely an illusion; humanistic–existential theorists begin with an assumption of personal freedom.
3. *Innovations in Therapy.* The humanistic–existential theorists we have discussed have made important innovations and contributions to the practice of psychotherapy. Of these, the best-known and most influential innovation is person-centered therapy, the type of therapy originated by Carl Rogers (see Chapter 14). According to a survey of clinical and counseling psychologists (Smith, 1982), Rogers is the single most influential psychotherapist of recent years.

   On the basis of his experiences, Frankl devised **logotherapy,** a form of psychotherapy that helps clients find meaningful ways of contemplating their lives. Logotherapy confronts clients with responsibility for their own lives, with the need to forge meaning and values, with their own capacity to make meaningful choices. Although few therapists practice logotherapy per se, the effort to help clients shape meaningful lives is widespread.

Weaknesses of Humanistic–Existential Approaches

1. *Focus on Conscious Experience.* Ironically, the primary strength of the humanistic–existential approaches—their focus on conscious experience—is also their primary weakness. Conscious experience is private and subjective. Therefore, the validity of formulating theories in terms of consciousness has been questioned.
2. *The Concept of Self-Actualization.* The concept of self-actualization—so important to Maslow and Rogers—cannot be proved or disproved. Like an id or a trait, a self-actualizing force cannot be observed or measured directly. It must be inferred from its supposed effects.

   Self-actualization, like trait theory, yields circular explanations for behavior. When we see someone engaged in what seems to be positive striving, we gain little insight by attributing this behavior to a self-actualizing force. We have done nothing to account for the origins of the self-actualizing force. And when

Logotherapy Frankl's psychotherapy method, which aims to help clients find meaning in their lives. (From the Greek *logos,* meaning "a word" and used to refer to the ways in which we talk about or study things—as in psycho*logy* and bio*logy.*)

Is this Test-Taker Telling the Truth? How can psychologists determine whether or not people are answering test items honestly? What are the validity scales of the MMPI?

we observe someone who is not engaged in growth-oriented striving, it seems arbitrary to "explain" this outcome by suggesting that the self-actualizing tendency has been blocked or frustrated. It could also be that self-actualization is an acquired need, rather than an innate need, and that it is found in some, but not all, of us.

3. *Failure to Account for Traits.* Humanistic–existential theories, like learning theories, have little to say about the development of traits and personality types. Humanistic–existential theorists assume that we are all unique, but they do not predict the sorts of traits, abilities, and interests we shall develop.

MEASUREMENT OF PERSONALITY

Measures of personality sample behavior, usually in the form of a self-report, to predict future behavior. Standardized interviews are often used, and many psychologists have some routine interviews carried out by computer (Erdman et al., 1985). Some measures of personality are **behavior-rating scales** which assess overt behavior in settings such as the classroom or mental hospital. With behavior-rating scales, trained observers usually check off each occurrence of a specific behavior within a certain time frame—say, a 15-minute period. Standardized objective and projective tests are used more frequently.

Measures of personality are used to make important decisions such as whether a person is suited for a certain type of work, for a particular class in school, or for a drug to reduce agitation. As part of their admissions process, graduate schools often ask professors to rate prospective students on scales that assess traits such as intelligence, emotional stability, and cooperation. Students may take tests of **aptitudes** and interests to gather insight into whether they are suited for certain occupations. It is assumed that students who share the aptitudes and interests of well-adjusted people in certain positions are also likely to be well-adjusted in those positions.

Objective Tests

Objective tests present respondents with a **standardized** group of test items in the form of a questionnaire. Respondents are limited to a specific range of answers. One test might ask respondents to indicate whether items are true or false for them. Another might ask respondents to select the preferred activity from groups of three.

Some tests have a **forced-choice format,** in which respondents are asked to indicate which of two statements is more true for them or which of several activities they prefer. The respondents are not given the option of answering "none of the above." Forced-choice formats are frequently used in interest inventories which help predict whether one would be well-adjusted in a certain occupation. The following item is similar to those found in interest inventories:

I would rather

a. be a forest ranger.
b. work in a busy office.
c. play a musical instrument.

A forced-choice format is also used in the Edwards Personal Preference Schedule, which measures the relative strength of social motives (such as achievement and affiliation) by pitting them against one another consecutively in groups of two. Objective-test items are often presented on a computer screen, and clients respond by using the keyboard.

Behavior-rating scale A systematic means for recording the frequency with which target behaviors occur.

Aptitude A natural ability or talent.

Objective tests Tests whose items must be answered in a specified, limited manner. Tests whose items have concrete answers that are considered correct.

Standardized Given to a large number of respondents so that data concerning the typical responses can be accumulated and analyzed.

Forced-choice format A method of presenting test questions that requires a respondent to select one of a number of possible answers.

TABLE 11.3: Commonly Used Validity and Clinical Scales of the MMPI

Scale	Abbreviation	Possible Interpretations
Validity Scales		
Question	?	Corresponds to number of items left unanswered
Lie	L	Lies or is highly conventional
Frequency	F	Exaggerates complaints or answers items haphazardly
Correction	K	Denies problems
Clinical Scales		
Hypochondriasis	Hs	Has bodily concerns and complaints
Depression	D	Is depressed, guilty; has feelings of guilt and helplessness
Hysteria	Hy	Reacts to stress by developing physical symptoms, lacks insight
Psychopathic deviate	Pd	Is immoral, in conflict with the law; has stormy relationships
Masculinity/femininity	Mf	High scores suggests interests and behavior patterns considered stereotypical of the opposite gender
Paranoia	Pa	Is suspicious and resentful, highly cynical about human nature
Psychasthenia	Pt	Is anxious, worried, high-strung
Schizophrenia	Sc	Is confused, disorganized, disoriented; has bizarre ideas
Hypomania	Ma	Is energetic, restless, active, easily bored
Social introversion	Si	Is introverted, timid, shy; lacks self-confidence

The Minnesota Multiphasic Personality Inventory. The Minnesota Multiphasic Personality Inventory (MMPI) contains hundreds of items presented in a true-false format. The MMPI was intended to be used by clinical and counseling psychologists to help diagnose abnormal behavior (see Chapter 13). Accurate measurement of clients' problems should point to appropriate treatment.

Psychologists can score tests by hand, send them to computerized scoring services, or have them scored by on-site computers. Computers generate reports by interpreting the test record according to certain rules or by comparing it to records in memory. Computer-based interpretations are efficient, but questions have been raised as to their validity (Butcher, 1987; Spielberger & Piotrowski, 1990).

The MMPI is usually scored for the four **validity scales** and ten **clinical scales** described in Table 11.3. The validity scales suggest whether answers are likely to represent the client's thoughts, emotions, and behaviors, although they cannot guarantee that deception will be disclosed.

It is *not* true that psychologists can invariably determine whether a person has told the truth on a personality test. But validity scales allow them to make educated guesses.

The validity scales in Table 11.3 assess different **response sets,** or biases in answering the questions. People with high L scores, for example, may be attempting to present themselves as excessively moral and well-behaved individuals. People with high F scores may be trying to seem bizarre or are answering haphazardly. In one study, F-scale scores were positively correlated with conceptual confusion, hostility, and presence of **hallucinations** and other unusual thought patterns as measured on a behavior-rating scale (Smith & Graham, 1981). Many personality measures have some kind of validity scale. The clinical scales of the MMPI assess the problems shown in Table 11.3, as well as stereotypical masculine or feminine interests and introversion.

Validity scales Groups of test items that indicate whether a person's responses accurately reflect that individual's traits.

Clinical scales Groups of test items that measure the presence of various abnormal behavior patterns.

Response set A tendency to answer test items according to a bias—for instance, to make oneself seem perfect or bizarre.

Hallucinations Perceptions in the absence of sensory stimulation that are confused with reality. See Chapter 13.

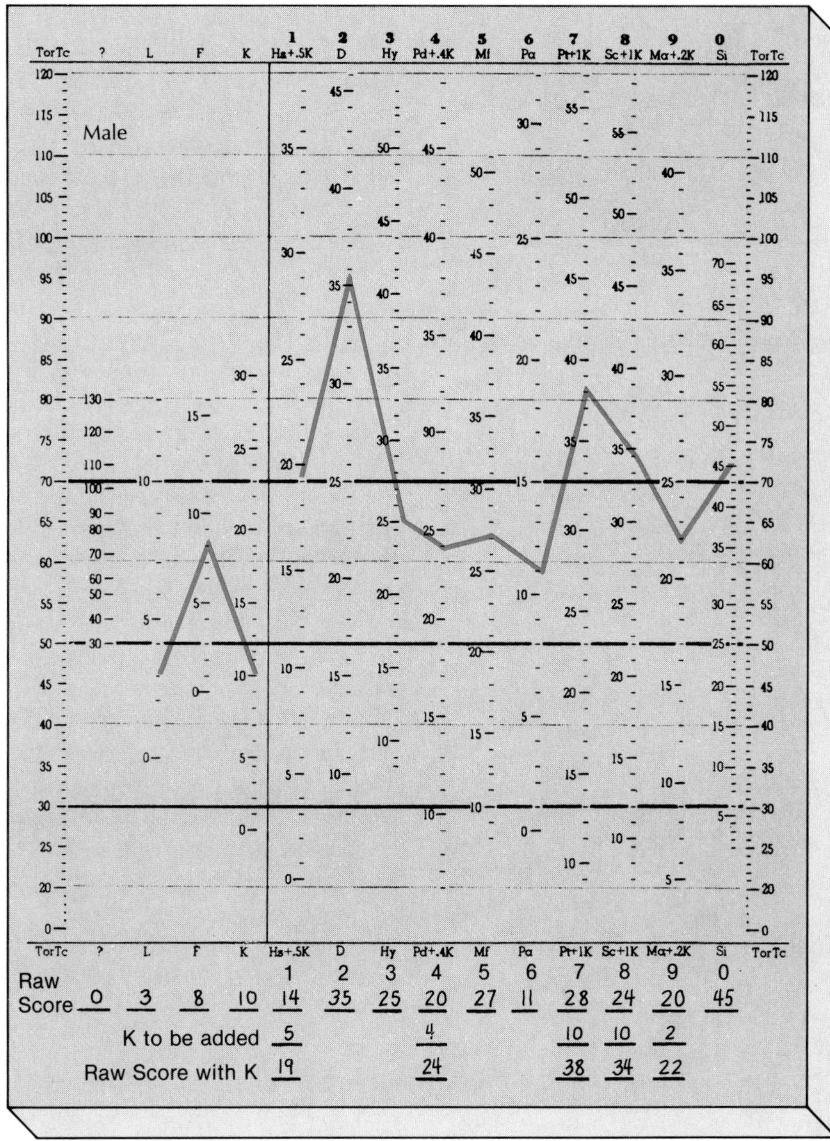

FIGURE 11.4
An MMPI Personality Profile. This profile was attained by a depressed barber. On this form, scores at the standard level of 50 are average for males, and scores above the standard score of 70 are considered abnormally high. The raw score is the number of items answered in a certain direction on a given MMPI scale. K is the correction scale. A certain percentage of the K-scale score is added onto several clinical scales to correct for denial of problems.

The MMPI scales were constructed empirically on the basis of actual clinical data rather than on the basis of psychological theory. A test-item bank of several hundred items was derived from questions often asked in clinical interviews. Here are some of the items that were used:

T F 1. My father was a good man.

T F 2. I am very seldom troubled by headaches.

T F 3. My hands and feet are usually warm enough.

T F 4. I have never done anything dangerous for the thrill of it.

T F 5. I work under a great deal of tension.

The items were administered to clients and psychiatric patients with previously identified symptoms such as depressive or **schizophrenic** symptoms. Items that successfully set apart people with these symptoms were included on scales named accordingly. Figure 11.4 shows the personality profile of a 27-year-old barber who consulted a psychologist because of depression and difficulty in making decisions. The barber scored abnormally high on the Hs, D, Pt, Sc, and Si scales,

Schizophrenic Characteristic of the thought disorder schizophrenia. See Chapter 13.

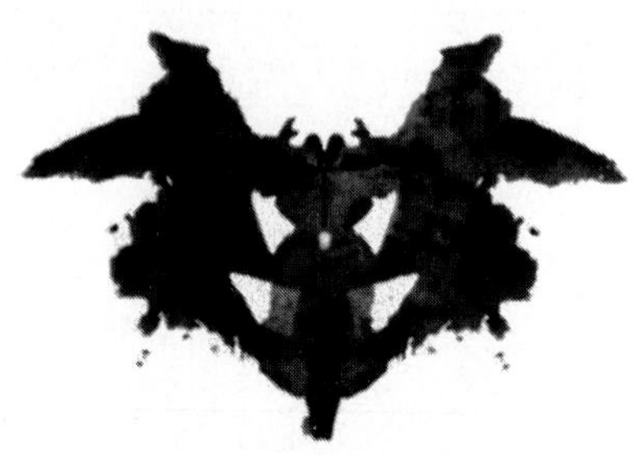

FIGURE 11.5
A Rorschach Inkblot. What does this look like? What could it be?

suggestive of concern with body functions (Hs), depression (D), persistent feelings of anxiety and tension (Pt), insomnia and fatigue, and some difficulties relating to other people (Sc, Si). Note that the high Sc score does not in itself indicate that the barber is schizophrenic.

In addition to the standard validity and clinical scales, investigators of personality have derived many experimental scales such as those that measure neuroticism, religious orthodoxy, assertiveness, substance abuse, and even well-being (Costa et al., 1985; Johnson et al., 1984; Snyder et al., 1985). The MMPI remains a rich mine for unearthing elements of personality.

The California Psychological Inventory. Another personality inventory, the California Psychological Inventory (CPI), is widely used in research to assess 18 dimensions of normal behavior such as achievement, dominance, flexibility, self-acceptance, and self-control.

Interest Inventories. Interest inventories can be of help to high school and college students who are uncertain about their future occupations. Tests such as the Strong-Campbell Interest Inventory (SCII) and the Kuder Occupational Interest Survey (KOIS) are used to predict adjustment in various occupations.

The SCII is used from high school to adulthood and is the most widely used test in counseling centers (Lubin et al., 1985). Most items on the SCII require test takers to indicate whether they like, are indifferent to, or dislike items chosen from the following: occupations (for example, actor/actress, architect), school subjects (algebra, art), activities (adjusting a carburetor, making a speech), amusements (golf, chess, jazz or rock concerts), and types of people (babies, nonconformists). The preferences of test takers are compared with those of people in various occupations. Areas of general interest (sales, science, teaching, agriculture) and specific interest (mathematician, guidance counselor, beautician) are derived from these comparisons.

The KOIS, like the SCII, is used from high school to adulthood. It consists of triads of activities such as the following:

a. write a story about a sports event
b. play in a baseball game
c. teach children to play a game

For each triad, the test taker indicates which activities he or she would like most and least. The KOIS predicts adjustment in college majors as well as occupations.

Projective Tests

You may have heard that there is a personality test that asks people what a drawing or inkblot looks like and that people commonly answer "a bat." There are a number of such tests, the best known of which is the Rorschach inkblot test, named after its originator, Swiss psychiatrist Hermann Rorschach (1884–1922).

The Rorschach Inkblot Test. The Rorschach test is a **projective test.** In projective techniques, there are no clear, specified answers. People are presented with **ambiguous** stimuli such as inkblots or vague drawings and may be asked to report what these stimuli look like to them or to tell stories about them. Because there is no one proper response, it is assumed that people *project* their own personalities into their responses. The meanings they attribute to these stimuli are assumed to reflect their personalities as well as the drawings or blots themselves.

Actually, the facts of the matter are slightly different. There may be no single "correct" response to the Rorschach inkblot shown in Figure 11.5, but some responses would clearly not be in keeping with the features of the blot. Figure 11.5

Projective test A psychological test that presents ambiguous stimuli onto which the test-taker projects his or her own personality in making a response.

Ambiguous Having two or more possible meanings.

could be a bat or a flying insect, the pointed face of an animal, the face of a jack o'lantern, or many other things. But responses like "an ice cream cone," "diseased lungs," or "a metal leaf in flames" are not suggested by the features of the blot and may suggest personality problems.

It is true that there is a psychological test made up of inkblots—the Rorschach inkblot test. And one of them does look somewhat like a bat.

The Thematic Apperception Test. The Thematic Apperception Test (TAT) was developed in the 1930s by psychologist Henry Murray at Harvard University. It consists of drawings like that shown in Figure 9.7 (see p. 343), that are open to a variety of interpretations. Subjects are given the cards one at a time and are asked to make up stories about them.

The TAT has been widely used in research into social motives as well as in clinical practice. In an experiment described in Chapter 9, need for achievement was assessed from subjects' responses to a picture of a boy and a violin. The notion is that we are likely to be preoccupied with our own needs to some degree and that our needs will be projected into our responses to ambiguous situations. The TAT is also widely used to assess attitudes toward other people, especially parents, lovers, and spouses.

Evaluation of Measures of Personality

Personality measures can provide useful information to help people make decisions about themselves and others. In general, however, psychological tests should not be the sole criteria for making important decisions.

For example, single scales of the MMPI are reasonably accurate measures of the presence of a trait such as depression. One could not justifiably hospitalize a person for fear of suicide solely on the basis of a high D-scale score on the MMPI, however. Similarly, combinations of high MMPI scale scores seem to reflect certain clinical pictures in some populations but not in others. A typical study found that a combination of high scores on the D, Pt, and Sc scales was likely to suggest severe disturbance in college males but not in college females (Kelley & King, 1979). Interpretation of the MMPI is further clouded by the fact that abnormal validity-scale scores do *not* necessarily invalidate the test for respondents who are highly disturbed.

The Rorschach inkblot test, for all its artistic appeal, has had major difficulties with validation. Although TAT has been consistently shown to be a useful research tool, its clinical validity has also met with criticism. Despite problems with projective techniques, they continue to be used regularly. The Rorschach inkblot test, in fact, remains the most widely used test in psychiatric hospitals (Lubin et al., 1985).

Psychological tests should not be used as the sole means for making important decisions. Tests that are carefully chosen and interpreted may provide useful information for supplementing other sources of information in making decisions, however.

STUDY GUIDE

EXERCISE: Matching Theorists and Concepts

In the column to the left are the names of personality theorists. In the column to the right is a list of personality-theory concepts. Match the concept with the theorist by writing the letter(s) of the appropriate theorist(s) in the blank space to the left of the concept.

	Concept	Theorist
____	1. Surface trait	A. Alfred Adler
____	2. Self	B. B. C. Skinner
____	3. Generalized expectancy	C. Albert Bandura
____	4. Id	D. Raymond Cattell
____	5. 16 PF Scale	E. Erik Erikson
____	6. Psychosocial development	F. Hans Eysenck
____	7. Frame of reference	G. Sigmund Freud
____	8. Behaviorism	H. Karen Horney
____	9. Inferiority complex	I. Carl Jung
____	10. Basic anxiety	J. Carl Rogers
____	11. Self-efficacy expectations	K. Julian Rotter
____	12. Introversion	L. John B. Watson
____	13. Trust vs. mistrust	
____	14. Latency	
____	15. Conditions of worth	
____	16. Electra complex	
____	17. Archetype	
____	18. Creative self	
____	19. Source trait	
____	20. Person variables	

Answers To Matching Exercise

1. D
2. A, I, J
3. K
4. G
5. D
6. E
7. J
8. B, L
9. A
10. H
11. C
12. I, F
13. E
14. G
15. J
16. G
17. I
18. A
19. D
20. C, K

ESL—BRIDGING THE GAP

This part is divided into

1. cultural references
2. phrases and expresssions in which words are used differently from their regular meaning, or are used as metaphors

Cultural References

Robert Louis Stevenson (413)—a Scots poet, novelist, and essayist who lived in Samoa

Byron (417)—One of the romantic English poets of the nineteenth century

Beethoven (417)—a German composer of great genius who lived from 1770 to 1827. He wrote nine symphonies, many sonatas and other musical works.

a date (425)—an invitation to another person to go to a social function

her serve (425)—refers to the game of tennis; the serve puts the ball in the game and there is an advantage to the server if she can hit a powerful and accurate serve

adjusting carburetor (436)—modifying the mixture between air and gasoline in the engine of a car in order to obtain better operation of the car

golf (436)—a sport requiring accurate hitting of a small ball over a large area of ground and ultimately hitting it into a hole

chess (436)—a game that is played on a board which requires a great amount of skill; a player needs to project future moves in order to capture the opponent's chess pieces

jack-o'-lantern 436)—at Hallowe'en, people often carve faces in pumpkins and then make a lamp shade (lantern) from it by putting a lighted candle inside

Phrases and Expressions (Different Usage)

After doing so (410)—After we do this

At a given moment (410)—A a specific moment

owes its origin (410)—has its origin, or beginning

shock of dark hair (411)—a lot of dark hair

forecasting good tidings then doom (411)—predicting good then bad

poked through (411)—went through to

shrouded in mystery (412)—unknown

a method of mental detective work (412)—a method of figuring out answers from evidence and clues

prodded to talk (412)—urged and encouraged to talk

that "pops" into their minds (412)—that enters their mind; that they think of

dwell side by side (412)—live or exist next to each other

be met (412)—be gratified

curbs the appetites (412)—restricts the desires

rising into awareness (412)—becoming known

holds forth shining examples (414)—displays excellent examples

hands out judgments (414)—dispenses judgments

floods the ego (414)—overwhelms the ego

stands between (414)—is in between

braving the arrows (414)—risking the criticisms and attacks

have a hard time of it (414)—encounter difficulty

stirred controversy (414)—evoked disagreement

fueled by (414)—caused to operate

clinging (415)—attaching physically and emotionally

"let it all hang out" (415)—display all feelings without any control

to handle (415)—to deal with; to cope with

inner circle (416)—the friends and colleagues who worked closely with Freud

fell into disfavor (416)—became disliked

render us (417)—cause us to be

shadowy parts (417)—unpleasant aspects

importance to conscious motives (417)—fully conscious functions must be considered important

spurred him on to (417)—caused him to work harder and achieve

in part (417)—not completely, but enough to be considered

harbor feelings (417)—have feelings and continue to have them

of paramount importance (417)—the most important

driving them away (418)—causing the parents to not care and respond

overly anxious to please (418)—eager, but with anxiety, to cause the other person to be happy

The price (418)—the negative emotional result

had placed undo emphasis on (418)—had considered much too emphatically the importance of (negative emphasis)

general climate (418)—general feeling

to a large degree (418)—to a great extent; almost completely

conscious architects (418)—conscious builders (we make our own personalities)

grants more powers to (418)—gives more powers to

forced upon us by intrapsychic warfare (418)—the compromises that we did not choose which result from the conflicts among the Ego, Superego and Id

polar opposites (418)—extreme opposites ("polar" refers to the North and South Poles)

mar the formation of (418)—obstruct or impede the formation of

short-sighted hedonism (419)—enjoying the moment without thinking about what the negative results might be

strike many psychologists as being (419)—are concepts that many psychologists think are

fought for the idea that (419)—tried to convince people that

far-reaching effects (419)—effects that will continue and also cause problems in the future

is also suspect (420)—is also questionable

address traits (420)—consider traits

"all across the board" (421)—in every situation; all the time

feel at home at gatherings (421)—feel comfortable with groups of people in a social context

that we "fit" our jobs (423)—that our jobs are appropriate to our abilities

suit us (423)—make us the right person

from situation to situation (423)—from one situation to another situation (behavior may be a particular way in one situation but it may be different in another situation)

hue and cry was (424)—ideas were

largely discard the notions (424)—almost completely dismiss the ideas

as surely as (424)—is the same way as

sidestep the roles of (424)—ignore the roles

are not so blindly ruled by pleasure and pain (424)—do not allow pleasure and pain to determine their actions without thinking about anything else

at the mercy of (425)—victims of
"calling out" (425)—speaking aloud without asking for permission to speak
"unladylike" (425)—not behaving like a lady should behave
codes of conduct (425)—rules for behavior
tossing a football properly (425)—throwing a football in the correct way in order to play football well
"made for each other" (426)—of compatible personality; personalities that are appropriate together
the broadest effect (427)—the widest effect; an effect on most of the issues
its intellectual forebear (428)—the theories that were before it and influenced it
getting in touch with (431)—becoming aware of
a carrot dangling from a stick (431)—something good which is not close enough to reach, but we are supposed to have it
cardinal role (432)—the most important role
victims of circumstance (432)—other situations and the environment affect us and we cannot control that
check off (433)—indicate that it occurred with a check(✓)
forced-choice format (433)—a form that requires that people answer something, even if none of the choices apply to that person
stormy relationships (434)—unstable relationships
for the thrill of it (435)—because I only wanted the exciting sensations
set apart people (435)—identified people
a rich mind (435)—an effective method
unearthing elements (435)—discovering elements
the facts of the matter (436)—the facts
inkblots (436)—large areas of ink on a piece of paper
make up stories (437)—create stories
sole criteria (437)—only criteria
for fear of (437)—because we are afraid the person might commit suicide
further clouded (437)—additionally unclear

CHAPTER REVIEW

SECTION 1: Introduction

Objective 1: Define *personality.*

Personality can be defined as the reasonably stable patterns of (1) be________________ that distinguish people from one another. Behavior, in this instance, includes thoughts and (2) ________________tions. These behavior patterns characterize a person's ways of (3) ________________ing to the demands of his or her life.

SECTION 2: Psychodynamic Theory

Objective 2: Describe the "mental structures" theorized by Sigmund Freud in his psychodynamic theory.

(4) Psycho________________ theories of personality teach that personality is characterized by a struggle between drives such as sex and aggression on the one hand, and laws, social rules, and moral codes on the other. The laws and social rules become (5) ________________lized; that is, we make them parts of ourselves.

Sigmund Freud labeled the clashing forces of personality (6) ________________ic structures. Psychodynamic theory assumes that we are driven largely by (7) ________________scious motives. Conflict is inevitable as basic instincts of hunger, (8) s________________, and (9) ag________________ come up against social pressures to follow laws, rules, and moral codes. The automatic ejection of anxiety-evoking ideas from awareness is called (10) ________________sion. Repression protects us from recognizing many impulses that are in conflict with our moral values.

Freud hypothesized the existence of (11: how many?) ________________ psychic structures. The unconscious (12) ________________ is the psychic structure present at birth. The id represents psychological drives and operates according to the (13) pl________________ principle, seeking instant gratification.

The psychic structure called the (14)________________ is the sense of self or "I." The ego develops through experience and operates according to the (15) re________________ principle. The ego takes into account what is practical and possible in gratifying the impulses of the (16) i________________. So-called (17) de________________ mechanisms protect the ego from anxiety by repressing unacceptable ideas or distorting reality.

The third psychic structure is the (18) ________________. The superego is the moral sense. It develops throughout early childhood, including the standards of parents and others by means of (19) ________________fication. The superego operates according to the (20) m________________ principle. The superego holds forth the example of the (21) i________________ self. It also acts like a (22) co________________, handing out judgments of right and wrong and flooding the ego with (23) g________________ and shame when the verdict is in the negative.

Objective 3: List Freud's stages of psychosexual development, and describe the major events that occur during each stage.

People undergo psychosexual development as psychosexual energy, or (24) l________________, is transferred from one (25) ________________nous zone to another during childhood. There are (26: how many?) ________________ stages of psychosexual development. They are the oral, (27) ________________, phallic, (28) ________________, and genital stages.

Freud believed that each stage would bring conflict. During the (29) ________________ stage, conflict would center on the nature and extent of oral gratification, and issues such as weaning. Conflict during the anal stage would concern (30) t________________ training and the general issue of (31) s________________-control. (32) Fi________________ in a stage may lead to the development of traits associated with that stage. Fixation in the oral stage, for example, may lead to oral traits such as (33) dep________________ and (34) g________________ility. Anal fixation may result in extremes of (35) cl________________ness versus messiness, or of (36) per________________ism versus carelessness.

The Oedipus and Electra complexes are conflicts of the (37) ________________ic stage. In these conflicts, children long to possess the parent of the (38: same or opposite?) gender and resent the parent of the (39: same or opposite?) gender. Under normal circumstances, these complexes eventually become resolved by identifying with the parent of the (40: same or opposite?) gender.

The (41) ________________cy stage is a period of life during which Freud believed sexual feelings remain largely unconscious. Freud believed that we enter the genital stage at (42) p________________. During the genital stage, the (43) i________________ taboo motivates us to displace sexual impulses onto adults or adolescents of the (44: same or opposite?) gender.

Objective 4: Describe the psychodynamic views of Carl Jung.

Carl Jung's psychodynamic theory is called (45) ________________cal psychology. Jung believed that in addition to a personal unconscious mind, we also have a (46) ________________tive unconscious, which contains primitive images or (47) ________________pes that are reflections of the history of our species. Jung downplayed the importance of the (48) ________________ual instinct. He also believed that one of the archetypes was the (49) ________________, a conscious, unifying force in personality that provides us with direction and purpose.

Objective 5: Describe the psychodynamic views of Alfred Adler.

Alfred Adler's psychodynamic theory is called (50) ________________ual psychology. Adler believed that people are basically motivated by an (51) ________________ity complex, and that this complex gave rise to a compensating drive for (52) ________________ity.

Objective 6: Describe the psychodynamic views of Karen Horney.

Karen (53) H________________, like Freud, saw parent–child relationships as paramount in importance. When parents treat children indifferently or harshly, the children develop feelings of insecurity that Horney labeled basic (54) ________________ty. Children also resent neglectful parents, giving rise to basic (55) ________________ty. Later in life, repressed hostility can lead us to relate to others in a (56) ________________tic manner.

Objective 7: Describe the psychodynamic views of Erik Erikson.

Erik Erikson's psychodynamic theory is called the theory of (57) psycho________________ development. Erikson highlights the importance of early (58) ________________al relationships rather than the gratification of childhood (59) ________________al impulses. Erikson extended Freud's five developmental stages to (60: how many?) ________________. Erikson's stages are characterized by certain life (61) ________________ses. These are the crises of (62) ________________ vs. mistrust, (63) ________________my vs. shame and doubt, initiative vs. (64)

g_______________, (65) _______________try vs. inferiority, identity vs. (66) _______________ diffusion, (67)_______________vity vs. stagnation, and integrity vs. (68) de_______________.

Objective 8: Evaluate psychodynamic theory.

Psychodynamic theory (69: advanced or contradicted?) the view that human behavior is subject to scientific analysis. Psychodynamic theory focused attention on the (70: importance or unimportance?) of childhood events. Freud also helped people (71: deny or recognize?) the importance of sexuality and aggressive impulses in their lives.

But Freud has been criticized by followers like Erik Erikson, Alfred Adler, and Erich Fromm for placing too much emphasis on sexual urges and (72: conscious or unconscious?) motives. Karl Popper criticizes Freud's psychodynamic theory because

(a) Freud's theoretical mental processes (73: can or cannot?) be observed;

(b) Freud's theory (74: does or does not?) predict behavior with precision; and

(c) Freud's views are not capable of being disproved.

SECTION 3: Trait Theory

Objective 9: Define *trait.*

Traits are personality elements that are inferred from (75) _______________or. Traits are said to endure and to account for behavioral (76) _______________ency.

Objective 10: Describe the contribution of Gordon Allport to trait theory.

Gordon Allport thought of traits as embedded in our (77) _______________us systems. Allport and Odbert catalogued 18,000 human traits from a search through word lists of the sort found in (78) _______________aries.

Objective 11: Describe the trait-theory views of Raymond Cattell.

According to Raymond Cattell, (79) s_______________ traits are characteristic ways of behaving that seem linked in an orderly manner. (80) S_______________ traits are underlying traits from which surface traits are derived. Cattell constructed the (81) S_______________ Personality Factors Scale, a test that measures source traits.

Objective 12: Describe the trait-theory views of Hans Eysenck.

Hans J. (82) E_______________ has focused on the relationships between two source traits introversion–extraversion and emotional stability–instability, otherwise known as (83) _______________ism. Eysenck notes that his scheme is reminiscent of that suggested by (84) _______________ates, the Greek physician. Hippocrates suggested that there are (85: how many?) _______________ basic personality types: (86) _______________ric (quick-tempered), sanguine (warm, cheerful, confident), (87) phl_______________ (sluggish, calm, cool), and (88) _______________lic (gloomy, pensive).

Objective 13: Evaluate trait theory.

Trait theory has contributed to the development of psychological tests. It has also given rise to theories concerning the (89) _______________t between personality and jobs. It has identified basic traits and pointed out that traits (90: are or are not?) generally stable. On the other hand, trait theories tend to describe rather than (91) ex_______________ behavior. Trait-theory explanations of behavior have been criticized as (92) _______________lar. Also, there is somewhat (93: more or less?) situational variability in behavior than trait theorists might allow, especially among people who are (94: high or low?) in private self-consciousness.

SECTION 4: Learning Theories

Objective 14: Describe the behaviorist approach to understanding personality.

Learning theorists of personality place more emphasis on (95) _______________nal variables than on internal, (96) p_______________ variables as the shapers of human preferences and behaviors. The behaviorists John B. Watson and B. F. (97) _______________ discarded notions of personal freedom, and argued that environmental contingencies can shape people into wanting to do the things that the physical environment and society requires of them.

Objective 15: Describe the social-learning-theory approach to understanding personality, emphasizing the roles of person and situational variables.

Modern social-learning theory, in contrast to behaviorism, has a strong (98) cog_______________ orientation and focuses on the importance of learning by (99) _______________tion. Rotter argues that behavior depends upon the person's (100) _______________ancies concerning the outcome of that behavior and the perceived or (101) _______________tive values of those outcomes. Social-learning theorists do not consider only situational rewards and (102) _______________ents important in the prediction of behavior. They also consider the roles of (103) p_______________ variables. Person variables include (104) co_______________cies, (105) en_______________ing strategies, expectancies, subjective values, and (106) self-_______________tory systems and plans. Competencies include (107) kn_______________ of rules that guide conduct; concepts about ourselves and other people; and (108) _______________lls. Expectancies are "if-then" statements or personal (109) _______________tions about the outcome (or [110] _______________cement contingencies) of engaging in a response. Bandura refers to beliefs that one can handle a task as (111) self-_______________ expectations. We are (112: more or less?) likely to persist at difficult tasks when we believe that we shall succeed at them.

Objective 16: Evaluate the learning theory of personality.

Learning theories have stimulated us to focus on (113: observable or unobservable?) behavior and on the (114: internal or situational?) determinants of behavior. They have led to innovations in therapy methods and had a (115: broad or limited?) impact on the science of psychology. Behaviorism fails to deal with human (116) cog_______________ processes. Social-learning theory has not yet derived satisfying statements about the development of (117) _______________ts and may not pay enough attention to (118) g_______________ic variation.

SECTION 5: Humanistic–Existential Theories

Humanists and (119) _______________lists dwell on the meaning of life. Their awareness of their existence—of their (120) _______________ing in the world—is the hub of the humanistic–existential search for meaning. Because of their focus on conscious, subjective experience, humanistic–existential theories have also been referred to as (121) _______________logical. The European existentialist philosophers Jean-Paul Sartre and Martin Heidegger saw human life as trivial in the grand scheme of things, leading to feelings of (122) _______________ation. Psychological "salvation" requires implanting personal (123) _______________ing on things and making personal (124) ch_______________s.

Objective 17: Describe Viktor Frankl's humanistic–existential views on personality.

Austrian psychiatrist Viktor Frankl's views were largely shaped by his experiences in Nazi (125) _______________ation camps. Frankl believed that his personal quest for (126) _______________ing helped him survive the ordeal. Without meaning, people are prone to (127) _______________tial frustration. Frankl believed that personal, (128) _______________tive experience is the significant facet of human nature. He also argued that people (129: are or are not?) experts on themselves, and that people become (130) _______________nated and apathetic when they are prevented from striving to reach their unique potentials.

Objective 18: Describe Abraham Maslow's humanistic–existential views on personality.

Abraham Maslow argued that people also have growth-oriented needs for (131) self-_______________ation. Self-actualization requires taking (132) _______________s.

Objective 19: Describe Carl Rogers' humanistic–existential views on personality.

Carl Rogers' theory begins with the assumption of the existence of the (133) s_______________. According to Carl (134) R_______________, the self is an organized and consistent way in which a person perceives his or her "I" to relate to others and the world.

The self is innate and will attempt to become actualized (develop its unique potential) when the person receives (135) _______________ional positive regard. We all have needs for self-esteem and see the world through unique frames of (136) _______________nce. Conditions of (137) w_______________lead to a distorted self-concept, to the disowning of parts of the self, and, often, to anxiety. When we accept our feelings as our own, there is a fit between our self-concepts and our behavior, thoughts, and emotions that Rogers calls psychological (138) _______________ence.

Objective 20: Evaluate humanistic–existential theory.

Some phenomenological theories focus on (139)

_______________ous experience and grant us the freedom to make choices But critics point out that conscious experience is private and (140) _______________tive, and thus not ideal subject matter for scientific investigation. Moreover, the concept of (141) self-_______________tion yields circular explanations for behavior.

SECTION 6: Measurement of Personality

Objective 21: Differentiate between objective and projective measures of personality.

In personality measurement, psychologists take a sample of (142) b_______________ in order to predict future behavior.

(143) _______________ive tests present test-takers with a standardized set of test items in the form of questionnaires. Respondents are limited to a specific range of answers, as in multiple-choice tests or true-false tests. A (144) fo_______________-_______________ format requires respondents to indicate which of two or more statements is true of them, or which of several activities they prefer. Projective tests present (145) _______________uous stimuli and permit the respondent a broad range of answers.

Objective 22: Describe some of the major objective measures of personality.

The (146) M_______________ (147) M_______________ Personality Inventory (MMPI) is the most widely used psychological test in the clinical setting. The MMPI is an (148) _______________ive personality test that uses a true-false format to assess (149) ab_______________ behavior. The MMPI contains (150) _______________ity scales as well as clinical scales and has been validated empirically.

Other widely used objective personality tests include the (151) C_______________ Psychological Inventory, which measures normal behavior patterns, and the (152) S_______________/C_______________ Interest Inventory, which helps adolescents and adults make occupational choices.

Objective 23: Describe some of the major projective measures of personality.

The foremost projective technique is the (153) R_______________ inkblot test, in which test-takers are asked to report what inkblots look like or could be. The (154) T_______________ (155) A_______________ Test (TAT) consists of ambiguous drawings that test-takers are asked to interpret. The TAT is widely used in research on social motives as well as in clinical practice.

Answers To Chapter Review

1. Behavior
2. Emotions
3. Adapting
4. Psychodynamic
5. Internalized
6. Psychic
7. Unconscious
8. Sex
9. Aggression
10. Repression
11. Three
12. Id
13. Pleasure
14. Ego
15. Reality
16. Id
17. Defense
18. Superego
19. Identification
20. Moral
21. Ideal
22. Conscience
23. Guilt
24. Libido
25. Erogenous
26. Five
27. Anal
28. Latency
29. Oral
30. Toilet
31. Self
32. Fixation
33. Dependence (or Depression)
34. Gullibility
35. Cleanliness
36. Perfectionism
37. Phallic
38. Opposite
39. Same
40. Same
41. Latency
42. Puberty
43. Incest
44. Opposite
45. Analytical
46. Collective
47. Archetypes
48. Sexual
49. Self
50. Individual
51. Inferiority
52. Superiority
53. Horney
54. Anxiety
55. Hostility
56. Neurotic
57. Psychosocial
58. Social
59. Sexual
60. Eight
61. Crises
62. Trust
63. Autonomy
64. Guilt
65. Industry
66. Role
67. Generativity
68. Despair
69. Advanced
70. Importance
71. Recognize
72. Unconscious
73. Cannot
74. Does not
75. Behavior
76. Consistency
77. Nervous
78. Dictionaries
79. Surface
80. Source
81. Sixteen
82. Eysenck
83. Neuroticism
84. Hippocrates
85. Four
86. Choleric
87. Phlegmatic
88. Melancholic
89. Fit
90. Are
91. Explain

92. Circular
93. More
94. High
95. Situational (or External)
96. Person
97. Skinner
98. Cognitive
99. Observation
100. Expectancies
101. Subjective
102. Punishments
103. Person
104. Competencies
105. Encoding
106. Regulatory
107. Knowledge
108. Skills
109. Predictions (or Expectations)
110. Reinforcement
111. Efficacy
112. More
113. Observable
114. Situational
115. Broad
116. Cognitive
117. Traits
118. Genetic
119. Existentialists
120. Being
121. Phenomenological
122. Alienation
123. Meaning
124. Choices
125. Concentration
126. Meaning
127. Existential
128. Subjective
129. Are
130. Alienated
131. Self-actualization
132. Risks
133. Self
134. Rogers
135. Unconditional
136. Reference
137. Worth
138. Congruence
139. Conscious
140. Subjective
141. Actualization
142. Behavior
143. Objective
144. Forced-choice
145. Ambiguous
146. Minnesota
147. Multiphasic
148. Objective
149. Abnormal
150. Validity
151. California
152. Strong/Campbell
153. Rorschach
154. Thematic
155. Apperception

POSTTEST

1. Freud labeled the clashing forces of personality
   (a) repression and resistance.
   (b) conscious and unconscious.
   (c) defense mechanisms.
   (d) psychic structures.

2. According to psychodynamic theory, the ________ follows the reality principle.
   (a) id
   (b) ego
   (c) superego
   (d) libido

3. According to psychodynamic theory, the superego usually incorporates the standards of parents through
   (a) identification.
   (b) repression.
   (c) unconditional positive regard.
   (d) classical and operant conditioning.

4. John throws his clothing and books all over the floor, leaves his hair unkempt, and rarely cleans his room. According to psychodynamic theory, John's behavior is suggestive of conflict during the ________ stage of psychosexual development.
   (a) genital
   (b) oral
   (c) phallic
   (d) anal

5. Alfred Adler believed that people are basically motivated by
   (a) the collective unconscious.
   (b) hostility.
   (c) biological and safety needs.
   (d) an inferiority complex.

6. Karen Horney agreed with Freud that
   (a) some women suffer from penis envy.
   (b) there are eight stages of psychosocial development.
   (c) parent–child relationships are very important.
   (d) sexual impulses are more important than social relationships.

7. According to the text, which of the following theorists believed that a basic element of personality was the Self?
   (a) John B. Watson
   (b) Carl Jung
   (c) Sigmund Freud
   (d) Hans J. Eysenck

8. Gordon Allport looked upon traits as
   (a) archetypes.
   (b) basic instincts.
   (c) generalized expectancies.
   (d) embedded in the nervous system.

9. Raymond Cattell hypothesized the existence of two types of traits: ________ traits and source traits.
   (a) surface
   (b) cardinal
   (c) secondary
   (d) central

10. The outlooks of John B. Watson and B. F. Skinner discarded all of the following notions, *with the exception of*
    (a) self-direction.
    (b) personal freedom.
    (c) learning.
    (d) choice.

11. ________ has argued for the inclusion of cognitive points of view within learning theory.
    (a) Carl Rogers
    (b) Albert Bandura
    (c) John. B. Watson
    (d) Carl Jung

12. Which of the following is a situational variable?
    (a) A self-efficacy expectation
    (b) The subjective value of a reward
    (c) A generalized expectancy
    (d) A reward

13. According to Carl Rogers, the sense of self
    (a) is an archetype.
    (b) develops as a result of conditions of worth.
    (c) is innate.
    (d) develops once biological and safety needs have been met.

14. A mother and father tell you that their most important goal for their new child is that she develop a strong sense of self-esteem. According to self theory, parents are likely to help their children develop self-esteem when they show them
    (a) conditional positive regard.
    (b) conditions of worth.
    (c) unconditional positive regard.
    (d) psychological congruence.

15. Which theorist has focused on the relationships between introversion–extraversion and neuroticism?
    (a) Carl Jung
    (b) Hans J. Eysenck
    (c) Raymond Cattell
    (d) Karen Horney

16. Which theorist explains stable behavior patterns in terms of generalized expectancies?
    (a) Julian Rotter
    (b) John B. Watson
    (c) Raymond Cattell
    (d) Walter Mischel

17. Which of the following personality theorists endured the hardships of Nazi concentration camps during World War II?
    (a) Viktor Frankl
    (b) Sigmund Freud
    (c) Karen Horney
    (d) Alfred Adler

18. Which of the following theorists would be most likely to agree that people are their own best experts on themselves?
    (a) B. F. Skinner
    (b) John Watson
    (c) Abraham Maslow
    (d) Sigmund Freud

19. Objective personality tests
    (a) all have forced-choice formats.
    (b) are easier to answer than projective tests.
    (c) limit respondents to a specific range of answers.
    (d) are less valid than projective personality tests.

20. Which of the following tests is used to help diagnose abnormal behavior?
    (a) Minnesota Multiphasic Personality Inventory
    (b) California Psychological Inventory
    (c) Edwards Personal Preference Schedule
    (d) Strong/Campbell Interest Inventory

Answers To Posttest

1. D
2. B
3. A
4. D
5. D
6. C
7. B
8. D
9. A
10. C
11. B
12. D
13. C
14. C
15. B
16. A
17. A
18. C
19. C
20. A

- Too much of a good thing can make you ill.
- A sense of humor can moderate the impact of stress.
- Single men live longer.
- Harvard University alumni who burn 2,000 calories a week in exercise live two years longer, on the average, than their sedentary counterparts.
- At any given moment, countless microscopic warriors within our bodies are carrying out search-and-destroy missions against foreign agents.
- Most headaches are caused by muscle tension.
- Stress can influence the course of cancer.
- Many people who are infected by the virus that causes AIDS have no symptoms for years.
- Only gay men and people who inject drugs are at serious risk for contracting AIDS.

12

Health Psychology

Learning Objectives

When you have finished studying Chapter 12, you should be able to:

Health Psychology

1. Define *health psychology*.
2. Define *stress*.

Sources of Stress

3. Enumerate sources of stress.

Moderators of Stress

4. Describe moderators of the impact of stress.

Physiological Responses to Stress

5. Describe the general adaptation syndrome.
6. Describe the functions of the immune system.

The Immune System

7. Describe the effects of stress on the immune system.

Factors in Physical Illness

8. Describe the relationships between psychological factors and illnesses such as headaches, cardiovascular disorders, cancer, and AIDS.

Compliance with Medical Advice

9. Describe factors that contribute to compliance with medical instructions and procedures.

Norman Cousins, former editor of the *Saturday Review,* was hospitalized for a rare and painful collagen illness that is somewhat similar to arthritis. He was not a "good patient." Right from the start he complained about hospital routines such as the low-calorie and tasteless diet, the indiscriminate taking of x-rays, and the heavy administration of drugs including pain-killers (analgesic drugs) and tranquilizers.

Even with all these procedures, his doctors gave him only a slim chance of a full recovery. Thus, as he related in his 1979 book, *Anatomy of an Illness,* Cousins decided to take things into his own hands. First, he moved from the hospital setting—which encourages passive compliance with the patient role—to a hotel room. Second, he traded the massive doses of analgesics and other drugs for laughter and vitamins. He watched films of the Marx Brothers and of his favorite TV comedy shows and focused on maintaining a positive attitude. To his physicians' amazement, he made a substantial recovery from his illness.

Later, at the age of 65, Cousins had a heart attack. He was brought to the hospital by ambulance, and the first thing he did was take charge of the ride. He refused the analgesic drug morphine and asked the driver to keep the siren off and remain within the speed limit. He declined routine medical tests and went home within a few days. As Cousins explained in *The Healing Heart: Antidote to Panic and Helplessness* (1983), he emphasized the use of diet, exercise, and a positive attitude in his return to health.

HEALTH PSYCHOLOGY

Cousins' ways of coping with illness are inspiring to anyone who has resented hospital routines or who has bridled at the physician's authority. They do not seem to have hurt Cousins; indeed, they may have helped him recover. Yet, we cannot uncritically endorse the notion that in rebellion lies the path to recovery; Cousins was more sophisticated about medicine and medical procedures than most of us. He also may have been lucky. His experiences provide us with a fascinating but scientifically uncontrolled case study.

Still, Cousins' experiences dramatize some of the relationships between psychological factors (in Cousins' case, taking control of the situation, maintaining a positive attitude, eating a nutritious diet, and exercising) and physical illness. His experience also seems to be consistent with folklore to the effect that we ought not "give in" to illness. Many of us have hardy relatives who, for example, "refuse" to get sick when people around them are succumbing to the flu.

These issues are also of vital concern to psychologists. The subfield of **health psychology** studies the relationships between psychological factors (for example, stress, attitudes, and behavior patterns) and the prevention and treatment of physical illness (Sheridan & Radmacher, 1992; Taylor, 1990). Some psychologists also consider sociocultural and environmental factors (Stokols, 1992). Cousins' own history is a useful springboard for a discussion of health psychology because, in recent years, health psychologists have been exploring the ways in which:

Health psychology The field of psychology that studies the relationships between psychological factors (e.g., attitudes, beliefs, situational influences, and behavior patterns) and the prevention and treatment of physical illness.

- stress, behavior patterns, and personality factors lead to or exacerbate physical illness (Blanchard, 1992a);
- people moderate the effects of stress;
- stress and **pathogens** interact to influence the immune system (Kiecolt-Glaser & Glaser, 1992);
- people decide to seek medical advice;
- people decide whether or not to comply with medical advice;
- psychological forms of intervention such as health education (for example, concerning nutrition, smoking, and exercise) and behavior modification contribute to physical health (Blanchard, 1992b; Dubbert, 1992; Lehrer et al., 1992).

In this chapter, we consider a number of issues in health psychology: sources of stress, factors that moderate the impact of stress, the body's response to stress, ways in which stress is related to physical illnesses, and the psychology of being sick.

SOURCES OF STRESS

In physics, stress is defined as a pressure or force exerted on a body. Tons of rock pressing on the earth, one car smashing into another, a rubber band stretching—all are types of physical stress. Psychological forces, or stresses, also "press," "push," or "pull." We may feel "crushed" by the "weight" of a big decision, "smashed" by adversity, or "stretched" to the point of "snapping."

In psychology, **stress** is the demand made on an organism to adapt, to cope, or to adjust. Some stress is healthful and necessary to keep us alert and occupied. Stress researcher Hans Selye (1980) referred to healthful stress as **eustress.** But stress that is too intense or prolonged can overtax our adjustive capacity, dampen our moods (Eckenrode, 1984; Stone & Neale, 1984), and have harmful physical effects.

Various sources of stress reflect external factors to some degree—daily hassles, life changes, pain and discomfort, frustration, and conflict. Others such as irrational beliefs and Type-A behavior are more self-imposed. Let us focus on daily hassles, life changes, and the Type-A behavior pattern.

Daily Hassles

It is the "last" straw that will break the camel's back—so goes the saying. Similarly, stresses can pile atop one another until we can no longer cope. Some of these stresses are **daily hassles,** or notable daily conditions and experiences that are threatening or harmful to a person's well-being (Lazarus, 1984a). Others are life changes. Lazarus and his colleagues (1985) analyzed a scale that measures daily hassles and found that they could be grouped as follows:

1. *Household hassles.* For example, preparing meals, shopping, and home maintenance
2. *Health hassles.* For example, physical illness, concern about medical treatment, and the side effects of medication
3. *Time-pressure hassles.* For example, having too many things to do, too many responsibilities, and not enough time
4. *Inner-concern hassles.* For example, being lonely and fearful of confrontation
5. *Environmental hassles.* For example, crime, neighborhood deterioration, and traffic noise

Pathogen A microscopic organism (e.g., bacterium or virus) that can cause disease.

Stress The demand that is made on an organism to adapt.

Eustress Stress that is healthful.

Daily hassles Notable daily conditions and experiences that are threatening or harmful to a person's well-being.

Daily Hassles. Daily hassles are notable daily conditions and experiences that are threatening or harmful to a person's well-being. The hassles shown in these photographs center around commuting. What are the daily hassles in your life?

6. *Financial-responsibility hassles.* For example, concern about owing money such as mortgage payments and loan installments
7. *Work hassles.* For example, job dissatisfaction, not liking one's work duties, and problems with co-workers
8. *Future-security hassles.* For example, concerns about job security, taxes, property investments, stock-market swings, and retirement

These hassles were linked to psychological variables such as nervousness, worrying, inability to get going, feelings of sadness, feelings of aloneness, and so on.

Life Changes: "Going Through Changes"

According to Holmes and Rahe (1967), too much of a good thing can make you ill. You might think that marrying Mr. or Ms. Right, finding a prestigious job, and moving to a better neighborhood all in the same year would propel you into a state of bliss. It might. But all these events, one on top of the other, may also lead to headaches, high blood pressure, and other ailments. As pleasant as they may be, they all entail major life changes, and life changes are another source of stress.

Life changes differ from daily hassles in two important ways: (1) Many life changes are positive and desirable, whereas all hassles, by definition, are negative. (2) Hassles tend to occur on a daily basis, whereas life changes are relatively more isolated.

Richard Lazarus and his colleagues (e.g., Kanner et al., 1981) constructed a list of 117 daily hassles for their research. They asked subjects to indicate which of these hassles the subjects had encountered and how intense they were. Holmes and Rahe (1967) constructed a scale to measure the impact of life changes by assigning marriage an arbitrary weight of 50 "life-change units." Then they asked subjects to assign units to other life changes, using marriage as the baseline. Most events were rated as less stressful than marriage, but a few were more stressful, such as the death of a spouse (100 units) and divorce (73 units). Changes in work hours and residence (20 units each) were included, regardless of whether they

Life Changes. Life changes differ from daily hassles in that they tend to be more episodic. Life changes can also be positive as well as negative. What is the relationship between life changes and illness? Is the relationship causal?

were negative or positive. Positive life changes such as an outstanding personal achievement (28 units) and going on vacation (13 units) also made the list.

Table 12.1 shows items from a Social Readjustment Rating Scale that is used with college students and the amount of life-change units associated with various life changes. Life changes with greater numbers of life-change units are considered more stressful by students.

Hassles, Life Changes, and Illness. It may seem reasonable enough that hassles and life changes—especially negative life changes—have a psychological effect on us. They may cause us to worry and may generally dampen our moods. Daily hassles (e.g., Kanner et al., 1981) and life changes also predict physical illness, even athletic injuries among adolescents (Smith et al., 1990). Holmes and Rahe found that people who "earned" more life-change units within a year according to their scale were at greater risk for illness. Other researchers have found that high numbers of life-change units amassed within a year are connected with physical and psychological problems ranging from heart disease and cancer to accidents, school failure, and relapses among persons who show abnormal behavior such as schizophrenia (Lloyd et al., 1980; Perkins, 1982; Rabkin, 1980; Thoits, 1983).

It is true that too much of a good thing—too many positive life changes—can contribute to illness. Changes are stressful and require adjustment.

Criticisms of the Research Links between Hassles, Life Changes, and Illness

Although the links between daily hassles, life changes, and illness seem to have been supported by a good deal of research, there are a number of limitations:

TABLE 12.1 Life Changes and the Number of Life-Change Units Assigned to Them by College Students

Life Changes/Life-Change Units
1. Death of a spouse, lover, or child / 94
2. Death of a parent or sibling / 88
3. Beginning formal higher education / 84
4. Death of a close friend / 83
5. Miscarriage or stillbirth of pregnancy of self, spouse, or lover / 83
6. Jail sentence / 82
7. Divorce or marital separation / 82
8. Unwanted pregnancy of self, spouse, or lover / 80
9. Abortion of unwanted pregnancy of self, spouse, or lover / 80
10. Detention in jail or other institution / 79
11. Change in dating activity / 79
12. Death of a close relative / 79
13. Change in marital situation other than divorce or separation / 78
14. Separation from significant other whom you like very much / 77
15. Change in health status or behavior of spouse or lover / 77
16. Academic failure / 77
17. Major violation of the law and subsequent arrest / 76
18. Marrying or living with lover against parents' wishes / 75
19. Change in love relationship or important friendship / 74
20. Change in health status or behavior of a parent or sibling / 73
21. Change in feelings of loneliness, insecurity, anxiety, boredom / 73
22. Change in marital status of parents / 73
23. Acquiring a visible deformity / 72
24. Change in ability to communicate with a significant other whom you like very much / 71
25. Hospitalization of a parent or sibling / 70
26. Reconciliation of marital or love relationship / 68
27. Release from jail or other institution / 68
28. Graduation from college / 68
29. Major personal injury or illness / 68
30. Wanted pregnancy of self, spouse, or lover / 67
31. Change in number or type of arguments with spouse or lover / 67
32. Marrying or living with lover with parents' approval / 66
33. Gaining a new family member through birth or adoption / 65
34. Preparing for an important exam or writing a major paper / 65
35. Major financial difficulties / 65
36. Change in the health status or behavior of a close relative or close friend / 65
37. Change in academic status / 64
38. Change in amount and nature of interpersonal conflicts / 63
39. Change in relationship with members of your immediate family / 62
40. Change in own personality / 62
41. Hospitalization of yourself or a close relative / 61
42. Change in course of study, major field, vocational goals, or work status / 60
43. Change in own financial status / 59
44. Change in status of divorced or widowed parent / 59
45. Change in number or type of arguments between parents / 59
46. Change in acceptance by peers, identification with peers, or social pressure by peers / 58
47. Change in general outlook on life / 57
48. Beginning or ceasing service in the armed forces / 57
49. Change in attitudes toward friends / 56
50. Change in living arrangements, conditions, or environment / 55
51. Change in frequency or nature of sexual experiences / 55
52. Change in parents' financial status / 55
53. Change in amount or nature of pressure from parents / 55
54. Change in degree of interest in college or attitudes toward education / 55
55. Change in the number of personal or social relationships you've formed or dissolved/ 55
56. Change in relationship with siblings / 54
57. Change in mobility or reliability of transportation / 54
58. Academic success / 54
59. Change to a new college or university / 54
60. Change in feelings of self-reliance, independence, or amount of self-discipline / 53
61. Change in number or type of arguments with roommate / 52
62. Spouse or lover beginning or ceasing work outside the home / 52
63. Change in frequency of use of amounts of drugs other than alcohol, tobacco, or marijuana / 51
64. Change in sexual morality, beliefs, or attitudes / 50
65. Change in responsibility at work / 50
66. Change in amount or nature of social activities / 50
67. Change in dependencies on parents / 50
68. Change from academic work to practical fieldwork experience or internship / 50
69. Change in amount of material possessions and concomitant responsibilities / 50
70. Change in routine at college or work / 49
71. Change in amount of leisure time / 49
72. Change in amount of in-law trouble / 49
73. Outstanding personal achievement / 49
74. Change in family structure other than parental divorce or separation / 48
75. Change in attitude toward drugs / 48
76. Change in amount and nature of competition with same sex / 48
77. Improvement of own health / 47
78. Change in responsibilities at home / 47
79. Change in study habits / 46
80. Change in number or type of arguments or close conflicts with close relatives / 46
81. Change in sleeping habits / 46
82. Change in frequency of use or amounts of alcohol / 45
83. Change in social status / 45
84. Change in frequency of use or amounts of tobacco / 45
85. Change in awareness of activities in external world / 45
86. Change in religious affiliation / 44
87. Change in type of gratifying activities / 43
88. Change in amount or nature of physical activities / 43
89. Change in address or residence / 43
90. Change in amount or nature of recreational activities / 43
91. Change in frequency of use or amounts of marijuana / 43
92. Change in social demands or responsibilities due to your age / 43
93. Court appearance for legal violation / 40
94. Change in weight or eating habits / 39
95. Change in religious activities / 37
96. Change in political views or affiliations / 34
97. Change in driving pattern or conditions / 33
98. Minor violation of the law / 31
99. Vacation or travel / 30
100. Change in number of family get-togethers / 30

Source: Peggy Blake, Robert Fry, and Michael Pesjack (1984). *Self-assessment and behavior change manual.* New York: Random House, pp. 43–47. Reprinted by permission of Random House, Inc.

Type-A Behavior. The Type-A behavior pattern is characterized by a sense of time urgency, competitiveness, and hostility.

1. *Correlational Evidence.* The links that have been uncovered between hassles, life changes, and illness are correlational rather than experimental (Dohrenwend et al., 1982; Monroe, 1982). It may seem logical that hassles and life changes cause such disorders, but people who are predisposed toward health problems may also encounter more hassles and amass more life-change units than other people do. Medical disorders, for example, may contribute to sexual problems, arguments with spouses or in-laws, changes in living conditions and personal habits, and changes in sleeping habits before they are diagnosed (Dohrenwend et al., 1984; Dohrenwend & Shrout, 1985; Monroe, 1983).
2. *Positive versus Negative Life Changes.* Positive life changes may be less disturbing than hassles and negative life changes, even when their number of life-change units is high (Lefcourt et al., 1981; Perkins, 1982; Thoits, 1983).
3. *Personality Differences.* People also respond to life stresses in different ways. For example, people who are easy-going and people who are psychologically hardy are less likely to become ill under the impact of stress.
4. *Cognitive Appraisal.* The stress linked to an event also reflects the meaning the event to the individual (Lazarus, 1991b). Pregnancy, for example, can be a positive or negative life change, depending on whether one wants and is prepared to have a child. We cognitively appraise hassles, traumatic experiences, and life changes (Creamer, 1992; Lazarus, 1991a). In responding to them, we consider their perceived danger, our values and goals, our beliefs in our coping ability, our social support, and so on.

Despite these questions concerning the links between hassles, life changes, and illness, hassles and life changes still require adjustments. It thus seems wise to be aware of the hassles and life changes in our lifestyles.

The Type-A Behavior Pattern

Some people create their own stress through the **Type-A behavior** pattern. Type-A people are highly driven, competitive, impatient, and aggressive (Thoresen & Powell, 1992). They feel rushed and under pressure and keep one eye glued firmly on the clock. They are not only prompt but often early for appointments. They eat, walk, and talk rapidly and become restless when others work slowly. They attempt to dominate group discussions. Type-A people find it difficult to surrender control or to share power. They are often reluctant to delegate authority in

Type-A behavior Behavior characterized by a sense of time urgency, competitiveness, and hostility.

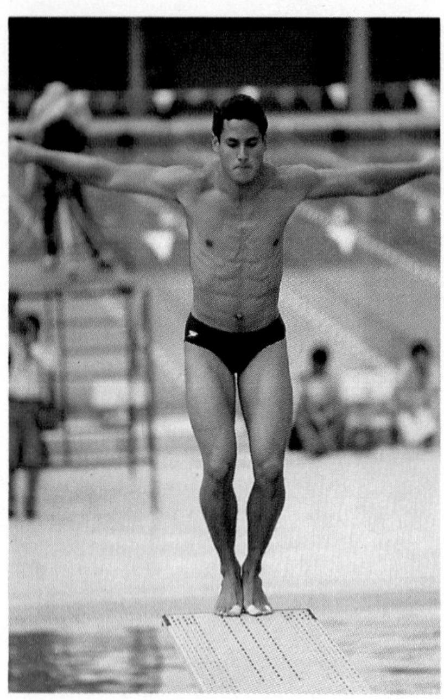
Self-Efficacy Expectancies and Performance. Outstanding athletes tend to have high self-efficacy expectancies. That is, they believe in themselves. High self-efficacy expectancies—beliefs that we can cope—moderate the amount of stress impacting upon us.

the workplace and thus increase their own workloads. Type-A people also "accentuate the negative": They are merciless in their self-criticism when they fail at a task (Moser & Dyck, 1989), and they seek out negative information about themselves in order to better themselves (Cooney & Zeichner, 1985).

Type-A people find it difficult just to go out on the tennis court and bat the ball back and forth. They watch their form, perfect their strokes, and demand regular self-improvement. The irrational belief that they must be perfectly competent and achieving in everything they undertake seems to be their motto.

Type-B people, in contrast, relax more readily and focus more on the quality of life. They are less ambitious and less impatient, and they pace themselves. Type-A people perceive time as passing more rapidly than do Type Bs, and they work more quickly (Yarnold & Grimm, 1982). Type-A people earn higher grades and more money than Type Bs of equal intelligence (Glass, 1977). Type-A people also seek greater challenges than Type Bs (Ortega & Pipal, 1984).

MODERATORS OF STRESS

There is no one-to-one relationship between a given quantity of stress and physical illness or psychological distress. Biological factors account for some of the variability in our responses. Some people inherit predispositions toward specific disorders, for example (Stokols, 1992). Psychological factors also play a role, however (Holahan & Moos, 1990). They can influence, or *moderate,* the effects of sources of stress. In this section, we discuss a number of moderators of stress: self-efficacy expectancies, psychological hardiness, a sense of humor, predictability, social support, and exercise—yes, exercise.

Self-Efficacy Expectancies: "The Little Engine That Could"?

Our **self-efficacy expectancies**—that is, our perceptions of our capacities to bring about change—have important influences on our abilities to withstand stress (Bandura, 1982, 1991). For example, when we are faced with fear-inducing objects, high self-efficacy expectancies are accompanied by *low* levels of adrenaline and noradrenaline in the bloodstream (Bandura et al., 1985). Adrenaline is secreted when we are under stress, and it arouses the body by means such as accelerating the heart rate and releasing glucose from the liver. As a result, we may have "butterflies in the stomach" and feelings of nervousness. Excessive arousal can impair our ability to manage stress by boosting our motivation beyond optimal levels and by distracting us from the tasks at hand. People with higher self-efficacy expectancies thus have biological as well as psychological reasons for remaining calmer.

Normal people have higher self-efficacy expectancies than psychiatric patients, further suggestive of the value of self-efficacy expectancies to psychological well-being (Rosenbaum & Hadari, 1985). People who are self-confident are less prone to become depressed in response to negative life events (Holahan & Moos, 1991). People with positive self-efficacy expectancies, moreover, respond more positively to treatment for depression (Hoberman et al., 1988; Steinmetz et al., 1983).

People with higher self-efficacy expectancies are more likely to lose weight or quit smoking and are less likely to relapse afterward (Condiotte & Lichtenstein, 1981; DiClemente et al., 1991; Marlatt & Gordon, 1980; Schifter & Ajzen, 1985). Women with higher self-efficacy expectancies are more likely to persist without medication in controlling pain during childbirth (Manning & Wright, 1983).

Self-efficacy expectancies Our beliefs that we can bring about desired changes through our own efforts.

The relationship between self-efficacy expectancies and performance is a two-way street. Although self-efficacy expectancies contribute to successful performance, Feltz (1982) found that success experiences (in women who were backdiving) heighten self-efficacy expectancies. There is thus something to be said for the value of giving our children (and ourselves) success experiences.

Psychological Hardiness

Psychological hardiness also helps people resist stress. The research on psychological hardiness is largely indebted to the pioneering work of Suzanne Kobasa (1979) and her colleagues, who studied business executives who resisted illness despite heavy loads of stress. In one phase of her research, Kobasa administered a battery of psychological tests to hardy and nonhardy executives and found that the hardy executives differed from the nonhardy in three important ways (Kobasa et al., 1982, pp. 169–170):

1. Hardy individuals were high in *commitment.* That is, they showed a tendency to involve themselves in, rather than experience alienation from, whatever they were doing or encountering.
2. Hardy individuals were high in *challenge.* They believed that change rather than stability was normal in life. They appraised change as an interesting incentive to personal growth, not as a threat to security.
3. Hardy individuals were also high in perceived *control* over their lives. They felt and behaved as though they were influential rather than helpless in facing the various rewards and punishments of life. Psychologically hardy people tend to have what Julian B. Rotter (1990) terms an internal **locus of control.**

According to Kobasa, hardy people are more resistant to stress because they see themselves as *choosing* to be in their stress-producing situations. They also interpret, or encode, the stress impacting upon them as making life more interesting, not as compounding the pressures to which they are subjected. Their activation of control allows them to regulate to some degree the amount of stress they will encounter at any given time (Maddi & Kobasa, 1984). Other researchers have found that even the *illusion* of being in control of one's situation tends to enhance one's mood in the face of stress (Alloy & Clements, 1992).

Kobasa and Pucetti (1983) suggest that psychological hardiness helps individuals resist stress by providing buffers between themselves and stressful life events. Buffering gives people the opportunity to draw on social supports (Ganellen & Blaney, 1984) and to use coping mechanisms such as controlling what they will be doing from day to day. Type-A individuals who show psychological hardiness are more resistant to illness, including coronary heart disease, than Type-A individuals who do not (Booth-Kewley & Friedman, 1987; Friedman & Booth-Kewley, 1987; Kobasa et al., 1983; Krantz et al., 1988; Rhodewalt & Agustsdottir, 1984).

Sense of Humor: Does "A Merry Heart Doeth Good Like a Medicine"?

The idea that humor lightens the burdens of the day and helps us cope with stress has been with us for millennia (Lefcourt & Martin, 1986). Consider the biblical maxim "a merry heart doeth good like a medicine" (Proverbs 17:22).

In *Anatomy of an Illness,* Norman Cousins (1979) reported that ten minutes of belly laughter had a powerful anesthetic effect on his pain. It allowed him to sleep for hours without analgesic medication. Laughter also might have reduced his inflammation, a finding that has led some writers to speculate that laughter

Psychological hardiness A cluster of traits that buffer stress and are characterized by commitment, challenge, and control.

Locus of control The place (locus) to which an individual attributes control over the receiving of reinforcers—either inside or outside the self.

might stimulate the output of endorphins. Benefits of humor might also result from the sudden cognitive shifts they entail and the emotional changes that accompany them.

Until recently, the benefits of humor were largely speculative and anecdotal. But an important psychological study of the moderating effects of humor on stress was run by Martin and Lefcourt (1983). The researchers administered a negative-life-events checklist and a measure of mood disturbance to college students. The mood-disturbance measure also yielded a stress score. The students were also given self-report scales concerning their sense of humor and behavioral assessments of their ability to produce humor under stressful conditions. Overall, there was a significant relationship between negative life events and stress scores: High accumulations of negative life events predicted higher levels of stress. However, students who had a greater sense of humor and who produced humor in difficult situations were less affected by negative life events than other students.

It is true that a sense of humor can moderate the impact of stress. In the experiment run by Martin and Lefcourt, humor apparently played its conjectured stress-buffering role.

Predictability

Ability to predict a stressor also moderates its impact. Predictability allows us to brace ourselves for the inevitable and, in many cases, to plan ways of coping with it. People who have accurate knowledge of medical procedures and what they will feel cope with pain more effectively than people who do not (Suls & Wan, 1989). Experiments also show that crowding is less aversive when we are forewarned about how crowding might make us feel (Baum et al., 1981; Paulus & Matthews, 1980).There is also a relationship between the desire to assume control over one's situation and the usefulness of information about impending stressors (Lazarus & Folkman, 1984). Predictability is of greater benefit to **"internals"**—that is, to people who wish to exercise control over their situations—than to **"externals"** (Affleck et al., 1987; Martelli et al., 1987).

Animal Research. Animal research tends to support the view that there are advantages to predictability, especially when predictability allows one to exercise direct control over a stressor (Weinberg & Levine, 1980). Providing laboratory rats with a signal that a stressor is approaching apparently buffers its impact.

In one study, Weiss (1972) placed three sets of rats matched according to age and weight into individual soundproof cages, as shown in Figure 12.1. The rat on the left received electric shock following a signal. It could then terminate the shock by turning the wheel. The rat in the center was shocked in tandem with the rat to the left, but it received no warning signal and could do nothing to terminate the shock. The rat to the right received no signal and no electric shock. However, it was placed in the identical apparatus, including having electrodes attached to its tail, to control for any effects of this unnatural environment.

As shown in Figure 12.2, shock led to ulceration in the rats—the definition of stressful experience in this study. The rats to the right, which received no signal and no shock, showed hardly any ulceration. Rats that received shock without warning showed the greatest amount of ulceration. Rats given warning signals and allowed to terminate the shock also developed ulcers, but less so.

The Weiss study suggests that inescapable stressors may be less harmful when they are predictable and when we act purposefully upon their arrival. The

"Internals" People who perceive the ability to attain reinforcements as being largely within themselves.

"Externals" People who perceive the ability to attain reinforcements as being largely outside themselves.

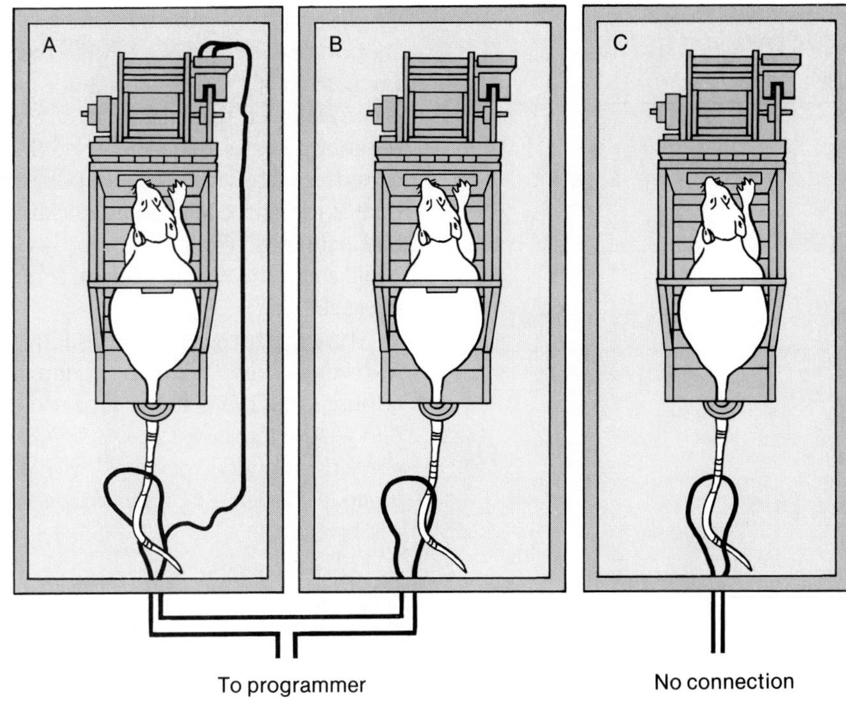

FIGURE 12.1
The Experimental Set-Up in the Weiss Study on Ulcer Formation in Rats. The rat to the left is signaled prior to receiving electric shock and can terminate the shock by turning the wheel. The rat in the center receives a shock of the same intensity and duration but is not warned of its onset and cannot terminate it. The rat to the right receives no signal and no shock.

predictability of a stressor is to some degree a situational variable. But if we learn what we can about the sources of stress in our lives—concurrent and impending—and commit ourselves to regulating them as best we can, we may, like Weiss's warned subjects, be able to brace ourselves and plan effective responses. We may not avert stress completely, but we may buffer its impact.

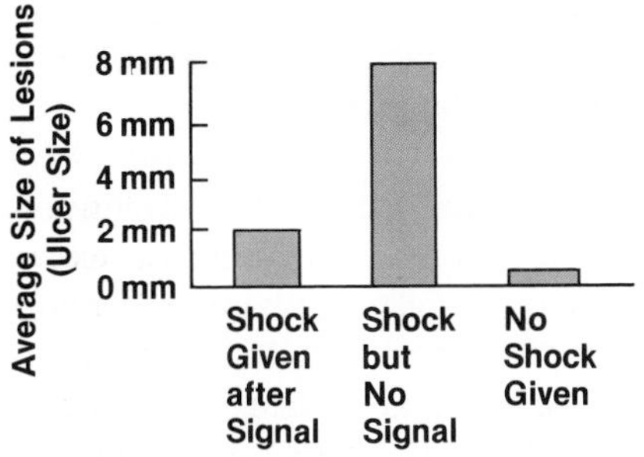

FIGURE 12.2
Effects of Predictability and Ability to Control a Stressor on Ulcer Formation in Rats. Rats who received no signals or shocks formed hardly any ulcers, as shown in Part C. Rats who received shocks but could not predict or terminate them showed the most ulcer formation. Part B shows that rats who were warned of impending shocks and could terminate them showed more ulcer formation than rats who were not shocked, but not nearly as much ulceration as rats who could not predict the onset of shocks.

Social Support

Social support, like psychological hardiness, seems to buffer the effects of stress (Burman & Margolin, 1992; Coyne & Downey, 1991; Holahan & Moos, 1990). Introverts, people who lack social skills, and people who live alone seem more prone to developing infectious diseases under stress (Cohen & Williamson, 1991). Although social support emanates from others, *we* choose whether to seek support or to try to develop social relationships.

Social supports include (Fiore, 1980; House, 1984):

1. *Emotional concern* (listening to people's problems and expressing feelings of sympathy, caring, understanding, and reassurance).
2. *Instrumental aid* (the material supports and services that facilitate adaptive behavior). For example, after a disaster, the government may arrange for low-interest loans so that survivors can rebuild. Relief organizations may provide foodstuffs, medicines, and temporary living quarters.
3. *Information* (guidance and advice that enhances people's ability to cope).
4. *Appraisal* (feedback from others as to how one is doing). This kind of support involves helping people interpret, or "make sense of," what has happened to them.
5. *Socializing* (simple conversation, recreation, even going shopping with another person). Beneficial effects are derived from socializing itself, even in ways that are not oriented toward solving problems.

Research supports the value of social support. Married people who have the support of their spouses tend to recover more rapidly from bouts of depression (McLeod et al., 1992). A study of men who were infected with the AIDS virus (H.I.V.) showed that men who received more satisfying social support were less depressed and found H.I.V.-related symptoms less stressful than men who received less satisfying social support (Hays et al., 1992). Following the nuclear accident at the Three Mile Island nuclear plant in Pennsylvania, nearby residents who had networks of social support—close relatives and friends with whom they could share the experience—reported less stress than those who did not (Fleming et al., 1982).

People who receive social support may even live longer, as found in studies of Alameda County, California (Berkman & Breslow, 1983), and Tecumseh, Michigan (House et al., 1982). In the Tecumseh study, adults were followed during a 12-year period. The mortality rate was significantly lower for men who were married, who regularly attended meetings of voluntary associations, and who frequently engaged in social leisure activities.

It is *not* true that single men live longer than married men. Actually, the reverse is true.

Exercise: Run for Your Life?

Exercise, particularly aerobic exercise, can enhance our psychological well being and help us cope with stress as well as foster physical health (Dubbert, 1992). *Aerobic exercise* is any kind of exercise that requires a sustained increase in the consumption of oxygen. Aerobic exercises include running and jogging, running in place, walking (at more than a "leisurely pace"), aerobic dancing, jumping rope, swimming, bicycle riding, basketball, racquetball, and cross-country skiing.

Anaerobic exercises, in contrast, involve short bursts of muscle activity, as in weight training, calisthenics (which usually allow rest periods between exercises), and sports such as baseball, in which there are infrequent bursts of strenuous activity. Anaerobic exercises can strengthen muscles and improve flexibility.

Physiological Benefits of Exercise. The major physiological effect of exercise is the promotion of *fitness.* Fitness is a complex concept that includes muscle strength; muscle endurance; suppleness or flexibility; cardiorespiratory, or aerobic, fitness; and changes in body composition so that the ratio of muscle to fat is increased, usually as a result of both building muscle and reducing fat.

Cardiovascular fitness, or "condition," means that the body can use greater amounts of oxygen during vigorous activity and pump more blood with each heartbeat. Because the conditioned athlete's heart pumps more blood with each beat, he or she usually has a slower pulse rate—that is, fewer heart beats per minute. During aerobic exercise, however, the person may double or triple her or his resting heart rate for many minutes at a time.

Stress has cardiovascular costs. Research suggests that sustained physical activity not only fosters fitness but also reduces the risks of cardiovascular disorders, as measured by incidence of heart attacks and mortality rates. A well-known English study by Morris and his colleagues (1953) correlated the incidence of cardiovascular disorders and physical activity among transportation and postal workers. Conductors aboard London's double-decker buses, who moved about the buses collecting fares, had about half the heart attacks of the more sedentary drivers. Among postal workers, mail carriers had significantly fewer heart attacks than clerks.

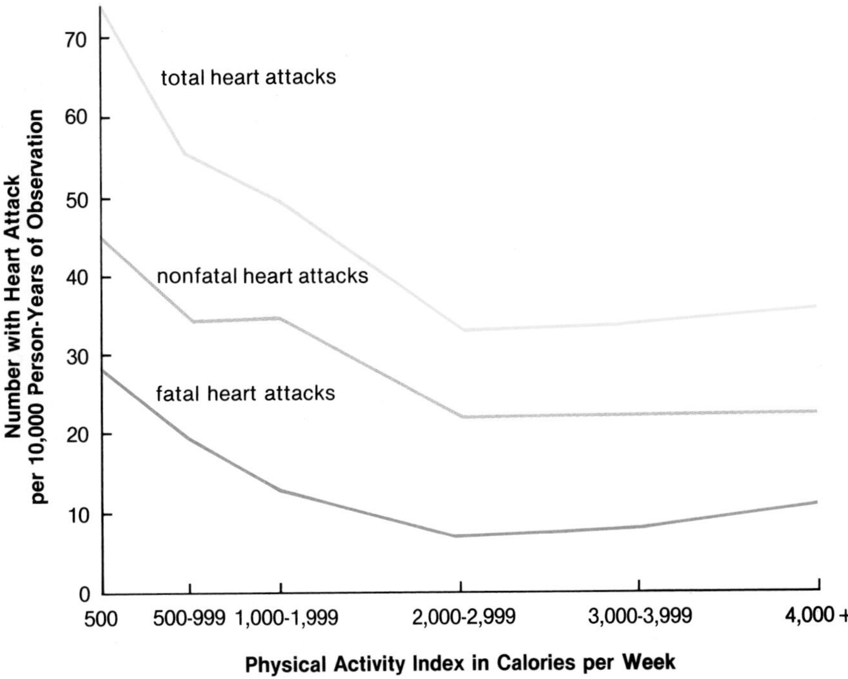

FIGURE 12.3
Incidence of Heart Attacks and Level of Physical Activity. Paffenbarger and his colleagues have correlated the incidence of heart attacks with level of physical activity among 17,000 Harvard alumni. The incidence of heart attacks declines as the activity level rises to burning about 2,000 calories a week by means of physical activity. Above 2,000 calories a week, however, the incidence of heart attacks begins to climb gradually again, although not steeply.

Paffenbarger (1972) and his colleagues surveyed some 3,700 San Francisco longshoremen and found that those who handled heavy cargo had only about 60 percent as many heart attacks as those engaged in less strenuous activity. To date, Paffenbarger and his colleagues (1978, 1984, 1986) have been tracking some 17,000 Harvard University alumni by means of university records and questionnaires and correlating the group's incidence of heart attacks with their levels of physical activity. As shown in Figure 12.3, the incidence of heart attacks among the alumni declines as the physical activity level rises to burning about 2,000 calories a week—the exercise equivalent of jogging about 20 miles a week. But above 2,000 calories, the incidence of heart attacks begins to climb again, although not steeply. Inactive alumni run the highest risks of heart attacks, and alumni who burn at least 2,000 calories a week through exercise live two years longer, on the average, than their less active counterparts.

Harvard University alumni who burn about 2,000 calories a week in exercise do live two years longer, on the average, than their sedentary counterparts.

Of course, there is an important limitation to the Morris and Paffenbarger studies: They are correlational, not experimental. It is possible that persons in better health choose to engage in, and enjoy, higher levels of physical activity. If such is the case, then their lower incidence of heart attacks and their lower mortality rates would be attributable to their initial superior health, not to physical activity.

An experiment with monkeys appears to confirm the cardiovascular benefits of sustained activity, however (Kramsch et al., 1981). Three groups of nine monkeys each were assigned at random to the following conditions: a sedentary group of monkeys who received a low-fat diet; another sedentary group switched to a diet high in fats and cholesterol after 12 months; and an active group of monkeys who gradually worked up to an hour of exercise on a treadmill three times weekly and who were also switched to the diet high in fats and cholesterol. The animals were monitored over a 42-month period. It turns out that the monkeys who exercised on the treadmill had lower levels of health-impairing cholesterol than their sedentary counterparts. Moreover, arteriosclerosis and sudden death were significantly more frequent occurrences within the sedentary groups.

Psychological Benefits of Exercise. Psychologists have been keenly interested in the effects of exercise on psychological variables such as depression. Articles have appeared on exercise as "therapy"—for example, "running therapy" (Greist, 1984).

Depression is characterized by inactivity and feelings of helplessness. Aerobic exercise is, in a sense, the "opposite" of inactivity, and success at it might also help alleviate feelings of helplessness. In a notable experiment, McCann and Holmes (1984) assigned mildly depressed college women at random to aerobic exercise, muscle relaxation group, or no treatment. The relaxation group showed some improvement, but aerobic exercise made dramatic inroads on students' depression. Other experiments also suggest that aerobic exercise alleviates feelings of depression, at least among mildly and moderately depressed individuals (Buffone, 1984; Greist, 1984).

Still other research suggests that sustained exercise alleviates feelings of anxiety (Long, 1984) and boosts feelings of self-esteem (Sonstroem, 1984). However, Sonstroem points out that in all these studies it might not be the exercise itself that is responsible for the psychological benefits. Sonstroem (1984) notes that the apparent benefits of exercise might also be attributed to the following:

1. feelings of physical well-being
2. improved physical health
3. achievement of (exercise) goals
4. an enhanced sense of control over one's body
5. the social support of fellow exercisers, or even
6. the attention of the researchers

Reasons 1 through 5 still provide very good reasons for exercising.

PHYSIOLOGICAL RESPONSES TO STRESS

How is it that too much of a good thing—or that anxiety, frustration, or conflict—can make us ill? We do not have all the answers yet, but those we have suggest that the body under stress is like a clock with an alarm system that does not shut off until its energy is dangerously depleted.

General Adaptation Syndrome

The body's response to different stressors shows some similarities, whether the stressor is a bacterial invasion, a perceived danger, a major life change, an inner conflict, or a wound. Selye (1976) has labeled this response the **general adaptation syndrome** (GAS). The GAS consists of three stages: an alarm reaction, a resistance stage, and an exhaustion stage.

The Alarm Reaction. The **alarm reaction** is triggered by perception of a stressor. This reaction mobilizes or arouses the body in preparation for defense. Cannon (1929) had earlier termed this alarm system the **fight-or-flight reaction.** The alarm reaction involves a number of body changes that are initiated by the brain and further regulated by the endocrine system and the sympathetic

General adaptation syndrome Selye's term for a hypothesized three-stage response to stress. Abbreviated *GAS.*

Alarm reaction The first stage of the GAS, which is triggered by the impact of a stressor and characterized by sympathetic activity.

Fight-or-flight reaction A hypothesized innate adaptive response to the perception of danger.

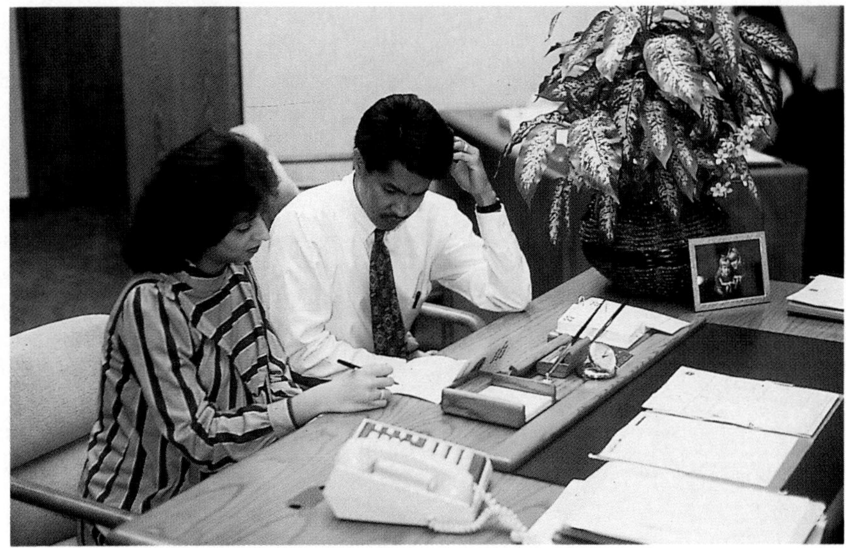

Are Their Alarm Systems Going Off? The alarm reaction of the general adaptation syndrome can be triggered by daily hassles and life changes—such as taking out a large loan—as well as by physical threats. When the stressor persists, diseases of adaptation may eventually develop.

division of the autonomic nervous system (ANS). Let us consider the roles of these two body systems.

There is a domino effect in the endocrine system when a stressor is perceived. The hypothalamus secretes corticotrophin-releasing hormone (CRH), which, in turn, stimulates the pituitary gland to secrete adrenocorticotrophic hormone (ACTH). ACTH then acts upon the adrenal cortex, causing it to release cortisol and other steroids that help the body respond to stress by fighting inflammation and allergic reactions (such as difficulty in breathing).

Two other hormones that play a major role in the alarm reaction are secreted by the adrenal medulla. The sympathetic division of the ANS activates the adrenal medulla, causing a mixture of adrenaline and noradrenaline to be released. The mixture arouses the body to cope with threats and stress by accelerating the heart rate and causing muscle tissue and the liver to release glucose (sugar). In this way, energy is provided for the fight-or-flight reaction, which was inherited from a time when many stressors were life threatening. This reaction activates the body so that it is prepared to fight or flee from a predator. Many of the bodily changes that occur in the fight-or-flight reaction are outlined in Table 12.2. Historically, the reaction was triggered by a predator at the edge of a thicket or by a sudden rustling in the undergrowth. Today, it is also aroused when you chafe at the bit in stop-and-go traffic or learn that your mortgage payments are going to be increased. Once the threat is removed, the body returns to a lower state of arousal.

Because cortisol and adrenaline are secreted in response to stress, the amount of these substances in the body serves as an objective measure of stress (see, for example, Brantley et al., 1988). In their research, psychologists frequently use the amount of cortisol in the saliva or urine and the amount of adrenaline in the urine as biological measures of stress.

TABLE 12.2: Components of the Alarm Reaction

Corticosteroids are secreted	Muscles tense
Adrenaline is secreted	Blood shifts from internal organs to the skeletal musculature
Noradrenaline is secreted	Digestion is inhibited
Respiration rate increases	Sugar is released from the liver
Heart rate increases	Blood coagulability increases
Blood pressure increases	

The alarm reaction is triggered by various types of stressors. It is defined by release of corticosteroids and adrenaline and by activity of the sympathetic branch of the autonomic nervous system. It prepares the body to fight or flee from a source of danger.

Our ancestors lived in situations in which the alarm reaction would not be activated for long. They fought or ran quickly or, to put it bluntly, they died. Sensitive alarm reactions contributed to survival.

Are sensitive alarm reactions still an advantage? Our ancestors did not spend years in the academic grind or carry 30-year mortgages. Contemporary pressures may activate our alarm systems for hours, days, or months at a time. For this reason, highly sensitive systems may now be a handicap. Pardine and Napoli (1983) administered a life-events questionnaire and found that students who reported high levels of recent stress showed higher heart rates and blood pressure levels in response to an experimentally induced stressor than students who reported low levels of stress. In other words, students with more sensitive alarm reactions recover less rapidly from stressors and find their lives generally more stressful. We cannot change our heredity—sensitive alarm systems tend to remain so. Later in the chapter, however, we shall explore methods for lowering our levels of arousal (turning the alarm system down or off).

The Resistance Stage. If the alarm reaction mobilizes the body and the stressor is not removed, we enter the adaptation stage, or **resistance stage,** of the GAS. The levels of endocrine and sympathetic activity are not as high as in the alarm reaction, but they are still greater than normal. In this stage, the body attempts to restore lost energy and repair bodily damage.

The Exhaustion Stage. If the stressor is still not adequately dealt with, we may enter the final or **exhaustion stage** of the GAS. Our individual capacities for resisting stress vary, but all of us, even the strongest of Richter's rats, eventually become exhausted when stress persists indefinitely. Our muscles become fatigued, and we deplete our bodies of resources required for combating stress. With exhaustion, the parasympathetic division of the ANS may predominate. As a result, our heartbeats and respiration rates slow down, and many of the body responses that had characterized sympathetic activity are reversed. It might sound as if we would profit from the respite, but remember that we are still under stress—and possibly an external threat. Continued stress in the exhaustion stage may lead to what Selye terms "diseases of adaptation"—from allergies and hives to ulcers and coronary heart disease—and, ultimately, to death.

Let us now consider the effects of stress on the body's immune system. Our discussion will pave the way for understanding the links between various psychological factors and physical illnesses.

THE IMMUNE SYSTEM

Given the complexities of our bodies and the fast pace of scientific change, it is common for us to think of ourselves as being highly dependent on trained professionals such as physicians to cope with illness. Yet, we actually do most of this coping by ourselves, by means of our **immune systems.**

Functions of the Immune System

The immune system has several functions that help us combat disease.

Destruction of Pathogens. One way in which we combat physical disorders is by producing white blood cells that routinely engulf and kill pathogens such as bacteria, fungi, and viruses; wornout body cells; even cells that have changed into cancerous cells. White blood cells are technically termed **leukocytes.** Leukocytes carry on microscopic warfare. They engage in search-and-destroy missions in which they "recognize" and then eliminate foreign agents and unhealthy cells.

Resistance stage The second stage of the GAS, characterized by prolonged sympathetic activity in an effort to restore lost energy and repair damage. Also called the *adaptation stage.*

Exhaustion stage The third stage of the GAS, characterized by weakened resistance and possible deterioration.

Immune system The system of the body that recognizes and destroys foreign agents (antigens) that invade the body.

Leukocytes White blood cells. (Derived from the Greek words *leukos,* meaning "white," and *kytos,* literally meaning "a hollow," but used to refer to cells.)

Recognition of Pathogens. Leukocytes recognize foreign agents by their surface fragments to enhance the effectiveness of future combat. The surface fragments are termed **antigens** because the body reacts to them by developing specialized proteins, or **antibodies,** that attach to the foreign bodies, inactivating them and marking them for destruction. The immune system "remembers" how to battle these antigens by maintaining them in the bloodstream, often for many years.[1]

Inflammation. **Inflammation** is a third function of the immune system. When injury occurs, blood vessels in the area first contract (to stem bleeding) but then dilate. Dilation increases the flow of blood to the damaged area, causing the redness and warmth that characterize inflammation. The increased blood supply also brings in large numbers of white blood cells to combat invading microscopic life forms such as bacteria that might otherwise use the local damage as a point of entry into the body.

It is true that countless microscopic warriors within our bodies are carrying out search-and-destroy missions against foreign agents at any given moment. They are white blood cells.

Effects of Stress on the Immune System

Psychologists, biologists, and medical researchers have recently been exploring the relationships between psychological factors such as stress, depression, and the immune system (Kiecolt-Glaser & Glaser, 1992; Weisse, 1992). One of the reasons that stress eventually exhausts us is that it stimulates us to produce steroids. Steroids suppress the functioning of the immune system. Suppression has negligible effects when steroids are secreted intermittently, but persistent secretion impairs the functioning of the immune system by decreasing inflammation and interfering with the formation of antibodies. As a consequence, susceptibility to various illnesses, including the common cold (Cohen et al., 1991), increases.

Empirical Findings Concerning Stress–Immune-System Relationships. Research shows that chronic stress suppresses the immune system (O'Leary, 1990). It also demonstrates the moderating effects of psychological factors such as control, the need for power, and social support.

An experiment with laboratory rats and electric shock mirrored the method of Weiss (1972), as described earlier. This time, however, the dependent variable was activity of the immune system, not ulcer formation (Laudenslager et al., 1983). The rats were exposed to inevitable electric shocks, but, as in the Weiss study, one group of rats could terminate the shock. Rats who could *not* exert control over the stressor showed immune-system deficits, but the rats who could terminate the shock showed no deficiency.

One study with people focused on dental students (Jemmott et al., 1983). Students showed lower immune-system functioning, as measured by lower levels of antibodies in the saliva, during stressful school periods than immediately following vacations. Moreover, students with many friends showed less suppression of the immune system than students with few friends. Social support apparently buffered school stresses.

[1]Vaccination is the introduction of a weakened form of an antigen (usually a bacteria or a virus) into the body to stimulate the production of antibodies. Antibodies can confer immunity for many years, in some cases for a lifetime. Smallpox has been eradicated by means of vaccination, and scientists are searching for a vaccine against the AIDS virus.

Antigen A substance that stimulates the body to mount an immune-system response to it. (The contraction of *anti*body *gen*erator.)

Antibodies Substances formed by white blood cells that recognize and destroy antigens.

Inflammation Increased blood flow to an injured area of the body, resulting in redness, warmth, and an increased supply of white blood cells.

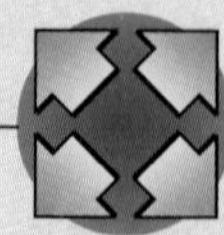

WORLD OF DIVERSITY

Health Psychology and Diversity

Recently, a cigarette company began to market a new brand, Uptown, which was specifically designed to appeal to African Americans. There was such a clamor from civil-rights groups and the media, however, that the ad campaign was canceled, and manufacture of the brand was discontinued.

Health psychologists have noted that health-related behaviors and illnesses have differential impacts on diverse segments of the community. Consider the following examples:

Forty percent of deaths from AIDS occur within ethnic minorities in the United States, predominantly among African and Hispanic Americans (USBC, 1990). Only 12 percent of the American population is African-American (Barringer, 1991), but African Americans yield over 20 percent of AIDS cases. Only .9 percent is Hispanic-American, but Hispanic Americans yield 14 percent of AIDS cases (Thompson, 1991). African- and Hispanic-American women are most likely to contract AIDS from sex with men who inject ("shoot up") drugs.

The incidence of sickle-cell anemia is highest among African and Hispanic Americans. The incidence of Tay-Sachs disease is greatest among Jews of East European origin.

The cigarette brand Virginia Slims is designed and marketed to appeal to women. A new brand, Dakota, will share this appeal (McCarthy, 1990). Note, too, that whereas most population groups are now smoking less than they did a generation ago, young career women are smoking more—accounting for a greater incidence of lung cancer and other smoking-related illnesses within this group.

African Americans are five to seven times more likely than non-Hispanic white Americans to suffer from hypertension (Leary, 1991). They are also more likely to suffer from hypertension than Black Africans, which leads many health professionals to believe that environmental factors such as stress, diet, and smoking contribute to high blood pressure in Black people who are genetically vulnerable to it (Leary, 1991).

Men are more likely to suffer from coronary (heart) disease than women—until menopause. After menopause, women—apparently no longer protected by high levels of estrogen—are dramatically more likely to incur heart disease.

At all ages, males are more likely to drink alcohol heavily than females. Heavy drinking is found less often among the elderly than among young and middle adults.

Another study with students found that the stress of examinations depressed immune-system response to the Epstein-Barr virus, which causes fatigue and other problems (Glaser et al., 1991). Moreover, students who were lonely showed greater suppression of the immune system than students who had more social support. In a study of elderly people, it was found that a combination of relaxation training, which decreases sympathetic activity, and training in coping skills *improves* immune-system functioning (Glaser et al., 1991).

Exercise and the Immune System. If stress suppresses the immune system, aerobic exercise appears to give the immune system a boost (Antoni et al., 1990, 1991; Dubbert, 1992). In one experiment, for example, people rode exercise bicycles for three 45-minute sessions a week over a ten-week period. After ten weeks of aerobic training, not only did they show a significantly increased volume of oxygen consumption, which is a measure of aerobic fitness, they also showed significant increases in their numbers of T_4 cells and other components of their immune systems (Laperriere et al., 1990, 1991).

FACTORS IN PHYSICAL ILLNESS

Physical illnesses ranging from heart disease to cancer can often only be understood in the context of many variables or factors (Stokols, 1992). Biological factors

The incidence of heavy drinking is highest in the nation's capitol—Washington, DC, and lowest in the states of Utah and West Virginia (CDC, 1990).

Anorexia and bulimia nervosa (described in Chapter 13) are uncommon among poor people, but obesity is most prevalent among them. The incidence of obesity is also greater among cultural groups in which many people associate obesity with happiness and health—as among some Haitian (Laguerre, 1981) and Puerto Rican groups (Harwood, 1981). The urban ghetto fosters obesity because junk food is heavily promoted and many residents eat as a way of coping with stress (Freeman, 1991).

African Americans are more likely than white Americans to contract most forms of cancer, and, once they contract cancer, African Americans are also more likely than white Americans to die from cancer (Andersen, 1992; Bal, 1992). The discouraging results for African Americans may be largely due to lower socioeconomic status (Baquet et al., 1991).

Death rates from cancer are higher in nations such as the Netherlands, Denmark, England, Canada, and—yes—the United States, where the population has a high daily fat intake (Cohen, 1987). Death rates from cancer are much lower in nations such as Thailand, the Philippines, and Japan, where the daily fat intake is markedly lower. Don't assume that the difference is racial just because Thailand, the Philippines, and Japan are Asian nations! The diets of Japanese Americans are similar in fat content to those of other Americans—and so are their death rates from cancer.

Because of dietary differences, Japanese-American men living in California and Hawaii are two to three times more likely to become obese than Japanese men who live in Japan (Curb & Marcus, 1991).

There are health-care "overusers" and "underusers" among diverse cultural groups and within each gender. By and large, however, women are more likely than men to regard unusual or painful sensations as symptoms and to seek health care. Men are more likely to ignore these sensations until they are forced to attend to them (Sheridan & Radmacher, 1992). Irish Americans are likely to stoically deny pain. Jews tend to practice prevention and to seek medical care rapidly. The nation's 20½ million Hispanic Americans visit physicians less often than African Americans and non-Hispanic white Americans because of lack of health insurance, difficulty speaking English, misgivings about medical technology, and—for illegal aliens—fear of deportation (Perez-Stable, 1991; Thompson, 1991).

such as family history of illness, pathogens, inoculations, injuries, age, and gender may strike us as the most obvious causes (or moderators) of illness. As shown in Table 12.3, however, psychological (personality and behavioral), social (socioeconomic and sociocultural), technological, and natural environmental factors also play key roles in health and illness.

This broad view of illness not only provides insight into the causes of illness, but also suggests avenues of prevention and treatment. In this section, we focus on the relationships between biological, psychological, and other factors and illnesses such as headaches, cardiovascular disorders, and cancer.

Headaches

Headaches are among the most common stress-related physical ailments. About one American in five suffers from severe headaches (Bonica, 1980).

Muscle-Tension Headache. The single most frequent kind of headache is the muscle-tension headache. We are likely to contract muscles in the shoulders, neck, forehead, and scalp during the first two stages of the GAS. Persistent stress can lead to persistent contraction of these muscles, giving rise to muscle-tension headaches. Such headaches usually come on gradually. They are most often characterized by dull, steady pain on both sides of the head and feelings of tightness or pressure.

TABLE 12.3: Factors in Health and Illness: Biological, Psychological, Social, Technological, and Natural Environmental

Biological	**Psychological** *Personality*	*Behavioral*	**Social: Socioeconomic and Sociocultural**	**Technological**	**Natural Environmental**
Family history of illness	Self-efficacy expectancies	Diet (intake of calories, fats, fiber, vitamins, etc.)	Socioeconomic status	Adequacy of available health care	Natural disasters (earthquakes, floods, hurricanes, drought, extremes of temperature, tornados)
Exposure to infectious pathogens (e.g., bacteria and viruses)	Psychological hardiness	Consumption of alcohol	Availability and use of social support	Vehicular safety	Radon
Functioning of the immune system	Optimism	Cigarette smoking	Social climate in the home environment and in the workplace	Architectural features (e.g., injury-resistant design, nontoxic construction materials, aesthetic design, air quality, noise insulation)	
Inoculations	Attributional style (how one explains one's failures to oneself)	Level of physical activity	Major life changes such as death of a spouse or divorce	Aesthetics of residential, workplace, and communal architecture and landscape architecture	
Medication history	Health locus of control (belief that one is in charge of one's own health)	Sleep patterns	Health-related cultural and religious beliefs and practices	Water quality	
Congenital disabilities	Introversion/ extraversion	Safety practices (e.g., driving with seat belts; careful driving; practice of sexual abstinence, monogamy, or "safe sex"; attaining of comprehensive prenatal care)	Major economic changes (e.g., taking out a large mortgage, losing one's job)	Solid waste treatment and sanitation	
Physiological conditions (e.g., hypertension, serum cholesterol level)	Coronary-prone (Type-A) personality	Regular medical and dental check-ups	Health promotion programs in the workplace or the community	Pollution	
Reactivity of the cardiovascular system (e.g., "hot reactor")	Tendencies to express feelings of anger and frustration	Compliance with medical and dental advice	Health-related legislation	Radiation	
Age	Depression/ anxiety	Interpersonal/ social skills	Availability of health insurance	Global warming	
Gender	Hostility/ suspiciousness			Ozone depletion	

This table incorporates elements from Table 2, p. 13 in D. Stokols. (1992). Establishing and maintaining healthy environments: Toward a social ecology of health promotion. *American Psychologist, 47,* 6–22.

Migraine Headache. Most other headaches, including the severe migraine headache, are vascular in nature—that is, stemming from changes in the blood supply to the head. **Migraine headaches** have preheadache phases during which the arteries that supply the head with blood are constricted, decreasing blood flow, and headache phases during which the arteries are dilated, increasing the blood flow. There is often a warning "aura" accompanying the preheadache phase that may be characterized by visual problems and perception of unusual odors. The attacks themselves are often attended by intensified sensitivity to light; loss of appetite, nausea, and vomiting; sensory and motor disturbances such as loss of balance; and changes in mood. The so-called common migraine headache is identified by sudden onset and throbbing on one side of the head. The so-called classic migraine is known by sensory and motor disturbances that precede the pain. The origins of migraine headaches are not clearly understood. It is believed, however, that they can be induced by barometric pressure; among women, the hormonal changes of the period prior to and during menstruation (Brody, 1992); pollen; certain drugs; the chemical monosodium glutamate (MSG), which is often used to enhance the flavor of food; chocolates; aged cheeses; and beer, champagne, and red wines. Type-A behavior may contribute to migraine headaches. In one study, 53 percent of 30 migraine sufferers showed the Type-A behavior pattern, as compared with 23 percent of 30 muscle-tension headache sufferers (Rappaport et al., 1988).

Regardless of the original source of the headache, we can unwittingly propel ourselves into a vicious cycle: Headache pain is a stressor that can lead us to increase, rather than relax, muscle tension in the neck, shoulders, scalp, and face.

Migraine headaches Throbbing headaches that are connected with changes in the supply of blood to the head.

It is true that most headaches are caused by muscle tension. And those that are not can be exacerbated by muscle tension.

Treatment. Aspirin and ibuprofen frequently decrease pain, including headache pain, by inhibiting the production of the prostaglandins that help initiate transmission of pain messages to the brain. Behavioral methods can also help. Progressive relaxation focuses on decreasing muscle tension and has been shown to be highly effective in relieving muscle-tension headaches (Blanchard, 1992b; Blanchard et al., 1990a, 1991). Biofeedback training that alters the flow of blood to the head has been used effectively to treat migraine headache (Blanchard, 1992b; Blanchard et al., 1990b). People who are sensitive to MSG or red wine can ask that MSG be left out of their dishes and can switch to a white wine.

Why, under stress, do some of us develop headaches, others develop hypertension, and still others suffer no physical problems? In the following sections, we see that there may be an interaction between stress and predisposing biological and psychological differences between individuals (Nevid et al., 1994; Walker, 1983).

Hypertension

About one American in five is afflicted by **hypertension,** or abnormally high blood pressure (Leary, 1991). When high blood pressure has no identifiable causes, it is referred to as *essential hypertension.* Arousal of the sympathetic division of the ANS heightens the blood pressure, and, when we are very stressed, we may believe that we can feel our blood pressure "pounding through the roof." Such ideas are usually misleading, however. Although most people believe that they would be able to recognize symptoms of hypertension, most of the time they cannot (Baumann & Leventhal, 1985; Meyer et al., 1985). It is thus important for us to check our blood pressure regularly.

Hypertension predisposes victims to other cardiovascular disorders such as arteriosclerosis, heart attacks, and strokes (Berkman et al., 1983). Blood pressure rises in situations in which people must be constantly on guard against threats, whether in combat, in the work place, or in the home.

Treatment. High blood pressure can frequently be controlled by medication, but because of lack of symptoms, many patients do not take medicine reliably. Dietary components, particularly sodium (salt), can heighten the blood pressure. African Americans, who are more susceptible to high blood pressure than white people, pay somewhat more attention to the salt in their diet (Burros, 1988).

Relaxation training (Agras et al., 1983), meditation (Benson et al., 1973), and aerobic exercise (Brownell & Wadden, 1992; Danforth et al., 1990) all show promise in the treatment of hypertension. So does dietary behavior modification, as highlighted in a study of 496 patients whose blood pressure had been normalized by medication for five years (Langford et al., 1985). The patients were taken off their medication and assigned to either a general weight-loss diet or a sodium-restricted diet. Seventy-two percent of those in the weight-loss group and 78 percent of those in the sodium-restricted group were able to maintain normal blood pressure without medication.

Cardiovascular Disorders

Cardiovascular disorders cause nearly half the deaths in the United States (USDHHS, 1984). Such disorders include heart disease and disorders of the circulatory system, the most common of which is stroke.

Hypertension High blood pressure.

Cardiovascular disorders Diseases of the cardiovascular system, including heart disease, hypertension, and arteriosclerosis.

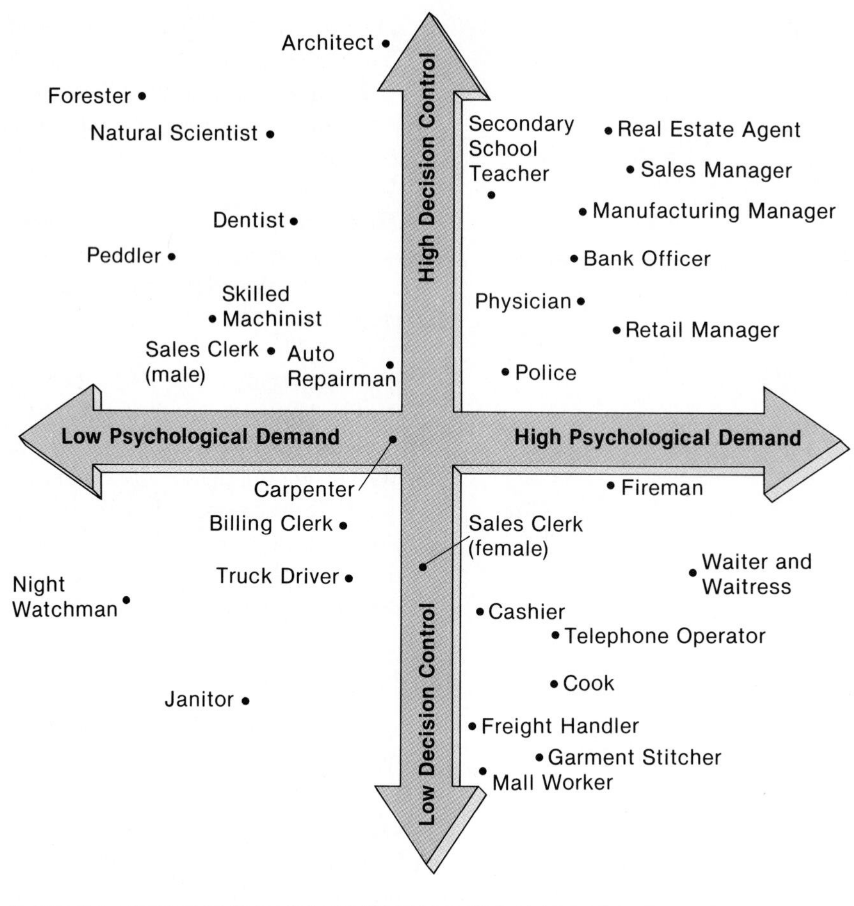

FIGURE 12.4
The Job-Strain Model. This model highlights the psychological demands made by various occupations and the amount of personal (decision) control they allow. Occupations characterized by both high demand and low decision control place workers at greatest risk for cardiovascular disorders.

There are several risk factors for cardiovascular disorders:

1. *Family history.* People whose families show a history of cardiovascular disease are more likely to develop cardiovascular disease themselves.
2. *Physiological conditions.* Obesity (Manson et al., 1990), hypertension, and high **serum cholesterol** levels (Rossouw et al., 1990; Stampfer et al., 1991) are examples.
3. *Patterns of consumption.* Patterns include heavy drinking, smoking (Epstein & Perkins, 1988; Eysenck, 1991), overeating, and eating food high in cholesterol, like saturated fats and tropical oils (Jeffery, 1988, 1991).
4. *Type-A behavior.* Evidence is mixed as to whether the Type-A behavior pattern—or one or more of its components—places people at risk for cardiovascular disorders. Still, most studies suggest that there is at least a modest relationship between Type-A behavior and cardiovascular disorders (Thoresen & Powell, 1992).
5. *Job strain.* Overtime work, assembly-line labor, and exposure to conflicting demands all make their contributions (Jenkins, 1988). So-called high-strain work, which makes high demands on workers but affords them little personal control, places workers at the highest risk (Karasek et al., 1982; Krantz et al., 1988). As shown in Figure 12.4, the work of waiters and waitresses may best fit this description.
6. *Chronic fatigue and emotional strain.*
7. *A physically inactive life-style* (Dubbert, 1992).

Serum cholesterol Cholesterol found in the blood.

Behavior Modification for Reducing Risk Factors. Once cardiovascular disease has been diagnosed, there are a number of medical treatments, including surgery and medication. However, persons who have not encountered cardiovascular disease (as well as those who have) can profit from behavior modification that is intended to reduce the risk factors. These methods include:

1. *Stopping smoking* (Lichtenstein & Glasgow, 1992).
2. *Weight control* (Brownell & Wadden, 1992).
3. *Reducing hypertension.*
4. *Lowering serum cholesterol.* The major method involves cutting down on foods high in cholesterol and saturated fats, but exercise can also help (Dubbert, 1992; Jeffery, 1988).
5. *Modifying type-A behavior* (Friedman & Ulmer, 1984).
6. *Exercise.* Aerobic exercise apparently raises blood levels of high-density lipoproteins (HDL, or "good cholesterol") (Wood et al., 1991). HDL lowers the amount of low-density lipoproteins (LDL, or "bad cholesterol") in the blood—another way in which exercise may lower the risk of heart attacks.

We end this section with good news. Many risk factors for cardiovascular disorders, such as smoking and diet, have been known for 25 years or more. Many people have responded to this knowledge by changing their lifestyles, and the incidence of coronary heart disease has declined (Pell & Fayerweather, 1985; Stamler, 1985a, 1985b). There is one particular message for readers of this book: *better-educated* individuals are more likely to modify health-impairing behavior patterns and reap the benefits of change (Johnston et al., 1992).

Asthma

> *Asthma doesn't seem to bother me anymore unless I'm around cigars or dogs. The thing that would bother me most would be a dog smoking a cigar.*
>
> Steve Allen

Asthma is a respiratory disorder characterized by episodic constriction of the main tubes of the windpipe (the bronchi), oversecretion of mucus, and inflammation of air passageways (Israel et al.,1990). Sufferers may wheeze and intermittently find it difficult to breathe. Asthma attacks can be triggered by an allergic reaction; by cold, dry air; by stress; by emotional responses such as anger; even by laughing too hard (Brody, 1988). Asthma has been linked to stress, but the link is controversial. In one study, for example, efforts to induce asthma attacks in sufferers by subjecting them to stress led to a slightly decreased air flow but not to an actual attack (Weiss et al., 1976). Other evidence suggests that asthma sufferers can experience attacks in response to the suggestion that their air flow will become constricted (Luparello et al., 1971), suggesting that the stress of worrying about an attack can help bring one on. A number of reports suggest that asthma sufferers can improve their breathing by muscle relaxation training (Lehrer et al., 1992), biofeedback that helps relax facial muscles (Klotses et al., 1991), and family therapy that reduces the interpersonal stresses that affect asthmatic children (Lehrer et al., 1992). Asthma has also been connected with maternal smoking during pregnancy (Martinez et al., 1992) and with respiratory infections (Alexander, 1981). Such evidence again suggests an interaction between the psychological and the biological.

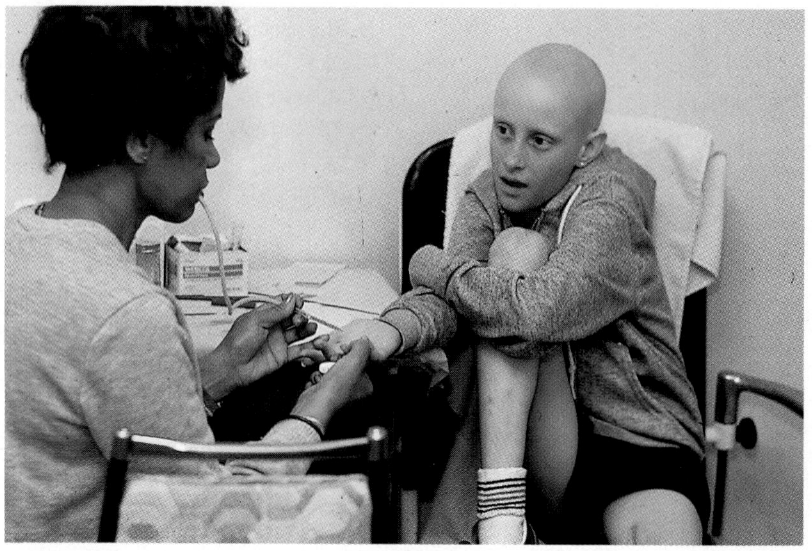

How Have Health Psychologists Helped This Young Cancer Patient? Cancer is a medical disorder, but psychologists have contributed to the treatment of cancer patients. For example, psychologists help cancer patients remain in charge of their lives, combat feelings of hopelessness and helplessness, cope with stress, and manage the side effects of chemotherapy.

Cancer

Cancer afflicts plants and animals as well as people. Cancer is characterized by the development of abnormal, or mutant, cells that reproduce rapidly and rob the body of nutrients. Cancerous cells may take root anywhere: in the blood (leukemia), bones, digestive tract, lungs, and genital organs. If not controlled early, the cancerous cells may metastasize (establish colonies elsewhere in the body). We apparently develop cancer cells quite frequently, but the immune system normally surveys the body and destroys cancer cells. Evidence suggests that people whose immune systems are compromised by physical or psychological factors are more likely to develop tumors (Antoni, 1987; Greenberg, 1987; Sheridan & Radmacher, 1992).

With all the talk of environmental toxins and the assorted hazards of contemporary life, one might expect that cancer rates have been skyrocketing. This is not the case. According to the National Institutes of Health (1985), cancers of the bladder, prostate, colon, and rectum have been stable since the 1940s. Cancer of the stomach has been declining. Lung cancer increased markedly between the 1940s and 1980 but has recently leveled off. However, a recent rise in cases among women has offset a decline among men. Smoking seems to be the culprit. Women who have entered the work force and taken managerial positions have increased their smoking. Men, however, have been smoking less.

Risk Factors. As with cardiovascular and many other disorders, people can inherit dispositions toward developing cancer (Eysenck, 1991; Moolgavkar, 1983). Many behavior patterns markedly heighten the risk for cancer, however, such as smoking, drinking alcohol (especially in women), ingesting animal fats (Willett et al., 1990), sunbathing (which because of ultraviolet light causes skin cancer [Levy, 1985]), and psychological conditions such as prolonged periods of depression or stress (Antoni, 1987; Sheridan & Radmacher, 1992).

Stress and Cancer. Researchers have also uncovered links between stress and cancer (Sheridan & Radmacher, 1992). A study of children with cancer by Jacob and Charles (1980) revealed that a significant percentage had encountered severe life changes within a year of the diagnosis, often involving the death of a loved one or the loss of a close relationship.

Numerous studies connect stressful life events to the onset of cancer among adults. However, this research has been criticized because it tends to be retrospective (Krantz et al., 1985). That is, cancer patients are interviewed about events preceding their diagnoses and about their psychological well-being prior to the onset of the disease. Self-reports are confounded by problems in memory and other inaccuracies. Moreover, the causal relationships in such research are clouded. For example, development of the illness might have precipitated many of the stressful events. Stress, in other words, might have been the result of the illness rather than the cause.

Experimental research that could not be conducted with humans has been conducted with rats and other animals. In one type of study, animals are injected with cancerous cells, or with viruses that cause cancer, and then exposed to various conditions. In this way, it can be determined which conditions influence the likelihood that the animals' immune systems will be able to fend off the antigens. Such experiments with rodents suggest that once cancer has affected the individual, stress can influence its course. In one study, for example, rats were implanted with small numbers of cancer cells so that their own immune systems would have a chance to successfully combat them (Visintainer et al., 1982). Some of the rats were then exposed to inescapable shocks, whereas others were exposed to escapable shocks or to no shock. The rats exposed to the most stressful condition—the inescapable shock—were half as likely as the other rats to reject the cancer and two times as likely to die from it.

In a study of this kind with mice, Riley (1981) studied the effects of a cancer-causing virus that can be passed from mothers to offspring by means of nursing. This virus typically produces breast cancer in 80 percent of female offspring by the time they have reached 400 days of age. Riley placed one group of female offspring at risk for cancer in a stressful environment of loud noises and noxious odors. Another group was placed in a less stressful environment. At the age of 400 days, 92 percent of the mice who developed under stressful conditions developed breast cancer, as compared to 7 percent of the controls. Moreover, the high-stress mice showed increases in levels of steroids, which depress the functioning of the body's immune system, and lower blood levels of disease-fighting antibodies. However, the "bottom line" in this experiment is of major interest: By the time another 200 days had elapsed, the low-stress mice had nearly caught up to their high-stress peers in the incidence of cancer. Stress appears to have hastened along the inevitable for many of these mice,but the ultimate outcomes were not overwhelmingly influenced by stress.

Although stress influences the timing of the onset of certain diseases such as cancer, genetic predispositions toward disease and powerful antigens may eventually do their damage. An extreme position along these lines was expressed in *The New England Journal of Medicine:* "The inherent biology of [cancer] alone determines the prognosis, overiding the potentially mitigating influence of psychosocial factors" (Cassileth et al., 1985, p. 1555).

It is true that stress can influence the course of cancer. Whether or not stress ever affects the ultimate outcome remains an open question.

Psychological Factors in the Treatment of Cancer. Cancer is a medical disorder, but health psychologists have made major improvements in the treatment of cancer patients. For example, a crisis like cancer can induce perceptions that life has spun out of control and become unpredictable. Control and predictability are factors in psychological hardiness, so perceptions of lack of control and unpredictability can lead to psychological vulnerability and heighten stress. Health psychologists therefore teach the value of encouraging cancer patients to remain in charge of their lives. Yes, cancer does require medical treatment and, in too many cases, there are few options for patients. Patients can still choose their attitudes, however, and a ten-year follow-up of breast cancer patients found a significantly higher survival rate for patients who met their diagnosis with anger and a "fighting spirit" rather than stoic acceptance (Pettingale et al., 1985). Emotional states like hostility, anxiety, even horror are all associated with increased rates of survival in breast cancer, suggesting that the desire to fight the illness is a vital treatment component.

Health psychologists have also found that the feelings of hopelessness and helplessness that often accompany the diagnosis of cancer can hinder recovery (Levy et al., 1985), perhaps by depressing the responsiveness of the patient's immune system. Hospitalization itself is stressful because it removes patients from their normal sources of social support and reduces their sense of control. If handled insensitively, hospitalization may further depress patients' own ability to fight illness. The traditional sick role requires passive compliance with medical routines and procedures. With cancer, it may be that a solid dose of nontraditional complaining is helpful.

Psychologists are also examining the value of teaching coping skills training to cancer patients to relieve psychological distress. In one study, cognitive-behavioral coping methods were found superior to supportive group therapy and a no-treatment control condition in reducing emotional distress and helping patients meet the demands of daily life (Telch & Telch, 1986). Coping-skills training included components such as relaxation training, stress management, assertive communication training, cognitive restructuring, problem-solving techniques, management of emotions, and engaging in pleasant activities. Coping skills are beneficial in themselves and also help patients regain a sense of control and mastery over their lives.

Another area of psychological intervention involves behavioral treatment of the nausea that often accompanies chemotherapy. Chemotherapy patients who receive relaxation training and guided imagery techniques have significantly less nausea and vomiting than no-treatment control subjects. Moreover, their blood pressure and pulse rates are lower, and their moods are less negative than those of control subjects (Burish et al., 1987). Studies with preteenagers and teenagers find that playing video games also lessens the discomfort of chemotherapy (Kolko & Rickard-Figueroa, 1985; Redd et al., 1987). The children focus on battling computer-generated monsters rather than the effects of the chemicals being injected.

Still another psychological application is helping chemotherapy patients keep up their strength by eating. The problem is that chemotherapy often causes nausea, and nausea becomes associated with foods eaten earlier in the day, causing enduring taste aversions in about 45 percent of patients (Carey & Burish, 1988). Cancer patients, who are often already losing weight because of their illness, may thus find that taste aversions exacerbate the problems caused by lack of appetite. To combat taste aversions in chemotherapy patients, Bernstein (1985) recommends feeding them atypical foods prior to chemotherapy. If taste aversions develop, they are associated with the unusual food, and patients' appetites for dietary staples may remain unaffected. Relaxation training also appears to increase food intake in cancer patients undergoing chemotherapy (Carey & Burish, 1987).

In sum, cancer is frightening and, in many cases, there may be little that we can do about its eventual outcome if we are afflicted. However, we are still not helpless in the face of cancer. We can take measures like the following:

1. We can limit our exposure to the behavioral risk factors for cancer.
2. We can modify our diets according to the suggestions in Table 12.4.
3. We can have regular medical checkups to detect cancer early.
4. We can regulate the amount of stress that affects us.
5. If we are struck by cancer, we can battle it energetically rather than assume the roles of passive victims.

Acquired immune deficiency syndrome A usually fatal disease thought to be caused by the human immunodeficiency virus (HIV). Abbreviated *AIDS*.

TABLE 12.4: Dietary Methods of Lowering Risk Factors for Cancer

Kinds Of Cancers	Recommendations
Colon, breast, uterus	Bring weight down to recommended range through dietary changes and exercise
Breast, colon, prostate	Reduce fat intake to less than 30% of daily calories by eating less high-fat foods
Colon	Increase intake of high-fiber foods and drink 6–8 cups of fluid a day to prevent constipation
Lungs, esophagus, larynx	Increase intake of dark green and deep yellow fruits and vegetables
Stomach, esophagus, larynx	Increase intake of vitamin C-rich fruits, vegetables, and juices

Vitamins, calcium, and fruits and vegetables appear to reduce the risk of cancer (Mevkens, 1990; Willett & MacMahon, 1984).

Acquired Immune Deficiency Syndrome (AIDS)

Many of us will remember where we were and what we were doing on November 7, 1991, when Los Angeles Laker Earvin "Magic" Johnson announced that he had been infected by the human immunodeficiency virus (H.I.V.). Johnson seemed in the best of health when he made his announcement. He also went on to star on the U.S. "Dream Team" at the Barcelona Olympic Games the following summer. Nevertheless, his future remained clouded, because H.I.V. is the virus that causes **acquired immune deficiency syndrome**—AIDS. Researchers estimate that it takes an average [median] of 10½ years for people who are infected with H.I.V. to develop full-blown cases of AIDS. AIDS is the fatal condition in which one's immune system is so weakened that it falls prey to "opportunistic" diseases. Johnson's infection also contributed to the shattering of the myth that young, strong, heterosexual males are invulnerable to H.I.V. (Specter, 1991). After all, Johnson had led the Lakers to five championships during his dozen years in the game, and his likeness had graced Wheaties boxes.

Magic Johnson on the Court and at His 1991 Press Conference. During his dozen years on the court, L.A. Laker Earvin "Magic" Johnson had led his team to five championships. In 1991, he announced that he had been infected by human immunodeficiency virus (H.I.V.), the virus that causes acquired immune deficiency syndrome (AIDS). Prior to Johnson's announcement, many Americans had believed that only homosexuals and injectable drug users were at serious risk of infection. Johnson's courageous public admission highlighted the fact that heterosexual, non-drug-abusing people are also at risk. One's behavior, and not one's group membership, places one at risk of H.I.V. infection and AIDS.

It is true that many people who are infected by H.I.V. go symptom-free for years. It may take more than a decade for infected people to develop full-blown cases of AIDS.

Why do we discuss AIDS in a chapter on health psychology? There are several reasons. AIDS, like cancer, is not a psychosomatic disorder. Stress does not directly cause either AIDS or cancer. Stress, however, may affect the course of AIDS in much the same way that stress is suspected to affect the course of cancer (Antoni et al., 1990, 1991). Psychologists have also become intensely interested in AIDS because our behavior patterns influence our risk for contracting AIDS, even more so than they affect our risk for contracting cancer. Moreover, AIDS, like cancer, has devastating psychological effects on victims, their families and friends, and on society at large. It is estimated that by the year 2000, 40 to 110 million people around the world will be infected by H.I.V. (Altman, 1991; Mann et al., 1992).

H.I.V. is transmitted by heterosexual vaginal intercourse, anal intercourse, sharing contaminated hypodermic needles (as when a group of people "shoots up" a drug), transfusions of contaminated blood (which is how former tennis player Arthur Ashe is reported to have been infected), and childbirth (Glasner & Kaslow, 1990). Small amounts of H.I.V. are found in victims' saliva (Glasner & Kaslow, 1990), which also raises concerns about deep ("French") kissing. There is no evidence, however, that public toilets, holding or hugging an infected person, or living or attending school with one transmit the virus.

H.I.V. has an affinity for, and kills, white blood cells called T_4 lymphocytes that are found in the immune system. T_4 lymphocytes recognize pathogens and "instruct" other white blood cells—called B lymphocytes—to make antibodies. As a result of depletion of T_4 lymphocytes, the body is left vulnerable to opportunistic diseases. Opportunistic diseases do not stand much chance of developing in people whose immune systems are intact (Antoni et al., 1990; Kiecolt-Glaser & Glaser, 1992).

People infected with H.I.V. may come down with a flu-like illness weeks or months after infection. Symptoms include fever, fatigue, and swollen glands. There may also be headaches, nausea, and a rash. These symptoms usually disappear within days or weeks. Years afterward, the person may develop full-blown AIDS, which is characterized by fatigue, fever, unexplained weight loss, swollen lymph nodes, diarrhea, and, in many cases, impairment in learning and memory (Grant & Heaton, 1990). Opportunistic infections may now take hold, such as an otherwise rare form of cancer (Kaposi's sarcoma, a cancer of the blood cells, has been seen in many gay males who contract AIDS) and a kind of pneumonia (*PCP*) that is characterized by coughing and shortness of breath.

In the United States, the following groups have been hardest hit by the AIDS epidemic (Coates, 1990; Glasner & Kaslow, 1990):

1. Gay males. The San Francisco and New York gay communities have been particularly hard hit. Nearly 75 percent of cases diagnosed in the early 1980s were among gay males, but the percentage of gays among new cases has declined dramatically in recent years.
2. People who inject drugs. Although people who inject ("shoot up") drugs accounted for only about 15 percent of cases in the early 1980s, they now account for about 30 percent of cases overall (Des Jarlais et al., 1990).
3. Sex partners of people who inject drugs.
4. Babies born to sex partners of people who inject drugs.
5. Prostitutes.
6. Men who visit prostitutes.

TABLE 12.5: Cause, Modes of Transmission, Symptoms, Diagnosis, and Treatment of H.I.V. Infection and AIDS

Pathogen Causing AIDS	Human immunodeficiency virus (H.I.V.)
Modes of Transmission	H.I.V. is transmitted by sexual contact, direct infusion of contaminated blood, from mother to fetus during pregnancy, or from mother to child through childbirth or breast-feeding
Symptoms	Infected people may initially be asymptomatic or develop mild flu-like symptoms which may then disappear for many years prior to the development of "full-blown" AIDS. Full-blown AIDS is symptomized by fever, weight loss, fatigue, diarrhea, and opportunistic infections such as rare forms of cancer (Kaposi's sarcoma) and pneumonia (PCP)
Diagnosis	A blood test (ELISA) detects H.I.V. antibodies in the bloodstream. The Western blot blood test may be used to confirm positive ELISA results. Diagnosis is usually made on the basis of H.I.V. antibodies, presence of indicator (opportunistic) diseases, and depletion of T_4* cells.
Treatment	There is no cure or effective vaccine for AIDS. The drug zidovudine apparently slows the progress of the disease, but it is unclear as to whether or not zidovudine prolongs the lives of people who are infected with H.I.V. Patients may profit from proper nutrition, exercise, counseling, and stress-management techniques.

*Also known as T-helper, CD_4, or CD_4+ cells.

7. Sex partners of men who visit infected prostitutes.
8. People receiving transfusions of blood—for example, surgery patients and hemophiliacs. This avenue of infection has become rare because the medical community routinely screens blood supplies (Busch et al., 1991).

Do not assume that you are invulnerable if you do not belong to one of these groups, however. Magic Johnson claimed to become infected through heterosexual relations and was more robust than most readers. When we take a global perspective, we find that most people are infected with H.I.V. through heterosexual intercourse (Mann et al., 1992; Rathus & Boughn, 1993).

It is not true that only gay men and people who inject drugs are at serious risk for contracting AIDS. One's behavior, and not one's group membership, places one at risk of being infected with H.I.V.

H.I.V. infection is generally diagnosed by blood tests that show antibodies to the virus (Jacobsen et al., 1990). (See Table 12.5.) It can take months after infection for antibodies to develop, however, so repeated tests may be in order. Unfortunately, there is not yet an effective vaccine for H.I.V. Nor is there a cure for AIDS. A number of antiviral drugs and behavioral interventions are under investigation, singly and in combination. Zidovudine (commonly called AZT), for example, appears to slow the progress of the disease (Graham et al., 1992; McKinney et al., 1991; Moore et al., 1991) and may prevent some infected people from developing full-blown cases of AIDS (McCutchan, 1990). The drug dideoxyinosine (DDI) also seems to hold some promise (Hilts, 1990). There is hope that behavioral interventions such as stress management techniques and aerobic exercise will help by increasing the numbers of T_4 cells in the immune system (Antoni et al., 1990, 1991). Behavioral interventions and drugs have not cured anyone to date, however, and drugs can have severe side effects. Clearly the best way to cope with AIDS is by *prevention*.

Preventing AIDS: It's More than Safe(r) Sex.

You're not just sleeping with one person, you're sleeping with everyone they *ever slept with.*

Dr. Theresa Crenshaw, President, American Association of Sex Educators, Counselors and Therapists

As shown by the remarks of one young woman, it can be clumsy to try to protect oneself from sexually transmitted diseases (STDs) such as AIDS:

It's one thing to talk about "being responsible about STD" and a much harder thing to do it at the very moment. It's just plain hard to say to someone I am feeling very erotic with, "Oh, yes, before we go any further, can we have a conversation about STD?" It's hard to imagine murmuring into someone's ear at a time of passion, "Would you mind slipping on this condom or using this cream just in case one of us has STD?" Yet it seems awkward to bring it up beforehand, if it's not yet clear between us that we want to make love with one another.

The New Our Bodies, Ourselves, 1993

Because of the difficulties in discussing STDs with sex partners, some people admit that they just "wing it" (Wallis, 1987). They assume that a partner does not have an STD, or they hope for the best—even in the age of AIDS. However, 52 percent of the single people aged 18 to 44 responding to a 1991 *New York Times*/CBS News survey reported that they had become more cautious about sex because of concern about AIDS (Kagay, 1991). The most common methods of behavior modification were use of condoms and limiting of the numbers of sex partners.

What can we do to prevent the transmission of H.I.V.? A number of things.

1. *Refuse to deny the prevalence and harmful nature of AIDS.* Many people try to put AIDS out of their minds and "wing it" when it comes to sex. The first and perhaps most important step in protecting oneself against AIDS is thus psychological: keeping it in mind—refusing to play the dangerous game that involves pretending (at least for the moment) that it does not exist. The other measures involve modifying our behavior.
2. *Remain abstinent.* One way of curtailing the sexual transmission of H.I.V. and other pathogens is sexual abstinence. Most people who remain abstinent do so while they are looking for Mr. or Ms. Right, of course. They thus eventually face the risk of engaging in sexual intercourse. Moreover, students want to know just what "abstinence" means (Rathus & Boughn, 1993). Does abstinence mean avoiding sexual intercourse (yes) or any form of sexual activity with another person (not necessarily)? Light kissing (without exchanging saliva), hugging, and petting to orgasm (without coming into contact with semen or vaginal secretions) are generally considered safe, although readers may argue about which of these behaviors is consistent with the definition of abstinence.
3. *Engage in a monogamous relationship with someone who is not infected.* Sexual activity within a monogamous relationship with an uninfected person is safe. The questions here are how certain one can be that one's partner is indeed uninfected and monogamous (Rathus & Boughn, 1993).

For those who do not abstain from sexual relationships or limit themselves to a monogamous relationship, some things can be done to make sex safer—though not perfectly safe:

4. *Be selective.* Engage in sexual activity only with people you know well and who are unlikely to have been infected with H.I.V.
5. *Wash one's own genitals before and after contact.* Washing beforehand helps protect one's partner, and washing promptly afterward with soap and water helps remove some H.I.V. Urinating afterward might be of some help, particularly to men, since the acidity of urine can kill H.I.V. in the urethra.
6. *Use spermicides.* Spermicides are marketed as birth-control devices, but many creams, foams, and jellies kill H.I.V. as well as sperm. Check with a pharmacist.
7. *Use condoms. Latex* condoms (but not condoms made from animal membrane) protect the man from vaginal (or other) body fluids and protect the woman from having infected semen enter the vagina (Rathus & Boughn, 1993). Combining condoms with spermicides is even more effective.
8. *When in doubt, stop.* If one is not sure that sex is safe, one can stop and mull things over or seek expert advice.

If you think about it, this last piece is some rather good general advice. When in doubt, why not stop and think regardless of whether the doubt is about one's sex partner, one's college major, or a financial investment? When playing cards, it is said that people who hesitate is making discards or making bets are "lost"; that is, they reveal their holdings to their adversaries. However, in sex and in most other areas of life, hesitating when in doubt pays off in many, many ways.

Health psychologists are also investigating the role of stress in inflammatory diseases such as arthritis, premenstrual distress, digestive diseases such as colitis, and metabolic diseases such as diabetes and hypoglycemia. The relationships among behavior patterns, attitudes, and illness are complex and under intense study. With some stress-related illnesses, it may be that stress determines whether or not the person will contract the disease at all. In others, it may be that an optimal environment merely delays the inevitable or that a stressful environment merely hastens the onset of the inevitable. Then, too, in different illnesses stress may have different effects on the patient's ability to recover.

Despite healthful behavior patterns, all of us become sick from time to time. In the following section, we explore what psychologists have learned about why people comply—or do not comply—with medical advice.

COMPLIANCE WITH MEDICAL ADVICE

Individual differences truly hit home when it comes to our behavior during illness. Some of us refuse to go to the doctor unless we are incapable of moving. Others rush off to the doctor at the drop of a hat. Some of us deny pain and other symptoms. Others exaggerate pain. Some of us view chronic disorders such as essential hypertension and diabetes as temporary setbacks. Others see them as the lingering problems that they are. Some of us make good use of visits to the doctor. Others do not. Some of us comply with medical advice. Others do not.

Once we have been to see the doctor, how many of us comply with medical instructions and procedures? In a review of the literature, Sackett and Snow (1979) concluded that about 75 percent of us keep appointments we have made, but only about half of us keep appointments scheduled by the professional. More of us will take medicines to cure illnesses than to prevent them: 77 percent of us will take medicine over the short term to cure an illness, whereas 63 percent of us will take medicine to prevent it. Over the long term, compliance drops to about 50 percent, which is especially troublesome for disorders such as hypertension, in which there may be no symptoms and protracted treatment can be required. Similarly, it has been found that only about 50 percent of patients stick to clinical exercise programs following the first six months (Dishman, 1982).

Some factors that determine compliance reside with the physician. Patients are more likely to adhere to advice from physicians who are perceived as being competent, friendly, warm, and concerned (DiNicola & DiMatteo, 1984). Patients are less likely to comply with instructions from physicians whom they perceive as being authoritarian and condescending (Gastorf & Galanos, 1983).

It is *not* true that patients are more likely to comply with "doctor's orders" when the orders are issued by an authoritarian physician.

There was a time when medical training was almost completely technical, but research findings like these have prompted medical schools to train students in ways of relating to patients as people.

Health psychologists have found that patients are more likely to comply with medical instructions when illness is severe (Becker & Maiman, 1980) and when they believe that the instructions will work. Women, for example, are more likely to engage in breast self-examination when they believe that they will really be able to detect abnormal growths (Alagna & Reddy, 1984). Diabetes patients are more likely to use insulin when they believe that their regimens will help control their blood-sugar levels (Brownlee-Duffeck et al., 1987).

Physicians often prescribe drugs and other treatment regimens without explaining to patients the purposes of the treatments and their possible complications. This approach can backfire. When it comes to taking prescribed drugs, patients frequently tend not to take them or to take them incorrectly (Haynes, 1979). Patients are particularly likely to discontinue medications when they encounter side effects, especially unexpected side effects. Therefore, specific instructions coupled with accurate information about potential side effects appears to be most useful in inducing compliance (Baron & Byrne, 1991; Keown et al., 1984).

Cultural factors are also involved in compliance. It has been shown, for example, that Hispanic Americans are more likely to comply with medical instructions when they are issued by personnel who have an understanding of Hispanic-American culture. A study in Zimbabwe, Africa, points out that some people do not comply with medical regimens because of belief in nonscientific, but traditional, methods of healing (Zyazema, 1984).

As in so many other areas of life, social support is helpful in fostering compliance with medical instructions and procedures. One study, for example, found that men with supportive spouses are more likely to change their nutritional and activity patterns to avert cardiovascular disorders (Doherty et al., 1983).

In this chapter, we have dealt primarily with physical disorders. In the following chapter, we turn our attention to psychological disorders—also referred to as patterns of abnormal behavior.

STUDY GUIDE

EXERCISE: True-False Questions

Directions: Consider each of the following statements. Circle the T if it is true and the F if it is false. Answers and explanations follow the exercise.
NOTE: I'm going to be impossibly tricky, so keep in mind that this is a learning exercise for you, and not a real test! The items should increase your test-wiseness.

T F 1. If we become ill and require hospitalization, we should, like Norman Cousins, refuse routine medical tests and leave the hospital as soon as we feel that we can.

T F 2. Daily hassles are the same as life changes.

T F 3. Life changes are to be avoided, if we wish to remain healthy.

T F 4. The research links between life changes and illness are correlational, not experimental.

T F 5. Type-A people become restless when they see others working slowly.

T F 6. Psychological factors can moderate the impact of sources of stress.

T F 7. It has been shown experimentally that high self-efficacy expectations are accompanied by *low* levels of adrenaline and norepinephrine in the bloodstream.

T F 8. People in whom high self-efficacy expectations are experimentally induced complete tasks more successfully than people of comparable ability but lower self-efficacy expectations.

T F 9. Psychologically hardy individuals show a tendency to involve themselves in, rather than experience alienation from, whatever they are doing or encountering.

T F 10. Of the three aspects of psychological hardiness that help people resist stress, Hull and his colleagues argue that commitment and challenge are the ones that make the most difference.

T F 11. Psychologically hardy people tend to have an external locus of control.

T F 12. In an important psychological study of the moderating effects of humor on stress by Canadian psychologists Rod Martin and Herbert Lefcourt, students with a greater sense of humor, and who produced humor in difficult situations, were less affected by negative life events than other students.

T F 13. In the Weiss study, rats that received shock without warning showed greatest ulceration.

T F 14. If you get married, you will live longer.

T F 15. The GAS consists of three stages: an adaptation stage, a resistance stage, and an exhaustion stage.

T F 16. The alarm reaction involves a number of body changes that are initiated by the brain and further regulated by the endocrine system and the sympathetic division of the autonomic nervous system.

T F 17. The hypothalamus secretes corticotrophin-releasing hormone, which, in turn, stimulates the pituitary gland to secrete adrenocorticotrophic hormone.

T F 18. The parasympathetic division of the ANS activates the adrenal medulla, causing a mixture of adrenaline and norepinephrine to be released.

T F 19. In their research, psychologists frequently use the amount of cortisol in the saliva or urine as a biological measure of stress.

T F 20. In their research, psychologists use the amount of cortisol in the adrenal glands as a biological measure of stress.

T F 21. One way in which we combat physical disorders is by producing white blood cells that routinely engulf and kill pathogens.

T F 22. The foreign agents that are recognized and destroyed by leucocytes are called antibodies.

T F 23. Steroids heighten the functioning of the immune system.

T F 24. The single most frequent kind of headache is the migraine headache.

T F 25. Arousal of the sympathetic division of the ANS heightens blood pressure.

T F 26. People whose families show a history of cardiovascular disease are more likely to develop cardiovascular disease themselves.

T F 27. According to the text, people with Type-A behavior are twice as likely as people with Type-B behavior to have heart attacks.

T F 28. Asthma attacks can be triggered by stress.

T F 29. Cancer rates have been skyrocketing.

T F 30. A study of children with cancer found that a significant percentage had encountered severe life changes within a year of the diagnosis, often involving the death of a loved one or the loss of a close relationship.

T F 31. Stress can cause cancer.

T F 32. Women are more likely to seek medical help than men.

Answer Key To True–False Exercise

	Answer	Comment
1.	F	Although Cousins' experiences are used to show how he took charge of his own treatment, the text warns readers that Cousins knew a great deal about medicine and that readers should not necessarily follow his example.
2.	F	The text points out that daily hassles differ from life changes in two ways. What are they?
3.	F	The text points out that *high numbers* of life changes place us in higher risk groups. Even so, there is no experimental evidence that high numbers of life changes directly cause illness in people.
4.	T	Again, this is why we cannot assume that life changes cause illness.
5.	T	This is one "side effect" of their sense of time urgency.
6.	T	Sure they can.
7.	T	Here the "trick" is to carefully check out the adjectives "high" and "low."
8.	T	Again, the task is the check out the relationships between the words "high," "more," and "lower."
9.	T	This is what is meant by their sense of commitment.
10.	F	Only half true! Hull argues that their senses of commitment and *control*—not challenge—make the difference.
11.	F	*Internal,* not *external.*
12.	T	You need to check out the names of the researchers (accurate) as well as the relationships between "greater" and "less" (all accurate).
13.	T	True in that the study was run by Weiss and the results are accurate.
14.	F	Again we have correlational evidence. Therefore, while it is true that married men live longer than single men, it may be that the factors that lead to the decision to get married, and not marriage itself, make the difference. Also, findings are less clear-cut for women.
15.	F	Tricky! Yes there are three stages, but the adaptation stage *is* the resistance stage; the alarm reaction has been erroneously omitted.
16.	T	All parts true (a difficult question!).
17.	T	Another difficult item, with all parts true. It may help to recall, from Chapter 3, that the hypothalamus secretes many releasing factors that cause the pituitary to secrete related hormones.
18.	F	The sympathetic division, not the parasympathetic division, does this.
19.	T	A simple statement of fact.
20.	T	False. Cortisol is produced by the adrenal glands.
21.	T	This is one of the functions of the immune system.
22.	F	They are called antigens, not antibodies.
23.	F	Steroids *suppress* the functioning of the immune system.
24.	F	The muscle-tension headache is more common.
25.	T	A simple statement of fact.
26.	T	There is a genetic risk factor.
27.	F	There is no statement in the text that twice as many Type-A people as Type-B people have heart attacks.
28.	T	A simple statement of fact.
29.	F	Actually, many better-educated people have been modifying their behavior and placing themselves in lower risk categories for many kinds of cancer.
30.	T	Stress appears to exacerbate the course of cancer.
31.	F	Although stress appears to exacerbate the course of cancer (see the previous item), there is no evidence that stress *causes* cancer.
32.	T	A factual gender difference related in the text.

ESL—BRIDGING THE GAP

This part is divided into

1. cultural references,
2. phrases and expressions in which words are used differently from their regular meaning, or are used as metaphors.

Cultural References

Saturday Review (450)—a national magazine of essays

loan installments (452)—monthly payments required to repay a loan

taxes (452)—the obligation of everyone to pay a portion of his or her income (earnings) or property to the government in order to finance it

property investments (452)—the purchase of property in order to receive income that ownership of the property will produce for the owner

stock-market swings (452)—the prices of stocks that are traded on the stock market tend to go up and go down together

retirement (452)—the period of life when a person stops his or her regular job and relies on his or her accumulated earnings (investments) and monthly social security payments for financial support
in-laws (455)—the parents of a spouse
low-interest loans (459)—loans made with low interest rates (the amount that a person pays in order to have the loan) so that the loans will be affordable (people can afford them)
Three Mile Island (460)—the name of a place where a nuclear reactor is situated
Overtime work (470)—additional hours of work for an employer for which an employee is paid more (sometimes a lot extra)
assembly-line labor (470)—work in a factory which entails a person standing in front of a moving table. Each person attaches a part to an item before the moving table carries the item to the next worker who adds another part; this continues until the item is assembled.
jumping rope (460)—an activity that involves causing a rope, each end of which is held by each hand, to move from the heels, over the head and to the toes. The person doing this jumps over the rope at this point. This is done rapidly.
cross-country skiing (460)—skiing is a sport; the feet are placed separately on long "boards" which rise at one end; the person moves down a long hill or mountain of snow; "cross-country" means that instead of moving down a mountain, the person moves on level ground covered with snow and moves in a "walking" fashion.
postal workers (460)—people who work for the U.S. Post Office
longshoremen (461)—people who are employed to unload cargo from ships

Phrases and Expressions (Different Usage)

Right from the start he (450)—He began in the beginning
gave him only a slim chance of a full recovery (450)—told him that he might not recover completely
has bridled at (450)—become very annoyed
uncritically endorse (450)—recommend without criticism
"give in" to illness (450)—allow ourselves to accept illness without fighting it
a springboard for discussion (450)—an illustration in order to initiate discussion
overtax (451)—put too large a burden upon (negative)
the last straw that will break the camel's back(451)—the final additional part of a load that causes a person to not be able to function
so goes the saying (451)—this is the expression
too much of a good thing (452)—attaining success in many areas in the same time period
marrying Mr. or Ms. Right (452)—marrying the perfect mate
propel you into a state of bliss (452)—make you extremely happy
one on top of the other (452)—one added to the other
baseline (453)—the same situation for all of them
dampen our moods (455)—depress us a little
easy-going (455)—relaxed and flexible
psychologically hardy (455)—psychologically strong
keep one eye glued firmly on the clock (455)—look at the clock continually in order to always know the time, and therefore not relax
bat the ball back and forth (456)—hit the ball over the net to someone who hits it back, without paying attention to the rules of the game
motto (456)—private rule
pace themselves (456)—ensure that there will be periods of time between stressful occurrences
no one-to-one relationship (456)—no relationship of amount of stress to the amount or kind of illness
to withstand stress (456)—to be able to endure stress; not be hurt by stress
hardy and nonhardy (457)—emotionally strong and emotionally weak
threat to security (457)—method of causing insecurity
buffers between themselves (457)—shields between themselves; a protection
"a merry heart doeth good like a medicine" (457)—a happy person is healthy
belly laughter (458)—strong, deep and continuous laughter
sudden cognitive shifts (458)—sudden cognitive change
a stressor (458)—the thing or occurrence or situation that causes the stress
to brace ourselves (458)—to be prepared
in tandem (458)—at the same time
foodstuffs (459)—food
pave the way for understanding (464)—help you to understand
Given . . . and fast pace of scientific change (464)—Because our bodies are so complex and because scientific changes are occurring very often
wornout body cells (464)—body cells that do not function anymore
mirrored the method of (465)—was the same as the method of
come on (467)—begin
unwittingly propel ourselves into (468)—unintentionally begin
"pounding through the roof" (469)—throbbing so hard in our heads that it feels that it will remove the top of our heads
on guard (469)—be conscious of protecting themselves
bring one on (471)—precipitate an attack
rob the body of nutrients (472)—remove vitamins that the body needs
skyrocketing (472)—rising quickly

the "bottom line" (473)—the important occurrence
remains an open question (473)—is not known
do not stand much chance of (476)—do not have an opportunity
from time to time (479)—sometimes
truly hit home (479)—are obvious
at the drop of a hat (479)—at the first suggestion that might indicate that an illness is beginning
temporary setbacks (479)—temporary and unexpected reverses
reside with (479)—remain with; the responsibility of
stick to (479)—stay with
backfire (480)—have the opposite effect of what was intended
short bursts (460)—short intensive periods
tracking (461)—researching
full-blown cases (475)—the completely developed illness
hard hit (476)—hurt a lot
singly and in combination (476)—one and combined
"wing it" (478)—do it without preparation or information
well-known people (478)—people whom you know well

CHAPTER REVIEW

SECTION 1: Health Psychology

Objective 1: Define *health psychology.*

The field of health psychology studies the relationships between (1) ________ical factors (e.g., stress, behavior, and attitudes) and the prevention and treatment of physical illness.

SECTION 2: Sources of Stress

Objective 2: Define *stress.*

In psychology, (2) s________ is the demand made on an organism to adapt, to cope, or to adjust. Some stress is healthful and keeps us alert and occupied.

Objective 3: Enumerate sources of stress.

Many sources of stress largely reflect external factors—daily (3) ________les, life changes, pain and discomfort, frustration, and conflict. Others such as Type-(4) ________ behavior are self-imposed.

(5) D________ hassles are notable daily conditions and experiences that are threatening or harmful to a person's well-being. Life changes differ from daily hassles in that many life changes are (6) ________ive and desirable, whereas hassles are all negative. (7) L________ changes are also more isolated than daily hassles. Holmes and Rahe constructed a scale to measure (8) life-________ units.

Type-A behavior is characterized by a sense of time (9) ________cy, competitiveness, and (10) ag________ness. Type-B people, by contrast, relax (11: less or more?) readily and focus (12: less or more?) on the quality of life.

SECTION 3: Moderators of Stress

Objective 4: Describe various moderators of the impact of stress.

There (13: is or is not?) a one-to-one relationship between the amount of stress we experience and physical illness or psychological distress. The following psychological moderators of stress are (14: person or situational?) variables: self-efficacy expectations, psychological hardiness, and a sense of humor. The following are (15: person or situational?) variables: predictability and social support.

Our (16) self-________ expectations are our perceptions of our capacities to bring about change. People with higher self-efficacy expectations tend to cope better with stress.

Kobasa and her colleagues have found that psychologically hardy executives differ from the nonhardy in three ways: Hardy individuals are high in (17) ________ment (they involve themselves in, rather than experience alienation from, what they are doing); hardy individuals are high in challenge; hardy individuals are (18: high or low?) in perceived control over their lives.

Being able to predict the onset of a stressor (19: increases or decreases?) its impact upon us.

Social support (20: does or does not?) buffer the effects of stress. Numerous studies have found a lower mortality rate for (21: single or married?) men.

Exercise, particularly (22) ________bic exercise, can enhance our psychological well being and help us cope with stress as well as foster physical health. Aerobic exercise is any kind of exercise that requires a sustained increase in the consumption of (23) o________. The major physiological effect of exercise is the promotion of (24) ______ness. (25) ______vascular fitness, or "condition," means that the body can use greater amounts of oxygen during vigorous activity and pump more blood with each heart beat. The benefits of exercise may also help people cope through enhancing feelings of physical well-being, improving physical health, and enhancing one's sense of (26) c______ over one's body.

SECTION 4: Physiological Responses to Stress

Objective 5: Describe the general adaptation syndrome.

The concept of the general adaptation syndrome (GAS) was originated by (27) S______. The GAS consists of (28: how many?) ______ stages. These stages are the (29) a______ reaction, a resistance stage, and the (30) ______tion stage. The alarm reaction (31) m______izes or arouses the body for defense. Cannon had earlier termed this alarm system the (32) ______-or-______ reaction.

The alarm reaction involves a number of body changes that are initiated by the brain and further regulated by the (33) ______rine system and the (34) ______etic division of the autonomic nervous system. Under stress, the hypothalamus secretes (35) ______trophin-releasing hormone (CRH), which, in turn, stimulates the pituitary gland to secrete (36) adr______cotrophic hormone (ACTH). ACTH then acts upon the adrenal cortex, causing it to release (37) ______sol and other steroids that help the body respond to stress by fighting (38) in______tion and allergic reactions. Two other hormones that play a major role in the alarm reaction are secreted by the adrenal medulla: (39) ad______ine and (40) nor______rine.

In the (41) ______tion stage, or resistance stage, of the GAS, the body attempts to restore lost energy and repair whatever damage has been done. All of us eventually reach the (42) ______tion stage when stress persists. With exhaustion, the (43) para______tic division of the ANS may become predominant.

SECTION 5: The Immune System

Objective 6: Describe the functions of the immune system.

The immune system has a number of functions that help us combat (44) ______ease. The immune system produces (45) ______ blood cells that routinely engulf and kill pathogens. White blood cells are technically termed (46) ______ytes. The immune system "remembers" foreign agents so that future combat will be more efficient. Pathogens that are recognized and destroyed by leucocytes are called (47) ______ens. Some leucocytes produce (48) ______dies, or specialized proteins that bind to their antigens and mark them for destruction. The immune system also causes (49) ______tion when injury occurs by increasing the flow of blood to the damaged area. The increased blood supply brings in large numbers of (50) ______blood cells to combat invading microscopic life forms.

Objective 7: Describe the effects of stress on the immune system.

One of the reasons that stress eventually exhausts us is that it stimulates us to produce (51) ______oids. Steroids (52: enhance or suppress?) the functioning of the immune system. Dental students in one study showed (53: higher or lower?) immune-system functioning during stressful school periods than immediately following vacations.

SECTION 6: Factors in Physical Illness

Objective 8: Describe the relationships between psychological factors and illnesses such as headaches, cardiovascular disorders, cancer, and AIDS.

The most common kind of headache is the (54) ______-______sion headache. Most other headaches, including the migraine, are vascular in nature—stemming from changes in the (55) b______ supply to the head. (56) Mi______ headaches have preheadache phases during which there is decreased blood supply to the head, followed by headaches phases, during which the (57) ______ries are dilated, increasing the flow of blood. Behavioral methods such as progressive (58) ______________tion help headaches by decreasing muscle tension. (59) ______________back training that alters the flow of blood to the head has been used effectively to treat migraine headache.

Arousal of the (60) ______________tic division of the ANS heightens the blood pressure. Hypertension predisposes victims to other (61) car______________lar disorders such as (62) art______________rosis, heart attacks, and strokes. Blood pressure (63: decreases or increases?) in situations in which people must be constantly on guard against threats. Blood pressure appears to be higher among (64: African Americans or whites?).

There are several risk factors for cardiovascular disease: family history; (65) phy______________gical conditions such as obesity, hypertension, and high levels of serum (66) ______________erol; patterns of consumption, such as heavy drinking and smoking; Type-(67) ______________ behavior; and work (68) o______________ (e.g., overtime work and assembly-line labor). We can profit from behavior modification that is intended to reduce the risk factors, such as stopping smoking; weight control; reducing (69) hy______________sion; lowering (70)s______________ cholesterol; modifying Type-A behavior; and exercise.

Asthma is a respiratory disorder which is often the result of an (71) ______________ic reaction in which the main tubes of the windpipe—the bronchi—contract, making it difficult to breathe. Asthma attacks (72: can or can not?) be triggered by stress.

People (73: can or can not?) inherit dispositions toward developing cancer, but many behavior patterns, such as smoking, drinking, and eating animal fats, heighten the risk for cancer. Numerous studies connect stressful life events to the onset of cancer in people, but this research has been criticized in that it is (74) ret______________tive. Experimental research with animals shows that once cancer has affected the individual, stress can (75: accelerate or retard?) its course.

H.I.V. is the virus that causes the disease called (76) ______________. H.I.V. (77: can or cannot) be transmitted by heterosexual vaginal intercourse. H.I.V. has an affinity for, and kills, (78: red or white?) blood cells called T_4 lymphocytes, thereby weakening the immune system. AIDS patients typically die from (79) ______________istic infections. In the United States, the two groups who have been hit hardest by the AIDS epidemic are (80) ______________ males and people who (81) ______________ drugs.

SECTION 7: Compliance with Medical Advice

Objective 9: Describe factors that contribute to compliance with medical instructions and procedures.

Patients are (82: less or more?) likely to comply with medical instructions when illness is severe. Patients are (83: less or more?) likely to comply with instructions when they believe that the instructions will work. Patients are likely to discontinue medications when they encounter (84) s______________ effects, especially when the side effects are (85: expected or unexpected?).

Answers To Chapter Review

1. Psychological
2. Stress
3. Hassles
4. A
5. Daily
6. Positive
7. Life
8. Life-change
9. Urgency
10. Aggressiveness
11. More
12. More
13. Is not
14. Person
15. Situational
16. Efficacy
17. Commitment
18. High
19. Decreases
20. Does
21. Married
22. Aerobic
23. Oxygen
24. Fitness
25. Cardiovascular
26. Control
27. Selye
28. Three
29. Alarm
30. Exhaustion
31. Mobilizes
32. Fight-or-flight
33. Endocrine
34. Sympathetic
35. Corticotrophin-releasing hormone
36. Adrenocorticotrophic hormone
37. Cortisol
38. Inflammation
39. Adrenaline
40. Norepinephrine
41. Adaptation
42. Exhaustion
43. Parasympathetic
44. Disease
45. White
46. Leucocytes
47. Antigens
48. Antibodies
49. Inflammation
50. White
51. Steroids
52. Suppress
53. Lower
54. Muscle-tension

55. Blood
56. Migraine
57. Arteries
58. Relaxation
59. Biofeedback
60. Sympathetic
61. Cardiovascular
62. Arteriosclerosis
63. Increases
64. African Americans
65. Physiological
66. Cholesterol
67. A
68. Overload
69. Hypertension
70. Serum
71. Allergic
72. Can
73. Can
74. Retrospective
75. Accelerate
76. AIDS
77. Is
78. White
79. Opportunistic
80. Gay (homosexual)
81. Inject
82. More
83. More
84. Side
85. Unexpected

POSTTEST

1. Which is the most accurate statement about stress?
   (a) Stress is the painful price we must pay for living.
   (b) The most stressed people are usually unaware of stress.
   (c) Some stress is necessary to keep us alert and occupied.
   (d) All stress is harmful to the body.

2. Hassles differ from life changes in that
   (a) hassles require adaptation.
   (b) hassles are a source of stress.
   (c) life changes occur more frequently.
   (d) life changes can be positive as well as negative.

3. Type-A people are characterized by
   (a) need for affiliation.
   (b) secretion of excessive ACTH.
   (c) competitiveness and impatience.
   (d) predisposition toward alcoholism.

4. As compared to Type-B people, Type-A people
   (a) perceive time as passing more rapidly.
   (b) earn less money.
   (c) smoke less frequently.
   (d) are better adjusted in their marriages.

5. Psychologically hardy individuals show all of the following, *with the exception of*
   (a) competitiveness.
   (b) commitment.
   (c) control.
   (d) challenge.

6. Nancy has just had a frightening experience in which she thought her car was going off the road. Which of the following is likely to be happening inside her?
   (a) Her respiration rate is decreasing.
   (b) Her blood pressure is decreasing.
   (c) Her digestive processes are speeding up.
   (d) Her blood flow is shifting away from her skeletal musculature.

7. Unrelieved stress during the _______ may lead to diseases of adaptation and death.
   (a) fight-or-flight reaction
   (b) exhaustion stage
   (c) resistance stage
   (d) alarm reaction

8. According to the text, people who inject drugs are at risk for contracting
   (a) AIDS.
   (b) cardiovascular disorders.
   (c) cancer.
   (d) headaches.

9. Hypertension predisposes victims to all of the following *with the exception of*
   (a) arteriosclerosis.
   (b) strokes.
   (c) heart attacks.
   (d) ulcers.

10. A vascular headache is caused by
   (a) muscle tension.
   (b) change in blood supply to the head.
   (c) injury.
   (d) chronic stress.

11. Which of the following is *not* a risk factor for cardiovascular disorders?
   (a) Low serum cholesterol
   (b) Family history of cardiovascular disease
   (c) Hypertension
   (d) Physical inactivity

12. The so-called common migraine headache is identified by
   (a) muscle tension in the shoulders and back of the neck.
   (b) hypertension.
   (c) sudden onset and throbbing on one side of the head.
   (d) sensory and motor disturbances that precede the pain.

13. Which of the following is a component of the alarm reaction?
   (a) Muscles relax.
   (b) Adrenaline is secreted.
   (c) Blood coagulability decreases.
   (d) Heart rate decreases.

14. According to the text, so-called diseases of adaptation are caused by
    (a) daily hassles and life changes.
    (b) fear that one will contract the disease.
    (c) genetic factors.
    (d) a combination of stress and some predisposing factor.

15. Bacteria and viruses are examples of
    (a) antigens.
    (b) antibodies.
    (c) leucocytes.
    (d) pathogens.

16. The immune system has all of the following functions, *with the exception of*
    (a) producing white blood cells.
    (b) producing red blood cells.
    (c) causing inflammation.
    (d) recognizing pathogens.

17. Which of the following suppresses the functioning of the immune system?
    (a) Leucocytes
    (b) Vaccination
    (c) Steroids
    (d) Relaxation

18. According to the text, which of the following is a reason that health psychologists study H.I.V. infection and AIDS?
    (a) They are of enormous concern to the public.
    (b) The costs of the AIDS epidemic have been skyrocketing.
    (c) Our behavior patterns place us at risk for being infected with H.I.V.
    (d) Stress-management techniques can cure AIDS.

19. The first and foremost recommendation in the chapter for preventing transmission of H.I.V. is to
    (a) refuse to deny the prevalence and harmful nature of AIDS.
    (b) use condoms.
    (c) abstain from sexual activity.
    (d) limit sexual activity to partners whom one knows very well.

20. People are least likely to comply with medical instructions when.
    (a) the physician is friendly.
    (b) the physician explains the rationale for the treatment.
    (c) symptoms are highly visible.
    (d) they believe that the treatment will not work.

Answers to Posttest

1. C
2. D
3. C
4. A
5. A
6. D
7. B
8. A
9. D
10. B
11. A
12. C
13. B
14. D
15. D
16. B
17. C
18. C
19. A
20. D

- A man shot the president of the United States in front of millions of television witnesses, yet was found not guilty by a court of law.

- In the Middle Ages, innocent people were drowned to prove that they were not possessed by the Devil.

- Stressful experiences can lead to recurrent nightmares.

- Some people have more than one personality, and the identities may have different allergies and eyeglass prescriptions.

- People have lost the use of their legs or eyes under stress, even though there was nothing medically wrong with them.

- You can never be too rich or too thin.

- Some college women control their weight by going on cycles of binge eating and self-induced vomiting.

- It is abnormal to feel depressed.

- African Americans are more likely than white Americans to commit suicide.

- People who threaten suicide are only seeking attention.

- In some abnormal behavior problems, people see and hear things that are not actually there.

13

Abnormal Behavior

Learning Objectives

When you have finished studying Chapter 13, you should be able to:

What Is Abnormal Behavior?

1. Define *abnormal behavior*.

Models of Abnormal Behavior

2. Explain and compare the following models for understanding abnormal behavior: the demonological, medical (organic and psychodynamic versions), learning, and cognitive models.

Anxiety Disorders

3. Describe the anxiety disorders and discuss their origins.

Dissociative Disorders

4. Describe the dissociative disorders and discuss their origins.

Somatoform Disorders

5. Describe the somatoform disorders and discuss their origins.

Eating Disorders

6. Describe the eating disorders and discuss their origins.

Mood Disorders

7. Describe the mood disorders and discuss their origins.
8. Explain who is likely to commit suicide, and discuss the factors that contribute to suicide.

Schizophrenia

9. Describe the schizophrenic disorders and discuss their origins.

Personality Disorders

10. Describe the personality disorders and discuss their origins.

The Ohio State campus lived in terror one long fall. Four college women were abducted, were forced to cash checks or obtain money with their automatic teller machine cards, then were raped. A mysterious phone call led to the arrest of a 23-year-old drifter, William, who had been dismissed from the Navy.

William was not the boy next door.

Psychologists and psychiatrists who interviewed William concluded that ten identities—eight male and two female—resided within him (Keyes, 1982). His personality had been "fractured" by an abusive childhood. The identities showed distinct facial expressions, vocal patterns, and memories. They even performed differently on personality and intelligence tests.

Arthur, the most rational identity, spoke with a British accent. Danny and Christopher were normal, quiet adolescents. Christene was a 3-year-old girl. It was Tommy, a 16-year-old, who had enlisted in the Navy. Allen was 18 and smoked. Adelena, a 19-year-old lesbian identity, had committed the rapes. Who had made the mysterious phone call? Probably David, aged 9, an anxious child identity.

The defense claimed that William was suffering from a psychological disorder: **dissociative identity disorder** (also referred to as **multiple personality disorder**). Several distinct identities or personalities dwelled within him. Some were aware of the others. Some believed that they were the sole occupants. Billy, the core identity, had learned to sleep as a child to avoid the abuse of his father. A psychiatrist asserted that Billy had also been "asleep," in a "psychological coma," during the abductions. Billy should therefore be found innocent by reason of **insanity.**

Billy was found not guilty. He was committed to a psychiatric institution and released six years later.

In 1982, John Hinckley was also found not guilty of the assassination attempt on President Ronald Reagan's life by reason of insanity. Expert witnesses testified that he was suffering from **schizophrenia.** Hinckley, too, was committed to a psychiatric institution.

It is true that a man shot the president of the United States in front of millions of television witnesses and was found not guilty by a court of law—not guilty by reason of insanity.

Dissociative identity disorder and schizophrenia are two patterns of abnormal behavior. In this chapter, we first define what is meant by abnormal behavior. We then examine various broad explanations for, or perspectives on, abnormal behavior. As we review the demonological perspective, we shall see that if William had lived in Salem, Massachusetts, in 1692—just 200 years after Columbus set foot in the New World—he might have been hanged or burned as a witch. At that time, most people assumed that abnormal behavior was caused by possession by the Devil. Nineteen people lost their lives that year in that colonial town for allegedly practicing the arts of Satan.

We then discuss various patterns of abnormal behavior including anxiety disorders, dissociative disorders, somatoform disorders, mood disorders, schizophrenia, and personality disorders.

Dissociative identity disorder A disorder in which a person appears to have two or more distinct identities or personalities which may alternately emerge. (A term first used in the DSM-IV)

Insanity A legal term descriptive of a person judged to be incapable of recognizing right from wrong or of conforming his or her behavior to the law.

Schizophrenia A psychotic disorder characterized by loss of control of thought processes and inappropriate emotional responses.

Hallucinations. Hallucinations are among the more flagrant features of schizophrenia. They are perceptions that occur in the absence of external stimulation that cannot be distinguished from real perceptions, as in "hearing voices" or "seeing things." Are the cats in this Sandy Skoglund photograph real or hallucinatory?

WHAT IS ABNORMAL BEHAVIOR?

There are various patterns of abnormal behavior. Some are characterized by anxiety or depression, but many of us are anxious or depressed now and then without being considered abnormal. It is normal to be anxious before a big date or on the eve of a midterm exam. It would be appropriate to be depressed if a friend is upset with you or if you have failed at a test or job.

When, then, are feelings like anxiety and depression deemed abnormal? For one thing, anxiety and depression may be abnormal when they are not appropriate to our situations. It is not normal to be depressed when everything is going well or to be distraught when entering an elevator or looking out of a fourth-story window. The magnitude of the problem may also suggest abnormality. Though some anxiety is to be expected before a job interview, feeling that your heart is pounding so intensely that it might leap out of your chest—and then avoiding the interview—are not. Nor is sweating so profusely that your clothing literally becomes soaked.

Most psychologists would agree that behavior is abnormal when it meets some combination of the following criteria:

1. *It is unusual.* Although people who show abnormal behavior are in a minority, uncommon behavior is not in itself abnormal. There is only one president of the United States, yet that person is not considered to be abnormal (usually). Only one person holds the record for running or swimming the fastest mile. That person is different from you and me, but is not abnormal.

   Rarity or statistical deviance may not be sufficient for behavior to be labeled abnormal, but it helps. Most people do not see or hear things that are not there, and "seeing things" and "hearing things" are considered abnormal. We must also consider the situation: although many of us feel "panicked" when we recall that a term paper or report is due, most of us do not have panic attacks "out of the blue." Unpredictable panic attacks may thus also be deemed abnormal.

2. *It suggests faulty perception or interpretation of reality.* It is considered normal to talk to God through prayer, but if you claim that God talks back, you may be committed to a psychiatric institution. Our society considers it normal

Exorcism. This medieval woodcut represents the practice of exorcism, in which a demon is expelled from a person who has been "possessed."

to be inspired by religious beliefs, but abnormal to believe that God is literally speaking to you. "Hearing voices" and "seeing things" are considered **hallucinations.** Similarly, **ideas of persecution** such as believing that the Mafia or the CIA are "out to get you," are considered signs of disorder. (Unless they *are* out to get you, of course.)

3. *It suggests severe personal distress.* Anxiety, depression, exaggerated fears, and other psychological states cause personal distress, and severe personal distress may be considered abnormal. Anxiety and depression may also be appropriate responses to one's situation, however, as in a real threat or loss. In such cases, they are not abnormal unless they persevere long after the source of distress has been removed or after most people would have adjusted.
4. *It is self-defeating.* Behavior that causes misery rather than happiness and fulfillment may be considered abnormal. Chronic drinking that impairs work and family life and cigarette smoking that impairs health may thus be deemed abnormal.
5. *It is dangerous.* Behavior that is hazardous to the self or others is considered abnormal. People who threaten or attempt suicide may be considered abnormal, as may people who threaten or attack others.
6. *It is socially unacceptable.*

PERSPECTIVES ON ABNORMAL BEHAVIOR

There are a number of perspectives on, or ways of explaining, abnormal behavior. In this section, we consider the demonological, medical (biological and psychodynamic versions), learning, and cognitive perspectives.

The Demonological Perspective: "The Devil Made Me Do It"

Throughout human history, the **demonological perspective** has been the prevalent perspective for explaining abnormal behavior. Archaeologists have unearthed Stone Age human skeletons with egg-sized holes in the skulls. The holes suggest that our ancestors believed that abnormal behavior reflected invasion by evil spirits, and **trephined**—broke a pathway through the skull of—the "patient" to provide those irascible spirits an outlet.

Did trephining work? Well, most of the time it terminated the disturbing behavior. And the patient. New bone growth suggests that some "patients" survived the ordeal, however. Fear of trephining probably also persuaded some people to conform to group or tribal norms as best they could.

The ancient Greeks by and large believed that the gods punished humans by causing confusion and madness. An exception was Hippocrates, the Greek physician of the Golden Age of art andliterature (fourth century B.C.). Hippocrates made the radical suggestion that abnormal behavior was caused by an abnormality of the brain. The notion that biology could affect thoughts, feelings, and behavior was to lie dormant for about 2,000 years.

During the Middle Ages in Europe, as well as during the early days of American civilization along the rocky coast of Massachusetts, the demonological perspective was in full sway. It was generally believed that abnormal behavior was a sign of possession by agents or spirits of the Devil. Possession could stem from retribution, or God's having the Devil possess your soul as punishment for sins. Agitation and confusion were ascribed to retribution. Possession was also believed to result from deals with the Devil, in which people traded their souls for earthly gains. Such traders were called witches. Witches were held responsible for unfortunate events ranging from a neighbor's infertility to a poor crop.

Hallucination A perception in the absence of sensory stimulation that is confused with reality.

Ideas of persecution Erroneous beliefs that one is being victimized or persecuted.

Paranoid Characterized by oversuspiciousness and delusions of grandeur or persecution.

Demonological perspective The view that abnormal behavior reflects invasion by evil spirits or demons.

Trephining The prehistoric practice of venting the skull, with the intention of providing evil spirits a passage out of the head.

In either case, you were in for it. An exorcist, whose function was to persuade these spirits to find better pickings elsewhere, might pray at your side and wave a cross at you. If the spirits didn't call it quits, you might be beaten or flogged. If your behavior was still unseemly, other remedies, such as the rack, might effect a change.

In the fifteenth century, Pope Innocent VIII ordered that witches be put to death. In the same century, two Dominican monks published a manual, *The Hammer of Witches,* that advised peasants about how they could recognize witches in their own neighborhoods. At least 200,000 accused witches were killed during the next two centuries. Europe was no place to practice strange ways. The goings-on at Salem were trivial by comparison.

There were ingenious "diagnostic" tests to ferret out possession. One was a water-float test. It was based on the principle that pure metals sink to the bottom during smelting, but impurities float to the surface. Suspects who sank to the bottom and drowned were judged to be pure. Suspects who managed to keep their heads above water were assumed to be "impure" and in league with the Devil. Then they were in real trouble. This ordeal is the origin of the phrase, "Damned if you do and damned if you don't."

It is true that innocent people were drowned in the Middle Ages as a way of proving that they were not possessed by the Devil.

Although contemporary perspectives on abnormal behavior may not have the curiosity of the demonological perspective, they have more scientific merit.

The Medical Perspective: Biological and Psychodynamic Versions

According to the **medical model,** abnormal behavior patterns are symptoms of underlying disorders. Symptoms are noted for diagnostic purposes, but the underlying disorders must be treated if abnormal behavior is to abate. There are two versions of the medical model: the biological version and the psychodynamic version.

Medical Model: Biological Version. According to the biological version, abnormal behavior reflects biological or biochemical problems, not evil spirits. In 1883, Emil Kraepelin published a textbook of psychiatry in which he argued that there were specific psychological disorders or, as they are called within the medical model, mental illnesses. (Table 13.1 lists common terms concerning psychological disorders that reflect the influence of the medical model.) Each mental illness was believed to have its own biological roots.

Investigators have speculated that abnormalities in various parts of the body might give rise to abnormal behavior. The ancient Greeks attributed premenstrual syndrome to a wandering uterus. In more recent years, researchers have looked,

Medical model The view that abnormal behavior is symptomatic of an underlying illness.

TABLE 13.1: Terms Concerning Abnormal Behavior that Are Derived from the Medical Model

Mental Illness	Diagnosis	Treatment
Mental Health	Mental Patient	Therapy
Symptoms	Mental Hospital	Cure
Syndrome	Prognosis	Relapse

often in vain, at the size of structures in the brain and at substances in the blood. Researchers today often look for such abnormalities in neurotransmitters, the chemicals that conduct "messages" from one cell in the nervous system, or neuron, to another.

Kraepelin argued that each mental illness, just like each physical illness, was typified by its own cluster of symptoms, or **syndrome.** Each mental illness or pattern of abnormal behavior had a specific outcome, or course, and would presumably respond to a specific form of therapy.

Contemporary supporters of the biological version of the medical model point to various sources of evidence. For one thing, some disorders run in families and may, therefore, be inherited by way of DNA, the material that contains our genetic codes. For another, chemical imbalances in the brain and elsewhere are connected with problems such as major depression and schizophrenia.

According to the biological version of the medical model, treatment requires medical expertise and control or cure of the underlying biological problem. The biological therapies discussed in Chapter 14 are largely based on the medical model.

The biological version of the medical model was a major advance over demonology. It led to the view that mentally ill people should be treated by qualified professionals rather than punished. Compassion replaced hatred, fear, and persecution.

There are some problems with the biological model, however. For one thing, there is no convincing role for biology in many disorders. For another, the medical model suggests that the mentally ill, like the physically ill, may not be responsible for their problems. In the past, this view often led to hospitalization and suspension of responsibility (as in work and maintenance of a family life) among the mentally ill. Thus removed from the real world, however, patients' abilities would often decline rather than return to normal. Today, most adherents to the medical model encourage patients to remain in the community and maintain as much responsibility as they can. Finally, treatments derived from other perspectives have been shown to be of help with several patterns of abnormal behavior, as we shall see in Chapter 14.

Medical Model: Psychodynamic Version. Whereas the biological version of the medical model suggests that abnormal behavior reflects biological problems, Sigmund Freud's psychodynamic perspective argues that abnormal behavior symptomizes *psychological* problems. In keeping with Freud's theory of psychosexual development, the underlying problem is usually assumed to be unconscious childhood conflict. The abnormal behavior is a "symptom" of the conflict. In persistent anxiety, abnormal behavior is thought to symptomize difficulty repressing primitive sexual and aggressive impulses.

Within Freudian theory, **neurotic** behavior and anxiety stem from the leakage of primitive impulses. Anxiety represents the impulse itself and fear of what might happen if the impulse were acted upon. In the case of **psychosis,** impulses are assumed to have broken through so that behavior falls under the control of the chaotic id. According to psychodynamic theory, treatment (other than a "Band-Aid" therapy) requires resolving the unconscious conflicts that underlie the behavior.

Syndrome A cluster or group of symptoms suggestive of a particular disorder.

Neurotic Of neurosis. Within psychodynamic theory, neuroses are a group of disorders theorized to stem from unconscious conflict.

Psychosis A major disorder in which a person lacks insight and has difficulty meeting the demands of daily life and maintaining contact with reality.

Learning Perspectives

Learning theorists do not necessarily see abnormal behavior as being symptomatic of underlying problems. Rather, abnormal behavior is itself the problem. Abnormal behavior may be acquired in the same ways normal behavior is acquired—for example, through conditioning and observational learning. Why, then, do some people show abnormal behavior? From the behaviorist perspective, one reason is found in situational variables. That is, the learning or reinforcement histories of persons with abnormal behavior might differ from those of most of us. But from the social-learning perspective, differences in person variables such as competencies, encoding strategies, self-efficacy expectations, and self-regulatory systems also play roles.

A person who lacks social skills may not have had the chance to observe skillful models. Or it might be that a minority subculture reinforced behaviors that are not approved by the majority. Punishment for early exploratory behavior or childhood sexual activity might lead to adult anxieties over independence or sexuality. Inconsistent discipline (haphazard rewarding of desirable behavior and unreliable punishment of misbehavior) might lead to antisocial behavior. Children whose parents ignore or abuse them may come to pay more attention to their fantasies than the outer world, leading to schizophrenic withdrawal and confusion of reality with fantasy.

Social-learning theorists, like Albert Bandura (1986) and Walter Mischel (1993), attribute importance to encoding strategies, self-regulatory systems, and expectancies in explaining behavior. For example, expectancies that we shall not be able to carry out our plans (low self-efficacy expectancies) sap motivation and generate feelings of hopelessness—two facets of depression (Bandura, 1982). Deficits in competencies, encoding strategies, and self-regulatory systems may heighten schizophrenic problems. Because learning theorists do not believe that behavior problems necessarily reflect biological problems or unconscious conflict, they often try to change or modify the problems directly, as with behavior therapy (see Chapter 14).

The Cognitive Perspective

Cognitive theorists focus on the cognitive events—such as thoughts, expectations, and attitudes—that accompany or give rise to abnormal behavior.

One cognitive approach to understanding abnormal behavior involves information processing. Information-processing theorists compare the processes of the mind to those of the computer. They think in terms of cycles of input (based on perception), storage, retrieval, manipulation, and output of information. They view psychological disorders as disturbances in the cycle. Disturbances might be caused by the blocking or distortion of input or by faulty storage, retrieval, or manipulation of information. Any of these can lead to lack of output or distorted output (for example, bizarre behavior). Schizophrenic individuals, for example, may chaotically jump from topic to topic, which is suggestive of problems in the manipulation of information.

Cognitive theorist Albert Ellis (1977, 1987) views anxiety as stemming from irrational beliefs such as an excessive want of social approval. Aaron Beck notes how "cognitive errors" like self-devaluation and pessimism can give rise to depression (Beck et al., 1979). Many cases of depression are connected with cognitions that one is helpless to improve one's lot.

Many psychologists look to more than one perspective to explain and treat abnormal behavior. They are labeled **eclectic** psychologists. Many social-learning theorists, for example, believe that some psychological disorders stem from biochemical factors or the interaction of biochemistry and learning. They are open to combining behavior therapy with drugs to treat problems such as schizophrenia and **bipolar disorder.** Psychoanalysts may believe that schizophrenia reflects control by the id and argue that only long-term psychotherapy can help the ego regain supremacy. But they may also be willing to use drugs to calm agitation on a temporary basis.

We now consider the major psychological disorders, using the classification provided by the American Psychiatric Association in the Fourth Edition of the Diagnostic and Statistical Manual (DSM-IV) of the Mental Disorders. We refer to the

Eclectic Selecting from various systems or theories.

Bipolar disorder A disorder in which the mood alternates between two extreme poles (elation and depression). Also referred to as *manic-depression.*

Panic Disorder. This man was overcome by feelings of panic as he was walking to his car. The physical aspects of panic attacks tend to be stronger than those of other kinds of anxiety, including shortness of breath, dizziness, and pounding of the heart. Many panic sufferers fear that they will have heart attacks.

DSM-IV because it is the most widely used system in the U.S. However, psychologists criticize it on many grounds, e.g., that it adheres too strongly to the medical model. So our use of the DSM is a convenience, not an endorsement.

ANXIETY DISORDERS

Anxiety disorders have subjective and physical features (Beck et al., 1988). Subjective features include fear of the worst happening, fear of losing control, nervousness, and inability to relax. Physical features reflect arousal of the sympathetic branch of the autonomic nervous system. They entail trembling, sweating, a pounding or racing heart, elevated blood pressure (a flushed face), and faintness. Anxiety is an appropriate response to a threat. Anxiety can be abnormal, however, when its extent is out of proportion to the threat or when it "comes out of the blue"—that is, when events do not seem to warrant it.

Types of Anxiety Disorders

The anxiety disorders include phobic, panic, generalized anxiety, obsessive–compulsive, and post-traumatic stress disorders.

Phobias. There are several types of phobias, including *specific phobia, social phobia,* and *agoraphobia.* **Specific phobias** are excessive, irrational fears of specific objects or situations. **Social phobias** are persistent fears of scrutiny by others or of doing something that will be humiliating or embarrassing. Stage fright and speech anxiety are common social phobias.

Some social phobics cannot sign their names in public, as in the case of Brett:

Brett was a signature phobic. She was literally terrified of signing her name in public. She had structured her life to avoid situations requiring a signature. She paid cash rather than by credit card. She filed documents by mail rather than in person. She even registered her car in her husband's name so that he would be responsible for signing the motor vehicle forms. Like many phobics, Brett was clever at restructuring her life so that she could avoid exposing herself to these fearful situations. She had even kept her phobia from her husband for 15 years.

Brett's phobia was maintained by an underlying fear of social embarrassment. She feared ridicule for an illegible or sloppy signature, or that authority figures like bank officers or motor vehicle officials would think that her signature was phony or a forgery. Brett knew that she could prove her identity by other means than her signature and also recognized that no one really cared whether or not her signature was legible. Brett had created a vicious cycle of anxiety: She felt she must prevent her hands from shaking so that she could write legibly. But her anxiety was so strong that she began to shake whenever her signature was required. The more she tried to fend off the anxiety, the stronger it became. Her anxiety confirmed her belief that her signature would be ridiculed.

Adapted from Nevid et al., 1994

One specific phobia is fear of elevators. Some people will not enter elevators despite the hardships they suffer (such as walking six flights of steps) as a result. Yes, the cable *could* break. The ventilation *could* fail. One *could* be stuck waiting in midair for repairs. These problems are uncommon, however, and it does not make sense for most of us to repeatedly walk flights of stairs to elude them. Similarly, some people with specific phobias for hypodermic needles will not receive injections, even when they are the advised remedy for profound illness. Injections can be painful, but most people with phobias for needles would gladly suffer an excruciating pinch if it would help them fight illness. Other specific phobias include **claustrophobia** (fear of tight or enclosed places), **acrophobia** (fear of heights), and fear of mice, snakes, and other creepy-crawlies.

Phobias can seriously disrupt one's life. A person may know that a phobia is irrational yet still experience acute anxiety and avoid the phobic article or circumstance.

Specific phobia Persistent fear of a specific object or situation. (Previously termed *simple phobia*)

Social phobia An irrational, excessive fear of public scrutiny.

Claustrophobia Fear of tight, small places.

Acrophobia Fear of high places.

Obsessive–Compulsive Disorder. This photograph, *Red Library #2,* by Laurie Simmons, is suggestive of certain features of obsessive–compulsive disorder. The "woman" in this compulsively neat room is apparently transfixed by the absence of perfection. It seems that one picture is missing. People with obsessive–compulsive disorder engage in repetitious behaviors as a way of managing troubling thoughts.

Fears of animals and imaginary creatures are common among children, and **agoraphobia** is among the most widespread phobias of adults. Agoraphobia is derived from the Greek meaning "fear of the marketplace," or of being out in open, busy areas. Persons with agoraphobia fear being in places from which it might be difficult to escape or in which help might be unavailable if they become disquieted. In practice, people who receive this label are often loath to venture out of their homes, especially when they are alone. They find it trying or infeasible to hold jobs or to sustain an ordinary social life.

Panic Disorder.

> *My heart would start pounding so hard I was sure I was having a heart attack. I used to go to the emergency room. Sometimes I felt dizzy, like I was going to pass out. I was sure I was about to die.*
>
> Kim Weiner (1992)

Panic disorder is an abrupt attack of acute anxiety that is not triggered by a specific object or situation. Panic sufferers experience strong physical sensations such as shortness of breath, heavy sweating, quaking, and pounding of the heart (Goleman, 1992). As was the case with Kim Weiner, they are particularly aware of cardiac sensations (Ehlers & Breuer, 1992). It is not unusual for them to think that they are having a heart attack. Sufferers may also experience choking sensations; nausea; numbness or tingling; flushes or chills; chest pain; and fear of dying, going crazy, or losing control. Panic attacks may last from a minute or two to an hour or more. Afterwards, victims usually feel spent.

Perhaps half of us panic now and then (Wilson et al., 1991). However, the diagnosis of panic disorder is reserved for people who undergo series of attacks or live in dread of attacks. Fewer than ten percent of us meet this standard (Wilson et al., 1992).

Because panic attacks seem to descend from nowhere, some sufferers remain in the home most of the time for fear of having an attack in public. In such cases, sufferers are diagnosed as having *panic disorder with agoraphobia.*

Generalized Anxiety Disorder. The central feature of **generalized anxiety disorder** is persistent anxiety. As in the panic disorder, the anxiety cannot be attributed to a phobic object, situation, or activity. Rather, it seems to be free floating. Features may include motor tension (shakiness, inability to relax, furrowed brow, fidgeting); autonomic overarousal (sweating, dry mouth, racing heart, light-headedness, frequent urinating, diarrhea); feelings of dread and foreboding; and excessive vigilance, as shown by distractibility, insomnia, and irritability.

Obsessive–Compulsive Disorder. **Obsessions** are recurrent thoughts or images that seem irrational and beyond control. The obsessions in obsessive–compulsive disorder are accompanied by anxiety (Foa, 1990). They are so compelling and recurrent that they disrupt daily life. They may include doubts about whether one has locked the doors and shut the windows; impulses such as the wish to strangle one's spouse; and images such as one mother's repeated fantasy that her children had been run over by traffic on the way home from school. In another case, a 16-year-old boy found "numbers in my head" whenever he was about to study or take a test. A housewife became obsessed with the idea that she had contaminated her hands with Sani-Flush and that the contamination was spreading to everything she touched.

Compulsions are thoughts or behaviors that tend to reduce the anxiety connected with obsessions (Foa, 1990). They are seemingly irresistible urges to engage in acts, often repeatedly, such as elaborate washing after using the bathroom. The impulse is recurrent and forceful, interfering with daily life. The woman who felt contaminated by Sani-Flush engaged in intricate hand-washing rituals to reduce the anxiety connected with the obsession. She spent three to four hours daily at the sink and complained, "My hands look like lobster claws."

Agoraphobia Fear of open, crowded places.

Panic disorder The recurrent experiencing of attacks of extreme anxiety in the absence of external stimuli that usually elicit anxiety.

Generalized anxiety disorder Feelings of dread and foreboding and sympathetic arousal of at least six months' duration.

Obsession A recurring thought or image that seems beyond control.

Compulsion An apparently irresistible urge to repeat an act or engage in ritualistic behavior such as hand-washing.

A Traumatic Experience from the Vietnam War. Physical threats and other traumatic experiences can lead to post-traumatic stress disorder (PTSD). PTSD is characterized by intrusive memories of the experience, recurrent dreams about it, and the sudden feeling that it is, in fact, recurring (as in "flashbacks").

Post-Traumatic Stress Disorder. **Post-traumatic stress disorder** (PTSD) is known by intense and persistent feelings of anxiety and helplessness that are caused by a traumatic experience such as a physical threat to oneself or one's family, destruction of one's community, or the witnessing of the death of another person. PTSD has troubled many Vietnam war veterans, victims of rape, and persons who have seen their homes and communities inundated by floods or swept away by tornadoes. In some cases, PTSD occurs many months after the event.

A traumatic event can give rise to intrusive memories, recurrent nightmares (Wood et al., 1992), and sudden feelings that the event is repeating (as in "flashbacks"). When Vietnam veterans with PTSD imagine the events of the battlefield, they show a great deal of muscle tension and other physiological signs of anxiety (Pitman et al., 1990).

It is true that stressful experiences can lead to recurrent nightmares.

The PTSD sufferer typically attempts to avoid thoughts and activities connected to the traumatic event. He or she may also display sleep problems, irritable outbursts, difficulty concentrating, extreme vigilance, and an intensified "startle" response.

The case of Margaret illustrates many of the features of PTSD:

Margaret was a 54-year-old woman who lived with her husband Travis in a small village in the hills to the east of the Hudson River. Two winters earlier, in the middle of the night, a fuel truck had skidded down one of the icy inclines that led into the village center. Two blocks away, Margaret was shaken from her bed by the explosion ("I thought the world was coming to an end. My husband said the Russians must've dropped the H-bomb.") when the truck slammed into the general store. The store and the apartments above were immediately engulfed in flames. The fire spread to the church next door. Margaret's first and most enduring visual impression was of shards of red and black that rose into the air in an eerie ballet. On their way down, they bathed the centuries-old tombstones in the church graveyard in hellish light. A dozen people died, mostly those who had lived above and in back of the general store. The old caretaker of the church and the truck driver were lost as well.

Post-traumatic stress disorder A disorder which follows a psychologically distressing event that is outside the range of normal human experience and which is characterized by features such as intense fear, avoidance of stimuli associated with the event, and reliving of the event.

Margaret shared the village's loss, took in the temporarily homeless, and did her share of what had to be done. Months later, after the general store had been leveled to a memorial park and the church was on the way toward being restored, Margaret started to feel that life was becoming strange, that the world outside was becoming a little unreal. She began to withdraw from her friends and scenes of the night of the fire would fill her mind. At night she now and then dreamt the scene. Her physician prescribed a sleeping pill which she discontinued because "I couldn't wake up out of the dream." Her physician turned to Valium, a minor tranquilizer, to help her get through the day. The pills helped for a while, but "I quit them because I needed more and more of the things and you can't take drugs forever, can you?"

Over the next year and a half, Margaret tried her best not to think about the disaster, but the intrusive recollections and the dreams came and went, apparently on their own. By the time Margaret sought help, her sleep had been seriously distressed for nearly two months and the recollections were as vivid as ever.

Adapted from Nevid et al., 1994

Theoretical Views

According to the psychodynamic perspective, phobias symbolize conflicts of childhood origin. Psychodynamic theory explains generalized anxiety as persistent difficulty in maintaining repression of primitive impulses. Psychoanalysts view obsessions as the leakage of unconscious impulses and compulsions as acts that allow people to keep such impulses partly repressed.

Some learning theorists suggest that phobias might be conditioned fears that were acquired in early childhood and whose origins are beyond memory. Avoidance of feared stimuli is reinforced by reduction of anxiety. In the case of rape victims, evidence suggests that exposure to a situation (for example, the neighborhood, one's place of employment) in which the attack occurred, in the absence of further attack, can extinguish some of the post-traumatic distress (Wirtz & Harrell, 1987).

Susan Mineka (1991) suggests that people (and nonhuman primates) are genetically predisposed to fear stimuli that may have once posed a threat to their ancestors. Evolutionary forces would have favored the survival of individuals who were predisposed toward acquiring fears of large animals, spiders, snakes, heights, entrapment, sharp objects, and strangers. In laboratory experiments, people have been shown photographs of various objects and then given electric shock (Hugdahl & Ohman, 1977; Ohman et al., 1976). Subjects more readily acquire fear reactions to some stimuli (e.g., spiders and snakes) than others (e.g., flowers and houses), as measured by sweat in the palm of the hand. These experiments, however, do not show that the subjects are genetically predisposed to develop fear responses to stimuli such as snakes and spiders. The subjects were reared in a society in which many people react negatively to these creepy-crawlies. Thus their learning experiences, and not genetic factors, may have predisposed them to fear these stimuli.

Similarly, social-learning theorists note a role for observational learning in acquiring fears (Bandura et al., 1969). If parents squirm, grimace, and shudder at mice, blood, or dirt on the kitchen floor, children might encode these stimuli as being awful and imitate their behavior. Learning theorists suggest that generalized anxiety is often nothing more than fear that has been associated with situations so broad that they are not readily identified such as social relationships or personal achievement. Social-learning and cognitive theorists suggest that anxiety can be maintained by thinking that one is in a terrible situation and is helpless to change it. Mineka (1991) argues that anxious people are cognitively biased toward paying more attention to threatening objects or situations. Psychoanalysts and learning theorists broadly agree that compulsive behavior reduces anxiety.

Cognitive theorists note that our appraisals of the magnitude of the threats in events help determine whether events are traumatic and lead to PTSD (Creamer et al., 1992). Obsessions and compulsions may serve to divert people's attention from more intimidating issues such as "What am I to do with my life?" When anxieties are acquired at a young age, we may later interpret them as enduring traits and label ourselves as "people who fear ________________"(you fill it in). We then live up to the labels. We also entertain thoughts that heighten and perpetuate anxiety (Meichenbaum & Jaremko, 1983) such as "I've got to get out of here," or "My heart is going to leap out of my chest." Such ideas intensify physical signs of anxiety, disrupt planning, magnify the aversiveness of stimuli, motivate avoidance, and decrease self-efficacy expectations about ability to manage the situation. Belief that we shall not be able to handle a threat heightens anxiety, whereas belief that we are in control lessens anxiety (Bandura et al., 1985; Miller, 1980).

Biological factors may play a role in anxiety disorders. For one thing, anxiety disorders tend to run in families (Turner et al., 1987). Scarr and her colleagues (1981) compared the **neuroticism** test scores of adopted adolescents to those of their natural and adoptive parents. She found that scores of parents and their natural children correlated more highly than those of parents and adopted children, suggestive of a stronger role for heredity than environmental influences. Twin studies also find the **concordance** rate for anxiety disorders higher among pairs of identical than fraternal twins (Torgersen, 1983).

Perhaps a predisposition toward anxiety—in the form of a highly reactive autonomic nervous system—can be inherited. What might make a nervous system "highly reactive"? One possibility is that receptor sites in the brain are not sensitive enough to **gamma-aminobutyric acid (GABA),** an inhibitory neurotransmitter that may help quell anxiety reactions. The **benzodiazepines,** a class of drugs that reduce anxiety, are thought to work by increasing the sensitivity of receptor sites to GABA.

Many cases of anxiety disorders might reflect the interaction of biological and psychological factors. In panic disorder, biological imbalances may initially trigger attacks, but subsequent fear of attacks—and of the bodily cues that signal the onset of attacks—may heighten their discomfort and give sufferers the idea that there is nothing they can do about them (McNally, 1990). Feelings of helplessness increase fear. Panic sufferers can thus be helped by psychological methods that provide ways of reducing physical discomfort—including regular breathing—and that show them that there are, after all, things they can do to cope with attacks (Barlow, 1986b; Klosko et al., 1990). The origins of many patterns of abnormal behavior seem quite complex, involving the interaction of biological and psychological factors.

DISSOCIATIVE DISORDERS

In the **dissociative disorders,** there is a separation of mental processes such as thoughts, emotions, identity, memory, or consciousness—the processes that make the person feel whole (Spiegel & Cardeña, 1991).

Types of Dissociative Disorders

The DSM-IV lists several dissociative disorders including *dissociative amnesia, dissociative fugue, dissociative identity disorder,* and *depersonalization.*

Dissociative Amnesia. In **dissociative amnesia,** there is sudden inability to recall important personal information. Memory loss cannot be attributed to organic problems such as a blow to the head or alcoholic intoxication. It is thus a *psycho*logical dissociative disorder, not an organic disorder. In the most common example, the person cannot recall events for a number of hours after a stressful incident, as in warfare or in the case of the uninjured survivor of an accident. In generalized amnesia, people forget their entire lives. Amnesia may last for hours or years. Termination of amnesia is also sudden.

Neuroticism A personality trait characterized largely by persistent anxiety.

Concordance Agreement.

Gamma-aminobutyric acid (GABA) An inhibitory neurotransmitter that is implicated in anxiety reactions.

Benzodiazepines A class of drugs that reduce anxiety; minor tranquilizers.

Dissociative disorders Disorders in which there are sudden, temporary changes in consciousness or self-identity.

Dissociative amnesia A dissociative disorder marked by loss of memory or self-identity; skills and general knowledge are usually retained. (Previously termed *psychogenic amnesia*)

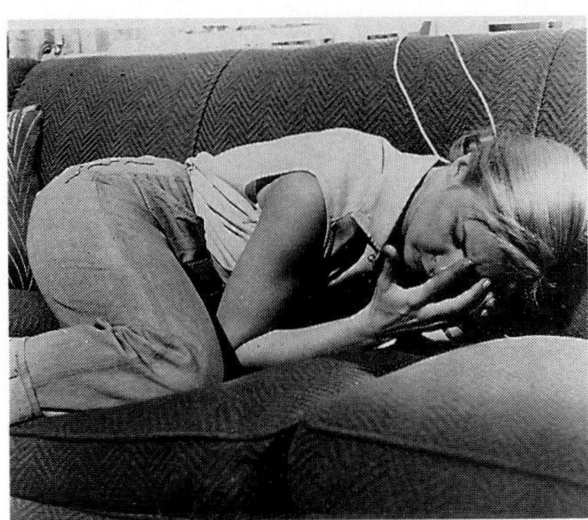
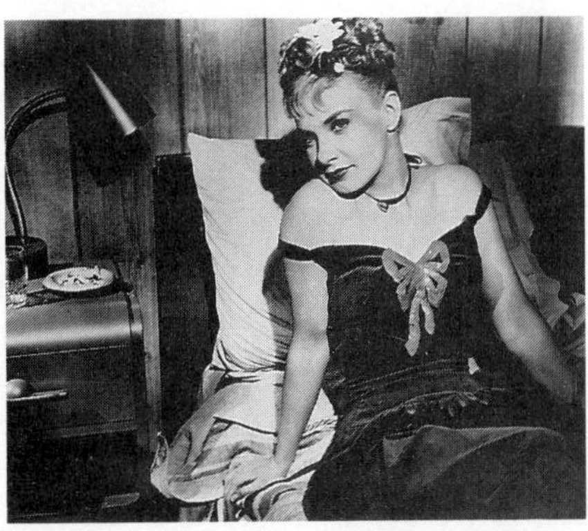

Dissociative Identity Disorder. In the film *The Three Faces of Eve,* Joanne Woodward played three identities in the same woman: the shy, inhibited Eve White (lying on couch); the flirtatious and promiscuous Eve Black (in the dark dress); and a third identity (Jane) who could accept her sexual and aggressive impulses and still maintain her sense of identity.

People sometimes claim that they cannot recall engaging in socially unacceptable behavior, promising to do something, and so on. Claiming to have a psychological problem such as amnesia in order to escape responsibility is known as **malingering.** Current research methods do not guarantee that we can distinguish malingerers from people with dissociative disorders.

Dissociative Fugue. In **dissociative fugue,** the person shows loss of memory for the past, travels abruptly from his or her home or place of work, and takes a new identity. Either the person does not think about the past, or that person reports a past filled with sham memories that are not known to be erroneous. Following recovery, the events that occurred during the fugue are not recalled.

Dissociative Identity Disorder. Dissociative identity disorder (formerly termed *multiple personality disorder*) is the name given to William's disorder, as described at the beginning of the chapter. In this disorder, two or more identities, or personalities, each with distinct traits and memories, "occupy" the same person, with or without awareness of the others. Different identities might even have different eyeglass prescriptions (Braun, 1988).

Braun reports cases in which assorted identities showed different allergic responses. In one patient, an identity named Timmy was not sensitive to orange juice. But when other identities who alternated control over him drank orange juice, they would break out with hives. Hives would also erupt after Timmy drank orange juice if another identitiy emerged while the juice was being digested. And if Timmy re-appeared when the allergic reaction was present, the itching of the hives would cease at once, and the water-filled blisters would start to subside. In other cases reported by Braun, different identities in one person might show various responses to the same medicine. Or one identity might exhibit color blindness while others had intact color vision. If such cases are accurately reported, they provide a fascinating demonstration of the varieties of behavior patterns and ways of perceiving the world that are possible for persons with comparable biological makeup.

It does seem to be true that some people do have more than one identity, with different allergies and eyeglass prescriptions.

A few celebrated cases have been portrayed in the popular media. In one that became the subject of the film *The Three Faces of Eve,* a timid housewife named

---

Malingering Pretending to be ill in order to escape duty or work.

Dissociative fugue A dissociative disorder in which one experiences amnesia, then flees to a new location and establishes a new life style. (Previously termed *psychogenic fugue*)

Feelings of Depersonalization. Episodes of depersonalization are typified by a sense of detachment from oneself. It may seem that one is outside of one's own body or walking in a dream.

Eve White harbored two other identities: Eve Black, a sexually aggressive, antisocial identity; and Jane, an emerging identity who was able to accept the existence of her primitive impulses, yet show socially appropriate behavior. Finally, the three faces merged into one—Jane. Ironically, Jane (Chris Sizemore, in real life) reportedly split into 22 identities later on. Another well-publicized case is that of Sybil, a woman with 16 identities whose case was also made into a film.

Depersonalization Disorder. **Depersonalization disorder** is characterized by persistent or recurrent feelings that one is detached from one's own body, as if one is observing one's thought processes from the outside. One may also feel as though he or she is functioning on automatic pilot, or as if in a dream.

The case of Richie illustrates a brief or transient (passing) episode of depersonalization:

"We went to Orlando with the children after school let out. I had also been driving myself hard, and it was time to let go. We spent three days 'doing' Disney World, and it got to the point where we were all wearing shirts with mice and ducks on them and singing Disney songs like 'Yo ho, yo ho, a pirate's life for me.' On the third day I began to feel unreal and ill at ease while we were watching these middle-American Ivory-soap teenagers singing and dancing in front of Cinderella's Castle. The day was finally cooling down, but I broke into a sweat. I became shaky and dizzy and sat down on the cement next to the 4-year-old's stroller without giving [my wife] an explanation. There were strollers and kids and [adults'] legs all around me, and for some strange reason I became fixated on the pieces of popcorn strewn on the ground. All of a sudden it was like the people around me were all silly mechanical creatures, like the dolls in the 'It's a Small World' [exhibit] or the animals on the 'Jungle Cruise.' Things sort of seemed to slow down, the way they do when you've smoked marijuana, and there was this invisible wall of cotton between me and everyone else.

"Then the concert was over and my wife was like 'What's the matter?' and did I want to stay for the Electrical Parade and the fireworks or was I sick? Now I was beginning to wonder if I was going crazy and I said I was sick, that my wife would have to take me by the hand and drive us back to the Sonesta Village [motel]. Somehow we got back to the monorail and turned in the strollers. I waited in the herd [of people] at the station like a dead person, my eyes glazed over, looking out over kids with Mickey Mouse ears and Mickey Mouse balloons. The mechanical voice on the monorail almost did me in and I got really shaky.

"I refused to go back to the Magic Kingdom. I went with the family to Sea World, and on another day I dropped [my wife] and the kids off at the Magic Kingdom and

Depersonalization disorder Persistent or recurrent feelings that one is not real or is detached from one's own experiences or body.

picked them up that night. My wife thought I was goldbricking or something, and we had a helluva fight about it, but we had a life to get back to and my sanity had to come first."

Nevid et al., 1994

Theoretical Views

According to psychodynamic theory, people with dissociative disorders use massive repression to avert recognition of improper impulses. In dissociative amnesia and fugue, the person forgets a profoundly disturbing event or impulse. In dissociative identity disorder, the person expresses unacceptable impulses through alternate identities. In depersonalization, the person stands outside—removed from the turmoil within.

According to learning theorists, in dissociative disorders people learn *not to think* about disturbing acts or impulses to avoid feelings of guilt and shame. Technically speaking, *not thinking about these matters* is reinforced[1] by *removal* of the aversive stimuli of guilt and shame.

Social-learning theory suggests that many people come to role-play dissociative identity disorder through observational learning—not quite the same thing as faking because people can "forget to tell themselves" that they have assumed a role. Reinforcers are made available by role-playing individuals with dissociative identity disorder: Drawing attention to oneself and escaping responsibility for unacceptable behavior are two (Spanos et al., 1985; Thigpen & Cleckley, 1984).

One cognitive perspective explains dissociative disorders in terms of deployment of attention. Perhaps all of us are capable of dividing our awareness so that we become unaware, at least temporarily, of events that we usually focus more attention on. Perhaps the marvel is *not* that attention can be divided, but that human consciousness normally integrates experience into a meaningful whole.

SOMATOFORM DISORDERS

In **somatoform disorders,** people show or complain of physical problems such as paralysis, pain, or the persistent belief that they have a serious disease, yet no evidence of a physical abnormality can be found.

Types of Somatoform Disorders

In this section, we discuss two somatoform disorders: *conversion disorder* and *hypochondriasis.*

Conversion Disorder. **Conversion disorder** is characterized by a major change in, or loss of, physical functioning, although there are no medical findings to explain the loss of functioning. The behaviors are not intentionally produced; that is, the person is not faking.

If you lost the ability to see at night, or if your legs became paralyzed, you would understandably show concern. But some victims of conversion disorder show indifference to their symptoms, a remarkable feature referred to as **la belle indifférence.** Conversion disorder is so named because it appears to "convert" a source of stress into a physical difficulty.

During World War II, a number of bomber pilots developed night blindness. They could not carry out their nighttime missions, although no damage to the optic nerves was found. In rare cases, women with large families have been reported to become paralyzed in the legs, again with no medical findings.

Somatoform disorders Disorders in which people complain of physical (somatic) problems, even though no physical abnormality can be found.

Conversion disorder A disorder in which anxiety or unconscious conflicts are "converted" into physical symptoms that often have the effect of helping the person cope with anxiety or conflict.

La belle indifférence A French term descriptive of the lack of concern sometimes shown by people with conversion disorders.

[1]This is an example of negative reinforcement, because the frequency of behavior—in this case, the frequency of diverting one's attention from a certain topic—is increased by *removal* of a stimulus—in this case, by removal of feelings of, say, guilt or shame.

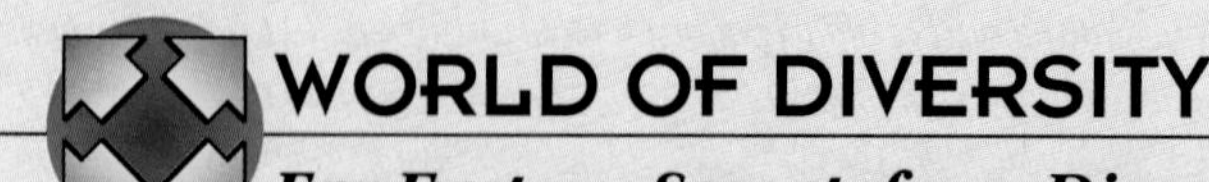

WORLD OF DIVERSITY

Far-Eastern Somatoform Disorders: Koro and Dhat Syndromes

It is common for American hypochondriacs to believe that they have grave illnesses, such as cancer. The Far-Eastern Koro and Dhat syndromes are similar to hypochondriasis, although they will seem "foreign" to many readers. Each syndrome is culture-related; each, that is, is connected with folklore in its culture.

Koro Syndrome

Koro syndrome is found primarily in China and some other nations in the Far East. People with the syndrome are afraid that their genital organs are shrinking in size and withdrawing into their bodies, a problem that they believe will cause their death (Fabian, 1991; Tseng et al., 1992). Koro syndrome is primarily found in young men, although some cases have been identified in women (Tseng et al, 1992). People with Koro syndrome often show physiological signs of anxiety that approach panic in proportion, such as heart palpitations, heavy sweating, and difficulty breathing (Devan & Ong-Seng-Hong, 1987; Tseng et al., 1992).

Epidemics of Koro syndrome involving thousands of people have been reported in Asian countries such as China, Singapore, Thailand, and India (Tseng et al., 1992), and can be traced back as far as 3000 B.C. An epidemic involving 2000 people occurred in China's Guangdong Province during the 1980s (Tseng, et al., 1992). Guangdong residents who did not fall victim to the Koro syndrome were apparently more likely to be critical thinkers; that is, they were less superstitious and less accepting of

It is true that some people have lost the use of their legs or eyes under stress, even though nothing was medically wrong with them.

Hypochondriasis. Persons with **hypochondriasis** insist that they are suffering from profound illness, even though no medical evidence can be found. They become preoccupied with minor physical sensations and maintain their belief despite medical reassurance. "Hypochondriacs" may run from doctor to doctor, seeking the one who will find the causes of the sensations. Fear may disrupt work or home life.

Hypochondriasis is supposed to be found more often among elderly people. As pointed out by Costa and McCrae (1985), however, real health changes occur with age, and most complaints are probably accurate reflections of people's changing health status.

Theoretical Views

Instances of conversion disorder are rare and short in duration, but their existence led the young Sigmund Freud to believe that subconscious processes were at work in people. The psychodynamic view of conversion disorders is that the symptoms produced by the victim protect the victim from feelings of guilt or shame or from another source of stress. Conversion disorders, like dissociative disorders, often seem to serve a purpose. The "blindness" of the pilots may have afforded them respite from stressful missions or may have allowed them to evade the guilt from bombing civilian populations. The paralysis of a woman who prematurely commits herself to a large family and a life at home may prevent her from doing housework or from engaging in sexual intercourse and becoming pregnant again. She "accomplishes" certain ends without having to identify them or make decisions.

There is evidence that some hypochondriacs use their complaints as a self-handicapping strategy (Smith et al., 1983). That is, they are more likely to com-

Hypochondriasis Persistent belief that one has a medical disorder despite lack of medical findings.

Koro-related folklore than were people who did fall victim to the epidemic (Tseng, et al., 1992). Although medical reassurance often fails to dent the concerns of hypochondriacs in the United States, it apparently often quells Koro episodes in the Far East (Devan & Ong-Seng-Hong, 1987). Koro episodes also tend to be transient among people who do not receive medical reassurance, but they are more likely to recur.

Many researchers have suggested that Koro syndrome should be listed in the DSM (Bernstein & Gaw, 1990; Fishbain, 1991).

Dhat Syndrome

Young Asian-Indian men are the ethnic group likely to experience another culture-related syndrome, Dhat syndrome, which involves unreasonable fears of loss of seminal fluid through nocturnal emissions (Akhtar, 1988). Some men with Dhat syndrome also believe (erroneously) that semen may mix with urine and be lost when they urinate. Like American hypochondriacs, men with Dhat syndrome may run from physician to physican for help. Within Indian and some other near- and Far-Eastern cultures, it is widely believed that the loss of semen depletes the body of physical and mental energy and is therefore harmful (Chadda & Ahuja, 1990). Akhtar (1988) notes that attitudes toward semen represent an "organized, deep-seated belief system that can be traced back" some 2500 years. "Semen is considered to be the elixir of life, in both a physical and mystical sense. Its perservation is supposed to guarantee health and longevity" (Akhtar, 1988, p. 71).

Dhat syndrome has also been connected with difficulty attaining erection, apparently because of excessive but unfounded concerns over loss of semen through ejaculation (Singh, 1985).

plain of feeling ill in situations in which illness can serve as an excuse for poor performance. In other cases, focusing on physical sensations and possible illness may take the person's mind off real problems—just like the obsessive–compulsive woman's focusing on her "contamination" by Sani-Flush might have diverted her thoughts from her unfulfilling lifestyle. Every effort should be made to uncover real medical problems among presumed hypochondriacs, however. Now and then, a supposed hypochondriac dies from something all too real.

EATING DISORDERS

Did you know that today the eating habits of the "average" American woman are characterized by dieting? For this reason, efforts to restrict the intake of food have become the norm. However, the eating disorders that we discuss here are characterized by gross disturbances in patterns of eating. They include *anorexia nervosa* and *bulimia nervosa.*

Anorexia Nervosa

Karen was the 22-year-old daughter of an English professor. She had begun her college career full of promise at the age of 17, but two years ago, after "social problems" occurred, she had returned to live at home and taken progressively lighter course loads at a local college. Karen had never been overweight, but about a year ago her mother noticed that she seemed to be gradually "turning into a skeleton."

Karen spent literally hours every day shopping at the supermarket, butcher, and bakeries; and in conjuring up gourmet treats for her parents and younger siblings. Arguments over her lifestyle and eating habits had divided the family into two camps. The camp led by her father called for patience; that headed by her mother demanded confrontation. Her mother feared that Karen's father would "protect her right into her grave" and wanted Karen placed in residential treatment "for her own good." The parents finally compromised on an outpatient evaluation.

At an even 5 feet, Karen looked like a prepubescent 11-year-old. Her nose and cheekbones protruded crisply, like those of an elegant young fashion model. Her lips were full, but the redness of the lipstick was unnatural, as if too much paint had been dabbed on a corpse for the funeral. Karen weighed only 78 pounds, but she had dressed in a stylish silk blouse, scarf, and baggy pants so that not one inch of her body was revealed. More striking than her mouth was the redness of her rouged cheeks. It was unclear whether she had used too much makeup or whether minimal makeup had caused the stark contrast between the parts of her face that were covered and those that were not.

Karen vehemently denied that she had a nutritional or psychological problem. Her figure was "just about where I want it to be" and she engaged in aerobic exercise daily. A deal was struck in which outpatient treatment would be tried as long as Karen lost no more weight and showed steady gains back to at least 90 pounds. Treatment included a day hospital with group therapy and two meals a day. But word came back that Karen was artfully toying with her food—cutting it up, sort of licking it, and moving it about her plate—rather than eating it. After three weeks Karen had lost another pound. At that point her parents were able to persuade her to enter a residential treatment program where her eating behavior could be more carefully monitored.

Nevid et al., 1994

There is a saying that you can never be too rich or too thin. Excess money may be pleasant enough,but as in the case of Karen, one can certainly be too thin. Karen was suffering from anorexia nervosa, a life-threatening disorder characterized by refusal to maintain a healthful body weight, intense fear of being overweight, a distorted body image, and, in females, lack of menstruation (amenorrhea.) Anorexic persons usually weigh less than 85 percent of their expected body weight.

I won't pass judgment on whether or not you can be too rich. You can clearly be too thin, however, as are people who are suffering from anorexia nervosa. People with this eating disorder show serious declines in health.

By and large, eating disorders afflict women during adolescence and young adulthood (Levine, 1987). Nearly 1 in 200 school-aged girls has trouble gaining or maintaining weight, and the incidences of anorexia nervosa and bulimia nervosa have increased markedly since the 1950s (Boskind-White & White, 1986; Strober, 1986). Anorexic women greatly outnumber anorexic men. Onset is most often in adolescence, between the ages of 12 and 18.

Anorexic women may be full height but weigh 60 pounds or less. They may drop 25 percent or more of their body weight in a year. Severe weight loss triggers amenorrhea (Sullivan, 1988). The girl's general health declines, and she may experience slowed heart rate, low blood pressure, constipation, and dehydration, among other problems (Kaplan & Woodside, 1987). About 4 percent of anorexic girls die from weight-loss-related problems such as weakness or severe imbalances in body chemistry (Herzog et al., 1988).

In the typical pattern, girls notice some weight gain after menarche and decide that it must come off. However, dieting—and, often, exercise—continue at a fever pitch. They go on long after girls reach normal body weights, even after family members and others have told them that they are losing too much. Anorexic girls almost always adamantly deny that they are wasting away. They may point to their fierce exercise regimens as proof. Their body images are distorted (Slade, 1985). Penner and his colleagues (1991) studied women who averaged 31 percent below their ideal bodyweights, according to Metropolitan Life Insurance Company charts. The women ironically overestimated the size of parts of their bodies to be 31 percent larger than they actually were! Whereas others perceive anorexic women as "skin and bones," the women frequently sit before the mirror and see themselves as they were, and not as they are.

Although the thought of eating can be odious to anorexic girls, now and then they may feel quite hungry. Many anorexics become obsessed with food and are constantly "around it." They may engross themselves in cookbooks, take on the family shopping chores, and prepare elaborate dinners for others.

Bulimia Nervosa

The case of Nicole provides a vivid account of a young woman with bulimia nervosa:

Nicole awakens in her cold dark room and already wishes it was time to go back to bed. She dreads the thought of going through this day, which will be like so many others in her recent past. She asks herself the question every morning, "Will I be able to make it through the day without being totally obsessed by thoughts of food, or will I blow it again and spend the day binging"? She tells herself that today she will begin a new life, today she will start to live like a normal human being. However, she is not at all convinced that the choice is hers. (Boskind-White & White, 1983, p. 29)

It turns out that this day Nicole begins by eating eggs and toast. Then she binges on cookies; doughnuts; bagels smothered with butter, cream cheese, and jelly; granola; candy bars; and bowls of cereal and milk—all within 45 minutes. Then she cannot take in any more food and turns her attention to purging what she has eaten. She goes to the bathroom, ties back her hair, turns on the shower to mask any noise she will make, drinks a glass of water, and makes herself vomit. Afterward she vows, "Starting tomorrow, I'm going to change." But she knows that tomorrow it will probably be the same story.

It is true that some college women do control their weight by going on cycles of binge eating followed by self-induced vomiting. They are said to have bulimia nervosa.

Bulimia nervosa is defined as recurrent cycles of binge eating, especially of foods rich in carbohydrates,[2] and the taking of dramatic measures to purge the food, once consumed. The binge involves the taking in of much larger-than-normal quantities of food and a sense of lack of control over eating (Wilson & Walsh, 1991). Purging includes self-induced vomiting, fasting or strict dieting, use of laxatives, and vigorous exercise. As with anorexia, there is overconcern about body shape and weight. The disorder usually begins in adolescence or early adulthood, and, like anorexia, it afflicts many more women than men.

Bulimia, like anorexia, predominantly affects females, the majority of whom are in their twenties. Most come from the middle or upper socioeconomic classes. About one-quarter are married (Fairburn et al., 1986). A review of the research suggests that 1 to 5 percent of the female college population, and perhaps 0.1 to 0.2 percent of the male, are bulimic (Nevid et al., 1994).

Bulimia is yet more common than anorexia. It has been estimated to affect 5 percent of the population (Nagelman et al., 1983). Bulimia has become of great concern on college campuses. About half of college women admit to at least an occasional cycle of binging and purging (Herzog, 1982a, 1982b).

Theoretical Views

Anorexia is found predominantly in females, by a ratio of about 20 to 1. Anorexia nervosa and bulimia nervosa were once considered very rare, but they are be-

[2]For example, candy, cookies, cakes. Meats contain protein and fat and are of relatively less interest to bulimic bingers.

coming increasingly common in the United States and other developed countries (Killen et al., 1986; Mitchell & Eckert, 1987; Pyle et al., 1986).

The typical anorexic or bulimic person is a young white female of higher socioeconomic status, although anorexia is also becoming more prevalent among other social groups and older age groups (Mitchell & Eckert, 1987). Anorexia and bulimia are relatively less common among African and Asian Americans (Jones et al., 1980).

Because anorexia is connected with amenorrhea, some psychodynamic theorists suggest that anorexia represents an effort by the girl to remain prepubescent. Anorexia allows the girl to avoid growing up, separating from the family, and assuming adult responsibilities. Because of the loss of fatty deposits, their breasts and hips flatten. In their fantasies, perhaps, anorexic women remain children, sexually undifferentiated.

Some psychoanalytically oriented theorists focus on family relationships as a causal factor and note that self-starvation has a brutal effect on parents. Do some adolescents use refusal to eat as a weapon against their parents? One study compared mothers of adolescents with eating disorders to mothers of adolescents without such problems. Mothers of adolescents with eating disorders were relatively more likely to be unhappy with their families' functioning, to have problems with eating and dieting themselves, to think that their daughters should lose weight, and to consider their daughters unattractive (Pike & Rodin, 1991). The researchers speculate that some adolescents develop eating disorders as ways of coping with feelings of loneliness and alienation they experience in the home. Could binge eating, as suggested by Humphrey (1986), be a metaphoric effort to gain nurturance and comfort not offered by the mother? Could purging be a symbolic ridding oneself of negative feelings toward the family?

Some learning theorists view anorexia as an irrational, culturally induced fear of gaining weight that reflects contemporary idealization of the slender female. College women generally see themselves as significantly heavier than the figure that is most attractive to males, and heavier, still, than the "ideal" female figure (Fallon & Rozin, 1985; Rozin & Fallon, 1987). College men actually prefer women to be heavier than women expect—about halfway between the girth of the average woman and what the woman thinks is most attractive. Even *children* express dissatisfaction with their body images. One study surveyed the body-figure preferences of 670 children between the ages of 10½ and 15 (Cohn et al., 1987). *Both* genders were generally dissatisfied with their bodies. Boys wanted to be heavier than they were and girls, thinner. As in the Fallon and Rozin studies, when girls were asked to describe the ideal female figure, they chose a figure that was thinner than theirs and also thinner than the figure preferred by boys. Boys, on the other hand, had an ideal body shape that was heavier than they were themselves and heavier than the figure they believed that girls would prefer.

Boys will naturally grow heavier as they mature and gain muscle mass. As a result, their bodies will conform more closely to their perceived ideal. Girls, unfortunately, are likely to experience a greater discrepancy between their own body shape and the cultural ideal as their busts fill out and their hips grow round. The discrepancy between the girl's perceived and ideal figures was in fact greater among the older girls in the study (Cohn et al., 1987). Even as they enter adolescence, contemporary girls have already developed a desire for thinness that sets many up for unhappiness and "failure."

As the cultural ideal grows slimmer, women with average or heavier-than-average figures come under more pressure to control their weight. Agras and Kirkley (1986) documented the interest in losing weight by counting the numbers of diet articles printed in three women's magazines since the year 1900: *Ladies' Home Journal, Good Housekeeping,* and *Harper's Bazaar.* Diet articles were absent until the 1930s. During the 1930s and 1940s, only about one article appeared in every ten issues. During the 1950s and 1960s, the number of diet articles jumped to about one in every other issue. During the 1980s, however, the number mushroomed to about 1.3 articles per issue. In recent years, that is, there has been an average of *more than one* diet article per issue!

MOOD DISORDERS

Mood disorders are characterized by disturbance in expressed emotions. The disruption generally involves depression or elation. As noted earlier, it must be kept in mind that most instances of depression are perfectly normal, or "run-of-the-mill." I am not suggesting that run-of-the-mill depression is to be ignored. My point is that if you have failed an important test, if a business investment has been lost, or if your closest friend becomes ill, it is understandable and fitting for you to be depressed about it. It would be odd, in fact, if you were *not* affected by adversity.

It is *not* abnormal to feel depressed when one's situation is depressing.

As with anxiety disorders, feelings of depression are considered abnormal when they are magnified far beyond one's circumstances or when there is no apparent justification for them.

Types of Mood Disorders

In this section, we discuss two mood disorders: *major depression* and *bipolar disorder,* which involves feelings of elation as well as depression.

Major Depression. Depression is the "common cold" of psychological problems, perhaps affecting upward of 10 percent of us at any given time (Alloy et al., 1990). People with run-of-the-mill depression may feel sad, blue, or "down in the dumps." They may complain of lack of energy, loss of self-esteem, difficulty concentrating, loss of interest in other people and usually enjoyable activities, pessimism, crying, and thoughts of suicide.

These feelings tend to be more intense among people with **major depression.** People with major depression may also show poor appetite and serious weight loss, agitation or **psychomotor retardation,** inability to concentrate and make decisions, complaints of "not caring" anymore, and recurrent suicide attempts.

Persons with major depression may also show faulty perception of reality—so-called psychotic behaviors. Psychotic behaviors include delusions of unworthiness, guilt for imagined wrongdoings, even ideas that one is rotting from disease. There may also be hallucinations such as of the Devil administering just punishment or of strange bodily sensations.

Bipolar Disorder. In bipolar disorder, formerly known as manic-depression, there are mood swings from elation to depression. These cycles seem to be unrelated to external events. In the elated, or **manic** phase, people may show excessive excitement or silliness, carrying jokes too far. They may show poor judgment, sometimes destroying property, and be argumentative. Roommates may avoid them, finding them abrasive. Manic people often speak rapidly ("pressured speech") and jump from topic to topic, showing **rapid flight of ideas.** It is hard to "get a word in edgewise." They may make extremely large contributions to charity or give away expensive possessions. They may not be able to sit still or to sleep restfully.

Major depression A severe depressive disorder in which the person may show loss of appetite, psychomotor behaviors, and impaired reality testing.

Psychomotor retardation Slowness in motor activity and (apparently) in thought.

Manic Elated, showing excessive excitement.

Rapid flight of ideas Rapid speech and topic changes, characteristic of manic behavior.

Depression is the other side of the coin. Bipolar-depressed people often sleep more than usual and are lethargic. People with major (or unipolar) depression are more likely to show insomnia and agitation. Bipolar-depressed individuals also exhibit social withdrawal and irritability.

Some people with bipolar disorder attempt suicide "on the way down" from the elated phase. They report that they will do almost anything to escape the depths of depression that they realize lie ahead.

Theoretical Views

Depression is a normal reaction to losses and unpleasant events. Problems such as marital discord, physical discomfort, incompetence, and failure or pressure at work all contribute to feelings of depression (Coyne et al., 1987; Eckenrode, 1984; Lewinsohn & Amenson, 1978; Stone & Neale, 1984). We are usually more depressed by things that we bring on ourselves, such as academic problems, financial problems, unwanted pregnancy, conflict with the law, arguments, and fights (Hammen & Mayol, 1982). Many people recover from such events less readily than others, however. Those who remain depressed are less likely to be able to solve social problems (Marx et al., 1992; Nezu & Ronan, 1985; Schotte & Clum, 1987) and have less social support (Asarnow et al., 1987; Billings et al., 1983; Pagel & Becker, 1987). Women are more likely than men to be diagnosed as showing major depression (Russo, 1990b). Belle (1990) points out that women—especially single mothers—have lower socioeconomic status than men in our society and that depression and other psychological disorders have traditionally been more common among poor people.

Psychodynamic Views. Psychoanalysts suggest various explanations for depression. In one, depressed people are overly concerned about hurting others' feelings or losing their approval. As a result, they hold in rather than express feelings of anger. Anger becomes turned inward and is experienced as misery and self-hatred. From the psychodynamic perspective, bipolar disorder may be seen as alternating dominance of the personality by the superego and the ego. In the depressive phase of the disorder, the superego dominates, flooding the individual with exaggerated ideas of wrongdoing and associated feelings of guilt and worthlessness. After a while, the ego defends itself by rebounding and asserting supremacy, accounting for the elation and self-confidence that in part characterize the manic phase. Later, in response to the excessive display of ego, feelings of guilt return, again plunging the person into depression.

Learning Views. Social-learning theorists note similarities in behavior between people who are depressed and laboratory animals who go unreinforced for instrumental behavior. Inactivity and loss of interest result in each. Lewinsohn (1975) theorizes that many depressed people lack skills that might lead to rewards. Some depressed people are nonassertive (Gotlib, 1984). Others do have the social skills of nondepressed people, but they do not reinforce (credit) themselves as much for showing these skills (Gotlib, 1982). In any event, social-skills training can ameliorate feelings of depression in many sufferers (Hersen et al., 1984).

Research has also found links between depression and **learned helplessness.** In one study, Seligman (1975) taught dogs that they were helpless to escape an electric shock by preventing them from leaving a cage in which they received repeated shock. Later a barrier to a safe compartment was removed, allowing the animals a way out. When they were shocked again, however, the dogs made no effort to escape. They had apparently learned that they were helpless. Seligman's dogs were also, in a sense, reinforced for doing nothing. That is, the shock *eventually* stopped when the dogs were showing helpless behavior—inactivity and withdrawal. "Reinforcement" might have increased the likelihood of repeating

Learned helplessness Seligman's model for the acquisition of depressive behavior, based on findings that organisms in aversive situations learn to show inactivity when their operants are not reinforced.

Why Did He Miss That Tackle? This football player is compounding his feelings of depression by attributing his shortcomings on the field to factors that he cannot change. For example, he tells himself that he missed the tackle because of stupidity and lack of athletic ability. He ignores the facts that his coaching was poor and that his teammates failed to come to his support.

their "successful behavior"—that is, doing nothing—in a similar situation. This helpless behavior resembles that of depressed people.

Cognitive Factors. The concept of learned helplessness bridges social-learning and cognitive approaches in that it is an attitude, a general expectation. Other cognitive factors also contribute to depression. For example, perfectionists set themselves up for depression through irrational self-demands. They are likely to fall short of their (unrealistic) expectations and, as a result, to feel depressed (Vestre, 1984).

Depressed people pay more attention to negative information (Mineka, 1991). They tend to be self-critical (Zuroff & Mongrain, 1987) and pessimistic about the future (Alloy & Ahrens, 1987; Pyszczynski et al., 1987). People, moreover, who respond to feelings of depression by focusing on their symptoms and the possible causes and effects of their symptoms tend to prolong depressive episodes (Nolen-Hoeksema, 1991). Susan Nolen-Hoeksema and her colleagues (1992) found that women are more likely than men to focus on their symptoms and thereby prolong feelings of depression. Men seem somewhat more likely to try to fight off negative feelings by distracting themselves (Parrot & Sabini, 1990). She points out that men are more likely to distract themselves by turning to alcohol, however, thus exposing themselves to additional problems (Nolen-Hoeksema, 1991).

Seligman and his colleagues note that when things go wrong, we may think of the causes of failure as *internal* or *external, stable* or *unstable, global* or *specific.* Let us explain these various **attributional styles** through the example of having a date that does not work out. An internal attribution involves self-blame, as in "I really loused it up," whereas an external attribution places the blame elsewhere (as in "Some couples just don't take to each other," or, "She was the wrong sign for me"). A stable attribution ("It's my personality") suggests a problem that cannot be changed, whereas an unstable attribution ("It was the head cold") suggests a temporary condition. A global attribution of failure ("I have no idea what to do when I'm with people") suggests that the problem is quite large. A specific attribution ("I have problems making small talk at the very outset of a relationship") chops the problem down to a manageable size.

Attributional style One's tendency to attribute one's behavior to internal or external factors, stable or unstable factors, and so on.

Research shows that depressed people are more likely than nondepressed people to attribute the causes of their failures to internal, stable, and global factors—factors that they are relatively helpless to change (Blumberg & Izard, 1985; Carver et al., 1985; Lam et al., 1987; Raps et al., 1982; Seligman et al., 1984).

Biological Factors. Researchers are also searching for biological factors in mood disorders. Mood swings tend to run in families, and there is a higher concordance rate for bipolar disorder among identical than fraternal twins (Goodwin & Jamison, 1990; Klein et al., 1985; Smith & Winokur, 1983). It has been estimated that about 80 percent of the risk of bipolar disorder may involve genetic factors (McGuffin & Katz, 1986), but the mode of genetic transmission remains unclear (Blehar et al., 1988; Kelsoe et al., 1989).

Other researchers focus on the actions of the neurotransmitters serotonin and noradrenaline. Deficiencies in serotonin may create a general disposition toward mood disorders. Serotonin deficiency *combined with* noradrenaline deficiency may be linked with depression. For example, rats with lowered levels of serotonin and noradrenaline show behavior similar to that of depressed people (Ellison, 1977). They are unaggressive, listless, apathetic, and withdrawn. Their appetites decrease, and they lose weight. A deficiency of serotonin combined with excessive levels of noradrenaline might produce manicky behavior, however. Other evidence for the roles of neurotransmitters in mood disorders is found in the fact that people with severe depression oftenrespond to antidepressant drugs that heighten the action of noradrenaline and serotonin. The metal lithium, moreover, which is the major chemical treatment for bipolar disorder, apparently flattens out manic-depressive cycles by moderating levels of noradrenaline.

Many cases of depression may reflect the interaction of biological factors (such as neurotransmitters) and psychological factors (such as learned helplessness). For example, Seligman (1975) and Weiss (1982) found that dogs who learn that they are helpless to escape electric shocks also have less noradrenaline available to the brain. Helplessness is thus linked to low noradrenaline levels. The relationship might be a vicious cycle: A depressing situation may decrease the action of noradrenaline, and this chemical change may aggravate depression.

Relationships between mood disorders and biological factors are complex and under intense study. Even if people are biologically predisposed toward depression, it seems that self-efficacy expectations and attitudes—particularly attitudes about whether or not one can change things for the better—may also play a role.

Suicide

About 13 people per 100,000 take their lives each year in the United States (Tolchin, 1989). Why? Most suicides are linked to feelings of depression and hopelessness (Beck et al., 1989, 1990; Cole, 1988; Petrie & Chamberlain, 1983; Schotte & Clum, 1982). Suicidal people find life more dull, empty, and boring than do nonsuicidal people. Suicidal people also feel more anxious, excitable, submissive, angry, guilt-ridden, helpless, and inadequate (Mehrabian & Weinstein, 1985; Neuringer, 1982). UCLA suicide scholar Edwin Shneidman (1985, 1987) notes that suicide attempters are usually trying to end extreme psychological anguish.

Suicide attempts are more frequent following stressful life events, especially "exit events" (Slater & Depue, 1981). Exit events entail loss of social support—as in the death of a spouse, friend, or relative; divorce or separation; a family member's leaving home; or the loss of a close friend. People under stress who consider suicide have also been found to be less capable of solving problems—particularly interpersonal problems—than nonsuicidal people (Rotheram-Borus et al., 1990; Schotte & Clum, 1987; Schotte et al., 1990). Suicidal people are thus less likely to find productive ways of changing the stressful situation.

Suicide, like so many other psychological problems, tends to run in families. Nearly one in four suicide attempters reports that a family member has committed suicide (Sorensen & Rutter, 1991). Mental disorders among family members also appear to make their contribution (Sorensen & Rutter, 1991; Wilson, 1991). However, the causal connections are unclear. Do suicide attempters inherit disorders that can lead to suicide? Does the family environment subject several family members to feeling of hopelessness? Does the suicide of a family member give one the idea of committing suicide, or create the impression that one is somehow fated to commit suicide? Perhaps these possibilities and others—such as poor problem solving ability—form a complex web of contributory factors.

Myths about Suicide. Some believe that people who threaten suicide are only seeking attention. The serious just "do it." Actually 70 to 80 percent of suicides gave clear clues concerning their intentions prior to the act (Cordes, 1985; Nevid et al., 1994).

It is *not* true that people who threaten suicide are only seeking attention. Many attempt to take their lives.

Some believe that those who fail at suicide attempts are only seeking attention. But 75 percent of successful suicides had made previous attempts (Nevid et al., 1994). Contrary to myth, discussion of suicide with a depressed person does not prompt suicide. In fact, extracting a promise that the person will not commit suicide before calling or visiting a helping professional seems to have prevented suicides.

Some believe that only "insane" people (meaning people who are out of touch with reality) would take their own lives. However, suicidal thinking is not necessarily a sign of psychosis, neurosis, or personality disorder. Instead, the contemplation of suicide reflects a narrowing of the range of options that people think are available to them (Rotheram-Borus et al., 1990; Schotte et al., 1990). As suggested by Figure 13.2, the elderly (people aged 65 and above) are relatively more likely to believe that there is little or nothing they can do to overcome their problems. Finally, most people with suicidal thoughts, contrary to myth, will *not* act on them. Suicidal thoughts are not an uncommon response to stress.

SCHIZOPHRENIA

Joyce was 19. Her boyfriend Ron brought her into the emergency room because she had slit her wrists. When she was interviewed, her attention wandered. She seemed distracted by things in the air, or something she might be hearing. It was as if she had an invisible earphone.

She explained that she had cut her wrists because the "hellsmen" had told her to. Then she seemed frightened. Later she said that the hellsmen had warned her not to reveal their existence. She had been afraid that they would punish her for talking about them.

Ron told the emergency-room physician that Joyce had been living with him for about a year. At first they had been together in a small apartment in town. But Joyce did not want to be near other people and had convinced him to rent a bungalow in the country. There she would make fantastic drawings of goblins and monsters during the days. Now and then she would become agitated and act as if invisible things were giving her instructions.

"I'm bad," Joyce would mutter, "I'm bad." She would begin to jumble her words. Ron would then try to convince her to go to the hospital, but she would refuse. Then the

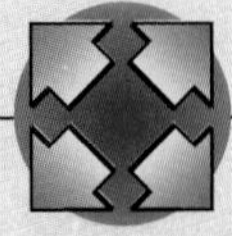

WORLD OF DIVERSITY

Who Commits Suicide?

Consider some facts about suicide:

Although African Americans are more likely than white Americans to live in poverty and suffer from discrimination, the suicide rate is about twice as high among white Americans (Figure 13.1).

White Americans are actually more likely than African Americans to commit suicide, despite African Americans' relatively greater socioeconomic and other burdens.

One in four Native-American teenagers has attempted suicide—a rate that is four times higher than that of other U.S. teenagers (Resnick et al., 1992). Among Zuni adolescents of New Mexico, the rate of completed suicides is more than twice the national rate (Howard-Pitney et al., 1992).

Suicide is more common among college students than among nonstudents. About 10,000 college students attempt suicide each year.

Suicide is the second leading cause of death among college students.

Nearly 200,000 people attempt suicide each year in the United States. About one in ten succeeds.

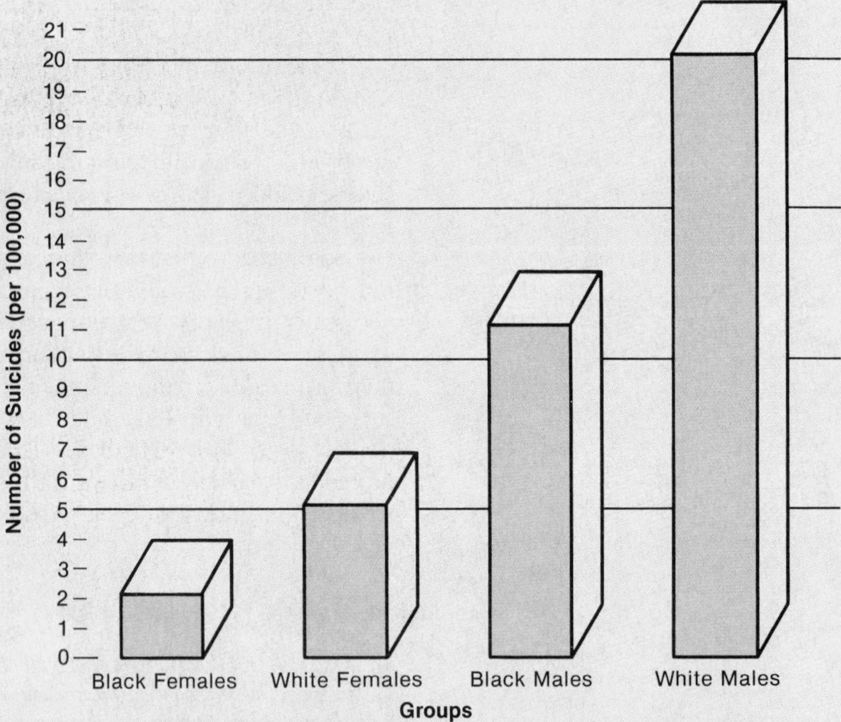

FIGURE 13.1
Suicide Rates According to Gender and Race. Men are more likely than women to commit suicide. Women, however, make more suicide attempts. How can we account for this discrepancy? Non-Hispanic white Americans are also more likely to commit suicide than African Americans. (Source of figure: U.S. Bureau of the Census, 1989.)

wrist-cutting would begin. Ron thought he had made the cottage safe by removing knives and blades. But Joyce would always find something.

Then Joyce would be brought to the hospital, have stitches put in, be kept under observation for a while, and medicated. She would explain that she cut herself because the hellsmen had told her that she was bad and must die. After a few days she would deny hearing the hellsmen, and she would insist on leaving the hospital.

Ron would take her home. The pattern continued.

When the emergency-room staff examined Joyce's wrists and heard that she believed she had been following the orders of "hellsmen," they suspected that she

FIGURE 13.2
Suicide Rates According to Age. The elderly (aged 65 and above) are more likely to commit suicide than the young and the middle-aged, yet suicide is the second leading cause of death among college students. (Source of figure: U.S. Bureau of the Census, 1989.)

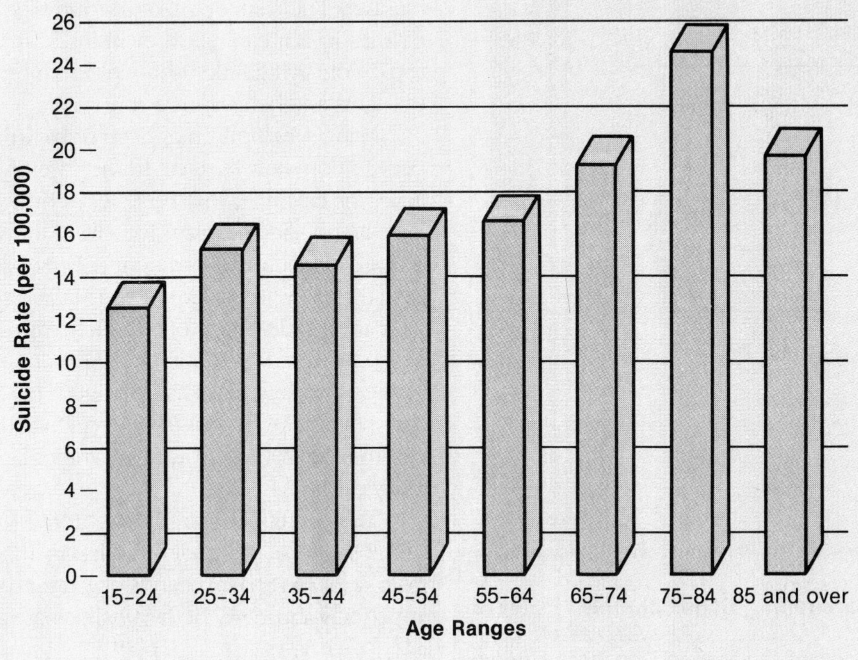

Three times as many women as men attempt suicide, but about four times as many men succeed (see Figure 13.1; Rich et al., 1988; CDC, 1985a).

Men prefer to use guns or to hang themselves, but women prefer to use sleeping pills. Males, that is, tend to choose quicker-acting and more-lethal means (Carlson & Miller, 1981). A study of 204 San Diego County suicides which took place in the early 1980s found that males who committed suicide were more likely to use guns (60 percent of the males versus 28 percent of the females) (Rich et al., 1988). Females who committed suicide more often used drugs or poisons (44% of the females versus 11% of the males).

Suicide is especially common among physicians, lawyers, and psychologists, although it is found among all occupational groups and at all age levels.

Teenage suicides loom large in the media spotlight, but the elderly are actually much more likely to commit suicide (Figure 13.2). The suicide rate among the elderly is nearly twice the national rate. Government statistics showed a 25 percent increase in the suicide rate among people 65 years of age and older during the period of 1981 to 1986 (Tolchin, 1989). Teenage suicides reached a peak in the late 1970s and have since declined (McIntosh & Osgood, 1986). Today's elderly are generally healthier and more financially secure than in earlier years, but some reasons have been suggested (Tolchin, 1989): for example, elongated lives may make the elderly more susceptible to diseases such as Alzheimer's which can leave them feeling helpless. Some suicides may thus stem from fear of impending helplessness. Or perhaps contemporary increased tolerance of suicide renders it a more attractive way to cope with exit events and loss of health. In any event, the elderly are clearly at greatest risk.

might be suffering from schizophrenia. Schizophrenia touches every aspect of victims' lives. Schizophrenia is characterized by disturbances in (1) thought and language, (2) perception and attention, (3) motor activity, and (4) mood and by (5) withdrawal and absorption in daydreams or fantasy.

Schizophrenia is known primarily by disturbances in thought, which are inferred from verbal and other behavior. Schizophrenic persons may show *loosening of associations.* Unless we are daydreaming or deliberately allowing our thoughts to "wander," our thinking is normally tightly knit. We start at a certain point, and the things that come to mind (the associations) tend to be logically and

Paranoid Schizophrenia. Paranoid schizophrenics hold systematized delusions, often involving ideas that they are being persecuted or are on a special mission. Although they cannot be argued out of their delusions, their cognitive functioning is relatively intact compared to that of disorganized and catatonic schizophrenics.

coherently connected. But schizophrenics often think in an illogical, disorganized manner. Their speech may be jumbled, combining parts of words or making rhymes in a meaningless fashion. Schizophrenics may also jump from topic to topic, conveying little useful information. They usually have no insight that their thoughts and behavior are abnormal.

Many schizophrenics have **delusions**—for example, delusions of grandeur, persecution, or reference. In the case of delusions of grandeur, a person may believe, for example, that he is Jesus or a person on a special mission, or he may have grand, illogical plans for saving the world. Delusions tend to be unshakable, despite disconfirming evidence. Persons with delusions of persecution may believe that they are sought by the Mafia, CIA, FBI, or some other group or agency. A woman with delusions of reference expressed the belief that national news broadcasts contained coded information about her. A man with such delusions complained that neighbors had "bugged" his walls with "radios." Other schizophrenics may have delusions to the effect that they have committed unpardonable sins, that they are rotting away from a hideous disease, or that they or the world do not really exist.

The perceptions of schizophrenics often include hallucinations—imagery in the absence of external stimulation that the schizophrenic cannot distinguish from reality. In Shakespeare's play, after the killing of King Duncan, feelings of guilt apparently cause Macbeth to hallucinate a knife:

> Is this a dagger which I see before me,
> The handle toward my hand? Come, let me clutch thee:
> I have thee not, and yet I see thee still.
> Art thou not, fatal vision, sensible
> To feeling as to sight? or art thou but
> A dagger of the mind, a false creation,
> Proceeding from the heat-oppressed brain?

Macbeth is a fictional character, of course. Joyce, however, the subject of a true case study, apparently believed that she heard "hellsmen." Other hallucinators may see colors or even obscene words spelled out in midair. Auditory hallucinations are most common.

It is true that in some abnormal behavior problems, people see and hear things that are not actually there. Schizophrenia is an example.

Motor activity may become wild and excited or may slow to a **stupor.** There may be strange gestures and peculiar facial expressions. Emotional response may be flat or blunted, or inappropriate—as in giggling at bad news. Schizophrenics tend to withdraw from social contacts and become wrapped up in their own thoughts and fantasies.

There are different kinds or types of schizophrenia, and different features predominate with each type.

Types of Schizophrenia

There are three major types of schizophrenia: *paranoid, disorganized,* and *catatonic.*

Paranoid Type. **Paranoid schizophrenics** have systematized delusions and, frequently, related auditory hallucinations. They usually show delusions of grandeur and persecution, but they may also show delusions of jealousy, in which they believe that a spouse or lover has been unfaithful. They may show agitation,

Delusions False, persistent beliefs that are unsubstantiated by sensory or objective evidence.

Stupor A condition in which the senses and thought are dulled.

Paranoid schizophrenia A type of schizophrenia characterized primarily by delusions—commonly of persecution—and by vivid hallucinations.

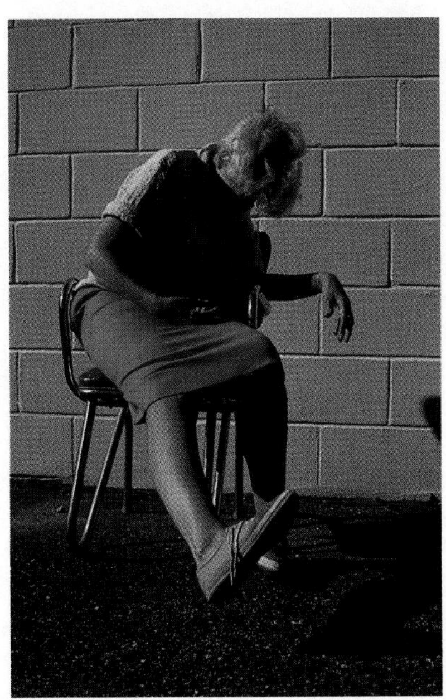

Catatonic schizophrenia. Catatonic schizophrenics show striking motor impairment and may hold unusual positions for hours at a time.

confusion, and fear, and may experience vivid hallucinations that are consistent with their delusions. The paranoid schizophrenic often constructs a complex or systematized delusion involving themes of wrongdoing or persecution.

The disorganized and catatonic subtypes are relatively rare (Andreasen, 1990).

Disorganized Type. **Disorganized schizophrenics** show incoherence, loosening of associations, disorganized behavior, disorganized delusions, fragmentary delusions or hallucinations, and flat or highly inappropriate emotional responses. Extreme social impairment is common among disorganized schizophrenics. They may also show silliness and giddiness of mood, giggling, and nonsensical speech. They may neglect their appearance and hygiene and lose control of their bladder and their bowels. Emilio showed some of these behaviors:

> *A 40-year-old man who looks more like 30 is brought to the hospital by his mother, who reports that she is afraid of him. It is his twelfth hospitalization. He is dressed in a tattered overcoat, baseball cap, and bedroom slippers, and sports several medals around his neck. His affect ranges from anger (hurling obscenities at his mother) to giggling. He speaks with a childlike quality and walks with exaggerated hip movements and seems to measure each step very carefully. Since stopping his medication about a month ago, . . . he has been hearing voices and looking and acting more bizarrely. He tells the interviewer he has been "eating wires" and lighting fires. His speech is generally incoherent and frequently falls into rhyme. . . .*
>
> Adapted from Spitzer et al., 1989, pp. 137-138.

Catatonic Type. **Catatonic schizophrenics** show striking impairment in motor activity. Impairment is characterized by slowing of activity into a stupor that may change suddenly into an agitated phase. Catatonic individuals may hold unusual, even difficult postures for hours, even as their limbs grow swollen or stiff. A striking feature is **waxy flexibility,** in which they maintain positions into which they have been manipulated by others. Catatonic individuals may also show **mutism,** but afterward they usually report that they heard what others were saying at the time.

People who show grossly psychotic characteristics such as hallucinations, delusions, incoherence, or disorganized behavior, but do not fit the definitions of these three types of schizophrenia, are considered to be of an *undifferentiated type.*

Theoretical Views

Psychologists have investigated various factors that may contribute to schizophrenia.

Psychodynamic Views. According to the psychodynamic perspective, schizophrenia is the overwhelming of the ego by sexual or aggressive impulses from the id. The impulses threaten the ego and cause intense intrapsychic conflict. Under this threat, the person regresses to an early phase of theoral stage in which the infant has not yet learned that it and the world are separate. Fantasies become confused with reality, giving birth to hallucinations and delusions. Primitive impulses may carry more weight than social norms.

Critics point out that schizophrenic behavior is not that similar to infantile behavior. Moreover, psychoanalysts have not been able to predict a schizophrenic outcome on the basis of theoretically predisposing childhoods.

Learning Views. Learning theorists explain schizophrenia through conditioning and observational learning. From this perspective, people show schizophrenic behavior when it is more likely than normal behavior to be reinforced. This may occur when the person is reared in a socially unrewarding or punitive situation; inner fantasies then become more reinforcing than social realities.

In the psychiatric hospital, patients may learn what is "expected" of them by observing other patients. Hospital staff may reinforce schizophrenic behavior by

Disorganized schizophrenics Schizophrenics who show disorganized delusions and vivid hallucinations.

Catatonic schizophrenics Schizophrenics who show striking impairment in motor activity.

Waxy flexibility A feature of catatonic schizophrenia in which persons maintain postures into which they are placed.

Mutism Refusal to talk.

paying more attention to patients who behave bizarrely. This view is consistent with folklore that the child who disrupts the class earns more attention from the teacher than the "good" child.

Critics note that many of us are reared in socially punitive settings but are apparently immune to extinction of socially appropriate behavior. Others develop schizophrenic behavior without the opportunity to observe other schizophrenics.

Genetic Factors. Schizophrenia, like many other psychological disorders, runs in families (Grove et al., 1991). Children of schizophrenic parents are at greater than average risk for showing certain problems at early ages. The children of schizophrenics have more problems in social relationships, more emotional instability, and less academic motivation than their age-mates (Goodman, 1987; Sameroff et al., 1987; Weintraub, 1987).

Schizophrenics constitute about 1 percent of the population, but children with one schizophrenic parent have a 10–15 percent chance of becoming schizophrenic. Children with two schizophrenic parents have about a 35 percent chance of doing so (Gottesman, 1991). Twin studies also find about a 45 percent concordance rate for the diagnosis among pairs of identical (MZ) twins, whose genetic codes are the same, as compared to a 13 percent rate among pairs of fraternal (DZ) twins (Gottesman, 1991; Murray & Reveley, 1986). Sharing genes with schizophrenics apparently places one at risk.

However, these kinship studies did not generally control for environmental influences. Adoptee studies do, and they find that the biological parent typically places the child at greater risk than the adoptive parent—even though the child has been reared by the adoptive parent (Gottesman, 1991; Mednick et al., 1987). A number of cases of schizophrenia have also been linked to an abnormally functioning gene or cluster of genes (Sherrington et al., 1988).

Whereas evidence for a genetic role in schizophrenia seems strong, heredity cannot be the sole factor. If it were, we might expect a 100-percent concordance rate for schizophrenia between pairs of identical twins, as opposed to the 45 percent rate found in research. Most investigators today favor a *multifactorial* model in which genetic factors create a predisposition toward schizophrenia. This predisposition, or genetic vulnerability, interacts with other factors such as the quality of parenting, birth complications, and stress to produce schizophrenic behavior (Asarnow & Goldstein, 1986; Gottesman, 1991). On the other hand, environmental factors such as help from additional caregivers, a nurturant family atmosphere, and the absence of problems during pregnancy and birth may help prevent genetically vulnerable children from developing schizophrenic behavior (Marcus et al., 1987; Mednick et al., 1987; Wynne et al., 1987).

The Dopamine Theory of Schizophrenia. Over the years, numerous substances have been thought to play a role in schizophrenic disorders. Much current theory and research focus on the neurotransmitter dopamine (Meltzer, 1987).

The dopamine theory of schizophrenia evolved from observation of the effects of **amphetamines,** a group of stimulants. Amphetamines apparently act by increasing the quantity of dopamine in the brain. High doses of amphetamines lead to behavior that mimics paranoid schizophrenia in normal people, and even low doses exacerbate the behaviors of schizophrenics (Snyder, 1980). A second source of evidence for the dopamine theory lies in that many drugs that are effective in treating schizophrenia apparently work by blocking the action of dopamine receptors (Creese et al., 1978; Turkington, 1983).

It does not appear that schizophrenic persons produce more dopamine than others but that they use more of the substance. Why? It could be that they have a greater number of dopamine receptors in the brain or that their dopamine receptors are hyperactive (Lee & Seeman, 1977; Mackay et al., 1982; Snyder, 1984). Postmortem studies of schizophrenics' brains have yielded evidence consistent with both possibilities.

Amphetamines Stimulants whose abuse can trigger behaviors that mimic schizophrenia.

Most researchers believe that dopamine plays a role in schizophrenia, but the dopamine hypothesis may apply mostly to schizophrenics who show bizarre, flagrant behavior patterns such as agitation, vivid hallucinations, and powerful delusions (Meltzer, 1987). Different mechanisms may be at work in people whose disorders are mainly characterized by behavioral deficits such as blunted emotions, narrowing or "poverty" of thought, and social withdrawal. Some investigators suggest that *deficit* forms of schizophrenia may be caused by structural defects in the brain rather than by imbalances in neurotransmitters (Andreasen, 1987; Buchsbaum & Haier, 1987; Meltzer, 1987).

PERSONALITY DISORDERS

Personality disorders, like personality traits, are characterized by enduring patterns of behavior. Personality disorders, however, are inflexible and maladaptive. They impair personal or social functioning and are a source of distress to the individual or to others.

Types of Personality Disorders

There are a number of personality disorders, including the *paranoid, schizotypal, schizoid,* and *antisocial personality disorders.* The defining trait of the **paranoid personality disorder** is the tendency to interpret other people's behavior as being deliberately threatening or demeaning. Although persons with the disorder do not show grossly disorganized thinking, they are mistrustful of others, and their social relationships suffer for it. They may be suspicious of coworkers and supervisors, but they can generally hold onto jobs.

Schizotypal personality disorder is characterized by pervasive peculiarities in thought, perception, and behavior such as excessive fantasy and suspiciousness, feelings of being unreal, or odd usage of words. The bizarre behaviors that characterize schizophrenia are absent, so this disorder is schizo*typal,* not schizophrenic. Because of their oddities, persons with the disorder are often maladjusted on the job.

The **schizoid personality** is defined by indifference to social relationships and flatness in emotional responsiveness. Schizoid personalities are "loners" who do not develop warm, tender feelings for others. They have few friends and rarely get married. Some schizoid personalities do very well on the job, as long as continuous social interaction is not required. Hallucinations and delusions are absent.

Persons with **antisocial personality disorder** persistently violate the rights of others and are in conflict with the law (Hare et al., 1991; see Table 13.2). They often show a superficial charm and are at least average in intelligence. Striking features are their lack of guilt or anxiety about their misdeeds and their failures to

TABLE 13.2: Characteristics of the Antisocial Personality

Persistent violation of the rights of others	Persistent lying
Irresponsibility	Sexual promiscuity
Lack of loyalty or of formation of enduring relationships	Substance abuse
Failure to maintain good job performance over the years	Impulsivity
Failure to develop or adhere to a life plan	Glibness; superficial charm
History of truancy	Exaggerated sense of self worth
History of delinquency	Inability to tolerate boredom
History of running away	At least 18 years of age

Personality disorders Enduring patterns of maladaptive behavior that are sources of distress to the individual or others.

Paranoid personality disorder A disorder characterized by persistent suspiciousness, but not involving the disorganization of paranoid schizophrenia.

Schizotypal personality disorder A disorder characterized by oddities of thought and behavior, but not involving bizarre psychotic behaviors.

Schizoid personality disorder A disorder characterized by social withdrawal.

Antisocial personality disorder The diagnosis given a person who is in frequent conflict with society, yet who is undeterred by punishment and experiences little or no guilt and anxiety.

Antisocial Personalities. Some antisocial personalities fit the stereotype of the amoral, violent career criminal. Gary Gilmore (left) was executed after being convicted of two murders. As a child, Gilmore showed conduct problems at home and in school. He began a violent career in adolescence. He never held a steady job or maintained a committed relationship. Though he was intentionally cruel, he never showed guilt or remorse for his misdeeds. As the fictional corporate raider Gordon Gekko in the film *Wall Street,* Michael Douglas (right) lied and cheated to gain insider information that enabled him to make millions and break up companies for profit. Motivated by the dollar sign, Gekko had no sympathy for the thousands of workers he dispossessed.

learn from punishment and form meaningful bonds with other people (Widiger, 1990). Though they have usually been heavily punished by parents and others for their misconduct, they carry on their impulsive, careless styles of life. Whereas women are more likely than men to be anxious and depressed, men are more likely to show antisocial personality disorder (Russo, 1990b).

Theoretical Views

Various factors appear to contribute to antisocial behavior, including an antisocial father, parental rejection, and inconsistent discipline (e.g., Magid, 1988; Nevid et al., 1994).

Antisocial personalities tend to run in families. Adoptee studies, for example, reveal higher incidences of antisocial behavior among the biological than the adoptive relatives of persons with the disorder (Cloninger & Gottesman, 1987). There is also evidence that genetic influences are moderate at best, however, and that the family environment is a crucial contributor to antisocial behavior (Carey, 1992).

One promising avenue of research concerns the observation that antisocial personalities are unlikely to show guilt for their misdeeds or be deterred by punishment. It is suggested that low levels of guilt and anxiety reflect lower-than-normal levels of arousal, which, in turn, have at least a partial genetic basis (Lykken, 1957, 1982). Experiments on this issue show, for example, that antisocial subjects do not learn as rapidly as others equal in intelligence when the payoff is avoidance of impending electric shock. But when the antisocial subjects' levels of arousal are increased by injections of adrenaline, they learn to avoid punishment as rapidly as others (Schachter & Latané, 1964; Chesno & Kilmann, 1975).

A lower-than-normal level of arousal does not guarantee the development of an antisocial personality. It might also be necessary for a person to be reared under conditions that do not foster the self-concept of one who abides by law and social custom. Punishment for deviation from the norm would then be unlikely to induce feelings of guilt and shame. The individual might be "undeterred" by punishment.

Cognitive psychologists find that antisocial adolescents encode social information in ways that bolster their misdeeds. For example, they tend to interpret other people's behavior as threatening, even when it is not (Dodge et al., 1990; Lochman, 1987). Perhaps family and community experiences contribute to their cynicism about human nature (Dodge & Frame, 1982; Jurovic, 1980). Cognitive therapists have encouraged some antisocial adolescents to view social provocations as problems to be solved rather than as threats to their "manhood," with some favorable initial results (Lochman et al., 1984).

Although the causes of many patterns of abnormal behavior remain in dispute, a number of therapy methods have been devised to deal with them. Those methods are the focus of Chapter 14.

STUDY GUIDE

EXERCISE: Matching Symptoms and Abnormal Behaviors

In the first column are a number of symptoms of types of abnormal behavior. In the second column are various types of abnormal behavior. Write the letter of the type of abnormal behavior in the appropriate blank space. Note that more than one type of abnormal behavior pattern may apply. Answers are given below.

_____ 1. Waxy flexibility
_____ 2. Flashbacks
_____ 3. Binge eating
_____ 4. Nervousness
_____ 5. Weight loss
_____ 6. Free-floating anxiety
_____ 7. Loss of a sense of one's personal identity
_____ 8. Pressured speech
_____ 9. Vivid, abundant hallucinations
_____ 10. Delusions of persecution
_____ 11. Delusions of unworthiness
_____ 12. Self-induced vomiting
_____ 13. Sudden anxiety attacks in the absence of threatening stimuli
_____ 14. Lack of guilt over misdeeds
_____ 15. Elation
_____ 16. Hallucinations
_____ 17. Lack of energy
_____ 18. Suspiciousness
_____ 19. La belle indifférence
_____ 20. Compulsive behavior
_____ 21. Social withdrawal
_____ 22. Fear of public scrutiny
_____ 23. Physical complaints
_____ 24. Loose associations
_____ 25. Giddiness

A. Phobic disorder
B. Panic disorder
C. Generalized anxiety disorder
D. Obsessive–compulsive disorder
E. Post-traumatic stress disorder
F. Dissociative amnesia
G. Dissociative identity disorder
H. Depersonalization disorder
I. Conversion disorder
J. Hypochondriasis
K. Anorexia nervosa
L. Bulimia nervosa
M. Major depression
N. Bipolar disorder
O. Disorganized schizophrenia
P. Catatonic schizophrenia
Q. Paranoid schizophrenia
R. Paranoid personality
S. Schizoid personality
T. Antisocial personality

Answers to Exercise

1. P
2. E
3. L
4. A, B, C, etc.
5. K, M
6. C
7. F, H
8. N
9. O
10. Q
11. M
12. L
13. B
14. T
15. N
16. O, P, Q
17. M
18. Q, R
19. I
20. D
21. M, S
22. A
23. J, I
24. O, P, Q
25. O

ESL—BRIDGING THE GAP

This part is divided into

1. cultural references,
2. words, phrases and expressions in which words are used differently from their regular meaning, or are used as metaphors.

Cultural References

automatic teller machine cards (492)—bank cards which can be used in bank machines to withdraw money from a person's account and receive the cash without the services of a teller (bank employee who sees customers)
The boy next door (492)—this is an expression used in the U.S. to refer to a nice, friendly, intelligent and perhaps naive young man, one who would never commit a crime
Salem, Massachusetts . . . burned as a witch (492)—a play called *The Crucible* has been written about the "witch trials" that occurred in Salem, Mass. It was written by Arthur Miller, an American playwright of this century.
Mafia (494)—an organized crime group
rocky coast of Massachusetts (494)—this refers to the town of Salem, Massachusetts
Sani-Flush (499)—the brand name for a chemical mixture which is used to clean toilets
The Three Faces of Eve (503)—This movie was being shown in the 1950s
can never be too rich or too thin (508)—This is an expression which reflects the culture in the U.S. in which money is important and youth (and thinness) is important. A person always needs more money and also needs to be "thinner," in this culture. (The "too" is negative.)
wrong sign (513)—refers to the astrological signs which indicate personality traits of people according to when they were born
co-workers (521)—people who work together in the same company

Phrases and Expressions (Different Usage)

by reason of (492)—because of
"out of the blue" (493)—unexpectedly; without warning
"out to get you" (494)—looking for you in order to kill you
And the "patient" (494)—And the patient died.
was to lie dormant (494)—was not to be considered
in full sway (494)—the accepted model
were in for it (495)—could expect the worst situation to happen to you
call it quits (495)—allow you to be free
goings-on (495)—occurrences
in league with (495)—acting in a way that the Devil wanted
a wandering uterus (495)—a uterus that moves inside the body
point to . . . evidence (496)—indicated . . . evidence as proof
Thus removed from the real world (496)—Removed from the real world this way
the leakage of (496)—slow withdrawing of
to have broken through (496)—to have traveled through
falls under the control of (496)—is controlled by
"band-aid" (496)—a superficial treatment that does not cure (a Band Aid is a small bandage)
jump from topic to topic (497)—move from one topic to another topic that is not relevant and continued to do this
racing heart (498)—a heart that feels as though it is beating more quickly than usual
out of proportion to (498)—not in proportion to
"comes out of the blue" (498)—occurs without warning
stage fright (498)—fear of being in front of or of performing in front of a group of people
midair (498)—between elevator stops
creepy-crawlies (498)—bugs
loath to venture out of (499)—afraid to go out of
feel spent (499)—feel extremely tired; exhausted
descend from nowhere (499)—occur without warning
free-floating (499)—without attachment
feel whole (502)—feel like one complete person
break out with hives (503)—have an allergic reaction consisting of red areas on the skin
stands outside (505)—feels as though he or she is outside of his or her personality
come to (505)—begin
meaningful whole (505)—a complete unified identity with meaning
run from doctor to doctor (506)—continuously search for a doctor by visiting one and then another, and then another
were at work (506)—were operating
to serve a purpose (506)—to accomplish something; to have a reason for occurring
certain ends (506)—specific results
taking a person's mind off (507)—redirecting; causing the person not to think about
something all too real (507)—an actual or real illness
at a fever pitch (508)—intensely and continually
wasting away (508)—becoming so thin that they look like they are going to die

"around it" (509)—where food is being prepared or being eaten
as a weapon against (510)—as a way of expressing anger at
run-of-the-mill (511)—common
fitting (511)—natural and appropriate
blue (511)—a little depressed
"down in the dumps" (511)—a little depressed
rotting away from disease (511)—slowly dying from a disease
carrying jokes too far (511)—allowing a joke to psychologically hurt someone
"get a word in edgewise" (511)—speak in a conversation because there is no space or time when the other person isn't talking
other side of the coin (512)—the other part of the same disorder
"on the way down" (512)—as they move into depression
overly concerned (512)—*too* concerned (negative)
becomes turned inward (512)—becomes directed toward the person himself or herself
bridges (513)—connects
to fall short (513)—to not reach
does not work out (513)—is not successful
"*. . . loused it up,"* (513)—caused, or was responsible for the bad experience
making small talk (513)—talking about things that are not serious, but are introductory at a gathering
chops the problem down to a manageable size (513)—causes the problem to be very specific and one that can be dealt with
out of touch with reality (515)—disconnected from the immediate circumstances, situation or environment
slit her wrists (515)—cut the place in the wrists where it is difficult to stop the bleeding and is an indication, therefore, of a wish to die
earphone (515)—telephone on her ear
tightly knit (517)—connected by associations
jumbled (518)—confused
"bugged" his walls with "radios" (518)—installed machines in his walls that could listen to and record what he was saying
wrapped up in (519)—focused only on
nonsensical speech (519)—speech that has no meaning
grossly disorganized (521)—extremely disorganized
hold onto jobs (521)—maintain their employment
"loners" (521)—people who prefer to be alone most of the time
striking feature (521)—their most noticeable characteristic
One promising avenue of research (522)—One direction of research that might be important
payoff (522)—positive result

CHAPTER REVIEW

SECTION 1: What Is Abnormal Behavior?

Objective 1: Define *abnormal behavior*.

The text lists (1: how many?) ________________ criteria for determining whether or not behavior is abnormal. Behavior tends to be labeled abnormal when it is unusual or (2)________________cally deviant; when it is socially (3) un________________ble; when it involves faulty (4) ________________tion of reality; when it is dangerous; when it is (5) self-________________ing; or when it is personally distressing.

SECTION 2: Models of Abnormal Behavior

Objective 2: Explain and compare the following models for understanding abnormal behavior: the demonological, medical (organic and psychodynamic versions), learning, and cognitive models.

There are several models for explaining abnormal behavior. The (6) ________________gical model has been the most prevalent model throughout history. According to the demonological model, people behave abnormally when they are (7) ________________sed by demons. Possession was believed to stem from (8) ________________tion for wrongdoing or from (9) ________________craft. Possession was "treated" by means of (10) ________________ism.

The medical model has two versions: the (11) o________________ and (12) ________________namic versions. The Greek physician (13) ________________tes was one of the earliest thinkers to suggest that there was a relationship between abnormal behavior and biological abnormality. Hippocrates believed that abnormal behavior frequently reflected an abnormality of the (14) b________________. In 1883, psychiatrist Emil (15) K________________ argued in his textbook that each form of abnormal behavior has a specific physiological origin—a view which is at the heart of the organic model. Sigmund Freud's (16) psycho________________ model argues that abnormal behavior is symptomatic of an underlying (17) ________________gical rather than biological disorder. This psychological disorder is presumed to be (18) ____________cious conflict of childhood origins.

According to learning models, abnormal behavior is not necessarily (19) ____________atic of any underlying problem; instead, the abnormal behavior *is* the problem. Abnormal behavior is assumed to be acquired in the same way (20) n____________ behavior is acquired: through processes of (21) ____________ning.

(22) ____________tive theorists focus on the cognitive events—thoughts, expectations, and attitudes—that accompany or underlie abnormal behavior. (23) In____________-processing theorists view abnormal behavior as disturbance in the cycle of perceiving, storing, and (24) ____________ing information. Cognitive theorist Albert Ellis views anxiety problems as reflecting (25) ____________nal beliefs and attitudes. Aaron Beck attributes numerous instances of depression to "cognitive (26) ____________rs" such as self-devaluation, interpretation of events in a negative light, and general (27: optimism or pessimism?).

SECTION 3: Anxiety Disorders

Objective 3: Describe the anxiety disorders and discuss their origins.

Anxiety disorders have subjective and (28) ____________cal features. (29) ____________tive features include fear of the worst happening, fear of losing control, nervousness, and inability to relax. Physical features reflect arousal of the (30) ____________tic branch of the autonomic nervous system. The anxiety disorders include irrational fears, or (31) ____________ias; panic disorder, which is characterized by sudden attacks in which people typically fear that they may be losing (32) con____________ or going crazy; free floating or (33) ____________zed anxiety; (34) obsessive–____________ disorder, in which people are troubled by intrusive thoughts or impulses to repeat some activity; and (35) post-____________ic stress disorder.

The most widespread phobia among adults is (36) ____________phobia, or fear of being out in open, busy areas. Stage fright and speech anxiety are examples of (37) ____________al phobias, in which people have excessive fear of public scrutiny. Panic disorder differs from other anxiety disorders in part because there is a stronger bodily component to the anxiety, including heavy (38) sw____________ing and pounding of the (39) h____________. An (40) ____________ion is a recurring thought or image that seems irrational and beyond control. A (41) ____________ion is a seemingly irresistible urge to engage in an act, often repeatedly. Post-traumatic (42) ____________ disorder (PTSD) involves intense and persistent feelings of anxiety and helplessness that are caused by a traumatic experience, such as a physical threat, destruction of one's community, or witnessing a death. The precipitating event is reexperienced, as in the form of intrusive memories, recurrent dreams, and (43) ____________cks, or the sudden feeling that the event is recurring.

Psychodynamic theory explains generalized anxiety as persistent difficulty in maintaining (44) ____________ion of primitive impulses. According to psychodynamic theory, phobias symbolize (45) ____________cious conflicts. From the behaviorist perspective, phobias are (46) ____________ned fears. Susan (47) M____________ suggests that people are genetically predisposed to fear stimuli that may have once posed a threat to their ancestors. (48) ____________nary forces would have favored the survival of individuals who were predisposed toward acquiring fears of large animals, spiders, snakes, heights, entrapment, sharp objects, and strangers. Given the apparent independence of panic attacks from (49: internal or external?) events, researchers are investigating possible organic causes for panic disorder. Psychoanalysts and learning theorists agree that compulsive behavior may be maintained because it reduces (50) ____________ty.

Anxiety disorders (51: do or do not?) tend to run in families. Sandra Scarr and her colleagues tested adolescents and their parents in biologically related and adoptive families and found that the neuroticism scores of parents and (52: natural or adopted?) children correlated more highly than those of parents and (53: natural or adopted?) children. Some people may have a biological predisposition to anxiety in that their receptors to (54) gamma-____________ric acid (GABA) may not be sensitive enough. GABA is an (55: excitatory or inhibitory?) neurotransmitter that may help quell anxiety reactions.

SECTION 4: Dissociative Disorders

Objective 4: Describe the dissociative disorders and discuss their origins.

Dissociative disorders are characterized by a sudden

temporary change in (56) co__________ness or self-identity. The dissociative disorders include (57) __________tive amnesia (motivated forgetting); dissociative fugue (forgetting plus fleeing), dissociative (58) i__________ disorder, identities in which a person behaves as if distinct identities occupied the body; and (59) de__________ disorder, in which people feel as if they are not themselves. One of the best-known cases of dissociative identity disorder was depicted in the film *The Three Faces of* (60) __________.

According to psychodynamic theory, dissociative disorders involve massive use of (61) __________sion. According to learning theory, dissociative disorders are conditions in which people learn not to (62) t__________ about disturbing acts or impulses in order to avoid feelings of guilt and shame. Cognitive theorists explain dissociative disorders in terms of where we focus our (63) __________ion at a given time.

SECTION 5: Somatoform Disorders

Objective 5: Describe the somatoform disorders and discuss their origins.

In (64) so__________ disorders, people show or complain of physical problems, such as paralysis, pain, or the persistent belief that they have a serious disease. Evidence of a medical problem (65: can or cannot?) be found.

The somatoform disorders include (66) con__________ disorder and (67) hypo__________is. In a conversion disorder, there is a major change in or loss of (68) p__________ functioning with no organic basis. Some victims of conversion disorder show a remarkable lack of concern over their loss of function, a symptom known as la (69) __________ indifférence. Persons with (70) __________iasis show consistent concern that they are suffering from illnesses, although there are no medical findings.

The (71) __________ic view of conversion disorders is that the symptoms produced by the victim protect the victim from guilt or another source of stress. There is evidence that some hypochondriacs use their complaints as a (72) self-__________ping strategy.

SECTION 6: Eating Disorders

Objective 6: Describe the eating disorders and discuss their origins.

The eating disorders discussed in the text include (73) an__________ nervosa and bulimia (74) n__________. Anorexia is characterized by refusal to maintain a healthful body weight, intense fear of being overweight, a distorted (75) __________ image, and, in females, (76) amen__________. Anorexia is more likely to afflict young (77: men or women?). Bulimia nervosa is defined as recurrent cycles of (78) b__________ eating, especially of foods rich in carbohydrates, and the taking of dramatic measures to (79) p__________ the food, such as self-induced vomiting. As with anorexia, there is overconcern about body shape and weight. Both disorders tend to begin in (80) __________ence.

Psychoanalysts suggest that anorexia may represent an unconscious effort by the girl to remain (81) pre__________. Some learning theorists have proposed that anorexia is a (82) ph__________ concerning the possibility of gaining weight. As noted by Polivy and Herman, cultural (83) __________zation of the slender female has become so ingrained that "normal" eating for American women today is characterized by dieting.

SECTION 7: Mood Disorders

Objective 7: Describe the mood disorders and discuss their origins.

Mood disorders are characterized by disturbance in expressed (84) __________ions. Mood disorders include major (85) __________sion, and (86) bi__________disorder.

Depression is characterized by sadness; lack of (87) __________gy; loss of self-esteem; difficulty in concentrating; loss of (88) in__________ in other people and activities that were enjoyable; (89: optimism or pessimism?); crying; and, sometimes, by thoughts of suicide. (90) M__________ depression can reach psychotic proportions, with grossly impaired reality testing. There may also be poor appetite and severe (91) w__________ loss; agitation or psychomotor (92) __________ation; delusions of (93) un__________ness and guilt; and suicide attempts.

(94) B________________ disorder was formerly known as manic-depression. In bipolar disorder there are mood swings from (95) ________________ion to depression and back. Manic people may show pressured speech, have grand, delusional schemes, and jump from topic to topic, a symptom called rapid (96) f________________ of (97) ________________s.

Depression is a(n) (98: normal or abnormal?) reaction to a loss or to exposure to unpleasant events. Recent research emphasizes the possible roles of learned helplessness, (99) attri________________al styles, and the roles of (100) neuro________________ters in prolonged depression.

According to psychodynamic theory, prolonged depression may reflect feelings of (101) ________________ that are turned inward rather than expressed. Learning theorists have noted similarities between depressed people and animals who are not (102) ________________ced for instrumental behavior. People and animals both show (103) in________________ty and loss of interest when they have repeatedly failed to receive reinforcement.

Martin (104) Se________________ and his colleagues have explored links between depression and learned helplessness. In experiments on learned (105) ________________ness, animals are eventually reinforced (by cessation of electric shock) for doing nothing. For this reason, they may learn to do nothing as a means of terminating discomfort. Depressed people are more likely than nondepressed people to make (106: internal or external?), (107: stable or unstable?), and (108: specific or global?) attributions for failures.

Research suggests that deficiencies in the neurotransmitter (109) ________________in may create a general predisposition toward affective disorders. A concurrent deficiency of the neurotransmitter (110: adrenaline or noradrenaline?) may then contribute to depression. Concurrent (111: excesses or deficiencies?) of noradrenaline may contribute to manic behavior. Antidepressant drugs work at least in part by (112: elevating or lowering?) the action of noradrenaline.

Objective 8: Explain who is likely to commit suicide, and discuss the factors that contribute to suicide.

Suicide is more common among (113: college students or nonstudents?). Three times as many (114: men as women? or women as men?) attempt suicide. Suicide is most often linked to feelings of (115) de________________ and hopelessness. According to Edwin Shneidman, people who attempt suicide are usually experiencing unendurable (116) ________________ical pain, and believe that their range of (117) ________________ons is narrowed. People who threaten suicide are (118: more or less?) likely to carry out the threat than people who do not.

SECTION 8: Schizophrenic Disorders

Objective 9: Describe the schizophrenic disorders and discuss their origins.

Schizophrenic disorders are characterized by disturbances in (119) th________________ and language (as found, for example, in the loosening of associations and in delusions); in (120) per________________ and attention (as found, for example, in hallucinations); in (121) m________________ activity (as found, for example, in a stupor or in excited behavior); in mood (as found, for example, in flat or inappropriate emotional responses); and by withdrawal and autism.

There are (122: how many?) ________________ major types of schizophrenia. These include (123) dis________________ schizophrenia; catatonic schizophrenia; and paranoid schizophrenia. Disorganized schizophrenia is characterized by disorganized (124) del________________s and vivid, abundant (125) ________________nations. Catatonic schizophrenia is characterized by impaired motor activity, as in a catatonic (126) ________________or, and by (127) w________________ flexibility. Paranoid schizophrenia is characterized by paranoid (128) ________________ions.

According to psychodynamic theory, schizophrenic behavior occurs when impulses of the (129: id, ego, or superego?) overwhelm the (130: id, ego, or superego?). Social-learning theorists have accounted for some schizophrenic behaviors by suggesting that inner (131) f________________ may become more reinforcing than outer reality when a person is in a nonrewarding situation.

Schizophrenia (132: does or does not?) tend to run in families. Children with two schizophrenic parents have about a (133) ________________ percent chance of becoming schizophrenic. Current theory and research concerning an organic basis for schizophrenia focus on the neurotransmitter (134) ________________ine. According to the dopamine theory of schizophrenia, schizophrenics may (135) u________________ more dopamine than normal people do. Overutilization stems from either a greater-than-normal number of dopamine (136) ______________ors in the brain, or from greater-than-normal sensitivity to dopamine. A group of drugs called the (137) ______________azines are often effective in treating schizophrenia. Researchers believe that phenothiazines work by blocking the action of (138) do______________ receptors.

SECTION 9: Personality Disorders

Objective 10: Describe the personality disorders and discuss their origins.

Personality disorders, like personality traits, are characterized by enduring patterns of (139) be______________. Personality disorders are inflexible, (140) mal______________ive behavior patterns that impair personal or social functioning and are a source of (141) dis______________ to the individual or to others.

The defining trait of the (142) ______________oid personality is suspiciousness. Persons with (143) sch______________ personality disorders show oddities of thought, perception, and behavior. However, schizotypal personalities do not show bizarre (144) ______________tic behavior. Social (145) ______________al is the major characteristic of the schizoid personality. Persons with (146) ______________oid personality prefer to be by themselves and do not develop warm, tender feelings for others.

Persons with (147) ______________ial personality disorders persistently violate the rights of others and encounter conflict with the (148) l______________. They show little or no (149) g______________ or shame over their misdeeds and are largely undeterred by (150) ______________ment.

Various factors seem to contribute to antisocial behavior. One is having an antisocial (151: mother or father?). Second is parental (152) re______________ion during childhood. Third is a pattern of inconsistent (153) ______________line. Fourth is an organic factor. Research suggests that persons with antisocial personalities have (154: higher or lower?)-than-normal levels of arousal, which might explain why they are undeterred by most forms of punishment. (155) ______________tive psychologists find that antisocial adolescents encode social information in ways that bolster their misdeeds. For example, antisocial adolescents tend to interpret other people's behavior as (156) ______________ning, even when it is not.

Answers to Chapter Review

1. Six
2. Statistically
3. Unacceptable
4. Perception (or Interpretation)
5. Self-defeating
6. Demonological
7. Possessed
8. Retribution
9. Witchcraft
10 Exorcism
11. Organic
12. Psychodynamic
13. Hippocrates
14. Brain
15. Kraepelin
16. Psychodynamic (or psychoanalytic)
17. Psychological
18. Unconscious
19. Symptomatic
20. Normal
21. Learning
22. Cognitive
23. Information
24. Retrieving (or Manipulating)
25. Irrational
26. Errors
27. Pessimism
28. Physical (physiological, biological)
29. Subjective
30. Sympathetic
31. Phobias
32. Control
33. Generalized
34. Obsessive–compulsive
35. Post-traumatic
36. Agoraphobia
37. Social
38. Sweating
39. Heart
40. Obsession
41. Compulsion
42. Stress
43. Flashbacks
44 Repression
45. Unconscious
46. Conditioned
47. Mineka
48. Evolutionary
49. External
50. Anxiety
51. Do
52. Natural
53. Adopted
54. Aminobutyric
55. Inhibitory
56. Consciousness
57. Dissociative
58. Identity
59. Depersonalization
60. *Eve*
61. Repression
62. Think
63. Attention
64. Somatoform
65. Cannot
66. Conversion
67. Hypochondriasis
68. Physical
69. Belle
70. Hypochondriasis
71. Psychodynamic (or psychoanalytic)
72. Self-handicapping
73. Anorexia
74. Nervosa
75. Body
76. Amenorrhea
77. Women
78. Binge
79. Purge
80. Adolescence
81. Prepubescent
82. Phobia
83. Idealization
84. Emotions
85. Depression
86. Bipolar
87. Energy
88. Interest
89. Pessimism
90. Major
91. Weight
92. Retardation
93. Unworthiness

94. Bipolar
95. Elation
96. Flight
97. Ideas
98. Normal
99. Attributional
100. Neurotransmitters
101. Anger
102. Reinforced
103. Inactivity
104. Seligman
105. Helplessness
106. Internal
107. Stable
108. Global
109. Serotonin
110. Noradrenaline
111. Excesses
112. Elevating
113. College students
114. Women as men
115. Depression
116. Psychological
117. Options
118. More
119. Thought
120. Perception
121. Motor
122. Three
123. Disorganized
124. Delusions
125. Hallucinations
126. Stupor
127. Waxy
128. Delusions
129. Id
130. Ego
131. Fantasy
132. Does
133. 35
134. Dopamine
135. Utilize
136. Receptors
137. Phenothiazines
138. Dopamine
139. Behavior
140. Maladaptive
141. Distress
142. Paranoid
143. Schizotypal
144. Psychotic
145. Withdrawal
146. Schizoid
147. Antisocial
148. Law
149. Guilt
150. Punishment
151. Father
152. Rejection
153. Discipline
154. Lower
155. Cognitive
156. Threatening

POSTTEST

1. A psychologist argues that patterns of normal and abnormal behavior are acquired by the same processes, although people who acquire abnormal behavior patterns have different experiences from those who acquire normal behavior patterns. This psychologist probably adheres to the _______ model of abnormal behavior.
   (a) learning
   (b) psychodynamic
   (c) organic
   (d) cognitive

2. The most widely used system of classification of patterns of abnormal behavior in the United States is written by the
   (a) American Psychiatric Association.
   (b) American Psychological Association.
   (c) American Medical Association.
   (d) World Health Organization.

3. According to the chapter, the most widespread phobia among adults is
   (a) speech anxiety.
   (b) claustrophobia.
   (c) agoraphobia.
   (d) fear of injections.

4. Dan has a problem in which he encounters heavy sweating and a pounding heart—both for no apparent reason. Dan would probably be diagnosed as having a(n)
   (a) phobic disorder.
   (b) panic disorder.
   (c) generalized anxiety disorder.
   (d) obsessive–compulsive disorder.

5. A difference between a phobic disorder and a fear is that the phobic response
   (a) is out of proportion to the actual danger.
   (b) involves cognitive as well as behavioral reactions.
   (c) is characterized by rapid heart rate.
   (d) encourages avoidance of the feared object or situation.

6. By definition, all dissociative disorders involve
   (a) massive repression of unacceptable impulses.
   (b) a sudden, temporary change in consciousness or identity.
   (c) the presence of at least two conflicting personalities.
   (d) malingering.

7. In which of the following does the individual feel unreal and separated from his or her body?
   (a) Depersonalization disorder
   (b) Schizotypal personality disorder
   (c) Dissociative identity disorder
   (d) Schizoid personality disorder

8. Mary believes that she is suffering from a serious stomach or intestinal disease because she has difficulty keeping food down and has unusual sensations in these regions of the body. However, repeated visits to physicians have not uncovered evidence of any medical disorder. Mary is most likely to be diagnosed as suffering from
   (a) bulima nervosa.
   (b) malingering.
   (c) anorexia nervosa.
   (d) hypochondriasis.

9. Mood disorders are primarily characterized by disturbance in
   (a) thought processes.
   (b) biological processes.
   (c) expressed emotions.
   (d) motor responses.

10. The symptom that differentiates bipolar disorder from other disorders is
   (a) suicide attempts.
   (b) severe bouts of depression.
   (c) delusional thinking.
   (d) rapid flight of ideas.

11. Deficiencies of _______ are most likely to be connected with both types of mood disorders discussed in the chapter.
   (a) adrenaline
   (b) noradrenaline
   (c) serotonin
   (d) dopamine

12. Schizophrenic disorders are known primarily by disturbances in
   (a) motor responses.
   (b) thought.
   (c) expressed emotions..
   (d) physical functioning

13. A person with _______ is most likely to show confused, jumbled thinking.
   (a) schizotypal personality disorder
   (b) paranoid schizophrenia
   (c) paranoid personality disorder
   (d) schizoid personality disorder

14. Evidence seems clearest that schizophrenics
   (a) produce more dopamine than normal people do.
   (b) have a greater number of dopamine receptors in the brain than normal people do.
   (c) are more sensitive to dopamine than normal people are.
   (d) utilize more dopamine than normal people do.

15. The defining trait of the paranoid personality disorder is
   (a) social withdrawal.
   (b) oddities of thought.
   (c) suspiciousness.
   (d) self-absorption.

16. According to Susan Nolen-Hoeksema, people who respond to feelings of depression by focusing on their symptoms and the possible causes and effects of their symptoms tend to
   (a) develop insight into the origins of their problems.
   (b) prolong depressive episodes.
   (c) increase the amount of noradrenaline available to the brain.
   (d) utilize lower-than-normal levels of dopamine.

17. As reported in the chapter, evidence suggests that there is a role for genetic factors in each of the following disorders, *with the exception of*
   (a) anxiety disorders.
   (b) schizophrenia.
   (c) bipolar disorder.
   (d) dissociative fugue.

18. So-called exit events contribute to
   (a) suicide attempts.
   (b) depersonalization disorder.
   (c) antisocial personality.
   (d) conversion disorder.

19. Emotional response tends to be flat or blunted in _______ disorders.
   (a) personality
   (b) anxiety
   (c) mood
   (d) schizophrenic

20. According to the chapter, adoptee studies show that the biological parent typically places the child at greater risk than the adoptive parent for _______, even when the child has been reared by the adoptive parent.
   (a) anxiety disorders
   (b) somatoform disorders
   (c) schizophrenic disorders
   (d) dissociative disorders

Answers to Posttest

1. A
2. A
3. C
4. B
5. A
6. B
7. A
8. D
9. C
10. D
11. C
12. B
13. B
14. D
15. C
16. B
17. D
18. A
19. D
20. C

- People in Merry Olde England used to visit the local insane asylum for a fun night out on the town.
- To be of help, psychotherapy must continue for months, perhaps years.
- Some psychotherapists interpret clients' dreams.
- Other psychotherapists encourage their clients to take the lead in the therapy session.
- Still other psychotherapists tell their clients precisely what to do.
- Lying around in your reclining chair and fantasizing can be an effective way of confronting your fears.
- Smoking cigarettes can be an effective treatment for helping people to . . . stop smoking cigarettes.
- You might be able to gain control over bad habits merely by keeping a record of where and when you practice them.
- Individual therapy is preferable to group therapy for people who can afford it.
- The originator of a surgical technique intended to reduce violence learned that it was not always successful—when one of his patients shot him.
- Drugs are never of help in treating people with abnormal behavior.

Methods of Therapy

Learning Objectives

When you have finished studying Chapter 14, you should be able to:

What is Therapy?

1. Define *psychotherapy*.
2. Trace the history of the treatment of abnormal behavior from ancient to contemporary times.

Psychodynamic Therapies

3. Describe the goals and methods of Freud's traditional psychoanalysis.
4. Compare and contrast traditional psychoanalysis with modern psychodynamic approaches.

Humanistic–Existential Therapies

5. Explain what the humanistic–existential therapies have in common.
6. Describe the goals and methods of Rogers' person-centered therapy.
7. Describe the goals and methods of Perls' Gestalt therapy.

Cognitive Therapies

8. Explain what the cognitive therapies have in common.
9. Describe the goals and methods of Ellis' rational-emotive therapy.
10. Describe the goals and methods of Beck's cognitive therapy.

Behavior Therapy

11. Describe the goals of behavior therapy.
12. Describe behavior-therapy methods of reducing fears.
13. Describe the behavior-therapy method of aversive conditioning.
14. Describe some behavior-therapy methods of operant conditioning.
15. Describe behavior-therapy self-control methods.

Group Therapies

16. Explain the advantages of group therapy.

Does Psychotherapy Work?

17. Evaluate methods of psychotherapy and behavior therapy.

Biological Therapies

18. Describe various methods of chemotherapy, and when they are used.
19. Describe electroconvulsive therapy, and when it is used.
20. Discuss psychosurgery.
21. Evaluate the biological therapies.

Brad is having an uplifting experience—literally. Six people who minutes ago were perfect strangers have cradled him in their arms and raised him into midair. His eyes are closed. They rock him gently back and forth and carry him about the room.

Brad is no paralyzed hospital patient. He has just joined an encounter group. He hopes to be able to learn to relate to other people as individuals, not as passing blurs on the street or as patrons asking him to cash payroll checks at the bank where he works as a teller. The group leader had directed that Brad be carried about to help him break down his defensive barriers and establish trust in others.

Brad had responded to a somewhat flamboyant ad in the therapy section of the classifieds in New York's *Village Voice:*

Come to life! Stop being a gray automaton in a mechanized society! Encounter yourself and others. New group forming. First meeting free. Call 212–555–0599. Qualified therapist.

Like many who seek personal help, Brad had little idea how to go about it. His group experience might or might not work out. For one thing, he has no idea about the qualifications of the group leader and did not know enough to ask. If he had answered other ads in the *Voice,* including some placed by highly qualified therapists, his treatment might have been quite different. Brad could have been:

- lying on a couch talking about anything that pops into awareness and exploring the hidden meanings of a recurrent dream.
- sitting face to face with a gentle, accepting therapist who places the major burden for what happens during therapy directly on Brad's shoulders.
- listening to a frank, straightforward therapist insist that his problems stem from self-defeating attitudes and beliefs such as an overriding need to be liked and approved of.
- role-playing the beginning of a social relationship, including smiling at a new acquaintance, making small talk, and looking the person squarely in the eye.

These methods, though different, all represent psychotherapies. To make sense of what is happening to Brad—and of all the things that are not happening to him—in this chapter, we first define *psychotherapy.* We consider the history of therapy and examine several of the major current psychotherapies including psychodynamic, humanistic–existential, cognitive, behavior, and group therapies. After exploring these approaches to psychotherapy, we shall turn our attention to *biological therapies* including drug therapy (also called *chemotherapy*), electroconvulsive shock therapy, and psychosurgery.

WHAT IS THERAPY?

The form of psychotherapy practiced by a psychologist or another helping professional is related to that practitioner's theory of personality or theoretical model of abnormal behavior. Treatment is not, or ought not to be, a matter of chance.

Although there are many different kinds of psychotherapy, they have a number of things in common. **Psychotherapy** is a systematic interaction between a therapist and a client that brings psychological principles to bear on influencing the client's thoughts, feelings, or behavior in order to help the client overcome abnormal behavior, adjust to problems in living, or develop as an individual.

Quite a mouthful? True. But note the essentials:

1. *Systematic Interaction.* Psychotherapy is a systematic interaction between a client and a therapist. The client's needs and goals and the therapist's theoretical point of view interact to determine how the therapist and client relate to one another.
2. *Psychological Principles.* Psychotherapy brings psychological principles to bear on the client's problems or goals. Psychotherapy is based on psychological theory and research in areas such as personality, learning, motivation, and emotion. Psychotherapy is not based on, say, religious or biological principles, although psychotherapy can be compatible with both.
3. *Thoughts, Feelings, and Behavior.* Psychotherapy influences clients' thoughts, feelings, and behavior. Psychotherapy can be aimed at any or all of these aspects of human psychology.
4. *Abnormal Behavior, Adjustment Problems, and Personal Growth.* Psychotherapy is used with at least three types of clients. First, there are people who have been diagnosed as showing patterns of abnormal behavior such as anxiety disorders, mood disorders, or schizophrenia. When these disorders are severe, as in the case of major depression or schizophrenia, biological therapies may play a role in treatment. Even so, psychotherapy is often used to help the individual in areas of personal, social, or vocational concern.

   Other people seek help in adjusting to problems such as social shyness, weight problems, loss of a spouse, or career confusion. Still others use psychotherapy, especially psychodynamic and humanistic–existential therapies, not because they are seeking help, but because they want to learn more about themselves and to reach their full potential as individuals, creative artists, parents, and members of social groups.

History of Therapies

Ancient and medieval "treatments" of psychological disorders often reflected the demonological model. As such, they tended to involve cruel practices such as exorcism and death by hanging or burning, as was practiced some 300 years ago. In Europe and the United States, some people who could not meet the demands of everyday life were also thrown into prisons. Others begged in city streets, stole produce and food animals from farms, or entered marginal societal niches occupied by prostitutes and petty thieves. A few might have found their ways to monasteries or other retreats that offered a kind word and some support. Generally speaking, they died early.

Asylums. **Asylums** often had their origins in European monasteries. They were the first institutions meant primarily for persons with psychological disorders. Their functions were human warehousing, not treatment. Asylums mushroomed in population until the daily stresses created by noise, overcrowding, and unsanitary conditions undoubtedly heightened the problems they were meant to ameliorate. Inmates were frequently chained and beaten. Some were chained for decades.

The word *bedlam* is derived from the name of the London asylum St. Mary's of Bethlehem, which opened its gates in 1547. Here, the unfortunate were chained between the inner and outer walls, whipped, and allowed to lie in their

Psychotherapy A systematic interaction between a therapist and a client that brings psychological principles to bear on influencing the client's thoughts, feelings, or behavior in order to help that client overcome abnormal behavior or adjust to problems in living.

Asylum An institution for the care of the mentally ill.

St. Mary's of Bethlehem. This famous London institution is the source of the term *bedlam.*

own waste. And here, the ladies and gentlemen of the British upper class might go for a stroll on a lazy afternoon to take in the sights. The admission for such amusement? One penny.

It is true that the English went to visit the local insane asylum as a source of entertainment. St. Mary's of Bethlehem was the best known.

Humanitarian reform movements began in the eighteenth century. In Paris, Philippe Pinel unchained the patients at the asylum known as La Bicêtre. The populace was amazed that most patients, rather than running amok, profited from kindness and greater freedom. Many could eventually function in society once more. Reform movements were later led by the Quaker William Tuke in England and by Dorothea Dix in America.

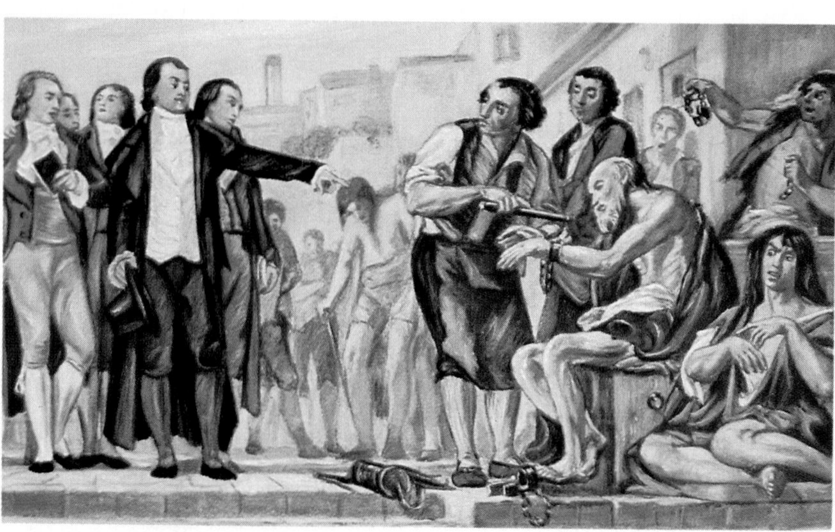

The Unchaining of the Patients at La Bicêtre. Frenchman Philippe Pinel sparked the humanitarian reform movement by unchaining the patients at this Paris asylum.

TABLE 14.1: Functions of the Community Mental Health Center

Outpatient treatment
Short-term hospitalization
Partial hospitalization (e.g., patient sleeps in the hospital and works outside during the day)
Crisis intervention
Community consultation and education about abnormal behavior

The Community Mental-Health Centers Act provided funds for community agencies that attempt to intervene in mental-health problems as early as possible and to maintain mental patients in the community.

Mental Hospitals. Mental hospitals gradually replaced asylums in the United States. In the mid-1950s, more than a million people resided in state, county, Veterans Administration, or private facilities. Treatment, not warehousing, is the function of the mental hospital. Still, because of high patient populations and understaffing, many patients have received little attention. Even today, with somewhat improved conditions, one psychiatrist may be responsible for the welfare of several hundred patients on a weekend.

The Community Mental-Health Movement. Since the 1960s, efforts have been made to maintain as many mental patients as possible in the community. The Community Mental-Health Centers Act of 1963 provided funds for creating hundreds of community mental-health centers, in which patients would be charged according to their ability to pay, in order to accomplish this goal. These centers attempt to maintain new patients as outpatients, to serve patients from mental hospitals who have been released into the community, and to provide other services as listed in Table 14.1. Today, about 63 percent of the nation's chronic mentally ill live in the community, not the hospital (Morganthau et al., 1986).

Critics note that many people who had resided in hospitals for decades were suddenly discharged to "home" communities that seemed foreign and frightening. Many discharged patients do not receive adequate follow-up care in the community (Morganthau et al., 1986). Many join the ranks of the nation's homeless (Carling, 1990; Levine & Rog, 1990). Some former hospital inhabitants try to return to the protected world of the hospital and become trapped in a "revolving door" between the hospital and the community.

The outlook for maintaining new patients in the community, rather than hospitalizing them, looks brighter. In a review of ten experiments in which seriously disturbed patients were randomly assigned either to hospitalization or outpatient care, Kiesler (1982) did not find one case in which the outcomes of hospitalization were superior. The outpatient alternative was usually superior in terms of the patient's maintaining independent living arrangements, staying in school, and finding employment.

Let us consider kinds of therapies that are available today.

PSYCHODYNAMIC THERAPIES

Psychodynamic therapies are based on the thinking of Sigmund Freud, the founder of psychodynamic theory. Broadly speaking, they are based on the view that our problems largely reflect early childhood experiences and internal conflicts. According to Freud, this internal conflict involves the shifting of psychic, or libidinal, energy among the three psychic structures—the id, ego, and superego. The sway of psychic energy determines our behavior, and, when primitive urges threaten to break through from the id or when the superego floods us with excessive guilt, it prompts the establishment of defenses and creates distress. Freud's psychodynamic therapy method—psychoanalysis—aims to modify the flow of energy among these structures, largely to bulwark the ego against the torrents of

A View of Freud's Consulting Room at Berggasse 19 in Vienna. Freud would sit in the chair by the head of the couch while a client free associated. The cardinal rule of free association is that no thought is to be censored.

energy loosed by the id and the superego. With impulses and feelings of guilt and shame placed under greater control, clients are emotionally freed to develop more adaptive behavior patterns.

Traditional Psychoanalysis: Where Id Was, There Shall Ego Be

> Canst thou not minister to a mind diseas'd,
> Pluck out from the memory a rooted sorrow,
> Raze out the written troubles of the brain,
> And with some sweet oblivious antidote
> Cleanse the stuff'd bosom of that perilous stuff
> Which weighs upon the heart?
>
> Shakespeare, *Macbeth*

In this passage, Macbeth asks a physician to minister to Lady Macbeth after she has gone mad. In the play, her madness is in part caused by current events—namely, her guilt for participating in murders designed to seat her husband on the throne of Scotland. There are also hints of more-deeply rooted and mysterious problems, however, such as conflicts about infertility.

If Lady Macbeth's physician had been a traditional psychoanalyst, he might have asked her to lie down on a couch in a slightly darkened room. He would have sat just behind her and encouraged her to talk about anything that came to mind, no matter how trivial, no matter how personal. To avoid interfering with her self-exploration, he might have said little or nothing for session after session. That would have been par for the course. A traditional **psychoanalysis,** you see, can extend for months, or years.

Psychoanalysis is the clinical method devised by Freud for plucking "from the memory a rooted sorrow," for razing "out the written troubles of the brain." Psychoanalysis is the method used by Freud and his followers to "cleanse . . . that perilous stuff which weighs upon the heart"—to provide insight into the conflicts presumed to lie at the roots of a person's problems. Insight involves a number of things: knowledge of the experiences that lead to conflicts and maladaptive be-

Psychoanalysis Freud's method of psychotherapy.

havior; identification and labeling of feelings and conflicts that lie below conscious awareness; and objective evaluation of one's beliefs and ideas, feelings, and overt behavior.

Psychoanalysis also seeks to allow the client to express emotions and impulses that are theorized to have been dammed up by the forces of repression. Freud was fond of saying, "Where id was, there shall ego be." In part, he meant that psychoanalysis could shed light on the inner workings of the mind. However, Freud did not believe that we ought, or needed, to become conscious of all of our conflicts and primitive impulses. Instead, he sought to replace impulsive and defensive behavior with coping behavior. He believed that impulsive behavior reflected the urges of the id. Defensive behavior such as timidly avoiding confrontations represented the ego's compromising efforts to protect the client from these impulses and the possibility of retaliation. Coping behavior would allow the client to partially express these impulses, but in socially acceptable ways. In so doing, the client would find gratification but avoid social and self-condemnation.

In this way, a man with a phobia for knives might discover that he had been repressing the urge to harm someone who had taken advantage of him. He might also find ways to confront his antagonist verbally. A woman with a conversion disorder—for example, paralysis of the legs—could see that her disability allowed her to avoid unwanted pregnancy without guilt. She might also realize her resentment at being pressed into a stereotypical feminine sex role and decide to expand her options.

Freud also believed that psychoanalysis permitted the client to spill forth the psychic energy theorized to have been repressed by conflicts and guilt. He called this spilling forth **abreaction,** or **catharsis.** Abreaction would provide feelings of relief by alleviating some of the forces assaulting the ego.

Free Association. Freud used **free association** as a gradual method of breaking down the walls of defense that blocked insight into unconscious processes. In free association, the client is made comfortable, as by lying on a couch, and is asked to talk about any topic that comes to mind. No thought is to be censored—that is the cardinal rule. Psychoanalysts ask their clients to wander "freely" from topic to topic, but they do not believe that the process *within* the client is fully free. Repressed impulses press for release. A client may begin to free associate with meaningless topics, but pertinent repressed material may eventually surface.

The ego persists in trying to repress unacceptable impulses and threatening conflicts. As a result, clients might show **resistance** to recalling and discussing threatening ideas. Clients might claim "My mind is blank" when they are about to entertain such thoughts. They might accuse the analyst of being demanding or inconsiderate. They might "forget" their appointment when threatening material is due to be uncovered.

The therapist observes the dynamic struggle between the compulsion to utter and resistance. Through discreet remarks, the analyst subtly tips the balance in favor of uttering. A gradual process of self-discovery and self-insight ensues. Now and then, the analyst offers an **interpretation** of an utterance, showing how it suggests resistance or deep-seated feelings and conflicts.

Dream Analysis.

Sometimes a cigar is just a cigar.

Sigmund Freud, on dream analysis

Freud considered dreams the "royal road to the unconscious" and often had clients jot down their dreams upon waking so that they could be interpreted in therapy. The psychodynamic theory of dreams holds that they are determined by unconscious processes as well as by the remnants, or "residues," of the day. Unconscious impulses tend to be expressed in dreams as a form of **wish fulfillment.**

Abreaction In psychoanalysis, expression of previously repressed feelings and impulses to allow the psychic energy associated with them to spill forth.

Catharsis Another term for *abreaction.*

Free association In psychoanalysis, the uncensored uttering of all thoughts that come to mind.

Resistance The tendency to block the free expression of impulses and primitive ideas—a reflection of the defense mechanism of repression.

Interpretation An explanation of a client's utterance according to psychoanalytic theory.

Wish fulfillment A primitive method used by the id to attempt to gratify basic instincts.

Unacceptable sexual and aggressive impulses are likely to be displaced onto objects and situations that reflect the client's era and culture. These objects become symbols of the unconscious wishes. For example, long, narrow dream objects might be **phallic symbols,** but whether the symbol takes the form of a spear, rifle, "stick shift," or spacecraft partially reflects one's cultural background.

In psychodynamic theory, the perceived content of the dream is called its shown or **manifest content.** Its presumed hidden or symbolic content is referred to as its **latent content.** A man might dream that he is flying. Flying is the manifest content of the dream. Freud usually interpreted flying as being symbolic of erection, so issues concerning sexual potency might make up the latent content of such a dream.

Transference. Freud found that his clients responded not only to his appearance and behavior but also to what these characteristics meant to clients. A young woman might see Freud as a father figure and displace, or transfer, her feelings toward her own father onto Freud. Another woman might view him as a lover and act seductively or suspiciously. Men also showed **transference.** A man, like a woman, might view Freud as a father figure, but a man also might respond to Freud as a competitor.

Freud discovered that transference was a two-way street. Freud could also transfer his feelings onto his clients—perhaps viewing a woman as a sex object or a young man as a rebellious son. He called this placing of clients into roles in his own life **countertransference.**

Transference and countertransference lead to unjustified expectations of new people and can foster maladaptive behavior. We might relate to our spouses as to our parents of the opposite gender and demand too much (or too little) from them. Or we might accuse them unfairly of harboring wishes and secrets we attribute to our parents. We might not give new friends or lovers "a chance" when we have been mistreated by someone who played a similar role in our lives or our fantasies.

In any event, psychoanalysts are trained to be **opaque** concerning their own behavior and feelings. Opaque therapists do not encourage client transference or express their own feelings of countertransference. Then, when the client acts accusingly, seductively, or otherwise inappropriately toward the analyst, the analyst can plead not guilty of encouraging the behavior and suggest that it reflects historical events and fantasies. In this way, transference behavior becomes grist for the therapeutic mill.

Analysis of client transference is an important element of therapy. It provides client insight and encourages more adaptive social behavior, as suggested in the following case dialogue:

PATIENT: . . . I continue to have success, but I have been feeling weak and tired. I saw my doctor yesterday and he said there's nothing organically wrong.

ANALYST: Does anything come to mind in relation to weak and tired feelings?

PATIENT: I'm thinking of the way you looked last year after you came out of the hospital [The patient was referring to a hospitalization that, in fact, I had the previous year during which time our treatment sessions were suspended].

ANALYST: Do you recall how you felt when you saw me looking that way?

PATIENT: It made me upset, even guilty.

ANALYST: But why guilty?

PATIENT: I'm not sure why I said that. There was nothing to feel guilty about.

ANALYST: Perhaps you had some other feelings.

Phallic symbol A sign that represents the penis.

Manifest content In psychodynamic theory, the reported content of dreams.

Latent content In psychodynamic theory, the symbolized or underlying content of dreams.

Transference In psychoanalysis, the generalization to the analyst of feelings toward a person in the client's life.

Countertransference In psychoanalysis, the generalization to the client of feelings toward a person in the analyst's life.

Opaque In psychoanalysis, descriptive of the analyst, who hides personal feelings.

PATIENT: Well it's true that at one point I felt faintly pleased that I was young and vigorous and you seemed to be going downhill. As a matter of fact I had the thought again last night when I thought of how well I have been doing.

ANALYST: Perhaps then . . . you imagined I felt [bad] because you were going uphill while I was going down.

PATIENT: That feels correct and I think that I may even want that to happen. [The patient looks distressed and then goes off on another topic.]

ANALYST: It's interesting how you felt what you were talking about after you said that you could sense wanting me to go downhill and you going up. Clearly you're not very comfortable when you contrast your state with mine—to your advantage.

PATIENT: Well you know I've never felt comfortable when thinking of myself outdoing you in any way. And when it comes to our states of health, the idea is particularly distressing.

ANALYST: I wonder now if the weak and tired feelings that you spoke about earlier . . . aren't related to what we're discussing now. Perhaps your weak and tired feeling represents an identification with me brought on by your feeling guilty about your successes, since that implies that you are outdoing me. Perhaps you felt that you were making me ill again with your wishes and thus you had to punish yourself by making yourself ill. Your discomfort with feeling that in certain respects you're surpassing me is posing a problem for you. (Silverman, 1984, pp. 226–227)

It can take months or years for transference to develop and be resolved, which is one reason that psychoanalysis can be a lengthy process.

Modern Psychodynamic Approaches

Some psychoanalysts adhere faithfully to Freud's protracted techniques. They continue to practice traditional psychoanalysis. In recent years, however, briefer, less intense forms of psychodynamic therapy have been devised (Koss et al., 1986; Zaiden, 1982). These methods are "psychoanalytically oriented." They make treatment available to clients who do not have the time or money for protracted therapy. Also, frankly, many of these therapists believe that protracted therapy is not needed or justifiable in terms of the ratio of cost to benefits.

It is *not* true that psychotherapy need go on for months or years in order to be of help.

Although some modern psychodynamic therapies continue to focus on revealing unconscious material and on breaking through psychological defenses or resistance, there are a number of differences from traditional psychoanalysis. One is that client and therapist usually sit face to face, as opposed to the client's reclining on a couch. The therapist is usually more directive than the traditional psychoanalyst. Modern therapists often suggest productive behavior instead of focusing solely on self-insight. Finally, there is usually more focus on the ego as the "executive" of personality. Accordingly, there is less emphasis on the role of the id. For this reason, many modern psychodynamic therapists are considered **ego analysts.**

Ego analyst A psychodynamically oriented therapist who focuses on the conscious, coping behavior of the ego instead of the hypothesized, unconscious functioning of the id.

Many of Freud's followers, the "second generation" of psychoanalysts—from Jung and Adler to Horney and Erikson—believed that Freud had placed too much

Person-Centered Therapy. By showing the qualities of unconditional positive regard, empathic understanding, genuineness, and congruence, person-centered therapists create an atmosphere in which clients can explore their feelings.

emphasis on sexual and aggressive impulses and underestimated the importance of the ego. Freud, for example, aimed to establish conditions under which clients could spill forth psychic energy and eventually shore up the position of the ego. Erikson, in contrast, spoke to clients directly about their values and concerns and encouraged them to consciously fashion desired traits and behavior patterns. Freud saw clients as perpetual victims of the past and doubted their ability to fully overcome childhood trauma. Karen Horney, on the other hand, deemed clients capable of overcoming early abuse and deprivation through self-understanding and adult relationships (Quinn, 1987). Even Freud's daughter, the psychoanalyst Anna Freud (1895–1982), was more concerned with the ego than with unconscious forces and conflicts.

Today, there are many psychodynamic therapies, many approaches that show the influence of Sigmund Freud. As a group they continue to use terms such as *conflict* and *ego,* but they differ in the prominence they ascribe to unconscious forces and in their perception of the role of the ego.

HUMANISTIC–EXISTENTIAL THERAPIES

Whereas psychodynamic therapies focus on internal conflicts and unconscious processes, humanistic–existential therapies focus on the quality of clients' subjective, conscious experience. Whereas psychodynamic therapies tend to focus on the past, and particularly on early childhood experiences, humanistic–existential therapies usually focus on what clients are experiencing today—on "the here and now."

Let us consider person-centered therapy and Gestalt therapy and discuss some of these ideas in more detail.

Person-Centered Therapy: Removing Roadblocks to Self-Actualization

Person-centered therapy was originated by Carl Rogers (1951), who was rated as the most influential psychotherapist in the Smith (1982) survey. Rogers believed that we are free to make choices and control our destinies, despite the burdens of the past.

Rogers also believed that we have natural tendencies toward health, growth, and fulfillment. Given this view, Rogers wrote that psychological problems arise

Person-centered therapy Carl Rogers' method of psychotherapy which emphasizes the creation of a warm, therapeutic atmosphere that frees clients to engage in self-exploration and self-expression.

from roadblocks placed in the path of our own self-actualization. Because others show us selective approval when we are young, we learn to disown the disapproved parts of ourselves. We don masks and façades to earn social approval. We may learn to be seen but not heard—not even heard, or examined fully, by ourselves. As a result, we might experience stress and discomfort and the feeling that we—or the world—are not real.

Person-centered therapy aims to provide insight into the parts of us that we have disowned so that we can feel whole. It stresses the importance of a warm, therapeutic atmosphere that encourages client self-exploration and self-expression. Therapist acceptance of the client is thought to foster client self-acceptance and self-esteem. Self-acceptance frees the client to make choices that develop his or her unique potential.

Person-centered therapy is nondirective. The client takes the lead, listing and exploring problems. The therapist reflects or paraphrases expressed feelings and ideas, helping the client to get in touch with deeper feelings and to follow the strongest leads in the quest for self-insight.

It is true that some psychotherapists encourage their clients to take the lead in the therapy session. Person-centered therapists provide an example.

Person-centered therapy is practiced widely in college and university counseling centers, not just to help students experiencing, say, anxieties or depression but also to help them make decisions. Many college students have not yet made career choices or wonder whether they should become involved with particular people or in sexual activity. Person-centered therapists provide an encouraging atmosphere in which clients can verbally explore choices and make decisions. Person-centered therapists do not tell clients what to do. Instead, they help clients arrive at their own decisions.

The effective person-centered therapist also shows four qualities: *unconditional positive regard, empathic understanding, genuineness,* and *congruence.* In showing **unconditional positive regard** for clients, person-centered therapists respect clients as important human beings with unique values and goals. Clients are provided with a sense of security that encourages them to follow their own feelings. Psychoanalysts might hesitate to encourage clients to freely express their impulses because of the fear that primitive sexual and aggressive forces might be unleashed. Person-centered therapists believe that people are basically *pro*social, however. If people follow their own feelings, rather than act defensively, they should not be abusive or *anti*social.

Empathic understanding is shown by accurately reflecting the client's experiences and feelings. Therapists try to view the world through their clients' **frames of reference** by setting aside their own values and listening closely.

Whereas psychoanalysts are trained to be opaque, person-centered therapists are trained to show **genuineness.** Person-centered therapists are open about their feelings. It would be harmful to clients if their therapists could not truly accept and like them, even though their values might differ from those of the therapists. Rogers admitted that he sometimes had negative feelings about clients, usually boredom. He usually expressed these feelings rather than hold them in (Bennett, 1985). Person-centered therapists must also be able to tolerate differentness, because they believe that every client is different in important ways.

Person-centered therapists also try to show **congruence,** or a fit between their thoughts, feelings, and behavior. Person-centered therapists serve as models of integrity to their clients.

Unconditional positive regard Acceptance of the value of another person, although not necessarily acceptance of everything the person does.

Empathic understanding Ability to perceive a client's feelings from the client's frame of reference. A quality of the good person-centered therapist.

Frame of reference One's unique patterning of perceptions and attitudes, according to which one evaluates events.

Genuineness Recognition and open expression of the therapist's own feelings.

Congruence A fit between one's self-concept and behaviors, thoughts, and emotions.

Gestalt Therapy: Getting It Together

Gestalt therapy was originated by Fritz Perls (1893–1970). Gestalt therapy, like person-centered therapy, aims to help individuals integrate conflicting parts of the personality. He aimed to make clients aware of inner conflict, accept its reality rather than deny it or keep it repressed, and make productive choices despite misgivings and fear.

Perls' ideas about conflicting personality elements owe much to psychodynamic theory. His form of therapy, unlike psychoanalysis, focuses on the here and now, however. Clients undergo planned experiences to heighten awareness of current feelings and behavior rather than explore the past. Perls believed, along with Carl Rogers, that people are free to make choices and to direct their personal growth. Unlike person-centered therapy, however, Gestalt therapy is highly directive.

In the Gestalt technique of the **dialogue,** clients express opposing wishes and ideas to increase awareness of conflict. Consider the example "top dog" and "underdog." One's top dog might conservatively suggest, "Don't take chances. Stick with what you have or you might lose it all." One's frustrated underdog might then rise up and assert, "You never try anything. How will you ever get out of this rut if you don't take on new challenges?" Heightened awareness of conflict can facilitate resolution, perhaps through compromise.

Body language also provides insight into conflicting feelings. Clients might be instructed to attend to the ways in which they furrow their eyebrows and tense their facial muscles when they express ideas that they think they support. In this way, they often find that their body language asserts feelings that they have been denying.

To increase clients' understanding of opposing points of view, Gestalt therapists might encourage them to argue in favor of ideas opposed to their own. They might also have clients role-play people who are important to them to become more in touch with their points of view.

Whereas psychodynamic theory views dreams as the "royal road to the unconscious," Perls saw the stuff of dreams as disowned parts of the personality.

It is true that some psychotherapists interpret clients' dreams. Psychoanalysts and Gestalt therapists are two examples.

Perls would often ask clients to role-play the elements in their dreams to get in touch with these parts. In *Gestalt Therapy Verbatim*, Perls describes a session in which a client, Jim, is reporting a dream:

JIM: I just have the typical recurring dream which I think a lot of people might have if they have a background problem, and it isn't of anything I think I can act out. It's the distant wheel—I'm not sure what type it is—it's coming towards me and ever-increasing in size. And then finally, it's just above me and it's no height that I can determine, it's so high. And that's—

[PERLS]: If you were this wheel, . . . what would you do with Jim?

JIM: I am just about to roll over Jim. (Perls, 1971, p. 127)

Jim learns that the wheel represents fears about taking decisive action. This insight renders the "wheel" more manageable in size, and Jim is able to use some of the "energy" that he might otherwise have spent in worrying to begin to take charge of his life.

Let us now turn our attention to another group of therapies that are concerned with subjective experience and the here and now—cognitive therapies.

Gestalt therapy Fritz Perls' form of psychotherapy which attempts to integrate conflicting parts of the personality through directive methods designed to help clients perceive their whole selves.

Dialogue A Gestalt therapy technique in which clients verbalize confrontations between conflicting parts of their personality.

Whereas humanistic–existential therapists tend to focus on clients' personalities, cognitive therapists focus on mental processes such as thoughts, strategies for interpreting experience, plans, problem-solving techniques, and attitudes—especially self-defeating attitudes.

COGNITIVE THERAPIES

There is nothing either good or bad, but thinking makes it so.
Shakespeare, *Hamlet*

In his lines from *Hamlet,* Shakespeare did not mean to suggest that injuries and misfortunes are painless or easy to manage. Rather, he meant that our cognitive appraisals of unfortunate circumstances can heighten our discomfort and impair our coping ability. In so doing, Shakespeare was providing a kind of motto for cognitive therapists.

Cognitive therapists generally agree with Carl Rogers that people are free to make choices and activate their concepts of what they are capable of being. Cognitive therapists would also agree with Perls that it is useful to focus on the here and now. Cognitive therapists, like Perls, are also reasonably directive in their approaches.

Cognitive therapists focus on the beliefs, attitudes, and automatic types of thinking that create and compound their clients' problems. Cognitive therapists, like psychodynamic and humanistic–existential therapists, are interested in fostering client self-insight, but they aim to heighten clients' insight into *current cognitions,* not those of the distant past. Cognitive therapists also aim to directly *change* maladaptive cognitions to reduce negative feelings, to provide more accurate perceptions of the self and others, and to orient the client toward solving problems.

Let us now look at some of the major cognitive therapists and at some of their approaches and methods.

Albert Ellis' Rational-Emotive Therapy: Shutting Ten Doorways to Distress

Albert Ellis is the founder of **rational-emotive therapy** and the second most influential psychotherapist in the Smith (1982) survey. Ellis (1977, 1985, 1987) points out that our beliefs about events, as well as the events themselves, shape our responses to them.

Consider a case in which one is fired from a job and is anxious and depressed about it. It may seem logical that losing the job is responsible for the misery, but Ellis points out how beliefs about the loss compound misery.

Let us examine this situation according to Ellis' A–B–C approach: Losing the job is an *activating event* (A). The eventual outcome, or *consequence* (C), is misery. Between the activating event (A) and the consequence (C), however, lie *beliefs* (B), such as: "This job was the most important thing in my life," "What a no-good failure I am," "My family will starve," "I'll never find a job as good," "There's nothing I can do about it." Beliefs such as these compound misery, foster helplessness, and divert us from planning and deciding what to do next. The belief "There's nothing I can do about it" fosters helplessness. The belief "What a no-good failure I am" internalizes the blame and may be an exaggeration. The belief "My family will starve" may also be an exaggeration.

We can diagram the situation like this:

Activating events → Beliefs → Consequences

Cognitive therapy A form of therapy that focuses on how clients' cognitions (expectations, attitudes, beliefs, etc.) lead to distress and may be modified to relieve distress and promote adaptive behavior.

Rational-emotive therapy Albert Ellis' form of cognitive psychotherapy which focuses on how irrational expectations create anxiety and disappointment and which encourages clients to challenge and correct these expectations.

Anxieties about the future and depression over a loss are normal enough. However, the beliefs of the person who lost the job tend to **catastrophize** the extent of the loss and to contribute to anxiety and depression. By heightening emotional reaction to the loss and fostering feelings of helplessness, these beliefs also impair coping ability. They lower self-efficacy expectations and divert attention from problem solving.

Ellis proposes that many of us harbor irrational beliefs. We carry them with us; they are our personal doorways to distress. They can give rise to problems in themselves, and, when problems assault us from other sources, these beliefs can magnify their effect. How many of these beliefs do you harbor? Are you sure?

Irrational Belief 1: You must have sincere love and approval almost all the time from the people who are important to you.

Irrational Belief 2: You must prove yourself to be thoroughly competent, adequate, and achieving at something important.

Irrational Belief 3: Things must go the way you want them to go. Life is awful when you don't get your first choice in everything.

Irrational Belief 4: Other people must treat everyone fairly and justly. When people act unfairly or unethically, they are rotten.

Irrational Belief 5: When there is danger or fear in your world, you must be preoccupied with and upset by it.

Irrational Belief 6: People and things should turn out better than they do. It's awful and horrible when you don't find quick solutions to life's hassles.

Irrational Belief 7: Your emotional misery stems from external pressures that you have little or no ability to control. Unless these external pressures change, you must remain miserable.

Irrational Belief 8: It is easier to evade life's responsibilities and problems than to face them and undertake more rewarding forms of self-discipline.

Irrational Belief 9: Your past influenced you immensely and must therefore continue to determine your feelings and behavior today.

Irrational Belief 10: You can achieve happiness by inertia and inaction, or by just enjoying yourself from day to day.

Ellis points out that it is understandable that we would want the approval of others but irrational to believe that we cannot survive without it. It would be nice to be competent in everything we do, but it's unreasonable to expect it. Sure, it would be nice to serve and volley like a tennis pro, but most of us haven't the time or natural ability to perfect the game. Demanding self-perfection prevents us from going out on the courts on weekends and batting the ball back and forth for fun. Belief 5 is a prescription for perpetual emotional upheaval. Beliefs 7 and 9 lead to feelings of helplessness and demoralization. Sure, Ellis might say, childhood experiences can explain the origins of irrational beliefs, but it is our own cognitive appraisal—here and now—that causes us misery.

Ellis's methods are active and directive. He urges clients to seek out their irrational beliefs, which can be fleeting and hard to catch. He shows clients how their beliefs lead to misery and challenges clients to change them.

Aaron Beck's Cognitive Therapy: Correcting Cognitive Errors

Psychiatrist Aaron Beck (1976, 1985) also focuses on clients' cognitive distortions. He encourages clients to see the irrationality of their own ways of thinking—how, for example, their minimizing of their accomplishments and their pessimistic assumptions that the worst will happen heightens feelings of depression. Beck, like

Catastrophize To exaggerate or magnify the noxious properties of negative events; to "blow out of proportion."

Ellis, notes that our cognitive distortions can be fleeting and automatic, difficult to detect. His therapy methods help clients pin down these self-defeating thoughts.

Beck notes in particular the pervasive influence of four basic types of cognitive errors that contribute to clients' miseries:

1. Clients may *selectively perceive* the world as a harmful place and ignore evidence to the contrary.
2. Clients may *overgeneralize* on the basis of a few examples. For example, they may perceive themselves as worthless because they were laid off at work or as grossly unattractive because they were refused a request for a date.
3. Clients may *magnify,* or blow out of proportion, the importance of negative events. As noted in the discussion of Ellis's views, clients may catastrophize flunking a test by assuming they will flunk out of college or catastrophize losing a job by believing that they will never work again and that serious harm will befall their families.
4. Clients may engage in *absolutist thinking,* or looking at the world in black and white rather than in shades of gray. In doing so, a rejection on a date takes on the meaning of a lifetime of loneliness; a discomforting illness takes on life-threatening proportions.

The concept of pinpointing and modifying errors may become more clear from reading an excerpt from a case in which a 53-year-old engineer was treated with cognitive therapy for severe depression. The engineer had left his job and become inactive. As reported by Beck and his colleagues, the first treatment goal was to foster physical activity—even things like raking leaves and preparing dinner—because activity is incompatible with depression. Then:

[The engineer's] cognitive distortions were identified by comparing his assessment of each activity with that of his wife. Alternative ways of interpreting his experiences were then considered.

In comparing his wife's résumé of his past experiences, he became aware that he had (1) undervalued his past by failing to mention many previous accomplishments, (2) regarded himself as far more responsible for his "failures" than she did, and (3) concluded that he was worthless since he had not succeeded in attaining certain goals in the past. When the two accounts were contrasted, he could discern many of his cognitive distortions. In subsequent sessions, his wife continued to serve as an "objectifier."

In midtherapy, [he] compiled a list of new attitudes that he had acquired since initiating therapy. These included:

1. *"I am starting at a lower level of functioning at my job, but it will improve if I persist."*
2. *"I know that once I get going in the morning, everything will run all right for the rest of the day."*
3. *"I can't achieve everything at once."*
4. *"I have my periods of ups and downs, but in the long run I feel better."*
5. *"My expectations from my job and life should be scaled down to a realistic level."*
6. *"Giving in to avoidance [e.g., staying away from work and social interactions] never helps and only leads to further avoidance."*

He was instructed to re-read this list daily for several weeks even though he already knew the content. (Rush et al., 1975)

Re-reading the list of productive attitudes is a variation of the cognitive technique of having clients rehearse or repeat accurate and rational ideas so that they come to replace cognitive distortions and irrational beliefs. The engineer gradually became less depressed in therapy and returned to work and an active social life. He learned to combat inappropriate self-blame, perfectionistic expectations, magnifications of failures, and overgeneralizations from failures.

Many theorists consider cognitive therapy to be a collection of techniques that belong within the province of behavior therapy, which is discussed in the following section. Some members of this group prefer the name "cognitive *behavior* therapy"; others argue that the term *behavior therapy* is broad enough to include cognitive techniques. Many cognitive therapists and behavior therapists differ in their focus, however. To behavior therapists, the purpose of dealing with client cognitions is to change *overt* behavior. Cognitive therapists agree that cognitive change leads to overt behavioral change and also see the value of tying treatment outcomes to observable behavior. Cognitive therapists tend to assert that cognitive change is in itself an important goal, however.

BEHAVIOR THERAPY

Behavior therapy—also called *behavior modification*—is the direct promotion of desired behavioral change by means of systematic application of principles of learning. Many behavior therapists incorporate cognitive processes in their theoretical outlook and cognitive procedures in their methodology (Wilson, 1982). Techniques such as systematic desensitization, covert sensitization, and covert reinforcement ask clients to focus on visual imagery. Behavior therapists insist that their methods be established by experimentation (Wolpe, 1985, 1990), however, and that therapeutic outcomes be assessed through observable, measurable behavior.

Behavior therapists rely on principles of conditioning and observational learning. They help clients discontinue self-defeating behavior patterns such as overeating, smoking, and phobic avoidance of harmless stimuli. They help clients acquire adaptive behavior patterns such as the social skills required to start social relationships and to say no to insistent salespeople. Behavior therapists, like other therapists, may also build warm, therapeutic relationships with clients, but they see the special strength of behavior therapy as deriving from specific, learning-based procedures (Wolpe, 1985, 1990).

About 17 percent of the clinical and counseling psychologists surveyed by Smith (1982) labeled themselves behavioral or cognitive-behavioral in orientation—the largest group of therapists who identified with an orientation. Behavior therapists Joseph Wolpe and Arnold Lazarus were ranked fourth and fifth among the ten most influential psychotherapists (Smith, 1982, p. 807).

Let us look at a number of behavior-therapy techniques.

Relaxation Training

Behavior therapists have developed many methods for helping people relax in the face of anxiety and stress. They include biofeedback training (discussed in the following pages) and **progressive relaxation.**

University of Chicago physician Edmund Jacobson (1938), the originator of progressive relaxation, noted that people tense their muscles when they are under stress, compounding their discomfort. Jacobson developed progressive relaxation to teach people how to relax these tensions. In this method, people purposefully tense a muscle group before relaxing it. This sequence allows them to (1) develop awareness of their muscle tensions and (2) differentiate between feelings of tension and relaxation. The method is "progressive" because people move on, or progress, from one muscle group to another. Progressive relaxation has been found useful in treating stress-related illnesses ranging from headaches (Blanchard et al., 1987; Teders et al., 1984) to hypertension (Agras et al., 1983; Taylor et al., 1977). You can experience muscle relaxation in the arms by doing the following:

Settle down in a reclining chair, dim the lights, and loosen any tight clothing. Use the instructions given below, which were written by Joseph Wolpe and Arnold Lazarus (1966, p. 177). The instructions can be memorized (slight variations from

Behavior therapy Systematic application of the principles of learning to the direct modification of a client's problem behaviors.

Progressive relaxation A method for inducing relaxation in which muscle groups are purposefully tensed, then relaxed.

the text will do no harm), tape-recorded, or read aloud by a friend. For instructions concerning relaxation of the entire body, consult a behavior therapist or other helping professional familiar with the technique.

Settle back as comfortably as you can. Let yourself relax to the best of your ability. . . . Now, as you relax like that, clench your right fist, just clench your fist tighter and tighter, and study the tension as you do so. Keep it clenched and feel the tension in your right fist, hand, forearm . . . and now relax. Let the fingers of your right hand become loose, and observe the contrast in your feelings. . . . Now, let yourself go and try to become more relaxed all over. . . . Once more, clench your right fist really tight . . . hold it, and notice the tension again. . . . Now let go, relax; your fingers straighten out, and you notice the difference once more. . . . Now repeat that with your left fist. Clench your left fist while the rest of your body relaxes; clench that fist tighter and feel the tension . . . and now relax. Again enjoy the contrast. . . . Repeat that once more, clench the left fist, tight and tense. . . . Now do the opposite of tension—relax and feel the difference. Continue relaxing like that for a while. . . . Clench both fists tighter and together, both fists tense, forearms tense, study the sensations . . . and relax; straighten out your fingers and feel that relaxation. Continue relaxing your hands and forearms more and more. . . . Now bend your elbows and tense your biceps, tense them harder and study the tension feelings . . . all right, straighten out your arms, let them relax and feel that difference again. Let the relaxation develop. . . . Once more, tense your biceps; hold the tension and observe it carefully. . . . Straighten the arms and relax; relax to the best of your ability. . . . Each time, pay close attention to your feelings when you tense up and when you relax. Now straighten your arms, straighten them so that you feel most tension in the triceps muscles along the back of your arms; stretch your arms and feel that tension. . . . And now relax. Get your arms back into a comfortable position. Let the relaxation proceed on its own. The arms should feel comfortably heavy as you allow them to relax. . . . Straighten the arms once more so that you feel the tension in the triceps muscles; straighten them. Feel that tension . . . and relax. Now let's concentrate on pure relaxation in the arms without any tension. Get your arms comfortable and let them relax further and further. Continue relaxing your arms even further. Even when your arms seem fully relaxed, try to go that extra bit further; try to achieve deeper and deeper levels of relaxation.

Overcoming Fear of Flying. This woman has undergone group systematic desensitization in order to overcome her fear of flying. For several sessions, she engaged in tasks such as viewing pictures of airplanes and imagining herself in one. Now in the final stages of her program, she actually flies in an airplane with the support of group members and her therapist.

Fear-Reduction Methods

Behavior therapists use many methods for reducing fears, including systematic desensitization and participant modeling.

Systematic Desensitization

Adam has a phobia for receiving injections. His behavior therapist treats him as he reclines in a comfortable padded chair. In a state of deep muscle relaxation, Adam observes slides projected on a screen. A slide of a nurse holding a needle has just been shown three times, 30 seconds at a time. Each time Adam has shown no anxiety. So now a slightly more discomforting slide is shown: one of the nurse aiming the needle toward someone's bare arm. After 15 seconds, our armchair adventurer notices twinges of discomfort and raises a finger as a signal (speaking might disturb his relaxation). The projector operator turns off the light, and Adam spends two minutes imagining his "safe scene"—lying on a beach beneath the tropical sun. Then the slide is shown again. This time Adam views it for 30 seconds before feeling anxiety.

Adam is undergoing **systematic desensitization,** a method for reducing phobic responses originated by psychiatrist Joseph Wolpe (1958, 1990) (Figure 14.1). Systematic desensitization is a gradual process. Clients learn to handle increasingly disturbing stimuli while anxiety to each one is being counterconditioned. About 10 to 20 stimuli are arranged in a sequence or **hierarchy** according to their capacity to elicit anxiety. In imagination or by being shown photos, the client travels gradually up through this hierarchy, approaching the target behavior. In Adam's case, the target behavior was the ability to receive an injection without undue anxiety.

Systematic desensitization Wolpe's method for reducing fears by associating a hierarchy of images of fear-evoking stimuli with deep muscle relaxation.

Hierarchy An arrangement of stimuli according to the amount of fear they evoke.

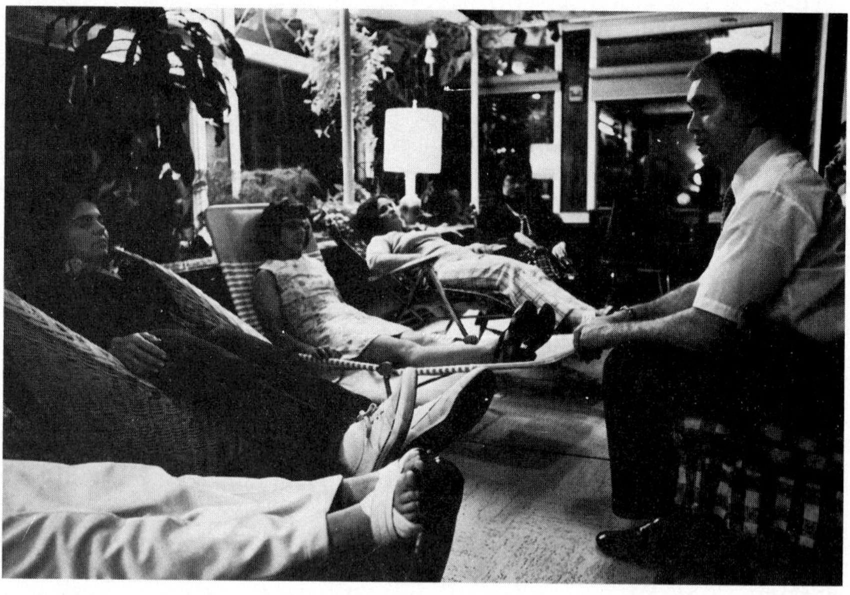

FIGURE 14.1
Systematic Desensitization. In systematic desensitization, clients engage in deep muscle relaxation while the therapist presents a graduated series of fear-evoking stimuli.

Joseph Wolpe developed systematic desensitization on the assumption that maladaptive anxiety responses, like other behaviors, are learned or conditioned. He reasoned that they can be unlearned by counterconditioning or by extinction. In counterconditioning, a response that is incompatible with anxiety is made to appear under conditions that usually elicit anxiety. Muscle relaxation is incompatible with anxiety. For this reason, Adam's therapist is teaching Adam to experience relaxation in the presence of (usually) anxiety-evoking slides of needles. Muscle relaxation is usually achieved by means of progressive relaxation.

Remaining in the presence of phobic imagery, rather than running from it, is also likely to enhance our self-efficacy expectations (Galassi, 1988). Self-efficacy expectations are negatively correlated with levels of adrenaline in the bloodstream (Bandura et al., 1985). Raising clients' self-efficacy expectations may thus help lower their adrenaline levels, counteract feelings of nervousness, and lessen the physical signs of anxiety.

It is true that lying around in your recliner and fantasizing can be an effective way of confronting your fears—if you are using the method of systematic desensitization.

Participant Modeling **Participant modeling** relies on observational learning. In this method, clients observe, then imitate, people who approach and cope with the objects or situations the clients fear. Bandura and his colleagues (1969) found that participant modeling worked as well as systematic desensitization—and more rapidly—in reducing fear of snakes (see Figure 14.2). Participant modeling, like systematic desensitization, is likely to increase self-efficacy expectations in coping with feared stimuli.

Participant modeling A behavior-therapy technique in which a client observes and imitates a person who approaches and copes with feared objects or situations.

Aversive Conditioning

You might have read or seen the filmed version of the futuristic Anthony Burgess novel, *A Clockwork Orange*. Alex, the antisocial "hero," finds violence and rape to be superb pastimes. When he is caught, he is given the chance to undergo an

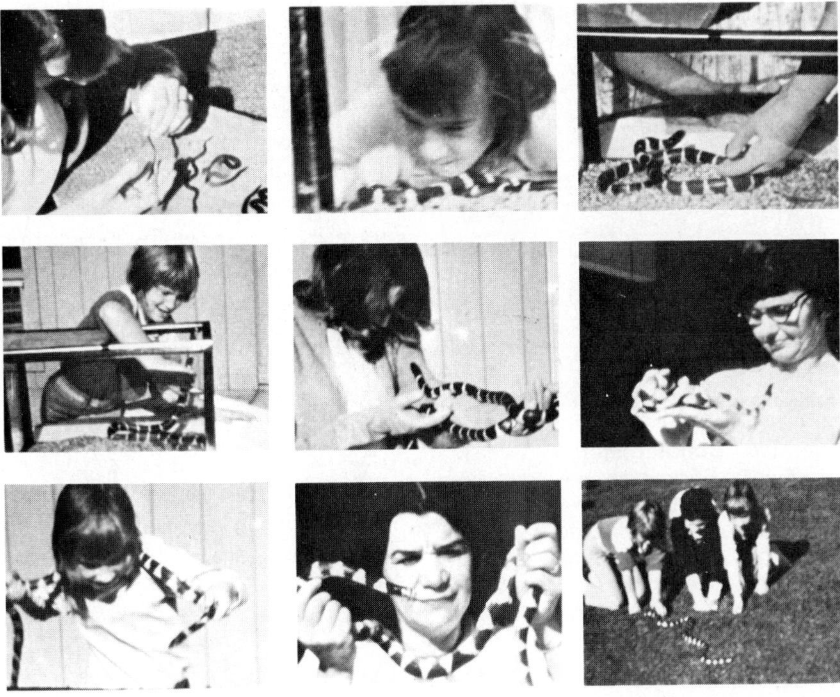

FIGURE 14.2
Participant Modeling. Participant modeling is a behavior-therapy technique that is based on principles of observational learning. In these photos, people with a fear of snakes observe, then imitate, models who are unafraid. Parents often try to convince children that something tastes good by eating it before them and saying "Mmm!"

experimental reconditioning program rather than serve a prison term. In this program, he watches films of violence and rape while vomiting under the influence of a nausea-inducing drug. After his release, he feels ill whenever he contemplates violence. Unfortunately, Beethoven's music, which he had previously enjoyed, accompanies the films and feelings of nausea. So Alex acquires an aversion for Beethoven as well.

In the novel, Alex undergoes a program of **aversive conditioning**—also called *aversion therapy*—which is actually used quite frequently today, although not in prisons. It is one of the more controversial procedures in behavior therapy. In aversive conditioning, painful or aversive stimuli are paired with unwanted impulses, such as desire for a cigarette or desire to engage in antisocial behavior, to make the goal less appealing. For example, to help people control alcohol intake, tastes of different alcoholic beverages can be paired with drug-induced nausea and vomiting or with electric shock.

Aversive conditioning has been used with problems as divergent as paraphilias (Rice et al., 1991), cigarette smoking (Lichtenstein, 1982; Walker & Franzoni, 1985), and retarded children's self-injurious behavior. In one study of aversive conditioning in the treatment of alcoholism, 63 percent of the 685 people treated remained abstinent for one year afterward, and about a third remained abstinent for at least three years (Wiens & Menustik, 1983). It may seem ironic that punitive aversive stimulation is sometimes used to stop children from punishing themselves, but people sometimes hurt themselves to obtain sympathy and attention from others. If self-injury leads to more pain than anticipated and no sympathy, it might be discontinued.

Aversive conditioning A behavior-therapy technique in which undesired responses are inhibited by pairing repugnant or offensive stimuli with them.

Using Aversive Conditioning to Help Clients Quit Smoking. Several aversive-conditioning techniques are used to help people quit smoking. In one, rapid smoking, the would-be quitter inhales every six seconds. In another, the hose of an everyday hair dryer is hooked up to a chamber with several lit cigarettes. Smoke is blown into the quitter's face as he or she also smokes a cigarette. In a third, branching pipes are used so that the smoker draws in smoke from two or more cigarettes simultaneously. In all of these methods, overexposure renders once-desirable cigarette smoke aversive. The quitter becomes motivated to avoid,

Aversive Conditioning. In aversive conditioning, unwanted behaviors take on a noxious quality as a result of pairing them repeatedly with aversive stimuli. Overexposure is making cigarette smoke aversive to the smoker in this photograph.

rather than seek, cigarettes and stops smoking on a preplanned date. Many reports have shown a quit rate of 60 percent or higher at six-month follow-ups.

Rapid smoking is the most widely researched aversion method for treating cigarette smoking (Lichtenstein, 1982). Rapid smoking is popular, because it is as effective as other methods and the apparatus—the quitter's own cigarettes—is readily available. Rapid smoking has "side effects," however. It raises the blood pressure, decreases the blood's capacity to carry oxygen, and produces heart abnormalities, as shown by the electrocardiogram (Lichtenstein & Glasgow, 1977). Nevertheless, a two-year follow-up study of cardiac and pulmonary patients found no negative effects from rapid smoking (Hall et al., 1984). When we consider the positive benefits of quitting smoking for these patients, rapid smoking thus elicits hope.

It is true that smoking cigarettes can be an effective treatment for helping people to stop smoking cigarettes. The trick is to inhale enough smoke so that it is aversive rather than enjoyable.

Operant Conditioning Procedures

We usually prefer to relate to people who smile at us rather than ignore us and to take courses in which we do well rather than fail. We tend to repeat behavior that is reinforced. Behavior that is not reinforced tends to become extinguished. Behavior therapists have used these principles of operant conditioning with psychotic patients as well as clients with milder problems.

The staff at one mental hospital was at a loss about how to encourage withdrawn schizophrenic patients to eat regularly. Ayllon and Haughton (1962) observed that staff members were exacerbating the problem by coaxing patients into the dining room, even feeding them. Increased staff attention apparently reinforced the patients' uncooperativeness. Some rules were changed. Patients who did not arrive at the dining hall within 30 minutes after serving were locked out. Staff could not interact with patients at mealtime. With uncooperative behavior no longer reinforced, patients quickly changed their eating habits. Patients were then required to pay one penny to enter the dining hall. Pennies were earned by interacting with other patients and showing other socially appropriate behaviors. These target behaviors also increased in frequency.

The Token Economy. Many psychiatric wards and hospitals now use **token economies** in which tokens such as poker chips must be used by patients to purchase TV-viewing time, extra visits to the canteen, or private rooms. The tokens are reinforcements for productive activities such as making beds, brushing teeth, and socializing. Whereas token economies have not eliminated all features of schizophrenia, they have enhanced patient activity and cooperation. Tokens have also been used successfully in programs designed to modify the behavior of children with conduct disorders. For example, Schneider and Byrne (1987) gave children tokens for helpful behaviors such as volunteering and removed tokens for behaviors such as arguing and inattention.

Successive Approximations. The operant-conditioning method of **successive approximations** is often used to help clients build good habits. Let us use a (not uncommon!) example: you wish to study three hours an evening but can only maintain concentration for half an hour. Rather than attempting to increase study time all at once, you could do so gradually, say, by five minutes an evening. After every hour or so of studying, you could reinforce yourself with five minutes of people-watching in a busy section of the library.

Token economy A controlled environment in which people are reinforced for desired behaviors with tokens (such as poker chips) that may be exchanged for privileges.

Successive approximations In operant conditioning, a series of behaviors that gradually become more similar to a target behavior.

Functional Analysis. Behavior therapists often help people modify problem behavior through functional analysis. This method helps people determine the stimuli that trigger the problem behavior and the reinforcers that maintain it. You can use a diary to jot down each instance of a problem behavior. Note the time of day, location, your activity (including your thoughts and feelings), and reactions (your and others'). Functional analysis makes you more aware of the environmental context of your behavior and can boost your motivation to change.

Social-Skills Training. In social-skills training, behavior therapists decrease social anxiety and build social skills through operant-conditioning procedures that employ **self-monitoring,** coaching, **modeling,** role playing, **behavior rehearsal,** and **feedback.** Social-skills training has been used to help formerly hospitalized mental patients maintain jobs and apartments in the community.

Assertiveness training is a kind of social-skills training that helps clients demand their rights and express their genuine feelings. Assertiveness training helps clients decrease social anxieties, but it has also been used to optimize the functioning of individuals without problems.

Social-skills training is effective in groups. Group members can role-play important people—such as parents, spouses, or potential dates—in the lives of other members. The trainee then can engage in behavior rehearsal with the role-player.

Biofeedback Training. Through **biofeedback training** (BFT), therapists help clients become more aware of, and gain control over, various bodily functions. Therapists attach clients to devices that measure bodily changes such as heart rate. "Bleeps" or other electronic signals are used to indicate (and thereby reinforce) bodily changes in the desired direction. (Knowledge of results is a powerful reinforcer.) The electromyograph (EMG), for example, monitors muscle tension. It has been used to augment control over muscle tension in the forehead and elsewhere, thereby alleviating anxiety and stress.

BFT also helps clients to voluntarily regulate functions such as heart rate and blood pressure that were once thought to be beyond conscious control. Hypertensive clients use a blood-pressure cuff and electronic signals to gain control over their blood pressure. The electroencephalograph (EEG) monitors brain waves and can be used to teach people how to produce alpha waves, which are associated with relaxation. Some people have overcome insomnia by learning to produce brain waves associated with sleep.

Self-Control Techniques

Do mysterious forces sometimes seem to be at work? Forces that delight in wreaking havoc on New Year's resolutions and other efforts to take charge of bad habits? Just when you go on a diet, that juicy pizza stares at you from the TV set. Just when you resolve to balance your budget, that sweater goes on sale. Behavior therapists have developed a number of self-control techniques to help people cope with such temptations.

Functional Analysis of Behavior. Behavior therapists usually begin with a **functional analysis** of the problem behavior to determine the stimuli that trigger problem behavior and the reinforcers that maintain it. Functional analysis makes clients more aware of the environmental context of behavior and can boost motivation to change. With highly motivated people, functional analysis alone can increase the amount of time spent studying (Johnson & White, 1971) and talking in a therapy group (Komaki & Dore-Boyce, 1978) and decrease cigarette consumption (Lipinski et al., 1975).

It is true that you may be able to gain control over bad habits by simply keeping a record of where and when you practice them. The record may help motivate you, make you more aware of the problems, and suggest strategies for behavior change.

Self-monitoring Keeping a record of one's own behavior to identify problems and record successes.

Model To engage in behavior patterns that are imitated by others.

Behavior rehearsal Practice.

Feedback In assertiveness training, information about the effectiveness of a response.

Biofeedback training The systematic feeding back to an organism of information about a bodily function so that the organism can gain control of that function. Abbreviated *BFT.*

Functional analysis A systematic study of behavior in which one identifies the stimuli that trigger problem behavior and the reinforcers that maintain it.

TABLE 14.2: Excerpts from Brian's Diary of Nail Biting for April 14

Incident	Time	Location	Activity (Thoughts, Feelings)	Reactions
1	7:45 A.M.	Freeway	Driving to work, bored, not thinking	Finger bleeds, pain
2	10:30 A.M.	Office	Writing report	Self-disgust
3	2:25 P.M.	Conference	Listening to dull financial report	Embarrassment
4	6:40 P.M.	Living room	Watching evening news	Self-disgust

A functional analysis of problem behavior like nail biting increases awareness of the environmental context in which it occurs, spurs motivation to change, and, in highly motivated people, might lead to significant behavioral change.

Brian used functional analysis to master his nail biting. Table 14.2 shows a few items from his notebook. He discovered that boredom and humdrum activities seemed to serve as triggers for nail biting. He began to watch for feelings of boredom as signs to practice self-control. He also made some changes in his life so that he would feel bored less often.

A number of self-control strategies are shown in Table 14.3.

TABLE 14.3: Behavior-Therapy Self-Control Strategies

Target of Strategies	Strategy	Example
Strategies Aimed at Stimuli that Trigger Behavior	Restriction of the stimulus field	Gradually exclude the problem behavior from more environments. For example, at first make smoking off limits in the car, then in the office. Or practice the habit only outside the environment in which it normally occurs. Smoke, for example, only in a "stimulus-deprived" (boring) corner of the basement.
	Avoidance of powerful stimuli that trigger habits	Avoid obvious sources of temptation. People who go window-shopping often wind up buying more than windows. If eating at The Pizza Glutton tempts you to forget your diet, eat at home or at The Celery Stalk instead.
	Stimulus control	Place yourself in an environment in which desirable behavior is likely to occur. Maybe it's difficult to lift your mood directly at times, but you can place yourself in the audience of that uplifting concert or film. It might be difficult to force yourself to study, but how about rewarding yourself for spending time in the library?
Strategies Aimed at Behavior	Response prevention	Make unwanted behavior difficult or impossible. Impulse buying is curbed when you shred your credit cards, leave your checkbook home, and carry only a couple of dollars. You can't reach for the strawberry cream cheese pie in your refrigerator if you have left it at the supermarket (that is, have not bought it).
	Competing responses	Engage in behaviors that are incompatible with the bad habits. It is difficult to drink a glass of water and a fattening milkshake simultaneously. Grasping something firmly is a useful competing response for nail biting or scratching.
	Chain breaking	Interfere with unwanted habitual behavior by complicating the process of engaging in it. Put your cigarette in the ashtray between puffs, or put your fork down between mouthfuls of dessert. Each time, ask yourself if you really want more.
Strategies Aimed at Reinforcements	Reinforcement of desired behavior	Make pleasant activities such as going to films, walking on the beach, or reading a new novel contingent upon meeting reasonable, daily behavioral goals. Put a few dollars away toward that camera or vacation trip each day you remain within your calorie limit.
	Response cost	Heighten awareness of the long-term reasons for dieting or cutting down on smoking by punishing yourself for not meeting a daily goal or for practicing a bad habit. Make out a check to your most hated cause and mail it at once if you bite your nails or inhale that cheesecake.
	"Grandma's method"	Remember Grandma's method for inducing children to eat their vegetables? Simple: no veggies, no dessert. In this method, desired behaviors such as studying and brushing teeth can be increased by insisting that they be done before you carry out a favored or frequently occurring activity. For example, don't watch television unless you have studied first. Don't leave the apartment until you've brushed your teeth.
	Covert sensitization	Create imaginary horror stories about problem behavior. Psychologists have successfully reduced overeating and smoking by having clients imagine that they become acutely nauseated at the thought of fattening foods or that a cigarette is made from vomit. Some horror stories are not so "imaginary." Deliberately focusing on heart strain and diseased lungs every time you overeat or smoke, rather than ignoring these long-term consequences, might also promote self-control.
	Covert reinforcement	Create rewarding imagery for desired behavior. When you have achieved a behavioral goal, fantasize about how wonderful you are. Imagine friends and family patting you on the back. Fantasize about the *Playboy* or *Playgirl* centerfold for a minute.

It is true that some psychotherapists outline behavioral prescriptions for their clients (or "tell their clients precisely what to do"). Behavior therapists as well as Gestalt therapists and some cognitive therapists provide examples.

GROUP THERAPIES

When a psychotherapist has several clients with similar problems—whether anxiety, depression, adjustment to divorce, or lack of social skills—it often makes sense to treat these clients in groups of 6 to 12 rather than conduct individual therapy sessions. Group methods will reflect the needs of the members and the theoretical orientation of the leader. For example, in group psychoanalysis, clients might interpret one anothers' dreams. In a person-centered group, they might provide an accepting atmosphere for self-exploration. Behavior-therapy groups might undergo joint desensitization to anxiety-evoking stimuli or model and rehearse social skills.

There are several advantages to group therapy:

1. Group therapy allows the therapist to work with several clients simultaneously.
2. Group therapy allows members to draw on the life experiences of many.
3. Appropriate behavior receives group support—an outburst of approval from peers.
4. Group members learn that other people have had similar problems, similar self-doubts, similar failure experiences.
5. Group members who show improvement provide hope for other members.
6. Members of groups have the opportunity to rehearse social skills with one another in a relatively nonthreatening atmosphere.

It is *not* true that individual therapy is always preferable to group therapy for people who can afford it. Group therapy offers advantages, such as the shared experience and support of group members.

Group Therapy. Group therapy has a number of advantages over individual therapy for many clients. It's economical, provides a fund of information and experience for clients to draw upon, elicits group support and reassurance, and provides the opportunity to relate to other people. On the other hand, some clients do require individual attention.

WORLD OF DIVERSITY

Multicultural Issues in Therapy

Kenyata, an African-American woman in her early twenties, was brought to the emergency room of a general hospital by the police. She physically resisted the police and the emergency-room attendants. Moreover, her speech seemed muddled, difficult to decipher. The attending psychiatrist thus had Kenyata restrained and gave her large doses of a major tranquilizer. The police explained that Kenyata had tried to knife her boyfriend, Jimmy. They had brought her to the hospital rather than arrested her, because she had a history of "mental problems."

Kenyata had been admitted to a hospital across the river on previous occasions. The psychiatrist telephoned that hospital and was told that Kenyata's diagnosis was schizophrenia. Since Kenyata was uncooperative during an attempted interview, he admitted her involuntarily to the hospital psychiatric unit and entered the reported diagnosis in her chart. (African Americans are more likely than whites to be committed involuntarily to mental institutions [Lindsey & Paul, 1989].) An admission note explained her violence and resistance as "schizophrenic negativism."

Kenyata was not schizophrenic. Her speech had been unintelligible in the emergency room, but she had been drinking and had used many Black-English expressions. Kenyata had grown up in the ghetto and dropped out of school early. She was hostile, mistrustful, and largely noncommunicative with white mental-health professionals. Yet she was "treated" for schizophrenia—that is, hospitalized and drugged.

Kenyata's case underscores some of the kinds of problems that can be encountered by ethnic minorities—especially poor people—when they come into contact with the mental-health system. Majority clinicians need to avoid stereotypes and to be sensitive to the languages, behavior patterns, and values of minority group members in making diagnoses and doing therapy (Comas-Diaz & Griffith, 1988; Greene, 1985, 1992; Lee & Richardson, 1991).

Kenyata's encounter with mental-health workers was involuntary. Minority group members are less likely than white Americans to voluntarily seek therapy (Ho, 1985; Lee & Richardson, 1991; Yamamoto, 1986). They are also more likely to quit therapy after a visit or two (Tharp, 1991). There are many reasons for this low participation rate, such as:

- lack of recognition that therapy is indicated.
- ignorance of the availability of mental-health services.
- distrust of mental-health workers, particularly white workers and (in the case of many women) male workers (Greene, 1992).
- language barriers (Martinez, 1986).
- reluctance to open up about personal matters to strangers—especially strangers who are not members of one's ethnic group (LaFromboise, 1988).

DOES PSYCHOTHERAPY WORK?

Many of us know people who swear by their therapists, but the evidence is often shaky—for example, "I was a wreck before, but now . . . ," or "I feel so much better now." Anecdotes like these are encouraging, but we do not know what would have happened to them if they had not sought help. Many people feel better about their problems as time goes on, with or without therapy. Sometimes, happily, problems seem to go away by themselves. Sometimes, people find solutions on their own. Then, too, we hear some stories about how therapy was to no avail and about people hopping fruitlessly from therapist to therapist.

Research into the effectiveness of therapy has been reasonably encouraging (Lambert et al., 1986; Smith et al., 1980). In an averaging technique referred to as *meta-analysis,* Mary Lee Smith and Gene Glass analyzed the results of dozens of outcome studies on types of therapies and concluded that people who received psychodynamic therapy showed greater well being, on the average, than 70 to 75 percent of those who were left untreated (Smith & Glass, 1977). Similarly, nearly 75 percent of the clients receiving person-centered therapy were better off than people who were left untreated. There also seems to be a consensus that psychodynamic and person-centered therapies are most effective with well-educated, verbal, strongly motivated clients who report problems with anxiety, depression

- cultural inclinations toward other approaches to problem solving, such as spiritual approaches.
- negative experiences with mental-health workers.

It might seem that it would be wisest for ethnic minorities to work only with therapists who share their ethnic backgrounds, and, perhaps, for women to work with female therapists. There are two problems with this approach, however. First, there are not enough minority therapists to go around (e.g., LaFromboise, 1988). Second, such limitations would unfairly stereotype white therapists as insensitive, particularly white male therapists. They would similarly unfairly characterize African-American therapists as sensitive. Neither stereotype is necessarily true. You cannot make assumptions about the racial sensitivity or comfort of the therapist simply on the basis of race (Greene, 1991).

A number of measures are suggested to enable majority therapists to treat minorities more effectively. Majority therapists—and their clients—can profit when therapists:

- become aware of and confront their own stereotypic beliefs about other cultural or ethnic groups, rather than deny their existence (Greene, 1985, 1992).
- become more aware of their own cultural and ethnic-based values and traditions (Greene, 1991).
- acquire training in cross-cultural therapy and information about the cultures from which their clients derive (Greene, 1991).
- not pretend to be colorblind, but are sensitive to the possible connections between clients' problems and their ethnicity (Greene, 1985; Tharp, 1991).
- interpret clients' problems in the light of their cultural backgrounds, values, *and* individual differences (Greene, 1992; Tharp, 1991).
- consider the possible impact of therapeutic goals and techniques on clients' values. (Clients are often caught between two cultures—the culture in the home or the neighborhood and the dominant culture.)
- call upon the skills of translators, as needed, to be certain that they understand the subtleties of clients' problems (Lee & Richardson, 1991).
- adopt approaches that are appropriate to the cultural group (Jenkins [1985] suggests that African Americans be approached in an egalitarian manner that reduces differences in status. Juarez [1985] suggests that Hispanic clients be approached in a firm, instructive manner. Isomura, Fine, and Lin [1987] suggest that the therapist take an authoritative, concrete, formal role with Japanese clients).
- cultivate relationships with minority members (not necessarily mental-health workers) who can be called upon for advice.
- recognize their limitations and, when necessary, refer the client elsewhere.

(of light to moderate proportions), and interpersonal relationships (Abramowitz et al., 1974; Wexler & Butler, 1976). Neither form of therapy appears to be successful with psychotic disorders such as major depression, bipolar disorder, and schizophrenia.

Smith and Glass (1977) found that people who received Gestalt therapy showed greater well-being than about 60 percent of those left untreated. The effectiveness of psychoanalysis and person-centered therapy was thus reasonably comparable. Gestalt therapy fell behind.

Other studies show that cognitive therapy of irrational beliefs decreases emotional distress (Lipsky et al., 1980; Smith, 1983) and helps people manage health problems such as headaches (Blanchard et al., 1990a, 1990b). Modifying self-defeating beliefs of the sort outlined by Beck frequently alleviates anxiety and depression (Beck, 1991; Whisman et al., 1991). Cognitive therapy apparently fosters greater improvements among anxious and depressed clients than psychodynamic and humanistic–existential approaches (Andrews & Harvey, 1981; Shapiro & Shapiro, 1982). Cognitive therapy may also be helpful in cases of severe depression that are usually considered responsive only to biological therapies (Hollon et al., 1991; Simons et al., 1986). Cognitive therapy has helped people with personality disorders (Beck & Freeman, 1990). It has helped schizophrenic outpatients (also using chemotherapy) modify delusional beliefs (Chadwick & Lowe, 1990).

Behavior therapy has provided strategies for treating anxiety, depression, social-skills deficits, and problems in self-control. These strategies have proved effective for most clients in terms of quantifiable behavioral change (Lazarus, 1990). Behavior therapists have also been innovative with a number of problems such as phobias and sexual dysfunctions for which there had not previously been effective treatments. Overall, Smith and Glass (1977) found behavior-therapy techniques to be somewhat more effective than psychodynamic or humanistic–existential methods. About 80 percent of those people receiving behavior-therapy treatments such as systematic desensitization and strategies for self-control showed greater well-being than people who were left untreated (as compared to percentages in the low to middle 70s for psychodynamic and humanistic–existential approaches).

Many studies that directly compare treatment techniques find behavior-therapy, psychodynamic, and humanistic–existential approaches to be about equal in overall effectiveness (Berman et al., 1985; Smith et al., 1980). Psychodynamic and humanistic–existential approaches seem to foster greater self-understanding, however, whereas behavior-therapy techniques (including cognitive-behavioral techniques) show superior results in treatment of specific problems such as phobias and sexual dysfunctions. Behavior therapy has also been effective in helping manage institutionalized populations, including schizophrenics and the mentally retarded. However, there is little evidence that behavior therapy alone is effective in treating the thought disorders involved in severe psychotic disturbance (Wolpe, 1985, 1990).

It is thus not enough to ask which type of therapy is most effective. We must ask, instead, which type of therapy is most effective for a particular problem (Beutler, 1991; Shoham-Salomon, 1991; Snow, 1991). What are its advantages? What are its limitations? Clients may successfully use systematic desensitization to overcome stage fright, as measured by actual ability to get up and talk before a group of people. If clients also want to know *why* they have stage fright, however, behavior therapy alone will not provide the answer.

BIOLOGICAL THERAPIES

In the 1950s, Fats Domino popularized the song "My Blue Heaven." Fats was singing about the sky and happiness. Today, "blue heavens" is one of the street names for the ten-milligram dose of one of the most widely prescribed drugs: Valium. The **minor tranquilizer** Valium became popular because it reduces feelings of anxiety and tension. The manufacturer also once claimed that people could not become addicted to Valium nor could they readily kill themselves with overdoses. Today, Valium appears to be more dangerous. Some people who have been used to taking high doses of Valium are reported to go into convulsions when use is suspended. And, now and then, someone dies from mixing Valium with alcohol, or someone shows unusual sensitivity to the drug.

Psychiatrists and other physicians prescribe Valium and other drugs as chemical therapy, or **chemotherapy,** for various forms of abnormal behavior. In this section, we discuss chemotherapy, *electroconvulsive therapy,* and *psychosurgery,* three biological or medical approaches to treating abnormal behavior.

Chemotherapy

Methods of chemotherapy include minor tranquilizers, major tranquilizers, antidepressants, and lithium.

Minor Tranquilizers. Valium (diazepam) is but one of many (many) minor tranquilizers. Some of the others are Librium, Miltown, Atarax, Serax, and Equanil. These drugs are usually prescribed for outpatients who complain of

Minor tranquilizer A drug that relieves feelings of anxiety and tension.

Chemotherapy The use of drugs to treat disordered behavior.

anxiety or tension, although many people also use them as sleeping pills. Valium and other tranquilizers are theorized to depress the activity of parts of the central nervous system (CNS). The CNS, in turn, decreases sympathetic activity reducing the heart rate, respiration rate, and feelings of nervousness and tension.

With regular usage, unfortunately, people come to tolerate small dosages of these drugs very quickly (Gillin, 1991). Dosages must be increased for the drug to remain effective. Some patients become embroiled in tugs-of-war with their physicians when the physicians become concerned about how much they are taking. Physicians typically want patients to cut down "for their own good." Patients typically resent physicians for getting them started with the drug and then playing moralist.

Another problem associated with many minor tranquilizers is **rebound anxiety.** Many patients who have been using these drugs regularly report that their anxiety returns in exacerbated form once they discontinue them. Some users might simply be experiencing fear of doing without the drugs. For others, rebound anxiety might reflect biochemical processes that are poorly understood (Chouinard et al., 1983).

Valium, interestingly, is usually ineffective with panic disorder, suggesting that panic has quite different bodily correlates than other anxiety disorders. Antidepressant medications, discussed later, do often help panic sufferers, giving rise to speculation that panic might involve faulty metabolism of noradrenaline.

Major Tranquilizers. Schizophrenic patients are likely to be treated with **major tranquilizers,** or "antipsychotic" drugs. Many of them, including Thorazine, Mellaril, Stelazine, and Clozaril are thought to act by blocking the action of dopamine in the brain.

In most cases, major tranquilizers reduce agitation, delusions, and hallucinations (Baldessarini, 1985; Gilman et al., 1990). Major tranquilizers account in large part for the lessened need for various forms of restraint and supervision (padded cells, straitjackets, hospitalization, and so on) used with schizophrenic patients. More than any other single form of treatment, major tranquilizers have allowed hundreds of thousands of patients to lead largely normal lives in the community, to hold jobs, and to maintain family lives.

Antidepressants. So-called **antidepressant** drugs are often given to patients with major depression, but they are also sometimes helpful with people who suffer from eating disorders (Craighead & Agras, 1991). Problems in the regulation of noradrenaline and serotonin may be involved in eating disorders as well as depression. Antidepressants are believed to work by increasing the amount of these neurotransmitters available in the brain, which can have an effect on both kinds of disorders.

There are various kinds of antidepressant drugs. Each type increases the brain concentrations of noradrenaline or serotonin (Potter et al., 1991). **Monoamine oxidase (MAO) inhibitors** block the activity of an enzyme that breaks down noradrenaline and serotonin. Nardil and Parnate are examples of MAO inhibitors. **Tricyclic antidepressants** such as Tofranil and Elavil prevent reuptake of noradrenaline and serotonin by the axon terminals of the transmitting neurons. Others such as fluoxetine hydrochloride (Prozac) block reuptake of serotonin. As a result, the neurotransmitters remain in the synaptic cleft for a greater amount of time, enhancing the probability that they will dock at receptor sites on receiving neurons.

Antidepressants tend to alleviate the physical aspects of depression. For example, they tend to increase the patient's activity level and to reduce eating and sleeping disturbances (Lyons et al., 1985; Weissman et al., 1981). In this way, patients may become more receptive to psychotherapy, which addresses the cognitive and social aspects of depression. A combination of chemotherapy and

---

Rebound anxiety Strong anxiety that can attend the suspension of usage of a tranquilizer.

Major tranquilizer A drug that decreases severe anxiety or agitation in psychotic patients or in violent individuals.

Antidepressant Acting to relieve depression.

Monoamine oxidase inhibitors Antidepressant drugs that work by blocking the action of an enzyme that breaks down noradrenaline and serotonin. Abbreviated *MAO inhibitors.*

Tricyclic antidepressants Antidepressant drugs that work by preventing the reuptake of noradrenaline and serotonin by transmitting neurons.

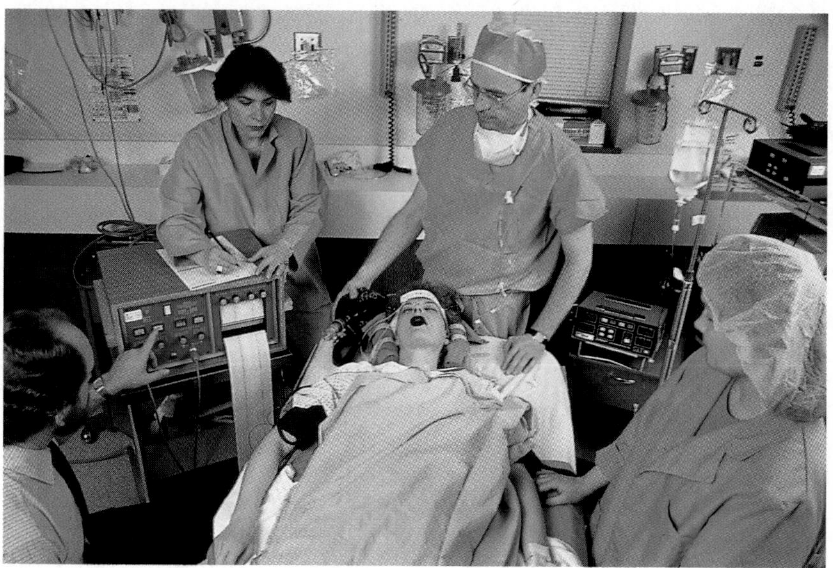

Electroconvulsive Therapy. In ECT, electrodes are placed on each side of the patient's head and a current is passed in between. A seizure is induced in this way. ECT is used mainly in cases of major depression when antidepressant drugs fail. ECT is quite controversial: Many believe that it is barbaric, and there are side effects.

psychotherapy may be more effective in treating depression than chemotherapy alone (Beckham & Leber, 1985; Conte et al., 1986).

Severely depressed people often have insomnia, and it is not unusual for antidepressant drugs, which have a strong **sedative** effect, to be given at bedtime. Typically, antidepressant drugs must "build up" to a therapeutic level, which may take several weeks. Because overdoses of antidepressants can be lethal, some patients are hospitalized during the build-up period to prevent suicide attempts.

Lithium. In a sense, the ancient Greeks and Romans were among the first to use the metal lithium as a psychoactive drug. They would prescribe mineral water for patients with bipolar disorder. They had no inkling as to why this treatment sometimes helped, but it might have been because mineral water contains lithium. A salt of the metal lithium (lithium carbonate), in tablet form, flattens out cycles of manic behavior and depression for most sufferers, apparently by moderating the level of noradrenaline available to the brain. Lithium has also shown some promise as a treatment for eating disorders (Mitchell & Eckert, 1987).

Because lithium is more toxic than most drugs, the dose must be carefully monitored during early phases of therapy by repeated analysis of blood samples. It might be necessary for persons with bipolar disorder to use lithium indefinitely, just as a medical patient with diabetes must continue insulin to control the illness. Lithium also has been shown to have the side effects of impairing memory and depressing motor speed (Shaw et al., 1987). Memory impairment is reported as the primary reason that patients discontinue lithium (Jamison & Akiskal, 1983).

Electroconvulsive Therapy

Electroconvulsive therapy (ECT) was introduced by Italian psychiatrist Ugo Cerletti in 1939 for use with psychiatric patients. Cerletti had noted that some slaughterhouses used electric shock to render animals unconscious. The shocks also produced convulsions, and Cerletti erroneously believed, as did other European researchers of the period, that convulsions were incompatible with schizophrenia and other major disorders.

ECT was originally used for a variety of psychological disorders. Because of the advent of major tranquilizers, however, the American Psychiatric Association (1990) now recommends ECT mainly for treatment of major depression among patients who are not responsive to antidepressants. ECT is still sometimes used to treat intense manicky episodes, schizophrenia, and other disorders, however (Sakheim, 1990).

Sedative Relieving nervousness or agitation.

Electroconvulsive therapy Treatment of disorders like major depression by passing an electric current (that causes a convulsion) through the head. Abbreviated *ECT.*

ECT patients typically receive one treatment three times a week for up to ten sessions. Electrodes are attached to the temples, or on one side of the head only (in "unilateral ECT"), and an electrical current strong enough to produce a convulsion is induced. The shock causes unconsciousness, so patients would not recall it. Still, patients are put to sleep with a sedative prior to treatment. In the past, ECT patients flailed about wildly during the convulsions, sometimes breaking bones. Today, they are given muscle-relaxing drugs, and convulsions are barely perceptible to onlookers. ECT is not given to patients with high blood pressure or heart ailments.

ECT is controversial for many reasons. First, many professionals are distressed by the thought of passing electric shock through the head and producing convulsions, even if they are suppressed by drugs. Second are the side effects. ECT disrupts recall of recent events. Although memory functioning usually seems near normal for most patients a few months after treatment, some patients appear to suffer permanent memory impairment (Coleman, 1990). Third, nobody knows *why* ECT works. For reasons such as these, ECT was outlawed in Berkeley, California, by voter referendum in 1982. This decision was later overturned in the courts, but it remains of interest because it marked the first time that a specific treatment found its way to the ballot box.

Psychosurgery

Psychosurgery is more controversial than ECT. The best-known modern technique, the **prefrontal lobotomy,** has been used with severely disturbed patients. In this method, a picklike instrument is used to crudely sever the nerve pathways that link the prefrontal lobes of the brain to the thalamus. The prefrontal lobotomy was pioneered by the Portuguese neurologist Antonio Egas Moniz and was brought to the United States in the 1930s. As pointed out by Valenstein (1986), the theoretical rationale for the operation was vague and misguided, and Moniz's reports of success were exaggerated. Nevertheless, the prefrontal lobotomy was performed on more than a thousand mental patients by 1950 in an effort to reduce violence and agitation. Anecdotal evidence of the method's unreliable outcomes is found in an ironic footnote to history: One of Dr. Moniz's failures shot him, leaving a bullet lodged in his spine and paralyzing his legs.

It is true that the originator of a surgical technique intended to reduce violence—the prefrontal lobotomy—was indeed shot by one of his patients.

The prefrontal lobotomy also has a host of side effects including hyperactivity and distractibility, impaired learning ability, overeating, apathy and withdrawal, epileptic-type seizures, reduced creativity, and, now and then, death. Because of these side effects, and because of the advent of major tranquilizers, the prefrontal lobotomy has been largely discontinued in the United States.

In recent years, a number of more refined psychosurgery techniques have been devised for various purposes. Generally speaking, they focus on smaller areas of the brain and leave less damage in their wake than does the prefrontal lobotomy. These operations have been performed to treat problems ranging from aggression to depression, psychotic behavior, chronic pain, and epilepsy (Valenstein, 1980). Follow-up studies of these contemporary procedures find that slightly more than half of them result in marked improvement (Corkin, 1980; Mirsky & Orzack, 1980). Moreover, no major neurological damage was attributable to these operations.

Psychosurgery Surgery intended to promote psychological changes or to relieve disordered behavior.

Prefrontal lobotomy The severing or destruction of a section of the frontal lobe of the brain.

Does Biological Therapy Work?

There is little question that major tranquilizers, antidepressants, and lithium help many people with severe psychiatric disorders. These drugs enable many patients to remain in, or return to, the community and lead productive lives. Most problems related to these drugs concern their side effects.

Minor tranquilizers are frequently abused by overuse. Many people request them to dull the arousal that stems from anxiety-producing lifestyles or interpersonal problems. Rather than make the often painful decisions required to confront their problems and change their lives, they find it easier to pop a pill. For a while. Then the dosage must be increased if the drug is to remain effective, and substance dependence becomes a possibility. Unfortunately, some family physicians, even some psychiatrists, find it easier to prescribe minor tranquilizers than to help patients examine their lives and change anxiety-evoking conditions. The physician's lot is not eased by the fact that many patients want pills, not conversation.

It is *not* true that drugs are never of help to people with abnormal behavior problems. They are of help to many people with schizophrenia and severe mood disorders. Psychologists nevertheless discourage use of drugs to cope with the anxieties, tensions, and problems of daily life.

In spite of the controversies that surround ECT, there is evidence that it brings many immobilized patients out of their depression when antidepressant drugs fail (Janicak et al., 1985; NIMH, 1985; Scovern & Kilmann, 1980). Moreover, ECT patients have a lower mortality rate following treatment than depressed people who do not receive ECT (Martin et al., 1985). This finding is in part attributable to a lower suicide rate. There are also suggestions that memory impairment is minimized by giving patients the lowest dose of electricity required to produce seizures (Daniel & Crovitz, 1983a; Sakheim et al., 1985).

In sum, chemotherapy and perhaps ECT seem to be desirable for some disorders that do not respond to psychotherapy alone. Yet common sense and research evidence suggest that psychotherapy is preferable for problems such as anxiety, mild depression, and interpersonal conflict. No chemical can show a client how to change an idea or solve an interpersonal problem. Chemicals can only dull the pain of failure and postpone the day when clients must seize control of their lives.

STUDY GUIDE

EXERCISE: Matching Therapy Methods and Kinds of Therapy

In the first column are a number of therapy methods. In the second column are the types of therapy discussed in the text. Match the method to the type of therapy by placing the letter of the type of therapy in the blank space to the left of the method. Answers are given below.

THERAPY METHODS

_____ 1. Dialogue
_____ 2. Showing genuineness
_____ 3. Lithium carbonate
_____ 4. Free association
_____ 5. Restriction of the stimulus field
_____ 6. Dream analysis
_____ 7. Prefrontal lobotomy
_____ 8. Empathic understanding
_____ 9. Phenothiazines
_____ 10. Interpretation
_____ 11. Aversive conditioning
_____ 12. Token economy
_____ 13. Challenging irrational beliefs
_____ 14. Showing congruence
_____ 15. Systematic desensitization
_____ 16. Resolving the transference relationship
_____ 17. Biofeedback training

KINDS OF THERAPY

A. Psychoanalysis
B. Person-centered therapy
C. Gestalt therapy
D. Cognitive therapy
E. Behavior therapy
F. Chemotherapy
G. Psychosurgery

Answers to Matching Exercise

1. C
2. B
3. F
4. A
5. E
6. A, C
7. G
8. B
9. F
10. A, C
11. E
12. E
13. D
14. B
15. E
16. A
17. E

EXERCISE: Matching Names and Kinds of Therapy

In the column to the left are the names of people who have made a contribution to the development of therapy methods. In the column to the right are the therapy methods. Match the person to the therapy method by writing the letter that signifies the method in the blank space to the left of the name.

PERSON	THERAPY METHOD
____ 1. Aaron Beck	A. Psychoanalysis
____ 2. Carl Rogers	B. Behavior therapy
____ 3. Fritz Perls	C. Cognitive therapy
____ 4. Albert Ellis	D. Family therapy
____ 5 Joseph Wolpe	E. Gestalt therapy
____ 6. Erik Erikson	F. Person-centered therapy
____ 7. Ugo Cerletti	G. Electroconvulsive therapy
____ 8. Arnold Lazarus	H. Psychosurgery
____ 9. Antonio Egas Moniz	
____ 10. Sigmund Freud	

Answers to Matching Exercise

1. C
2. F
3. E
4. C
5. B
6. A
7. G
8. B
9. H
10. A

ESL—BRIDGING THE GAP

This part is divided into

1. cultural references
2. phrases and expresssions in which words are used differently from their regular meaning, or are used as metaphors

Cultural References

Voice (536)—*The Village Voice* is a New York City newspaper. It has a large section of personal and business advertisements.

Quakers (538)—a religious group which originated in England in 1620. The actual name is *Society of Friends.* Friends are known for their active concern for humanitarian issues.

Fats Domino (560)—a popular singer and piano player

voter referendum (563)—a vote of "yes" or "no" on a proposed law by the registered voters in the election district

found its way to the ballot box (563)—became an issue that the public would vote on in local elections

Phrases and Expressions (Different Usage)

out on the town (534)—going places for entertainment

to take the lead (534)—to direct the discussion and emphasis themselves

uplifting experience (536)—exciting and happy experience

is no (536)—is not a

passing blurs on the street (536)—people with no feelings or personalities

break down his defensive barriers (536)—destroy his defensive barriers

somewhat flamboyant ad (536)—an advertisement that was excessive in its explanation of services

a gray automaton in a mechanized society (536)—a robot in an impersonal society

to go about it (536)—to do it; to find help

not work out (536)—not be successful

For one thing (536)—There were many problems, and this is one of them

pops into (536)—enters
face to face (536)—the front of one person directly in front of the front of the other person
places major burden . . . on . . . shoulders (536)—expects Brad to direct his own therapy
Role-playing (536)—Imagining a social situation and acting it; acting
squarely in the eye (536)—directly
a matter of chance (536)—not carefully planned
brings . . . to bear on influencing (537)—using . . . in order to influence
quite a mouthful (537)—This is an overwhelming statement, isn't it?
not based on, say, (537)—not based on, for example
aimed at (537)—relevant to
As such, (537)—As this,
not meet demands . . . life (537)—not function in terms of supporting themselves and, therefore, not having money for food and shelter
human warehousing (537)—to provide only a place to stay; to provide "storage space" (no care)
mushroomed in population (537)—increased in number
go for a stroll on a lazy afternoon (538)—walk slowly and leisurely on an afternoon in which they did not have to work
to take in the sights (538)—to look at the "entertainment"
running amok (538)—becoming confused, disorganized and more insane or troubled in their actions and in their thinking
seemed foreign and frightening (539)—appeared too unfamiliar (negative) and scary (they were afraid)
follow-up care (539)—care which followed their release on a continuous and consistent basis
a "revolving door" (539)—a situation in which they left the hospital feeling all right, became disturbed again and therefore returned to the hospital, and this cycle continued
outlook (539)—prospect
looks brighter (539)—appears optimistic
to bulwark the ego against (539)—to protect the ego from
torrents of energy (539–540)—large amounts of energy
loosed by the id (540)—released by the id
no matter how trivial . . . personal (540)—it did not matter how trivial . . . or personal
par for the course (540)—what was expected
plucking (540)—taking; pulling
weighs upon the heart (540)—causes depression
to have been dammed up (541)—to have been restrained
the inner workings of (541)—the operation of
to spill forth (541)—to release
blocked insight (541)—stopped; insight that cannot occur
may eventually surface (541)—may eventually be revealed
"My mind is blank" (541)—There are no thoughts in my mind.
compulsion to utter (541)—compulsion to say something that reveals a hidden feeling
tips the balance in favor of (541)—changes the balance so that the person speaks about it
deep-seated feelings (541)—feelings that are very deep and entrenched
the "royal road . . . " (541)—the best way
a father figure (542)—a substitute for a father
a two-way street (542)—the feelings are from the client to the therapist and they are also from the therapist to the client
sex object (542)—an impersonalized person to enjoy sexually
not give new . . . "a chance" (542)—not allow time and experience to know the new person and refuse to continue to develop the relationship
plead not guilty of encouraging (542)—say that he or she did not encourage
grist for the therapeutic mill (542)—information for the therapist to use in treatment
a lengthy process (543)—a long process
frankly (543)—candidly; I shall be direct and say this, even though it may be negative
ratio of cost to benefits (543)—the relationship of the cost to the results received
fashioned desired traits (544)—create the traits that they want
Given this view (544)—Accepting this opinion
roadblocks placed in the path of (545)—hindrances that are preventing
don masks and façades (544)—act falsely
seen but not heard (545)—be quiet and unobtrusive and not express or feelings (an expression referring to children—that they are not to make noise and only speak when an adult speaks to them)
might be unleashed (545)—might be released
by setting aside (545)—by not considering
"top dog" (546)—a boss
"underdog" (546)—a person who has nothing
Don't take chances . . . (546)—Don't experiment
Stick with what you have (546)—Remain the way you are
get out of this rut (546)—remove yourself from the boring routine
spent in worrying (546)—used in worrying
shape our responses to them (547)—are responsible for what we do about them
be fleeting (548)—quick in appearing and quick in disappearing
hard to catch (548)—hard to notice
the worst will happen (548)—the worst event will happen
pin down (549)—notice and pay attention
were laid off at work (549)—lost their jobs; were told they could not work there anymore
blow out of proportion (549)—exaggerate
get going in the morning (549)—start to function in the morning
run all right (549)—be all right
in the long run (549)—most of the time
scaled down (549)—reduced

build . . . relationships (550)—develop relationships
armchair adventurer (551)—one who satisfies the need for adventure vicariously, e.g., sitting and reading or watching TV
twinges of discomfort (551)—feelings of discomfort; uncomfortable
would-be quitters (553)—the people who are trying to stop
an everyday hair dryer (553)—an ordinary hair dryer (a common appliance that most people have)
at six-month follow-ups (554)—every six months (an analysis in September, for example, and another analysis in March
swear by (558)—were very happy about
as time goes on (558)—as time passes
on their own (558)—without help
but one of many (many) (560)—there are very many and Valium is only but one of them
come to tolerate (561)—become able to tolerate
padded cells, straitjackets (561)—rooms with pads on the walls for protection against injury to the person in the room; jackets that tie a person's arms so they cannot be used to hurt themselves or someone else
a host of (563)—a great number of
in their wake (563)—afterward
to pop a pill (564)—to take a pill
The physician's lot is not eased (564)—The physician's work is not made easier

CHAPTER REVIEW

SECTION 1: What Is Therapy?

Objective 1: Define *psychotherapy.*

The text defines psychotherapy as a systematic interaction between a therapist and a client that brings (1) ______ical principles to bear on influencing the client's thoughts, feelings, or behavior. Psychotherapy helps the client overcome (2) ab______ behavior or adjust to problems in living.

Objective 2: Trace the history of the treatment of abnormal behavior from ancient to contemporary times.

Ancient and medieval treatments of abnormal behavior often reflected the (3) ______gical model. They involved cruel practices such as the (4) ex______ of the Middle Ages. The first institutions intended primarily for the mentally ill were called (5) ______ms. Asylums often had their origins in European (6) ______aries. St. Mary's of (7) Be______ is the name of a well-known London asylum.

Humanitarian reform movements began in the (8) ______eenth century. Philippe (9) P______ unchained the patients at the asylum called La Bicêtre. The reform movement in the United States was led by schoolteacher Dorothea (10) ______. Mental (11) ______tals replaced asylums in the United States. Today as many patients as possible are maintained in the community. The community movement was in part stimulated by the Community (12) M______-______ Centers Act of 1963.

SECTION 2: Psychodynamic Therapies

Objective 3: Describe the goals and methods of Freud's traditional psychoanalysis.

Psychodynamic therapies are based on the thinking of Sigmund (13) ______. They are based on the view that our problems largely reflect early childhood experiences and internal (14) con______s. Freud's method of psychoanalysis attempts to shed light on (15) ______cious conflicts that are presumed to lie at the roots of clients' problems. Freud also sought to replace impulsive and defensive behavior with (16) ______ng behavior. Freud also believed that psychoanalysis would allow clients to engage in (17) ______sis or abreaction—that is, to spill forth the (18) ______ic energy theorized to have been repressed by conflicts and guilt.

The chief psychoanalytic method is (19) ______ association. The cardinal rule of free association is that no thought is to be (20) ______ed. In this way, material that has been (21) ______sed should eventually come to the surface of awareness. But the ego's continuing tendency to repress threatening material leads to the countervailing force of (22) ______nce.

Freud considered (23) ______s to be the "royal road to the unconscious." In dreams, unconscious impulses were expressed as a form of wish (24) ____________ment. Objects in dreams were thought to be (25) ____________s of unconscious wishes. The perceived content of a dream is termed its (26) ____________t content. The presumed symbolic content of a dream is termed its hidden or (27) ____________t content.

Freud also found that people generalized feelings toward other men onto him, and Freud termed this generalization of feelings (28) ____________ence. Freud termed the analyst's transference of feelings onto clients (29) ____________ference.

Objective 4: Compare and contrast traditional psychoanalysis with modern psychodynamic approaches.

Contemporary psychodynamic approaches tend to be (30: longer or briefer?) and (31: more or less?) intense than Freud's. However, many of them still focus on revealing (32) un____________ conflicts and on breaking down psychological resistance. Modern psychodynamic therapists focus more on the (33) e____________ as the "executive" of personality. For this reason, many modern psychodynamic therapists are considered ego (34) ____________sts.

SECTION 3: Humanistic–Existential Therapies

Objective 5: Explain what the humanistic–existential therapies have in common.

Humanistic–existential therapies focus on the quality of clients' (35) ____________tive, conscious experience. (36) Psy____________ therapies tend to focus on the past, and particularly on early childhood experiences. (37) Humanistic–____________ therapies, however, focus on what clients are experiencing today—on "the here and now."

Objective 6: Describe the goals and treatment methods of Rogers' person-centered therapy.

Person-centered therapy was originated by (38) ____________s. Person-centered therapy is a (39: directive or nondirective?) method that provides clients with a warm, accepting atmosphere that enables them to explore and overcome roadblocks to self-actualization. The characteristics shown by the person-centered therapist include (40: conditional or unconditional?) positive regard, (41) em____________ understanding, (42) gen____________, and (43) ____________ence.

The goals of person-centered therapy include (44) self-es____________, self-acceptance, and (45) self-ac____________ation.

Objective 7: Describe the goals and methods of Perls' Gestalt therapy.

Gestalt therapy was originated by (46) ____________s. Gestalt therapy provides (47: directive or nondirective?) methods that are designed to help clients integrate conflicting parts of the (48) ____________ity. In the Gestalt technique of the (49) d____________, people undertake a verbal confrontation between conflicting parts of the personality. Clients are instructed to pay attention to their body (50) l____________, such as their facial expressions, in order to gain insight into their true feelings. Perls saw the content of dreams as (51) ____________ned parts of the personality.

SECTION 4: Cognitive Therapies

Objective 8: Explain what the cognitive therapies have in common.

Cognitive therapists focus on the (52) be____________s, attitudes, and (53) ____________tic types of thinking that create and compound their clients' problems.

Objective 9: Describe the goals and methods of Ellis' rational-emotive therapy.

(54) Rational-____________ therapy is one type of cognitive therapy. It was originated by (55) ____________. Rational-emotive therapy confronts clients with the ways in which (56) ____________nal beliefs contribute to problems such as anxiety, depression, and feelings of hopelessness. Ellis' methods are (57: nondirective or directive?).

Objective 10: Describe the goals and methods of Beck's cognitive therapy.

Psychiatrist Aaron Beck has focused on ways in which cognitive errors of (58) dis____________s heighten feelings of (59) de____________. Beck notes the pervasive influence of four basic types of cognitive errors that contribute to clients' miseries: selective (60) ____________tion of the world as a harmful place; (61) over____________zation on the basis of a few examples; (62) mag____________tion of the significance of negative events; and (63)__________tist thinking, or looking at the world in black and white rather than in shades of gray. Beck also encourages clients to see how their (64: exaggerating or minimizing?) of accomplishments and their (65: optimism or pessimism?) are self-defeating.

Many theorists consider cognitive therapy to be a collection of techniques that belong within the province of (66) be__________ therapy. Some members of this group prefer the name (67) "cog__________ __________ior therapy." However, there is a difference in focus between many cognitive therapists and behavior therapists. To behavior therapists, the purpose of dealing with client cognitions is to change overt (68) be__________. Cognitive therapists assert that (69) __________tive change is in and of itself an important goal.

SECTION 5: Behavior Therapy

Objective 11: Describe the goals of behavior therapy.

Behavior therapy is also referred to as behavior (70) __________tion. Behavior therapy is defined as the systematic application of principles of (71) __________ing to bring about desired behavioral changes. Behavior therapists insist that their methods be established by (72) __________tation and that therapeutic outcomes be assessed in terms of (73) ob__________ble, mesuable behavior. Behavior therapists attempt to help clients discontinue self-defeating, (74) mal__________ive behavior patterns and to acquire (75)__________ive behavior patterns.

Objective 12: Describe behavior-therapy methods of reducing fears.

The text describes two behavior-therapy methods for reducing fears: systematic (76) de__________tion, in which a client is gradually exposed to more fear-arousing stimuli; and (77) p__________ modeling, in which a client observes and then imitates a model who handles fear-arousing stimuli. Systematic desensitization was developed by (78) __________, who assumed that maladaptive anxiety responses are learned or conditioned. Wolpe reasoned that these anxiety responses could be unlearned by means of (79) __________conditioning or extinction. In counterconditioning, a response that is (80: compatible or incompatible?) with anxiety is made to occur under conditions that usually elicit anxiety. Muscle (81) __________ation is incompatible with anxiety. In systematic desensitization, clients confront a (82) h__________y of anxiety-evoking stimuli while they remain relaxed.

Objective 13: Describe the behavior-therapy method of aversive conditioning.

In the behavior-therapy method of aversive conditioning, undesired responses are decreased in frequency by being associated with (83) __________ive stimuli. An example of aversive conditioning is (84) r__________ smoking, in which cigarette smoke is made aversive by means of puffing every six seconds.

Objective 14: Describe some behavior-therapy methods of operant conditioning.

In behavior-therapy operant-conditioning methods, desired responses are (85) __________ced and undesired responses are (86) __________shed. Two examples are the use of the (87) t__________ economy and of successive approximations.

In social-skills training, behavior therapists decrease social anxiety and build social skills through operant-conditioning procedures that employ (88) __________-monitoring, coaching, modeling, (89) __________ playing, (90) __________ rehearsal, and (91) __________back.

Through (92) __________back training (BFT), therapists help clients become more aware of, and gain control over, various bodily functions. "Bleeps" or other electronic signals are used to (93) r__________ bodily changes in the desired direction. The (94) __________ograph (EMG) monitors muscle tension. The (95)__________ograph (EEG) monitors brain waves and can be used to teach people how to produce (96) __________a waves, which are associated with relaxation.

Objective 15: Describe behavior-therapy self-control methods.

In behavior-therapy self-control methods, clients first engage in a (97) __________nal analysis of their problem behavior. A functional analysis helps them learn what stimuli trigger and (98) __________ain the behavior. Then clients are taught how to manipulate the antecedents and (99) __________nces of their behavior, and the behavior itself, to increase the frequency of desired responses and decrease the frequency of undesired responses.

SECTION 6: Group Therapy

Objective 16: Explain the advantages of group therapy.

The methods and characteristics of group therapy reflect the clients' needs and the (100) ____________ical orientation of the group leader. There are a number of advantages to group therapy. Group therapy can be more (101) ____________ical than individual therapy, allowing several clients to be seen at once. Clients may draw upon the (102) exp____________ of other group members as well as the knowledge of the therapist. Too, clients can receive (103) em____________al support from other group members.

SECTION 7: Does Psychotherapy Work?

Objective 17: Evaluate methods of psychotherapy and behavior therapy.

Smith and Glass found that people who receive psychoanalysis show greater well-being than (104) ____________ percent of those who are left untreated. Psychoanalysis is most effective with clients who are (105: well- or poorly?) educated, highly verbal, and (106: highly or poorly?) motivated. About (107) ____________ percent of clients receiving person-centered therapy were better off than people left untreated.

SECTION 8: Biological Therapies

Objective 18: Describe various methods of chemotherapy, and when they are used.

The use of drugs in the treatment of abnormal behavior is termed (108) ____________rapy. (109: Minor or major?) tranquilizers are usually prescribed for outpatients who complain of anxiety or tension. (110) V____________ and other minor tranquilizers are theorized to depress the activity of the (111) ____________ nervous system, which, in turn, decreases sympathetic activity.

Major tranquilizers are sometimes referred to as (112) anti____________ drugs. In most cases, major tranquilizers reduce agitation, (113) del____________s, and hallucinations. Major tranquilizers that belong to the chemical class of (114) ____________iazines are thought to work by blocking the action of the neurotransmitter (115) ____________ine in the brain. (116: Minor or major?) tranquilizers have permitted thousands of schizophrenics to lead productive lives in the community.

(117) Anti____________ drugs have relieved many instances of major depression. Antidepressants are believed to work by increasing the amounts of the neurotransmitters (118) nor____________ine and (119) ____________nin available in the brain. Antidepressants have also been found useful in many instances of the anxiety disorder called (120) p____________ disorder and in some cases of (121) e____________ing disorders.

Lithium helps flatten out the cycles of (122) m____________ behavior and depression found in (123) ____________ar disorder. Lithium appears to moderate the level of (124) ____________line available to the brain.

Objective 19: Describe electroconvulsive therapy, and when it is used.

Electroconvulsive therapy (ECT) was introduced by Ugo (125) C____________ in 1939. ECT uses electric shock to produce (126) ____________ions. Since the advent of major tranquilizers, use of ECT has been generally limited to patients with (127) ____________ ____________sion. ECT is controversial because it impairs (128) m____________ and nobody knows why it works. Today, ECT tends to be used only when (129) anti____________ drugs fail. (130) Uni____________ ECT appears to have relatively fewer side effects.

Objective 20: Discuss psychosurgery.

Psychosurgery was pioneered by Antonio Egas (131) M____________. The best-known technique is called the (132) pre____________ ____________omy. The prefrontal lobotomy has been used with severely disturbed patients and severs the nerve pathways that link the prefrontal (133) ____________s of the brain to the (134) ____________mus. Today, the prefrontal lobotom has been largely discontinued because of the advent of major tranquilizers and because of (135) s____________ effects.

Objective 21: Evaluate the biological therapies.

(136) Chemo____________ has a distinct place in the treatment of abnormal behavior. Unfortunately, (137: minor

or major?) tranquilizers, used for common anxiety and tension, are frequently abused. Patients rapidly develop (138) ____________ance for these drugs, and the drugs do nothing to show them how to manage their problems in more productive ways. In spite of the controversies that surround ECT, supporters note that there is evidence that it brings many immobilized patients out of their depression when (139) anti____________ drugs fail. ECT patients have a (140: higher or lower?) mortality rate following treatment than depressed people who do not receive ECT.

Answers to Chapter Review

1. Psychological
2. Abnormal
3. Demonological
4. Exorcism
5. Asylums
6. Monasteries
7. Bethlehem
8. Eighteenth
9. Pinel
10. Dix
11. Hospitals
12. Mental-Health
13. Freud
14. Conflicts
15. Unconscious
16. Coping
17. Catharsis
18. Psychic
19. Free
20. Censored
21. Repressed
22. Resistance
23. Dreams
24. Fulfillment
25. Symbols
26. Manifest
27. Latent
28. Transference
29. Countertransference
30. Briefer
31. Less
32. Unconscious
33. Ego
34. Analysts
35. Subjective
36. Psychodynamic (or psychoanalytic)
37. Humanistic–existential
38. Carl Rogers
39. Nondirective
40. Unconditional
41. Empathic
42 Genuineness
43. Congruence
44. Self-esteem
45. Self-actualization
46 Fritz Perls
47. Directive
48. Personality
49. Dialogue
50. Language
51. Disowned
52. Beliefs
53. Automatic
54. Rational-emotive
55. Albert Ellis
56. Irrational
57. Directive
58. Distortions
59. Depression
60. Perception
61. Overgeneralization
62. Magnification
63. Absolutist
64. Minimizing
65. Pessimism
66. Behavior
67. Cognitive behavior
68. Behavior
69. Cognitive
70. Modification
71. Learning
72. Experimentation
73. Observable
74. Maladaptive
75. Adaptive
76. Desensitization
77. Participant
78. Joseph Wolpe
79. Counterconditioning
80. Incompatible
81. Relaxation
82. Hierarchy
83. Aversive
84. Rapid
85. Reinforced
86. Extinguished
87. Token
88. Self
89. Role
90. Behavior
91. Feedback
92. Biofeedback
93. Reinforce
94. Electromyograph
95. Electroencephalograph
96. Alpha
97. Functional
98. Maintain
99. Consequences
100. Theoretical
101. Economical
102. Experiences
103. Emotional
104. 70–75
105. Well
106. Highly
107. 75
108. Chemotherapy
109. Minor
110. Valium
111. Central
112. Antipsychotic
113. Delusions
114. Phenothiazines
115. Dopamine
116. Major
117. Antidepressant
118. Noradrenaline
119. Serotonin
120. Panic
121. Eating
122. Manic
123. Bipolar
124. Noradrenaline
125. Cerletti
126. Convulsions
127. Major depression
128. Memory
129. Antidepressant
130. Unilateral
131. Moniz
132. Prefrontal lobotomy
133. Lobes
134. Thalamus
135. Side
136. Chemotherapy
137. Minor
138. Tolerance
139. Antidepressant
140. Lower

POSTTEST

1. A leader of the humanitarian reform movement in the United States was
(a) Philippe Pinel.
(b) Dorothea Dix.
(c) Sigmund Freud.
(d) William Tuke.

2. A woman client complains to her therapist, "Who do you think you are—my father?" Sigmund Freud would probably characterize her behavior as an example of
(a) transference.
(b) reaction formation.
(c) projection.
(d) resistance.

3. Sigmund Freud remarked, "Where id was, there shall ego be." According to the text, Freud meant that
(a) all unconscious ideas should be made conscious.
(b) feelings of guilt should be removed.
(c) coping behavior should replace impulsive behavior.
(d) defense mechanisms should be destroyed.

4. A person has a dream in which she is flying. According to Sigmund Freud, the perceived subject matter of a dream—in this case, flying—is its
(a) manifest content.
(b) objective content.
(c) symbolic content.
(d) latent content.

5. Congruence may be defined as
   (a) honesty in interpersonal relationships.
   (b) a fit between one's behavior and feelings.
   (c) ability to perceive the world from a client's frame of reference.
   (d) genuine acceptance of the client as a person.

6. A relative of yours is considering seeing a person-centered therapist, but wonders if person-centered therapy is right for him. You note that person-centered therapy seems to be most effective with ________ clients.
   (a) psychotic (c) middle-class
   (b) poorly motivated (d) well-educated

7. According to Albert Ellis, the central factors in our problems are
   (a) genetic factors.
   (b) maladaptive habits.
   (c) unconscious conflicts.
   (d) irrational beliefs.

8. Behavior rehearsal is most similar in meaning to
   (a) practice.
   (b) role playing.
   (c) modeling.
   (d) countertransference.

9. According to the text, the technique of modeling is connected with
   (a) person-centered therapy.
   (b) traditional psychoanalysis.
   (c) social-skills training.
   (d) Gestalt therapy.

10. The technique called ________ is an example of aversive conditioning.
    (a) "Grandma's method"
    (b) restriction of the stimulus field
    (c) operant conditioning
    (d) rapid smoking

11. Tom cut down on his cigarette intake by simply pausing between puffs. This technique is an example of
    (a) successive approximations.
    (b) chain breaking.
    (c) response prevention.
    (d) avoiding stimuli that trigger unwanted behavior.

12. Which of the following forms of therapy is nondirective?
    (a) Gestalt therapy
    (b) Behavior therapy
    (c) Cognitive therapy
    (d) Person-centered therapy

13. According to the studies analyzed by Smith and Glass, the *least* effective form of therapy is
    (a) Gestalt therapy.
    (b) psychoanalysis,.
    (c) cognitive therapy.
    (d) behavior therapy.

14. Valium and other minor tranquilizers are thought to depress the activity of the ________, which, in turn, decreases sympathetic activity.
    (a) central nervous system
    (b) parasympathetic nervous system
    (c) adrenal medulla
    (d) adrenal cortex

15. Major tranquilizers are thought to work by blocking the action of
    (a) acetylcholine. (c) dopamine.
    (b) noradrenaline. (d) serotonin.

16. Which of the following is an antidepressant drug?
    (a) Clozaril
    (b) Valium
    (c) Thorazine
    (d) Prozac

17. Which of the following is likely to be recommended for treating depression when antidepressant drugs fail?
    (a) Librium
    (b) ECT
    (c) Tofranil
    (d) psychosurgery

18. According to the text, the person who wrote that many people are depressed because they are pessimistic and tend to minimize their own accomplishments is a
    (a) cognitive therapist.
    (b) traditional psychoanalyst.
    (c) behavior therapist.
    (d) transactional analyst.

19. Psychosurgery was pioneered by
    (a) Wolpe. (c) Moniz.
    (b) Dix. (d) Perls.

20. The self-control technique of ________ is a strategy that is aimed at the reinforcements that maintain behavior.
    (a) response prevention
    (b) stimulus control
    (c) successive approximations
    (d) covert sensitization

Answers to Posttest

1. B	**6.** D	**11.** B	**16.** D
2. A	**7.** D	**12.** D	**17.** B
3. C	**8.** A	**13.** A	**18.** A
4. A	**9.** C	**14.** A	**19.** C
5. B	**10.** D	**15.** C	**20.** D

- Airing a television commercial repeatedly hurts sales.
- We value things more when we have to work for them.
- First impressions have powerful effects on our social relationships.
- We take others to task for their misdeeds but tend to see ourselves as victims of circumstances when our conduct falls short of our ideals.
- Beauty is in the eye of the beholder.
- People are perceived as being more attractive when they are smiling.
- Most people would refuse to deliver painful electric shock to an innocent party, even under strong social pressure.
- Many people are late to social gatherings because they are conforming to a social norm.
- Group decisions tend to represent conservative compromises of the opinions of the group members.
- Nearly 40 people stood by and did nothing while a woman was being stabbed to death.

Social Psychology

Learning Objectives

When you have finished studying Chapter 15, you should be able to:

1. Define *social psychology*.

Attitudes

2. Define *attitude* and explain what is meant by the A–B problem.
3. Discuss the origins of attitudes.
4. Discuss ways in which attitudes may be changed by means of persuasion.
5. Discuss the roles of balance theory and cognitive dissonance in changing attitudes.
6. Define *prejudice* and discuss the origins of prejudice.

Social Perception

7. Explain the primacy and recency effects on social perception.
8. Differentiate between dispositional and situational attributions, and explain the biases that are found in the attribution process.
9. Explain the role of body language in social perception.

Interpersonal Attraction

10. Discuss factors that contribute to interpersonal attraction.

Social Influence

11. Describe the Milgram studies on obedience to authority, and discuss factors that contribute to obedience.
12. Describe the Asch studies on conformity, and discuss factors that contribute to conformity.

Group Behavior

13. Discuss factors that contribute to social facilitation and social loafing.
14. Discuss social-decision schemes in group decision making.
15. Discuss these factors as they contribute to the group decision-making process: polarization and the risky shift.
16. Discuss the factors that contribute to groupthink.
17. Discuss the factors that contribute to helping behavior.
18. Discuss the factors that contribute to the bystander effect.

Candy and Stretch. A new technique for controlling weight gains? No, these are the names Bach and Deutsch (1970) give two people who have just met at a camera club that doubles as a meeting place for singles.

Candy and Stretch stand above the crowd—literally. Candy, an attractive woman in her early thirties, is almost 6 feet tall. Stretch is more plain-looking, but wholesome, in his late thirties, and 6 feet 5 inches.

Stretch has been in the group for some time. Candy is a new member. Let's listen in on them as they make conversation during a coffee break. As you will see, there are some differences between what they say and what they are thinking:

	THEY SAY	**THEY THINK**
Stretch:	Well you're certainly a welcome addition to our group.	(Can't I ever say something clever?)
Candy:	Thank you. It certainly is friendly and interesting.	(He's cute.)
Stretch:	My friends call me Stretch. It's left over from my basketball days. Silly, but I'm used to it.	(It's safer than saying my name is David Stein.)
Candy:	My name is Candy.	(At least my nickname is. He doesn't have to hear Hortense O'Brien.)
Stretch:	What kind of camera is that?	(Why couldn't a girl named Candy be Jewish? It's only a nickname, isn't it?)
Candy:	Just this old German one of my uncle's. I borrowed it from the office.	(He could be Irish. And that camera looks expensive.)
Stretch:	May I? (He takes her camera, brushing her hand and then tingling with the touch.) Fine lens. You work for your uncle?	(Now I've done it. Brought up work.)
Candy:	Ever since college. It's more than being just a secretary. I get into sales, too.	(So okay, what if I only went for a year. If he asks what I sell, I'll tell him anything except underwear.)
Stretch:	Sales? That's funny. I'm in sales, too, but mainly as an executive. I run our department. I started using cameras on trips. Last time I was in the Bahamas. I took—	(Is there a nice way to say used cars? I'd better change the subject.) (Great legs! And the way her hips move—)
Candy:	Oh! Do you go to the Bahamas, too? I love those islands.	(So I went just once, and it was for the brassiere manufacturers' convention. At least we're off the subject of jobs.)

Stretch:		(She's probably been around. Well, at least we're off the subject of jobs.)
	I did a little underwater work there last summer. Fantastic colors. So rich in life.	(And lonelier than hell.)
Candy:		(Look at that build. He must swim like a fish. I should learn.)
	I wish I'd had time when I was there. I love the water.	(Well, I do. At the beach, anyway, where I can wade in and not go too deep.)

Thus begins a relationship. Candy and Stretch have a drink and talk, sharing their likes and dislikes. Amazingly, they seem to agree on everything—from cars to clothing to politics. The attraction is very strong, and neither is willing to risk turning the other off by disagreeing.

Soon they feel that they have fallen in love. They still agree on everything they discuss, but they scrupulously avoid one topic: religion. Their religious differences became apparent when they exchanged last names. That doesn't mean they have to talk about it.

They also put off introducing each other to their parents. The O'Briens and the Steins are narrow-minded about religion. If the truth be known, so are Candy and Stretch. They narrow their outside relationships to avoid tension with one another, and as the romance develops, they feel progressively isolated from family and friends.

What happens in this tangled web of deception? Candy becomes pregnant. After some deliberation, and not without misgivings, the couple decides to get married. Do they live happily ever after? We cannot say—"ever after" isn't here yet.

We do not have all the answers, but we have some questions. Candy and Stretch's relationship began with a powerful attraction. What is *attraction?* How do we determine who is attractive? Candy and Stretch pretended to share each other's attitudes? What are *attitudes?* Why were they so reluctant to disagree?

Candy and Stretch were both prejudiced about religion. What is *prejudice?* Why didn't they introduce each other to their parents? Did they fear that their parents would want them to *conform* to their own standards? Would their parents try to *persuade* them to limit dating to people of their own religions? Would they *obey?*

Attraction, attitudes, prejudice, conformity, persuasion, obedience—these topics are the province of the branch of psychology called **social psychology.** Social psychologists study the nature and causes of our behavior and mental processes in social situations (Baron & Byrne, 1991). The social psychological topics we discuss in this chapter include attitudes, social perception, attraction, social influence, and group behavior.

ATTITUDES

How do you feel about abortion, Japanese cars, and the Republican party? The only connection I draw among these items is that people tend to have strong *attitudes* toward them. They each tend to elicit cognitive evaluations (such as approval or disapproval), feelings (liking, disliking, or something stronger), and behavioral tendencies (as of approach or avoidance). Although I asked you how you "feel," attitudes are not just feelings or emotions (Pratkanis et al., 1989). Thinking is primary, according to most contemporary psychologists, and feelings and behavior follow (Baron & Byrne, 1991; Breckler & Wiggins, 1989; Petty & Cacioppo, 1986).

Social psychology The field of psychology that studies the nature and causes of individual thoughts, feelings, and overt behavior in social situations.

Attitudes are enduring mental representations of people, places, or things that evoke feelings and influence behavior. Attitudes are learned and have major impacts on behavior (Shavitt, 1990; Snyder & DeBono, 1989). Attitudes can foster love or hatred. They can give rise to helping behavior or to mass destruction. They can lead to social conflict or to conflict resolution. Attitudes can change, but they tend to remain stable unless shoved. Most people do not change their religion or political affiliation without serious reflection or, perhaps, coercion.

The A–B Problem

Our definition of attitude implies that our behavior is consistent with our beliefs and our feelings. When we are free to do as we wish, it often is. But, as indicated by the term **A–B problem,** the link between attitudes (A) and behavior (B) tends to be weak. In their review of the literature, General attitudes toward groups of people, politics, and religion (such as whether one is prejudiced toward African Americans or whether one is a Republican or a Christian) apparently do not predict specific behavior patterns very well (Azjen & Fishbein, 1977). Knowing that James is a Republican does not guarantee that he will vote invariably for Republicans, or that he will bother to vote. We would be better able to predict James's voting behavior if we knew whether he places party loyalty ahead of the excellence of individuals and if we knew how committed he was to expressing his political views, as by voting.

A number of factors affect the prediction of from attitudes:

1. *Specificity.* We can better predict specific behavior from specific attitudes than from global attitudes (Baron & Byrne, 1991). We can better predict church attendance by knowing people's attitudes toward regular church attendance than by knowing whether they are Christian.
2. *Strength of attitudes.* Strong attitudes are more likely to determine behavior than weak attitudes (Fazio et al., 1982). A person who believes that the nation's destiny depends on Republicans taking control of Congress is more likely to vote than a person who does not believe that the outcome of elections makes much difference.
3. *Vested interest.* People are more likely to act on their attitudes when they have a vested interest in the outcome (Johnson & Eagly, 1989). People are more likely to vote for (or against) unionization of their workplace, for example, when they believe that their job security depends on the outcome.
4. *Accessibility.* People are more likely to express their attitudes when they are accessible—that is, when they are brought to mind (Fazio, 1989; Krosnick, 1989). This is why politicians attempt to "get out the vote" by means of media blitzes just prior to an election. It does politicians little good to have supporters who forget them on election day.

Candy and Stretch avoided discussing matters on which they differed. One motive might have been to avoid heightening the *accessibility* of their clashing attitudes. By keeping them under the table, perhaps Candy and Stretch would be less likely to act on them and go their separate ways.

Origins of Attitudes

You were not born a Republican or a Democrat. You were not born a Catholic or a Jew—although your parents may have practiced one of these religions when you came along. Political, religious, and other attitudes are learned.

Conditioning. Conditioning may play a role in acquiring attitudes. Laboratory experiments have shown that attitudes toward national groups can be

Attitude An enduring mental representation of a person, place, or thing that evokes an emotional response and affected behavior.

A–B problem The issue of how well we can predict behavior on the basis of attitudes.

influenced simply by associating them with positive words (such as *gift* or *happy*) or negative words (such as *ugly* and *failure*) (Lohr & Staats, 1973). President George Bush's repeated references to Iraq's Saddam Hussein as "another Hitler" prior to 1991's War in the Gulf encouraged people to associate the hatred they felt for Hitler with Hussein. Parents often reward children for saying and doing things that are consistent with their own attitudes.

Observational Learning. Attitudes formed through direct experience may be stronger and easier to recall (Fazio & Cooper, 1983), but we also acquire attitudes from friends and the mass media. The approval or disapproval of peers molds adolescents to prefer short or long hair, blue jeans, or preppy sweaters. Television shows us that body odor, bad breath, and the frizzies are dreaded diseases—and, perhaps, that people who use harsh toilet paper are somehow un-American.

Cognitive Appraisal. All is not mechanical, however. We now and then evaluate information and attitudes on the basis of evidence. We may revise stereotypes on the basis of new information (Weber & Crocker, 1983).

Still, initial attitudes tend to serve as cognitive anchors. They help mold the ways in which we perceive the world and interpret events. Attitudes we encounter later are thus often judged in terms of how much they "deviate" from the initial set. Accepting larger deviations appears to require greater adjustments in information processing (Quattrone, 1982). However, attitudes can be changed by persuasion.

Changing Attitudes through Persuasion

Let advertisers spend the same amount of money improving their product that they do on advertising and they wouldn't have to advertise it.
Will Rogers

Rogers' humorous social comment sounds on the mark, but he was probably wrong. It does little good to have a wonderful product if its existence remains a secret.

Petty and Cacioppo (1986) have devised the **elaboration likelihood model** for understanding the processes by which people examine the information in persuasive messages. According to this view, there are at least two routes to persuading others to change attitudes—that is, two ways of responding to, or elaborating, persuasive messages. The first, or central route, involves thoughtful consideration of arguments and evidence. The second, or peripheral route, involves associating objects with positive or negative cues. When politicians avow that, "This bill is supported by Jesse Jackson (or Jesse Helms)," they are seeking predictable, "knee-jerk" reactions, not careful consideration of a bill's merits. Other cues are rewards (such as a smile or a hug), punishments (such as parental disapproval), and factors such as the trustworthiness and attractiveness of the communicator.

Advertisements, which are a form of persuasive communication, also rely on central and peripheral routes. Some ads focus on the quality of the product (central route), whereas others attempt to associate the product with appealing images (peripheral route). Ads that highlight the nutritional benefits of food products provide information about their quality (Snyder & DeBono, 1985). So do the "Pepsi challenge" taste-test ads, which claim that Pepsi tastes better than Coca-Cola. The Marlboro cigarette ads, in contrast, focus on the masculine, rugged image of the "Marlboro man"[1] and offer no information about the product itself (Snyder & DeBono, 1985).

Elaboration likelihood model The view that persuasive messages are evaluated (elaborated) on the basis of central and peripheral cues.

[1]The rugged actor in the original TV commercials died from lung cancer. Cigarettes were apparently more rugged than he.

Can You Take Beauty to the Bank? Advertisers use both central and peripheral cues to hawk their wares. What factors contribute to the persuasiveness of messages? To the persuasiveness of communicators?

The success of most persuasive communications often relies on a combination of central and peripheral cues such as speech content and voice quality (O'Sullivan et al., 1985). In this section, we shall examine one central factor in persuasion—the nature of the message—and three peripheral factors: (1) the person delivering the message, (2) the context in which the message is delivered, and (3) the audience. We shall also examine a method of persuasion used frequently by persons seeking charitable contributions: the foot-in-the-door technique.

The Persuasive Message: Say What? Say How? Say How Often?

How do we respond when TV commercials are repeated until we have memorized every dimple on the actors' faces? Research suggests that familiarity breeds content, not contempt.

You might not be crazy about *zebulons* and *afworbu's* at first, but Zajonc (1968) found that people began to react favorably toward these bogus words[2] on the basis of repeated exposure. Political candidates who become well known to the public through regular TV commercials attain more votes (Grush, 1980). People respond more favorably to abstract art (Heingartner & Hall, 1974), classical music (Smith & Dorfman, 1975), and photographs of African Americans (Hamm et al., 1975) and college students (Moreland & Zajonc, 1982) on the basis of repetition. Love for classical art and music may begin through exposure in the nursery, not the college appreciation course.

It is *not* true that airing a commercial repeatedly hurts sales. Repeated exposure frequently leads to liking and acceptance.

The more complex the stimuli, the more likely it is that frequent exposure will have favorable effects (Saegert & Jellison, 1970; Smith & Dorfman, 1975). The one-hundredth playing of a Bach concerto may thus be less tiresome than the one-hundredth performance of a pop tune.

[2]*Zebulun,* it happens, is the name of Jacob's tenth son, as reported in *Genesis.* Driving through the Carolinas one summer, your author noted a town named Zebulon. (I'm a respository of useless information.)

Bill Cosby Sells Coca-Cola. Why do companies like Coca-Cola pay millions to recruit celebrities to endorse their products? What accounts for the appeal of Bill Cosby?

Two-sided arguments, in which the communicator recounts the arguments of the opposition in order to refute them, can be especially effective when the audience is at first uncertain about its position (Sorrentino et al., 1988). Theologians and politicians sometimes expose their followers to the arguments of the opposition. By refuting them one by one, they impart to their followers a kind of psychological immunity to them. Swinyard found that two-sided product claims, in which advertisers admitted their product's weak points in addition to highlighting its strengths, were most credible (Bridgwater, 1982).

It would be nice to think that people are too sophisticated to be persuaded by an **emotional appeal.** However, grisly films of operations on cancerous lungs are more effective than matter-of-fact presentations for changing attitudes toward smoking (Leventhal et al., 1972). Films of bloodied gums and decayed teeth are also more effective than logical discussions for boosting toothbrushing (Dembroski et al., 1978). Fear appeals are most effective when they are strong, when the audience believes the dire consequences, and when the recommendations seem sensible (Robberson & Rogers, 1988).

Audiences also tend to believe arguments that appear to run counter to the vested interests of the communicator (Wood & Eagly, 1981). People may pay more attention to a whaling-fleet owner's claim than to a conservationist's that whales are becoming extinct. If the president of Chrysler or General Motors conceded that Toyotas and Hondas were superior, you can bet that we would prick up our ears.

The Persuasive Communicator: Whom Do You Trust? Would you buy a used car from a person convicted of larceny? Would you attend weight-control classes run by a 350-pound leader? Would you leaf through fashion magazines featuring homely models? Probably not. Research shows that persuasive communicators show expertise (Hennigan et al., 1982), trustworthiness, attractiveness, or similarity to their audiences (Baron & Byrne, 1991).

Television news anchorpersons enjoy high prestige. One study (Mullen et al., 1987) found that before the 1984 presidential election, Peter Jennings of ABC News had shown significantly more favorable facial expressions when reporting on Ronald Reagan than on Walter Mondale. Tom Brokaw of NBC and Dan Rather of CBS had not shown favoritism. The researchers also found that viewers of ABC News voted for Reagan in greater proportions than viewers of NBC or CBS News. It is tempting to conclude that viewers were subtly persuaded by Jennings to vote for Reagan—and maybe this happened in a number of cases. But Sweeney and Gruber (1984) have shown that viewers do not simply absorb, spongelike, whatever the tube feeds them. Instead, they show **selective avoidance** and **selective exposure.** They tend to switch channels when they are faced with news coverage that counters their own attitudes. They also seek communicators whose outlooks coincide with their own. And so, Jennings may have swayed his audience's attitudes toward Reagan, but it may also be that Reaganites favored Jennings over Brokaw and Rather.

The Context of the Message: "Get 'Em in a Good Mood." You are too shrewd to let someone persuade you by buttering you up, but perhaps someone you know would be influenced by a sip of wine, a bite of cheese, and a sincere compliment. Seduction attempts usually come at the tail-end of a date—after the Szechuan tidbits, the nouveau Fresno film, the disco party, and the wine that was sold at its time. An assault at the outset of a date would be viewed as . . . well, an assault. Experiments suggest that food and pleasant music boost acceptance of persuasive messages (Galizio & Hendrick, 1972; Janis et al., 1965). When we are in a good mood, we are apparently less likely to carefully evaluate the situation (Mackie & Worth, 1989).

It is also counterproductive to call your dates fools when they differ with you—even though their ideas are bound to be foolish if they do not concur with

Emotional appeal A type of persuasive communication that influences behavior on the basis of feelings that are aroused instead of rational analysis of the issues.

Selective avoidance Diverting one's attention from information that is inconsistent with one's attitudes.

Selective exposure Deliberately seeking and attending to information that is consistent with one's attitudes.

yours. Agreement and praise are more effective at encouraging others to embrace your views. Appear sincere or else your compliments will look manipulative. (It seems unsporting to divulge this information.)

The Persuaded Audience: Are You a Person Who Can't Say No? Why do some people have "sales resistance," whereas others enrich the lives of every door-to-door salesperson? It may be that people with high self-esteem and low social anxiety are more likely to resist social pressure (Santee & Maslach, 1982). Baumeister and Covington (1985) challenge the view that persons with low self-esteem are more open to persuasion, however. Persons with high self-esteem may also be persuaded, but they may be less willing to confess that others have influenced them. Knowledge of the areas that a communicator is addressing also tends to lessen persuadability (Wood, 1982).

A study by Schwartz and Gottman (1976) reveals the cognitive nature of the social anxiety that can make it hard for some of us to refuse requests. Schwartz and Gottman found that people who comply with unreasonable requests are more apt to report thinking, "I was worried about what the other person would think of me if I refused," "It is better to help others than to be self-centered," or "The other person might be hurt or insulted if I refused." People who did not comply reported thoughts such as, "It doesn't matter what the other person thinks of me," "I am perfectly free to say no," or "This request is an unreasonable one" (p. 916).

The Foot-in-the-Door Technique. You might suppose that giving money to door-to-door solicitors for charity will get you off the hook—i.e., they'll take the cash and leave you alone for a while. Actually, the opposite is true: The next time they mount a campaign, they may call on generous you to go door to door! Organizations compile lists of persons they can rely on. Giving an inch apparently encourages others to go for a yard. They have gotten their "foot in the door."

Consider a classic experiment on the **foot-in-the-door technique** by Freedman and Fraser (1966). Groups of women received phone calls from a consumer group requesting that they let a six-man crew drop by their homes to catalog their household products. The job could take hours. Only 22 percent of one group acceded to this irksome entreaty. But 53 percent of another group of women assented to a visit from this wrecking crew. Why was the second group more compliant? The pliant group had been phoned a few days earlier and had agreed to answer a few questions about the soap products they used. They had been primed for the second request. The caller had gotten a "foot in the door." The foot-in-the-door technique has also been shown to be effective in persuading people to do things such as making charitable contributions and signing petitions (Beaman et al., 1983).

Research suggests that people who accede to small requests become more amenable to larger ones because they come to see themselves as the kind of people who help out in this way (DeJong & Musilli, 1982; Eisenberg et al., 1987). Regardless of how the foot-in-the-door technique works, if you want to say no, it may be easier to do so (and stick to your guns) the first time a request is made rather than later.

The foot-in-the-door technique may place us in cognitive conflict. We may have made a commitment to help but might prefer not to. Let us elaborate the role of cognitive conflict by considering balance theory and cognitive-dissonance theory.

Foot-in-the-door technique A method for inducing compliance in which a small request is followed by a larger request.

Balance theory The view that people have a need to organize their perceptions, opinions, and beliefs in a harmonious manner.

Balance Theory

According to **balance theory,** we are motivated to maintain harmony among our perceptions, beliefs, and attitudes (Heider, 1958). When people we like share our attitudes, there is balance and all is well. It works the other way as well: If we like Peter Jennings and he expresses an attitude, our own cognitions will remain in balance if we agree with him. For this reason, we are likely to develop favorable attitudes toward unfamiliar objects that Jennings seems to endorse. If we dislike other people, we might not care very much about their attitudes. They may disagree with us, but this state of **nonbalance** leaves us indifferent (Newcomb, 1981).

When someone we care about expresses a discrepant attitude, however, we *are* likely to be concerned (Orive, 1988). The relationship will survive if we like chocolate and our friend prefers vanilla, but what if the discrepancy concerns religion, politics, or childrearing? A state of **imbalance** now exists. What if Peter Jennings, whom we like, reports favorably on an object we dislike? There is now an uncomfortable state of imbalance. Candy was Catholic and Stretch was Jewish. Each was painfully aware of the imbalance in religious choice. How did they handle the imbalance? At first, they misperceived the other's religion. Later, they tried to sweep it under the rug.

What else can people do to end a state of imbalance? We can try to induce others to change their attitudes. (Candy and Stretch could have asked each other to change religions.) Or we can change our feelings about the other person. (Candy or Stretch might have "realized" that the other was unworthy, after all.) Cognitive-dissonance theory, however, suggests that Candy and Stretch's feelings for each other might grow *stronger* as a result of discovering their religious differences, as we shall see.

Cognitive-Dissonance Theory

Do I contradict myself?
Very well then I contradict myself,
(I am large, I contain multitudes.)

Walt Whitman, *Song of Myself*

Most of us are unlike Walt Whitman, according to **cognitive-dissonance theory** (Festinger, 1957; Festinger & Carlsmith, 1959). Whitman may not have minded contradicting himself, but most people do not like their attitudes (cognitions) to be inconsistent. Awareness that two cognitions are dissonant, or that our attitudes are incompatible with our behavior, is sufficient to motivate us to reduce the discrepancy. Cognitive dissonance is unpleasant (Fazio & Cooper, 1983) and accompanied by heightened arousal (Croyle & Cooper, 1983). One motive for eliminating cognitive dissonance may thus be to reduce uncomfortable arousal.

In a classic study on cognitive dissonance, one group of subjects received $1.00 for telling someone else that a boring task was interesting (Festinger & Carlsmith, 1959). A second group of subjects received $20.00 to describe the chore positively. Both groups were paid to engage in **attitude-discrepant behavior**—that is, behavior that ran counter to their cognitions. After "selling" the job to others, the subjects were asked to rate their own liking for it. Ironically, the group paid *less* rated the task as more interesting. *Why?*

According to learning theory, the result would be confusing. After all, shouldn't we learn to like that which is highly rewarding? But cognitive-dissonance theory would predict this "less-leads-to-more effect" for the following reason: The cognitions "I was paid very little" and "I told someone that this assignment was interesting" are dissonant. People tend to engage in **effort justification;** they usually explain their behavior to themselves in such a way that unpleasant undertakings seem worth it. Subjects paid only $1.00 may have justified their lie by concluding that they may not have been lying in the first place. Similarly, we appreciate things more when they are more difficult to obtain.

Nonbalance In balance theory, a condition in which persons whom we dislike do not agree with us.

Imbalance In balance theory, a condition in which persons whom we like disagree with us.

Cognitive-dissonance theory The view that people strive to reduce the discomfort that is produced by the recognition that their cognitions are inconsistent.

Attitude-discrepant behavior Behavior that runs counter to one's thoughts and feelings.

Effort justification The tendency to seek justification (reasons) for strenuous efforts.

It is true that we tend to appreciate things more when we have to work for them. This is another example of the principle of effort justification.

Consider another situation. Cognitive dissonance would be created if we were to believe that our preferred candidate was unlikely to win the American presidential election. One cognition would be that our candidate is better for the country or, at an extreme, would "save" the country from harmful forces. A second, and dissonant, cognition would be that our candidate does not have a chance to win. Research shows that in the presidential elections from 1952 to 1980, people by a four-to-one margin helped reduce such dissonance by expressing the belief that their candidate would win (Granberg & Brent, 1983). They frequently held these beliefs despite lopsided polls to the contrary. Among highly involved but poorly informed people, the margin of self-deception was still higher.

Consider Candy and Stretch. Cognitive-dissonance theory might predict that their discovery of different religious backgrounds would *strengthen* rather than hurt their relationship. Why? After discovering the other's religion, each might have thought, "Stretch (Candy) must be *very* important to me if I can feel this way about him (her), knowing that he (she) is Jewish (Catholic)."

Cognitive-dissonance theory leads to the hypothesis that we can change people's attitudes by somehow getting them to behave in a manner consistent with the attitudes we wish to promote. Research shows that people may indeed change attitudes when attitude-discrepant behavior is rewarded (Calder et al., 1973; Cooper, 1980). It is at once a frightening and promising concept. For instance, it sounds like a prescription for totalitarianism. Yet it also suggests that prejudiced individuals who are prevented from discriminating—who are compelled, for example, by open-housing laws to allow people from different ethnic backgrounds to buy homes in their neighborhoods—may actually become less prejudiced.

In the following section we discuss one particularly troubling kind of attitude: prejudice.

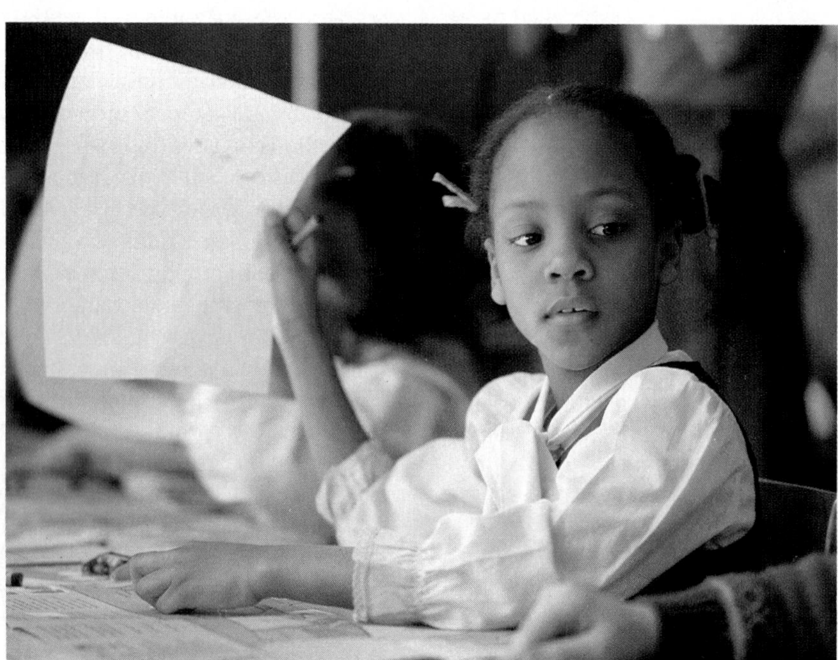

Stereotyping. How well is this child performing on her test? An experiment by Darley and Gross showed that our expectations concerning a child's performance on a test are linked to our awareness of that child's socioeconomic background.

TABLE 15.1: Some Stereotypes of Cultural and Ethnic Groups Within the United States

African Americans	Irish Americans	Jewish Americans
Physically powerful and well-coordinated	Sexually repressed	Cheap, shrewd in business
Unclean	Heavy drinkers	Clannish
Unintelligent and superstitious	Overly religious	Control banks, Wall Street, and the media
Musically talented	Political and nationalistic	Wealthy and showy
Excellent as lovers	Outgoing, witty, and literary	Big-nosed
Lazy	Hot-tempered ("fighting Irish")	Pushy
Emotional and aggressive		Smothering mother
Flashy (gaudy clothes and big cars)	**Italian Americans**	
	Overly interested in food	**Polish Americans**
Chinese Americans	Ignorant, suspicious of education	Unintelligent and uneducated
Deceitful	Clannish	Overly religious
Inscrutable	Great singers	Dirty
Wise	Great shoemakers and barbers	Racist, bigoted
Cruel	Hot-tempered and violent	Boorish, uncultured
Polite, quiet, and deferential	Connected to the Mafia	
Possessing strong family ties	Talk with their hands	**"White Anglo-Saxon Protestants" ("WASPs")**
Law-abiding	Cowardly in battle	Hardworking, ambitious, thrifty
		Honorable
Hispanic Americans	**Japanese Americans**	Wealthy, powerful
Macho	Ambitious, hardworking, and competitive	Insensitive, emotionally cold
Unwilling to learn English	Intelligent, well-educated	Polite, well-mannered, genteel
Disinterested in education	Obedient, servile women	Snobbish
Not concerned about being on welfare	Sneaky	Guilt-ridden do-gooders
Warm, expressive	Poor lovers	
Lazy	Possessing strong family ties	
Hot-tempered and violent	Great imitators, not originators	
	Law-abiding	

Stereotypes are fixed, conventional ideas about groups of people and can give rise to prejudice and discrimination. Do you believe the stereotypes listed in this table? What is the evidence for your beliefs?

Sources of stereotypes: Kornblum, W. (1991). *Sociology in a changing world,* 2d ed. Fort Worth: Holt, Rinehart and Winston; Rathus, S. A., & Fichner-Rathus, L. (1994). *Making the most of college,* 2d ed. Englewood Cliffs, NJ: Prentice Hall.

Prejudice

People have condemned billions of other people. Without ever meeting them. Without ever learning their names.

Prejudice is an attitude toward a group that leads people to evaluate members of that group negatively. On a cognitive level, prejudice is linked to expectations that the target group will behave poorly, say, in the workplace or by engaging in criminal behavior. On an affective level, prejudice is associated with negative feelings such as dislike or hatred. Behaviorally, prejudice is connected with avoidance, aggression, and discrimination. There is an interaction among our cognitions, emotional responses, and behavior patterns.

Discrimination. One form of negative behavior that results from prejudice is called **discrimination.** Many groups have been discriminated against in the United States—women, Jews, Catholics, African Americans, Native Americans, Hispanic Americans, Asian Americans, Arab Americans, homosexuals, and the elderly, to name a few. Discrimination takes many forms including denial of access to jobs, housing, and the voting booth—even failing to make eye contact (Neuberg, 1989). Many people have forgotten that African-American men gained the right to vote decades before women did.

Stereotypes. Are Jews shrewd and ambitious? Are African Americans superstitious and musical? Are Hispanic men macho? If you believe such ideas, you are falling for a **stereotype**—a prejudice about a group that can lead you to interpret observations in a biased fashion. In Chapter 7 we noted that stereotypes of African

Prejudice The belief that a person or group, on the basis of assumed racial, ethnic, sexual, or other features, will possess negative characteristics or perform inadequately.

Discrimination The denial of privileges to a person or group because of prejudice.

Stereotype A fixed, conventional idea about a group.

WORLD OF DIVERSITY

*Machismo/Marianismo Stereotypes and Hispanic Culture**

People who are unfamiliar with the diversity that exists among the Spanish-speaking peoples of Latin America tend to perceive all Hispanics as part of a single culture. The term *Hispanic* is generally used to describe Spanish-speaking peoples of Latin America whose cultures were influenced by a mixture of Spanish and Native American (Indian) cultures. Although Hispanic peoples do share some common cultural traditions, most notably the Spanish language and devotion to Christianity, each Spanish-speaking nation in Latin America has its own cultural tradition, as well as distinct subcultures. The differences between the peoples of Latin America can be seen in their dress styles, their use of language, and their music and literary traditions. Argentinians, for example, tend to be more Europeanized in their style of dress and tastes in music. In the Dominican Republic and Puerto Rico, the influence of African and Native Carib Indian cultures blossoms forth in the colorful style of dress and in the use of percussion instruments in music.

Machismo

Machismo is a cultural stereotype that defines masculinity in terms of an idealized view of manliness. To be *macho* is to be strong, virile, and dominant. Each Hispanic culture puts its own particular cultural stamp on the meaning of machismo, however. In the Spanish-speaking cultures of the Caribbean and Central America, the macho code encourages men to restrain their feelings and maintain an emotional distance. In my travels in Argentina and some other Latin American countries, however, I have observed that men who are sensitive and emotionally expressive are not perceived as compromising their macho code. More research is needed into differences in cultural conceptions of machismo and other gender roles among various Hispanic groups.

Marianismo

In counterpoint to the macho ideal among Hispanic peoples is the cultural idealization of femininity embodied in the concept of *marianismo.* The marianismo stereotype, which derives its name from the Virgin Mary, refers to the ideal of the virtuous woman as one who "suffers in silence," submerging her needs and desires to those of her husband and children. With the marianismo stereotype, the image of a woman's role as a martyr is raised to the level of a cultural ideal. According to this cultural stereotype, a woman is expected to demonstrate her love for her husband by waiting patiently at home and having dinner

Americans led observers of a film to remember an African American as wielding a knife that was actually being held by a white man. Table 15.1 shows common stereotypes about cultural and ethnic groups. Do you believe any of these stereotypes? What is the evidence for your beliefs?

Sources of Prejudice. The sources of prejudice are many and varied. Let us briefly consider several possible contributors:

1. *Assumptions of dissimilarity.* We are apt to like people who share our attitudes. In forming impressions of others, we are influenced by attitudinal similarity and dissimilarity as well as by race (Goldstein & Davis, 1972). People of different religions and races often have different backgrounds, however, giving rise to dissimilar attitudes. Even when people of different races share important values, they may assume that they do not.

2. *Social conflict.* There is also a lengthy history of social and economic conflict between people of different races and religions. For example, Southern whites and African Americans have competed for jobs, giving rise to negative attitudes, even lynchings (Hepworth & West, 1988).

3. *Authoritarianism.* Based on psychoanalytic theory and their interpretation of the **Holocaust,** some social scientists (e.g., Adorno et al., 1950) have argued that racial and religious minorities serve as **scapegoats** for majority groups. The Germans, for instance, submitted to Nazi **authoritarianism** because they had been reared to submit to authority figures. They then displaced unconscious hostility toward their fathers onto Jews. These Freudian concepts have been criticized by many psychologists, but authoritarian people do appear to

Holocaust The name given the Nazi murder of millions of Jews during World War II.

Scapegoat A person or group on whom the blame for the mistakes or crimes of others is cast.

Authoritarianism Belief in the importance of unquestioning obedience to authority.

prepared for him at any time of day or night he happens to come home, to have his slippers ready for him, and so on. The feminine ideal is one of suffering in silence and being the provider of joy, even in the face of pain. Strongly influenced by the partriarchal Spanish tradition, the marianismo stereotype has historically been used to maintain women in a subordinate position in relation to men.

Acculturation: When Traditional Stereotypes Meet the Financial Realities of Life in the United States

Acculturation—the merging of cultures that occurs when immigrant groups become assimilated into the mainstream culture—has challenged this traditional machismo/marianismo division of marital roles among Hispanic couples in the United States. I have seen in my own work in treating Hispanic-American couples in therapy that marriages are under increasing strain from the conflict between traditional and modern expectations about marital roles. Hispanic-American women have been entering the work force in increasing numbers, usually in domestic or childcare positions, but they are still expected to assume responsibility for tending their own children, keeping the house, and serving their husbands' needs when they return home. In many cases, a reversal of traditional roles occurs in which the wife works and supports the family, while the husband remains at home because he is unable to find or maintain employment.

It is often the Hispanic-American husband who has the greater difficulty accepting a more flexible distribution of roles within the marriage and giving up a rigid set of expectations tied to traditional machismo/marianismo gender expectations. Although some couples manage to reshape their expectations and marital roles in the face of changing conditions, many relationships buckle under the strain and are terminated in divorce. While I do not expect either the machismo or marianismo stereotype to disappear entirely, I would not be surprised to find a greater flexibility in gender role expectations as a product of continued acculturation.

*This guest feature was written by Rafael Art. Javier, Ph.D. Dr. Javier is Associate Clinical Professor of Psychology and Director of the Center for Psychological Services and Clinical Studies at St. John's University in Jamaica, NY. Dr. Javier was born in the Dominican Republic and educated in philosophy in the Dominican Republic, Puerto Rico, and Venezuela, and in psychology and psychoanalysis at New York University. Dr. Javier is a practicing psychoanalyst and maintains a research interest in psycholinguistic research and psychotherapy with ethnic minorities.

harbor more prejudices than nonauthoritarians (e.g., Stephan & Rosenfield, 1978).

4. *Social learning.* Children acquire some attitudes from others, especially parents, through identification and socialization. Children often broadly imitate their parents, and parents reinforce their children for doing so. In this way, prejudices can be transmitted from generation to generation.

5. *Information processing.* As attitudes, prejudices act as cognitive filters through which we perceive the social world. Prejudice is a way of processing social information. It is easier to attend to, and remember, instances of behavior that are consistent with our prejudices than it is to reconstruct our mental categories (Bodenhausen, 1988; Devine, 1989; Dovidio et al., 1986; Fiske, 1989). If you believe that Jews are stingy, it is easier to recall a Jew's negotiation of a price than a Jew's charitable donation. If you believe that Californians are "airheads," it may be easier to recall TV images of surfing than of scientific conferences at Caltech and Berkeley.

People also tend to divide the social world into two categories: "us" and "them." People usually view those who belong to their own groups—the "in-group"—more favorably than those who do not—the "out-group" (Linville et al., 1989; Schaller & Maas, 1989). Moreover, there is a tendency for us to assume that out-group members are more alike, or homogeneous, in their attitudes and behaviors than members of our own groups (Judd & Park, 1988; Wilder, 1986). Our isolation from out-group members makes it easier to maintain our stereotypes.

First Impressions. Why is it important to make a good first impression? What are some ways of doing so?

Let us now turn our attention to some of the factors involved in the formation of our impressions of other people.

SOCIAL PERCEPTION

Getting to know you,
Getting to know all about you. . . .

So goes the song from *The King and I.* How do we get to know other people, get to know all about them? In this section, we shall explore some factors that contribute to **social perception:** primacy and recency effects, attribution theory, and body language. Then, we shall survey the determinants of interpersonal attraction.

Primacy and Recency Effects: The Importance of First Impressions

Why do you wear your best outfit to a job interview? Why do defense attorneys dress their clients neatly and cut their hair before they are seen by the jury? Because first impressions are important and reasonably accurate (Burnstein & Schul, 1982; Wyer, 1988).

When I was a teenager, a young man was accepted or rejected by his date's parents the first time they were introduced. If he was considerate and made small talk, her parents would allow the couple to stay out past curfew, even to watch submarine races at the beach during the early morning hours. If he was boorish or uncommunicative, he was a cad forever. Her parents would object to him, no matter how hard he worked to gain their favor later on.

First impressions often make or break us. This is the **primacy effect.** People infer traits from behavior. If we act considerately at first, we are labeled considerate. The trait of consideration is used to explain and predict our future behavior. If, after being labeled considerate, one keeps a date out past curfew, this lapse is likely to be seen as an exception to a rule—as excused by circumstances or external causes. If one is first seen as inconsiderate, however, several months of considerate behavior may be perceived as a cynical effort to "make up for it."

In a classic experiment on the primacy effect, Luchins (1957) had subjects read different stories about "Jim." The stories consisted of one or two paragraphs. One-paragraph stories portrayed Jim as friendly or unfriendly. These paragraphs

---

Social perception A subfield of social psychology that studies the ways in which we form and modify impressions of others.

Primacy effect The tendency to evaluate others in terms of first impressions.

were also used in the two-paragraph stories but were presented to different subjects in opposite order. Of subjects reading only the "friendly" paragraph, 95 percent rated Jim as friendly. Of those who read just the "unfriendly" paragraph, 3 percent rated him as friendly. Seventy-eight percent of those who read two-paragraph stories in the "friendly-unfriendly" order labeled Jim as friendly. When they read the paragraphs in the reverse order, only 18 percent rated Jim as friendly.

It is true that first impressions have powerful effects on our social relationships.

How can we encourage people to pay more attention to more recent impressions? Luchins accomplished this by allowing time to elapse between presenting the paragraphs. In this way, fading memories allowed more recent information to take precedence. This is the **recency effect.** Luchins found a second way to counter first impressions: He simply counseled subjects to avoid snap judgments and to weigh all the evidence.

Attribution Theory

At the age of 3, one of my daughters believed that a friend's son was a boy because he *wanted* to be a boy. Since she was 3 at the time, this error in my daughter's **attribution** for the boy's gender is understandable. Adults tend to make somewhat similar attribution errors, however. No, adults do not believe that people's preferences have much to do with their gender. Adults—as we shall see—may tend to exaggerate the role of conscious choice in other aspects of their behavior, however.

An assumption about why people do things is called an attribution for behavior (Jones, 1990). Our inference of the motives and traits of others through the observation of their behavior is called the **attribution process.** We now focus on attribution theory, or the processes by which people draw conclusions about the factors that influence one another's behavior.

Attribution theory is very important, because our attributions lead us to perceive others either as purposeful actors or as victims of circumstances.

Dispositional and Situational Attributions. Social psychologists describe two types of attributions—dispositional attributions and situational attributions. In making **dispositional attributions,** we ascribe a person's behavior to internal factors, such as personality traits and free will. In making **situational attributions,** we attribute a person's actions to external factors such as social influence or socialization.

The Fundamental Attribution Error. We have a tendency to attribute too much of other people's behavior to internal factors such as choice. This bias in the attribution process is what social psychologists refer to as the **fundamental attribution error.** Apparently, when we observe the behavior of others, we focus excessively on their actions and too little on the contexts within which their actions take place. But we do tend to be more aware of the networks of forces acting on ourselves.

One reason for the fundamental attribution error is that we tend to infer traits from behavior. When we overhear a woman screaming at her husband in a supermarket, we tend to assume that she is impulsive and boisterous. We are usually not aware of the many things that her husband might have done to infuriate her.

Recency effect The tendency to evaluate others in terms of the most recent impression.

Attribution A belief concerning why people behave in a certain way.

Attribution process The process by which people draw inferences about the motives and traits of others.

Dispositional attribution An assumption that a person's behavior is determined by internal causes such as personal attitudes or goals.

Situational attribution An assumption that a person's behavior is determined by external circumstances such as the social pressure found in a situation.

Fundamental attribution error The tendency to assume that others act predominantly on the basis of their dispositions, even when there is evidence suggesting the importance of their situations.

The Actor–Observer Effect. Who is at fault here? When parents and teenagers argue about the teenagers' choice of friends or dates, the parents tend to perceive the teenagers as stubborn and independent. But the children may perceive their parents as bossy and controlling. Parents and children alike make dispositional attributions for each others' behavior. But the parents and teenagers both tend to see their own behavior as being motivated by situational factors. Teenagers often see themselves as being caught between peer pressures and parental restrictiveness. Parents, on the other hand, tend to see themselves as being forced to act out of love, and fear for what might happen to, their impetuous children.

The fundamental attribution error is linked to another bias in the attribution process: the actor–observer effect.

The Actor–Observer Effect. When we see ourselves and others engaging in behavior that we do not like, we tend to see the others as willful actors but to perceive ourselves as victims of circumstances (Fiske & Taylor, 1984). The tendency to attribute the behavior of others to dispositional factors and our own behavior to situational influences is termed the **actor–observer effect** (Jellison & Green, 1981; Reeder, 1982; Safer, 1980).

Consider an example of the actor–observer effect. When parents and children argue about the children's choice of friends or dates, the parents infer traits from behavior and tend to perceive their children as stubborn, difficult, and independent. The children also infer traits from behavior, and they may perceive their parents as bossy and controlling. Parents and children alike attribute the others' behavior to internal causes. They both make dispositional attributions about other people's behavior, that is.

How do the parents and children perceive themselves? The parents probably see themselves as being forced into combat by their children's foolishness. If they become insistent, it is in response to their children's stubbornness. The children probably see themselves as responding to peer pressures and, perhaps, to sexual urges that may have come from within but do not seem "of their own making." The parents and the children both tend to see their own behavior as being motivated by external factors. That is, they make situational attributions for their own behavior.

It is true that we tend to hold others responsible for their misdeeds but to see ourselves as victims of circumstances when our conduct falls short of our ideals. This bias in the attribution process is referred to as the actor–observer effect.

The actor–observer effect extends to our perceptions of the in-group (an extension of ourselves) and the out-group. Consider conflicts between nations. Both sides may engage in brutal acts of violence. Each side usually considers the other to be calculating, inflexible, and—not infrequently—sinister. Each side also typically views its own people as victims of circumstances and its own violent actions as being vindicated or dictated by the situation. After all, we may look at the other side as being in the wrong, but can we expect the out-group to agree with us?[3]

The Self-Serving Bias. There is also a **self-serving bias** in the attribution process. We are likely to ascribe our successes to internal, dispositional factors but our failures to external, situational influences (Baumgardner et al., 1986; O'Malley & Becker, 1984; Van der Plight & Eiser, 1983). When we have done well on a test or impressed a date, we are likely to credit these outcomes to our intelligence and charm. When we fail, we are likely to ascribe them to bad luck, an unfairly demanding test, or our date's bad mood.

We apparently extend the self-serving bias to others in our perceptions of why we win or lose when we gamble. When we win bets on football games, we tend to attribute our success to the greater ability of the winning team—a

Actor–observer effect The tendency to attribute our own behavior to situational factors but to attribute the behavior of others to dispositional factors.

Self-serving bias The tendency to view one's successes as stemming from internal factors and one's failures as stemming from external factors.

[3] I am not suggesting that all nations are equally blameless (or blameworthy) for their brutality toward other nations. I am merely pointing out that there is a tendency for the people of a nation to perceive themselves as being driven to unwanted behavior. Yet they are also likely to perceive other nations' negative behavior as willful and directed by national dispositions.

dispositional factor (Gilovich, 1983). When we lose our bets, we tend to ascribe the game's outcome to a fluke, such as an error by a referee—to some unforeseeable external factor.

An ironic twist to the self-serving bias is that we tend to see ourselves as less self-centered than others (Rempel et al., 1985).

There are exceptions to the self-serving bias. We are more likely to own up to our responsibility for our failures when we think that other people will not accept situational attributions (Reiss et al., 1981). Depressed people are also more likely than nondepressed people to ascribe their failures to internal factors, even when dispositional attributions are not justified (see Chapter 13).

Another interesting attribution bias is a gender difference in attributions for friendly behavior. Men are more likely than women to interpret a woman's friendliness toward men as flirting (Abbey, 1987). Perhaps gender roles still lead men to expect that "decent" women are passive.

Body Language

Body language is important in our perception of others. Nonverbal behavior can express internal states, such as people's feelings. It can regulate social interactions (Patterson, 1991). People sometimes try to use their body language to deceive other people as to how they really feel (DePaulo, 1992).

At an early age, we learn that the ways people carry themselves provide cues to how they feel and are likely to behave (Saarni, 1990). You may have noticed that when people are "uptight," their bodies may also be rigid and straight-backed. People who are relaxed are more likely, literally, to "hang loose." It seems that various combinations of eye contact, posture, and distance between people provide broadly recognized cues to their moods and feelings toward their companions (Schwartz et al., 1983).

When people face us and lean toward us, we may assume that they like us or are interested in what we are saying. If we are privy to a conversation between a couple and observe that the woman is leaning toward the man, but that the man is sitting back and toying with his hair, we are likely to infer that he is not having any of what she is selling (Clore et al., 1975; DePaulo et al., 1978).

Touching also communicates. Women are more likely than men to touch other people when they are interacting with them (Stier & Hall, 1984). In one touching experiment, Kleinke (1977) showed that appeals for help can be more effective when the distressed person engages in physical contact with people being asked for aid. A woman received more dimes for phone calls when she touched the person she was asking for money on the arm. In another experiment, waitresses received higher tips when they touched patrons on the hand or the shoulder while making change (Crusco & Wetzel, 1984).

Body language can also be used to establish and maintain territorial control (Brown & Altman, 1981), as anyone who has had to step aside because a football player was walking down the hall can testify. Werner and her colleagues (1981) found that players in a game arcade used touching as a way of signaling others to keep their distance. Solo players engaged in more touching than did groups, perhaps because they were surrounded by strangers.

Gazing and Staring: The Eyes Have It. We usually feel that we can learn much from eye contact. When others "look us squarely in the eye," we may assume that they are being assertive or open with us. Avoidance of eye contact may suggest deception or depression. In a study designed to validate a scale to measure romantic love, Rubin (1970) found that couples who attained higher "love scores" also spent more time gazing into each other's eyes. Gazing is interpreted as a sign of liking or friendliness (Kleinke, 1986). In one penetrating study, as a matter of fact, male and female subjects were instructed to gaze into each

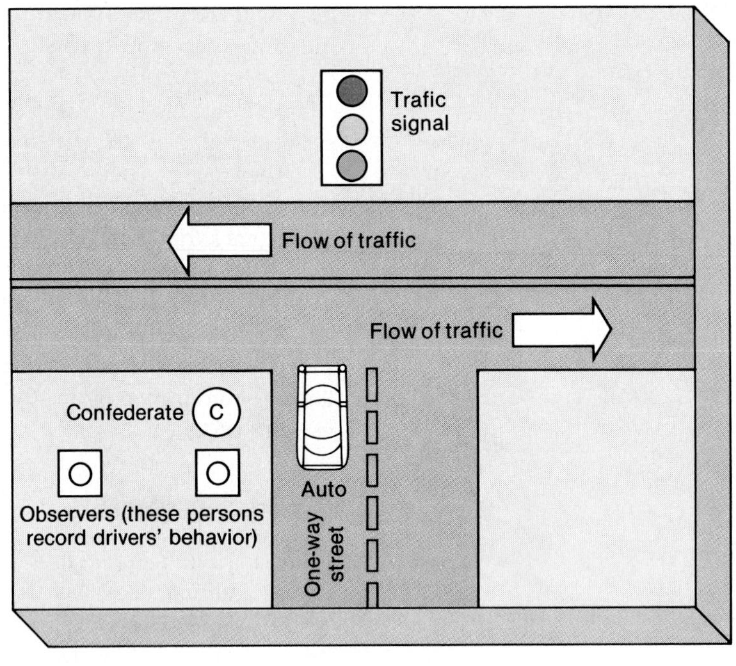

FIGURE 15.1
Diagram of an Experiment in Hard Staring and Avoidance. In the Greenbaum and Rosenfeld study, the confederate of the experimenter stared at some drivers and not at others. Recipients of the stares drove across the intersection more rapidly once the light turned green. Why?

other's eyes for two minutes (Kellerman et al., 1989). Afterward, they reported passionate feelings toward one another! (Watch out.)

Gazes differ, of course, from persistent hard stares. Hard stares are interpreted as provocations or signs of anger (Ellsworth & Langer, 1976). Adolescent males sometimes engage in staring contests as an assertion of dominance. The male who looks away first loses.

In a series of field experiments, Phoebe Ellsworth and her colleagues (1972) subjected drivers stopped at red lights to hard stares from riders of motor scooters (see Figure 15.1). Recipients of the stares crossed the intersection more rapidly than nonrecipients when the light changed. Greenbaum and Rosenfeld (1978) found that recipients of hard stares from a man seated near an intersection also drove off more rapidly after the light turned green. Other research shows that recipients of hard stares show higher levels of physiological arousal than people who do not receive the stares (Strom & Buck, 1979). Did you ever leave a situation in which you were stared at in order to lower feelings of arousal and avoid the threat of danger?

INTERPERSONAL ATTRACTION

Whether we are discussing the science of physics, a pair of magnetic toy dogs, or a couple in a singles bar, **attraction** is a force that draws bodies together. In psychology, attraction is also thought of as a force that draws bodies, or people, together—an attitude of liking or disliking (Berscheid, 1976). Magnetic "kissing" dogs are usually constructed so that the heads attract one another, but (unlike their flesh-and-blood counterparts) a head and tail repel one another. We shall see that when there is a matching of the heads—that is, a meeting of the minds—people are also attracted to one another. And, as with the toy dogs, when we believe that another person's opinions are, well, asinine, we are repelled.

Let us consider some factors that contribute to interpersonal attraction.

Attraction In social psychology, an attitude of liking or disliking.

"Looking Good." Actors Julia Roberts and Mel Gibson are among those who set the standards for beauty in contemporary American culture. How important is physical attractiveness? What are our stereotypes of attractive people? Do we see them as being more successful? As making better spouses and parents?

Physical Attractiveness: How Important Is Looking Good?

You might like to think that we are all so intelligent and sophisticated that we rank physical appearance low on the roster of qualities we seek in a date—below sensitivity and warmth, for example. But in experimental "Coke dates" and computer dates, physical appearance has been found to be the central factor in attraction and consideration of partners for future dates, sexual activity, and marriage (Byrne et al., 1971; Green et al., 1984).

Is Beauty in the Eye of the Beholder? What determines physical allure? Are our standards subjective—that is, "in the eye of the beholder"—or is there agreement on what is appealing?

There may be no universal yardsticks for beauty, but our society has some collective standards. Tallness is an asset for men (Lynn & Shurgot, 1984), although college women favor dates who are medium in height (Graziano et al., 1978). Tall women are beheld less positively (Sheppard & Strathman, 1989). College women prefer their dates to be about six inches taller than they are, whereas college men tend to fancy women who are about 4½ inches shorter (Gillis & Avis, 1980).

Stretch and Candy were tall. Since we tend to connect tallness with social dominance, many women of Candy's height may be concerned that their stature will compromise their femininity. Some fear that shorter men are disinclined to ask them out. A few walk with a hunch, trying to downplay their height.

Plumpness is valued in many cultures. Grandmothers who worry that their granddaughters are starving themselves often come from cultures in which stoutness is acceptable or desirable.[4] In current Western society, both genders find

[4]The other side of the coin, as noted in Chapter 13's discussion of anorexia nervosa, is that some granddaughters *are* literally starving themselves today.

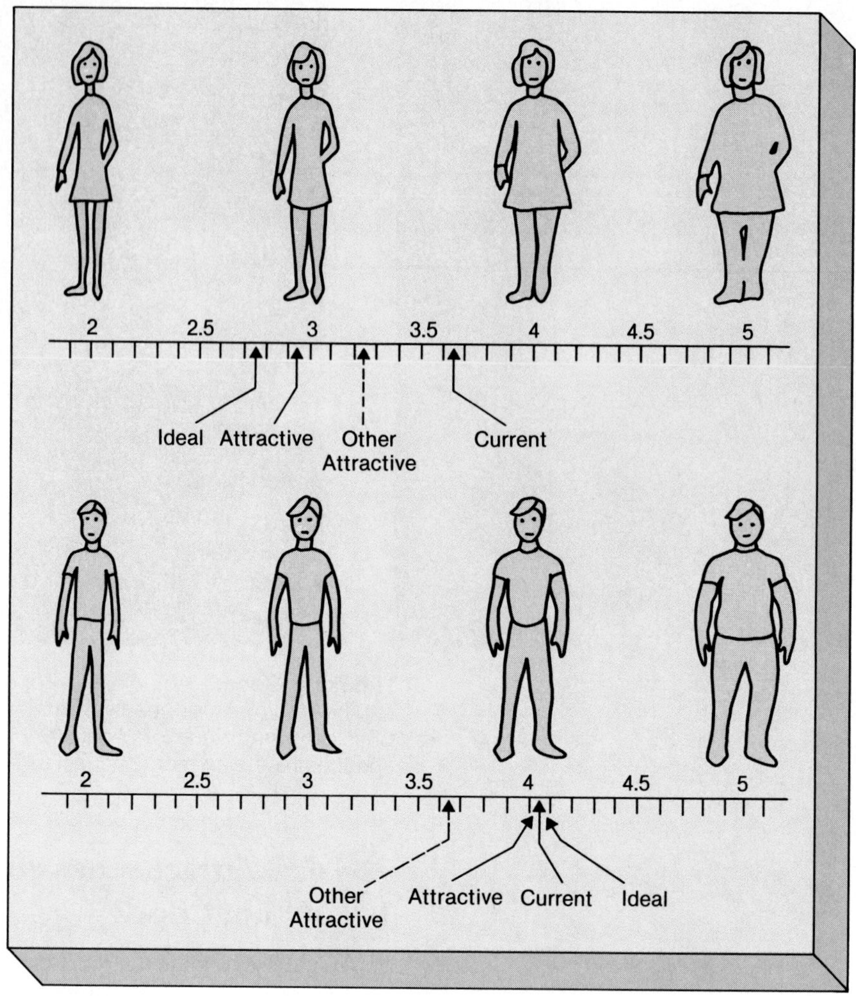

FIGURE 15.2
Can You Ever Be Too Thin? Research suggests that most college women believe that they are heavier than they ought to be. However, men actually prefer women to be a bit heavier than women assume the men would like them to be.

slenderness engaging (Franzoi & Herzog, 1987). Women generally favor men with a V-taper (Horvath, 1981).

It is *not* true that beauty is in the eye of the beholder, despite the familiarity of the adage. There are actually cultural standards for beauty that are adhered to rather strongly.

Although both genders perceive overweight people as unappealing, there are fascinating gender differences in perceptions of desirable body shapes. College men generally find their current physique similar to the ideal male build and to the one that women find most appealing (Fallon & Rozin, 1985). College women, in contrast, generally see themselves as markedly heavier than the figure that is most appealing to men and heavier still than the ideal (see Figure 15.2). Both mothers and fathers of college students see themselves as heavier than their ideal weights (Rozin & Fallon, 1988). Both genders err in their estimates of the other's likes, however. Men of both generations actually prefer women to be heavier than women presume, and women of both generations fancy men who are slimmer than the men imagine.

Beauty Is As Beauty Does. Men and women are both perceived as more attractive when they pose happy faces rather than sad faces (Mueser et al., 1984). There is thus ample reason to, as the song goes, "put on a happy face" when you are meeting people or looking for a date.

It is true that people are perceived as being more attractive when they are smiling.

Other aspects of behavior also affect interpersonal attraction. Women shown videotapes of prospective dates prefer men who act outgoing and self-expressive (Riggio & Wolf, 1984). College men who show dominance (operationally defined as control over a social interaction with a professor) in a videotape are rated as more attractive by women (Sadalla et al., 1987). College men respond negatively to women who show self-assertion and social dominance, however (Riggio & Wolf, 1984; Sadalla et al., 1987). Despite the liberating forces of recent years, the cultural stereotype of the ideal woman still finds a place for demureness. I am not suggesting that self-assertive, expressive women take a back seat to make themselves appealing to traditional men; assertive women might find nothing but conflict with such men anyhow.

Stereotypes of Attractive People: Do Good Things Come in Pretty Packages? By and large, we rate what is beautiful as good. We expect physically attractive people to be poised, sociable, popular, intelligent, mentally healthy, fulfilled, persuasive, and successful in their jobs and marriages (Feingold, 1992). Unattractive people are more likely to be judged as outside of the mainstream—for example, politically radical, homosexual, or mentally ill (Brigham, 1980; O'Grady, 1982; Unger et al., 1982). Unattractive college students are also more apt to rate themselves as susceptible to personal problems.

These stereotypes seem to have some basis in reality. For one thing, attractive people *do* seem less likely to develop psychological disorders, and the disorders of unattractive people are more severe (e.g., Archer & Cash, 1985; Farina et al., 1986; Burns & Farina, 1987). For another, attractiveness correlates positively with popularity, social skills, and sexual experience (Feingold, 1992). The correlations between physical attractiveness and most measures of mental ability and personality are trivial, however (Feingold, 1992).

One way to interpret the data on the correlates of beauty is to assume that they are all innate. In other words, we can believe that beauty and social competence go genetically hand in hand. We can believe that biology is destiny and throw up our hands in despair. Another (more adaptive!) interpretation is that we can do things to make ourselves more attractive and also more successful and fulfilled. Smiling, for example, is linked to attractiveness. So is having a decent physique or figure (which we can work on) and attending to grooming and dress. So don't abandon ship.

Attractive people are also more likely to be judged innocent of crimes in mock jury experiments and observational studies (Michelini & Snodgrass, 1980). When found guilty, they are handed down less severe sentences (Efran, 1974; Stewart, 1980). Perhaps we assume that attractive people have less need to resort to deviant behavior to achieve their goals. Even when they have erred, perhaps they will have more opportunity for personal growth and be more likely to change their evil ways.

The Matching Hypothesis: Who Is "Right" for You? Have you ever refrained from asking out an extremely attractive person for fear of rejection? Do you feel more comfortable when you approach someone who is a bit less attractive?

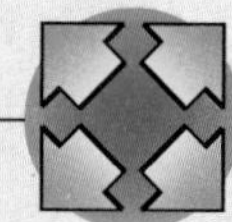

WORLD OF DIVERSITY

*Interracial Relationships: Race, Sex, and Stereotypes**

Interracial relationships remain a controversial issue for U.S. society, despite our passage through the liberal, civil rights era of the 1960s (Kroll et al., 1991). Consider Spike Lee's movie, *Jungle Fever,* as a revisit of Stanley Kramer's *Guess Who's Coming to Dinner?* and the whole issue of interracial sexual pairings and the associated taboos. For those of you who are not movie buffs, both Kramer's and Lee's movies dealt with a romantic relationship between an African-American man and a white woman and its repercussions. The murder of Yusuf Hawkins in Bensonhurst, Brooklyn, is a real-life reflection of the intensity of some of these feelings. Hawkins was killed by a group of white youth because he was mistaken as the African-American boyfriend of one of the local white women living there. "Protecting one's woman" has a long history and in fact serves as a common battle cry for wars (that is, to protect our homes and our women from the enemies).

The psychological dynamics and motivations associated with interracial relationships are extremely complex and diverse. We are dealing with the forces of history, sociology, family dynamics, personal value systems, and sometimes psychopathology. However, there are some stereotypes regarding interracial sexual relationships which we can explore briefly. First of all, Madison Avenue and all of its other manifestations created and maintained the image of the slim, blonde white woman as the epitome of sexual beauty. If you doubt the veracity of this proposition, pause and analyze some of the more sexually-oriented TV commercials the next time you are watching. Alternatively, you can check out the last few swimsuit issues of *Sports Illustrated.* Some minority men buy into these images and will only date white women. Conversely, there is a common stereotype that African-American men have sexual prowess which white men lack. Some white women believe this, or are at least curious enough to cross the invisible racial boundaries. Relatedly, Asian women are particularly attractive to some white men because they are stereotyped as "exotic" and/or "submissive" (Walsh, 1990). Russian and other Eastern European women, on the other hand, are stereotyped as "huge, bear-like, and manly."

What are some of the consequences of these stereotypes? One is that 71 percent of African-American–white

The Matching Hypothesis. Do opposites attract, or do we tend to pair off with people who look and think as we do? As suggested by these photographs, similarity often runs at least skin-deep.

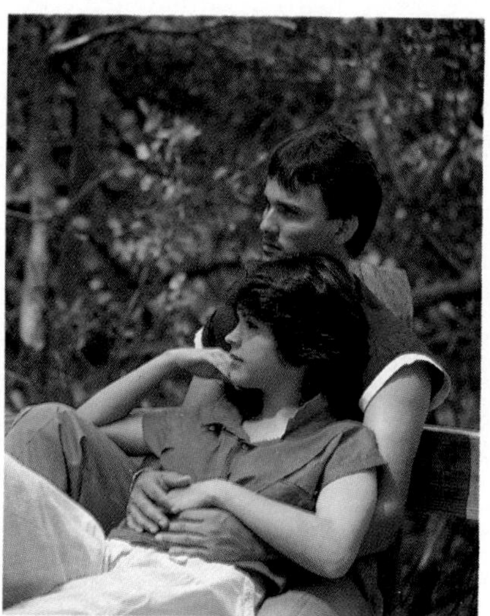

If so, you're not alone. Although we may rate highly attractive people as being most desirable, we will not necessarily be left to blend in with the wallpaper. According to the **matching hypothesis,** we tend to ask out people who are similar to ourselves in physical attractiveness rather than the local Mel Gibson or Julia Roberts look-alike. The central motive for asking out "matches" seems to be fear of rejection by more attractive people (Bernstein et al., 1983).

The matching hypothesis does not apply to physical appeal only. We are also more likely to get married to people who are similar to us in their psychological needs (Meyer & Pepper, 1977), personality traits (Buss, 1984; Caspi & Herbener, 1990; Lesnik-Oberstein & Cohen, 1984), and attitudes.

Matching hypothesis The view that people tend to choose persons similar to themselves in attractiveness and attitudes in the formation of interpersonal relationships.

marriages in the United States are between African-American men and white women, whereas only 29 percent are between white men and African-American women (Kroll et al., 1991). Apparently, Madison Avenue is succeeding in its campaign. However, the pattern is reversed with Asian Americans. A review of the marriage record in San Francisco County revealed that "four times as many Asian women as Asian men married whites" (Walsh, 1990). What might account for this reversal? If white women represent the epitome of sexual beauty, why are there not more Asian men who marry white women than the reverse? Any ideas?

Shinagawa (cited in Walsh, 1990), an Ethnic Studies professor at University of California at Berkeley, has one theory. He maintains that "hiergamy" is responsible for some of this pattern of "outmarriage" (that is, marrying into another racial group) and interracial relationships. According to Shinagawa, hiergamy is the process whereby individuals use marriage to maximize their status opportunities in a society that is stratified by race, class, and gender—namely, marriage as a means of upward mobility. Yet, Shinagawa's notion of hiergamy accounts for only part of the pattern; otherwise, there would be as many African-American women who marry white men as there are African-American men who marry white women. If upward mobility is the main process, and presumably both Asian men and Asian women have the same level of aspirations, then just as many Asian men should be marrying whites as Asian women, but that is not true.

Perhaps sexual stereotypes are also operating. For example, white women are stereotyped as the epitome of beauty and sexuality for African-American men, whereas African-American women lack this stereotype to attract white men. Conversely, Asian women are stereotyped as exotic and submissive, whereas Asian men lack any alluring stereotype for white women. If we assume that popular images are reflections of stereotypes, then Asian women are represented by the "Suzy Wongs" and "Saigon Sallys," whereas Asian men are represented by the "Charlie Chans" and the "Fu Manchus."

What is your theory?

*This guest feature was written by Frederick T. L. Leong, Ph.D., of the Department of Psychology at The Ohio State University.

Attitudinal Similarity: Do "Opposites Attract" or Do "Birds of a Feather Flock Together"?

Do "opposites attract," or are "birds of a feather" more likely to "flock together"? The weight of psychological research suggests that attitudinal similarity buttresses friendships and love relationships (Griffin & Sparks, 1990; Park & Flink, 1989). Candy and Stretch's physical attraction motivated them to pretend that their preferences, tastes, and opinions coincided. They made a tacit agreement not to discuss their religious differences. Attitudes toward religion and children are more important in mate selection than characteristics like kindness and professional status (e.g., Buss & Barnes, 1986; Howard et al., 1987).

We also tend to *assume* that alluring people share our attitudes (Dawes, 1989; Marks et al., 1981). Is this wish fulfillment? When sexual attraction is strong, as with Candy and Stretch, perhaps we want to think that the kinks in the relationship will be small or that we can iron them out. Similarly, we tend to assume that our presidential choices share our political views (Brent & Granberg, 1982). We may even forget public statements that conflict with our views (Johnson & Judd, 1983). Then, once they are in office, we may be disillusioned when they swerve from our expectations.

Reciprocity: If You Like Me, You Must Have Excellent Judgment

Has anyone told you how good-looking, brilliant, and mature you are? That your taste is refined? That all in all, you are really something special? If so, have you been impressed by his or her fine judgment?

Reciprocity is also an extremely powerful determinant of attraction (Condon & Crano, 1988). When we feel admired and complimented, we tend to return these feelings and behaviors. We tend to be more open, warm, and helpful when we are interacting with strangers who seem to like us (Clark et al., 1989; Curtis & Miller, 1986). Men tend to be attracted to women who engage them in conversation, maintain eye contact, and lean toward them while speaking, even when their attitudes are dissimilar (Gold et al., 1984).

Now that we have seen how our feelings of attraction are influenced by physical attractiveness, attitudinal similarity, and so on, let us consider the psychology of social influence.

SOCIAL INFLUENCE

Most of us would be reluctant to wear blue jeans to a funeral, to walk naked on city streets, or, for that matter, to wear clothes at a nudist colony. Other people and groups can exert enormous pressure on us to behave according to their wishes or according to group norms. **Social influence** is the area of social psychology that studies the ways in which people alter the thoughts, feelings, and behavior of others. We already learned how attitudes can be changed through persuasion. We also know a good deal about the ways in which people try to manipulate one another. For example, we are more likely to use "charm" to elicit desired behavior than to suppress behavior, and we are more likely to use force or the "silent treatment" to discourage unwanted behavior (Buss et al., 1987). In this section, we shall describe a couple of classic experiments to show various ways in which people influence others to engage in destructive obedience and conform to social norms.

Obedience to Authority

Richard Nixon resigned the presidency of the United States in August, 1974. For two years, the business of the nation had almost ground to a halt while Congress investigated the 1972 burglary of a Democratic party campaign office in the Watergate office and apartment complex. It turned out that Nixon supporters had authorized the break-in. Nixon himself might have been involved in the cover-up of this connection later on. For two years, Nixon and his aides had been investigated by the press and by Congress. Now it was over. Some of the bad guys were thrown in jail. Nixon was exiled to the beaches of southern California. The nation returned to work. The new president, Gerald Ford, declared, "Our national nightmare is over."

But was it over? Have we come to grips with the implications of the Watergate affair?

According to the late Stanley Milgram ((*APA Monitor,* January 1978), a Yale University psychologist, the Watergate cover-up, like the Nazi slaughter of the Jews, was made possible through the compliance of people who were more concerned about the approval of their supervisors than about their own morality. Otherwise they would have refused to abet these crimes. The broad question is: How pressing is the need to obey authority figures at all costs?

Reciprocity In interpersonal attraction, the tendency to return feelings and attitudes that are expressed about us.

Social influence The area of social psychology that studies the ways in which people influence the thoughts, feelings, and behavior of others.

The Milgram Studies: Shocking Stuff at Yale

Stanley Milgram also wondered how many of us would resist authority figures who made immoral requests. To find out, he ran a series of experiments at Yale University. In an early phase of his work, Milgram (1963) placed ads in New Haven newspapers for subjects for studies on learning and memory. He enlisted 40 men

FIGURE 15.3
The "Aggression Machine." In the Milgram studies on obedience to authority, pressing levers on the "aggression machine" was the operational definition of aggression.

ranging in age from 20 to 50—teachers, engineers, laborers, salespeople, men who had not completed elementary school, men with graduate degrees. The sample was a cross-section of the male population of this Connecticut city.

Let us suppose you had answered an ad. You would have shown up at the university for a fee of $4.50, for the sake of science and your own curiosity. You might have been impressed. After all, Yale was a venerable institution that dominated the city. You would not have been less impressed by the elegant labs where you would have met a distinguished behavioral scientist dressed in a white laboratory coat and another newspaper recruit—like you. The scientist would have explained that the purpose of the experiment was to study the *effects of punishment on learning.* The experiment would require a "teacher" and a "learner." By chance you would be appointed the teacher and the other recruit the learner.

You, the scientist, and the learner would enter a laboratory room with a rather threatening-looking chair with dangling straps. The scientist would secure the learner's cooperation and strap him in. The learner would express some concern, but this was, after all, for the sake of science. And this was Yale University, was it not? What could happen to a person at Yale?

You would follow the scientist to an adjacent room from which you would do your "teaching." This teaching promised to be effective. You would punish the learner's errors by pressing levers marked from 15 to 450 volts on a fearsome-looking console (see Figure 15.3). Labels described 28 of the 30 levers as running the gamut from "Slight Shock" to "Danger: Severe Shock." The last two levers resembled a film unfit for anyone under age 17: They were rated "XXX." Just in case you had no idea what electric shock felt like, the scientist gave you a sample 45-volt shock. It stung. You pitied the fellow who might receive more.

Your learner was expected to learn word pairs. Pairs of words would be read from a list. After hearing the list once, the learner would have to produce the word that was paired with the stimulus word. He would do so by pressing a switch that would signify his choice from a list of four alternatives. The switch would light one of four panels in your room. If it was the correct panel, you would proceed to the next stimulus word. If not, you would deliver an electric shock. With each error, you would increase the voltage of the shock (Figure 15.4).

FIGURE 15.4
The Experimental Set-Up in the Milgram Studies. When the "learner" makes an error, the experimenter prods the "teacher" to deliver a painful electric shock.

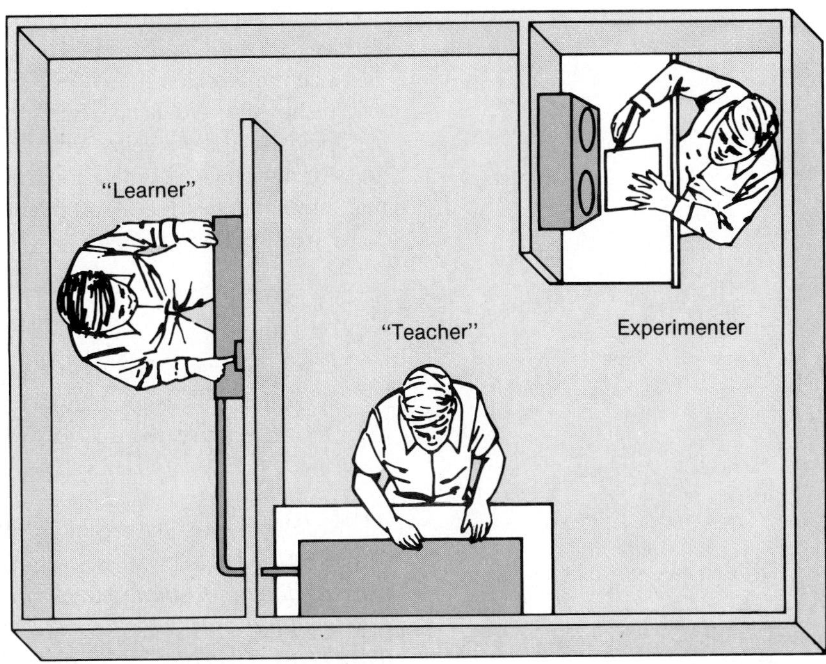

You would probably have some misgivings. Electrodes had been strapped to the learner's wrists, and the scientist had applied electrode paste to "avoid blisters and burns." You were also told that the shocks would cause "no permanent tissue damage," although they might be extremely painful. Still, the learner was going along, and after all, this was Yale.

The learner answered some items correctly and then made some errors. With mild concern you pressed the levers up through 45 volts. You had tolerated that much yourself. Then a few more mistakes were made. You pressed the 60-volt lever, then 75. The learner made another mistake. You paused and looked at the scientist. He was reassuring: "Although the shocks may be painful, there is no permanent tissue damage, so please go on." Further errors were made, and quickly you were up to a shock of 300 volts. But now the learner was pounding on the other side of the wall! Your chest tightened and you began to perspire. Damn science and the $4.50, you thought. You hesitated and the scientist said, "The experiment requires that you continue." After the delivery of the next stimulus word, there was no answer at all. What were you to do? "Wait for five to ten seconds," the scientist instructed, "and then treat no answer as a wrong answer." But after the next shock, there was again that pounding on the wall! Now your heart was racing and you were convinced that you were causing extreme pain and discomfort. Was it possible that no lasting damage was being done? Was the experiment that important, after all? What to do? You hesitated again. The scientist said, "It is absolutely essential that you continue." His voice was very convincing. "You have no other choice," he said, "you *must* go on." You could barely think straight, and for some unaccountable reason you felt laughter rising in your throat. Your finger shook above the lever. What were you to do?

On Truth at Yale. Milgram (1963, 1974) found out what most people would do. Of the 40 men in this phase of his research, only 5 refused to go beyond the 300-volt level, at which the learner first pounded the wall. Nine more "teachers" defied the scientist within the 300-volt range. But 65 percent of the participants complied with the scientist throughout the series, believing that they were delivering 450-volt, XXX-rated shocks.

Were these newspaper recruits simply unfeeling? Not at all. Milgram was impressed by their signs of stress. They trembled, they stuttered, they bit their lips. They groaned, they sweated, they dug their fingernails into their flesh. There were fits of laughter, though laughter was inappropriate. One salesperson's laughter was so convulsive that he could not continue with the experiment.

Milgram wondered if college students, heralded for independent thinking, would show more defiance. But a replication of the study with Yale undergraduates yielded similar results. What about women, who were supposedly less aggressive than men? Women, too, shocked the learners—and all this in a nation that values independence and the free will of the individual. Our "national nightmare" may not be over at all.

It is *not* true that most people would refuse to deliver distressing electric shocks to an innocent party. When they are under strong social pressure, the majority will deliver such shocks.

Nor should we take too much comfort in the finding that a minority of individuals refused to follow the experimenter's orders. *Not one teacher attempted to extricate the unfortunate learner from the experiment. Not one teacher barged into the administrative offices at Yale and demanded that they investigate and put an end to the experiment* (Ross, 1988).

On Deception at Yale. You are probably skeptical enough to wonder whether the teachers in the Milgram study actually shocked the learners when they pressed the levers on the console. They didn't. The only real shock in this experiment was the 45-volt sample given to the teachers. Its purpose was to lend credibility to the procedure.

The learners in the experiment were actually confederates of the experimenter. They had not answered the newspaper ads but were in on the truth from the start. Teachers were the only real subjects. They were led to believe that they were chosen at random for the teacher role, but the choosing was rigged so that newspaper recruits would always become teachers.

As you can imagine, many psychologists have questioned the ethics of deceiving participants in the Milgram studies. Psychologists use deception only when research could not be run without it and when they believe that the benefits of the research outweigh potential harm (see Chapter 2). Regardless of the propriety of Milgram's research, we must acknowledge that it has highlighted some hard truths about human nature.

The Big Question: Why? We have shown that most people obey the commands of others, even when pressed to perform immoral tasks. But we have not answered the most pressing question: *Why?* Why did Germans "just follow orders" and commit atrocities? Why did "teachers" obey orders from the experimenter? We do not have all the answers, but we can offer a number of hypotheses:

1. *Socialization.* Despite the expressed American ideal of independence, we are socialized to obey others (such as parents and teachers) from the time we are little children.
2. *Lack of social comparison.* In Milgram's experimental settings, experimenters showed command of the situation, whereas teachers (subjects) were on the experimenter's ground and very much on their own. Being on their own, they did not have the opportunity to compare their ideas and feelings with those of people in the same situation. They were thus less likely to have a clear impression of what to do.
3. *Perception of legitimate authority.* The phase of Milgram's research just described took place within the hallowed halls of Yale University. Subjects there might have been overpowered by the reputation and authority of the setting. An experimenter at Yale might have appeared to be very much the legitimate authority figure—as might a government official or a high-ranking officer in the military. Further research showed that the university setting contributed to compliance but was not fully responsible for it. The percentage of subjects complying with the experimenter's demands dropped from 65 percent to 48 percent when Milgram (1974) replicated the study in a dingy storefront in a nearby town. In the less prestigious setting, slightly fewer than half the subjects were willing to administer the highest levels of shock. At first glance, this finding might seem encouraging. But the main point of the Milgram studies is precisely that most of us remain willing to engage in morally reprehensible acts at the behest of a legitimate-looking authority figure. Hitler and his henchmen were very much the legitimate authority figures in Nazi Germany. Nixon was very much the authority figure in the White House of the early 1970s. "Science" and Yale University legitimized the authority of the experimenters in the Milgram studies. The problem of acquiescence to authority figures remains.
4. *The foot-in-the-door technique.* The foot-in-the-door technique might also have contributed to the obedience of the teachers (Gilbert, 1981). That is, after they had begun the process of delivering graduated shocks to learners, perhaps they found it progressively more difficult to extricate themselves from the project. Soldiers, similarly, are first taught to obey unquestioningly in innocuous matters such as dress and drill. By the time they are ordered to risk

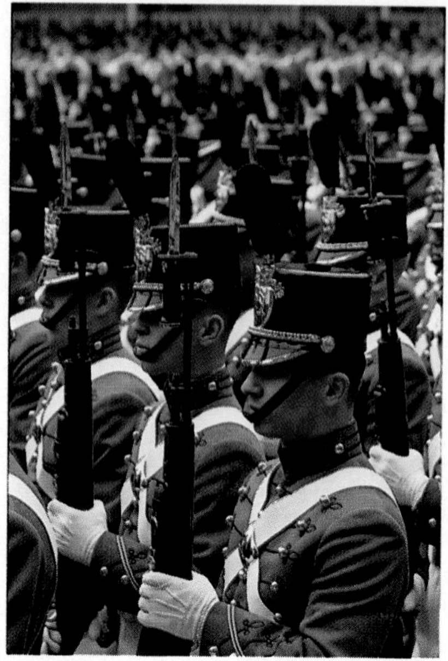

Conformity. In the military, individuals are taught to conform until the group functions in machine-like fashion. What pressures toward conformity do you experience? From whom? Do you accede to them? Are you aware of doing so?

their lives, they have been saluting smartly and following commands for quite some time.

5. *Inaccessibility of values.* People are more likely to act in accord with their attitudes when their attitudes are readily available, or accessible. Most people believe that it is wrong to harm innocent people. But as the subjects in the Milgram experiments became more and more aroused, their attitudes might have become less accessible. As a consequence, it might have become progressively more difficult for them to behave in ways that were consistent with them.
6. *Buffers.* Several buffers decreased the effect of the learners' suffering on the teachers. Learners (confederates of the experimenter), for example, were in another room. When they were in the same room with teachers—that is, when subjects had full view of their victims—the compliance rate dropped from 65 to 40 percent (Miller, 1986). Moreover, when the subject was given the duty of holding the learner's hand on the shock plate, the compliance rate dropped to 30 percent. In modern warfare, opposing soldiers tend to be separated by great distances. It is one thing to press a button to launch a missile or to aim a piece of artillery at a distant troop carrier or a distant ridge. It is another to hold the weapon to the victim's throat.

There are thus numerous theoretical explanations for obedience. Regardless of the exact nature of the forces that acted on the subjects in the Milgram studies, Milgram's research has alerted us to a real and present danger—the tendency of most people to obey an authority figure even when the figure's demands contradict the person's own moral attitudes and values. It has happened before. Unhappily, unless we remain alert, it may happen again. Who are the authority figures in your life? How do you think you would have behaved if you had been a teacher in the Milgram studies? Are you sure?

In the section on conformity, we describe another classic study, and you may again try to imagine how you would behave if you were involved in it.

Conformity

We are said to **conform** when we change our behavior to adhere to social norms. **Social norms** are widely accepted rules that indicate how we are expected to behave under certain circumstances (Moscovici, 1985). Rules that require us to whisper in libraries and to slow down when driving past a school are examples of explicit social norms. Other social norms are unspoken, or implicit (Zuckerman et al., 1983). One unspoken social norm is to face front in elevators. Another is to be fashionably late for social gatherings.

It is true that many people are late to social gatherings because they are conforming to a social norm—in this case, the norm of "fashionable lateness."

The tendency to conform to social norms is often a good thing. Many norms have evolved because they favor comfort and survival. Group pressure can also promote maladaptive behavior, however, as in the group pressure to wear coats and ties during summer in buildings cooled only to, say, 78 degrees Fahrenheit. At that high temperature, the only motive for conforming to a dress code may be to show that we have been adequately socialized and are not threats to social rules.

Let us look at a classic experiment on conformity run by Solomon Asch in the early 1950s. We shall then examine factors that promote conformity.

Conform To changes one's attitudes or overt behavior to adhere to social norms.

Social norms Explicit and implicit rules that reflect social expectations and influence the ways people behave in social situations.

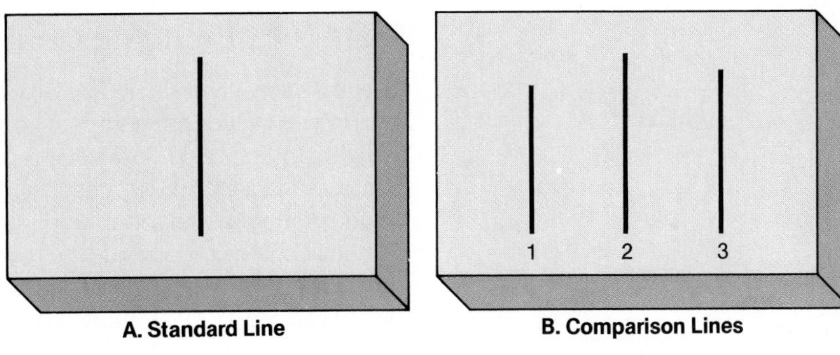

FIGURE 15.5
Cards Used in the Asch Study on Conformity. Which line on card B—1, 2, or 3— is the same length as the line on card A? Line 2, right? But would you say "2" if you were a member of a group and six people answering ahead of you all said "3"? Are you sure?

Seven Line Judges Can't Be Wrong: The Asch Study

Do you believe what you see with your own eyes? Seeing is believing, is it not? Not if you were a participant in the Asch (1952) study.

You would enter a laboratory room with seven other subjects for an experiment on visual discrimination. If you were familiar with psychology experiments, you might be surprised: There were no rats and no electric-shock apparatus in sight, only a man at the front of a room with some cards with lines drawn on them.

The eight of you would be seated in a series. You would be given the seventh seat, a minor fact at the time. The man would explain the task. There was a single line on the card on the left. Three lines were drawn on the card at the right (Figure 15.5). One line was the same length as the line on the other card. You and the other subjects need only call out, one at a time, which of the three lines—1, 2, or 3—was the same length. Simple.

You would try it out. Those to your right spoke out in order: "3," "3," "3," "3," "3," "3." Now it was your turn. Line 3 was clearly the same length as the line on the first card, so you said "3." The fellow after you then chimed in: "3." That's all there was to it. Two other cards were then set up in the front of the room. This time line 2 was clearly the same length as the line on the first card. The answers: "2," "2," "2," "2," "2," "2." Your turn again: "2," you said, and perhaps your mind began to wander. Your stomach was gurgling a bit. That night you would not even mind dorm food particularly. The fellow after you said, "2."

Another pair of cards was held up. Line 3 was clearly the correct answer. The six people on your right spoke in turn: "1," "1 . . ." Wait a second! ". . . 1," "1—" You forgot about dinner and studied the lines briefly. No, 1 was too short, by a good half an inch. But ". . . 1," "1," and suddenly it was your turn. Your hands had quickly become sweaty and there was a lump in your throat. You wanted to say 3, but was it right? There was really no time and you had already paused noticeably: "1," you said, "1," the last fellow confirmed matter-of-factly.

Now your attention was riveted on the chore. Much of the time you agreed with the other seven line judges, but sometimes you did not. And for some reason beyond your understanding, they were in perfect agreement, even when they were wrong—assuming that you could trust your eyes. The experiment was becoming an uncomfortable experience, and you began to doubt your judgment.

The discomfort in the Asch study was caused by the pressure to conform. Actually, the other seven recruits were confederates of the experimenter. They prearranged a number of incorrect responses. The sole purpose of the study was to see whether you would conform to the erroneous group judgments.

How many of Asch's subjects caved in? How many went along with the crowd rather than assert what they thought to be the right answer? Seventy-five percent. *Three of four agreed with the majority wrong answer at least once.*

What about you? Would you wear blue jeans if everyone else wore slacks and skirts?

Factors Influencing Conformity

Several personal and situational factors prompt conformity to social norms. Personal factors include the desires to be liked by other members of the group and to be right (Insko, 1985), low self-esteem, high self-consciousness, social shyness (Santee & Maslach, 1982), gender, and familiarity with the job. Situational factors include group size and social support.

Situational factors include the number of people who hold the majority opinion and the presence of at least one other person who shares the discrepant opinion. Likelihood of conformity, even to incorrect group judgments, increases rapidly as a group grows to five members, then rises more slowly to about eight members (Tanford & Penrod, 1984). At about that point, the maximum chance of conformity is reached.

Finding just one other person who supports your minority opinion is apparently enough to encourage you to stick to your guns (Morris et al., 1977). In a variation of the Asch experiment, recruits were provided with just one confederate who agreed with their minority judgments (Allen & Levine, 1971). Even though this confederate seemed to have a visual impairment, as evidenced by thick glasses, his support was sufficient to lead actual subjects not to conform to incorrect majority opinions.

A final note: It has been shown that people who value being right more than being liked by others are less likely to conform to group pressure (Insko et al., 1985). Which is more important to you?

Studies in conformity highlight some of the ways in which we are influenced by groups. In the following section, we discuss other aspects of group behavior.

GROUP BEHAVIOR

To be human is to belong to groups. Groups help us satisfy the needs for affection, attention, and belonging (Robbins, 1989). They empower us to do things we could not manage by ourselves. Families, classes, religious groups, political parties, nations, circles of friends, bowling teams, sailing clubs, conversation groups, therapy groups—to how many groups do you belong? How do groups influence the behavior of individuals?

In this section, we look at a number of aspects of group behavior: social facilitation, group decision making, mob behavior, and the bystander effect.

Social Facilitation

One effect of groups on individual behavior is **social facilitation,** or the effects on performance that result from the presence of others. Bicycle riders and runners tend to move more rapidly when they are members of a group. This effect is not limited to humans: Dogs and cats eat more rapidly when others are present. Even roaches—yes, roaches—run more rapidly when other roaches are present (Zajonc, 1980).

According to Robert Zajonc (1980), the presence of others influences us by increasing our levels of arousal, or motivation. When our levels of arousal are highly increased, our performance of simple, dominant responses is facilitated. Our performance of complex, recently acquired responses may be impaired, however. For this reason, a well-rehearsed speech may be delivered more masterfully before a larger audience, but an offhand speech or a question-and-answer session may be hampered by a large audience.

Social facilitation may be influenced by **evaluation apprehension** as well as level of arousal (Bray & Sugarman, 1980; Sanna & Shotland, 1990). Our performance before a group is not only affected by the presence of others, but also by

Social facilitation The process by which a person's performance is increased when other members of a group engage in similar behavior.

Evaluation apprehension Concern that others are evaluating our behavior.

Social Facilitation. Runners tend to move more rapidly when they are members of a group. Does the presence of others raise our levels of arousal or give rise to evaluation apprehension?

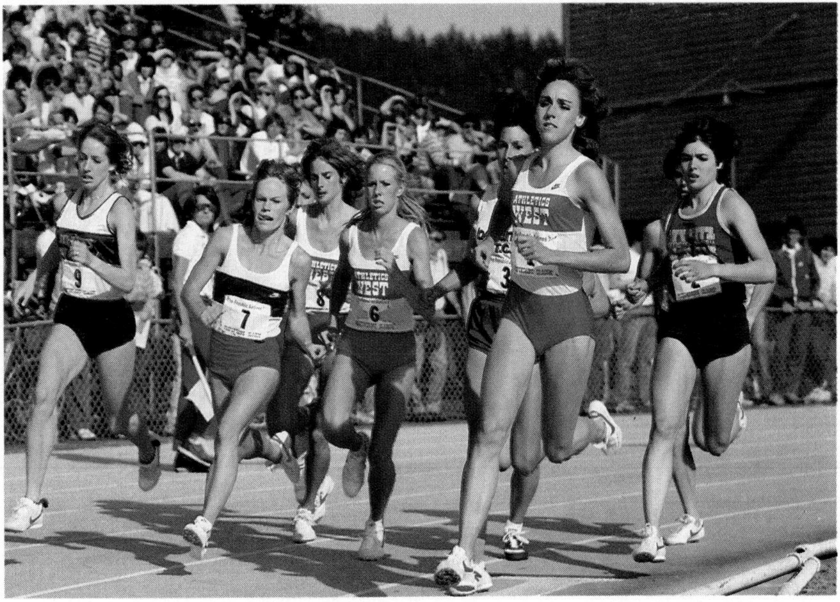

concern that they are evaluating us. When giving a speech, we may "lose our thread" if we are distracted by the audience and focus too much on their apparent reactions to us (Seta, 1982). If we believe that we have begun to flounder, evaluation apprehension may skyrocket. As a result, our performance may falter further.

The presence of others can also impair performance—not when we are acting *before* a group, but when we are anonymous members *of* a group (Harkins, 1987; Latané et al., 1979). Workers, for example, may "goof off" or engage in "social loafing" on humdrum jobs when they believe that they will not be found out and held accountable. There is then no evaluation apprehension. There may also be **diffusion of responsibility** in groups. Each person may feel less obligation to help because others are present. Group members may also reduce their efforts if an apparently capable member makes no contribution but "rides free" on the efforts of others (Kerr, 1983).

Group Decision-Making

In 1986 and 1987, President Ronald Reagan's popularity took a drubbing when it was alleged that he had authorized the sale of American weapons to Iran to try to gain the release of American hostages being held by pro-Iranian groups in Lebanon. This occurred at a time when the American public was very hostile toward Iran. Reagan had also sworn he would never negotiate with terrorists and had branded Iran a "terrorist nation." The decision to trade weapons for hostages apparently resulted from heated discussions in the White House during which the secretaries of state and defense took one position and the national security adviser took another position.

How do group decisions get made? Social psychologists have discovered a number of "rules," or **social decision schemes,** that govern much of group decision making (Davis et al., 1984; Kerr & MacCoun, 1985; Stasser et al., 1989). Note some examples:

1. *The majority-wins scheme.* In this commonly used scheme, the group arrives at the decision that was initially supported by the majority. This scheme appears to guide decision making most often when there is no objectively correct decision. An example would be a decision about which car models to build when their popularity has not been tested in the "court" of public opinion.

Diffusion of responsibility The spreading or sharing of responsibility for a decision or behavior within a group.

Social decision schemes Rules for predicting the final outcome of group decision-making on the basis of the members' initial positions.

2. *The truth-wins scheme.* In this scheme, as more information is provided and opinions are discussed, the group comes to recognize that one approach is objectively correct. For example, a group deciding whether to use SAT scores in admitting students to college would profit from information about whether these scores actually predict college success.
3. *The two-thirds majority scheme.* This scheme is frequently adopted by juries, who tend to convict defendants when two-thirds of the jury initially favors conviction.
4. *The first-shift rule.* In this scheme, the group tends to adopt the decision that reflects the first shift in opinion expressed by any group member. If a car-manufacturing group is equally divided on whether or not to produce a convertible, it may opt to do so after one group member initially opposed to the idea changes her mind. If a jury is deadlocked, the members may eventually follow the lead of the first juror to switch his position.

Now let us consider whether group members are likely to make compromise decisions or to take relatively extreme viewpoints as a result of diverse initial positions.

Polarization and the Risky Shift

We might think that a group decision would be more conservative than an individual decision. After all, shouldn't there be an effort to compromise, to "split the differences"? We might also expect that a few mature individuals would be able to balance the opinions of daredevils. Groups do not generally seem to work in these ways, however.

Consider the **polarization** effect. As an individual, you might recommend that your company risk $500,000 to develop or market a new product. Other company executives, polled individually, might risk similar amounts. If you were gathered for a group decision, however, you would probably recommend either an amount well above this figure or nothing at all (Burnstein, 1983). This group effect is called polarization, or the taking of an extreme position. If you had to gamble on which way the decision would go, however, you would do better to place your money on movement toward the higher sum—that is, to bet on a **risky shift.** Why?

One possibility is that a group member may reveal information the others had not been aware of and that this information clearly points in one direction or the other. With doubts removed, the group becomes polarized, moving decidedly in the appropriate direction. It may also be that social facilitation occurs in the group setting and that increased motivation prompts more extreme decisions.

Why, however, do groups tend to take greater, not smaller, risks than those that would be ventured by their members as individuals? One answer is diffusion of responsibility (Burnstein, 1983; Myers, 1983). If the venture flops, it will not be you alone to blame. Remember the self-serving bias: You can always say (and tell yourself) that the failure was, after all, a group decision. If the venture pays off handsomely, on the other hand, you can attribute the outcome to your cool analysis and trumpet abroad your influential role in the group decision-making process.

It is not true that group decisions are conservative. Group decisions actually tend to be riskier than the average decision that would be made by each group member acting as an individual—probably because of diffusion of responsibility.

Polarization In social psychology, taking an extreme position or attitude on an issue.

Risky shift The tendency to make riskier decisions as a member of a group than as an individual acting independently.

Groupthink

A problem that sometimes arises in group-decision making is called **groupthink.** Groupthink is usually instigated by a dynamic group leader. As noted by the originator of the term, Irving Janis (1982), groupthink is usually unrealistic and fueled by the perception of external threats to the group or to those the group wishes to protect. The perception of external threat heightens group cohesiveness and serves as a source of stress. When under stress, group members tend not to consider all their options carefully (Keinan, 1987). Flawed decisions are therefore a common outcome.

Baron and Byrne (1991) attribute a number of historic mistakes to groupthink such as President Kennedy's decision to support the Bay of Pigs invasion of Cuba, the illegal cover-up of a break-in to Democratic campaign headquarters we refer to as the Watergate affair, and NASA's decision to launch the *Challenger* space shuttle despite engineers' warnings that low ambient temperatures might make the launching hazardous. The Iran–Contra affair of the mid-1980s, which made Colonel Oliver North a household phrase, offers another example. Five characteristics of groupthink are noted by Janis to play roles in such flawed group decisions:

1. *Feelings of invulnerability.* Each decision-making group might have believed that it was beyond the reach of critics or the law—in some cases, because the groups consisted of powerful individuals close to the president of the United States.
2. *Group belief in its rightness.* These groups apparently believed in the rightness of what they were doing. In some cases, the groups were carrying out the president's wishes. In the case of the *Challenger* launch, NASA had a track record of nearly unblemished success.
3. *The discrediting of information opposed to the group's decision.* At the time that Oliver North's group decided to divert funds from (secret) sales of arms to Iran to the Contras, it was illegal for the U.S. government to do so. The group apparently discredited the law by (1) deciding that it was inconsistent with the best interests of the United States and (2) enlisting private citizens to divert profits from sales to the Contras so that the U.S. government was not directly involved.
4. *Pressures on group members to conform.* Groupthink pressures group members to conform (McCauley, 1989). Pressure to conform can lead to **deindividuation,** a state of reduced self-awareness and lowered concern for social evaluation (Mann et al., 1982). Many factors lead to deindividuation, including anonymity, diffusion of responsibility, arousal due to noise and crowding (Zimbardo, 1969), and focus of individual attention on the group process (Diener, 1980).
5. *Stereotyping of members of the outgroup.* Oliver North's group reportedly stereotyped persons who would oppose them as communist "sympathizers"; "knee-jerk liberals"; and, in the case of the Congress that had made helping the contras illegal, "slow-acting," "vacillating" (i.e., voting to aid the contras in one bill and prohibiting aid to the contras in another), and "irresolute."

Groupthink can be averted when group leaders encourage group members to remain skeptical about options and to feel free to ask probing questions and disagree with other members.

Groupthink A process in which group members are influenced by cohesiveness and a dynamic leader to ignore external realities as they make decisions.

Deindividuation The process by which group members may discontinue self-evaluation and adopt group norms and attitudes.

Altruism and the Bystander Effect: Some Watch While Others Die

In 1964, the nation was shocked by the murder of 28-year-old Kitty Genovese in New York City. Murder was not unheard of in the Big Apple, but Kitty had screamed for help as her killer had repeatedly stabbed her. Nearly 40 neighbors heard the commotion. Many watched. Nobody helped. Why? As a nation, are we a callous bunch who would rather watch than help when others are in trouble? Since the murder, more than 1,000 books and articles have been written attempting to explain the behavior of bystanders in crises (Dowd, 1984). According to Stanley Milgram, the Genovese case "touched on a fundamental issue of the human condition. If we need help, will those around us stand around and let us be destroyed or will they come to our aid?" (Dowd, 1984).

Whom Do You Help? Psychologists have dressed the same person in different ways in experiments to determine how appearance influences our decisions to help others.

It is true that some 40 people stood by and did nothing while a woman was being stabbed to death. Their failure to come to her aid has been termed the *bystander effect.*

What factors determine whether we help others who are in trouble?

The Helper: Who Helps? Some theorists (e.g., Hoffman, 1981; Rushton, 1989) suggest that **altruism** is a part of human nature. In keeping with sociobiological theory, they argue that self-sacrifice sometimes helps close relatives or others who are similar to us to survive. Ironically, self-sacrifice is selfish from a genetic point of view: It helps us perpetuate a genetic code similar to our own.

Most psychologists focus on the roles of a helper's mood and personality traits. By and large, we are more likely to help others when we are in a good mood (Berkowitz, 1987; Manucia et al., 1984), perhaps because good moods impart a sense of personal power (Cunningham et al., 1990). We may help others when we are miserable ourselves, however, if our own problems work to increase our empathy or sensitivity to the plights of others (Thompson et al., 1980). People with a high need for approval may help others to earn social approval (Satow, 1975). People who are empathic, who can take the perspective of others, are also likely to help (Batson et al., 1989).

There are many reasons why bystanders are reluctant to aid people in distress. First, bystanders may not fully understand what they are seeing and fail to recognize that an emergency exists. The more ambiguous the situation, that is, the less likely bystanders are to help (Shotland & Heinold, 1985). Second, the presence of others may lead to diffusion of responsibility, so that no one assumes responsibility for helping. Third, bystanders who are not certain that they possess the competencies to take charge of the situation may stay on the sidelines for fear of making a social blunder and being subject to ridicule (Pantin & Carver, 1982)—or for fear of getting hurt themselves.

Bystanders who believe that others get what they deserve may rationalize not helping by thinking that a person would not be in trouble unless this outcome was just (Lerner et al., 1975). A sense of personal responsibility increases the likelihood of helping. Such responsibility may stem from having made a verbal commitment to help (e.g., Moriarty, 1975) or from having been designated by others as being responsible for carrying out a helping chore (Maruyama et al., 1982).

The Victim: Who Is Helped? Although gender roles have been changing, it is traditional for men to help women in our society. Women are more likely than men to receive help, especially from men, when they dropped coins in Atlanta (a southern city) than in Seattle or Columbus (northern cities) (Latané & Dabbs, 1975). The researchers suggest that traditional gender roles persevere more strongly in the South.

Women are also more likely than men to be helped when their cars have broken down on the highway or they are hitchhiking (Pomazal & Clore, 1973). There

Altruism Unselfish concern for the welfare of others.

may be sexual overtones to some of this "altruism." Attractive and unaccompanied women are most likely to be helped by men (Benson et al., 1976; Snyder et al., 1974).

As in the research on interpersonal attraction, similarity also seems to promote helping behavior. Poorly dressed people are more likely to succeed in requests for a dime with poorly dressed strangers, and well-dressed people are more likely to get money from well-dressed strangers (Hensley, 1981).

Situational Determinants of Helping: "Am I the Only One Here?" It may seem logical that a group of people would be more likely to have come to the aid of Kitty Genovese than a lone person. After all, a group could more effectively have overpowered her attacker. Research by Darley and Latané (1968) suggests that a lone person may have been more likely to try to help her, however.

In their classic experiment, male subjects were performing meaningless tasks in cubicles when they heard a (convincing) recording of a person apparently having an epileptic seizure. When the subjects thought that four other persons were immediately available to help, only 31 percent made an effort to help the victim. When they thought that no one else was available, however, 85 percent of them tried to offer aid. As in other areas of group behavior, it seems that diffusion of responsibility inhibits helping behavior in groups or crowds. When we are in a group, we are often willing to let George (or Georgette) do it. When George isn't around, we are more willing to help others ourselves.

Note that in most studies on the bystander effect, the bystanders are strangers (Latané & Nida, 1981). Research shows that bystanders who are acquainted with victims are more likely to respond to the social norm of helping others in need (Rutkowski et al., 1983). Aren't we also more likely to give to charity when asked directly by a co-worker or supervisor in the socially exposed situation of the office as compared to a letter received in the privacy of our own homes?

We are more likely to help when we understand what is happening (for instance, if we clearly see that the woman whose car has broken down is alone), when the environment is familiar (when we are in our home town rather than a strange city), and when we have the competencies. Registered nurses, for example, are likely to come to the aid of accident victims (Cramer et al., 1988).

Altruism and the bystander effect highlight the fact that we are members of a vast, interdependent social fabric. The next time you see a stranger who is in need of help, what will you do? Are you sure?

STUDY GUIDE

EXERCISE: Matching Concepts and Examples

In the first column are a number of concepts in social psychology. In the second column are instances of behavior that serve as examples of these concepts. Match the example with the appropriate concept by writing the letter of the example in the blank space to the left of the concept. Answers are given below.

CONCEPT

_____ 1. Prejudice
_____ 2. Bystander effect
_____ 3. Cognitive dissonance
_____ 4. Discrimination
_____ 5. Conformity
_____ 6. Dispositional attribution
_____ 7. Emotional appeal
_____ 8. Foot-in-the-door technique
_____ 9. Matching hypothesis
_____ 10. Nonbalance
_____ 11. Primacy effect
_____ 12. Evaluation apprehension
_____ 13. Effort justification
_____ 14. Risky shift
_____ 15. Situational attribution
_____ 16. Deindividuation
_____ 17. Diffusion of responsibility
_____ 18. Fundamental attribution error
_____ 19. The first-shift rule
_____ 20. Buffer
_____ 21. Inaccessibility of attitudes
_____ 22. A–B problem
_____ 23. Groupthink

EXAMPLES

A. A person assumes that someone who bumped into him did so on purpose.
B. A man does not ask a beautiful woman out for fear of rejection.
C. A committee takes a greater gamble than any member would take acting alone.
D. A person asks a small favor to prepare someone to grant a larger favor later.
E. A new worker is late and the boss conceptualizes him as "a late person."
F. John blames his mood on the weather.
G. A person does not come to the aid of a crime because many people surround the victim.
H. A man changes his beliefs after he is coerced into attitude-discrepant behavior.
I. A mob member adopts the norms of the crowd.
J. A person is paid too little for his work and begins to think that his work has high intrinsic value because of the low pay.
K. A student wears blue jeans because "everyone" is wearing them.
L. An athlete runs faster because he is concerned that fellow racers are aware of his performance.
M. A man assumes that a woman will not be assertive in the business world.
N. The man in item M, above, chooses not to hire a woman.
O. A dentist shows photos of diseased gums to convince patients to improve their oral hygiene.
P. Jim disagrees with Joan, but Joan doesn't care because she is indifferent toward Jim.
Q. A group with a dynamic leader ignores the evidence and makes foolish decisions.
R. A person becomes so aroused as a member of a mob that he completely forgets his personal moral values.
S. A psychologist cannot predict a voter's behavior because the voter's political beliefs are very generalized.
T. A "teacher" in the Milgram study shocks the "learner" because the learner is out of sight, behind a wall.
U. A deadlocked jury votes to convict a defendant after one person who had previously thought the defendant not guilty changes his mind.

Answers to Matching Exercise

1. M
2. G
3. H, J
4. N
5. K
6. A
7. O
8. D
9. B
10. P
11. E
12. L
13. J
14. C
15. F
16. I
17. G
18. A
19. U
20. T
21. R
22. S
23. Q

ESL—BRIDGING THE GAP

This part is divided into

1. cultural references
2. phrases and expresssions in which words are used differently from their regular meaning, or are used as metaphors.

Cultural References

blue jeans (579)—the most common, universal and informal clothing in the U.S. culture

preppy sweaters (579)—sweaters that are often thought to be worn by people who have been educated in "prep" schools (private and expensive high schools) and "ivy league" colleges (specific private and expensive colleges in the northeast part of the U.S.)

frizzies (579)—split ends in the hair

college appreciation course (580)—college music appreciation course

pop tune (580)—popular music (as opposed to classical music)

Chrysler or General Motors . . . Toyotas and Hondas (581)—manufacturers of automobiles

Peter Jennings . . . Tom Brokaw . . . Dan Rather (581)—news commentators on the three primary network news broadcasting systems

Szechuan tidbits, the nouveau Fresno film, the disco party (581)—special Chinese food, the new and important movie, the party at the discoteque; (an impressive evening of entertainment)

signing petitions (582)—requests by citizens to other citizens that they sign their names on a piece of paper which has on it a statement about an issue; this "petition" would indicate that those people who signed want the government to act in a particular manner about that issue

voting booth (585)—the designated area of privacy where a person casts his or her vote (votes)

The King and I (588)—a musical comedy popular in the 1950s

defense attorneys (588)—the lawyers responsible for defending the accused person in a court of law

jury (588)—a group of citizens selected to make judgments as to the innocence or responsibility of a defendant in a court of law

curfew (588)—the time when the person is supposed to be home

Mel Gibson or Julia Roberts (593)—current movie stars

Madison Avenue (596)—the advertising industry

Suzy Wongs, Charlie Chans, and Fu Manchus (597)—stereotyped Asian characters in American movies

dorm food (603)—food available in the college dormitory cafeteria as opposed to food in a restaurant or home

car model (605)—each car manufacturer makes several different styles of cars each year and then chooses the most popular ones to manufacture and sell

SAT scores (606)—Scholastic Aptitude Test scores

Big Apple (607)—a nickname (short and affectionate name) for New York City

Atlanta . . . Seattle or Columbus . . . the South (608)—The south (east) is a geographical area in the U.S. which has specific characteristics. The people tend to be more conservative than in some other areas (but this is a generalization); Atlanta is in the state of Georgia; Seattle is in the state of Washington which is in the northwest; Columbus is in the state of Ohio which is in the midwest (north)

our home town (609)—the town (small city) where a person was born and lived when he or she was a child and maybe as an adult too

Phrases and Expressions (Different Usage)

hurts sales (574)—has a negative effect on selling the product; the product won't sell well

take others to task (574)—criticize others

falls short of our ideals (574)—is not what we think it should be

Beauty is in the eye of the beholder (574)—A person is beautiful because another person believes it

social norm (574)—what is normal for the culture

doubles as (574)—also has the function of being

make conversation (576)—talk to each other for the purpose of getting to know each other, not to give information or to solve problems

been around (577)—had a very active social life; known a lot of people of the opposite sex

thus begins a relationship (577)—And the relationship begins.

turning the other off (577)—saying or doing something that will cause the other person to not be interested anymore

narrow-minded (577)—believe that their religion is the only true religion

If the truth be known (577)—If you want to know the truth

tangled web of deception (577)—confusing situation in which each person is deceiving the other
ever after? (577)—forever?
makes much difference (578)—will cause changes in what the government does (both the Democrats and the Republicans will act in the same way)
"get out the vote" (578)—encourage people to vote
media blitzes (578)—a great number of advertisements very close together on radio, TV, and in the newspapers
It does . . . little good (578)—politicians may have supporters, but if the supporters don't vote, their "support" does not help them
by keeping them under the table (578)—by not discussing them; by not acknowledging that they have different attitudes
go their separate ways (578)—part; not see each other anymore
somehow un-American (579)—they are not respecting the American ideals, but it is not clear how they are not
cognitive anchors (579)—cognitive bases
mold the ways (579)—create the ways
So do (579)—Also, the . . . ads do that
familiarity breeds content, not contempt (580)—The expression is "familiarity breeds contempt", which means that we become bored or indifferent with what we know very well.
grisly films (581)—terrible, horrible, bloody films
vested interests (581)—the beliefs a person has which he or she has for selfish reasons
prick up our ears (581)—listen in a very interested manner
homely models? (581)—ugly or unattractive models
spongelike (581)—like a sponge (a "sponge" is a material which absorbs liquid)
tube feeds them (581)—is on the television
by buttering you up (581)—by flattering you; by telling you wonderful things about yourself, which may or may not be true for an ulterior purpose or to persuade you to say or do something
a sip of wine (581)—a small drink of wine
tail end of a date (581)—the last few minutes of a date
wine that was sold at its time (581)—wine that was sold at the time when the taste is the best
enrich the lives of every door-to-door salesperson (582)—always buy something from salespeople who come to the home (and thus help them to live better)
get you off the hook (582)—you will not be asked or required to do anything else
mount a campaign (582)—begin a campaign
Giving an inch . . . to go for a yard (582)—If you give or do a little, the other people expect you to give or do a lot more
wrecking crew (582)—people whose job it is to destroy a building
primed for (582)—prepared for
and stick to your guns (582)—and not change your mind; not waiver
it works the other way (583)—it is also the reverse
leaves us (583)—causes us to be
to sweep it under the rug (583)—to hide it
not have a chance to win (584)—cannot win (emphatic)
despite lopsided polls to the contrary (584)—even though the answers to the questions that had been distributed (polls) did not indicate that the candidate would win
a prescription for totalitarianism (584)—a plan which indicates how to establish totalitarianism
falling for (585)—believing
charitable donation (587)—an amount of money that a person gives to a charity (an organization which helps people in trouble
"airheads" (587)—not intelligent, or people who don't think a lot
boorish (588)—awkward and clumsy; not socially skilled
was a cad forever (588)—would always be socially unskilled
make or break us (588)—establish us as wonderful or establish us as unattractive and awful
an exception to a rule (588)—not part of our real character or personality
to "make up for it" (588)—to compensate for it; to create a better image
to take precedence (589)—to be what we think of; to be more important
snap judgments (589)—opinions that a person forms quickly and without thinking
networks of forces acting on ourselves (589)—pressures that affect us
as being forced into combat (590)—having to argue, disagree and disapprove
"of their own making" (590)—to be their responsibility
to a fluke (591)—to an accidental incident that appears unrelated to the actual outcome
ironic twist (591)—an outcome that you did not expect
"uptight" (591)—tense and worried
"hang loose" (591)—be flexible and not worry
privy to a conversation (591)—overhear a conversation; hear a conversation that is between others that we are not involved in
toying with his hair (591)—playing with his hair
is not having any of what she is selling (591)—does not want what she has to offer; is not interested in her
hard stares (592)—unrelenting stares
that is, a meeting of the minds (592)—that is, when two people have similar opinions and ideas; when they agree
a hunch (593)—their backs bent forward a little
fancy men (595)—like men
outside of the mainstream (595)—not among the accepted groups in the society; separate from most people

go hand in hand (595)—coincide in the same person
throw up our hands in despair (595)—not care about changing or improving ourselves anymore
So don't abandon ship (596)—Therefore don't stop trying to change or improve; continue to try
you're not alone (596)—you're not the only person who feels that way
left to blend in with the wallpaper (596)—be on a less equal basis with
look-alike (596)—imitation
movie buffs (596)—fans who know a lot about movies
kinks in a relationship (597)—disagreements and unresolved issues
of being ironed out (597)—reconciled; made "smooth" (without flaws)
swerve from our expectations (597)—do not do what we expect
ground to a halt (598)—stopped
break-in (598)—use of force to enter a locked building
cover-up (598)—concealment
come to grips with (598)—tried to understand
for the sake of science (599)—because you wanted to help science
running the gamut (599)—being all degrees
Fearsome looking console (599)—a console, or cabinet, that is intimidating
having some misgivings (600)—think that maybe it wasn't a good idea
What to do? (600)—You thought, "What should I do?"
What were you to do? (600)—You thought, "What should I do?"
Not at all (600)—No, that was not true (emphatic)
barged into (600)—went into, quickly and with anger
were in on (600)—knew
hard truths (601)—unfortunate facts
experimenter's ground (601)—the experiment's territory
on their own (601)—alone
dingy storefront (601)—small, unpainted, unrepaired and unoccupied store (did not have a business in it)
at the behest of (603)—at the request of; for someone else, because someone wants us to
gurgling a bit (603)—making hunger noises
was riveted on the chore (603)—directed at the task
trust your eyes (603)—trust what you were seeing
caved in? (603)—stopped participating in the experiment
went along with (603)—continued to do what everyone was expecting him or her to do
What about you? (603)—What would you do?
offhand speech (604)—informal, not practiced speech
"lose our thread" (605)—forget what we planned to say next
have begun to flounder (605)—have become disorganized or confused
"goof off" (605)—not work when they should be working
"rides free" (605)—obtain credit for what other members of the group have done
took a drubbing (605)—decreased a lot
first shift in opinion (606)—first change in opinion
changes her mind (606)—expresses a different opinion from the one previously expressed
daredevils (606)—reckless people
fueled by (607)—caused and maintained by
"knee-jerk liberals" (607)—people whose political positions are not based on analysis of facts but who have automatic reactions of sympathy for the underdog (person without job, food, and shelter)
a callous bunch (608)—an unfeeling group of people
". . . come to our aid?" (608)—help us?
stay on the sidelines (608)—stay on the side
making a social blunder (608)—doing something that would be socially wrong
subject to ridicule (608)—be the recipient of ridicule

CHAPTER REVIEW

SECTION 1: Introduction

Objective 1: Define *social psychology*.

Social psychology is the study of the nature and causes of our behavior and (1) m__________ processes in (2) __________al situations.

SECTION 2: Attitudes

Objective 2: Define *attitude* and explain what is meant by the A–B problem.

Attitudes can be defined as enduring mental (3) __________ations of people, places, or things that evoke feelings and influence (4) __________vior. When we are free to do as we wish, our behavior (5: is or is not?) most often consistent with our attitudes. According to the (6) A__________ problem, the link between attitudes and behavior tends to be weak. Factors that influence the predictability of behavior from attitudes include the attitudes' specificity and strength, whether people have a (7) v__________ed interest in the outcome of behavior based on their attitudes, and the (8) __________ility of the attitudes.

Objective 3: Discuss the origins of attitudes.

Attitudes may be acquired through conditioning, observational learning, and (9) cog__________ appraisal. Attitudes toward national groups can be influenced by (10) ________ing them with positive or negative words. Parents often (11) re________ children for doing or saying things that are consistent with their own attitudes. We also acquire attitudes by observing friends and the mass media. Early attitudes tend to serve as cognitive (12) ________ors; we judge later points of view in terms of how much they (13) d________ from the first set.

Objective 4: Discuss ways in which attitudes may be changed by means of persuasion.

Petty and Cacioppo have devised the (14) ________tion ________hood model for understanding the processes by which people examine the information in persuasive messages. According to this view, there are central and (15) ________ral routes to persuading others to change attitudes. That is, there are two ways of responding to, or (16) ________ting, persuasive messages. The (17) ________ral route views elaboration and possible attitudinal change as resulting from conscientious consideration of arguments and evidence. The (18) ________ral route involves elaboration of the objects of attitudes by associating them with positive or negative cues.

Repeated messages generally "sell" (19: better or worse?) than messages delivered once. (20) Two-________d arguments, in which the communicator recounts the arguments of the opposition in order to (21) re________ them, can be especially effective when the audience is at first uncertain about its position. People tend to show greater response to (22) e________al appeals than to purely factual presentations, especially when emotional appeals offer concrete advice for avoiding negative consequences. Audiences also tend to believe arguments that appear to (23: be in agreement with, or run counter to?) the personal interests of the communicator.

Persuasive communicators tend to show (24) ex________, trustworthiness, attractiveness, or (25) ________ity to the audience. People show selective avoidance of and selective (26) ex________ to communicators. They avoid communicators whose messages (27: agree or disagree?) with their own attitudes. They seek communicators whose outlooks (28: agree or disagree?) with their own. People are more readily persuaded when they are in a (29: good or bad?) mood. People who are easily persuaded frequently show (30: high or low?) self-esteem and (31: high or low?) social anxiety. They also tend (32: to be, or not to be?) highly concerned with what the persuader might think of them if they fail to comply.

According to the (33) ________-in-the-door effect, people are more likely to accede to large requests after they have acceded to smaller requests. Perhaps initial compliance causes them to view themselves as people who help under these sorts of circumstances.

Objective 5: Discuss the roles of balance theory and cognitive dissonance in changing attitudes.

According to (34) b________ theory, we are motivated to maintain harmony among our perceptions, beliefs, and attitudes. When people we care about express attitudes that differ from ours, we are in an uncomfortable state of (35) ________ance, and we are motivated to try to restore the balance. When we are disinterested in people who disagree with us, we are said to be in a state of (36) ________ance.

According to (37) cog________-________ theory, which is similar to balance theory, people dislike inconsistency between their attitudes and their behavior. Behavior that is (38) att________-________pant apparently induces cognitive dissonance, which people can then reduce by changing their attitudes. People also engage in effort (39) ________tion; that is, people tend to justify (40)________tude-dis________ behavior to themselves by concluding that their attitudes might differ from what they thought they were.

Objective 6: Define *prejudice* and discuss the origins of prejudice.

Prejudice is an (41) at________ toward a group. Prejudice can involve negative (42) ev________tion, negative affect; avoidance behavior; and denial of access to privileges, which is termed (43) ________nation. A (44) ________type is a fixed, conventional idea about a group that can lead us to make certain assumptions about group members we have not met.

Sources of prejudice include attitudinal (45: similarity or dissimilarity?). We tend to assume that members of outgroups hold attitudes that are (46: similar or dissimilar?) to our own. Other sources may include social and (47) ec_______________ conflict; an authoritarian society in which minority group members serve as (48) _______________goats; social learning from parents; and the tendency to divide the social world into two categories: "us" and "them." We also tend to assume that members of out-groups are (49: more or less?) similar to one another in their attitudes than are the members of our own in-groups.

SECTION 3: Social Perception.

Objective 7: Explain the primacy and recency effects on social perception.

The psychology of social (50) _______________tion concerns our perception of others. We often perceive others in terms of first impressions; this is an example of the (51) _______________cy effect. In a classic experiment on the primacy effect, (52) L_______________ had subjects read different stories about "Jim." However, fading memories sometimes allow more recent information to take precedence; this is the so-called (53) _______________cy effect.

Objective 8: Differentiate between dispositional and situational attributions, and explain the biases that are found in the attribution process.

Our inference of the motives and traits of others through the observation of their behavior is called the (54) _______________tion process. When we make dispositional attributions, we attribute people's behavior to (55: internal or external?) factors, such as their personality traits and decisions. When we make (56) _______________nal attributions, we attribute people's behavior to their circumstances or external forces.

Certain biases operate in the attribution (57) _______________ss. The so-called (58) _______________tal attribution error is the tendency to attribute too much of other people's behavior to dispositional factors. Another is the (59) actor–_______________er effect. According to the actor–observer effect, we tend to attribute the behavior of others to internal, (60) _______________nal factors, whereas we tend to attribute our own behavior to external, (61) _______________nal factors. According to the (62) self-_______________ing bias, we are more likely to ascribe our successes to internal, dispositional factors but our failures to external, (63) _______________nal influences.

Objective 9: Explain the role of body language in social perception.

At an early age we learn to "read" body language. People who feel (64: positively or negatively?) toward one another tend to position themselves close together and to touch. Women are (65: more or less?) likely than men to touch other people when they are interacting with them. Waitresses in one study received (66: higher or lower?) tips when they touched patrons on the hand or the shoulder while making change. Gazing into another's eyes can be a sign of love, but a so-called (67) h_______________ stare is an aversive challenge.

SECTION 4: Interpersonal Attraction

Objective 10: Discuss factors that contribute to interpersonal attraction.

In social psychology, (68) _______________tion has been defined as an attitude of liking (positive attraction) or disliking. In our culture, (69: obesity or slenderness?) is found attractive in both men and women, and tallness is valued in (70: men or women?). Women generally see themselves as (71: slimmer or heavier?) than the figure that is attractive to most males. Men actually prefer women to be somewhat (72: slimmer or heavier?) than women expect. Women prefer men to be somewhat (73: slimmer or heavier?) than men expect. We tend to find the same people (74: more or less?) attractive when they are smiling. Socially dominant college men are rated as being (75: attractive or unattractive) by college women. Assertive college women (76: are or are not) rated as being attractive by most college men.

We are more attracted to good-looking people. We tend to assume that attractive people are (77: more or less?) likely to be talented and (78: more or less?) likely to engage in criminal behavior. (79: Attractive or Unattractive?) college students are more likely to rate themselves as prone toward developing problems and psychological disorders. According to the (80) _______________ing hypothesis, we tend to seek dates and mates at our own level of attractiveness. The matching tendency seems to be motivated largely by fear of (81) _______________tion.

We are (82: more or less?) attracted to people who share our attitudes.

SECTION 5: Social Influence

Objective 11: Describe the Milgram studies on obedience to authority, and discuss factors that contribute to obedience.

Social (83) in_______________ is the area of social psychology that studies the ways in which people alter the thoughts, feelings, and behavior of others. Areas within the study of social influence include (84) ob_______________ and conformity.

Most people comply with the demands of authority figures, even when these demands seem immoral, as shown in the studies on obedience run by Stanley (85) M_______________ at (86) _______________e University. Of 40 men participating in an early phase of his research, (87) _______________ percent complied with the authority figure's demands all the way up to the highest level of electric shock. It turns out that the only people who received electric shock during Milgram's studies were the (88) "_______________ers."

The following factors appear to have contributed to obedience in the Milgram studies: subjects' history of socialization, lack of (89) _______________al comparison, perception of experimenters as being legitimate (90) _______________ity figures, the (91) foot-in-the-_______________ technique, inaccessibility of values, and the presence of (92) _______________ers that separated "teachers" from their victims.

Objective 12: Describe the Asch studies on conformity, and discuss factors that contribute to conformity.

In Asch's studies of conformity to group pressure, (93) _______________ percent of the subjects agreed with an incorrect majority judgment at least once. People experience increasing pressure to conform to group norms and opinions as groups grow to (94: how many?) _______________ people. (95: Men or Women?) are more likely to conform. The presence of at least (96: how many?) _______________ person(s) who share(s) one's minority view, and familiarity with the tasks at hand, decrease conforming behavior.

SECTION 6: Group Behavior

Objective 13: Discuss factors that contribute to social facilitation and social loafing.

Social (97) _______________tion refers to the effects on performance that result from the presence of others. According to Zajonc, the presence of others influences us by increasing our levels of (98) _______________sal. We may also be concerned that the other people present are evaluating our performance—a phenomenon termed (99) ev_______________ _______________sion. However, Latané and other researchers have found that task performance may decline when we are (100) _______________mous members of a group. This phenomenon is referred to as social (101) _______________ing.

Objective 14: Discuss social-decision schemes in group decision making.

Social psychologists have discovered a number of rules, or (102) so_______________-_______________sion schemes, that seem to govern group decision making. In the (103) _______________-wins scheme, the group arrives at the decision that was initially supported by the majority. In the (104) _______________-wins scheme, the group comes to recognize that one approach is objectively correct as more information is provided and opinions are discussed. The (105) _______________-_______________ds majority scheme is frequently adopted by juries, who tend to convict defendants when two-thirds of the jury initially favors conviction. In the (106) _______________-shift rule, the group tends to adopt the decision that reflects the first shift in opinion expressed by any group member. According to the first-shift rule, a deadlocked jury may eventually follow the lead of the (107) _______________st juror to change his position.

Objective 15: Discuss these factors as they contribute to the group decision-making process: polarization and the risky shift.

A number of phenomena tend to occur during group decision-making processes. One is termed (108) _______________ation, or the taking of extreme positions by group members. Another is the tendency for groups to take (109: more or less?) risky actions than the average group member would take if he or she were acting as an individual. This phenomenon is known as the (110) _______________-_______________ft. Groups may take riskier actions than individual group members would because of diffusion of (111)_______________ility.

Objective 16: Discuss the factors that contribute to groupthink.

Groupthink is usually (112: realistic or unrealistic?) and can lead to flawed decisions. Groupthink is usually instigated by a dynamic group leader. It tends to be fueled by the perception of (113) ______________nal threats to the group or to those the group wishes to protect. The perception of external threat heightens group (114) co______________ness and serves as a source of stress. When under stress, group members (115: tend or tend not?) to weigh carefully all their options.

The following factors contribute to groupthink: feelings of (116: vulnerability or invulnerability?), group belief in its rightness, discrediting of (117) ______________tion opposed to the group's decision, pressures on group members to conform, and stereotyping of members of the (118) out______________. As members of a group, we may experience (119) ______________duation, which is a state of reduced self-awareness and lowered concern for social (120) ev______________tion. Factors that lead to deindividuation include anonymity, (121) ______________sion of responsibility, a high level of (122) ar______________ due to noise and crowding, and focusing of individual attention on the group process.

Objective 17: Discuss the factors that contribute to helping behavior.

Helping behavior is otherwise termed (123) ______________ism. We are more likely to help others when we are in a (124: good or bad?) mood.

Objective 18: Discuss the factors that contribute to the bystander effect.

According to the (125) ______________der effect, people are less likely to aid others in distress when they are members of crowds. A powerful case in point is the tragedy of Kitty (126) Ge______________, who was stabbed to death while some 40 neighbors did nothing to help. One reason for failure to help is that in a crowd there is diffusion of (127) re______________ity. We are more likely to help people in need when we think we are the only one available, when we have a (128: clear or unclear?) view of the situation, and when we (129: are or are not?) afraid that we shall be committing a social blunder.

Answers to Chapter Review

1. Mental
2. Social
3. Representations
4. Behavior
5. Is
6. A–B
7. Vested
8. Accessibility
9. Cognitive
10. Associating (or Pairing)
11. Reinforce (or Reward)
12. Anchors
13. Deviate
14. Elaboration likelihood
15. Peripheral
16. Elaborating
17. Central
18. Peripheral
19. Better
20. Sided
21. Refute
22. Emotional
23. Run counter to
24. Expertise
25. Similarity
26. Exposure
27. Disagree
28. Agree
29. Good
30. Low
31. High
32. To be
33. Foot
34. Balance
35. Imbalance
36. Nonbalance
37. Cognitive-dissonance
38. Attitude-discrepant
39. Justification
40. Attitude-discrepant
41. Attitude
42. Evaluation
43. Discrimination
44. Stereotype
45. Dissimilarity
46. Dissimilar
47. Economic
48. Scapegoats
49. More
50. Perception
51. Primacy
52. Luchins
53. Recency
54. Attribution
55. Internal
56. Situational
57. Process
58. Fundamental
59. Observer
60. Dispositional
61. Situational
62. Serving
63. Situational
64. Positively
65. More
66. Higher
67. Hard
68. Attraction
69. Slenderness
70. Men
71. Heavier
72. Heavier
73. Slimmer
74. More
75. Attractive
76. Are not
77. More
78. Less
79. Unattractive
80. Matching
81. Rejection
82. More
83. Influence
84. Obedience
85. Milgram
86. Yale
87. 65
88. Teachers
89. Social
90. Authority
91. Door
92. Buffers
93. 75
94. Eight
95. Women
96. One
97. Facilitation
98. Arousal
99. Evaluation apprehension
100. Anonymous
101. Loafing
102. Social decision
103. Majority
104. Truth
105. Two-thirds
106. First-shift
107. First
108. Polarization

109. More
110. Risky shift
111. Responsibility
112. Unrealistic
113. External
114. Cohesiveness
115. Tend not
116. Invulnerability
117. Information
118. Outgroup
119. Deindividuation
120. Evaluation
121. Diffusion
122. Arousal
123. Altruism
124. Good
125. Bystander
126. Genovese
127. Responsibility
128. Clear
129. Are not

POSTTEST

1. Which of the following most nearly expresses the relationship between attitudes and behaviors?
   (a) People always behave in ways that are consistent with their attitudes.
   (b) People always change their attitudes so that they are consistent with their behavior.
   (c) There is no relationship between attitudes and behaviors.
   (d) People are likely to act in accord with strong, specific attitudes.

2. Which of the following is a central cue for persuading people to drink Coke or Pepsi?
   (a) Providing information about the taste of the drink.
   (b) Having a rock star deliver a television commercial.
   (c) Showing attractive, slender people drinking the soda.
   (d) Using a person with a fine voice to sell the product.

3. People tend to be easy to persuade when they
   (a) have high self-esteem.
   (b) focus on the needs and feelings of the persuader.
   (c) have low social anxiety.
   (d) focus on their own needs and feelings.

4. Mary and John like one another very much. However, they disagree on their choice of friends. According to the text, Mary and John are each in a state of
   (a) balance.
   (b) dissonance.
   (c) imbalance.
   (d) nonbalance.

5. According to balance theory, we experience indifference when we are in a state of
   (a) imbalance.
   (b) nonbalance.
   (c) balance.
   (d) evaluation apprehension.

6. Which of the following is a concept in cognitive-dissonance theory?
   (a) Diffusion of responsibility
   (b) Evaluation apprehension
   (c) Effort justification
   (d) Imbalance

7. Which of the following sources of prejudice is reflected in the statement that "It is easier to attend to, and remember, instances of behavior that are consistent with our prejudices than it is to reconstruct our mental categories"?
   (a) Assumptions of dissimilarity
   (b) Social conflict
   (c) Authoritarianism
   (d) Information processing

8. One form of behavior that results from prejudice is called
   (a) authoritarianism.
   (b) deindividuation.
   (c) attitude-discrepant behavior.
   (d) discrimination.

9. Which of the following statements reflects a clear dispositional attribution?
   (a) "Something got the best of him."
   (b) "He did what he thought was right."
   (c) "He did it that way because of the weather."
   (d) "He could not refuse the money."

10. Attributing too much of other people's behavior to dispositional factors is called
    (a) the fundamental attribution error.
    (b) the actor-observer effect.
    (c) internalization.
    (d) evaluation apprehension.

11. Which of the following is true about standards for attractiveness in our culture?
    (a) Tallness is an asset for women.
    (b) Women prefer their dates to be about the same height as they are.
    (c) Women prefer their men somewhat heavier than men expect.
    (d) Men prefer their women somewhat heavier than women expect.

12. In their dating practices, people tend to ask out persons who are similar in attractiveness largely because of
    (a) fairness.
    (b) fear of rejection.
    (c) balance theory.
    (d) evaluation apprehension.

13. Important experiments on obedience to authority were carried out by
    (a) Stanley Milgram.
    (b) Solomon Asch.
    (c) Abraham Luchins.
    (d) John Dollard.

14. In the experiments on obedience to authority run at Yale University, who received electric shock?
    (a) Learners
    (b) Teachers
    (c) Experimenters
    (d) Confederates of the experimenters

15. Conformity is defined as
    (a) obedience to authority.
    (b) deindividuation.
    (c) behavior in accordance with social norms.
    (d) diffusion of responsibility.

16. When we are members of a group, we are most likely to engage in social loafing when
    (a) we experience evaluation apprehension.
    (b) our level of arousal increases.
    (c) we are anonymous.
    (d) the leader is an authority figure.

17. When juries are deadlocked, they are most likely to arrive at a verdict by means of the
    (a) two-thirds rule.
    (b) majority-wins scheme.
    (c) first-shift rule.
    (d) truth-wins scheme.

18. Groups are thought to make risky decisions because
    (a) needed information is rarely shared in the group process.
    (b) group members experience evaluation apprehension in regard to other group members.
    (c) strong group leaders tend to have their way.
    (d) responsibility for the decisions is diffused.

19. All of the following appear to lead to deindividuation, with the exception of
    (a) a low level of arousal.
    (b) anonymity.
    (c) diffusion of responsibility.
    (d) focusing of individual attention on the group process.

20. The case of Kitty Genovese illustrates
    (a) cognitive-dissonance theory.
    (b) group decision-making.
    (c) the bystander effect.
    (d) the principle of social loafing.

Answers to Posttest

1. D
2. A
3. B
4. C
5. B
6. C
7. D
8. D
9. B
10. A
11. D
12. B
13. A
14. B
15. C
16. C
17. C
18. D
19. A
20. C

Appendix: Statistics

Imagine that some visitors from outer space arrive outside Madison Square Garden in New York City. Their goal this dark and numbing winter evening is to learn all they can about the inhabitants of planet Earth. They are drawn inside the Garden by lights, shouts, and warmth. The spotlighting inside rivets their attention to a wood-floored arena where the New York Apples are hosting the California Quakes in a briskly contested basketball game.

Our visitors use their sophisticated instruments to take some measurements of the players. Some surprising statistics are sent back to the planet of their origin: It appears that (1) 100 percent of Earthlings are male, and (2) the height of Earthlings ranges from six feet one inch to seven feet two inches.

Statistics is the name given the science concerned with obtaining and organizing numerical measurements or information. Our imagined visitors have sent home some statistics about the sex and size of human beings that are at once accurate and misleading. Although they accurately measured the basketball players, their small **sample** of Earth's **population** was quite distorted. Fortunately for us Earthlings, about half of us are female. And the **range** of heights observed by the aliens, of six feet one to seven feet two, is both restricted and too high. People vary in height by more than one foot and one inch. And our **average** height is not between six one and seven two but a number of inches below.

Psychologists, like our imagined visitors, are vitally concerned with measuring human as well as animal characteristics and traits—not just physical characteristics like sex and height but also psychological traits like intelligence, aggressiveness, anxiety, or self-assertiveness. By observing the central tendencies (averages) and variations in measurements from person to person, psychologists can state that some person is average or above average in intelligence or that another person is less assertive than, say, 60 percent of the population.

But psychologists, unlike our aliens, are careful in their attempts to select a sample that accurately represents the entire population. Professional basketball players do not represent the human species. They are taller, stronger, and more agile than the rest of us, and they make more shaving-cream commercials.

In this appendix, we shall survey some of the statistical methods used by psychologists to draw conclusions about the measurements they take in research activities. First, we shall discuss *descriptive statistics* and learn what types of statements we can make about the height of basketball players and some other human traits. Then, we shall discuss the *normal curve* and learn

Statistics • Numerical facts assembled in such a manner that they provide significant information about measures or scores. (From the Latin word *status*, meaning "standing" or "position.")

Sample • Part of a population.

Population • A complete group from which a sample is selected.

Range • A measure of variability; the distance between extreme measures or scores.

Average • Central tendency of a group of measures, expressed as means, median, and mode.

why basketball players are abnormal—at least in terms of height. We shall explore *correlation coefficients* and provide you with some less-than-shocking news: More intelligent people attain higher grades than less intelligent people. Finally, we shall have a brief look at *inferential statistics* and see why we can be bold enough to say that the difference in height between basketball players and other people is not just a chance accident, or fluke. Basketball players are in fact *statistically significantly* taller than the general population.

Descriptive Statistics

Being told that someone is a "ten" is not very descriptive unless you know something about how possible scores are distributed and how frequently one finds a ten. Fortunately—for tens, if not for the rest of us—one is usually informed that someone is a ten on a scale of one to ten and that ten is the positive end of the scale. If this is not sufficient, one will also be told that tens are few and far between—rather unusual statistical events.

This business of a scale from one to ten is not very scientific, to be sure, but it does suggest something about **descriptive statistics**. We can use descriptive statistics to clarify our understanding of a distribution of scores such as heights, test grades, IQs, or increases or decreases in measures of sexual arousal following the drinking of alcohol. For example, descriptive statistics can help us to determine measures of central tendency, or averages, and to determine how much variability there is in the scores. Being a ten loses some of its charm if the average score is an eleven. Being a ten is more remarkable in a distribution whose scores range from one to ten than in one that ranges from nine to ten.

Let us now examine some of the concerns of descriptive statistics: the *frequency distribution, measures of central tendency* (types of averages), and *measures of variability.*

Descriptive statistics · The branch of statistics that is concerned with providing information about a distribution of scores.

Frequency distribution · An ordered set of data that indicates how frequently scores appear.

The Frequency Distribution. A **frequency distribution** takes scores or items of raw data, puts them into order as from lowest to highest, and groups them according to class intervals. Table A.1 shows the rosters for a recent California Quakes–New York Apples basketball game. The members of each team are listed according to the numbers on their uniforms. Table

Table A.1: Rosters of Quakes versus Apples at New York

California		New York	
2 Callahan	6′-7″	3 Roosevelt	6′-1″
5 Daly	6′-11″	12 Chaffee	6′-5″
6 Chico	6′-2″	13 Baldwin	6′-9″
12 Capistrano	6′-3″	25 Delmar	6′-6″
21 Brentwood	6′-5″	27 Merrick	6′-8″
25 Van Nuys	6′-3″	28 Hewlett	6′-6″
31 Clemente	6′-9″	33 Hollis	6′-9″
32 Whittier	6′-8″	42 Bedford	6′-5″
41 Fernando	7′-2″	43 Coram	6′-2″
43 Watts	6′-9″	45 Hampton	6′-10″
53 Huntington	6′-6″	53 Ardsley	6′-10″

A glance at the rosters for a recent California Quakes–New York Apples basketball game shows you that the heights of the team members, combined, ranged from six feet one inch to seven feet two inches. Are the heights of the team members representative of those of the general male population?

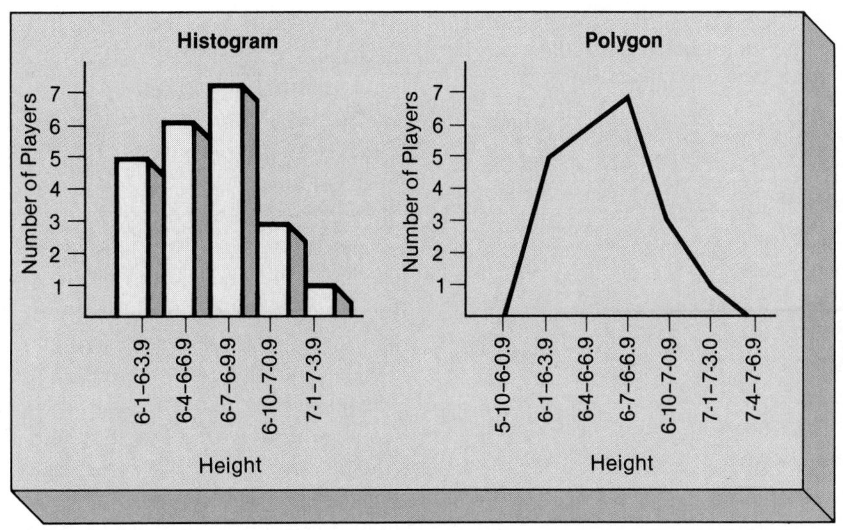

Figure A.1 Two Graphical Representations of the Data in Table A.3

A.2 shows a frequency distribution of the heights of the players of both teams combined, with a class interval of one inch.

It would also be possible to use three-inch class intervals, as in Table A.3. In determining how large a class interval should be, a researcher attempts to collapse that data into a small enough number of classes to ensure that they will appear meaningful at a glance. But the researcher also attempts to maintain a large enough number of categories to ensure that important differences are not obscured.

Table A.3 obscures the fact that no players are six feet four inches tall. If the researcher believes that this information is extremely important, a class interval of one inch may be maintained.

Figure A.1 shows two methods for representing the information in Table A.3 with graphs. Both in frequency **histograms** and frequency **polygons**, the class intervals are typically drawn along the horizontal line, or X-axis, and the number of scores (persons, cases, or events) in each class is drawn along the vertical line, or Y-axis. In a histogram, the number of scores in each class interval is represented by a rectangular solid so that the graph resembles a series of steps. In a polygon, the number of scores in each class interval is plotted as a point, and the points are then connected to form a many-sided geometric figure. Note that class intervals were added at both ends of the horizontal axis of the frequency polygon so that the lines could be brought down to the axis to close the geometric figure.

Histogram • A graphic representation of a frequency distribution that uses rectangular solids. (From the Greek *historia*, meaning "narrative," and *gramma*, meaning "writing" or "drawing.")

Polygon • A closed figure. (From the Greek *polys*, meaning "many," and *gōnia*, meaning "angle.")

Mean • A type of average calculated by dividing the sum of scores by the number of scores. (From the Latin *medius*, meaning "middle.")

Measures of Central Tendency. There are three types of measures of central tendency, or averages: *mean*, *median*, and *mode*. Each tells us something about the way in which the scores in a distribution may be summarized by a typical or representative number.

The **mean** is what most people think of as "the average." The mean is obtained by adding up all the scores in a distribution and then dividing this sum by the number of scores. In the case of our basketball players, it would be advisable first to convert all heights into one unit, such as inches (6′1″ becomes 73″, and so on). If we add all the heights in inches, then divide by the number of players, or 22, we obtain a mean height of 78.73″, or 6′6.73″.

Table A.2: Frequency Distribution of Heights of Basketball Players, with a One-inch Class Interval

Class Interval	Number of Players in Class
6-1 to 6-1.9	1
6-2 to 6-2.9	2
6-3 to 6-3.9	2
6-4 to 6-4.9	0
6-5 to 6-5.9	3
6-6 to 6-6.9	3
6-7 to 6-7.9	1
6-8 to 6-8.9	2
6-9 to 6-9.9	4
6-10 to 6-10.9	2
6-11 to 6-11.9	1
7-0 to 7-0.9	0
7-1 to 7-1.9	0
7-2 to 7-2.9	0

Table A.3: Frequency Distribution of Heights of Basketball Players, with a Three-inch Class Interval

Class Interval	Number of Players in Class
6-1 to 6-3.9	5
6-4 to 6-6.9	6
6-7 to 6-9.9	7
6-10 to 7-0.9	3
7-1 to 7-3.9	1

The **median** is the score of the middle case in a frequency distribution. It is the score beneath which 50 percent of the cases fall. In a distribution with an even number of cases, such as the distribution of the heights of the 22 basketball players in Table A.2, the median is determined by finding the mean of the two middle cases. Listing these 22 cases in ascending order, we find that the eleventh case is 6′6″ and the twelfth case is 6′7″. Thus the median is (6′6″ + 6′7″)/2, or 6′6½″.

In the case of the heights of the basketball players, the mean and the median are similar, and either serves as a useful indicator of the central tendency of the data. But suppose we are attempting to determine the average savings of 30 families living on a suburban block. Let us assume that 29 of the 30 families have savings between $8,000 and $12,000, adding up to $294,000. But the thirtieth family has savings of $1,400,000! The mean savings for a family on this block would thus be $56,467. A mean can be greatly distorted by one or two extreme scores, and for such distributions the median is a better indicator of the central tendency. The median savings on our hypothetical block would lie between $8,000 and $12,000 and so would be more representative of the central tendency of savings. Studies of the incomes of American families usually report median rather than mean incomes just to avoid the distortions that would result from treating incomes of the small numbers of multimillionaires in the same way as other incomes.

The **mode** is simply the most frequently occurring score in a distribution. The mode of the data in Table A.1 is 6′9″ because this height occurs most often. The median class interval for the data in Table A.3 is 6′6½″ to 6′9½″. In these cases, the mode is somewhat higher than the mean or median height.

In some cases, the mode is a more appropriate description of a distribution than the mean or median. Figure A.2 shows a **bimodal** distribution, or a distribution with two modes. In this hypothetical distribution of the test scores, the mode at the left indicates the most common class interval for students who did not study, and the mode at the right indicates the most frequent class interval for students who did. The mean and median test scores would probably lie within the 55–59 class interval, yet use of that interval as a measure of central tendency would not provide very meaningful information about the distribution of scores. It might suggest that the test was too hard, not that a number of students chose not to study. One would be better able to visualize the distribution of scores if it is reported as a bimodal distribution. Even in similar cases in which the modes are not exactly equal, it might be more appropriate to describe a distribution as being bimodal or even multimodal.

Median • The score beneath which 50 percent of the class fall. (From the Latin *medius*, meaning "middle.")

Mode • The most frequently occurring number or score in a distribution. (From the Latin *modus*, meaning "measure.")

Bimodal • Having two modes.

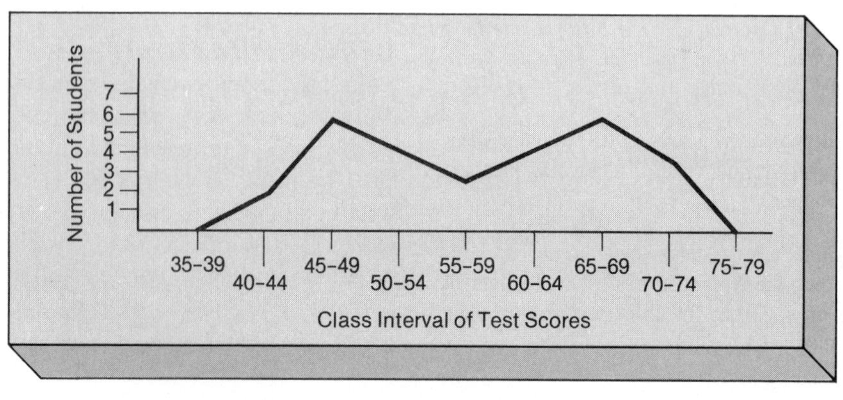

Figure A.2
A Bimodal Distribution This hypothetical distribution represents students' scores on a test. The mode at the left represents the central tendency of students who did not study, and the mode at the right represents the mode of students who did study.

Table A.4: Hypothetical Scores Attained from an IQ Testing

IQ Score	*d* (Deviation Score)	d^2 (Deviation Score Squared)
85	15	225
87	13	169
89	11	121
90	10	100
93	7	49
97	3	9
97	3	9
100	0	0
101	−1	1
104	−4	16
105	−5	25
110	−10	100
112	−12	144
113	−13	169
117	−17	289

Sum of IQ scores = 1,500

Sum of d^2 scores = 1,426

$$\text{Mean} = \frac{\text{Sum of scores}}{\text{Number of scores}} = \frac{1{,}500}{15} = 100$$

Standard Deviation (S.D.)

$$= \sqrt{\frac{\text{Sum of } d^2}{\text{Number of Scores}}}$$

$$= \sqrt{\frac{1{,}426}{15}} = \sqrt{95.07} = 9.75$$

Range • The difference between the highest and the lowest scores in a distribution.

Standard deviation • A measure of the variability of a distribution, attained by the formula

$$\sqrt{\frac{\text{Sum of } d^2}{N}}$$

Measures of Variability. Measures of variability of a distribution inform us about the spread of scores, or about the typical distances of scores from the average score. Measures of variability include the *range* of scores and the *standard deviation.*

The **range** of scores in a distribution is defined as the difference between the highest score and the lowest score, and it is obtained by subtracting the lowest score from the highest score. The range of heights in Table A.2 is 7′2″ minus 6′1″, or 1′1″. It is important to know the range of temperatures if we move to a new climate so that we may anticipate the weather and dress appropriately. A teacher must have some understanding of the range of abilities or skills in a class in order to teach effectively. Classes of gifted students or slow learners are formed so that teachers may attempt to devise a level of instruction that will better meet the needs of all members of a particular class.

The range is an imperfect measure of variability because of the manner in which it is influenced by extreme scores. In our earlier discussion of the savings of 30 families on a suburban block, the range of savings is \$1,400,000 to \$8,000, or \$1,392,000. This tells us little about the typical variability of savings accounts, which lie within a restricted range of \$8,000 to \$12,000. The **standard deviation** is a statistic that indicates how scores are distributed about a mean of a distribution.

The standard deviation considers every score in a distribution, not just the extreme scores. Thus, the standard deviation for the distribution on the right in Figure A.3 would be smaller than that of the distribution on the left. Note that each distribution has the same number of scores, the same mean, and the same range of scores. But the standard deviation for the distribution on the right is smaller than that of the distribution on the left, because the scores tend to cluster more closely about the mean.

The standard deviation (S.D.) is calculated by the following formula:

$$\text{S.D.} = \sqrt{\frac{\text{Sum of } d^2}{N}}$$

where *d* equals the deviation of each score from the mean of the distribution, and *N* equals the number of scores in the distribution.

Let us find the mean and standard deviation of the IQ scores listed in column 1 of Table A.4. To obtain the mean, we add all the scores, attain 1,500, and then divide by the number of scores (15) to obtain a mean of 100. We obtain the deviation score (*d*) for each IQ score by subtracting the score from 100. The *d* for an IQ of 85 equals 100 minus 85, or 15, and so on. Then

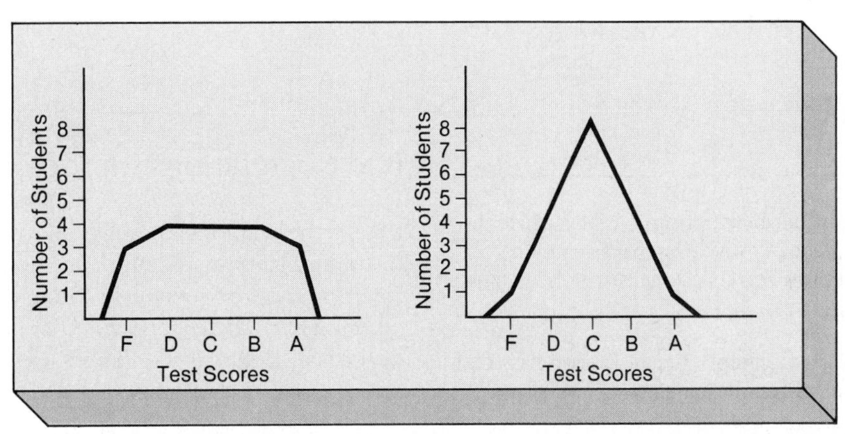

Figure A.3
Hypothetical Distributions of Student Test Scores Each distribution has the same number of scores, the same mean, and even the same range, but the standard deviation is greater for the distribution on the left because the scores tend to be farther from the mean.

Table A.5: Computation of Standard Deviations for Test-score Distributions in Figure A.3

Distribution at Left:			Distribution at Right:		
Grade	d	d^2	Grade	d	d^2
A (4)	2	4	A (4)	2	4
A (4)	2	4	B (3)	1	1
A (4)	2	4	B (3)	1	1
B (3)	1	1	B (3)	1	1
B (3)	1	1	B (3)	1	1
B (3)	1	1	C (2)	0	0
B (3)	1	1	C (2)	0	0
C (2)	0	0	C (2)	0	0
C (2)	0	0	C (2)	0	0
C (2)	0	0	C (2)	0	0
C (2)	0	0	C (2)	0	0
D (1)	−1	1	C (2)	0	0
D (1)	−1	1	C (2)	0	0
D (1)	−1	1	D (1)	−1	1
D (1)	−1	1	D (1)	−1	1
F (0)	−2	4	D (1)	−1	1
F (0)	−2	4	D (1)	−1	1
F (0)	−2	4	F (0)	−2	4
Sum of grades = 36			Sum of grades = 36		
Mean grade = 36/18 = 2			Mean grade = 36/18 = 2		
Sum of d^2 = 32			Sum of d^2 = 16		
S.D. = $\sqrt{32/18}$ = 1.33			S.D. = $\sqrt{16/18}$ = 0.94		

we square each *d* and add these squares. The S.D. equals the square root of the sum of squares (1,426) divided by the number of scores (15), or 9.75.

As an additional exercise, we can show that the S.D. of the test scores on the left (in Figure A.3) is greater than that for the scores on the right by assigning the grades points according to a 4.0 system. Let A = 4, B = 3, C = 2, D = 1, and F = 0. The S.D. for each distribution of test scores is computed in Table A.5. The greater S.D for the distribution on the left indicates that the scores in that distribution are more variable, or tend to be farther from the mean.

The Normal Curve

Many human traits and characteristics such as height and intelligence seem to be distributed in a pattern known as a normal distribution. In a **normal distribution**, the mean, median, and mode all fall at the same data point or score. Scores cluster most heavily about the mean, fall off rapidly in either direction at first (as shown in Figure A.4), and then taper off more gradually.

The curve in Figure A.4 is bell shaped. This type of distribution is also called a **normal curve**. It is hypothesized to reflect the distribution of variables in which different scores are determined by chance variation. Height is thought to be largely determined by chance combinations of genetic material. A distribution of the heights of a random sample of the population approximates normal distributions for men and women, with the mean of the distribution for men a few inches higher than the mean for women.

Test developers traditionally assumed that intelligence was also randomly or normally distributed among the population. For that reason, they constructed intelligence tests so that scores would be distributed as close to "normal" as possible. In actuality, IQ scores are also influenced by enironmental factors and chromosomal abnormalities, so the resultant curves are not perfectly normal. Most IQ tests have means defined as scores of 100 points, and the Wechsler scales are constructed to have standard deviations of 15 points, as shown in Figure A.4. This means that 50 percent of the Wechsler scores fall between 90 and 100 (the "broad average" range), about 68 percent (or two of three) fall between 85 and 115, and more than 95 percent fall between 70 and 130—that is, within two S.D.s of the mean. The Stanford-Binet Intelligence Scale has an S.D. of 16 points.

The Scholastic Aptitude Test (SATs) were constructed so that the mean scores would be 500 points, and an S.D. would be 100 points. Thus, a score of 600 would equal or excel that of some 84 to 85 percent of the test-takers. Because of the complex interaction of variables determining SAT scores, the distribution of SAT scores is not exactly normal either. The normal curve is an idealized curve.

Normal distribution • A symmetrical distribution in which approximately 68 percent of cases lie within a standard deviation of the mean.

Normal curve • Graphic presentation of a normal distribution, showing a bell shape.

The Correlation Coefficient

What is the relationship between intelligence and educational achievement? Between cigarette smoking and lung cancer in human beings? Between introversion and frequency of dating among college students? We cannot run experiments to determine whether the relationships between these variables are causal, because we cannot manipulate the independent variable. For example, we cannot randomly assign a group of people to cigarette smoking

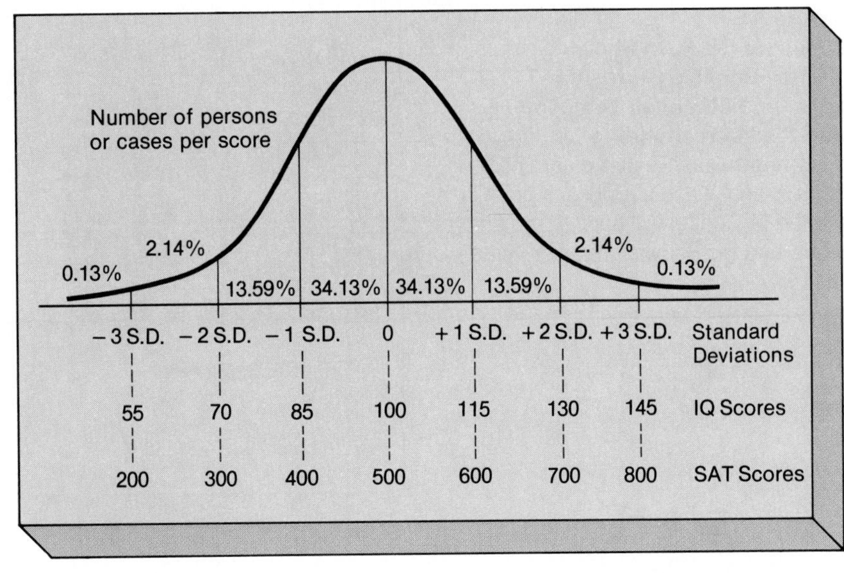

Figure A.4
A Bell-Shaped or Normal Curve
In a normal curve, approximately 68 percent of the cases lie within a standard deviation (S.D.) from the mean, and the mean, median, and mode all lie at the same score. IQ tests and Scholastic Aptitude Tests have been constructed so that distributions of scores approximate the normal curve.

and another group to nonsmoking. People must be permitted to make their own choices, and so it is possible that the same factors that lead people to choose to smoke may also lead to lung cancer. However, the **correlation coefficient** may be used to show that there is a relationship between smoking and cancer. If a strong correlation is shown between the two variables, and we add supportive experimental evidence with laboratory animals who are assigned to conditions in which they inhale tobacco smoke, we wind up with a rather convincing indictment of smoking as a determinant of lung cancer.

The correlation coefficient is a statistic that describes the relationship between two variables. It varies from +1.00 to −1.00; therefore, a correlation coefficient of +1.00 is called a perfect positive correlation, a coefficient of −1.00 is a perfect negative correlation, and a coefficient of 0.00 shows no correlation between variables. To examine the meanings of different correlation coefficients, let us first discuss the *scatter diagram.*

The Scatter Diagram. A **scatter diagram**, or scatter plot, is a graphic representation of the relationship between two variables. As shown in Figure A.5, a scatter diagram is typically drawn with an *X* axis (horizontal) and *Y* axis (vertical).

Let us assume that we have two thermometers. One measures temperature according to the Fahrenheit scale and one measures temperature according to the centrigrade scale. Over a period of several months, we record the temperatures Fahrenheit and centigrade at various times of the day. Then we randomly select a sample of eight Fahrenheit readings and jot down the corresponding centigrade readings, as shown in Figure A.5.

Figure A.5 shows a perfect positive correlation. One variable increases as the other increases, and the points on the scatter diagram may be joined to form a straight line. We usually do not find variables forming a perfect positive (or perfect negative) correlation, unless they are related according to a specific mathematical formula. The temperatures Fahrenheit and centigrade are so related (degrees Fahrenheit = 9/5 degrees centigrade + 32).

Correlation coefficient • A number between −1.00 and +1.00 that indicates the degree of relationship between two variables.

Scatter diagram • A graphic presentation showing the plotting of points defined by the intersections of two variables.

Figure A.5
A Scatter Diagram Showing the Perfect Positive Correlation between Fahrenheit Temperatures and the Corresponding Centigrade Temperatures Scatter diagrams have *X* and *Y* axes, and each point is plotted by finding the spot where an *X* value and the corresponding *Y* value meet.

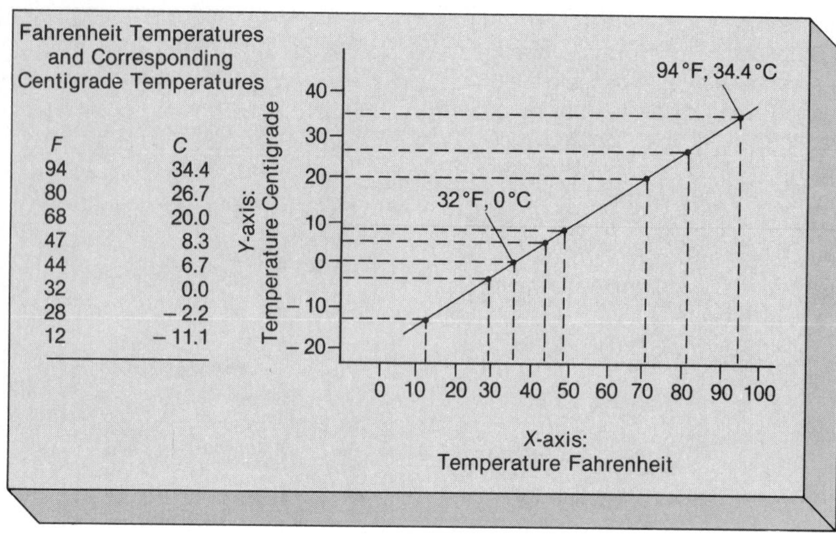

Figure A.6
A Hypothetical Scatter Diagram Showing the Relationship between IQ Scores and Academic Averages
Such correlations usually fall between +0.60 and +0.70, which is considered an adequate indication of validity for intelligence tests, since such tests are intended to predict academic performance.

Figure A.7
A Scatter Diagram Showing a Correlation Coefficient of 0.00 between the *X* and *Y* Variables.

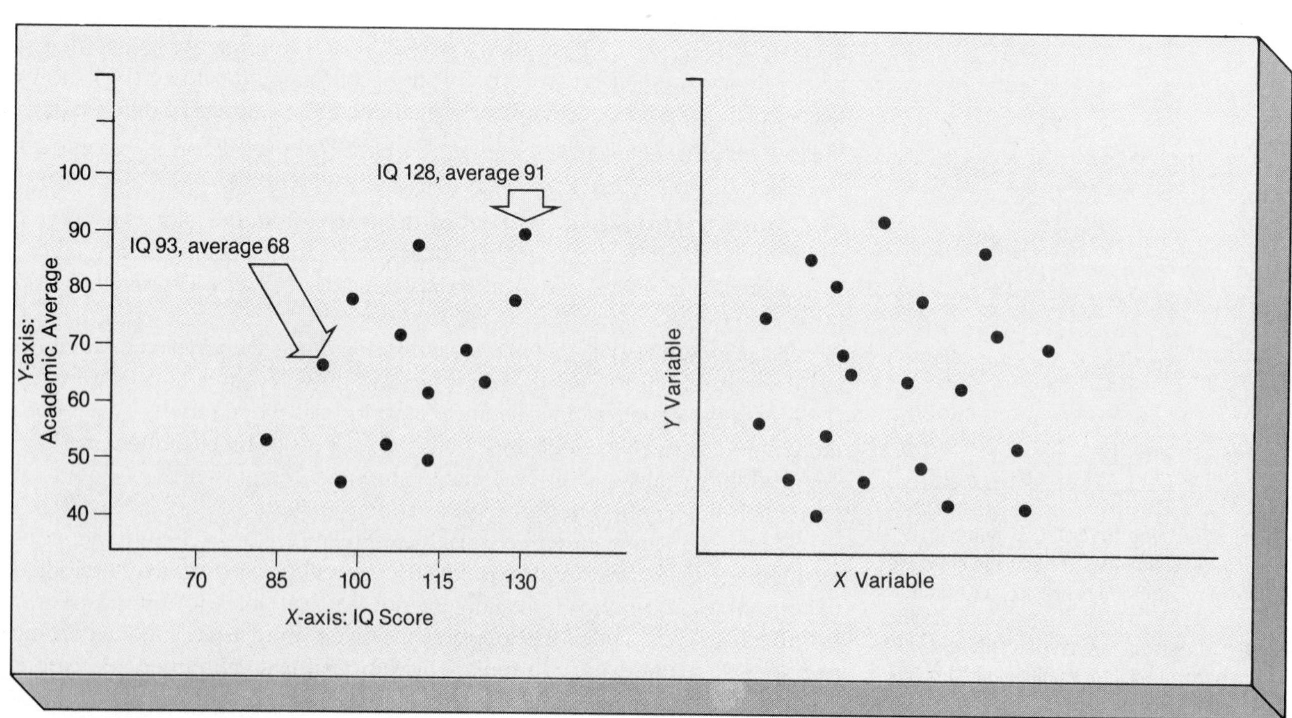

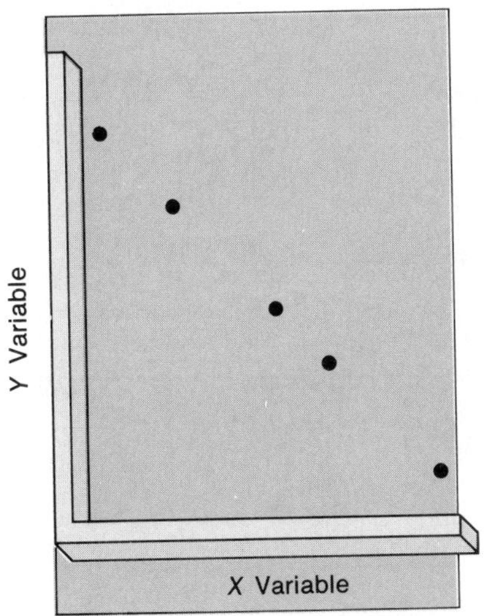

Figure A.8
A Scatter Diagram Showing a Correlation Coefficient of −1.00 between the *X* and *Y* Variables, or a Perfect Negative Relationship.

A positive correlation of about +0.80 to +0.90, or higher, between scores attained on separate testings is usually required to determine the **reliability** of psychological tests. Intelligence tests such as the Stanford-Binet Intelligence Scale and the Wechsler scales have been found to yield **test–retest reliabilities** that meet these requirements. Somewhat lower correlation coefficients are usually accepted as indicators that a psychological test is **valid** when test scores are correlated with scores on an external criterion. Figure A.6 shows a hypothetical scatter diagram that demonstrates the relationship between IQ scores and academic averages for children in grade school. The correlation coefficient that would be derived by mathematical formula would be between +0.60 and +0.70. Remember that correlation does not show cause and effect. Figure A.6 suggests a relationship between the variables but cannot be taken as evidence that intelligence causes achievement.

Figure A.7 shows a scatter diagram in which there is a correlation coefficient of about 0.00 between the *X* and *Y* variables, suggesting that they are fully independent of each other. A person's scores on spelling quizzes taken in California ought to be independent of the daily temperatures in Bolivia. Thus we would expect a correlation coefficient of close to 0.00 between the variables.

Figure A.8 shows a scatter diagram in which there is a perfect negative correlation between two variables: As one variable increases, the other decreases systematically.

Correlations between 0.80 and 1.00 are considered to be very high (whether they are positive or negative). Correlations between 0.60 and 0.80 are high, between 0.40 and 0.60 moderate, from 0.20 to 0.40 weak, and between 0.00 and 0.20 very weak.

It cannot be overemphasized that correlation coefficients do not show cause and effect. For instance, a relationship between intelligence and academic performance, as shown in Figure A.9, could be explained by suggesting that the same cultural factors that lead some children to do well on intelligence tests also lead them to do well on academic tasks. According to this view, intelligence does not cause high academic performance. Instead, a third variable determines both intelligence and academic performance.

However, many psychologists undertake correlational research as a first step in attempting to determine causal relationships between variables. Correlation does not show cause and effect; yet a lack of correlation between two variables suggests that it may be fruitless to undertake experimental research to determine whether they are causally related.

Inferential Statistics

In a study reported in Chapter 6, children enrolled in a Head Start program earned a mean IQ score of 99, whereas children similar in background who were not enrolled in Head Start earned a mean IQ score of 93. Is this difference of six points in IQ significant, or does it represent chance fluctuation of scores? In a study reported in Chapter 1, subjects who believed they had drunk alcohol chose higher levels of electric shock to be applied to persons who had provoked them than did subjects who believed they had not drunk alcohol. Did the difference in level of shock chosen reflect an actual difference between the two groups of subjects, or could it have been a chance fluctuation? Inferential statistics help us make decisions about whether differences found between such groups reflect real differences or just fluctuations.

Reliability • Consistency; see Chapter 6.

Test–retest reliability • Consistency of a test as determined by a comparison of scores on repeated testings.

Validity • The degree to which a test measures what it is supposed to measure; see Chapter 6.

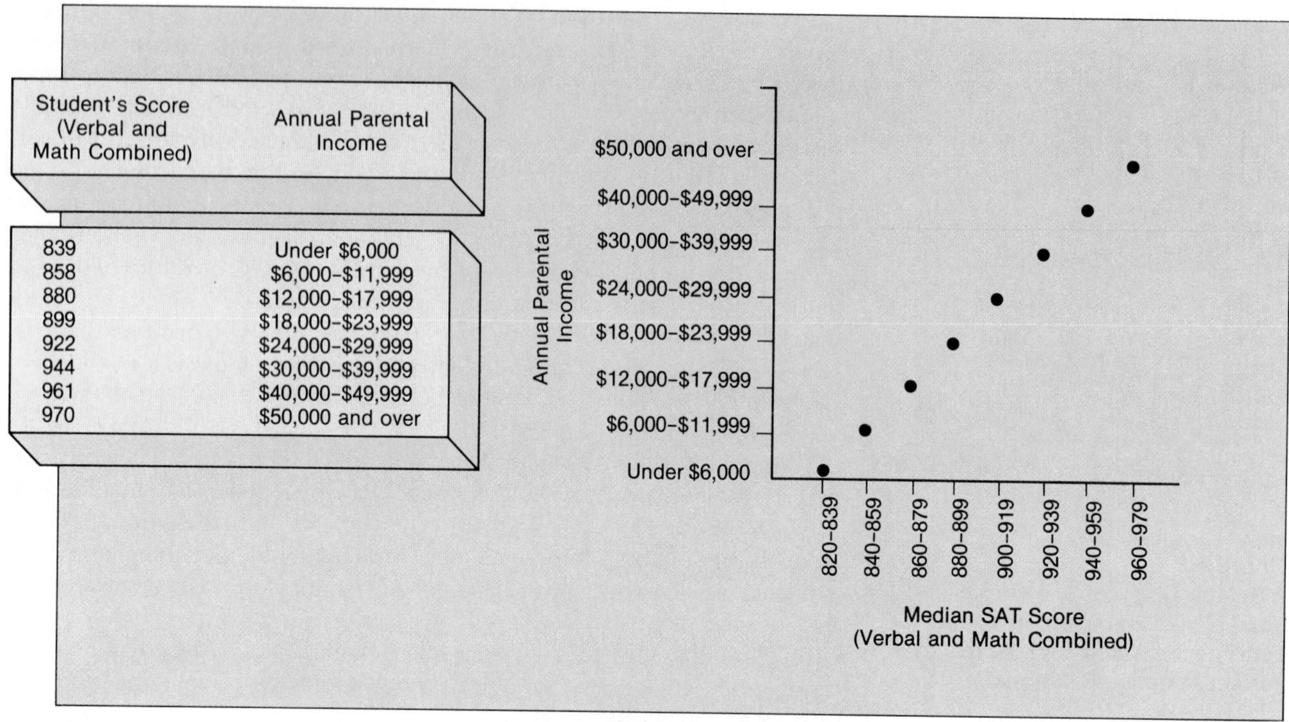

Figure A.9
A Scatter Diagram Showing the Relationship between the Income of a Student's Family and the Student's Score on the Scholastic Aptitude Test (SAT) Taken during 1980–1981.

Scores are a combination of scores on the Verbal and Mathematics subtests and may vary from 400–1600. Scores shown are for white students only. SAT scores predict performance in college. Notê the strong positive correlation between SAT scores and parental income. Does the relationship show that a high-income family is better able to expose children to concepts and skills measured on the SAT? Or that families who transmit genetic influences that may contribute to high test performance also tend to earn high incomes? Correlation is *not* cause and effect. For this reason, the data cannot answer these questions.

Figure A.9 shows the distribution of heights of a thousand men and a thousand women selected at random. The mean height for men is greater than the mean height for women. Can we draw the conclusion, or **infer**, that this difference in heights represents the general population of men and women? Or must we avoid such an inference and summarize our results by stating only that the sample of a thousand men in the study had a higher mean height than that of the sample of a thousand women in the study?

If we could not draw inferences about populations from studies of samples, our research findings would be very limited indeed—limited only to the specific subjects studied. However, the branch of statistics known as **inferential statistics** uses mathematical techniques in such a way that we can make statements about populations from which samples have been drawn, with a certain level of confidence.

Infer • To draw a conclusion, to conclude. (From the Latin *in*, meaning "in," and *ferre*, meaning "to bear.")

Inferential statistics • The branch of statistics concerned with the confidence with which conclusions drawn about samples may be extended to the populations from which they were drawn.

Statistically Significant Differences. In determining whether differences in measures taken of research samples may be applied to the populations from which they were drawn, psychologists use mathematical techniques that indicate whether differences are statistically significant. Was the difference in IQ scores for children attending and those not attending Head Start significant? Did it represent only the children participating in the study,

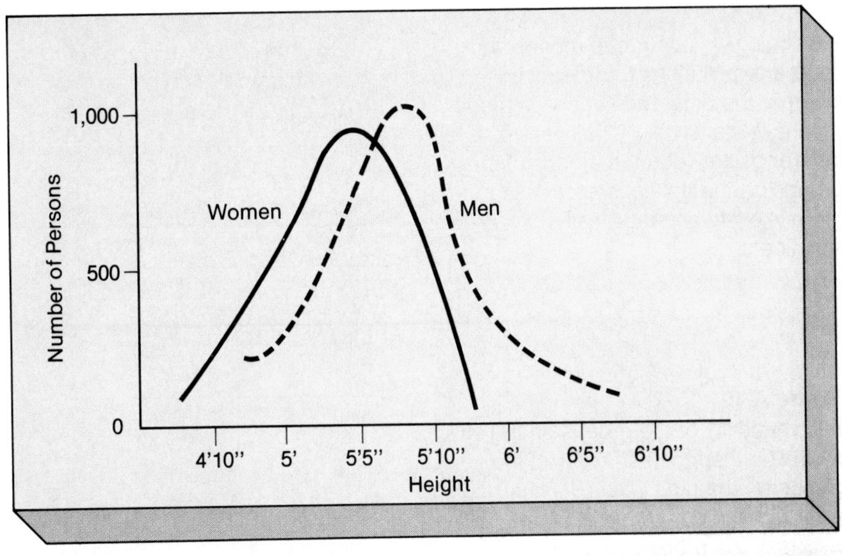

Figure A.10
Distribution of Heights for Random Samples of Men and Women
Inferential statistics permit us to apply our findings to the populations sampled.

or can it be applied to all children represented by the sample? Is the difference between the height of men and the height of women in Figure A.10 statistically significant? Can we apply our findings to all men and women?

Psychologists use formulas involving the means and standard deviations of sample groups to determine whether group differences are statistically significant. As you can see in Figure A.11, the farther apart the group means are, the more likely it is that the difference between them is statistically significant. This makes a good deal of common sense. After all, if you were told that your neighbor's car had gotten one-tenth of a mile more per gallon of gasoline than your car had last year, you might assume that this was a chance difference. But if the differences were farther apart, say 14 miles per gallon, you might readily believe that this difference reflected an actual difference in driving habits or efficiency of the automobiles.

As you can see in Figure A.12, the smaller the standard deviations (a measure of variability) of the two groups, the more likely it is that the difference of the means is statistically significantly. As an extreme example, if all women sampled were exactly 5′5″ tall, and all men sampled were exactly 5′10″, we would be highly likely to assume that the difference of five inches in group means is statistically significant. But if the heights of women varied from 2′ to 14′, and the heights of men varied from 2′1″ to 14′3″, we might be more likely to assume that the five-inch difference in group means could be attributed to chance fluctuation.

Samples and Populations. Inferential statistics are mathematical tools that psychologists apply to samples of scores to determine whether they can generalize their findings to populations of scores. Thus, they must be quite certain that the samples involved actually represent the populations from which they were drawn.

As you learned in Chapter 1, psychologists often use the techniques of random sampling and stratified sampling of populations in order to draw representative samples. If the samples studied do not accurately represent their intended populations, it matters very little how sophisticated the statis-

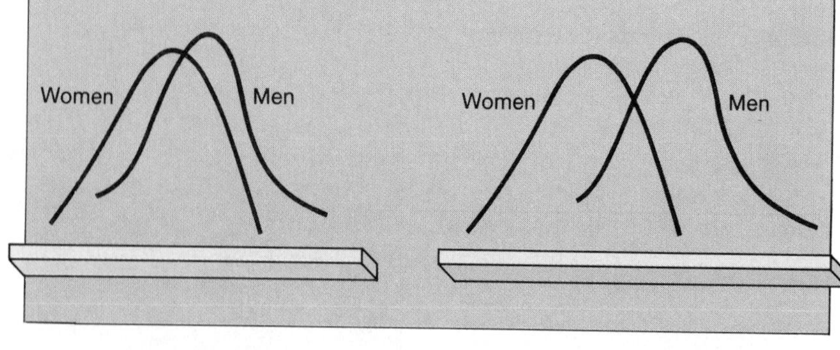

Figure A.11
Psychologists use group means and standard deviations to determine whether the difference between group means is statistically significant. The difference between the means of the groups on the right is greater and thus more likely to be statistically significant.

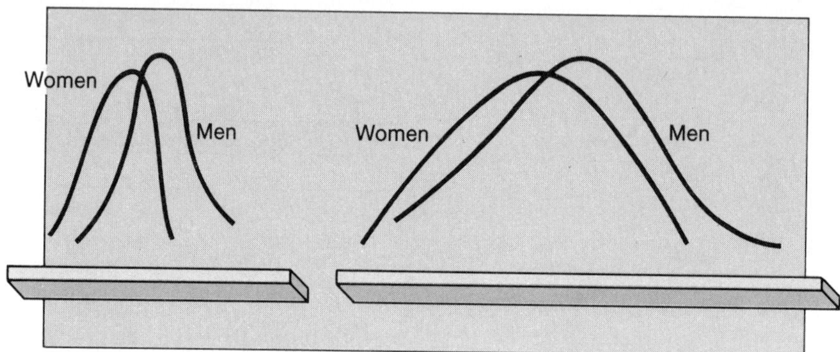

Figure A.12
The variability of the groups on the left is smaller than the variability of the groups on the right. Thus, it is more likely that the difference between the means of the groups on the left is statistically significant.

tical techniques of the psychologist may be. We could use a variety of statistical techniques on the heights of the New York Apples and California Quakes, but none would tell us much about the height of the general population.

GLOSSARY

A

A–B problem The issue of how well we can predict behavior on the basis of attitudes.

Abreaction In psychodynamic theory, the expression of previously repressed feelings and impulses in order to allow the psychic energy associated with them to spill forth.

Absolute refractory period A phase following a neuron's firing during which an action potential cannot be triggered.

Absolute threshold The minimal amount of energy that can produce a sensation.

Abstinence syndrome A characteristic cluster of symptoms that results from sudden decrease in the level of usage of a drug on which one is physiologically dependent.

Accommodation According to Piaget, the modification of existing concepts or schemas so that new information can be integrated or understood.

Acculturation The process of becoming adapted to a new or different culture, according to such factors as the language of the culture and relationships with people from that culture.

Acetylcholine A neurotransmitter that controls muscle contractions. Abbreviated *ACh.*

Achievement Accomplishment; that which is attained by one's efforts and presumed to be made possible by one's abilities.

Acoustic code Mental representation of information as a sequence of sounds.

Acquired drives Drives that are acquired through experience, or learned.

Acquired immune deficiency syndrome A usually fatal disease caused by the human immunodeficiency virus (H.I.V.) that destroys cells of the immune system, leaving the body vulnerable to opportunistic diseases. Abbreviated *AIDS.*

Acquisition trial In conditioning, a presentation of stimuli such that a new response is learned and strengthened.

Acronym A word that is composed of the first letters of the elements of a phrase.

Acrophobia Fear of high places.

Action potential The electrical impulse that provides the basis for the conduction of a neural impulse along an axon of a neuron.

Activating effects The arousal-producing effects of sex hormones that increase the likelihood of dominant sexual responses.

Activation–synthesis model The view that dreams reflect activation by the reticular activating system and synthesis by the cerebral cortex.

Active coping A response to stress that manipulates the environment or changes the response patterns of the individual to permanently remove the stressor or to render it harmless.

Actor–observer effect In attribution theory, the tendency to attribute our own behavior to situational factors but to attribute the behavior of others to dispositional factors.

Acupuncture The ancient Chinese practice of piercing parts of the body with needles to deaden pain and treat illness.

Adaptation stage See *resistance stage.*

ADH Abbreviation of antidiuretic hormone.

Adipose tissue Tissue that contains fat.

Adjustment The process of responding to stress.

Adolescence The stage of development bounded by the advent of puberty and the capacity to assume adult responsibilities.

Adrenal cortex The outer part of the adrenal gland, which produces steroids.

Adrenaline A hormone produced by the adrenal medulla that stimulates the sympathetic division of the autonomic nervous system. Also called *epinephrine.*

Adrenal medulla The inner part of the adrenal gland, which produces adrenaline.

Adrenocorticotrophic hormone A pituitary hormone that regulates the adrenal cortex. Abbreviated *ACTH.*

Aerobic exercise Exercise that requires sustained increase in oxygen consumption.

Affective disorders Disorders characterized primarily by prolonged disturbances of mood or emotional response. (Now referred to as *mood disorders.*

Afferent neuron A neuron that transmits messages from sensory receptors to the spinal cord and brain. Also called *sensory neuron.*

Affiliation The social motive to be with others and to cooperate.

Afterimage The lingering impression made by a stimulus that has been removed.

Age regression In hypnosis, taking on the role of childhood, frequently accompanied by vivid recollections of the early years.

Agoraphobia Fear of open, crowded places.

AIDS Acronym for *Acquired Immune Deficiency Syndrome.* A disorder of the immune system caused by human immunodeficiency virus (H.I.V.) and characterized by suppression of the immune response, leaving the body prey to opportunistic diseases.

Alarm reaction The first stage of the general adaptation syndrome, which is triggered by the impact of a stressor and characterized by heightened sympathetic activity.

Alcoholism Drinking that persistently impairs personal, social, or physical well-being.

Algorithm A specific procedure such as a formula for solving a problem that will work invariably if it is applied correctly.

All-or-none principle The principle that a neuron fires an impulse of the same strength whenever its action potential has been triggered.

Alpha waves Rapid, low-amplitude brain waves that have been linked to feelings of relaxation.

Altered states of consciousness States other than the normal waking state, including sleep, meditation, the hypnotic trance, and the distorted perceptions that can be caused by use of certain drugs.

Alternate-form reliability The consistency of a test as determined by correlating scores attained on one form of the test with scores attained on another form. The Scholastic Aptitude Test and Graduate Record Exam, for example, have many forms.

Altruism Selflessness; unselfish concern for the welfare of others.

Alzheimer's disease A progressive disease that is associated with degeneration of hippocampal cells that produce acetylcholine. It is symptomized by the inability to form new memories and the loss of other cognitive functions.

Ambiguous Having two or more possible meanings.

Amenorrhea Absence of menstruation.

American Sign Language A sign language for the deaf comprised of a system of hand gestures which convey specific meanings. Abbreviated *ASL*.

Amino acid Protein involved in metabolism.

Amniocentesis A prenatal test which consists of tapping amniotic fluid and examining fetal chromosomes that have been sloughed off, making it possible to determine the presence of genetic abnormalities and the sex of the fetus.

Amniotic fluid Fluid within the amniotic sac, formed largely from the fetus's urine, that protects the fetus from jarring or injury.

Amniotic sac A sac within the uterus that contains the embryo or fetus.

Amotivational syndrome Loss of ambition or motivation to achieve.

Amphetamines Stimulants such as Dexedrine and Benzedrine that are derived from *a*lpha-*m*ethyl-beta-*ph*enyl-*et*hyl-*amine*. Abuse can trigger symptoms that mimic schizophrenia.

Amplitude Height. The extreme range of a variable quantity.

Amygdala A part of the limbic system that apparently facilitates stereotypical aggressive responses.

Anabolic steroids Steroids, the chief of which is testosterone, that promote the growth of muscle tissue by creating protein and other substances. Anabolic steroids also foster feelings of invincibility. See also *corticosteroids*.

Anaerobic exercise Exercise that does not require sustained increase in oxygen consumption, such as weight lifting.

Anal expulsive A Freudian personality type characterized by unregulated self-expression such as messiness.

Anal fixation In psychodynamic theory, attachment to objects and behaviors characteristic of the anal stage.

Analgesia (1) A conscious state in which pain is reduced or terminated. (2) A method for inducing such a state.

Analogous hues Colors that lie next to one another on the color wheel, forming families of harmonious colors such as yellow and orange, and green and blue.

Anal retentive A Freudian personality type characterized by self-control such as excessive neatness and punctuality.

Anal stage In psychodynamic theory, the second stage of psychosexual development, in which gratification is obtained through anal activities like eliminating wastes.

Analyst A person who practices psychoanalysis, Freud's method of psychotherapy.

Analytical psychology Jung's psychodynamic theory which emphasizes archetypes, a collective unconscious, and a unifying force of personality called the Self.

Androgen Male sex hormone.

Androgenital syndrome A hormonal disorder in which prenatal exposure to androgens masculinizes the external genitals of genetic females.

Anger (1) A negative emotion frequently characterized by a provocation, cognitions that one has been taken advantage of and should seek revenge, and aggressive behavioral tendencies. (2) The second stage in Kübler-Ross's theory of dying.

Angiotensin A kidney hormone that signals the hypothalamus of depletion of body fluids.

Anima Jung's feminine archetype.

Animism The belief, characteristic of preoperational thought, that inanimate objects move because of will or spirit.

Animus Jung's masculine archetype.

Anorexia nervosa An eating disorder characterized by maintenance of an abnormally low body weight, intense fear of weight gain, a distorted body image, and, in females, amenorrhea.

Anosmia Lack of sensitivity to a specific odor.

ANS Abbreviation for *autonomic nervous system*.

Antecedent An event or thing that occurs before another.

Anterograde amnesia Failure to remember events that occur after physical trauma because of the effects of the trauma.

Antibodies Substances formed by white blood cells that recognize and destroy antigens.

Antidepressant drug A drug that acts to relieve depression.

Antidiuretic hormone A pituitary hormone that conserves body fluids by increasing the reabsorption of urine. Abbreviated *ADH*.

Antigen A substance that stimulates the body to mount an immune-system response to it. (The contraction for *anti*body *gen*erator.)

Antisocial personality disorder The diagnosis given a person who is in frequent conflict with society yet is undeterred by punishment and experiences little or no guilt and anxiety. Also referred to as psychopathy or sociopathy.

Anvil A bone of the middle ear.

Anxiety A psychological state characterized by tension and apprehension, foreboding and dread.

Aphagic Characterized by undereating.

Aphasia Impaired ability to comprehend or express oneself through speech.

Apnea Temporary discontinuation of breathing during sleep.

Applied psychology The application of fundamental psychological methods and knowledge to the investigation and solution of human problems.

Applied research Research conducted in an effort to find solutions to particular problems.

Approach–approach conflict Conflict involving two positive but mutually exclusive goals.

Approach–avoidance conflict Conflict involving a goal with positive and negative features.

Aptitude A natural ability or talent.

Archetypes In Jung's personality theory, primitive images or concepts that reside in the collective unconscious.

Arousal (1) A general level of activity or preparedness for activity in an organism. (2) A general level of motivation in an organism.

Arteriosclerosis A disease characterized by thickening and hardening of the arteries.

Artificialism The belief, characteristic of preoperational thought, that natural objects have been created by human beings.

Assertiveness training A form of social-skills training including techniques such as coaching, modeling, feedback, and behavior rehearsal that teaches clients to express their feelings and seek fair treatment.

Assimilation According to Piaget, the inclusion of a new event into an existing concept or schema.

Association areas Parts of the cerebral cortex involved in learning, thought, memory, and language.

Asthma Recurrent attacks of difficult breathing and wheezing.

Astigmatism A visual disorder in which vertical and horizontal contours cannot be focused on simultaneously.

Asylum (1) An early institution for the care of the mentally ill. (2) A safe place, or refuge.

Attachment The enduring affectional tie that binds one person to another.

Attachment-in-the-making phase The second phase in forming bonds of attachment, characterized by preference for familiar figures.

Attitude An enduring mental representation of people, places, or things that evokes feelings and influences behavior.

Attitude-discrepant behavior Behavior that is inconsistent with an attitude and may have the effect of modifying an attitude.

Attraction A force that draws bodies or people together. In social psychology, an attitude of liking (positive attraction) or disliking (negative attraction).

Attribution A belief about why people behave in a certain way.

Attributional style One's tendency to attribute one's behavior to internal or external factors, stable or unstable factors, and so on.

Attribution process The process by which people draw conclusions about the motives and traits of others.

Auditory Having to do with hearing.

Auditory nerve The axon bundle that transmits neural impulses from the organ of Corti to the brain.

Authoritarianism Belief in the importance of unquestioning obedience to authority.

Autism (1) Self-absorption. Absorption in daydreaming and fantasy. (2) A childhood disorder marked by problems such as failure to relate to others, lack of speech, and intolerance of change.

Autogenic training A method for reducing tension involving repeated suggestions that the limbs are becoming warmer and heavier and that one's breathing is becoming more regular.

Autokinetic effect The tendency to perceive a stationary point of light in a dark room as moving.

Autonomic nervous system The division of the peripheral nervous system that regulates glands and involuntary activities like heartbeat, respiration, digestion, and dilation of the pupils. Abbreviated *ANS.* Also see *sympathetic* and *parasympathetic* branches of the ANS.

Autonomy Self-direction. The social motive to be free, unrestrained, and independent.

Autonomy versus shame and doubt Erikson's second stage of psychosocial development, during which the child develops (or does not develop) the wish to make choices and the capacity to exercise self-control.

Autosomes Chromosomes that look alike and possess information about the same sets of traits. One autosome is received from the father and the corresponding autosome is received from the mother.

Average The central tendency of a group of measures, expressed as *mean, median,* or *mode.*

Aversive conditioning A behavior-therapy technique in which a previously desirable or neutral stimulus is made obnoxious by being paired repeatedly with a repugnant or offensive stimulus.

Avoidance–avoidance conflict Conflict involving two negative goals in which avoidance of one requires approach of the other.

Avoidance learning An operant conditioning procedure in which an organism learns to exhibit an operant that permits it to avoid an aversive stimulus.

Axon A long, thin part of a neuron that transmits impulses to other neurons from branching structures called terminals.

B

B lymphocytes The white blood cells of the immune system that produce antibodies.

Babbling The child's first verbalizations that have the sound of speech.

Babinski reflex An infant's fanning of the toes in response to stimulation of the sole of the foot.

Backward conditioning A classical conditioning procedure in which the unconditioned stimulus is presented prior to the conditioned stimulus.

Balance sheet An outline of positive and negative expectations concerning a course of action. An aid to effective decision-making.

Balance theory The view that people have a need to organize their perceptions, opinions, and beliefs in a harmonious manner.

Barbiturate An addictive depressant used to relieve anxiety or induce sleep.

Bargaining The third stage in Kübler-Ross's theory of dying, in which the terminally ill try to bargain with God to postpone death, usually by offering to do good deeds in exchange for time.

Barnum effect The tendency to believe in the accuracy of a generalized personality report or prediction about oneself.

Basal ganglia Ganglia located in the brain between the thalamus and the cerebrum that are involved in motor coordination.

Basic anxiety Horney's term for enduring feelings of insecurity that stem from harsh or indifferent parental treatment.

Basic hostility Horney's term for enduring feelings of anger that accompany basic anxiety but that are directed toward nonfamily members in adulthood.

Basilar membrane A membrane to which the organ of Corti is attached. The basilar membrane lies coiled within the cochlea.

Behavior The observable or measurable actions of people and lower animals.

Behavioral competencies Skills.

Behavioral medicine An interdisciplinary field in which psychological principles are applied to the treatment of health problems.

Behavior genetics The study of the genetic transmission of structures and traits that give rise to behavior.

Behaviorism The school of psychology that defines psychology as the study of observable behavior and investigates the relationships between stimuli and responses.

Behaviorist A psychologist who believes that psychology should address observable behavior and the relationships between stimuli and responses.

Behavior modification Use of principles of learning to change behavior in desired directions.

Behavior rating scale A systematic means of recording the frequency with which target behaviors occur. (An alternative to self-report methods of personality testing.)

Behavior rehearsal Practice.

Behavior therapy Use of the principles of learning in the direct modification of problem behavior.

Benzodiazepines A class of drugs that reduce anxiety. Minor tranquilizers.

Bimodal Having two modes.

Binocular cues Stimuli that suggest depth by means of simultaneous perception by both eyes. Examples: retinal disparity and convergence.

Biofeedback training The systematic feeding back to an organism of information about a body function so that the organism can gain control of that function. Abbreviated *BFT.*

Biological psychologist A psychologist who studies the relationships between biological processes and behavior.

Bipolar cells Neurons that conduct neural impulses from rods and cones to ganglion cells.

Bipolar disorder A disorder in which the mood inappropriately alternates between extremes of elation and depression. Formerly called *manic-depression.*

Blind In experimental terminology, unaware of whether one has received a treatment.

Blind spot The area of the retina where axons from ganglion cells meet to form the optic nerve. It is insensitive to light.

Blocking In conditioning, the phenomenon whereby a new stimulus fails to gain the capacity to signal an unconditioned stimulus (US) when the new stimulus is paired repeatedly with a stimulus that already effectively foretells the US.

Bottom-up processing The organization of the parts of a pattern to recognize, or form an image of, the pattern they compose.

Breathalyzer A device that measures the quantity of alcohol in the body by analyzing the breath.

Brief reactive psychosis A psychotic episode of less than two weeks in duration that follows a known stressful event.

Brightness constancy The tendency to perceive an object as being just as bright even though lighting conditions change the intensity with which it impacts on the eye.

Broca's aphasia A speech disorder caused by damage to Broca's area of the brain. It is characterized by slow, laborious speech and by difficulty articulating words and forming grammatical sentences.

Bulimia nervosa An eating disorder characterized by recurrent episodes of binge eating followed by purging and by persistent overconcern with body shape and weight.

C

Cannon-Bard theory The theory of emotion that holds that events are processed by the brain and that the brain induces patterns of activity and autonomic arousal *and* cognitive activity—that is, the experiencing of the appropriate emotion.

Carcinogen An agent that gives rise to cancerous changes.

Cardinal trait Allport's term for pervasive traits that steer practically all of a person's behavior.

Cardiovascular disorders Diseases of the cardiovascular system, including heart disease, hypertension, and arteriosclerosis.

Case study A carefully drawn biography that may be obtained through interviews, questionnaires, psychological tests, and, sometimes, historical records.

Catalyst An agent that hastens or facilitates a reaction. (A term borrowed from chemistry.)

Catastrophize To exaggerate or magnify the noxious properties of negative events; to "blow out of proportion."

Catatonic schizophrenia A subtype of schizophrenia characterized by striking impairment in motor activity.

Catch Thirties Sheehy's term for the fourth decade of life, which is frequently characterized by major reassessment of one's accomplishments and goals.

Catecholamines A number of chemical substances produced from an amino acid that are important as neurotransmitters (dopamine and norepinephrine) and as hormones (adrenaline and norepinephrine).

Catharsis The free expression or spilling forth of feelings. Also called *abreaction.*

Cellular-aging theory The view that aging occurs because body cells lose the capacity to reproduce and maintain themselves.

Center According to Piaget, to focus one's attention.

Central fissure The valley in the cerebral cortex that separates the frontal and parietal lobes.

Central nervous system The brain and spinal cord.

Central traits Characteristics that are outstanding and noticeable but not necessarily all-pervasive.

Cephalocaudal Proceeding from top to bottom.

Cerebellum A part of the hindbrain involved in muscle coordination and balance.

Cerebral cortex The wrinkled surface area of the cerebrum, often called "gray matter" because of the appearance afforded by the many cell bodies.

Cerebrum The large mass of the forebrain, which consists of two hemispheres.

Chain breaking A behavior-therapy self-control technique in which one disrupts problematic behavior by complicating its execution.

Chemotherapy The use of drugs to treat abnormal behavior patterns.

Childhood amnesia Inability to recall events that occurred before the age of 3.

Chorionic villus sampling The detection of genetic abnormalities by sampling the membrane that envelopes the amniotic sac and the fetus within. Abbreviated *CVS.*

Chromosomes Genetic structures consisting of genes that are found in the nuclei of the body's cells.

Chronological age A person's actual age—as contrasted to *mental age.*

Chunk A stimulus or group of stimuli that are perceived or encoded as a discrete piece of information.

Circular explanation An explanation that merely repeats its own concepts instead of offering additional information.

Cirrhosis of the liver A disease caused by protein deficiency in which connective fibers replace active liver cells, impairing circulation of the blood. Alcohol does not contain protein; therefore, people who drink excessively may be prone to acquiring this disease.

Classic organization theories Theories that hold that organizations should be structured from the skeleton (governing body) outward.

Classical conditioning (1) According to cognitive theorists, the learning of relations among events so as to allow an organism to represent its environment. (2) According to behaviorists, a form of learning in which one stimulus comes to evoke the response usually evoked by a second stimulus by being paired repeatedly with the second stimulus. Also referred to as *respondent conditioning* or *Pavlovian conditioning.*

Claustrophobia Fear of tight, small places.

Clearcut-attachment phase The third phase in forming bonds of attachment, characterized by intensified dependence on the primary caregiver.

Client-centered therapy See *person-centered therapy.*

Clinical scales Groups of test items that measure the presence of various abnormal behavior patterns, as on the Minnesota Multiphasic Personality Inventory (MMPI).

Closure The tendency to perceive a broken figure as being complete or whole.
Cocaine A powerful stimulant derived from coca leaves that is usually snorted, brewed, or injected.
Cochlea The inner ear; the bony tube that contains the basilar membrane and the organ of Corti.
Cognitive Having to do with mental processes such as sensation and perception, memory, intelligence, language, thought, and problem-solving.
Cognitive dissonance theory The view that we are motivated to make our cognitions or beliefs consistent.
Cognitive map A mental representation or picture of the elements in a learning situation, such as a maze.
Cognitive therapy A form of psychotherapy that focuses on how clients' cognitions (expectations, attitudes, beliefs, etc.) lead to distress and may be modified to relieve distress and promote adaptive behavior.
Collective unconscious Jung's hypothesized store of vague racial memories and archetypes.
Color constancy The tendency to perceive an object as being the same color even as lighting conditions change its appearance.
Comatose In a coma, a state resembling sleep from which it is difficult to be aroused.
Common fate The tendency to perceive elements that move together as belonging together.
Community psychology A field of psychology, related to clinical psychology, that focuses on the prevention of psychological problems and the maintenance of distressed persons in the community.
Companionate love A type of nonpassionate love characterized by intimacy, respect, trust, and commitment.
Competencies Within social-learning theory, knowledge and skills.
Competing response In behavior therapy, a response that is incompatible with an unwanted response.
Complementary (1) In sensation and perception, descriptive of colors of the spectrum which, when combined, produce white or nearly white light. (2) In transactional analysis, descriptive of a transaction in which the ego states of two people interact harmoniously.
Componential level According to Sternberg, the level of intelligence that consists of metacomponents, performance components, and knowledge-acquisition components.
Compulsion An apparently irresistible urge to repeat an act or engage in ritualistic behavior, such as hand-washing.
Computerized axial tomography Formation of a computer-generated image of the anatomical details of the brain by passing a narrow X-ray beam through the head and measuring from different angles the amount of radiation that passes through. Abbreviated *CAT scan.*
Concept A symbol that stands for a group of objects, events, or ideas that share common properties.
Concordance Agreement.
Concrete operational stage Piaget's third stage of cognitive development, characterized by logical thought processes concerning tangible objects, conservation, reversibility, and subjective morality.
Conditional positive regard In self theory, judgment of another person's basic value as a human being on the basis of the acceptability of that person's behaviors.
Conditioned reinforcer Another term for *secondary reinforcer.*
Conditioned response In classical conditioning, a learned response to a previously neutral stimulus. A response to a conditioned stimulus. Abbreviated *CR.*
Conditioned stimulus A previously neutral stimulus that elicits a conditioned response because it has been paired repeatedly with a stimulus that had already elicited that response. Abbreviated *CS.*
Conditioning A simple form of learning in which responses become associated with stimuli. See *classical conditioning* and *operant conditioning.*
Conditions of worth Standards by which the value of a person, or the self, is judged.
Conduction deafness The forms of deafness in which there is loss of conduction of sound through the middle ear.
Cone A cone-shaped photoreceptor in the eye that transmits sensations of color.
Confederate In experimental terminology, a person who pretends to be a subject in a study but who is in league with the experimenter.
Confidential Secret, not to be disclosed.
Conflict (1) Being torn in different directions by opposing motives. (2) Feelings produced by being in conflict.
Conform To change one's attitudes or overt behavior to adhere to social norms.
Conformity Behavior that is in accordance with group norms and expectations.
Congruence In self-theory, a fit between one's self-concept and one's behaviors, thoughts, and feelings. A quality shown by the person-centered therapist.
Conscious Aware, in the normal waking state.
Consciousness A complex and controversial concept in psychology. Consciousness has several meanings in addition to the normal waking state; see *sensory awareness, direct inner awareness,* and *self.*
Consensus General agreement.
Conservation According to Piaget, recognition that certain properties of substances remain constant even though their appearance may change. For example, the weight and mass of a ball of clay remain constant (are conserved) even if the ball is flattened into a pancake.
Consolidation The fixing of information in long-term memory.
Consonant In harmony.
Construe Interpret.
Consultation The provision of professional advice or services.
Consumer psychology The field of psychology that studies the nature, causes, and modification of consumer behavior and mental processes.
Consummate love In Sternberg's triangular model, the kind of love characterized by passion, intimacy, and commitment.
Contact comfort (1) The pleasure attained from physical contact with another. (2) A hypothesized primary drive to seek physical comfort through physical contact with another.
Context-dependent memory Information that is better retrieved in the context in which it was encoded and stored, or learned.
Contextual level According to Sternberg, those aspects of intelligent behavior that permit people to adapt to their environment.
Contiguous Next to one another.
Contingency theory (1) In conditioning, the view that learning occurs when stimuli provide information about the likelihood of the occurrence of other stimuli. (2) In industrial/organizational psychology, a theory that holds that organizational structure should depend on factors such as goals, workers' characteristics, and the overall economic or political environment.

Continuity As a rule of perceptual organization, the tendency to perceive a series of stimuli as having unity.

Continuous reinforcement A schedule of reinforcement in which every correct response is reinforced. See *partial reinforcement.*

Control subject A participant in an experiment who does not receive the experimental treatment but for whom all other conditions are comparable to those of experimental subjects.

Conventional level According to Kohlberg, a period of moral development during which moral judgments largely reflect social conventions. A "law-and-order" approach to morality.

Convergence A binocular cue for depth based on the inward movement of the eyes as they attempt to focus on an object that is drawing nearer.

Convergent thinking A thought process that attempts to narrow in on the single best solution to a problem.

Conversion disorder A disorder in which anxiety or unconscious conflicts are "converted" into physical symptoms that often have the effect of helping the person cope with the anxiety or conflicts.

Cooing Prelinguistic, articulated, vowel-like sounds that appear to reflect feelings of positive excitement.

Copulate To engage in sexual intercourse.

Cornea Transparent tissue that forms the outer surface of the eyeball.

Corpus callosum A thick bundle of fibers that connects the two hemispheres of the cerebrum.

Correlational research A method of scientific investigation that studies the relationships between variables. Correlational research can imply but cannot show cause and effect, because no experimental treatment is introduced.

Correlation coefficient A number ranging from +1.00 to –1.00 that expresses the strength and direction (positive or negative) of the relationship between two variables.

Corticosteroids Steroids, produced by the adrenal cortex, that regulate carbohydrate metabolism and increase resistance to stress by fighting inflammation and allergic reactions. Also called *cortical steroids.*

Cortisol A hormone (steroid) produced by the adrenal cortex that helps the body cope with stress by counteracting inflammation and allergic reactions.

Counterconditioning A behavior-therapy technique which involves the repeated pairing of a stimulus that elicits a problematic response (such as fear) with a stimulus that elicits an antagonistic response (such as relaxation instructions) so that the first stimulus loses the capacity to evoke the problematic response. See also *systematic desensitization* and *aversive conditioning.*

Countertransference In psychoanalysis, the generalization to the client of feelings toward another person in the analyst's life.

Covert reinforcement A behavior-therapy self-control technique in which one creates pleasant imagery to reward desired behavior.

Covert sensitization A behavior-therapy self-control technique in which one creates aversive imagery and associates it with undesired behavior.

CR Conditioned response.

Creative self According to Adler, the self-aware aspect of personality that strives to achieve its full potential.

Creativity The ability to generate novel solutions to problems. A trait characterized by originality, ingenuity, and flexibility.

Cretinism A condition caused by thyroid deficiency in childhood and characterized by mental retardation and stunted growth.

Criteria Plural of *criterion.*

Criterion A standard; a means for making a judgment.

Criterion-referenced testing A testing approach in which scores are based on whether or not one can perform up to a set standard.

Critical period A period in an organism's development during which it is capable of certain types of learning.

CS Conditioned stimulus.

Cultural bias A factor hypothesized to be present in intelligence tests that provides an advantage for test-takers from certain cultural or ethnic backgrounds but that does not reflect actual intelligence.

Culture-fair Describing a test in which there are no cultural biases. On such a test, test-takers from different cultural backgrounds would have an equal opportunity to earn scores that reflect their true abilities.

Cumulative incidence The occurrence of an event or act by a given time or age.

Cumulative recorder An instrument used in operant conditioning laboratory procedures to automatically record the frequency of targeted responses.

D

Daily hassles Notable daily conditions and experiences that are threatening or harmful to a person's well-being.

Dark adaptation The process of adjusting to conditions of lower lighting by increasing the sensitivity of rods and cones.

Debrief To receive information about a procedure that has been completed.

Decibel A unit expressing the loudness of a sound. Abbreviated *dB.*

Deep structure The underlying meaning of a sentence as determined by interpretation of the meanings of the words.

Defense mechanisms In psychodynamic theory, unconscious functions of the ego that protect it from anxiety-evoking material by preventing accurate recognition of this material.

Defensive coping A response to stress that reduces the stressor's immediate effect but frequently at some cost to the individual. Defensive coping may involve self-deception and does not change the environment or the person's response patterns to permanently remove or modify the effects of the stressor. Contrast with *active coping.*

Deindividuation The process by which group members may discontinue self-evaluation and adopt group norms and attitudes.

Delayed conditioning A classical conditioning procedure in which the CS is presented several seconds before the US and left on until the response occurs.

Delirium tremens A condition characterized by sweating, restlessness, disorientation, and hallucinations that occurs in some chronic users of alcohol when there is a sudden decrease in the level of drinking. Abbreviated *DTs.*

Delta-9-tetrahydrocannabinol The major active ingredient in marijuana. Abbreviated *THC.*

Delta waves Strong, slow brain waves usually emitted during stage 4 sleep.

Delusions False, persistent beliefs that are unsubstantiated by sensory or objective evidence.

Delusions of grandeur Erroneous beliefs that one is a grand person, like Jesus or a secret agent on a special mission.

Delusions of persecution Erroneous beliefs that one is being threatened or persecuted.

Dendrites Rootlike structures attached to the soma of a neuron that receive impulses from other neurons.

Denial (1) A defense mechanism in which threatening events are misperceived to be harmless. (2) The first stage in Kübler-Ross's theory of the dying process.

Dependent variable A measure of an assumed effect of an independent variable. An outcome measure in a scientific study.

Depersonalization disorder Persistent or recurrent feelings that one is not real or is detached from one's own experiences or body.

Depolarization The reduction of the resting potential of a cell membrane from about −70 millivolts toward zero.

Depressant A drug that lowers the nervous system's rate of activity.

Depression (1) A negative emotion frequently characterized by sadness, feelings of helplessness, and a sense of loss. (2) The fourth stage in Kübler-Ross's theory of the dying process.

Descriptive statistics The branch of statistics that is concerned with providing descriptive information about a distribution of scores.

Desensitization The type of sensory adaptation in which we become less sensitive to constant stimuli. Also called *negative adaptation.*

Determinant A factor that defines or sets limits.

Deviation IQ A score on an intelligence test that is derived by determining how far an individual's score deviates from the norm. On the Wechsler scales, the mean IQ score is defined as 100, and approximately two of three scores fall between 85 and 115.

Diabetes A disorder caused by inadequate secretion or utilization of insulin and characterized by excess sugar in the blood.

Diagnosis A decision or opinion about the nature of a diseased condition.

Dialogue A Gestalt therapy technique in which clients verbalize confrontations between conflicting parts of their personality.

Dichromat A person who is sensitive to the intensity of light and to red and green or blue and yellow and who thus is partially color-blind.

Difference threshold The minimal difference in intensity that is required between two sources of energy so that they will be perceived as being different.

Differentiation The modification of tissues and organs in structure, function, or both during the course of development.

Diffusion of responsibility The spreading or sharing of responsibility for a decision or behavior among the members of a group.

Direct coping See *active coping.*

Direct inner awareness One of the definitions of consciousness: Knowledge of one's own thoughts, feelings, and memories, without use of sensory organs.

Discovery learning Bruner's view that children should work on their own to discover basic principles.

Discrimination (1) In conditioning, the tendency for an organism to distinguish between a conditioned stimulus and similar stimuli that do not forecast an unconditioned stimulus. (2) In social psychology, the denial of privileges to a person or a group on the basis of prejudice.

Discrimination training Teaching an organism to show a conditioned response to only one of a series of similar stimuli by pairing that stimulus with the unconditioned stimulus and presenting similar stimuli in the absence of the unconditioned stimulus.

Discriminative stimulus In operant conditioning, a stimulus that indicates that reinforcement is available.

Disinhibit In social learning theory, to trigger a response that is usually inhibited, generally as a consequence of observing a model engage in the behavior without negative consequences.

Disorganized schizophrenia A subtype of schizophrenia characterized by disorganized delusions and vivid hallucinations. Formerly *hebephrenic schizophrenia.*

Disorientation Gross confusion. Loss of awareness of time, place, and the identity of people.

Displacement (1) In information processing, the causing of chunks of information to be lost from short-term memory by adding too many new items. (2) In psychodynamic theory, a defense mechanism that involves the transference of feelings or impulses from threatening or unacceptable objects onto unthreatening or acceptable objects. (3) As a property of language, the ability to communicate information about events in other times and places.

Dispositional attribution An assumption that a person's behavior is determined by internal causes such as personal attitudes or goals. Contrast with *situational attribution.*

Dissociative disorder A disorder in which there is a sudden, temporary change in consciousness or self-identity, such as psychogenic amnesia, or psychogenic fugue, or multiple personality.

Dissonant Incompatible, discordant.

Divergent thinking A thought process that attempts to generate multiple solutions to problems. Free and fluent associations to the elements of a problem.

Dizygotic twins Twins who develop from separate zygotes. Fraternal twins. Abbreviated *DZ twins.* Contrast with *monozygotic twins.*

DNA Deoxyribonucleic acid. The substance that carries the genetic code and makes up genes and chromosomes.

Dominant trait In genetics, a trait that is expressed. See *recessive trait.*

Dopamine A neurotransmitter that is involved in Parkinson's disease and theorized to play a role in schizophrenia.

Double approach–avoidance conflict Conflict involving two goals, each of which has positive and negative aspects.

Double-blind study A study in which neither the subjects nor the persons measuring results know who has received the treatment.

Down syndrome A chromosomal abnormality caused by an extra chromosome in the 21st pair ("trisomy 21") and characterized by slanted eyelids and mental retardation. Also called *mongolism.*

Dream A form of cognitive activity—usually a sequence of images or thoughts—that occurs during sleep. Dreams may be vague and loosely plotted or vivid and intricate.

Drive A condition of arousal within an organism that is associated with a need.

Drive for superiority Adler's term for the desire to compensate for feelings of inferiority.

Drive-reduction theory The view that organisms are motivated to learn to engage in behaviors that have the effect of reducing drives.

DSM The *Diagnostic and Statistical Manual of the Mental Disorders,* published by the American Psychiatric Association. A frequently used compendium of psychological disorders.

Duct Passageway.

Duplicity theory A combination of the place and frequency theories of pitch discrimination.

Dyslexia A severe reading disorder characterized by problems such as letter reversals, reading as if one were seeing words reflected in a mirror, slow reading, and reduced comprehension.

Dyspareunia Persistent or recurrent pain during or after sexual intercourse.

E

Eardrum A thin membrane that vibrates in response to sound waves, transmitting them from the outer ear to the middle and inner ears.

Echo A mental representation of an auditory stimulus that is held briefly in sensory memory.

Echoic memory The sensory register that briefly holds mental representations of auditory stimuli.

Eclectic Selecting from various systems or theories.

ECT Acronym for *electroconvulsive therapy.*

Educational psychology The field of psychology that studies the nature, causes, and enhancement of teaching and learning.

Efferent neuron A neuron that transmits messages from the brain or spinal cord to muscles or glands. Also called *motor neuron.*

Effort justification In cognitive-dissonance theory, the tendency to seek justification (acceptable reasons) for strenuous efforts.

Ego In psychodynamic theory, the second psychic structure to develop. The ego is governed by the reality principle and its functioning is characterized by self-awareness, planning, and capacity to tolerate frustration and delay gratification.

Ego analyst A psychodynamically oriented therapist who focuses on the conscious, coping behavior of the ego instead of the hypothesized unconscious functioning of the id.

Egocentric According to Piaget, assuming that others view the world as oneself does. Unable or unwilling to view the world as through the eyes of others.

Ego-dystonic homosexuality Homosexuality that is inconsistent with one's self-concept and therefore causes personal distress.

Ego identity Erikson's term for the sense of who one is and what one stands for.

Ego identity versus role diffusion Erikson's fifth stage of psychosocial development, which challenges the adolescent to connect skills and social roles to career objectives.

Ego integrity Erikson's term for a firm sense of identity during the later years, characterized by the wisdom to accept the fact that life is limited and the ability to let go.

Ego integrity versus despair Erikson's eighth stage of psychosocial development, which challenges persons to accept the limits of their own life cycles during the later years.

Eidetic imagery The maintenance of detailed visual memories over several minutes.

Elaboration likelihood model The view that persuasive messages are evaluated (elaborated) on the basis of central and peripheral cues.

Elaborative rehearsal A method for increasing retention of new information by relating it to information that is well-known.

Electra complex In psychodynamic theory, a conflict of the phallic stage in which the girl longs for her father and resents her mother.

Electroconvulsive therapy Treatment of disorders like major depression by passing an electric current through the head, causing a convulsion. Abbreviated *ECT.*

Electroencephalograph An instrument that measures electrical activity of the brain (brain waves). Abbreviated *EEG.*

Electromyograph An instrument that measures muscle tension. Abbreviated *EMG.*

Elicit To bring forth, evoke.

Embryo The developing organism from the third through the eighth weeks following conception, during which time the major organ systems undergo rapid differentiation.

Embryonic period The period of prenatal development between the period of the ovum and fetal development, approximately from the third through the eighth weeks following conception.

Embryo transfer Transfer of an embryo from the fallopian tube of its mother into the uterus of another woman, where it becomes implanted and develops.

Emetic Causing vomiting.

Emotion A state of feeling that has cognitive, physiological, and behavioral components.

Emotional appeal A type of persuasive communication that influences behavior on the basis of feelings that are aroused instead of rational analysis of the issues.

Empathic understanding Ability to perceive a client's feelings from the client's frame of reference. A quality of a good person-centered therapist.

Empathy Ability to understand and share another person's feelings.

Empirical Experimental. Emphasizing or based on observation and measurement, in contrast to theory and deduction.

Empty-nest syndrome A sense of depression and loss of purpose felt by some parents when the youngest child leaves home.

Encoding Modifying information so that it can be placed in memory. The first stage of information processing.

Encounter group A structured group process that aims to foster self-awareness by focusing on how group members relate to each other in a setting that encourages frank expression of feelings.

Endocrine system The body's system of ductless glands that secrete hormones and release them directly into the bloodstream.

Endorphins Neurotransmitters that are composed of amino acids and are functionally similar to morphine.

Engram (1) An assumed electrical circuit in the brain that corresponds to a memory trace. (2) An assumed chemical change in the brain that accompanies learning.

Enkephalins Types of endorphins that are weaker and shorter-acting than beta-endorphin.

Enuresis Lack of bladder control at an age by which control is normally attained.

Environmental psychology The field of psychology that studies the ways in which people and the physical environment influence one another.

Epilepsy Temporary disturbances of brain functions that involve sudden neural discharges.

Epinephrine A hormone produced by the adrenal medulla that stimulates the sympathetic division of the ANS. Also called *adrenaline.*

Episodic memory Memories of incidents experienced by a person; of events that occur to a person or take place in the person's presence.

Equilibrium Another term for the vestibular sense.

Erogenous zone An area of the body that is sensitive to sexual sensations.

Eros In psychodynamic theory, the basic

life instinct, which aims toward the preservation and perpetuation of life.

Erotica Sexual material that stimulates a sexual response.

Estrogen A generic term for several female sex hormones that promote growth of female sexual characteristics and regulate the menstrual cycle.

Estrus The periodic sexual excitement of many female mammals, during which they are capable of conceiving and are receptive to sexual advances by males.

Ethical Moral; referring to one's system of deriving standards for determining what is moral.

Ethologist A scientist who studies behavior patterns that are characteristic of various species.

Euphoria Feelings of extreme well-being, elation.

Eustress Stress that is healthful.

Evaluation apprehension Concern that others are evaluating our behavior.

Exaltolide A musky substance that is suspected to be a sexual pheromone.

Exceptional students The term applied to students whose educational needs are special because of physical and health problems, communication problems, behavior disorders, specific learning disabilities, mental retardation, or intellectual giftedness.

Excitatory synapse A synapse that influences receiving neurons in the direction of firing by increasing depolarization of their cell membranes.

Excitement phase The first phase of the sexual response cycle, characterized by erection in the man and by vaginal lubrication and clitoral swelling in the woman.

Exhaustion stage The third stage of the general adaptation syndrome, characterized by parasympathetic activity, weakened resistance, and possible deterioration.

Exhibitionism A paraphilia in which a person feels the compulsion to seek sexual excitement by exposing his genitals in public.

Existentialism The view that people are completely free and responsible for their own behavior.

Expectancies A person variable in social-learning theory. Personal predictions about the outcomes of potential behaviors—"if–then" statements.

Experiential level According to Sternberg, those aspects of intelligence that permit people to cope with novel situations and process information automatically.

Experiment A scientific method that seeks to discover cause-and-effect relationships by introducing independent variables and observing their effects on dependent variables.

Experimental subject (1) A subject receiving a treatment in an experiment, in contrast to a *control subject.* (2) More generally, a participant in an experiment.

Explicit Frank, revealing; leaving nothing implied or to the imagination.

Expository teaching Ausubel's method of presenting material in an organized form, moving from broad to specific concepts.

Expressive vocabulary The sum total of the words that one can use in the production of language.

External eater A person who eats predominantly in response to external stimuli, such as the time of day, the smell of food, or the presence of people who are eating. See *internal eater.*

"Externals" People who have an external locus of control—who perceive the ability to attain reinforcements as largely outside themselves.

Extinction An experimental procedure in which stimuli lose their ability to evoke learned responses because the events that had followed the stimuli no longer occur. (The learned responses are said to be *extinguished.*)

Extinction trial In conditioning, a performance of a learned response in the absence of its predicted consequences so that the learned response becomes inhibited.

Extrasensory perception Perception of external objects and events without sensation. Abbreviated *ESP.* A controversial area of investigation.

Extraversion A source trait in which one's attention is directed to persons and things outside the self, often associated with a sociable, outgoing approach to others and the free expression of feelings and impulses. Opposite of *introversion.*

F

Facial-feedback hypothesis The view that stereotypical facial expressions can contribute to the experiencing of stereotypical emotions.

Factor A cluster of related items such as those found on an intelligence test.

Factor analysis A statistical technique that allows researchers to determine the relationships among large numbers of items such as test questions.

Fallopian tube A tube that conducts ova from an ovary to the uterus.

Family therapy A form of therapy in which the family unit is treated as the client.

Farsighted Capable of seeing distant objects with greater acuity than nearby objects.

Fat cells Cells that store fats. Also called *adipose tissue.*

Fear A negative emotion characterized by perception of a threat, sympathetic nervous system activity, and avoidance tendencies.

Feature detectors Neurons in the visual cortex that fire in response to specific features of visual information, such as lines or edges presented at particular angles.

Feedback Information about one's own behavior.

Feeling-of-knowing experience See *tip-of-the-tongue phenomenon.*

Feminists People (of both genders) who seek social change and legislation to reverse discrimination against women and to otherwise advance the concerns of women.

Fetishism A paraphilia; a variation of choice of sexual object in which the person prefers a body part (such as a foot) or an inanimate object (such as an undergarment) to sexual relations with another person.

Fetus The developing organism from the third month following conception through childbirth, during which time there are maturation of organ systems and dramatic gains in length and weight.

Fight-or-flight reaction Cannon's term for a hypothesized innate adaptive response to the perception of danger.

Final acceptance The fifth stage in Kübler-Ross's theory of the dying process, which is characterized by lack of feeling.

Fissure Valley—referring to the valleys in the wrinkled surface of the cerebral cortex.

Fixation In psychodynamic theory, arrested development. Attachment to objects of an earlier stage.

Fixation time The amount of time spent looking at a visual stimulus. A measure of interest in infants.

Fixed-action pattern An instinct; abbreviated *FAP.*

Fixed-interval schedule A partial

reinforcement schedule in which a fixed amount of time must elapse between the previous and subsequent times that reinforcement is made available.

Fixed-ratio schedule A partial reinforcement schedule in which reinforcement is made available after a fixed number of correct responses.

Flashbacks Distorted perceptions or hallucinations that occur days or weeks after usage of a hallucinogenic drug (usually LSD) but that mimic the effects of the drug.

Flashbulb memories Memories that are preserved in great detail because they reflect intense emotional experiences.

Flat affect Monotonous, dull emotional response.

Flextime A modification of one's work schedule from the standard 9:00 to 5:00 in order to enable one to better meet personal needs.

Flooding A behavioral fear-reduction technique that is based on principles of classical conditioning. Fear-evoking stimuli (CSs) are presented continuously in the absence of actual harm so that fear responses (CRs) are extinguished.

Foot-in-the-door technique A method of persuasion in which compliance with a large request is encouraged by first asking the recipient of the request to comply with a smaller request.

Forced-choice format A method of presenting test questions that requires a respondent to select one of a number of possible answers.

Forensic psychology The field that applies psychological knowledge within the criminal-justice system.

Formal operational stage Piaget's fourth stage of cognitive development, characterized by abstract logical and theoretical thought and deduction from principles.

Fovea A rodless area near the center of the retina where vision is most acute.

Frame of reference In self theory, one's unique patterning of perceptions and attitudes, according to which one evaluates events.

Free association In psychoanalysis, the uncensored uttering of all thoughts that come to mind.

Free-floating anxiety Chronic, persistent anxiety. Anxiety that is not tied to particular events.

Frequency distribution An ordered set of data that indicates how frequently scores appear.

Frequency theory The theory that the pitch of a sound is reflected in the frequency of the neural impulses that are generated in response.

Frontal lobe The lobe of the cerebral cortex that is involved with movement and that lies to the front of the central fissure.

Frustration (1) The thwarting of a motive. (2) The emotion produced by the thwarting of a motive.

Functional analysis A systematic study of behavior in which one identifies the stimuli that trigger it (antecedents) and the reinforcers that maintain it (consequences).

Functional fixedness The tendency to view an object in terms of its name or familiar usage; an impediment to creative problem-solving.

Functionalism The school of psychology founded by William James that emphasizes the uses or functions of the mind.

Functional psychosis A psychotic disorder that is hypothesized to stem from psychological conflict.

Fundamental attribution error A bias in social perception characterized by the tendency to assume that others act predominantly on the basis of their dispositions, even when there is evidence suggesting the importance of their situations.

G

g Spearman's symbol for general intelligence, a general factor that he hypothesized underlay more specific abilities.

Galvanic skin response A sign of sympathetic arousal detected by the amount of sweat in the hand. The greater the amount of sweat, the more electricity is conducted across the skin, suggesting greater sympathetic arousal. Abbreviated *GSR.*

Ganglia Plural of *ganglion.* A group of neural cell bodies found elsewhere in the body other than the brain or spinal cord.

Ganglion See *ganglia.*

Ganglion cells Neurons whose axons form the optic fiber.

GAS Abbreviation for general adaptation syndrome.

Gay male A male homosexual.

Gender The state of being male or female.

Gender constancy The concept that one's gender remains the same, despite superficial changes in appearance or behavior.

Gender identity One's sense of being male or female. (The first stage in the cognitive-developmental theory of the assumption of sex roles.)

Gender-identity disorder A disorder in which a person's anatomic sex is inconsistent with his or her sense of being male or female.

Gender role A complex cluster of behaviors that characterizes traditional male or female behaviors.

Gender-schema theory The view that gender identity plus knowledge of the distribution of behavior patterns into masculine and feminine roles motivates and guides the sex typing of the child.

Gender stability The concept that one's gender is a permanent feature.

Gender typing The process by which people acquire a sense of being male or female and acquire the traits considered typical of males or females.

Gene The basic building block of heredity, which consists of deoxyribonucleic acid (DNA).

General adaptation syndrome Selye's term for a theoretical three-stage response to stress. Abbreviated *GAS.*

General anesthetics Methods that control pain by putting a person to sleep.

Generalization (1) The process of going from the particular to the general. (2) In conditioning, the tendency for a conditioned response to be evoked by stimuli that are similar to the stimulus to which the response was conditioned.

Generalized anxiety disorder Feelings of dread and foreboding and sympathetic arousal of at least six months' duration.

Generalized expectancies In social-learning theory, broad expectations that reflect extensive learning and that are relatively resistant to change.

Generativity versus stagnation Erikson's seventh stage of psychosocial development; the middle years during which persons find (or fail to find) fulfillment in expressing creativity and in guiding and encouraging the younger generation.

Genetic counseling Advice or counseling that concerns the probability that a couple's offspring will have genetic abnormalities.

Genetics The branch of biology that studies heredity.

Genital stage In psychodynamic theory, the fifth and mature stage of psychosexual development, characterized by preferred expression of libido through intercourse with an adult of the opposite sex.

Genuineness Recognition and open expression of one's feelings. A quality of the good person-centered therapist.

Germinal stage The first stage of prenatal development during which the dividing mass of cells has not become implanted in the uterine wall.

Gestalt psychology The school of psychology that emphasizes the tendency to organize perceptions into wholes, to integrate separate stimuli into meaningful patterns.

Gestalt therapy Fritz Perls's form of psychotherapy which attempts to integrate conflicting parts of the personality through directive methods designed to help clients perceive their whole selves.

Glaucoma An eye disease characterized by increased fluid pressure within the eye. A cause of blindness.

Glial cells Cells that nourish and insulate neurons, direct their growth, and remove waste products from the nervous system.

Glucagon A pancreatic hormone that increases the levels of sugar and fat in the blood.

Gout A disease characterized by swelling of joints and severe pain, especially in the big toe.

Grasp reflex An infant reflex in which an object placed on the palms or soles is grasped. Also called *palmar* or *plantar reflex.*

Gray matter In the spinal cord, the neurons and neural segments that are involved in spinal reflexes. They are gray in appearance. Also see *white matter.*

Groupthink A process in which group members, as they make decisions, are influenced by cohesiveness and a dynamic leader to ignore external realities.

Growth hormone A pituitary hormone that regulates growth.

Growth hormone releasing factor A hormone produced by the hypothalamus that causes the pituitary to secrete growth hormone.

GSR Abbreviation for galvanic skin response.

H

Habit A response to a stimulus that becomes automatic with repetition.

Habituate To become accustomed to a stimulus, as determined by no longer showing a response to the stimulus.

Hallucination A sensory experience in the absence of sensory stimulation that is confused with reality.

Hallucinogenic Giving rise to hallucinations.

Halo effect The tendency for one's general impression of a person to influence one's perception of aspects of, or performances by, that person.

Hammer A bone of the middle ear.

Hashish A psychedelic drug derived from the resin of *Cannabis sativa.* Often called "hash."

Hassle A source of annoyance or aggravation.

Health psychology The field of psychology that studies the relationships between psychological factors (e.g., attitudes, beliefs, situational influences, and overt behavior patterns) and the prevention and treatment of physical illness.

Hebephrenic schizophrenia See *disorganized schizophrenia.*

Hemoglobin The substance in the blood that carries oxygen.

Heredity The transmission of traits from one generation to another through genes.

Heritability The percentage of the variation in a trait among people can be attributed to, or explained by, heredity.

Heroin A powerful opiate that provides a euphoric "rush" and feelings of well-being.

Hertz A unit expressing the frequency of sound waves. One Hertz, or *1 Hz,* equals one cycle per second.

Heterosexual A person whose sexual orientation is characterized by preference for sexual activity and the formation of romantic relationships with members of the opposite sex.

Heuristic device A rule of thumb that helps us simplify and solve problems.

Higher-order conditioning (1) According to cognitive psychologists, the learning of relations among events, none of which evokes an unlearned response. (2) According to behaviorists, a classical conditioning procedure in which a previously neutral stimulus comes to elicit the response brought forth by a *conditioned* stimulus by being paired repeatedly with that conditioned stimulus.

Hippocampus A part of the *limbic system* of the brain that plays an important role in the formation of new memories.

Histogram A graphic representation of a frequency distribution that uses rectangular solids.

H.I.V. See *Human immunodeficiency virus.*

Holocaust The name given the Nazi murder of millions of Jews during World War II.

Holophrase A single word used to express complex meanings.

Homeostasis The tendency of the body to maintain a steady state, such as body temperature or level of sugar in the blood.

Homosexuality The sexual orientation characterized by preference for sexual activity and the formation of romantic relationships with members of one's own gender.

Homunculus Latin for "little man." A homunculus within the brain was once thought to govern human behavior.

Hormone A substance secreted by an endocrine gland that promotes development of body structures or regulates bodily functions.

Hot reactors People who respond to stress with accelerated heart rate and constriction of blood vessels in peripheral areas of the body.

Hue The color of light, as determined by its wavelength.

Human immunodeficiency virus The virus that gives rise to acquired immune deficiency syndrome (AIDS) by destroying cells of the immune system and leaving the body prey to opportunistic diseases. Abbreviated *H.I.V.* Sometimes referred to as "the AIDS virus."

Humanism The philosophy (and school of psychology) that asserts that that people are conscious, self-aware, and capable of free choice, self-fulfillment, and ethical behavior.

Humanistic psychology The school of psychology that assumes the existence of the self and emphasizes the importance of consciousness, self-awareness, and the freedom to make choices.

Human-relations theories Theories that hold that efficient organizations are structured according to the characteristics and needs of the individual worker.

Hydrocarbons Chemical compounds consisting of hydrogen and carbon.

Hyperactive More active than normal.

Hyperactivity A disorder found most frequently in young boys, characterized by restlessness and short attention span. It is thought to reflect immaturity of the nervous system.

Hyperglycemia A disorder caused by excess sugar in the blood that can lead to coma and death.

Hypermnesia Greatly enhanced memory.
Hyperphagic Characterized by excessive eating.
Hypertension High blood pressure.
Hyperthyroidism A condition caused by excess thyroxin and characterized by excitability, weight loss, and insomnia.
Hypnagogic state The drowsy interval between waking and sleeping, characterized by brief, hallucinatory, dreamlike experiences.
Hypnosis A condition in which people appear to be highly suggestible and behave as though they are in a trance.
Hypoactive sexual desire disorder Persistent or recurrent lack of sexual fantasies and of interest in sexual activity.
Hypochondriasis Persistent belief that one has a medical disorder despite the lack of medical findings.
Hypoglycemia A metabolic disorder that is characterized by shakiness, dizziness, and lack of energy. It is caused by a low level of sugar in the blood.
Hypothalamus A bundle of nuclei below the thalamus involved in the regulation of body temperature, motivation, and emotion.
Hypothesis An assumption about behavior that is tested through research.
Hypothesis testing In concept formation, an active process in which we try to ferret out the meanings of concepts by testing our assumptions.
Hypothyroidism A condition caused by a deficiency of thyroxin and characterized by sluggish behavior and a low metabolic rate.
Hysterical disorder, conversion type Former term for *conversion disorder.*

I

Icon A mental representation of a visual stimulus that is held briefly in sensory memory.
Iconic memory The sensory register that briefly holds mental representations of visual stimuli.
Id In psychodynamic theory, the psychic structure that is present at birth and that is governed by the pleasure principle. The id represents physiological drives and is fully unconscious.
Idealize To think of as being perfect, without flaws.
Ideas of persecution Erroneous beliefs (delusions) that one is being victimized or persecuted.
Identification (1) In psychodynamic theory, unconscious incorporation of the personality of another person. (2) In social-learning theory, a broad, continuous process of imitation during which children strive to become like role models.
Identity achievement Resolution of an identity crisis through development of a stable set of beliefs or a course of action.
Identity crisis According to Erikson, a period of inner conflict during which one examines his or her values and makes decisions about life roles.
Identity diffusion See *role diffusion.*
Illusions Sensations that give rise to misperceptions.
Imbalance In balance theory, an uncomfortable condition in which persons whom we like disagree with us.
Immune system The system of the body that recognizes and destroys foreign agents (antigens) that invade the body.
Imprinting A process that occurs during a critical period in an organism's development, in which that organism forms an attachment that will afterward be difficult to modify.
Incentive An object, person, or situation perceived as being capable of satisfying a need.
Incest taboo The cultural prohibition against marrying or having sexual relations with a close blood relative.
Incidence The extent to which an event occurs.
Incubation In problem solving, a hypothetical process that sometimes occurs when we stand back from a frustrating problem for a while and the solution suddenly occurs to us.
Incubus (1) A spirit or demon thought in medieval times to lie on sleeping people, especially on women, for sexual purposes. (2) A nightmare.
Incus A bone of the middle ear. Latin for "anvil."
Independent variable A condition in a scientific study that is manipulated so that its effects may be observed.
Indiscriminate attachment The showing of attachment behaviors toward any person.
Individual psychology Adler's psychodynamic theory which emphasizes feelings of inferiority and the creative self.
Individuation The process by which one separates from others and gains control over one's own behavior.
Inductive Going from the particular to the general; for example, descriptive of a disciplinary technique in which the individual is taught the principle involved and not merely punished.
Industrial psychology The field of psychology that studies the relationships between people and work.
Industry versus inferiority Erikson's fourth stage of psychosocial development in which the child is challenged to master the fundamentals of technology during the primary school years.
Infant A very young organism, a baby.
Infantile autism A developmental disorder of childhood, characterized by extreme aloneness, communication problems, preservation of sameness, and ritualistic behavior.
Infer Draw a conclusion.
Inference Conclusion.
Inferential statistics The branch of statistics concerned with the confidence with which conclusions drawn about samples may be extended to the populations from which they were drawn.
Inferiority complex Feelings of inferiority hypothesized by Adler to serve as a central source of motivation.
Inflammation Increased blood flow to an injured area of the body, resulting in redness, warmth, and increased supply of white blood cells.
Inflections Grammatical markers that change the forms of words to indicate grammatical relationships such as number and tense.
Information processing The processes by which information is encoded, stored, and retrieved.
Informed consent Agreement to participate in research after receiving information about the purposes of the study and the nature of the treatments.
Inhibitory synapse A synapse that influences receiving neurons in the direction of not firing by encouraging changes in their membrane permeability in the direction of the resting potential.
Initial-preattachment phase The first phase in forming bonds of attachment, characterized by indiscriminate attachment.
Initiative versus guilt Erikson's third stage of psychosocial development, during which the child is challenged to add planning and "attacking" to the exercise of choice.
Innate Existing at birth. Unlearned, natural.
Innate fixed-action pattern An instinct.
Inner ear The cochlea.

Insanity A legal term descriptive of a person judged to be incapable of recognizing right from wrong or of conforming his or her behavior to the law.

Insecure attachment A negative type of attachment, in which children show indifference or ambivalence toward attachment figures.

Insight (1) In Gestalt psychology, the sudden perception of relationships among elements of the perceptual field, allowing the sudden solution of a problem. (2) In psychotherapy, awareness of one's genuine motives and feelings.

Insomnia A term for three types of sleeping problems: (1) difficulty falling asleep; (2) difficulty remaining asleep; and (3) waking early.

Instinct An inherited disposition to activate specific behavior patterns that are designed to reach certain goals.

Instinctive Inborn, natural, unlearned.

Instructional objective A clear statement of what is to be learned.

Instrumental conditioning Another term for operant conditioning, reflecting the fact that in operant conditioning, the learned behavior is instrumental in achieving certain effects.

Instrumental learning See instrumental conditioning.

Insulin A pancreatic hormone that stimulates the metabolism of sugar.

Intellectualization A defense mechanism in which threatening events are viewed with emotional detachment.

Intelligence A complex and controversial concept: (1) Learning ability, as contrasted with achievement. (2) Defined by David Wechsler as the capacity ". . . to understand the world [and the] resourcefulness to cope with its challenges." (3) Defined operationally as the trait or traits required to perform well on an intelligence test.

Intelligence quotient (1) Originally, a ratio obtained by dividing a child's mental age on an intelligence test by his or her chronological age. (2) Generally, a score on an intelligence test. Abbreviated *IQ*.

Interactionism An approach to understanding behavior that emphasizes specification of the relationships among the various determinants of behavior instead of seeking the first cause of behavior.

Interference theory The view that we may forget stored material because other learning interferes with it.

Internal eaters People who eat predominantly in response to internal stimuli, like hunger pangs. See *external eater.*

"Internals" People who have an internal locus of control—who perceive the ability to attain reinforcements as being largely within themselves.

Interneuron A neuron that transmits a neural impulse from a sensory neuron to a motor neuron.

Interpersonal attraction See *attraction.*

Interposition A monocular cue for depth based on the fact that closer objects obscure vision of objects behind them.

Interpretation In psychoanalysis, an analyst's explanation of a client's utterance according to psychodynamic theory.

Intimacy versus isolation Erikson's sixth stage of psychosocial development; the young adult years during which persons are challenged to commit themselves to intimate relationships with others.

Intonation The use of pitches of varying levels to help communicate meaning.

Intoxication Drunkenness.

Intrapsychic Referring to the psychodynamic movement of psychic energy among the psychic structures hypothesized by Sigmund Freud.

Introjection In psychodynamic theory, the bringing within oneself of the personality of another individual.

Introspection An objective approach to describing one's mental content.

Introversion A trait characterized by intense imagination and the tendency to inhibit impulses. Opposite of *extraversion.*

Intuitive The direct learning or knowing of something without conscious use of reason.

In utero A Latin phrase meaning "in the uterus."

Involuntary Automatic, not consciously controlled—referring to functions like heartbeat and dilation of the pupils.

IQ Intelligence quotient. A score on an intelligence test.

Iris A muscular membrane whose dilation regulates the amount of light that enters the eye.

J

James-Lange theory The theory that certain external stimuli trigger stereotypical patterns of activity and autonomic arousal. Emotions are the cognitive representations of this behavior and arousal.

Job sharing Sharing of a full-time job by two or more workers.

Just noticeable difference The minimal amount by which a source of energy must be increased or decreased so that a difference in intensity will be perceived.

K

Kinesthesis The sense that provides information about the position and motion of parts of the body.

Knobs Swellings at the ends of axon terminals. Also referred to as *bulbs* or *buttons.*

Knowledge-acquisition components According to Sternberg, components of intelligence that are used in gaining knowledge, such as encoding and relating new knowledge to existing knowledge.

Korsakoff's syndrome See *Wernicke-Korsakoff's syndrome.*

L

La belle indifférence A French term descriptive of the lack of concern shown by some persons with conversion disorder.

LAD Acronym for *language acquisition device.*

Language The communication of information through symbols that are arranged according to rules of grammar.

Language acquisition device In psycholinguistic theory, neural "prewiring" that is theorized to facilitate the child's learning of grammar.

Larynx The structure in the throat that contains the vocal cords.

Latency stage In psychodynamic theory, the fourth stage of psychosexual development during which sexual impulses are repressed.

Latent content In psychodynamic theory, the symbolized or underlying content of dreams.

Latent learning Learning that is not exhibited at the time of learning but is shown when adequate reinforcement is introduced.

Lateral fissure The valley in the cerebral cortex that separates the temporal lobe from the frontal and parietal lobes.

Lateral hypothalamus An area at the side of the hypothalamus that appears to function as a start-eating center.

Law of effect Thorndike's principle that responses are "stamped in" by rewards and "stamped out" by punishments.

Leadership-motive syndrome A cluster of needs that includes strong needs for power and self-control and a low need for affiliation.

Learned helplessness Seligman's model for the acquisition of depressive behavior, based on findings that organisms in aversive situations learn to show inactivity when their operants are not reinforced.

Learning (1) According to cognitive theorists, the process by which organisms make relatively permanent changes in the way they represent the environment because of experience. These changes influence the organism's behavior. (2) According to behaviorists, a relatively permanent change in behavior that results from experience.

Lens A transparent body between the iris and the vitreous humor of the eye that focuses an image onto the retina.

Lesbian Female homosexual.

Lesion An injury that results in impaired behavior or loss of a function.

Leukocytes The white blood cells of the immune system.

Libido (1) In psychodynamic theory, the energy of Eros, the sexual instinct. (2) Generally, sexual interest or drive.

Lie detector See *polygraph*.

Life-change units Numbers assigned to various life events that indicate the degree of stress they cause.

Light Electromagnetic energy of various wavelengths. The part of the spectrum of energy that stimulates the eye and produces visual sensations.

Limbic system A group of brain structures that form a fringe along the inner edge of the cerebrum. These structures are involved in memory and motivation.

Linguistic relativity hypothesis The view that language structures the way in which we perceive the world. As a consequence, our thoughts would be limited by the concepts available in our languages.

Linguists Scientists who study the structure, functions, and origins of language.

Locus of control The place (locus) to which an individual attributes control over the receiving of reinforcements—either inside or outside the self.

Long-term memory The type or stage of memory capable of relatively permanent storage.

Love A strong, positive emotion with many meanings. See, for example, *romantic love* and *attachment*.

Low-balling A sales method in which extremely attractive terms are offered to induce a person to make a commitment. Once the commitment is made, the terms are revised.

LSD Lysergic acid diethylamide. A hallucinogenic drug.

Lucid dream A dream in which we seem to be awake and aware that we are dreaming.

Lysergic acid diethylamide A hallucinogenic drug. Abbreviated *LSD*.

M

Maintenance rehearsal Mental repetition of information in order to keep it in memory.

Major depression A severe mood disorder in which the person may show loss of appetite, psychomotor symptoms, and impaired reality testing.

Major tranquilizer A drug that decreases severe anxiety or agitation in psychotic patients or in violent individuals.

Malingering Pretending to be ill in order to escape duty or work.

Malleus A bone of the middle ear. Latin for "hammer."

Mania A state characterized by elation and restlessness. (A Greek word meaning "madness.")

Manic-depression Former term for *bipolar disorder*.

Manifest content In the psychodynamic theory of dreams, the reported or perceived content of dreams.

Mantra A word or sound that is repeated in transcendental meditation as a means of narrowing consciousness and inducing relaxation.

Marijuana The dried vegetable matter of the *Cannabis sativa* plant. A mild hallucinogenic drug that is most frequently taken in by smoking.

Matching hypothesis The view that people tend to choose persons similar to themselves in attractiveness and attitudes in the formation of interpersonal relationships.

Maturation Changes that result from heredity and minimal nutrition but that do not appear to require learning or exercise. A gradual, orderly unfolding or developing of new structures or behaviors as a result of heredity.

Mean A type of average calculated by dividing the sum of scores by the number of scores.

Means–end analysis A heuristic device in which we try to solve a problem by evaluating the difference between the current situation and the goal.

Median A type of average defined as the score beneath which 50 percent of the cases fall.

Mediation In information processing, a method of improving memory by linking two items with a third that ties them together.

Medical model The view that abnormal behavior is symptomatic of underlying illness.

Meditation A systematic narrowing of attention that slows the metabolism and helps produce feelings of relaxation.

Medulla An oblong-shaped area of the hindbrain involved in heartbeat and respiration.

Meiosis A process of reduction division in which sperm and ova are formed, each of which contains 23 chromosomes.

Memory The processes by which information is encoded, stored, and retrieved.

Memory trace An assumed change in the nervous system that reflects the impression made by a stimulus. Memory traces are said to be "held" in sensory registers.

Menarche The onset of menstruation.

Menopause The cessation of menstruation.

Menstrual synchrony The convergence of the menstrual cycles of women who spend time in close quarters.

Menstruation The monthly shedding of the uterine lining by nonpregnant women.

Mental age The accumulated months of credit that a test-taker earns on the Stanford-Binet Intelligence Scale.

Mental set (1) Readiness to respond to a situation in a set manner. (2) In problem-solving, a tendency to respond to a new problem with an approach that was successful with problems similar in appearance.

Mescaline A hallucinogenic drug derived from the mescal (peyote) cactus. In religious ceremonies, Mexican Indians chew the buttonlike structures at the tops of the rounded stems of the plant.

Metabolism In organisms, a continuous process that converts food into energy.

Metacognition Awareness and control of one's cognitive abilities, as shown by the intentional use of cognitive strategies in solving problems.

Metacomponents According to Sternberg, components of intelligence that are based on self-awareness of our intellectual processes.

Metamemory Self-awareness of the ways in which memory functions, as shown by use of cognitive strategies to foster the effective encoding, storing, and retrieval of information.

Metaphor The use of words or phrases characteristic of one situation in another situation. A figure of speech that dramatizes a description by applying imagery from another situation.

Methadone An artificial narcotic that is slower acting than, and does not provide the rush of, heroin. Methadone allows heroin addicts to abstain from heroin without experiencing an abstinence syndrome.

Methaqualone An addictive depressant often referred to as "ludes."

Method of constant stimuli A psychophysical method for determining thresholds in which the researcher presents stimuli of various magnitudes and asks the subject to report detection.

Method of loci A method of retaining information in which chunks of new material are related to a series of well-established or well-known images.

Method of savings A measure of retention in which the difference between the number of repetitions originally required to learn a list and the number of repetitions required to relearn the list after a certain amount of time has elapsed is calculated.

Microspectrophotometry A method for analyzing the sensitivity of single cones to lights of different wavelengths.

Middle ear The central part of the ear that contains three small bones, the "hammer," "anvil," and "stirrup."

Midlife crisis A crisis felt by many people at about age 40 when they realize that life may be halfway over and they feel trapped in meaningless life roles.

Migraine headache A throbbing headache, usually occurring on one side of the head, that stems from change in the blood supply to the head. It is often accompanied by nausea and impaired vision.

Mind That part of consciousness involved in perception and awareness.

Minor tranquilizer A drug that relieves feelings of anxiety and tension.

Mitosis The process of cell division by which the identical genetic code is carried into new cells in the body.

Mnemonics A system for remembering in which items are related to easily recalled sets of symbols such as acronyms, phrases, or jingles.

Mode A type of average defined as the most frequently occurring score in a distribution.

Model In social-learning theory: (1) As a noun, an organism that engages in a response that is imitated by another organism. (2) As a verb, to engage in behavior patterns that are imitated by others.

Modeling A behavior therapy technique in which the therapist or a group member engages in a behavior that is imitated by a client.

Modifier genes Genes that alter the action of the phenotypical expression of other genes.

Monoamine oxidase inhibitors Antidepressant drugs that work by blocking the action of an enzyme that breaks down norepinephrine and serotonin. Abbreviated *MAO inhibitors.*

Monochromat A person who is sensitive to the intensity of light only and thus color-blind.

Monocular cues Stimuli that suggest depth and that can be perceived with only one eye, such as perspective and interposition.

Monozygotic twins Twins who develop from the same zygote, thus carrying the same genetic instructions. Identical twins. Abbreviated *MZ twins.* See *dizygotic twins.*

Moral principle In psychodynamic theory, the governing principle of the superego, which sets moral standards and enforces adherence to them.

Moro reflex An infant reflex characterized by arching of the back and drawing up of the legs in response to a sudden, startling stimulus. Also called the *startle reflex.*

Morpheme The smallest unit of meaning in a language.

Morphine A narcotic derived from opium that reduces pain and produces feelings of well-being.

Morphology The study of the units of meaning in a language.

Motion parallax A monocular cue for depth based on the perception that nearby objects appear to move more rapidly in relation to our own motion.

Motive A hypothetical state within an organism that propels the organism toward a goal.

Motor cortex The section of cerebral cortex that lies in the frontal lobe, just across the central fissure from the sensory cortex. Neural impulses in the motor cortex are linked to muscular responses.

Multiple approach–avoidance conflict A type of conflict in which a number of goals each produces approach and avoidance motives.

Multiple orgasms The experiencing of one or more additional orgasms as a result of sexual stimulation during the resolution phase. Two or more orgasms in rapid succession.

Multiple personality A dissociative disorder in which a person has two or more distinct personalities.

Mutation Sudden variations in the genetic code that usually occur as a result of environmental influences.

Mutism Refusal to talk.

Myelination The process by which the axons of neurons become coated with a fatty, insulating substance.

Myelin sheath A fatty substance that encases and insulates axons, permitting more rapid transmission of neural impulses.

Myotonia Muscle tension.

N

***n* Ach** The need for achievement; the need to master, to accomplish difficult things.

***n* Aff** The need for affiliation; the need to be associated with groups.

Narcolepsy A sleep disorder characterized by uncontrollable seizures of sleep during the waking state.

Narcotics Drugs used to relieve pain and induce sleep. The term is usually reserved for opiates.

Native-language approach A method of teaching a second language in which children are at first taught in the language spoken in the home.

Naturalistic observation A method of scientific investigation in which organisms are observed carefully and unobtrusively in their natural environments.

Nature In behavior genetics, inherited influences on behavior, as contrasted with *nurture.*

Nearsightedness Inability to see distant objects with the acuity with which a person with normal vision can see distant objects.

Need A state of deprivation.

Need for achievement The need to master, to accomplish difficult things.

Need for affiliation The need for affiliation; the need to be associated with groups.

Negative correlation A relationship between two variables in which one variable increases as the other variable decreases.

Negative feedback Descriptive of a system in which information that a quantity (e.g., of a hormone) has reached a set point suspends action of the agency (e.g., a gland) that gives rise to that quantity.

Negative instance In concept formation, events that are *not* examples of a concept.

Negative reinforcer A reinforcer that increases the frequency of operant behavior when it is removed. Pain, anxiety, and disapproval usually, but not always, function as negative reinforcers. See *positive reinforcer.*

Neodissociation theory A theory that explains hypnotic events in terms of an ability to divide our awareness so that we can focus on hypnotic instructions and, at the same time, perceive outside sources of stimulation.

Neo-Freudians Theorists in the psychodynamic tradition who usually place less emphasis than Freud did on the importance of sexual impulses and unconscious determinants of behavior. Instead, they place more emphasis than Freud did on conscious motives and rational decision-making.

Neonate A newborn child.

Nerve A bundle of axons from many neurons.

Neural impulse The electrochemical discharge of a neuron, or nerve cell.

Neuroendocrine reflex A reflex that involves the nervous system and the endocrine system, such as the ejection of milk.

Neuron A nerve cell.

Neuropeptide A short chain of amino acids (peptide) that functions as a neurotransmitter.

Neurosis One of a number of disorders characterized chiefly by anxiety, feelings of dread and foreboding, and avoidance behavior and theorized to stem from unconscious conflict. (Contemporary systems of classifying abnormal behavior de-emphasize this concept.)

Neuroticism (1) A trait in which a person is given to anxiety, feelings of foreboding, inhibition of impulses, and avoidance behavior. (2) Eysenck's term for emotional instability—a definition that is not fully consistent with other usages of the word.

Neurotransmitter A chemical substance that is involved in the transmission of neural impulses from one neuron to another.

Nicotine A stimulant found in tobacco smoke.

Nightmare A frightening dream that usually occurs during rapid-eye-movement (REM) sleep.

Night terrors See *sleep terrors.*

Node of Ranvier A noninsulated segment of an otherwise myelinated axon.

Noise (1) In signal-detection theory, any unwanted signal that interferes with perception of the desired signal. (2) More generally, a combination of dissonant sounds.

Non-rapid-eye-movement sleep Stages 1 through 4 of sleep, which are not characterized by rapid eye movements. Abbreviated *NREM sleep.*

Nonbalance In balance theory, a condition in which persons whom we dislike do not agree with us.

Nonconscious Descriptive of bodily processes, such as the growing of hair, of which we cannot become conscious. We may know that our hair is growing, but we cannot directly experience the biological process.

Nonsense syllables Meaningless sets of two consonants, with a vowel sandwiched in between, that are used to study memory.

Norepinephrine A neurotransmitter whose action is similar to that of the hormone *epinephrine* and which may play a role in depression.

Normal curve A graphic presentation of a normal distribution, showing a bell shape.

Normal distribution A symmetrical distribution in which approximately two-thirds of the cases lie within a standard deviation of the mean. A distribution that represents chance deviations of a variable.

Normative data Information concerning the behavior of a population.

Norm-referenced testing A testing approach in which scores are derived by comparing the number of items answered correctly with the average performance of others.

Novel stimulation (1) New or different stimulation. (2) A hypothesized primary drive to experience new or different stimulation.

Noxious Harmful, injurious.

Nuclear magnetic resonance Formation of a computer-generated image of the anatomical details of the brain by measuring the signals that these structures emit when the head is placed in a strong magnetic field.

Nuclei Plural of *nucleus.* A group of neural cell bodies found in the brain or spinal cord.

Nurturance The quality of nourishing, rearing, and fostering the development of children, animals, or plants.

Nurture In behavior genetics, environmental influences on behavior, including factors such as nutrition, culture, socioeconomic status, and learning. Contrast with *nature.*

O

Objective Of known or perceived objects rather than existing only in the mind; real.

Objective morality According to Piaget, objective moral judgments assign guilt according to the amount of damage done rather than on the motives of the actor.

Objective tests Tests whose items must be answered in a specified, limited manner. Tests that have concrete answers that are considered to be correct.

Object permanence Recognition that objects removed from sight still exist, as demonstrated in young children by continued pursuit.

Observational learning In social-learning theory, the acquisition of expectations and skills by observing the behavior of others. As opposed to operant conditioning, skill acquisition by means of observational learning occurs without the emission and reinforcement of a response.

Obsession A recurring thought or image that seems to be beyond control.

Occipital lobe The lobe of the cerebral cortex that is involved in vision. It lies below and behind the parietal lobe and behind the temporal lobe.

Odor The characteristic of a substance that makes it perceptible to the sense of smell. An odor is a sample of the molecules of the substance being sensed.

Oedipus complex In psychodynamic theory, a conflict of the phallic stage in which the boy wishes to possess his mother sexually and perceives his father as a rival in love.

Olfactory Having to do with the sense of smell.

Olfactory membrane A membrane high in each nostril that contains receptor neurons for the sense of smell.

Olfactory nerve The nerve that transmits information about odors from olfactory receptors to the brain.

Opaque (1) Not permitting the passage of light. (2) In psychoanalysis, descriptive of the analyst, who is expected to hide his or her own feelings from the client.

Operant behavior Voluntary responses that are reinforced.

Operant conditioning A simple form of learning in which an organism learns to engage in behavior because it is reinforced.

Operational definition A definition of a variable in terms of the methods used to create or measure the variable.

Opiate An addictive drug derived from the opium poppy that provides a euphoric rush and depresses the nervous system.

Opioid A synthetic (artificial) drug similar in chemical structure and effects to opiates.

Opponent-process theory The theory that color vision is made possible by three types of cones, some of which respond to red or green light, some to blue or yellow light, and some to the intensity of light only.

Optic nerve The nerve that transmits sensory information from the eye to the brain.

Optimal arousal A level of arousal at which an organism has the greatest feelings of well-being or functions most efficiently.

Oral fixation In psychodynamic theory, attachment to objects and behaviors characteristic of the oral stage.

Oral stage The first stage in Freud's theory of psychosexual development, during which gratification is obtained primarily through oral activities like sucking and biting.

Organic psychosis A psychotic disorder that is known to stem from biochemical abnormalities.

Organic model The view that abnormal behavior is caused by biochemical or physiological abnormalities.

Organizational analysis Evaluation of the goals and resources of an organization.

Organizational psychology The field of psychology that studies the structure and functions of organizations.

Organizing effects The directional effects of sex hormones—for example, along stereotypical masculine or feminine lines.

Organ of Corti The receptor for hearing, which lies on the basilar membrane in the cochlea. Called the command post of hearing, it contains the receptor cells that transmit auditory information to the auditory nerve.

Orgasm The height or climax of sexual excitement, involving involuntary muscle contractions, release of sexual tensions, and, usually, intense subjective feelings of pleasure.

Orienting reflex An unlearned response in which an organism attends to a stimulus.

Osmoreceptors Receptors in the hypothalamus that are sensitive to depletion of fluid in the body.

Osteoporosis A condition caused by calcium deficiency and characterized by brittleness of the bones.

Outer ear The funnel-shaped outer part of the ear that transmits sound waves to the eardrum.

Oval window A membrane that transmits vibrations from the stirrup of the middle ear to the inner ear.

Ovaries The female reproductive organs located in the abdominal cavity. The ovaries produce egg cells (ova) and the hormones estrogen and progesterone.

Overextension Overgeneralizing the use of words into situations in which they do not apply (characteristic of the speech of young children).

Overregularization The formation of plurals and past tenses of irregular nouns and verbs according to rules of grammar that apply to regular nouns and verbs (characteristic of the speech of young children).

Overtones Tones higher in frequency than those played on an instrument. Overtones result from vibrations throughout the instrument.

Ovulation The releasing of an egg cell (ovum) from an ovary.

Oxytocin A pituitary hormone that stimulates labor (childbirth).

P

Paired associates Nonsense syllables presented in pairs in experiments that measure recall. After viewing pairs, participants are shown one member of each pair and asked to recall the other.

Palmar reflex See *grasp reflex.*

Pancreas A gland behind the stomach whose secretions, including insulin, influence the level of sugar in the blood.

Panic disorder The recurrent experiencing of attacks of extreme anxiety in the absence of external stimuli that usually elicit anxiety.

Paradoxical intention Achieving one's goals by undertaking an apparently opposing course of action.

Paradoxical sleep Another term for rapid-eye-movement sleep, reflecting the fact that brain waves found during REM sleep suggest a level of arousal similar to that shown during the waking state.

Paranoia A rare psychotic disorder in which a person shows a persistent delusional system but not the confusion of the paranoid schizophrenic.

Paranoid personality disorder A disorder characterized by persistent suspiciousness but not the disorganization of paranoid schizophrenia.

Paranoid schizophrenia A subtype of schizophrenia characterized primarily by delusions—commonly of persecution—and by vivid hallucinations.

Paraphilia A disorder in which the person shows sexual arousal in response to unusual or bizarre objects or situations.

Parasympathetic nervous system The branch of the autonomic nervous system that is most active during processes such as digestion and relaxation that restore the body's reserves of energy. See *sympathetic division.*

Parietal lobe The lobe of the cerebral cortex that lies behind the central fissure and that is involved in body senses.

Partial reinforcement One of several types of reinforcement schedules in which correct responses receive intermittent reinforcement, as opposed to *continuous reinforcement.*

Participant modeling A behavior-therapy technique in which a client observes and imitates a person who approaches and copes with feared objects or situations.

Passionate love See *romantic love.*

Pathogen An organism such as a bacterium or virus that can cause disease.

Pathological gambler A person who gambles habitually despite consistent losses. A compulsive gambler.

PCP Phencyclidine; a hallucinogenic drug.

Peak experience In humanistic theory, a brief moment of rapture that stems from the realization that one is on the path toward self-actualization.

Penis envy In psychodynamic theory, jealousy of the male sexual organ attributed to girls in the phallic stage.

Pepsinogen A substance that helps the body digest proteins.

Perceived self-efficacy In social-learning theory, a person's belief that he or she can achieve goals through his or her own efforts.

Perception The process by which sensations are organized into an inner representation of the world—a psychological process through which we interpret sensory information.

Perceptual organization The tendency to integrate perceptual elements into meaningful patterns.

Performance anxiety Fear concerning whether or not one will be able to perform adequately.

Performance components According to Sternberg, the mental operations used in processing information.

Period of the ovum Up to the first two weeks following conception, before the developing ovum (now fertilized) has become securely implanted in the uterine wall. Another term for the *germinal stage.*

Peripheral nervous system The part of the nervous system consisting of the somatic nervous system and the autonomic nervous system.

Permeability The degree to which a membrane allows a substance to pass through it.

Personality The distinct patterns of behaviors, including thoughts and feelings, that characterize a person's adaptation to the demands of life.

Personality disorder An enduring pattern of maladaptive behavior that is a source of distress to the individual or to others.

Personality structure One's total pattern of traits.

Person-centered therapy Carl Rogers' method of psychotherapy, which emphasizes the creation of a warm, therapeutic atmosphere that frees clients to engage in self-expression and self-exploration.

Person variables In social-learning theory, determinants of behavior that lie within the person, including competencies, encoding strategies, expectancies, subjective values, and self-regulatory systems and plans.

Perspective A monocular cue for depth based on the convergence (coming together) of parallel lines as they recede into the distance.

pH A chemical symbol expressing the acidity of a solution.

Phallic stage In psychodynamic theory, the third stage of psychosexual development, characterized by shifting of libido to the phallic region and by the Oedipus and Electra complexes.

Phallic symbol In psychodynamic theory, an object that represents the penis.

Phencyclidine A hallucinogenic drug whose name is an acronym for its chemical structure. Abbreviated *PCP.*

Phenomenological Having to do with subjective, conscious experience.

Phenothiazines Drugs that act as major tranquilizers and that are effective in treating many cases of schizophrenic disorders.

Phenylketonuria A genetic abnormality transmitted by a recessive gene, in which one is unable to metabolize phenylpyruvic acid, leading to mental retardation. Abbreviated *PKU.*

Pheromones Chemical secretions detected by the sense of smell that stimulate stereotypical behaviors in other members of the same species.

Phi phenomenon The perception of movement as a result of sequential presentation of visual stimuli, as with lights going on and off in a row on a theater marquee.

Phobic disorder Excessive, irrational fear. Fear that is out of proportion to the actual danger and that interferes with one's life. Formerly called *phobic neurosis.*

Phobic neurosis See *phobic disorder.*

Phoneme A basic sound in a language.

Phonology The study of the basic sounds in a language.

Photographic memory See *iconic memory.*

Photoreceptors Cells that respond to light. See *rod* and *cone.*

Phrenology An unscientific method of analyzing personality by measurement of the shapes and protuberances of the skull.

Physiological Having to do with the biological functions and vital processes of organisms.

Physiological dependence Addiction to a drug.

Physiological drives Unlearned drives with a biological basis, such as hunger, thirst, and avoidance of pain. Also called *primary drives.*

Physiological psychologists Same as biological psychologists.

Pitch The highness or lowness of a sound, as determined by the frequency of the sound waves.

Pituitary gland The body's master gland, located in the brain, that secretes growth hormone, prolactin, antidiuretic hormone, and others.

Placebo A bogus treatment that controls for the effects of expectations. A so-called "sugar pill."

Placenta A membrane that permits the exchange of nutrients and waste products between the mother and the fetus but that does not allow the maternal and fetal bloodstreams to mix.

Place theory The theory that the pitch of a sound is determined by the section of the basilar membrane that vibrates in response to it.

Plantar reflex See *grasp reflex.*

Plateau phase An advanced state of sexual arousal that precedes orgasm.

Pleasure principle In psychodynamic theory, the principle that governs the id; the demanding of immediate gratification of instinctive needs.

Polarization (1) In physiological psychology, the readying of a neuron for firing by creating an internal negative charge in relation to the body fluid outside the cell membrane. (2) In social psychology, the taking of an extreme position or attitude on an issue.

Polygenic Determined by more than one gene.

Polygraph An instrument that is theorized to be sensitive to whether or not an individual is telling lies by assessing four measures of arousal: heart rate, blood pressure, respiration rate, and galvanic skin response (GSR). Also called a *lie detector.*

Pons A structure of the hindbrain involved in respiration.

Population A complete group of organisms or events.

Positive correlation A relationship between variables in which one variable increases as the other variable also increases.

Positive instance In concept formation, an example of a concept.

Positive reinforcer A reinforcer that increases the frequency of operant behavior when it is presented. Food and approval are usually, but not always, positive reinforcers. See *negative reinforcer.*

Positron-emission tomography Formation of a computer-generated image of the neural activity of parts of the brain by tracing the amount of glucose used by the various parts. Abbreviated *PET scan.*

Possession According to superstitious belief, a psychological state in which a person shows abnormal behavior induced by demons or the Devil as a result of retribution or of making a pact with the Devil.

Postconventional level According to Kohlberg, a period of moral development during which moral judgments are derived from moral principles and people look to themselves to set moral standards.

Posthypnotic amnesia Inability to recall material presented while hypnotized, following the suggestion of the hypnotist.

Post-traumatic stress disorder A disorder that follows a psychologically distressing event that is outside the range of normal human experience. It is characterized by symptoms such as intense fear, avoidance of stimuli associated with the event, and reliving of the event.

Pragmatics The practical aspects of communication. Adaptation of language to fit the social context.

Preconscious In psychodynamic theory, descriptive of material of which one is not currently aware but which can be brought into awareness by focusing one's attention. Also see *unconscious.*

Preconventional level According to Kohlberg, a period of moral development during which moral judgments are based largely on expectation of rewards and punishments.

Prefrontal lobotomy A form of psychosurgery in which a section of the frontal lobe of the brain is severed or destroyed.

Pregenital In psychodynamic theory, characteristic of stages less mature than the genital stage.

Prejudice The unfounded belief that a person or group—on the basis of assumed racial, ethnic, sexual, or other features—will possess negative characteristics or perform inadequately.

Prelinguistic Prior to the development of language.

Premenstrual syndrome A cluster of symptoms—which may include tension, irritability, depression, and fatigue—that some women experience before menstruating.

Prenatal Prior to birth.

Preoperational stage The second of Piaget's stages of cognitive development, characterized by illogical use of words and symbols, egocentrism, animism, artificialism, and objective moral judgments.

Presbyopia Brittleness of the lens, a condition that impairs visual acuity for nearby objects.

Primacy effect (1) In information processing, the tendency to recall the initial items in a series of items. (2) In social psychology, the tendency to evaluate others in terms of first impressions.

Primary colors Colors that we cannot produce by mixing other hues; colors from which other colors are derived.

Primary drives Unlearned drives; physiological drives.

Primary mental abilities According to Thurstone, the basic abilities that compose human intelligence.

Primary narcissism In psychodynamic theory, the type of autism that describes the newborn child who has not learned that he or she is separate from the rest of the world.

Primary prevention In community psychology, the deterrence of psychological problems before they start.

Primary reinforcer A stimulus that has reinforcement value without learning. Examples: food, water, warmth, and pain. See *secondary reinforcer.*

Primary sex characteristics Physical traits that distinguish the sexes and that are directly involved in reproduction.

Primate A member of an order of mammals including monkeys, apes, and human beings.

Prism A transparent triangular solid that breaks down visible light into the colors of the spectrum.

Private self-consciousness The tendency to take critical note of one's own behavior even when unobserved by others.

Proactive interference Interference from previously learned material in one's ability to retrieve or recall recently learned material. See *retroactive interference.*

Proband The family member first studied or tested.

Procedural memory Knowledge of ways of doing things; skill memory.

Productivity A property of language; the ability to combine words into unlimited, novel sentences.

Progesterone A sex hormone that promotes growth of the sexual organs and helps maintain pregnancy.

Prognosis A prediction of the probable course of a disease.

Programmed learning A method of learning, based on operant conditioning principles, in which complex tasks are broken down into simple steps. The proper performance of each step is reinforced. Incorrect responses go unreinforced but are not punished.

Progressive relaxation Jacobson's method for reducing muscle tension, which involves alternate tensing and relaxing of muscle groups throughout the body.

Projection In psychodynamic theory, a defense mechanism in which unacceptable ideas and impulses are cast out or attributed to others.

Projective test A psychological test that presents questions to which there is no single correct response. A test that presents ambiguous stimuli into which the test-taker projects his or her own personality in making a response.

Prolactin A pituitary hormone that regulates production of milk and, in lower animals, maternal behavior.

Propinquity Nearness.

Prosocial Behavior that is characterized by helping others and making a contribution to society.

Prototype A concept of a category of objects or events that serves as a good example of the category.

Proximity Nearness. The perceptual tendency to group together objects that are near one another.

Proximodistal Proceeding from near to far.

Psychedelic Causing hallucinations or delusions, or heightening perceptions.

Psychiatrist A physician who specializes in the application of medical treatments to abnormal behavior.

Psychic structure In psychodynamic theory, a hypothesized mental structure that helps explain various aspects of behavior. See *id, ego,* and *superego.*

Psychoactive Describing drugs that give rise to psychological effects.

Psychoanalysis The school of psychology, founded by Sigmund Freud, that emphasizes the importance of unconscious motives and conflicts as determinants of human behavior. Also the name of Freud's methods of psychotherapy and clinical investigation.

Psychodynamic Descriptive of Freud's

view that various forces move within the personality, frequently clashing, and that the outcome of these clashes determines behavior.

Psychogenic amnesia A dissociative disorder marked by loss of episodic memory or self-identity. Skills and general knowledge are usually retained.

Psychogenic fugue A dissociative disorder in which one experiences amnesia, then flees to a new location and establishes a new identity and life-style.

Psycholinguist A psychologist who studies how we perceive and acquire language.

Psycholinguistic theory The view that language learning involves an interaction between environmental influences and an inborn tendency to acquire language. The emphasis is on the innate tendency.

Psychological dependence Repeated use of a substance as a way of dealing with stress.

Psychological hardiness A cluster of traits that buffer stress and that are characterized by commitment, challenge, and control.

Psychology The science that studies behavior and mental processes.

Psychomotor retardation Slowness in motor activity and, apparently, in thought.

Psychoneuroimmunology The field that studies the relationships between psychological factors (e.g., attitudes and overt behavior patterns) and the functioning of the immune system.

Psychopath Another term for a person who shows an antisocial personality disorder.

Psychophysics The study of the relationships between physical stimuli, such as light and sound, and their perception.

Psychophysiological Psychosomatic.

Psychosexual development In psychodynamic theory, the process by which libidinal energy is expressed through different erogenous zones during different stages of development.

Psychosexual trauma A distressing sexual experience that may have lingering psychological effects.

Psychosis A major psychological disorder in which a person shows impaired reality testing and has difficulty meeting the demands of everyday life.

Psychosocial development Erikson's theory of personality and development, which emphasizes the importance of social relationships and conscious choice throughout eight stages of development, including three stages of adult development.

Psychosomatic Having to do with physical illnesses that have psychological origins or that are intensified by stress.

Psychosurgery Biological treatments in which specific areas or structures of the brain are destroyed in order to promote psychological changes or to relieve disordered behavior.

Psychotherapy A systematic interaction between a therapist and a client that brings psychological principles to bear on influencing the client's thoughts, feelings, or behaviors in order to help that client overcome abnormal behavior or adjust to problems in living.

Puberty The period of early adolescence during which hormones spur rapid physical development.

Punishment An unpleasant stimulus that suppresses the frequency of the behavior it follows.

Pupil The apparently black opening in the center of the iris, through which light enters the eye.

Pupillary reflex The automatic adjusting of the irises to permit more or less light to enter the eye.

Pure research Research conducted without concern for immediate applications.

R

Radical behaviorist A person who does not believe in the existence of mind, consciousness, and other mentalistic concepts.

Rage response Stereotypical aggressive behavior that can be brought forth in lower animals by electrical stimulation of the brain.

Random sample A sample drawn in such a manner that every member of a population has an equal chance of being selected.

Random trial-and-error In operant conditioning, refers to behavior that occurs prior to learning what behavior is reinforced. The implication is that in a novel situation, the organism happens upon the first correct (reinforced) response by chance.

Range A measure of variability; the distance between extreme measures or scores in a distribution.

Rapid-eye-movement sleep A stage of sleep characterized by rapid eye movements that have been linked to dreaming. Abbreviated *REM sleep.* Also called *paradoxical sleep.*

Rapid flight of ideas Rapid speech and topic changes, characteristic of manic behavior.

Rapid smoking A type of aversive conditioning in which cigarettes are inhaled every six seconds, making the smoke aversive.

Rational–emotive therapy Albert Ellis's form of cognitive psychotherapy, which focuses on how irrational expectations create negative feelings and maladaptive behavior, and which encourages clients to challenge and correct these expectations.

Rationalization In psychodynamic theory, a defense mechanism in which an individual engages in self-deception, finding justifications for unacceptable ideas, impulses, or behaviors.

Reaction formation In psychodynamic theory, a defense mechanism in which unacceptable impulses and ideas are kept unconscious through the exaggerated expression of opposing ideas and impulses.

Reaction time The amount of time required to respond to a stimulus.

Readiness In developmental psychology, referring to a stage in the maturation of an organism when it is capable of engaging in a certain response.

Reality principle In psychodynamic theory, the principle that guides ego functioning; consideration of what is practical and possible in gratifying needs.

Reality testing The capacity to form an accurate mental representation of the world, including socially appropriate behavior, reasonably accurate knowledge of the motives of others, undistorted sensory impressions, and self-insight.

Rebound anxiety Strong anxiety that can attend the suspension of usage of a tranquilizer.

Recall Retrieval or reconstruction of learned material.

Recency effect (1) In information processing, the tendency to recall the last items in a series of items. (2) In social psychology, the tendency to evaluate others in terms of the most recent impression.

Receptive vocabulary The extent of one's knowledge of the meanings of words that are communicated to one by others.

Receptor site A location on a dendrite of

a receiving neuron that is tailored to receive a neurotransmitter.

Recessive trait In genetics, a trait that is not expressed when the gene or genes involved have been paired with *dominant* genes. However, recessive traits are transmitted to future generations and expressed if paired with other recessive genes. See *dominant trait.*

Reciprocity (1) Mutual action. Treating others as one is treated. (2) In interpersonal attraction, the tendency to return feelings and attitudes that are expressed about us.

Recitation A teaching format in which teachers pose questions that are answered by students.

Recognition In information processing, a relatively easy memory task in which one identifies objects or events as having been encountered previously.

Reconstructive memories Memories that are based on the piecing together of memory fragments with general knowledge and expectations rather than a precise picture of the past.

Reflex A simple, unlearned response to a stimulus.

Refractory period (1) In a discussion of the nervous system, a period following firing during which a neuron's action potential cannot be triggered. (2) In human sexuality, a period following orgasm when a male is insensitive to further sexual stimulation.

Regression In psychodynamic theory, return to a form of behavior characteristic of an earlier stage of development. As a defense mechanism, regression to less-mature behavior is a means of coping with stress.

Reinforcement A stimulus that follows a response and increases the frequency of that response. See *positive* and *negative, primary* and *secondary* reinforcers.

Relative refractory period A phase following the absolute refractory period during which a neuron will fire in response to stronger-than-usual messages from other neurons.

Relaxation response Benson's term for a cluster of responses brought about by meditation that lower the activity of the sympathetic division of the autonomic nervous system.

Relearning A measure of retention. Material is usually relearned more quickly than it is learned initially.

Releaser In ethology, a stimulus that elicits an instinctive response.

Reliability In psychological measurement, consistency. Also see *validity.*

Remediation The process of helping people overcome deficiencies.

Replication The repetition or duplication of scientific studies in order to double-check their results.

Repression In psychodynamic theory, the ejection of anxiety-provoking ideas, impulses, or images from awareness, without the awareness that one is doing so. A defense mechanism.

Resistance During psychoanalysis, a blocking of thoughts the awareness of which could cause anxiety. The client may miss sessions or verbally abuse the analyst as threatening material is about to be unearthed.

Resistance stage The second stage of the general adaptation syndrome, characterized by prolonged sympathetic activity in an effort to restore lost energy and repair damage. Also called the *adaptation stage.*

Resolution phase The final stage of the sexual response cycle, during which the body returns gradually to its resting state.

Response A movement or other observable reaction to a stimulus.

Response cost A behavior-therapy self-control technique in which one uses self-punishment for practicing a bad habit or failing to meet a goal.

Response prevention A behavior-therapy self-control technique in which one makes unwanted behaviors difficult or impossible.

Response set A tendency to answer test items according to a bias—for example, with the intention of making oneself appear perfect or bizarre.

Resting potential The electrical potential across the neural membrane when it is not responding to other neurons.

Restriction of the stimulus field A behavior-therapy self-control technique in which a problem behavior is gradually restricted from more environments.

Reticular activating system A part of the brain involved in attention, sleep, and arousal. Abbreviated *RAS.*

Retina The area of the inner surface of the eye that contains rods and cones.

Retinal disparity A binocular cue for depth based on the difference of the image cast by an object on the retinas of the eyes as the object moves closer or farther away.

Retrieval The location of stored information and its return to consciousness. The third stage of information processing.

Retroactive interference The interference by new learning in one's ability to retrieve material learned previously. See *proactive interference.*

Retrograde amnesia Failure to remember events that occur prior to physical trauma because of the effects of the trauma.

Reversibility According to Piaget, recognition that processes can be undone, leaving things as they were before.

follows.

Risky shift The tendency to make riskier decisions as a member of a group than as an individual acting independently.

Rod A rod-shaped photoreceptor in the eye that is sensitive to the intensity of light. Rods permit "black-and-white" vision.

Role diffusion According to Erikson, a state of confusion, insecurity, and susceptibility to the suggestions of others; the probable outcome if ego identity is not established during adolescence.

Role theory A theory that explains hypnotic events in terms of the person's ability to act *as though* he or she were hypnotized. Role theory differs from faking in that subjects cooperate and focus on hypnotic suggestions instead of cynically pretending to be hypnotized.

Romantic love An intense, positive emotion that involves arousal, a cultural setting that idealizes love, feelings of caring, and the belief that one is in love. Also called *passionate love.* Within Sternberg's triangular model, the kind of love that is characterized by passion and intimacy.

Rooting (1) A reflex in which an infant turns its head toward a touch, such as by the mother's nipple. (2) In adult development, the process of establishing a home, which frequently occurs in the second half of the thirties.

Rorschach Inkblot Test A projective personality test that presents test-takers the task of interpreting inkblots.

Rote Mechanical associative learning that is based on repetition.

"Roy G. Biv" A mnemonic device for

remembering the colors of the visible spectrum, in order: red, orange, yellow, green, blue, indigo, violet.

Rumination Turning or chewing over thoughts repeatedly in one's mind.

S

s Spearman's symbol for specific or "s" factors, which he believed accounted for individual abilities.

Saccadic eye movement The rapid jumps made by a reader's eyes as they fixate on different points in the text.

"SAME" The mnemonic device for remembering that *s*ensory neurons are called *a*fferent neurons and that *m*otor neurons are termed *e*fferent neurons.

Sample Part of a population.

Satiety The state of being satisfied; fullness.

Saturation The degree of purity of a color, as measured by its freedom from mixture with white or black.

Savings The difference between the number of repetitions originally required to learn a list and the number of repetitions required to relearn the list after a certain amount of time has elapsed.

Scapegoat A person or group upon whom the blame for the mistakes or crimes of others is cast.

Scatter diagram A graphic presentation formed by plotting the points defined by the intersections of two variables.

Schachter-Singer theory The theory of emotion that holds that emotions have generally similar patterns of bodily arousal, and that the label we attribute to an emotion depends on our level of arousal and our cognitive appraisal of our situation.

Schema A way of mentally representing the world, such as a belief or an expectation, that can influence perception of persons, objects, and situations.

Schizoid personality disorder A disorder characterized by social withdrawal.

Schizophrenic disorder A psychotic disorder of at least six months' duration in which thought processes and reality testing are impaired and emotions are not appropriate to one's situation. Also see *schizophreniform disorder, brief reactive psychosis,* and *schizotypal personality.*

Schizophreniform disorder A disorder whose symptoms resemble schizophrenia but that is relatively brief (two weeks to less than six months in duration).

Schizotypal personality disorder A disorder characterized by oddities of thought and behavior but not involving bizarre psychotic symptoms. Formerly called *simple schizophrenia.*

Scientific method A method for obtaining scientific evidence in which a hypothesis is formed and tested.

Secondary colors Colors derived by mixing primary colors.

Secondary prevention In community psychology, the early detection and treatment of psychological problems.

Secondary reinforcer A stimulus that gains reinforcement value through association with other, established reinforcers. Money and social approval are secondary reinforcers. Also called *conditioned reinforcer.* See *primary reinforcer.*

Secondary sex characteristics Physical traits that differentiate the genders, such as the depth of the voice, but that are not directly involved in reproduction.

Secondary traits Allport's term for traits that appear in a limited number of situations and govern a limited number of responses.

Secure attachment A type of attachment characterized by positive feelings toward attachment figures and feelings of security.

Sedative A drug that soothes or quiets restlessness or agitation.

Selective attention The focus of consciousness on a particular stimulus.

Selective avoidance Diverting one's attention from information that is inconsistent with one's attitudes.

Selective exposure The deliberate seeking of, and attending to, information that is consistent with one's attitudes.

Self The totality of one's impressions, thoughts, and feelings. The center of consciousness that organizes sensory impressions and governs one's perceptions of the world.

Self-actualization According to Maslow and other humanistic psychologists, self-initiated striving to become what one is capable of being. The motive to reach one's full potential, to express one's unique capabilities.

Self-efficacy expectations Our beliefs that we can bring about desired changes through our own efforts.

Self-esteem One's evaluation of, and the placement of value on, oneself.

Self-fulfilling prophecy An expectation that is confirmed because of the behavior of those who hold the expectation.

Self-ideal A mental image of what we believe we ought to be.

Self-insight In psychodynamic theory, accurate awareness of one's own motives and feelings.

Self-monitoring A behavior-therapy technique in which one keeps a record of his or her behavior in order to identify problems and record successes.

Self-report (1) A subject's testimony about his or her own thoughts, feelings, or behaviors. (2) A method of investigation in which information is obtained through the report of the subject.

Self-serving bias The tendency to view one's successes as stemming from internal factors and one's failures as stemming from external factors.

Self theory The name of Carl Rogers' theory of personality, which emphasizes the importance of self-awareness, choice, and self-actualization.

Semantic code Mental representation of information according to its meaning.

Semanticity Meaning. The property of language in which words are used as symbols for objects, events, or ideas.

Semantic memory General knowledge, as opposed to episodic memory.

Semantics The study of the relationships between language and objects or events. The study of the meaning of language.

Semicircular canals Structures of the inner ear that monitor body movement and position.

Sensation The stimulation of sensory receptors and the transmission of sensory information to the central nervous system.

Sensitive period In linguistic theory, the period from about 18 months to puberty when the brain is thought to be particularly capable of learning language because of plasticity.

Sensitization The type of sensory adaptation in which we become more sensitive to stimuli that are low in magnitude. Also called *positive adaptation.*

Sensorimotor stage The first of Piaget's stages of cognitive development, characterized by coordination of sensory information and motor activity, early exploration of the environment, and lack of language.

Sensory adaptation The processes by which organisms become more sensitive to stimuli that are low in magnitude and less sensitive to stimuli that are constant or ongoing in magnitude.

Sensory awareness One of the definitions of consciousness: Knowledge of the environment through perception of sensory stimulation.

Sensory cortex The section of the cerebral cortex that lies in the parietal lobe, just behind the central fissure. Sensory stimulation is projected in this section of cortex.

Sensory deprivation (1) In general, insufficient sensory stimulation. (2) A research method for systematically decreasing the stimuli that impinge on sensory receptors.

Sensory memory The type or stage of memory first encountered by a stimulus. Sensory memory holds impressions briefly, but long enough so that series of perceptions are psychologically continuous.

Sensory-neural deafness The forms of deafness that result from damage to hair cells or the auditory nerve.

Sensory register A system of memory that holds information briefly, but long enough so that it can be processed further. There may be a sensory register for every sense.

Septum A part of the limbic system that apparently restrains stereotypically aggressive responses.

Serial position effect The tendency to recall more accurately the first and last items in a series.

Serotonin A neurotransmitter, deficiencies of which have been linked to affective disorders, anxiety, and insomnia.

Serotonin reuptake inhibitor An antidepressant medication that works by slowing the re-uptake of serotonin in the synaptic cleft.

Serum cholesterol A fatty substance (cholesterol) in the blood (serum) that has been linked to heart disease.

Set point A value that the body attempts to maintain. For example, the body tries to maintain a certain weight by adjusting the metabolism.

Sex chromosomes The 23rd pair of chromosomes, which determine whether a child will be male or female.

Sexism The prejudgment that a person, on the basis of his or her sex, will possess negative traits or perform inadequately.

Sex norms Social rules or conventions that govern the ways in which males and females interact.

Sex role See gender role.

Sex typing See gender typing.

Shadowing A monocular cue for depth based on the fact that opaque objects block light and produce shadows.

Shape constancy The tendency to perceive an object as being the same shape even though its retinal images changes in shape as the object rotates.

Shaping In operant conditioning, a procedure for teaching complex behaviors that at first reinforces approximations to these behaviors.

Short-term memory The type or stage of memory that can hold information for up to a minute or so after the trace of the stimulus decays. Also called *working memory.*

Siblings Brothers and sisters.

Signal-detection theory In psychophysics, the view that the perception of sensory stimuli is influenced by the interaction of physical, biological, and psychological factors.

Significant others Persons who have a major influence on one's psychosocial development, including parents, peers, lovers, and children.

Similarity As a rule of perceptual organization, the tendency to group together objects that are similar in appearance.

Simple phobia Persistent fear of a specific object or situation.

Simple schizophrenia See *schizotypal personality disorder.*

Simultaneous conditioning A classical conditioning procedure in which the CS and US are presented at the same time, and the CS is left on until the response occurs.

Situational attribution An assumption that a person's behavior is determined by external circumstances, such as social pressure. Contrast with *dispositional attribution.*

Situational variables In social-learning theory, external determinants of behavior, such as rewards and punishments.

Size constancy The tendency to perceive an object as being the same size even as the size of its retinal image changes according to its distance.

Skewed distribution A slanted distribution, drawn out toward the low or high scores.

Sleep-onset insomnia Difficulty falling asleep.

Sleep spindles Short bursts of rapid brain waves that occur during stage 2 sleep.

Sleep terrors Frightening, dreamlike experiences that usually occur during deep stage 4 sleep.

Social-comparison theory The view that people look to others for cues about how to behave in confusing situations.

Social decision schemes Rules for predicting the final outcome of group decision-making on the basis of the initial positions of the members.

Social facilitation The process by which a person's performance is increased when other members of a group engage in similar behavior.

Social influence The area of social psychology that studies the ways in which people influence the thoughts, feelings, and behavior of others.

Socialization Guidance of people—and children in particular—into socially desirable behavior by means of verbal messages, the systematic use of rewards and punishments, and other methods of teaching.

Social-learning theory A cognitively-oriented learning theory that emphasizes observational learning and the roles of person and situational variables in determining behavior.

Social loafing The process by which a person's performance is decreased as a function of being a member of a group.

Social motives Learned or acquired motives such as the needs for achievement and affiliation.

Social norms Explicit and implicit rules that reflect social expectations and influence the ways people behave in social situations.

Social perception A subfield of social psychology that studies the ways in which we form and modify impressions of others.

Social phobias Irrational fears that involve themes of public scrutiny.

Social psychology The field of psychology that studies the nature and causes of people's thoughts, feelings, and behavior in social situations.

Sociobiology A biological theory of social behavior that assumes that the underlying purpose of behavior is to ensure the transmission of an organism's genes from generation to generation.

Sociopath Another term for a person who shows an antisocial personality disorder.

Soma A cell body.

Somatic nervous system The division of the peripheral nervous system that connects the central nervous system (brain and spinal cord) with sensory receptors, muscles, and the surface of the body.

Somatoform disorders Disorders in which people complain of physical (somatic) problems, although no physical abnormality can be found. See *conversion disorder* and *hypochondriasis.*

Source traits Cattell's term for underlying traits from which surface traits are derived.

Spectrograph An instrument that converts sounds to graphs or pictures according to their acoustic qualities.

Sphincter A ringlike muscle that circles a body opening such as the anus. An infant will exhibit the sphincter reflex (have a bowel movement) in response to intestinal pressure.

Spinal cord A column of nerves within the spine that transmits messages from the sensory receptors to the brain and from the brain to muscles and glands throughout the body.

Spinal reflex A simple, unlearned response to a stimulus that may involve only two neurons.

Split-brain operation An operation in which the corpus callosum is severed, usually in an effort to control epileptic seizures.

Split-half reliability A method for determining the internal consistency of a test (an index of reliability) by correlating scores attained on half the items with scores attained on the other half of the items.

Spontaneous recovery Generally, the recurrence of an extinguished response as a function of the passage of time. In classical conditioning, the eliciting of a conditioned response by a conditioned stimulus after some time has elapsed following the extinction of the conditioned response. In operant conditioning, the performance of an operant in the presence of discriminative stimuli after some time has elapsed following the extinction of the operant.

Sports psychology The field of psychology that studies the nature, causes, and modification of the behavior and mental processes of people involved in sports.

Stage In developmental psychology, a distinct period of life that is qualitatively different from other stages. Stages follow one another in an orderly sequence.

Standard deviation A measure of the variability of a distribution, obtained by taking the square root of the sum of difference scores squared divided by the number of scores.

Standardization The process of setting standards for a psychological test, accomplished by determining how a population performs on it. Standardization permits psychologists to interpret individual scores as deviations from a norm.

Standardized tests Tests for which norms are based on the performance of a range of individuals.

Stapes A bone of the middle ear. Latin for "stirrup."

Startle reflex See Moro reflex.

State anxiety A temporary condition of anxiety that may be attributed to one's situation. Contrast with *trait anxiety.*

State-dependent memory Information that is better retrieved in the physiological or emotional state in which it was encoded (stored) or learned.

Statistically significant difference As indicated by inferential statistics, a difference between two groups that is not likely to result from chance fluctuation.

Statistics Numerical facts assembled in such a manner that they provide useful information about measures or scores.

Stereotype A fixed, conventional idea about a group.

Steroids A family of hormones that includes testosterone, estrogen, progesterone, and corticosteroids.

Stimulant A drug that increases the activity of the nervous system.

Stimulation deafness The forms of deafness that result from exposure to excessively loud sounds.

Stimuli Plural of *stimulus.*

Stimulus (1) A feature in the environment that is detected by an organism or that leads to a change in behavior (a response). (2) A form of physical energy, such as light or sound that impinges on the sensory receptors.

Stimulus control A behavior-therapy self-control technique in which one places oneself in an environment in which desired responses are likely to occur.

Stimulus discrimination The eliciting of a conditioned response by only one of a series of similar stimuli.

Stimulus generalization The eliciting of a conditioned response by stimuli that are similar to the conditioned stimulus.

Stimulus motives Motives to increase the stimulation impinging on an organism.

Stirrup A bone of the middle ear.

Storage The maintenance of information over time. The second stage of information processing.

Strabismus A visual disorder in which the eyes point in different directions and thus do not focus simultaneously on the same point.

Stratified sample A sample drawn in such a way that known subgroups within a population are represented in proportion to their numbers in the population.

Stress The demand made on an organism to adjust or adapt.

Stressor An event or stimulus that acts as a source of stress.

Stroboscopic motion A visual illusion in which the perception of motion is generated by presentation of a series of stationary images in rapid succession.

Structuralism The school of psychology, founded by Wilhelm Wundt, that argues that the mind consists of three basic elements—sensations, feelings, and images—which combine to form experience.

Stupor A condition in which the senses and thought processes are dulled.

Subject A participant in a scientific study. Many psychologists consider this term dehumanizing and no longer use it in reference to human participants.

Subjective Of the mind; personal; determined by thoughts and feelings rather than by external objects.

Subjective morality According to Piaget, subjective moral judgments assign guilt according to the motives of the actor. See *objective morality.*

Subjective value The desirability of an object or event.

Sublimation In psychodynamic theory, a defense mechanism in which primitive impulses—usually sexual or aggressive—are channeled into positive, constructive activities.

Subordinate Descriptive of a lower (included) class or category in a hierarchy, contained by another class; opposite of *superordinate.*

Substance abuse Persistent use of a

substance despite the fact that it is disrupting one's life.

Substance dependence A term whose definition is in flux: Substance dependence is characterized by loss of control over use of a substance, but some professionals consider that *physiological* dependence, as typified by tolerance, withdrawal, or both, is essential to the definition.

Successive approximations In operant conditioning, a series of behaviors that gradually become more similar to a target behavior.

Superego In psychodynamic theory, the psychic structure that is governed by the moral principle, it sets forth high standards for behavior, and floods the ego with feelings of guilt and shame when it falls short.

Superordinate Descriptive of a higher (including) class or category in a hierarchy, containing another class; opposite of *subordinate.*

Suppression The deliberate, or conscious, placing of certain ideas, impulses, or images out of awareness. Contrast with *repression.*

Surface structure The superficial construction of a sentence as defined by the placement of words.

Surface traits Cattell's term for characteristic, observable ways of behaving. See *source traits.*

Surrogate Substitute.

Survey A method of scientific investigation in which large samples of people are questioned.

Syllogism A form of reasoning in which a conclusion is drawn from two statements or premises.

Symbol Something that stands for or represents another thing.

Sympathetic nervous system The branch of the autonomic nervous system that is most active when the person is engaged in behavior or experiencing feeling states that spend the body's reserves of energy, such as fleeing or experiencing fear or anxiety.

Symptom substitution The exchange of one symptom for another. The term refers to the psychodynamic argument that a phobia is a symptom of an underlying disorder (that is, unconscious conflict) and that the removal of the phobia through behavioral techniques may lead to the emergence of another symptom of the disorder.

Synapse A junction between a terminal knob of a transmitting neuron and a dendrite or soma of a receiving neuron.

Syndrome A cluster of symptoms characteristic of a disorder.

Syntax The rules in a language for placing words in proper order to form meaningful sentences.

Systematic desensitization A behavior-therapy fear-reduction technique in which a hierarchy of fear-evoking stimuli are presented while the person remains in a state of deep muscle relaxation.

T

Tactile Of the sense of touch.

Target behavior Goal.

Taste aversion A kind of classical conditioning in which a previously desirable or neutral food comes to be perceived as repugnant because it is associated with aversive stimulation.

Taste buds The sensory organs for taste. They contain taste cells and are located on the tongue.

Taste cells Receptor cells that are sensitive to taste.

TAT Thematic Apperception Test.

Telegraphic speech Speech in which only the essential words are used, as in a telegram.

Temporal lobe The lobe of the cerebral cortex that is involved in hearing. It lies below the lateral fissure, near the temples.

Terminal A small branching structure found at the tip of an axon.

Territory In sociobiology, the particular area acquired and defended by an animal, or pair of animals, for purposes of feeding and breeding.

Tertiary colors Colors derived by mixing primary and adjoining secondary colors.

Tertiary prevention In community psychology, the treatment of ripened psychological problems. (See *primary* and *secondary prevention.*)

Testes The male reproductive organs that produce sperm and the hormone testosterone.

Testosterone A male sex hormone (steroid) that is produced by the testes and promotes growth of male sexual characteristics and sperm.

Test–retest reliability A method for determining the reliability of a test by comparing (correlating) test-takers' scores on separate occasions.

Texture gradient A monocular cue for depth based on the perception that nearby objects appear to have rougher or more detailed surfaces.

Thalamus An area near the center of the brain that is involved in the relay of sensory information to the cortex and in the functions of sleep and attention.

Thanatos In psychodynamic theory, the death instinct.

THC Delta-9-tetrahydrocannabinol. The major active ingredient in marijuana.

The Dream Levinson's term for the overriding drive of youth to become someone important, to leave one's mark on history.

T-helper lymphocytes The white blood cells of the immune system that recognize invading pathogens. Also called *T_4-helper lymphocytes.*

Thematic Apperception Test A projective test devised by Henry Murray to measure needs through the production of fantasy.

Theory A formulation of relationships underlying observed events. A theory involves assumptions and logically derived explanations and predictions.

Theory of social comparison The view that people look to others for cues about how to behave when they are in confusing or unfamiliar situations.

Theta waves Slow brain waves produced during the hypnagogic state.

Threshold The point at which a stimulus is just strong enough to produce a response.

Thyroxin The thyroid hormone that increases the metabolic rate.

Timbre The quality or richness of a sound. The quality that distinguishes the sounds of one musical instrument from those of another.

Time out In operant conditioning, a method for decreasing the frequency of undesired behaviors by removing an organism from a situation in which reinforcement is available as a consequence of showing the undesired behavior.

Tip-of-the-tongue phenomenon The feeling that information is stored in memory although it cannot be readily retrieved. Also called the *feeling-of-knowing experience.*

TM Transcendental meditation.

Token economy A controlled environment in which people are reinforced for desired behaviors with tokens (such as poker chips) that may be exchanged for privileges.

Tolerance Habituation to a drug, with

the result that increasingly higher doses of the drug are required to achieve similar effects.

Tolerance for frustration Ability to delay gratification, to maintain self-control when a motive is thwarted.

Top-down processing The use of contextual information or knowledge of a pattern in order to organize parts of the pattern.

Total immersion A method of teaching a second language in which all instruction is carried out in the second language.

Trace conditioning A classical conditioning procedure in which the CS is presented and then removed before the US is presented.

Trait A distinguishing quality or characteristic of personality that is inferred from behavior and assumed to account for consistency in behavior.

Trait anxiety Anxiety as a personality variable, or persistent trait. Contrast with *state anxiety.*

Tranquilizers Drugs used to reduce anxiety and tension. See *minor* and *major* tranquilizer.

Transaction In transactional analysis, an exchange between two people.

Transactional analysis A form of psychotherapy that deals with how people interact and how their interactions reinforce attitudes, expectations, and "life positions." Abbreviated *TA.*

Transcendental meditation The simplified form of meditation brought to the United States by the Maharishi Mahesh Yogi in which one focuses on a repeated mantra. Abbreviated *TM.*

Transference In psychoanalysis, the generalization to the analyst of feelings toward another person in the client's life.

Transsexualism A gender identity disorder in which the person feels trapped inside a body of the wrong sex.

Trauma An injury or wound.

Treatment In experiments, a condition received by participants so that its effects may be observed.

Trial In conditioning, a presentation of the stimuli.

Triangular model Sternberg's model of love, which refers to combinations of passion, intimacy, and decision/commitment.

Triarchic Governed by three. (Referring to Sternberg's triarchic theory of intelligence.)

Trichromat A person with normal color vision.

Trichromatic theory The theory that color vision is made possible by three types of cones, some of which respond to red light, some to green, and some to blue.

Tricyclic antidepressants Antidepressant drugs that work by preventing the reuptake of norepinephrine and serotonin by transmitting neurons.

Trimester A period of three months.

Trisomy 21 Another term for Down syndrome.

Trust versus mistrust The first of Erikson's stages of psychosocial development, during which the child comes to (or not to) develop a basic sense of trust in others.

Trying Twenties Sheehy's term for the third decade of life, which is frequently characterized by preoccupation with advancement in the career world.

Two-point threshold The least distance by which two rods touching the skin must be separated before the subject will report that there are two rods, not one, on 50 percent of occasions.

Type In personality theory, a group of traits that cluster in a meaningful way.

Type A behavior Behavior characterized by a sense of time urgency, competitiveness, and hostility.

U

Ulcer An open sore, as in the lining of the stomach.

Umbilical cord A tube between the mother and her fetus through which nutrients and waste products are conducted.

Unconditional positive regard In self theory, a consistent expression of esteem for the basic value of a person, but not necessarily an unqualified endorsement of all that person's behaviors. A quality shown by the person-centered therapist.

Unconditioned response An unlearned response. A response to an unconditioned stimulus. Abbreviated *UR.*

Unconditioned stimulus A stimulus that elicits a response from an organism without learning. Abbreviated *US.*

Unconscious In psychodynamic theory, descriptive of ideas and feelings that are not available to awareness, in many instances because of the *defense mechanism* of *repression.*

Unobtrusive Not interfering.

Uplifts Notable pleasant daily conditions and experiences.

UR Unconditioned response.

US Unconditioned stimulus.

Uterus The hollow organ within women in which the embryo and fetus develop.

V

Validity The degree to which a test or instrument measures or predicts what it is supposed to measure or predict. Also see *reliability.*

Validity scale A group of test items that suggests whether or not the results of a test are valid—whether a person's test responses accurately reflect his or her traits.

Variable A condition that is measured or controlled in a scientific study. A variable can be altered in a measurable manner.

Variable-interval schedule A partial reinforcement schedule in which a variable amount of time must elapse between the previous and subsequent times that reinforcement is available.

Variable-ratio schedule A partial reinforcement schedule in which reinforcement is provided after a variable number of correct responses.

Vasopressin Another term for *antidiuretic hormone.*

Ventromedial nucleus A central area on the underside of the hypothalamus that appears to function as a stop-eating center. Abbreviated *VMN.*

Vestibular sense The sense that provides information about the position of the body relative to gravity. Also referred to as the sense of equilibrium.

Vicarious Taking the place of another person or thing. In vicarious learning, we learn from the experiences of others.

Visible light The band of electromagnetic energy that produces visual sensations.

Visual accommodation Automatic adjustment of the thickness of the lens in order to focus on objects.

Visual acuity Keenness or sharpness of vision.

Visual capture The tendency of vision to dominate the other senses.

Visual code Mental representation of information as a picture.

Volley principle A modification of the *frequency theory* of pitch perception. The hypothesis that groups of neurons may be able to achieve the effect of firing at very high frequencies by "taking turns" firing—that is, by firing in volleys.

Volt A unit of electrical potential.

Voyeurism A paraphilia in which the

person prefers to seek sexual excitement through secret observation of others undressing or engaged in sexual activity.

W

Waxy flexibility A symptom of catatonic schizophrenia in which the person maintains a posture or position into which he or she is placed.

Weaning Accustoming the child not to suck the mother's breast or a baby bottle.

Weber's constant The fraction of the intensity by which a source of physical energy must be increased or decreased so that a difference in intensity will be perceived.

Wernicke-Korsakoff's syndrome An alcohol-related disorder that is characterized by loss of memory and that is thought to reflect nutritional deficiency.

Wernicke's aphasia An aphasia caused by damage to Wernicke's area of the brain. It is characterized by difficulty comprehending the meaning of spoken language and by the production of language that is grammatically correct but confused or meaningless in content.

White matter In the spinal cord, axon bundles that carry messages back and forth from and to the brain.

White noise Discordant sounds of many frequencies, which often produce a lulling effect.

Wish fulfillment In psychodynamic theory, a primitive method used by the id—such as in fantasy and dreams—to attempt to gratify basic impulses.

Working memory See *short-term memory.*

Y

Yerkes-Dodson law The principle that a high level of arousal increases performance on a relatively simple task, whereas a low level of arousal increases performance on a relatively complex task.

Z

Zygote A fertilized egg cell or ovum.

REFERENCES

A

AAUW (1992). See American Association of University Women.

Abbey, A. (1987). Misperceptions of friendly behavior as sexual interest: A survey of naturally occurring incidents. *Psychology of Women Quarterly, 11,* 173–194.

Abikoff, H. , & Gittelman, R. (1985). The normalizing effects of methylphenidate on the classroom behavior of ADDH children. *Journal of Abnormal Child Psychology, 13,* 33–44.

Abramowitz, C. V., Abramowitz, S. I., Roback, H. B., & Jackson, C. (1974). Differential effectiveness of directive and nondirective group therapies as a function of client internal-external control. *Journal of Consulting and Clinical Psychology, 42,* 849–853.

Abrams, D. B., & Wilson, G. T. (1983). Alcohol, sexual arousal, and self-control. *Journal of Personality and Social Psychology, 45,* 188–198.

Abravanel, E., & Gingold, H. (1985). Learning via observation during the second year of life. *Developmental Psychology, 21,* 614–623.

Abravanel, E., & Sigafoos, A. D. (1984). Exploring the presence of imitation during early infancy. *Child Development, 55,* 381–392.

Ackerman, D. (1990). *A natural history of the senses.* New York: Random House.

Adair, J. G., Dushenko, T. W., & Lindsay, R. C. L. (1985). Ethical regulations and their impact on research practice. *American Psychologist, 40,* 59–72.

Adelson, A. (1988, March 9). Women still finding bias in engineering. *The New York Times,* p. D6.

Adelson, A. (1990, November 19). Study attacks women's roles in TV. *The New York Times,* p. C18.

Adelson, J. (1982). Still vital after all these years. *Psychology Today, 16*(4), 52–59.

Adler, T. (1990). Distraction, relaxation can help "shut off" pain. *APA Monitor, 21*(9), 11.

Adorno, T. W., Frenkel-Brunswick, E., & Levinson, D. J. (1950). *The authoritarian personality.* New York: Harper.

Affleck, G., Tennen, H., Pfeiffer, C., & Fifield, J. (1987). Appraisals of control and predictability in adapting to chronic disease. *Journal of Personality and Social Psychology, 53,* 273–279.

Agras, W. S., & Kirkley, B. G. (1986). Bulimia: Theories of etiology. In K. D. Brownell & J. P. Foreyt (Eds.), *Handbook of eating disorders.* New York: Basic Books.

Agras, W. S., Southam, M. A., & Taylor, C. B. (1983). Long-term persistence of relaxation-induced blood pressure lowering during the working day. *Journal of Consulting and Clinical Psychology, 51,* 792–794.

Ainsworth, M. D. S. (1984). Attachment. In N. S. Endler & J. McV. Hunt (Eds.), *Personality and the behavioral disorders,* Vol. 1, 2d ed. New York: Wiley.

Ainsworth, M. D. S. (1985). Patterns of infant-mother attachments: Antecedents and effects on development. *Bulletin of the New York Academy of Medicine, 61,* 771–791

Ainsworth, M. D. S. (1989). Attachments beyond infancy. *American Psychologist, 44,* 709–716.

Ainsworth, M. D. S., & Bowlby, J. (1991). An ethological approach to personality development. *American Psychologist, 46,* 333–341.

Akil, H. (1978). Endorphins, beta-LPH, and ACTH: Biochemical pharmacological and anatomical studies. *Advances in Biochemical Psychopharmacology, 18,* 125–139.

Albert, M. S. (1981). Geriatric neuropsychology. *Journal of Consulting and Clinical Psychology, 49,* 835–850.

Alexander, A. B. (1981). Asthma. In S. N. Haynes & L. Gannon (Eds.), *Psychosomatic disorders: A psychophysiological approach to etiology and treatment.* New York: Praeger Books.

Alicke, M. D., Smith, R. H., & Klotz, M. L. (1986). Judgments of physical attractiveness: The role of faces and bodies. *Personality and Social Psychology Bulletin, 12,* 381–389.

Allen, V. L., & Levine, J. M. (1971). Social support and conformity: The role of independent assessment of reality. *Journal of Experimental Social Psychology, 7,* 48–58.

Alloy, L. B., & Ahrens, A. H. (1987). Depression and pessimism for the future: Biased use of statistically relevant information in predictions for self versus others. *Journal of Personality and Social Psychology, 52,* 366–378.

Alloy, L. B., Abramson, L. Y., & Dykman, B. M. (1990). Depressive realism and nondepressive optimistic illusions: The role of the self. In R. E. Ingram (Ed.), *Contemporary psychological approaches to depression.* New York: Plenum.

Alloy, L. B., & Clements, C. M. (1992). Illusion of control: Invulnerability to negative affect and depressive symptoms after laboratory and natural stressors. *Journal of Abnormal Psychology, 101,* 234–245.

Allport, G. W. (1937). *Personality: A psychological interpretation.* New York: Holt, Rinehart and Winston.

Allport, G. W. (1961). *Pattern and growth in personality.* New York: Holt, Rinehart and Winston.

Allport, G. W., & Odbbert, H. S. (1936). Trait names: A psycholexical study. *Psychological Monographs, 47,* 2–11.

Altman, L. K. (1988, January 26). Cocaine's many dangers: The evidence mounts. *The New York Times,* p. C3.

Altman, L. K. (1991, June 18). W.H.O. says 40 million will be infected with AIDS virus by 2000. *The New York Times,* p. C3.

Amabile, T. M. (1982). Social psychology of creativity: A consensual assessment technique. *Journal of Personality and Social Psychology, 43,* 997–1013.

Amabile, T. M. (1983). The social psychology of creativity: A componential conceptualization. *Journal of Personality and Social Psychology, 45,* 357–376.

Amato, P. R. (1983). Helping behavior in urban and rural environments: Field studies based on taxonomic organization of helping episodes. *Journal of Personality and Social Psychology, 45,* 571–586.

American Association of University Women (1992). *How schools shortchange women: The A.A.U.W. report.* Washington, DC: A.A.U.W. Educational Foundation.

American Psychiatric Association (1990). *The practice of electroconvulsive therapy.* Washington, DC: American Psychiatric Press, Inc.

American Psychological Association (1990). *Ethical principles of psychologists.* American Psychologist, 45, 390–395.

American Psychological Association (1992). Draft revision of the Guidelines on ethical conduct in the care and use of animals. *APA Monitor, 23*(8), 25–26.

Amoore, J. E. (1970). *The molecular basis of odor.* Springfield, IL: Thomas.

Anastasi, A. (1983). Evolving trait concepts. *American Psychologist, 38,* 175–184.

Anastasiow, N. J., & Hanes, M. L. (1976). *Language patterns of children in poverty.* Springfield, IL: Charles C Thomas.

Andersen, B. L. (1992). Psychological interventions for cancer patients to enhance the quality of life. *Journal of Consulting and Clinical Psychology, 60,* 552–568.

Anderson, J. R. (1976). *Language, memory, and thought.* Hillsdale, NJ: Erlbaum.

Anderson, J. R. (1985). *Cognitive psychology and its implications,* 2d ed. San Francisco: W. H. Freeman.

Andreasen, N. C. (1987). The diagnosis of schizophrenia. *Schizophrenia Bulletin, 13,* 1–8.

Andreasen, N. C. (1990, August/September). Schizophrenia. In American Psychiatric Association, *DSM–IV Update.* Washington, DC: American Psychiatric Association.

Andrews, G., & Harvey, R. (1981). Does psychotherapy benefit neurotic patients? *Archives of General Psychiatry, 38,* 1203–1208.

Aneshensel, C. S., & Huba, G. J. (1983). Depression, alcohol use, and smoking over one year: A four-wave longitudinal causal model. *Journal of Abnormal Psychology, 92,* 134–150.

Angier, N. (1990, March 29). New antidepressant is acclaimed but not perfect. *The New York Times,* p. B9.

Angier, N. (1992, August 1). Researchers find a second anatomical idiosyncrasy in brains of homosexual men. *The New York Times,* p. A7.

Antoni, M. H. (1987). Neuroendocrine influences in psychoimmunology and neoplasia: A review. *Psychology and Health, 1,* 3–24.

Antoni, M. H. (1990). Psychoneuroimmunology and HIV-1. *Journal of Consulting and Clinical Psychology, 58,* 38–49.

Antoni, M. H. (1991). Cognitive-behavioral stress management intervention buffers distress responses and immunologic changes following notification of HIV-1 seroposivity. *Journal of Consulting and Clinical Psychology, 59,* 906–915.

APA Monitor, February 1978, p. 4.

APA Monitor, January 1978, pp. 5, 23.

Archer, R. P., & Cash, T. F. (1985). Physical attractiveness and maladjustment among psychiatric patients. *Journal of Social and Clinical Psychology, 3,* 170–180.

Arkin, R. M., Detchon, C. S., & Maruyama, G. M. (1982). Roles of attribution, affect, and cognitive interference in test anxiety. *Journal of Personality and Social Psychology, 43,* 1111–1124.

Asarnow, J. R., Carlson, G. A., & Guthrie, D. (1987). Coping strategies, self-perceptions, hopelessness, and perceived family environments in depressed and suicidal children. *Journal of Consulting and Clinical Psychology, 55,* 361–366.

Asarnow, J. R., & Goldstein, M. J. (1986). Schizophrenia during adolescence and early adulthood: A developmental perspective on risk research. *Clinical Psychology Review, 6,* 211–235.

Asch, S. E. (1952). *Social psychology.* Englewood Cliffs, NJ: Prentice-Hall.

Aslin, R. N., & Banks, M. S. (1978). Early visual experience in humans: Evidence for a critical period in the development of binocular vision. In S. Schneider, H. Liebowitz, H. Pick, & H. Stevenson (Eds.), *Psychology: From basic research to practice.* New York: Plenum Publishing Co.

Aslin, R. N., Pisoni, D. B., & Jusczyk, P. W. (1983). Auditory development and speech perception in infancy. In P. H. Mussen (Ed.), *Handbook of child psychology, 4th ed.* New York: Wiley.

Atkins, C. J., Kaplan, R. M., Timms, R. M., Reinsch, S., & Lofback, K. (1984). Behavioral exercise programs in the management of chronic obstructive pulmonary disease. *Journal of Consulting and Clinical Psychology, 52,* 591–603.

Atkinson, J., & Huston, T. L. (1984). Sex role orientation and division of labor early in marriage. *Journal of Personality and Social Psychology, 46,* 330–345.

Atkinson, R. C. (1975). Mnemotechnics in second-language learning. *American Psychologist, 30,* 821–828.

Atkinson, R. C., & Shiffrin, R. M. (1968). Human memory: A proposed system and its control processes. In K. Spence (Ed.), *The psychology of learning and motivation,* Vol. 2. New York: Academic Press.

Ayllon, T., & Haughton, E. (1962). Control of the behavior of schizophrenic patients by food. *Journal of the Experimental Analysis of Behavior, 5,* 343–352.

Azjen, I., & Fishbein, M. (1977). Attitude-behavior relations: A theoretical analysis and review of empirical research. *Psychological Bulletin, 84,* 888–918.

Azjen, I., & Fishbein, M. (1980). *Understanding attitudes and predicting social behavior.* Englewood Cliffs, NJ: Prentice-Hall.

B

Bach, G. R., & Deutsch, R. M. (1970). *Pairing.* New York: Peter H. Wyden.

Bagozzi, R. P. (1981). Attitudes, intentions, and behaviors: A test of some key hypotheses. *Journal of Personality and Social Psychology, 41,* 607–627.

Bahrick, H. P., Bahrick, P. O., & Wittlinger, R. P. (1975).

Fifty years of memory for names and faces: A cross-sectional approach. *Journal of Experimental Psychology: General, 104,* 54–75.

Bailey, J. M., & Pillard, R. C. (1991). A genetic study of male sexual orientation. *Archives of General Psychiatry, 48,* 1089–1096.

Baker, L. A., DeFries, J. C., & Fulker, D. W. (1983). Longitudinal stability of cognitive ability in the Colorado adoption project. *Child Development, 54,* 290–297.

Bal, D. G. (1992). Cancer in African Americans. *Ca-A Cancer Journal for Clinicians, 42,* 5–6.

Baldessarini, R. J. (1985). *Chemotherapy in psychiatry.* Cambridge, MA: Harvard University Press.

Baldessarini, R. J., & Frankenburg, F. R. (1991). Clozapine: A novel antipsychotic agent. *The New England Journal of Medicine, 324,* 746–754.

Bales, J. (1986). New studies cite drug use dangers. *APA Monitor, 17*(11), 26.

Bandura, A. (1973). *Aggression: A social learning analysis.* Englewood Cliffs, NJ: Prentice-Hall.

Bandura, A. (1977). *Social learning theory.* Englewood Cliffs, NJ: Prentice-Hall.

Bandura, A. (1981). Self-referrant thought: A developmental analysis of self-efficacy. In J. H. Flavell & L. Ross (Eds.), *Social cognitive development: Frontiers and possible futures.* Cambridge: Cambridge University Press.

Bandura, A. (1982). Self-efficacy mechanism in human agency. *American Psychologist, 37,* 122–147.

Bandura, A. (1986). *Social foundations of thought and action: A social-cognitive theory.* Englewood Cliffs, NJ: Prentice-Hall.

Bandura, A. (1989). Human agency in social cognitive theory. *American Psychologist, 44,* 1175–1184.

Bandura, A. (1991). Human agency: The rhetoric and the reality. *The American Psychologist, 46,* 157–162.

Bandura, A., Blanchard, E. B., & Ritter, B. (1969). The relative efficacy of desensitization and modeling approaches for inducing behavioral, affective, and cognitive changes. *Journal of Personality and Social Psychology, 13,* 173–199.

Bandura, A., & McDonald, F. J. (1963). Influence of social reinforcement and the behavior of models in shaping children's moral judgments. *Journal of Abnormal and Social Psychology, 67,* 274–281.

Bandura, A., Reese, L., & Adams, N. E. (1982). Microanalysis of action and fear arousal as a function of differential levels of perceived self-efficacy. *Journal of Personality and Social Psychology, 43,* 5–21.

Bandura, A., & Rosenthal, T. L. (1966). Vicarious classical conditioning as a function of fear arousal. *Journal of Personality and Social Psychology, 3,* 54–62.

Bandura, A., Ross, D., & Ross, S. A. (1963a). A comparative test of the status envy, and the secondary reinforcement theories of identificatory learning. *Journal of Abnormal and Social Psychology, 67,* 527–534.

Bandura, A., Ross, S. A., & Ross, D. (1963b). Imitation of film-mediated aggressive models. *Journal of Abnormal and Social Psychology, 66,* 3–11.

Bandura, A., Taylor, C. B., Williams, S. L., Medford, I. N., & Barchas, J. D. (1985). Catecholamine secretion as a function of perceived coping self-efficacy. *Journal of Consulting and Clinical Psychology, 53,* 406–414.

Banks, M. S., & Salapatek, P. (1981). Infant pattern vision: A new approach based on the contrast selectivity function. *Journal of Experimental Child Psychology, 31,* 1–45.

Banks, M. S., & Salapatek, P. (1983). Infant visual perception. In M. M. Haith & J. J. Campos (Eds.), *Handbook of child psychology,* Vol. 2. New York: Wiley.

Banyai, E. I., & Hilgard, E. R. (1976). A comparison of active-alert hypnotic induction with traditional relaxation induction. *Journal of Abnormal Psychology, 85,* 218–224.

Baquet, C. R., Horm, J. W., Gibbs, T., & Greenwald, P. (1991). Socioeconomic factors and cancer incidence among Blacks and Whites. *Journal of the National Cancer Institute, 83,* 551–557.

Barber, T. X. (1970). *LSD, marihuana, yoga, and hypnosis.* Chicago: Aldine.

Barber, T. X. (1982). Hypnosuggestive procedures in the treatment of clinical pain: Implications for theories of hypnosis and suggestive therapy. In T. Millon, C. J. Green, & R. B. Meagher, Jr. (Eds.), *Handbook of clinical health psychology.* New York: Plenum Publishing Co.

Barber, T. X. (1984). Hypnosis, deep relaxation, and active relaxation: Data, theory, and clinical applications. In R. L. Woolfolk & P. M. Lehrer (Eds.), *Principles and practice of stress management.* New York: Guilford Press.

Barber, T. X., Spanos, N. P., & Chaves, J. F. (1974). *Hypnosis, imagination, and human potentialities.* New York: Pergamon Press.

Bard, P. (1934). The neurohumoral basis of emotional reactions. In C. A. Murchison (Ed.), *Handbook of general experimental psychology.* Worcester, MA: Clark University Press.

Bardwick, J. M. (1980). The seasons of a woman's life. In D. G. McGuigan (Ed.), *Women's lives: New theory, research, and policy.* Ann Arbor: University of Michigan, Center for Continuing Education of Women.

Barkley, R. A. (1989). Attention-deficit hyperactivity disorder. In E. J. Mash & R. A. Barkley (Eds.), *Treatment of childhood disorders.* New York: Guilford Press.

Barlow, D. H. (1986). Behavioral conception and treatment of panic. *Psychopharmacology Bulletin, 22,* 802–806.

Barlow, D. H. (1991). Introduction to the special issue on diagnoses, definitions, and *DSM-IV:* The science of classification. *Journal of Abnormal Psychology, 100,* 243–244.

Barnes, M. L., & Buss, D. M. (1985). Sex differences in the interpersonal behavior of married couples. *Journal of Personality and Social Psychology, 48,* 654–661.

Barnett, W. S., & Escobar, C. M. (1990). Economic costs and benefits of early intervention. In S. J. Meisels & J. P. Shonkoff (Eds.), *Handbook of early childhood intervention,* New York: Cambridge University Press.

Baron, R. A., & Byrne, D. (1991). *Social psychology: Understanding human interaction,* 6th ed. Boston: Allyn and Bacon.

Barringer, F. (1991, March 11). Census shows profound change in racial makeup of the nation. *The New York Times,* pp. A1, B8.

Barrow, G. M., & Smith, P. A. (1983). *Aging, the individual, and society,* 2d ed. St. Paul: West.

Barry, M. (1991). The influence of the U.S. tobacco industry on the health, economy, and environment of developing countries. *The New England Journal of Medicine, 324,* 917–920.

Bartus, R. T. (1982). The cholinergic hypothesis of geriatric memory dysfunction. *Science, 217,* 408–417.

Basham, R. B. (1986). Scientific and practical advantages of comparative design in psychotherapy outcome research. *Journal of Consulting and Clinical Psychology, 54,* 88–94.

Bates, E., Bretherton, I., Beeghly-Smith, M., & McNew, S. (1982). Social bases of language development: A reassessment. In H. W. Reese & L. P. Lipsitt (Eds.), *Advances in child development and behavior,* Vol. 16. New York: Academic Press.

Batson, C. D. (1989). Negative state relief and the empathy-altruism hypothesis. *Journal of Personality and Social Psychology, 56,* 922–933.

Batson, C. D.. (1989). Religious prosocial motivation: Is it altruistic or egoistic? *Journal of Personality and Social Psychology, 57,* 873–884.

Baucom, D. H., & Aiken, P. A. (1981). Effect of depressed mood on eating among obese and nonobese dieting and nondieting persons. *Journal of Personality and Social Psychology, 41,* 577–585.

Baucom, D. H., & Danker-Brown, P. (1979). Influence of sex roles on the development of learned helplessness. *Journal of Consulting and Clinical Psychology, 47,* 928–936.

Baucom, D. H., & Danker-Brown, P. (1983). Peer ratings of males and females possessing different sex role identities. *Journal of Personality Assessment, 44,* 334–343.

Bauer, R. H., & Fuster, J. M. (1976). Delayed-matching and delayed-response deficit from cooling dorsolateral prefrontal cortex in monkeys. *Journal of Comparative and Physiological Psychology, 90,* 293–302.

Baum, A., Fisher, J. D., & Solomon, S. (1981). Type of information, familiarity, and the reduction of crowding stress. *Journal of Personality and Social Psychology, 40,* 11–23.

Baumann, L. J., & Leventhal, H. (1985). "I can tell when my blood pressure is up, can't I?" *Health Psychology, 4,* 203–218.

Baumeister, R. F., & Covington, M. V. (1985). Self-esteem, persuasion, and retrospective distortion of initial attitudes. *Electronic Social Psychology, 1,* 1–22.

Baumgardner, A. H., Heppner, P. P., & Arkin, R. M. (1986). Role of causal attribution in personal problem solving. *Journal of Personality and Social Psychology, 50,* 636–643.

Baumrind, D. (1985). Research using intentional deception: Ethical issues revisited. *American Psychologist, 40,* 165–174.

Baumrind, D. (1986). Sex differences in moral reasoning: Response to Walker's (1984) conclusion that there are none. *Child Development, 57,* 511–521.

Beal, C. R., & Flavell, J. H. (1983). Young speakers' evaluation of their listeners' comprehensions in a referential communication task. *Child Development, 54,* 148–153.

Beal, C. R., & Flavell, J. H. (1984). Development of the ability to distinguish communicative attention and literal message meaning. *Child Development, 55,* 920–928.

Beaman, A. L., Cole, M., Preston, M., Klentz, B., & Steblay, N. M. (1983). Fifteen years of foot-in-the-door research: A meta-analysis. *Personality and Social Psychology Bulletin, 9,* 181–186.

Beardslee, W. R., Bemporad, J., Keller, M. B., & Klerman, G. L. (1983). Children of parents with major affective disorder: A review. *American Journal of Psychiatry, 140,* 825–832.

Beatty, W. W. (1979). Gonadal hormones and sex differences in nonreproductive behaviors in rodents: Organizational and activational influences. *Hormones and Behavior, 12,* 112–163.

Beck, A. T. (1976). *Cognitive therapy and the emotional disorders.* New York: International Universities Press.

Beck, A. T. (1985). Theoretical perspectives on clinical anxiety. In A. H. Tuma, & J. D. Maser (Eds.), *Anxiety and the anxiety disorders.* Hillsdale, NJ: Erlbaum.

Beck, A. T. (1991). Cognitive therapy: A 30-year retrospective. *American Psychologist, 46,* 368–375.

Beck, A. T., Brown, G., Berchick, R. J., Stewart, B. L., & Steer, R. A. (1990). Relationship between hopelessness and ultimate suicide. *American Journal of Psychiatry, 147,* 190–195.

Beck, A. T., Brown, G., & Steer, R. A. (1989). Prediction of eventual suicide in psychiatric inpatients by clinical ratings of hopelessness. *Journal of Consulting and Clinical Psychology, 57,* 309–310.

Beck, A. T., Epstein, N., Brown, G., & Steer, R. A. (1988). An inventory for measuring clinical anxiety: Psychometric properties. *Journal of Consulting and Clinical Psychology, 56,* 893–897.

Beck, A. T., & Freeman, A. (1990). *Cognitive therapy of personality disorders.* New York: Guilford.

Beck, A. T., Rush, A. J., Show, B. F., & Emery, G. (1979). *Cognitive therapy of depression.* New York: Guilford Press.

Beck, J., Elsner, A., & Silverstein, C. (1977). Position uncertainty and the perception of apparent movement. *Perception and psychophysics, 21,* 33–38.

Beck, R. C. (1978). *Motivation: Theories and principles.* Englewood Cliffs, NJ: Prentice-Hall.

Becker, K. L. (1990). *Principles and practice of endocrinology and metabolism.* Philadelphia: Lippincott.

Becker, M. H., & Maiman, L. A. (1980). Strategies for enhancing patient compliance. *Journal of Community Health, 6,* 113–135.

Beckham, E. E., & Leber, W. R. (1985). The comparative efficacy of psychotherapy and pharmacotherapy for depression. In E. E. Beckham & W. R. Leber (Eds.), *Handbook of depression: Treatment, assessment, and research.* Homewood, IL: Dorsey Press.

Beckwith, L., & Parmelee, A. H., Jr. (1986). EEG patterns of preterm infants, home environment, and later IQ. *Child Development, 57,* 777–789.

Bee, H. L. (1982). Prediction of IQ and language skill from perinatal status, child performance, family characteristics, and mother-infant interaction. *Child Development, 53,* 1134–1156.

Bell, A. P., Weinberg, M. S., & Hammersmith, S. K. (1981). *Sexual preference: Its development in men and women.* Bloomington, IN: University of Indiana Press.

Belle, D. (1990). Poverty and women's mental health. *American Psychologist, 45,* 385–389.

Belsky, J. (1984). The determinants of parenting: A process model. *Child Development, 55,* 83–96.

Belsky, J. (1984). *The psychology of aging: Theory, research, and practice.* Monterey, CA: Brooks/Cole.

Belsky, J., Gilstrap, B., & Rovine, M. (1984). The Pennsylvania and infant family development project, I: Stability and change in mother-infant and father-infant interaction in a family setting at one, three, and nine months. *Child Development, 55,* 692–705.

Bem, D. J. (1972). Self-perception theory. In L. Berkowitz (Ed.), *Advances in experimental social psychology,* Vol. 6. New York: Academic Press.

Bem, D. J., & Allen, A. (1974). On predicting some of the people some of the time: The search for cross-situational consistencies in behavior. *Psychological Review, 81,* 506–520.

Bem, S. L. (1981). Gender schema theory: A cognitive account of sex typing. *Psychological Review, 88,* 354–364.

Bem, S. L. (1983). Gender schema theory and its implications for child development: Raising gender-aschematic children in a gender-schematic society. *Signs: Journal of Women in Culture and Society, 8,* 598–616.

Bem, S. L. (1985). Androgyny and gender schema theory: A conceptual and empirical integration. In T. B. Sonderegger (Ed.), *Nebraska symposium on motivation.* Lincoln, NE: University of Nebraska Press.

Benbow, C. P., & Stanley, J. C. (1980). Sex differences in mathematical ability: Fact or artifact? *Science, 210,* 1029–1031.

Benbow, C. P., & Stanley, J. C. (1983). Sex differences in mathematical reasoning ability: More facts. *Science, 229,* 1029–1030.

Bennett, W., & Gurin, J. (1982). *The dieter's dilemma: Eating less and weighing more.* New York: Basic Books.

Benson, H. (1975). *The relaxation response.* New York: Morrow.

Benson, H., Manzetta, B. R., & Rosner, B. (1973). Decreased systolic blood pressure in hypertensive subjects who practiced meditation. *Journal of Clinical Investigation, 52,* 8.

Benson, P. L., Karabenick, S. A., & Lerner, R. M. (1976). Pretty pleases: The effects of physical attractiveness, race, and sex on receiving help. *Journal of Experimental Social Psychology, 12,* 409–415.

Bentler, P. M., & Speckart, G. (1981). Attitudes "cause" behaviors: A structural equation analysis. *Journal of Personality and Social Psychology, 40,* 226–238.

Berkman, L. F., & Breslow, L. (1983). *Health and ways of living: The Alameda County Study.* New York: Oxford University Press.

Berkowitz, L. (1987). Mood, self-awareness, and willingness to help. *Journal of Personality and Social Psychology, 52,* 721–729.

Berkowitz, L. (1988). Frustrations, appraisals, and aversively stimulated aggression. *Aggressive Behavior, 14,* 3–11.

Berkowitz, L. (1989). Frustration-aggression hypothesis: Examination and reformulation. *Psychological Bulletin, 106,* 59–73.

Berman, J. S., Miller, R. C., & Massman, P. J. (1985). Cognitive therapy versus systematic desensitization: Is one therapy superior? *Psychological Bulletin, 97,* 451–461.

Berns, R. M. (1989). *Child, family, community, 2d ed.* New York: Holt, Rinehart and Winston.

Bernstein, I. L. (1985). Learned food aversions in the progression of cancer and its treatment. In N. S. Braverman & P. Bernstein (Eds.), *Experimental assessments and clinical application of conditioned food aversions. Annals of the New York Academy of Sciences, 443.*

Bernstein, W. M., Stephenson, B. O., Snyder, M. L., & Wicklund, R. A. (1983). Causal ambiguity and heterosexual affiliation. *Journal of Experimental Social Psychology, 19,* 78–92.

Berntzen, D., & Götestam, K. G. (1987). Effects of on-demand versus fixed-interval schedules in the treatment of chronic pain with analgesic compounds. *Journal of Consulting and Clinical Psychology, 55,* 213–217.

Berquier, A., & Ashton, R. (1992). Characteristics of the frequent nightmare sufferer. *Journal of Abnormal Psychology, 101,* 246–250.

Berscheid, E. (1976). Theories of interpersonal attraction. In B. B. Wolman & L. R. Pomeroy (Eds.), *International encyclopaedia of neurology, psychiatry, psychoanalysis, and psychology.* New York: Springer.

Bersoff, D. N. (1981). Testing and the law. *American Psychologist, 36,* 1159–1166.

Bertelson, A. D., Marks, P. A., & May, G. D. (1982). MMPI and race: A controlled study. *Journal of Consulting and Clinical Psychology, 50,* 316–318.

Betz, N. E., & Hackett, G. (1981). The relationships of career-related self-efficacy expectations to perceived career options in college women and men. *Journal of Counseling Psychology, 28,* 399–410.

Beutler, L. E. (1991). Have all won and must all have prizes? *Journal of Consulting and Clinical Psychology, 59,* 226–232.

Beutler, L. E., & Kendall, P. C. (1991). Ethical dilemmas. *Journal of Consulting and Clinical Psychology, 59,* 245–245.

Bexton, W. H., Heron, W., & Scott, T. H. (1954). Effects of decreased variation in the sensory environment. *Canadian Journal of Psychology, 8,* 70–76.

Billings, A. G., Cronkite, R. C., & Moos, R. H. (1983). Social-environmental factors in unipolar depression: Comparisons of depressed patients and nondepressed controls. *Journal of Abnormal Psychology, 92,* 119–133.

Biran, M., & Wilson, G. T. (1981). Treatment of phobic disorders using cognitive and exposure methods: A self-efficacy analysis. *Journal of Consulting and Clinical Psychology, 49,* 886–899.

Birch, H. G., & Rabinowitz, H. S. (1951). The negative effect of previous experience on productive thinking. *Journal of Experimental Psychology, 42,* 121–125.

Birren, J. E. (1983). Aging in America: Roles for psychology. *American Psychologist, 38,* 298–299.

Bisanz, G. L., & Rule, B. G. (1989). Gender and the persuasion schema: A search for cognitive invariants. *Personality and Social Psychology Bulletin, 15,* 4–18.

Bjorklund, A., & Stenevi, U. (1984). Intracerebral neural implants: Neuronal replacement and reconstruction of damaged circuitries. *Annual Review of Neuroscience, 7,* 279–308.

Bjorklund, D. F., & de Marchena, M. R. (1984). Developmental shifts in the basis of organization in memory: The role of associative versus categorical relatedness in children's free recall. *Child Development, 55,* 952–962.

Blakeslee, S. (1992, January 7). Scientists unraveling chemistry of dreams. *The New York Times,* pp. C1, C10.

Blanchard, E. B. (1992a). Introduction to the special issue on behavioral medicine: An update for the 1990s. *Journal of Consulting and Clinical Psychology, 60,* 491–492.

Blanchard, E. B. (1992b). Psychological treatment of benign headache disorders. *Journal of Consulting and Clinical Psychology, 60,* 537–551.

Blanchard, E. B. (1990a). Placebo-controlled evaluation of abbreviated progressive muscle relaxation and of relaxation combined with cognitive therapy in the treatment of tension headache. *Journal of Consulting and Clinical Psychology, 58,* 210–215.

Blanchard, E. B. (1990b). A controlled evaluation of thermal biofeedback and thermal feedback combined with cognitive therapy in the treatment of vascular headache. *Journal of Consulting and Clinical Psychology, 58,* 216–224.

Blanchard, E. B. (1991). The role of regular home practice in the relaxation treatment of tension headache. *Journal of Consulting and Clinical Psychology, 59,* 467–470.

Blanck, P. D., Bellack, A. S., Rosnow, R. L., Rotheram-Borus, M. J., & Schooler, N. R. (1992). Scientific rewards and conflicts of ethical choices in human subjects research. *American Psychologist, 47,* 959–965.

Blasi, A. (1980). Bridging moral cognition and moral action: A critical review of the literature. *Psychological Bulletin, 88,* 1–45.

Blehar, M. C. (1988). Family and genetic studies of affective disorders. *Archives of Gneral Psychiatry, 45,* 289–292.

Blittner, M., Goldberg, J., & Merbaum, M. (1978). Cognitive self-control factors in the reduction of smoking behavior. *Behavior Therapy, 9,* 553–561.

Bloom, L., Lahey, L., Hood, L., Lifter, K., & Fiess, K. (1980). Complex sentences: Acquisition of syntactic connectives and the semantic relations they encode. *Journal of Child Language, 7,* 235–261.

Bloom, L., Merkin, S., & Wootten, J. (1982). *Wh*-questions: Linguistic factors that contribute to the sequence of acquisition. *Child Development, 53,* 1084–1092.

Blumberg, S. H., & Izard, C. E. (1985). Affective and cognitive characteristics of depression in 10- and 11-year-old children. *Journal of Personality and Social Psychology, 49,* 194–202.

Blumenthal, D. (1988, October 9). Dieting reassessed. *The New York Times Magazine. Part 2: The Good Health Magazine,* pp. 24–25, 53–54.

Bodenhausen, G. V. (1988). Stereotypic biases in social decision making and memory. *Journal of Personality and Social Psychology, 55,* 726–737.

Bolles, R. C., & Faneslow, M. S. (1982). Endorphins and behavior. *Annual Review of Psychology, 33,* 87–101.

Bonica, J. J. (Ed.) (1980). *Pain.* New York: Raven Press.

Bonvillian, J. D., Orlansky, M. D., & Novack, L. L. (1983). Developmental milestones: Sign language acquisition and motor development. *Child Development, 54,* 1435–1445.

Booth, A., & Edwards, J. N. (1985). Age at marriage and marital instability. *Journal of Marriage and the Family, 47,* 67–75.

Booth-Kewley, S., & Friedman, H. S. (1987). Psychological predictors of heart disease: A quantitative review. *Psychological Bulletin, 101,* 343–362.

Bootzin, R. R., Epstein, D., & Wood, J. N. (1991). Stimulus control instructions. In P. Hauri (Ed.), *Case studies in insomnia.* New York: Plenum Press.

Borgida, E., & Campbell, B. (1982). Belief relevance and attitude-behavior consistency: The moderating role of personal experience. *Journal of Personality and Social Psychology, 42,* 239–247.

Borkan, G. A. (1986). Body weight and coronary heart disease risk: Patterns of risk factor change associated with long-term weight change. The Normative Aging Study. *American Journal of Epidemiology, 124,* 410–419.

Bornstein, M. H., Kessen, W., & Weiskopf, S. (1976). The categories of hue in infancy. *Science, 191,* 201–202.

Bornstein, M. H., & Marks, L. E. (1982). Color revisionism. *Psychology Today, 16*(1), 64–73.

Borod, J. C. (1992). Interhemispheric and intrahemispheric control of emotion: A focus on unilateral brain damage. *Journal of Consulting and Clinical Psychology, 60,* 339–348.

Boskind-White, M., & White, W. C. (1983). *Bulimarexia: The binge/purge cycle.* New York: W. W. Norton.

Boskind-White, M., & White, W. C. (1986). Bulimarexia: A historical-sociocultural perspective. In K. D. Brownell & J. P. Foreyt (Eds.), *Handbook of eating disorders.* New York: Basic Books.

Bothwell, R. K., Deffenbacher, K. A., & Brigham, J. C. (1987). Correlation of eyewitness accuracy and confidence: Optimality hypothesis revisited. *Journal of Applied Psychology, 72,* 691–695.

Botvin, G. J. (1990). Preventing adolescent drug abuse through a multimodal cognitive-behavioral approach: Results of a 3-year study. *Journal of Consulting and Clinical Psychology, 58,* 437–446.

Bouchard, C. (1991). Is weight fluctuation a risk factor? *The New England Journal of Medicine, 324,* 1887–1889.

Bouchard, T. J., Jr., Lykken, D. T., McGue, M., Segal, N. L., & Tellegen, A. (1990). Sources of human psychological differences: The Minnesota study of twins reared apart. *Science, 250,* 223–228.

Bower, G. H. (1981). Mood and memory. *American Psychologist, 36,* 129–148.

Bowerman, M. F. (1982). Starting to talk worse: Clues to language acquisition from children's late speech errors. In S. Strauss (Ed.), *U-shaped behavioral growth.* New York: Academic Press.

Bowlby, J. (1973). Separation. *Attachment and loss,* Vol. 2. New York: Basic Books.

Bowlby, J. (1988). *A secure base.* New York: Basic Books.

Boyatzis, R. E. (1974). The effect of alcohol consumption on the aggressive behavior of men. *Quarterly Journal for the Study of Alcohol, 35,* 959–972.

Bradley, R. H., & Caldwell, B. M. (1976). The relation of infants' home environments to mental test performance at 54 months: A follow-up study. *Child Development, 47,* 1172–1174.

Bradley, R. H., & Caldwell, B. M. (1984). The relation of infants' home environments to achievement test performance in first grade: A follow-up study. *Child Development, 55,* 803–809.

Braitman, L. E., Adlin, E. V., & Stanton, J. L., Jr. (1985). Obesity and caloric intake. *Journal of Chronic Diseases, 38,* 727–732.

Brantley, P. J., McKnight, G. T., Jones, G. N., Dietz, L. S., & Tulley, R. (1988). Convergence between the daily stress inventory and endocrine measures of stress. *Journal of Consulting and Clinical Psychology, 56,* 549–551.

Braun, B. G. (1988). *Treatment of multiple personality disorder.* Washington, DC: American Psychiatric Press.

Bray, N. W., Hersh, R. E., & Turner, L. A. (1985). Selective remembering during adolescence. *Developmental Psychology, 21,* 290–294.

Bray, R. M., & Sugarman, R. (1980). Social facilitation among interaction groups: Evidence for the evaluation-apprehension hypothesis. *Personality and Social Psychology Bulletin, 6,* 137–142.

Breckler, S. J., & Wiggins, E. C. (1989). Affect versus evaluation in the structure of attitudes. *Journal of Experimental Social Psychology, 25,* 253–271.

Brent, E., & Granberg, D. (1982). Subjective agreement with the presidential candidates of 1976 and 1980. *Journal of Personality and Social Psychology, 42,* 393–403.

Bretherton, I., & Waters, E. (1985). Growing points of attachment theory and research. *Monographs of the Society for Research in Child Development, 50* (1, 2, Serial No. 209).

Brewer, W. F., & Pani, J. R. (1984). The structure of human memory. In G. H. Bower (Ed.), *The psychology of learning and motivation,* Vol. 17. New York: Academic Press.

Bridges, K. (1932). Emotional development in early infancy. *Child Development, 3,* 324–341.

Bridgwater, C. A. (1982). What candor can do. *Psychology Today, 16*(5), 16.

Brigham, J. C. (1980). Limiting conditions of the "physical attractiveness stereotype": Attributions about divorce. *Journal of Research in Personality, 14,* 365–375.

Brigham, T. A., Hopper, C., Hill, B., DeArmas, A., & Newsom, P. (1985). A self-management program for disruptive adolescents in the school: A clinical replication analysis. *Behavior Therapy, 16,* 99–115.

Brim, O. G., & Kagan, J. (1980). *Continuity and change in human development.* Cambridge, MA: Harvard University Press.

Brody, J. E. (1988, May 5). Sifting fact from myth in the face of asthma's growing threat to American children. *The New York Times,* p. B19.

Brody, J. E. (1991, April 9). Not just music, bird song is a means of courtship and defense. *The New York Times,* C1, C9.

Brody, J. E. (1992, January 8). Migraines and the estrogen connection. *The New York Times,* p. C12.

Brody, J. E. (1992, August 4). How the taste bud translates between tongue and brain. *The New York Times,* pp. C1, C8.

Broman, S. H., Nichols, P. L., & Kennedy, N. A. (1975). *Preschool IQ: Prenatal and early developmental correlates.* Hillsdale, NJ: Erlbaum.

Brooks, J. (1985). Polygraph testing: Thoughts of a skeptical legislator. *American Psychologist, 40,* 348–354.

Brooks, V. R. (1982). Sex differences in student dominance behavior in female and male professors' classrooms. *Sex Roles, 8,* 683–690.

Brooks-Gunn, J., & Ruble, D. N. (1980). The menstrual attitude questionnaire. *Psychosomatic Medicine, 42,* 503–511.

Brown, A. L., Bransford, J. D., Ferrara, R. A., & Campione, J. C. (1983). Learning, remembering, and understanding. In J. H. Flavell & E. M. Markman (Eds.), *Handbook of child psychology: Vol. 3. Cognitive development.* New York: Wiley.

Brown, B. B., & Altman, J. (1981). Territoriality and residential crime. In P. A. Brantingham & P. L. Brantingham (Eds.), *Urban crime and environmental criminology.* Beverly Hills, CA: Sage Press.

Brown, E. L., & Deffenbacher, K. (1979). *Perception and the senses.* Oxford: Oxford University Press.

Brown, P. L. (1987, September 14). Studying seasons of a woman's life. *The New York Times,* p. B17.

Brown, R. (1970). The first sentences of child and chimpanzee. In R. Brown (Ed.), *Psycholinguistics.* New York: Free Press.

Brown, R. (1973). *A first language: The early stages.* Cambridge, MA: Harvard University Press.

Brown, R., & Hanlon, C. (1970). Derivational complexity and order of acquisition in child speech. In J. R. Hayes (Ed.), *Cognition and the development of language.* New York: Wiley.

Brown, R., & Kulik, J. (1977). Flashbulb memories. *Cognition, 5,* 73–99.

Brown, R., & McNeill, D. (1966). The tip-of-the-tongue phenomenon. *Journal of Verbal Learning and Verbal Behavior, 5,* 325–337.

Brown, S. A. (1985). Expectancies versus background in the prediction of college drinking patterns. *Journal of Consulting and Clinical Psychology, 53,* 123–130.

Brown, S. A., Goldman, M. S., & Christiansen, B. A. (1985). Do alcohol expectancies mediate drinking patterns of adults? *Journal of Consulting and Clinical Psychology, 53,* 512–519.

Brown, W. A., Monti, P. M., & Corriveau, D. P. (1978). Serum testosterone and sexual activity and interest in men. *Archives of Sexual Behavior, 7,* 97–103.

Brownell, K. D. (1988). Yo-yo dieting. *Psychology Today, 22*(1), 20–23.

Brownell, K. D., & Wadden, T. A. (1986). Behavior therapy for obesity: Modern approaches and better results. In K. D. Brownell & J. P. Foreyt (Eds.), *Handbook of eating disorders: Physiology, psychology, and treatment of obesity, anorexia, and bulimia.* New York: Basic Books.

Brownell, K. D., & Wadden, T. A. (1992). Obesity: Understanding a serious, prevalent, and refractory disorder. *Journal of Consulting and Clinical Psychology, 60,* 505–517.

Brownell, W. E. (1992). Cited in Browne, M. W. (1992, June 9). Ear's own sounds may underlie its precision. *The New York Times,* pp. C1, C8.

Brownlee-Duffeck, M. (1987). The role of health beliefs in the regimen adherence and metabolic control of adolescents and adults with diabetes mellitus. *Journal of Consulting and Clinical Psychology, 55,* 139–144.

Bruner, J. S. (1983). *Child's talk: Learning to use language.* New York: W. W. Norton.

Bryant, P. (1982). Piaget's questions. *British Journal of Psychology, 73,* 157–163.

Buchanan, C. M., Eccles, J. S., & Becker, J. B. (1992). Are adolescents the victims of raging hormones? Evidence for activational effects of hormones on moods and behavior at adolescence. *Psychological Bulletin, 111,* 62–107.

Buchsbaum, M. S., & Haier, R. J. (1987). Functional and anatomical brain imaging: Impact on schizophrenia research. *Schizophrenia Bulletin, 13,* 115–132.

Budzynski, T. H., & Stoyva, J. M. (1984). Biofeedback methods in the treatment of anxiety and stress. In R. L. Woolfolk & P. M. Lehrer (Eds.), *Principles and practice of stress management.* New York: Guilford Press.

Buffone, G. W. (1980). Exercise as therapy: A closer look. *Journal of Counseling and Psychotherapy, 3,* 101–115.

Buffone, G. W. (1984). Running and depression. In M. L. Sachs & G. W. Buffone (Eds.), *Running as therapy: An integrated approach.* Lincoln, NE: University of Nebraska Press.

Bullock, M. (1985). Animism in childhood thinking: A new look at an old question. *Developmental Psychology, 21,* 217–225.

Bulman, R. J., & Wortman, C. B. (1977). Attribution of blame and coping in the "real world": Severe accident victims react to their lot. *Journal of Personality and Social Psychology, 35,* 351–363.

Burns, G. L., & Farina, A. (1987). Physical attractiveness and self-perception of mental disorder. *Journal of Abnormal Psychology, 96,* 161–163.

Burnstein, E. (1983). Persuasion as argument processing. In M. Brandstatter, J. H. Davis, & G. Stocker-Kreichgauer (Eds.), *Group decision processes.* London: Academic Press.

Burish, T. G., Carey, M. P., Krozely, M. G., & Greco, F. A. (1987). Conditioned side effects induced by cancer chemotherapy: Prevention through behavioral treatment. *Journal of Consulting and Clinical Psychology, 55,* 42–48.

Burish, T. G., Snyder, S. L., & Jenkins, R. A. (1991). Preparing patients for cancer chemotherapy: Effect of coping preparation and relaxation interventions. *Journal of Consulting and Clinical Psychology, 59,* 518–525.

Burman, B., & Margolin, G. (1992). Analysis of the association between marital relationships and health problems: An interactional perspective. *Psychological Bulletin, 112,* 39–63.

Burns, D. D., & Nolen-Hoeksema, S. (1992). Therapeutic empathy and recovery from depression in cognitive-behavioral therapy: A structural equation model. *Journal of Consulting and Clinical Psychology, 60,* 441–449.

Burnstein, E., & Schul, Y. (1982). The informational basis of social judgments: Operations in forming an impression of another person. *Journal of Experimental Social Psychology, 18,* 217–234.

Burros, M. (1988, January 6). What Americans really eat: Nutrition can wait. *The New York Times,* pp. C1, C6.

Busch, M. P. (1991). Evaluation of screened blood donations for HIV-1 infection by culture and DNA amplification of pooled cells. *The New England Journal of Medicine, 325,* 1–5.

Bushnell, E. W., Shaw, L., & Strauss, D. (1985). Relationship between visual and tactual exploration by 6-month-olds. *Developmental Psychology, 21,* 591–600.

Buss, A. H. (1983). Social rewards and personality. *Journal of Personality and Social Psychology, 44,* 553–563.

Buss, A. H. (1986). *Social behavior and personality.* Hillsdale, NJ: Erlbaum.

Buss, D. M. (1984). Toward a psychology of person–environment (PE) correlation: The role of spouse selection. *Journal of Personality and Social Psychology, 47,* 361–377.

Buss, D. M. (1989). Sex differences in human mate preferences: Evolutionary hypotheses tested in 37 cultures. *Behavioral and Brain Sciences, 12,* 1–49.

Buss, D. M., & Barnes, M. (1986). Preferences in human mate selection. *Journal of Personality and Social Psychology, 50,* 559–570.

Butcher, J. N., Braswell, L., & Raney, D. (1983). A cross-cultural comparison of American Indian, black, and white inpatients on the MMPI and presenting symptoms. *Journal of Consulting and Clinical Psychology, 51,* 587–594.

Butcher, J. N., Dahlstrom, W. G., Graham, J. R., Tellegen, A., & Kaemmer, B. (1989). *MMPI-2: Manual for administration and scoring.* Minneapolis: University of Minnesota Press.

Byrne, D., & Murnen, S. (1987). Maintaining love relationships. In R. J. Sternberg & M. L. Barnes (Eds.), *The anatomy of love.* New Haven: Yale University Press.

C

Cacioppo, J. T., Martzke, J. S, Petty, R. E., & Tassinary, L. G. (1988). Specific forms of facial EMG response index emotions during an interview. *Journal of Personality and Social Psychology, 54,* 552–604.

Cadoret, R. J., Cain, C. A., & Grove, W. M. (1980). Development of alcoholism in adoptees raised apart from alcoholic biologic relatives. *Archives of General Psychiatry, 37,* 561–563.

Calder, B. J., Ross, M., & Inkso, C. A. (1973). Attitude change and attitude attribution: Effects of incentive, choice, and consequences. *Journal of Personality and Social Psychology, 25,* 84–99.

Campos, J. J., Hiatt, S., Ramsey, D., Henderson, C., & Svejda, M. (1978). The emergence of fear on the visual cliff. In M. Lewis & L. Rosenblum (Eds.), *The origins of affect.* New York: Plenum Publishing Co.

Campos, J. J., Langer, A., & Krowitz, A. (1970). Cardiac responses on the visual cliff in prelocomotor infants. *Science, 170,* 196–197.

Campos, J. J., & Stenberg, C. R. (1981). Perception, appraisal, and emotion: The onset of social referencing. In M. Lamb & L. Sherrod (Eds.), *Infant social cognition.* Hillsdale, NJ: Erlbaum.

Cannon, D. S., & Baker, T. B. (1981). Emetic and electric shock alcohol aversion therapy. *Journal of Consulting and Clinical Psychology, 49,* 20–33.

Cannon, W. B. (1927). The James-Lange theory of emotions: A critical examination and an alternative theory. *American Journal of Psychology, 39,* 106–124.

Cannon, W. B. (1929). *Bodily changes in pain, hunger, fear, and rage.* New York: Appleton.

Caplan, P. J., MacPherson, G. M., & Tobin, P. (1985). Do sex-related differences in spatial abilities exist? A multilevel critique with new data. *American Psychologist, 40,* 786–799.

Carey, G. (1992). Twin imitation for antisocial behavior: Implications for genetic and family environment research. *Journal of Abnormal Psychology, 101,* 18–25.

Carey, M. P., & Burish, T. G. (1987). Providing relaxation training to cancer chemotherapy patients: A comparison of three delivery techniques. *Journal of Consulting and Clinical Psychology, 55,* 732–737.

Carey, M. P., & Burish, T. G. (1988). Etiology and treatment of the psychological side effects associated with cancer chemotherapy: A critical review and discussion. *Psychological Bulletin, 104,* 307–325.

Carling, P. J. (1990). Major mental illness, housing, and supports: The promise of community integration. *American Psychologist, 45,* 969–975.

Carlson, G. A., & Miller, D. C. (1981). Suicide affective disorder and women physicians. *American Journal of Psychiatry, 138,* 1330–1335.

Carlson, J. G., & Hatfield, E. (1992). *Psychology of emotion.* Fort Worth: Harcourt Brace Jovanovich.

Carlson, N. R. (1988). *Foundations of physiological psychology.* Boston: Allyn & Bacon.

Carmichael, L. L., Hogan, H. P., & Walter, A. A. (1932). An experimental study of the effect of language on the reproduction of visually perceived form. *Journal of Experimental Psychology, 15,* 73–86.

Carmody, D. (1988, September 20). Blacks gain again in college admission tests. *The New York Times,* p. A30.

Caro, R. A. (1989). *The years of Lyndon Johnson: Means of ascent.* New York: Knopf.

Carr, D. B. (1981). Physical conditioning facilitates the exercise-induced secretion of beta-endorphins and beta-lipotropin in women. *New England Journal of Medicine, 305,* 560–563.

Carroll, D. (1985). *Living with dying.* New York: McGraw-Hill.

Carson, R. C., Butcher, J. N., & Coleman, J. C. (1988). *Abnormal psychology and modern life,* 8th ed. Glenview, IL: Scott, Foresman and Company.

Cartwright, R. D., Lloyd, S., Nelson, J. B., & Bass, S. (1983). The traditional-liberated woman dimension: Social stereotype and self-concept. *Journal of Personality and Social Psychology, 44,* 581–588.

Carver, C. S., & Gaines, J. G. (1987). Optimism, pessimism, and postpartum depression. *Cognitive Therapy and Research, 11,* 449–462.

Carver, C. S., Ganellen, R. J., & Behar-Mitrani, V. (1985). Depression and cognitive style: Comparisons between measures. *Journal of Personality and Social Psychology, 49,* 722–728.

Cash, T. F., & Kilcullen, R. N. (1985). The age of the beholder: Susceptibility to sexism and beautyism in the evaluation of managerial applicants. *Journal of Applied Social Psychology, 15,* 591–605.

Caspi, A., & Herbener, E. S. (1990). Continuity and change: Assortative marriage and the consistency of personality in adulthood. *Journal of Personality and Social Psychology, 58,* 250–258.

Cassileth, B. R. (1985). Psychosocial correlates of survival in advanced malignant diseases? *New England Journal of Medicine, 312,* 1551–1555.

Cattell, R. B. (1949). *The culture-free intelligence test.* Champaign, IL: Institute for Personality and Ability Testing.

Cattell, R. B. (1965). *The scientific analysis of personality.* Baltimore: Penguin Books.

Cattell, R. B. (1973). Personality pinned down. *Psychology Today, 7,* 40–46.

CDC (Centers for Disease Control). (1985). *Suicide surveillance: 1970–1980.* Washington, DC: USDHHS.

CDC (Centers for Disease Control). (1991). Mortality attributable to HIV infection/AIDS—United States, 1981–1990. *Journal of the American Medical Association, 265,* 848.

CDC (Centers for Disease Control). (1992). Cited in *The New York Times* (1992, May 22). Smoking declines at a faster pace. *The New York Times,* p. A17.

Celis, W. (1993, January 10). College curriculums shaken to the core. *Education Life (The New York Times),* Section 4A, pp. 16–18.

Center for Women in Government (1992). Women in Public Service Survey. Rockefeller College of Public Affairs and Policy. Cited in Associated Press (1992, January 3). Few women found in top public jobs. *The New York Times,* p. A12.

Cermak, L. (1978). *Improving your memory.* New York: McGraw-Hill.

Cernoch, J., & Porter, R. (1985). Recognition of maternal axillary odors by infants. *Child Development, 56,* 1593–1598.

Chadwick, P. D. J., & Lowe, C. F. (1990). Measurement and modification of delusional beliefs. *Journal of Consulting and Clinical Psychology, 58,* 225–232.

Chaiken, S., & Eagly, A. H. (1983). Communication modality as a determinant of persuasion: The role of communicator salience. *Journal of Personality and Social Psychology, 45,* 241–256.

Chassin, L., Mann, L. M., & Sher, K. J. (1988). Self-awareness theory, family history of alcoholism, and adolescent alcohol involvement. *Journal of Abnormal Psychology, 97,* 206–217.

Chesno, F. A., & Kilmann, P. R. (1975). Effects of stimulation intensity on sociopathic avoidance learning. *Journal of Abnormal Psychology, 84,* 144–151.

Chouinard, G. (1983). New concepts on benzodiazepine therapy: Rebound anxiety and new indications for the more potent benzodiazepines. *Progress in Neuro-Psychopharmacology and Biological Psychiatry, 7,* 669–673.

Chronicle of Higher Education (1992, March 18). Pp. A35–A44.

Chwalisz, K., Diener, E., & Gallagher, D. (1988). Autonomic arousal feedback and emotional experience: Evidence from the spinal-cord injured. *Journal of Personality and Social Psychology, 54,* 820–828.

Cialdini, R. B., & Fultz, J. (1990). Interpreting the negative mood-helping literature via "mega"-analysis: A contrary view. *Psychological Bulletin, 107,* 210–214.

Clark, M. S., Mills, J. R., & Corcoran, D. M. (1989). Keeping track of needs and inputs of friends and strangers. *Personality and Social Psychology Bulletin, 15,* 533–542.

Cline, V. B., Croft, R. C., & Courrier, S. (1973). The desensitization of children to television violence. *Journal of Personality and Social Psychology, 27,* 360–365.

Clkurel, K., & Gruzelier, J. (1990). The effects of active alert hypnotic induction on lateral haptic processing. *British Journal of Experimental and Clinical Hypnosis, 11,* 17–25.

Cloninger, C. R., & Gottesman, I. I. (1987). Genetic and environmental factors in antisocial behavior disorders. In S. A. Mednick et al. (Eds.), *The causes of crime: New biological approaches.* New York: Cambridge University Press.

Clore, G. L., Wiggins, N. H., & Itkin, S. (1975). Gain and loss in attraction: Attributions from nonverbal behavior. *Journal of Personality and Social Psychology, 31,* 706–712.

Coates, T. J. (1990). Strategies for modifying sexual behavior for primary and secondary prevention of HIV disease. *Journal of Consulting and Clinical Psychology, 58,* 57–69.

Coe, W. C., & Yaskinski, E. (1985). Volitional experiences associated with breaching posthypnotic amnesia. *Journal of Personality and Social Psychology, 48,* 716–722.

Cohen, L. A. (1987, November). Diet and cancer. *Scientific American,* pp. 42–48, 533–534.

Cohen, S., Evans, G. W., Stokols, D., & Krantz, D. S. (1986). *Behavior, health, and environmental stress.* New York: Plenum Publishing Co.

Cohen, S., Tyrrell, D. A. J., & Smith, A. P. (1991). Psychological stress and susceptibility to the common cold. *The New England Journal of Medicine, 325,* 606–612.

Cohen, S., & Williamson, G. M. (1991). Stress and infectious disease in humans. *Psychological Bulletin, 109,* 5–24.

Cohn, L. D. (1987). Body-figure preferences in male and female adolescents. *Journal of Abnormal Psychology, 96,* 276–279.

Colby, A., Kohlberg, L., Gibbs, J., & Lieberman, M. (1983). A longitudinal study of moral judgment. *Monographs of the Society for Research in Child Development, 48* (Serial No. 200).

Colby, C. Z., Lanzetta, J. T., & Kleck, R. E. (1977). Effects of the expression of pain on autonomic and pain tolerance response to subject-controlled pain. *Psychophysiology, 14,* 537–540.

Cole, D. A. (1988). Hopelessness, social desirability, depression, and parasuicide in two college student samples. *Journal of Consulting and Clinical Psychology, 56,* 131–136.

Coleman, L. (1990). Cited in Goleman, G. (1990, August 2). The quiet comeback of electroshock therapy. *The New York Times,* p. B5.

Collins, R. L., Parks, G. A., & Marlatt, G. A. (1985). Social determinants of alcohol consumption: The effects of social interaction and model status on the self-administration of alcohol. *Journal of Consulting and Clinical Psychology, 53,* 189–200.

Comas-Diaz, L., & Griffith, E. (1988). Introduction: On culture and psychotherapeutic care. In L. Comas-Diaz & E. Griffith (Eds.), *Clinical guidelines in cross-cultural mental health.* New York: Wiley.

Conant, M. (1986). Condoms prevent transmission of the AIDS-associated retrovirus. *Journal of the American Medical Association, 255,* 1706.

Condiotte, M. M., & Lichtenstein, E. (1981). Self-efficacy and relapse in smoking cessation programs. *Journal of Consulting and Clinical Psychology, 49,* 648–658.

Condon, J. W., & Crano, W. D. (1988). Inferred evaluation and the relation between attitude similarity and interpersonal attraction. *Journal of Personality and Social Psychology, 54,* 789–797.

Conger, J. J., & Petersen, A. (1984). *Adolescence and youth: Psychological development in a changing world.* New York: Harper and Row.

Conley, J. J. (1984). Longitudinal consistency of adult personality: Self-reported psychological characteristics across 45 years. *Journal of Personality and Social Psychology, 47,* 1325–1333.

Conley, J. J. (1985). Longitudinal stability of personality traits: A multitrait-multimethod-multioccasion analysis. *Journal of Personality and Social Psychology, 49,* 1266–1282.

Conn, P. M., & Crowley, W. F., Jr. (1991). Gonadotropin-releasing hormone and its analogues. *The New England Journal of Medicine, 324,* 93–103.

Connor, J. (1972). Olfactory control of aggressive and sexual behavior in the mouse. *Psychonomic Science, 27,* 1–3.

Conover, M. R. (1982). Modernizing the scarecrow to protect crops from birds. *Frontiers of Plant Science, 35,* 7–8.

Conte, H. R., Plutchik, R., Wild, K. V., & Karasu, T. B. (1986). Combined psychotherapy and pharmacotherapy for depression: A systematic analysis of the evidence. *Archives of General Psychiatry, 43,* 471–479.

Cools, J., Schotte, D. E., & McNally, R. J. (1992). Emotional arousal and overeating in restrained eaters. *Journal of Abnormal Psychology, 101,* 348–351.

Coon, H., Fulker, D. W., DeFries, J. C., & Plomin, R. (1990). Home environment and cognitive ability of 7-year-old children in the Colorado Adoption Project: Genetic and environmental etiologies. *Developmental Psychology, 26,* 459–468.

Cooney, J. L., & Zeichner, A. (1985). Selective attention to negative feedback in Type A and Type B individuals. *Journal of Abnormal Psychology, 94,* 110–112.

Cooper, A. J. (1978). Neonatal olfactory bulb lesions: Influences on subsequent behavior of male mice. *Bulletin of the Psychonomic Society, 11,* 53–56.

Cooper, J. (1980). Reducing fears and increasing assertiveness: The role of dissonance reduction. *Journal of Experimental Social Psychology, 16,* 199–213.

Cooper, M. L., Russell, M., & George, W. H. (1988). Coping, expectancies, and alcohol abuse: A test of social learning formulations. *Journal of Abnormal Psychology, 97,* 218–230.

Cooper, R., & Zubek, J. (1958). Effects of enriched and restricted early environments on the learning ability of bright and dull rats. *Canadian Journal of Psychology, 12,* 159–164.

Cordes, C. (1985). Common threads found in suicide. *APA Monitor, 16*(10), 11.

Corkin, S. (1980). A prospective study of cingulotomy. In E. S. Valenstein (Ed.), *The psychosurgery debate.* San Francisco: W. H. Freeman.

Corkin, S. (1985). Analyses of global memory impairments of different etiologies. In D. S. Olton, E. Gamzu, & S. Corkin (Eds.), *Memory dysfunction.* New York: New York Academy of Sciences.

Corter, J. E., & Gluck, M. A. (1992). Explaining basic categories: Feature predictability and information. *Psychological Bulletin, 111,* 291–303.

Costa, E. (1985). Benzodiazepine/GABA interactions: A model to investigate the neurobiology of anxiety. In A. H. Tuma & J. D. Maser (Eds.), *Anxiety and the anxiety disorders.* Hillsdale, NJ: Erlbaum.

Costa, P. T., Jr., & McCrae, R. R. (1984). Personality as a lifelong determinant of wellbeing. In C. Z. Malatesta & C. E. Izard (Eds.), *Emotion in adult development.* Beverly Hills: Sage Publications.

Costa, P. T., Jr., & McCrae, R. R. (1985). Hypochondriasis, neuroticism, and aging: When are somatic complaints unfounded? *American Psychologist, 40,* 19–28.

Costa, P. T., Jr., Zonderman, A. B., McCrae, R. R., & Williams, R. B., Jr. (1985). Content and comprehensiveness in the MMPI: An item factor analysis in a normal adult sample. *Journal of Personality and Social Psychology, 48,* 925–933.

Cournoyer, D., & Caskey, C. T. (1990). Gene transfer into humans—A first step. *The New England Journal of Medicine, 323,* 601–603.

Cowen, E. L. (1983). Primary prevention: Past, present, and future. In R. D. Felner (Eds.), *Preventive psychology: Theory, research, and practice.* New York: Pergamon Press.

Cox, W. M., & Klinger, E. (1988). A motivational model of alcohol use. *Journal of Abnormal Psychology, 97,* 168–180.

Coyle, J. T., Price, D. L., & DeLong, M. R. (1983). Alzheimer's disease: A disorder of cortical cholinergic innervation. *Science, 219,* 1184–1190.

Coyne, J. C. (1987). Living with a depressed person. *Journal of Consulting and Clinical Psychology, 55,* 347–352.

Coyne, J. C., & Downey, G. (1991). Social factors and psychopathology: Stress, social support, and coping processes. *Annual Review of Psychology, 42,* 401–425.

Craighead, L. W., & Agras, W. S. (1991). Mechanisms of action in cognitive-behavioral and pharmacological interventions for obesity and bulimia nervosa. *Journal of Consulting and Clinical Psychology, 59,* 115–125.

Craik, F. I. M., & Lockhart, R. S. (1972). Levels of processing: A framework for memory research. *Journal of Verbal Learning and Verbal Behavior, 11,* 671–684.

Craik, F. I. M., & Watkins, M. J. (1973). The role of rehearsal in short-term memory. *Journal of Verbal Learning and Verbal Behavior, 12,* 599–607.

Cramer, R. E., McMaster, M. R., Bartell, P. A., & Dragna, M. (1988). Subject competence and minimization of the bystander effect. *Journal of Applied Social Psychology, 18,* 1133–1148.

Crawford, C. (1979). George Washington, Abraham Lincoln, and Arthur Jensen: Are they compatible? *American Psychologist, 34,* 664–672.

Crawford, H. J. (1982). Hypnotizability, daydreaming styles, imagery vividness, and absorption: A multidimensional study. *Journal of Personality and Social Psychology, 42,* 915–926.

Creamer, M., Burgess, P., & Pattison, P. (1992). Reaction to trauma: A cognitive processing model. *Journal of Abnormal Psychology, 101,* 452–459.

Creese, I., Burt, D. R., & Snyder, S. H. (1978). Biochemical actions of neuroleptic drugs. In L. L. Iverson, S. D. Iverson, & S. H. Snyder (Eds.), *Handbook of psychopharmacology,* Vol. 10. New York: Plenum Publishing Co.

Crews, D., & Moore, M. C. (1986). Evolution of mechanisms controlling mating behavior. *Science, 231,* 121–125.

Crits-Christoph, P., & Mintz, J. (1991). Implications of therapist effects for the design and analysis of comparative studies of psychotherapies. *Journal of Consulting and Clinical Psychology, 59,* 20–26.

Cronbach, L. J. (1975). Five decades of public controversy over mental testing. *American Psychologist, 30,* 1–14.

Croyle, R. T., & Cooper, J. (1983). Dissonance arousal: Physiological evidence. *Journal of Personality and Social Psychology, 45,* 782–791.

Crusco, A. H., & Wetzel, C. G. (1984). The midas touch: The effects of interpersonal touch on restaurant tipping. *Personality and Social Psychology Bulletin, 10,* 512–517.

Cummings, E. M., Iannotti, R. J., & Zahn-Waxler, C. (1985). Influence of conflict between adults on the emotions and aggression of young children. *Developmental Psychology, 21,* 495–507.

Cunningham, M. R., Shaffer, D. R., Barbee, A. P., Wolff, P. L., & Kelley, D. J. (1990). Separate processes in the relation of elation and depression to helping: Social versus personal concerns. *Journal of Experimental Social Psychology, 26,* 13–33.

Curb, J. D., & Marcus, E. B. (1991). Body fat and obesity in Japanese Americans. *American Journal of Clinical Nutrition, 53,* 1552S–1555S.

Curry, S. J., Wagner, E. H., & Grothaus, L. C. (1991). Evaluation of intrinsic and extrinsic motivation interventions with a self-help smoking cessation program. *Journal of Consulting and Clinical Psychology, 59,* 318–324.

Curtis, R. C., & Miller, K. (1986). Believing another likes or dislikes you: Behavior making the beliefs come true. *Journal of Personality and Social Psychology, 51,* 284–290.

Curtiss, S. R. (1977). *Genie: A psycholinguistic study of a modern-day "wild child."* New York: Academic Press.

Cutler, B. L., Penrod, S. D., & Martens, T. K. (1987). Improving the reliability of eyewitness identification: Putting content into context. *Journal of Applied Psychology, 72,* 629–637.

Cutrona, C. E., & Troutman, B. R. (1986). Social support, infant temperament, and parenting self-efficacy: A mediational model of postpartum depression. *Child Development, 57,* 1507–1518.

D

Danforth, J. S. (1990). Exercise as a treatment for hypertension in low-socioeconomic-status black children. *Journal of Consulting and Clinical Psychology, 58,* 237–239.

Daniel, W. F., & Crovitz, H. F. (1983a). Acute memory impairment following electroconvulsive therapy: 1. Effects of electrical stimulus and number of treatments. *Acta Psychiatrica Scandinavica, 67,* 1–7.

Daniel, W. F., & Crovitz, H. F. (1983b). Acute memory impairment following electroconvulsive therapy: 2. Effects of electrode placement. *Acta Psychiatrica Scandinavica, 67,* 57–68.

Daniels, D., & Plomin, R. (1985). Origins of individual differences in infant shyness. *Developmental Psychology, 21,* 118–121.

Darley, J. M., & Latané, B. (1968). Bystander intervention in emergencies: Diffusion of responsibility. *Journal of Personality and Social Psychology, 8,* 377–383.

Darwin, C. A. (1872). *The expression of the emotions in man and animals.* London: J. Murray.

Dauber, R. B. (1984). Subliminal psychodynamic activation in depression: On the role of autonomy issues in depressed college women. *Journal of Abnormal Psychology, 93,* 9–18.

Davidson, J. M. (1982). Hormonal replacement and sexuality in men. *Clinics in endocrinology and metabolism, 11,* 599–623.

Davidson, T. M., & Bowers, K. S. (1991). Selective hypnotic amnesia: It it a successful attempt to forget or an unsuccessful attempt to remember? *Journal of Abnormal Psychology, 100,* 133–143.

Davis, J. H., Tindale, R. S., Nagao, D. H., Hinsz, V. B., & Robertson, B. (1984). Order effects in multiple decisions by groups: A demonstration with mock juries and trial procedures. *Journal of Personality and Social Psychology, 47,* 1003–1012.

Davison, G. C., & Neale, J. M. (1990). *Abnormal psychology,* 5th ed. New York: Wiley.

Davitz, J. R. (1969). *The language of emotion.* New York: Academic Press.

Dawes, R. M. (1989). Statistical criteria for establishing a truly false consensus effect. *Journal of Experimental Social Psychology, 25,* 1–17.

DeAngelis, T. (1991,). Hearing pinpoints gaps in research on women. *APA Monitor,*, p. 8.

Deaux, K. (1984). From individual differences to social categories: Analysis of a decade's research on gender. *American Psychologist, 39,* 105–116.

DeCasper, A. J., & Fifer, W. P. (1980). Of human bonding: Newborns prefer their mothers' voices. *Science, 208,* 1174–1176.

DeFries, J. C., Fulker, D. W., & LaBuda, M. C. (1987). Reading disability in twins: Evidence for a genetic etiology. *Nature, 329,* 537–539.

DeFries, J. C., Plomin, R., & LaBuda, M. C. (1987). Genetic stability of cognitive development from childhood to adulthood. *Developmental Psychology, 23,* 4–12.

DeGree, C. E., & Snyder, C. R. (1985). Adler's psychology (of use) today: Personal history of traumatic life events as a self-handicapping strategy. *Journal of Personality and Social Psychology, 48,* 1512–1519.

DeJong, W., & Musilli, L. (1982). External pressure to comply: Handicapped versus nonhandicapped requesters and the foot-in-the-door phenomenon. *Personality and Social Psychology Bulletin, 8,* 522–527.

Delanoy, R. L., Merrin, J. S., & Gold, P. E. (1982). Moderation of long-term potentiation (LTP) by adrenergic agonists. *Neuroscience Abstracts, 8,* 316.

Delgado, J. M. R. (1969). *Physical control of the mind.* New York: Harper & Row.

Dembroski, T. M., Lasater, T. M., & Ramirez, A. (1978). Communicator similarity, fear-arousing communications, and compliance with health care recommendations. *Journal of Applied Social Psychology, 8,* 254–269.

Dement, W. (1972). Sleep and dreams. In A. M. Freedman & H. I. Kaplan (Eds.), *Human behavior: Biological, psychological, and sociological.* New York: Atheneum.

Denton, L. (1988). Memory: Not place, but process. *APA Monitor,* p. 4.

DePaulo, B. M. (1992). Nonverbal behavior and self-presentation. *Psychological Bulletin, 111,* 203–243.

DePaulo, B. M., Rosenthal, R., Eisenstat, R. A., Rogers, P. L., & Finkelstein, S. (1978). Decoding discrepant nonverbal cues. *Journal of Personality and Social Psychology, 38,* 313–323.

Depue, R. A. (1981). A behavioral paradigm for identifying persons at risk for bipolar depressive disorder. *Journal of Abnormal Psychology, 90,* 381–438.

Derryberry, D., & Tucker, D. M. (1992). Neural mechanisms of emotion. *Journal of Consulting and Clinical Psychology, 60,* 329–338.

Des Jarlais, D. C., Friedman, S. R., & Casriel, C. (1990). Target groups for preventing AIDS among intravenous drug users: 2. The "hard" data studies. *Journal of Consulting and Clinical Psychology, 58,* 50–56.

Dethier, V. G. (1978). Other tastes, other worlds. *Science, 201,* 224–228.

DeValois, R. L., & Jacobs, G. H. (1984). Neural mechanisms of color vision. In I. Darian-Smith (Ed.), *Handbook of physiology, Vol. 3.* Bethesda, MD: American Physiological Society.

Devine, P. G. (1989). Stereotypes and prejudice: Their automatic and controlled components. *Journal of*

Personality and Social Psychology, 56, 5–18.

Dewsbury, D. A. (1991). "Psychobiology." *American Psychologist, 46,* 198–205.

Diamond, M. (1977). Human sexual development: Biological foundations for social development. In F. A. Beach (Ed.), *Human sexuality in four perspectives.* Baltimore: Johns Hopkins University Press.

Diamond, M. (1978,). Aging and cell loss: Calling for an honest count. *Psychology Today,* p. 126.

Diamond, M. (1984). A love affair with the brain. *Psychology Today,* pp. 62–73.

Diaz, R. M. (1985). Bilingual cognitive development: Addressing three gaps in current research. *Child Development, 56,* 1376–1388.

DiClemente, C. C. (1991). The process of smoking cessation. *Journal of Consulting and Clinical Psychology, 59,* 295–304.

Diener, E. (1980). Deindividuation: The absence of self-awareness and self-regulation in group members. In P. Paulus (Ed.), *The psychology of group influence.* Hillsdale, NJ: Erlbaum.

Digman, J. M. (1990). Personality structure: Emergence of the five-factor model. *Annual Review of Psychology, 41,* 417–440.

DiLalla, L. F., & Gottesman, I. I. (1991). Biological and genetic contributors to violence—Widom's untold tale. *Psychological Bulletin, 109,* 125–129.

Dill, C. A., Gilden, E. R., Hill, P. C., & Hanselka, L. L. (1982). Federal human subjects regulations: A methodological artifact. *Personality and Social Psychology Bulletin, 8,* 417–425.

DiMatteo, M. R., & DiNicola, D. D. (1982). *Achieving patient compliance: The psychology of the medical practitioner's role.* New York: Pergamon Press.

Dimsdale, J. E., & Moss, J. (1980). Plasma catecholamines in stress and exercise. *Journal of the American Medical Association, 243,* 340–342.

DiNicola, D. D., & DiMatteo, M. R. (1984). Practitioners, patients, and compliance with medical regimens: A social psychological perspective. In A. Baum, S. E. Taylor, & J. E. Singer (Eds.), *Handbook of psychology and health: Vol. 4. Social psychological aspects of health.* Hillsdale, NJ: Erlbaum.

Dishman, R. K. (1982). Compliance/adherence in health-related exercise. *Health Psychology, 1,* 237–267.

Divorce may be the price of living together first. *The New York Times* (1987, December 7), p. A25.

Doctorow, M., Wittrock, M. C., & Marks, C. (1978). Generative processes in reading comprehension. *Journal of Educational Psychology, 70,* 109–118.

Dodge, K. A., & Frame, C. L. (1982). Social cognitive biases and deficits in aggressive boys. *Child Development, 53,* 620–635.

Dodge, K. A., Price, J. M., Bachorowski, J., & Newman, J. P. (1990). Hostile attributional biases in severely aggressive adolescents. *Journal of Abnormal Psychology, 99,* 385–392.

Doherty, W. J., Schrott, H. G., Metcalf, L., & Iasiello-Vailas, L. (1983). Effects of spouse support and health beliefs on medication adherence. *Journal of Family Practice, 17,* 837–841.

Dohrenwend, B. P., & Shrout, P. E. (1985). "Hassles" in the conceptualization and measurement of life stress variables. *American Psychologist, 40,* 780–785.

Dohrenwend, B. S., Dohrenwend, B. P., Dodson, M., & Shrout, P. E. (1984). Symptoms, hassles, social supports and life events: The problem of confounded measures. *Journal of Abnormal Psychology, 93,* 222–230.

Dohrenwend, B. S., Krasnoff, L., Askenasy, A. R., & Dohrenwend, B. P. (1982). The psychiatric epidemiology research interview life events scale. In L. Goldberger & S. Breznitz (Eds.), *Handbook of stress: Theoretical and clinical aspects.* New York: Free Press.

Doll, R., & Peto, R. (1981). *The causes of cancer.* New York: Oxford University Press.

Dollard, J., Doob, L. W., Miller, N. E., Mowrer, O. H., & Sears, R. R. (1939). *Frustration and aggression.* New Haven, CT: Yale University Press.

Donatelle, R. J., Davis, L. G., & Hoover, C. F. (1991). *Access to health.* Englewood Cliffs, NJ: Prentice-Hall.

Dovidio, J. H., Evans, N., & Tyler, R. B. (1986). Racial stereotypes: The contents of their cognitive representations. *Journal of Experimental Social Psychology, 22,* 22–37.

Dowd, M. (1984, March 12). Twenty years after the murder of Kitty Genovese, the question remains: Why? *The New York Times,* pp. B1, B4.

Doyne, E. J., Chambless, D. L., & Bentler, L. E. (1983). Aerobic exercise as treatment for depression in women. *Behavior Therapy, 14,* 434–440.

Doyne, E. J. (1987). Running versus weight lifting in the treatment of depression. *Journal of Consulting and Clinical Psychology, 55,* 748–754.

Dubbert, P. M. (1992). Exercise in behavioral medicine. *Journal of Consulting and Clinical Psychology, 60,* 613–618.

Dugan, K. W. (1989). Ability and effort attributions: Do they affect how managers communicate performance feedback information? *Academy of Management Journal, 32,* 87–114.

Dywan, J., & Bowers, K. S. (1983). The use of hypnosis to enhance recall. *Science, 222,* 184–185.

E

Eagly, A. H. (1974). Comprehensibility of persuasive arguments as a determinant of opinion change. *Journal of Personality and Social Psychology, 29,* 758–773.

Eagly, A. H. (1983). Gender and social influence: A social psychological analysis. *American Psychologist, 38,* 971–981.

Eagly, A. H. (1987). *Sex differences in social behavior: A social-role interpretation.* Hillsdale, NJ: Erlbaum.

Eagly, A. H., & Johnson, B. T. (1990). Gender and leadership style: A meta-analysis. *Psychological Bulletin, 108,* 233–256.

Eagly, A. H., & Steffen, V. J. (1984). Gender stereotypes stem from the distribution of men and women into social roles. *Journal of Personality and Social Psychology, 46,* 735–754.

Eagly, A. H., Wood, W., & Chaiken, S. (1978). Causal inferences about communicators and their effect on opinion change. *Journal of Personality and Social Psychology, 36,* 424–435.

Eagly, A. H., Wood, W., & Fishbaugh, L. (1981). Sex differences in conformity: Surveillance by the group as a determinant of male conformity. *Journal of Personality and Social Psychology, 40,* 384–394.

Ebbeson, E. B., & Bowers, J. B. (1974). Proportion of risky to conservative arguments in a group discussion and choice shift. *Journal of Personality and Social Psychology, 29,* 316–327.

Ebbinghaus, H. (1913). *Memory: A contribution to experimental psychology.* (H. A. Roger & C. E. Bussenius, trans.). New York: Columbia University Press. (Original work published 1885).

Eccles, J. S., & Hoffman, L. W. (1984). Sex roles, socialization, and occupational behavior. In H. W. Stevenson & A. E. Siegel (Eds.), *Research in child development and social policy,* Vol. 1. Chicago: University of Chicago Press.

Eckenrode, J. (1984). Impact of chronic and acute stressors on daily reports of mood. *Journal of Personality and Social Psychology, 46,* 907–918.

Eckert, E. D. (1986). Homosexuality in monozygotic twins reared apart. *British Journal of Psychiatry, 148,* 421–425.

Edgley, C. (1989). Commercial sex: Pornography, prostitution, and advertising. In K. McKinney & S. Sprecher (Eds.), *Human sexuality: The societal and interpersonal context.* Norwood, NJ: Ablex Publishing Corporation

Edwards, D. J. A. (1972). Approaching the unfamiliar: A study of human interaction differences. *Journal of Behavioral Sciences, 1,* 249–250.

Efran, M. G. (1974). The effect of physical appearance on the judgment of guilt, interpersonal attraction, and severity of recommended punishment in a simulated jury task. *Journal of Research in Personality, 8,* 45–54.

Ehlers, A., & Breuer, P. (1992). Increased cardiac awareness in panic disorder. *Journal of Abnormal Psychology, 101,* 371–382.

Ehrhardt, A. A., & Baker, S. W. (1975). Hormonal aberrations and their implications for the understanding of normal sex differentiation. In P. H. Mussen, J. J. Conger, & J. Kagan (Eds.), *Basic and contemporary issues in developmental psychology.* New York: Harper & Row.

Eibl-Eibesfeldt, I. (1974). *Love and hate: The natural history of behavior patterns.* New York: Schocken Books.

Eidelson, R. J., & Epstein, N. (1982). Cognition and relationship maladjustment: Development of a measure of dysfunctional relationship beliefs. *Journal of Consulting and Clinical Psychology, 50,* 715–720.

Eisenberg, N., Cialdini, R. B., McCreath, H., & Shell, R. (1987). Consistency-based compliance: When and why do children become vulnerable? *Journal of Personality and Social Psychology, 52,* 1174–1181.

Eisenman, R. (1985). Marijuana use and attraction: Support for Byrne's similarity-attraction paradigm. *Perceptual and Motor Skills, 61,* 582.

Ekman, P. (1980). *The face of man.* Garland STPM Press.

Ekman, P. (1985). Cited in B. Bower (1985, July 6). The face of emotion. *Science News, 128,* 12–13.

Ekman, P., Davidson, R. J., & Friesen, W. V. (1990). The Duchenne smile: Emotional expression and brain physiology II. *Journal of Personality and Social Psychology, 58,* 342–353.

Ekman, P. (1987). Universals and cultural differences in the judgments of facial expressions of emotion. *Journal of Personality and Social Psychology, 53,* 712–717.

Ekman, P., Levenson, R. W., & Friesen, W. V. (1983). Autonomic nervous system activity distinguishes among emotions. *Science, 221,* 1208–1210.

Ekman, P., & Oster, H. (1979). Facial expressions of emotion. *Annual Review of Psychology, Vol. 30.* Palo Alto, CA: Annual Reviews.

Elardo, R., Bradley, R. H., & Caldwell, B. M. (1975). The relation of infants' home environments to mental test performance from 6 to 36 months: A longitudinal analysis. *Child Development, 46,* 71–76.

Elardo, R., Bradley, R. H., & Caldwell, B. M. (1977). A longitudinal study of the relation of infants' home environments to language development at age 3. *Child Development, 48,* 595–603.

Elkin, I. (1985). NIMH treatment of depression collaborative research program. *Archives of General Psychiatry, 42,* 305–316

Elkins, R. L. (1980). Covert sensitization treatment of alcoholism. *Addictive Behaviors, 5,* 67–89.

Ellickson, P. L., Hays, R. D., & Bell, R. M. (1992). Stepping through the drug use sequence: Longitudinal scalogram analysis of initiation and regular use. *Journal of Abnormal Psychology, 101,* 441–451.

Ellis, A. (1977). The basic clinical theory or rational-emotive therapy. In A. Ellis & R. Grieger (Eds.), *Handbook of rational-emotive therapy.* New York: Springer.

Ellis, A. (1985). Cognition and affect in emotional disturbance. *American Psychologist, 40,* 471–472.

Ellis, A. (1987). The impossibility of achieving consistently good mental health. *American Psychologist, 42,* 364–375.

Ellis, L. (1990). Prenatal stress may effect sex-typical behaviors of a child. *Brown University Child Behavior and Development Letter, 6*(1), pp. 1–3.

Ellis, L., & Ames, M. A. (1987). Neurohormonal functioning and sexual orientation: A theory of homosexuality–heterosexuality. *Psychological Bulletin, 101,* 233–258.

Ellison, G. D. (1977). Animal models of psychopathology: The low-norepinephrine and low-serotonin rat. *American Psychologist, 32,* 1036–1045.

Ellsworth, P. C., Carlsmith, J. M., & Henson, A. (1972). The stare as a stimulus to flight in human subjects. *Journal of Personality and Social Psychology, 21,* 302–311.

Ellsworth, P. C., & Langer, E. J. (1976). Staring and approach: An interpretation of the stare as a nonspecific activator. *Journal of Personality and Social Psychology, 33,* 117–122.

Engen, T. (1991). *Odor sensation and memory.* New York: Praeger.

Epstein, L. H., & Perkins, K. A. (1988). Smoking, stress, and coronary heart disease. *Journal of Consulting and Clinical Psychology, 56,* 342–349.

Epstein, L. H., & Wing, R. R. (1980). Aerobic exercise and weight. *Addictive Behaviors, 5,* 371–388.

Epstein, L. H., Wing, R. R., Koeske, R., & Valoski, A. (1984). Effects of diet plus exercise on weight change in parents and children. *Journal of Consulting and Clinical Psychology, 52,* 429–437.

Erikson, E. H. (1963). *Childhood and society.* New York: W. W. Norton.

Erikson, E. H. (1975). *Life history and the historical moment.* New York: W. W. Norton.

Erikson, E. H. (1983). Cited in E. Hall (1983). A conversation with Erik Erikson. *Psychology Today, 17*(6), 22–30.

Ernst, N. D., & Harlan, W. R. (1991). Obesity and cardiovascular disease in minority populations: Executive summary. *American Journal of Clinical Nutrition, 53,* 1507S–1511S.

Eron, L. D. (1982). Parent–child interaction, television violence, and aggression of children. *American Psychologist, 37,* 197–211.

Eron, L. D. (1987). The development of aggressive behavior from the perspective of a developing behaviorism. *American Psychologist, 42,* 435–442.

Erwin, J., Maple, T., Mitchell, G., & Willott, J. (1974). Follow-up study of isolation-reared rhesus monkeys paired with preadolescent cospecifics in late infancy: Cross-sex pairings. *Developmental Psychology, 6,* 808–814.

Estes, W. K. (1972). An associative basis for coding and organization in memory. In A. W. Melton & E. Martin (Eds.), *Coding processes in human memory.* Washington, DC: Winston.

Evans, D. A. (1989). Prevalence of Alzheimer's disease in a community population of older persons. *Journal of the American Medical Association, 262,* 2551–2556.

Eysenck, H. J. (1991). *Smoking, personality, and stress: Psychosocial factors in the prevention of cancer and coronary heart disease.* New York: Springer-Verlag.

Eysenck, H. J., & Eysenck, M. W. (1985). *Personality and individual differences.* New York: Plenum.

F

Fabian, W. D., Jr., & Fishkin, S. M. (1981). A replicated study of self-reported changes in psychological absorption with marijuana intoxication. *Journal of Abnormal Psychology, 90,* 546–553.

Fabricius, W. V., & Wellman, H. M. (1983). Children's understanding of retrieval cue utilization. *Developmental Psychology, 19,* 15–21.

Fagen, J. W. (1980). Stimulus preference, reinforcer effectiveness, and relational responding in infants. *Child Development, 51,* 372–378.

Fagot, B. I. (1982). Adults as socializing agents. In T. M. Field (Ed.), *Review of human development.* New York: Wiley.

Fairbanks, L. A., McGuire, M. T., & Harris, C. J. (1982). Nonverbal interaction of patients and therapists during psychiatric interviews. *Journal of Abnormal Psychology, 91,* 109–119.

Fairburn, C. G., Cooper, Z., & Cooper, P. J. (1986). The clinical features and maintenance of bulimia nervosa. In K. D. Brownell & J. P. Foreyt (Eds.), *Handbook of eating disorders.* New York: Basic Books.

Fallon, A. E., & Rozin, P. (1985). Sex differences in perceptions of desirable body shape. *Journal of Abnormal Psychology, 94,* 102–105.

Fantz, R. L. (1961). The origin of form perception. *Scientific American, 204*(5), 66–72.

Farina, A., Burns, G. L., Austad, C., Bugglin, C. S., & Fischer, E. H. (1986). The role of physical attractiveness in the readjustment of discharged psychiatric patients. *Journal of Abnormal Psychology, 95,* 139–143.

Farthing, G. W., Venturino, M., & Brown, S. W. (1984). Suggestion and distraction in the control of pain: Test of two hypotheses. *Journal of Abnormal Psychology, 93,* 266–276.

Fazio, R. H. (1989). In M. P. Zanna (Ed.), *Advances in experimental social psychology.* New York: Academic Press.

Fazio, R. H., & Cooper, J. (1983). Arousal in the dissonance process. In J. T. Cacioppo & R. E. Petty (Eds.), *Social psychophysiology.* New York: Guilford Press.

Fazio, R. H., Sherman, S. J., & Herr, P. M. (1982). The feature-positive effect in the self-perception process: Does not doing matter as much as doing? *Journal of Personality and Social Psychology, 42,* 404–411.

Feder, H. H. (1984). Hormones and sexual behavior. *Annual Review of Psychology, 35,* 165–200.

Feingold, A. (1992). Good-looking people are not what we think. *Psychological Bulletin, 111,* 304–341.

Feist, J., & Brannon, L. (1988). *Health psychology.* Belmont, CA: Wadsworth Publishing Co.

Feldman, D. (1980). *Beyond universals in cognitive development.* Norwood, NJ: Ablex.

Feldman, J. (1966). *The dissemination of health information.* Chicago: Aldine.

Felsenthal, N. (1976). *Orientations to mass communications.* Chicago: Science Research.

Feltz, D. L. (1982). Path analysis of the causal elements in Bandura's theory of self-efficacy and an anxiety-based model of avoidance behavior. *Journal of Personality and Social Psychology, 42,* 764–781.

Fenigstein, A. (1979). Does aggression cause a preference for viewing media violence? *Journal of Personality and Social Psychology, 37,* 2307–2317.

Fenigstein, A., Scheier, M. F., & Buss, A. H. (1975). Public and private self-consciousness: Assessment and theory. *Journal of Consulting and Clinical Psychology, 43,* 522–527.

Ferguson, C. A., & Farwell, C. (1975). Words and sounds in early language acquisition: English consonants in the first 50 words. *Language, 51,* 419–439.

Festinger, L. (1957). *A theory of cognitive dissonance.* Evanston, IL: Row, Peterson.

Festinger, L., & Carlsmith, J. M. (1959). Cognitive consequences of forced compliance. *Journal of Abnormal and Social Psychology, 58,* 203–210.

Fielding, J. E. (1985). Smoking: Health effects and control. *New England Journal of Medicine, 313,* 491–498, 555–561.

Finchilescu, G. (1988). Interracial contact in South Africa within the nursing context. *Journal of Applied Social Psychology, 18,* 1207–1221.

Findley, M. J., & Cooper, H. M. (1983). Locus of control and academic achievement: A literature review. *Journal of Personality and Social Psychology, 44,* 419–427.

Fiore, J. (1980). *Global satisfaction scale.* Unpublished manuscript, University of Washington, Department of Psychiatry and Behavioral Sciences, Seattle.

Fischer, K. W., Shaver, P. R., & Carochan, P. (1990). How emotions develop and how they organize development. *Cognition and Emotion, 4,* 81–127.

Fisher, K. (1984). Family violence cycle questioned. *APA Monitor, 15*(12), 30.

Fiske, S. T. (1989). *Interdependence and stereotyping: From the laboratory to the Supreme Court (and back).* Paper presented to the annual meeting of the American Psychological Association, New Orleans.

Fiske, S. T., & Taylor, S. E. (1984). *Social cognition.* Reading, MA: Addison-Wesley.

Fitch, G. (1970). Effects of self-esteem, perceived performance, and choice of causal attribution. *Journal of Personality and Social Psychology, 16,* 311–315.

Flaskerud, J. H., & Hu, L. (1992). Relationship of ethnicity to psychiatric diagnosis. *Journal of Nervous & Mental Disease, 180,* 296–303.

Flavell, J. H. (1982). Structures, stages, and sequences in cognitive development. In W. A. Collins (Ed.), *The concept of development: The Minnesota symposia on child psychology,* Vol. 15. Hillsdale, NJ: Erlbaum.

Flavell, J. H. (1985). *Cognitive development.* Englewood Cliffs, NJ: Prentice-Hall.

Flavell, J. H., Speer, J. R., Green, F. L., & August, D. L. (1981). The development of comprehension monitoring and knowledge about communication. *Monographs of the Society for Research in Child Development, 46*(5, Serial No. 192).

Flavell, J. H., & Wellman, H. M. (1976). Metamemory. In R. V. Kail & J. W. Hagen (Eds.), *Perspectives on the development of memory and cognition.* Hillsdale, NJ: Erlbaum.

Fleming, R., Baum, A., Gisriel, M. M., & Gatchel, R. J. (1982). Mediation of stress at Three Mile Island by social support. *Journal of Human Stress, 8*(3), 14–22.

Floderus-Myrhed, B., Pederson, N., & Rasmuson, I. (1980). Assessment of heritability for personality based on a short form of the Eysenck Personality Inventory: A study of 12,898 twin pairs. *Behavior Genetics, 10,* 153–162.

Foa, E. B. (1990, August/September). Obsessive-compulsive disorder. In American Psychiatric Association, *DSM–IV Update.* Washington, DC: American Psychiatric Association.

Fodor, E. M. (1984). The power motive and reactivity to power stresses. *Journal of Personality and Social Psychology, 47,* 853–859.

Fodor, E. M. (1985). The power motive, group conflict, and physiological arousal. *Journal of Personality and Social Psychology, 49,* 1408–1415.

Fodor, E. M., & Smith, T. (1982). The power motive as an influence on group decision making. *Journal of Personality and Social Psychology, 42,* 178–185.

Fodor, J. A., Bever, T. G., & Garrett, M. F. (1974). *The psychology of language.* New York: McGraw-Hill.

Folkins, C. H., & Sime, W. E. (1981). Physical fitness training and mental health. *American Psychologist, 36,* 373–389.

Folkman, S., & Lazarus, R. S. (1985). If it changes it must be a process: Study of emotion and coping during three stages of a college examination. *Journal of Personality and Social Psychology, 48,* 150–170.

Ford, C. S., & Beach, F. A. (1951). *Patterns of sexual behavior.* New York: Harper & Row.

Foreyt, J. P. (1986). Treating the diseases of the 1980s: Eating disorders. *Contemporary Psychology, 31,* 658–660.

Fowler, R. D. (1992). Solid support needed for animal research. *APA Monitor, 23*(6), 2.

Fox, S. (1984). *The mirror makers.* New York: Morrow.

Foy, D. W., Nunn, L. B., & Rychtarik, R. G. (1984). Broad-spectrum behavioral treatment for chronic alcoholics: Effects of training controlled drinking skills. *Journal of Consulting and Clinical Psychology, 52,* 218–230.

Francis, D. (1984). *Will you still need me, will you still feed me, when I'm 84?* Bloomington: Indiana University Press.

Franck, K. D., Unseld, C. T., & Wentworth, W. E. (1974). Adaptation of the newcomer: A process of construction. Unpublished manuscript, City University of New York.

Frankl, V. (1959). *Man's search for meaning.* Boston: Beacon Press.

Franzoi, S. L., & Herzog, M. E. (1987). Judging physical attractiveness: What body aspects do we use? *Personality and Social Psychology Bulletin, 13,* 19–33.

Freedman, J. L., & Fraser, S. C. (1966). Compliance without pressure: The foot-in-the-door technique. *Journal of Personality and Social Psychology, 4,* 195–202.

Freedman, J. L., Wallington, S. A., & Bless, E. (1967). Compliance without pressure: The effect of guilt. *Journal of Personality and Social Psychology, 7,* 117–124.

Freeman, A. M. (1991, December 18). Deadly diet. *The Wall Street Journal,* pp. 1, B1.

French, G. M., & Harlow, H. F. (1962). Variability of delayed-reaction performance in normal and brain-damaged rhesus monkeys. *Journal of Neurophysiology, 25,* 585–599.

Freud, S. (1909). Analysis of a phobia in a 5-year-old boy. In *Collected papers,* Vol. 3, trans. A. & J. Strachey. New York: Basic Books, 1959.

Freud, S. (1927). A religious experience. In *Standard edition of the complete psychological works of Sigmund Freud,* Vol. 21. London: Hogarth Press, 1964.

Freud, S. (1961). *Civilization and its discontents.* (J. Strachey, Trans.) New York: W. W. Norton. (Original work published 1930)

Freud, S. (1933). New introductory lectures. In *Standard edition of the complete psychological works of Sigmund Freud,* Vol. 22. London: Hogarth Press, 1964.

Friedman, H. S., & Booth-Kewley, S. (1987). Personality, Type A behavior, and coronary heart disease: The role of emotional expression. *Journal of Personality and Social Psychology, 53,* 783–792.

Friedman, M., & Rosenman, R. H. (1974). *Type A behavior and your heart.* New York: Harper & Row.

Friedman, M., & Ulmer, D. (1984). *Treating Type A behavior and your heart.* New York: Fawcett Crest.

Friedman, M. I., & Stricker, E. M. (1976). The physiological psychology of hunger: A physiological perspective. *Psychological Review, 83,* 409–431.

Friman, P. C., & Christopherson, E. R. (1983). Behavior therapy and hyperactivity: A brief review of therapy for a big problem. *The Behavior Therapist, 6,* 175–176.

Frodi, A. M., Bridges, L., & Grolnick, W. (1985). Correlates of master-related behavior: A short-term longitudinal study of infants in their second year. *Child Development, 56,* 1291–1298.

Frodi, A. M., Macauley, J., & Thome, P. R. (1977). Are women always less aggressive than men? A review of the experimental literature. *Psychological Bulletin, 84,* 634–660.

Furedy, J. J. (1990, July). *Experimental psychophysiology and pseudoscientific polygraphy: Conceptual concerns and practical problems.* Symposium at the 5th International Congress of Psychophysiology, Budapest, Hungary.

Furumoto, L. (1992). Joining separate spheres—Christine Ladd-Franklin, woman–scientist. *American Psychologist, 47,* 175–182.

G

Gaertner, S. L., Mann, J., Murrell, A., & Dovidio, J. F. (1989). Reducing intergroup bias: The benefits of recategorization. *Journal of Personality and Social Psychology, 57,* 239–249.

Galanter, E. (1962). Contemporary psychophysics. In R. Brown et al. (Eds.), *New directions in psychology.* New York: Holt, Rinehart and Winston.

Galassi, J. P. (1988). Four cognitive-behavioral approaches: Additional considerations. *The Counseling Psychologist, 16*(1), 102–105.

Galassi, J. P., Frierson, H. T., & Sharer, R. (1981). Behavior of high, moderate, and low test anxious students during an actual test situation. *Journal of Consulting and Clinical Psychology, 49,* 51–62.

Galassi, J. P., Frierson, H. T., Jr., & Siegel, R. G. (1984). Cognitions, test anxiety, and test performance: A closer look. *Journal of Consulting and Clinical Psychology, 52,* 319–320.

Galizio, M., & Hendrick, C. (1972). Effect of musical accompaniment on attitude: The guitar as a prop for persuasion. *Journal of Applied Social Psychology, 2,* 350–359.

Ganellen, R. J., & Blaney, P. H. (1984). Hardiness and social support as moderators of the effects of life stress. *Journal of Personality and Social Psychology, 47,* 156–163.

Garcia, J. (1981). The logic and limits of mental aptitude testing. *American Psychologist, 36,* 1172–1180.

Garcia, J., Brett, L. P., & Rusiniak, K. W. (1989). Limits of Darwinian conditioning. In S. B. Klein & R. R. Mowrer (Eds.), *Contemporary learning theories: Instrumental conditioning theory and the impact of biological constraints on learning.* Hillsdale, NJ: Erlbaum.

Garcia, J., & Koelling, R. A. (1966). Relation of cue to consequences in avoidance learning. *Psychonomic Science, 4,* 123–124.

Gardner, H. (1983). *Frames of mind: The theory of multiple intelligences.* New York: Basic Books.

Gastorf, J. W., & Galanos, A. N. (1983). Patient compliance and physicians' attitude. *Family Practice Research Journal, 2,* 190–198.

Gatchel, R. J., & Proctor, J. D. (1976). Effectiveness of voluntary heart rate control in reducing speech anxiety. *Journal of Consulting and Clinical Psychology, 44,* 381–389.

Gatto, G. J. (1987). Persistence of tolerance to a single dose of ethanol in the selectively bred alcohol-preferring P rat. *Pharmacology, Biochemistry, and Behavior, 28,* 105–110.

Gayle, H. D. (1990). Prevalence of human immunodeficiency virus among university students. *The New England Journal of Medicine, 323,* 1538–1541.

Gazzaniga, M. S. (1972). One brain—two minds? *American Science, 60,* 311–317.

Gazzaniga, M. S. (1983). Right hemisphere language following brain bisection: A 20-year perspective. *American Psychologist, 38,* 525–537.

Gazzaniga, M. S. (1985). The social brain. *Psychology Today, 19*(11), 29–38.

Geen, R. G. (1981). Behavioral and physiological reactions to observed violence: Effects of prior exposure to aggressive stimuli. *Journal of Personality and Social Psychology, 40,* 868–875.

Geen, R. G., Stonner, D., & Shope, G. L. (1975). The facilitation of aggression by aggression. Evidence against the catharsis hypothesis. *Journal of Personality and Social Psychology, 31,* 721–726.

Geer, J. T., O'Donohue, W. T., & Schorman, R. H. (1986). Sexuality. In M. G. H. Coles et al. (Eds.), *Psychophysiology: Systems, processes, and applications.* New York: Guilford Press.

Gelman, R., & Baillargeon, R. (1983). A review of some Piagetan concepts. In J. Flavell & E. Markman (Eds.), *Handbook of child psychology.* New York: Wiley.

Gerbner, G., & Gross, L. (1976, September). The scary world of TV's heavy viewer. *Psychology Today,* pp. 41–45.

Gerrard, G. (1986). Are men and women really different? In K. Kelley (Ed.), *Females, males, and sexuality.* Albany, NY: State University of New York at Albany Press.

Getzels, J. W., & Jackson, P. W. (1962). *Creativity and intelligence: Explorations with gifted students.* New York: Wiley.

Gfeller, J. D., Lynn, S. J., & Pribble, W. E. (1987). Enhancing hypnotic susceptibility: Interpersonal and rapport factors. *Journal of Personality and Social Psychology, 52,* 586–595.

Gibson, E. J., & Walk, R. D. (1960, April). The visual cliff. *Scientific American, 202,* 64–71.

Gibson, M., & Ogbu, J. (Eds.). (1991). *Minority status and schooling: A comparative study of immigrant and involuntary minorities.* New York: Garland Press.

Gilbert, S. J. (1981). Another look at the Milgram obedience studies: The role of the gradated series of shocks. *Personality and Social Psychology Bulletin, 7,* 690–695.

Gill, J. S. (1986). Stroke and alcohol consumption. *New England Journal of Medicine, 315,* 1041–1046.

Gillen, B. (1981). Physical attractiveness: A determinant of two types of goodness. *Personality and Social Psychology Bulletin, 7,* 277–281.

Gilligan, C. G. (1982). *In a different voice.* Cambridge, MA: Harvard University Press.

Gilligan, C. G., Ward, J. V., & Taylor, J. M. (1989). *Mapping the moral domain: A contribution of women's thinking to psychological theory and education.* Cambridge, MA: Harvard University Press.

Gillin, J. C. (1991). The long and the short of sleeping pills. *The New England Journal of Medicine, 324,* 1735–1736.

Gillin, J. C., & Byerley, W. F. (1990). The diagnosis and management of insomnia. *The New England Journal of Medicine, 322,* 239–248.

Gillis, J. S., & Avis, W. E. (1980). The male-taller norm in mate selection. *Personality and Social Psychology Bulletin, 6,* 396–401.

Gilman, A. G. (1990). *Goodman and Gilman's the pharmacological basis of therapeutics,* 8th ed. New York: Pergamon Press.

Gilovich, T. (1983). Biased evaluation and persistence in gambling. *Journal of Personality and Social Psychology, 44,* 1110–1126.

Glaser, R. (1991). Stress-related activation of Epstein-Barr virus. *Brain, Behavior, and Immunity, 5,* 219–232.

Glasner, P. D., & Kaslow, R. A. (1990). The epidemiology of human immunodeficiency virus infection. *Journal of Consulting and Clinical Psychology, 58,* 13–21.

Glass, D. C. (1977). *Stress and coronary-prone behavior.* Hillsdale, NJ: Erlbaum.

Glass, D. C., & Singer, J. E. (1972). *Urban stress.* New York: Academic Press.

Glover, J. A., Ronning, R. R., & Bruning, R. H. (1990). *Cognitive psychology for teachers.* New York: Macmillan.

Goddard, H. H. (1917). Mental tests and the immigrant. *The Journal of Delinquency, 2,* 243–277.

Godden, D. R., & Baddeley, A. D. (1975). Context-dependent memory in two natural environments: On land and underwater. *British Journal of Psychology, 66,* 325–331.

Goeders, N. E., & Smith, J. E. (1983). Cortical dopaminergic involvement in cocaine reinforcement. *Science, 221,* 773–775.

Goelet, P. (1986). The long and the short of long-term memory—A molecular framework. *Nature, 322,* 419–422.

Gold, J. A., Ryckman, R. M., & Mosley, N. R. (1984). Romantic mood induction and attraction to a dissimilar other: Is love blind? *Personality and Social Psychology Bulletin, 10,* 358–368.

Gold, P. E., & King, R. A. (1974). Retrograde amnesia: Storage failure versus retrieval failure. *Psychological Review, 81,* 465–469.

Goldberg, L. W. (1978). Differential attribution of trait-descriptive terms to oneself as compared to well-liked, neutral, and disliked others. *Journal of Personality and Social Psychology, 36,* 1012–1028.

Goldberg, S. (1983). Parent–infant bonding: Another look. *Child Development, 54,* 1355–1382.

Goldberg, S., & Lewis, M. (1969). Play behavior in the year-old infant: Early sex differences. *Child Development, 40,* 21–31.

Goldfoot, D. A. (1978). Anosmia in male rhesus monkeys does not alter copulatory activity with cycling females. *Science, 199,* 1095–1096.

Goldfried, M. R. (1988). Application of rational restructuring to anxiety disorders. *The Counseling Psychologist, 16*(1), 50–68.

Goldfried, M. R., Linehan, M. M., & Smith, J. L. (1978). Reduction of test anxiety through cognitive restructuring. *Journal of Consulting and Clinical Psychology, 46,* 32–39.

Goldsmith, H. H. (1983). Genetic influences on personality from infancy to adulthood. *Child Development, 54,* 331–355.

Goldstein, M., & Davis, E. E. (1972). Race and belief: A further analysis of the social determinants of behavioral intentions. *Journal of Personality and Social Psychology, 22,* 345–355.

Goldstein, T. (1988, February 12). Women in the law aren't yet equal partners. *The New York Times,* p. B7.

Goleman, D. J. (1982,). Staying up. *Psychology Today, 16*(3), pp. 24–35.

Goleman, D. J. (1985, January 15). Pressure mounts for analysts to prove theory is scientific. *The New York Times,* pp. C1, C9.

Goleman, D. J. (1992, January 8). Heart seizure or panic attack? Disorder is a terrifying mimic. *The New York Times,* p. C12.

Goodman, S. H. (1987). Emory University project on children of disturbed parents. *Schizophrenia Bulletin, 13,* 411–423.

Goodwin, D. W. (1979). Alcoholism and heredity. *Archives of General Psychiatry, 36,* 57–61.

Goodwin, D. W. (1985). Alcoholism and genetics. *Archives of General Psychiatry, 42,* 171–174.

Goodwin, D. W. (1973). Alcohol problems in adoptees raised apart from alcoholic biological parents. *Archives of General Psychiatry, 30,* 239–243.

Goodwin, F. K., & Jamison, K. R. (1990). *Manic-depressive illness.* New York: Oxford University Press.

Gordon, E. W., & Terrell, M. D. (1981). The changed social context of testing. *American Psychologist, 36,* 1167–1171.

Gotlib, I. H. (1982). Self-reinforcement and depression in interpersonal interaction: The role of performance level. *Journal of Abnormal Psychology, 91,* 3–13.

Gotlib, I. H. (1984). Depression and general psychopathology in university students. *Journal of Abnormal Psychology, 93,* 19–30.

Gottesman, I. I. (1991). *Schizophrenia genesis: The origins of madness.* New York: Freeman.

Gottfried, A. W. (1984). Home environment and early cognitive development: Integration, meta-analyses, and conclusions. In A. W. Gottfried (Ed.), *Home environment and early cognitive development.* San Francisco: Academic Press.

Gould, R. (1975, August). Adult life stages: Growth toward self-tolerance. *Psychology Today,* pp. 74–81.

Goy, R. W., & Goldfoot, D. A. (1976). Neuroendocrinology: Animal models and problems of human sexuality. In E. A. Rubenstein et al. (Eds.), *New directions in sex research.* New York: Plenum Publishing Co.

Goy, R. W., & McEwen, B. S. (1982). *Sexual differentia-*

tion of the brain. Cambridge, MA: MIT Press.

Graesser, A. C., & Nakamura, G. V. (1982). The impact of a schema on comprehension and memory. In G. H. Bower (Ed.), *The psychology of learning and motivation,* Vol. 16. New York: Academic Press.

Graham, J. R. (1990). *MMPI-2: Assessing personality and psychopathology.* New York: Oxford University Press.

Graham, N. M. H. (1992). The effects on survival of early treatment of human immunodeficiency virus infection. *The New England Journal of Medicine, 326,* 1037–1042.

Granberg, D., & Brent, E. (1983). When prophecy bends: The preference–expectation link in U.S. presidential elections. *Journal of Personality and Social Psychology, 45,* 477–491.

Grant, I., & Heaton, R. K. (1990). Human immunodeficiency virus-type 1 (HIV-1) and the brain. *Journal of Consulting and Clinical Psychology, 58,* 22–30.

Gray, V. R. (1984). The psychological response of the dying patient. In P. S. Chaney (Ed.), *Dealing with death and dying,* 2d ed. Springhouse, PA: International Communications.

Green, J. A., Jones, L. E., & Gustafson, G. E. (1987). Perception of cries by parents and nonparents: Relation to cry acoustics. *Developmental Psychology, 23,* 370–382.

Green, R. (1987). *The "sissy boy syndrome" and the development of homosexuality.* New Haven: Yale University Press.

Green, S. K., Buchanan, D. R., & Heuer, S. K. (1984). Winners, losers, and choosers: A field investigation of dating initiation. *Personality and Social Psychology Bulletin, 10,* 502–511.

Greenbaum, P., & Rosenfeld, H. M. (1978). Patterns of avoidance in response to interpersonal staring and proximity: Effects of bystanders on drivers at a traffic intersection. *Journal of Personality and Social Psychology, 36,* 575–587.

Greenberg, P. D. (1987). Tumor immunology. In D. P. Stites et al. (Eds.), *Basic and clinical immunology,* 6th ed. Norwalk, CT: Appleton & Lange.

Greenberg, R., Pearlman, C., Schwartz, W. R., & Grossman, H. Y. (1983). Memory, emotion, and REM sleep. *Journal of Abnormal Psychology, 92,* 378–381.

Greene, A. S., & Saxe, L. (1990). *Tall tales told to teachers.* Unpublished manuscript, Brandeis University.

Greene, B. A. (1985). Considerations in the treatment of black patients by white therapists. *Psychotherapy, 22,* 389–393.

Greene, B. A. (1991). Personal communication.

Greene, B. A. (1992). Still here: A perspective on psychotherapy with African American women. In J. Chrisler & D. Howard (Eds.), *New directions in feminist psychology.* New York: Springer.

Greene, J. (1982). The gambling trap. *Psychology Today, 16*(9), pp. 50–55.

Greenwald, A. G. (1992). New Look 3: Unconscious cognition reclaimed. *American Psychologist, 47,* 766–779.

Gregory, R. L. (1973). *Eye and brain,* 2d ed. New York: World Universities Library.

Greist, J. H. (1984). Exercise in the treatment of depression. *Coping with mental stress: The potential and limits of exercise intervention.* Washington, DC: National Institute of Mental Health.

Griffin, E., & Sparks, G. G. (1990). Friends forever: A longitudinal exploration of intimacy in same-sex friends and platonic pairs. *Journal of Social and Personal Relationships, 7,* 29–46.

Grinspoon, L. (1987, July 28). Cancer patients should get marijuana. *The New York Times,* p. A23.

Gronlund, N. E. (1985). *Measurement and evaluation in teaching,* 5th ed. New York: Macmillan.

Grosjean, F. (1982). *Life with two languages: An introduction to bilingualism.* Cambridge, MA: Harvard University Press.

Grove, W. M. (1991). Familial prevalence and coaggregation of schizotypy indicators: A multitrait family study. *Journal of Abnormal Psychology, 100,* 115–121.

Grünbaum, A. (1985). Cited in Goleman, D. J. (1985, January 15). Pressure mounts for analyst to prove theory is scientific. *The New York Times,* pp. C1, C9.

Grush, J. E. (1980). The impact of candidate expenditures, regionality, and prior outcomes on the 1976 Democratic presidential primaries. *Journal of Personality and Social Psychology, 38,* 337–347.

Guilford, J. P. (1959). Traits of creativity. In H. H. Anderson (Ed.), *Creativity and its cultivation.* New York: Harper & Row.

Guilford, J. P. (1982). Cognitive psychology's ambiguities: Some suggested remedies. *Psychological Review, 89,* 48–49.

Guthrie, R. V. (1990). Cited in Korn, J. H., Davis, R., & Davis, S. F. (1991). Historians' and chairpersons' judgments of eminence among psychologists. *American Psychologist, 46,* 789–792.

H

Haaf, R. A., Smith, P. H., & Smitley, S. (1983). Infant response to facelike patterns under fixed trial and infant-control procedures. *Child Development, 54,* 172–177.

Haaland, K. Y. (1992). Introduction to the special section on the emotional concomitants of brain damage. *Journal of Consulting and Clinical Psychology, 60,* 327–328.

Haber, R. N. (1969). Eidetic images. *Scientific American, 220,* 36–55.

Haber, R. N. (1980,). Eidetic images are not just imaginary. *Psychology Today,* pp. 72–82.

Haber, R. N., & Hershenson, M. (1980). *The psychology of visual perception.* New York: Holt, Rinehart and Winston.

Haley, J. (1987). *Problem-solving therapy,* 2d ed. San Francisco: Jossey-Bass.

Hall, C. S. (1984). "A ubiquitous sex difference in dreams" revisited. *Journal of Personality and Social Psychology, 46,* 1109–1117.

Hall, J. (1989). *Learning and memory,* 2d ed. Boston: Allyn & Bacon.

Hall, R. G., Sachs, D. P. L., Hall, S. M., & Benowitz, N. L. (1984). Two-year efficacy and safety of rapid smoking therapy in patients with cardiac and pulmonary disease. *Journal of Consulting and Clinical Psychology, 52,* 574–581.

Hall, S. M., Havassy, B. E., & Wasserman, D. A. (1990). Commitment to abstinence and acute stress in relapse to alcohol, opiates, and nicotine. *Journal of Consulting and Clinical Psychology, 58,* 175–181.

Hall, S. M., Rugg, D., Tunstall, C., & Jones, R. T. (1984). Preventing relapse to cigarette smoking by behavioral skill training. *Journal of Consulting and Clinical Psychology, 52,* 372–382.

Hall, S. M., Tunstall, C., Rugg, D., Jones, R. T., & Benowitz, N. (1985). Nicotine gum and behavioral treatment in smoking cessation. *Journal of Consulting and Clinical Psychology, 53,* 256–258.

Halldin, M. (1985). Alcohol consumption and alcoholism in an urban population in central Sweden. *Acta Psychiatrica Scadinavica, 71,* 128–140.

Halmi, K. A., Eckert, E., LaDu, T. J., & Cohen, J. (1986). Treatment efficacy of cyproheptadine and amitriptyline. *Archives of General Psychiatry, 43,* 177–181.

Halperin, K. M., & Snyder, C. R. (1979). Effects of enhanced psychological test feedback on treatment outcome: Therapeutic implications of the Barnum effect. *Journal of Consulting and Clinical Psychology, 47,* 140–146.

Hamamy, H. (1990). Consanguinity and the genetic control of Down syndrome. *Clinical Genetics, 37,* 24–29.

Hamilton, R. J. (1985). A framework for the evaluation of the effectiveness of adjunct questions and objectives. *Review of Educational Research, 55,* 47–86.

Hamm, N. M., Baum, M. R., & Nikels, K. W. (1975). Effects of race and exposure on judgments of interpersonal favorability. *Journal of Experimental Social Psychology, 11,* 14–24.

Hammen, C., & Mayol, A. (1982). Depression and cognitive characteristics of stressful life-event types. *Journal of Abnormal Psychology, 91,* 165–174.

Harackiewicz, J. M., Sansone, C., Blair, L. W., Epstein, J. A., & Harder, D. W., Gift, T. E., Strauss, J. S., Ritzler, B. A., & Kokes, R. F. (1981). Life events and two-year outcome in schizophrenia. *Journal of Consulting and Clinical Psychology, 49,* 619–626.

Hardy, J. (1991). *Nature,* February 21.

Hardy-Brown, K., & Plomin, R. (1985). Infant communicative development: Evidence from adoptive and biological families for genetic and environmental influences on rate differences. *Developmental Psychology, 21,* 378–385.

Hare, R. D., Hart, S. D., & Harpur, T. J. (1991). Psychopathy and the *DSM-IV* criteria for antisocial personality disorder. *Journal of Abnormal Psychology, 100,* 391–398.

Hare-Mustin, R. (1983). An appraisal of the relationship between women and psychotherapy: 80 years after the case of Dora. *American Psychologist, 38,* 593–601.

Harkins, S. (1987). Social loafing and social facilitation. *Journal of Experimental Social Psychology, 23,* 1–18.

Harlow, H. F. (1959). Love in infant monkeys. *Scientific American, 200,* 68–86.

Harlow, H. F. (1965). Sexual behavior in the rhesus monkey. In F. A. Beach (Ed.), *Sex and behavior.* New York: Wiley.

Harlow, H. F., & Harlow, M. K. (1966). Learning to love. *American Scientist, 54,* 244–272.

Harlow, H. F., Harlow, M. K., & Meyer, D. R. (1950). Learning motivated by a manipulation drive. *Journal of Experimental Psychology, 40,* 228–234.

Harlow, H. F., & Zimmermann, R. R. (1959). Affectional responses in the infant monkey. *Science, 130,* 421–432.

Harlow, M. K., & Harlow, H. F. (1966). Affection in primates. *Discovery, 27,* 11–17.

Harrell, T. W., & Harrell, M. S. (1945). Army General Classification Test scores for civilian occupations. *Educational and Psychological Measurement, 5,* 229–239.

Harris, D. K., & Cole, W. E. (1980). *Sociology of aging.* Boston: Houghton Mifflin.

Harris, G. W., & Levine, S. (1965). Sexual differentiation of the brain and its experimental control. *Journal of Physiology, 181,* 379–400.

Harris, L. (1988). *Inside America.* New York: Vintage.

Hartz, A. J. (1984). The association of girth measurements with disease in 32,856 women. *American Journal of Epidemiology, 119,* 71–80.

Harvey, J. H., Ickes, W. J., & Kidd, R. F. (Eds.) (1976). *New directions in attributional research,* Vol. 1. Hillsdale, NJ: Erlbaum.

Harvey, J. H., Ickes, W. J., & Kidd, R. F. (Eds.) (1978). *New directions in attributional research,* Vol. 2. Hillsdale, NJ: Erlbaum.

Harwood, A. (1981). Mainland Puerto Ricans. In A. Harwood (Ed.), *Ethnicity and medical care.* Cambridge, MA: Harvard University Press.

Hatfield, E. (1983). What do women and men want from love and sex? In E. R. Allgeier & N. B. McCormick (Eds.), *Changing boundaries: Gender roles and sexual behavior.* Palo Alto, CA: Mayfield.

Hatfield, E. (1988). Passionate and companionate love. In R. J. Sternberg & M. L. Barnes (Eds.), *The psychology of love.* New Haven, CT: Yale University Press.

Hauser-Cram, P., Pierson, D. E., Walker, D. K., & Tivnan, T. (1991). *Early education in the public schools.* San Francisco: Jossey-Bass.

Hayse, S. C. (Ed.). (1989). *Rule-governed behavior: Cognition, contingencies, and instructional control.* New York: Plenum.

Hayes, S. L. (1981). Single case design and empirical clinical practice. *Journal of Consulting and Clinical Psychology, 49,* 193–211.

Haynes, R. B. (1976). A critical review of the determinants of patient compliance with therapeutic regimens. In D. L. Sackett & R. B. Haynes (Eds.), *Compliance with therapeutic regimens.* Baltimore: Johns Hopkins University Press.

Haynes, R. B. (1979). Determinants of compliance: The disease and the mechanics of treatment. In R. B. Haynes, D. W. Taylor, & D. L. Sackett (Eds.), *Compliance in health care.* Baltimore: Johns Hopkins University Press.

Hays, R. B., Turner, H., & Coates, T. J. (1992). Social support, AIDS-related symptoms, and depression among gay men. *Journal of Consulting and Clinical Psychology, 60,* 463–469.

Heaton, R. K., & Victor, R. G. (1976). Personality characteristics associated with psychedelic flashbacks in natural and experimental settings. *Journal of Abnormal Psychology, 85,* 83–90.

Hefferline, R. F., & Keenan, B. (1963). Amplitude-induction gradient of a small-scale (covert) operant. *Journal of the Experimental Analysis of Behavior, 6,* 307–315.

Heider, F. (1958). *The psychology of interpersonal relations.* New York: Wiley.

Heingartner, A., & Hall, J. V. (1974). Affective consequences in adults and children of repeated exposure to auditory stimuli. *Journal of Personality and Social Psychology, 29,* 719–723.

Helmreich, R. L., Spence, J. T., & Holahan, C. J. (1979). Psychological androgyny and sex-role flexibility: A test of two hypotheses. *Journal of Personality and Social Psychology, 37,* 1631–1644.

Helms, J. E. (1992). Why is there no study of cultural equivalence of standardized cognitive ability testing? *American Psychologist, 47,* 1083–1101.

Helson, R., & Moane, G. (1987). Personality change in women from college to midlife. *Journal of Personality and Social Psychology, 53,* 176–186.

Helzer, J. E. (1987). Epidemiology of alcoholism. *Journal of Consulting and Clinical Psychology, 55,* 284–292.

Helzer, J. E., & Schuckit, M. A. (1990, August/September). Substance use disorders. In American Psychiatric Association, *DSM–IV Update.* Washington, DC: American Psychiatric Association.

Hendrick, C. D., Wells, K. S., & Faletti, M. V. (1982). Social and emotional effects of geographical relocation on elderly retirees. *Journal of Personality and Social Psychology, 42,* 951–962.

Hendrick, S. S., & Hendrick, C. (1977). *Aging in mass society: Myths and realities.* Cambridge, MA: Winthrop.

Hendrick, S. S., Hendrick, C., Slapion-Foote, M. J., & Foote, F. H. (1985). Gender differences in sexual attitudes. *Journal of Personality and Social Psychology, 48,* 1630–1642.

Hennigan, K. M., Cook, T. D., & Gruder, C. L. (1982). Cognitive tuning set, source credibility, and the temporal persistence of attitude change. *Journal of Personality and Social Psychology, 42,* 412–425.

Hennigan, K. M. (1982). Impact of the introduction of television on crime in the United States. *Journal of Personality and Social Psychology, 42,* 461–477.

Hensley, W. E. (1981). The effects of attire, location, and sex on aiding behavior: A similarity explanation. *Journal of Nonverbal Behavior, 6,* 3–11.

Hepworth, J. T., & West, S. G. (1988). Lynchings and the economy: A time-series reanalysis of Hovland and Sears (1940). *Journal of Personality and Social Psychology, 55,* 239–247.

Hersen, M., Bellack, A. S., Himmelhoch, J. M., & Thase, M. E. (1984). Effect of social skill training, amitriptyline, and psychotherapy in unipolar depressed women. *Behavior Therapy, 15,* 21–40.

Herzog, D. B., Keller, M.B., & Lavori, P.W. (1988). Outcome in anorexia and bulimia nervosa: A review of the literature. *The Journal of Nervous and Mental Disease, 176,* 131–143.

Heuch, I. (1983). Use of alcohol, tobacco and coffee, and risk of pancreatic cancer. *British Journal of Cancer, 48,* 637–643.

Hilgard, E. R. (1977). *Divided consciousness: Multiple controls in human thought and action.* New York: Wiley.

Hilgard, E. R. (1978). Hypnosis and pain. In R. A. Sternbach (Ed.), *The psychology of pain.* New York: Raven Press.

Hill, C. (1987). Affiliation motivation: People who need people . . . but in different ways. *Journal of Personality and Social Psychology, 52,* 1008–1018.

Hilts, P. J. (1990, August 31). Drug is found to delay progression to AIDS. *The New York Times,* p. A15.

Hinds, M. W. (1984). Dietary vitamin A, carotene, vitamin C and risk of lung cancer in Hawaii. *American Journal of Epidemiology, 119,* 227–237.

Hirsch, J. (1975). Jensenism: The bankruptcy of "science" without scholarship. *Educational Theory, 25,* 3–28.

Ho, D. Y. F. (1985). Cultural values and professional issues in clinical psychology: Implications from the Hong Kong experience. *American Psychologist, 40,* 1212–1218.

Hobbs, N., & Robinson, S. (1982). Adolescent development and public policy. *American Psychologist, 37,* 212–223.

Hoberman, H. M., Lewinsohn, P. M., & Tilson, M. (1988). Group treatment of depression: Individual predictors of outcome. *Journal of Consulting and Clinical Psychology, 56,* 393–398.

Hobson, J. A. (1992). Cited in Blakeslee, S. (1992, January 7). Scientists unraveling chemistry of dreams. *The New York Times,* pp. C1, C10.

Hobson, J. A., & McCarley, R. W. (1977). The brain as a dream state generator: An activation-synthesis hypothesis of the dream process. *American Journal of Psychiatry, 134,* 1335–1348.

Hoffman, C., & Hurst, N. (1990). Gender stereotypes: Perception or rationalization? *Journal of Personality and Social Psychology, 58,* 197–208.

Hoffman, L. W. (1985). The changing genetics/socialization balance. *Journal of Social Issues, 41,* 127–148.

Hoffman, M. L. (1981). Is altruism part of human nature? *Journal of Personality and Social Psychology, 40,* 121–137.

Holahan, C. J., & Moos, R. H. (1985). Life stress and health: Personality, coping, and family support in stress resistance. *Journal of Personality and Social Psychology, 49,* 739–747.

Holahan, C. J., & Moos, R. H. (1990). Life stressors, resistance factors, and psychological health: An extension of the stress-resistance paradigm. *Journal of Personality and Social Psychology, 58,* 909–917.

Holahan, C. J., & Moos, R. H. (1991). Life stressors, personal and social resources, and depression: A 4-year structural model. *Journal of Abnormal Psychology, 100,* 31–38.

Hollon, S. D, & Beck, A. T. (1986). Research on cognitive therapies. In S. L. Garfield & A. E. Bergin (Eds.), *Handbook of psychotherapy and behavior change,* 3d ed. New York: Wiley.

Hollon, S. D., Shelton, R. C., & Loosen, P. T. (1991). Cognitive therapy and pharmacotherapy for depression. *Journal of Consulting and Clinical Psychology, 59,* 88–99.

Holmes, D. S. (1984). Meditation and somatic arousal reduction: A review of the experimental evidence. *American Psychologist, 39,* 1–10.

Holmes, D. S. (1985). To meditate or to simply rest, that is the question: A response to the comments of Shapiro. *American Psychologist, 40,* 722–725.

Holmes, D. S., Solomon, S., Cappo, B. M., & Greenberg, J. L. (1983). Effects of transcendental meditation versus resting on physiological and subjective arousal. *Journal of Personality and Social Psychology, 44,* 1244–1252.

Holmes, T. H., & Rahe, R. H. (1967). The social readjustment rating scale. *Journal of Psychosomatic Research, 11,* 213–218.

Holroyd, K. A., Westbrook, T., Wolf, M., & Badhorn, E. (1978). Performance, cognition, and physiological responding in test anxiety. *Journal of Abnormal Psychology, 87,* 442–451.

Holyoak, K., Koh, K., & Nisbett, R. E. (1989). A theory of conditioning: Inductive learning within rule-based default hierarchies. *Psychological Review, 96,* 315–340.

Horn, J. M. (1983). The Texas adoption project: Adopted children and their intellectual resemblance to biological and adoptive parents. *Child Development, 54,* 268–275.

Horney, K. (1967). *Feminine psychology.* New York: W. W. Norton.

Horvath, T. (1981). Physical attractiveness: The influence of selected torso parameters. *Archives of Sexual Behavior, 10,* 21–24.

House, J. S. (1981). *Work stress and social support.* Reading, MA: Addison-Wesley.

House, J. S. (1984). Barriers to work stress: I. Social support. In W. D. Gentry, H. Benson, & C. deWolff (Eds.), *Behavioral medicine: Work, stress, and health.* The Hague: Nijhoff.

House, J. S., Robbins, C., & Metzner, H. L. (1982). The association of social relationships and activities with mortality: Prospective evidence from the Tecumseh Community Health Study. *American Journal of Epidemiology, 116,* 123–140.

Howard, D. V. (1983). *Cognitive psychology.* New York: Macmillan.

Howard, J. A., Blumstein, P., & Schwartz, P. (1987). Social or evolutionary theories: Some observations on preferences in mate selection. *Journal of Personality and Social Psychology, 53,* 194–200.

Howard, K. I., Kopta, S. M., Krause, M. S., & Orlinksy, D. E. (1986). The dose-effect relationship in psychotherapy. *American Psychologist, 41,* 159–164.

Howard, L., & Polich, J. (1985). P300 latency and memory span development. *Developmental Psychology, 21,* 283–289.

Howard-Pitney, B., LaFramboise, T. D., Basil, M., September, B., & Johnson, M. (1992). Psychological and social indicators of suicide ideation and suicide attempots in Zuni adolescents. *Journal of Consulting and Clinical Psychology, 60,* 473–476.

Howes, M. J., Hokanson, J. E., & Loewenstein, D. A. (1985). Induction to depressive affect after prolonged exposure to a mildly depressed individual. *Journal of Personality and Social Psychology, 49,* 1110–1113.

Hrncir, E. J., Speller, G. M., & West, M. (1985). What are we testing? *Developmental Psychology, 21,* 226–232.

Hsu, L. K. G. (1986). The treatment of anorexia nervosa. *American Journal of Psychiatry, 143,* 573–581.

Hubel, D. H., & Wiesel, T. N. (1979). Brain mechanisms of vision. *Scientific American, 241,* 150–162.

Huesmann, L. R. (1988). An information processing model for the development of aggression. *Aggressive Behavior, 14,* 13–24.

Huesmann, L. R., Eron, L. D., Klein, R., Brice, P., & Fischer, P. (1983). Mitigating the imitation of aggressive behaviors by changing children's attitudes about media violence. *Journal of Personality and Social Psychology, 44,* 899–910.

Hugdahl, K., & Ohman, A. (1977). Effects of instruction on acquisition and extinction of electrodermal response to fear-relevant stimuli. *Journal of Experimental Psychology: Human Learning and Memory, 3,* 608–618.

Hughes, J. R. (1986). Genetics of smoking: A brief review. *Behavior Therapy, 17,* 335–345.

Hughes, P. L. (1986). Treating bulimia with desipramine. *Archives of General Psychiatry, 43,* 182–186.

Hull, J. G., Levenson, R. W., Young, R. D., & Sher, K. J. (1983). Self-awareness-reducing effects of alcohol consumption. *Journal of Personality and Social Psychology, 44,* 461–473.

Humphrey, L. L. (1986). Family dynamics in bulimia. In S. C. Feinstein et al. (Eds.), *Adolescent psychiatry.* Chicago: University of Chicago Press.

Humphreys, L. G. (1981). The primary mental ability. In M. P. Friedman, J. P. Das, & N. O'Connor (Eds.), *Intelligence and learning.* New York: Plenum Publishing Co.

Hunter, J. E., & Schmidt, F. L. (1983). Quantifying the effects of psychological interventions on employee job performance and work-force productivity. *American Psychologist, 38,* 473–478.

Huntley, C. W., & Davis, F. (1983). Undergraduate study of value scores as predictors of occupation 25 years later. *Journal of Personality and Social Psychology, 45,* 1148–1155.

Hurvich, L. M. (1981). *Color vision.* Sunderland, MA: Sinauer Associates.

Huxley, A. (1939). *Brave new world.* New York: Harper & Row.

Hyde, J. S. (1981). How large are cognitive gender differences? *American Psychologist, 36,* 892–901.

Hyde, J. S., Fennema, E., & Lamon, S. J. (1990). Gender differences in mathematics performance: A meta-analysis. *Psychological Bulletin, 107,* 139–155.

I

Insko, C. A. (1985). Balance theory, the Jordan paradigm, and the Wiest tetrahedron. In L. Berkowitz (Ed.), *Advances in experimental social psychology.* New York: Academic Press.

Insko, C. A., Smith, R. H., Alicke, M. D., Wade, J., & Taylor, S. (1985). Conformity and group size: The concern with being right and the concern with being liked. *Personality and Social Psychology Bulletin, 11,* 41–50.

Isomura, T., Fine, S., & Lin, T. (1987). Two Japanese families: A cultural perspective. *Canadian Journal of Psychiatry, 32,* 282–286.

Israel, E. (1990). The effects of a 5-lipoxygenase inhibitor on asthma induced by cold, dry air. *The New England Journal of Medicine, 323,* 1740–1744.

Izard, C. E. (1978). On the development of emotions and emotion-cognition relationships in infancy. In M. Lewis & L. Rosenblum (Eds.), *The development of affect.* New York: Plenum Publishing Co.

Izard, C. E. (Ed.) (1982). *Measuring emotions in infants and children.* New York: Cambridge University Press.

Izard, C. E. (1984). Emotion-cognition relationships and human development. In C. E. Izard, J. Kagan, & R. B. Zajonc (Eds.), *Emotions, cognition, and behavior.* New York: Cambridge University Press.

Izard, C. E. (1990). Facial expression and the regulation of emotions. *Journal of Personality and Social Psychology, 58,* 487–498.

J

Jacklin, C. N., & Maccoby, E. E. (1983). Issues of gender differentiation. In M. D. Levine (Eds.), *Developmental-behavioral pediatrics.* Philadelphia: W. B. Saunders.

Jacob, T., Krahn, G. L., & Leonard, K. (1991). Parent-child interactions in families with alcoholic fathers. *Journal of Consulting and Clinical Psychology, 59,* 176–181.

Jacobs, T. J., & Charles, E. (1980). Life events and the occurrence of cancer in children. *Psychosomatic Medicine, 42,* 11–24.

Jacobsen, P. B., Perry, S. W., & Hirsch, D. (1990). Behavioral and psychological responses to HIV antibody testing. *Journal of Consulting and Clinical Psychology, 58,* 31–37.

Jacobson, E. (1938). *Progressive relaxation.* Chicago: University of Chicago Press.

Jacobson, N. S., & Truax, P. (1991). Clinical significance: A statistical approach to defining meaningful changes in psychotherapy research. *Journal of Consulting and Clinical Psychology, 59,* 12–19.

James, W. (1890). *The principles of psychology.* New York: Henry Holt and Company.

James, W. (1904). Does "consciousness" exist? *Journal of Philosophy, Psychology, and Scientific Methods, 1,* 477–491.

Jamison, K. K., & Akiskal, H. S. (1983). Medication compliance in patients with bipolar disorder. *Psychiatric Clinics of North America, 6,* 175–192.

Janerich, D. T. (1990). Lung cancer and exposure to tobacco smoke in the household. *The New England Journal of Medicine, 323,* 632–636.

Janicak, P. G. (1985). Efficacy of ECT: A meta-analysis. *American Journal of Psychiatry, 142,* 297–302.

Janis, I. L. (1982). *Groupthink: Psychological studies of policy decisions and fiascoes,* 2d ed. Boston: Houghton Mifflin.

Janis, I. L., Kaye, D., & Kirschner, P. (1965). Facilitating effects of "eating while reading" on responsiveness to persuasive communications. *Journal of Personality and Social Psychology, 1,* 181–186.

Jannoun, L., Oppenheimer, C., & Gelder, M. (1982). A self-help treatment program for anxiety state patients. *Behavior Therapy, 13,* 103–111.

Janowitz, H. D., & Grossman, M. I. (1949). Effects of variations in nutritive density on intake of food in dogs and cats. *American Journal of Physiology, 158,* 184–193.

Jeavons, C. M., & Taylor, S. P. (1985). The control of alcohol-related aggression: Redirecting the inebriate's attention to socially appropriate conduct. *Aggressive Behavior, 11,* 93–101.

Jeffery, R. W. (1988). Dietary risk factors and their modification in cardiovascular disease. *Journal of Consulting and Clinical Psychology, 56,* 350–357.

Jeffery, R. W. (1991). Population perspectives on the prevention and treatment of obesity in minority populations. *American Journal of Clinical Nutrition, 53,* 1621S–1624S.

Jellison, J. M., & Green, J. (1981). A self-presentation approach to the fundamental attribution error: The norm of internality. *Journal of Personality and Social Psychology, 40,* 643–649.

Jemmott, J. B. (1990). Motivational syndromes associated with natural killer cell activity. *Journal of Behvaioral Medicine, 13,* 53–73.

Jenkins, A. H. (1985). Attending to self-activity in the Afro-American client. *Psychotherapy, 22,* 335–341.

Jenkins, C. D. (1988). Epidemiology of cardiovascular diseases. *Journal of Consulting and Clinical Psychology, 56,* 324–332.

Jensen, A. R. (1969). How much can we boost IQ and scholastic achievement? *Harvard Educational Review, 39,* 1–123.

Jensen, A. R. (1980). *Bias in mental testing.* New York: Free Press.

Jensen, A. R. (1985). The nature of the black-white difference on various psychometric tests: Spearman's hypothesis. *The Behavioral and Brain Sciences, 8* (2), 193–219.

Jensen, M. P., & Karoly, P. (1991). Control beliefs, coping efforts, and adjustment to chronic pain. *Journal of Consulting and Clinical Psychology, 59,* 431–438.

Johnson, B. T., & Eagly, A. H. (1989). Effects of involvement on persuasion: A meta-analysis. *Psychological Bulletin, 106,* 290–314.

Johnson, C. A. (1990). Relative effectiveness of comprehensive community programming for drug abuse prevention with high-risk and low-risk adolescents. *Journal of Consulting and Clinical Psychology, 58,* 447–457.

Johnson, D. (1990, March 8). AIDS clamor at colleges muffling older dangers. *The New York Times,* A18.

Johnson, J. H., Butcher, J. N., Null, C., & Johnson, K. N. (1984). Replicated item level factor analysis of the full MMPI. *Journal of Personality and Social Psychology, 48,* 105–114.

Johnson, J. T., Cain, L. M., Falke, T. L., Hayman, J., & Perillo, E. (1985). The "Barnum effect" revisited: Cognitive and motivational factors in the acceptance of personality descriptions. *Journal of Personality and Social Psychology, 49,* 1378–1391.

Johnson, J. T., & Judd, C. M. (1983). Overlooking the incongruent: Categorization biases in the identification of political statements. *Journal of Personality and Social Psychology, 45,* 978–996.

Johnson, P. B. (1981). Achievement motivation and success: Does the end justify the means? *Journal of Personality and Social Psychology, 40,* 374–375.

Johnson, S. M., & White, G. (1971). Self-observation as an agent of behavioral change. *Behavior Therapy, 2,* 488–497.

Johnston, J., & Ettema, J. S. (1982). *Positive images: Breaking stereotypes with children's television.* Beverly Hills, CA: Sage.

Johnston, L. D., Bachman, J. G., & O'Malley, P. M. (1992, January 25). Monitoring the future: A continuing study of the lifestyles and values of youth. The University of Michigan News and Information Services: Ann Arbor, MI.

Johnston, W., & Dark, V. (1986). Selective attention. *Annual Review of Psychology, 37,* 43–75.

Jones, D. J., Fox, M. M., Babigan, H. M., & Hutton, H. E. (1980). Epidemiology of anorexia nervosa in Monroe County, New York, 1960–1976. *Psychosomatic Medicine, 42,* 551–558.

Jones, E. E. (1961). *The life and work of Sigmund Freud.* New York: Basic Books.

Jones, E. E. (1990). *Interpersonal perception.* New York: W. H. Freeman.

Jones, J. (1991). Personal communication from the American Psychological Association. Washington, DC: American Psychological Association.

Jones, M. (1975). Community care for chronic mental patients: The need for a reassessment. *Hospital and Community Psychiatry, 26,* 94–98.

Jones, M. C. (1924). Elimination of children's fears. *Journal of Experimental Psychology, 7,* 381–390.

Josephson, W. D. (1987). Television violence and children's aggression: Testing the priming, social script, and disinhibition prediction. *Journal of Personality and Social Psychology, 53,* 882–890.

Juarez, R. (1985). Core issue in psychotherapy with the Hispanic child. *Psychotherapy, 22,* 441–448.

Julien, R. M. (1988). *A primer of drug action,* 2d ed. San Francisco: Freeman.

Judd, C. M., & Park, B. (1988). Out-group homogeneity: Judgments of variability at the individual and group levels. *Journal of Personality and Social Psychology, 54,* 778–788.

Jung, C. G. (1964). *Man and his symbols.* Garden City, NY: Doubleday.

Jurkovic, G. J. (1980). The juvenile delinquent as a moral philosopher: A structural-developmental perspective. *Psychological Bulletin, 88,* 709–727.

K

Kagan, J. (1972). The plasticity of early intellectual development. Paper presented at the meeting of the Association for the Advancement of Science, Washington, DC.

Kagan, J. (1984). *The nature of the child.* New York: Basic Books.

Kagan, J., Kearsley, R. B., & Zelazo, P. R. (1980). *Infancy: Its place in human development.* Cambridge, MA: Harvard University Press.

Kagay, M. R. (1991, June 18). Poll finds AIDS causes single people to alter behavior. *The New York Times,* p. C3.

Kahle, L. R., & Beatty, S. E. (1987). Cognitive consequences of post-purchase behavior. *Journal of Applied Social Psychology, 17,* 828–843.

Kahn, S., Zimmerman, G., Csikszentmihalyi, M., & Getzels, J. W. (1985). Relations between identity in young adulthood and intimacy at midlife. *Journal of Personality and Social Psychology, 49,* 1316–1322.

Kail, R., & Nippold, M. A. (1984). Unrestrained retrieval from semantic memory. *Child Development, 55,* 944–951.

Kalish, R. A. (1985). *Death, grief, and caring relationships,* 2d ed. Monterey, CA: Brooks/Cole.

Kalish, R. A., & Reynolds, D. K. (1976). *Death and ethnicity: A psycho-cultural study.* Los Angeles: University of Southern California Press.

Kallmann, F. J. (1952). Comparative twin study on the genetic aspects of male homosexuality. *Journal of Nervous and Mental Disease, 115,* 283–298.

Kamin, L. J. (1982). Mental testing and immigration. *American Psychologist, 37,* 97–98.

Kammeyer, K. C. W., Ritzer, G., & Yetman, N. R. (1990). *Sociology: Experiencing changing societies.* Boston: Allyn & Bacon.

Kandel, E. R., & Schwartz, J. H. (1982). Molecular biology of learning: Modulation of neurotransmitter release. *Science, 218,* 433–443.

Kanfer, F., & Goldfoot, D. (1966). Self-control and tolerance of noxious stimulation. *Psychological Reports, 18,* 79–85.

Kanner, A. D., Coyne, J. C., Schaefer, C., & Lazarus, R. S. (1981). Comparison of two modes of stress measurement: Daily hassles and uplifts versus major life events. *Journal of Behavioral Medicine, 4,* 1–39.

Kaplan, A. S., & Woodside, D. B. (1987). Biological aspects of anorexia nervosa and bulimia nervosa. *Journal of Consulting and Clinical Psychology, 55,* 645–653.

Kaplan, R. M., & Singer, R. D. (1976). Television violence and viewer aggression: A reexamination of the evidence. *Journal of Social Issues, 32,* 35–70.

Karasek, R. A. (1982). Job, psychological factors and coronary heart disease. *Advances in Cardiology, 29,* 62–67.

Kastenbaum, R. (1977). *Death, society, and human behavior.* St. Louis: Mosby.

Kazdin, A. E. (1981). Drawing valid inferences from case studies. *Journal of Consulting and Clinical Psychology, 49,* 183–192.

Kazdin, A. E., Moser, J., Colbus, D., & Bell, R. (1985). Depressive symptoms among physically abused and psychiatrically disturbed children. *Journal of Abnormal Psychology, 94,* 298–307.

Kazdin, A. E., & Wilcoxin, L. A. (1976). Systematic desensitization and nonspecific treatment effects: A methodological evaluation. *Psychological Bulletin, 83,* 729–758.

Keating, C. F. (1985). Psychosocial enhancement of immunocompetence in a geriatric population. *Health Psychology, 4,* 25–41.

Keefe, F. J. (1987). Pain coping strategies in osteoarthritis patients. *Journal of Consulting and Clinical Psychology, 55,* 208–212.

Keefe, F. J., Dunsmore, J., & Burnett, R. (1992). Behavioral and cognitive-behavioral approaches to chronic pain. *Journal of Consulting and Clinical Psychology, 60,* 528–536.

Keesey, R. E. (1986). A set-point theory of obesity. In K. D. Brownell & J. P. Foreyt (Eds.). *Handbook of eating disorders: Physiology, psychology, and treatment of obesity, anorexia, and bulimia.* New York: Basic Books.

Keesey, R. E., & Powley, T. L. (1986). The regulation of body weight. *Annual Review of Psychology, 37,* 109–133.

Keinan, G. (1987). Decision making under stress: Scanning of alternatives under controllable and uncontrollable threats. *Journal of Personality and Social Psychology, 52,* 639–644.

Keller, M. B., First, M., & Koscis, J. H. (1990, August/September). Major depression and dysthymia. In American Psychiatric Association, *DSM–IV Update.* Washington, DC: American Psychiatric Association.

Kellerman, J., Lewis, J., & Laird, J. D. (1989). Looking and loving: The effects of mutual gaze on feelings of romantic love. *Journal of Research in Personality, 23,* 145–161.

Kelley, C. K., & King, G. D. (1979). Behavioral correlates of the 2-7-8 MMPI profile type in students at a university mental health center. *Journal of Consulting and Clinical Psychology, 47,* 679–685.

Kelley, H. H. (1973). The processes of causal attribution. *American Psychologist, 28,* 107–128.

Kelley, H. H. (1979). *Personal relationships: Their structure and processes.* Hillsdale, NJ: Erlbaum.

Kelley, H. H., & Michela, J. L. (1980). Attribution theory and research. *Annual Review of Psychology, 31,* 457–501.

Kelly, G. A. (1955). *The psychology of personal constructs, Vols. 1 & 2.* New York: W. W. Norton.

Kelsoe, J. R. (1989). Re-evaluation of the linkage relationship between chromosome 11p loci and the gene for bipolar affective disorder in the Old Order Amish. *Nature, 342,* 238–243.

Kemper, P., & Murtaugh, C. M. (1991). Lifetime use of nursing home care. *The New England Journal of Medicine, 324,* 595–600.

Kendall, P. C., & Norton-Ford, J. D. (1982). Therapy outcome research methods. In P. C. Kendall & J. N. Butcher (Eds.), *Handbook of research methods in clinical psychology.* New York: Wiley.

Kent, M. R. (1991). Women and AIDS. *The New England Journal of Medicine, 324,* 1442.

Kerr, N. L. (1983). Motivation losses in small groups: A social dilemma analysis. *Journal of Personality and Social Psychology, 45,* 819–828.

Kerr, N. L., & MacCoun, R. J. (1985). The effects of jury size and polling method on the process and product of jury deliberation. *Journal of Personality and Social Psychology, 48,* 349–363.

Kershner, J. R., & Ledger, G. (1985). Effect of sex, intelligence, and style of thinking on creativity: A comparison of gifted and average IQ children. *Journal of Personality and Social Psychology, 48,* 1033–1040.

Kesey, K. (1962). *One flew over the cuckoo's nest.* New York: Viking.

Kety, S. (1980). The syndrome of schizophrenia: Unresolved questions and opportunities for research. *British Journal of Psychiatry, 136,* 421–436.

Keyes, D. (1982). *The minds of Billy Milligan.* New York: Bantam Books.

Kiecolt-Glaser, J. K., & Glaser, R. (1992). Psychoneuroimmunology: Can psychological interventions modulate immunity? *Journal of Consulting and Clinical Psychology, 60,* 569–575.

Kiesler, C. A. (1982). Mental hospitalization and alternative care. *American Psychologist, 37,* 349–360.

Kihlstrom, J. F. (1980). Posthypnotic amnesia for recently learned material: Interactions with "episodic" and "semantic" memory. *Cognitive Psychology, 12,* 227–251.

Kihlstrom, J. F., Brenneman, H. A., Pistole, D. D., & Shor, R. E. (1985). Hypnosis as a retrieval cue in posthypnotic amnesia. *Journal of Abnormal Psychology, 94,* 264–271.

Kilbride, J. E., Komin, S., Leahy, P., Thurman, B., & Wirsing, R. (1981). Culture and the perception of social dominance from facial expression. *Journal of Personality and Social Psychology, 40,* 615–626.

Killen, J. D. (1986). Self-induced vomiting and laxative and diuretic use among teenagers. *Journal of the American Medical Association, 225,* 1417–1449.

Killen, J. D., Fortmann, S. P., Newman, B., & Varady, A. (1990). Evaluation of a treatment approach combining nicotine gum with self-guided behavioral treatments for smoking relapse prevention. *Journal of Consulting and Clinical Psychology, 58,* 85–92.

Kimble, D. P. (1988). *Biological psychology.* New York: Holt, Rinehart and Winston.

Kimble, D. P., BreMiller, R., & Stickrod, G. (1986). Fetal brain implants improve maze performance in hippocampal-lesioned rats. *Brain Research, 363,* 358–363.

Kimble, G. A. (1989). Psychology from the standpoint of a generalist. *American Psychologist, 44,* 491–499.

Kimmel, A. J. (1991). Predictable biases in the ethical decision making of American psychologists. *American Psychologist, 46,* 786–788.

Kimmel, D. C. (1974). *Adulthood and aging: An interdisciplinary developmental view.* New York: Wiley.

Kimura, D. (1988, November). Paper presented to the Society for Neuroscience, Toronto, Canada.

Kinsey, A. C., Pomeroy, W. B., & Martin, C. E. (1948). *Sexual behavior in the human male.* Philadelphia: W. B. Saunders Co.

Kinsey, A. C., Pomeroy, W. B., Martin, C. E., & Gebhard, P. H. (1953). *Sexual behavior in the human female.* Philadelphia: W. B. Saunders Co.

Klatzky, R. L. (1980). *Human memory: Structures and processes,* 2d ed. San Francisco: W. H. Freeman.

Klatzky, R. L. (1983). The icon is dead: Long live the icon. *Behavioral and Brain Sciences, 6,* 27–28.

Klein, D. F., & Rabkin, J. G. (1984). Specificity and strategy in psychotherapy research and practice. In R. L. Spitzer & J. R. W. Williams (Eds.), *Psychotherapy research: Where are we and where should we go?* New York: Guilford Press.

Klein, D. N., & Depue, R. A. (1985). Obsessional personality traits and risk for bipolar affective disorder: An offspring study. *Journal of Abnormal Psychology, 94,* 291–297.

Klein, D. N., Depue, R. A., & Slater, J. F. (1985). Cyclothymia in the adolescent offspring of parents with bipolar affective disorder. *Journal of Abnormal Psychology, 94,* 115–127.

Klein, M. H. (1985). A comparative outcome study of group psychotherapy versus exercise treatments for depression. *International Journal of Mental Health, 13,* 148–175.

Kleinke, C. L. (1977). Compliance to requests made by gazing and touching experimenters in field settings. *Journal of Experimental Social Psychology, 13,* 218–223.

Kleinke, C. L. (1986). Gaze and eye contact: A research review. *Psychological Review, 100,* 78–100.

Kleinke, C. L., & Staneski, R. A. (1980). First impressions of female bust size. *Journal of Social Psychology, 110,* 123–134.

Kleinke, C. L., & Walton, J. H. (1982). Influence of reinforced smiling on affective responses in an interview. *Journal of Personality and Social Psychology, 42,* 557–565.

Kleinmuntz, B. (1982). *Personality and psychological assessment.* New York: St. Martin's Press.

Kleinmuntz, B., & Szucko, J. J. (1984). Lie detection in ancient and modern times: A call for contemporary scientific study. *American Psychologist, 39,* 766–776.

Klesges, R. C., Klesges, L. M., & Meyers, A. W. (1991). Relationship of smoking status, energy balance, and body weight: Analysis of the Second National Health and Nutrition Examination Survey. *Journal of Consulting and Clinical Psychology, 59,* 899–905.

Klosko, J. S., Barlow, D. H., Tassinari, R., & Cerny, J. A. (1990). A comparison of alprazolam and behavior therapy in treatment of panic disorder. *Journal of Consulting and Clinical Psychology, 58,* 77–84.

Kobasa, S. C. (1979). Stressful life events, personality, and health: An inquiry into hardiness. *Journal of Personality and Social Psychology, 37,* 1–11.

Kobasa, S. C. (1985). Personality and health: Specifying and strengthening the conceptual links. In P. Shaver (Ed.), *Self, situations, and social behavior.* Beverly Hills, CA: Sage Press.

Kobasa, S. C., Maddi, S. R., & Kahn, S. (1982). Hardiness and health: A prospective study. *Journal of Personality and Social Psychology, 42,* 168–177.

Kobasa, S. C., Maddi, S. R., & Zola, M. A. (1983). Type A and hardiness. *Journal of Behavioral Medicine, 6,* 41–51.

Kobasa, S. C., & Puccetti, M. C. (1983). Personality and social resources in stress resistance. *Journal of Personality and Social Psychology, 45,* 839–850.

Koffka, K. (1925). *The growth of the mind.* New York: Harcourt Brace Jovanovich.

Kohen, W., & Paul, G. L. (1976). Current trends and recommended changes in extended care placements of mental patients: The Illinois system as a case in point. *Schizophrenia Bulletin, 2,* 575–594.

Kohlberg, L. (1969). *Stages in the development of moral thought and action.* New York: Holt, Rinehart and Winston.

Kohlberg, L. (1981). *The philosophy of moral development: Moral stages and the idea of justice.* San Francisco: Harper & Row.

Kihler, W. (1925). *The mentality of apes.* New York: Harcourt Brace Jovanovich.

Kolata, G. (1988, August 30). Latest surgery for Parkinson's is disappointing. *The New York Times,* pp. C1, C3.

Kolata, G. (1991, November 8). Studies cite 10.5 years from infection to illness. *The New York Times,* p. B12.

Kolko, D. J., & Rickard-Figueroa, J. L. (1985). Effects of video games on the adverse corollaries of chemotherapy in pediatric oncology patients: A single-case analysis. *Journal of Consulting and Clinical Psychology, 53,* 223–228.

Komacki, J., & Dore-Boyce, K. (1978). Self-recording: Its effects on individuals high and low in motivation. *Behavior Therapy, 9,* 65–72.

Koocher, G. P. (1991). Questionable methods in alcoholism research. *Journal of Consulting and Clinical Psychology, 59,* 246–248.

Korn, J. H., Davis, R., & Davis, S. F. (1991). Historians' and chairpersons' judgments of eminence among psychologists. *American Psychologist, 46,* 789–792.

Kornblum, W. (1991). *Sociology in a changing world,* 2d ed. Ft. Worth: Holt, Rinehart and Winston.

Koss, M. P., Butcher, J. L., & Strupp, H. H. (1986). Brief psychotherapy methods in clinical research. *Journal of Consulting and Clinical Psychology, 54,* 60–67.

Kramsch, D. M. (1981). Reduction of coronary atherosclerosis by moderate conditioning exercise in monkeys on an atherogenic diet. *New England Journal of Medicine, 305,* 1483–1489.

Krantz, D. S., Contrada, R. J., Hill, D. R., & Friedler, E. (1988). Environmental stress and biobehavioral antecedents of coronary heart disease. *Journal of Consulting and Clinical Psychology, 56,* 333–341.

Krantz, D. S., Grunberg, N. E., & Baum, A. (1985). Health psychology. *Annual Review of Psychology, 36,* 349–383.

Krieger, D. T. (1983). Brain peptides: What, where, and why? *Science, 222,* 975–985.

Kroll, J., Smith, V., & Murr, A. (1991, June 10). A black–white affair is the catalyst for Spike Lee's panoramic view of a culture in a color bind. *Newsweek.*

Kromhout, D., Bosschieter, E. B., & de Lezenne Coulander, C. (1985). The inverse relation between fish consumption and 20-year mortality from coronary heart disease. *New England Journal of Medicine, 312,* 1205–1209.

Krosnick, J. A. (1989). Attitude importance and attitude accessibility. *Personality and Social Psychology Bulletin, 15,* 297–308.

Kübler-Ross, E. (1969). *On death and dying.* New York: Macmillan.

Kuczmarski, R. J. (1992). Prevalence of overweight and weight gain in the United States. *American Journal of Clinical Nutrition, 55*(Suppl.), 495S–502S.

Kuhn, D., Kohlberg, L., Langer, J., & Haan, N. (1977). The development of formal operations in logical and moral judgment. *Genetic Psychology Monographs.*

Kushler, M. G. (1989). Use of evaluation to improve energy conservation programs. *Journal of Social Issues, 45,* 153–168.

L

LaBerge, S. P. (1988). In Blakeslee, S. (1988, August 11). New methods help researchers explore the dark world of dreams. *The New York Times*, p. B5.

Labov, W. (1972). The study of language in its social context. In W. Labov (Ed.), *Sociolinguistic patterns*. Philadelphia: University of Pennsylvania Press.

Lacks, P., & Morin, C. M. (1992). Recent advances in the assessment and treatment of insomnia. *Journal of Consulting and Clinical Psychology, 60*, 586–594.

LaCroix, A. Z., & Haynes, S. G. (1987). Gender differences in the stressfulness of workplace roles: A focus on work and health. In R. Barnett, G. Baruch, & L. Biener (Eds.), *Gender and stress*. New York: The Free Press.

LaCroix, A. Z. (1991). Smoking and mortality among older men and women in three communities. *The New England Journal of Medicine, 324*, 1619–1625.

LaFreniere, P. J., & Sroufe, L. A. (1985). Profiles of peer competence in the preschool: Interrelations between measures, influence of social ecology, and relation to attachment history. *Developmental Psychology, 21*, 56–69.

LaFromboise, T. D. (1988). American Indian mental health policy. *American Psychologist, 43*, 388–397.

Laguerre, M. S. (1981). Haitian Americans. In A. Harwood (Ed.), *Ethnicity and medical care*. Cambridge, MA: Harvard University Press.

Lahey, B. B., & Drabman, R. S. (1981). Behavior modification in the classroom. In W. E. Craighead, A. E. Kazdin, & M. J. Mahoney (Eds.), *Behavior modification: Principles, issues and applications*, 2d ed. Boston: Houghton Mifflin.

Laird, J. D. (1974). Self-attribution of emotion: The effects of expressive behavior on the quality of emotional experience. *Journal of Personality and Social Psychology, 29*, 475–486.

Laird, J. D. (1984). The real role of facial response in the experience of emotion: A reply to Tourangeau and Ellsworth, and others. *Journal of Personality and Social Psychology, 47*, 909–917.

Lam, D. H., Brewin, C. R., Woods, R. T., & Bebbington, P. E. (1987). Cognition and social adversity in the depressed elderly. *Journal of Abnormal Psychology, 96*, 23–26.

Lamb, M. E., Easterbrooks, M. A., & Holden, G. W. (1980). Reinforcement and punishment among preschoolers: Characteristics, effects, and correlates. *Child Development, 51*, 1230–1236.

Lambert, M. J., Shapiro, D. A., & Bergin, A. E. (1986). The effectiveness of psychotherapy. In S. L. Garfield & A. E. Bergin (Eds.), *Handbook of psychotherapy and behavior change*, 3d ed. New York: Wiley.

Landreth, C. (1967). *Early childhood*. New York: Knopf.

Lang, A. R., Goeckner, D. J., Adesso, V. J., & Marlatt, G. A. (1975). Effects of alcohol on aggression in male social drinkers. *Journal of Abnormal Psychology, 84*, 508–518.

Lang, A. R., Searles, J., Lauerman, R., & Adesso, V. J. (1980). Expectancy, alcohol, and sex guilt as determinants of interest in and reaction to sexual stimuli. *Journal of Abnormal Psychology, 89*, 644–653.

Lang, P. J., & Melamed, B. B. (1969). Case report: Avoidance conditioning therapy of an infant with chronic ruminative vomiting. *Journal of Abnormal Psychology, 74*, 1–8.

Langer, E. J., Bashner, R. S., & Chanowitz, B. (1985). Decreasing prejudice by increasing discrimination. *Journal of Personality and Social Psychology, 49*, 113–120.

Langer, E. J., Rodin, J., Beck, P., Weinan, C., & Spitzer, L. (1979). Environmental determinants of memory improvement in late adulthood. *Journal of Personality and Social Psychology, 37*, 2003–2013.

Langford, H. G. (1985). Dietary therapy slows the return of hypertension after stopping prolonged medication. *Journal of the American Medical Association, 253*, 657–664.

Lansky, D., & Wilson, G. T. (1981). Alcohol, expectations, and sexual arousal. *Journal of Abnormal Psychology, 90*, 35–45.

Lanzetta, J. T., Cartwright-Smith, J., & Kleck, R. E. (1976). Effects of nonverbal dissimulation on emotional experience and autonomic arousal. *Journal of Personality and Social Psychology, 33*, 354–370.

LaPerriere, A. R. (1990). Exercise intervention attenuates emotional distress and natural killer cell decrements following notification of positive serologic status for HIV-1. *Biofeedback and Self-Regulation, 15*, 229–242.

LaPerriere, A. R. (1991). Aerobic exercise training in an AIDS risk group. *International Journal of Sports Medicine, 12*, S53–S57.

Laroche, S., & Bloch, V. (1982). Conditioning of hippocampal cells and long-term potentiation: An approach to mechanisms of posttrial memory facilitation. In C. Ajmone Marsan & H. Matthies (Eds.), *Neuronal plasticity and memory formation*. New York: Raven Press.

Latané, B., & Dabbs, J. M. (1975). Sex, group size, and helping in three cities. *Sociometry, 38*, 180–194.

Latané, B., & Nida, S. (1981). Ten years of research on group size and helping. *Psychological Bulletin, 89*, 308–324.

Latané, B., Williams, K., & Harkins, S. (1979). Many hands make light the work: The causes and consequences of social loafing. *Journal of Personality and Social Psychology, 37*, 822–832.

Lau, R. R., & Hartman, K. A. (1983). Common sense representations of common illnesses. *Health Psychology, 2*, 167–185.

Lau, R. R., & Russell, D. (1980). Attributions in the sports pages. *Journal of Personality and Social Psychology, 39*, 29–38.

Laudenslager, M. L. (1983). Coping and immunosuppression: Inescapable but not escapable shock suppresses lymphocyte proliferation. *Science, 221*, 568–570.

Lax, E. (1991, February 24). Woody & Mia: A New York story. *The New York Times Magazine*, pp. 30–32, 72–75.

Layne, C. (1979). The Barnum effect: Rationality versus gullibility? *Journal of Consulting and Clinical Psychology, 47*, 219–221.

Lazar, I., & Darlington, R. (1982). Lasting effects of early education: A report from the Consortium of Longitudinal Studies. *Monographs of the Society for Research in Child Development, 47*(2–3), Serial No. 195.

Lazarus, A. A. (1990). If this be research. . . . *American Psychologist, 45*, 670–671.

Lazarus, R. S. (1984). Puzzles in the study of daily hassles. *Journal of Behavioral Medicine, 7*, 375–389.

Lazarus, R. S. (1984). The trivialization of distress. In B. L. Hammonds & C. J. Scheirer (Eds.), *Psychology and health: The master lecture series*. Washington, DC: American Psychological Association.

Lazarus, R. S. (1991a). Cognition and motivation in emotion. *American Psychologist, 46*, 352–367.

Lazarus, R. S. (1991b). *Emotion and adaptation*. New York: Oxford University Press.

Lazarus, R. S., DeLongis, A., Folkman, S., & Gruen, R. (1985). Stress and adaptational outcomes: The problem of confounded measures. *American Psychologist, 40*, 770–779.

Lazarus, R. S., & Folkman, S. (1984). *Stress, appraisal, and coping*. New York: Springer.

Leary, W. E. (1990, June 9). Gloomy report on the health of teenagers. *The New York Times*, p. 24.

Leary, W. E. (1991, October 22). Black hypertension may reflect other ills. *The New York Times*, p. C3.

LeDoux, J. E. (1986). The neurobiology of emotion. In J. E. LeDoux & W. Hirst (Eds.), *Mind and brain: Dialogues in cognitive neuroscience*. Cambridge: Cambridge University Press.

Lee, C. C., & Richardson, B. L. (1991). *Multicultural issues in counseling: New approaches to diversity*. Alexandria, VA: AACD.

Lee, T., & Seeman, P. (1977). Dopamine receptors in normal and schizophrenic human brains. *Proceedings of the Society of Neurosciences, 3*, 443.

Lefcourt, H. M., & Martin, R. A. (1986). *Humor and life stress: Antidote to adversity*. New York: Springer-Verlag.

Lefcourt, H. M., Miller, R. S., Ware, E. E., & Sherk, D. (1981). Locus of control as a modifier of the relationship between stressors and moods. *Journal of Personality and Social Psychology, 41*, 357–369.

Lehrer, P. M., Sargunaraj, D., & Hochron, S. (1992). Psychological approaches to the treatment of asthma. *Journal of Consulting and Clinical Psychology, 60*, 639–643.

Leibowitz, S. F. (1986). Brain monoamines and peptides: Role in the control of eating behavior. *Federation Proceedings, 45*, 599–615.

Leippe, M. R. (1985). The influence of eyewitness nonidentifications on mock-jurors' judgments of a court case. *Journal of Applied Social Psychology, 15*, 656–672.

Lenneberg, E. H. (1967). *Biological foundations of language*. New York: Wiley.

Lenneberg, E. H. (1969). On explaining language. *Science, 164*, 635–643.

Lerner, M. J., Miller, D. T., & Holmes, J. G. (1975). Deserving versus justice: A contemporary dilemma. In L. Berkowitz & E. Walster (Eds.), *Advances in experimental social psychology*, Vol. 12. New York: Academic Press.

Lesnik-Oberstein, M., & Cohen, L. (1984). Cognitive style, sensation seeking, and assortive mating. *Journal of Personality and Social Psychology, 46*, 112–117.

Lester, B. M., Als, H., & Brazelton, T. B. (1982). Regional obstetric anesthesia and newborn behavior: A reanalysis toward synergistic effects. *Child Development, 53*, 687–692.

Leventhal, H. (1970). Findings and theory in the study of fear communication. In L. Berkowitz (Ed.), *Advances in experimental social psychology*, Vol. 5. New York: Academic Press.

Leventhal, H., Meyer, D., & Nerenz, D. R. (1980). The commonsense representation of illness danger. In S. Rachman (Ed.), *Medical psychology*, Vol. 2. New York: Pergamon Press.

Leventhal, H., Nerenz, D. R., & Steele, D. J. (1984). Illness representations and coping with health threats. In A. Baum, S. E. Taylor, & J. E. Singer (Eds.), *Handbook of psychology and health: Vol. 4. Social psychological aspects of health*. Hillsdale, NJ: Erlbaum.

Leventhal, H., Watts, J. C., & Paogano, F. (1967). Effects of fear and instructions on how to cope with danger. *Journal of Personality and Social Psychology, 6*, 313–321.

Levine, I. S., & Rog, D. J. (1990). Mental health services for homeless mentally ill: Federal initiatives and current service trends. *American Psychologist, 45*, 963–968.

Levine, J. D., Gordon, N. C., & Fields, H. L. (1979). Naloxone dose dependently produces analgesia and hyperalgesia in post-operative pain. *Nature, 278*, 740–741.

Levine, M. P. (1987). *Student eating disorders: Anorexia nervosa and bulimia*. Washington, DC: National Education Association.

Levine, S. R. (1990). Cerebrovascular complications of the use of the "crack" form of alkaloidal cocaine. *The New England Journal of Medicine, 323*, 699–704.

Levinson, D. J., Darrow, C. N., Klein, E. B., Levinson, M. H., & McKee, B. (1978). *The seasons of a man's life*. New York: Knopf.

Levitt, R. A. (1981). *Physiological psychology*. New York: Holt, Rinehart and Winston.

Levy, J. (1985,). Right brain, left brain: Fact and fiction. *Psychology Today, 19*(5), pp. 38–44.

Levy, S. M. (1985). *Behavior and cancer: Life-style and psychosocial factors in the initiation and progression of cancer*. San Francisco: Jossey-Bass.

Levy, S. M., Herberman, R. B., Maluish, A. M., Schlien, B., & Lippman, M. (1985). Prognostic risk assessment in the primary breast cancer by behavioral and immunological parameters. *Health Psychology, 4*, 99–113.

Lewinsohn, P. M. (1975). The behavioral study and treatment of depression. In M. Hersen, R. M. Eisler, & P. M. Miller (Eds.), *Progress in behavior modification*, Vol. 1. New York: Academic Press.

Lewinsohn, P. M., & Amenson, C. S. (1978). Some relations between pleasant and unpleasant mood-related events and depression. *Journal of Abnormal Psychology, 87*, 644–654.

Lex, B. W. (1987). Review of alcohol problems in ethnic minority groups. *Journal of Consulting and Clinical Psychology, 55*, 293–300.

Lichtenstein, E., & Glasgow, R. E. (1977). Rapid smoking: Side effects and safeguards. *Journal of Consult-*

ing and Clinical Psychology, 45, 815–821.

Lichtenstein, E., & Glasgow, R. E. (1992). Smoking cessation: What have we learned in the past decade? *Journal of Consulting and Clinical Psychology, 60,* 518–527.

Lieber, C. S. (1990, January 14). Cited in Barroom biology: How alcohol goes to a woman's head, *The New York Times,* E24.

Lieberman, M. A., Yalom, I. D., & Miles, M. (1973). *Encounter groups: First facts.* New York: Basic Books.

Liebert, R. M., Sprafkin, J. N., & Davidson, E. S. (1989). *The early window: Effects of television on children and youth,* 3rd ed. New York: Pergamon.

Lindsay, D. S., & Johnson, M. K. (1989). The reversed eyewitness suggestibility effect. *Bulletin of the Psychonomic Society, 27,* 111–113.

Lindsay, R. C. L., Lim, R., Marando, L., & Culley, D. (1986). Mock-juror evaluations of eyewitness testimony: A test of metamemory hypotheses. *Journal of Applied Social Psychology, 16,* 447–459.

Lindsey, K. P., & Paul, G. L. (1989). Involuntary commitments to public mental institutions: Issues involving the overrepresentation of blacks and assessment of relevant functioning. *Psychological Bulletin, 106,* 171–183.

Ling, G. S. F. (1984). Separation of morphine analgesia from physical dependence. *Science, 226,* 462–464.

Linville, P. W., Fischer, G. W., & Salovey, P. (1989). Perceived distribution of the characteristics of in-group and out-group members. *Journal of Personality and Social Psychology, 57,* 165–188.

Lipinski, D. P., Black, J. L., Nelson, R. O., & Ciminero, A. R. (1975). Influence of motivational variables on the reactivity and reliability of self-recording. *Journal of Consulting and Clinical Psychology, 43,* 637–646.

Lipsky, M., Kassinove, H., & Miller, N. (1980). Effects of rational-emotive therapy, rational role reversal, and rational-emotive imagery on the emotional adjustment of community-mental-health-center patients. *Journal of Consulting and Clinical Psychology, 48,* 366–374.

Lipton, D. N., McDonel, E. C., & McFall, R. M. (1987). Heterosocial perception in rapists. *Journal of Consulting and Clinical Psychology, 55,* 17–21.

Lissner, L. (1991). Variability of body weight and health outcomes in the Framingham population. *The New England Journal of Medicine, 324,* 1839–1844.

Lloyd, C., Alexander, A. A., Rice, D. G., & Greenfield, N. S. (1980). Life events as predictors of academic performance. *Journal of Human Stress, 6,* 15–25.

Loftus, E. F. (1979). *Eyewitness testimony.* Cambridge, MA: Harvard University Press.

Loftus, E. F. (1983). Silence is not golden. *American Psychologist, 38,* 564–572.

Loftus, E. F., & Burns, T. E. (1982). Mental shock can produce retrograde amnesia. *Memory and Cognition, 10,* 318–323.

Loftus, E. F., & Klinger, M. A. (1992). Is the unconscious smart or dumb? *American Psychologist, 47,* 761–765.

Loftus, E. F., & Loftus, G. R. (1980). On the permanence of stored information in the brain. *American Psychologist, 35,* 409–420.

Loftus, E. F., & Palmer, J. C. (1974). Reconstruction of automobile destruction: An example of interaction between language and memory. *Journal of Verbal Learning and Verbal Behavior, 13,* 585–589.

Loftus, G. R. (1983). The continuing persistence of the icon. *Behavioral and Brain Sciences, 6,* 28.

Loftus, G. R., & Loftus, E. F. (1976). *Human memory: The processing of information.* Hillsdale, NJ: Erlbaum.

Lohr, J. M., & Staats, A. (1973). Attitude conditioning in Sino-Tibetan languages. *Journal of Personality and Social Psychology, 26,* 196–200.

Lonergan, E. T., & Krevans, J. R. (1991). A national agenda for research on aging. *The New England Journal of Medicine, 324,* 1825–1828.

Long, B. C. (1984). Aerobic conditioning and stress inoculation: A comparison of stress-management interventions. *Cognitive Therapy and Research, 8,* 517–542.

Long, G. M., & Beaton, R. J. (1982). The case for peripheral persistence: Effects of target and background luminance on a partial-report task. *Journal of Experimental Psychology: Human Perception and Performance, 8,* 383–391.

Long, M. E. (1987, December). What is this thing called sleep? *National Geographic,* pp. 787–821.

Loomis, J. M., & Lederman, S. J. (1986). Tactual perception. In K. Boff, L. Kaufman, & J. Thomas (Eds.), *Handbook of perception and human performance,* Vol. 1. New York: Wiley.

Lorenz, K. Z. (1966). *On aggression.* New York: Harcourt Brace Jovanovich.

Lorenz, K. Z. (1981). *The foundations of ethology.* New York: Springer-Verlag.

Lowenthal, M. F., & Haven, C. (1981). Interaction and adaptation: Intimacy as a critical variable. In L. D. Steinberg (Ed.), *The life cycle.* New York: Columbia University Press.

Lubin, B., Larsen, R. M., Matarazzo, J. D., & Seever, M. (1985). Psychological test usage patterns in five professional settings. *American Psychologist, 40,* 857–861.

Lublin, J. S. (1984, March 8). Couples working different shifts take on new duties and pressures. *The Wall Street Journal,* p. 33.

Luborsky, L., & DeRubeis, R. J. (1984). The use of psychotherapy treatment manuals: A small revolution in psychotherapy research style. *Clinical Psychology Review, 4,* 5–15.

Lucariello, J., & Nelson, K. (1985). Slot-filler categories as memory organizers for young children. *Developmental Psychology, 21,* 272–281.

Luchins, A. S. (1957). Primacy-recency in impression formation. In C. I. Hovland (Ed.), *The order of presentation in persuasion.* New Haven, CT: Yale University Press.

Luparello, T. J. (1971). Psychologic factors and bronchial asthma. *New York State Journal of Medicine, 71,* 2161–2165.

Lykken, D. T. (1957). A study of anxiety in the sociopathic personality. *Journal of Abnormal and Social Psychology, 55,* 6–10.

Lykken, D. T. (1982). Fearlessness: Its carefree charm and deadly risks. *Psychology Today, 16*(9), pp. 20–28.

Lynn, M., & Shurgot, B. A. (1984). Responses to lonely hearts advertisements: Effects of reported physical attractiveness, physique, and coloration. *Personality and Social Psychology Bulletin, 10,* 349–357.

Lynn, R. (1977). The intelligence of the Japanese. *Bulletin of the British Psychological Society, 30,* 69–72.

Lynn, R. (1982). IQ in Japan and the United States shows a growing disparity. *Nature, 297,* 222–223.

Lynn, R. (1991). Educational achievements of Asian Americans. *American Psychologist, 46,* 875–876.

Lyons, J. S., Rosen, A. J., & Dysken, M. W. (1985). Behavioral effects of tricyclic drugs in depressed patients. *Journal of Consulting and Clinical Psychology, 53,* 17–24.

M

Maccoby, E. E. (1988). Gender as a social category. *Developmental Psychology, 24,* 755–765.

Maccoby, E. E. (1990). Gender and relationships: A developmental account. *American Psychologist, 45,* 513–520.

Maccoby, E. E., & Feldman, S. S. (1972). Mother-attachment and stranger reactions in the third year of life. *Monographs of the Society for Research in Child Development, 37* (No. 1).

Maccoby, E. E., & Jacklin, C. N. (1974). *The psychology of sex differences.* Stanford, CA: Stanford University Press.

Maccoby, E. E., & Jacklin, C. N. (1980). Sex differences in aggression: A rejoinder and reprise. *Child Development, 51,* 964–980.

Macfarlane, J. A. (1975). Olfaction in the development of social preferences in the human neonate. In M. A. Hofer (Ed.), *Parent–infant interaction.* Amsterdam: Elsevier.

Mackay, A. V. P. (1982). Increased brain dopamine and dopamine receptors in schizophrenia. *Archives of General Psychiatry, 39,* 991–997.

Mackenzie, B. (1984). Explaining race differences in IQ: The logic, the methodology, and the evidence. *American Psychologist, 39,* 1214–1233.

Mackie, D. M., & Worth, L. T. (1989). Processing deficits and the mediation of positive affect in persuasion. *Journal of Personality and Social Psychology, 57,* 27–40.

Macmillan, N. A., & Creelman, C. D. (1991). *Signal detection theory.* New York: Cambridge University Press.

Maddi, S. R. (1980). *Personality theories: A comparative analysis.* Homewood, IL: Dorsey Press.

Maddi, S. R., & Kobasa, S. C. (1984). *The hardy executive: Health under stress.* Homewood, IL: Dow Jones-Irwin.

Maddison, S., Wood, R. J., Rolls, E. T., Rolls, B. J., & Gibbs, J. (1980). Drinking in the rhesus monkey: Peripheral factors. *Journal of Comparative and Physiological Psychology, 94,* 365–374.

Madigan, S., & O'Hara, R. (1992). Short-term memory at the turn of the century: Mary Whiton Calkin's memory research. *American Psychologist, 47,* 170–174.

Madsen, C. H., Becker, W. C., & Thomas, D. R. (1968). Rules, praise, and ignoring: Elements of elementary classroom control. *Journal of Applied Behavior Analysis, 1,* 139–150.

Magid, K. (1988). *High risk: Children without a conscience.* New York: Bantam Books.

Maier, N. R. F., & Schneirla, T. C. (1935). *Principles of animal psychology.* New York: McGraw-Hill.

Malatesta, V. J., Sutker, P. B., & Treiber, F. A. (1981). Sensation seeking and chronic public drunkenness. *Journal of Consulting and Clinical Psychology, 49,* 282–294.

Mandler, G. (1984). *Mind and body: The psychology of emotion and stress.* New York: W. W. Norton.

Mankiewicz, F., & Swerdlow, J. (1977). *Remote control.* New York: Quadrangle.

Mann, J., Tarantola, D., & Netter, T. W. (1992). *AIDS in the world 1992.* Cambridge, MA: Harvard University Press.

Mann, L., Newton, J. W., & Innes, J. M. (1982). A test between deindividuation and emergent norm theories of crowd aggression. *Journal of Personality and Social Psychology, 42,* 260–272.

Manning, M. M., & Wright, T. L. (1983). Self-efficacy expectancies, outcome expectancies, and the persistence of pain control in childbirth. *Journal of Personality and Social Psychology, 45,* 421–431.

Manson, J. E. (1990). A prospective study of obesity and risk of coronary heart disease in women. *The New England Journal of Medicine, 322,* 882–889.

Manucia, G. K., Baumann, D. J., & Cialdini, R. B. (1984). Mood influences on helping: Direct effects or side effects? *Journal of Personality and Social Psychology, 46,* 357–364.

Marcus, J. (1987). Review of the NIMH Israeli kibbutz–city study and the Jerusalem infant development study. *Schizophrenia Bulletin, 13,* 425–438.

Margraf, J. (1991). How "blind" are double-blind studies? *Journal of Consulting and Clinical Psychology, 59,* 184–187.

Marin, P. (1983,). A revolution's broken promises. *Psychology Today, 17*(7), pp. 50–57.

Markman, H. J. (1981). Prediction of marital distress: A five-year follow-up. *Journal of Consulting and Clinical Psychology, 49,* 760–762.

Marks, G., Miller, N., & Maruyama, G. (1981). Effect of targets' physical attractiveness on assumption of similarity. *Journal of Personality and Social Psychology, 41,* 198–206.

Marks, I. M. (1982). Toward an empirical clinical science: Behavioral psychotherapy in the 1980s. *Behavior Therapy, 13,* 63–81.

Marlatt, G. A., & Gordon, J. R. (1980). Determinants of relapse: Implications for the maintenance of behavior change. In P. O. Davidson & S. M. Davidson (Eds.), *Behavioral medicine: Changing health lifestyles.* New York: Brunner/Mazel.

Martelli, M. F., Auerbach, S. M., Alexander, J., & Mercuri, L. G. (1987). Stress management in the health care setting: Matching interventions with patient coping styles. *Journal of Consulting and Clinical Psychology, 55,* 201–207.

Martin, R. A., & Lefcourt, H. M. (1983). Sense of humor as a moderator of the relation between stressors and moods. *Journal of Personality and Social Psychology, 45,* 1313–1324.

Martin, R. L. (1985). Mortality in a follow-up of 500 psychiatric outpatients: I. Total mortality. *Archives of General Psychiatry, 42,* 47–54.

Martinez, C. (1986). Hispanics: Psychiatric issues. In C. B. Wilkinson (Ed.), *Ethnic psychiatry.* New York: Academic Press.

Martinez, F. D., Cline, M., & Burrows, B. (1992). Increased incidence of asthma in children of smoking mothers. *Pediatrics, 89,* 21–26.

Martinez, J. (1992). Personal communication.

Maruyama, G., Fraser, S. C., & Miller, N. (1982). Personal responsibility and altruism in children. *Journal of Personality and Social Psychology, 42,* 658–664.

Marx, E. M., Williams, J. M. G., & Claridge, G. C. (1992). Depression and social problem solving. *Journal of Abnormal Psychology, 101,* 78–86.

Maser, J. D., Kaelber, C., & Weise, R. E. (1991). International use and attitudes toward *DSM-III* and *DSM-III-R:* Growing consensus in psychiatric classification. *Journal of Abnormal Psychology, 100,* 271–279.

Maslach, C. (1978). Emotional consequences of arousal without reason. In C. E. Izard (Ed.), *Emotions and psychopathology.* New York: Plenum Publishing Co.

Maslow, A. H. (1963). The need to know and the fear of knowing. *Journal of General Psychology, 68,* 111–124.

Maslow, A. H. (1970). *Motivation and personality,* 2d ed. New York: Harper & Row.

Maslow, A. H. (1971). *The farther reaches of human nature.* New York: Viking.

Masters, W. H., & Johnson, V. E. (1966). *Human sexual response.* Boston: Little, Brown.

Masters, W. H., & Johnson, V. E. (1970). *Human sexual inadequacy.* Boston: Little, Brown.

Masters, W. H., & Johnson, V. E. (1979). *Homosexuality in perspective.* Boston: Little, Brown.

Masters, W. H., Johnson, V. E., & Kolodny, R. C. (1991). *Human sexuality,* 4th ed. New York: HarperCollins.

Matarazzo, J. D. (1990). Psychological assessment versus psychological testing. *American Psychologist, 45,* 999–1017.

Matefy, R. (1980). Role-playing theory of psychedelic flashbacks. *Journal of Consulting and Clinical Psychology, 48,* 551–553.

Mathes, E. W., Adams, H. E., & Davies, R. M. (1985). Jealousy: Loss of relationship rewards, loss of self-esteem, depression, anxiety, and anger. *Journal of Personality and Social Psychology, 48,* 1552–1561.

Matlin, M. (1983). *Cognition.* New York: Holt, Rinehart and Winston.

Matlin, M. (1987). *The psychology of women.* New York: Holt, Rinehart and Winston.

Matsumoto, D. (1987). The role of facial response in the experience of emotion: More methodological problems and a meta-analysis. *Journal of Personality and Social Psychology, 52,* 769–774.

Mattes, J. A., & Gittelman, R. (1983). Growth of hyperactive children on maintenance regimen of methylphenidate. *Archives of General Psychiatry, 40,* 317–321.

Maugh, T. H. (1982). Marijuana "justifies serious concern." *Science, 215,* 1488–1489.

May, J. L., & Hamilton, P. A. (1980). Effects of musically evoked affect on women's interpersonal attraction toward and perceptual judgments of physical attractiveness of men. *Motivation and Emotion, 4,* 217–228.

May, R. (1958). Contributions of existential psychotherapy. In R. May et al., *Existence.* New York: Simon & Schuster.

McBurney, D. H., & Collings, V. (1977). *Introduction to sensation/perception.* Englewood Cliffs, NJ: Prentice-Hall.

McBurney, D. H., Levine, J. M., & Cavanaugh, P. H. (1977). Psychophysical and social ratings of human body odor. *Personality and Social Psychology Bulletin, 3,* 135–138.

McCall, R. B. (1977). Children's IQ as predictors of adult educational and occupational status. *Science, 297,* 482–483.

McCann, I. L., & Holmes, D. S. (1984). Influence of aerobic exercise on depression. *Journal of Personality and Social Psychology, 46,* 1142–1147.

McCanne, T. R., & Anderson, J. A. (1987). Emotional responding following manipulation of facial electromyographic activity. *Journal of Personality and Social Psychology, 52,* 759–768.

McCarley, R. W. (1992). Cited in Blakeslee, S. (1992, January 7). Scientists unraveling chemistry of dreams. *The New York Times,* pp. C1, C10.

McCarthy, M. J. (1990, February 26). Anti-smoking groups grow more sophisticated in tactics used to put heat on tobacco firms. *The Wall Street Journal,* pp. B1, B3.

McCartney, K., Harris, M. J., & Bernieri, F. (1990). Growing up and growing apart: A developmental meta-analysis of twin studies. *Psychological Bulletin, 107,* 226–237.

McCaul, K. D., & Haugvedt, C. (1982). Attention, distraction, and cold-pressor pain. *Journal of Personality and Social Psychology, 43,* 154–162.

McCaul, K. D., Holmes, D. S., & Solomon, S. (1982). Voluntary expressive changes and emotion. *Journal of Personality and Social Psychology, 42,* 145–152.

McCauley, C. (1989). The nature of social influence in groupthink: Compliance and internalization. *Journal of Personality and Social Psychology, 57,* 250–260.

McCauley, C., Woods, K., Coolidge, C., & Kulick, W. (1983). More aggressive cartoons are funnier. *Journal of Personality and Social Psychology, 44,* 817–823.

McClelland, D. C. (1958). Methods of measuring human motivation. In J. W. Atkinson (Ed.), *Motives in fantasy, action, and society.* Princeton, NJ: Van Nostrand.

McClelland, D. C. (1965). Achievement and entrepreneurship: A longitudinal study. *Journal of Personality and Social Psychology, 1,* 389–392.

McClelland, D. C. (1979). Inhibited power motivation and high blood pressure in man. *Journal of Abnormal Psychology, 88,* 182–190.

McClelland, D. C. (1985). How motives, skills, and values determine what people do. *American Psychologist, 40,* 812–825.

McClelland, D. C., Alexander, C., & Marks, E. (1982). The need for power, stress, immune functions, and illness among male prisoners. *Journal of Abnormal Psychology, 91,* 61–70.

McClelland, D. C., Atkinson, J. W., Clark, R. A., & Lowell, E. L. (1953). *The achievement motive.* New York: Appleton.

McClelland, D. C., Davidson, R. J., Floor, E., & Saron, C. (1980). Stressed power motivation, sympathetic activation, immune function and illness. *Journal of Human Stress, 6*(2), 11–19.

McClelland, D. C., & Jemmott, J. B., III (1980). Power motivation, stress and physical illness. *Journal of Human Stress, 6*(4), 6–15.

McConaghy, N., & Blaszczynski, A. (1980). A pair of monozygotic twins discordant for homosexuality: Sex-dimorphic behavior and penile volume responses. *Archives of Sexual Behavior, 9,* 123–124.

McCutchan, J. A. (1990). Virology, immunology, and clinical course of HIV infection. *Journal of Consulting and Clinical Psychology, 58,* 5–12.

McDougall, W. (1904). The sensations excited by a single momentary stimulation of the eye. *British Journal of Psychology, 1,* 78–113.

McDougall, W. (1908). *An introduction to social psychology.* London: Methuen.

McFadden, D., & Wightman, F. L. (1983). Audition. *Annual Review of Psychology, 34,* 95–128.

McGaugh, J. L. (1983). Preserving the presence of the past: Hormonal influences on memory storage. *American Psychologist, 38,* 161–174.

McGaugh, J. L., Martinez, J. L., Jr., Jensen, R. A., Messing, R. B., & Vasquez, B. J. (1980). Central and peripheral catecholamine function in learning and memory processes. In *Neural mechanisms of goal-directed behavior and learning.* New York: Academic Press.

McGoldrick, M., & Carter, E. A. (1982). *The family life cycle in normal family processes.* London: Guilford Press.

McGovern, T. V., Furumoto, L., Halpern, D. F., Kimble, G. A., & McKeachie, W. J. (1991). Liberal education, study in depth, and the arts and sciences major—psychology. *American Psychologist, 46,* 598–605.

McGowan, R. J., & Johnson, D. L. (1984). The mother-child relationship and other antecedents of childhood intelligence: A causal analysis. *Child Development, 55,* 810–820.

McGrath, J. J., & Cohen, D. B. (1978). REM sleep facilitation of adaptive waking behavior: A review of the literature. *Psychological Bulletin, 85,* 24–57.

McGuffin, P., & Katz, R. (1986). Nature, nurture, and affective disorder. In J. W. W. Deakin (Ed.), *The biology of depression.* Washington, DC: American Psychiatric Press.

McGurk, H., Turnura, C., & Creighton, S. J. (1977). Auditory-visual coordination in neonates. *Child Development, 48,* 138–143.

McIntosh, J. L. (1985). Suicide among the elderly: levels and trends. *American Journal of Orthopsychiatry, 55,* 288–293.

McIntyre, K. O., Lichtenstein, E., & Mermelstein, R. J. (1983). Self-efficacy and relapse in smoking cessation: A replication and extension. *Journal of Consulting and Clinical Psychology, 51,* 632–633.

McKinney, R. E. (1991). A multicenter trial of oral zidovudine in children with advanced human immunodeficiency virus disease. *The New England Journal of Medicine, 324,* 1018–1025.

McLaughlin, B. (1984). *Second language acquisition in childhood: Vol. 1. Preschool children,* 2d ed. Hillsdale, NJ: Erlbaum.

McLaughlin, F. J. (1992). Randomized trial of comprehensive prenatal care for low-income women: Effect on infant birth weight. *Pediatrics, 89,* 128–132.

McLeod, J. D., Kessler, R. C., & Landis, K. R. (1992). Speed of recovery from major depressive episodes in a community sample of married men and women. *Journal of Abnormal Psychology, 101,* 277–286.

McNally, R. J. (1990). Psychological approaches to panic disorder: A review. *Psychological Bulletin, 108,* 403–419.

Mead, M. (1935). *Sex and temperament in three primitive societies.* New York: Morrow.

Mechanic, D. (1978). *Medical sociology.* New York: Free Press.

Mednick, S. A. (1962). The associative basis of the creative process. *Psychological Review, 69,* 220–232.

Mednick, S. A., Moffitt, T. E., & Stack, S. (1987). *The causes of crime: New biological approaches.* New York: Cambridge University Press.

Mednick, S. A., Parnas, J., & Schulsinger, F. (1987). The Copenhagen high-risk project, 1962–1986. *Schizophrenia Bulletin, 13,* 485–495.

Meer, J. (1985,). Turbulent teens: The stress factors. *Psychology Today, 19*(5), pp. 15–16.

Mehrabian, A., & Weinstein, L. (1985). Temperament characteristics of suicide attempters. *Journal of Consulting and Clinical Psychology, 53,* 544–546.

Meichenbaum, D. (1976). Toward a cognitive theory of self-control. In G. Schwartz & D. Shapiro (Eds.), *Consciousness and self-regulation: Advances in research.* New York: Plenum Publishing Co.

Meichenbaum, D. (1977). *Cognitive behavior modification: An integrative approach.* New York: Plenum Publishing Co.

Meichenbaum, D., & Butler, L. (1980). Toward a conceptual model for the treatment of test anxiety: Implications for research and treatment. In I. G. Sarason (Ed.), *Test anxiety: Theory, research, and application.* Hillsdale, NJ: Erlbaum.

Meichenbaum, D. H., & Deffenbacher, J. L. (1988). Stress inoculation training. *The Counseling Psychologist, 16*(1), 69–90.

Meichenbaum, D., & Jaremko, M. E. (Eds.) (1983). *Stress reduction and prevention.* New York: Plenum Publishing Co.

Meikle, S., Peitchinis, J. A., & Pearce, K. (1985). *Teenage sexuality.* San Diego: College-Hill Press.

Mellstrom, M., Jr., Cicala, G. A., & Zuckerman, M. (1976). General versus specific trait anxiety measures in the prediction of fear of snakes, heights, and darkness. *Journal of Consulting and Clinical Psychology, 44,* 83–91.

Meltzer, H. Y. (1987). Biological studies in schizophrenia. *Schizophrenia Bulletin, 13,* 77–111.

Melzack, R. (1973). *The puzzle of pain.* New York: Basic Books.

Melzack, R. (1980). Psychological aspects of pain. In J. J. Bonica (Ed.), *Pain.* New York: Raven Press.

Melzack, R., & Scott, T. H. (1957). The effects of early experience on the response to pain. *Journal of Com-*

parative and Physiological Psychology, 50, 155–161.
Mendelson, J. H., Rossi, A. M., & Meyer, R. E. (Eds.) (1974). *The use of marihuana: A psychological and physiological inquiry.* New York: Plenum Publishing Co.
Mevkens, F. L. (1990). Coming of age—The chemoprevention of cancer. *The New England Journal of Medicine, 323,* 825–827.
Meyer, D., Leventhal, H., & Gutman, M. (1985). Common-sense models of illness: The example of hypertension. *Health Psychology, 4,* 115–135.
Michelini, R. L., & Snodgrass, S. R. (1980). Defendant characteristics and juridic decisions. *Journal of Research in Personality, 14,* 340–350.
Mider, P. A. (1984). Failures in alcoholism and drug dependence prevention and learning from the past. *American Psychologist, 39,* 183.
Milgram, S. (1963). Behavioral study of obedience. *Journal of Abnormal and Social Psychology, 67,* 371–378.
Milgram, S. (1974). *Obedience to authority.* New York: Harper & Row.
Miller, A. G. (1986). *The obedience experiments: A case study of controversy in social science.* New York: Praeger.
Miller, G. A. (1956). The magical number seven, plus or minus two: Some limits on our capacity for processing information. *Psychological Review, 63,* 81–97.
Miller, M. F., Barabasz, A. F., & Barabasz, M. (1991). Effects of active alert and relaxation hypnotic inductions on cold-pressor pain. *Journal of Abnormal Psychology, 100,* 223–226.
Miller, N. E. (1969). Learning of visceral and glandular responses. *Science, 163,* 434–445.
Miller, N. E. (1985,). Rx: Biofeedback. *Psychology Today, 19*(2), pp. 54–59.
Miller, N. E. (1985). The value of behavioral research on animals. *American Psychologist, 40,* 423–440.
Miller, P. H., Heldmeyer, K. H., & Miller, S. A. (1975). Facilitation of conservation of number in young children. *Developmental Psychology, 11,* 253.
Miller, S. M. (1980). Why having control reduces stress: If I can stop the roller coaster I don't want to get off. In J. Garber & M. E. P. Seligman (Eds.), *Human helplessness: Theory and research.* New York: Academic Press.
Millette, B., & Hawkins, J. (1983). *The passage through menopause.* Reston, VA: Reston Publishing.
Millon, T. (1991). Classification in psychopathology: Rationale, alternatives, and standards. *Journal of Abnormal Psychology, 100,* 245–261.
Mills, J., & Harvey, J. (1972). Opinion change as a function of when information about the communicator is received and whether he is attractive or expert. *Journal of Personality and Social Psychology, 21,* 52–55.
Milner, B. R. (1966). Amnesia following operation on temporal lobes. In C. W. M. Whitty & O. L. Zangwill (Eds.), *Amnesia.* London: Butterworth.
Mineka, S. (1991, August). Paper presented to the annual meeting of the American Psychological Association, San Francisco. (Cited in Turkington, C. [1991, November]. Evolutionary memories may have phobia role. *APA Monitor,* p. 14.)
Mirsky, A. F., & Orzack, M. H. (1980). Two retrospective studies of psychosurgery. In E. S. Valenstein (Ed.), *The psychosurgery debate.* San Francisco: W. H. Freeman.
Mischel, W. (1977). On the future of personality measurement. *American Psychologist, 32,* 246–254.
Mischel, W. (1993). *Introduction to personality,* 5th ed. Fort Worth: Harcourt Brace Jovanovich.
Mishkin, M., & Appenzeller, T. (1987). The anatomy of memory. *Scientific American, 256,* 80–89.
Mitchell, J. E., & Eckert, E. D. (1987). Scope and significance of eating disorders. *Journal of Consulting and Clinical Psychology, 55,* 628–634.
Molfese, D. L., & Molfese, V. J. (1979). Hemisphere and stimulus differences as reflected in the cortical responses of newborn infants to speech stimuli. *Developmental Psychology, 15,* 505–511.
Moncher, M. S., Holden, G. W., & Trimble, J. E. (1990). Substance abuse among Native-American youth. *Journal of Consulting and Clinical Psychology, 58,* 408–415.
Money, J. (1987). Sin, sickness, or status? Homosexual gender identity and psychoneuroendocrinology. *American Psychologist, 42,* 384–399.
Money, J., & Ehrhardt, A. (1972). *Man and woman, boy and girl.* Baltimore, MD: The Johns Hopkins University Press.
Monmaney, T. (1988, January 18). Heredity and drinking: How strong is the link? *Newsweek,* pp. 66–67.
Monroe, S. M. (1982). Life events and disorder: Event-symptom associations and the course of disorder. *Journal of Abnormal Psychology, 91,* 14–24.
Monroe, S. M. (1983). Major and minor life events as predictors of psychological distress: Further issues and findings. *Journal of Behavioral Medicine, 6,* 189–205.
Monte, C. F. (1980). *Beneath the mask: An introduction to theories of personality.* New York: Holt, Rinehart and Winston.
Moolgavkar, S. H. (1983). A model for human carcinogenesis: Hereditary cancers and premalignant lesions. In R. G. Crispen (Ed.), *Cancer: Etiology and prevention.* New York: Elsevier Biomedical.
Moon, J. R., & Eisler, R. M. (1983). Anger control: An experimental comparison of three behavioral treatments. *Behavior Therapy, 14,* 493–505.
Moore, J. E., & Chaney, E. F. (1985). Outpatient group treatment of chronic pain: Effects of spouse involvement. *Journal of Consulting and Clinical Psychology, 53,* 325–334.
Moore, R. D. (1991). Zidovudine and the natural history of the acquired immunodeficiency syndrome. *The New England Journal of Medicine, 324,* 1412–1416.
Moran, J., & Desimone, R. (1985). Selective attention gates visual processing in the extrastriate cortex. *Science, 229,* 782–784.
Morganthau, T. (1986, January 6). Abandoned: The chronic mentally ill. *Newsweek,* pp. 14–19.
Moriarty, T. (1975). Crimes, commitment, and the responsive bystander: Two field experiments. *Journal of Personality and Social Psychology, 31,* 370–376.
Morin, C. M., & Azrin, N. H. (1987). Stimulus control and imagery training in treating sleep-maintenance insomnia. *Journal of Consulting and Clinical Psychology, 55,* 260–262.
Morris, J. N. (1953). Coronary heart disease and physical activity of work. *Lancet, 2,* 1053–1057, 1111–1120.
Morris, W. N., Miller, R. S., & Spangenberg, S. (1977). The effects of dissenter position and task difficulty on conformity and response conflict. *Journal of Personality, 45,* 251–256.
Morrison, A. M., & Von Glinow, M. A. (1990). Women and minorities in management. *American Psychologist, 45,* 200–209.
Moscovici, S. (1985). Social influence and conformity. In G. Lindzey & E. Aronson (Eds.), *Handbook of social psychology,* Vol. 2. New York: Random House.
Moser, C. G., & Dyck, D. G. (1989). Type A behavior, uncontrollability, and the activation of hostile self-schema responding. *Journal of Research in Personality, 23,* 248–267.
Mowrer, O. H. (1947). On the dual nature of learning—a reinterpretation of "conditioning" and "problem-solving." *Harvard Educational Review, 17,* 102–148.
Mueser, K. T., Grau, B. W., Sussman, S., & Rosen, A. J. (1984). You're only as pretty as you feel: Facial expression as a determinant of physical attractiveness. *Journal of Personality and Social Psychology, 46,* 469–478.
Mullen, B. (1987). Newscasters' facial expressions and voting behavior of viewers: Can a smile elect a president? *Journal of Personality and Social Psychology, 53,* in press.
Murphy, M. R., & Gilmore, M. M. (1989). Quality-specific effects of aging on the human taste system. *Perception and Psychophysics, 45,* 121–128.
Murray, A. D. (1985). Aversiveness is in the mind of the beholder. In B. M. Lester & C. F. Z. Boukydis (Eds.), *Infant crying.* New York: Plenum Publishing Co.
Murray, E. A., & Mishkin, M. (1985). Amygdalectomy impairs cross-modal association in monkeys. *Science, 228,* 604–606.
Murray, H. A. (1938). *Explorations in personality.* New York: Oxford University Press.
Murray, R. M., & Reveley, A. M. (1986). Genetic aspects of schizophrenia: Overview. In A. Kerr & P. Snaith (Eds.), *Contemporary issues in schizophrenia.* (pp. 261–267). Avon, England: The Bath Press.
Myers, D. G. (1983). Polarizing effects of social interaction. In H. Brandstatter, J. H. Davis, & G. Stocker-Kreichgauer (Eds.), *Group decision processes.* London: Academic Press.

N

Nathan, P. (1991). Substance use disorders in the *DSM-IV. Journal of Abnormal Psychology, 100,* 356–361.
Nathans, J., Thomas, D., & Hogness, D. S. (1986). Molecular genetics of human color vision: The genes encoding blue, green, and red pigments. *Science, 232,* 193–202.
National Institute of Mental Health. (1982). Television and behavior: Ten years of scientific progress and implications for the eighties. Washington, DC: National Institute of Mental Health.
National Institute of Mental Health. (1985). *Electroconvulsive therapy: Consensus Development Conference statement.* Bethesda, MD: U.S. Department of Health and Human Services.
National Institute of Occupational Safety and Health. (1990). *A proposal: National strategy for the prevention of psychological disorders* (Draft paper provided to the U. S. Senate Appropriations Subcommittee on Labor, Health and Human Services, and Education and Related Agencies by NIOSH).
National Institutes of Health. (1985). *National cancer program: 1983–1984 director's report and annual plan, FY 1986–1990.* (NIH Publication No. 85-2765). Washington, DC: U.S. Government Printing Office.
Neimark, E. D., Slotnik, N., & Ulrich, T. (1971). Development of memorization strategies. *Developmental Psychology, 5,* 427–432.
Nelson, K. (1973). Structure and strategy in learning to talk. *Monographs for the Society for Research in Child Development, 38* (Whole No. 149).
Neuberg, S. L. (1989). The goal of forming accurate impressions during social interactions: Attenuating the impact of negative expectancies. *Journal of Personality and Social Psychology, 56,* 374–386.
Neuringer, C. (1982). Affect configurations and changes in women who threaten suicide following a crisis. *Journal of Consulting and Clinical Psychology, 50,* 182–186.
Nevid, J. S. (1984). Sex differences in factors of romantic attraction. *Sex Roles, 11*(5/6), 401–411.
Nevid, J. S. (1992). Extremely condescending personal communication.
Nevid, J. S., & Rathus, S. A. (1978). Multivariate and normative data pertaining to the RAS with the college population. *Behavior Therapy, 9,* 675.
Nevid, J. S., Rathus, S. A., & Greene, B. (1994). *Abnormal Psychology,* 2d ed. Englewood Cliffs, NJ: Prentice Hall.
Newberne, P. M., & Suphakarn, V. (1983). Nutrition and cancer: A review, with emphasis on the role of vitamins C and E and selenium. *Nutrition and Cancer, 5,* 107–119.
Newcomb, M., & Bentler, P. (1980). Assessment of personality and demographic aspects of cohabitation and marital success. *Journal of Personality Development, 4,* 11–24.
Newcomb, T. M. (1971). Dyadic balance as a source of clues about interpersonal attraction. In B. I. Murstein (Ed.), *Theories of attraction and love.* New York: Springer.
Newcomb, T. M. (1981). Heiderian balance as a group phenomenon. *Journal of Personality and Social Psychology, 40,* 862–867.
Newcombe, N., & Bandura, M. M. (1983). The effect of age at puberty on spatial ability in girls: A question of mechanism. *Developmental Psychology, 19,* 215–224.
Newcombe, N., Bandura, M. M., & Taylor, D. G. (1983). Sex differences in spatial ability and spatial activity. *Sex Roles, 9,* 377–386.
Newlin, D. B., & Thomson, J. B. (1990). Alcohol challenge with sons of alcoholics: A critical review and analysis. *Psychological Bulletin, 108,* 383–402.
Newman, F. L., & Howard, K. I. (1991). Introduction to the special section on seeking new clinical research methods. *Journal of Consulting and Clinical Psychology, 59,* 8–11.

Nezu, A. M., & Ronan, G. F. (1985). Life stress, current problems, problem solving, and depressive symptoms: An integrative model. *Journal of Consulting and Clinical Psychology, 53,* 693–697.

Niaura, R. S. (1988). Relevance of cue reactivity to understanding alcohol and smoking relapse. *Journal of Abnormal Psychology, 97,* 133–152.

Nicassio, P., & Bootzin, R. (1974). A comparison of progressive relaxation and autogenic training as treatments for insomnia. *Journal of Abnormal Psychology, 83,* 253–260.

Nicholson, R. A., & Berman, J. S. (1983). Is follow-up necessary in evaluating psychotherapy? *Psychological Bulletin, 93,* 261–278.

Nickerson, R. A., & Adams, N. J. (1979). Long-term memory for a common object. *Cognitive Psychology, 11,* 287–307.

Niemark, J. (1986). Her nose knows best. *American Health, 5*(5), 36–40.

NIMH. See National Institute of Mental Health.

Nisan, M. (1984). Distributive justice and social norms. *Child Development, 55,* 1020–1029.

Nogrady, H., McConkey, K. M., & Perry, C. (1985). Enhancing visual memory: Trying hypnosis, trying imagination, and trying again. *Journal of Abnormal Psychology, 94,* 195–204.

Nolen-Hoeksema, S. (1991). Responses to depression and their effects on the duration of depressive episodes. *Journal of Abnormal Psychology, 100,* 569–582.

Nolen-Hoeksema, S., Morrow, J., & Fredrickson, B. L. (1992). *The effects of response styles on the duration of depressed mood: A field study.* Manuscript submitted for publication.

Novin, D. (1983). Is there a role for the liver in the control of food intake? *American Journal of Clinical Nutrition, 9,* 233–246.

Novin, D., Wyrwick, W., & Bray, G. A. (1976). *Hunger: Basic mechanisms and clinical implications.* New York: Raven Press.

Nowlis, G. H., & Kessen, W. (1976). Human newborns differentiate differing concentrations of sucrose and glucose. *Science, 191,* 865–866.

Nussbaum, M. (1985). Follow-up investigation of patients with anorexia nervosa. *The Journal of Pediatrics, 106,* 835–840.

O

Oetting, E. R., & Beauvais, F. (1990). Adolescent drug use: Findings of national and local surveys. *Journal of Consulting and Clinical Psychology, 58,* 385–394.

O'Grady, K. E. (1982). Sex, physical attractiveness, and perceived risk for mental illness. *Journal of Personality and Social Psychology, 43,* 1064–1071.

O'Hara, M. W., Neunaber, D. J., & Zekoski, E. M. (1984). Prospective study of postpartum depression: Prevalence, course, and predictive factors. *Journal of Abnormal Psychology, 93,* 158–171.

Ohman, A., Fredrikson, M., Hugdahl, K., & Rimmo, P. (1976). The premise of equipotentiality in human classical conditioning: Conditioned electrodermal responses to potentially phobic stimuli. *Journal of Experimental Psychology: General, 105,* 313–337.

O'Leary, A. (1990). Stress, emotion, and human immune function. *Psychological Bulletin, 108,* 363–382.

Olds, J. (1969). The central nervous system and the reinforcement of behavior. *American Psychologist, 24,* 114–132.

Olds, J., & Milner, P. (1954). Positive reinforcement produced by electrical stimulation of the septal area and other regions of the rat brain. *Journal of Comparative and Physiological Psychology, 47,* 419–427.

Oller, D. K. (1981). Infant vocalizations: Exploration and reflectivity. In R. E. Stark (Ed.), *Language behavior in infancy and early childhood.* New York: Elsevier.

Olson, R. P., Ganley, R., Devine, D. T., & Dorsey, G. (1981). Long-term effects of behavior versus insight-oriented therapy with inpatient alcoholics. *Journal of Consulting and Clinical Psychology, 49,* 866–877.

O'Malley, M. N., & Becker, L. A. (1984). Removing the egocentric bias: The relevance of distress cues to evaluation of fairness. *Personality and Social Psychology Bulletin, 10,* 235–242.

Opstad, P. K. (1978). Performance, mood and clinical symptoms in men exposed to prolonged, severe physical work and sleep deprivation. *Aviation, Space and Environmental Medicine, 49,* 1065–1073.

Orive, R. (1988). Social projective and social comparison of opinion. *Journal of Personality and Social Psychology, 54,* 953–964.

Orme-Johnson, D. (1973). Autonomic stability and transcendental meditation. *Psychosomatic Medicine, 35,* 341–349.

Orne, M. T., Soskis, D. A., & Dinges, D. F. (1984). Hypnotically-induced testimony and the criminal justice system. In G. L. Wells & E. F. Loftus (Eds.), *Eyewitness testimony: Psychological perspectives.* New York: Cambridge University Press.

Ortega, D. F., & Pipal, J. E. (1984). Challenge seeking and the Type A coronary-prone behavior pattern. *Journal of Personality and Social Psychology, 46,* 1328–1334.

Osborn, D. K., & Endsley, R. C. (1971). Emotional reactions of young children to TV violence. *Child Development, 42,* 321–331.

O'Sullivan, M., Ekman, P., Friesen, W., & Scherer, K. (1985). What you say and how you say it: The contribution of speech quality and voice content to judgments of others. *Journal of Personality and Social Psychology, 48,* 54–62.

P

Paffenbarger, R. S., Jr. (1972). Factors predisposing to fatal stroke in longshoremen. *Preventive Medicine, 1,* 522–527.

Paffenbarger, R. S., Jr. (1978). Physical activity as an index of heart attack risk in college alumni. *American Journal of Epidemiology, 108,* 161–175.

Paffenbarger, R. S., Jr. (1984). A natural history of athleticism and cardiovascular health. *Journal of the American Medical Association, 252,* 491–495.

Paffenbarger, R. S., Jr. (1986). Physical activity, all-cause mortality, and longevity of college alumni. *New England Journal of Medicine, 314,* 605–613.

Pandurangi, A. K. et al. (1988). Schizophrenic symptoms and deterioration: Relation to computerized tomographic findings. *The Journal of Nervous and Mental Disease, 176,* 200–206.

Pantin, H. M., & Carver, C. S. (1982). Induced competence and the bystander effect. *Journal of Applied Social Psychology, 12,* 100–111.

Pardes, H. (1991). Physicians and the animal-rights movement. *The New England Journal of Medicine, 324,* 1640–1643.

Pardine, P., & Napoli, A. (1983). Physiological reactivity and recent life-stress experience. *Journal of Consulting and Clinical Psychology, 51,* 467–469.

Paris, S. G., Newman, R. S., & McVey, K. A. (1982). Learning the functional significance of mnemonic actions: A microgenetic study of strategy acquisition. *Journal of Experimental Child Psychology, 34,* 490–509.

Park, B., & Flink, C. (1989). A social relations analysis of agreement in liking judgments. *Journal of Personality and Social Psychology, 56,* 506–518.

Parloff, M. B. (1986). Placebo controls in psychotherapy research: A sine qua non or a placebo for research problems? *Journal of Consulting and Clinical Psychology, 54,* 79–87.

Parloff, M. B., Waskow, I. E., & Wolfe, B. E. (1978). Research on therapist variables in relation to process and outcome. In S. L. Garfield & A. E. Bergin (Eds.), *Handbook of psychotherapy and behavior change,* 2d ed. New York: Wiley.

Parron, D. L., Solomon, F., & Jenkins, C. D. (Eds.) (1982). *Behavior, health risks, and social disadvantage.* Washington, DC: National Academy Press.

Parrot, W. G., & Sabini, J. (1990). Mood and memory under natural conditions: Evidence for mood incongruent recall. *Journal of Personality and Social Psychology, 59,* 321–336.

Parsons, T. (1978). *Action theory and the human condition.* New York: Free Press.

Patterson, M. L. (1991). Functions of nonverbal behavior in interpersonal interaction. In R. S. Feldman & B. Rime (Eds.), *Fundamentals of nonverbal behavior.* Cambridge, England: Cambridge University Press.

Pattison, E. M. (1977). *The experience of dying.* Englewood Cliffs, NJ: Prentice-Hall.

Pavlov, I. (1927). *Conditioned reflexes.* London: Oxford University Press.

Pearl, D., Bouthilet, L., & Lazar, J. (Eds.) (1982). *Television and behavior: Ten years of scientific progress and implications for the eighties,* Vols. 1 & 2. Washington, DC: U.S. Government Printing Office.

Pedersen, N. L., Plomin, R., McClearn, G. E., & Friberg, L. (1988). Neuroticism, extraversion, and related traits in adult twins reared apart and reared together. *Journal of Personality and Social Psychology, 55,* 950–957.

Pelham, W. E., Jr., & Murphy, H. A. (1986). Attention deficit and conduct disorders. In M. Hersen (Ed.), *Pharmacological and behavioral treatment: An integrative approach.* New York: Wiley.

Pell, S., & Fayerweather, W. E. (1985). Trends in the incidence of myocardial infarction and in associated mortality and morbidity in a large employed population, 1957–1983. *New England Journal of Medicine, 312,* 1005–1011.

Penfield, W. (1969). Consciousness, memory, and man's conditioned reflexes. In K. H. Pribram (Ed.), *On the biology of learning.* New York: Harcourt Brace Jovanovich.

Pennebaker, J. W., & Skelton, J. A. (1981). Selective monitoring of physical sensations. *Journal of Personality and Social Psychology, 41,* 213–223.

Penner, L. A., Thompson, J. K., & Coovert, D. L. (1991). Size overestimation among anorexics: Much ado about very little? *Journal of Abnormal Psychology, 100,* 90–93.

Pennington, B. F., & Smith, S. D. (1988). Genetic influences on lerning disabilities: An update. *Journal of Consulting and Clinical Psychology, 56,* 817–823.

Perez-Stable, E. (1991, May). *Health promotion among Latinos: What are the priorities?* Chancellor's Distinguished Lecture, University of California, Irvine.

Perkins, D. (1982). The assessment of stress using life events scales. In L. Goldberger & S. Brenitz (Eds.), *Handbook of stress: Theoretical and clinical aspects.* New York: Free Press.

Perls, F. S. (1971). *Gestalt therapy verbatim.* New York: Bantam Books.

Perri, M. G. (1988). Effects of four maintenance programs on the long-term management of obesity. *Journal of Consulting and Clinical Psychology, 56,* 529–534.

Perri, M. G., Richards, C. S., & Schultheis, K. R. (1977). Behavioral self-control and smoking reduction: A study of self-initiated attempts to reduce smoking. *Behavior Therapy, 8,* 360–365.

Perry, D. G., & Bussey, K. (1979). The social learning theory of sex differences: Imitation is alive and well. *Journal of Personality and Social Psychology, 37,* 1699–1712.

Petersen, S. E. (1988). Positron emission tomograph studies of the cortical anatomy of single-word processing. *Nature, 331,* 585–589.

Peterson, L. R., & Peterson, M. J. (1959). Short-term retention of individual verbal items. *Journal of Experimental Psychology, 58,* 193–198.

Peto, R. (1981). Can dietary beta-carotene materially reduce human cancer rates? *Nature, 290,* 201–208.

Petrie, K., & Chamberlain, K. (1983). Hopelessness and social desirability as moderator variables in predicting suicidal behavior. *Journal of Consulting and Clinical Psychology, 51,* 485–487.

Pettingale, K. W. (1985). Mental attitudes to cancer: An additional prognostic factor. *Lancet, 1,* 750.

Pettit, G. S., & Bates, J. E. (1984). Continuity in individual differences in the mother–infant relationship from six to thirteen months. *Child Development, 55,* 729–739.

Petty, R. E., & Cacioppo, J. T. (1986). The elaboration-likelihood model of persuasion. In L. Berkowitz (Ed.), *Advances in experimental social psychology,* Vol. 19. New York: Academic Press.

Peyser, H. (1982). Stress and alcohol. In L. Goldberger & S. Brenitz (Eds.), *Handbook of stress: Theoretical and clinical aspects.* New York: Free Press.

Piaget, J. (1962). *The moral judgment of the child.* New York: Collier.

Piaget, J. (1963). *The origins of intelligence in children.* New York: W. W. Norton.

Piaget, J. (1971). *The construction of reality in the child.*

New York: Ballantine Books.

Piaget, J. (1976). *The grasp of consciousness.* Cambridge, MA: Harvard University Press.

Pihl, R. O., Peterson, J., & Finn, P. (1990). Inherited predisposition to alcoholism: Characteristics of sons of male alcoholics. *Journal of Abnormal Psychology, 99,* 291–301.

Pike, K. M., & Rodin, J. (1991). Mothers, daughters, and disordered eating. *Journal of Abnormal Psychology, 100,* 198–204.

Pine, C. J. (1985). Anxiety and eating behavior in obese and nonobese American Indians and White Americans. *Journal of Personality and Social Psychology, 49,* 774–780.

Piotrowski, C., & Keller, J. W. (1989). Psychological testing in outpatient mental health facilities. *Professional Psychology: Research and Practice, 20,* 423–425.

Pipp, S., Shaver, P., Jennings, S., Lamborn, S., & Fischer, K. W. (1985). Adolescents' theories about the development of their relationships with parents. *Journal of Personality and Social Psychology, 48,* 991–1001.

Pitman, R. K. (1990). Psychophysiologic responses to combat imagery of Vietnam veterans with posttraumatic stress disorder versus other anxiety disorders. *Journal of Abnormal Psychology, 99,* 49–54.

Platz, S. G., & Hosch, H. M. (1988). Cross-racial/ethnic eyewitness identification: A field study. *Journal of Applied Social Psychology, 18,* 972–984.

Plomin, R. (1989). Environment and genes: Determinants of behavior. *American Psychologist, 44,* 105–111.

Plomin, R., & DeFries, J. C. (1980). Genetics and intelligence: Recent data. *Intelligence, 4,* 15–24.

Plutchik, R. (1984). A general psychoevolutionary theory. In K. Scherer & P. Ekman (Eds.), *Approaches to emotion.* Hillsdale, NJ: Erlbaum.

Polivy, J., & Herman, C. P. (1987). Diagnosis and treatment of normal eating. *Journal of Consulting and Clinical Psychology, 55,* 635–644.

Poll finds many women seek marriage plus jobs. *The New York Times* (1985, May 12), p. 19.

Pomazal, R. J., & Clore, G. L. (1973). Helping on the highway: The effects of dependency and sex. *Journal of Applied Social Psychology, 3,* 150–164.

Popham, R. E., Schmidt, W., & Israelstam, S. (1984). Heavy alcohol consumption and physical health problems: A review of the epidemiologic evidence. In R. G. Smart et al. (Eds.), *Research advances in alcohol and drug problems,* Vol. 8. New York: Plenum Publishing Co.

Popper, K. (1985). Cited in Goleman (1985).

Postman, L. (1975). Verbal learning and memory. *Annual Review of Psychology, 26,* 291–335.

Potter, W. Z., Rudorfer, M. V., & Manji, H. (1991). Drug therapy: The pharmacologic treatment of depression. *The New England Journal of Medicine, 325,* 633–642.

Pratkanis, A. R., Breckler, S. J., & Greenwald, A. G. (1989). *Attitude structure and function.* Hillsdale, NJ: Erlbaum.

Premack, A. J., & Premack, D. (1975). Teaching language to an ape. In R. C. Atkinson (Ed.), *Psychology in Progress.* San Francisco: W. H. Freeman.

Premack, D. (1970). Mechanisms of self-control. In W. A. Hunt (Ed.), *Learning mechanisms in smoking.* Chicago: Aldine.

Press, A. (1981, October 19). The trials of hypnosis. *Newsweek,* p. 96.

Press, A. (1985, March 18). The war against pornography. *Newsweek,* pp. 58–66.

Prewett, M. J., van Allen, P. K., & Milner, J. S. (1978). Multiple electroconvulsive shocks and feeding and drinking behavior in the rat. *Bulletin of the Psychonomic Society, 12,* 137–139.

Price, D. D. (1984). A psychophysical analysis of acupuncture analgesia. *Pain, 19,* 27–42.

Prigatano, G. P. (1992). Personality disturbances associated with traumatic brain injury. *Journal of Consulting and Clinical Psychology, 60,* 360–368.

Pritchard, D., & Rosenblatt, A. (1980). Racial bias in the MMPI: A methodological review. *Journal of Consulting and Clinical Psychology, 48,* 129–142.

Pyle, R. L., Halvorson, P.A., & Goff, G. M. (1986). The increasing prevalence of bulimia in freshman college students. *International Journal of Eating Disorders, 5,* 631–647.

Pyszczynski, T., Holt, K., & Greenberg, J. (1987). Depression, self-focused attention, and expectancies for positive and negative future life events for self and others. *Journal of Personality and Social Psychology, 52,* 994–1001.

Q

Qualls, P. J., & Sheehan, P. W. (1981). Imagery encouragement, absorption capacity, and relaxation during electromyographic feedback. *Journal of Personality and Social Psychology, 41,* 370–379.

Quattrone, G. A. (1982). Overattribution and unit formation: When behavior engulfs the person. *Journal of Personality and Social Psychology, 42,* 593–607.

Quinn, S. (1987). *A mind of her own: The life of Karen Horney.* New York: Summit Books.

R

Rabkin, J. G. (1980). Stressful life events and schizophrenia: A review of the literature. *Psychological Bulletin, 87,* 408–425.

Rajecki, D. J. (1989). *Attitudes.* Sunderland, MA: Sinauer Associates.

Rao, S. M., Huber, S. J., & Bornstein, R. B. (1992). Emotional changes with multiple sclerosis and Parkinson's disease. *Journal of Consulting and Clinical Psychology, 60,* 369–378.

Rangel, C. B. (1990). Cited in Berke, R. L. (1990, February 14). Survey shows use of drugs by students fell last year. *The New York Times,* p. A16.

Rappaport, N. B., McAnulty, D. P., & Brantley, P. J. (1988). Exploration of the Type A-behavior pattern in chronic headache sufferers. *Journal of Consulting and Clinical Psychology, 56,* 621–623.

Rapport, M. D. (1987). Attention deficit disorder with hyperactivity. In M. Hersen & V. B. VanHasselt (Eds.), *Behavior therapy with children and adolescents: A clinical approach.* New York: Wiley.

Raps, C. S., Peterson, C., Reinhard, K. E., Abramson, L. Y., & Seligman, M. E. P. (1982). Attributional style among depressed patients. *Journal of Abnormal Psychology, 91,* 102–108.

Rasmussen, T., & Milner, B. (1977). Clinical and surgical studies of the cerebral speech areas in man. In K. J. Zulch (Eds.), *Cerebral localization.* Berlin: Springer-Verlag.

Rathus, S. A. (1973). A 30-item schedule for assessing assertive behavior. *Behavior Therapy, 4,* 398–406.

Rathus, S. A. (1975). Principles and practices of assertive training: An eclectic overview. *The Counseling Psychologist, 5*(4), 9–20.

Rathus, S. A. (1978). Assertiveness training: Rationales, procedures, and controversies. In J. M. Whiteley & J. V. Flowers (Eds.), *Approaches to assertion training.* Monterey, CA: Brooks/Cole.

Rathus, S. A. (1988). *Understanding child development.* New York: Holt, Rinehart and Winston.

Rathus, S. A., & Boughn, S. (1993) *AIDS—What every student needs to know.* Fort Worth: Harcourt Brace Jovanovich.

Rathus, S. A., & Fichner-Rathus, L. (1991). *Making the most of college.* Englewood Cliffs, NJ: Prentice-Hall.

Rathus, S. A., & Nevid, J. S. (1977). *Behavior therapy.* Garden City, NY: Doubleday.

Rathus, S. A., & Nevid, J. S. (1992). *Adjustment and growth: The challenges of life,* 5th Ed. Fort Worth: Harcourt Brace Jovanovich.

Rathus, S. A., Nevid, J. S., & Fichner-Rathus, L. (1993). *Human sexuality in a world of diversity.* Boston: Allyn & Bacon.

Rebok, G. (1987). *Life-span cognitive development.* New York: Holt, Rinehart and Winston.

Redd, W. H. (1987). Cognitive/attentional distraction in the control of conditioned nausea in pediatric cancer patients receiving chemotherapy. *Journal of Consulting and Clinical Psychology, 55,* 391–395.

Reeder, G. D. (1982). Let's give the fundamental attribution error another chance. *Journal of Personality and Social Psychology, 43,* 341–344.

Reeder, G. D., Henderson, D. J., & Sullivan, J. J. (1982). From dispositions to behaviors: The flip side of attribution. *Journal of Research in Personality, 16,* 355–375.

Reeder, G. D., & Spores, J. M. (1983). The attribution of morality. *Journal of Personality and Social Psychology, 44,* 736–745.

Regan, D. T., Williams, M., & Sparling, S. (1972). Voluntary expiation of guilt: A field experiment. *Journal of Personality and Social Psychology, 24,* 42–45.

Rehm, L. P. (1978). Mood, pleasant events, and unpleasant events. *Journal of Consulting and Clinical Psychology, 46,* 854–859.

Reich, J. W., & Zautra, A. (1981). Life events and personal causation: Some relationships with satisfaction and distress. *Journal of Personality and Social Psychology, 41,* 1002–1012.

Reinke, B. J., Holmes, D. S., & Harris, R. L. (1985). The timing of psychosocial changes in women's lives. *Journal of Personality and Social Psychology, 48,* 1353–1364.

Reis, H. T., Senchak, M., & Solomon, B. (1985). Sex differences in the intimacy of social interaction. *Journal of Personality and Social Psychology, 48,* 1205–1217.

Reiser, M. (1992). *Memory and mind and brain: What dream imagery reveals.* New York: Basic Books.

Reiss, M., Rosenfeld, P., Melburg, V., & Tedeschi, J. T. (1981). Self-serving attributions: Biased private perceptions and distorted public descriptions. *Journal of Personality and Social Psychology, 41,* 224–231.

Remafedi, G. (1990). Study group report on the impact of television portrayals of gender roles on youth. *Journal of Adolescent Health Care, 11*(1), 59–61.

Rempel, J. K., Holmes, J. G., & Zanna, M. P. (1985). Trust in close relationships. *Journal of Personality and Social Psychology, 49,* 95–112.

Renninger, K. A., & Wozniak, R. H. (1985). Effect of interest on attentional shift, recognition, and recall in young children. *Developmental Psychology, 21,* 624–632.

Reschly, D. J. (1981). Psychological testing in educational testing and placement. *American Psychologist, 36,* 1094–1102.

Rescorla, R. A. (1967). Pavlovian conditioning and its proper control procedures. *Psychological Review, 74,* 71–80.

Rescorla, R. A. (1988). Pavlovian conditioning: It's not what you think it is. *American Psychologist, 43,* 151–160.

Rescorla, R. A., & Holland, P. C. (1982). Behavioral studies of associative learning in animals. *Annual Review of Psychology, 33,* 265–308.

Rescorla, R. A., & Solomon, R. L. (1967). Two-process learning theory: Relationships between Pavlovian conditioning and instrumental learning. *Psychological Review, 74,* 151–182.

Resnick, M. (1992, March 24). *Journal of the American Medical Association.* Cited in Young Indians prone to suicide, study finds. *The New York Times,* March 25, 1992, p. D24.

Rest, J. R. (1983). Morality. In P. H. Mussen, J. Flavell, & E. Markman (Eds.), *Handbook of child psychology, Vol. 3: Cognitive development.* New York: Wiley.

Rest, J. R., & Thoma, S. J. (1985). Relation of moral judgment development to formal education. *Developmental Psychology, 21,* 709–714.

Restak, R. (1975, August 9). José Delgado: Exploring inner space. *Saturday Review.*

Reuman, D. A., Alwin, D. F., & Veroff, J. (1984). Assessing the validity of the achievement motive in the presence of random measurement error. *Journal of Personality and Social Psychology, 47,* 1347–1362.

Rhodes, J. E., & Jason, L. A. (1990). A social stress model of substance abuse. *Journal of Consulting and Clinical Psychology, 58,* 395–401.

Rhodewalt, F., & Agustsdottir, S. (1984). On the relationship of hardiness to the Type A-behavior pattern: Perception of life events versus coping with life events. *Journal of Research in Personality, 18,* 212–223.

Rice, B. (1979, September). Brave new world of intelligence testing. *Psychology Today,* p. 27.

Rice, M. E., Quinsey, V. L., & Harris, G. T. (1991). Sexual recidivism among child molesters released from a maximum security psychiatric institution. *Journal of Consulting and Clinical Psychology, 59,* 381–386.

Rich, C. L., Ricketts, J. E., Thaler, R. C., & Young, D. (1988). Some differences between men and women who commit suicide. *American Journal of Psychiatry, 145,* 718–722.

Richardson, D. C., Bernstein, S., & Taylor, S. P. (1979). The effect of situational contingencies on female retaliative behavior. *Journal of Personality and Social Psychology, 37,* 2044–2048.

Richter, C. P. (1957). On the phenomenon of sudden death in animals and man. *Psychosomatic Medicine, 19,* 191–198.

Ridon, J., & Langer, E. J. (1977). Long-term effects of control-relevant intervention with the institutionalized aged. *Journal of Personality and Social Psychology, 35,* 897–902.

Rieser, J., Yonas, A., & Wilkner, K. (1976). Radial localization of odors by human newborns. *Child Development, 47,* 856–859.

Riggio, R. E., & Woll, S. B. (1984). The role of nonverbal cues and physical attractiveness in the selection of dating partners. *Journal of Social and Personal Relationships, 1,* 347–357.

Riley, V. (1981). Psychoneuroendocrine influences on immunocompetence and neoplasia. *Science, 212,* 1100–1109.

Rimm, E. B. (1991, August 24). *Lancet.*

Ringler, N. (1975). Mother-to-child speech at 2 years—Effects of early postnatal contact. *Journal of Pediatrics, 86*(1), 141–144.

Rinn, W. E. (1991). Neuropsychology of facial expression. In R. S. Feldman & B. Rime (Eds.), *Fundamentals of nonverbal behavior.* Cambridge, England: Cambridge University Press.

Rizley, R. (1978). Depression and distortion in the attribution of causality. *Journal of Abnormal Psychology, 87,* 32–48.

Robberson, M. R., & Rogers, R. W. (1988). Beyond fear appeals: Negative and positive persuasive appeals to health and self-esteem. *Journal of Applied Social Psychology, 18,* 277–287.

Rock, I., & Victor, J. (1964). Vision and touch: An experimentally created conflict between the two senses. *Science, 143,* 594–596.

Rodgers, J. L., Billy, J. O., & Udry, J. R. (1984). A model of friendship similarity in mildly deviant behaviors. *Journal of Applied Social Psychology, 14,* 413–425.

Rodin, J. (1986). Aging and health: Effects of the sense of control. *Science, 233,* 1271–1276.

Rogers, C. R. (1951). *Client-centered therapy.* Boston: Houghton Mifflin.

Rogers, C. R. (1959). A theory of therapy, personality and interpersonal relationships, as developed in the client-centered framework. In S. Koch (Ed.), *Psychology: A study of science,* Vol. 3. New York: McGraw-Hill.

Rogers, C. R. (1974). In retrospect: 46 years. *American Psychologist, 29,* 115–123.

Rogers, C. R. (1985). Cited in S. Cunningham (1985, May). Humanists celebrate gains, goals. *APA Monitor,* pp. 16, 18.

Rogers, C. R., & Dymond, R. F. (Eds.) (1954). *Psychotherapy and personality change.* Chicago: University of Chicago Press.

Rogers, R. W. (1983). Preventive health psychology: An interface of social and clinical psychology. *Journal of Social and Clinical Psychology, 1,* 120–127.

Rogers, R. W., & Deckner, C. W. (1975). Effects of fear appeals and physiological arousal upon emotions, attitudes, and cigarette smoking. *Journal of Personality and Social Psychology, 32,* 222–230.

Rohsenow, D. J. (1983). Drinking habits and expectancies about alcohol's effects for self versus others. *Journal of Consulting and Clinical Psychology, 51,* 752–756.

Rorschach, H. (1921). *Psychodiagnostics.* Bern, Switzerland: Hans Huber.

Rosch, E. H. (1974). Linguistic relativity. In A. Silverstein (Ed.), *Human communication: Theoretical perspectives.* New York: Halsted Press.

Rosch, E. H. (1975). Cognitive representations of semantic categories. *Journal of Experimental Psychology: General, 104,* 192–233.

Rosch, E. (1978). Principles of categorization. In E. Rosch & B. L. Lloyd (Eds.), *Cognition and categorization.* Hillsdale, NJ: Erlbaum.

Rose, S. A. (1983). Differential rates of visual information processing in full-term and preterm infants. *Child Development, 54,* 1189–1198.

Rosenbaum, M., & Hadari, D. (1985). Personal efficacy, external locus of control, and perceived contingency of parental reinforcement among depressed, paranoid, and normal subjects. *Journal of Personality and Social Psychology, 49,* 539–547.

Rosenblum, L. A., & Paully, G. S. (1984). The effects of varying environmental demands on maternal and infant behavior. *Child Development, 55,* 305–314.

Rosenthal, D. M. (1980). The modularity and maturation of cognitive capacities. *Behavior and Brain Science, 3,* 32–34.

Rosenthal, E. (1990, August 28). The spread of AIDS: A mystery unravels. *The New York Times,* C1–C2.

Rosenthal, E. (1991, December 3). Study of canine genes seeks hints on behavior. *The New York Times,* pp. C1, C12.

Rosenzweig, M. R. (1969). Effects of heredity and environment on brain chemistry, brain anatomy, and learning ability in the rat. In M. Manosovitz (Eds.), *Behavioral genetics.* New York: Appleton.

Rosenzweig, M. R., Bennett, E. L., & Diamond, M. C. (1972). Brain changes in response to experience. *Scientific American, 226,* 22–29.

Roskies, E. (1986). The Montreal Type A Intervention Project: Major findings. *Health Psychology, 5,* 45–69.

Ross, L. D. (1988). Situationist perspectives on the obedience experiments. *Contemporary Psychology, 33,* 101–104.

Rossouw, J. E. (1990). The value of lowering cholesterol after myocardial infarction. *The New England Journal of Medicine, 323,* 1112–1119.

Rotberg, I. C. (1982). Some legal and research considerations in establishing federal policy in bilingual education. *Harvard Educational Review, 52,* 149–168.

Rotheram-Borus, M. J., Trautman, P. D., Dopkins, S. C., & Shrout, P. E. (1990). Cognitive style and pleasant activities among female adolescent suicide attempters. *Journal of Consulting and Clinical Psychology, 58,* 554–561.

Rotter, J. B. (1972). Beliefs, social attitudes, and behavior: A social learning analysis. In J. B. Rotter, J. E. Chance, & E. J. Phares (Eds.), *Applications of a social learning theory of personality.* New York: Holt, Rinehart and Winston.

Rotter, J. B. (1975). Some problems and misconceptions related to the construct of internal versus external control of reinforcement. *Journal of Consulting and Clinical Psychology, 43,* 56–67.

Rotter, J. B. (1990). Internal versus external control of reinforcement. *American Psychologist, 45,* 489–493.

Rounsaville, B. J. (1987). The relation between specific and general dimensions of the psychotherapy process in interpersonal psychotherapy of depression. *Journal of Consulting and Clinical Psychology, 55,* 379–384.

Rozin, P., & Fallon, A. (1988). Body image, attitudes to weight, and misperceptions of figure preferences of the opposite sex: A comparison of men and women in two generations. *Journal of Abnormal Psychology, 97,* 342–345.

Rubinstein, E. A. (1983). Television and behavior: Research conclusions of the 1982 NIMH report and their policy implications. *American Psychologist, 38,* 820–825.

Ruderman, A. J. (1985). Dysphoric mood and overeating: A test of restraint theory's disinhibition hypothesis. *Journal of Abnormal Psychology, 94,* 78–85.

Rudman, D. (1990). Effects of human growth hormone in men over 60 years old. *The New England Journal of Medicine, 323*(1), 1–6.

Ruiz, P., & Ruiz, P. P. (1983). Treatment compliance among Hispanics. *Journal of Operational Psychiatry, 14,* 112–114.

Rule, B. G., Taylor, B. R., & Dobbs, A. R. (1987). Priming effects of heat on aggressive thoughts. *Social cognition, 5,* 131–143.

Rundus, D. (1971). Analysis of rehearsal processes in free recall. *Journal of Experimental Psychology, 89,* 63–77.

Ruppenthal, G. C., Arling, G. L., Harlow, H. F., Sackett, G. P., & Suomi, S. J. (1976). A ten-year perspective on motherless-mother monkey behavior. *Journal of Abnormal Psychology, 85,* 341–349.

Rush, A. J., Khatami, M., & Beck, A. T. (1975). Cognitive and behavior therapy in chronic depression. *Behavior Therapy, 6,* 398–404.

Rushton, J. P. (1989). Genetic similarity, human altruism, and group selection. *Behavioral and Brain Sciences, 12,* 503–559.

Russell, J. A., & Mehrabian, A. (1977). Evidence for a three-factor theory of emotions. *Journal of Research in Personality, 11,* 273–294.

Russo, N. F. (1990a). Cited in Korn, J. H., Davis, R., & Davis, S. F. (1991). Historians' and chairpersons' judgments of eminence among psychologists. *American Psychologist, 46,* 789–792.

Russo, N. F. (1990b). Overview: Forging research priorities for women's mental health. *American Psychologist, 45,* 368–373.

Rutkowski, G. K., Gruder, C. L., & Romer, D. (1983). Group cohesiveness, social norms, and bystander intervention. *Journal of Personality and Social Psychology, 44,* 545–552.

Rymer, R. (1992, April 20). Annals of science (A silent childhood—Part II). *The New Yorker,* pp. 43–77.

S

Saarni, C. (1990). Emotional competence: How emotions and relationships become integrated. In R. Thompson (Ed.), *Nebraska symposium on motivation: Vol. 36. Socioemotional development.* Lincoln: University of Nebraska Press.

Sackett, D. L., & Snow, J. C. (1979). The magnitude of compliance and noncompliance. In R. B. Haynes (Eds.), *Compliance in health care.* Baltimore: Johns Hopkins University Press.

Sackheim, H. A. (1990). Cited in Goleman, G. (1990, August 2). The quiet comeback of electroshock therapy. *The New York Times,* p. B5.

Sackheim, H. A. (1985). Cognitive consequences of low dosage ECT. In S. Malitz & H. A. Sakheim (Eds.), *Electroconvulsive therapy: Clinical and basic research issues.* New York: Annals of the New York Academy of Science.

Sacks, O. (1985). *The man who mistook his wife for a hat and other clinical tales.* New York: Summit Books.

Sadalla, E. K., Kenrick, D. T., & Vershure, B. (1987). Dominance and heterosexual attraction. *Journal of Personality and Social Psychology, 52,* 730–738.

Sadker, M., & Sadker, D. (1985, March). Sexism in the schoolroom of the 1980s. *Psychology Today,* pp. 54–57.

Saegert, S. C., & Jellison, J. M. (1970). Effects of initial level of response competition and frequency of exposure to liking and exploratory behavior. *Journal of Personality and Social Psychology, 16,* 553–558.

Safer, M. A. (1980). Attributing evil to the subject, not the situation: Student reactions to Milgram's film on obedience. *Personality and Social Psychology Bulletin, 6,* 205–209.

Salgado de Snyder, V. N., Cervantes, R. C., & Padilla, A. M. (1990). Gender and ethnic differences in psychosocial stress and generalized distress among Hispanics. *Sex Roles, 22,* 441–453.

Sameroff, A. et al. (1987). Early indicators of developmental risk: Rochester Longitudinal Study. *Schizophrenia Bulletin, 13,* 526–529.

Sanders, B., & Soares, M. P. (1986). Sexual maturation and spatial ability in college students. *Developmental Psychology, 22,* 199–203.

Sanders, B., Soares, M. P., & D'Aquila, J. M. (1982). The sex difference on one test of spatial visualization: A nontrivial difference. *Child Development, 53,* 1106–1110.

Sanders, G. S. (1984). Effects of context cues on eyewitness identification responses. *Journal of Applied Social Psychology, 14,* 386–397.

Sanders, G. S., & Chiu, W. (1988). Eyewitness errors in the free recall of actions. *Journal of Applied Social Psychology, 18,* 1241–1259.

Sanna, L. J., & Shotland, R. L. (1990). Valence of anticipated evaluation and social facilitation. *Journal of Experimental Social Psychology, 26,* 82–92.

Santee, R. T., & Maslach, C. (1982). To agree or not to agree: Personal dissent amid social pressure to conform. *Journal of Personality and Social Psychology, 42,* 690–700.

Sarbin, T. R., & Coe, W. C. (1972). *Hypnosis.* New York: Holt, Rinehart and Winston.

Sarbin, T. R., & Nucci, L. P. (1973). Self-reconstitution processes: A proposal for reorganizing the conduct of confirmed smokers. *Journal of Abnormal Psychology, 81,* 182–195.

Satir, V. (1967). *Conjoint family therapy.* Palo Alto, CA: Science and Behavior Books.

Satow, K. L. (1975). Social approval and helping. *Journal of Experimental Social Psychology, 11,* 501–509.

Sattler, J. M. (1988). *Assessment of children.* San Diego: Jerome M. Sattler.

Sauer, M. V., Paulson, R. J., & Lobo, R. A. (1990). A preliminary report on oocyte donation extending reproductive potential to women over 40. *The New England Journal of Medicine, 323,* 1157–1160.

Saunders, C. (1984). St. Christopher's hospice. In E. S. Shneidman (Ed.), *Death: Current perspectives,* 3rd ed. Palo Alto, CA: Mayfield.

Saxe, L. (1991a). Lying. *American Psychologist, 46,* 409–415.

Saxe, L. (1991b). Science and the CQT polygraph: a theoretical critique. *Integration of Physiological and Behavioral Sciences,* 26, 223–231.

Scarr, S. (1981a). Testing *for* children: Assessment and the many determinants of intellectual competence. *American Psychologist, 36,* 1159–1166.

Scarr, S. (1981b). *Race, social class, and individual differences in IQ.* Hillsdale, NJ: Erlbaum.

Scarr, S., & Kidd, K. K. (1983). Developmental behavior genetics. In M. Haith & J. J. Campos (Eds.), *Handbook of child psychology.* New York: Wiley.

Scarr, S., Webber, P. L., Weinberg, R. A., & Wittig, M. A. (1981). Personality resemblance among adolescents and their parents in biologically related and adoptive families. *Journal of Personality and Social Psychology, 41,* 885–898.

Scarr, S., & Weinberg, R. A. (1976). IQ test performance of black children adopted by white families. *American Psychologist, 31,* 726–739.

Scarr, S., & Weinberg, R. A. (1977). Intellectual similarities within families of both adopted and biological children. *Intelligence, 1,* 170–191.

Scarr, S., & Weinberg, R. A. (1983). The Minnesota adoption studies: Genetic differences and malleability. *Child Development, 54,* 260–267.

Schachter, S. (1959). *The psychology of affiliation.* Stanford, CA: Stanford University Press.

Schachter, S. (1982). Recidivism and self-cure of smoking and obesity. *American Psychologist, 37,* 436–444.

Schachter, S., Kozlowski, L. T., & Silverstein, B. (1977). Effects of urinary pH on cigarette smoking. *Journal of Experimental Psychology: General, 106,* 13–19.

Schachter, S., & Latané, B. (1964). Crime, cognition, and the autonomic nervous system. In D. Levine (Ed.), *Nebraska symposium on motivation.* Lincoln, NE: University of Nebraska Press.

Schachter, S., & Rodin, J. (1974). *Obese humans and rats.* Washington, DC: Erlbaum/Halsted.

Schachter, S., & Singer, J. E. (1962). Cognitive, social, and physiological determinants of emotional state. *Psychological Review, 69,* 379–399.

Schaeffer, J., Andrysiak, T., & Ungerleider, J. T. (1981). Cognition and long-term use of ganja (cannabis). *Science, 213,* 465–466.

Schafer, J., & Brown, S. A. (1991). Marijuana and cocaine effect expectancies and drug use patterns. *Journal of Consulting and Clinical Psychology, 59,* 558–565.

Schaller, M., & Maas, A. (1989). Illusory correlation and social categorization: Toward an integration of motivational and cognitive factors in stereotype formation. *Journal of Personality and Social Psychology, 56,* 709–721.

Scheier, M. F., Buss, A. H., & Buss, D. M. (1978). Self-consciousness, self-report of aggressiveness, and aggression. *Journal of Research in Personality, 12,* 133–140.

Scheier, M. F., & Carver, C. S. (1985). Optimism, coping, and health: Assessment and implications of generalized outcome expectancies. *Health Psychology, 4,* 219–247.

Scheier, M. F. (1989). Dispositional optimism and recovery from coronary artery bypass surgery: The beneficial effects on physical and psychological well-being. *Journal of Personality and Social Psychology, 57,* 1024–1040.

Schiavi, R. C. (1977). Luteinizing hormone and testosterone during nocturnal sleep: Relation to penile tumescent cycles. *Archives of Sexual Behavior, 6,* 97–104.

Schiedel, D. G., & Marcia, J. E. (1985). Ego identity, intimacy, sex-role orientation, and gender. *Developmental Psychology, 21,* 149–160.

Schiffman, H. R. (1990). *Sensation and perception,* 3d ed. New York: Wiley.

Schifter, D. E., & Ajzen, I. (1985). Intention, perceived control, and weight loss: An application of the theory of planned behavior. *Journal of Personality and Social Psychology, 49,* 843–851.

Schleidt, M., & Hold, B. (1981). Paper presented to the Conference on the Determination of Behavior by Chemical Stimuli. Hebrew University, Jerusalem.

Schmauk, F. J. (1970). Punishment, arousal, and avoidance learning in sociopaths. *Journal of Abnormal Psychology, 76,* 443–453.

Schmeck, H. M., Jr. (1988, May 5). Expert panel affirms success of ear implants for the profoundly deaf. *The New York Times,* p. B19.

Schneider, B. H., & Byrne, B. M. (1987). Individualizing social skills training for behavior-disordered children. *Journal of Consulting and Clinical Psychology, 55,* 444–445.

Schotte, D. E., & Clum, G. A. (1982). Suicide ideation in a college population: A test of a model. *Journal of Consulting and Clinical Psychology, 50,* 690–696.

Schotte, D. E., & Clum, G. A. (1987). Problem-solving skills in suicidal psychiatric patients. *Journal of Consulting and Clinical Psychology, 55,* 49–54.

Schotte, D. E., Cools, J., & Payvar, S. (1990). Problem-solving deficits in suicidal patients: Trait vulnerability or state phenomenom? *Journal of Consulting and Clinical Psychology, 58,* 562–564.

Schuckit, M. A. (1987). Biological vulnerability to alcoholism. *Journal of Consulting and Clinical Psychology, 55,* 301–309.

Schuckit, M. A. (1990, January/February). Substance use disorders. In American Psychiatric Association: DSM–IV update. Washington, D.C.: American Psychiatric Association.

Schultz, N. R., Jr., & Moore, D. W. (1984). Loneliness: Correlates, attributions, and coping among older adults. *Personality and Social Psychology Bulletin, 10,* 67–77.

Schutte, N. S., Malouff, J. M., Post-Gorden, J. C., & Rodasts, A. L. (1988). Effect of playing videogames on children's aggressive and other behavior. *Journal of Applied Social Psychology, 18,* 454–460.

Schwartz, L. M., Foa, U. G., & Foa, E. B. (1983). Multichannel nonverbal communication: Evidence for combinatory rules. *Journal of Personality and Social Psychology, 45,* 274–281.

Schwartz, M. F., Saffran, E. M., & Marin, O. S. M. (1980). The word order problem in agrammatism: I: Comprehension. *Brain and Language, 10,* 249–262.

Schwartz, R. M. (1982). Cognitive behavior modification: A conceptual review. *Clinical Psychology Review, 2,* 267–293.

Schwartz, R. M., & Gottman, J. M. (1976). Toward a task analysis of assertive behavior. *Journal of Consulting and Clinical Psychology, 44,* 910–920.

Scovern, A. W., & Kilmann, P. R. (1980). Status of electroconvulsive therapy: A review of the outcome literature. *Psychological Bulletin, 87,* 260–303.

Sears, R. R., Maccoby, E. E., & Levin, H. (1957). *Patterns of child rearing.* New York: Harper & Row.

Segalowitz, N. S. (1981). Issues in the cross-cultural study of bilingual development. In H. C. Triandis & A. Heron (Eds.), *Handbook of cross-cultural psychology: Vol. 4. Developmental psychology.* Boston: Allyn & Bacon.

Seligman, M. E. P. (1984). Attributional style and depressive symptoms among children. *Journal of Abnormal Psychology, 93,* 235–238.

Selye, H. (1976). *The stress of life,* rev. ed. New York: McGraw-Hill.

Selye, H. (1980). The stress concept today. In I. L. Kutash (Eds.), *Handbook on stress and anxiety.* San Francisco: Jossey-Bass.

Serlin, E. (1980). Emptying the nest: Women in the launching stage. In D. G. McGuigan (Ed.), *Women's lives: New theory, research, and policy.* Ann Arbor: University of Michigan, Center for Continuing Education of Women.

Seta, J. J. (1982). The impact of comparison processes on coactors' task performance. *Journal of Personality and Social Psychology, 42,* 281–291.

Severn, J., Belch, G. E., & Belch, M. A. (1990). The effects of sexual and non-sexual advertising appeals and information level on cognitive procesing and communication effectiveness. *Journal of Advertising, 19,* 14–22.

Shadish, W. R., Hickman, D., & Arrick, M. C. (1981). Psychological problems of spinal injury patients: Emotional distress as a function of time and locus of control. *Journal of Consulting and Clinical Psychology, 49,* 297.

Shapiro, D. (1985). Clinical use of meditation as a self-regulation strategy: Comments on Holmes' conclusions and implications. *American Psychologist, 40,* 719–722.

Shapiro, D., & Goldstein, I. B. (1982). Behavioral perspectives on hypertension. *Journal of Consulting and Clinical Psychology, 50,* 841–859.

Shapiro, D. A., & Shapiro, D. (1982). Meta-analysis of comparative therapy outcome studies: A replication and refinement. *Psychological Bulletin, 92,* 581–594.

Shapley, R., & Enroth-Cugell, C. (1984). Visual adaptation and retinal gain controls. In N. Osborne & G. Chaders (Eds.), *Progress in retinal research,* Vol. 3. Oxford: Pergamon Press.

Shavitt, S. (1990). The role of attitude objects in attitude functions. *Journal of Experimental Social Psychology, 26,* 124–148.

Shaw, E. D., Stokes, P. E., Mann, J. J., & Manevitz, A. Z. A. (1987). Effects of lithium carbonate on the memory and motor speed of bipolar patients. *Journal of Abnormal Psychology, 96,* 64–69.

Shaw, J. S. (1982). Psychological androgyny and stressful life events. *Journal of Personality and Social Psychology, 43,* 145–153.

Sheehy, G. (1976). *Passages: Predictable crises of adult life.* New York: Dutton.

Sheehy, G. (1981). *Pathfinders.* New York: Morrow.

Sheingold, K., & Tenney, Y. J. (1982). Memory for a salient childhood event. In U. Niesser (Ed.), *Memory observed: Remembering in natural contexts.* San Francisco: Freeman.

Sheppard, J. A., & Strathman, A. J. (1989). Attractiveness and height: The role of stature in dating preference, frequency of dating, and perceptions of attractiveness. *Personality and Social Psychology Bulletin, 15,* 617–627.

Sher, K. J., Walitzer, K. S., Wood, P. K., & Brent, E. E. (1991). Characteristics of children of alcoholics: Putative risk factors, substance use and abuse, and psychopathology. *Journal of Abnormal Psychology, 100,* 427–448.

Sheraton, M. (1984, June 4). You can argue with taste. *Time,* pp. 74–75.

Sheridan, C. L., & Radmacher, S. A. (1992). *Health psychology: Challenging the biomedical model.* New York: Wiley.

Sherrington, R. (1988). Localization of a susceptibility locus for schizophrenia on chromosome 5. *Nature, 336,* 164–167.

Sherwin, B. B., Gelfand, M. M., & Brender, W. (1985). Androgen enhances sexual motivation in females: A prospective crossover study of sex steroid medication in the surgical menopause. *Psychosomatic Medicine, 47,* 339–351.

Sherwin, R., & Sherry, C. (1985). Campus sexual norms and lasting relationships: A trend analysis. *Journal of Sex Research, 21,* 258–274.

Shiffman, S. (1982). Relapse following smoking cessation: A situational analysis. *Journal of Consulting and Clinical Psychology, 50,* 71–86.

Shiffman, S. (1984). Coping with temptations to smoke. *Journal of Consulting and Clinical Psychology, 52,* 261–267.

Shipley, R. H. (1981). Maintenance of smoking cessation: Effect of follow-up letters, smoking motivation, muscle tension, and health locus of control. *Journal of Consulting and Clinical Psychology, 49,* 982–984.

Shneidman, E. S. (Ed.) (1984). *Death: Current perspectives,* 3rd ed. Palo Alto, CA: Mayfield.

Shneidman, E. S. (1985). *Definition of suicide.* New York: Wiley.

Shneidman, E. S. (1987). A psychological approach to suicide. In G. R. VanderBos & B. K. Bryant (Eds.), *Cataclysms, cries, and catastrophes: Psychology in action* (Master Lecture Series, Vol. 6, pp. 151–183). Washington, DC: American Psychological Association.

Shoham-Salomon, V. (1991). Introduction to special section on client-therapy interaction research. *Journal of Consulting and Clinical Psychology, 59,* 203–204.

Shotland, R. L., & Heinold, W. D. (1985). Bystander response to arterial bleeding: Helping skills, the decision-making process, and differentiating the helping response. *Journal of Personality and Social Psychology, 49,* 347–356.

Shusterman, G., & Saxe, L. (1990). *Deception in romantic relationships.* Unpublished manuscript, Brandeis University.

Siegler, R. S., & Liebert, R. M. (1972). Effects of presenting relevant rules and complete feedback on the conservation of liquid quantity task. *Developmental Psychology, 7,* 133–138.

Signorielli, N. (1990). Children, television, and gender roles: Messages and impact. *Journal of Adolescent Health Care, 11*(1), 50–58.

Silverman, L. H. (1984). Beyond insight: An additional necessary step in redressing intrapsychic conflict. *Psychoanalytic Psychology, 1,* 215–234.

Silverstein, B. (1982). Cigarette smoking, nicotine addiction, and relaxation. *Journal of Personality and Social Psychology, 42,* 946–950.

Silverstein, B., Koslowski, L. T., & Schachter, S. (1977). Social life, cigarette smoking, and urinary pH. *Journal of Experimental Psychology: General, 106,* 20–23.

Simone, C. B. (1983). *Cancer and nutrition.* New York: McGraw-Hill.

Simons, A. D. (1985). Exercise as a treatment for depression: An update. *Clinical Psychology Review, 5,* 553–568.

Simons, A. D. (1986). Cognitive therapy and pharmacotherapy for depression: Sustained improvement over one year. *Archives of General Psychiatry, 43,* 43–48.

Singer, D. G. (1983). A time to reexamine the role of television in our lives. *American Psychologist, 38,* 815–816.

Singer, J. L. (1975). *The inner world of daydreaming.* New York: Harper & Row.

Singer, J. L., & Singer, D. G. (1981). *Television, imagination, and aggression: A study of preschoolers.* Hillsdale, NJ: Erlbaum.

Singer, J. L., & Singer, D. G. (1983). Psychologists look at television: Cognitive, developmental, personality, and social policy implications. *American Psychologist, 38,* 826–834.

Sistrunk, F., & McDavid, J. W. (1971). Sex variable in conforming behavior. *Journal of Personality and Social Psychology, 17,* 200–207.

Skinner, B. F. (1938). *The behavior of organisms: An experimental analysis.* New York: Appleton.

Skinner, B. F. (1948). *Walden Two.* New York: Macmillan.

Skinner, B. F. (1960). Pigeons in a pelican. *American Psychologist, 15,* 28–37.

Skinner, B. F. (1972). *Beyond freedom and dignity.* New York: Knopf.

Skinner, B. F. (1979). *The shaping of a behaviorist.* New York: Knopf.

Skinner, B. F. (1987). Whatever happened to psychology as the science of behavior? *American Psychologist, 42,* 780–786.

Slade, P. D. (1985). A review of body-image studies in anorexia nervosa and bulimia nervosa. *Psychological Medicine, 7,* 245–252.

Slater, J. F., & Depue, R. A. (1981). The contribution of environmental events and social support to serious suicide attempts in primary depressive disorder. *Journal of Abnormal Psychology, 90,* 275–285.

Sloane, B. (1983). Health care: Physical and mental. In D. S. Woodruff & J. E. Birren (Eds.), *Aging: Scientific perspectives and social issues.* Monterey, CA: Brooks/Cole.

Slobin, D. I. (1971). *Psycholinguistics.* Glenview, IL: Scott, Foresman.

Slobin, D. I. (1973). Cognitive prerequisites for the development of grammar. In C. A. Ferguson & D. I. Slobin (Eds.), *Studies of child development.* New York: Holt, Rinehart and Winston.

Slobin, D. I. (1978). A case study of early language awareness. In A. Sinclair, R. J. Jarvella, & W. J. M. Levelt (Eds.), *The child's conception of language.* Berlin: Springer-Verlag.

Slobin, D. I. (1983). Crosslinguistic evidence for basic child grammar. Paper presented to the biennial meeting of the Society for Research in Child Development, Detroit.

Smith, B., & Sechrest, L. (1991). Treatment of aptitude by treatment interactions. *Journal of Consulting and Clinical Psychology, 1991,* 233–244.

Smith, C. P., & Graham, J. R. (1981). Behavioral correlates for the MMPI *F* scale and for a modified *F* scale for black and white psychiatric patients. *Journal of Consulting and Clinical Psychology, 49,* 455–459.

Smith, D. (1982). Trends in counseling and psychotherapy. *American Psychologist, 37,* 802–809.

Smith, D., King, M., & Hoebel, B. G. (1970). Lateral hypothalamic control of killing: Evidence for a cholinoceptive mechanism. *Science, 167,* 900–901.

Smith, G. F., & Dorfman, D. (1975). The effect of stimulus uncertainty on the relationship between frequency of exposure and liking. *Journal of Personality and Social Psychology, 31,* 150–155.

Smith, M. L., & Glass, G. V. (1977). Meta-analysis of psychotherapy outcome studies. *American Psychologist, 32,* 752–760.

Smith, M. L., Glass, G. V., & Miller, T. I. (1980). *The benefits of psychotherapy.* Baltimore, MD: The Johns Hopkins University Press.

Smith, R. E., Smoll, F. L., & Ptacek, J. T. (1990). Conjunctive moderator variables in vulnerability and resiliency research: Life stress, social support and coping skills, and adolescent sport injuries. *Journal of Personality and Social Psychology, 58,* 360–370.

Smith, R. E., & Winokur, G. (1983). Affective disorders. In R. E. Tarter (Ed.), *The child at psychiatric risk.* New York: Oxford University Press.

Smith, S. M., Glenberg, A. M., & Bjork, R. A. (1978). Environmental context and human memory. *Memory and Cognition, 6,* 342–355.

Smith, S. S., & Richardson, D. (1983). Amelioration of deception and harm in psychological research: The important role of debriefing. *Journal of Personality and Social Psychology, 44,* 1075–1082.

Smith, T. W. (1983). Change in irrational beliefs and the outcome of rational-emotive psychotherapy. *Journal of Consulting and Clinical Psychology, 51,* 156–157.

Smith, T. W., & Pope, M. K. (1990). Cynical hostility as a health risk: Current status and future directions. *Journal of Social Behavior and Personality, 5,* 77–88.

Smith, T. W., Snyder, C. R., & Handelsman, M. M. (1982). On the self-serving function of an academic wooden leg: Test anxiety as a self-handicapping strategy. *Journal of Personality and Social Psychology, 42,* 314–321.

Smith, T. W., Snyder, C. R., & Perkins, S. C. (1983). The self-serving function of hypochondriacal complaints: Physical symptoms as self-handicapping strategies. *Journal of Personality and Social Psychology, 44,* 787–797.

Smoking declines at a faster pace. *The New York Times* (1992, May 22), p. A17.

Smoking vs. life expectancy. *The New York Times* (1987, November 1), p. 19.

Snarey, J. R. (1987, June). A question of morality. *Psychology Today,* pp. 6–8.

Snarey, J. R., Reimer, J., & Kohlberg, L. (1985). Development of social-moral reasoning among kibbutz adolescents: A longitudinal cross-cultural study. *Developmental Psychology, 21,* 3–17.

Snow, R. E. (1991). Aptitude–treatment interaction as a framework for research on individual differences in psychotherapy. *Journal of Consulting and Clinical Psychology, 59,* 205–216.

Snyder, D. K., Kline, R. B., & Podany, E. C. (1985). Comparison of external correlates of MMPI substance abuse scales across sex and race. *Journal of Consulting and Clinical Psychology, 53,* 520–525.

Snyder, M., & DeBono, G. (1985). Appeals to image and claims about quality: Understanding the psychology of advertising. *Journal of Personality and Social Psychology, 49,* 586–597.

Snyder, M., & DeBono, G. (1989). Understanding the functions of attitudes. In A. R. Pratkanis (Eds.), *Attitude structure and function.* Hillsdale, NJ: Erlbaum.

Snyder, M., Grether, J., & Keller, K. (1974). Staring and compliance: A field experiment on hitchhiking. *Journal of Applied Social Psychology, 4,* 165–170.

Snyder, S. H. (1977). Opiate receptors and internal opiates. *Scientific American, 236,* 44–56.

Snyder, S. H. (1980). *Biological aspects of mental disorder.* New York: Oxford University Press.

Snyder, S. H. (1984). Drug and neurotransmitter receptors in the brain. *Science, 224,* 22–31.

Snyderman, M., & Rothman, S. (1987). Survey of expert opinion on intelligence and aptitude testing. *American Psychologist, 42,* 137–144.

Snyderman, M., & Rothman, S. (1990). *The I.Q. controversy.* New Brunswick, NJ: Transaction Publishers.

Sommer, R. (1991). James V. McConnell (1925–1990). *American Psychologist, 46,* 650.

Sommers, S. (1981). Emotionality reconsidered: The role of cognition in emotional responsiveness. *Journal of Personality and Social Psychology, 41,* 553–561.

Sonstroem, R. J. (1984). Exercise and self-esteem. *Exercise and Sport Sciences Reviews, 12,* 123–155.

Sorce, J. F., Emde, R. N., Campos, J. J., & Klinnert, M. D. (1985). Maternal emotional signaling: Its effect on the visual-cliff behavior of 1-year-olds. *Developmental Psychology, 21,* 195–200.

Sorensen, S. B., & Rutter, C. M. (1991). Transgenerational patterns of suicide attempt. *Journal of Consulting and Clinical Psychology, 59,* 861–866.

Sorlie, P., Gordon, T., & Kannel, W. B. (1980). Body build and mortality—The Framingham Study. *Journal of the American Medical Association, 243,* 1828–1831.

Sorrentino, R. M. (1988). Uncertainty orientation and persuasion. *Journal of Personality and Social Psychology, 55,* 371–375.

Spanos, N. P., Jones, B., & Malfara, A. (1982). Hypnotic deafness: Now you hear it—now you still hear it. *Journal of Abnormal Psychology, 91,* 75–77.

Spanos, N. P., McNeil, C., Gwynn, M. I., & Stam, H. J. (1984). Effects of suggestion and distraction on reported pain in subjects high and low on hypnotic suggestibility. *Journal of Abnormal Psychology, 93,* 277–284.

Spanos, N. P., Radtke, H. L., & Dubreuil, D. L. (1982). Episodic and semantic memory in posthypnotic amnesia: A reevaluation. *Journal of Personality and Social Psychology, 43,* 565–573.

Spanos, N. P., & Radtke-Bodorik, H. L. (1980, April). Integrating hypnotic phenomena with cognitive psychology: An illustration using suggested amnesia. *Bulletin of the British Society for Experimental and Clinical Hypnosis,* pp. 4–7.

Spanos, N. P., Weekes, J. R., & Bertrand, L. D. (1985). Multiple personality: A social psychological perspective. *Journal of Abnormal Psychology, 94,* 362–376.

Specter, M. (1991, November 8). Magic's loud message for young black men. *The New York Times,* p. B12.

Spence, J. T., Helmreich, R., & Stapp, J. (1975). Ratings of self and peers on sex-role attributes and their relation to self-esteem and concepts of masculinity and femininity. *Journal of Personality and Social Psychology, 32,* 29–39.

Sperling, G. (1960). The information available in brief visual presentations. *Psychological Monographs, 74,* 1–29.

Sperry, R. W. (1974). Lateral specialization in the surgically separated hemispheres. In F. O. Schmitt & F. G. Worden (Eds.), *The neurosciences: Third study program.* Cambridge, MA: MIT Press.

Spiegel, D., & Cardeña, E. (1991). Disintegrated experience. The dissociative disorders revisited. *Journal of Abnormal Psychology, 100,* 366–378.

Spielberger, C. D., & Piotrowski, C. (1990). Clinicians' attitudes toward computer-based testing. *The Clinical Psychologist, 43,* 60–63.

Spinhoven, P. (1989). Pain coping strategies in a Dutch population of chronic low back pain patients. *Pain, 37,* 77–83.

Spitzer, R. L., Forman, J. B. W., & Nee, J. (1979). DSM-III field trials: Initial interrater diagnostic reliability. *American Journal of Psychiatry, 136,* 815–817.

Spitzer, R. L., Gibbon, M., Skodol, A. E., Williams, J. B. W., & First, M. B. (1989). *DSM-III-R casebook.* Washington, DC: American Psychiatric Press.

Squire, L. R. (1977). ECT and memory loss. *American Journal of Psychiatry, 134,* 997–1001.

Squire, L. R. (1986). Mechanisms of memory. *Science, 232,* 1612–1619.

Squire, L. R., Cohen, N. J., & Nadel, L. (1984). The medial temporal region and memory consolidations: A new hypothesis. In H. Weingartner & E. Parker (Eds.), *Memory consolidation.* Hillsdale, NJ: Erlbaum.

Squire, L. R., & Slater, P. C. (1978). Bilateral and unilateral ECT: Effects on verbal and nonverbal memory. *American Journal of Psychiatry, 135,* 1316–1320.

Sroufe, L. A. (1979). Socioemotional development. In J. Osofsky (Ed.), *Handbook of infant development.* New York: Wiley.

Sroufe, L. A. (1983). Individual patterns of adaptation from infancy to preschool. In M. Perlmutter (Ed.), *Minnesota symposium on child psychology,* Vol. 16. Hillsdale, NJ: Erlbaum.

Sroufe, L. A. (1985). Attachment classification from the perspective of infant-caregiver relationships and infant temperament. *Child Development, 56,* 1–14.

Staats, A. W., & Burns, G. L. (1981). Intelligence and child development: What intelligence is and how it is learned and functions. *Genetic Psychology Monographs, 104,* 237–301.

Stacy, A. W., Newcomb, M. D., & Bentler, P. M. (1991). Cognitive motivation and drug use: A 9-year longitudinal study. *Journal of Abnormal Psychology, 100,* 502–515.

Stamler, J. (1985a). Coronary heart disease: Doing the "right things." *New England Journal of Medicine, 312,* 1053–1055.

Stamler, J. (1985b). The marked decline in coronary heart disease mortality rates in the United States, 1968–1981: Summary of findings and possible explanations. *Cardiology, 72,* 11–12.

Stamler, J. (1986). Is the relationship between serum cholesterol and risk of premature death from coronary heart disease continuous and graded? Findings in 356,222 primary screenees of the Multiple Risk Factor Intervention Trial (MRFIT). *Journal of the American Medical Association, 256,* 2823–2828.

Stampfer, M. J. (1991). A prospective study of cholesterol, apolipoproteins, and the risk of myocardial infarction. *The New England Journal of Medicine, 325,* 373–381.

Stapp, J., Tucker, A. M., & VandenBos, G. R. (1985). Census of psychological personnel: 1983. *American Psychologist, 40,* 1317–1351.

Stark, E. (1984, February). Hypnosis on trial. *Psychology Today,* pp. 34–36.

Stasser, G., Taylor, L. A., & Hanna, C. (1989). Information sampling in structured and unstructured discussion of three- and six-person groups. *Journal of Personality and Social Psychology, 57,* 67–78.

Steck, L., Levitan, D., McLane, D., & Kelley, H. H. (1982). Care, need, and conceptions of love. *Journal of Personality and Social Psychology, 43,* 481–491.

Steele, C. M., & Josephs, R. A. (1990). Alcohol myopia: Its prized and dangerous effects. *American Psychologist, 45,* 921–933.

Stehr, P. A. (1985). Dietary vitamin A deficiencies and stomach cancer. *American Journal of Epidemiology, 121,* 65–70.

Steinberg, L., Dornbusch, S. M., & Brown, B. B. (1992). Ethnic differences in adolescent achievement. *American Psychologist, 47,* 723–729.

Steinbrook, R. (1992). The polygraph test—A flawed diagnostic method. *The New England Journal of Medicine, 327,* 122–123.

Steiner, J. E. (1979). Facial expressions in response to taste and smell discrimination. In H. W. Reese & L. P. Lipsitt (Eds.), *Advances in child development and behavior,* Vol. 13. New York: Academic Press.

Steinmetz, J. L., Lewinsohn, P. M., & Antonuccio, D. O. (1983). Prediction of individual outcome in a group intervention for depression. *Journal of Consulting and Clinical Psychology, 51,* 331–337.

Stenberg, C. R., & Campos, J. J. (1990). The development of anger expressions in infancy. In N. Stein, B. Leventhal, & T. Trabasso (Eds.), *Psychological and biological approaches to emotion.* Hillsdale, NJ: Erlbaum.

Stenberg, C. R., Campos, J. J., & Emde, R. N. (1983). The facial expression of anger in 7-month-old infants. *Child Development 54,* 178–184.

Stephan, W. G., & Rosenfield, D. (1978). Effects of desegregation on racial attitudes. *Journal of Personality and Social Psychology, 36,* 795–804.

Steriade, M. (1992). Cited in Blakeslee, S. (1992, January 7). Scientists unraveling chemistry of dreams. *The New York Times,* pp. C1, C10.

Stericker, A., & LeVesconte, S. (1982). Effect of brief training on sex-related differences in visual-spatial skill. *Journal of Personality and Social Psychology, 43,* 1018–1029.

Stern, L. (1985). *The structures and strategies of human memory.* Homewood, IL: Dorsey Press.

Sternberg, R. J. (1979, September) Stalking the IQ quark. *Psychology Today,* pp. 42–54.

Sternberg, R. J. (1982, April). Who's intelligent? *Psychology Today,* pp. 30–39.

Sternberg, R. J. (1985). *Beyond IQ: A triarchic theory of human intelligence.* New York: Cambridge University Press.

Sternberg, R. J., Conway, B. E., Ketron, J. L., & Bernstein, M. (1981). People's conception of intelligence. *Journal of Personality and Social Psychology, 41,* 37–55.

Sternberg, R. J. (1986). A triangular theory of love. *Psychological Review, 93,* 119–135.

Sternberg, R. J. (1988). Triangulating love. In R. J. Sternberg & M. J. Barnes (Eds.), *The psychology of love.* New Haven, CT: Yale University Press.

Stevenson, H. W., Lee, S. Y., & Stigler, J. W. (1986). Mathematics achievement of Chinese, Japanese, and American children. *Science, 231,* 693–699.

Stevenson, R. W. (1991, November 8). Magic Johnson ends his career, saying he has AIDS infection. *The New York Times,* pp. A1, B12.

Stewart, J. E., II. (1980). Defendant's attractiveness as a factor in the outcome of criminal trials: An observational study. *Journal of Applied Social Psychology, 10,* 348–361.

Stier, D. S., & Hall, J. A. (1984). Gender differences in touch: An empirical and theoretical review. *Journal of Personality and Social Psychology, 47,* 440–459.

Stillman, M. J. (1977). Women's health beliefs about cancer and breast self-examination. *Nursing Research, 26,* 121–127.

Stokols, D. (1992). Establishing and maintaining healthy environments: Toward a social ecology of health promotion. *American Psychologist, 47,* 6–22.

Stone, A. A., & Neale, J. M. (1984). Effects of severe daily events on mood. *Journal of Personality and Social Psychology, 46,* 137–144.

Storandt, M. (1983). Psychology's response to the graying of America. *American Psychologist, 38,* 323–326.

Storms, M. D. (1980). Theories of sexual orientation. *Journal of Personality and Social Psychology, 38,* 783–792.

Strack, F., Martin, L. L., & Stepper, S. (1988). Inhibiting and facilitating conditions of the human smile: A nonobtrusive test of the facial feedback hypothesis. *Journal of Personality and Social Psychology, 54,* 768–777.

Stretch, R. H. (1986). Posttraumatic stress disorder among Vietnam and Vietnam-era veterans. In C. R. Figley (Ed.), *Trauma and its wake: Vol. 2. Traumatic stress theory, research, and intervention.* New York: Brunner/Mazel.

Stretch, R. H. (1987). Posttraumatic stress disorder among U.S. army reservists: Reply to Nezu and Carnevale. *Journal of Consulting and Clinical Psychology, 55,* 272–273.

Stricker, G. (1991). Ethical concerns in alcohol research. *Journal of Consulting and Clinical Psychology, 59,* 256–257.

Strickland, B. (1991). Cited in DeAngelis, T. Hearing pinpoints gaps in research on women. *APA Monitor,* p. 8.

Strober, M. (1986). Anorexia nervosa: History and psychological concepts. In K. D. Brownell & J. P. Foreyt (Eds.), *Handbook of eating disorders.* New York: Basic Books.

Strom, J. C., & Buck, R. W. (1979). Staring and participants' sex: Physiological and subjective reactions. *Personality and Social Psychology Bulletin, 5,* 114–117.

Strube, M. J., Berry, J. M., Goza, B. K., & Fennimore, D. (1985). Type A-behavior, age, and psychological well being. *Journal of Personality and Social Psychology, 49,* 203–218.

Strube, M. J., & Werner, C. (1985). Relinquishment of control and the Type-A behavior pattern. *Journal of Personality and Social Psychology, 48,* 688–701.

Strupp, H. H. (1990). Rejoinder to Arnold Lazarus. *American Psychologist, 45,* 671–672.

Stunkard, A. J., Harris, J. R., Pedersen, N. L., & McLearn, G. E. (1990). A separated twin study of the body mass index. *New England Journal of Medicine, 322,* 1483–1487.

Sue, S. (1988). Psychotherapeutic services for ethnic minorities: Two decades of research findings. *American Psychologist, 43,* 301–308.

Sue, S., & Okazaki, S. (1990). Asian-American educational achievements. *American Psychologist, 45,* 913–920.

Suler, J. R. (1985). Meditation and somatic arousal: A comment on Holmes's review. *American Psychologist, 40,* 717.

Suls, J., & Fletcher, B. (1985). The relative efficacy of avoidant and nonavoidant coping strategies: A meta-analysis. *Health Psychology, 4,* 249–288.

Suls, J., & Wan, C. K. (1989). The effects of sensory and procedural information on coping with stressful medical procedures and pain: A meta-analysis. *Journal of Consulting and Clinical Psychology, 57,* 372–379.

Sunday, S., & Lewin, M. (1985). Integrating nuclear issues into the psychology curriculum. Paper presented to the meeting of the Eastern Psychological Association.

Sweeney, P. D., & Gruber, K. L. (1984). Selective exposure: Voter information preferences and the Watergate affair. *Journal of Personality and Social Psychology, 46,* 1208–1221.

Symons, D. (1979). *The evolution of human sexuality.* New York: Oxford University Press.

Szasz, T. S. (1984). *The therapeutic state: Psychiatry in the mirror of current events.* Buffalo: Prometheus.

Szmukler, G. I., & Russell, G. F. M. (1986). Outcome and prognosis of anorexia nervosa. In K. D. Brownell & J. P. Foreyt (Eds.), *Handbook of eating disorders.* New York: Basic Books.

Szucko, J. J., & Kleinmuntz, B. (1981). Statistical versus clinical lie detection. *American Psychologist, 36,* 488–496.

T

Tanford, S., & Penrod, S. (1984). Social influence model: A formal integration of research on majority and minority influence processes. *Psychological Bulletin, 95,* 189–225.

Tavris, C., & Sadd, S. (1977). *The Redbook report on female sexuality.* New York: Delacorte.

Taylor, C. B. (1977). Relaxation therapy and high blood pressure. *Archives of General Psychiatry, 34,* 339–343.

Taylor, S. E. (1983). Adjustment to threatening events: A theory of cognitive adaptation. *American Psychologist, 38,* 1161–1173.

Taylor, S. E. (1990). Health psychology: The science and the field. *American Psychologist, 45,* 40–50.

Taylor, S. P., & Sears, J. D. (1988). The effects of alcohol and persuasive social pressure on human physical aggression. *Aggressive Behavior, 14,* 237–243.

Taylor, W. N. (1985). Super athletes made to order. *Psychology Today, 19*(5), pp. 62–66.

Telch, C. F., & Telch, M. J. (1986). Group coping skills instruction and supportive group therapy for cancer patients: A comparison of strategies. *Journal of Consulting and Clinical Psychology, 54,* 802–808.

Télégdy, G. (1977). Prenatal androgenization of primates

and humans. In J. Money & H. Musaph (Eds.), *Handbook of sexology.* Amsterdam: Excerpta Medica.

Tellegen, A. (1988). Personality similarity in twins reared apart and together. *Journal of Personality and Social Psychology, 54,* 1031–1039.

Teri, L., & Wagner, A. (1992). Alzheimer's disease and depression. *Journal of Consulting and Clinical Psychology, 60,* 379–391.

Terkel, J., & Rosenblatt, J. S. (1972). Humoral factors underlying maternal behavior at parturition: Cross transfusion between freely moving rats. *Journal of Comparative and Physiological Psychology, 80,* 365–371.

Terrace, H. S. (1987). *Nim,* 2d ed. New York: Knopf.

Tesser, A., Campbell, J., & Smith, M. (1984). Friendship choice and performance: Self-evaluation maintenance in children. *Journal of Personality and Social Psychology, 46,* 561–574.

Tharp, R. G. (1991). Cultural diversity and treatment of children. *Journal of Consulting and Clinical Psychology, 59,* 799–812.

Thigpen, C. H., & Cleckley, H. M. (1984). On the incidence of multiple personality disorder. *International Journal of Clinical and Experimental Hypnosis, 32,* 63–66.

Thoits, P. A. (1983). Dimensions of life events as influences upon the genesis of psychological distress and associated conditions: An evaluation and synthesis of the literature. In H. B. Kaplan (Ed.), *Psychosocial stress: Trends in theory and research.* New York: Academic Press.

Thomas, M. H., Horton, R. W., Lippincott, E. C., & Drabman, R. S. (1977). Desensitization to portrayals of real-life aggression as a function of exposure to television violence. *Journal of Personality and Social Psychology, 35,* 450–458.

Thomas, R. M. (1991, April 10). Bucks too big, a majority tells poll. *The New York Times,* p. B7.

Thompson, C. P., & Cowan, T. (1986). The neurobiology of learning and memory. *Science, 233,* 941–947.

Thompson, L. (1991, January, 15). Health status of Hispanics: Nation's fastest-growing minority lacks access to medical care. *The Washington Post.*

Thompson, P. D. (1982). Cardiovascular hazards of physical activity. *Exercise and Sport Sciences Reviews, 10,* 208–235.

Thompson, S. (1988, August). An intervention to increase physician-patient communication. Paper presented to the American Psychological Association, Atlanta.

Thompson, T. (1988). *Benedictus* behavior analysis: B. F. Skinner's magnum opus at fifty. *Contemporary Psychology, 33,* 397–402.

Thompson, W. C., Cowan, C. L., & Rosenhan, D. L. (1980). Focus of attention mediates the impact of negative affect on altruism. *Journal of Personality and Social Psychology, 38,* 291–300.

Thoresen, C., & Powell, L. H. (1992). Type A-behavior pattern: New perspectives on theory, assessment, and intervention. *Journal of Consulting and Clinical Psychology, 60,* 595–604.

Thornton, D., & Reid, R. L. (1982). Moral reasoning and type of criminal offense. *British Journal of Social Psychology, 21,* 231–238.

Thurstone, L. L. (1938). Primary mental abilities. *Psychometric Monographs, 1.*

Thurstone, L. L., & Thurstone, T. G. (1963). *SRA primary abilities.* Chicago: SRA.

Tobias, S. (1982, January). Sexist equations. *Psychology Today,* pp. 14–17.

Tolchin, M. (1989, July, 19). When long life is too much: Suicide rises among elderly. *The New York Times,* pp. A1, A15.

Tolman, E. C., & Honzik, C. H. (1930). Introduction and removal of reward, and maze performance in rats. *University of California Publications in Psychology, 4,* 257–275.

Tolstedt, B., & Stokes, J. (1983). Relation of verbal, affective, and physical intimacy to marital satisfaction. *Journal of Counseling Psychology, 30,* 573–580.

Torgersen, S. (1983). Genetic factors in anxiety disorders. *Archives of General Psychiatry, 40,* 1085–1089.

Toufexis, A., Garcia, C., & Kalb, B. (1986, January 20). Dieting: The losing game. *Time,* pp. 54–60.

Trull, T. J. (1992). *DSM–III–R* personality disorders and the five-factor model of personality. *Journal of Abnormal Psychology, 101,* 553–560.

Tryon, R. C. (1940). Genetic differences in maze learning in rats. *Yearbook of the National Society for Studies in Education, 39,* 111–119.

Tulving, E. (1972). Episodic and semantic memory. In E. Tulving & W. Donaldson (Eds.), *Organization of memory.* New York: Academic Press.

Tulving, E. (1974). Cue-dependent forgetting. *American Scientist, 62,* 74–82.

Tulving, E. (1982). *Elements of episodic memory.* New York: Oxford University Press.

Tulving, E. (1985). How many memory systems are there? *American Psychologist, 40,* 385–398.

Turk, D. C., Meichenbaum, D., & Genest, M. (1983). *Pain and behavioral medicine: A cognitive behavioral perspective.* New York: Guilford Press.

Turkington, C. (1983,). Drugs found to block dopamine receptors. *APA Monitor,* p. 11.

Turkington, C. (1984,). Hormones in rats found to control sexual behavior. *APA Monitor,* pp. 40–41.

Turkington, C. (1985,). Taste inhibitors. *APA Monitor,* p. 3.

Turnbull, C. M. (1961). Notes and discussion: Some observations regarding the experiences and behavior of the Bambute pygmies. *American Journal of Psychology, 7,* 304–308.

Turner, A. M., Greenough, W. T. (1985). Differential rearing effects on rat visual cortex synapses: I. Synaptic and neuronal density and synapses per neuron. *Brain Research, 329,* 195–203.

Turner, J. A., & Chapman, C. R. (1982a). Psychological interventions for chronic pain: A critical review: I. Relaxation training and biofeedback. *Pain, 12,* 1–21.

Turner, J. A., & Chapman, C. R. (1982b). Psychological interventions for chronic pain: A critical review: II. Operant conditioning, hypnosis, and cognitive-behavior therapy. *Pain, 12,* 23–46.

Turner, S. M. (1987). Psychopathology in the offspring of anxiety disorders patients. *Journal of Consulting and Clinical Psychology, 55,* 229–235.

Turner, J. W., Jr. (1987). Effects of biobehaviorally assisted relaxation training on blood pressure and hormone levels and their variation in normotensives and essential hypertensives. Paper presented at the 4th Internation Conference on REST, Toledo, OH.

Tversky, A., & Kahneman, D. (1974). Judgment under uncertainty: Heuristics and biases. *Science, 185,* 1124–1131.

Tzuriel, D. (1984). Sex role typing and ego identity in Israeli, Oriental, and Western adolescents. *Journal of Personality and Social Psychology, 46,* 440–457.

U

Ugwuegbu, D. C. E. (1979). Racial and evidential factors in juror attribution of legal responsibility. *Journal of Experimental Social Psychology, 15,* 133–146.

Underwood, B., & Moore, B. S. (1981). Sources of behavioral consistency. *Journal of Personality and Social Psychology, 40,* 780–785.

Unger, R. K., Hilderbrand, M., & Madar, T. (1982). Physical attractiveness and assumptions about social deviance: Some sex-by-sex comparisons. *Personality and Social Psychology Bulletin, 8,* 293–301.

USBC (U.S. Bureau of the Census). (1985). *Statistical abstract of the United States,* 105th ed. Washington, DC: U.S. Government Printing Office.

USBC (U.S. Bureau of the Census). (1990). *Statistical abstract of the United States,* 110th ed. Washington, DC: U.S. Government Printing Office.

U.S. Congress (1983, November). *Scientific validity of polygraph testing: A research review and evaluation* (OTA-TM-H-15). Washington, DC: Office of Technology Assessment.

U.S. Department of Health, Education, and Welfare. (1979). *Smoking and health: A report of the Surgeon General.* (DHEW Publication No. 79-50066). Washington, DC: U.S. Government Printing Office.

U.S. Department of Health and Human Services (1984). *The 1984 report of the Joint National Committee on Detection, Evaluation, and Treatment of High Blood Pressure.* (DHHS Publication No. NIH: 84-1088). Washington, DC: U.S. Government Printing Office.

U.S. Department of Health and Human Services (1991, June). *Environmental tobacco smoke in the workplace* (DHHS Publication No. 91-108). Cincinnati, OH: Centers for Disease Control, National Institute for Occupational Safety and Health.

V

Vaillant, G. E. (1982). *The natural history of alcoholism.* Cambridge, MA: Harvard University Press.

Vaillant, G. E., & Milofsky, E. S. (1982). The etiology of alcoholism. *American Psychologist, 37,* 494–503.

Valenstein, E. S. (1978, July). Science-fiction fantasy and the brain. *Psychology Today, 12*(7), 28–39.

Valenstein, E. S. (1980). *The psychosurgery debate.* San Francisco: W. H. Freeman.

Valenstein, E. S. (1986). *Great and desperate cures: The rise and decline of psychosurgery and other radical treatments for mental illness.* New York: Basic Books.

Vallis, M., McCabe, S. B., & Shaw, B. F. (1986, June). The relationships between therapist skill in cognitive therapy and general therapy skill. Paper presented to the Society for Psychotherapy Research, Wellesley, MA.

Vance, M. L. (1990). Cited in Angier, N. (1990, July 5). Human growth hormone reverses effects of aging. *The New York Times,* pp. A1, B6.

Vandenberg, S. G., Singer, S. M., & Pauls, D. L. (1986). *The heredity of behavior disorders in adults and children.* New York: Plenum Press.

Van der Pligt, J., & Eiser, J. R. (1983). Actors' and observers' attributions, self-serving bias, and positivity bias. *European Journal of Social Psychology, 13,* 95–104.

Van Dyke, C., & Byck, R. (1982). Cocaine. *Scientific American, 44*(3), 128–141.

Van Itallie, T. B. (1985). Health implications of overweight and obesity in the United States. *Annals of Internal Medicine, 103,* 983–988.

Van Toller, C., Dodd, G. H., & Billing, A. (1985). *Aging and the sense of smell.* Springfield, IL: Charles C Thomas.

Velicer, W. F., DiClemente, C. C., Prochaska, J. O., & Brandenburg, N. (1985). Decisional balance measure for predicting smoking status. *Journal of Personality and Social Psychology, 48,* 1279–1289.

Verbrugge, L. M. (1983). Multiple roles and physical health of women and men. *Journal of Health and Social Behavior, 24,* 16–30.

Vestre, N. D. (1984). Irrational beliefs and self-reported depressed mood. *Journal of Abnormal Psychology, 93,* 239–241.

Visintainer, M. A., Volpicelli, J. R., & Seligman, M. E. P. (1982). Tumor rejection in rats after inescapable or escapable shock. *Science, 216*(23), 437–439.

Vogler, G. P., DeFries, J. C., & Decker, S. N. (1985). Family history as an indicator of risk for reading disability. *Journal of Learning Disabilities, 18,* 419–421.

Von Békésy, G. (1957, August). The ear. *Scientific American,* 66–78.

W

Waber, D. P., Mann, M. B., Merola, J., & Moylan, P. M. (1985). Physical maturation rate and cognitive performance in early adolescence: A longitudinal examination. *Developmental Psychology, 21,* 666–681.

Wachtel, P. L. (1982). What can dynamic therapies contribute to behavior therapy? *Behavior Therapy, 13,* 594–609.

Wagner, R. K., & Sternberg, R. J. (1985). Practical intelligence in real-world pursuits: The role of tacit knowledge. *Journal of Personality and Social Psychology, 49,* 436–458.

Wagner, R. K., & Torgesen, J. K. (1987). The nature of phonological processing and its causal role in the acquisition of reading skills. *Psychological Bulletin, 101,* 192–212.

Walker, A. M., Rablen, R. A., & Rogers, C. R. (1960). Development of a scale to measure process changes in psychotherapy. *Journal of Clinical Psychology, 16,* 79–85.

Walker, B. B. (1983). Treating stomach disorders: Can we reinstate regulatory processes? In W. E. Whitehead &

R. Holzl (Eds.), *Psychophysiology of the gastrointestinal tract.* New York: Plenum Publishing Co.

Walker, L. J. (1984). Sex differences in the development of moral reasoning: A critical review. *Child Development, 55,* 677–691.

Walker, W. B., & Franzini, L. R. (1985). Low-risk aversive group treatments, physiological feedback, and booster treatments for smoking cessation. *Behavior Therapy, 16,* 263–274.

Wallington, S. A. (1973). Consequences of transgression: Self-punishment and depression. *Journal of Personality and Social Psychology, 29,* 1–7.

Wallston, B. S., & Wallston, K. A. (1984). Social psychological models of health behavior: An examination and integration. In A. Baum, S. E. Taylor, & J. E. Singer (Eds.), *Handbook of psychology and health: Vol. 4. Social psychological aspects of health.* Hillsdale, NJ: Erlbaum.

Walsh, B. T. (1984). Treatment of bulimia with phenelzine: A double-blind, placebo-controlled study. *Archives of General Psychiatry, 41,* 1105–1109.

Walsh, J. (1990, December 2). Asian women, Caucasian men. *The San Francisco Examiner, Image Magazine.*

Walstedt, J. J., Geis, F. L., & Brown, V. (1980). Influence of television commercials on women's self-confidence and independent judgment. *Journal of Personality and Social Psychology, 38,* 203–210.

Walster, E., Aronson, E., & Abrahams, D. (1966a). On increasing the persuasiveness of a low-prestige communicator. *Journal of Experimental Social Psychology, 2,* 325–342.

Walster, E., Aronson, E., Abrahams, D., & Rottman, L. (1966b). Importance of physical attractiveness in dating behavior. *Journal of Personality and Social Psychology, 4,* 508–516.

Wardlaw, G. M., & Insel, P. M. (1990). *Perspectives in nutrition.* St. Louis: Times Mirror/Mosby College Publishing.

Watkins, M. J., Ho, E., & Tulving, E. (1976). Context effects on recognition memory for faces. *Journal of Verbal Learning and Verbal Behavior, 15,* 505–518.

Watson, J. B. (1913). Psychology as the behaviorist views it. *Psychological Review, 20,* 158–177.

Watson, J. B. (1924). *Behaviorism.* New York: Norton.

Watson, J. B., & Rayner, R. (1920). Conditioned emotional reactions. *Journal of Experimental Psychology, 3,* 1–14.

Watt, N. F., Grubb, T. W., & Erlenmeyer-Kimling, L. (1982). Social, emotional, and intellectual behavior among children at high risk for schizophrenia. *Journal of Consulting and Clinical Psychology, 50,* 171–181.

Weber, R., & Crocker, J. (1983). Cognitive processes in the revision of stereotypic beliefs. *Journal of Personality and Social Psychology, 45,* 961–977.

Wechsler, D. (1975). Intelligence defined and undefined: A relativistic appraisal. *American Psychologist, 30,* 135–139.

Weekes, J. R., Lynn, S. J., Green, J. P., & Brentar, J. T. (1992). Pseudomemory in hypnotized and task-motivated subjects. *Journal of Abnormal Psychology, 101,* 356–360.

Wegner, D. M. (1979). Hidden Brain Damage Scale. *American Psychologist, 34,* 192–193.

Weidner, G., Istvan, J., & McKnight, J. D. (1989). Clusters of behavioral coronary risk factors in employed women and men. *Journal of Applied Social Psychology, 19,* 468–480.

Weinberg, J., & Levine, S. (1980). Psychobiology of coping in animals: The effects of predictability. In S. Levine & H. Ursin (Eds.), *Coping and health.* New York: Plenum Publishing Co.

Weinberg, R. S., Yukelson, S., & Jackson, A. (1980). Effect of public and private efficacy expectations on competitive performance. *Journal of Sport Psychology, 2,* 340–349.

Weinberg, S. L., & Richardson, M. S. (1981). Dimensions of stress in early parenting. *Journal of Consulting and Clinical Psychology, 49,* 688–693.

Weiner, B. (1991). Metaphors in motivation and attribution. *American Psychologist, 46,* 921–930.

Weiner, K. (1992). Cited in Goleman, D. J. (1992, January 8). Heart seizure or panic attack? Disorder is a terrifying mimic. *The New York Times,* p. C12.

Weiner, M. J., & Wright, F. E. (1973). Effects of undergoing arbitrary discrimination upon subsequent attitudes toward a minority group. *Journal of Applied Social Psychology, 3,* 94–102.

Weinraub, M., & Wolf, B. M. (1983). Effects of stress and social supports on mother-child interactions in single- and two-parent families. *Child Development, 54,* 1297–1311.

Weinstein, N. D. (1980). Unrealistic optimism about future life events. *Journal of Personality and Social Psychology, 39,* 806–820.

Weinstein, N. D. (1984). Why it won't happen to me: Perceptions of risk factors and susceptibility. *Health Psychology, 3,* 431–457.

Weintraub, S. (1987). Risk factors in schizophrenia: The Stony Brook high-risk project. *Schizophrenia Bulletin, 13,* 439–450.

Weiss, J. M. (1972). Psychological factors in stress and disease. *Scientific American, 226*(6), 104–113.

Weiss, J. M., Glazer, H. I., & Pohorecky, L. A. (1976). Coping behavior and neurochemical changes: An alternative explanation for the original "learned helplessness" experiments. In G. Serban & A. Kling (Eds.), *Animal models of human psychobiology.* New York: Plenum Publishing Co.

Weisse, C. S. (1992). Depression and immunocompetence: A review of the literature. *Psychological Bulletin, 11,* 475–489.

Weissman, M. (1981). Depressed outpatients. Results one year after treatment with drugs and/or interpersonal psychotherapy. *Archives of General Psychology, 18,* 51–55.

Wells, G. L., & Luus, C. A. E. (1990). Police lineups as experiments: Social methodology as a framework for properly conducted lineups. *Personality and Social Psychology Bulletin, 16,* 106–117.

Werner, C. M., Brown, B. B., & Damron, G. (1981). Territorial marking in a game arcade. *Journal of Personality and Social Psychology, 41,* 1094–1104.

Werth, B. (1991, June 16). How short is too short? *The New York Times Magazine,* pp. 14–18, 28–29, 47.

West, M. A. (1985). Meditation and somatic arousal reduction. *American Psychologist, 40,* 717–719.

Wetzler, S. E., & Sweeney, J. A. (1986). Childhood amnesia. In D. C. Rubin (Ed.), *Autobiographical memory.* New York: Cambridge University Press.

Wexler, D. A., & Butler, J. M. (1976). Therapist modification of client expressiveness in client-centered therapy. *Journal of Consulting and Clinical Psychology, 44,* 261–265.

Whalen, C. K., & Henker, B. (1991). Therapies for hyperactive children: Comparisons, combinations, and compromises. *Journal of Consulting and Clinical Psychology, 59,* 126–137.

Whisman, M. A., Miller, I. W., Norman, W. H., & Keitner, G. I. (1991). Cognitive therapy with depressed inpatients: Specific effects on dysfunctional cognitions. *Journal of Consulting and Clinical Psychology, 59,* 282–288.

White, J. L., & Nicassio, P. M. (1990, November). The relationship between daily stress, pre-sleep arousal and sleep disturbance in good and poor sleepers. Paper presented at the annual meeting of the Association for the Advancement of Behavior Therapy. San Francisco.

Whorf, B. (1956). *Language, thought, and reality.* New York: Wiley.

Widiger, T. A. (1990, August/September). Antisocial personality disorder. In American Psychiatric Association, *DSM-IV Update.* Washington, DC: American Psychiatric Association.

Widiger, T. A. (1991). Toward an empirical classification for the *DSM-IV. Journal of Abnormal Psychology, 100,* 280–288.

Widom, C. S. (1991, June). Cited in Freiberg, P. More long-term problems seen for abused kids. *APA Monitor,* pp. 18–19.

Wiens, A. N., & Menustik, C. E. (1983). Treatment outcome and patient characteristics in an aversion therapy program for alcoholism. *American Psychologist, 38,* 1089–1096.

Wilcox, B. L. (1981). Social support, life stress, and psychological adjustment. *American Journal of Community Psychology, 9*(4), 371–386.

Wilder, D. A. (1986). Social categorization: Implications for creation and reduction of intergroup bias. In L. Berkowitz (Ed.), *Advances in experimental social psychology.* Orlando, FL: Academic Press.

Willerman, L. (1977). *The psychology of individual and group differences.* San Francisco: Freeman.

Willett, W. C., & MacMahon, B. (1984). Diet and cancer—an overview. *The New England Journal of Medicine, 310,* 633–638.

Willett, W. C. (1990). Relation of meat, fat, and fiber intake to the risk of colon cancer in a prospective study among women. *The New England Journal of Medicine, 323,* 1664–1672.

Williams, J. G., & Solano, C. H. (1983). The social reality of feeling lonely: Friendship and reciprocation. *Personality and Social Psychology Bulletin, 9,* 237–242.

Williams, R. L. (1974,). Scientific racism and IQ: The silent mugging of the black community. *Psychology Today.*

Williams, R. M., Goldman, M. S., & Williams, D. L. (1981). Expectancy and pharmacological effects of alcohol on human cognitive and motor performance: The compensation for alcohol effect. *Journal of Abnormal Psychology, 90,* 267–270.

Williamson, D. F. (1991). Smoking cessation and severity of weight gain in a national cohort. *The New England Journal of Medicine, 324,* 739–745.

Wills, T. A. (1986). Stress and coping in adolescence: Relationships to substance use in urban school samples. *Health Psychology, 5,* 503–530.

Wilson, G. L. (1991). Comment: Transgenerational patterns of suicide attempt. *Journal of Consulting and Clinical Psychology, 59,* 869–873.

Wilson, G. T. (1982). Psychotherapy process and procedure: The behavioral mandate. *Behavior Therapy, 13,* 291–312.

Wilson, G. T., Leaf, R. C., & Nathan, P. E. (1975). The aversive control of excessive alcohol consumption by chronic alcoholics in the laboratory setting. *Journal of Applied Behavior Analysis, 8,* 13–26.

Wilson, G. T., & Walsh, T. (1991). Eating disorders in the *DSM-IV. Journal of Abnormal Psychology, 100,* 362–365.

Wilson, K. G. (1991). Effects of instructional set on self-reports of panic attacks. *Journal of Anxiety Disorders, 5,* 43–63.

Wilson, K. G. (1992). Panic attacks in the nonclinical population: An empirical approach to case identification. *Journal of Abnormal Psychology, 101,* 460–468.

Wilson, R. S. (1983). The Louisville twin study: Developmental synchronies in behavior. *Child Development, 54,* 298–316.

Wilson, T. D., & Linville, P. W. (1982). Improving the performance of college freshmen: Attribution therapy revisited. *Journal of Personality and Social Psychology, 42,* 367–376.

Wing, R. R., Epstein, L. H., & Shapira, B. (1982). The effect of increasing initial weight loss with the Scarsdale diet on subsequent weight loss in a behavioral treatment program. *Journal of Consulting and Clinical Psychology, 50,* 446–447.

Wingard, D. L., Berkman, L. F., & Brand, R. J. (1982). A multivariate analysis of health-related practices: A nine-year mortality follow-up of the Alameda County Study. *American Journal of Epidemiology, 116,* 765–775.

Winson, J. (1992). Cited in Blakeslee, S. (1992, January 7). Scientists unraveling chemistry of dreams. *The New York Times,* pp. C1, C10.

Winterbottom, M. (1958). The relation of need for achievement to learning experiences in independence and mastery. In J. Atkinson (Ed.), *Motives in fantasy, action, and society.* Princeton, NJ: Van Nostrand.

Wirtz, P. W., & Harrell, A. V. (1987). Effects of postassault exposure to attack-similar stimuli on long-term recovery of victims. *Journal of Consulting and Clinical Psychology, 55,* 10–16.

Wittig, M. A. (1985). Metatheoretical dilemmas in the psychology of gender. *American Psychologist, 40,* 800–811.

Wlodkowski, R. J. (1982). Making sense out of motivation. *Educational Psychologist, 16,* 101–110.

Wolf, S., & Bugaj, A. M. (1990). The social impact of courtroom witnesses. *Social Behaviour, 5,* 1–13.

Wolfe, L. (1981). *The Cosmo report.* New York: Arbor House.

Wolinsky, J. (1982,). Responsibility can delay aging. *APA Monitor,* pp. 14, 41.

Wolpe, J. (1958). *Psychotherapy by reciprocal inhibition.* Stanford, CA: Stanford University Press.

Wolpe, J. (1985). Existential problems and behavior therapy. *The Behavior Therapist, 8*(7), 126–127.

Wolpe, J. (1990). *The practice of behavior therapy,* 4th ed. New York: Pergamon Press.

Wolpe, J., & Lazarus, A. A. (1966). *Behavior therapy techniques.* New York: Pergamon Press.

Wolpe, J., & Rachman, S. (1960). Psychoanalytic "evidence": A critique based on Freud's case of Little Hans. *Journal of Nervous and Mental Disease, 131,* 135–147.

Wolraich, M. L. (1990). Stimulant medication use by primary care physicians in the treatment of attention-deficit hyperactivity disorder. *Pediatrics, 86,* 95–101.

Women's Programs Office. (1988). *Women in the American Psychological Association.* Washington, DC: American Psychological Association.

Wong, P. K. H. (1991). *Introduction to brain topography.* New York: Plenum.

Wood, J. M., & Bootzin, R. R. (1990). The prevalence of nightmares and their independence from anxiety. *Journal of Abnormal Psychology, 99,* 64–68.

Wood, J. M., Bootzin, R. R., Rosenhan, D., Nolen-Hoeksema, S., & Jourden, F. (1992). Effects of the 1989 San Francisco earthquake on frequency and content of nightmares. *Journal of Abnormal Psychology, 101,* 219–224.

Wood, P. D. (1991). The effects on plasma lipoproteins of a prudent weight-reducing diet, with or without exercise, in overweight men and women. *The New England Journal of Medicine, 325,* 461–466.

Wood, W. (1982). Retrieval of attitude-relevant information from memory: Effects on susceptibility to persuasion and on intrinsic motivation. *Journal of Personality and Social Psychology, 42,* 798–810.

Wood, W., & Eagly, A. H. (1981). Steps in the positive analysis of causal attributions and message comprehension. *Journal of Personality and Social Psychology, 40,* 246–259.

Woods, S. W. (1987). Situational panic attacks: Behavioral, physiologic, and biochemical characterization. *Archives of General Psychiatry, 44,* 365–375.

Woolfolk, R. L., & McNulty, T. F. (1983). Relaxation treatment for insomnia: A component analysis. *Journal of Consulting and Clinical Psychology, 51,* 495–503.

Worchel, S., & Brown, E. H. (1984). The role of plausibility in influencing environmental attributions. *Journal of Experimental Social Psychology, 20,* 86–96.

Wright, J. C., & Huston, A. C. (1983). A matter of form: Potentials of television for young viewers. *American Psychologist, 38,* 835–843.

Wu, C., & Shaffer, C. R. (1987). Susceptibility to persuasive appeals as a function of source credibility and prior experience with the attitude object. *Journal of Personality and Social Psychology, 52,* 677–688.

Wyatt, G. E. (1989). Re-examining factors predicting Afro-American and white American women's age at first coitus. *Archives of Sexual Behavior, 18,* 271–298.

Wyatt, G. E. (1990). The aftermath of child sexual abuse of African-American and White American Women: The victim's experience. *Journal of Family Violence, 5,* 61–81.

Wyatt, G. E., & Lyons-Rowe, S. (1990). African-American women's sexual satisfaction as a dimension of their sex roles. *Sex Roles, 22,* 509–524.

Wyatt, G. E., & Newcomb, M. (1990). Internal and external mediators of women's sexual abuse in childhood. *Journal of Consulting and Clinical Psychology, 58,* 758–767.

Wyatt, G. E., Notgrass, C. M., & Newcomb, M. (1990). Internal and external mediators of women's rape experiences. *Psychology of Women Quarterly, 14,* 153–176.

Wyatt, G. E., Peters, S. D., & Guthrie, D. (1988a). Kinsey revisited, Part I: Comparisons of the sexual socialization and sexual behavior of white women over 33 years. *Archives of Sexual Behavior, 17, 3,* 201–209.

Wyatt, G. E., Peters, S. D., & Guthrie, D. (1988b). Kinsey revisited, Part II: Comparisons of the sexual socialization and sexual behavior of black women over 33 years. *Archives of Sexual Behavior, 17, 4,* 289–332.

Wyer, R. S., Jr. (1988). Social memory and social judgment. In P. R. Solomon et al. (Eds.), *Perspectives on memory research.* New York: Springer-Verlag.

Wynne, L. C., Cole, R. E., & Perkins, P. (1987). University of Rochester child and family study: Risk research in progress. *Schizophrenia Bulletin, 13,* 463–476.

Y

Yamamoto, J. (1986). Therapy for Asian Americans and Pacific Islanders. In C. B. Wilkinson (Ed.), *Ethnic psychiatry.* New York: Academic Press.

Yarmey, D. A. (1986). Verbal, visual, and voice identification of a rape suspect under different levels of illumination. *Journal of Applied Psychology, 71,* 363–370.

Yarnold, P. R., & Grimm, L. G. (1982). Time urgency among coronary-prone individuals. *Journal of Abnormal Psychology, 91,* 175–177.

Yates, A. (1983). Running—An analogue of anorexia? *New England Journal of Medicine, 308,* 251–255.

Yeates, K. O., MacPhee, D., Campbell, F. A., & Ramey, C. T. (1983). Maternal IQ and home environment as determinants of early childhood intellectual competence: A developmental analysis. *Developmental Psychology, 19,* 731–739.

Ying, Y. (1988). Depressive symptomatology among Chinese-Americans as measured by the CES-D. *Journal of Clinical Psychology, 44,* 739–746.

Yonas, A., Granrud, C. E., & Pettersen, L. (1985). Infants' sensitivity to relative size information for distance. *Developmental Psychology, 21,* 161–167.

Yost, W. A., & Nielson, D. W. (1985). *Fundamentals of hearing,* 2d ed. New York: Holt, Rinehart and Winston.

Yu, B. (1985). STM capacity for Chinese and English language materials. *Memory and Cognition, 13,* 202–207.

Z

Zaiden, J. (1982). Psychodynamic therapy: Clinical applications. In A. J. Rush (Ed.), *Short-term psychotherapies for depression.* New York: Guilford Press.

Zajonc, R. B. (1965). Social facilitation. *Science, 149,* 269–274.

Zajonc, R. B. (1968). Attitudinal effects of mere exposure. *Journal of Personality and Social Psychology, Monograph Supplement 2, 9,* 1–27.

Zajonc, R. B. (1980). Compresence. In P. Paulus (Ed.), *The psychology of group influence.* Hillsdale, NJ: Erlbaum.

Zajonc, R. B. (1984). On the primacy of affect. *American Psychologist, 39,* 117–123.

Zajonc, R. B. (1985). Cited in B. Bower (1985). The face of emotion. *Science News, 128,* 12–13.

Zamansky, H. S., & Bartis, S. P. (1985). The dissociation of an experience. *Journal of Abnormal Psychology, 94,* 243–248.

Zane, N., & Sue, S. (1991). Culturally responsive mental health services for Asian Americans: Treatment and training issues. In H. F. Myers (Eds.), *Ethnic minority perspectives on clinical training and services in psychology* (pp. 49–58). Washington, D.C.: American Psychological Association.

Zatz, S., & Chassin, L. (1985). Cognitions of test-anxious children under naturalistic test-taking conditions. *Journal of Consulting and Clinical Psychology, 53,* 393–401.

Zigler, E., Abelson, W. D., Trickett, P. K., & Seitz, V. (1982). Is an intervention program necessary to improve economically disadvantaged children's IQ scores? *Child Development, 53,* 340–348.

Zigler, E., & Butterfield, E. C. (1968). Motivational aspects of change in IQ test performance of culturally deprived nursery school children. *Child Development, 39,* 1–14.

Zigler, E., Taussig, C., & Black, K. (1992). Early childhood intervention: A promising preventative for juvenile delinquency. *American Psychologist, 47,* 997–1006.

Zimbardo, P. G. (1969). The human choice: Individuation, reason, and order versus deindividuation, impulse, and chaos. In W. J. Arnold & D. Levine (Eds.), *Nebraska symposium on motivation,* Vol. 17. Lincoln, NE: University of Nebraska Press.

Zimbardo, P. G., Ebbeson, E. B., & Maslach, C. (1977). *Influencing attitudes and changing behavior.* Reading, MA: Addison-Wesley.

Zimmer, D. (1983). Interaction patterns and communication skills in sexually distressed, maritally distressed, and normal couples: Two experimental studies. *Journal of Sex and Marital Therapy, 9,* 251–265.

Zuckerman, M. (1974). The sensation-seeking motive. In B. Maher (Ed.), *Progress in experimental personality research, 7.* New York: Academic Press.

Zuckerman, M. (1980). Sensation seeking. In H. London & J. Exner (Eds.), *Dimensions of personality.* New York: Wiley.

Zuckerman, M. (1987). Cited in D. J. Goleman (1987, November 24). Teen-age risk-taking: Rise in deaths prompts new research effort. *The New York Times,* p. C17.

Zuckerman, M., Eysenck, S., & Eysenck, H. J. (1978). Sensation seeking in England and America: Cross-cultural, age, and sex comparisons. *Journal of Consulting and Clinical Psychology, 46,* 139–149.

Zuckerman, M., Klorman, R., Larrance, D. T., & Spiegel, N. H. (1981). Facial, autonomic, and subjective components of emotion. *Journal of Personality and Social Psychology, 41,* 929–944.

Zuckerman, M., Miserandino, M., & Bernieri, F. (1983). Civil inattention exists—in elevators. *Personality and Social Psychology Bulletin, 9,* 578–586.

Zuger, B. (1976). Monozygotic twins discordant for homosexuality: Report of a pair and significance of the phenomenon. *Comprehensive Psychiatry, 17,* 661–669.

Zuroff, D. C., & Mongrain, M. (1987). Dependency and self-criticism: Vulnerability factors for depressive affective states. *Journal of Abnormal Psychology, 96,* 14–22

Zyazema, N. Z. (1984). Toward better patient drug compliance and comprehension: A challenge to medical and pharmaceutical services in Zimbabwe. *Social Science and Medicine, 18,* 551–554.

PHOTO CREDITS

COVER, ii Ed Sheckman/Liaison International.

CHAPTER ONE **xxviii**: ©1992 Laurie A. Watters. **7:** ©Ray Morsch/The Stock Market. **8:** ©Ken Robert Buck/The Picture Cube. **11:** ©Archives of the History of American Psychology. **12 (top):** ©Archives of the History of American Psychology. **12 (btm):** ©Archives of the History of American Psychology. **13 (left):** ©Yale Joel/Life Picture Services. **13 (rt):** ©Animal Behavior Enterprises. **14:** ©Archives of the History of American Psychology. **15 (top):** ©SuperStock, Inc. **15 (btm):** ©Bettmann Archive. **17 (both):** ©Archives of General Psychiatry. **25 (mid):** ©Courtesy of Dr. Kenneth B. Clark. **25 (top upper left):** ©Robert Brenner/PhotoEdit. **25 (top upper right):** ©Tony Freeman/PhotoEdit. **25 (top lower left):** ©Robert Brenner/PhotoEdit. **25 (top lower right):** ©Tony Freeman/PhotoEdit. **25 (middle):** ©Archives of the History of American Psychology. **27:** ©1993 Terry Wild Studio.

CHAPTER TWO **38:** ©Laurie A. Watters. **43:** ©Courtesy University of the Fine Arts, Philadelphia. Photography: Tom Crane ©1993. **45:** ©1992 Jon Feingersh/The Stock Market. **50 (L):** ©Jane Goodall Institute. **50 (R):** ©Hugo Van Lawick/National Geographic. **51:** ©William Edward Smith. **52:** Comstock. **54:** ©Jeff Albertson/Stock, Boston.

CHAPTER THREE **68:** ©Laurie A. Watters. **71:** ©Jon Mili/Life Magazine. **78:** ©SuperStock, Inc. **82 (top):** ©Dan McCoy/Rainbow. **82 (btm):** ©Palmer/Kane, Inc./The Stock Market. **83:** ©Brookhaven National Laboratory and New York University Medical Center. **84:** ©G. Zimbel/Monkmeyer Press. **101:** ©Porterfield-Chickering/Photo Researchers, Inc.

CHAPTER FOUR **114:** ©Laurie A. Watters. **117:** ©UPI/Bettmann. **120:** ©H. Abernathy/H. Armstrong Roberts. **120:** ©David Dempster/Offshoot. **125:** ©Frank Werbin and Edward Lewis--UC. Berkeley. **128 (btm):** ©Courtesy of the Inmont Corporation. **129:** ©George Seurat, "Sunday Afternoon on the Island of La Grande Jatte," 1884–86, oil on canvas, 207.6 308.0 cm, Helen Birch Bartlett Memorial Collection, 1926.224. **132:** The Psychological Corporation. **133:** ©Man Ray/Museum of Modern Art. **134:** ©Courtesy of the Escher Estate. **137 (top):** ©Abe Rezny/The Image Works. **137 (btm):** ©Courtesy of New York Stock Exchange. **138 (L):** ©Courtesy of the Escher Estate. **138 (R):** ©Hogarth/Bettman Archive. **139:** ©Art Resource, NY/Vasarely, Vega Tek, wool Aubosson tapestry, 1969. Private collection. **140:** ©David Dempster/Offshoot. **149:** ©David Dempster/Offshoot. **153:** ©Andy Levin/Photo Researchers, Inc.

CHAPTER FIVE **154:** ©Richard Steedman/The Stock Market. **167:** ©Fred Boden/Offshoot. **170:** Holt, Rinehart and Winston. **174:** ©Superstock, Inc. **176:** ©Art Resource. **180 (L):** ©David Schafer/The Picture Cube. **180 (R):** ©Tim Eagan/Woodfin Camp & Associates. **182:** ©Jane Schreibman/Photo Researchers, Inc. **184:** ©Ray Morsch/The Stock Market. **185:** ©Joel Gordon 1987. **186:** ©Used by permission of the American Cancer Society. **188:** ©Anne Marie Rousseau/The Image Works. **190:** ©Joel Gordon 1984. **191:** ©Dan McCoy/Rainbow. **192:** ©David Parker/Photo Researchers, Inc.

CHAPTER SIX **204:** ©Michal Heron/The Stock Market. **207:** ©Richard Hutchings/InfoEdit. **209:** ©Bettmann Archive. **212:** ©Susan McElhimery/Archive Photos. **214:** ©Dennis O'Clair/Tony Stone Images. **217:** ©1990 Comstock. **220:** ©Walter Dawn/Photo Researchers, Inc. **222:** ©King Features Syndicate, Inc. **224:** ©Hank Morgan/Rainbow. **226:** ©Erickson Photography. **228:** ©Tony Freeman/PhotoEdit. **232:** ©David Dempster/Offshoot.

CHAPTER SEVEN **246:** Fernando Bueno/The Image Bank. **250:** ©Yves De Braine/Black Star. **256:** ©David Dempster/Offshoot. **259:** ©Blumebild/H. Armstrong Roberts. **262:** ©George Goodwin/Monkmeyer Press. **264:** ©Rainbow/NASA. **265:** ©Russ Kinner/Photo Researchers, Inc. **272:** ©Mimi Forsyth/Monkmeyer Press.

CHAPTER EIGHT **286:** ©Laurie A Watters. **288:** Duane Rumbaugh, Dept. of Psychology, Georgia State University. **289:** ©Frank Siteman/The Picture Cube. **301:** ©Tony Howarth/Woodfin Camp & Associates. **302:** NASA. **307:** David Dempster/Offshoot. **314:** Elizabeth Crews/The Image Works. **303:** ©SuperStock, Inc. **311:** ©Bonnie Kamin/Comstock.

CHAPTER NINE **322:** ©1989 Jose Azel/Contact Press Images. **325 (L):** ©Mark S. Levine/New York Mets. **325 (R):** ©Michael Zagaris 1991/Oakland As. **327:** ©1987, Comstock. **330:** ©Tony Freeman/PhotoEdit. **331:** ©Courtesy of Dr. Neal Miller/Yale University. **340 (L):** ©Harlow Primate Lab/University of Wisconsin. **340 (R):** ©Yerkes Regional Primate Center. **342:** ©AP/Wide World Photos. **346:** ©David Dempster/Offshoot. **347:** ©Human Interaction Laboratory.

CHAPTER TEN **360:** ©Jim Cummins/ALLSTOCK. **363:** ©Steven Jones, 1990. **365 (top):** ©Bill Bachmann/The Image Works. **365 (btm):** ©Suzanne Arms-Wimberley/Jeroboam. **366:** ©Courtesy of Creative Playthings. **368:** ©Enrico Ferorelli/DOT. **369:** ©1989 Robert Brenner/PhotoEdit. **371:** ©Harlow Primate Lab/University of Wisconsin. **372 (top):** ©Harlow Primate Lab/University of Wisconsin. **372 (btm):** ©Nina Leen/Life Magazine. **375 (top, L):** ©Doug Goodman/Monkmeyer Press. **375 (top, R):** ©Doug Goodman/Monkmeyer Press. **375 (btm, L):** ©George Zimbel/Monkmeyer Press. **375 (btm, M):** ©George Zimbel/Monkmeyer Press. **375 (btm, R):** George Zimbel/Monkmeyer Press. **377:** ©Richard Steedman/The Stock Market. **381:** ©AP/Wide World Photos. **386:** ©Richard Steedman/The Stock Market. **389:** ©John Curtis/Offshoot. **391:** ©Rene Sheret/Tony Stone Images. **392:** ©Lou Adamski Peck/Tony Stone Images.

CHAPTER ELEVEN **408:** ©Russell R. Grundke/Unicorn Stock Photos. **413:** ©MOMA Film Stills Archives. **414:** ©The Image Works. **425:** ©Focus on Sports. **430:** ©E. Doris Lee. **433:** ©Bob Daemmrich/The Image Works. **436:** ©Courtesy of Harvard University.

CHAPTER TWELVE **448:** ©Tom Rosenthal/SuperStock, Inc. **452 (L):** ©John Spragens, Jr./Photo Researchers, Inc. **452 (R):** ©Roy Morsch/The Stock Market. **453 (L):** ©Alan Oddie/PhotoEdit. **453 (R):** ©John Coletti/Stock, Boston. **455:** ©Gabe Palmer/The Stock Market. **456:** ©Focus on Sports. **463:** ©David Young-Wolff/PhotoEdit. **472:** ©Louise Gubb/Gamma-Liaison. **475 (L):** ©Focus on Sports. **475 (R):** ©Richard Mackson/Sports Illustrated.

CHAPTER THIRTEEN **490:** ©1992 Laurie A. Watters. **493:** ©Sandy Skoglund/Janet Borden, Inc. **494:** ©The Granger Collection. **498:** ©David Dempster/Offshoot. **499:** ©Laurie Simmons (photographer): "Red Library #2 (1983). Collection of the Artist, courtesy Metro Pictures, New York. **500:** ©Robert Ellison/Black Star. **503:** ©MOMA Film Stills Archives. **504:** ©AP/Wide World Photos. **513:** ©Four by Five/SuperStock, Inc. **519:** ©Grunnitus/Monkmeyer Press. **518:** ©Mitchell Funk/The Image Bank. **522 (L):** ©UPI/Bettmann. **522 (R):** ©Andy Schwartz/PhotoFest.

CHAPTER FOURTEEN **534:** ©1992 Laurie A. Watters. **538 (top):** ©Bettmann Archive. **538 (btm):** ©Bettmann Archive. **540:** ©AP/Wide World. **544:** ©Erich Hartmann/Magnum Photos. **551:** ©Rick Friedman/Black Star. **552:** ©Rick Friedman/Black Star. **553:** ©Courtesy of Albert Bandura. **554:** ©Lester Sloan/Woodfin Camp & Associates. **555:** ©Elaine Sulle/The Image Bank. **557:** ©Jim Pickerell/Stock, Boston. **562:** ©James D. Wilson/Woodfin Camp & Associates.

CHAPTER FIFTEEN **574:** ©Sund/The Image Bank. **580:** ©Robert V. Eckert/EKM Nepenthe. **581:** ©Courtesy of Coca Cola USA. **584:** ©Richard Hutchings/Photo Researchers. **588:** David Dempster. **590:** ©Tony Freeman/PhotoEdit. **593 (L):** ©AP/Wide World. **593 (R):** ©AP/Wide World. **596 (L):** ©Willie Hill Jr./The Image Works. **596 (R):** ©Bill Aron/PhotoEdit. **599:** ©Courtesy of the Estate of Stanley Milgram. **602:** ©Dan McCoy/Rainbow. **605:** ©Michael Kevin Daly/The Stock Market. **608:** ©David Dempster/Offshoot.

Literary Credits

Table 1.2, p. 16: Korn, J.H., Davis, R., and Davis, S.F. Historians' and chairpersons' judgement of eminence among psychologists. *American Psychologist,* 46, 789–792. Copyright ©1991 by the American Psychological Association. Reprinted by permission.

Table 8.1, p. 296: Adapted from Abraham S. Luchins and Edith H. Luchins, *Rigidity of Behavior* (Eugene: University of Oregon Press, 1959), p. 109.

Table 10.2, p. 376: Table from *Piaget: With Feeling: Cognitive, Social, and Emotional Dimensions* by Philip A. Cowen, copyright ©1978 by Holt, Rinehart and Winston, Inc., reprinted by permission of the publisher. **Table 10.3, p. 380:** J.R. Rest, "Hierarchical Nature of Moral Judgement." *Journal of Personality,* 41:1, p. 92–93. Copyright Duke University Press, 1974. Reprinted with permission of the publisher.

Table 11.2, p. 419: Adapted from *Childhood and Society,* 2nd edition, by Erik H. Erikson, by permission of W.W. Norton and Company, Inc. Copyright ©1950, 1963 by W.W. Norton and Company, Inc. Copyright renewed 1978, 1991 by Erik H. Erikson. **Table 12.1, p. 454:** Peggy Blake, Robert Fry, and Michael Pesjack (1984). *Self-Assessment and Behavior Change Manual.* New York: Random House, pp. 43–47. Reprinted by permission of Random House, Inc. **Table 12.3, p. 468:** Adapted from Stokols, D. Establishing and maintaining healthy environments: Toward a social ecology of health promotion. *American Psychologist,* 47, 6–22. Copyright ©1992 by the American Psychological Association. Reprinted by permission.

Chapter 13: Excerpts, pp. 498, 501, 504, 507, 515: From *Abnormal Psychology* by Spencer A. Rathus and Jeffrey Nevid. Copyright ©1991 by Prentice Hall, Englewood Cliffs, New Jersey. Reprinted by permission of Prentice Hall.

NAME INDEX

SUBJECT INDEX

Note: **Location of running glossary items (i.e., in the margins) are indicated by page numbers in boldface type.**

A

Q

R